BUTTERWORTHS INSOLVENCY LAW HANDBOOK

Editor

MICHAEL CRYSTAL, QC

LONDON
BUTTERWORTHS
1987

United Kingdom	Butterworth & Co (Publishers) Ltd, 88 Kingsway, LONDON WC2B 6AB and 61A North Castle Street, EDINBURGH EH2 3LJ
Australia	Butterworths Pty Ltd, SYDNEY, MELBOURNE, BRISBANE, ADELAIDE, PERTH, CANBERRA and HOBART
Canada	Butterworths. A division of Reed Inc, TORONTO and VANCOUVER
New Zealand	Butterworths of New Zealand Ltd, WELLINGTON and AUCKLAND
Singapore	Butterworth & Co (Asia) Pte Ltd, SINGAPORE
South Africa	Butterworth Publishers (Pty) Ltd, DURBAN and PRETORIA
USA	Butterworths Legal Publishers, ST PAUL, Minnesota, SEATTLE, Washington, BOSTON, Massachusetts, AUSTIN, Texas and D & S Publishers, CLEARWATER, Florida

© Butterworth & Co (Publishers) Ltd 1987

ISBN 0 406 50006 1

Typeset, printed and bound in Great Britain by
William Clowes Limited, Beccles and London

EDITOR'S INTRODUCTION

The publication of this handbook has been prompted by the recent sweeping changes in insolvency law. The handbook is intended to make available to those interested in insolvency law and practice a similar technical apparatus to that provided by Butterworths in other fields such as Revenue Law. The aim of the handbook is to provide in one volume the text of major current insolvency legislation and practice directions. For reasons of space it has not proved practicable to include statutory forms in the handbook.

The handbook is divided into five parts:

Part I—Insolvency Act 1986
Part II—Company Directors Disqualification Act 1986
Part III—Bankruptcy (Scotland) Act 1985
Part IV—Insolvency Statutory Instruments
Part V—Miscellaneous

Part IV contains the primary insolvency statutory instruments presently in force in relation to both England and Wales and Scotland. Part V contains selected primary and secondary legislation of importance in the insolvency field in England and Wales and also English Court Practice Directions made in connection with the new legislation.

The contents of the handbook attempt to take into account legislation and Practice Directions available as at 1 May 1987.

The editor is grateful to Mr Mark Phillips, of the Inner Temple, Barrister for his assistance in connection with the compilation of the materials for inclusion in this handbook.

May 1987   MICHAEL CRYSTAL QC

CONTENTS

Editor's Introduction   p iii

PART I   INSOLVENCY ACT 1986   *para*

Insolvency Act 1986 (c 45)   .   .   .   .   [1]

PART II   COMPANY DIRECTORS DISQUALIFICATION ACT 1986

Company Directors Disqualification Act 1986 (c 46)   .   .   .   [469]

PART III   BANKRUPTCY (SCOTLAND) ACT 1985

Bankruptcy (Scotland) Act 1985 (c 46)   .   .   .   .   .   .   [501]

PART IV   INSOLVENCY STATUTORY INSTRUMENTS

Section A   Insolvency Rules 1986
Insolvency Rules 1986 (SI 1986 No 1925)   .   .   .   .   [591]

Section B   Other Statutory Instruments—England and Wales
Companies (Winding Up) Rules 1949 (SI 1949 No 330)   .   .   [1347A]
Administrative Receivers (Value Added Tax Certificates) Rules
  1986 (SI 1986 No 385)   .   .   .   .   [1348]
Insolvent Companies (Disqualification of Unfit Directors) Pro-
  ceedings Rules 1986 (SI 1986 No 612)   .   .   .   .   .   [1354]
Insolvency Practitioners Tribunal (Conduct of Investigations)
  Rules 1986 (SI 1986 No 952)   .   .   .   .   .   .   [1368]
Insolvency Practitioners (Recognised Professional Bodies) Order
  1986 (SI 1986 No 1764)   .   .   .   .   [1384]
Insolvency Regulations 1986 (SI 1986 No 1994)   .   .   .   [1387]
Insolvency Practitioners Regulations 1986 (SI 1986 No 1995)   . [1424]
Insolvency Proceedings (Monetary Limits) Order 1986 (SI 1986
  No 1996)   .   .   .   .   [1448]
Administration of Insolvent Estates of Deceased Persons Order
  1986 (SI 1986 No 1999)   .   .   .   .   [1454]
Insolvency Fees Order 1986 (SI 1986 No 2030).   .   .   .   [1472]
Companies (Disqualification Orders) Regulations (SI 1986
  No 2067)   .   .   .   .   [1487]
Co-operation of Insolvency Courts (Designation of Relevant
  Countries and Territories) Order 1986 (SI 1986 No 2123)   .   [1494]
Insolvent Companies (Reports on Conduct of Directors) No 2
  Rules 1986 (SI 1986 No 2134)   .   .   .   .   .   .   [1497]
Insolvent Partnerships Order 1986 (SI 1986 No 2142)   .   .   [1504]

Section C   Insolvency (Scotland) Rules 1986
Insolvency (Scotland) Rules 1986 (SI 1986 No 1915 (S139))   .   [1524]

v

para

Section D   Other Statutory Instruments—Scotland

Bankruptcy (Scotland) Regulations 1985 (SI 1985 No 1925
(S147)) . . . . [1707A]
Administrative Receivers (Value Added Tax Certificates) (Scotland) Rules 1986 (SI 1986 No 304 (S23)) . . . . [1708]
Bankruptcy (Scotland) Amendment Regulations 1986 (SI 1986
No 1914 (S138)) . . . . [1717]
Insolvent Companies (Reports on Conduct of Directors) (No 2)
(Scotland) Rules 1986 (SI 1986 No 1916 (S140)) . . . [1721]
Receivers (Scotland) Regulations 1986 (SI 1986 No 1917 (S141)) . [1727]
Insurance Companies (Winding Up) (Scotland) Rules 1986 (SI
1986 No 1918 (S142)) . . . . [1735]

PART V   MISCELLANEOUS

Section A   Other Legislation

Deeds of Arrangement Act 1914 (c 47) . . . . . [1767]
Third Parties (Rights Against Insurers) Act 1930 (c 25) . . [1795]
Matrimonial Causes Act 1973 (c 18) (s 39) . . . . [1799]
Powers of Criminal Courts Act 1973 (c 62) (s 39) . . . [1800]
Employment Protection (Consolidation) Act 1978 (c 44) (ss 122–
127) . . . . [1801]
Banking Act 1979 (c 37) (ss 18, 28, 31) . . . . [1807]
Insurance Companies Act 1982 (c 50) (ss 53–59, 95–96) . . [1810]
Financial Services Act 1986 (c 60) (ss 72–74) . . . [1829]

Section B   Other Statutory Instruments

Deeds of Arrangement Rules 1925 (SI 1925 No 795) . . . [1834]
Deeds of Arrangement (Fees) Order 1984 (SI 1984 No 887) . [1877]
Insurance Companies (Winding-Up) Rules 1985 (SI 1985 No 95) [1884]
Insurance Companies (Winding-Up) Rules 1986 (SI 1986 No
2002) . . . . [1917]

Section C   Practice Directions

Companies Court: Petitions [1986] 1 WLR 1428 . . . [1937]
Companies Court: Insolvency [1987] 1 WLR 53 . . . [1938]
Bankruptcy Court: Petition [1987] 1 WLR 81 . . . [1939]
Bankruptcy Court: Service [1987] 1 WLR 82 . . . . [1940]
Bankruptcy Court: Service [1987] 1 WLR 85 . . . . [1941]
Bankruptcy Court: Statutory demand [1987] 1 WLR 119 . . [1942]
Bankruptcy Court: Proof of debt [1987] 1 WLR 120 . . [1943]

PART I

INSOLVENCY ACT 1986

INSOLVENCY ACT 1986
(c 45)

ARRANGEMENT OF SECTIONS

THE FIRST GROUP OF PARTS

COMPANY INSOLVENCY; COMPANIES WINDING UP

PART I

COMPANY VOLUNTARY ARRANGEMENTS

The proposal

Section		Para
1	Those who may propose an arrangement ..	[1]
2	Procedure where nominee is not the liquidator or administrator	[2]
3	Summoning of meetings	[3]

Consideration and implementation of proposal

4	Decisions of meetings	[4]
5	Effect of approval ..	[5]
6	Challenge of decisions	[6]
7	Implementation of proposal	[7]

PART II

ADMINISTRATION ORDERS

Making etc of administration order

8	Power of court to make order	[8]
9	Application for order	[9]
10	Effect of application	[10]
11	Effect of order	[11]
12	Notification of order	[12]

Administrators

13	Appointment of administrator	[13]
14	General powers	[14]
15	Power to deal with charged property, etc ..	[15]
16	Operation of s 15 in Scotland	[16]
17	General duties	[17]
18	Discharge or variation of administration order ..	[18]
19	Vacation of office ..	[19]
20	Release of administrator ..	[20]

Ascertainment and investigation of company's affairs

21	Information to be given by administrator	[21]
22	Statement of affairs to be submitted to administrator	[22]

Administrator's proposals

23	Statement of proposals	[23]
24	Consideration of proposals by creditors' meeting	[24]
25	Approval of substantial revisions ..	[25]

Miscellaneous

26	Creditors' committee	[26]
27	Protection of interests of creditors and members	[27]

Section   Para

PART III

RECEIVERSHIP

CHAPTER I

RECEIVERS AND MANAGERS (ENGLAND AND WALES)

Preliminary and general provisions

28 Extent of this Chapter .. .. [28]
29 Definitions .. .. [29]
30 Disqualification of body corporate from acting as receiver .. .. .. [30]
31 Disqualification of undischarged bankrupt .. .. [31]
32 Power for court to appoint official receiver .. .. [32]

Receivers and managers appointed out of court

33 Time from which appointment is effective .. .. [33]
34 Liability for invalid appointment .. .. [34]
35 Application to court for directions .. .. [35]
36 Court's power to fix remuneration .. .. [36]
37 Liability for contracts, etc .. .. [37]
38 Receivership accounts to be delivered to registrar .. .. [38]

Provisions applicable to every receivership

39 Notification that receiver or manager appointed .. .. [39]
40 Payment of debts out of assets subject to floating charge .. .. .. [40]
41 Enforcement of duty to make returns .. .. [41]

Administrative receivers : general

42 General powers .. .. [42]
43 Power to dispose of charged property, etc .. .. [43]
44 Agency and liability for contracts .. .. [44]
45 Vacation of office .. .. [45]

*Administrative receivers : ascertainment and
investigation of company's affairs*

46 Information to be given by administrative receiver .. .. [46]
47 Statement of affairs to be submitted .. .. [47]
48 Report by administrative receiver .. .. [48]
49 Committee of creditors .. .. [49]

CHAPTER II

RECEIVERS (SCOTLAND)

50 Extent of this Chapter .. .. [50]
51 Power to appoint receiver .. .. [51]
52 Circumstances justifying appointment .. .. [52]
53 Mode of appointment by holder of charge .. .. [53]
54 Appointment by court .. .. [54]
55 Powers of receiver .. .. [55]
56 Precedence among receivers .. .. [56]
57 Agency and liability of receiver for contracts .. .. [57]
58 Remuneration of receiver .. .. [58]
59 Priority of debts .. .. [59]
60 Distribution of moneys .. .. [60]
61 Disposal of interest in property .. .. [61]
62 Cessation of appointment of receiver .. .. [62]
63 Powers of court .. .. [63]
64 Notification that receiver appointed .. .. [64]
65 Information to be given by receiver .. .. [65]
66 Company's statement of affairs .. .. [66]
67 Report by receiver .. .. [67]

Section		Para
68	Committee of creditors	[68]
69	Enforcement of receiver's duty to make returns, etc	[69]
70	Interpretation for Chapter II	[70]
71	Prescription of forms etc; regulations	[71]

CHAPTER III

RECEIVERS' POWERS IN GREAT BRITAIN AS A WHOLE

72	Cross-border operation of receivership provisions	[72]

PART IV

WINDING UP OF COMPANIES REGISTERED UNDER THE COMPANIES ACTS

CHAPTER I

PRELIMINARY

Modes of winding up

73	Alternative modes of winding up	[73]

Contributories

74	Liability as contributories of present and past members	[74]
75	Directors, etc with unlimited liability	[75]
76	Liability of past directors and shareholders	[76]
77	Limited company formerly unlimited	[77]
78	Unlimited company formerly limited	[78]
79	Meaning of "contributory"	[79]
80	Nature of contributory's liability	[80]
81	Contributories in case of death of a member	[81]
82	Effect of contributory's bankruptcy	[82]
83	Companies registered under Companies Act, Part XXII, Chapter II	[83]

CHAPTER II

VOLUNTARY WINDING UP (INTRODUCTORY AND GENERAL)

Resolutions for, and commencement of, voluntary winding up

84	Circumstances in which company may be wound up voluntarily	[84]
85	Notice of resolution to wind up	[85]
86	Commencement of winding up	[86]

Consequences of resolution to wind up

87	Effect on business and status of company..	[87]
88	Avoidance of share transfers, etc after winding-up resolution	[88]

Declaration of solvency

89	Statutory declaration of solvency	[89]
90	Distinction between "members'" and "creditors'" voluntary winding up	[90]

CHAPTER III

MEMBERS' VOLUNTARY WINDING UP

91	Appointment of liquidator..	[91]
92	Power to fill vacancy in office of liquidator	[92]
93	General company meeting at each year's end	[93]
94	Final meeting prior to dissolution	[94]

Section Para
95 Effect of company's insolvency .. .. [95]
96 Conversion to creditors' voluntary winding up .. .. [96]

CHAPTER IV

CREDITORS' VOLUNTARY WINDING UP

97 Application of this Chapter .. .. [97]
98 Meeting of creditors .. .. [98]
99 Directors to lay statement of affairs before creditors .. .. [99]
100 Appointment of liquidator.. .. .. [100]
101 Appointment of liquidation committee .. .. [101]
102 Creditors' meeting where winding up converted under s 96 .. .. .. [102]
103 Cesser of directors' powers.. .. .. [103]
104 Vacancy in office of liquidator .. .. [104]
105 Meetings of company and creditors at each year's end .. .. [105]
106 Final meeting prior to dissolution .. .. [106]

CHAPTER V

PROVISIONS APPLYING TO BOTH KINDS OF
VOLUNTARY WINDING UP

107 Distribution of company's property .. .. [107]
108 Appointment or removal of liquidator by the court .. .. [108]
109 Notice by liquidator of his appointment .. .. [109]
110 Acceptance of shares, etc, as consideration for sale of company property .. .. [110]
111 Dissent from arrangement under s 110 .. .. [111]
112 Reference of questions to court .. .. [112]
113 Court's power to control proceedings (Scotland).. .. .. [113]
114 No liquidator appointed or nominated by company .. .. [114]
115 Expenses of voluntary winding up .. .. [115]
116 Saving for certain rights .. .. [116]

CHAPTER VI

WINDING UP BY THE COURT

Jurisdiction (England and Wales)

117 High Court and county court jurisdiction.. .. .. [117]
118 Proceedings taken in wrong court.. .. .. [118]
119 Proceedings in county court; case stated for High Court .. .. .. [119]

Jurisdiction (Scotland)

120 Court of Session and sheriff court jurisdiction .. .. [120]
121 Power to remit winding up to Lord Ordinary .. .. [121]

Grounds and effect of winding-up petition

122 Circumstances in which company may be wound up by the court .. .. [122]
123 Definition of inability to pay debts .. .. [123]
124 Application for winding up .. .. [124]
125 Powers of court on hearing of petition .. .. [125]
126 Power to stay or restrain proceedings against company .. .. [126]
127 Avoidance of property dispositions, etc .. .. [127]
128 Avoidance of attachments, etc .. .. [128]

Commencement of winding up

129 Commencement of winding up by the court .. .. [129]
130 Consequences of winding-up order .. .. [130]

Section   Para

Investigation procedures

131 Company's statement of affairs   ..   .. [131]
132 Investigation by official receiver ..   .. [132]
133 Public examination of officers   ..   .. [133]
134 Enforcement of s 133   ..   .. [134]

Appointment of liquidator

135 Appointment and powers of provisional liquidator   ..   .. [135]
136 Functions of official receiver in relation to office of liquidator ..   ..   .. [136]
137 Appointment by Secretary of State   ..   .. [137]
138 Appointment of liquidator in Scotland   ..   .. [138]
139 Choice of liquidator at meetings of creditors and contributories   ..   .. [139]
140 Appointment by the court following administration or voluntary arrangement   .. [140]

Liquidation committees

141 Liquidation committee (England and Wales)   ..   .. [141]
142 Liquidation committee (Scotland)   ..   .. [142]

The liquidator's functions

143 General functions in winding up by the court   ..   .. [143]
144 Custody of company's property   ..   .. [144]
145 Vesting of company property in liquidator   ..   .. [145]
146 Duty to summon final meeting   ..   .. [146]

General powers of court

147 Power to stay or sist winding up   ..   .. [147]
148 Settlement of list of contributories and application of assets   ..   ..   .. [148]
149 Debts due from contributory to company..   ..   .. [149]
150 Power to make calls   ..   .. [150]
151 Payment into bank of money due to company   ..   .. [151]
152 Order on contributory to be conclusive evidence..   ..   .. [152]
153 Power to exclude creditors not proving in time   ..   .. [153]
154 Adjustment of rights of contributories   ..   .. [154]
155 Inspection of books by creditors, etc   ..   .. [155]
156 Payment of expenses of winding up   ..   .. [156]
157 Attendance at company meetings (Scotland)   ..   .. [157]
158 Power to arrest absconding contributory ..   .. [158]
159 Powers of court to be cumulative ..   .. [159]
160 Delegation of powers to liquidator (England and Wales)   ..   .. [160]

Enforcement of, and appeal from, orders

161 Orders for calls on contributions (Scotland)   ..   .. [161]
162 Appeals from orders in Scotland ..   .. [162]

CHAPTER VII

LIQUIDATORS

Preliminary

163 Style and title of liquidators   ..   .. [163]
164 Corrupt inducement affecting appointment   ..   .. [164]

Liquidator's powers and duties

165 Voluntary winding up   ..   .. [165]
166 Creditors' voluntary winding up ..   .. [166]
167 Winding up by the court ..   .. [167]
168 Supplementary powers (England and Wales)   ..   .. [168]
169 Supplementary powers (Scotland)..   ..   .. [169]
170 Enforcement of liquidator's duty to make returns, etc ..   .. [170]

Section   Para
Removal ; vacation of office

171   Removal, etc (voluntary winding up)   ..   ..   [171]
172   Removal, etc (winding up by the court) ..   ..   [172]

Release of liquidator

173   Release (voluntary winding up) ..   ..   [173]
174   Release (winding up by the court) ..   ..   [174]

CHAPTER VIII

PROVISIONS OF GENERAL APPLICATION IN WINDING UP

Preferential debts

175   Preferential debts (general provision) ..   ..   [175]
176   Preferential charge on goods distrained ..   ..   [176]

Special managers

177   Power to appoint special manager   ..   ..   [177]

Disclaimer (England and Wales only)

178   Power to disclaim onerous property   ..   ..   [178]
179   Disclaimer of leaseholds   ..   ..   [179]
180   Land subject to rentcharge..   ..   ..   [180]
181   Powers of court (general)   ..   ..   [181]
182   Powers of court (leaseholds)   ..   ..   [182]

Execution, attachment and the Scottish equivalents

183   Effect of execution or attachment (England and Wales)..   ..   ..   [183]
184   Duties of sheriff (England and Wales)   ..   ..   [184]
185   Effect of diligence (Scotland)   ..   ..   [185]

Miscellaneous matters

186   Rescission of contracts by the court   ..   ..   [186]
187   Power to make over assets to employees ..   ..   [187]
188   Notification that company is in liquidation   ..   ..   [188]
189   Interest on debts   ..   ..   [189]
190   Documents exempt from stamp duty   ..   ..   [190]
191   Company's books to be evidence   ..   ..   [191]
192   Information as to pending liquidations   ..   ..   [192]
193   Unclaimed dividends (Scotland)   ..   ..   [193]
194   Resolutions passed at adjourned meetings   ..   ..   [194]
195   Meetings to ascertain wishes of creditors or contributories   ..   ..   [195]
196   Judicial notice of court documents   ..   ..   [196]
197   Commission for receiving evidence   ..   ..   [197]
198   Court order for examination of persons in Scotland   ..   ..   [198]
199   Costs of application for leave to proceed (Scottish companies) ..   ..   [199]
200   Affidavits etc in United Kingdom and overseas ..   ..   [200]

CHAPTER IX

DISSOLUTION OF COMPANIES AFTER WINDING UP

201   Dissolution (voluntary winding up)   ..   ..   [201]
202   Early dissolution (England and Wales)   ..   ..   [202]
203   Consequence of notice under s 202   ..   ..   [203]
204   Early dissolution (Scotland)   ..   ..   [204]
205   Dissolution otherwise than under ss 202–204   ..   ..   [205]

Section   Para

CHAPTER X

MALPRACTICE BEFORE AND DURING LIQUIDATION;
PENALISATION OF COMPANIES AND COMPANY OFFICERS;
INVESTIGATIONS AND PROSECUTIONS

Offences of fraud, deception, etc

206   Fraud, etc in anticipation of winding up ..   .. [206]
207   Transactions in fraud of creditors ..   .. [207]
208   Misconduct in course of winding up   ..   .. [208]
209   Falsification of company's books ..   .. [209]
210   Material omissions from statement relating to company's affairs   ..   ..   .. [210]
211   False representations to creditors ..   .. [211]

Penalisation of directors and officers

212   Summary remedy against delinquent directors, liquidators, etc   ..   ..   .. [212]
213   Fraudulent trading ..   .. [213]
214   Wrongful trading ..   .. [214]
215   Proceedings under ss 213, 214   ..   .. [215]
216   Restriction on re-use of company names ..   .. [216]
217   Personal liability for debts, following contravention of s 216   ..   ..   .. [217]

Investigation and prosecution of malpractice

218   Prosecution of delinquent officers and members of company ..   .. [218]
219   Obligations arising under s 218   ..   .. [219]

PART V

WINDING UP OF UNREGISTERED COMPANIES

220   Meaning of "unregistered company"   ..   .. [220]
221   Winding up of unregistered companies   ..   .. [221]
222   Inability to pay debts: unpaid creditor for £750 or more   ..   .. [222]
223   Inability to pay debts: debt remaining unsatisfied after action brought   ..   .. [223]
224   Inability to pay debts: other cases ..   .. [224]
225   Oversea company may be wound up though dissolved ..   .. [225]
226   Contributories in winding up of unregistered company ..   .. [226]
227   Power of court to stay, sist or restrain proceedings   ..   .. [227]
228   Actions stayed on winding-up order   ..   .. [228]
229   Provisions of this Part to be cumulative ..   .. [229]

PART VI

MISCELLANEOUS PROVISIONS APPLYING TO COMPANIES
WHICH ARE INSOLVENT OR IN LIQUIDATION

Office-holders

230   Holders of office to be qualified insolvency practitioners   ..   .. [230]
231   Appointment to office of two or more persons ..   .. [231]
232   Validity of office-holder's acts   ..   .. [232]

Management by administrators, liquidators, etc

233   Supplies of gas, water, electricity, etc   ..   .. [233]
234   Getting in the company's property   ..   .. [234]
235   Duty to co-operate with office-holder   ..   .. [235]
236   Inquiry into company's dealings, etc   ..   .. [236]
237   Court's enforcement powers under s 236 ..   .. [237]

Section   Para

Adjustment of prior transactions (administration and liquidation)

238   Transactions at an undervalue (England and Wales)   ..   .. [238]
239   Preferences (England and Wales) ..   .. [239]
240   "Relevant time" under ss 238, 239   ..   .. [240]
241   Orders under ss 238, 239   ..   .. [241]
242   Gratuitous alienations (Scotland) ..   .. [242]
243   Unfair preferences (Scotland)   ..   .. [243]
244   Extortionate credit transactions   ..   .. [244]
245   Avoidance of certain floating charges   ..   .. [245]
246   Unenforceability of liens on books, etc   ..   .. [246]

PART VII

INTERPRETATION FOR FIRST GROUP OF PARTS

247   "Insolvency" and "go into liquidation"   ..   .. [247]
248   "Secured creditor", etc   ..   .. [248]
249   "Connected" with a company   ..   .. [249]
250   "Member" of a company   ..   .. [250]
251   Expressions used generally   ..   .. [251]

THE SECOND GROUP OF PARTS

INSOLVENCY OF INDIVIDUALS; BANKRUPTCY

PART VIII

INDIVIDUAL VOLUNTARY ARRANGEMENTS

Moratorium for insolvent debtor

252   Interim order of court   ..   .. [252]
253   Application for interim order   ..   .. [253]
254   Effect of application   ..   .. [254]
255   Cases in which interim order can be made   ..   .. [255]
256   Nominee's report on debtor's proposal   ..   .. [256]
257   Summoning of creditors' meeting ..   .. [257]

Consideration and implementation of debtor's proposal

258   Decisions of creditors' meeting   ..   .. [258]
259   Report of decisions to court   ..   .. [259]
260   Effect of approval ..   .. [260]
261   Effect where debtor an undischarged bankrupt ..   .. [261]
262   Challenge of meeting's decision   ..   .. [262]
263   Implementation and supervision of approved voluntary arrangement ..   ..   .. [263]

PART IX

BANKRUPTCY

CHAPTER I

BANKRUPTCY PETITIONS; BANKRUPTCY ORDERS

Preliminary

264   Who may present a bankruptcy petition ..   .. [264]
265   Conditions to be satisfied in respect of debtor   ..   .. [265]
266   Other preliminary conditions   ..   .. [266]

Creditor's petition

267   Grounds of creditor's petition   ..   .. [267]
268   Definition of "inability to pay", etc; the statutory demand   ..   ..   .. [268]
269   Creditor with security   ..   .. [269]

Section   Para
270   Expedited petition ..   ..   [270]
271   Proceedings on creditor's petition ..   ..   [271]

Debtor's petition

272   Grounds of debtor's petition   ..   ..   [272]
273   Appointment of insolvency practitioner by the court   ..   ..   [273]
274   Action on report of insolvency practitioner   ..   ..   [274]
275   Summary administration ..   ..   [275]

Other cases for special consideration

276   Default in connection with voluntary arrangement   ..   ..   [276]
277   Petition based on criminal bankruptcy order   ..   ..   [277]

Commencement and duration of bankruptcy; discharge

278   Commencement and continuance..   ..   ..   [278]
279   Duration   ..   ..   [279]
280   Discharge by order of the court   ..   ..   [280]
281   Effect of discharge ..   ..   [281]
282   Court's power to annul bankruptcy order..   ..   ..   [282]

CHAPTER II

PROTECTION OF BANKRUPT'S ESTATE AND INVESTIGATION OF HIS AFFAIRS

283   Definition of bankrupt's estate   ..   ..   [283]
284   Restrictions on dispositions of property ..   ..   [284]
285   Restriction on proceedings and remedies..   ..   ..   [285]
286   Power to appoint interim receiver..   ..   ..   [286]
287   Receivership pending appointment of trustee   ..   ..   [287]
288   Statement of affairs..   ..   ..   [288]
289   Investigatory duties of official receiver   ..   ..   [289]
290   Public examination of bankrupt ..   ..   [290]
291   Duties of bankrupt in relation to official receiver   ..   ..   [291]

CHAPTER III

TRUSTEES IN BANKRUPTCY

Tenure of office as trustee

292   Power to make appointments   ..   ..   [292]
293   Summoning of meeting to appoint first trustee   ..   ..   [293]
294   Power of creditors to requisition meeting..   ..   ..   [294]
295   Failure of meeting to appoint trustee   ..   ..   [295]
296   Appointment of trustee by Secretary of State   ..   ..   [296]
297   Special cases   ..   ..   [297]
298   Removal of trustee; vacation of office   ..   ..   [298]
299   Release of trustee ..   ..   [299]
300   Vacancy in office of trustee   ..   ..   [300]

Control of trustee

301   Creditors' committee   ..   ..   [301]
302   Exercise by Secretary of State of functions of creditors' committee   ..   ..   ..   [302]
303   General control of trustee by the court ..   ..   [303]
304   Liability of trustee ..   ..   [304]

CHAPTER IV

ADMINISTRATION BY TRUSTEE

Preliminary

305   General functions of trustee   ..   ..   [305]

Section   Para

Acquisition, control and realisation of bankrupt's estate

306   Vesting of bankrupt's estate in trustee .. .. [306]
307   After-acquired property .. .. [307]
308   Vesting in trustee of certain items of excess value .. .. [308]
309   Time-limit for notice under s 307 or 308 .. .. [309]
310   Income payments orders .. .. [310]
311   Acquisition by trustee of control .. .. [311]
312   Obligation to surrender control to trustee.. .. .. [312]
313   Charge on bankrupt's home .. .. [313]
314   Powers of trustee .. .. [314]

Disclaimer of onerous property

315   Disclaimer (general power) .. .. [315]
316   Notice requiring trustee's decision .. .. [316]
317   Disclaimer of leaseholds .. .. [317]
318   Disclaimer of dwelling house .. .. [318]
319   Disclaimer of land subject to rentcharge .. .. [319]
320   Court order vesting disclaimed property .. .. [320]
321   Order under s 320 in respect of leaseholds .. .. [321]

Distribution of bankrupt's estate

322   Proof of debts .. .. [322]
323   Mutual credit and set-off .. .. [323]
324   Distribution by means of dividend .. .. [324]
325   Claims by unsatisfied creditors .. .. [325]
326   Distribution of property in specie .. .. [326]
327   Distribution in criminal bankruptcy .. .. [327]
328   Priority of debts .. .. [328]
329   Debts to spouse .. .. [329]
330   Final distribution .. .. [330]
331   Final meeting .. .. [331]
332   Saving for bankrupt's home .. .. [332]

Supplemental

333   Duties of bankrupt in relation to trustee .. .. [333]
334   Stay of distribution in case of second bankruptcy .. .. [334]
335   Adjustment between earlier and later bankruptcy estates .. .. .. [335]

CHAPTER V

EFFECT OF BANKRUPTCY ON CERTAIN RIGHTS, TRANSACTIONS, ETC

Rights of occupation

336   Rights of occupation etc of bankrupt's spouse .. .. [336]
337   Rights of occupation of bankrupt .. .. [337]
338   Payments in respect of premises occupied by bankrupt .. .. .. [338]

Adjustment of prior transactions, etc

339   Transactions at an undervalue .. .. [339]
340   Preferences .. .. [340]
341   "Relevant time" under ss 339, 340 .. .. [341]
342   Orders under ss 339, 340 .. .. [342]
343   Extortionate credit transactions .. .. [343]
344   Avoidance of general assignment of book debts .. .. [344]
345   Contracts to which bankrupt is a party .. .. [345]
346   Enforcement procedures .. .. [346]
347   Distress, etc .. .. [347]
348   Apprenticeships, etc .. .. [348]
349   Unenforceability of liens on books, etc .. .. [349]

Section   Para

CHAPTER VI

BANKRUPTCY OFFENCES

Preliminary

350	Scheme of this Chapter	[350]
351	Definitions	[351]
352	Defence of innocent intention	[352]

Wrongdoing by the bankrupt before and after bankruptcy

353	Non-disclosure	[353]
354	Concealment of property	[354]
355	Concealment of books and papers; falsification	[355]
356	False statements	[356]
357	Fraudulent disposal of property	[357]
358	Absconding	[358]
359	Fraudulent dealing with property obtained on credit	[359]
360	Obtaining credit; engaging in business	[360]
361	Failure to keep proper accounts of business	[361]
362	Gambling	[362]

CHAPTER VII

POWERS OF COURT IN BANKRUPTCY

363	General control of court	[363]
364	Power of arrest	[364]
365	Seizure of bankrupt's property	[365]
366	Inquiry into bankrupt's dealings and property	[366]
367	Court's enforcement powers under s 366	[367]
368	Provision corresponding to s 366, where interim receiver appointed	[368]
369	Order for production of documents by inland revenue	[369]
370	Power to appoint special manager	[370]
371	Re-direction of bankrupt's letters, etc	[371]

PART X

INDIVIDUAL INSOLVENCY: GENERAL PROVISIONS

372	Supplies of gas, water, electricity, etc	[372]
373	Jurisdiction in relation to insolvent individuals	[373]
374	Insolvency districts	[374]
375	Appeals etc from courts exercising insolvency jurisdiction	[375]
376	Time-limits	[376]
377	Formal defects	[377]
378	Exemption from stamp duty	[378]
379	Annual report	[379]

PART XI

INTERPRETATION FOR SECOND GROUP OF PARTS

380	Introductory	[380]
381	"Bankrupt" and associated terminology	[381]
382	"Bankruptcy debt", etc	[382]
383	"Creditor", "security", etc	[383]
384	"Prescribed" and "the rules"	[384]
385	Miscellaneous definitions	[385]

Section Para

THE THIRD GROUP OF PARTS

MISCELLANEOUS MATTERS BEARING ON BOTH
COMPANY AND INDIVIDUAL INSOLVENCY; GENERAL
INTERPRETATION; FINAL PROVISIONS

PART XII

PREFERENTIAL DEBTS IN COMPANY AND
INDIVIDUAL INSOLVENCY

386 Categories of preferential debts .. .. [386]
387 "The relevant date" .. .. [387]

PART XIII

INSOLVENCY PRACTITIONERS AND THEIR
QUALIFICATION

*Restrictions on unqualified persons acting as
liquidator, trustee in bankruptcy, etc*

388 Meaning of "act as insolvency practitioner" .. .. [388]
389 Acting without qualification an offence .. .. [389]

*The requisite qualification, and the
means of obtaining it*

390 Persons not qualified to act as insolvency practitioners .. .. [390]
391 Recognised professional bodies .. .. [391]
392 Authorisation by competent authority .. .. [392]
393 Grant, refusal and withdrawal of authorisation .. .. [393]
394 Notices .. .. [394]
395 Right to make representations .. .. [395]
396 Reference to Tribunal .. .. [396]
397 Action of Tribunal on reference .. .. [397]
398 Refusal or withdrawal without reference to Tribunal .. .. [398]

PART XIV

PUBLIC ADMINISTRATION (ENGLAND AND WALES)

Official receivers

399 Appointment, etc of official receivers .. .. [399]
400 Functions and status of official receivers .. .. [400]
401 Deputy official receivers and staff .. .. [401]

The Official Petitioner

402 Official Petitioner .. .. [402]

Insolvency Service finance, accounting and investment

403 Insolvency Services Account .. .. [403]
404 Investment Account .. .. [404]
405 Application of income in Investment Account; adjustment of balances .. .. [405]
406 Interest on money received by liquidators and invested .. .. [406]
407 Unclaimed dividends and undistributed balances .. .. [407]
408 Recourse to Consolidated Fund .. .. [408]
409 Annual financial statement and audit .. .. [409]

Supplementary

410 Extent of this Part .. .. [410]

Section   Para

PART XV

SUBORDINATE LEGISLATION

General insolvency rules

411 Company insolvency rules ..   .. [411]
412 Individual insolvency rules (England and Wales)   ..   .. [412]
413 Insolvency Rules Committee   ..   .. [413]

Fees orders

414 Fees orders (company insolvency proceedings) ..   .. [414]
415 Fees orders (individual insolvency proceedings in England and Wales)   .. [415]

*Specification, increase and reduction of money sums
relevant in the operation of this Act*

416 Monetary limits (companies winding up)..   ..   .. [416]
417 Money sum in s 222   ..   .. [417]
418 Monetary limits (bankruptcy)   ..   .. [418]

Insolvency practice

419 Regulations for purposes of Part XIII   ..   .. [419]

Other order-making powers

420 Insolvent partnerships   ..   .. [420]
421 Insolvent estates of deceased persons   ..   .. [421]
422 Recognised banks, etc   ..   .. [422]

PART XVI

PROVISIONS AGAINST DEBT AVOIDANCE
(ENGLAND AND WALES ONLY)

423 Transactions defrauding creditors   ..   .. [423]
424 Those who may apply for an order under s 423 ..   .. [424]
425 Provision which may be made by order under s 423   ..   .. [425]

PART XVII

MISCELLANEOUS AND GENERAL

426 Co-operation between courts exercising jurisdiction in relation to insolvency ..   .. [426]
427 Parliamentary disqualification   ..   .. [427]
428 Exemptions from Restrictive Trade Practices Act   ..   .. [428]
429 Disabilities on revocation of administration order against an individual   .. [429]
430 Provision introducing Schedule of punishments ..   .. [430]
431 Summary proceedings   ..   .. [431]
432 Offences by bodies corporate   ..   .. [432]
433 Admissibility in evidence of statements of affairs, etc   ..   ..   .. [433]
434 Crown application ..   .. [434]

PART XVIII

INTERPRETATION

435 Meaning of "associate"   ..   .. [435]
436 Expressions used generally   ..   .. [436]

PART XIX

FINAL PROVISIONS

437 Transitional provisions, and savings .. .. [437]
438 Repeals .. .. [438]
439 Amendment of enactments .. .. [439]
440 Extent (Scotland) .. .. [440]
441 Extent (Northern Ireland) .. .. [441]
442 Extent (other territories) .. .. [442]
443 Commencement .. .. [443]
444 Citation .. .. [444]

SCHEDULES

Schedule 1—Powers of administrator or administrative receiver .. .. .. [445]
Schedule 2—Powers of a Scottish receiver (additional to those conferred on him by
    the instrument of charge) .. .. [446]
Schedule 3—Orders in course of winding up pronounced in vacation (Scotland) .. [447]
Schedule 4—Powers of liquidator in a winding up .. .. [449]
Schedule 5—Powers of trustee in bankruptcy .. .. [452]
Schedule 6—The categories of preferential debts .. .. [455]
Schedule 7—Insolvency Practitioners Tribunal .. .. [456]
Schedule 8—Provisions capable of inclusion in company insolvency rules .. [457]
Schedule 9—Provisions capable of inclusion in individual insolvency rules .. [458]
Schedule 10—Punishment of offences under this Act .. .. [459]
Schedule 11—Transitional provisions and savings .. .. [460]
Schedule 12—Enactments repealed .. .. [463]
Schedule 13—Consequential amendments of Companies Act 1985 .. .. [464]
Schedule 14—Consequential amendments of other enactments .. .. .. [465]

An Act to consolidate the enactments relating to company insolvency and winding up (including the winding up of companies that are not insolvent, and of unregistered companies); enactments relating to the insolvency and bankruptcy of individuals; and other enactments bearing on those two subject matters, including the functions and qualification of insolvency practitioners, the public administration of insolvency, the penalisation and redress of malpractice and wrongdoing, and the avoidance of certain transactions at an undervalue

[25 July 1986]

This Act came into force on 29 December 1986 by virtue of s 443 post and the Insolvency Act 1985 (Commencement No 5) Order 1986, SI 1986 No 1924, art 3.

THE FIRST GROUP OF PARTS

COMPANY INSOLVENCY; COMPANIES WINDING UP

PART I

COMPANY VOLUNTARY ARRANGEMENTS

The proposal

1. Those who may propose an arrangement

(1) The directors of a company (other than one for which an administration order is in force, or which is being wound up) may make a proposal under this Part to the company and to its creditors for a composition in satisfaction of its debts or a scheme of arrangement of its affairs (from here on referred to, in either case, as a "voluntary arrangement").

(2) A proposal under this Part is one which provides for some person ("the

nominee") to act in relation to the voluntary arrangement either as trustee or otherwise for the purpose of supervising its implementation; and the nominee must be a person who is qualified to act as an insolvency practitioner in relation to the company.

(3) Such a proposal may also be made—

 (a) where an administration order is in force in relation to the company, by the administrator, and

 (b) where the company is being wound up, by the liquidator.   **[1]**

NOTES
  Commencement: 29 December 1986.
  This section derived from the Insolvency Act 1985, s 20.

2. Procedure where nominee is not the liquidator or administrator

(1) This section applies where the nominee under section 1 is not the liquidator or administrator of the company.

(2) The nominee shall, within 28 days (or such longer period as the court may allow) after he is given notice of the proposal for a voluntary arrangement, submit a report to the court stating—

 (a) whether, in his opinion, meetings of the company and of its creditors should be summoned to consider the proposal, and

 (b) if in his opinion such meetings should be summoned, the date on which, and time and place at which, he proposes the meetings should be held.

(3) For the purposes of enabling the nominee to prepare his report, the person intending to make the proposal shall submit to the nominee—

 (a) a document setting out the terms of the proposed voluntary arrangement, and

 (b) a statement of the company's affairs containing—

  (i) such particulars of its creditors and of its debts and other liabilities and of its assets as may be prescribed, and

  (ii) such other information as may be prescribed.

(4) The court may, on an application made by the person intending to make the proposal, in a case where the nominee has failed to submit the report required by this section, direct that the nominee be replaced as such by another person qualified to act as an insolvency practitioner in relation to the company.

[2]

NOTES
  Commencement: 29 December 1986.
  This section derived from the Insolvency Act 1985, s 21.

3. Summoning of meetings

(1) Where the nominee under section 1 is not the liquidator or administrator, and it has been reported to the court that such meetings as are mentioned in section 2(2) should be summoned, the person making the report shall (unless the court otherwise directs) summon those meetings for the time, date and place proposed in the report.

(2) Where the nominee is the liquidator or administrator, he shall summon meetings of the company and of its creditors to consider the proposal for such a time, date and place as he thinks fit.

(3) The persons to be summoned to a creditors' meeting under this section are every creditor of the company of whose claim and address the person summoning the meeting is aware.   **[3]**

NOTES
Commencement: 29 December 1986.
This section derived from the Insolvency Act 1985, s 22.

Consideration and implementation of proposal

4. Decisions of meetings

(1) The meetings summoned under section 3 shall decide whether to approve the proposed voluntary arrangement (with or without modifications).

(2) The modifications may include one conferring the functions proposed to be conferred on the nominee on another person qualified to act as an insolvency practitioner in relation to the company.

But they shall not include any modification by virtue of which the proposal ceases to be a proposal such as is mentioned in section 1.

(3) A meeting so summoned shall not approve any proposal or modification which affects the right of a secured creditor of the company to enforce his security, except with the concurrence of the creditor concerned.

(4) Subject as follows, a meeting so summoned shall not approve any proposal or modification under which—

  (*a*) any preferential debt of the company is to be paid otherwise than in priority to such of its debts as are not preferential debts, or
  (*b*) a preferential creditor of the company is to be paid an amount in respect of a preferential debt that bears to that debt a smaller proportion than is borne to another preferential debt by the amount that is to be paid in respect of that other debt.

However, the meeting may approve such a proposal or modification with the concurrence of the preferential creditor concerned.

(5) Subject as above, each of the meetings shall be conducted in accordance with the rules.

(6) After the conclusion of either meeting in accordance with the rules, the chairman of the meeting shall report the result of the meeting to the court, and, immediately after reporting to the court, shall give notice of the result of the meeting to such persons as may be prescribed.

(7) References in this section to preferential debts and preferential creditors are to be read in accordance with section 386 in Part XII of this Act.   **[4]**

NOTES
Commencement: 29 December 1986.
This section derived from the Insolvency Act 1985, s 23(1)–(6), (7) (part).

5. Effect of approval

(1) This section has effect where each of the meetings summoned under section 3 approves the proposed voluntary arrangement either with the same modifications or without modifications.

(2) The approved voluntary arrangement—

    (*a*) takes effect as if made by the company at the creditors' meeting, and

    (*b*) binds every person who in accordance with the rules had notice of, and was entitled to vote at, that meeting (whether or not he was present or represented at the meeting) as if he were a party to the voluntary arrangement.

(3) Subject as follows, if the company is being wound up or an administration order is in force, the court may do one or both of the following, namely—

    (*a*) by order stay or sist all proceedings in the winding up or discharge the administration order;

    (*b*) give such directions with respect to the conduct of the winding up or the administration as it thinks appropriate for facilitating the implementation of the approved voluntary arrangement.

(4) The court shall not make an order under subsection (3)(*a*)—

    (*a*) at any time before the end of the period of 28 days beginning with the first day on which each of the reports required by section 4(6) has been made to the court, or

    (*b*) at any time when an application under the next section or an appeal in respect of such an application is pending, or at any time in the period within which such an appeal may be brought.   **[5]**

NOTES
Commencement: 29 December 1986.
This section derived from the Insolvency Act 1985, s 24.

6. Challenge of decisions

(1) Subject to this section, an application to the court may be made, by any of the persons specified below, on one or both of the following grounds, namely—

    (*a*) that a voluntary arrangement approved at the meetings summoned under section 3 unfairly prejudices the interests of a creditor, member or contributory of the company;

    (*b*) that there has been some material irregularity at or in relation to either of the meetings.

(2) The persons who may apply under this section are—

    (*a*) a person entitled, in accordance with the rules, to vote at either of the meetings;

    (*b*) the nominee or any person who has replaced him under section 2(4) or 4(2); and

    (*c*) if the company is being wound up or an administration order is in force, the liquidator or administrator.

(3) An application under this section shall not be made after the end of the period of 28 days beginning with the first day on which each of the reports required by section 4(6) has been made to the court.

(4) Where on such an application the court is satisfied as to either of the grounds mentioned in subsection (1), it may do one or both of the following, namely—

    (*a*) revoke or suspend the approvals given by the meetings or, in a case falling within subsection (1)(*b*), any approval given by the meeting in question;

    (*b*) give a direction to any person for the summoning of further meetings to consider any revised proposal the person who made the original proposal may make or, in a case falling within subsection (1)(*b*), a further company or (as the case may be) creditors' meeting to reconsider the original proposal.

(5) Where at any time after giving a direction under subsection (4)(*b*) for the summoning of meetings to consider a revised proposal the court is satisfied that the person who made the original proposal does not intend to submit a revised proposal, the court shall revoke the direction and revoke or suspend any approval given at the previous meetings.

(6) In a case where the court, on an application under this section with respect to any meeting—

(*a*) gives a direction under subsection (4)(*b*), or
(*b*) revokes or suspends an approval under subsection (4)(*a*) or (5),

the court may give such supplemental directions as it thinks fit and, in particular, directions with respect to things done since the meeting under any voluntary arrangement approved by the meeting.

(7) Except in pursuance of the preceding provisions of this section, an approval given at a meeting summoned under section 3 is not invalidated by any irregularity at or in relation to the meeting. **[6]**

NOTES
Commencement: 29 December 1986.
This section derived from the Insolvency Act 1985, s 25.

7. Implementation of proposal

(1) This section applies where a voluntary arrangement approved by the meetings summoned under section 3 has taken effect.

(2) The person who is for the time being carrying out in relation to the voluntary arrangement the functions conferred—

(*a*) by virtue of the approval on the nominee, or
(*b*) by virtue of section 2(4) or 4(2) on a person other than the nominee, ·

shall be known as the supervisor of the voluntary arrangement.

(3) If any of the company's creditors or any other person is dissatisfied by any act, omission or decision of the supervisor, he may apply to the court; and on the application the court may—

(*a*) confirm, reverse or modify any act or decision of the supervisor,
(*b*) give him directions, or
(*c*) make such other order as it thinks fit.

(4) The supervisor—

(*a*) may apply to the court for directions in relation to any particular matter arising under the voluntary arrangement, and
(*b*) is included among the persons who may apply to the court for the winding up of the company or for an administration order to be made in relation to it.

(5) The court may, whenever—

(*a*) it is expedient to appoint a person to carry out the functions of the supervisor, and
(*b*) it is inexpedient, difficult or impracticable for an appointment to be made without the assistance of the court,

make an order appointing a person who is qualified to act as an insolvency practitioner in relation to the company, either in substitution for the existing supervisor or to fill a vacancy.

(6) The power conferred by subsection (5) is exercisable so as to increase the number of persons exercising the functions of supervisor or, where there is more than one person exercising those functions, so as to replace one or more of those persons. **[7]**

NOTES
Commencement: 29 December 1986.
This section derived from the Insolvency Act 1985, s 26.

PART II

ADMINISTRATION ORDERS

Making etc of administration order

8. Power of court to make order

(1) Subject to this section, if the court—
- (*a*) is satisfied that a company is or is likely to become unable to pay its debts (within the meaning given to that expression by section 123 of this Act), and
- (*b*) considers that the making of an order under this section would be likely to achieve one or more of the purposes mentioned below,

the court may make an administration order in relation to the company.

(2) An administration order is an order directing that, during the period for which the order is in force, the affairs, business and property of the company shall be managed by a person ("the administrator") appointed for the purpose by the court.

(3) The purposes for whose achievement an administration order may be made are—
- (*a*) the survival of the company, and the whole or any part of its undertaking, as a going concern;
- (*b*) the approval of a voluntary arrangement under Part 1;
- (*c*) the sanctioning under section 425 of the Companies Act of a compromise or arrangement between the company and any such persons as are mentioned in that section; and
- (*d*) a more advantageous realisation of the company's assets than would be effected on a winding up;

and the order shall specify the purpose or purposes for which it is made.

(4) An administration order shall not be made in relation to a company after it has gone into liquidation, nor where it is—
- (*a*) an insurance company within the meaning of the Insurance Companies Act 1982, or
- (*b*) a recognised bank or licensed institution within the meaning of the Banking Act 1979, or an institution to which sections 16 and 18 of that Act apply as if it were a licensed institution. **[8]**

NOTES
Commencement: 29 December 1986.

This section derived from the Insolvency Act 1985, s 27.

9. Application for order

(1) An application to the court for an administration order shall be by petition presented either by the company or the directors, or by a creditor or creditors (including any contingent or prospective creditor or creditors), or by all or any of those parties, together or separately.

(2) Where a petition is presented to the court—

(*a*) notice of the petition shall be given forthwith to any person who has appointed, or is or may be entitled to appoint, an adminstrative receiver of the company, and to such other persons as may be prescribed, and

(*b*) the petition shall not be withdrawn except with the leave of the court.

(3) Where the court is satisfied that there is an administrative receiver of the company, the court shall dismiss the petition unless it is also satisfied either—

(*a*) that the person by whom or on whose behalf the receiver was appointed has consented to the making of the order, or

(*b*) that, if an administration order were made, any security by virtue of which the receiver was appointed would—

(i) be liable to be released or discharged under sections 238 to 240 in Part VI (transactions at an undervalue and preferences),

(ii) be avoided under section 245 in that Part (avoidance of floating charges), or

(iii) be challengeable under section 242 (gratuitous alienations) or 243 (unfair preferences) in that Part, or under any rule of law in Scotland.

(4) Subject to subsection (3), on hearing a petition the court may dismiss it, or adjourn the hearing conditionally or unconditionally, or make an interim order or any other order that it thinks fit.

(5) Without prejudice to the generality of subsection (4), an interim order under that subsection may restrict the exercise of any powers of the directors or of the company (whether by reference to the consent of the court or of a person qualified to act as an insolvency practitioner in relation to the company, or otherwise). [9]

NOTES
Commencement: 29 December 1986.
This section derived from the Insolvency Act 1985, s 28.

10. Effect of application

(1) During the period beginning with the presentation of a petition for an administration order and ending with the making of such an order or the dismissal of the petition—

(*a*) no resolution may be passed or order made for the winding up of the company;

(*b*) no steps may be taken to enforce any security over the company's property, or to repossess goods in the company's possession under any hire-purchase agreement, except with the leave of the court and subject to such terms as the court may impose; and (*c*) no other proceedings and no execution or other legal process may be commenced or continued, and no distress may be levied, against the company or its property except with the leave of the court and subject to such terms as aforesaid.

(2) Nothing in subsection (1) requires the leave of the court—

     (*a*) for the presentation of a petition for the winding up of the company,

     (*b*) for the appointment of an administrative receiver of the company, or

     (*c*) for the carrying out by such a receiver (whenever appointed) of any of his functions.

(3) Where—

     (*a*) a petition for an administration order is presented at a time when there is an administrative receiver of the company, and

     (*b*) the person by or on whose behalf the receiver was appointed has not consented to the making of the order,

the period mentioned in subsection (1) is deemed not to begin unless and until that person so consents.

(4) References in this section and the next to hire-purchase agreements include conditional sale agreements, chattel leasing agreements and retention of title agreements.

(5) In the application of this section and the next to Scotland, references to execution being commenced or continued include references to diligence being carried out or continued, and references to distress being levied shall be omitted.   **[10]**

NOTES

Commencement: 29 December 1986.

This section derived from the Insolvency Act 1985, s 29.

11. Effect of order

(1) On the making of an administration order—

     (*a*) any petition for the winding up of the company shall be dismissed, and

     (*b*) any administrative receiver of the company shall vacate office.

(2) Where an administration order has been made, any receiver of part of the company's property shall vacate office on being required to do so by the administrator.

(3) During the period for which an administration order is in force—

     (*a*) no resolution may be passed or order made for the winding up of the company;

     (*b*) no administrative receiver of the company may be appointed;

     (*c*) no other steps may be taken to enforce any security over the company's property, or to repossess goods in the company's possession under any hire-purchase agreement, except with the consent of the administrator or the leave of the court and subject (where the court gives leave) to such terms as the court may impose; and

     (*d*) no other proceedings and no execution or other legal process may be commenced or continued, and no distress may be levied, against the company or its property except with the consent of the administrator or the leave of the court and subject (where the court gives leave) to such terms as aforesaid.

(4) Where at any time an administrative receiver of the company has vacated office under subsection (1)(*b*), or a receiver of part of the company's property has vacated office under subsection (2)—

  (*a*) his remuneration and any expenses properly incurred by him, and
  (*b*) any indemnity to which he is entitled out of the assets of the company,

shall be charged on and (subject to subsection (3) above) paid out of any property of the company which was in his custody or under his control at that time in priority to any security held by the person by or on whose behalf he was appointed.

(5) Neither an administrative receiver who vacates office under subsection (1)(*b*) nor a receiver who vacates office under subsection (2) is required on or after so vacating office to take any steps for the purpose of complying with any duty imposed on him by section 40 or 59 of this Act (duty to pay preferential creditors). **[11]**

NOTES
  Commencement: 29 December 1986.
  This section derived from the Insolvency Act 1985, s 30.

12. Notification of order

(1) Every invoice, order for goods or business letter which, at a time when an administration order is in force in relation to a company, is issued by or on behalf of the company or the administrator, being a document on or in which the company's name appears, shall also contain the administrator's name and a statement that the affairs, business and property of the company are being managed by the administrator.

(2) If default is made in complying with this section, the company and any of the following persons who without reasonable excuse authorises or permits the default, namely, the administrator and any officer of the company, is liable to a fine. **[12]**

NOTES
  Commencement: 29 December 1986.
  This section derived from the Insolvency Act 1985, s 31.

Administrators

13. Appointment of administrator

(1) The administrator of a company shall be appointed either by the administration order or by an order under the next subsection.

(2) If a vacancy occurs by death, resignation or otherwise in the office of the administrator, the court may by order fill the vacancy.

(3) An application for an order under subsection (2) may be made—

  (*a*) by any continuing administrator of the company; or
  (*b*) where there is no such administrator, by a creditors' committee established under section 26 below; or
  (*c*) where there is no such administrator and no such committee, by the company or the directors or by any creditor or creditors of the company. **[13]**

NOTES
  Commencement: 29 December 1986.

This section derived from the Insolvency Act 1985, s 32.

14. General powers

(1) The administrator of a company—

    (a) may do all such things as may be necessary for the management of the affairs, business and property of the company, and

    (b) without prejudice to the generality of paragraph (a), has the powers specified in Schedule 1 to this Act;

and in the application of that Schedule to the administrator of a company the words "he" and "him" refer to the administrator.

(2) The administrator also has power—

    (a) to remove any director of the company and to appoint any person to be a director of it, whether to fill a vacancy or otherwise, and

    (b) to call any meeting of the members or creditors of the company.

(3) The administrator may apply to the court for directions in relation to any particular matter arising in connection with the carrying out of his functions.

(4) Any power conferred on the company or its officers, whether by this Act or the Companies Act or by the memorandum or articles of association, which could be exercised in such a way as to interfere with the exercise by the administrator of his powers is not exercisable except with the consent of the administrator, which may be given either generally or in relation to particular cases.

(5) In exercising his powers the administrator is deemed to act as the company's agent.

(6) A person dealing with the administrator in good faith and for value is not concerned to inquire whether the administrator is acting within his powers. **[14]**

NOTES
Commencement: 29 December 1986.
This section derived from the Insolvency Act 1985, s 33.

15. Power to deal with charged property, etc

(1) The administrator of a company may dispose of or otherwise exercise his powers in relation to any property of the company which is subject to a security to which this subsection applies as if the property were not subject to the security.

(2) Where, on an application by the administrator, the court is satisfied that the disposal (with or without other assets) of—

    (a) any property of the company subject to a security to which this subsection applies, or

    (b) any goods in the possession of the company under a hire-purchase agreement,

would be likely to promote the purpose or one or more of the purposes specified in the administration order, the court may by order authorise the administrator to dispose of the property as if it were not subject to the security or to dispose of the goods as if all rights of the owner under the hire-purchase agreement were vested in the company.

(3) Subsection (1) applies to any security which, as created, was a floating charge; and subsection (2) applies to any other security.

(4) Where property is disposed of under subsection (1), the holder of the security has the same priority in respect of any property of the company directly or indirectly representing the property disposed of as he would have had in respect of the property subject to the security.

(5) It shall be a condition of an order under subsection (2) that—

    (a) the net proceeds of the disposal, and
    (b) where those proceeds are less than such amount as may be determined by the court to be the net amount which would be realised on a sale of the property or goods in the open market by a willing vendor, such sums as may be required to make good the deficiency,

shall be applied towards discharging the sums secured by the security or payable under the hire-purchase agreement.

(6) Where a condition imposed in pursuance of subsection (5) relates to two or more securities, that condition requires the net proceeds of the disposal and, where paragraph (b) of that subsection applies, the sums mentioned in that paragraph to be applied towards discharging the sums secured by those securities in the order of their priorities.

(7) An office copy of an order under subsection (2) shall, within 14 days after the making of the order, be sent by the administrator to the registrar of companies.

(8) If the administrator without reasonable excuse fails to comply with subsection (7), he is liable to a fine and, for continued contravention, to a daily default fine.

(9) References in this section to hire-purchase agreements include conditional sale agreements, chattel leasing agreements and retention of title agreements. **[15]**

NOTES
Commencement: 29 December 1986.
This section derived from the Insolvency Act 1985, s 34(1)–(8), (12).

16. Operation of s 15 in Scotland

(1) Where property is disposed of under section 15 in its application to Scotland, the administrator shall grant to the disponee an appropriate document of transfer or conveyance of the property, and—

    (a) that document, or
    (b) where any recording, intimation or registration of the document is a legal requirement for completion of title to the property, that recording, intimation or registration,

has the effect of disencumbering the property of or, as the case may be, freeing the property from the security.

(2) Where goods in the possession of the company under a hire-purchase agreement, conditional sale agreement, chattel leasing agreement or retention of title agreement are disposed of under section 15 in its application to Scotland, the disposal has the effect of extinguishing, as against the disponee, all rights of the owner of the goods under the agreement. **[16]**

NOTES
Commencement: 29 December 1986.
This section derived from the Insolvency Act 1985, s 34(9), (10).

17. General duties

(1) The administrator of a company shall, on his appointment, take into his custody or under his control all the property to which the company is or appears to be entitled.

(2) The administrator shall manage the affairs, business and property of the company—

(a) at any time before proposals have been approved (with or without modifications) under section 24 below, in accordance with any directions given by the court, and

(b) at any time after proposals have been so approved, in accordance with those proposals as from time to time revised, whether by him or a predecessor of his.

(3) The administrator shall summon a meeting of the company's creditors if—

(a) he is requested, in accordance with the rules, to do so by one-tenth, in value, of the company's creditors, or

(b) he is directed to do so by the court.   **[17]**

NOTES
Commencement: 29 December 1986.
This section derived from the Insolvency Act 1985, s 35.

18. Discharge or variation of administration order

(1) The administrator of a company may at any time apply to the court for the administration order to be discharged, or to be varied so as to specify an additional purpose.

(2) The administrator shall make an application under this section if—

(a) it appears to him that the purpose or each of the purposes specified in the order either has been achieved or is incapable of achievement; or

(b) he is required to do so by a meeting of the company's creditors summoned for the purpose in accordance with the rules.

(3) On the hearing of an application under this section, the court may by order discharge or vary the administration order and make such consequential provision as it thinks fit, or adjourn the hearing conditionally or unconditionally, or make an interim order or any other order it thinks fit.

(4) Where the administration order is discharged or varied the administrator shall, within 14 days after the making of the order effecting the discharge or variation, send an office copy of that order to the registrar of companies.

(5) If the administrator without reasonable excuse fails to comply with subsection (4), he is liable to a fine and, for continued contravention, to a daily default fine.   **[18]**

NOTES
Commencement: 29 December 1986.
This section derived from the Insolvency Act 1985, s 36.

19. Vacation of office

(1) The administrator of a company may at any time be removed from office by order of the court and may, in the prescribed circumstances, resign his office by giving notice of his resignation to the court.

(2) The administrator shall vacate office if—

(*a*) he ceases to be qualified to act as an insolvency practitioner in relation to the company, or

(*b*) the administration order is discharged.

(3) Where at any time a person ceases to be administrator, the next two subsections apply.

(4) His remuneration and any expenses properly incurred by him shall be charged on and paid out of any property of the company which is in his custody or under his control at that time in priority to any security to which section 15(1) then applies.

(5) Any sums payable in respect of debts or liabilities incurred, while he was administrator, under contracts entered into or contracts of employment adopted by him or a predecessor of his in the carrying out of his or the predecessor's functions shall be charged on and paid out of any such property as is mentioned in subsection (4) in priority to any charge arising under that subsection.

For this purpose, the administrator is not to be taken to have adopted a contract of employment by reason of anything done or omitted to be done within 14 days after his appointment. **[19]**

NOTES
Commencement: 29 December 1986.
This section derived from the Insolvency Act 1985, s 37(1)–(3).

20. Release of administrator

(1) A person who has ceased to be the administrator of a company has his release with effect from the following time, that is to say—

(*a*) in the case of a person who has died, the time at which notice is given to the court in accordance with the rules that he has ceased to hold office;

(*b*) in any other case, such time as the court may determine.

(2) Where a person has his release under this section, he is, with effect from the time specified above, discharged from all liability both in respect of acts or omissions of his in the administration and otherwise in relation to his conduct as administrator.

(3) However, nothing in this section prevents the exercise, in relation to a person who has had his release as above, of the court's powers under section 212 in Chapter X of Part IV (summary remedy against delinquent directors, liquidators, etc). **[20]**

NOTES
Commencement: 29 December 1986.
This section derived from the Insolvency Act 1985, s 37(4), (5).

Ascertainment and investigation of company's affairs

21. Information to be given by administrator

(1) Where an administration order has been made, the administrator shall—

(a) forthwith send to the company and publish in the prescribed manner a notice of the order, and

(b) within 28 days after the making of the order, unless the court otherwise directs, send such a notice to all creditors of the company (so far as he is aware of their addresses).

(2) Where an administration order has been made, the administrator shall also, within 14 days after the making of the order, send an office copy of the order to the registrar of companies and to such other persons as may be prescribed.

(3) If the administrator without reasonable excuse fails to comply with this section, he is liable to a fine and, for continued contravention, to a daily default fine. **[21]**

NOTES

Commencement: 29 December 1986.

This section derived from the Insolvency Act 1985, s 38.

22. Statement of affairs to be submitted to administrator

(1) Where an administration order has been made, the administrator shall forthwith require some or all of the persons mentioned below to make out and submit to him a statement in the prescribed form as to the affairs of the company.

(2) The statement shall be verified by affidavit by the persons required to submit it and shall show—

(a) particulars of the company's assets, debts and liabilities;

(b) the names and addresses of its creditors;

(c) the securities held by them respectively;

(d) the dates when the securities were respectively given; and

(e) such further or other information as may be prescribed.

(3) The persons referred to in subsection (1) are—

(a) those who are or have been officers of the company;

(b) those who have taken part in the company's formation at any time within one year before the date of the administration order;

(c) those who are in the company's employment or have been in its employment within that year, and are in the administrator's opinion capable of giving the information required;

(d) those who are or have been within that year officers of or in the employment of a company which is, or within that year was, an officer of the company.

In this subsection "employment" includes employment under a contract for services.

(4) Where any persons are required under this section to submit a statement of affairs to the administrator, they shall do so (subject to the next subsection) before the end of the period of 21 days beginning with the day after that on which the prescribed notice of the requirement is given to them by the administrator.

(5) The administrator, if he thinks fit, may—

  (*a*) at any time release a person from an obligation imposed on him under subsection (1) or (2), or

  (*b*) either when giving notice under subsection (4) or subsequently, extend the period so mentioned;

and where the administrator has refused to exercise a power conferred by this subsection, the court, if it thinks fit, may exercise it.

(6) If a person without reasonable excuse fails to comply with any obligation imposed under this section, he is liable to a fine and, for continued contravention, to a daily default fine. **[22]**

NOTES
Commencement: 29 December 1986.
This section derived from the Insolvency Act 1985, s 39.

Administrator's proposals

23. Statement of proposals

(1) Where an administration order has been made, the administrator shall, within 3 months (or such longer period as the court may allow) after the making of the order—

  (*a*) send to the registrar of companies and (so far as he is aware of their addresses) to all creditors a statement of his proposals for achieving the purpose or purposes specified in the order, and

  (*b*) lay a copy of the statement before a meeting of the company's creditors summoned for the purpose on not less than 14 days' notice.

(2) The administrator shall also, within 3 months (or such longer period as the court may allow) after the making of the order, either—

  (*a*) send a copy of the statement (so far as he is aware of their addresses) to all members of the company, or

  (*b*) publish in the prescribed manner a notice stating an address to which members of the company should write for copies of the statement to be sent to them free of charge.

(3) If the administrator without reasonable excuse fails to comply with this section, he is liable to a fine and, for continued contravention, to a daily default fine. **[23]**

NOTES
Commencement: 29 December 1986.
This section derived from the Insolvency Act 1985, s 40.

24. Consideration of proposals by creditors' meeting

(1) A meeting of creditors summoned under section 23 shall decide whether to approve the administrator's proposals.

(2) The meeting may approve the proposals with modifications, but shall not do so unless the administrator consents to each modification.

(3) Subject as above, the meeting shall be conducted in accordance with the rules.

(4) After the conclusion of the meeting in accordance with the rules, the administrator shall report the result of the meeting to the court and shall give

notice of that result to the registrar of companies and to such persons as may be prescribed.

(5) If a report is given to the court under subsection (4) that the meeting has declined to approve the administrator's proposals (with or without modifications), the court may by order discharge the administration order and make such consequential provision as it thinks fit, or adjourn the hearing conditionally or unconditionally, or make an interim order or any other order that it thinks fit.

(6) Where the administration order is discharged, the administrator shall, within 14 days after the making of the order effecting the discharge, send an office copy of that order to the registrar of companies.

(7) If the administrator without reasonable excuse fails to comply with subsection (6), he is liable to a fine and, for continued contravention, to a daily default fine.   **[24]**

NOTES
Commencement: 29 December 1986.
This section derived from the Insolvency Act 1985, s 41.

25. Approval of substantial revisions

(1) This section applies where—

- (a) proposals have been approved (with or without modifications) under section 24, and
- (b) the administrator proposes to make revisions of those proposals which appear to him substantial.

(2) The administrator shall—

- (a) send to all creditors of the company (so far as he is aware of their addresses) a statement in the prescribed form of his proposed revisions, and
- (b) lay a copy of the statement before a meeting of the company's creditors summoned for the purpose on not less than 14 days' notice;

and he shall not make the proposed revisions unless they are approved by the meeting.

(3) The administrator shall also either—

- (a) send a copy of the statement (so far as he is aware of their addresses) to all members of the company, or
- (b) publish in the prescribed manner a notice stating an address to which members of the company should write for copies of the statement to be sent to them free of charge.

(4) The meeting of creditors may approve the proposed revisions with modifications, but shall not do so unless the administrator consents to each modification.

(5) Subject as above, the meeting shall be conducted in accordance with the rules.

(6) After the conclusion of the meeting in accordance with the rules, the administrator shall give notice of the result of the meeting to the registrar of companies and to such persons as may be prescribed.   **[25]**

NOTES
Commencement: 29 December 1986.
This section derived from the Insolvency Act 1985, s 42.

Miscellaneous

26. Creditors' committee

(1) Where a meeting of creditors summoned under section 23 has approved the administrator's proposals (with or without modifications), the meeting may, if it thinks fit, establish a committee ("the creditors' committee") to exercise the functions conferred on it by or under this Act.

(2) If such a committee is established, the committee may, on giving not less than 7 days' notice, require the administrator to attend before it at any reasonable time and furnish it with such information relating to the carrying out of his functions as it may reasonably require. **[26]**

NOTES
Commencement: 29 December 1986.
This section derived from the Insolvency Act 1985, s 43.

27. Protection of interests of creditors and members

(1) At any time when an administration order is in force, a creditor or member of the company may apply to the court by petition for an order under this section on the ground—

(*a*) that the company's affairs, business and property are being or have been managed by the administrator in a manner which is unfairly prejudicial to the interests of its creditors or members generally, or of some part of its creditors or members (including at least himself), or

(*b*) that any actual or proposed act or omission of the administrator is or would be so prejudicial.

(2) On an application for an order under this section the court may, subject as follows, make such order as it thinks fit for giving relief in respect of the matters complained of, or adjourn the hearing conditionally or unconditionally, or make an interim order or any other order that it thinks fit.

(3) An order under this section shall not prejudice or prevent—

(*a*) the implementation of a voluntary arrangement approved under section 4 in Part I, or any compromise or arrangement sanctioned under section 425 of the Companies Act; or

(*b*) where the application for the order was made more than 28 days after the approval of any proposals or revised proposals under section 24 or 25, the implementation of those proposals or revised proposals.

(4) Subject as above, an order under this section may in particular—

(*a*) regulate the future management by the administrator of the company's affairs, business and property;

(*b*) require the administrator to refrain from doing or continuing an act complained of by the petitioner, or to do an act which the petitioner has complained he has omitted to do;

(*c*) require the summoning of a meeting of creditors or members for the purpose of considering such matters as the court may direct;

(*d*) discharge the administration order and make such consequential provision as the court thinks fit.

(5) Nothing in section 15 or 16 is to be taken as prejudicing applications to the court under this section.

(6) Where the administration order is discharged, the administrator shall, within 14 days after the making of the order effecting the discharge, send an office copy of that order to the registrar of companies; and if without reasonable excuse he fails to comply with this subsection, he is liable to a fine and, for continued contravention, to a daily default fine.   **[27]**

NOTES
Commencement: 29 December 1986.
This section derived from the Insolvency Act 1985, ss 34(11), 44.

PART III

RECEIVERSHIP

CHAPTER 1

RECEIVERS AND MANAGERS (ENGLAND AND WALES)

Preliminary and general provisions

28. Extent of this Chapter

This Chapter does not apply to receivers appointed under Chapter II of this Part (Scotland).   **[28]**

NOTES
Commencement: 29 December 1986.
This section derived from the Companies Act 1985, s 488, and the Insolvency Act 1985, s 45(1).

29. Definitions

(1) It is hereby declared that, except where the context otherwise requires—

  (a) any reference in the Companies Act or this Act to a receiver or manager of the property of a company, or to a receiver of it, includes a receiver or manager, or (as the case may be) a receiver of part only of that property and a receiver only of the income arising from the property or from part of it; and

  (b) any reference in the Companies Act or this Act to the appointment of a receiver or manager under powers contained in an instrument includes an appointment made under powers which, by virtue of an enactment, are implied in and have effect as if contained in an instrument.

(2) In this Chapter "administrative receiver" means—

  (a) a receiver or manager of the whole (or substantially the whole) of a company's property appointed by or on behalf of the holders of any debentures of the company secured by a charge which, as created, was a floating charge, or by such a charge and one or more other securities; or

  (b) a person who would be such a receiver or manager but for the appointment of some other person as the receiver of part of the company's property.   **[29]**

NOTES
Commencement: 29 December 1986.

This section derived from the Companies Act 1985, s 500, and the Insolvency Act 1985, s 45(2).

30. Disqualification of body corporate from acting as receiver

A body corporate is not qualified for appointment as receiver of the property of a company, and any body corporate which acts as such a receiver is liable to a fine. **[30]**

NOTES
Commencement: 29 December 1986.
This section derived from the Companies Act 1985, s 489.

31. Disqualification of undischarged bankrupt

If a person being an undischarged bankrupt acts as receiver or manager of the property of a company on behalf of debenture holders, he is liable to imprisonment or a fine, or both.

This does not apply to a receiver or manager acting under an appointment made by the court. **[31]**

NOTES
Commencement: 29 December 1986.
This section derived from the Companies Act 1985, s 490.

32. Power for court to appoint official receiver

Where application is made to the court to appoint a receiver on behalf of the debenture holders or other creditors of a company which is being wound up by the court, the official receiver may be appointed. **[32]**

NOTES
Commencement: 29 December 1986.
This section derived from the Companies Act 1985, s 491.

Receivers and managers appointed out of court

33. Time from which appointment is effective

(1) The appointment of a person as a receiver or manager of a company's property under powers contained in an instrument—

   (*a*) is of no effect unless it is accepted by that person before the end of the business day next following that on which the instrument of appointment is received by him or on his behalf, and

   (*b*) subject to this, is deemed to be made at the time at which the instrument of appointment is so received.

(2) This section applies to the appointment of two or more persons as joint receivers or managers of a company's property under powers contained in an instrument, subject to such modifications as may be prescribed by the rules.**[33]**

NOTES
Commencement: 29 December 1986.
This section derived from the Insolvency Act 1985, s 46.

34. Liability for invalid appointment

Where the appointment of a person as the receiver or manager of a company's property under powers contained in an instrument is discovered to be invalid (whether by virtue of the invalidity of the instrument or otherwise), the court may order the person by whom or on whose behalf the appointment was made to indemnify the person appointed against any liability which arises solely by reason of the invalidity of the appointment. **[34]**

NOTES
Commencement: 29 December 1986.
This section derived from the Insolvency Act 1985, s 47.

35. Application to court for directions

(1) A receiver or manager of the property of a company appointed under powers contained in an instrument, or the persons by whom or on whose behalf a receiver or manager has been so appointed, may apply to the court for directions in relation to any particular matter arising in connection with the performance of the functions of the receiver or manager.

(2) On such an application, the court may give such directions, or may make such order declaring the rights of persons before the court or otherwise, as it thinks just. **[35]**

NOTES
Commencement: 29 December 1986.
This section derived from the Companies Act 1985, s 492(1), (2), and the Insolvency Act 1985, Sch 6, para 16(2).

36. Court's power to fix remuneration

(1) The court may, on an application made by the liquidator of a company, by order fix the amount to be paid by way of remuneration to a person who, under powers contained in an instrument, has been appointed receiver or manager of the company's property.

(2) The court's power under subsection(1), where no previous order has been made with respect thereto under the subsection—

    (a) extends to fixing the remuneration for any period before the making of the order or the application for it,

    (b) is exercisable notwithstanding that the receiver or manager has died or ceased to act before the making of the order or the application, and

    (c) where the receiver or manager has been paid or has retained for his remuneration for any period before the making of the order any amount in excess of that so fixed for that period, extends to requiring him or his personal representatives to account for the excess or such part of it as may be specified in the order.

But the power conferred by paragraph (c) shall not be exercised as respects any period before the making of the application for the order under this section, unless in the court's opinion there are special circumstances making it proper for the power to be exercised.

(3) The court may from time to time on an application made either by the liquidator or by the receiver or manager, vary or amend an order made under subsection (1). **[36]**

NOTES
Commencement: 29 December 1986.
This section derived from the Companies Act 1985, s 494.

37. Liability for contracts, etc

(1) A receiver or manager appointed under powers contained in an instrument (other than an administrative receiver) is, to the same extent as if he had been appointed by order of the court—

    (*a*) personally liable on any contract entered into by him in the performance of his functions (except in so far as the contract otherwise provides) and on any contract of employment adopted by him in the performance of those functions, and

    (*b*) entitled in respect of that liability to indemnity out of the assets.

(2) For the purposes of subsection (1)(*a*), the receiver or manager is not to be taken to have adopted a contract of employment by reason of anything done or omitted to be done within 14 days after his appointment.

(3) Subsection (1) does not limit any right to indemnity which the receiver or manager would have apart from it, nor limit his liability on contracts entered into without authority, nor confer any right to indemnity in respect of that liability.

(4) Where at any time the receiver or manager so appointed vacates office—

    (*a*) his remuneration and any expenses properly incurred by him, and

    (*b*) any indemnity to which he is entitled out of the assets of the company,

shall be charged on and paid out of any property of the company which is in his custody or under his control at that time in priority to any charge or other security held by the person by or on whose behalf he was appointed. **[37]**

NOTES
    Commencement: 29 December 1986.
    This section derived from the Companies Act 1985, s 492(3), and the Insolvency Act 1985, Sch 6, para 16(3), (4).

38. Receivership accounts to be delivered to registrar

(1) Except in the case of an administrative receiver, every receiver or manager of a company's property who has been appointed under powers contained in an instrument shall deliver to the registrar of companies for registration the requisite accounts of his receipts and payments.

(2) The accounts shall be delivered within one month (or such longer period as the registrar may allow) after the expiration of 12 months from the date of his appointment and of every subsequent period of 6 months, and also within one month after he ceases to act as receiver or manager.

(3) The requisite accounts shall be an abstract in the prescribed form showing—

    (*a*) receipts and payments during the relevant period of 12 or 6 months, or

    (*b*) where the receiver or manager ceases to act, receipts and payments during the period from the end of the period of 12 or 6 months to which the last preceding abstract related (or, if no preceding abstract has been delivered under this section, from the date of his appointment) up to the date of his so ceasing, and the aggregate amount of receipts and payments during all preceding periods since his appointment.

(4) In this section "prescribed" means prescribed by regulations made by statutory instrument by the Secretary of State.

(5) A receiver or manager who makes default in complying with this section is liable to a fine and, for continued contravention, to a daily default fine.   **[38]**

NOTES
Commencement: 29 December 1986.
This section derived from the Companies Act 1985, s 498, and the Insolvency Act 1985, Sch 6, para 17.

Provisions applicable to every receivership

39. Notification that receiver or manager appointed

(1) When a receiver or manager of the property of a company has been appointed, every invoice, order for goods or business letter issued by or on behalf of the company or the receiver or manager or the liquidator of the company, being a document on or in which the company's name appears, shall contain a statement that a receiver or manager has been appointed.

(2) If default is made in complying with this section, the company and any of the following persons, who knowingly and wilfully authorises or permits the default, namely, any officer of the company, any liquidator of the company and any receiver or manager, is liable to a fine.   **[39]**

NOTES
Commencement: 29 December 1986.
This section derived from the Companies Act 1985, s 493.

40. Payment of debts out of assets subject to floating charge

(1) The following applies, in the case of a company, where a receiver is appointed on behalf of the holders of any debentures of the company secured by a charge which, as created, was a floating charge.

(2) If the company is not at the time in course of being wound up, its preferential debts (within the meaning given to that expression by section 386 in Part XII) shall be paid out of the assets coming to the hands of the receiver in priority to any claims for principal or interest in respect of the debentures.

(3) Payments made under this section shall be recouped, as far as may be, out of the assets of the company available for payment of general creditors. **[40]**

NOTES
Commencement: 29 December 1986.
This section derived from the Companies Act 1985, s 196 (part), and the Insolvency Act 1985, Sch 6, para 15(2), (3).

41. Enforcement of duty to make returns

(1) If a receiver or manager of a company's property—

(*a*) having made default in filing, delivering or making any return, account or other document, or in giving any notice, which a receiver or manager is by law required to file, deliver, make or give, fails to make good the default within 14 days after the service on him of a notice requiring him to do so, or

(*b*) having been appointed under powers contained in an instrument, has, after being required at any time by the liquidator of the company to do so, failed to render proper accounts of his receipts and payments and to vouch them and pay over to the liquidator the amount properly payable to him,

the court may, on an application made for the purpose, make an order directing the receiver or manager (as the case may be) to make good the default within such time as may be specified in the order.

(2) In the case of the default mentioned in subsection (1)(*a*), application to the court may be made by any member or creditor of the company or by the registrar of companies; and in the case of the default mentioned in subsection (1)(*b*), the application shall be made by the liquidator.

In either case the court's order may provide that all costs of and incidental to the application shall be borne by the receiver or manager, as the case may be.

(3) Nothing in this section prejudices the operation of any enactment imposing penalties on receivers in respect of any such default as is mentioned in subsection (1).   [41]

NOTES
Commencement: 29 December 1986.
This section derived from the Companies Act 1985, s 499.

Administrative receivers: general

42. General powers

(1) The powers conferred on the administrative receiver of a company by the debentures by virtue of which he was appointed are deemed to include (except in so far as they are inconsistent with any of the provisions of those debentures) the powers specified in Schedule 1 to this Act.

(2) In the application of Schedule 1 to the administrative receiver of a company—

    (*a*) the words "he" and "him" refer to the administrative receiver, and
    (*b*) references to the property of the company are to the property of which he is or, but for the appointment of some other person as the receiver of part of the company's property, would be the receiver or manager.

(3) A person dealing with the administrative receiver in good faith and for value is not concerned to inquire whether the receiver is acting within his powers.   [42]

NOTES
Commencement: 29 December 1986.
This section derived from the Insolvency Act 1985, s 48.

43. Power to dispose of charged property, etc

(1) Where, on an application by the administrative receiver, the court is satisfied that the disposal (with or without other assets) of any relevant property which is subject to a security would be likely to promote a more advantageous realisation of the company's assets than would otherwise be effected, the court may by order authorise the administrative receiver to dispose of the property as if it were not subject to the security.

(2) Subsection (1) does not apply in the case of any security held by the person by or on whose behalf the administrative receiver was appointed, or of any security to which a security so held has priority.

(3) It shall be a condition of an order under this section that—

    (*a*) the net proceeds of the disposal, and

    (*b*) where those proceeds are less than such amount as may be determined by the court to be the net amount which would be realised on a sale of the property in the open market by a willing vendor, such sums as may be required to make good the deficiency,

shall be applied towards discharging the sums secured by the security.

(4) Where a condition imposed in pursuance of subsection (3) relates to two or more securities, that condition shall require the net proceeds of the disposal and, where paragraph (*b*) of that subsection applies, the sums mentioned in that paragraph to be applied towards discharging the sums secured by those securities in the order of their priorities.

(5) An office copy of an order under this section shall, within 14 days of the making of the order, be sent by the administrative receiver to the registrar of companies.

(6) If the administrative receiver without reasonable excuse fails to comply with subsection (5), he is liable to a fine and, for continued contravention, to a daily default fine.

(7) In this section "relevant property", in relation to the administrative receiver, means the property of which he is or, but for the appointment of some other person as the receiver of part of the company's property, would be the receiver or manager.   **[43]**

NOTES
Commencement: 29 December 1986.
This section derived from the Insolvency Act 1985, s 49.

44. Agency and liability for contracts

(1) The administrative receiver of a company—

    (*a*) is deemed to be the company's agent, unless and until the company goes into liquidation;

    (*b*) is personally liable on any contract entered into by him in the carrying out of his functions (except in so far as the contract otherwise provides) and on any contract of employment adopted by him in the carrying out of those functions; and

    (*c*) is entitled in respect of that liability to an indemnity out of the assets of the company.

(2) For the purposes of subsection (1)(*b*) the administrative receiver is not to be taken to have adopted a contract of employment by reason of anything done or omitted to be done within 14 days after his appointment.

(3) This section does not limit any right to indemnity which the administrative receiver would have apart from it, nor limit his liability on contracts entered into or adopted without authority, nor confer any right to indemnity in respect of that liability.   **[44]**

NOTES
Commencement: 29 December 1986.
This section derived from the Insolvency Act 1985, s 50.

45. Vacation of office

(1) An administrative receiver of a company may at any time be removed from office by order of the court (but not otherwise) and may resign his office by giving notice of his resignation in the prescribed manner to such persons as may be prescribed.

(2) An administrative receiver shall vacate office if he ceases to be qualified to act as an insolvency practitioner in relation to the company.

(3) Where at any time an administrative receiver vacates office—

    (*a*) his remuneration and any expenses properly incurred by him, and

    (*b*) any indemnity to which he is entitled out of the assets of the company,

shall be charged on and paid out of any property of the company which is in his custody or under his control at that time in priority to any security held by the person by or on whose behalf he was appointed.

(4) Where an administrative receiver vacates office otherwise than by death, he shall, within 14 days after his vacation of office, send a notice to that effect to the registrar of companies.

(5) If an administrative receiver without reasonable excuse fails to comply with subsection (4), he is liable to a fine and, for continued contravention, to a daily default fine. **[45]**

NOTES

Commencement: 29 December 1986.

This section derived from the Insolvency Act 1985, s 51.

Administrative receivers: ascertainment and investigation of company's affairs

46. Information to be given by administrative receiver

(1) Where an administrative receiver is appointed, he shall—

    (*a*) forthwith send to the company and publish in the prescribed manner a notice of his appointment, and

    (*b*) within 28 days after his appointment, unless the court otherwise directs, send such a notice to all the creditors of the company (so far as he is aware of their addresses).

(2) This section and the next do not apply in relation to the appointment of an administrative receiver to act—

    (*a*) with an existing administrative receiver, or

    (*b*) in place of an administrative receiver dying or ceasing to act,

except that, where they apply to an administrative receiver who dies or ceases to act before they have been fully complied with, the references in this section and the next to the administrative receiver include (subject to the next subsection) his successor and any continuing administrative receiver.

(3) If the company is being wound up, this section and the next apply notwithstanding that the administrative receiver and the liquidator are the same person, but with any necessary modifications arising from that fact.

(4) If the administrative receiver without reasonable excuse fails to comply with this section, he is liable to a fine and, for continued contravention, to a daily default fine. **[46]**

NOTES
    Commencement: 29 December 1986.
    This section derived from the Insolvency Act 1985, s 52.

47. Statement of affairs to be submitted

(1) Where an administrative receiver is appointed, he shall forthwith require some or all of the persons mentioned below to make out and submit to him a statement in the prescribed form as to the affairs of the company.

(2) A statement submitted under this section shall be verified by affidavit by the persons required to submit it and shall show—

    (a) particulars of the company's assets, debts and liabilities;
    (b) the names and addresses of its creditors;
    (c) the securities held by them respectively;
    (d) the dates when the securities were respectively given; and
    (e) such further or other information as may be prescribed.

(3) The persons referred to in subsection (1) are—

    (a) those who are or have been officers of the company;
    (b) those who have taken part in the company's formation at any time within one year before the date of the appointment of the administrative receiver;
    (c) those who are in the company's employment, or have been in its employment within that year, and are in the administrative receiver's opinion capable of giving the information required;
    (d) those who are or have been within that year officers of or in the employment of a company which is, or within that year was, an officer of the company.

In this subsection "employment" includes employment under a contract for services.

(4) Where any persons are required under this section to submit a statement of affairs to the administrative receiver, they shall do so (subject to the next subsection) before the end of the period of 21 days beginning with the day after that on which the prescribed notice of the requirement is given to them by the administrative receiver.

(5) The administrative receiver, if he thinks fit, may—

    (a) at any time release a person from an obligation imposed on him under subsection (1) or (2), or
    (b) either when giving notice under subsection (4) or subsequently, extend the period so mentioned;

and where the administrative receiver has refused to exercise a power conferred by this subsection, the court, if it thinks fit, may exercise it.

(6) If a person without reasonable excuse fails to comply with any obligation imposed under this section, he is liable to a fine and, for continued contravention, to a daily default fine.   [47]

NOTES
    Commencement: 29 December 1986.
    This section derived from the Insolvency Act 1985, s 53.

48. Report by administrative receiver

(1) Where an administrative receiver is appointed, he shall, within 3 months (or such longer period as the court may allow) after his appointment, send to the registrar of companies, to any trustees for secured creditors of the company and (so far as he is aware of their addresses) to all such creditors a report as to the following matters, namely—

    (a) the events leading up to his appointment, so far as he is aware of them;

    (b) the disposal or proposed disposal by him of any property of the company and the carrying on or proposed carrying on by him of any business of the company;

    (c) the amounts of principal and interest payable to the debenture holders by whom or on whose behalf he was appointed and the amounts payable to preferential creditors; and

    (d) the amount (if any) likely to be available for the payment of other creditors.

(2) The administrative receiver shall also, within 3 months (or such longer period as the court may allow) after his appointment, either—

    (a) send a copy of the report (so far as he is aware of their addresses) to all unsecured creditors of the company; or

    (b) publish in the prescribed manner a notice stating an address to which unsecured creditors of the company should write for copies of the report to be sent to them free of charge,

and (in either case), unless the court otherwise directs, lay a copy of the report before a meeting of the company's unsecured creditors summoned for the purpose on not less than 14 days' notice.

(3) The court shall not give a direction under subsection (2) unless—

    (a) the report states the intention of the administrative receiver to apply for the direction, and

    (b) a copy of the report is sent to the persons mentioned in paragraph (a) of that subsection, or a notice is published as mentioned in paragraph (b) of that subsection, not less than 14 days before the hearing of the application.

(4) Where the company has gone or goes into liquidation, the administrative receiver—

    (a) shall, within 7 days after his compliance with subsection (1) or, if later, the nomination or appointment of the liquidator, send a copy of the report to the liquidator, and

    (b) where he does so within the time limited for compliance with subsection (2), is not required to comply with that subsection.

(5) A report under this section shall include a summary of the statement of affairs made out and submitted to the administrative receiver under section 47 and of his comments (if any) upon it.

(6) Nothing in this section is to be taken as requiring any such report to include any information the disclosure of which would seriously prejudice the carrying out by the administrative receiver of his functions.

(7) Section 46(2) applies for the purposes of this section also.

(8) If the administrative receiver without reasonable excuse fails to comply with this section, he is liable to a fine and, for continued contravention, to a daily default fine. **[48]**

NOTES
Commencement: 29 December 1986.
This section derived from the Insolvency Act 1985, s 54.

49. Committee of creditors

(1) Where a meeting of creditors is summoned under section 48, the meeting may, if it thinks fit, establish a committee ("the creditors' committee") to exercise the functions conferred on it by or under this Act.

(2) If such a committee is established, the committee may, on giving not less than 7 days' notice, require the administrative receiver to attend before it at any reasonable time and furnish it with such information relating to the carrying out by him of his functions as it may reasonably require. **[49]**

NOTES
Commencement: 29 December 1986.
This section derived from the Insolvency Act 1985, s 55.

CHAPTER II

RECEIVERS (SCOTLAND)

50. Extent of this Chapter

This Chapter extends to Scotland only. **[50]**

NOTES
Commencement: 29 December 1986.
This section derived from the Companies Act 1985, s 487.

51. Power to appoint receiver

(1) It is competent under the law of Scotland for the holder of a floating charge overall or any part of the property (including uncalled capital), which may from time to time be comprised in the property and undertaking of an incorporated company (whether a company within the meaning of the Companies Act or not) which the Court of Session has jurisdiction to wind up, to appoint a receiver of such part of the property of the company as is subject to the charge.

(2) It is competent under the law of Scotland for the court, on the application of the holder of such a floating charge, to appoint a receiver of such part of the property of the company as is subject to the charge.

(3) The following are disqualified from being appointed as receiver—

    (*a*) a body corporate;
    (*b*) an undischarged bankrupt; and
    (*c*) a firm according to the law of Scotland.

(4) A body corporate or a firm according to the law of Scotland which acts as a receiver is liable to a fine.

(5) An undischarged bankrupt who so acts is liable to imprisonment or a fine, or both.

(6) In this section, "receiver" includes joint receivers. **[51]**

NOTES
Commencement: 29 December 1986.
This section derived from the Companies Act 1985, s 467.

52. Circumstances justifying appointment

(1) A receiver may be appointed under section 51(1) by the holder of the floating charge on the occurrence of any event which, by the provisions of the instrument creating the charge, entitles the holder of the charge to make that appointment and, in so far as not otherwise provided for by the instrument, on the occurrence of any of the following events, namely—

(a) the expiry of a period of 21 days after the making of a demand for payment of the whole or any part of the principal sum secured by the charge, without payment having been made;

(b) the expiry of a period of 2 months during the whole of which interest due and payable under the charge has been in arrears;

(c) the making of an order or the passing of a resolution to wind up the company;

(d) the appointment of a receiver by virtue of any other floating charge created by the company.

(2) A receiver may be appointed by the court under section 51(2) on the occurrence of any event which, by the provisions of the instrument creating the floating charge, entitles the holder of the charge to make that appointment, on the occurrence of any of the following events, namely—

(a) where the court, on the application of the holder of the charge, pronounces itself satisfied that the position of the holder of the charge is likely to be prejudiced if no such appointment is made;

(b) any of the events referred to in paragraphs (a) to (c) of subsection (1).

[52]

NOTES
Commencement: 29 December 1986.
This section derived from the Companies Act 1985, s 468.

53. Mode of appointment by holder of charge

(1) The appointment of a receiver by the holder of the floating charge under section 51(1) shall be by means of a validly executed instrument in writing ("the instrument of appointment"), a copy (certified in the prescribed manner to be a correct copy) whereof shall be delivered by or on behalf of the person making the appointment to the registrar of companies for registration within 7 days of its execution and shall be accompanied by a notice in the prescribed form.

(2) If any person without reasonable excuse makes default in complying with the requirements of subsection (1), he is liable to a fine and, for continued contravention, to a daily default fine.

(3) The instrument of appointment is validly executed—

(a) by a company, if it is executed in accordance with the provisions of section 36 of the Companies Act as if it were a contract, and

(b) by any other person, if it is executed in the manner required or permitted by the law of Scotland in the case of an attested deed.

(4) The instrument may be executed on behalf of the holder of the floating charge by virtue of which the receiver is to be appointed—

(a) by any person duly authorised in writing by the holder to execute the instrument, and

(b) in the case of an appointment of a receiver by the holders of a series of secured debentures, by any person authorised by resolution of the debenture-holders to execute the instrument.

(5) On receipt of the certified copy of the instrument of appointment in accordance with subsection (1), the registrar shall, on payment of the prescribed fee, enter the particulars of the appointment in the register of charges.

(6) The appointment of a person as a receiver by an instrument of appointment in accordance with subsection (1)—

(a) is of no effect unless it is accepted by that person before the end of the business day next following that on which the instrument of appointment is received by him or on his behalf, and

(b) subject to paragraph (a), is deemed to be made on the day on and at the time at which the instrument of appointment is so received, as evidence by a written docquet by that person or on his behalf;

and this subsection applies to the appointment of joint receivers subject to such modifications as may be prescribed.

(7) On the appointment of a receiver under this section, the floating charge by virtue of which he was appointed attaches to the property then subject to the charge; and such attachment has effect as if the charge was a fixed security over the property to which it has attached. **[53]**

NOTES
    Commencement: 29 December 1986.
    This section derived from the Companies Act 1985, s 469, and the Insolvency Act 1985, s 56 (part).

54. Appointment by court

(1) Application for the appointment of a receiver by the court under section 51(2) shall be by petition to the court, which shall be served on the company.

(2) On such an application, the court shall, if it thinks fit, issue an interlocutor making the appointment of the receiver.

(3) A copy (certified by the clerk of the court to be a correct copy) of the court's interlocutor making the appointment shall be delivered by or on behalf of the petitioner to the registrar of companies for registration, accompanied by a notice in the prescribed form within 7 days of the date of the interlocutor or such longer period as the court may allow.
    If any person without reasonable excuse makes default in complying with the requirements of this subsection, he is liable to a fine and, for continued contravention, to a daily default fine.

(4) On receipt of the certified copy interlocutor in accordance with subsection (3), the registrar shall, on payment of the prescribed fee, enter the particulars of the appointment in the register of charges.

(5) The receiver is to be regarded as having been appointed on the date of his being appointed by the court.

(6) On the appointment of a receiver under this section, the floating charge by virtue of which he was appointed attaches to the property then subject to the charge; and such attachment has effect as if the charge were a fixed security over the property to which it has attached.

(7) In making rules of court for the purposes of this section, the Court of Session shall have regard to the need for special provision for cases which appear to the court to require to be dealt with as a matter of urgency. **[54]**

NOTES
Commencement: 29 December 1986.
This section derived from the Companies Act 1985, s 470.

55. Powers of receiver

(1) Subject to the next subsection, a receiver has in relation to such part of the property of the company as is attached by the floating charge by virtue of which he was appointed, the powers, if any, given to him by the instrument creating that charge.

(2) In addition, the receiver has under this Chapter the powers as respects that property (in so far as these are not inconsistent with any provision contained in that instrument) which are specified in Schedule 2 to this Act.

(3) Subsections (1) and (2) apply—

(a) subject to the rights of any person who has effectually executed diligence on all or any part of the property of the company prior to the appointment of the receiver, and

(b) subject to the rights of any person who holds over all or any part of the property of the company a fixed security or floating charge having priority over, or ranking pari passu with, the floating charge by virtue of which the receiver was appointed.

(4) A person dealing with a receiver in good faith and for value is not concerned to enquire whether the receiver is acting within his powers. **[55]**

NOTES
Commencement: 29 December 1986.
This section derived from the Companies Act 1985, s 471, and the Insolvency Act 1985, s 57.

56. Precedence among receivers

(1) Where there are two or more floating charges subsisting over all or any part of the property of the company, a receiver may be appointed under this Chapter by virtue of each such charge; but a receiver appointed by, or on the application of, the holder of a floating charge having priority of ranking over any other floating charge by virtue of which a receiver has been appointed has the powers given to a receiver by section 55 and Schedule 2 to the exclusion of any other receiver.

(2) Where two or more floating charges rank with one another equally, and two or more receivers have been appointed by virtue of such charges, the receivers so appointed are deemed to have been appointed as joint receivers.

(3) Receivers appointed, or deemed to have been appointed, as joint receivers shall act jointly unless the instrument of appointment or respective instruments of appointment otherwise provide.

(4) Subject to subsection (5) below, the powers of a receiver appointed by, or on the application of, the holder of a floating charge are suspended by, and as from the date of, the appointment of a receiver by, or on the application of, the holder of a floating charge having priority of ranking over that charge to such extent as may be necessary to enable the receiver second mentioned to exercise his powers under section 55 and Schedule 2; and any powers so

suspended take effect again when the floating charge having priority of ranking ceases to attach to the property then subject to the charge, whether such cessation is by virtue of section 62(6) or otherwise.

(5) The suspension of the powers of a receiver under subsection (4) does not have the effect of requiring him to release any part of the property (including any letters or documents) of the company from his control until he receives from the receiver superseding him a valid indemnity (subject to the limit of the value of such part of the property of the company as is subject to the charge by virtue of which he was appointed) in respect of any expenses, charges and liabilities he may have incurred in the performance of his functions as receiver.

(6) The suspension of the powers of a receiver under subsection (4) does not cause the floating charge by virtue of which he was appointed to cease to attach to the property to which it attached by virtue of section 53(7) or 54(6).

(7) Nothing in this section prevents the same receiver being appointed by virtue of two or more floating charges. **[56]**

NOTES
    Commencement: 29 December 1986.
    This section derived from the Companies Act 1985, s 472.

57. Agency and liability of receiver for contracts

(1) A receiver is deemed to be the agent of the company in relation to such property of the company as is attached by the floating charge by virtue of which he was appointed.

(2) A receiver (including a receiver whose powers are subsequently suspended under section 56) is personally liable on any contract entered into by him in the performance of his functions, except in so far as the contract otherwise provides, and on any contract of employment adopted by him in the carrying out of those functions.

(3) A receiver who is personally liable by virtue of subsection (2) is entitled to be indemnified out of the property is respect of which he was appointed.

(4) Any contract entered into by or on behalf of the company prior to the appointment of a receiver continues in force (subject to its terms) notwithstanding that appointment, but the receiver does not by virtue only of his appointment incur any personal liability on any such contract.

(5) For the purposes of subsection (2), a receiver is not to be taken to have adopted a contract of employment by reason of anything done or omitted to be done within 14 days after his appointment.

(6) This section does not limit any right to indemnity which the receiver would have apart from it, nor limit his liability on contracts entered into or adopted without authority, nor confer any right to indemnity in respect of that liability.

(7) Any contract entered into by a receiver in the performance of his functions continues in force (subject to its terms) although the powers of the receiver are subsequently suspended under section 56. **[57]**

NOTES
    Commencement: 29 December 1986.
    This section derived from the Companies Act 1985, s 473, and the Insolvency Act 1985, s 58.

58. Remuneration of receiver

(1) The remuneration to be paid to a receiver is to be determined by agreement between the receiver and the holder of the floating charge by virtue of which he was appointed.

(2) Where the remuneration to be paid to the receiver has not been determined under subsection (1), or where it has been so determined but is disputed by any of the persons mentioned in paragraphs (*a*) to (*d*) below, it may be fixed instead by the Auditor of the Court of Session on application made to him by—

    (*a*) the receiver;
    (*b*) the holder of any floating charge or fixed security over all or any part of the property of the company;
    (*c*) the company; or
    (*d*) the liquidator of the company.

(3) Where the receiver has been paid or has retained for his remuneration for any period before the remuneration has been fixed by the Auditor of the Court of Session under subsection (2) any amount in excess of the remuneration so fixed for that period, the receiver or his personal representatives shall account for the excess. **[58]**

NOTES
    Commencement: 29 December 1986.
    This section derived from the Companies Act 1985, s 474.

59. Priority of debts

(1) Where a receiver is appointed and the company is not at the time of the appointment in course of being wound up, the debts which fall under subsection (2) of this section shall be paid out of any assets coming to the hands of the receiver in priority to any claim for principal or interest by the holder of the floating charge by virtue of which the receiver was appointed.

(2) Debts falling under this subsection are preferential debts (within the meaning given by section 386 in Part XII) which, by the end of a period of 6 months after advertisement by the receiver for claims in the Edinburgh Gazette and in a newspaper circulating in the district where the company carries on business either—

    (i) have been intimated to him, or
    (ii) have become known to him.

(3) Any payments made under this section shall be recouped as assets of the company available for payment of ordinary creditors. **[59]**

NOTES
    Commencement: 29 December 1986.
    This section derived from the Companies Act 1985, s 475, and the Insolvency Act 1985, Sch 6, para 20(1), (2).

60. Distribution of moneys

(1) Subject to the next section, and to the rights of any of the following categories of persons (which rights shall, except to the extent otherwise provided in any instrument, have the following order of priority), namely—

(a) the holder of any fixed security which is over property subject to the floating charge and which ranks prior to, or pari passu with, the floating charge;

(b) all persons who have effectually executed diligence on any part of the property of the company which is subject to the charge by virtue of which the receiver was appointed;

(c) creditors in respect of all liabilities, charges and expenses incurred by or on behalf of the receiver;

(d) the receiver in respect of his liabilities, expenses and remuneration, and any indemnity to which he is entitled out of the property of the company; and

(e) the preferential creditors entitled to payment under section 59,

the receiver shall pay moneys received by him to the holder of the floating charge by virtue of which the receiver was appointed in or towards satisfaction of the debt secured by the floating charge.

(2) Any balance of moneys remaining after the provisions of subsection (1) and section 61 below have been satisfied shall be paid in accordance with their respective rights and interests to the following persons, as the case may require—

(a) any other receiver;

(b) the holder of a fixed security which is over property subject to the floating charge;

(c) the company or its liquidator, as the case may be.

(3) Where any question arises as to the person entitled to a payment under this section, or where a receipt or a discharge of a security shall consign the amount of such payment in any joint stock bank of issue in Scotland in name of the Accountant of Court for behoof of the person or persons entitled thereto.

[60]

NOTES
Commencement: 29 December 1986.
This section derived from the Companies Act 1985, s 476, and the Insolvency Act 1985, Sch 6, para 21.

61. Disposal of interest in property

(1) Where the receiver sells or disposes, or is desirous of selling or disposing, of any property or interest in property of the company which is subject to the floating charge by virtue of which the receiver was appointed and which is—

(a) subject to any security or interest of, or burden or encumbrance in favour of, a creditor the ranking of which is prior to, or pari passu with, or postponed to the floating charge, or

(b) property or an interest in property affected or attached by effectual diligence executed by any person,

and the receiver is unable to obtain the consent of such creditor or, as the case may be, such person to such a sale or disposal, the receiver may apply to the court for authority to sell or dispose of the property or interest in property free of such security, interest, burden, encumbrance or diligence.

(2) Subject to the next subsection, on such an application the court may, if it thinks fit, authorise the sale or disposal of the property or interest in question free of such security, interest, burden, encumbrance or diligence, and such authorisation may be on such terms or conditions as the court thinks fit.

(3) In the case of an application where a fixed security over the property or

interest in question which ranks prior to the floating charge has not been met or provided for in full, the court shall not authorise the sale or disposal of the property or interest in question unless it is satisfied that the sale or disposal would be likely to provide a more advantageous realisation of the company's assets than would otherwise be effected.

(4) It shall be a condition of an authorisation to which subsection (3) applies that—

    (*a*) the net proceeds of the disposal, and

    (*b*) where those proceeds are less than such amount as may be determined by the court to be the net amount which would be realised on a sale of the property or interest in the open market by a willing seller, such sums as may be required to make good the deficiency,

shall be applied towards discharging the sums secured by the fixed security.

(5) Where a condition imposed in pursuance of subsection (4) relates to two or more such fixed securities, that condition shall require the net proceeds of the disposal and, where paragraph (*b*) of that subsection applies, the sums mentioned in that paragraph to be applied towards discharging the sums secured by those fixed securities in the order of their priorities.

(6) A copy of an authorisation under subsection (2) certified by the clerk of court shall, within 14 days of the granting of the authorisation, be sent by the receiver to the registrar of companies.

(7) If the receiver without reasonable excuse fails to comply with subsection (6), he is liable to a fine and, for continued contravention, to a daily default fine.

(8) Where any sale or disposal is effected in accordance with the authorisation of the court under subsection (2), the receiver shall grant to the purchaser or disponee an appropriate document of transfer or conveyance of the property or interest in question, and that document has the effect, or, where recording, intimation or registration of that document is a legal requirement for completion of title to the property or interest, then that recording, intimation or registration (as the case may be) has the effect, of—

    (*a*) disencumbering the property or interest of the security, interest, burden or encumbrance affecting it, and

    (*b*) freeing the property or interest from the diligence executed upon it.

(9) Nothing in this section prejudices the right of any creditor of the company to rank for his debt in the winding up of the company.   **[61]**

NOTES
    Commencement: 29 December 1986.
    This section derived from the Companies Act 1985, s 477, and the Insolvency Act 1985, s 59.

62. Cessation of appointment of receiver

(1) A receiver may be removed from office by the court under subsection (3) below and may resign his office by giving notice of his resignation in the prescribed manner to such persons as may be prescribed.

(2) A receiver shall vacate office if he ceases to be qualified to act as an insolvency practitioner in relation to the company.

(3) Subject to the next subsection, a receiver may, on application to the court by the holder of the floating charge by virtue of which he was appointed, be removed by the court on cause shown.

(4) Where at any time a receiver vacates office—

(a) his remuneration and any expenses properly incurred by him, and
(b) any indemnity to which he is entitled out of the property of the company,

shall be paid out of the property of the company which is subject to the floating charge and shall have priority as provided for in section 60(1).

(5) When a receiver ceases to act as such otherwise than by death he shall, and, when a receiver is removed by the court, the holder of the floating charge by virtue of which he was appointed shall, within 14 days of the cessation or removal (as the case may be) give the registrar of companies notice to that effect, and the registrar shall enter the notice in the register of charges.

If the receiver or the holder of the floating charge (as the case may require) makes default in complying with the requirements of this subsection, he is liable to a fine and, for continued contravention, to a daily fine.

. (6) If by the expiry of a period of one month following upon the removal of the receiver or his ceasing to act as such no other receiver has been appointed, the floating charge by virtue of which the receiver was appointed—

(a) thereupon ceases to attach to the property then subject to the charge, and
(b) again subsists as a floating charge;

and for the purposes of calculating the period of one month under this subsection no account shall be taken of any period during which an administration order under Part II of this Act is in force. **[62]**

NOTES
Commencement: 29 December 1986.
This section derived from the Companies Act 1985, s 478, and the Insolvency Act 1985, s 60, Sch 6, para 13.

63. Powers of court

(1) The court on the application of—

(a) the holder of a floating charge by virtue of which a receiver was appointed, or
(b) a receiver appointed under section 51.

may give directions to the receiver in respect of any matter arising in connection with the performance by him of his functions.

(2) Where the appointment of a person as a receiver by the holder of a floating charge is discovered to be invalid (whether by virtue of the invalidity of the instrument or otherwise), the court may order the holder of the floating charge to indemnify the person appointed against any liability which arises solely by reason of the invalidity of the appointment. **[63]**

NOTES
Commencement: 29 December 1986.
This section derived from the Companies Act 1985, s 479, and the Insolvency Act 1985, s 61.

64. Notification that receiver appointed

(1) Where a receiver has been appointed, every invoice, order for goods or business letter issued by or on behalf of the company or the receiver or the liquidator of the company, being a document on or in which the name of the company appears, shall contain a statement that a receiver has been appointed.

(2) If default is made in complying with the requirements of this section, the company and any of the following persons who knowingly and wilfully authorises or permits the default, namely any officer of the company, any liquidator of the company and any receiver, is liable to a fine. **[64]**

NOTES

Commencement: 29 December 1986.

This section derived from the Companies Act 1985, s 480.

65. Information to be given by receiver

(1) Where a receiver is appointed, he shall—

    (a) forthwith send to the company and publish notice of his appointment, and

    (b) within 28 days after his appointment, unless the court otherwise directs, send such notice to all the creditors of the company (so far as he is aware of their addresses).

(2) This section and the next do not apply in relation to the appointment of a receiver to act—

    (a) with an existing receiver, or

    (b) in place of a receiver who has died or ceased to act,

except that, where they apply to a receiver who dies or ceases to act before they have been fully complied with, the references in this section and the next to the receiver include (subject to subsection (3) of this section) his successor and any continuing receiver.

(3) If the company is being wound up, this section and the next apply notwithstanding that the receiver and the liquidator are the same person, but with any necessary modifications arising from that fact.

(4) If a person without reasonable excuse fails to comply with this section, he is liable to a fine and, for continued contravention, to a daily default fine. **[65]**

NOTES

Commencement: 29 December 1986.

This section derived from the Companies Act 1985, s 481, and the Insolvency Act 1985, s 62.

66. Company's statement of affairs

(1) Where a receiver of a company is appointed, the receiver shall forthwith require some or all of the persons mentioned in subsection (3) below to make out and submit to him a statement in the prescribed form as to the affairs of the company.

(2) A statement submitted under this section shall be verified by affidavit by the persons required to submit it and shall show—

    (a) particulars of the company's assets, debts and liabilities;

    (b) the names and addresses of its creditors;

    (c) the securities held by them respectively;

    (d) the dates when the securities were respectively given; and

    (e) such further or other information as may be prescribed.

(3) The persons referred to in subsection (1) are—

    (a) those who are or have been officers of the company;

(b) those who have taken part in the company's formation at any time within one year before the date of the appointment of the receiver;

(c) those who are in the company's employment or have been in its employment within that year, and are in the receiver's opinion capable of giving the information required;

(d) those who are or have been within that year officers of or in the employment of a company which is, or within that year was, an officer of the company.

In this subsection "employment" includes employment under a contract for services.

(4) Where any persons are required under this section to submit a statement of affairs to the receiver they shall do so (subject to the next subsection) before the end of the period of 21 days beginning with the day after that on which the prescribed notice of the requirement is given to them by the receiver.

(5) The receiver, if he thinks fit, may—

(a) at any time release a person from an obligation imposed on him under subsection (1) or (2), or

(b) either when giving the notice mentioned in subsection (4) or subsequently extend the period so mentioned,

and where the receiver has refused to exercise a power conferred by this subsection, the court, if it thinks fit, may exercise it.

(6) If a person without reasonable excuse fails to comply with any obligation imposed under this section, he is liable to a fine and, for continued contravention to a daily default fine.   **[66]**

NOTES
Commencement: 29 December 1986.
This section derived from the Companies Act 1985, s 482, and the Insolvency Act 1985, s 63.

67. Report by receiver

(1) Where a receiver is appointed under section 51, he shall within 3 months (or such longer period as the court may allow) after his appointment, send to the registrar of companies, to the holder of the floating charge by virtue of which he was appointed and to any trustees for secured creditors of the company and (so far as he is aware of their addresses) to all such creditors a report as to the following matters, namely—

(a) the events leading up to his appointment, so far as he is aware of them;

(b) the disposal or proposed disposal by him of any property of the company and the carrying on or proposed carrying on by him of any business of the company;

(c) the amounts of principal and interest payable to the holder of the floating charge by virtue of which he was appointed and the amounts payable to preferential creditors; and

(d) the amount (if any) likely to be available for the payment of other creditors.

(2) The receiver shall also, within 3 months (or such longer period as the court may allow) after his appointment, either—

(a) send a copy of the report (so far as he is aware of their addresses) to all unsecured creditors of the company, or

(b) publish in the prescribed manner a notice stating an address to which unsecured creditors of the company should write for copies of the report to be sent to them free of charge,

and (in either case), unless the court otherwise directs, lay a copy of the report before a meeting of the company's unsecured creditors summoned for the purpose on not less than 14 days' notice.

(3) The court shall not give a direction under subsection (2) unless—

(a) the report states the intention of the receiver to apply for the direction, and

(b) a copy of the report is sent to the persons mentioned in paragraph (a) of that subsection, or a notice is published as mentioned in paragraph (b) of that subsection, not less than 14 days before the hearing of the application.

(4) Where the company has gone or goes into liquidation, the receiver—

(a) shall, within 7 days after his compliance with subsection (1) or, if later, the nomination or appointment of the liquidator, send a copy of the report to the liquidator, and

(b) where he does so within the time limited for compliance with subsection (2), is not required to comply with that subsection.

(5) A report under this section shall include a summary of the statement of affairs made out and submitted under section 66 and of his comments (if any) on it.

(6) Nothing in this section shall be taken as requiring any such report to include any information the disclosure of which would seriously prejudice the carrying out by the receiver of his functions.

(7) Section 65(2) applies for the purposes of this section also.

(8) If a person without reasonable excuse fails to comply with this section, he is liable to a fine and, for continued contravention, to a daily default fine.

(9) In this section "secured creditor", in relation to a company, means a creditor of the company who holds in respect of his debt a security over property of the company, and "unsecured creditor" shall be construed accordingly.   [67]

NOTES
Commencement: 29 December 1986.
This section derived from the Companies Act 1985, s 482A, and the Insolvency Act 1985, s 64.

68. Committee of creditors

(1) Where a meeting of creditors is summoned under section 67, the meeting may, if it thinks fit, establish a committee ("the creditors' committee") to exercise the functions conferred on it by or under this Act.

(2) If such a committee is established, the committee may on giving not less than 7 days' notice require the receiver to attend before it at any reasonable time and furnish it with such information relating to the carrying out by him of his functions as it may reasonably require.   [68]

NOTES
Commencement: 29 December 1986.
This section derived from the Companies Act 1985, s 482B, and the Insolvency Act 1985, s 65.

69. Enforcement of receiver's duty to make returns, etc.

(1) If any receiver—

> (*a*) having made default in filing, delivering or making any return, account or other document, or in giving any notice, which a receiver is by law required to file, deliver, make or give, fails to make good the default within 14 days after the service on him of a notice requiring him to do so; or

> (*b*) has, after being required at any time by the liquidator of the company so to do, failed to render proper accounts of his receipts and payments and to vouch the same and to pay over to the liquidator the amount properly payable to him,

the court may, on an application made for the purpose, make an order directing the receiver to make good the default within such time as may be specified in the order.

(2) In the case of any such default as is mentioned in subsection (1)(*a*), an application for the purposes of this section may be made by any member or creditor of the company or by the registrar of companies; and, in the case of any such default as is mentioned in subsection (1)(*b*), the application shall be made by the liquidator; and, in either case, the order may provide that all expenses of and incidental to the application shall be borne by the receiver.

(3) Nothing in this section prejudices the operation of any enactments imposing penalties on receivers in respect of any such default as is mentioned in subsection (1).   **[69]**

NOTES
> Commencement: 29 December 1986.
> This section derived from the Companies Act 1985, s 483.

70. Interpretation for Chapter II

(1) In this Chapter, unless the contrary intention appears, the following expressions have the following meanings respectively assigned to them—

> "company" means an incorporated company (whether or not a company within the meaning of the Companies Act) which the Court of Session has jurisdiction to wind up;

> "fixed security", in relation to any property of a company, means any security, other than a floating charge or a charge having the nature of a floating charge, which on the winding up of the company in Scotland would be treated as an effective security over that property, and (without prejudice to that generality) includes a security over that property, being a heritable security within the meaning of the Conveyancing and Feudal Reform (Scotland) Act 1970;

> "instrument of appointment" has the meaning given by section 53(1);

> "prescribed" means prescribed by regulations made under this Chapter by the Secretary of State;

> "receiver" means a receiver of such part of the property of the company as is subject to the floating charge by virtue of which he has been appointed under section 51;

> "register of charges" means the register kept by the registrar of companies for the purposes of Chapter II of Part XII of the Companies Act;

> "secured debenture" means a bond, debenture, debenture stock or other security which, either itself or by reference to any other instrument, creates a floating charge over all or any part of the property of the

company, but does not include a security which creates no charge other than a fixed security; and

"series of secured debentures" means two or more secured debentures created as a series by the company in such a manner that the holders thereof are entitled pari passu to the benefits of the floating charge.

(2) Where a floating charge, secured debenture or series of secured debentures has been created by the company, then, except where the context otherwise requires, any reference in this Chapter to the holder of the floating charge shall—

    (a) where the floating charge, secured debenture or series of secured debentures provides for a receiver to be appointed by any person or body, be construed as a reference to that person or body;

    (b) where, in the case of a series of secured debentures, no such provision has been made therein but—

        (i) there are trustees acting for the debenture-holders under and in accordance with a trust deed, be construed as a reference to those trustees, and

        (ii) where no such trustees are acting, be construed as a reference to—

            (aa) a majority in nominal value of those present or represented by proxy and voting at a meeting of debenture-holders at which the holders of at least one-third in nominal value of the outstanding debentures or the series are presented or so represented, or

            (bb) where no such meeting is held, the holders of at least one-half in nominal value of the outstanding debentures of the series.

(3) Any reference in this Chapter to a floating charge, secured debenture, series of secured debentures or instrument creating a charge includes, except where the context otherwise requires, a reference to that floating charge, debenture, series of debentures or instrument as varied by any instrument.

(4) References in this Chapter to the instrument by which a floating charge was created are, in the case of a floating charge created by words in a bond or other written acknowledgement, references to the bond or, as the case may be, the other written acknowledgement. **[70]**

NOTES
    Commencement: 29 December 1986.
    This section derived from the Companies Act 1985, ss 462(4), 484, 486 (part).

71. Prescription of forms, etc; regulations

(1) The notice referred to in section 62(5), and the notice referred to in section 65(1)(a) shall be in such form as may be prescribed.

(2) Any power conferred by this Chapter on the Secretary of State to make regulations is exercisable by statutory instrument; and a statutory instrument made in the exercise of the power so conferred to prescribe a fee is subject to annulment in pursuance of a resolution of either House of Parliament. **[71]**

NOTES
    Commencement: 29 December 1986.
    This section derived from the Companies Act 1985, s 485.

CHAPTER III

RECEIVERS' POWERS IN GREAT BRITAIN AS A WHOLE

72. Cross-border operation of receivership provisions

(1) A receiver appointed under the law of either part of Great Britain in respect of the whole or any part of any property or undertaking of a company and in consequence of the company having created a charge which, as created, was a floating charge may exercise his powers in the other part of Great Britain so far as their exercise is not inconsistent with the law applicable there.

(2) In subsection (1) "receiver" includes a manager and a person who is appointed both receiver and manager.   **[72]**

NOTES
> Commencement: 29 December 1986.
>> This section derived from the Companies Act 1985, s 724.

PART IV

WINDING UP OF COMPANIES REGISTERED
UNDER THE COMPANIES ACTS

CHAPTER I

PRELIMINARY

Modes of winding up

73. Alternative modes of winding up

(1) The winding up of a company, within the meaning given to that expression by section 735 of the Companies Act, may be either voluntary (Chapters II, III, IV and V in this Part) or by the court (Chapter VI).

(2) This Chapter, and Chapters VII to X, relate to winding up generally, except where otherwise stated.   **[73]**

NOTES
> Commencement: 29 December 1986.
>> This section derived from the Companies Act 1985, s 501.

Contributories

74. Liability as contributories of present and past members

(1) When a company is wound up, every present and past member is liable to contribute to its assets to any amount sufficient for payment of its debts and liabilities, and the expenses of the winding up, and for the adjustment of the rights of the contributories among themselves.

(2) This is subject as follows—
  (a) a past member is not liable to contribute if he has ceased to be a member for one year or more before the commencement of the winding up;
  (b) a past member is not liable to contribute in respect of any debt or liability of the company contracted after he ceased to be a member;
  (c) a past member is not liable to contribute, unless it appears to the court that the existing members are unable to satisfy the contributions

required to be made by them in pursuance of the Companies Act and this Act;

(*d*) in the case of a company limited by shares, no contribution is required from any member exceeding the amount (if any) unpaid on the shares in respect of which he is liable as a present or past member;

(*e*) nothing in the Companies Act or this Act invalidates any provision contained in a policy of insurance or other contract whereby the liability of individual members on the policy or contract is restricted, or whereby the funds of the company are alone made liable in respect of the policy or contract;

(*f*) a sum due to any member of the company (in his character of a member) by way of dividends, profits or otherwise is not deemed to be a debt of the company, payable to that member in a case of competition between himself and any other creditor not a member of the company, but any such sum may be taken into account for the purpose of the final adjustment of the rights of the contributories among themselves.

(3) In the case of a company limited by guarantee, no contribution is required from any member exceeding the amount undertaken to be contributed by him to the company's assets in the event of its being wound up; but if it is a company with a share capital, every member of it is liable (in addition to the amount so undertaken to be contributed to the assets), to contribute to the extent of any sums unpaid on shares held by him.   [74]

NOTES
Commencement: 29 December 1986.
This section derived from the Companies Act 1985, s 502.

75. Directors, etc with unlimited liability

(1) In the winding up of a limited company, any director or manager (whether past or present) whose liability is under the Companies Act unlimited is liable, in addition to his liability (if any) to contribute as an ordinary member, to make a further contribution as if he were at the commencement of the winding up a member of an unlimited company.

(2) However—

(*a*) a past director or manager is not liable to make such further contribution if he has ceased to hold office for a year or more before the commencement of the winding up;

(*b*) a past director or manager is not liable to make such further contribution in respect of any debt or liability of the company contracted after he ceased to hold office;

(*c*) subject to the company's articles, a director or manager is not liable to make such further contribution unless the court deems it necessary to require that contribution in order to satisfy the company's debts and liabilities, and the expenses of the winding up.   [75]

NOTES
Commencement: 29 December 1986.
This section derived from the Companies Act 1985, s 503.

76. Liability of past directors and shareholders

(1) This section applies where a company is being wound up and—

(*a*) it has under Chapter VII of Part V of the Companies Act (redeemable shares; purchase by a company of its own shares) made a payment out of capital in respect of the redemption or purchase of any of its own shares (the payment being referred to below as "the relevant payment"), and

(*b*) the aggregate amount of the company's assets and the amounts paid by way of contribution to its assets (apart from this section) is not sufficient for payment of its debts and liabilities, and the expenses of the winding up.

(2) If the winding up commenced within one year of the date on which the relevant payment was made, then—

(*a*) the person from whom the shares were redeemed or purchased, and

(*b*) the directors who signed the statutory declaration made in accordance with section 173(3) of the Companies Act for purposes of the redemption or purchase (except a director who shows that he had reasonable grounds for forming the opinion set out in the declaration),

are, so as to enable that insufficiency to be met, liable to contribute to the following extent to the company's assets.

(3) A person from whom any of the shares were redeemed or purchased is liable to contribute an amount not exceeding so much of the relevant payment as was made by the company in respect of his shares; and the directors are jointly and severally liable with that person to contribute that amount.

(4) A person who has contributed any amount to the assets in pursuance of this section may apply to the court for an order directing any other person jointly and severally liable in respect of that amount to pay him such amount as the court thinks just and equitable.

(5) Sections 74 and 75 do not apply in relation to liability accruing by virtue of this section.

(6) This section is deemed included in Chapter VII of Part V of the Companies Act for the purposes of the Secretary of State's power to make regulations under section 179 of that Act.　　　　　　　　　　**[76]**

NOTES
　Commencement: 29 December 1986.
　This section derived from the Companies Act 1985, s 504.

77. Limited company formerly unlimited

(1) This section applies in the case of a company being wound up which was at some former time registered as unlimited but has re-registered—

(*a*) as a public company under section 43 of the Companies Act (or the former corresponding provision, section 5 of the Companies Act 1980), or

(*b*) as a limited company under section 51 of the Companies Act (or the former corresponding provision, section 44 of the Companies Act 1967).

(2) Notwithstanding section 74(2)(*a*) above, a past member of the company who was a member of it at the time of re-registration, if the winding up commences within the period of 3 years beginning with the day on which the company was re-registered, is liable to contribute to the assets of the company in respect of debts and liabilities contracted before that time.

(3) If no persons who were members of the company at that time are existing members of it, a person who at that time was a present or past member is liable to contribute as above notwithstanding that the existing members have satisfied the contributions required to be made by them under the Companies Act and this Act.

This applies subject to section 74(2)(*a*) above and to subsection (2) of this section, but notwithstanding section 74(2)(*c*).

(4) Notwithstanding section 74(2)(*d*) and (3), there is no limit on the amount which a person who, at that time, was a past or present member of the company is liable to contribute as above. **[77]**

NOTES
    Commencement: 29 December 1986.
    This section derived from the Companies Act 1985, s 505.

78. Unlimited company formerly limited

(1) This section applies in the case of a company being wound up which was at some former time registered as limited but has been re-registered as unlimited under section 49 of the Companies Act (or the former corresponding provision, section 43 of the Companies Act 1967).

(2) A person who, at the time when the application for the company to be re-registered was lodged, was a past member of the company and did not after that again become a member of it is not liable to contribute to the assets of the company more than he would have been liable to contribute had the company not been re-registered. **[78]**

NOTES
    Commencement: 29 December 1986.
    This section derived from the Companies Act 1985, s 506.

79. Meaning of "contributory"

(1) In this Act and the Companies Act the expression "contributory" means every person liable to contribute to the assets of a company in the event of its being wound up, and for the purposes of all proceedings for determining, and all proceedings prior to the final determination of, the persons who are to be deemed contributories, includes any person alleged to be a contributory.

(2) The reference in subsection (1) to persons liable to contribute to the assets does not include a person so liable by virtue of a declaration by the court under section 213 (imputed responsibility for company's fraudulent trading) or section 214 (wrongful trading) in Chapter X of this Part.

(3) A reference in a company's articles to a contributory does not (unless the context requires) include a person who is a contributory only by virtue of section 76.

This subsection is deemed included in Chapter VII of Part V of the Companies Act for the purposes of the Secretary of State's power to make regulations under section 179 of that Act. **[79]**

NOTES
    Commencement: 29 December 1986.
    This section derived from the Companies Act 1985, s 507, and the Insolvency Act 1985, Sch 6, para 5.

80. Nature of contributory's liability

The liability of a contributory creates a debt (in England and Wales in the nature of a specialty) accruing due from him at the time when his liability commenced, but payable at the times when calls are made for enforcing the liability.   **[80]**

NOTES
Commencement: 29 December 1986.
This section derived from the Companies Act 1985, s 508.

81. Contributories in case of death of a member

(1) If a contributory dies either before or after he has been placed on the list of contributories, his personal representatives, and the heirs and legatees of heritage of his heritable estate in Scotland, are liable in a due course of administration to contribute to the assets of the company in discharge of his liability and are contributories accordingly.

(2) Where the personal representatives are placed on the list of contributories, the heirs or legatees of heritage need not be added, but they may be added as and when the court thinks fit.

(3) If in England and Wales the personal representatives make default in paying any money ordered to be paid by them, proceedings may be taken for administering the estate of the deceased contributory and for compelling payment out of it of the money due.   **[81]**

NOTES
Commencement: 29 December 1986.
This section derived from the Companies Act 1985, s 509.

82. Effect of contributory's bankruptcy

(1) The following applies if a contributory becomes bankrupt, either before or after he has been placed on the list of contributories.

(2) His trustee in bankruptcy represents him for all purposes of the winding up, and is a contributory accordingly.

(3) The trustee may be called on to admit to proof against the bankrupt's estate, or otherwise allow to be paid out of the bankrupt's assets in due course of law, any money due from the bankrupt in respect of his liability to contribute to the company's assets.

(4) There may be proved against the bankrupt's estate the estimated value of his liability to future calls as well as calls already made.   **[82]**

NOTES
Commencement: 29 December 1986.
This section derived from the Companies Act 1985, s 510.

83. Companies registered under Companies Act, Part XXII, Chapter II

(1) The following applies in the event of a company being wound up which has been registered under section 680 of the Companies Act (or previous corresponding provisions in the Companies Act 1948 or earlier Acts).

(2) Every person is a contributory, in respect of the company's debts and liabilities contracted before registration, who is liable—

(*a*) to pay, or contribute to the payment of, any debt or liability so contracted, or

(*b*) to pay, or contribute to the payment of, any sum for the adjustment of the rights of the members among themselves in respect of any such debt or liability, or

(*c*) to pay, or contribute to the amount of, the expenses of winding up the company, so far as relates to the debts or liabilities above-mentioned.

(3) Every contributory is liable to contribute to the assets of the company, in the course of the winding up, all sums due from him in respect of any such liability.

(4) In the event of the death, bankruptcy or insolvency of any contributory, provisions of this Act, with respect to the personal representatives, to the heirs and legatees of heritage of the heritable estate in Scotland of deceased contributories and to the trustees of bankrupt or insolvent contributories respectively, apply. **[83]**

NOTES
Commencement: 29 December 1986.
This section derived from the Companies Act 1985, s 511.

CHAPTER II

VOLUNTARY WINDING UP (INTRODUCTORY AND GENERAL)

Resolutions for, and commencement of, voluntary winding up

84. Circumstances in which company may be wound up voluntarily

(1) A company may be wound up voluntarily—

(*a*) when the period (if any) fixed for the duration of the company by the articles expires, or the event (if any) occurs, on the occurrence of which the articles provide that the company is to be dissolved, and the company in general meeting has passed a resolution requiring it to be wound up voluntarily;

(*b*) if the company resolves by special resolution that it be wound up voluntarily;

(*c*) if the company resolves by extraordinary resolution to the effect that it cannot by reason of its liabilities continue its business, and that it is advisable to wind up.

(2) In this Act the expression "a resolution for voluntary winding up" means a resolution passed under any of the paragraphs of subsection (1).

(3) A resolution passed under paragraph (*a*) of subsection (1), as well as a special resolution under paragraph (*b*) and an extraordinary resolution under paragraph (*c*), is subject to section 380 of the Companies Act (copy of resolution to be forwarded to registrar of companies within 15 days). **[84]**

NOTES
Commencement: 29 December 1986.
This section derived from the Companies Act 1985, s 572.

85. Notice of resolution to wind up

(1) When a company has passed a resolution for voluntary winding up, it shall, within 14 days after the passing of the resolution, give notice of the resolution by advertisement in the Gazette.

(2) If default is made in complying with this section, the company and every officer of it who is in default is liable to a fine and, for continued contravention, to a daily default fine.

For purposes of this subsection the liquidator is deemed an officer of the company.   [85]

NOTES
Commencement: 29 December 1986.
This section derived from the Companies Act 1985, s 573.

86. Commencement of winding up

A voluntary winding up is deemed to commence at the time of the passing of the resolution for voluntary winding up.   [86]

NOTES
Commencement: 29 December 1986.
This section derived from the Companies Act 1985, s 574.

Consequences of resolution to wind up

87. Effect on business and status of company

(1) In case of a voluntary winding up, the company shall from the commencement of the winding up cease to carry on its business, except so far as may be required for its beneficial winding up.

(2) However, the corporate state and corporate powers of the company, notwithstanding anything to the contrary in its articles, continue until the company is dissolved.   [87]

NOTES
Commencement: 29 December 1986.
This section derived from the Companies Act 1985, s 575.

88. Avoidance of share transfers, etc after winding-up resolution

Any transfer of shares, not being a transfer made to or with the sanction of the liquidator, and any alteration in the status of the company's members, made after the commencement of a voluntary winding up, is void.   [88]

NOTES
Commencement: 29 December 1986.
This section derived from the Companies Act 1985, s 576.

Declaration of solvency

89. Statutory declaration of solvency

(1) Where it is proposed to wind up a company voluntarily, the directors (or, in the case of a company having more than two directors, the majority of them) may at a directors' meeting make a statutory declaration to the effect that they have made a full inquiry into the company's affairs and that, having done so, they have formed the opinion that the company will be able to pay its debts in full, together with interest at the official rate (as defined in section 251), within such period, not exceeding 12 months from the commencement of the winding up, as may be specified in the declaration.

(2) Such a declaration by the directors has no effect for purposes of this Act unless—

(*a*) it is made within the 5 weeks immediately preceding the date of the passing of the resolution for winding up, or on that date but before the passing of the resolution, and

(*b*) it embodies a statement of the company's assets and liabilities as at the latest practicable date before the making of the declaration.

(3) The declaration shall be delivered to the registrar of companies before the expiration of 15 days immediately following the date on which the resolution for winding up is passed.

(4) A director making a declaration under this section without having reasonable grounds for the opinion that the company will be able to pay its debts in full, together with interest at the official rate, within the period specified is liable to imprisonment or a fine, or both.

(5) If the company is wound up in pursuance of a resolution passed within 5 weeks after the making of the declaration, and its debts (together with interest at the official rate) are not paid or provided for in full within the period specified, it is to be presumed (unless the contrary is shown) that the director did not have reasonable grounds for his opinion.

(6) If a declaration required by subsection (3) to be delivered to the registrar is not so delivered within the time prescribed by that subsection, the company and every officer in default is liable to a fine and, for continued contravention, to a daily default fine. **[89]**

NOTES
Commencement: 29 December 1986.
This section derived from the Companies Act 1985, s 577, and the Insolvency Act 1985, Sch 6, para 35.

90. Distinction between "members'" and "creditors'" voluntary winding up

A winding up in the case of which a directors' statutory declaration under section 89 has been made is a "members' voluntary winding up"; and a winding up in the case of which such a declaration has not been made is a "creditors' voluntary winding up". **[90]**

NOTES
Commencement: 29 December 1986.
This section derived from the Companies Act 1985, s 578.

CHAPTER III
MEMBERS' VOLUNTARY WINDING UP

91. Appointment of liquidator

(1) In a members' voluntary winding up, the company in general meeting shall appoint one or more liquidators for the purpose of winding up the company's affairs and distributing its assets.

(2) On the appointment of a liquidator all the powers of the directors cease, except so far as the company in general meeting or the liquidator sanctions their continuance. **[91]**

NOTES
  Commencement: 29 December 1986.
  This section derived from the Companies Act 1985, s 580.

92. Power to fill vacancy in office of liquidator

(1) If a vacancy occurs by death, resignation or otherwise in the office of liquidator appointed by the company, the company in general meeting may, subject to any arrangement with its creditors, fill the vacancy.

(2) For that purpose a general meeting may be convened by any contributory or, if there were more liquidators than one, by the continuing liquidators.

(3) The meeting shall be held in manner provided by this Act or by the articles, or in such manner as may, on application by any contributory or by the continuing liquidators, be determined by the court.   **[92]**

NOTES
  Commencement: 29 December 1986.
  This section derived from the Companies Act 1985, s 581.

93. General company meeting at each year's end

(1) Subject to sections 96 and 102, in the event of the winding up continuing for more than one year, the liquidator shall summon a general meeting of the company at the end of the first year from the commencement of the winding up, and of each succeeding year, or at the first convenient date within 3 months from the end of the year or such longer period as the Secretary of State may allow.

(2) The liquidator shall lay before the meeting an account of his acts and dealings, and of the conduct of the winding up, during the preceding year.

(3) If the liquidator fails to comply with this section, he is liable to a fine.

[93]

NOTES
  Commencement: 29 December 1986.
  This section derived from the Companies Act 1985, s 584, and the Insolvency Act 1985, Sch 6, para 36.

94. Final meeting prior to dissolution

(1) As soon as the company's affairs are fully wound up, the liquidator shall make up an account of the winding up, showing how it has been conducted and the company's property has been disposed of, and thereupon shall call a general meeting of the company for the purpose of laying before it the account, and giving an explanation of it.

(2) The meeting shall be called by advertisement in the Gazette, specifying its time, place and object and published at least one month before the meeting.

(3) Within one week after the meeting, the liquidator shall send to the registrar of companies a copy of the account, and shall make a return to him of the holding of the meeting and of its date.

(4) If the copy is not sent or the return is not made in accordance with subsection (3), the liquidator is liable to a fine and, for continued contravention, to a daily default fine.

(5) If a quorum is not present at the meeting, the liquidator shall, in lieu of

the return mentioned above, make a return that the meeting was duly summoned and that no quorum was present; and upon such a return being made, the provisions of subsection (3) as to the making of the return are deemed complied with.

(6) If the liquidator fails to call a general meeting of the company as required by subsection (1), he is liable to a fine. **[94]**

NOTES
Commencement: 29 December 1986.
This section derived from the Companies Act 1985, s 585(1)–(4), (7).

95. Effect of company's insolvency

(1) This section applies where the liquidator is of the opinion that the company will be unable to pay its debts in full (together with interest at the official rate) within the period stated in the directors' declaration under section 89.

(2) The liquidator shall—

(a) summon a meeting of creditors for a day not later than the 28th day after the day on which he formed that opinion;

(b) send notices of the creditors' meeting to the creditors by post not less than 7 days before the day on which that meeting is to be held;

(c) cause notice of the creditors' meeting to be advertised once in the Gazette and once at least in 2 newspapers circulating in the relevant locality (that is to say the locality in which the company's principal place of business in Great Britain was situated during the relevant period); and

(d) during the period before the day on which the creditors' meeting is to be held, furnish creditors free of charge with such information concerning the affairs of the company as they may reasonably require;

and the notice of the creditors' meeting shall state the duty imposed by paragraph (d) above.

(3) The liquidator shall also—

(a) make out a statement in the prescribed form as to the affairs of the company;

(b) lay that statement before the creditors' meeting; and

(c) attend and preside at that meeting.

(4) The statement as to the affairs of the company shall be verified by affidavit by the liquidator and shall show—

(a) particulars of the company's assets, debts and liabilities;

(b) the names and addresses of the company's creditors;

(c) the securities held by them respectively;

(d) the dates when the securities were respectively given; and

(e) such further or other information as may be prescribed.

(5) Where the company's principal place of business in Great Britain was situated in different localities at different times during the relevant period, the duty imposed by subsection (2)(c) applies separately in relation to each of those localities.

(6) Where the company had no place of business in Great Britain during the relevant period, references in subsections (2)(c) and (5) to the company's principal place of business in Great Britain are replaced by references to its registered office.

(7) In this section "the relevant period" means the period of 6 months immediately preceding the day on which were sent the notices summoning the company meeting at which it was resolved that the company be wound up voluntarily.

(8) If the liquidator without reasonable excuse fails to comply with this section, he is liable to a fine. **[95]**

NOTES
Commencement: 29 December 1986.
This section derived from the Insolvency Act 1985, s 83(1)–(6), (9), (10).

96. Conversion to creditors' voluntary winding up

As from the day on which the creditors' meeting is held under section 95, this Act has effect as if—

 (a) the directors' declaration under section 89 had not been made; and
 (b) the creditors' meeting and the company meeting at which it was resolved that the company be wound up voluntarily were the meetings mentioned in section 98 in the next Chapter;

and accordingly the winding up becomes a creditors' voluntary winding up. **[96]**

NOTES
Commencement: 29 December 1986.
This section derived from the Insolvency Act 1985, s 83(7) (part).

CHAPTER IV
CREDITORS' VOLUNTARY WINDING UP

97. Application of this Chapter

(1) Subject as follows, this Chapter applies in relation to a creditors' voluntary winding up.

(2) Sections 98 and 99 do not apply where, under section 96 in Chapter III, a members' voluntary winding up has become a creditors' voluntary winding up. **[97]**

NOTES
Commencement: 29 December 1986.
This section derived from the Companies Act 1985, s 587, and the Insolvency Act 1985, s 85(1).

98. Meeting of creditors

(1) The company shall—

 (a) cause a meeting of its creditors to be summoned for a day not later than the 14th day after the day on which there is to be held the company meeting at which the resolution for voluntary winding up is to be proposed;
 (b) cause the notices of the creditors' meeting to be sent by post to the creditors not less than 7 days before the day on which that meeting is to be held; and
 (c) cause notice of the creditors' meeting to be advertised once in the Gazette and once at least in two newspapers circulating in the relevant locality (that is to say the locality in which the company's principal place of business in Great Britain was situated during the relevant period).

(2) The notice of the creditors' meeting shall state either—

(*a*) the name and address of a person qualified to act as an insolvency practitioner in relation to the company who, during the period before the day on which that meeting is to be held, will furnish creditors free of charge with such information concerning the company's affairs as they may reasonably require; or

(*b*) a place in the relevant locality where, on the two business days falling next before the day on which that meeting is to be held, a list of the names and addresses of the company's creditors will be available for inspection free of charge.

(3) Where the company's principal place of business in Great Britain was situated in different localities at different times during the relevant period, the duties imposed by subsections (1)(*c*) and (2)(*b*) above apply separately in relation to each of those localities.

(4) Where the company had no place of business in Great Britain during the relevant period, references in subsections (1)(*c*) and (3) to the company's principal place of business in Great Britain are replaced by references to its registered office.

(5) In this section "the relevant period" means the period of 6 months immediately preceding the day on which were sent the notices summoning the company meeting at which it was resolved that the company be wound up voluntarily.

(6) If the company without reasonable excuse fails to comply with subsection (1) or (2), it is guilty of an offence and liable to a fine.   [98]

NOTES

Commencement: 29 December 1986.

This section derived from the Insolvency Act 1985, s 85(2), (3), (6)–(8), (9)(*a*), (10).

---

99. Directors to lay statement of affairs before creditors

(1) The directors of the company shall—

(*a*) make out a statement in the prescribed form as to the affairs of the company;

(*b*) cause that statement to be laid before the creditors' meeting under section 98; and

(*c*) appoint one of their number to preside at that meeting;

and it is the duty of the director so appointed to attend the meeting and preside over it.

(2) The statement as to the affairs of the company shall be verified by affidavit by some or all of the directors and shall show—

(*a*) particulars of the company's assets, debts and liabilities;

(*b*) the names and addresses of the company's creditors;

(*c*) the securities held by them respectively;

(*d*) the dates when the securities were respectively given; and

(*e*) such further or other information as may be prescribed.

(3) If—

(*a*) the directors without reasonable excuse fail to comply with subsection (1) or (2); or (*b*) any director without reasonable excuse fails to comply with subsection (1), so far as requiring him to attend and preside at the creditors' meeting,

the directors are or (as the case may be) the director is guilty of an offence and liable to a fine. **[99]**

NOTES
Commencement: 29 December 1986.
This section derived from the Insolvency Act 1985, s 85(4), (5), (9)(*b*), (*c*), (10).

100. Appointment of liquidator

(1) The creditors and the company at their respective meetings mentioned in section 98 may nominate a person to be liquidator for the purpose of winding up the company's affairs and distributing its assets.

(2) The liquidator shall be the person nominated by the creditors or, where no person has been so nominated, the person (if any) nominated by the company.

(3) In the case of different persons being nominated, any director, member or creditor of the company may, within 7 days after the date on which the nomination was made by the creditors, apply to the court for an order either—

(*a*) directing that the person nominated as liquidator by the company shall be liquidator instead of or jointly with the person nominated by the creditors, or

(*b*) appointing some other person to be liquidator instead of the person nominated by the creditors. **[100]**

NOTES
Commencement: 29 December 1986.
This section derived from the Companies Act 1985, s 589, and the Insolvency Act 1985, Sch 6, para 37(1), (2).

101. Appointment of liquidation committee

(1) The creditors at the meeting to be held under section 98 or at any subsequent meeting may, if they think fit, appoint a committee ("the liquidation committee") of not more than 5 persons to exercise the functions conferred on it by or under this Act.

(2) If such a committee is appointed, the company may, either at the meeting at which the resolution for voluntary winding up is passed or at any time subsequently in general meeting, appoint such number of persons as they think fit to act as members of the committee, not exceeding 5.

(3) However, the creditors may, if they think fit, resolve that all or any of the persons so appointed by the company ought not to be members of the liquidation committee; and if the creditors so resolve—

(*a*) the persons mentioned in the resolution are not then, unless the court otherwise directs, qualified to act as members of the committee; and

(*b*) on any application to the court under this provision the court may, if it thinks fit, appoint other persons to act as such members in place of the persons mentioned in the resolution.

(4) In Scotland, the liquidation committee has, in addition to the powers

and duties conferred and imposed on it by this Act, such of the powers and duties of commissioners on a bankrupt estate as may be conferred and imposed on liquidation committees by the rules. **[101]**

NOTES
Commencement: 29 December 1986.
This section derived from the Companies Act 1985, s 590, and the Insolvency Act 1985, Sch 6, para 38(2)–(4).

102. Creditors' meeting where winding up converted under s 96

Where, in the case of a winding up which was, under section 96 in Chapter III, converted to a creditors' voluntary winding up, a creditors' meeting is held in accordance with section 95, any appointment made or committee established by that meeting is deemed to have been made or established by a meeting held in accordance with section 98 in this Chapter. **[102]**

NOTES
Commencement: 29 December 1986.
This section derived from the Insolvency Act 1985, s 83(7) (part).

103. Cesser of directors' powers

On the appointment of a liquidator, all the powers of the directors cease, except so far as the liquidation committee (or, if there is no such committee, the creditors) sanction their continuance. **[103]**

NOTES
Commencement: 29 December 1986.
This section derived from the Companies Act 1985, s 591(2), and the Insolvency Act 1985, Sch 6, para 39.

104. Vacancy in office of liquidator

If a vacancy occurs, by death, resignation or otherwise, in the office of a liquidator (other than a liquidator appointed by, or by the direction of, the court), the creditors may fill the vacancy. **[104]**

NOTES
Commencement: 29 December 1986.
This section derived from the Companies Act 1985, s 592.

105. Meetings of company and creditors at each year's end

(1) If the winding up continues for more than one year, the liquidator shall summon a general meeting of the company and a meeting of the creditors at the end of the first year from the commencement of the winding up, and of each succeeding year, or at the first convenient date within 3 months from the end of the year or such longer period as the Secretary of State may allow.

(2) The liquidator shall lay before each of the meetings an account of his acts and dealings and of the conduct of the winding up during the preceding year.

(3) If the liquidator fails to comply with this section, he is liable to a fine.

(4) Where under section 96 a members' voluntary winding up has become a creditors' voluntary winding up, and the creditors' meeting under section 95 is

held 3 months or less before the end of the first year from the commencement of the winding up, the liquidator is not required by this section to summon a meeting of creditors at the end of that year.   **[105]**

NOTES
    Commencement: 29 December 1986.
    This section derived from the Companies Act 1985, s 594, and the Insolvency Act 1985, s 83(8).

106. Final meeting prior to dissolution

(1) As soon as the company's affairs are fully wound up, the liquidator shall make up an account of the winding up, showing how it has been conducted and the company's property has been disposed of, and thereupon shall call a general meeting of the company and a meeting of the creditors for the purpose of laying the account before the meetings and giving an explanation of it.

(2) Each such meeting shall be called by advertisement in the Gazette specifying the time, place and object of the meeting, and published at least one month before it.

(3) Within one week after the date of the meetings (or, if they are not held on the same date, after the date of the later one) the liquidator shall send to the registrar of companies a copy of the account, and shall make a return to him of the holding of the meetings and of their dates.

(4) If the copy is not sent or the return is not made in accordance with subsection (3), the liquidator is liable to a fine and, for continued contravention, to a daily default fine.

(5) However, if a quorum is not present at either such meeting, the liquidator shall, in lieu of the return required by subsection (3), make a return that the meeting was duly summoned and that no quorum was present; and upon such return being made the provisions of that subsection as to the making of the return are, in respect of that meeting, deemed complied with.

(6) If the liquidator fails to call a general meeting of the company or a meeting of the creditors as required by this section, he is liable to a fine.   **[106]**

NOTES
    Commencement: 29 December 1986.
    This section derived from the Companies Act 1985, s 595(1)–(5), (8).

CHAPTER V

PROVISIONS APPLYING TO BOTH KINDS OF
VOLUNTARY WINDING UP

107. Distribution of company's property

Subject to the provisions of this Act as to preferential payments, the company's property in a voluntary winding up shall on the winding up be applied in satisfaction of the company's liabilities pari passu and, subject to that application, shall (unless the articles otherwise provide) be distributed among the members according to their rights and interests in the company.   **[107]**

NOTES
    Commencement: 29 December 1986.
    This section derived from the Companies Act 1985, s 597.

108. Appointment or removal of liquidator by the court

(1) If from any cause whatever there is no liquidator acting, the court may appoint a liquidator.

(2) The court may, on cause shown, remove a liquidator and appoint another. **[108]**

NOTES
Commencement: 29 December 1986.
This section derived from the Companies Act 1985, s 599.

109. Notice by liquidator of his appointment

(1) The liquidator shall, within 14 days after his appointment, publish in the Gazette and deliver to the registrar of companies for registration a notice of his appointment in the form prescribed by statutory instrument made by the Secretary of State.

(2) If the liquidator fails to comply with this section, he is liable to a fine and, for continued contravention, to a daily default fine. **[109]**

NOTES
Commencement: 29 December 1986.
This section derived from the Companies Act 1985, s 600.

110. Acceptance of shares, etc, as consideration for sale of company property

(1) This section applies, in the case of a company proposed to be, or being, wound up voluntarily, where the whole or part of the company's business or property is proposed to be transferred or sold to another company ("the transferee company"), whether or not the latter is a company within the meaning of the Companies Act.

(2) With the requisite sanction, the liquidator of the company being, or proposed to be, wound up ("the transferor company") may receive, in compensation or part compensation for the transfer or sale, shares, policies or other like interests in the transferee company for distribution among the members of the transferor company.

(3) The sanction requisite under subsection (2) is—

   (a) in the case of a members' voluntary winding up, that of a special resolution of the company, conferring either a general authority on the liquidator or an authority in respect of any particular arrangement, and

   (b) in the case of a creditors' voluntary winding up, that of either the court or the liquidation committee.

(4) Alternatively to subsection (2), the liquidator may (with that sanction) enter into any other arrangement whereby the members of the transferor company may, in lieu of receiving cash, shares, policies or other like interests (or in addition thereto), participate in the profits of, or receive any other benefit from, the transferee company.

(5) A sale or arrangement in pursuance of this section is binding on members of the transferor company.

(6) A special resolution is not invalid for purposes of this section by reason that it is passed before or concurrently with a resolution for voluntary winding

up or for appointing liquidators; but, if an order is made within a year for winding up the company by the court, the special resolution is not valid unless sanctioned by the court. **[110]**

NOTES
Commencement: 29 December 1986.
This section derived from the Companies Act 1985, ss 582(1)–(4), (7), 593, and the Insolvency Act 1985, Sch 6, para 40.

111. Dissent from arrangement under s 110

(1) This section applies in the case of a voluntary winding up where, for the purposes of section 110(2) or (4), there has been passed a special resolution of the transferor company providing the sanction requisite for the liquidator under that section.

(2) If a member of the transferor company who did not vote in favour of the special resolution expresses his dissent from it in writing, addressed to the liquidator and left at the company's registered office within 7 days after the passing of the resolution, he may require the liquidator either to abstain from carrying the resolution into effect or to purchase his interest at a price to be determined by agreement or by arbitration under this section.

(3) If the liquidator elects to purchase the member's interest, the purchase money must be paid before the company is dissolved and be raised by the liquidator in such manner as may be determined by special resolution.

(4) For purposes of an arbitration under this section, the provisions of the Companies Clauses Consolidation Act 1845 or, in the case of a winding up in Scotland, the Companies Clauses Consolidation (Scotland) Act 1845 with respect to the settlement of disputes by arbitration are incorporated with this Act, and—

    (*a*) in the construction of those provisions this Act is deemed the special Act and "the company" means the transferor company, and

    (*b*) any appointment by the incorporated provisions directed to be made under the hand of the secretary or any two of the directors may be made in writing by the liquidator (or, if there is more than one liquidator, then any two or more of them). **[111]**

NOTES
Commencement: 29 December 1986.
This section derived from the Companies Act 1985, s 582(5), (6), (8).

112. Reference of questions to court

(1) The liquidator or any contributory or creditor may apply to the court to determine any question arising in the winding up of a company, or to exercise, as respects the enforcing of calls or any other matter, all or any of the powers which the court might exercise if the company were being wound up by the court.

(2) The court, if satisfied that the determination of the question or the required exercise of power will be just and beneficial, may accede wholly or partially to the application on such terms and conditions as it thinks fit, or may make such other order on the application as it thinks just.

(3) A copy of an order made by virtue of this section staying the proceedings

in the winding up shall forthwith be forwarded by the company, or otherwise as may be prescribed, to the registrar of companies, who shall enter it in his records relating to the company. **[112]**

NOTES
Commencement: 29 December 1986.
This section derived from the Companies Act 1985, s 602.

113. Court's power to control proceedings (Scotland)

If the court, on the application of the liquidator in the winding up of a company registered in Scotland, so directs, no action or proceeding shall be proceeded with or commenced against the company except by leave of the court and subject to such terms as the court may impose. **[113]**

NOTES
Commencement: 29 December 1986.
This section derived from the Companies Act 1985, s 603.

114. No liquidator appointed or nominated by company

(1) This section applies where, in the case of a voluntary winding up, no liquidator has been appointed or nominated by the company.

(2) The powers of the directors shall not be exercised, except with the sanction of the court or (in the case of a creditors' voluntary winding up) so far as may be necessary to secure compliance with sections 98 (creditors' meeting) and 99 (statement of affairs), during the period before the appointment or nomination of a liquidator of the company.

(3) Subsection (2) does not apply in relation to the powers of the directors—

    (*a*) to dispose of perishable goods and other goods the value of which is likely to diminish if they are not immediately disposed of, and
    (*b*) to do all such other things as may be necessary for the protection of the company's assets.

(4) If the directors of the company without reasonable excuse fail to comply with this section, they are liable to a fine. **[114]**

NOTES
Commencement: 29 December 1986.
This section derived from the Insolvency Act 1985, s 82.

115. Expenses of voluntary winding up

All expenses properly incurred in the winding up, including the remuneration of the liquidator, are payable out of the company's assets in priority to all other claims. **[115]**

NOTES
Commencement: 29 December 1986.
This section derived from the Companies Act 1985, s 604.

116. Saving for certain rights

The voluntary winding up of a company does not bar the right of any creditor or contributory to have it wound up by the court; but in the case of an application by a contributory the court must be satisfied that the rights of the contributories will be prejudiced by a voluntary winding up. **[116]**

NOTES
Commencement: 29 December 1986.
This section derived from the Companies Act 1985, s 605.

CHAPTER VI

WINDING UP BY THE COURT

Jurisdiction (England and Wales)

117. High Court and county court jurisdiction

(1) The High Court has jurisdiction to wind up any company registered in England and Wales.

(2) Where the amount of a company's share capital paid up or credited as paid up does not exceed £120,000, then (subject to this section) the county court of the district in which the company's registered office is situated has concurrent jurisdiction with the High Court to wind up the company.

(3) The money sum for the time being specified in subsection (2) is subject to increase or reduction by order under section 416 in Part XV.

(4) The Lord Chancellor may by order in a statutory instrument exclude a county court from having winding-up jurisdiction, and for the purposes of that jurisdiction may attach its district, or any part thereof, to any other county court, and may by statutory instrument revoke or vary any such order.

In exercising the powers of this section, the Lord Chancellor shall provide that a county court is not to have winding-up jurisdiction unless it has for the time being jurisdiction for the purposes of Parts VIII to XI of this Act (individual insolvency).

(5) Every court in England and Wales having winding-up jurisdiction has for the purposes of that jurisdiction all the powers of the High Court; and every prescribed officer of the court shall perform any duties which an officer of the High Court may discharge by order of a judge of that court or otherwise in relation to winding up.

(6) For the purposes of this section, a company's "registered office" is the place which has longest been its registered office during the 6 months immediately preceding the presentation of the petition for winding up.   **[117]**

NOTES
Commencement: 29 December 1986.
This section derived from the Companies Act 1985, s 512, and the Insolvency Act 1985, Sch 6, paras 25, 26.

118. Proceedings taken in wrong court

(1) Nothing in section 117 invalidates a proceeding by reason of its being taken in the wrong court.

(2) The winding up of a company by the court in England and Wales, or any proceedings in the winding up, may be retained in the court in which the proceedings were commenced, although it may not be the court in which they ought to have been commenced.   **[118]**

NOTES
Commencement: 29 December 1986.

This section derived from the Companies Act 1985, s 513.

119. Proceedings in county court; case stated for High Court

(1) If any question arises in any winding-up proceedings in a county court which all the parties to the proceedings, or which one of them and the judge of the court, desire to have determined in the first instance in the High Court, the judge shall state the facts in the form of a special case for the opinion of the High Court.

(2) Thereupon the special case and the proceedings (or such of them as may be required) shall be transmitted to the High Court for the purposes of the determination.   **[119]**

NOTES
Commencement: 29 December 1986.
This section derived from the Companies Act 1985, s 514.

Jurisdiction (Scotland)

120. Court of Session and sheriff court jurisdiction

(1) The Court of Session has jurisdiction to wind up any company registered in Scotland.

(2) When the Court of Session is in vacation, the jurisdiction conferred on that court by this section may (subject to the provisions of this Part) be exercised by the judge acting as vacation judge in pursuance of section 4 of the Administration of Justice (Scotland) Act 1933.

(3) Where the amount of a company's share capital paid up or credited as paid up does not exceeed £120,000, the sheriff court of the sheriffdom in which the company's registered office is situated has concurrent jurisdiction with the Court of Session to wind up the company; but—

    (*a*) the Court of Session may, if it thinks expedient having regard to the amount of the company's assets to do so—

        (i) remit to a sheriff court any petition presented to the Court of Session for winding up such a company, or

        (ii) require such a petition presented to a sheriff court to be remitted to the Court of Session; and

    (*b*) the Court of Session may require any such petition as above-mentioned presented to one sheriff court to be remitted to another sheriff court; and

    (*c*) in a winding up in the sheriff court the sheriff may submit a stated case for the opinion of the Court of Session on any question of law arising in that winding up.

(4) For purposes of this section, the expression "registered office" means the place which has longest been the company's registered office during the 6 months immediately preceding the presentation of the petition for winding up.

(5) The money sum for the time being specified in subsection (3) is subject to increase or reduction by order under section 416 in Part XV.   **[120]**

NOTES
Commencement: 29 December 1986.
This section derived from the Companies Act 1985, s 515, and the Insolvency Act 1985, Sch 6, para 25.

121. Power to remit winding up to Lord Ordinary

(1) The Court of Session may, by Act of Sederunt, make provision for the taking of proceedings in a winding up before one of the Lords Ordinary; and, where provision is so made, the Lord Ordinary has, for the purposes of the winding up, all the powers and jurisdiction of the court.

(2) However, the Lord Ordinary may report to the Inner House any matter which may arise in the course of a winding up.   **[121]**

NOTES
Commencement: 29 December 1986.
This section derived from the Companies Act 1985, s 516.

Grounds and effect of winding-up petition

122. Circumstances in which company may be wound up by the court

(1) A company may be wound up by the court if—

    (*a*) the company has by special resolution resolved that the company be wound up by the court,

    (*b*) being a public company which was registered as such on its original incorporation, the company has not been issued with a certificate under section 117 of the Companies Act (public company share capital requirements) and more than a year has expired since it was so registered,

    (*c*) it is an old public company, within the meaning of the Consequential Provisions Act,

    (*d*) the company does not commence its business within a year from its incorporation or suspends its business for a whole year,

    (*e*) the number of members is reduced below 2,

    (*f*) the company is unable to pay its debts,

    (*g*) the court is of the opinion that it is just and equitable that the company should be wound up.

(2) In Scotland, a company which the Court of Session has jurisdiction to wind up may be wound up by the Court if there is subsisting a floating charge over property comprised in the company's property and undertaking, and the court is satisfied that the security of the creditor entitled to the benefit of the floating charge is in jeopardy.

For this purpose a creditor's security is deemed to be in jeopardy if the Court is satisfied that events have occurred or are about to occur which render it unreasonable in the creditor's interests that the company should retain power to dispose of the property which is subject to the floating charge.   **[122]**

NOTES
Commencement: 29 December 1986.
This section derived from the Companies Act 1985, s 517.

123. Definition of inability to pay debts

(1) A company is deemed unable to pay its debts—

    (*a*) if a creditor (by assignment or otherwise) to whom the company is indebted in a sum exceeding £750 then due has served on the company, by leaving it at the company's registered office, a written demand (in the prescribed form) requiring the company to pay the sum so due and the company has for 3 weeks thereafter neglected to pay the sum

or to secure or compound for it to the reasonable satisfaction of the creditor, or
(b) if, in England and Wales, execution or other process issued on a judgment, decree or order of any court in favour of a creditor of the company is returned unsatisfied in whole or in part, or
(c) if, in Scotland, the induciae of a charge for payment on an extract decree, or an extracted registered bond, or an extract registered protest, have expired without payment being made, or
(d) if, in Northern Ireland, a certificate of unenforceability has been granted in respect of a judgment against the company, or
(e) if it is proved to the satisfaction of the court that the company is unable to pay its debts as they fall due.

(2) A company is also deemed unable to pay its debts if it is proved to the satisfaction of the court that the value of the company's assets is less than the amount of its liabilities, taking into account its contingent and prospective liabilities.

(3) The money sum for the time being specified in subsection (1)(*a*) is subject to increase or reduction by order under section 416 in Part XV.   **[123]**

NOTES
Commencement: 29 December 1986.
This section derived from the Companies Act 1985, s 518, and the Insolvency Act 1985, Sch 6, paras 25, 27.

124. Application for winding up

(1) Subject to the provisions of this section, an application to the court for the winding up of a company shall be by petition presented either by the company, or the directors, or by any creditor or creditors (including any contingent or prospective creditor or creditors), contributory or contributories, or by all or any of those parties, together or separately.

(2) Except as mentioned below, a contributory is not entitled to present a winding-up petition unless either—
(a) the number of members is reduced below 2, or
(b) the shares in respect of which he is a contributory, or some of them, either were originally allotted to him, or have been held by him, and registered in his name, for at least 6 months during the 18 months before the commencement of the winding up, or have devolved on him through the death of a former holder.

(3) A person who is liable under section 76 to contribute to a company's assets in the event of its being wound up may petition on either of the grounds set out in section 122(1)(*f*) and (*g*), and subsection (2) above does not then apply; but unless the person is a contributory otherwise than under section 76, he may not in his character as contributory petition on any other ground.

This subsection is deemed included in Chapter VII of Part V of the Companies Act (redeemable shares; purchase by a company of its own shares) for the purposes of the Secretary of State's power to make regulations under section 179 of that Act.

(4) A winding-up petition may be presented by the Secretary of State—
(a) if the ground of the petition is that in section 122(1)(*b*) or (*c*), or
(b) in a case falling within section 440 of the Companies Act (expedient in the public interest, following report of inspectors, etc).

(5) Where a company is being wound up voluntarily in England and Wales, a winding-up petition may be presented by the official receiver attached to the court as well as by any other person authorised in that behalf under the other provisions of this section; but the court shall not make a winding-up order on the petition unless it is satisfied that the voluntary winding up cannot be continued with due regard to the interests of the creditors or contributories.

[124]

NOTES
Commencement: 29 December 1986.
This section derived from the Companies Act 1985, s 519, and the Insolvency Act 1985, Sch 6, para 28.

125. Powers of court on hearing of petition

(1) On hearing a winding-up petition the court may dismiss it, or adjourn the hearing conditionally or unconditionally, or make an interim order, or any other order that it thinks fit; but the court shall not refuse to make a winding-up order on the ground only that the company's assets have been mortgaged to an amount equal to or in excess of those assets, or that the company has no assets.

(2) If the petition is presented by members of the company as contributories on the ground that it is just and equitable that the company should be wound up, the court, if it is of opinion—

(a) that the petitioners are entitled to relief either by winding up the company or by some other means, and
(b) that in the absence of any other remedy it would be just and equitable that the company should be wound up,

shall make a winding-up order; but this does not apply if the court is also of the opinion both that some other remedy is available to the petitioners and that they are acting unreasonably in seeking to have the company wound up instead of pursuing that other remedy.   **[125]**

NOTES
Commencement: 29 December 1986.
This section derived from the Companies Act 1985, s 520.

126. Power to stay or restrain proceedings against company

(1) At any time after the presentation of a winding-up petition, and before a winding-up order has been made, the company, or any creditor or contributory, may—

(a) where any action or proceeding against the company is pending in the High Court or Court of Appeal in England and Wales or Northern Ireland, apply to the court in which the action or proceeding is pending for a stay of proceedings therein, and
(b) where any other action or proceeding is pending against the company, apply to the court having jurisdiction to wind up the company to restrain further proceedings in the action or proceeding;

and the court to which application is so made may (as the case may be) stay, sist or restrain the proceedings accordingly on such terms as it thinks fit.

(2) In the case of a company registered under section 680 of the Companies Act (pre-1862 companies; companies formed under legislation other than the

Companies Acts) or the previous corresponding legislation, where the application to stay, sist or restrain is by a creditor, this section extends to actions and proceedings against any contributory of the company.　　**[126]**

NOTES
　　Commencement: 29 December 1986.
　　This section derived from the Companies Act 1985, s 521.

127. Avoidance of property dispositions, etc

In a winding up by the court, any disposition of the company's property, and any transfer of shares, or alteration in the status of the company's members, made after the commencement of the winding up is, unless the court otherwise orders, void.　　**[127]**

NOTES
　　Commencement: 29 December 1986.
　　This section derived from the Companies Act 1985, s 522.

128. Avoidance of attachments, etc

(1) Where a company registered in England and Wales is being wound up by the court, any attachment, sequestration, distress or execution put in force against the estate or effects of the company after the commencement of the winding up is void.

(2) This section, so far as relates to any estate or effects of the company situated in England and Wales, applies in the case of a company registered in Scotland as it applies in the case of a company registered in England and Wales.　　**[128]**

NOTES
　　Commencement: 29 December 1986.
　　This section derived from the Companies Act 1985, s 523.

Commencement of winding up

129. Commencement of winding up by the court

(1) If, before the presentation of a petition for the winding up of a company by the court, a resolution has been passed by the company for voluntary winding up, the winding up of the company is deemed to have commenced at the time of the passing of the resolution; and unless the court, on proof of fraud or mistake, directs otherwise, all proceedings taken in the voluntary winding up are deemed to have been validly taken.

(2) In any other case, the winding up of a company by the court is deemed to commence at the time of the presentation of the petition for winding up.
　　[129]

NOTES
　　Commencement: 29 December 1986.
　　This section derived from the Companies Act 1985, s 524.

130. Consequences of winding-up order

(1) On the making of a winding-up order, a copy of the order must forthwith be forwarded by the company (or otherwise as may be prescribed) to the registrar of companies, who shall enter it in his records relating to the company.

(2) When a winding-up order has been made or a provisional liquidator has been appointed, no action or proceeding shall be proceeded with or commenced against the company or its property, except by leave of the court and subject to such terms as the court may impose.

(3) When an order has been made for winding up a company registered under section 680 of the Companies Act, no action or proceeding shall be commenced or proceeded with against the company or its property or any contributory of the company, in respect of any debt of the company, except by leave of the court, and subject to such terms as the court may impose.

(4) An order for winding up a company operates in favour of all the creditors and of all contributories of the company as if made on the joint petition of a creditor and of a contributory.   **[130]**

NOTES
Commencement: 29 December 1986.
This section derived from the Companies Act 1985, s 525, and the Insolvency Act 1985, Sch 6, para 29.

Investigation procedures

131. Company's statement of affairs

(1) Where the court has made a winding-up order or appointed a provisional liquidator, the official receiver may require some or all of the persons mentioned in subsection (3) below to make out and submit to him a statement in the prescribed form as to the affairs of the company.

(2) The statement shall be verified by affidavit by the persons required to submit it and shall show—

    (*a*) particulars of the company's assets and liabilities;
    (*b*) the names and addresses of the company's creditors;
    (*c*) the securities held by them respectively;
    (*d*) the dates when the securities were respectively given; and
    (*e*) such further or other information as may be prescribed or as the official receiver may require.

(3) The persons referred to in subsection (1) are—

    (*a*) those who are or have been officers of the company;
    (*b*) those who have taken part in the formation of the company at any time within one year before the relevant date;
    (*c*) those who are in the company's employment, or have been in its employment within that year, and are in the official receiver's opinion capable of giving the information required;
    (*d*) those who are or have been within that year officers of, or in the employment of, a company which is, or within that year was, an officer of the company.

(4) Where any persons are required under this section to submit a statement of affairs to the official receiver, they shall do so (subject to the next subsection) before the end of the period of 21 days beginning with the day after that on which the prescribed notice of the requirement is given to them by the official receiver.

(5) The official receiver, if he thinks fit, may—

(*a*) at any time release a person from an obligation imposed on him under subsection (1) or (2) above; or

(*b*) either when giving the notice mentioned in subsection (4) or subsequently, extend the period so mentioned;

and where the official receiver has refused to exercise a power conferred by this subsection, the court, if it thinks fit, may exercise it.

(6) In this section—

"employment" includes employment under a contract for services; and "the relevant date" means—

(*a*) in a case where a provisional liquidator is appointed, the date of his appointment; and

(*b*) in a case where no such appointment is made, the date of the winding-up order.

(7) If a person without reasonable excuse fails to comply with any obligation imposed under this section, he is liable to a fine and, for continued contravention, to a daily default fine.

(8) In the application of this section to Scotland references to the official receiver are to the liquidator or, in the case where a provisional liquidator is appointed, the provisional liquidator. **[131]**

NOTES

Commencement: 29 December 1986.

This section derived from the Insolvency Act 1985, s 66.

132. Investigation by official receiver

(1) Where a winding-up order is made by the court in England and Wales, it is the duty of the official receiver to investigate—

(*a*) if the company has failed, the causes of the failure; and

(*b*) generally, the promotion, formation, business, dealings and affairs of the company,

and to make such report (if any) to the court as he thinks fit.

(2) The report is, in any proceedings, prima facie evidence of the facts stated in it. **[132]**

NOTES

Commencement: 29 December 1986.

This section derived from the Insolvency Act 1985, s 67.

133. Public examination of officers

(1) Where a company is being wound up by the court, the official receiver or, in Scotland, the liquidator may at any time before the dissolution of the company apply to the court for the public examination of any person who—

(*a*) is or has been an officer of the company; or

(*b*) has acted as liquidator or administrator of the company or as receiver or manager or, in Scotland, receiver of its property; or

(*c*) not being a person falling within paragraph (*a*) or (*b*), is or has been concerned, or has taken part, in the promotion, formation or management of the company.

(2) Unless the court otherwise orders, the official receiver or, in Scotland,

the liquidator shall make an application under subsection (1) if he is requested in accordance with the rules to do so by—

    (*a*) one-half, in value, of the company's creditors; or

    (*b*) three-quarters, in value, of the company's contributories.

(3) On an application under subsection (1), the court shall direct that a public examination of the person to whom the application relates shall be held on a day appointed by the court; and that person shall attend on that day and be publicly examined as to the promotion, formation or management of the company or as to the conduct of its business and affairs, or his conduct or dealings in relation to the company.

(4) The following may take part in the public examination of a person under this section and may question that person concerning the matters mentioned in subsection (3), namely—

    (*a*) the official receiver;

    (*b*) the liquidator of the company;

    (*c*) any person who has been appointed as special manager of the company's property or business;

    (*d*) any creditor of the company who has tendered a proof or, in Scotland, submitted a claim in the winding up;

    (*e*) any contributory of the company.   **[133]**

NOTES
Commencement: 29 December 1986.
This section derived from the Insolvency Act 1985, s 68(1)–(4).

134. Enforcement of s 133

(1) If a person without reasonable excuse fails at any time to attend his public examination under section 133, he is guilty of a contempt of court and liable to be punished accordingly.

(2) In a case where a person without reasonable excuse fails at any time to attend his examination under section 133 or there are reasonable grounds for believing that a person has absconded, or is about to abscond, with a view to avoiding or delaying his examination under that section, the court may cause a warrant to be issued to a constable or prescribed officer of the court—

    (*a*) for the arrest of that person; and

    (*b*) for the seizure of any books, papers, records, money or goods in that person's possession.

(3) In such a case the court may authorise the person arrested under the warrant to be kept in custody, and anything seized under such a warrant to be held, in accordance with the rules, until such time as the court may order. **[134]**

NOTES
Commencement: 29 December 1986.
This section derived from the Insolvency Act 1985, s 68(5), (6).

Appointment of liquidator

135. Appointment and powers of provisional liquidator

(1) Subject to the provisions of this section, the court may, at any time after the presentation of a winding-up petition, appoint a liquidator provisionally.

(2) In England and Wales, the appointment of a provisional liquidator may

be made at any time before the making of a winding-up order; and either the official receiver or any other fit person may be appointed.

(3) In Scotland, such an appointment may be made at any time before the first appointment of liquidators.

(4) The provisional liquidator shall carry out such functions as the court may confer on him.

(5) When a liquidator is provisionally appointed by the court, his powers may be limited by the order appointing him. **[135]**

NOTES
Commencement: 29 December 1986.
This section derived from the Companies Act 1985, s 532, and the Insolvency Act 1985, s 69(3).

136. Functions of official receiver in relation to office of liquidator

(1) The following provisions of this section have effect, subject to section 140 below, on a winding-up order being made by the court in England and Wales.

(2) The official receiver, by virtue of his office, becomes the liquidator of the company and continues in office until another person becomes liquidator under the provisions of this Part.

(3) The official receiver is, by virtue of his office, the liquidator during any vacancy.

(4) At any time when he is the liquidator of the company, the official receiver may summon separate meetings of the company's creditors and contributories for the purpose of choosing a person to be liquidator of the company in place of the official receiver.

(5) It is the duty of the official receiver—

(a) as soon as practicable in the period of 12 weeks beginning with the day on which the winding-up order was made, to decide whether to exercise his power under subsection (4) to summon meetings, and

(b) if in pursuance of paragraph (a) he decides not to exercise that power, to give notice of his decision, before the end of that period, to the court and to the company's creditors and contributories, and

(c) (whether or not he has decided to exercise that power) to exercise his power to summon meetings under subsection (4) if he is at any time requested, in accordance with the rules, to do so by one-quarter, in value, of the company's creditors;

and accordingly, where the duty imposed by paragraph (c) arises before the official receiver has performed a duty imposed by paragraph (a) or (b), he is not required to perform the latter duty.

(6) A notice given under subsection (5)(b) to the company's creditors shall contain an explanation of the creditors' power under subsection (5)(c) to require the official receiver to summon meetings of the company's creditors and contributories. **[136]**

NOTES
Commencement: 29 December 1986.
This section derived from the Insolvency Act 1985, s 70(1)–(3), (4)(a), (5), (6).

137. Appointment by Secretary of State

(1) In a winding up by the court in England and Wales the official receiver may, at any time when he is the liquidator of the company, apply to the Secretary of State for the appointment of a person as liquidator in his place.

(2) If meetings are held in pursuance of a decision under section 136(5)(*a*), but no person is chosen to be liquidator as a result of those meetings, it is the duty of the official receiver to decide whether to refer the need for an appointment to the Secretary of State.

(3) On an application under subsection (1), or a reference made in pursuance of a decision under subsection (2), the Secretary of State shall either make an appointment or decline to make one.

(4) Where a liquidator has been appointed by the Secretary of State under subsection (3), the liquidator shall give notice of his appointment to the company's creditors or, if the court so allows, shall advertise his appointment in accordance with the directions of the court.

(5) In that notice or advertisement the liquidator shall—

   (*a*) state where he proposes to summon a general meeting of the company's creditors under section 141 below for the purpose of determining (together with any meeting of contributories) whether a liquidation committee should be established under that section, and

   (*b*) if he does not propose to summon such a meeting, set out the power of the company's creditors under that section to require him to summon one.   **[137]**

NOTES
Commencement: 29 December 1986.
This section derived from the Insolvency Act 1985, s 70(4)(*b*), (7)–(9).

138. Appointment of liquidator in Scotland

(1) Where a winding-up order is made by the court in Scotland, a liquidator shall be appointed by the court at the time when the order is made.

(2) The liquidator so appointed (here referred to as "the interim liquidator") continues in office until another person becomes liquidator in his place under this section or the next.

(3) The interim liquidator shall (subject to the next subsection) as soon as practicable in the period of 28 days beginning with the day on which the winding-up order was made or such longer period as the court may allow, summon separate meetings of the company's creditors and contributories for the purpose of choosing a person (who may be the person who is the interim liquidator of the company) in place of the interim liquidator.

(4) If it appears to the interim liquidator, in any case where a company is being wound up on grounds including its inability to pay its debts, that it would be inappropriate to summon under subsection (3) a meeting of the company's contributories, he may summon only a meeting of the company's creditors for the purpose mentioned in that subsection.

(5) If one or more meetings are held in pursuance of this section but no person is appointed or nominated by the meeting or meetings, the interim liquidator shall make a report to the court which shall appoint either the interim liquidator or some other person to a liquidator of the company.

(6) A person who becomes liquidator of the company in place of the interim liquidator shall, unless he is appointed by the court, forthwith notify the court of that fact.   **[138]**

NOTES
Commencement: 29 December 1986.
This section derived from the Companies Act 1985, s 535, and the Insolvency Act 1985, s 71, Sch 6, para 30.

139. Choice of liquidator at meetings of creditors and contributories

(1) This section applies where a company is being wound up by the court and separate meetings of the company's creditors and contributories are summoned for the purpose of choosing a person to be liquidator of the company.

(2) The creditors and the contributories at their respective meetings may nominate a person to be liquidator.

(3) The liquidator shall be the person nominated by the creditors or, where no person has been so nominated, the person (if any) nominated by the contributories.

(4) In the case of different persons being nominated, any contributory or creditor may, within 7 days after the date on which the nomination was made by the creditors, apply to the court for an order either—

> (*a*) appointing the person nominated as liquidator by the contributories to be a liquidator instead of, or jointly with, the person nominated by the creditors; or
> (*b*) appointing some other person to be liquidator instead of the person nominated by the creditors.   **[139]**

NOTES
Commencement: 29 December 1986.
This section derived from the Insolvency Act 1985, s 72.

140. Appointment by the court following administration or voluntary arrangement

(1) Where a winding-up order is made immediately upon the discharge of an administration order, the court may appoint as liquidator of the company the person who has ceased on the discharge of the administration order to be the administrator of the company.

(2) Where a winding-up order is made at a time when there is a supervisor of a voluntary arrangement approved in relation to the company under Part I, the court may appoint as liquidator of the company the person who is the supervisor at the time when the winding-up order is made.

(3) Where the court makes an appointment under this section, the official receiver does not become the liquidator as otherwise provided by section 136(2), and he has no duty under section 136(5)(*a*) or (*b*) in respect of the summoning of creditors' or contributories' meetings.   **[140]**

NOTES
Commencement: 29 December 1986.
This section derived from the Insolvency Act 1985, s 73.

Liquidation committees

141. Liquidation committee (England and Wales)

(1) Where a winding-up order has been made by the court in England and Wales and separate meetings of creditors and contributories have been summoned for the purpose of choosing a person to be liquidator, those meetings may establish a committee ("the liquidation committee") to exercise the functions conferred on it by or under this Act.

(2) The liquidator (not being the official receiver) may at any time, if he thinks fit, summon separate general meetings of the company's creditors and contributories for the purpose of determining whether such a committee should be established and, if it is so determined, of establishing it.

The liquidator (not being the official receiver) shall summon such a meeting if he is requested, in accordance with the rules, to do so by one-tenth, in value, of the company's creditors.

(3) Where meetings are summoned under this section, or for the purpose of choosing a person to be liquidator, and either the meeting of creditors or the meeting of contributories decides that a liquidation committee should be established, but the other meeting does not so decide or decides that a committee should not be established, the committee shall be established in accordance with the rules, unless the court otherwise orders.

(4) The liquidation committee is not to be able or required to carry out its functions at any time when the official receiver is liquidator; but at any such time its functions are vested in the Secretary of State except to the extent that the rules otherwise provide.

(5) Where there is for the time being no liquidation committee, and the liquidator is a person other than the official receiver, the functions of such a committee are vested in the Secretary of State except to the extent that the rules otherwise provide.   **[141]**

NOTES
    Commencement: 29 December 1986.
    This section derived from the Insolvency Act 1985, s 74.

142. Liquidation committee (Scotland)

(1) Where a winding-up order has been made by the court in Scotland and separate meetings or creditors and contributories have been summoned for the purpose of choosing a person to be liquidator or, under section 138(4), only a meeting of creditors has been summoned for that purpose, those meetings or (as the case may be) that meeting may establish a committee ("the liquidation committee") to exercise the functions conferred on it by or under this Act.

(2) The liquidator may at any time, if he thinks fit, summon separate general meetings of the company's creditors and contributories for the purpose of determining whether such a committee should be established and, if it is so determined, of establishing it.

(3) The liquidator, if appointed by the court otherwise than under section 139(4)(a), is required to summon meetings under subsection (2) if he is requested, in accordance with the rules, to do so by one-tenth, in value, of the company's creditors.

(4) Where meetings are summoned under this section, or for the purpose of

choosing a person to be liquidator, and either the meeting of creditors or the meeting of contributories decides that a liquidation committee should be established, but the other meeting does not so decide that a committee should not be established, the committee shall be established in accordance with the rules, unless the court otherwise orders.

(5) Where in the case of any winding up there is for the time being no liquidation committee, the functions for such a committee are vested in the court except to the extent that the rules otherwise provide.

(6) In addition to the powers and duties conferred and imposed on it by this Act, a liquidation committee has such of the powers and duties of commissioners in a sequestration as may be conferred and imposed on such committees by the rules. **[142]**

NOTES
> Commencement: 29 December 1986.
> This section derived from the Insolvency Act 1985, s 75.

The liquidator's functions

143. General functions in winding up by the court

(1) The functions of the liquidator of a company which is being wound up by the court are to secure that the assets of the company are got in, realised and distributed to the company's creditors and, if there is a surplus, to the persons entitled to it.

(2) It is the duty of the liquidator of a company which is being wound up by the court in England and Wales, if he is not the official receiver—

    (*a*) to furnish the official receiver with such information,
    (*b*) to produce to the official receiver, and permit inspection by the official receiver of, such books, papers and other records, and
    (*c*) to give the official receiver such other assistance,

as the official receiver may reasonably require for the purposes of carrying out his functions in relation to the winding up. **[143]**

NOTES
> Commencement: 29 December 1986.
> This section derived from the Insolvency Act 1985, s 69(1), (2).

144. Custody of company's property

(1) When a winding-up order has been made, or where a provisional liquidator has been appointed, the liquidator or the provisional liquidator (as the case may be) shall take into his custody or under his control all the property and things in action to which the company is or appears to be entitled.

(2) In a winding up by the court in Scotland, if and so long as there is no liquidator, all the property of the company is deemed to be in the custody of the court. **[144]**

NOTES
> Commencement: 29 December 1986.
> This section derived from the Companies Act 1985, s 537.

145. Vesting of company property in liquidator

(1) When a company is being wound up by the court, the court may on the application of the liquidator by order direct that all or any part of the property of whatsoever description belonging to the company or held by trustees on its behalf shall vest in the liquidator by his official name; and thereupon the property to which the order relates vests accordingly.

(2) The liquidator may, after giving such indemnity (if any) as the court may direct, bring or defend in his official name any action or other legal proceeding which relates to that property or which it is necessary to bring or defend for the purpose of effectually winding up the company and recovering its property.   **[145]**

NOTES
    Commencement: 29 December 1986.
    This section derived from the Companies Act 1985, s 538.

146. Duty to summon final meeting

(1) Subject to the next subsection, if it appears to the liquidator of a company which is being wound up by the court that the winding up of the company is for practical purposes complete and the liquidator is not the official receiver, the liquidator shall summon a final general meeting of the company's creditors which—

    (*a*) shall receive the liquidator's report of the winding up, and
    (*b*) shall determine whether the liquidator should have his release under
        section 174 in Chapter VII of this Part.

(2) The liquidator may, if he thinks fit, give the notice summoning the final general meeting at the same time as giving notice of any final distribution of the company's property but, if summoned for an earlier date, that meeting shall be adjourned (and, if necessary, further adjourned) until a date on which the liquidator is able to report to the meeting that the winding up of the company is for practical purposes complete.

(3) In the carrying out of his functions in the winding up it is the duty of the liquidator to retain sufficient sums from the company's property to cover the expenses of summoning and holding the meeting required by this section. **[146]**

NOTES
    Commencement: 29 December 1986.
    This section derived from the Insolvency Act 1985, s 78.

General powers of court

147. Power to stay or sist winding up

(1) The court may at any time after an order for winding up, on the application either of the liquidator or the official receiver or any creditor or contributory, and on proof to the satisfaction of the court that all proceedings in the winding up ought to be stayed or sisted, make an order staying or sisting the proceedings, either altogether or for a limited time, on such terms and conditions as the court thinks fit.

(2) The court may, before making an order, require the official receiver to furnish to it a report with respect to any facts or matters which are in his opinion relevant to the application.

(3) A copy of every order made under this section shall forthwith be forwarded by the company, or otherwise as may be prescribed, to the registrar of companies, who shall enter it in his records relating to the company.   **[147]**

NOTES
Commencement: 29 December 1986.
This section derived from the Companies Act 1985, s 549.

148. Settlement of list of contributories and application of assets

(1) As soon as may be after making a winding-up order, the court shall settle a list of contributories, with power to rectify the register of members in all cases where rectification is required in pursuance of the Companies Act or this Act, and shall cause the company's assets to be collected, and applied in discharge of its liabilities.

(2) If it appears to the court that it will not be necessary to make calls on or adjust the rights of contributories, the court may dispense with the settlement of a list of contributories.

(3) In settling the list, the court shall distinguish between persons who are contributories in their own right and persons who are contributories as being representatives of or liable for the debts of others.   **[148]**

NOTES
Commencement: 29 December 1986.
This section derived from the Companies Act 1985, s 550.

149. Debts due from contributory to company

(1) The court may, at any time after making a winding-up order, make an order on any contributory for the time being on the list of contributories to pay, in manner directed by the order, any money due from him (or from the estate of the person whom he represents) to the company, exclusive of any money payable by him or the estate by virtue of any call in pursuance of the Companies Act or this Act.

(2) The court in making such an order may—

   (*a*) in the case of an unlimited company, allow to the contributory by way of set-off any money due to him or the estate which he represents from the company on any independent dealing or contract with the company, but not any money due to him as a member of the company in respect of any dividend or profit, and
   (*b*) in the case of a limited company, make to any director or manager whose liability is unlimited or to his estate the like allowance.

(3) In the case of any company, whether limited or unlimited, when all the creditors are paid in full (together with interest at the official rate), any money due on any account whatever to a contributory from the company may be allowed to him by way of set-off against any subsequent call.   **[149]**

NOTES
Commencement: 29 December 1986.
This section derived from the Companies Act 1985, s 552, and the Insolvency Act 1985, Sch 6, para 32.

150. Power to make calls

(1) The court may, at any time after making a winding-up order, and either before or after it has ascertained the sufficiency of the company's assets, make calls on all or any of the contributories for the time being settled on the list of the contributories to the extent of their liability, for payment of any money which the court considers necessary to satisfy the company's debts and liabilities, and the expenses of winding up, and for the adjustment of the rights of the contributories among themselves, and make an order for payment of any calls so made.

(2) In making a call the court may take into consideration the probability that some of the contributories may partly or wholly fail to pay it.   **[150]**

NOTES
Commencement: 29 December 1986.
This section derived from the Companies Act 1985, s 553.

151. Payment into bank of money due to company

(1) The court may order any contributory, purchaser or other person from whom money is due to the company to pay the amount due into the Bank of England (or any branch of it) to the account of the liquidator instead of to the liquidator, and such an order may be enforced in the same manner as if it had directed payment to the liquidator.

(2) All money and securities paid or delivered into the Bank of England (or branch) in the event of a winding up by the court are subject in all respects to the orders of the court.   **[151]**

NOTES
Commencement: 29 December 1986.
This section derived from the Companies Act 1985, s 554.

152. Order on contributory to be conclusive evidence

(1) An order made by the court on a contributory is conclusive evidence that the money (if any) thereby appearing to be due or ordered to be paid is due, but subject to any right of appeal.

(2) All other pertinent matters stated in the order are to be taken as truly stated as against all persons and in all proceedings except proceedings in Scotland against the heritable estate of a deceased contributory; and in that case the order is only prima facie evidence for the purpose of charging his heritable estate, unless his heirs or legatees of heritage were on the list of contributories at the time of the order being made.   **[152]**

NOTES
Commencement: 29 December 1986.
This section derived from the Companies Act 1985, s 555.

153. Power to exclude creditors not proving in time

The court may fix a time or times within which creditors are to prove their debts or claims or to be excluded from the benefit of any distribution made before those debts are proved.   **[153]**

NOTES
Commencement: 29 December 1986.
This section derived from the Companies Act 1985, s 557.

154. Adjustment of rights of contributories

The court shall adjust the rights of the contributories among themselves and distribute any surplus among the persons entitled to it. **[154]**

NOTES
    Commencement: 29 December 1986.
    This section derived from the Companies Act 1985, s 558.

155. Inspection of books by creditors, etc

(1) The court may, at any time after making a winding-up order, make such order for inspection of the company's books and papers by creditors and contributories as the court thinks just; and any books and papers in the company's possession may be inspected by creditors and contributories accordingly, but not further or otherwise.

   (2) Nothing in this section excludes or restricts any statutory rights of a government department or person acting under the authority of a government department. **[155]**

NOTES
    Commencement: 29 December 1986.
    This section derived from the Companies Act 1985, s 559.

156. Payment of expenses of winding up

The court may, in the event of the assets being insufficient to satisfy the liabilities, make an order as to the payment out of the assets of the expenses incurred in the winding up in such order of priority as the court thinks just.
[156]

NOTES
    Commencement: 29 December 1986.
    This section derived from the Companies Act 1985, s 560.

157. Attendance at company meetings (Scotland)

In the winding up by the court of a company registered in Scotland, the court has power to require the attendance of any officer of the company at any meeting of creditors or of contributories, or of a liquidation committee, for the purpose of giving information as to the trade, dealings, affairs or property of the company. **[157]**

NOTES
    Commencement: 29 December 1986.
    This section derived from the Companies Act 1985, s 562, and the Insolvency Act 1985, Sch 6, para 33.

158. Power to arrest absconding contributory

The court, at any time either before or after making a winding-up order, on proof of probable cause for believing that a contributory is about to quit the United Kingdom or otherwise to abscond or to remove or conceal any of his property for the purpose of evading payment of calls, may cause the contributory to be arrested and his books and papers and moveable personal property to be seized and him and them to be kept safely until such time as the court may order. **[158]**

NOTES
    Commencement: 29 December 1986.
    This section derived from the Companies Act 1985, s 565.

159. Powers of court to be cumulative

Powers conferred by this Act and the Companies Act on the court are in addition to, and not in restriction of, any existing powers of instituting proceedings against a contributory or debtor of the company, or the estate of any contributory or debtor, for the recovery of any call or other sums.   **[159]**

NOTES
    Commencement: 29 December 1986.
    This section derived from the Companies Act 1985, s 566.

160. Delegation of powers to liquidator (England and Wales)

(1) Provision may be made by rules for enabling or requiring all or any of the powers and duties conferred and imposed on the court in England and Wales by the Companies Act and this Act in respect of the following matters—

    (*a*) the holding and conducting of meetings to ascertain the wishes of creditors and contributories,

    (*b*) the settling of lists of contributories and the rectifying of the register of members where required, and the collection and application of the assets,

    (*c*) the payment, delivery, conveyance, surrender or transfer of money, property, books or papers to the liquidator,

    (*d*) the making of calls,

    (*e*) the fixing of a time within which debts and claims must be proved,

to be exercised or performed by the liquidator as an officer of the court, and subject to the court's control.

    (2) But the liquidator shall not, without the special leave of the court, rectify the register of members, and shall not make any call without either that special leave or the sanction of the liquidation committee.   **[160]**

NOTES
    Commencement: 29 December 1986.
    This section derived from the Companies Act 1985, s 567, and the Insolvency Act 1985, Sch 6, para 34.

Enforcement of, and appeal from, orders

161. Orders for calls on contributories (Scotland)

(1) In Scotland, where an order, interlocutor or decree has been made for winding up a company by the court, it is competent to the court, on production by the liquidators of a list certified by them of the names of the contributories liable in payment of any calls, and of the amount due by each contributory, and of the date when that amount became due, to pronounce forthwith a decree against those contributories for payment of the sums so certified to be due, with interest from that date until payment (at 5 per cent. per annum) in the same way and to the same effect as if they had severally consented to registration for execution, on a charge of 6 days, of a legal obligation to pay those calls and interest.

(2) The decree may be extracted immediately, and no suspension of it is competent, except on caution or consignation, unless with special leave of the court. **[161]**

NOTES
Commencement: 29 December 1986.
This section derived from the Companies Act 1985, s 569.

162. Appeals from orders in Scotland

(1) Subject to the provisions of this section and to rules of court, an appeal from any order or decision made or given in the winding up of a company by the court in Scotland under this Act lies in the same manner and subject to the same conditions as an appeal from an order or decision of the court in cases within its ordinary jurisdiction.

(2) In regard to orders or judgments pronounced by the judge acting as vacation judge in pursuance of section 4 of the Administration of Justice (Scotland) Act 1933—

(a) none of the orders specified in Part I of Schedule 3 to this Act are subject to review, reduction, suspension or stay of execution, and

(b) every other order or judgment (except as mentioned below) may be submitted to review by the Inner House by reclaiming motion enrolled within 14 days from the date of the order or judgement.

(3) However, an order being one of those specified in Part II of that Schedule shall, from the date of the order and notwithstanding that it has been submitted to review as above, be carried out and receive effect until the Inner House have disposed of the matter.

(4) In regard to orders or judgments pronounced in Scotland by a Lord Ordinary before whom proceedings in a winding up are being taken, any such order or judgment may be submitted to review by the Inner House by reclaiming motion enrolled within 14 days from its date; but should it not be so submitted to review during sessions, the provisions of this section in regard to orders or judgments pronounced by the judge acting as vacation judge apply.

(5) Nothing in this section affects provisions of the Companies Act or this Act in reference to decrees in Scotland for payment of calls in the winding up of companies, whether voluntary or by the court. **[162]**

NOTES
Commencement: 29 December 1986.
This section derived from the Companies Act 1985, s 571.

CHAPTER VII

LIQUIDATORS

Preliminary

163. Style and title of liquidators

The liquidator of a company shall be described—

(a) where a person other than the official receiver is liquidator, by the style of "the liquidator" of the particular company, or

(b) where the official receiver is liquidator, by the style of "the official receiver and liquidator" of the particular company;

and in neither case shall he be described by an individual name.   **[163]**

NOTES
Commencement: 29 December 1986.
This section derived from the Insolvency Act 1985, s 94.

164. Corrupt inducement affecting appointment

A person who gives, or agrees or offers to give, to any member or creditor of a company any valuable consideration with a view to securing his own appointment or nomination, or to securing or preventing the appointment or nomination of some person other than himself, as the company's liquidator is liable to a fine.   **[164]**

NOTES
Commencement: 29 December 1986.
This section derived from the Companies Act 1985, s 635.

Liquidator's powers and duties

165. Voluntary winding up

(1) This section has effect where a company is being wound up voluntarily, but subject to section 166 below in the case of a creditors' voluntary winding up.

(2) The liquidator may—

(*a*) in the case of a members' voluntary winding up, with the sanction of an extraordinary resolution of the company, and

(*b*) in the case of a creditors' voluntary winding up, with the sanction of the court or the liquidation committee (or, if there is no such committee, a meeting of the company's creditors),

exercise any of the powers specified in Part I of Schedule 4 to this Act (payment of debts, compromise of claims, etc).

(3) The liquidator may, without sanction, exercise either of the powers specified in Part II of that Schedule (institution and defence of proceedings; carrying on the business of the company) and any of the general powers specified in Part III of that Schedule.

(4) The liquidator may—

(*a*) exercise the court's power of settling a list of contributories (which list is prima facie evidence of the liability of the persons named in it to be contributories),

(*b*) exercise the court's power of making calls,

(*c*) summon general meetings of the company for the purpose of obtaining its sanction by special or extraordinary resolution or for any other purpose he may think fit.

(5) The liquidator shall pay the company's debts and adjust the rights of the contributories among themselves.

(6) Where the liquidator in exercise of the powers conferred on him by this Act disposes of any property of the company to a person who is connected with the company (within the meaning of section 249 in Part VII), he shall, if there is for the time being a liquidation committee, give notice to the committee of that exercise of his powers.   **[165]**

NOTES
Commencement: 29 December 1986.
This section derived from the Companies Act 1985, ss 539(1)(*d*), (*e*), (*f*), 598, and the Insolvency Act 1985, s 84(1), Sch 6, para 41.

166. Creditors' voluntary winding up

(1) This section applies where, in the case of a creditors' voluntary winding up, a liquidator has been nominated by the company.

(2) The powers conferred on the liquidator by section 165 shall not be exercised, except with the sanction of the court, during the period before the holding of the creditors' meeting under section 98 in Chapter IV.

(3) Subsection (2) does not apply in relation to the power of the liquidator—

    (*a*) to take into his custody or under his control all the property to which the company is or appears to be entitled;

    (*b*) to dispose of perishable goods and other goods the value of which is likely to diminish if they are not immediately disposed of; and

    (*c*) to do all such other things as may be necessary for the protection of the company's assets.

(4) The liquidator shall attend the creditors' meeting held under section 98 and shall report to the meeting on any exercise by him of his powers (whether or not under this section or under section 112 or 165).

(5) If default is made—

    (*a*) by the company in complying with subsection (1) or (2) of section 98, or

    (*b*) by the directors in complying with subsection (1) or (2) of section 99,

the liquidator shall, within 7 days of the relevant day, apply to the court for directions as to the manner in which that default is to be remedied.

(6) "The relevant day" means the day on which the liquidator was nominated by the company or the day on which he first became aware of the default, whichever is the later.

(7) If the liquidator without reasonable excuse fails to comply with this section, he is liable to a fine. **[166]**

NOTES
Commencement: 29 December 1986.
This section derived from the Insolvency Act 1985, s 84.

167. Winding up by the court

(1) Where a company is being wound up by the court, the liquidator may—

    (*a*) with the sanction of the court or the liquidation committee, exercise any of the powers specified in Parts I and II of Schedule 4 to this Act (payment of debts; compromise of claims, etc; institution and defence of proceedings; carrying on of the business of the company), and

    (*b*) with or without that sanction, exercise any of the general powers specified in Part III of that Schedule.

(2) Where the liquidator (not being the official receiver), in exercise of the powers conferred on him by this Act—

    (*a*) disposes of any property of the company to a person who is connected with the company (within the meaning of section 249 in Part VII), or

(b) employs a solicitor to assist him in the carrying out of his functions,

he shall, if there is for the time being a liquidation committee, give notice to the committee of that exercise of his powers.

(3) The exercise by the liquidator in a winding up by the court of the powers conferred by this section is subject to the control of the court, and any creditor or contributory may apply to the court with respect to any exercise or proposed exercise of any of those powers.   **[167]**

NOTES
  Commencement: 29 December 1986.
  This section derived from the Companies Act 1985, s 539(1), (2), (2A), (3), and the Insolvency Act 1985, Sch 6, para 31(2), (3).

168. Supplementary powers (England and Wales)

(1) This section applies in the case of a company which is being wound up by the court in England and Wales.

(2) The liquidator may summon general meetings of the creditors or contributories for the purpose of ascertaining their wishes; and it is his duty to summon meetings at such times as the creditors or contributories by resolution (either at the meeting appointing the liquidator or otherwise) may direct, or whenever requested in writing to do so by one-tenth in value of the creditors or contributories (as the case may be).

(3) The liquidator may apply to the court (in the prescribed manner) for directions in relation to any particular matter arising in the winding up.

(4) Subject to the provisions of this Act, the liquidator shall use his own discretion in the management of the assets and their distribution among the creditors.

(5) If any person is aggrieved by an act or decision of the liquidator, that person may apply to the court; and the court may confirm, reverse or modify the act or decision complained of, and make such order in the case as it thinks just.   **[168]**

NOTES
  Commencement: 29 December 1986.
  This section derived from the Companies Act 1985, s 540(3)–(6).

169. Supplementary powers (Scotland)

(1) In the case of a winding up in Scotland, the court may provide by order that the liquidator may, where there is no liquidation committee, exercise any of the following powers, namely—

  (a) to bring or defend any action or other legal proceedings in the name and on behalf of the company, or
  (b) to carry on the business of the company so far as may be necessary for its beneficial winding up,

without the sanction or intervention of the court.

(2) In a winding up by the court in Scotland, the liquidator has (subject to the rules) the same powers as a trustee on a bankrupt estate.   **[169]**

NOTES
Commencement: 29 December 1986.
This section derived from the Companies Act 1985, s 539(4), (5), and the Insolvency Act 1985,
Sch 6, para 31(4).

170. Enforcement of liquidator's duty to make returns, etc

(1) If a liquidator who has made any default—

   (a) in filing, delivering or making any return, account or other document, or

   (b) in giving any notice which he is by law required to file, deliver, make or give,

fails to make good the default within 14 days after the service on him of a notice requiring him to do so, the court has the following powers.

(2) On an application made by any creditor or contributory of the company, or by the registrar of companies, the court may make an order directing the liquidator to make good the default within such time as may be specified in the order.

(3) The court's order may provide that all costs of and incidental to the application shall be borne by the liquidator.

(4) Nothing in this section prejudices the operation of any enactment imposing penalties on a liquidator in respect of any such default as is mentioned above. **[170]**

NOTES
Commencement: 29 December 1986.
This section derived from the Companies Act 1985, s 636.

Removal; vacation of office

171. Removal, etc (voluntary winding up)

(1) This section applies with respect to the removal from office and vacation of office of the liquidator of a company which is being wound up voluntarily.

(2) Subject to the next subsection, the liquidator may be removed from office only by an order of the court or—

   (a) in the case of a members' voluntary winding up, by a general meeting of the company summoned specially for that purpose, or

   (b) in the case of a creditors' voluntary winding up, by a general meeting of the company's creditors summoned specially for that purpose in accordance with the rules.

(3) Where the liquidator was appointed by the court under section 108 in Chapter V, a meeting such as is mentioned in subsection (2) above shall be summoned for the purpose of replacing him only if he thinks fit or the court so directs or the meeting is requested, in accordance with the rules—

   (a) in the case of a members' voluntary winding up, by members representing not less than one-half of the total voting rights of all the members having at the date of the request a right to vote at the meeting, or

   (b) in the case of a creditors' voluntary winding up, by not less than one-half, in value, of the company's creditors.

(4) A liquidator shall vacate office if he ceases to be a person who is qualified to act as an insolvency practitioner in relation to the company.

(5) A liquidator may, in the prescribed circumstances, resign his office by giving notice of his resignation to the registrar of companies.

(6) Where—

(a) in the case of a members' voluntary winding up, a final meeting of the company has been held under section 94 in Chapter III, or

(b) in the case of a creditors' voluntary winding up, final meetings of the company and of the creditors have been held under section 106 in Chapter IV,

the liquidator whose report was considered at the meeting or meetings shall vacate office as soon as he has complied with subsection (3) of that section and has given notice to the registrar of companies that the meeting or meetings have been held and of the decisions (if any) of the meeting or meetings.　　　**[171]**

NOTES

Commencement: 29 December 1986.

This section derived from the Insolvency Act 1985, s 86.

172. Removal, etc (winding up by the court)

(1) This section applies with respect to the removal from office and vacation of office of the liquidator of a company which is being wound up by the court, or of a provisional liquidator.

(2) Subject as follows, the liquidator may be removed from office only by an order of the court or by a general meeting of the company's creditors summoned specially for that purpose in accordance with the rules; and a provisional liquidator may be removed from office only by an order of the court.

(3) Where—

(a) the official receiver is liquidator otherwise than in succession under section 136(3) to a person who held office as a result of a nomination by a meeting of the company's creditors or contributories, or

(b) the liquidator was appointed by the court otherwise than under section 139(4)(a) or 140(1), or was appointed by the Secretary of State,

a general meeting of the company's creditors shall be summoned for the purpose of replacing him only if he thinks fit, or the court so directs, or the meeting is requested, in accordance with the rules, by not less than one-quarter, in value, of the creditors.

(4) If appointed by the Secretary of State, the liquidator may be removed from office by a direction of the Secretary of State.

(5) A liquidator or provisional liquidator, not being the official receiver, shall vacate office if he ceases to be a person who is qualified to act as an insolvency practitioner in relation to the company.

(6) A liquidator may, in the prescribed circumstances, resign his office by giving notice of his resignation to the court.

(7) Where an order is made under section 204 (early dissolution in Scotland) for the dissolution of the company, the liquidator shall vacate office when the dissolution of the company takes effect in accordance with that section.

(8) Where a final meeting has been held under section 146 (liquidator's

report on completion of winding up), the liquidator whose report was considered at the meeting shall vacate office as soon as he has given notice to the court and the registrar of companies that the meeting has been held and of the decisions (if any) of the meeting. **[172]**

NOTES
Commencement: 29 December 1986.
This section derived from the Insolvency Act 1985, s 79.

Release of liquidator

173. Release (voluntary winding up)

(1) This section applies with respect to the release of the liquidator of a company which is being wound up voluntarily.

(2) A person who has ceased to be a liquidator shall have his release with effect from the following time, that is to say—

  (a) in the case of a person who has been removed from office by a general meeting of the company or by a general meeting of the company's creditors that has not resolved against his release or who has died, the time at which notice is given to the registrar of companies in accordance with the rules that that person has ceased to hold office;

  (b) in the case of a person who has been removed from office by a general meeting of the company's creditors that has resolved against his release, or by the court, or who has vacated office under section 171(4) above, such time as the Secretary of State may, on the application of that person, determine;

  (c) in the case of a person who has resigned, such time as may be prescribed;

  (d) in the case of a person who has vacated office under subsection (6)(a) of section 171, the time at which he vacated office;

  (e) in the case of a person who has vacated office under subsection (6)(b) of that section—

    (i) if the final meeting of the creditors referred to in that subsection has resolved against that person's release, such time as the Secretary of State may, on an application by that person, determine, and

    (ii) if that meeting has not resolved against that person's release, the time at which he vacated office.

(3) In the application of subsection (2) to the winding up of a company registered in Scotland, the references to a determination by the Secretary of State as to the time from which a person who has ceased to be liquidator shall have his release are to be read as references to such a determination by the Accountant of Court.

(4) Where a liquidator has his release under subsection (2), he is, with effect from the time specified in that subsection, discharged from all liability both in respect of acts or omissions of his in the winding up and otherwise in relation to his conduct as liquidator.

But nothing in this section prevents the exercise, in relation to a person who has had his release under subsection (2), of the court's powers under section 212 of this Act (summary remedy against delinquent directors, liquidators, etc).

[173]

NOTES
Commencement: 29 December 1986.
This section derived from the Insolvency Act 1985, s 87.

174. Release (winding up by the court)

(1) This section applies with respect to the release of the liquidator of a company which is being wound up by the court, or of a provisional liquidator.

(2) Where the official receiver has ceased to be liquidator and a person becomes liquidator in his stead, the official receiver has his release with effect from the following time, that is to say—

    (*a*) in a case where that person was nominated by a general meeting of creditors or contributories, or was appointed by the Secretary of State, the time at which the official receiver gives notice to the court that he has been replaced;

    (*b*) in a case where that person is appointed by the court, such time as the court may determine.

(3) If the official receiver while he is a liquidator gives notice to the Secretary of State that the winding up is for practical purposes complete, he has his release with effect from such time as the Secretary of State may determine.

(4) A person other than the official receiver who has ceased to be a liquidator has his release with effect from the following time, that is to say—

    (*a*) in the case of a person who has been removed from office by a general meeting of creditors that has not resolved against his release or who has died, the time at which notice is given to the court in accordance with the rules that that person has ceased to hold office;

    (*b*) in the case of a person who has been removed from office by a general meeting of creditors that has resolved against his release, or by the court or the Secretary of State, or who has vacated office under section 172(5) or (7), such time as the Secretary of State may, on an application by that person, determine;

    (*c*) in the case of a person who has resigned, such time as may be prescribed;

    (*d*) in the case of a person who has vacated office under section 172(8)—

        (i) if the final meeting referred to in that subsection has resolved against that person's release, such time as the Secretary of State may, on an application by that person, determine, and

        (ii) if that meeting has not so resolved, the time at which that person vacated office.

(5) A person who has ceased to hold office as a provisional liquidator has his release with effect from such time as the court may, on an application by him, determine.

(6) Where the official receiver or a liquidator or provisional liquidator has his release under this section, he is, with effect from the time specified in the preceding provisions of this section, discharged from all liability both in respect of acts or omissions of his in the winding up and otherwise in relation to his conduct as liquidator or provisional liquidator.

But nothing in this section prevents the exercise, in relation to a person who has had his release under this section, of the court's powers under section 212 (summary remedy against delinquent directors, liquidators, etc).

(7) In the application of this section to a case where the order for winding up has been made by the court in Scotland, the references to a determination by the Secretary of State as to the time from which a person who has ceased to be liquidator has his release are to such a determination by the Accountant of Court. **[174]**

NOTES

Commencement: 29 December 1986.
This section derived from the Insolvency Act 1985, s 80.

CHAPTER VIII

PROVISIONS OF GENERAL APPLICATION IN WINDING UP

Preferential debts

175. Preferential debts (general provision)

(1) In a winding up the company's preferential debts (within the meaning given by section 386 in Part XII) shall be paid in priority to all other debts.

(2) Preferential debts—

    (*a*) rank equally among themselves after the expenses of the winding up and shall be paid in full, unless the assets are insufficient to meet them, in which case they abate in equal proportions; and

    (*b*) so far as the assets of the company available for payment of general creditors are insufficient to meet them, have priority over the claims of holders of debentures secured by, or holders of, any floating charge created by the company, and shall be paid accordingly out of any property comprised in or subject to that charge. **[175]**

NOTES

Commencement: 29 December 1986.
This section derived from the Insolvency Act 1985, s 89(1), (2).

176. Preferential charge on goods distrained

(1) This section applies where a company is being wound up by the court in England and Wales, and is without prejudice to section 128 (avoidance of attachments, etc).

(2) Where any person (whether or not a landlord or person entitled to rent) has distrained upon the goods or effects of the company in the period of 3 months ending with the date of the winding-up order, those goods or effects, or the proceeds of their sale, shall be charged for the benefit of the company with the preferential debts of the company to the extent that the company's property is for the time being insufficient for meeting them.

(3) Where by virtue of a charge under subsection (2) any person surrenders any goods or effects to a company or makes a payment to a company, that person ranks, in respect of the amount of the proceeds of sale of those goods or effects by the liquidator or (as the case may be) the amount of the payment, as a preferential creditor of the company, except as against so much of the company's property as is available for the payment of preferential creditors by virtue of the surrender or payment. **[176]**

NOTES

Commencement: 29 December 1986.

This section derived from the Insolvency Act 1985, s 89(3), (4).

Special managers

177. Power to appoint special manager

(1) Where a company has gone into liquidation or a provisional liquidator has been appointed, the court may, on an application under this section, appoint any person to be the special manager of the business or property of the company.

(2) The application may be made by the liquidator or provisional liquidator in any case where it appears to him that the nature of the business or property of the company, or the interests of the company's creditors or contributories or members generally, require the appointment of another person to manage the company's business or property.

(3) The special manager has such powers as may be entrusted to him by the court.

(4) The court's power to entrust powers to the special manager includes power to direct that any provision of this Act that has effect in relation to the provisional liquidator or liquidator of a company shall have the like effect in relation to the special manager for the purposes of the carrying out by him of any of the functions of the provisional liquidator or liquidator.

(5) The special manager shall—

    (*a*) give such security or, in Scotland, caution as may be prescribed;

    (*b*) prepare and keep such accounts as may be prescribed; and

    (*c*) produce those accounts in accordance with the rules to the Secretary of State or to such other persons as may be prescribed.   **[177]**

NOTES
Commencement: 29 December 1986.
This section derived from the Insolvency Act 1985, s 90.

Disclaimer (England and Wales only)

178. Power to disclaim onerous property

(1) This and the next two sections apply to a company that is being wound up in England and Wales.

(2) Subject as follows, the liquidator may, by the giving of the prescribed notice, disclaim any onerous property and may do so notwithstanding that he has taken possession of it, endeavoured to sell it, or otherwise exercised rights of ownership in relation to it.

(3) The following is onerous property for the purposes of this section—

    (*a*) any unprofitable contract, and

    (*b*) any other property of the company which is unsaleable or not readily saleable or is such that it may give rise to a liability to pay money or perform any other onerous act.

(4) A disclaimer under this section—

    (*a*) operates so as to determine, as from the date of the disclaimer, the rights, interests and liabilities of the company in or in respect of the property disclaimed; but (*b*) does not, except so far as is necessary for the purpose of releasing the company from any liability, affect the rights or liabilities of any other person.

(5) A notice of disclaimer shall not be given under this section in respect of any property if—

 (*a*) a person interested in the property has applied in writing to the liquidator or one of his predecessors as liquidator requiring the liquidator or that predecessor to decide whether he will disclaim or not, and

 (*b*) the period of 28 days beginning with the day on which that application was made, or such longer period as the court may allow, has expired without a notice of disclaimer having been given under this section in respect of that property.

(6) Any person sustaining loss or damage in consequence of the operation of a disclaimer under this section is deemed a creditor of the company to the extent of the loss or damage and accordingly may prove for the loss or damage in the winding up. **[178]**

NOTES
Commencement: 29 December 1986.
This section derived from the Insolvency Act 1985, s 91(1)–(4), (8).

179. Disclaimer of leaseholds

(1) The disclaimer under section 178 of any property of a leasehold nature does not take effect unless a copy of the disclaimer has been served (so far as the liquidator is aware of their addresses) on every person claiming under the company as underlessee or mortgagee and either—

 (*a*) no application under section 181 below is made with respect to that property before the end of the period of 14 days beginning with the day on which the last notice served under this subsection was served; or

 (*b*) where such an application has been made, the court directs that the disclaimer shall take effect.

(2) Where the court gives a direction under subsection (1)(*b*) it may also, instead of or in addition to any order it makes under section 181, make such orders with respect to fixtures, tenant's improvements and other matters arising out of the lease as it thinks fit. **[179]**

NOTES
Commencement: 29 December 1986.
This section derived from the Insolvency Act 1985, s 91(5), (6).

180. Land subject to rentcharge

(1) The following applies where, in consequence of the disclaimer under section 178 of any land subject to a rentcharge, that land vests by operation of law in the Crown or any other person (referred to in the next subsection as "the proprietor").

(2) The proprietor and the successors in title of the proprietor are not subject to any personal liability in respect of any sums becoming due under the

rentcharge except sums becoming due after the proprietor, or some person claiming under or through the proprietor, has taken possession or control of the land or has entered into occupation of it.   **[180]**

NOTES
Commencement: 29 December 1986.
This section derived from the Insolvency Act 1985, s 91(7).

181. Powers of court (general)

(1) This section and the next apply where the liquidator has disclaimed property under section 178.

   (2) An application under this section may be made to the court by—

   (a) any person who claims an interest in the disclaimed property, or
   (b) any person who is under any liability in respect of the disclaimed property, not being a liability discharged by the disclaimer.

   (3) Subject as follows, the court may on the application make an order, on such terms as it thinks fit, for the vesting of the disclaimed property in, or for its delivery to—

   (a) a person entitled to it or a trustee for such a person, or
   (b) a person subject to such a liability as is mentioned in subsection (2)(b) or a trustee for such a person.

   (4) The court shall not make an order under subsection (3)(b) except where it appears to the court that it would be just to do so for the purpose of compensating the person subject to the liability in respect of the disclaimer.

   (5) The effect of any order under this section shall be taken into account in assessing for the purpose of section 178(6) the extent of any loss or damage sustained by any person in consequence of the disclaimer.

   (6) An order under this section vesting property in any person need not be completed by conveyance, assignment or transfer.   **[181]**

NOTES
Commencement: 29 December 1986.
This section derived from the Insolvency Act 1985, s 92(1)–(4), (9), (10).

182. Powers of court (leaseholds)

(1) The court shall not make an order under section 181 vesting property of a leasehold nature in any person claiming under the company as underlessee or mortgagee except on terms making that person—

   (a) subject to the same liabilities and obligations as the company was subject to under the lease at the commencement of the winding up, or
   (b) if the court thinks fit, subject to the same liabilities and obligations as that person would be subject to if the lease had been assigned to him at the commencement of the winding up.

   (2) For the purposes of an order under section 181 relating to only part of any property comprised in a lease, the requirements of subsection (1) apply as if the lease comprised only the property to which the order relates.

   (3) Where subsection (1) applies and no person claiming under the company as underlessee or mortgagee is willing to accept an order under section 181 on the terms required by virtue of that subsection, the court may, by order under that section, vest the company's estate or interest in the property in any person

who is liable (whether personally or in a representative capacity, and whether alone or jointly with the company) to perform the lessee's covenants in the lease.

The court may vest that estate and interest in such a person freed and discharged from all estates, incumbrances and interests created by the company.

(4) Where subsection (1) applies and a person claiming under the company as underlessee or mortgagee declines to accept an order under section 181, that person is excluded from all interest in the property. **[182]**

NOTES
Commencement: 29 December 1986.
This section derived from the Insolvency Act 1985, s 92(5)–(8).

Execution, attachment and the Scottish equivalents

183. Effect of execution or attachment (England and Wales)

(1) Where a creditor has issued execution against the goods or land of a company or has attached any debt due to it, and the company is subsequently wound up, he is not entitled to retain the benefit of the execution or attachment against the liquidator unless he has completed the execution or attachment before the commencement of the winding up.

(2) However—

(a) if a creditor has had notice of a meeting having been called at which a resolution for voluntary winding up is to be proposed, the date on which he had notice is substituted, for the purpose of subsection (1), for the date of commencement of the winding up;

(b) a person who purchases in good faith under a sale by the sheriff any goods of a company on which execution has been levied in all cases acquires a good title to them against the liquidator; and

(c) the rights conferred by subsection (1) on the liquidator may be set aside by the court in favour of the creditor to such extent and subject to such terms as the court thinks fit.

(3) For purposes of this Act—

(a) an execution against goods is completed by seizure and sale, or by the making of a charging order under section 1 of the Charging Orders Act 1979;

(b) an attachment of a debt is completed by receipt of the debt; and

(c) an execution against land is completed by seizure, by the appointment of a receiver, or by the making of a charging order under section 1 of the Act above-mentioned.

(4) In this section, "goods" includes all chattels personal; and "the sheriff" includes any officer charged with the execution of a writ or other process.

(5) This section does not apply in the case of a winding up in Scotland.**[183]**

NOTES
Commencement: 29 December 1986.
This section derived from the Companies Act 1985, s 621.

184. Duties of sheriff (England and Wales)

(1) The following applies where a company's goods are taken in execution and, before their sale or the completion of the execution (by the receipt or recovery of the full amount of the levy), notice is served on the sheriff that a provisional

liquidator has been appointed or that a winding-up order has been made, or that a resolution for voluntary winding up has been passed.

(2) The sheriff shall, on being so required, deliver the goods and any money seized or received in part satisfaction of the execution to the liquidator; but the costs of execution are a first charge on the goods or money so delivered, and the liquidator may sell the goods, or a sufficient part of them, for the purpose of satisfying the charge.

(3) If under an execution in respect of a judgment for a sum exceeding [£500] a company's goods are sold or money is paid in order to avoid sale, the sheriff shall deduct the costs of the execution from the proceeds of sale or the money paid and retain the balance for 14 days.

(4) If within that time notice is served on the sheriff of a petition for the winding up of the company having been presented, or of a meeting having been called at which there is to be proposed a resolution for voluntary winding up, and an order is made or a resolution passed (as the case may be), the sheriff shall pay the balance to the liquidator, who is entitled to retain it as against the execution creditor.

(5) The rights conferred by this section on the liquidator may be set aside by the court in favour of the creditor to such extent and subject to such terms as the court thinks fit.

(6) In this section, "goods" includes all chattels personal; and "the sheriff" includes any officer charged with the execution of a writ or other process.

(7) The money sum for the time being specified in subsection (3) is subject to increase or reduction by order under section 416 in Part XV.

(8) This section does not apply in the case of a winding up in Scotland.**[184]**

NOTES
  Commencement: 29 December 1986.
  This section derived from the Companies Act 1985, s 622, and the Insolvency Act 1985, Sch 6, para 25.
  Sub-s (3): amended by SI 1986 No 1996, art 2, Schedule, Pt I.

185. Effect of diligence (Scotland)

(1) In the winding up of a company registered in Scotland, the following provisions of the Bankruptcy (Scotland) Act 1985—

  (a) subsections (1) to (6) of section 37 (effect of sequestration on diligence); and
  (b) subsections (3), (4), (7) and (8) of section 39 (realisation of estate),

apply, so far as consistent with this Act, in like manner as they apply in the sequestration of a debtor's estate, with the substitutions specifed below and with any other necessary modifications.

(2) The substitutions to be made in those sections of the Act of 1985 are as follows—

  (a) for references to the debtor, substitute references to the company;
  (b) for references to the sequestration, substitute references to the winding up;
  (c) for references to the date of sequestration, substitute references to the commencement of the winding up of the company; and
  (d) for references to the permanent trustee, substitute references to the liquidator.

(3) In this section, "the commencement of the winding up of the company" means, where it is being wound up by the court, the day on which the winding-up order is made.

(4) This section, so far as relating to any estate or effects of the company situated in Scotland, applies in the case of a company registered in England and Wales as in the case of one registered in Scotland. **[185]**

NOTES
Commencement: 29 December 1986.
This section derived from the Companies Act 1985, s 623, and the Bankruptcy (Scotland) Act 1985, Sch 7, para 21.

Miscellaneous matters

186. Rescission of contracts by the court

(1) The court may, on the application of a person who is, as against the liquidator, entitled to the benefit or subject to the burden of a contract made with the company, make an order rescinding the contract on such terms as to payment by or to either party of damages for the non-performance of the contract, or otherwise as the court thinks just.

(2) Any damages payable under the order to such a person may be proved by him as a debt in the winding up. **[186]**

NOTES
Commencement: 29 December 1986.
This section derived from the Companies Act 1985, s 619(4).

187. Power to make over assets to employees

(1) On the winding up of a company (whether by the court or voluntarily), the liquidator may, subject to the following provisions of this section, make any payment which the company has, before the commencement of the winding up, decided to make under section 719 of the Companies Act (power to provide for employees or former employees on cessation or transfer of business).

(2) The power which a company may exercise by virtue only of that section may be exercised by the liquidator after the winding up has commenced if, after the company's liabilities have been fully satisfied and provision has been made for the expenses of the winding up, the exercise of that power has been sanctioned by such a resolution of the company as would be required of the company itself by section 719(3) before that commencement, if paragraph (*b*) of that subsection were omitted and any other requirement applicable to its exercise by the company had been met.

(3) Any payment which may be made by a company under this section (that is, a payment after the commencement of its winding up) may be made out of the company's assets which are available to the members on the winding up.

(4) On a winding up by the court, the exercise by the liquidator of his powers under this section is subject to the court's control, and any creditor or contributory may apply to the court with respect to any exercise or proposed exercise of the power.

(5) Subsections (1) and (2) above have effect notwithstanding anything in any rule of law or in section 107 of this Act (property of company after satisfaction of liabilities to be distributed among members). **[187]**

NOTES
    Commencement: 29 December 1986.
    This section derived from the Companies Act 1985, s 659, and the Insolvency Act 1985, Sch 6,
para 48.

188. Notification that company is in liquidation

(1) When a company is being wound up, whether by the court or voluntarily,
every invoice, order for goods or business letter issued by or behalf of the
company, or a liquidator of the company, or a receiver or manager of the
company's property, being a document on or in which the name of the company
appears, shall contain a statement that the company is being wound up.

(2) If default is made in complying with this section, the company and any
of the following persons who knowingly and wilfully authorises or permits the
default, namely, any officer of the company, any liquidator of the company and
any receiver or manager, is liable to a fine.   **[188]**

NOTES
    Commencement: 29 December 1986.
    This section derived from the Companies Act 1985, s 637.

189. Interest on debts

(1) In a winding up interest is payable in accordance with this section on any
debt proved in the winding up, including so much of any such debt as represents
interest on the remainder.

(2) Any surplus remaining after the payment of the debts proved in a
winding up shall, before being applied for any other purpose, be applied in
paying interest on those debts in respect of the periods during which they have
been outstanding since the company went into liquidation.

(3) All interest under this section ranks equally, whether or not the debts on
which it is payable rank equally.

(4) The rate of interest payable under this section in respect of any debt
("the official rate" for the purposes of any provision of this Act in which that
expression is used) is whichever is the greater of—

   (*a*) the rate specified in section 17 of the Judgments Act 1838 on the day
          on which the company went into liquidation, and
   (*b*) the rate applicable to that debt apart from the winding up.

(5) In the application of this section to Scotland—

   (*a*) references to a debt proved in a winding up have effect as references
          to a claim accepted in a winding up, and
   (*b*) the reference to section 17 of the Judgments Act 1838 has effect as a
          reference to the rules.   **[189]**

NOTES
    Commencement: 29 December 1986.
    This section derived from the Insolvency Act 1985, s 93.

190. Documents exempt from stamp duty

(1) In the case of a winding up by the court, or of a creditors' voluntary winding
up, the following has effect as regards exemption from duties chargeable under
the enactments relating to stamp duties.

(2) If the company is registered in England and Wales, the following documents are exempt from stamp duty—

> (*a*) every assurance relating solely to freehold or leasehold property, or to any estate, right or interest in, any real or personal property, which forms part of the company's assets and which, after the execution of the assurance, either at law or in equity, is or remains part of those assets, and
>
> (*b*) every writ, order, certificate, or other instrument or writing relating solely to the property of any company which is being wound up as mentioned in subsection (1), or to any proceeding under such a winding up.

"Assurance" here includes deed, conveyance, assignment and surrender.

(3) If the company is registered in Scotland, the following documents are exempt from stamp duty—

> (*a*) every conveyance relating solely to property which forms part of the company's assets and which, after the execution of the conveyance, is or remains the company's property for the benefit of its creditors,
>
> (*b*) any article of roup or sale, submission and every other instrument and writing whatsoever relating solely to the company's property, and
>
> (*c*) every deed or writing forming part of the proceedings in the winding up.

"Conveyance" here includes assignation, instrument, discharge, writing and deed. **[190]**

NOTES
  Commencement: 29 December 1986.
  This section derived from the Companies Act 1985, s 638.

191. Company's books to be evidence

Where a company is being wound up, all books and papers of the company and of the liquidators are, as between the contributories of the company, prima facie evidence of the truth of all matters purporting to be recorded in them.

[191]

NOTES
  Commencement: 29 December 1986.
  This section derived from the Companies Act 1985, s 639.

192. Information as to pending liquidations

(1) If the winding up of a company is not concluded within one year after its commencement, the liquidator shall, at such intervals as may be prescribed, until the winding up is concluded, send to the registrar of companies a statement in the prescribed form and containing the prescribed particulars with respect to the proceedings in, and position of, the liquidation.

(2) If a liquidator fails to comply with this section, he is liable to a fine and, for continued contravention, to a daily default fine. **[192]**

NOTES
  Commencement: 29 December 1986.
  This section derived from the Companies Act 1985, s 641.

193. Unclaimed dividends (Scotland)

(1) The following applies where a company registered in Scotland has been wound up, and is about to be dissolved.

(2) The liquidator shall lodge in an appropriate bank or institution as defined in section 73(1) of the Bankruptcy (Scotland) Act 1985 (not being a bank or institution in or of which the liquidator is acting partner, manager, agent or cashier) in the name of the Accountant of Court the whole unclaimed dividends and unapplied or undistributable balances, and the deposit receipts shall be transmitted to the Accountant of Court.

(3) The provisions of section 58 of the Bankruptcy (Scotland) Act 1985 (so far as consistent with this Act and the Companies Act) apply with any necessary modifications to sums lodged in a bank or institution under this section as they apply to sums deposited under section 57 of the Act first mentioned.   **[193]**

NOTES
    Commencement: 29 December 1986.
    This section derived from the Companies Act 1985, s 643, and the Bankruptcy (Scotland) Act 1985, Sch 7, para 22.

194. Resolutions passed at adjourned meetings

Where a resolution is passed at an adjourned meeting of a company's creditors or contributories, the resolution is treated for all purposes as having been passed on the date on which it was in fact passed, and not as having been passed on any earlier date.   **[194]**

NOTES
    Commencement: 29 December 1986.
    This section derived from the Companies Act 1985, s 644.

195. Meetings to ascertain wishes of creditors or contributories

(1) The court may—
    (*a*) as to all matters relating to the winding up of a company, have regard to the wishes of the creditors or contributories (as proved to it by any sufficient evidence), and
    (*b*) if it thinks fit, for the purpose of ascertaining those wishes, direct meetings of the creditors or contributories to be called, held and conducted in such manner as the court directs, and appoint a person to act as chairman of any such meeting and report the result of it to the court.

(2) In the case of creditors, regard shall be had to the value of each creditor's debt.

(3) In the case of contributories, regard shall be had to the number of votes conferred on each contributory by the Companies Act or the articles.   **[195]**

NOTES
    Commencement: 29 December 1986.
    This section derived from the Companies Act 1985, s 645.

196. Judicial notice of court documents

In all proceedings under this Part, all courts, judges and persons judicially acting, and all officers, judicial or ministerial, of any court, or employed in enforcing the process of any court shall take judicial notice—

(*a*) of the signature of any officer of the High Court or of a county court in England and Wales, or of the Court of Session or a sheriff court in Scotland, or of the High Court in Northern Ireland, and also

(*b*) of the official seal or stamp of the several offices of the High Court in England and Wales or Northern Ireland, or of the Court of Session, appended to or impressed on any document made, issued or signed under the provisions of this Act or the Companies Act, or any official copy of such a document. **[196]**

NOTES
Commencement: 29 December 1986.
This section derived from the Companies Act 1985, s 646.

197. Commission for receiving evidence

(1) When a company is wound up in England and Wales or in Scotland, the court may refer the whole or any part of the examination of witnesses—

(*a*) to a specified county court in England and Wales, or to the sheriff principal for a specified sheriffdom in Scotland, or

(*c*) to the High Court in Northern Ireland or a specified Northern Ireland County Court,

("specified" meaning specified in the order of the winding-up court).

(2) Any person exercising jurisdiction as a judge of the court to which the reference is made (or, in Scotland, the sheriff principal to whom it is made) shall then, by virtue of this section, be a commissioner for the purpose of taking the evidence of those witnesses.

(3) The judge or sheriff principal has in the matter referred the same power of summoning and examining witnesses, of requiring the production and delivery of documents, of punishing defaults by witnesses, and of allowing costs and expenses to witnesses, as the court which made the winding-up order.

These powers are in addition to any which the judge or sheriff principal might lawfully exercise apart from this section.

(4) The examination so taken shall be returned or reported to the court which made the order in such manner as the court requests.

(5) This section extends to Northern Ireland. **[197]**

NOTES
Commencement: 29 December 1986.
This section derived from the Companies Act 1985, s 647.

198. Court order for examination of persons in Scotland

(1) The court may direct the examination in Scotland of any person for the time being in Scotland (whether a contributory of the company or not), in regard to the trade, dealings, affairs or property of any company in course of being wound up, or of any person being a contributory of the company, so far as the company may be interested by reason of his being a contributory.

(2) The order or commission to take the examination shall be directed to the sheriff principal of the sheriffdom in which the person to be examined is residing or happens to be for the time; and the sheriff principal shall summon the person to appear before him at a time and place to be specified in the summons for examination on oath as a witness or as a haver, and to produce any books or papers called for which are in his possession or power.

(3) The sheriff principal may take the examination either orally or on written interrogatories, and shall report the same in writing in the usual form to the court, and shall transmit with the report the books and papers produced, if the originals are required and specified by the order or commission, or otherwise copies or extracts authenticated by the sheriff.

(4) If a person so summoned fails to appear at the time and place specified, or refuses to be examined or to make the production required, the sheriff principal shall proceed against him as a witness or have duly cited; and failing to appear or refusing to give evidence or make production may be proceeded against by the law of Scotland.

(5) The sheriff principal is entitled to such fees, and the witness is entitled to such allowances, as sheriffs principal when acting as commissioners under appointment from the Court of Session and as witnesses and havers are entitled to in the like cases according to the law and practice of Scotland.

(6) If any objection is stated to the sheriff principal by the witness, either on the ground of his incompetency as a witness, or as to the production required, or on any other ground, the sheriff principal may, if he thinks fit, report the objection to the court, and suspend the examination of the witness until it has been disposed of by the court.   **[198]**

NOTES
Commencement: 29 December 1986.
This section derived from the Companies Act 1985, s 648.

199. Costs of application for leave to proceed (Scottish companies)

Where a petition or application for leave to proceed with an action or proceeding against a company which is being wound up in Scotland is unopposed and is granted by the court, the costs of the petition or application shall, unless the court otherwise directs, be added to the amount of the petitioner's or applicant's claim against the company.   **[199]**

NOTES
Commencement: 29 December 1986.
This section derived from the Companies Act 1985, s 649.

200. Affidavits etc in United Kingdom and overseas

(1) An affidavit required to be sworn under or for the purposes of this Part may be sworn in the United Kingdom, or elsewhere in Her Majesty's dominions, before any court, judge or person lawfully authorised to take and receive affidavits, or before any of Her Majesty's consuls or vice-consuls in any place outside Her dominions.

(2) All courts, judges, justices, commissioners and persons acting judicially shall take judicial notice of the seal or stamp or signature (as the case may be) of any such court, judge, person, consul or vice-consul attached, appended or subscribed to any such affidavit, or to any other document to be used for the purposes of this Part.   **[200]**

NOTES
Commencement: 29 December 1986.
This section derived from the Companies Act 1985, s 650.

CHAPTER IX

DISSOLUTION OF COMPANIES AFTER WINDING UP

201. Dissolution (voluntary winding up)

(1) This section applies, in the case of a company wound up voluntarily, where the liquidator has sent to the registrar of companies his final account and return under section 94 (members' voluntary) or section 106 (creditors' voluntary).

(2) The registrar on receiving the account and return shall forthwith register them; and on the expiration of 3 months from the registration of the return the company is deemed to be dissolved.

(3) However, the court may, on the application of the liquidator or any other person who appears to the court to be interested, make an order deferring the date at which the dissolution of the company is to take effect for such time as the court thinks fit.

(4) It is the duty of the person on whose application an order of the court under this section is made within 7 days after the making of the order to deliver to the registrar an office copy of the order for registration; and if that person fails to do so he is liable to a fine and, for continued contravention, to a daily default fine.   **[201]**

NOTES
   Commencement: 29 December 1986.
   This section derived from the Companies Act 1985, ss 585(5), (6), 595(6), (7).

202. Early dissolution (England and Wales)

(1) This section applies where an order for the winding up of a company has been made by the court in England and Wales.

(2) The official receiver, if—

   (a) he is the liquidator of the company, and
   (b) it appears to him—

      (i) that the realisable assets of the company are insufficient to cover the expenses of the winding up, and
      (ii) that the affairs of the company do not require any further investigation,

may at any time apply to the registrar of companies for the early dissolution of the company.

(3) Before making that application, the official receiver shall give not less than 28 days' notice of his intention to do so to the company's creditors and contributories and, if there is an administrative receiver of the company, to that receiver.

(4) With the giving of that notice the official receiver ceases (subject to any directions under the next section) to be required to perform any duties imposed on him in relation to the company, its creditors or contributories by virtue of any provision of this Act, apart from a duty to make an application under subsection (2) of this section.

(5) On the receipt of the official receiver's application under subsection (2) the registrar shall forthwith register it and, at the end of the period of 3 months

beginning with the day of the registration of the application, the company shall be dissolved.

However, the Secretary of State may, on the application of the official receiver or any other person who appears to the Secretary of State to be interested, give directions under section 203 at any time before the end of that period.   **[202]**

NOTES
Commencement: 29 December 1986.
This section derived from the Insolvency Act 1985, s 76(1)–(3), (6).

203. Consequence of notice under s 202

(1) Where a notice has been given under section 202(3), the official receiver or any creditor or contributory of the company, or the administrative receiver of the company (if there is one) may apply to the Secretary of State for directions under this section.

(2) The grounds on which that application may be made are—

 (a) that the realisable assets of the company are sufficient to cover the expenses of the winding up;
 (b) that the affairs of the company do require further investigation; or
 (c) that for any other reason the early dissolution of the company is inappropriate.

(3) Directions under this section—

 (a) are directions making such provision as the Secretary of State thinks fit for enabling the winding up of the company to proceed as if no notice had been given under section 202(3), and
 (b) may, in the case of an application under section 202(5), include a direction deferring the date at which the dissolution of the company is to take effect for such period as the Secretary of State thinks fit.

(4) An appeal to the court lies from any decision of the Secretary of State on an application for directions under this section.

(5) It is the duty of the person on whose application any directions are given under this section, or in whose favour an appeal with respect to an application for such directions is determined, within 7 days after the giving of the directions or the determination of the appeal, to deliver to the registrar of companies for registration such a copy of the directions or determination as is prescribed.

(6) If a person without reasonable excuse fails to deliver a copy as required by subsection (5), he is liable to a fine and, for continued contravention, to a daily default fine.   **[203]**

NOTES
Commencement: 29 December 1986.
This section derived from the Insolvency Act 1985, s 76(4), (5), (7)–(10).

204. Early dissolution (Scotland)

(1) This section applies where a winding-up order has been made by the court in Scotland.

(2) If after a meeting or meetings under section 138 (appointment of liquidator in Scotland) it appears to the liquidator that the realisable assets of

the company are insufficient to cover the expenses of the winding up, he may apply to the court for an order that the company be dissolved.

(3) Where the liquidator makes that application, if the court is satisfied that the realisable assets of the company are insufficient to cover the expenses of the winding up and it appears to the court appropriate to do so, the court shall make an order that the company be dissolved in accordance with this section.

(4) A copy of the order shall within 14 days from its date be forwarded by the liquidator to the registrar of companies, who shall forthwith register it; and, at the end of the period of 3 months beginning with the day of the registration of the order, the company shall be dissolved.

(5) The court may, on an application by any person who appears to the court to have an interest, order that the date at which the dissolution of the company is to take effect shall be deferred for such period as the court thinks fit.

(6) It is the duty of the person on whose application an order is made under subsection (5), within 7 days after the making of the order, to deliver to the registrar of companies such a copy of the order as is prescribed.

(7) If the liquidator without reasonable excuse fails to comply with the requirements of subsection (4), he is liable to a fine and, for continued contravention, to a daily default fine.

(8) If a person without reasonable excuse fails to deliver a copy as required by subsection (6), he is liable to a fine and, for continued contravention, to a daily default fine. **[204]**

NOTES

Commencement: 29 December 1986.

This section derived from the Insolvency Act 1985, s 77.

205. Dissolution otherwise than under ss 202–204

(1) This section applies where the registrar of companies receives—

(*a*) a notice served for the purposes of section 172(8) (final meeting of creditors and vacation of office by liquidator), or

(*b*) a notice from the official receiver that the winding up of a company by the court is complete.

(2) The registrar shall, on receipt of the notice, forthwith register it; and, subject as follows, at the end of the period of 3 months beginning with the day of the registration of the notice, the company shall be dissolved.

(3) The Secretary of State may, on the application of the official receiver or any other person who appears to the Secretary of State to be interested, give a direction deferring the date at which the dissolution of the company is to take effect for such period as the Secretary of State thinks fit.

(4) An appeal to the court lies from any decision of the Secretary of State on an application for a direction under subsection (3).

(5) Subsection (3) does not apply in a case where the winding-up order was made by the court in Scotland, but in such a case the court may, on an application by any person appearing to the court to have an interest, order that the date at which the dissolution of the company is to take effect shall be deferred for such period as the court thinks fit.

(6) It is the duty of the person—

    (*a*) on whose application a direction is given under subsection (3);

    (*b*) in whose favour an appeal with respect to an application for such a direction is determined; or

    (*c*) on whose application an order is made under subsection (5),

within 7 days after the giving of the direction, the determination of the appeal or the making of the order, to deliver to the registrar for registration such a copy of the direction, determination or order as is prescribed.

(7) If a person without reasonable excuse fails to deliver a copy as required by subsection (6), he is liable to a fine and, for continued contravention, to a daily default fine. **[205]**

NOTES

    Commencement: 29 December 1986.

    This section derived from the Insolvency Act 1985, s 81.

CHAPTER X

MALPRACTICE BEFORE AND DURING LIQUIDATION; PENALISATION
OF COMPANIES AND COMPANY OFFICERS; INVESTIGATIONS
AND PROSECUTIONS

Offences of fraud, deception, etc

206. Fraud, etc in anticipation of winding up

(1) When a company is ordered to be wound up by the court, or passes a resolution for voluntary winding up, any person, being a past or present officer of the company, is deemed to have committed an offence if, within the 12 months immediately preceding the commencement of the winding up, he has—

    (*a*) concealed any part of the company's property to the value of [£500] or more, or concealed any debt due to or from the company, or

    (*b*) fraudulently removed any part of the company's property to the value of [£500] or more, or

    (*c*) concealed, destroyed, mutilated or falsified any book or paper affecting or relating to the company's property or affairs, or

    (*d*) made any false entry in any book or paper affecting or relating to the company's property or affairs, or

    (*e*) fraudulently parted with, altered or made any omission in any document affecting or relating to the company's property or affairs, or

    (*f*) pawned, pledged or disposed of any property of the company which has been obtained on credit and has not been paid for (unless the pawning, pledging or disposal was in the ordinary way of the company's business).

(2) Such a person is deemed to have committed an offence if within the period above mentioned he has been privy to the doing by others of any of the things mentioned in paragraphs (*c*), (*d*) and (*e*) of subsection (1); and he commits an offence if, at any time after the commencement of the winding up, he does any of the things mentioned in paragraphs (*a*) to (*f*) of that subsection, or is privy to the doing by others of any of the things mentioned in paragraphs (*c*) to (*e*) of it.

(3) For purposes of this section, "officer" includes a shadow director.

(4) It is a defence—

(*a*) for a person charged under paragraph (*a*) or (*f*) of subsection (1) (or under subsection (2) in respect of the things mentioned in either of those two paragraphs) to prove that he had no intent to defraud, and

(*b*) for a person charged under paragraph (*c*) or (*d*) of subsection (1) (or under subsection (2) in respect of the things mentioned in either of those two paragraphs) to prove that he had no intent to conceal the state of affairs of the company or to defeat the law.

(5) Where a person pawns, pledges or disposes of any property in circumstances which amount to an offence under subsection (1)(*f*), every person who takes in pawn or pledge, or otherwise receives, the property knowing it to be pawned, pledged or disposed of in such circumstances, is guilty of an offence.

(6) A person guilty of an offence under this section is liable to imprisonment or a fine, or both.

(7) The money sums specified in paragraphs (*a*) and (*b*) of subsection (1) are subject to increase or reduction by order under section 416 in Part XV.   **[206]**

NOTES
    Commencement: 29 December 1986.
    This section derived from the Companies Act 1985, s 624, and the Insolvency Act 1985, Sch 6, para 25.
    Sub-s (1): amended by SI 1986 No 1996, art 2, Schedule, Pt I.

207. Transactions in fraud of creditors

(1) When a company is ordered to be wound up by the court or passes a resolution for voluntary winding up, a person is deemed to have committed an offence if he, being at the time an officer of the company—

(*a*) has made or caused to be made any gift or transfer of, or charge on, or has caused or connived at the levying of any execution against, the company's property, or

(*b*) has concealed or removed any part of the company's property since, or within 2 months before, the date of any unsatisfied judgment or order for the payment of money obtained against the company.

(2) A person is not guilty of an offence under this section—

(*a*) by reason of conduct constituting an offence under subsection (1)(*a*) which occurred more than 5 years before the commencement of the winding up, or

(*b*) if he proves that, at the time of the conduct constituting the offence, he had no intent to defraud the company's creditors.

(3) A person guilty of an offence under this section is liable to imprisonment or a fine, or both.   **[207]**

NOTES
    Commencement: 29 December 1986.
    This section derived from the Companies Act 1985, s 625, and the Insolvency Act 1985, Sch 6, para 42.

208. Misconduct in course of winding up

(1) When a company is being wound up, whether by the court or voluntarily, any person, being a past or present officer of the company, commits an offence if he—

(a) does not to the best of his knowledge and belief fully and truly discover to the liquidator all the company's property, and how and to whom and for what consideration and when the company disposed of any part of that property (except such part as has been disposed of in the ordinary way of the company's business), or

(b) does not deliver up to the liquidator (or as he directs) all such part of the company's property as is in his custody or under his control, and which he is required by law to deliver up, or

(c) does not deliver up to the liquidator (or as he directs) all books and papers in his custody or under his control belonging to the company and which he is required by law to deliver up, or

(d) knowing or believing that a false debt has been proved by any person in the winding up, fails to inform the liquidator as soon as practicable, or

(e) after the commencement of the winding up, prevents the production of any book or paper affecting or relating to the company's property or affairs.

(2) Such a person commits an offence if after the commencement of the winding up he attempts to account for any part of the company's property by fictitious losses or expenses; and he is deemed to have committed that offence if he has so attempted at any meeting of the company's creditors within the 12 months immediately preceding the commencement of the winding up.

(3) For purposes of this section, "officer" includes a shadow director.

(4) It is a defence—

(a) for a person charged under paragraph (a), (b) or (c) of subsection (1) to prove that he had no intent to defraud, and

(b) for a person charged under paragraph (e) of that subsection to prove that he had no intent to conceal the state of affairs of the company or to defeat the law.

(5) A person guilty of an offence under this section is liable to imprisonment or a fine, or both.   **[208]**

NOTES
Commencement: 29 December 1986.
This section derived from the Companies Act 1985, s 626, and the Insolvency Act 1985, Sch 6, para 43.

209. Falsification of company's books

(1) When a company is being wound up, an officer or contributory of the company commits an offence if he destroys, mutilates, alters or falsifies any books, papers or securities, or makes or is privy to the making of any false or fraudulent entry in any register, book of account or document belonging to the company with intent to defraud or deceive any person.

(2) A person guilty of an offence under this section is liable to imprisonment or a fine, or both.   **[209]**

NOTES
Commencement: 29 December 1986.
This section derived from the Companies Act 1985, s 627.

210. Material omissions from statement relating to company's affairs

(1) When a company is being wound up, whether by the court or voluntarily, any person, being a past or present officer of the company, commits an offence if he makes any material omission in any statement relating to the company's affairs.

(2) When a company has been ordered to be wound up by the court, or has passed a resolution for voluntary winding up, any such person is deemed to have committed that offence if, prior to the winding up, he has made any material omission in any such statement.

(3) For purposes of this section, "officer" includes a shadow director.

(4) It is a defence for a person charged under this section to prove that he had no intent to defraud.

(5) A person guilty of an offence under this section is liable to imprisonment or a fine, or both. **[210]**

NOTES
Commencement: 29 December 1986.
This section derived from the Companies Act 1985, s 628.

211. False representations to creditors

(1) When a company is being wound up, whether by the court or voluntarily, any person, being a past or present officer of the company—

    (*a*) commits an offence if he makes any false representation or commits any other fraud for the purpose of obtaining the consent of the company's creditors or any of them to an agreement with reference to the company's affairs or to the winding up, and

    (*b*) is deemed to have committed that offence if, prior to the winding up, he has made any false representation, or committed any other fraud, for that purpose.

(2) For purposes of this section, "officer" includes a shadow director.

(3) A person guilty of an offence under this section is liable to imprisonment or a fine, or both. **[211]**

NOTES
Commencement: 29 December 1986.
This section derived from the Companies Act 1985, s 629.

Penalisation of directors and officers

212. Summary remedy against delinquent directors, liquidators, etc

(1) This section applies if in the course of the winding up of a company it appears that a person who—

    (*a*) is or has been an officer of the company,

    (*b*) has acted as liquidator, administrator or administrative receiver of the company, or

    (*c*) not being a person falling within paragraph (*a*) or (*b*), is or has been concerned, or has taken part, in the promotion, formation or management of the company,

has misapplied or retained, or become accountable for, any money or other property of the company, or been guilty of any misfeasance or breach of any fiduciary or other duty in relation to the company.

(2) The reference in subsection (1) to any misfeasance or breach of any fiduciary or other duty in relation to the company includes, in the case of a person who has acted as liquidator or administrator of the company, any misfeasance or breach of any fiduciary or other duty in connection with the carrying out of his functions as liquidator or administrator of the company.

(3) The court may, on the application of the official receiver or the liquidator, or of any creditor or contributory, examine into the conduct of the person falling within subsection (1) and compel him—

> (a) to repay, restore or account for the money or property or any part of it, with interest at such rate as the court thinks just, or
> (b) to contribute such sum to the company's assets by way of compensation in respect of the misfeasance or breach of fiduciary or other duty as the court thinks just.

(4) The power to make an application under subsection (3) in relation to a person who has acted as liquidator or administrator of the company is not exercisable, except with the leave of the court, after that person has had his release.

(5) The power of a contributory to make an application under subsection (3) is not exercisable except with the leave of the court, but is exercisable notwithstanding that he will not benefit from any order the court may make on the application.   **[212]**

NOTES

Commencement: 29 December 1986.
This section derived from the Insolvency Act 1985, s 19.

213. Fraudulent trading

(1) If in the course of the winding up of a company it appears that any business of the company has been carried on with intent to defraud creditors of the company or creditors of any other person, or for any fraudulent purpose, the following has effect.

(2) The court, on the application of the liquidator may declare that any persons who were knowingly parties to the carrying on of the business in the manner above-mentioned are to be liable to make such contributions (if any) to the company's assets as the court thinks proper.   **[213]**

NOTES

Commencement: 29 December 1986.
This section derived from the Companies Act 1985, s 630(1), (2), and the Insolvency Act 1985, Sch 6, para 6(1).

214. Wrongful trading

(1) Subject to subsection (3) below, if in the course of the winding up of a company it appears that subsection (2) of this section applies in relation to a person who is or has been a director of the company, the court, on the application of the liquidator, may declare that that person is to be liable to make such contribution (if any) to the company's assets as the court thinks proper.

(2) This subsection applies in relation to a person if—

> (a) the company has gone into insolvent liquidation,

(*b*) at some time before the commencement of the winding up of the company, that person knew or ought to have concluded that there was no reasonable prospect that the company would avoid going into insolvent liquidation, and

(*c*) that person was a director of the company at that time;

but the court shall not make a declaration under this section in any case where the time mentioned in paragraph (*b*) above was before 28th April 1986.

(3) The court shall not make a declaration under this section with respect to any person if it is satisfied that after the condition specified in subsection (2)(*b*) was first satisfied in relation to him that person took every step with a view to minimising the potential loss to the company's creditors as (assuming him to have known that there was no reasonable prospect that the company would avoid going into insolvent liquidation) he ought to have taken.

(4) For the purposes of subsections (2) and (3), the facts which a director of a company ought to know or ascertain, the conclusions which he ought to reach and the steps which he ought to take are those which would be known or ascertained, or reached or taken, by a reasonably diligent person having both—

(*a*) the general knowledge, skill and experience that may reasonably be expected of a person carrying out the same functions as are carried out by that director in relation to the company, and

(*b*) the general knowledge, skill and experience that that director has.

(5) The reference in subsection (4) to the functions carried out in relation to a company by a director of the company includes any functions which he does not carry out but which have been entrusted to him.

(6) For the purposes of this section a company goes into insolvent liquidation if it goes into liquidation at a time when its assets are insufficient for the payment of its debts and other liabilities and the expenses of the winding up.

(7) In this section "director" includes a shadow director.

(8) This section is without prejudice to section 213.   **[214]**

NOTES

Commencement: 29 December 1986.

This section derived from the Insolvency Act 1985, ss 12(9), 15(1)–(5), (7), Sch 9, para 4.

215. Proceedings under ss 213, 214

(1) On the hearing of an application under section 213 or 214, the liquidator may himself give evidence or call witnesses.

(2) Where under either section the court makes a declaration, it may give such further directions as it thinks proper for giving effect to the declaration; and in particular, the court may—

(*a*) provide for the liability of any person under the declaration to be a charge on any debt or obligation due from the company to him, or on any mortgage or charge or any interest in a mortgage or charge on assets of the company held by or vested in him, or any person on his behalf, or any person claiming as assignee from or through the person liable or any person acting on his behalf, and

(*b*) from time to time make such further order as may be necessary for enforcing any charge imposed under this subsection.

(3) For the purposes of subsection (2), "assignee"—

(*a*) includes a person to whom or in whose favour, by the directions of the person made liable, the debt, obligation, mortgage or charge was created, issued or transferred or the interest created, but

(*b*) does not include an assignee for valuable consideration (not including consideration by way of marriage) given in good faith and without notice of any of the matters on the ground of which the declaration is made.

(4) Where the court makes a declaration under either section in relation to a person who is a creditor of the company, it may direct that the whole or any part of any debt owed by the company to that person and any interest thereon shall rank in priority after all other debts owed by the company and after any interest on those debts.

(5) Sections 213 and 214 have effect notwithstanding that the person concerned may be criminally liable in respect of matters on the ground of which the declaration under the section is to be made.   **[215]**

NOTES
   Commencement: 29 December 1986.
   This section derived from the Companies Act 1985, s 630(3)–(6), and the Insolvency Act 1985, s 15(6), Sch 6, para 6(2), (3).

216. Restriction on re-use of company names

(1) This section applies to a person where a company ("the liquidating company") has gone into insolvent liquidation on or after the appointed day and he was a director or shadow director of the company at any time in the period of 12 months ending with the day before it went into liquidation.

(2) For the purposes of this section, a name is a prohibited name in relation to such a person if—

(*a*) it is a name by which the liquidating company was known at any time in that period of 12 months, or

(*b*) it is a name which is so similar to a name falling within paragraph (*a*) as to suggest an association with that company.

(3) Except with leave of the court or in such circumstances as may be prescribed, a person to whom this section applies shall not at any time in the period of 5 years beginning with the day on which the liquidating company went into liquidation—

(*a*) be a director of any other company that is known by a prohibited name, or

(*b*) in any way, whether directly or indirectly, be concerned or take part in the promotion, formation or management of any such company, or

(*c*) in any way, whether directly or indirectly, be concerned or take part in the carrying on of a business carried on (otherwise than by a company) under a prohibited name.

(4) If a person acts in contravention of this section, he is liable to imprisonment or a fine, or both.

(5) In subsection (3) "the court" means any court having jurisdiction to wind up companies; and on an application for leave under that subsection, the Secretary of State or the official receiver may appear and call the attention of the court to any matters which seem to him to be relevant.

(6) References in this section, in relation to any time, to a name by which a

company is known are to the name of the company at that time or to any name under which the company carries on business at that time.

(7) For the purposes of this section a company goes into insolvent liquidation if it goes into liquidation at a time when its assets are insufficient for the payment of its debts and other liabilities and the expenses of the winding up.

(8) In this section "company" includes a company which may be wound up under Part V of this Act.   **[216]**

NOTES
Commencement: 29 December 1986.
This section derived from the Insolvency Act 1985, s 17, Sch 9, para 5.

217. Personal liability for debts, following contravention of s 216

(1) A person is personally responsible for all the relevant debts of a company if at any time—

  (a) in contravention of section 216, he is involved in the management of the company, or

  (b) as a person who is involved in the management of the company, he acts or is willing to act on instructions given (without the leave of the court) by a person whom he knows at that time to be in contravention in relation to the company of section 216.

(2) Where a person is personally responsible under this section for the relevant debts of a company, he is jointly and severally liable in respect of those debts with the company and any other person who, whether under this section or otherwise, is so liable.

(3) For the purposes of this section the relevant debts of a company are—

  (a) in relation to a person who is personally responsible under paragraph (a) of subsection (1), such debts and other liabilities of the company as are incurred at a time when that person was involved in the management of the company, and

  (b) in relation to a person who is personally responsible under paragraph (b) of that subsection, such debts and other liabilities of the company as are incurred at a time when that person was acting or was willing to act on instructions given as mentioned in that paragraph.

(4) For the purposes of this section, a person is involved in the management of a company if he is a director of the company or if he is concerned, whether directly or indirectly, or takes part, in the management of the company.

(5) For the purposes of this section a person who, as a person involved in the management of a company, has at any time acted on instructions given (without the leave of the court) by a person whom he knew at that time to be in contravention in relation to the company of section 216 is presumed, unless the contrary is shown, to have been willing at any time thereafter to act on any instructions given by that person.

(6) In this section "company" includes a company which may be wound up under Part V.   **[217]**

NOTES
Commencement: 29 December 1986.
This section derived from the Insolvency Act 1985, s 18(1), (part), (2)–(6).

Investigation and prosecution of malpractice

218. Prosecution of delinquent officers and members of company

(1) If it appears to the court in the course of a winding up by the court that any past or present officer, or any member, of the company has been guilty of any offence in relation to the company for which he is criminally liable, the court may (either on the application of a person interested in the winding up or of its own motion) direct the liquidator to refer the matter to the prosecuting authority.

(2) "The prosecuting authority" means—

> (a) in the case of a winding up in England and Wales, the Director of Public Prosecutions, and
> (b) in the case of a winding up in Scotland, the Lord Advocate.

(3) If in the case of a winding up by the court in England and Wales it appears to the liquidator, not being the official receiver, that any past or present officer of the company, or any member of it, has been guilty of an offence in relation to the company for which he is criminally liable, the liquidator shall report the matter to the official receiver.

(4) If it appears to the liquidator in the course of a voluntary winding up that any past or present officer of the company, or any member of it, has been guilty of an offence in relation to the company for which he is criminally liable, he shall—

> (a) forthwith report the matter to the prosecuting authority, and
> (b) furnish to that authority such information and give to him such access to and facilities for inspecting and taking copies of documents (being information or documents in the possession or under the control of the liquidator and relating to the matter in question) as the authority requires.

(5) Where a report is made to him under subsection (4), the prosecuting authority may, if he thinks fit, refer the matter to the Secretary of State for further enquiry; and the Secretary of State—

> (a) shall thereupon investigate the matter, and
> (b) for the purpose of his investigation may exercise any of the powers which are exercisable by inspectors appointed under section 431 or 432 of the Companies Act to investigate a company's affairs.

(6) If it appears to the court in the course of a voluntary winding up that—

> (a) any past or present officer of the company, or any member of it, has been guilty as above-mentioned, and
> (b) no report with respect to the matter has been made by the liquidator to the prosecuting authority under subsection (4),

the court may (on the application of any person interested in the winding up or of its own motion) direct the liquidator to make such a report.

On a report being made accordingly, this section has effect as though the report had been made in pursuance of subsection (4).   **[218]**

NOTES

Commencement: 29 December 1986.

This section derived from the Companies Act 1985, s 632, and the Insolvency Act 1985, Sch 6, para 44.

219. Obligations arising under s 218

(1) For the purpose of an investigation by the Secretary of State under section 218(5), any obligation imposed on a person by any provision of the Companies Act to produce documents or give information to, or otherwise to assist, inspectors appointed as mentioned in that subsection is to be regarded as an obligation similarly to assist the Secretary of State in his investigation.

(2) An answer given by a person to a question put to him in exercise of the powers conferred by section 218(5) may be used in evidence against him.

(3) Where criminal proceedings are instituted by the prosecuting authority or the Secretary of State following any report or reference under section 218, it is the duty of the liquidator and every officer and agent of the company past and present (other than the defendant or defender) to give to that authority or the Secretary of State (as the case may be) all assistance in connection with the prosecution which he is reasonably able to give.

For this purpose "agent" includes any banker or solicitor of the company and any person employed by the company as auditor, whether that person is or is not an officer of the company.

(4) If a person fails or neglects to give assistance in the manner required by subsection (3), the court may, on the application of the prosecuting authority or the Secretary of State (as the case may be) direct the person to comply with that subsection; and if the application is made with respect to a liquidator, the court may (unless it appears that the failure or neglect to comply was due to the liquidator not having in his hands sufficient assets of the company to enable him to do so) direct that the costs shall be borne by the liquidator personally.

[219]

NOTES
Commencement: 29 December 1986.
This section derived from the Companies Act 1985, s 633.

PART V

WINDING UP OF UNREGISTERED COMPANIES

220. Meaning of "unregistered company"

(1) For the purposes of this Part, the expression "unregistered company" includes *any trustee savings bank certified under the enactments relating to such banks*, any association and any company, with the following exceptions—

(a) a railway company incorporated by Act of Parliament,
(b) a company registered in any part of the United Kingdom under the Joint Stock Companies Acts or under the legislation (past or present) relating to companies in Great Britain.

(2) On such day as the Treasury appoints by order under section 4(3) of the Trustee Savings Banks Act 1985, the words in subsection (1) from "any trustee" to "banks" cease to have effect and are hereby repealed. **[220]**

NOTES
Commencement: 29 December 1986.
This section derived from the Companies Act 1985, s 665.
The words "any trustee savings bank certified under the enactments relating to such banks", formerly in the Companies Act 1985, s 665(1), and an additional word "and" following the word "banks" which is not reproduced in sub-s (1) above, were repealed by the Trustee Savings Banks Act 1985, ss 4(3), 7(3), Sch 4. The repeal of those words was brought into force on 21 July 1986 by

virtue of the Trustee Savings Banks Act 1985 (Appointed Day) (No 4) Order 1986, SI 1986/1223 (made under s 4(3) of that Act). It is thought, therefore, that, as construed in accordance with s 437, Sch 11, para 27 post, the words specified in sub-s (1) by sub-s (2) above have ceased to have effect and are thus repealed.

221. Winding up of unregistered companies

(1) Subject to the provisions of this Part, any unregistered company may be wound up under this Act; and all the provisions of this Act and the Companies Act about winding up apply to an unregistered company with the exceptions and additions mentioned in the following subsections.

(2) If an unregistered company has a principal place of business situated in Northern Ireland, it shall not be wound up under this Part unless it has a principal place of business situated in England and Wales or Scotland, or in both England and Wales and Scotland.

(3) For the purpose of determining a court's winding-up jurisdiction, an unregistered company is deemed—

    (a) to be registered in England and Wales or Scotland, according as its principal place of business is situated in England and Wales or Scotland, or

    (b) if it has a principal place of business situated in both countries, to be registered in both countries;

and the principal place of business situated in that part of Great Britain in which proceedings are being instituted is, for all purposes of the winding up, deemed to be the registered office of the company.

(4) No unregistered company shall be wound up under this Act voluntarily.

(5) The circumstances in which an unregistered company may be wound up are as follows—

    (a) if the company is dissolved, or has ceased to carry on business, or is carrying on business only for the purpose of winding up its affairs;

    (b) if the company is unable to pay its debts;

    (c) if the court is of opinion that it is just and equitable that the company should be wound up.

(6) *A petition for winding up a trustee savings bank may be presented by the Trustee Savings Banks Central Board or by a commissioner appointed under section 35 of the Trustee Savings Banks Act 1981 as well as by any person authorised under Part IV of this Act to present a petition for the winding up of a company.*

On such day as the Treasury appoints by order under section 4(3) of the Trustee Savings Banks Act 1985, this subsection ceases to have effect and is hereby repealed.

(7) In Scotland, an unregistered company which the Court of Session has jurisdiction to wind up may be wound up by the court if there is subsisting a floating charge over property comprised in the company's property and undertaking, and the court is satisfied that the security of the creditor entitled to the benefit of the floating charge is in jeopardy.

For this purpose a creditor's security is deemed to be in jeopardy if the court is satisfied that events have occurred or are about to occur which render it unreasonable in the creditor's interests that the company should retain power to dispose of the property which is subject to the floating charge.   **[221]**

NOTES
Commencement: 29 December 1986.
This section derived from the Companies Act 1985, s 666.
The Companies Act 1985, s 666(6), from which sub-s (6) above is principally derived, was repealed by the Trustee Savings Banks Act 1985, ss 4(3), 7(3), Sch 4, as from 21 July 1986 by virtue of the Trustee Savings Banks Act 1985 (Appointed Day) (No 4) Order 1986, SI 1986/1223 (made under s 4(3) of that Act). It is thought, therefore, that, as construed in accordance with s 437, Sch 11, para 27 post, sub-s (6) above has ceased to have effect and is thus repealed.

222. Inability to pay debts; unpaid creditor for £750 or more

(1) An unregistered company is deemed (for the purposes of section 221) unable to pay its debts if there is a creditor, by assignment or otherwise, to whom the company is indebted in a sum exceeding £750 then due and—

(*a*) the creditor has served on the company, by leaving at its principal place of business, or by delivering to the secretary or some director, manager or principal officer of the company, or by otherwise serving in such manner as the court may approve or direct, a written demand in the prescribed form requiring the company to pay the sum due, and

(*b*) the company has for 3 weeks after the service of the demand neglected to pay the sum or to secure or compound for it to the creditor's satisfaction.

(2) The money sum for the time being specified in subsection (1) is subject to increase or reduction by regulations under section 417 in Part XV; but no increase in the sum so specified affects any case in which the winding-up petition was presented before the coming into force of the increase. **[222]**

NOTES
Commencement: 29 December 1986.
This section derived from the Companies Act 1985, s 667, and the Insolvency Act 1985, Sch 6, para 50.

223. Inability to pay debts: debt remaining unsatisfied after action brought

An unregistered company is deemed (for the purposes of section 221) unable to pay its debts if an action or other proceeding has been instituted against any member for any debt or demand due, or claimed to be due, from the company, or from him in his character of member, and—

(*a*) notice in writing of the institution of the action or proceeding has been served on the company by leaving it at the company's principal place of business (or by delivering it to the secretary, or some director, manager or principal officer of the company, or by otherwise serving it in such manner as the court may approve or direct), and

(*b*) the company has not within 3 weeks after service of the notice paid, secured or compounded for the debt or demand, or procured the action or proceeding to be stayed or sisted, or indemnified the defendant or defender to his reasonable satisfaction against the action or proceeding, and against all costs, damages and expenses to be incurred by him because of it. **[223]**

NOTES
Commencement: 29 December 1986.
This section derived from the Companies Act 1985, s 688, and the Insolvency Act 1985, Sch 6, para 51.

224. Inability to pay debts: other cases

(1) An unregistered company is deemed (for purposes of section 221) unable to pay its debts—

(a) if in England and Wales execution or other process issued on a judgment, decree or order obtained in any court in favour of a creditor against the company, or any member of it as such, or any person authorised to be sued as nominal defendant on behalf of the company, is returned unsatisfied;

(b) if in Scotland the induciae of a charge for payment on an extract decree, or an extract registered bond, or an extract registered protest, have expired without payment being made;

(c) if in Northern Ireland a certificate of unenforceability has been granted in respect of any judgment, decree or order obtained as mentioned in paragraph (a);

(d) if it is otherwise proved to the satisfaction of the court that the company is unable to pay its debts as they fall due.

(2) An unregistered company is also deemed unable to pay its debts if it is proved to the satisfaction of the court that the value of the company's assets is less than the amount of its liabilities, taking into account its contingent and prospective liabilities. **[224]**

NOTES
Commencement: 29 December 1986.
This section derived from the Companies Act 1985, s 669, and the Insolvency Act 1985, Sch 6, para 52.

225. Oversea company may be wound up though dissolved

Where a company incorporated outside Great Britain which has been carrying on business in Great Britain ceases to carry on business in Great Britain, it may be wound up as an unregistered company under this Act, notwithstanding that it has been dissolved or otherwise ceased to exist as a company under or by virtue of the laws of the country under which it was incorporated. **[225]**

NOTES
Commencement: 29 December 1986.
This section derived from the Companies Act 1985, s 670.

226. Contributories in winding up of unregistered company

(1) In the event of an unregistered company being wound up, every person is deemed a contributory who is liable to pay or contribute to the payment of any debt or liability of the company, or to pay or contribute to the payment of any sum for the adjustment of the rights of members among themselves, or to pay or contribute to the payment of the expenses of winding up the company.

(2) Every contributory is liable to contribute to the company's assets all sums due from him in respect of any such liability as is mentioned above.

(3) In the case of an unregistered company engaged in or formed for working mines within the stannaries, a past member is not liable to contribute to the assets if he has ceased to be a member for 2 years or more either before the mine ceased to be worked or before the date of the winding-up order.

(4) In the event of the death, bankruptcy or insolvency of any contributory, the provisions of this Act with respect to the personal representatives, to the heirs and legatees of heritage of the heritable estate in Scotland of deceased contributories, and to the trustees of bankrupt or insolvent contributories, respectively apply. **[226]**

227. Power of court to stay, sist or restrain proceedings

The provisions of this Part with respect to staying, sisting or restraining actions and proceedings against a company at any time after the presentation of a petition for winding up and before the making of a winding-up order extend, in the case of an unregistered company, where the application to stay, sist or restrain is presented by a creditor, to actions and proceedings against any contributory of the company.   **[227]**

228. Actions stayed on winding-up order

Where an order has been made for winding up an unregistered company, no action or proceeding shall be proceeded with or commenced against any contributory of the company in respect of any debt of the company, except by leave of the court, and subject to such terms as the court may impose.   **[228]**

229. Provisions of this Part to be cumulative

(1) The provisions of this Part with respect to unregistered companies are in addition to and not in restriction of any provisions in Part IV with respect to winding up companies by the court; and the court or liquidator may exercise any powers or do any act in the case of unregistered companies which might be exercised or done by it or him in winding up companies formed and registered under the Companies Act.

(2) However, an unregistered company is not, except in the event of its being wound up, deemed to be a company under the Companies Act, and then only to the extent provided by this Part of this Act.   **[229]**

PART VI

MISCELLANEOUS PROVISIONS APPLYING TO COMPANIES WHICH ARE INSOLVENT OR IN LIQUIDATION

Office-holders

230. Holders of office to be qualified insolvency practitioners

(1) Where an administration order is made in relation to a company, the administrator must be a person who is qualified to act as an insolvency practitioner in relation to the company.

(2) Where an administrative receiver of a company is appointed, he must be a person who is so qualified.

(3) Where a company goes into liquidation, the liquidator must be a person who is so qualified.

(4) Where a provisional liquidator is appointed, he must be a person who is so qualified.

(5) Subsections (3) and (4) are without prejudice to any enactment under which the official receiver is to be, or may be, liquidator or provisional liquidator.   **[230]**

NOTES
Commencement: 29 December 1986.
This section derived from the Insolvency Act 1985, ss 95(1), (2), 96(1).

231. Appointment to office of two or more persons

(1) This section applies if an appointment or nomination of any person to the office of administrator, administrative receiver, liquidator or provisional liquidator—

  (*a*) relates to more than one person, or
  (*b*) has the effect that the office is to be held by more than one person.

(2) The appointment or nomination shall declare whether any act required or authorised under any enactment to be done by the administrator, administrative receiver, liquidator or provisional liquidator is to be done by all or any one or more of the persons for the time being holding the office in question.   **[231]**

NOTES
Commencement: 29 December 1986.
This section derived from the Insolvency Act 1985, ss 95(1), (2), 96(2).

232. Validity of office-holder's acts

The acts of an individual as administrator, administrative receiver, liquidator or provisional liquidator of a company are valid notwithstanding any defect in his appointment, nomination or qualifications.   **[232]**

NOTES
Commencement: 29 December 1986.
This section derived from the Insolvency Act 1985, ss 95(1), (2), 96(3).

Management by administrators, liquidators, etc

233. Supplies of gas, water, electricity, etc

(1) This section applies in the case of a company where—

  (*a*) an administration order is made in relation to the company, or
  (*b*) an administrative receiver is appointed, or
  (*c*) a voluntary arrangement under Part I, approved by meetings summoned under section 3, has taken effect, or
  (*d*) the company goes into liquidation, or
  (*e*) a provisional liquidator is appointed;

and "the office-holder" means the administrator, the administrative receiver, the supervisor of the voluntary arrangement, the liquidator or the provisional liquidator, as the case may be.

(2) If a request is made by or with the concurrence of the office-holder for the giving, after the effective date, of any of the supplies mentioned in the next subsection, the supplier—

(a) may make it a condition of the giving of the supply that the office-holder personally guarantees the payment of any charges in respect of the supply, but

(b) shall not make it a condition of the giving of the supply, or do anything which has the effect of making it a condition of the giving of the supply, that any outstanding charges in respect of a supply given to the company before the effective date are paid.

(3) The supplies referred to in subsection (2) are—

(a) a public supply of gas,

(b) a supply of electricity by an Electricity Board,

(c) a supply of water by statutory water undertakers or, in Scotland, a water authority,

(d) a supply of telecommunication services by a public telecommunications operator.

(4) "The effective date" for the purposes of this section is whichever is applicable of the following dates—

(a) the date on which the administration order was made,

(b) the date on which the administrative receiver was appointed (or, if he was appointed in succession to another administrative receiver, the date on which the first of his predecessors was appointed),

(c) the date on which the voluntary arrangement was approved by the meetings summoned under section 3,

(d) the date on which the company went into liquidation,

(e) the date on which the provisional liquidator was appointed.

(5) The following applies to expressions used in subsection (3)—

(a) "public supply of gas" means a supply of gas by the British Gas Corporation or a public gas supplier within the meaning of Part I of the Gas Act 1986,

(b) "Electricity Board" means the same as in the Energy Act 1983,

(c) "water authority" means the same as in the Water (Scotland) Act 1980, and

(d) "telecommunication services" and "public telecommunications operator" mean the same as in the Telecommunications Act 1984, except that the former does not include services consisting in the conveyance of programmes included in cable programme services (within the meaning of the Cable and Broadcasting Act 1984). **[233]**

NOTES

Commencement: 29 December 1986.

This section derived from the Insolvency Act 1985, ss 95, 97.

234. Getting in the company's property

(1) This section applies in the case of a company where—

(a) an administration order is made in relation to the company, or

(b) an administrative receiver is appointed, or

(c) the company goes into liquidation, or

(*d*) a provisional liquidator is appointed;

and "the office-holder" means the administrator, the administrative receiver, the liquidator or the provisional liquidator, as the case may be.

(2) Where any person has in his possession or control any property, books, papers or records to which the company appears to be entitled, the court may require that person forthwith (or within such period as the court may direct) to pay, deliver, convey, surrender or transfer the property, books, papers or records to the office-holder.

(3) Where the office-holder—

    (*a*) seizes or disposes of any property which is not property of the company, and

    (*b*) at the time of seizure or disposal believes, and has reasonable grounds for believing, that he is entitled (whether in pursuance of an order of the court or otherwise) to seize or dispose of that property,

the next subsection has effect.

(4) In that case the office-holder—

    (*a*) is not liable to any person in respect of any loss or damage resulting from the seizure or disposal except in so far as that loss or damage is caused by the office-holder's own negligence, and

    (*b*) has a lien on the property, or the proceeds of its sale, for such expenses as were incurred in connection with the seizure or disposal.   **[234]**

NOTES

    Commencement: 29 December 1986.

    This section derived from the Insolvency Act 1985, ss 95(1), (2), 98.

235. Duty to co-operate with office-holder

(1) This section applies as does section 234; and it also applies, in the case of a company in respect of which a winding-up order has been made by the court in England and Wales, as if references to the office-holder included the official receiver, whether or not he is the liquidator.

(2) Each of the persons mentioned in the next subsection shall—

    (*a*) give to the office-holder such information concerning the company and its promotion, formation, business, dealings, affairs or property as the office-holder may at any time after the effective date reasonably require, and

    (*b*) attend on the office-holder at such times as the latter may reasonably require.

(3) The persons referred to above are—

    (*a*) those who are or have at any time been officers of the company.

    (*b*) those who have taken part in the formation of the company at any time within one year before the effective date,

    (*c*) those who are in the employment of the company, or have been in its employment (including employment under a contract for services) within that year, and are in the office-holder's opinion capable of giving information which he requires,

    (*d*) those who are, or have within that year been, officers of, or in the employment (including employment under a contract for services) of, another company which is, or within that year was, an officer of the company in question, and (*e*) in the case of a company being wound up by the court, any person who has acted as administrator, administrative receiver or liquidator of the company.

(4) For the purposes of subsections (2) and (3), "the effective date" is whichever is applicable of the following dates—

(*a*) the date on which the administration order was made,

(*b*) the date on which the administrative receiver was appointed or, if he was appointed in succession to another administrative receiver, the date on which the first of his predecessors was appointed,

(*c*) the date on which the provisional liquidator was appointed, and

(*d*) the date on which the company went into liquidation.

(5) If a person without reasonable excuse fails to comply with any obligation imposed by this section, he is liable to a fine and, for continued contravention, to a daily default fine. **[235]**

NOTES

Commencement: 29 December 1986.

This section derived from the Insolvency Act 1985, ss 95(1), (2), 99.

236. Inquiry into company's dealings, etc

(1) This section applies as does section 234; and it also applies in the case of a company in respect of which a winding-up order has been made by the court in England and Wales as if references to the office-holder included the official receiver, whether or not he is the liquidator.

(2) The court may, on the application of the office-holder, summon to appear before it—

(*a*) any officer of the company,

(*b*) any person known or suspected to have in his possession any property of the company or supposed to be indebted to the company, or

(*c*) any person whom the court thinks capable of giving information concerning the promotion, formation, business, dealings, affairs or property of the company.

(3) The court may require any such person as is mentioned in subsection (2)(*a*) to (*c*) to submit an affidavit to the court containing an account of his dealings with the company or to produce any books, papers or other records in his possession or under his control relating to the company or the matters mentioned in paragraph (*c*) of the subsection.

(4) The following applies in a case where—

(*a*) a person without reasonable excuse fails to appear before the court when he is summoned to do so under this section, or

(*b*) there are reasonable grounds for believing that a person has absconded, or is about to abscond, with a view to avoiding his appearance before the court under this section.

(5) The court may, for the purpose of bringing that person and anything in his possession before the court, cause a warrant to be issued to a constable or prescribed officer of the court—

(*a*) for the arrest of that person, and

(*b*) for the seizure of any books, papers, records, money or goods in that person's possession.

(6) The court may authorise a person arrested under such a warrant to be kept in custody, and anything seized under such a warrant to be held, in accordance with the rules, until that person is brought before the court under the warrant or until such other time as the court may order.   **[236]**

NOTES
Commencement: 29 December 1986.
This section derived from the Insolvency Act 1985, ss 95(1), (2), 100(1), (2), (6).

237. Court's enforcement powers under s 236

(1) If it appears to the court, on consideration of any evidence obtained under section 236 or this section, that any person has in his possession any property of the company, the court may, on the application of the office-holder, order that person to deliver the whole or any part of the property to the officer-holder at such time, in such manner and on such terms as the court thinks fit.

(2) If it appears to the court, on consideration of any evidence so obtained, that any person is indebted to the company, the court may, on the application of the office-holder, order that person to pay to the office-holder, at such time and in such manner as the court may direct, the whole or any part of the amount due, whether in full discharge of the debt or otherwise, as the court thinks fit.

(3) The court may, if it thinks fit, order that any person who if within the jurisdiction of the court would be liable to be summoned to appear before it under section 236 or this section shall be examined in any part of the United Kingdom where he may for the time being be, or in a place outside the United Kingdom.

(4) Any person who appears or is brought before the court under section 236 or this section may be examined on oath, either orally or (except in Scotland) by interrogatories, concerning the company or the matters mentioned in section 236(2)(*c*).   **[237]**

NOTES
Commencement: 29 December 1986.
This section derived from the Insolvency Act 1985, s 100(3)–(5), (7).

Adjustment of prior transactions (administration and liquidation)

238. Transactions at an undervalue (England and Wales)

(1) This section applies in the case of a company where—
   (*a*) an administration order is made in relation to the company, or
   (*b*) the company goes into liquidation;
and "the office-holder" means the administrator or the liquidator, as the case may be.

(2) Where the company has at a relevant time (defined in section 240) entered into a transaction with any person at an undervalue, the office-holder may apply to the court for an order under this section.

(3) Subject as follows, the court shall, on such an application, make such order as it thinks fit for restoring the position to what it would have been if the company had not entered into that transaction.

(4) For the purposes of this section and section 241, a company enters into a transaction with a person at an undervalue if—

    (*a*) the company makes a gift to that person or otherwise enters into a transaction with that person on terms that provide for the company to receive no consideration, or

    (*b*) the company enters into a transaction with that person for a consideration the value of which, in money or money's worth, is significantly less than the value, in money or money's worth, of the consideration provided by the company.

(5) The court shall not make an order under this section in respect of a transaction at an undervalue if it is satisfied—

    (*a*) that the company which entered into the transaction did so in good faith and for the purpose of carrying on its business, and

    (*b*) that at the time it did so there were reasonable grounds for believing that the transaction would benefit the company. **[238]**

NOTES

    Commencement: 29 December 1986.

    This section derived from the Insolvency Act 1985, ss 95(1)(*a*), (*b*), 101(1) (part)–(3).

239. Preferences (England and Wales)

(1) This section applies as does section 238.

(2) Where the company has at a relevant time (defined in the next section) given a preference to any person, the office-holder may apply to the court for an order under this section.

(3) Subject as follows, the court shall, on such an application, make such order as it thinks fit for restoring the position to what it would have been if the company had not given that preference.

(4) For the purposes of this section and section 241, a company gives a preference to a person if—

    (*a*) that person is one of the company's creditors or a surety or guarantor for any of the company's debts or other liabilities, and

    (*b*) the company does anything or suffers anything to be done which (in either case) has the effect of putting that person into a position which, in the event of the company going into insolvent liquidation, will be better than the position he would have been in if that thing had not been done.

(5) The court shall not make an order under this section in respect of a preference given to any person unless the company which gave the preference was influenced in deciding to give it by a desire to produce in relation to that person the effect mentioned in subsection (4)(*b*).

(6) A company which has given a preference to a person connected with the company (otherwise than by reason only of being its employee) at the time the preference was given is presumed, unless the contrary is shown, to have been influenced in deciding to give it by such a desire as is mentioned in subsection (5).

(7) The fact that something has been done in pursuance of the order of a court does not, without more, prevent the doing or suffering of that thing from constituting the giving of a preference. **[239]**

NOTES
Commencement: 29 December 1986.
This section derived from the Insolvency Act 1985, ss 95(1)(*a*), (*b*), 101(1) (part), (4)–(7), (11).

240. "Relevant time" under ss 238, 239

(1) Subject to the next subsection, the time at which a company enters into a transaction at an undervalue or gives a preference is a relevant time if the transaction is entered into, or the preference given—

    (*a*) in the case of a transaction at an undervalue or of a preference which is given to a person who is connected with the company (otherwise than by reason only of being its employee), at a time in the period of 2 years ending with the onset of insolvency (which expression is defined below),

    (*b*) in the case of a preference which is not such a transaction and is not so given, at a time in the period of 6 months ending with the onset of insolvency, and

    (*c*) in either case, at a time between the presentation of a petition for the making of an administration order in relation to the company and the making of such an order on that petition.

(2) Where a company enters into a transaction at an undervalue or gives a preference at a time mentioned in subsection (1)(*a*) or (*b*), that time is not a relevant time for the purposes of section 238 or 239 unless the company—

    (*a*) is at that time unable to pay its debts within the meaning of section 123 in Chapter VI of Part IV, or

    (*b*) becomes unable to pay its debts within the meaning of that section in consequence of the transaction or preference;

but the requirements of this subsection are presumed to be satisfied, unless the contrary is shown, in relation to any transaction at an undervalue which is entered into by a company with a person who is connected with the company.

(3) For the purposes of subsection (1), the onset of insolvency is—

    (*a*) in a case where section 238 or 239 applies by reason of the making of an administration order or of a company going into liquidation immediately upon the discharge of an administration order, the date of the presentation of the petition on which the administration order was made, and

    (*b*) in a case where the section applies by reason of a company going into liquidation at any other time, the date of the commencement of the winding up.   **[240]**

NOTES
Commencement: 29 December 1986.
This section derived from the Insolvency Act 1985, s 101(8)–(11).

241. Orders under ss 238, 239

(1) Without prejudice to the generality of sections 238(3) and 239(3), an order under either of those sections with respect to a transaction or preference entered into or given by a company may (subject to the next subsection)—

    (*a*) require any property transferred as part of the transaction, or in connection with the giving of the preference, to be vested in the company,

(b) require any property to be so vested if it represents in any person's hands the application either of the proceeds of sale of property so transferred or of money so transferred,

(c) release or discharge (in whole or in part) any security given by the company,

(d) require any person to pay, in respect of benefits received by him from the company, such sums to the office-holder as the court may direct,

(e) provide for any surety or guarantor whose obligations to any person were released or discharged (in whole or in part) under the transaction, or by the giving of the preference, to be under such new or revived obligations to that person as the court thinks appropriate,

(f) provide for security to be provided for the discharge of any obligation imposed by or arising under the order, for such an obligation to be charged on any property and for the security or charge to have the same priority as a security or charge released or discharged (in whole or in part) under the transaction or by the giving of the preference, and

(g) provide for the extent to which any person whose property is vested by the order in the company, or on whom obligations are imposed by the order, is to be able to prove in the winding up of the company for debts or other liabilities which arose from, or were released or discharged (in whole or in part) under or by, the transaction or the giving of the preference.

(2) An order under section 238 or 239 may affect the property of, or impose any obligation on, any person whether or not he is the person with whom the company in question entered into the transaction or (as the case may be) the person to whom the preference was given; but such an order—

(a) shall not prejudice any interest in property which was acquired from a person other than the company and was acquired in good faith, for value and without notice of the relevant circumstances, or prejudice any interest deriving from such an interest, and

(b) shall not require a person who received a benefit from the transaction or preference in good faith, for value and without notice of the relevant circumstances to pay a sum to the office-holder, except where that person was a party to the transaction or the payment is to be in respect of a preference given to that person at a time when he was a creditor of the company.

(3) For the purposes of this section the relevant circumstances, in relation to a transaction or preference, are—

(a) the circumstances by virtue of which an order under section 238 or (as the case may be) 239 could be made in respect of the transaction or preference if the company were to go into liquidation, or an administration order were made in relation to the company, within a particular period after the transaction is entered into or the preference given, and

(b) if that period has expired, the fact that the company has gone into liquidation or that such an order has been made.

(4) The provisions of sections 238 to 241 apply without prejudice to the availability of any other remedy, even in relation to a transaction or preference which the company had no power to enter into or give. **[241]**

NOTES

Commencement: 29 December 1986.

This section derived from the Insolvency Act 1985, ss 95(1), 102.

242. Gratuitous alienations (Scotland)

(1) Where this subsection applies and—

  (*a*) the winding up of a company has commenced, alienation by the company is challengeable by—

   (i) any creditor who is a creditor by virtue of a debt incurred on or before the date of such commencement, or
   (ii) the liquidator;

  (*b*) an administration order is in force in relation to a company is challengeable by the administrator.

(2) Subsection (1) applies where—

  (*a*) by the alienation, whether before or after 1st April 1986 (the coming into force of section 75 of the Bankruptcy (Scotland) Act 1985), any part of the company's property is transferred or any claim or right of the company is discharged or renounced, and

  (*b*) the alienation takes place on a relevant day.

(3) For the purposes of subsection (2)(*b*), the day on which an alienation takes place is the day on which it becomes completely effectual; and in that subsection "relevant day" means, if the alienation has the effect of favouring—

  (*a*) a person who is an associate (within the meaning of the Bankruptcy (Scotland) Act 1985) of the company, a day not earlier than 5 years before the date on which—

   (i) the winding up of the company commences, or
   (ii) as the case may be, the administration order is made; or

  (*b*) any other person, a day not earlier than 2 years before that date.

(4) On a challenge being brought under subsection (1), the court shall grant decree of reduction or for such restoration of property to the company's assets or other redress as may be appropriate; but the court shall not grant such a decree if the person seeking to uphold the alienation establishes—

  (*a*) that immediately, or at any other time, after the alienation the company's assets were greater than its liabilities, or

  (*b*) that the alienation was made for adequate consideration, or

  (*c*) that the alienation—

   (i) was a birthday, Christmas or other conventional gift, or
   (ii) was a gift made, for a charitable purpose, to a person who is not an associate of the company,

  which, having regard to all the circumstances, it was reasonable for the company to make:

Provided that this subsection is without prejudice to any right or interest acquired in good faith and for value from or through the transferee in the alienation.

(5) In subsection (4) above, "charitable purpose" means any charitable, benevolent or philanthropic purpose, whether or not it is charitable within the meaning of any rule of law.

(6) For the purposes of the foregoing provisions of this section, an alienation

in implementation of a prior obligation is deemed to be one for which there was no consideration or no adequate consideration.

(7) A liquidator and an administrator have the same right as a creditor has under any rule of law to challenge an alienation of a company made for no consideration or no adequate consideration.

This section applies to Scotland only. **[242]**

NOTES
Commencement: 29 December 1986.
This section derived from the Companies Act 1985, s 615A, and the Bankruptcy (Scotland) Act 1985, Sch 7, para 20.

243. Unfair preferences (Scotland)

(1) Subject to subsection (2) below, subsection (4) below applies to a transaction entered into by a company, whether before or after 1st April 1986, which has the effect of creating a preference in favour of a creditor to the prejudice of the general body of creditors, being a preference created not earlier than 6 months before the commencement of the winding up of the company or the making of an administration order in relation to the company.

(2) Subsection (4) below does not apply to any of the following transactions—

(*a*) a transaction in the ordinary course of trade or business;

(*b*) a payment in cash for a debt which when it was paid had become payable, unless the transaction was collusive with the purpose of prejudicing the general body of creditors;

(*c*) a transaction whereby the parties to it undertake reciprocal obligations (whether the performance by the parties of their respective obligations occurs at the same time or at different times) unless the transaction was collusive as aforesaid;

(*d*) the granting of a mandate by a company authorising an arrestee to pay over the arrested funds or part thereof to the arrester where—

(i) there has been a decree for payment or a warrant for summary diligence, and

(ii) the decree or warrant has been preceded by an arrestment on the dependence of the action or followed by an arrestment in execution.

(3) For the purposes of subsection (1) above, the day on which a preference was created is the day on which the preference became completely effectual.

(4) A transaction to which this subsection applies is challengeable by—

(*a*) in the case of a winding up—

(i) any creditor who is a creditor by virtue of a debt incurred on or before the date of commencement of the winding up, or

(ii) the liquidator; and

(*b*) in the case of an administration order, the administrator.

(5) On a challenge being brought under subsection (4) above, the court, if satisfied that the transaction challenged is a transaction to which this section applies, shall grant decree of reduction or for such restoration of property to the company's assets or other redress as may be appropriate:

Provided that this subsection is without prejudice to any right or interest acquired in good faith and for value from or through the creditor in whose favour the preference was created.

(6) A liquidator and an administrator have the same right as a creditor has under any rule of law to challenge a preference created by a debtor.

(7) This section applies to Scotland only.   **[243]**

NOTES
Commencement: 29 December 1986.
This section derived from the Companies Act 1985, s 615B, and the Bankruptcy (Scotland) Act 1985, Sch 7, para 20.

244. Extortionate credit transactions

(1) This section applies as does section 238, and where the company is, or has been, a party to a transaction for, or involving, the provision of credit to the company.

(2) The court may, on the application of the office-holder, make an order with respect to the transaction if the transaction is or was extortionate and was entered into in the period of 3 years ending with the day on which the administration order was made or (as the case may be) the company went into liquidation.

(3) For the purposes of this section a transaction is extortionate if, having regard to the risk accepted by the person providing the credit—

(*a*) the terms of it are or were such as to require grossly exorbitant payments to be made (whether unconditionally or in certain contingencies) in respect of the provision of the credit, or

(*b*) it otherwise grossly contravened ordinary principles of fair dealing;

and it shall be presumed, unless the contrary is proved, that a transaction with respect to which an application is made under this section is or, as the case may be, was extortionate.

(4) An order under this section with respect to any transaction may contain such one or more of the following as the court thinks fit, that is to say—

(*a*) provision setting aside the whole or part of any obligation created by the transaction,

(*b*) provision otherwise varying the terms of the transaction or varying the terms on which any security for the purposes of the transaction is held,

(*c*) provision requiring any person who is or was a party to the transaction to pay to the office-holder any sums paid to that person, by virtue of the transaction, by the company,

(*d*) provision requiring any person to surrender to the office-holder any property held by him as security for the purposes of the transaction,

(*e*) provision directing accounts to be taken between any persons.

(5) The powers conferred by this section are exercisable in relation to any transaction concurrently with any powers exercisable in relation to that transaction as a transaction at an undervalue or under section 242 (gratuitous alienations in Scotland).   **[244]**

NOTES
Commencement: 29 December 1986.
This section derived from the Insolvency Act 1985, ss 95(1)(*a*), (*b*), 103.

245. Avoidance of certain floating charges

(1) This section applies as does section 238, but applies to Scotland as well as to England and Wales.

(2) Subject as follows, a floating charge on the company's undertaking or property created at a relevant time is invalid except to the extent of the aggregate of—

    (a) the value of so much of the consideration for the creation of the charge as consists of money paid, or goods or services supplied, to the company at the same time as, or after, the creation of the charge,

    (b) the value of so much of that consideration as consists of the discharge or reduction, at the same time as, or after, the creation of the charge, of any debt of the company, and

    (c) the amount of such interest (if any) as is payable on the amount falling within paragraph (a) or (b) in pursuance of any agreement under which the money was so paid, the goods or services were so supplied or the debt was so discharged or reduced.

(3) Subject to the next subsection, the time at which a floating charge is created by a company is a relevant time for the purposes of this section if the charge is created—

    (a) in the case of a charge which is created in favour of a person who is connected with the company, at a time in the period of 2 years ending with the onset of insolvency,

    (b) in the case of a charge which is created in favour of any other person, at a time in the period of 12 months ending with the onset of insolvency, or

    (c) in either case, at a time between the presentation of a petition for the making of an administration order in relation to the company and the making of such an order on that petition.

(4) Where a company creates a floating charge at a time mentioned in subsection (3)(b) and the person in favour of whom the charge is created is not connected with the company, that time is not a relevant time for the purposes of this section unless the company—

    (a) is at that time unable to pay its debts within the meaning of section 123 in Chapter VI of Part IV, or

    (b) becomes unable to pay its debts within the meaning of that section in consequence of the transaction under which the charge is created.

(5) For the purposes of subsection (3), the onset of insolvency is—

    (a) in a case where this section applies by reason of the making of an administration order, the date of the presentation of the petition on which the order was made, and

    (b) in a case where this section applies by reason of a company going into liquidation, the date of the commencement of the winding up.

(6) For the purposes of subsection (2)(a) the value of any goods or services supplied by way of consideration for a floating charge is the amount in money which at the time they were supplied could reasonably have been expected to be obtained for supplying the goods or services in the ordinary course of business and on the same terms (apart from the consideration) as those on which they were supplied to the company. **[245]**

NOTES

Commencement: 29 December 1986.

This section derived from the Insolvency Act 1985, ss 95(1)(*a*), (*b*), 104.

246. Unenforceability of liens on books, etc

(1) This section applies in the case of a company where—

   (*a*) an administration order is made in relation to the company, or
   (*b*) the company goes into liquidation, or
   (*c*) a provisional liquidator is appointed;

and "the office-holder" means the administrator, the liquidator or the provisional liquidator, as the case may be.

(2) Subject as follows, a lien or other right to retain possession of any of the books, papers or other records of the company is unenforceable to the extent that its enforcement would deny possession of any books, papers or other records to the office-holder.

(3) This does not apply to a lien on documents which give a title to property and are held as such.   **[246]**

NOTES
Commencement: 29 December 1986.
This section derived from the Insolvency Act 1985, ss 95(1)(*a*), (*b*), (2), 105.

PART VII

INTERPRETATION FOR FIRST GROUP OF PARTS

247. "Insolvency" and "go into liquidation"

(1) In this Group of Parts, except in so far as the context otherwise requires, "insolvency", in relation to a company, includes the approval of a voluntary arrangement under Part I, the making of an administration order or the appointment of an administrative receiver.

(2) For the purposes of any provision in this Group of Parts, a company goes into liquidation if it passes a resolution for voluntary winding up or an order for its winding up is made by the court at a time when it has not already gone into liquidation by passing such a resolution.   **[247]**

NOTES
Commencement: 29 December 1986.
This section derived from the Insolvency Act 1985, s 108(3) (part), (4).

248. "Secured creditor", etc

In this Group of Parts, except in so far as the context otherwise requires—

   (*a*) "secured creditor", in relation to a company, means a creditor of the company who holds in respect of his debt a security over property of the company, and "unsecured creditor" is to be read accordingly; and
   (*b*) "security" means—

       (i) in relation to England and Wales, any mortgage, charge, lien or other security, and
       (ii) in relation to Scotland, any security (whether heritable or moveable), any floating charge and any right of lien or preference and any right of retention (other than a right of compensation or set off).   **[248]**

NOTES
Commencement: 29 December 1986.
This section derived from the Insolvency Act 1985, s 108(3) (part).

249. "Connected" with a company

For the purposes of any provision in this Group of Parts, a person is connected with a company if—

    (*a*) he is a director or shadow director of the company or an associate of such a director or shadow director, or

    (*b*) he is an associate of the company;

and "associate" has the meaning given by section 435 in Part XVIII of this Act. **[249]**

NOTES
Commencement: 29 December 1986.
This section derived from the Insolvency Act 1985, s 108(5).

250. "Member" of a company

For the purposes of any provision in this Group of Parts, a person who is not a member of a company but to whom shares in the company have been transferred, or transmitted by operation of law, is to be regarded as a member of the company, and references to a member or members are to be read accordingly. **[250]**

NOTES
Commencement: 29 December 1986.
This section derived from the Insolvency Act 1985, s 108(6).

251. Expressions used generally

In this Group of Parts, except in so far as the context otherwise requires—

    "administrative receiver" means—

        (*a*) an administrative receiver as defined by section 29(2) in Chapter I of Part III, or

        (*b*) a receiver appointed under section 51 in Chapter II of that Part in a case where the whole (or substantially the whole) of the company's property is attached by the floating charge;

    "business day" means any day other than a Saturday, a Sunday, Christmas Day, Good Friday or a day which is a bank holiday in any part of Great Britain;

    "contributory" has the meaning given by section 79;

    "chattel leasing agreement" means an agreement for the bailment or, in Scotland, the hiring of goods which is capable of subsisting for more than 3 months;

    "floating charge" means a charge which, as created, was a floating charge and includes a floating charge within section 462 of the Companies Act (Scottish floating charges);

    "office copy", in relation to Scotland, means a copy certified by the clerk of court;

    "the official rate", in relation to interest, means the rate payable under section 189(4);

    "prescribed" means prescribed by the rules;

"receiver", in the expression "receiver or manager", does not include a receiver appointed under section 51 in Chapter II of Part III;

"retention of title agreement" means an agreement for the sale of goods to a company, being an agreement—

(a) which does not constitute a charge on the goods, but

(b) under which, if the seller is not paid and the company is wound up, the seller will have priority over all other creditors of the company as respects the goods or any property representing the goods;

"the rules" means rules under section 411 in Part XV; and

"shadow director", in relation to a company, means a person in accordance with whose directions or instructions the directors of the company are accustomed to act (but so that a person is not deemed a shadow director by reason only that the directors act on advice given by him in a professional capacity);

and any expression for whose interpretation provision is made by Part XXVI of the Companies Act, other than an expression defined above in this section, is to be construed in accordance with that provision. **[251]**

NOTES
Commencement: 29 December 1986.
This section derived from the Insolvency Act 1985, s 108(3) (part).

THE SECOND GROUP OF PARTS

INSOLVENCY OF INDIVIDUALS; BANKRUPTCY

PART VIII

INDIVIDUAL VOLUNTARY ARRANGEMENTS

Moratorium for insolvent debtor

252. Interim order of court

(1) In the circumstances specified below, the court may in the case of a debtor (being an individual) make an interim order under this section.

(2) An interim order has the effect that, during the period for which it is in force—

(a) no bankruptcy petition relating to the debtor may be presented or proceeded with, and

(b) no other proceedings, and no execution or other legal process, may be commenced or continued against the debtor or his property except with the leave of the court. **[252]**

NOTES
Commencement: 29 December 1986.
This section derived from the Insolvency Act 1985, s 112(1) (part), (3).

253. Application for interim order

(1) Application to the court for an interim order may be made where the debtor intends to make a proposal to his creditors for a composition in satisfaction of his debts or a scheme of arrangement of his affairs (from here on referred to, in either case, as a "voluntary arrangement").

(2) The proposal must provide for some person ("the nominee") to act in relation to the voluntary arrangement either as trustee or otherwise for the purpose of supervising its implementation.

(3) Subject as follows, the application may be made—

(a) if the debtor is an undischarged bankrupt, by the debtor, the trustee of his estate, or the official receiver, and

(b) in any other case, by the debtor.

(4) An application shall not be made under subsection (3)(a) unless the debtor has given notice of his proposal (that is, the proposal to his creditors for a voluntary arrangement) to the official receiver and, if there is one, the trustee of his estate.

(5) An application shall not be made while a bankruptcy petition presented by the debtor is pending, if the court has, under section 273 below, appointed an insolvency practitioner to inquire into the debtor's affairs and report. **[253]**

NOTES
Commencement: 29 December 1986.
This section derived from the Insolvency Act 1985, ss 110, 111(1), (2), (3) (part).

254. Effect of application

(1) At any time when an application under section 253 for an interim order is pending, the court may stay any action, execution or other legal process against the property or person of the debtor.

(2) Any court in which proceedings are pending against an individual may, on proof that an application under that section has been made in respect of that individual, either stay the proceedings or allow them to continue on such terms as it thinks fit. **[254]**

NOTES
Commencement: 29 December 1986.
This section derived from the Insolvency Act 1985, s 111(4), (5).

255. Cases in which interim order can be made

(1) The court shall not make an interim order on an application under section 253 unless it is satisfied—

(a) that the debtor intends to make such a proposal as is mentioned in that section;

(b) that on the day of the making of the application the debtor was an undischarged bankrupt or was able to petition for his own bankruptcy;

(c) that no previous application has been made by the debtor for an interim order in the period of 12 months ending with that day; and

(d) that the nominee under the debtor's proposal to his creditors is a person who is for the time being qualified to act as an insolvency practitioner in relation to the debtor, and is willing to act in relation to the proposal.

(2) The court may make an order if it thinks that it would be appropriate to do so for the purpose of facilitating the consideration and implementation of the debtor's proposal.

(3) Where the debtor is an undischarged bankrupt, the interim order may contain provision as to the conduct of the bankruptcy, and the administration of the bankrupt's estate, during the period for which the order is in force.

(4) Subject as follows, the provision contained in an interim order by virtue of subsection (3) may include provision staying proceedings in the bankruptcy or modifying any provision in this Group of Parts, and any provision of the rules in their application to the debtor's bankruptcy.

(5) An interim order shall not, in relation to a bankrupt, make provision relaxing or removing any of the requirements of provisions in this Group of Parts, or of the rules, unless the court is satisfied that that provision is unlikely to result in any significant diminution in, or in the value of, the debtor's estate for the purposes of the bankruptcy.

(6) Subject to the following provisions of this Part, an interim order made on an application under section 253 ceases to have effect at the end of the period of 14 days beginning with the day after the making of the order. **[255]**

NOTES
Commencement: 29 December 1986.
This section derived from the Insolvency Act 1985, s 112(1) (part), (2), (4)–(7)(*a*).

256. Nominee's report on debtor's proposal

(1) Where an interim order has been made on an application under section 253, the nominee shall, before the order ceases to have effect, submit a report to the court stating—

  (*a*) whether, in his opinion, a meeting of the debtor's creditors should be summoned to consider the debtor's proposal, and
  (*b*) if in his opinion such a meeting should be summoned, the date on which, and time and place at which, he proposes the meeting should be held.

(2) For the purpose of enabling the nominee to prepare his report the debtor shall submit to the nominee—

  (*a*) a document setting out the terms of the voluntary arrangement which the debtor is proposing, and
  (*b*) a statement of his affairs containing—

     (i) such particulars of his creditors and of his debts and other liabilities and of his assets as may be prescribed, and
     (ii) such other information as may be prescribed.

(3) The court may, on an application made by the debtor in a case where the nominee has failed to submit the report required by this section, do one or both of the following, namely—

  (*a*) direct that the nominee shall be replaced as such by another person qualified to act as an insolvency practitioner in relation to the debtor;
  (*b*) direct that the interim order shall continue, or (if it has ceased to have effect) be renewed, for such further period as the court may specify in the direction.

(4) The court may, on the application of the nominee, extend the period for which the interim order has effect so as to enable the nominee to have more time to prepare his report.

(5) If the court is satisfied on receiving the nominee's report that a meeting of the debtor's creditors should be summoned to consider the debtor's proposal, the court shall direct that the period for which the interim order has effect shall be extended, for such further period as it may specify in the direction, for the

purpose of enabling the debtor's proposal to be considered by his creditors in accordance with the following provisions of this Part.

(6) The court may discharge the interim order if it is satisfied, on the application of the nominee—

(a) that the debtor has failed to comply with his obligations under subsection (2), or

(b) that for any other reason it would be inappropriate for a meeting of the debtor's creditors to be summoned to consider the debtor's proposal. **[256]**

NOTES
Commencement: 29 December 1986.
This section derived from the Insolvency Act 1985, s 113.

257. Summoning of creditors' meeting

(1) Where it has been reported to the court under section 256 that a meeting of the debtor's creditors should be summoned, the nominee (or his replacement under section 256(3)(a)) shall, unless the court otherwise directs, summon that meeting for the time, date and place proposed in his report.

(2) The persons to be summoned to the meeting are every creditor of the debtor of whose claim and address the person summoning the meeting is aware.

(3) For this purpose the creditors of a debtor who is an undischarged bankrupt include—

(a) every person who is a creditor of the bankrupt in respect of a bankruptcy debt, and

(b) every person who would be such a creditor if the bankruptcy had commenced on the day on which notice of the meeting is given. **[257]**

NOTES
Commencement: 29 December 1986.
This section derived from the Insolvency Act 1985, s 114(1) (part), (2), (3).

Consideration and implementation of debtor's proposal

258. Decisions of creditors' meeting

(1) A creditors' meeting summoned under section 257 shall decide whether to approve the proposed voluntary arrangement.

(2) The meeting may approve the proposed voluntary arrangement with modifications, but shall not do so unless the debtor consents to each modification.

(3) The modifications subject to which the proposed voluntary arrangement may be approved may include one conferring the functions proposed to be conferred on the nominee on another person qualified to act as an insolvency practitioner in relation to the debtor.

But they shall not include any modification by virtue of which the proposal ceases to be a proposal such as is mentioned in section 253.

(4) The meeting shall not approve any proposal or modification which affects the right of a secured creditor of the debtor to enforce his security, except with the concurrence of the creditor concerned.

(5) Subject as follows, the meeting shall not approve any proposal or modification under which—

    (*a*) any preferential debt of the debtor is to be paid otherwise than in priority to such of his debts as are not preferential debts, or

    (*b*) a preferential creditor of the debtor is to be paid an amount in respect of a preferential debt that bears to that debt a smaller proportion than is borne to another preferential debt by the amount that is to be paid in respect of that other debt.

However, the meeting may approve such a proposal or modification with the concurrence of the preferential creditor concerned.

(6) Subject as above, the meeting shall be conducted in accordance with the rules.

(7) In this section "preferential debt" has the meaning given by section 386 in Part XII; and "preferential creditor" is to be construed accordingly.   **[258]**

NOTES
Commencement: 29 December 1986.
This section derived from the Insolvency Act 1985, s 115(1)–(6), (9), (10).

259. Report of decisions to court

(1) After the conclusion in accordance with the rules of the meeting summoned under section 257, the chairman of the meeting shall report the result of it to the court and, immediately after so reporting, shall give notice of the result of the meeting to such persons as may be prescribed.

(2) If the report is that the meeting has declined (with or without modifications) to approve the debtor's proposal, the court may discharge any interim order which is in force in relation to the debtor.   **[259]**

NOTES
Commencement: 29 December 1986.
This section derived from the Insolvency Act 1985, s 115(7), (8).

260. Effect of approval

(1) This section has effect where the meeting summoned under section 257 approves the proposed voluntary arrangement (with or without modifications).

(2) The approved arrangement—

    (*a*) takes effect as if made by the debtor at the meeting, and

    (*b*) binds every person who in accordance with the rules had notice of, and was entitled to vote at, the meeting (whether or not he was present or represented at it) as if he were a party to the arrangement.

(3) The Deeds of Arrangement Act 1914 does not apply to the approved voluntary arrangement.

(4) Any interim order in force in relation to the debtor immediately before the end of the period of 28 days beginning with the day on which the report with respect to the creditors' meeting was made to the court under section 259 ceases to have effect at the end of that period.

This subsection applies except to such extent as the court may direct for the purposes of any application under section 262 below.

(5) Where proceedings on a bankruptcy petition have been stayed by an interim order which ceases to have effect under subsection (4), that petition is deemed, unless the court otherwise orders, to have been dismissed.   **[260]**

NOTES
Commencement: 29 December 1986.
This section derived from the Insolvency Act 1985, s 116(1)–(3), (6), (7).

261. Effect where debtor an undischarged bankrupt

(1) Subject as follows, where the creditors' meeting summoned under section 257 approves the proposed voluntary arrangement (with or without modifications) and the debtor is an undischarged bankrupt, the court may do one or both of the following, namely—

(a) annul the bankruptcy order by which he was adjudged bankrupt;

(b) give such directions with respect to the conduct of the bankruptcy and the administration of the bankrupt's estate as it thinks appropriate for facilitating the implementation of the approved voluntary arrangement.

(2) The court shall not annul a bankruptcy order under subsection (1)—

(a) at any time before the end of the period of 28 days beginning with the day on which the report of the creditors' meeting was made to the court under section 259, or

(b) at any time when an application under section 262 below, or an appeal in respect of such an application, is pending or at any time in the period within which such an appeal may be brought.   **[261]**

NOTES
Commencement: 29 December 1986.
This section derived from the Insolvency Act 1985, s 116(4), (5).

262. Challenge of meeting's decision

(1) Subject to this section, an application to the court may be made, by any of the persons specified below, on one or both of the following grounds, namely—

(a) that a voluntary arrangement approved by a creditor's meeting summoned under section 257 unfairly prejudices the interests of a creditor of the debtor;

(b) that there has been some material irregularity at or in relation to such a meeting.

(2) The persons who may apply under this section are—

(a) the debtor;

(b) a person entitled, in accordance with the rules, to vote at the creditors' meeting;

(c) the nominee (or his replacement under section 256(3)(a) or 258(3)); and

(d) if the debtor is an undischarged bankrupt, the trustee of his estate or the official receiver.

(3) An application under this section shall not be made after the end of the period of 28 days beginning with the day on which the report of the creditors' meeting was made to the court under section 259.

(4) Where on an application under this section the court is satisfied as to

either of the grounds mentioned in subsection (1), it may do one or both of the following, namely—

(*a*) revoke or suspend any approval given by the meeting;
(*b*) give a direction to any person for the summoning of a further meeting of the debtor's creditors to consider any revised proposal he may make or, in a case falling within subsection (1)(*b*), to reconsider his original proposal.

(5) Where at any time after giving a direction under subsection (4)(*b*) for the summoning of a meeting to consider a revised proposal the court is satisfied that the debtor does not intend to submit such a proposal, the court shall revoke the direction and revoke or suspend any approval given at the previous meeting.

(6) Where the court gives a direction under subsection (4)(*b*), it may also give a direction continuing or, as the case may require, renewing, for such period as may be specified in the direction, the effect in relation to the debtor of any interim order.

(7) In any case where the court, on an application made under this section with respect to a creditors' meeting, gives a direction under subsection (4)(*b*) or revokes or suspends an approval under subsection (4)(*a*) or (5), the court may give such supplemental directions as it thinks fit and, in particular, directions with respect to—

(*a*) things done since the meeting under any voluntary arrangement approved by the meeting, and
(*b*) such things done since the meeting as could not have been done if an interim order had been in force in relation to the debtor when they were done.

(8) Except in pursuance of the preceding provisions of this section, an approval given at a creditors' meeting summoned under section 257 is not invalidated by any irregularity at or in relation to the meeting.   **[262]**

NOTES
Commencement: 29 December 1986.
This section derived from the Insolvency Act 1985, s 117.

---

263. Implementation and supervision of approved voluntary arrangement

(1) This section applies where a voluntary arrangement approved by a creditors' meeting summoned under section 257 has taken effect.

(2) The person who is for the time being carrying out, in relation to the voluntary arrangement, the functions conferred by virtue of the approval on the nominee (or his replacement under section 256(3)(*a*) or 258(3)) shall be known as the supervisor of the voluntary arrangement.

(3) If the debtor, any of his creditors or any other person is dissatisfied by any act, omission or decision of the supervisor, he may apply to the court; and on such an application the court may—

(*a*) confirm, reverse or modify any act or decision of the supervisor,
(*b*) give him directions, or
(*c*) make such other order as it thinks fit.

(4) The supervisor may apply to the court for directions in relation to any particular matter arising under the voluntary arrangement.

(5) The court may, whenever—

(a) it is expedient to appoint a person to carry out the functions of the supervisor, and

(b) it is inexpedient, difficult or impracticable for an appointment to be made without the assistance of the court,

make an order appointing a person who is qualified to act as an insolvency practitioner in relation to the debtor, either in substitution for the existing supervisor or to fill a vacancy.

This is without prejudice to section 41(2) of the Trustee Act 1925 (power of court to appoint trustees of deeds of arrangement).

(6) The power conferred by subsection (5) is exercisable so as to increase the number of persons exercising the functions of the supervisor or, where there is more than one person exercising those functions, so as to replace one or more of those persons.   **[263]**

NOTES
Commencement: 29 December 1986.
This section derived from the Insolvency Act 1985, s 118.

PART IX

BANKRUPTCY

CHAPTER I

BANKRUPTCY PETITIONS; BANKRUPTCY ORDERS

Preliminary

264. Who may present a bankruptcy petition

(1) A petition for a bankruptcy order to be made against an individual may be presented to the court in accordance with the following provisions of this Part—

(a) by one of the individual's creditors or jointly by more than one of them,

(b) by the individual himself,

(c) by the supervisor of, or any person (other than the individual) who is for the time being bound by, a voluntary arrangement proposed by the individual and approved under Part VIII, or

(d) where a criminal bankruptcy order has been made against the individual, by the Official Petitioner or by any person specified in the order in pursuance of section 39(3)(b) of the Powers of Criminal Courts Act 1973.

(2) Subject to those provisions, the court may make a bankruptcy order on any such petition.   **[264]**

NOTES
Commencement: 29 December 1986.
This section derived from the Insolvency Act 1985, s 119(1).

265. Conditions to be satisfied in respect of debtor

(1) A bankruptcy petition shall not be presented to the court under section 264(1)(a) or (b) unless the debtor—

(a) is domiciled in England and Wales,

(b) is personally present in England and Wales on the day on which the petition is presented, or (*c*) at any time in the period of 3 years ending with that day—

        (i) has been ordinarily resident, or has had a place of residence, in England and Wales, or

        (ii) has carried on business in England and Wales.

    (2) The reference in subsection (1)(*c*) to an individual carrying on business includes—

    (*a*) the carrying on of business by a firm or partnership of which the individual is a member, and

    (*b*) the carrying on of business by an agent or manager for the individual or for such a firm or partnership. **[265]**

NOTES
Commencement: 29 December 1986.
This section derived from the Insolvency Act 1985, s 119(2), (3).

266. Other preliminary conditions

(1) Where a bankruptcy petition relating to an individual is presented by a person who is entitled to present a petition under two or more paragraphs of section 264(1), the petition is to be treated for the purposes of this Part as a petition under such one of those paragraphs as may be specified in the petition.

    (2) A bankruptcy petition shall not be withdrawn without the leave of the court.

    (3) The court has a general power, if it appears to it appropriate to do so on the grounds that there has been a contravention of the rules or for any other reason, to dismiss a bankruptcy petition or to stay proceedings on such a petition; and, where it stays proceedings on a petition, it may do so on such terms and conditions as it thinks fit.

    (4) Without prejudice to subsection (3), where a petition under section 264(1)(*a*), (*b*) or (*c*) in respect of an individual is pending at a time when a criminal bankruptcy order is made against him, or is presented after such an order has been so made, the court may on the application of the Official Petitioner dismiss the petition if it appears to it appropriate to do so. **[266]**

NOTES
Commencement: 29 December 1986.
This section derived from the Insolvency Act 1985, s 119(4)–(7).

Creditor's petition

267. Grounds of creditor's petition

(1) A creditor's petition must be in respect of one or more debts owed by the debtor, and the petitioning creditor or each of the petitioning creditors must be a person to whom the debt or (as the case may be) at least one of the debts is owed.

    (2) Subject to the next three sections, a creditor's petition may be presented to the court in respect of a debt or debts only if, at the time the petition is presented—

    (*a*) the amount of the debt, or the aggregate amount of the debts, is equal to or exceeds the bankruptcy level, (*b*) the debt, or each of the debts, is for a liquidated sum payable to the petitioning creditor, or one or more of the petitioning creditors, either immediately or at some certain, future time, and is unsecured,

    (*c*) the debt, or each of the debts, is a debt which the debtor appears either to be unable to pay or to have no reasonable prospect of being able to pay, and

    (*d*) there is no outstanding application to set aside a statutory demand served (under section 268 below) in respect of the debt or any of the debts.

(3) A debt is not to be regarded for the purposes of subsection (2) as a debt for a liquidated sum by reason only that the amount of the debt is specified in a criminal bankruptcy order.

(4) "The bankruptcy level" is £750; but the Secretary of State may by order in a statutory instrument substitute any amount specified in the order for that amount or (as the case may be) for the amount which by virtue of such an order is for the time being the amount of the bankruptcy level.

(5) An order shall not be made under subsection (4) unless a draft of it has been laid before, and approved by a resolution of, each House of Parliament.

                                                                                           [267]

NOTES

Commencement: 29 December 1986.

This section derived from the Insolvency Act 1985, s 120(1), (2), (7)–(9).

268. Definition of "inability to pay", etc; the statutory demand

(1) For the purposes of section 267(2)(*c*), the debtor appears to be unable to pay a debt if, but only if, the debt is payable immediately and either—

    (*a*) the petitioning creditor to whom the debt is owed has served on the debtor a demand (known as "the statutory demand") in the prescribed form requiring him to pay the debt or to secure or compound for it to the satisfaction of the creditor, at least 3 weeks have elapsed since the demand was served and the demand has been neither complied with nor set aside in accordance with the rules, or

    (*b*) execution or other process issued in respect of the debt on a judgment or order of any court in favour of the petitioning creditor, or one or more of the petitioning creditors to whom the debt is owed, has been returned unsatisfied in whole or in part.

(2) For the purposes of section 267(2)(*c*) the debtor appears to have no reasonable prospect of being able to pay a debt if, but only if, the debt is not immediately payable and—

    (*a*) the petitioning creditor to whom it is owed has served on the debtor a demand (also known as "the statutory demand") in the prescribed form requiring him to establish to the satisfaction of the creditor that there is a reasonable prospect that the debtor will be able to pay the debt when it falls due,

    (*b*) at least 3 weeks have elapsed since the demand was served, and

    (*c*) the demand has been neither complied with nor set aside in accordance with the rules.   [268]

NOTES

Commencement: 29 December 1986.

This section derived from the Insolvency Act 1985, s 120(3), (4).

269. Creditor with security

(1) A debt which is the debt, or one of the debts, in respect of which a creditor's petition is presented need not be unsecured if either—

    (*a*) the petition contains a statement by the person having the right to enforce the security that he is willing, in the event of a bankruptcy order being made, to give up his security for the benefit of all the bankrupt's creditors, or

    (*b*) the petition is expressed not to be made in respect of the secured part of the debt and contains a statement by that person of the estimated value at the date of the petition of the security for the secured part of the debt.

(2) In a case falling within subsection (1)(*b*) the secured and unsecured parts of the debt are to be treated for the purposes of sections 267 to 270 as separate debts.   **[269]**

NOTES
    Commencement: 29 December 1986.
    This section derived from the Insolvency Act 1985, s 120(5).

270. Expedited petition

In the case of a creditor's petition presented wholly or partly in respect of a debt which is the subject of a statutory demand under section 268, the petition may be presented before the end of the 3-week period there mentioned if there is a serious possibility that the debtor's property or the value of any of his property will be significantly diminished during that period and the petition contains a statement to that effect.   **[270]**

NOTES
    Commencement: 29 December 1986.
    This section derived from the Insolvency Act 1985, s 120(6).

271. Proceedings on creditor's petition

(1) The court shall not make a bankruptcy order on a creditor's petition unless it is satisfied that the debt, or one of the debts, in respect of which the petition was presented is either—

    (*a*) a debt which, having been payable at the date of the petition or having since become payable, has been neither paid nor secured or compounded for, or

    (*b*) a debt which the debtor has no reasonable prospect of being able to pay when it falls due.

(2) In a case in which the petition contains such a statement as is required by section 270, the court shall not make a bankruptcy order until at least 3 weeks have elapsed since the service of any statutory demand under section 268.

(3) The court may dismiss the petition if it is satisfied that the debtor is able to pay all his debts or is satisfied—

    (*a*) that the debtor has made an offer to secure or compound for a debt in respect of which the petition is presented,

    (*b*) that the acceptance of that offer would have required the dismissal of the petition, and

(c) that the offer has been unreasonably refused;

and, in determining for the purposes of this subsection whether the debtor is able to pay all his debts, the court shall take into account his contingent and prospective liabilities.

(4) In determining for the purposes of this section what constitutes a reasonable prospect that a debtor will be able to pay a debt when it falls due, it is to be assumed that the prospect given by the facts and other matters known to the creditor at the time he entered into the transaction resulting in the debt was a reasonable prospect.

(5) Nothing in sections 267 to 271 prejudices the power of the court, in accordance with the rules, to authorise a creditor's petition to be amended by the omission of any creditor or debt and to be proceeded with as if things done for the purposes of those sections had been done only by or in relation to the remaining creditors or debts. **[271]**

NOTES
Commencement: 29 December 1986.
This section derived from the Insolvency Act 1985, s 121.

Debtor's petition

272. Grounds of debtor's petition

(1) A debtor's petition may be presented to the court only on the grounds that the debtor is unable to pay his debts.

(2) The petition shall be accompanied by a statement of the debtor's affairs containing—

    (a) such particulars of the debtor's creditors and of his debts and other liabilities and of his assets as may be prescribed, and

    (b) such other information as may be prescribed. **[272]**

NOTES
Commencement: 29 December 1986.
This section derived from the Insolvency Act 1985, s 122.

273. Appointment of insolvency practitioner by the court

(1) Subject to the next section, on the hearing of a debtor's petition the court shall not make a bankruptcy order if it appears to the court—

    (a) that if a bankruptcy order were made the aggregate amount of the bankruptcy debts, so far as unsecured, would be less than the small bankruptcies level,

    (b) that if a bankruptcy order were made, the value of the bankrupt's estate would be equal to or more than the minimum amount,

    (c) that within the period of 5 years ending with the presentation of the petition the debtor has neither been adjudged bankrupt nor made a composition with his creditors in satisfaction of his debts or a scheme of arrangement of his affairs, and

    (d) that it would be appropriate to appoint a person to prepare a report under section 274.

"The minimum amount" and "the small bankruptcies level" mean such amounts as may for the time being be prescribed for the purposes of this section.

(2) Where on the hearing of the petition, it appears to the court as mentioned

in subsection (1), the court shall appoint a person who is qualified to act as an insolvency practitioner in relation to the debtor—

  (a) to prepare a report under the next section, and
  (b) subject to section 258(3) in Part VIII, to act in relation to any voluntary arrangement to which the report relates either as trustee or otherwise for the purpose of supervising its implementation.   **[273]**

NOTES
  Commencement: 29 December 1986.
  This section derived from the Insolvency Act 1985, s 123(1), (2), (8).

274. Action of report of insolvency practitioner

(1) A person appointed under section 273 shall inquire into the debtor's affairs and, within such period as the court may direct, shall submit a report to the court stating whether the debtor is willing, for the purposes of Part VIII, to make a proposal for a voluntary arrangement.

(2) A report which states that the debtor is willing as above mentioned shall also state—

  (a) whether, in the opinion of the person making the report, a meeting of the debtor's creditors should be summoned to consider the proposal, and
  (b) if in that person's opinion such a meeting should be summoned, the date on which, and time and place at which, he proposes the meeting should be held.

(3) On considering a report under this section the court may—

  (a) without any application, make an interim order under section 252, if it thinks that it is appropriate to do so for the purpose of facilitating the consideration and implementation of the debtor's proposal, or
  (b) if it thinks it would be inappropriate to make such an order, make a bankruptcy order.

(4) An interim order made by virtue of this section ceases to have effect at the end of such period as the court may specify for the purpose of enabling the debtor's proposal to be considered by his creditors in accordance with the applicable provisions of Part VIII.

(5) Where it has been reported to the court under this section that a meeting of the debtor's creditors should be summoned, the person making the report shall, unless the court otherwise directs, summon that meeting for the time, date and place proposed in his report.

The meeting is then deemed to have been summoned under section 257 in Part VIII, and subsections (2) and (3) of that section, and sections 258 to 263 apply accordingly.   **[274]**

NOTES
  Commencement: 29 December 1986.
  This section derived from the Insolvency Act 1985, ss 111(3) (part), 112(1) (part), (7)(b), 114(1) (part), 123(3)–(5).

275. Summary administration

(1) Where on the hearing of a debtor's petition the court makes a bankruptcy order and the case is as specified in the next subsection, the court shall, if it

appears to it appropriate to do so, issue a certificate for the summary administration of the bankrupt's estate.

(2) That case is where it appears to the court—

    (*a*) that if a bankruptcy order were made the aggregate amount of the bankruptcy debts so far as unsecured would be less than the small bankruptcies level (within the meaning given by section 273), and

    (*b*) that within the period of 5 years ending with the presentation of the petition the debtor has neither been adjudged bankrupt nor made a composition with his creditors in satisfaction of his debts or a scheme of arrangement of his affairs,

whether the bankruptcy order is made because it does not appear to the court as mentioned in section 273(1)(*b*) or (*d*), or it is made because the court thinks it would be inappropriate to make an interim order under section 252.

(3) The court may at any time revoke a certificate issued under this section if it appears to it that, on any grounds existing at the time the certificate was issued, the certificate ought not to have been issued. **[275]**

NOTES

Commencement: 29 December 1986.

This section derived from the Insolvency Act 1985, s 123(6), (7).

Other cases for special consideration

276. Default in connection with voluntary arrangement

(1) The court shall not make a bankruptcy order on a petition under section 264(1)(*c*) (supervisor of, or person bound by, voluntary arrangement proposed and approved) unless it is satisfied—

    (*a*) that the debtor has failed to comply with his obligations under the voluntary arrangement, or

    (*b*) that information which was false or misleading in any material particular or which contained material omissions—

        (i) was contained in any statement of affairs or other document supplied by the debtor under Part VIII to any person, or

        (ii) was otherwise made available by the debtor to his creditors at or in connection with a meeting summoned under that Part, or

    (*c*) that the debtor has failed to do all such things as may for the purposes of the voluntary arrangement have been reasonably required of him by the supervisor of the arrangement.

(2) Where a bankruptcy order is made on a petition under section 264(1)(*c*), any expenses properly incurred as expenses of the administration of the voluntary arrangement in question shall be a first charge on the bankrupt's estate. **[276]**

NOTES

Commencement: 29 December 1986.

This section derived from the Insolvency Act 1985, s 124.

277. Petition based on criminal bankruptcy order

(1) Subject to section 266(3), the court shall make a bankruptcy order on a petition under section 264(1)(*d*) on production of a copy of the criminal bankruptcy order on which the petition is based.

This does not apply if it appears to the court that the criminal bankruptcy order has been rescinded on appeal.

(2) Subject to the provisions of this Part, the fact that an appeal is pending against any conviction by virtue of which a criminal bankruptcy order was made does not affect any proceedings on a petition under section 264(1)(*d*) based on that order.

(3) For the purposes of this section, an appeal against a conviction is pending—

> (*a*) in any case, until the expiration of the period of 28 days beginning with the date of conviction;
> (*b*) if notice of appeal to the Court of Appeal is given during that period and during that period the appellant notifies the official receiver of it, until the determination of the appeal and thereafter for so long as an appeal to the House of Lords is pending within the meaning of section 40(5) of the Powers of Criminal Courts Act 1973.   **[277]**

NOTES
Commencement: 29 December 1986.
This section derived from the Insolvency Act 1985, s 125.

Commencement and duration of bankruptcy; discharge

278. Commencement and continuance

The bankruptcy of an individual against whom a bankruptcy order has been made—

> (*a*) commences with the day on which the order is made, and
> (*b*) continues until the individual is discharged under the following provisions of this Chapter.   **[278]**

NOTES
Commencement: 29 December 1986.
This section derived from the Insolvency Act 1985, s 126(1).

279. Duration

(1) Subject as follows, a bankrupt is discharged from bankruptcy—

> (*a*) in the case of an individual who was adjudged bankrupt on a petition under section 264(1)(*d*) or who had been an undischarged bankrupt at any time in the period of 15 years ending with the commencement of the bankruptcy, by an order of the court under the section next following, and
> (*b*) in any other case, by the expiration of the relevant period under this section.

(2) That period is as follows—

> (*a*) where a certificate for the summary administration of the bankrupt's estate has been issued and is not revoked before the bankrupt's discharge, the period of 2 years beginning with the commencement of the bankruptcy, and
> (*b*) in any other case, the period of 3 years beginning with the commencement of the bankruptcy.

(3) Where the court is satisfied on the application of the official receiver that an undischarged bankrupt in relation to whom subsection (1)(*b*) applies

has failed or is failing to comply with any of his obligations under this Part, the court may order that the relevant period under this section shall cease to run for such period, or until the fulfilment of such conditions (including a condition requiring the court to be satisfied as to any matter), as may be specified in the order.

(4) This section is without prejudice to any power of the court to annul a bankruptcy order.   **[279]**

NOTES
Commencement: 29 December 1986.
This section derived from the Insolvency Act 1985, s 126(2)–(5).

280. Discharge by order of the court

(1) An application for an order of the court discharging an individual from bankruptcy in a case falling within section 279(1)(*a*) may be made by the bankrupt at any time after the end of the period of 5 years beginning with the commencement of the bankruptcy.

(2) On an application under this section the court may—

(*a*) refuse to discharge the bankrupt from bankrutpcy,
(*b*) make an order discharging him absolutely, or
(*c*) make an order discharging him subject to such conditions with respect to any income which may subsequently become due to him, or with respect to property devolving upon him, or acquired by him, after his discharge, as may be specified in the order.

(3) The court may provide for an order falling within subsection (2)(*b*) or (*c*) to have immediate effect or to have its effect suspended for such period, or until the fulfilment of such conditions (including a condition requiring the court to be satisfied as to any matter), as may be specified in the order.   **[280]**

NOTES
Commencement: 29 December 1986.
This section derived from the Insolvency Act 1985, s 127.

281. Effect of discharge

(1) Subject as follows, where a bankrupt is discharged, the discharge releases him from all the bankruptcy debts, but has no effect—

(*a*) on the functions (so far as they remain to be carried out) of the trustee of his estate, or
(*b*) on the operation, for the purposes of the carrying out of those functions, of the provisions of this Part;

and, in particular, discharge does not affect the right of any creditor of the bankrupt to prove in the bankruptcy for any debt from which the bankrupt is released.

(2) Discharge does not affect the right of any secured creditor of the bankrupt to enforce his security for the payment of a debt from which the bankrupt is released.

(3) Discharge does not release the bankrupt from any bankruptcy debt which he incurred in respect of, or forbearance in respect of which was secured by means of, any fraud or fraudulent breach of trust to which he was a party.

(4) Discharge does not release the bankrupt from any liability in respect of

a fine imposed for an offence or from any liability under a recognisance except, in the case of a penalty imposed for an offence under an enactment relating to the public revenue or of a recognisance, with the consent of the Treasury.

(5) Discharge does not, except to such extent and on such conditions as the court may direct, release the bankrupt from any bankruptcy debt which—

> (a) consists in a liability to pay damages for negligence, nuisance or breach of a statutory, contractual or other duty, being damages in respect of personal injuries to any person, or
> (b) arises under any order made in family proceedings or in domestic proceedings.

(6) Discharge does not release the bankrupt from such other bankruptcy debts, not being debts provable in his bankruptcy, as are prescribed.

(7) Discharge does not release any person other than the bankrupt from any liability (whether as partner or co-trustee of the bankrupt or otherwise) from which the bankrupt is released by the discharge, or from any liability as surety for the bankrupt or as a person in the nature of such a surety.

(8) In this section—

> "domestic proceedings" means domestic proceedings within the meaning of the Magistrates' Courts Act 1980 and any proceedings which would be such proceedings but for section 65(1)(ii) of that Act (proceedings for variation of order for periodical payments);
> "family proceedings" means the same as in Part V of the Matrimonial and Family Proceedings Act 1984;
> "fine" means the same as in the Magistrates' Courts Act 1980; and
> "personal injuries" includes death and any disease or other impairment of a person's physical or mental condition.   **[281]**

NOTES
  Commencement: 29 December 1986.
  This section derived from the Insolvency Act 1985, s 128.

282. Court's power to annul bankruptcy order

(1) The court may annul a bankruptcy order if it at any time appears to the court—

> (a) that, on the grounds existing at the time the order was made, the order ought not to have been made, or
> (b) that, to the extent required by the rules, the bankruptcy debts and the expenses of the bankruptcy have all, since the making of the order, been either paid or secured for to the satisfaction of the court.

(2) The court may annul a bankruptcy order made against an individual on a petition under paragraph (a), (b) or (c) of section 264(1) if it at any time appears to the court, on an application by the Official Petitioner—

> (a) that the petition was pending at a time when a criminal bankruptcy order was made against the individual or was presented after such an order was so made, and
> (b) no appeal is pending (within the meaning of section 277) against the individual's conviction of any offence by virtue of which the criminal bankruptcy order was made;

and the court shall annul a bankruptcy order made on a petition under section 264(1)(d) if it at any time appears to the court that the criminal bankruptcy order on which the petition was based has been rescinded in consequence of an appeal.

(3) The court may annul a bankruptcy order whether or not the bankrupt has been discharged from the bankruptcy.

(4) Where the court annuls a bankruptcy order (whether under this section or under section 261 in Part VIII)—

> (*a*) any sale or other disposition of property, payment made or other thing duly done, under any provision in this Group of Parts, by or under the authority of the official receiver or a trustee of the bankrupt's estate or by the court is valid, but
>
> (*b*) if any of the bankrupt's estate is then vested, under any such provision, in such a trustee, it shall vest in such person as the court may appoint or, in default of any such appointment, revert to the bankrupt on such terms (if any) as the court may direct;

and the court may include in its order such supplemental provisions as may be authorised by the rules.

(5) In determining for the purposes of section 279 whether a person was an undischarged bankrupt at any time, any time when he was a bankrupt by virtue of an order that was subsequently annulled is to be disregarded. **[282]**

NOTES
> Commencement: 29 December 1986.
> This section derived from the Insolvency Act 1985, s 129.

Chapter II

Protection of Bankrupt's Estate and Investigation of His Affairs

283. Definition of bankrupt's estate

(1) Subject as follows, a bankrupt's estate for the purposes of any of this Group of Parts comprises—

> (*a*) all property belonging to or vested in the bankrupt at the commencement of the bankruptcy, and
>
> (*b*) any property which by virtue of any of the following provisions of this Part is comprised in that estate or is treated as falling within the preceding paragraph.

(2) Subsection (1) does not apply to—

> (*a*) such tools, books, vehicles and other items of equipment as are necessary to the bankrupt for use personally by him in his employment, business or vocation;
>
> (*b*) such clothing, bedding, furniture, household equipment and provisions as are necessary for satisfying the basic domestic needs of the bankrupt and his family.

This subsection is subject to section 308 in Chapter IV (certain excluded property reclaimable by trustee).

(3) Subsection (1) does not apply to—

> (*a*) property held by the bankrupt on trust for any other person, or
>
> (*b*) the right of nomination to a vacant ecclesiastical benefice.

(4) References in any of this Group of Parts to property, in relation to a bankrupt, include references to any power exercisable by him over or in respect of property except in so far as the power is exercisable over or in respect of property not for the time being comprised in the bankrupt's estate and—

(a) is so exercisable at a time after either the official receiver has had his release in respect of that estate under section 299(2) in Chapter III or a meeting summoned by the trustee of that estate under section 331 in Chapter IV has been held, or

(b) cannot be so exercised for the benefit of the bankrupt;

and a power exercisable over or in respect of property is deemed for the purposes of any of this Group of Parts to vest in the person entitled to exercise it at the time of the transaction or event by virtue of which it is exercisable by that person (whether or not it becomes so exercisable at that time).

(5) For the purposes of any such provision in this Group of Parts, property comprised in a bankrupt's estate is so comprised subject to the rights of any person other than the bankrupt (whether as a secured creditor of the bankrupt or otherwise) in relation thereto, but disregarding—

(a) any rights in relation to which a statement such as is required by section 269(1)(a) was made in the petition on which the bankrupt was adjudged bankrupt, and

(b) any rights which have been otherwise given up in accordance with the rules.

(6) This section has effect subject to the provisions of any enactment not contained in this Act under which any property is to be excluded from a bankrupt's estate.   **[283]**

NOTES
Commencement: 29 December 1986.
This section derived from the Insolvency Act 1985, s 130.

284. Restrictions on dispositions of property

(1) Where a person is adjudged bankrupt, any disposition of property made by that person in the period to which this section applies is void except to the extent that it is or was made with the consent of the court, or is or was subsequently ratified by the court.

(2) Subsection (1) applies to a payment (whether in cash or otherwise) as it applies to a disposition of property and, accordingly, where any payment is void by virtue of that subsection, the person paid shall hold the sum paid for the bankrupt as part of his estate.

(3) This section applies to the period beginning with the day of the presentation of the petition for the bankruptcy order and ending with the vesting, under Chapter IV of this Part, of the bankrupt's estate in a trustee.

(4) The preceding provisions of this section do not give a remedy against any person—

(a) in respect of any property or payment which he received before the commencement of the bankruptcy in good faith, for value and without notice that the petition had been presented, or

(b) in respect of any interest in property which derives from an interest in respect of which there is, by virtue of this subsection, no remedy.

(5) Where after the commencement of his bankruptcy the bankrupt has incurred a debt to a banker or other person by reason of the making of a

payment which is void under this section, that debt is deemed for the purposes of any of this Group of Parts to have been incurred before the commencement of the bankruptcy unless—

> (*a*) that banker or person had notice of the bankruptcy before the debt was incurred, or
>
> (*b*) it is not reasonably practicable for the amount of the payment to be recovered from the person to whom it was made.

(6) A disposition of property is void under this section notwithstanding that the property is not or, as the case may be, would not be comprised in the bankrupt's estate; but nothing in this section affects any disposition made by a person of property held by him on trust for any other person.　　　　**[284]**

NOTES

Commencement: 29 December 1986.

This section derived from the Insolvency Act 1985, s 131.

285. Restriction on proceedings and remedies

(1) At any time when proceedings on a bankruptcy petition are pending or an individual has been adjudged bankrupt the court may stay any action, execution or other legal process against the property or person of the debtor or, as the case may be, of the bankrupt.

(2) Any court in which proceedings are pending against any individual may, on proof that a bankruptcy petition has been presented in respect of that individual or that he is an undischarged bankrupt, either stay the proceedings or allow them to continue on such terms as it thinks fit.

(3) After the making of a bankruptcy order no person who is a creditor of the bankrupt in respect of a debt provable in the bankruptcy shall—

> (*a*) have any remedy against the property or person of the bankrupt in respect of that debt, or
>
> (*b*) before the discharge of the bankrupt, commence any action or other legal proceedings against the bankrupt except with the leave of the court and on such terms as the court may impose.

This is subject to sections 346 (enforcement procedures) and 347 (limited right to distress).

(4) Subject as follows, subsection (3) does not affect the right of a secured creditor of the bankrupt to enforce his security.

(5) Where any goods of an undischarged bankrupt are held by any person by way of pledge, pawn or other security, the official receiver may, after giving notice in writing of his intention to do so, inspect the goods.

Where such a notice has been given to any person, that person is not entitled, without leave of the court, to realise his security unless he has given the trustee of the bankrupt's estate a reasonable opportunity of inspecting the goods and of exercising the bankrupt's right of redemption.

(6) References in this section to the property or goods of the bankrupt are to any of his property or goods, whether or not comprised in his estate.　　　**[285]**

NOTES

Commencement: 29 December 1986.

This section derived from the Insolvency Act 1985, s 132.

286. Power to appoint interim receiver

(1) The court may, if it is shown to be necessary for the protection of the debtor's property, at any time after the presentation of a bankruptcy petition and before making a bankruptcy order, appoint the official receiver to be interim receiver of the debtor's property.

(2) Where the court has, on a debtor's petition, appointed an insolvency practitioner under section 273 and it is shown to the court as mentioned in subsection (1) of this section, the court may, without making a bankruptcy order, appoint that practitioner, instead of the official receiver, to be interim receiver of the debtor's property.

(3) The court may by an order appointing any person to be an interim receiver direct that his powers shall be limited or restricted in any respect; but, save as so directed, an interim receiver has, in relation to the debtor's property, all the rights, powers, duties and immunities of a receiver and manager under the next section.

(4) An order of the court appointing any person to be an interim receiver shall require that person to take immediate possession of the debtor's property or, as the case may be, the part of it to which his powers as interim receiver are limited.

(5) Where an interim receiver has been appointed, the debtor shall give him such inventory of his property and such other information, and shall attend on the interim receiver at such times, as the latter may for the purpose of carrying out his functions under this section reasonably require.

(6) Where an interim receiver is appointed, section 285(3) applies for the period between the appointment and the making of a bankruptcy order on the petition, or the dismissal of the petition, as if the appointment were the making of such an order.

(7) A person ceases to be interim receiver of a debtor's property if the bankruptcy petition relating to the debtor is dismissed, if a bankruptcy order is made on the petition or if the court by order otherwise terminates the appointment.

(8) References in this section to the debtor's property are to all his property, whether or not it would be comprised in his estate if he were adjudged bankrupt.   **[286]**

NOTES
    Commencement: 29 December 1986.
    This section derived from the Insolvency Act 1985, s 133.

287. Receivership pending appointment of trustee

(1) Between the making of a bankruptcy order and the time at which the bankrupt's estate vests in a trustee under Chapter IV of this Part, the official receiver is the receiver and (subject to section 370 (special manager)) the manager of the bankrupt's estate and is under a duty to act as such.

(2) The function of the official receiver while acting as receiver or manager of the bankrupt's estate under this section is to protect the estate; and for this purpose—

(*a*) he has the same powers as if he were a receiver or manager appointed
by the High Court, and

(*b*) he is entitled to sell or otherwise dispose of any perishable goods
comprised in the estate and any other goods so comprised the value of
which is likely to diminish if they are not disposed of.

(3) The official receiver while acting as receiver or manager of the estate
under this section—

(*a*) shall take all such steps as he thinks fit for protecting any property
which may be claimed for the estate by the trustee of that estate,

(*b*) is not, except in pursuance of directions given by the Secretary of
State, required to do anything that involves his incurring expenditure,

(*c*) may, if he thinks fit (and shall, if so directed by the court) at any time
summon a general meeting of the bankrupt's creditors.

(4) Where—

(*a*) the official receiver acting as receiver or manager of the estate under
this section seizes or disposes of any property which is not comprised
in the estate, and

(*b*) at the time of the seizure or disposal the official receiver believes, and
has reasonable grounds for believing, that he is entitled (whether in
pursuance of an order of the court or otherwise) to seize or dispose of
that property,

the official receiver is not to be liable to any person in respect of any loss or
damage resulting from the seizure or disposal except in so far as that loss or
damage is caused by his negligence; and he has a lien on the property, or the
proceeds of its sale, for such of the expenses of the bankruptcy as were incurred
in connection with the seizure or disposal.

(5) This section does not apply where by virtue of section 297 (appointment
of trustee; special cases) the bankrupt's estate vests in a trustee immediately on
the making of the bankruptcy order.   [287]

NOTES
Commencement: 29 December 1986.
This section derived from the Insolvency Act 1985, s 134.

288. Statement of affairs

(1) Where a bankruptcy order has been made otherwise than on a debtor's
petition, the bankrupt shall submit a statement of his affairs to the official
receiver before the end of the period of 21 days beginning with the
commencement of the bankruptcy.

(2) The statement of affairs shall contain—

(*a*) such particulars of the bankrupt's creditors and of his debts and other
liabilities and of his assets as may be prescribed, and

(*b*) such other information as may be prescribed.

(3) The official receiver may, if he thinks fit—

(*a*) release the bankrupt from his duty under subsection (1), or

(*b*) extend the period specified in that subsection;

and where the official receiver has refused to exercise a power conferred by this
section, the court, if it thinks fit, may exercise it.

(4) A bankrupt who—

(a) without reasonable excuse fails to comply with the obligation imposed
   by this section, or

(b) without reasonable excuse submits a statement of affairs that does not
   comply with the prescribed requirements,

is guilty of a contempt of court and liable to be punished accordingly (in addition
to any other punishment to which he may be subject).   **[288]**

NOTES
   Commencement: 29 December 1986.
   This section derived from the Insolvency Act 1985, s 135.

289. Investigatory duties of official receiver

(1) Subject to subsection (5) below, it is the duty of the official receiver to
investigate the conduct and affairs of every bankrupt and to make such report
(if any) to the court as he thinks fit.

(2) Where an application is made by the bankrupt under section 280 for his
discharge from bankruptcy, it is the duty of the official receiver to make a report
to the court with respect to the prescribed matters; and the court shall consider
that report before determining what order (if any) to make under that section.

(3) A report by the official receiver under this section shall, in any
proceedings, be prima facie evidence of the facts stated in it.

(4) In subsection (1) the reference to the conduct and affairs of a bankrupt
includes his conduct and affairs before the making of the order by which he was
adjudged bankrupt.

(5) Where a certificate for the summary administration of the bankrupt's
estate is for the time being in force, the official receiver shall carry out an
investigation under subsection (1) only if he thinks fit.   **[289]**

NOTES
   Commencement: 29 December 1986.
   This section derived from the Insolvency Act 1985, s 136.

290. Public examination of bankrupt

(1) Where a bankruptcy order has been made, the official receiver may at any
time before the discharge of the bankrupt apply to the court for the public
examination of the bankrupt.

(2) Unless the court otherwise orders, the official receiver shall make an
application under subsection (1) if notice requiring him to do so is given to him,
in accordance with the rules, by one of the bankrupt's creditors with the
concurrence of not less than one-half, in value, of those creditors (including the
creditor giving notice).

(3) On an application under subsection (1), the court shall direct that a
public examination of the bankrupt shall be held on a day appointed by the
court; and the bankrupt shall attend on that day and be publicly examined as to
his affairs, dealings and property.

(4) The following may take part in the public examination of the bankrupt
and may question him concerning his affairs, dealings and property and the
causes of his failure, namely—

(a) the official receiver and, in the case of an individual adjudged
   bankrupt on a petition under section 264(1)(d), the Official Petitioner,

(b) the trustee of the bankrupt's estate, if his appointment has taken effect,

(c) any person who has been appointed as special manager of the bankrupt's estate or business,

(d) any creditor of the bankrupt who has tendered a proof in the bankruptcy.

(5) If a bankrupt without reasonable excuse fails at any time to attend his public examination under this section he is guilty of a contempt of court and liable to be punished accordingly (in addition to any other punishment to which he may be subject). **[290]**

NOTES
    Commencement: 29 December 1986.
    This section derived from the Insolvency Act 1985, s 137.

291. Duties of bankrupt in relation to official receiver

(1) Where a bankruptcy order has been made, the bankrupt is under a duty—

  (a) to deliver possession of his estate to the official receiver, and

  (b) to deliver up to the official receiver all books, papers and other records of which he has possession or control and which relate to his estate and affairs (including any which would be privileged from disclosure in any proceedings).

(2) In the case of any part of the bankrupt's estate which consists of things possession of which cannot be delivered to the official receiver, and in the case of any property that may be claimed for the bankrupt's estate by the trustee, it is the bankrupt's duty to do all such things as may reasonably be required by the official receiver for the protection of those things or that property.

(3) Subsections (1) and (2) do not apply where by virtue of section 297 below the bankrupt's estate vests in a trustee immediately on the making of the bankruptcy order.

(4) The bankrupt shall give the official receiver such inventory of his estate and such other information, and shall attend on the official receiver at such times, as the official receiver may for any of the purposes of this Chapter reasonably require.

(5) Subsection (4) applies to a bankrupt after his discharge.

(6) If the bankrupt without reasonable excuse fails to comply with any obligation imposed by this section, he is guilty of a contempt of court and liable to be punished accordingly (in addition to any other punishment to which he may be subject). **[291]**

NOTES
    Commencement: 29 December 1986.
    This section derived from the Insolvency Act 1985, s 138.

CHAPTER III

TRUSTEES IN BANKRUPTCY

Tenure of office as trustee

292. Power to make appointments

(1) The power to appoint a person as trustee of a bankrupt's estate (whether the first such trustee or a trustee appointed to fill any vacancy) is exercisable—

(*a*) except at a time when a certificate for the summary administration of the bankrupt's estate is in force, by a general meeting of the bankrupt's creditors;

(*b*) under section 295(2), 296(2) or 300(6) below in this Chapter, by the Secretary of State; or

(*c*) under section 297, by the court.

(2) No person may be appointed as trustee of a bankrupt's estate unless he is, at the time of the appointment, qualified to act as an insolvency practitioner in relation to the bankrupt.

(3) Any power to appoint a person as trustee of a bankrupt's estate includes power to appoint two or more persons as joint trustees; but such an appointment must make provision as to the circumstances in which the trustees must act together and the circumstances in which one or more of them may act for the others.

(4) The appointment of any person as trustee takes effect only if that person accepts the appointment in accordance with the rules. Subject to this, the appointment of any person as trustee takes effect at the time specified in his certificate of appointment.

(5) This section is without prejudice to the provisions of this Chapter under which the official receiver is, in certain circumstances, to be trustee of the estate.   **[292]**

NOTES

Commencement: 29 December 1986.

This section derived from the Insolvency Act 1985, s 139.

293. Summoning of meeting to appoint first trustee

(1) Where a bankruptcy order has been made and no certificate for the summary administration of the bankrupt's estate has been issued, it is the duty of the official receiver, as soon as practicable in the period of 12 weeks beginning with the day on which the order was made, to decide whether to summon a general meeting of the bankrupt's creditors for the purpose of appointing a trustee of the bankrupt's estate.

This section does not apply where the bankruptcy order was made on a petition under section 264(1)(*d*) (criminal bankruptcy); and it is subject to the provision made in sections 294(3) and 297(6) below.

(2) Subject to the next section, if the official receiver decides not to summon such a meeting, he shall, before the end of the period of 12 weeks above mentioned, give notice of his decision to the court and to every creditor of the bankrupt who is known to the official receiver or is identified in the bankrupt's statement of affairs.

(3) As from the giving to the court of a notice under subsection (2), the official receiver is the trustee of the bankrupt's estate.   **[293]**

NOTES

Commencement: 29 December 1986.

This section derived from the Insolvency Act 1985, s 140.

294. Power of creditors to requisition meeting

(1) Where in the case of any bankruptcy—

(*a*) the official receiver has not yet summoned, or has decided not to summon, a general meeting of the bankrupt's creditors for the purpose of appointing the trustee, and

(*b*) a certificate for the summary administration of the estate is not for the time being in force,

any creditor of the bankrupt may request the official receiver to summon such a meeting for that purpose.

(2) If such a request appears to the official receiver to be made with the concurrence of not less than one-quarter, in value, of the bankrupt's creditors (including the creditor making the request), it is the duty of the official receiver to summon the requested meeting.

(3) Accordingly, where the duty imposed by subsection (2) has arisen, the official receiver is required neither to reach a decision for the purposes of section 293(1) nor (if he has reached one) to serve any notice under section 293(2). **[294]**

NOTES
Commencement: 29 December 1986.
This section derived from the Insolvency Act 1985, s 141.

295. Failure of meeting to appoint trustee

(1) If a meeting summoned under section 293 or 294 is held but no appointment of a person as trustee is made, it is the duty of the official receiver to decide whether to refer the need for an appointment to the Secretary of State.

(2) On a reference made in pursuance of that decision, the Secretary of State shall either make an appointment or decline to make one.

(3) If—

(*a*) the official receiver decides not to refer the need for an appointment to the Secretary of State, or

(*b*) on such a reference the Secretary of State declines to make an appointment,

the official receiver shall give notice of his decision or, as the case may be, of the Secretary of State's decision to the court.

(4) As from the giving of notice under subsection (3) in a case in which no notice has been given under section 293(2), the official receiver shall be trustee of the bankrupt's estate. **[295]**

NOTES
Commencement: 29 December 1986.
This section derived from the Insolvency Act 1985, s 142.

296. Appointment of trustee by Secretary of State

(1) At any time when the official receiver is the trustee of a bankrupt's estate by virtue of any provision of this Chapter (other than section 297(1) below) he may apply to the Secretary of State for the appointment of a person as trustee instead of the official receiver.

(2) On an application under subsection (1) the Secretary of State shall either make an appointment or decline to make one.

(3) Such an application may be made notwithstanding that the Secretary of State has declined to make an appointment either on a previous application

under subsection (1) or on a reference under section 295 or under section 300(4) below.

(4) Where the trustee of a bankrupt's estate has been appointed by the Secretary of State (whether under this section or otherwise), the trustee shall give notice to the bankrupt's creditors of his appointment or, if the court so allows, shall advertise his appointment in accordance with the court's directions.

(5) In that notice or advertisement the trustee shall—

    (*a*) state whether he proposes to summon a general meeting of the bankrupt's creditors for the purpose of establishing a creditors' committee under section 301, and

    (*b*) if he does not propose to summon such a meeting, set out the power of the creditors under this Part to require him to summon one.   **[296]**

NOTES
    Commencement: 29 December 1986.
    This section derived from the Insolvency Act 1985, s 143.

297. Special cases

(1) Where a bankruptcy order is made on a petition under section 264(1)(*d*) (criminal bankruptcy), the official receiver shall be trustee of the bankrupt's estate.

(2) Subject to the next subsection, where the court issues a certificate for the summary administration of a bankrupt's estate, the official receiver shall, as from the issue of that certificate, be the trustee.

(3) Where such a certificate is issued or is in force, the court may, if it thinks fit, appoint a person other than the official receiver as trustee.

(4) Where a bankruptcy order is made in a case in which an insolvency practitioner's report has been submitted to the court under section 274 but no certificate for the summary admininstration of the estate is issued, the court, if it thinks fit, may on making the order appoint the person who made the report as trustee.

(5) Where a bankruptcy order is made (whether or not on a petition under section 264(1)(*c*)) at a time when there is a supervisor of a voluntary arrangement approved in relation to the bankrupt under Part VIII, the court, if it thinks fit, may on making the order appoint the supervisor of the arrangement as trustee.

(6) Where an appointment is made under subsection (4) or (5) of this section, the official receiver is not under the duty imposed by section 293(1) (to decide whether or not to summon a meeting of creditors).

(7) Where the trustee of a bankrupt's estate has been appointed by the court, the trustee shall give notice to the bankrupt's creditors of his appointment or, if the court so allows, shall advertise his appointment in accordance with the directions of the court.

(8) In that notice or advertisement he shall—

    (*a*) state whether he proposes to summon a general meeting of the bankrupt's creditors for the purpose of establishing a creditors' committee under section 301 below, and

    (*b*) if he does not propose to summon such a meeting, set out the power of the creditors under this Part to require him to summon one.   **[297]**

NOTES

Commencement: 29 December 1986.

This section derived from the Insolvency Act 1985, s 144.

298. Removal of trustee; vacation of office

(1) Subject as follows, the trustee of a bankrupt's estate may be removed from office only by an order of the court or by a general meeting of the bankrupt's creditors summoned specially for that purpose in accordance with the rules.

(2) Where the official receiver is trustee by virtue of section 297(1), he shall not be removed from office under this section.

(3) A general meeting of the bankrupt's creditors shall not be held for the purpose of removing the trustee at any time when a certificate for the summary administration of the estate is in force.

(4) Where the official receiver is trustee by virtue of section 293(3) or 295(4) or a trustee is appointed by the Secretary of State or (otherwise than under section 297(5)) by the court, a general meeting of the bankrupt's creditors shall be summoned for the purpose of replacing the trustee only if—

    (*a*) the trustee thinks fit, or

    (*b*) the court so directs, or

    (*c*) the meeting is requested by one of the bankrupt's creditors with the concurrence of not less than one-quarter, in value, of the creditors (including the creditor making the request).

(5) If the trustee was appointed by the Secretary of State, he may be removed by a direction of the Secretary of State.

(6) The trustee (not being the official receiver) shall vacate office if he ceases to be a person who is for the time being qualified to act as an insolvency practitioner in relation to the bankrupt.

(7) The trustee may, in the prescribed circumstances, resign his office by giving notice of his resignation to the court.

(8) The trustee shall vacate office on giving notice to the court that a final meeting has been held under section 331 in Chapter IV and of the decision (if any) of that meeting.

(9) The trustee shall vacate office if the bankruptcy order is annulled. **[298]**

NOTES

Commencement: 29 December 1986.

This section derived from the Insolvency Act 1985, s 145.

299. Release of trustee

(1) Where the official receiver has ceased to be the trustee of a bankrupt's estate and a person is appointed in his stead, the official receiver shall have his release with effect from the following time, that is to say—

    (*a*) where that person is appointed by a general meeting of the bankrupt's creditors or by the Secretary of State, the time at which the official receiver gives notice to the court that he has been replaced, and

    (*b*) where that person is appointed by the court, such time as the court may determine.

(2) If the official receiver while he is the trustee gives notice to the Secretary of State that the administration of the bankrupt's estate in accordance with

Chapter IV of this Part is for practical purposes complete, he shall have his release with effect from such time as the Secretary of State may determine.

(3) A person other than the official receiver who has ceased to be the trustee shall have his release with effect from the following time, that is to say—

    (*a*) in the case of a person who has been removed from office by a general meeting of the bankrupt's creditors that has not resolved against his release or who has died, the time at which notice is given to the court in accordance with the rules that that person has ceased to hold office;

    (*b*) in the case of a person who has been removed from office by a general meeting of the bankrupt's creditors that has resolved against his release, or by the court, or by the Secretary of State, or who has vacated office under section 298(6), such time as the Secretary of State may, on an application by that person, determine;

    (*c*) in the case of a person who has resigned, such time as may be prescribed;

    (*d*) in the case of a person who has vacated office under section 298(8)—

        (i) if the final meeting referred to in that subsection has resolved against that person's release, such time as the Secretary of State may, on an application by that person, determine; and

        (ii) if that meeting has not so resolved, the time at which the person vacated office.

(4) Where a bankruptcy order is annulled, the trustee at the time of the annulment has his release with effect from such time as the court may determine.

(5) Where the official receiver or the trustee has his release under this section, he shall, with effect from the time specified in the preceding provisions of this section, be discharged from all liability both in respect of acts or omissions of his in the administration of the estate and otherwise in relation to his conduct as trustee.

But nothing in this section prevents the exercise, in relation to a person who has had his release under this section, of the court's powers under section 304.

[299]

NOTES

    Commencement: 29 December 1986.

    This section derived from the Insolvency Act 1985, s 146.

300. Vacancy in office of trustee

(1) This section applies where the appointment of any person as trustee of a bankrupt's estate fails to take effect or, such an appointment having taken effect, there is otherwise a vacancy in the office of trustee.

(2) The official receiver shall be trustee until the vacancy is filled.

(3) The official receiver may summon a general meeting of the bankrupt's creditors for the purpose of filling the vacancy and shall summon such a meeting if required to do so in pursuance of section 314(7) (creditors' requisition).

(4) If at the end of the period of 28 days beginning with the day on which the vacancy first came to the official receiver's attention he has not summoned, and is not proposing to summon, a general meeting of creditors for the purpose of filling the vacancy, he shall refer the need for an appointment to the Secretary of State.

(5) Where a certificate for the summary administration of the estate is for the time being in force—

 (a) the official receiver may refer the need to fill any vacancy to the court or, if the vacancy arises because a person appointed by the Secretary of State has ceased to hold office, to the court or the Secretary of State, and

 (b) subsections (3) and (4) of this section do not apply.

(6) On a reference to the Secretary of State under subsection (4) or (5) the Secretary of State shall either make an appointment or decline to make one.

(7) If on a reference under subsection (4) or (5) no appointment is made, the official receiver shall continue to be trustee of the bankrupt's estate, but without prejudice to his power to make a further reference.

(8) References in this section to a vacancy include a case where it is necessary, in relation to any property which is or may be comprised in a bankrupt's estate, to revive the trusteeship of that estate after the holding of a final meeting summoned under section 331 or the giving by the official receiver of notice under section 299(2). **[300]**

NOTES
Commencement: 29 December 1986.
This section derived from the Insolvency Act 1985, s 147.

Control of trustee

301. Creditors' committee

(1) Subject as follows, a general meeting of a bankrupt's creditors (whether summoned under the preceding provisions of this Chapter or otherwise) may, in accordance with the rules, establish a committee (known as "the creditors' committee") to exercise the functions conferred on it by or under this Act.

(2) A general meeting of the bankrupt's creditors shall not establish such a committee, or confer any functions on such a committee, at any time when the official receiver is the trustee of the bankrupt's estate, except in connection with an appointment made by that meeting of a person to be trustee instead of the official receiver. **[301]**

NOTES
Commencement: 29 December 1986.
This section derived from the Insolvency Act 1985, s 148.

302. Exercise by Secretary of State of functions of creditors' committee

(1) The creditors' committee is not to be able or required to carry out its functions at any time when the official receiver is trustee of the bankrupt's estate; but at any such time the functions of the committee under this Act shall be vested in the Secretary of State, except to the extent that the rules otherwise provide.

(2) Where in the case of any bankruptcy there is for the time being no creditors' committee and the trustee of the bankrupt's estate is a person other than the official receiver, the functions of such a committee shall be vested in the Secretary of State, except to the extent that the rules otherwise provide.

[302]

NOTES
   Commencement: 29 December 1986.
   This section derived from the Insolvency Act 1985, s 149.

303. General control of trustee by the court

(1) If a bankrupt or any of his creditors or any other person is dissatisfied by any act, omission or decision of a trustee of the bankrupt's estate, he may apply to the court; and on such an application the court may confirm, reverse or modify any act or decision of the trustee, may give him directions or may make such other order as it thinks fit.

(2) The trustee of a bankrupt's estate may apply to the court for directions in relation to any particular matter arising under the bankruptcy.   **[303]**

NOTES
   Commencement: 29 December 1986.
   This section derived from the Insolvency Act 1985, s 150.

304. Liability of trustee

(1) Where on an application under this section the court is satisfied—

  (a) that the trustee of a bankrupt's estate has misapplied or retained, or become accountable for, any money or other property comprised in the bankrupt's estate, or

  (b) that a bankrupt's estate has suffered any loss in consequence of any misfeasance or breach of fiduciary or other duty by a trustee of the estate in the carrying out of his functions,

the court may order the trustee, for the benefit of the estate, to repay, restore or account for money or other property (together with interest at such rate as the court thinks just) or, as the case may require, to pay such sum by way of compensation in respect of the misfeasance or breach of fiduciary or other duty as the court thinks just.

This is without prejudice to any liability arising apart from this section.

(2) An application under this section may be made by the official receiver, the Secretary of State, a creditor of the bankrupt or (whether or not there is, or is likely to be, a surplus for the purposes of section 330(5) (final distribution)) the bankrupt himself.

But the leave of the court is required for the making of an application if it is to be made by the bankrupt or if it is to be made after the trustee has had his release under section 299.

(3) Where—

  (a) the trustee seizes or disposes of any property which is not comprised in the bankrupt's estate, and

  (b) at the time of the seizure or disposal the trustee believes, and has reasonable grounds for believing, that he is entitled (whether in pursuance of an order of the court or otherwise) to seize or dispose of that property,

the trustee is not liable to any person (whether under this section or otherwise) in respect of any loss or damage resulting from the seizure or disposal except in so far as that loss or damage is caused by the negligence of the trustee; and he has a lien on the property, or the proceeds of its sale, for such of the expenses of the bankruptcy as were incurred in connection with the seizure or disposal.

[304]

NOTES
Commencement: 29 December 1986.
This section derived from the Insolvency Act 1985, s 151.

CHAPTER IV

ADMINISTRATION BY TRUSTEE

Preliminary

305. General functions of trustee

(1) This Chapter applies in relation to any bankruptcy where either—

(*a*) the appointment of a person as trustee of a bankrupt's estate takes effect, or

(*b*) the official receiver becomes trustee of a bankrupt's estate.

(2) The function of the trustee is to get in, realise and distribute the bankrupt's estate in accordance with the following provisions of this Chapter; and in the carrying out of that function and in the management of the bankrupt's estate the trustee is entitled, subject to those provisions, to use his own discretion.

(3) It is the duty of the trustee, if he is not the official receiver—

(*a*) to furnish the official receiver with such information,

(*b*) to produce to the official receiver, and permit inspection by the official receiver of, such books, papers and other records, and

(*c*) to give the official receiver such other assistance,

as the official receiver may reasonably require for the purpose of enabling him to carry out his functions in relation to the bankruptcy.

(4) The official name of the trustee shall be "the trustee of the estate of ...., a bankrupt" (inserting the name of the bankrupt); but he may be referred to as "the trustee in bankruptcy" of the particular bankrupt. **[305]**

NOTES
Commencement: 29 December 1986.
This section derived from the Insolvency Act 1985, s 152.

Acquisition, control and realisation of bankrupt's estate

306. Vesting of bankrupt's estate in trustee

(1) The bankrupt's estate shall vest in the trustee immediately on his appointment taking effect or, in the case of the official receiver, on his becoming trustee.

(2) Where any property which is, or is to be, comprised in the bankrupt's estate vests in the trustee (whether under this section or under any other provision of this Part), it shall so vest without any conveyance, assignment or transfer. **[306]**

NOTES
Commencement: 29 December 1986.
This section derived from the Insolvency Act 1985, s 153.

307. After-acquired property

(1) Subject to this section and section 309, the trustee may by notice in writing claim for the bankrupt's estate any property which has been acquired by, or has devolved upon, the bankrupt since the commencement of the bankruptcy.

(2) A notice under this section shall not be served in respect of—

   (a)   any property falling within subsection (2) or (3) of section 283 in Chapter II,

   (b)   any property which by virtue of any other enactment is excluded from the bankrupt's estate, or

   (c)   without prejudice to section 280(2)(c) (order of court on application for discharge), any property which is acquired by, or devolves upon, the bankrupt after his discharge.

(3) Subject to the next subsection, upon the service on the bankrupt of a notice under this section the property to which the notice relates shall vest in the trustee as part of the bankrupt's estate; and the trustee's title to that property has relation back to the time at which the property was acquired by, or devolved upon, the bankrupt.

(4) Where, whether before or after service of a notice under this section—

   (a)   a person acquires property in good faith, for value and without notice of the bankruptcy, or

   (b)   a banker enters into a transaction in good faith and without such notice,

the trustee is not in respect of that property or transaction entitled by virtue of this section to any remedy against that person or banker, or any person whose title to any property derives from that person or banker.

(5) References in this section to property do not include any property which, as part of the bankrupt's income, may be the subject of an income payments order under section 310.   [307]

NOTES
   Commencement: 29 December 1986.
   This section derived from the Insolvency Act 1985, s 154(1)–(4), (7).

308. Vesting in trustee of certain items of excess value

(1) Subject to the next section, where—

   (a)   property is excluded by virtue of section 283(2) (tools of trade, household effects, etc) from the bankrupt's estate, and

   (b)   it appears to the trustee that the realisable value of the whole or any part of that property exceeds the cost of a reasonable replacement for that property or that part of it,

the trustee may by notice in writing claim that property or, as the case may be, that part of it for the bankrupt's estate.

(2) Upon the service on the bankrupt of a notice under this section, the property to which the notice relates vests in the trustee as part of the bankrupt's estate; and, except against a purchaser in good faith, for value and without notice of the bankruptcy, the trustee's title to that property has relation back to the commencement of the bankruptcy.

(3) The trustee shall apply funds comprised in the estate to the purchase by or on behalf of the bankrupt of a reasonable replacement for any property

vested in the trustee under this section; and the duty imposed by this subsection has priority over the obligation of the trustee to distribute the estate.

(4) For the purposes of this section property is a reasonable replacement for other property if it is reasonably adequate for meeting the needs met by the other property. **[308]**

NOTES
Commencement: 29 December 1986.
This section derived from the Insolvency Act 1985, s 155(1), (2), (4), (5).

309. Time-limit for notice under s 307 or 308

(1) Except with the leave of the court, a notice shall not be served—

    (*a*) under section 307, after the end of the period of 42 days beginning with the day on which it first came to the knowledge of the trustee that the property in question had been acquired by, or had devolved upon, the bankrupt;

    (*b*) under section 308, after the end of the period of 42 days beginning with the day on which the property in question first came to the knowledge of the trustee.

(2) For the purposes of this section—

    (*a*) anything which comes to the knowledge of the trustee is deemed in relation to any successor of his as trustee to have come to the knowledge of the successor at the same time; and

    (*b*) anything which comes (otherwise than under paragraph (*a*)) to the knowledge of a person before he is the trustee is deemed to come to his knowledge on his appointment taking effect or, in the case of the official receiver, on his becoming trustee. **[309]**

NOTES
Commencement: 29 December 1986.
This section derived from the Insolvency Act 1985, ss 154(5), (6), 155(3).

310. Income payments orders

(1) The court may, on the application of the trustee, make an order ("an income payments order") claiming for the bankrupt's estate so much of the income of the bankrupt during the period for which the order is in force as may be specified in the order.

(2) The court shall not make an income payments order the effect of which would be to reduce the income of the bankrupt below what appears to the court to be necessary for meeting the reasonable domestic needs of the bankrupt and his family.

(3) An income payments order shall, in respect of any payment of income to which it is to apply, either—

    (*a*) require the bankrupt to pay the trustee an amount equal to so much of that payment as is claimed by the order, or

    (*b*) require the person making the payment to pay so much of it as is so claimed to the trustee, instead of to the bankrupt.

(4) Where the court makes an income payments order it may, if it thinks fit, discharge or vary any attachment of earnings order that is for the time being in force to secure payments by the bankrupt.

(5) Sums received by the trustee under an income payments order form part of the bankrupt's estate.

(6) An income payments order shall not be made after the discharge of the bankrupt, and if made before, shall not have effect after his discharge except—

(a) in the case of a discharge under section 279(1)(a) (order of court), by virtue of a condition imposed by the court under section 280(2)(c) (income, etc after discharge), or

(b) in the case of a discharge under section 279(1)(b) (expiration of relevant period), by virtue of a provision of the order requiring it to continue in force for a period ending after the discharge but no later than 3 years after the making of the order.

(7) For the purposes of this section the income of the bankrupt comprises every payment in the nature of income which is from time to time made to him or to which he from time to time becomes entitled, including any payment in respect of the carrying on of any business or in respect of any office or employment. **[310]**

NOTES
Commencement: 29 December 1986.
This section derived from the Insolvency Act 1985, s 156.

311. Acquisition by trustee of control

(1) The trustee shall take possession of all books, papers and other records which relate to the bankrupt's estate or affairs and which belong to him or are in his possession or under his control (including any which would be privileged from disclosure in any proceedings).

(2) In relation to, and for the purpose of acquiring or retaining possession of, the bankrupt's estate, the trustee is in the same position as if he were a receiver of property appointed by the High Court; and the court may, on his application, enforce such acquisition or retention accordingly.

(3) Where any part of the bankrupt's estate consists of stock or shares in a company, shares in a ship or any other property transferable in the books of a company, office or person, the trustee may exercise the right to transfer the property to the same extent as the bankrupt might have exercised it if he had not become bankrupt.

(4) Where any part of the estate consists of things in action, they are deemed to have been assigned to the trustee; but notice of the deemed assignment need not be given except in so far as it is necessary, in a case where the deemed assignment is from the bankrupt himself, for protecting the priority of the trustee.

(5) Where any goods comprised in the estate are held by any person by way of pledge, pawn or other security and no notice has been served in respect of those goods by the official receiver under subsection (5) of section 285 (restriction on realising security), the trustee may serve such a notice in respect of the goods; and whether or not a notice has been served under this subsection or that subsection, the trustee may, if he thinks fit, exercise the bankrupt's right of redemption in respect of any such goods.

(6) A notice served by the trustee under subsection (5) has the same effect as a notice served by the official receiver under section 285(5). **[311]**

NOTES
Commencement: 29 December 1986.
This section derived from the Insolvency Act 1985, s 157.

312. Obligation to surrender control to trustee

(1) The bankrupt shall deliver up to the trustee possession of any property, books, papers or other records of which he has possession or control and of which the trustee is required to take possession.

This is without prejudice to the general duties of the bankrupt under section 333 in this Chapter.

(2) If any of the following is in possession of any property, books, papers or other records of which the trustee is required to take possession, namely—

(*a*) the official receiver,
(*b*) a person who has ceased to be trustee of the bankrupt's estate, or
(*c*) a person who has been the supervisor of a voluntary arrangement approved in relation to the bankrupt under Part VIII,

the official receiver or, as the case may be, that person shall deliver up possession of the property, books, papers or records to the trustee.

(3) Any banker or agent of the bankrupt or any other person who holds any property to the account of, or for, the bankrupt shall pay or deliver to the trustee all property in his possession or under his control which forms part of the bankrupt's estate and which he is not by law entitled to retain as against the bankrupt or trustee.

(4) If any person without reasonable excuse fails to comply with any obligation imposed by this section, he is guilty of a contempt of court and liable to be punished accordingly (in addition to any other punishment to which he may be subject). **[312]**

NOTES
Commencement: 29 December 1986.
This section derived from the Insolvency Act 1985, s 158.

313. Charge on bankrupt's home

(1) Where any property consisting of an interest in a dwelling house which is occupied by the bankrupt or by his spouse or former spouse is comprised in the bankrupt's estate and the trustee is, for any reason, unable for the time being to realise that property, the trustee may apply to the court for an order imposing a charge on the property for the benefit of the bankrupt's estate.

(2) If on an application under this section the court imposes a charge on any property, the benefit of that charge shall be comprised in the bankrupt's estate and is enforceable, up to the value from time to time of the property secured, for the payment of any amount which is payable otherwise than to the bankrupt out of the estate and of interest on that amount at the prescribed rate.

(3) An order under this section made in respect of property vested in the trustee shall provide, in accordance with the rules, for the property to cease to be comprised in the bankrupt's estate and, subject to the charge (and any prior charge), to vest in the bankrupt.

(4) Subsections (1) and (2) and (4) to (6) of section 3 of the Charging Orders

Act 1979 (supplemental provisions with respect to charging orders) have effect in relation to orders under this section as in relation to charging orders under that Act. **[313]**

NOTES
Commencement: 29 December 1986.
This section derived from the Insolvency Act 1985, s 159.

314. Powers of trustee

(1) The trustee may—

    (*a*) with the permission of the creditors' committee or the court, exercise any of the powers specified in Part I of Schedule 5 to this Act, and

    (*b*) without that permission, exercise any of the general powers specified in Part II of that Schedule.

(2) With the permission of the creditors' committee or the court, the trustee may appoint the bankrupt—

    (*a*) to superintend the management of his estate or any part of it,

    (*b*) to carry on his business (if any) for the benefit of his creditors, or

    (*c*) in any other respect to assist in administering the estate in such manner and on such terms as the trustee may direct.

(3) A permission given for the purposes of subsection (1)(*a*) or (2) shall not be a general permission but shall relate to a particular proposed exercise of the power in question; and a person dealing with the trustee in good faith and for value is not to be concerned to enquire whether any permission required in either case has been given.

(4) Where the trustee has done anything without the permission required by subsection (1)(*a*) or (2), the court or the creditors' committee may, for the purpose of enabling him to meet his expenses out of the bankrupt's estate, ratify what the trustee has done.

But the committee shall not do so unless it is satisfied that the trustee has acted in a case of urgency and has sought its ratification without undue delay.

(5) Part III of Schedule 5 to this Act has effect with respect to the things which the trustee is able to do for the purposes of, or in connection with, the exercise of any of his powers under any of this Group of Parts.

(6) Where the trustee (not being the official receiver) in exercise of the powers conferred on him by any provision in this Group of Parts—

    (*a*) disposes of any property comprised in the bankrupt's estate to an associate of the bankrupt, or

    (*b*) employs a solicitor,

he shall, if there is for the time being a creditors' committee, give notice to the committee of that exercise of his powers.

(7) Without prejudice to the generality of subsection (5) and Part III of Schedule 5, the trustee may, if he thinks fit, at any time summon a general meeting of the bankrupt's creditors.

Subject to the preceding provisions in this Group of Parts, he shall summon such a meeting if he is requested to do so by a creditor of the bankrupt and the request is made with the concurrence of not less than one-tenth, in value, of the bankrupt's creditors (including the creditor making the request).

(8) Nothing in this Act is to be construed as restricting the capacity of the trustee to exercise any of his powers outside England and Wales. **[314]**

NOTES
Commencement: 29 December 1986.
This section derived from the Insolvency Act 1985, s 160.

Disclaimer of onerous property

315. Disclaimer (general power)

(1) Subject as follows, the trustee may, by the giving of the prescribed notice, disclaim any onerous property and may do so notwithstanding that he has taken possession of it, endeavoured to sell it or otherwise exercised rights of ownership in relation to it.

(2) The following is onerous property for the purposes of this section, that is to say—

(*a*) any unprofitable contract, and
(*b*) any other property comprised in the bankrupt's estate which is unsaleable or not readily saleable, or is such that it may give rise to a liability to pay money or perform any other onerous act.

(3) A disclaimer under this section—

(*a*) operates so as to determine, as from the date of the disclaimer, the rights, interests and liabilities of the bankrupt and his estate in or in respect of the property disclaimed, and
(*b*) discharges the trustee from all personal liability in respect of that property as from the commencement of his trusteeship,

but does not, except so far as is necessary for the purpose of releasing the bankrupt, the bankrupt's estate and the trustee from any liability, affect the rights or liabilities of any other person.

(4) A notice of disclaimer shall not be given under this section in respect of any property that has been claimed for the estate under section 307 (after-acquired property) or 308 (personal property of bankrupt exceeding reasonable replacement value), except with the leave of the court.

(5) Any person sustaining loss or damage in consequence of the operation of a disclaimer under this section is deemed to be a creditor of the bankrupt to the extent of the loss or damage and accordingly may prove for the loss or damage as a bankruptcy debt. **[315]**

NOTES
Commencement: 29 December 1986.
This section derived from the Insolvency Act 1985, s 161(1)–(4), (10).

316. Notice requiring trustee's decision

(1) Notice of disclaimer shall not be given under section 315 in respect of any property if—

(*a*) a person interested in the property has applied in writing to the trustee or one of his predecessors as trustee requiring the trustee or that predecessor to decide whether he will disclaim or not, and

(b) the period of 28 days beginning with the day on which that application was made has expired without a notice of disclaimer having been given under section 315 in respect of that property.

(2) The trustee is deemed to have adopted any contract which by virtue of this section he is not entitled to disclaim.   **[316]**

NOTES
Commencement: 29 December 1986.
This section derived from the Insolvency Act 1985, s 161(5).

317. Disclaimer of leaseholds

(1) The disclaimer of any property of a leasehold nature does not take effect unless a copy of the disclaimer has been served (so far as the trustee is aware of their addresses) on every person claiming under the bankrupt as underlessee or mortgagee and either—

(a) no application under section 320 below is made with respect to the property before the end of the period of 14 days beginning with the day on which the last notice served under this subsection was served, or

(b) where such an application has been made, the court directs that the disclaimer is to take effect.

(2) Where the court gives a direction under subsection (1)(b) it may also, instead of or in addition to any order it makes under section 320, make such orders with respect to fixtures, tenant's improvements and other matters arising out of the lease as it thinks fit.   **[317]**

NOTES
Commencement: 29 December 1986.
This section derived from the Insolvency Act 1985, s 161(6), (7).

318. Disclaimer of dwelling house

Without prejudice to section 317, the disclaimer of any property in a dwelling house does not take effect unless a copy of the disclaimer has been served (so far as the trustee is aware of their addresses) on every person in occupation of or claiming a right to occupy the dwelling house and either—

(a) no application under section 320 is made with respect to the property before the end of the period of 14 days beginning with the day on which the last notice served under this section was served, or

(b) where such an application has been made, the court directs that the disclaimer is to take effect.   **[318]**

NOTES
Commencement: 29 December 1986.
This section derived from the Insolvency Act 1985, s 161(8).

319. Disclaimer of land subject to rentcharge

(1) The following applies where, in consequence of the disclaimer under section 315 of any land subject to a rentcharge, that land vests by operation of law in the Crown or any other person (referred to in the next subsection as "the proprietor").

(2) The proprietor, and the successors in title of the proprietor, are not subject to any personal liability in respect of any sums becoming due under the

rentcharge, except sums becoming due after the proprietor, or some person claiming under or through the proprietor, has taken possession or control of the land or has entered into occupation of it. **[319]**

NOTES
Commencement: 29 December 1986.
This section derived from the Insolvency Act 1985, s 161(9).

320. Court order vesting disclaimed property

(1) This section and the next apply where the trustee has disclaimed property under section 315.

(2) An application may be made to the court under this section by—

    (*a*) any person who claims an interest in the disclaimed property,

    (*b*) any person who is under any liability in respect of the disclaimed property, not being a liability discharged by the disclaimer, or

    (*c*) where the disclaimed property is property in a dwelling house, any person who at the time when the bankruptcy petition was presented was in occupation of or entitled to occupy the dwelling house.

(3) Subject as follows in this section and the next, the court may, on an application under this section, make an order on such terms as it thinks fit for the vesting of the disclaimed property in, or for its delivery to—

    (*a*) a person entitled to it or a trustee for such a person,

    (*b*) a person subject to such a liability as is mentioned in subsection (2)(*b*) or a trustee for such a person, or

    (*c*) where the disclaimed property is property in a dwelling house, any person who at the time when the bankruptcy petition was presented was in occupation of or entitled to occupy the dwelling house.

(4) The court shall not make an order by virtue of subsection (3)(*b*) except where it appears to the court that it would be just to do so for the purpose of compensating the person subject to the liability in respect of the disclaimer.

(5) The effect of any order under this section shall be taken into account in assessing for the purposes of section 315(5) the extent of any loss or damage sustained by any person in consequence of the disclaimer.

(6) An order under this section vesting property in any person need not be completed by any conveyance, assignment or transfer. **[320]**

NOTES
Commencement: 29 December 1986.
This section derived from the Insolvency Act 1985, s 162(1)–(4), (9), (10).

321. Order under s 320 in respect of leaseholds

(1) The court shall not make an order under section 320 vesting property of a leasehold nature in any person, except on terms making that person—

    (*a*) subject to the same liabilities and obligations as the bankrupt was subject to under the lease on the day the bankruptcy petition was presented, or

    (*b*) if the court thinks fit, subject to the same liabilities and obligations as that person would be subject to if the lease had been assigned to him on that day.

(2) For the purposes of an order under section 320 relating to only part of

any property comprised in a lease, the requirements of subsection (1) apply as if the lease comprised only the property to which the order relates.

(3) Where subsection (1) applies and no person is willing to accept an order under section 320 on the terms required by that subsection, the court may (by order under section 320) vest the estate or interest of the bankrupt in the property in any person who is liable (whether personally or in a representative capacity and whether alone or jointly with the bankrupt) to perform the lessee's covenants in the lease.

The court may by virtue of this subsection vest that estate and interest in such a person freed and discharged from all estates, incumbrances and interests created by the bankrupt.

(4) Where subsection (1) applies and a person declines to accept any order under section 320, that person shall be excluded from all interest in the property. **[321]**

NOTES
Commencement: 29 December 1986.
This section derived from the Insolvency Act 1985, s 162(5)–(8).

Distribution of bankrupt's estate

322. Proof of debts

(1) Subject to this section and the next, the proof of any bankruptcy debt by a secured or unsecured creditor of the bankrupt and the admission or rejection of any proof shall take place in accordance with the rules.

(2) Where a bankruptcy debt bears interest, that interest is provable as part of the debt except in so far as it is payable in respect of any period after the commencement of the bankruptcy.

(3) The trustee shall estimate the value of any bankruptcy debt which, by reason of its being subject to any contingency or contingencies or for any other reason, does not bear a certain value.

(4) Where the value of a bankruptcy debt is estimated by the trustee under subsection (3) or, by virtue of section 303 in Chapter III, by the court, the amount provable in the bankruptcy in respect of the debt is the amount of the estimate. **[322]**

NOTES
Commencement: 29 December 1986.
This section derived from the Insolvency Act 1985, s 163.

323. Mutual credit and set-off

(1) This section applies where before the commencement of the bankruptcy there have been mutual credits, mutual debts or other mutual dealings between the bankrupt and any creditor of the bankrupt proving or claiming to prove for a bankruptcy debt.

(2) An account shall be taken of what is due from each party to the other in respect of the mutual dealings and the sums due from one party shall be set off against the sums due from the other.

(3) Sums due from the bankrupt to another party shall not be included in the account taken under subsection (2) if that other party had notice at the time

they became due that a bankruptcy petition relating to the bankrupt was pending.

(4) Only the balance (if any) of the account taken under subsection (2) is provable as a bankruptcy debt or, as the case may be, to be paid to the trustee as part of the bankrupt's estate. **[323]**

NOTES
Commencement: 29 December 1986.
This section derived from the Insolvency Act 1985, s 164.

324. Distribution by means of dividend

(1) Whenever the trustee has sufficient funds in hand for the purpose he shall, subject to the retention of such sums as may be necessary for the expenses of the bankruptcy, declare and distribute dividends among the creditors in respect of the bankruptcy debts which they have respectively proved.

(2) The trustee shall give notice of his intention to declare and distribute a dividend.

(3) Where the trustee has declared a dividend, he shall give notice of the dividend and of how it is proposed to distribute it; and a notice given under this subsection shall contain the prescribed particulars of the bankrupt's estate.

(4) In the calculation and distribution of a dividend the trustee shall make provision—

(a) for any bankruptcy debts which appear to him to be due to persons who, by reason of the distance of their place of residence, may not have had sufficient time to tender and establish their proofs,

(b) for any bankruptcy debts which are the subject of claims which have not yet been determined, and

(c) for disputed proofs and claims. **[324]**

NOTES
Commencement: 29 December 1986.
This section derived from the Insolvency Act 1985, s 165(1)–(4).

325. Claims by unsatisfied creditors

(1) A creditor who has not proved his debt before the declaration of any dividend is not entitled to disturb, by reason that he has not participated in it, the distribution of that dividend or any other dividend declared before his debt was proved, but—

(a) when he has proved that debt he is entitled to be paid, out of any money for the time being available for the payment of any further dividend, any dividend or dividends which he has failed to receive; and

(b) any dividend or dividends payable under paragraph (a) shall be paid before that money is applied to the payment of any such further dividend.

(2) No action lies against the trustee for a dividend, but if the trustee refuses to pay a dividend the court may, if it thinks fit, order him to pay it and also to pay, out of his own money—

(a) interest on the dividend, at the rate for the time being specified in section 17 of the Judgments Act 1838, from the time it was withheld, and

(b) the costs of the proceedings in which the order to pay is made.   **[325]**

NOTES
Commencement: 29 December 1986.
This section derived from the Insolvency Act 1985, s 165(5), (6).

326. Distribution of property in specie

(1) Without prejudice to sections 315 to 319 (disclaimer), the trustee may, with the permission of the creditors' committee, divide in its existing form amongst the bankrupt's creditors, according to its estimated value, any property which from its peculiar nature or other special circumstances cannot be readily or advantageously sold.

(2) A permission given for the purposes of subsection (1) shall not be a general permission but shall relate to a particular proposed exercise of the power in question; and a person dealing with the trustee in good faith and for value is not to be concerned to enquire whether any permission required by subsection (1) has been given.

(3) Where the trustee has done anything without the permission required by subsection (1), the court or the creditors' committee may, for the purpose of enabling him to meet his expenses out of the bankrupt's estate, ratify what the trustee has done.

But the committee shall not do so unless it is satisfied that the trustee acted in a case of urgency and has sought its ratification without undue delay.   **[326]**

NOTES
Commencement: 29 December 1986.
This section derived from the Insolvency Act 1985, s 165(7), (8).

327. Distribution in criminal bankruptcy

Where the bankruptcy order was made on a petition under section 264(1)(d) (criminal bankruptcy), no distribution shall be made under sections 324 to 326 so long as an appeal is pending (within the meaning of section 277) against the bankrupt's conviction of any offence by virtue of which the criminal bankruptcy order on which the petition was based was made.   **[327]**

NOTES
Commencement: 29 December 1986.
This section derived from the Insolvency Act 1985, s 165(9).

328. Priority of debts

(1) In the distribution of the bankrupt's estate, his preferential debts (within the meaning given by section 386 in Part XII) shall be paid in priority to other debts.

(2) Preferential debts rank equally between themselves after the expenses of the bankruptcy and shall be paid in full unless the bankrupt's estate is insufficient for meeting them, in which case they abate in equal proportions between themselves.

(3) Debts which are neither preferential debts nor debts to which the next section applies also rank equally between themselves and, after the preferential debts, shall be paid in full unless the bankrupt's estate is insufficient for meeting them, in which case they abate in equal proportions between themselves.

(4) Any surplus remaining after the payment of the debts that are preferential or rank equally under subsection (3) shall be applied in paying interest on those debts in respect of the periods during which they have been outstanding since the commencement of the bankrutpcy; and interest on preferential debts ranks equally with interest on debts other than preferential debts.

(5) The rate of interest payable under subsection (4) in respect of any debt is whichever is the greater of the following—

    (*a*) the rate specified in section 17 of the Judgments Act 1838 at the commencement of the bankruptcy, and

    (*b*) the rate applicable to that debt apart from the bankruptcy.

(6) This section and the next are without prejudice to any provision of this Act or any other Act under which the payment of any debt or the making of any other payment is, in the event of bankruptcy, to have a particular priority or to be postponed.　　　　　　　　　　　　　　　　　　　　　　　　　**[328]**

NOTES
Commencement: 29 December 1986.
This section derived from the Insolvency Act 1985, s 166(1)–(5), (7).

329. Debts to spouse

(1) This section applies to bankruptcy debts owed in respect of credit provided by a person who (whether or not the bankrupt's spouse at the time the credit was provided) was the bankrupt's spouse at the commencement of the bankruptcy.

(2) Such debts—

    (*a*) rank in priority after the debts and interest required to be paid in pursuance of section 328(3) and (4), and

    (*b*) are payable with interest at the rate specified in section 328(5) in respect of the period during which they have been outstanding since the commencement of the bankruptcy;

and the interest payable under paragraph (*b*) has the same priority as the debts on which it is payable.　　　　　　　　　　　　　　　　　　　　　　**[329]**

NOTES
Commencement: 29 December 1986.
This section derived from the Insolvency Act 1985, s 166(6).

330. Final distribution

(1) When the trustee has realised all the bankrupt's estate or so much of it as can, in the trustee's opinion, be realised without needlessly protracting the trusteeship, he shall give notice in the prescribed manner either—

    (*a*) of his intention to declare a final dividend, or

    (*b*) that no dividend, or further dividend, will be declared.

(2) The notice under subsection (1) shall contain the prescribed particulars and shall require claims against the bankrupt's estate to be established by a date ("the final date") specified in the notice.

(3) The court may, on the application of any person, postpone the final date.

(4) After the final date, the trustee shall—

    (*a*) defray any outstanding expenses of the bankruptcy out of the bankrupt's estate, and (*b*) if he intends to declare a final dividend, declare and distribute that dividend without regard to the claim of any person in respect of a debt not already proved in the bankruptcy.

(5) If a surplus remains after payment in full and with interest of all the bankrupt's creditors and the payment of the expenses of the bankruptcy, the bankrupt is entitled to the surplus.   **[330]**

NOTES
Commencement: 29 December 1986.
This section derived from the Insolvency Act 1985, s 167.

331. Final meeting

(1) Subject as follows in this section and the next, this section applies where—

(*a*) it appears to the trustee that the administration of the bankrupt's estate in accordance with this Chapter is for practical purposes complete, and
(*b*) the trustee is not the official receiver.

(2) The trustee shall summon a final general meeting of the bankrupt's creditors which—

(*a*) shall receive the trustee's report of his administration of the bankrupt's estate, and
(*b*) shall determine whether the trustee should have his release under section 299 in Chapter III.

(3) The trustee may, if he thinks fit, give the notice summoning the final general meeting at the same time as giving notice under section 330(1); but, if summoned for an earlier date, that meeting shall be adjourned (and, if necessary, further adjourned) until a date on which the trustee is able to report to the meeting that the administration of the bankrupt's estate is for practical purposes complete.

(4) In the administration of the estate it is the trustee's duty to retain sufficient sums from the estate to cover the expenses of summoning and holding the meeting required by this section.   **[331]**

NOTES
Commencement: 29 December 1986.
This section derived from the Insolvency Act 1985, s 168(1), (2), (4).

332. Saving for bankrupt's home

(1) This section applies where—

(*a*) there is comprised in the bankrupt's estate property consisting of an interest in a dwelling house which is occupied by the bankrupt or by his spouse or former spouse, and
(*b*) the trustee has been unable for any reason to realise that property.

(2) The trustee shall not summon a meeting under section 331 unless either—

(*a*) the court has made an order under section 313 imposing a charge on that property for the benefit of the bankrupt's estate, or
(*b*) the court has declined, on an application under that section, to make such an order, or

(*c*) the Secretary of State has issued a certificate to the trustee stating that it would be inappropriate or inexpedient for such an application to be made in the case in question. **[332]**

NOTES
Commencement: 29 December 1986.
This section derived from the Insolvency Act 1985, s 168(3).

Supplemental

333. Duties of bankrupt in relation to trustee

(1) The bankrupt shall—

(*a*) give to the trustee such information as to his affairs,
(*b*) attend on the trustee at such times, and
(*c*) do all such other things,

as the trustee may for the purposes of carrying out his functions under any of this Group of Parts reasonably require.

(2) Where at any time after the commencement of the bankruptcy any property is acquired by, or devolves upon, the bankrupt or there is an increase of the bankrupt's income, the bankrupt shall, within the prescribed period, give the trustee notice of the property or, as the case may be, of the increase.

(3) Subsection (1) applies to a bankrupt after his discharge.

(4) If the bankrupt without reasonable excuse fails to comply with any obligation imposed by this section, he is guilty of a contempt of court and liable to be punished accordingly (in addition to any other punishment to which he may be subject). **[333]**

NOTES
Commencement: 29 December 1986.
This section derived from the Insolvency Act 1985, s 169.

334. Stay of distribution in case of second bankruptcy

(1) This section and the next apply where a bankruptcy order is made against an undischarged bankrupt; and in both sections—

(*a*) "the later bankruptcy" means the bankruptcy arising from that order,
(*b*) "the earlier bankruptcy" means the bankruptcy (or, as the case may be, most recent bankruptcy) from which the bankrupt has not been discharged at the commencement of the later bankruptcy, and
(*c*) "the existing trustee" means the trustee (if any) of the bankrupt's estate for the purposes of the earlier bankruptcy.

(2) Where the existing trustee has been given the prescribed notice of the presentation of the petition for the later bankruptcy, any distribution or other disposition by him of anything to which the next subsection applies, if made after the giving of the notice, is void except to the extent that it was made with the consent of the court or is or was subsequently ratified by the court.

This is without prejudice to section 284 (restrictions on dispositions of property following bankruptcy order).

(3) This subsection applies to—

(*a*) any property which is vested in the existing trustee under section 307(3) (after-acquired property);

(b) any money paid to the existing trustee in pursuance of an income payments order under section 310; and

(c) any property or money which is, or in the hands of the existing trustee represents, the proceeds of sale or application of property or money falling within paragraph (a) or (b) of this subsection. **[334]**

NOTES
Commencement: 29 December 1986.
This section derived from the Insolvency Act 1985, s 170(1)–(3).

335. Adjustment between earlier and later bankruptcy estates

(1) With effect from the commencement of the later bankruptcy anything to which section 334(3) applies which, immediately before the commencement of that bankruptcy, is comprised in the bankrupt's estate for the purposes of the earlier bankruptcy is to be treated as comprised in the bankrupt's estate for the purposes of the later bankruptcy and, until there is a trustee of that estate, is to be dealt with by the existing trustee in accordance with the rules.

(2) Any sums which in pursuance of an income payments order under section 310 are payable after the commencement of the later bankruptcy to the existing trustee shall form part of the bankrupt's estate for the purposes of the later bankruptcy; and the court may give such consequential directions for the modification of the order as it thinks fit.

(3) Anything comprised in a bankrupt's estate by virtue of subsection (1) or (2) is so comprised subject to a first charge in favour of the existing trustee for any bankruptcy expenses incurred by him in relation thereto.

(4) Except as provided above and in section 334, property which is, or by virtue of section 308 (personal property of bankrupt exceeding reasonable replacement value) is capable of being, comprised in the bankrupt's estate for the purposes of the earlier bankruptcy, or of any bankruptcy prior to it, shall not be comprised in his estate for the purposes of the later bankruptcy.

(5) The creditors of the bankrupt in the earlier bankruptcy and the creditors of the bankrupt in any bankruptcy prior to the earlier one, are not to be creditors of his in the later bankruptcy in respect of the same debts; but the existing trustee may prove in the later bankruptcy for—

(a) the unsatisfied balance of the debts (including any debt under this subsection) provable against the bankrupt's estate in the earlier bankruptcy;

(b) any interest payable on that balance; and

(c) any unpaid expenses of the earlier bankruptcy.

(6) Any amount provable under subsection (5) ranks in priority after all the other debts provable in the later bankruptcy and after interest on those debts and, accordingly, shall not be paid unless those debts and that interest have first been paid in full. **[335]**

NOTES
Commencement: 29 December 1986.
This section derived from the Insolvency Act 1985, s 170(4)–(9).

CHAPTER V

EFFECT OF BANKRUPTCY ON CERTAIN RIGHTS,
TRANSACTIONS, ETC

Rights of occupation

336. Rights of occupation etc of bankrupt's spouse

(1) Nothing occurring in the initial period of the bankruptcy (that is to say, the period beginning with the day of the presentation of the petition for the bankruptcy order and ending with the vesting of the bankrupt's estate in a trustee) is to be taken as having given rise to any rights of occupation under the Matrimonial Homes Act 1983 in relation to a dwelling house comprised in the bankrupt's estate.

(2) Where a spouse's rights of occupation under the Act of 1983 are a charge on the estate or interest of the other spouse, or of trustees for the other spouse, and the other spouse is adjudged bankrupt—

    (*a*) the charge continues to subsist notwithstanding the bankruptcy and, subject to the provisions of that Act, binds the trustee of the bankrupt's estate and persons deriving title under that trustee, and

    (*b*) any application for an order under section 1 of that Act shall be made to the court having jurisdiction in relation to the bankruptcy.

(3) Where a person and his spouse or former spouse are trustees for sale of a dwelling house and that person is adjudged bankrupt, any application by the trustee of the bankrupt's estate for an order under section 30 of the Law of Property Act 1925 (powers of court where trustees for sale refuse to act) shall be made to the court having jurisdiction in relation to the bankruptcy.

(4) On such an application as is mentioned in subsection (2) or (3) the court shall make such order under section 1 of the Act of 1983 or section 30 of the Act of 1925 as it thinks just and reasonable having regard to—

    (*a*) the interests of the bankrupt's creditors,

    (*b*) the conduct of the spouse or former spouse, so far as contributing to the bankruptcy,

    (*c*) the needs and financial resources of the spouse or former spouse,

    (*d*) the needs of any children, and

    (*e*) all the circumstances of the case other than the needs of the bankrupt.

(5) Where such an application is made after the end of the period of one year beginning with the first vesting under Chapter IV of this Part of the bankrupt's estate in a trustee, the court shall assume, unless the circumstances of the case are exceptional, that the interests of the bankrupt's creditors outweigh all other considerations. **[336]**

NOTES
Commencement: 29 December 1986.
This section derived from the Insolvency Act 1985, s 171.

337. Rights of occupation of bankrupt

(1) This section applies where—

    (*a*) a person who is entitled to occupy a dwelling house by virtue of a beneficial estate or interest is adjudged bankrupt, and (*b*) any persons under the age of 18 with whom that person had at some time occupied that dwelling house had their home with that person at the time when the bankruptcy petition was presented and at the commencement of the bankruptcy.

(2) Whether or not the bankrupt's spouse (if any) has rights of occupation under the Matrimonial Homes Act 1983—

(*a*) the bankrupt has the following rights as against the trustee of his estate—

    (i) if in occupation, a right not to be evicted or excluded from the dwelling house or any part of it, except with the leave of the court,

    (ii) if not in occupation, a right with the leave of the court to enter into and occupy the dwelling house, and

(*b*) the bankrupt's rights are a charge, having the like priority as an equitable interest created immediately before the commencement of the bankruptcy, on so much of his estate or interest in the dwelling house as vests in the trustee.

(3) The Act of 1983 has effect, with the necessary modifications, as if—

(*a*) the rights conferred by paragraph (*a*) of subsection (2) were rights of occupation under that Act,

(*b*) any application for leave such as is mentioned in that paragraph were an application for an order under section 1 of that Act, and

(*c*) any charge under paragraph (*b*) of that subsection on the estate or interest of the trustee were a charge under that Act on the estate or interest of a spouse.

(4) Any application for leave such as is mentioned in subsection (2)(*a*) or otherwise by virtue of this section for an order under section 1 of the Act of 1983 shall be made to the court having jurisdiction in relation to the bankruptcy.

(5) On such an application the court shall make such order under section 1 of the Act of 1983 as it thinks just and reasonable having regard to the interests of the creditors, to the bankrupt's financial resources, to the needs of the children and to all the circumstances of the case other than the needs of the bankrupt.

(6) Where such an application is made after the end of the period of one year beginning with the first vesting (under Chapter IV of this Part) of the bankrupt's estate in a trustee, the court shall assume, unless the circumstances of the case are exceptional, that the interests of the bankrupt's creditors outweigh all other considerations. **[337]**

NOTES
Commencement: 29 December 1986.
This section derived from the Insolvency Act 1985, s 172.

338. Payments in respect of premises occupied by bankrupt

Where any premises comprised in a bankrupt's estate are occupied by him (whether by virtue of the preceding section or otherwise) on condition that he makes payments towards satisfying any liability arising under a mortgage of the premises or otherwise towards the outgoings of the premises, the bankrupt does not, by virtue of those payments, acquire any interest in the premises. **[338]**

NOTES
Commencement: 29 December 1986.
This section derived from the Insolvency Act 1985, s 173.

Adjustment of prior transactions, etc

339. Transactions at an undervalue

(1) Subject as follows in this section and sections 341 and 342, where an individual is adjudged bankrupt and he has at a relevant time (defined in section 341) entered into a transaction with any person at an undervalue, the trustee of the bankrupt's estate may apply to the court for an order under this section.

(2) The court shall, on such an application, make such order as it thinks fit for restoring the position to what it would have been if that individual had not entered into that transaction.

(3) For the purposes of this section and sections 341 and 342, an individual enters into a transaction with a person at an undervalue if—

(a) he makes a gift to that person or he otherwise enters into a transaction with that person on terms that provide for him to receive no consideration,

(b) he enters into a transaction with that person in consideration of marriage, or

(c) he enters into a transaction with that person for a consideration the value of which, in money or money's worth, is significantly less than the value, in money or money's worth, of the consideration provided by the individual. **[339]**

NOTES
Commencement: 29 December 1986.
This section derived from the Insolvency Act 1985, s 174(1) (part), (2).

340. Preferences

(1) Subject as follows in this and the next two sections, where an individual is adjudged bankrupt and he has at a relevant time (defined in section 341) given a preference to any person, the trustee of the bankrupt's estate may apply to the court for an order under this section.

(2) The court shall, on such an application, make such order as it thinks fit for restoring the position to what it would have been if that individual had not given that preference.

(3) For the purposes of this and the next two sections, an individual gives a preference to a person if—

(a) that person is one of the individual's creditors or a surety or guarantor for any of his debts or other liabilities, and

(b) the individual does anything or suffers anything to be done which (in either case) has the effect of putting that person into a position which, in the event of the individual's bankruptcy, will be better than the position he would have been in if that thing had not been done.

(4) The court shall not make an order under this section in respect of a preference given to any person unless the individual who gave the preference was influenced in deciding to give it by a desire to produce in relation to that person the effect mentioned in subsection (3)(b) above.

(5) An individual who has given a preference to a person who, at the time the preference was given, was an associate of his (otherwise than by reason only of being his employee) is presumed, unless the contrary is shown, to have been influenced in deciding to give it by such a desire as is mentioned in subsection (4).

(6) The fact that something has been done in pursuance of the order of a court does not, without more, prevent the doing or suffering of that thing from constituting the giving of a preference.   **[340]**

NOTES
Commencement: 29 December 1986.
This section derived from the Insolvency Act 1985, s 174(1) (part), (3)–(6), (12) (part).

341. "Relevant time" under ss 339, 340

(1) Subject as follows, the time at which an individual enters into a transaction at an undervalue or gives a preference is a relevant time if the transaction is entered into or the preference given—

> (a) in the case of a transaction at an undervalue, at a time in the period of 5 years ending with the day of the presentation of the bankruptcy petition on which the individual is adjudged bankrupt,
> (b) in the case of a preference which is not a transaction at an undervalue and is given to a person who is an associate of the individual (otherwise than by reason only of being his employee), at a time in the period of 2 years ending with that day, and
> (c) in any other case of a preference which is not a transaction at an undervalue, at a time in the period of 6 months ending with that day.

(2) Where an individual enters into a transaction at an undervalue or gives a preference at a time mentioned in paragraph (a), (b) or (c) of subsection (1) (not being, in the case of a transaction at an undervalue, a time less than 2 years before the end of the period mentioned in paragraph (a)), that time is not a relevant time for the purposes of sections 339 and 340 unless the individual—

> (a) is insolvent at that time, or
> (b) becomes insolvent in consequence of the transaction or preference;

but the requirements of this subsection are presumed to be satisfied, unless the contrary is shown, in relation to any transaction at an undervalue which is entered into by an individual with a person who is an associate of his (otherwise than by reason only of being his employee).

(3) For the purposes of subsection (2), an individual is insolvent if—

> (a) he is unable to pay his debts as they fall due, or
> (b) the value of his assets is less than the amount of his liabilities, taking into account his contingent and prospective liabilities.

(4) A transaction entered into or preference given by a person who is subsequently adjudged bankrupt on a petition under section 264(1)(d) (criminal bankruptcy) is to be treated as having been entered into or given at a relevant time for the purposes of sections 339 and 340 if it was entered into or given at any time on or after the date specified for the purposes of this subsection in the criminal bankruptcy order on which the petition was based.

(5) No order shall be made under section 339 or 340 by virtue of subsection

(4) of this section where an appeal is pending (within the meaning of section 277) against the individual's conviction of any offence by virtue of which the criminal bankruptcy order was made. **[341]**

NOTES
Commencement: 29 December 1986.
This section derived from the Insolvency Act 1985, s 174(7)–(11), (12) (part).

342. Orders under ss 339, 340

(1) Without prejudice to the generality of section 339(2) or 340(2), an order under either of those sections with respect to a transaction or preference entered into or given by an individual who is subsequently adjudged bankrupt may (subject as follows)—

(a) require any property transferred as part of the transaction, or in connection with the giving of the preference, to be vested in the trustee of the bankrupt's estate as part of that estate;

(b) require any property to be so vested if it represents in any person's hands the application either of the proceeds of sale of property so transferred or of money so transferred;

(c) release or discharge (in whole or in part) any security given by the individual;

(d) require any person to pay, in respect of benefits received by him from the individual, such sums to the trustee of his estate as the court may direct;

(e) provide for any surety or guarantor whose obligations to any person were released or discharged (in whole or in part) under the transaction or by the giving of the preference to be under such new or revived obligations to that person as the court thinks appropriate;

(*f*) provide for security to be provided for the discharge of any obligation imposed by or arising under the order, for such an obligation to be charged on any property and for the security or charge to have the same priority as a security or charge released or discharged (in whole or in part) under the transaction or by the giving of the preference; and

(g) provide for the extent to which any person whose property is vested by the order in the trustee of the bankrupt's estate, or on whom obligations are imposed by the order, is to be able to prove in the bankruptcy for debts or other liabilities which arose from, or were released or discharged (in whole or in part) under or by, the transaction or the giving of the preference.

(2) An order under section 339 or 340 may affect the property of, or impose any obligation on, any person whether or not he is the person with whom the individual in question entered into the transaction or, as the case may be, the person to whom the preference was given; but such an order—

(a) shall not prejudice any interest in property which was acquired from a person other than that individual and was acquired in good faith, for value and without notice of the relevant circumstances, or prejudice any interest deriving from such an interest, and

(b) shall not require a person who received a benefit from the transaction or preference in good faith, for value and without notice of the relevant circumstances to pay a sum to the trustee of the bankrupt's estate, except where he was a party to the transaction or the payment is to be in respect of a preference given to that person at a time when he was a creditor of that individual.

(3) Any sums required to be paid to the trustee in accordance with an order under section 339 or 340 shall be comprised in the bankrupt's estate.

(4) For the purposes of this section the relevant circumstances, in relation to a transaction or preference, are—

    (*a*) the circumstances by virtue of which an order under section 339 or 340 could be made in respect of the transaction or preference if the individual in question were adjudged bankrupt within a particular period after the transaction is entered into or the preference given, and

    (*b*) if that period has expired, the fact that that individual has been adjudged bankrupt within that period. **[342]**

<hr>

NOTES
Commencement: 29 December 1986.
This section derived from the Insolvency Act 1985, s 175.

343. Extortionate credit transactions

(1) This section applies where a person is adjudged bankrupt who is or has been a party to a transaction for, or involving, the provision to him of credit.

(2) The court may, on the application of the trustee of the bankrupt's estate, make an order with respect of the transaction if the transaction is or was extortionate and was not entered into more than 3 years before the commencement of the bankruptcy.

(3) For the purposes of this section a transaction is extortionate if, having regard to the risk accepted by the person providing the credit—

    (*a*) the terms of it are or were such as to require grossly exorbitant payments to be made (whether unconditionally or in certain contingencies) in respect of the provision of the credit, or

    (*b*) it otherwise grossly contravened ordinary principles of fair dealing;

and it shall be presumed, unless the contrary is proved, that a transaction with respect to which an application is made under this section is or, as the case may be, was extortionate.

(4) An order under this section with respect to any transaction may contain such one or more of the following as the court thinks fit, that is to say—

    (*a*) provision setting aside the whole or part of any obligation created by the transaction;

    (*b*) provision otherwise varying the terms of the transaction or varying the terms on which any security for the purposes of the transaction is held;

    (*c*) provision requiring any person who is or was party to the transaction to pay to the trustee any sums paid to that person, by virtue of the transaction, by the bankrupt;

    (*d*) provision requiring any person to surrender to the trustee any property held by him as security for the purposes of the transaction;

    (*e*) provision directing accounts to be taken between any persons.

(5) Any sums or property required to be paid or surrendered to the trustee in accordance with an order under this section shall be comprised in the bankrupt's estate.

(6) Neither the trustee of a bankrupt's estate nor an undischarged bankrupt is entitled to make an application under section 139(1)(*a*) of the Consumer

Credit Act 1974 (re-opening of extortionate credit agreements) for any agreement by which credit is or has been provided to the bankrupt to be re-opened.

But the powers conferred by this section are exercisable in relation to any transaction concurrently with any powers exercisable under this Act in relation to that transaction as a transaction at an undervalue. **[343]**

NOTES

Commencement: 29 December 1986.

This section derived from the Insolvency Act 1985, s 176.

344. Avoidance of general assignment of book debts

(1) The following applies where a person engaged in any business makes a general assignment to another person of his existing or future book debts, or any class of them, and is subsequently adjudged bankrupt.

(2) The assignment is void against the trustee of the bankrupt's estate as regards book debts which were not paid before the presentation of the bankruptcy petition, unless the assignment has been registered under the Bills of Sale Act 1878.

(3) For the purposes of subsections (1) and (2)—

    (*a*) "assignment" includes an assignment by way of security or charge on book debts, and

    (*b*) "general assignment" does not include—

        (i) an assignment of book debts due at the date of the assignment from specified debtors or of debts becoming due under specified contracts, or

        (ii) an assignment of book debts included either in a transfer of a business made in good faith and for value or in an assignment of assets for the benefit of creditors generally.

(4) For the purposes of registration under the Act of 1878 an assignment of book debts is to be treated as if it were a bill of sale given otherwise than by way of security for the payment of a sum of money; and the provisions of that Act with respect to the registration of bills of sale apply accordingly with such necessary modifications as may be made by rules under that Act. **[344]**

NOTES

Commencement: 29 December 1986.

This section derived from the Insolvency Act 1985, s 177.

345. Contracts to which bankrupt is a party

(1) The following applies where a contract has been made with a person who is subsequently adjudged bankrupt.

(2) The court may, on the application of any other party to the contract, make an order discharging obligations under the contract on such terms as to payment by the applicant or the bankrupt of damages for non-performance or otherwise as appear to the court to be equitable.

(3) Any damages payable by the bankrupt by virtue of an order of the court under this section are provable as a bankruptcy debt.

(4) Where an undischarged bankrupt is a contractor in respect of any contract jointly with any person, that person may sue or be sued in respect of the contract without the joinder of the bankrupt.   **[345]**

NOTES
Commencement: 29 December 1986.
This section derived from the Insolvency Act 1985, s 178.

346. Enforcement procedures

(1) Subject to section 285 in Chapter II (restrictions on proceedings and remedies) and to the following provisions of this section, where the creditor of any person who is adjudged bankrupt has, before the commencement of the bankruptcy—

(*a*) issued execution against the goods or land of that person, or
(*b*) attached a debt due to that person from another person,

that creditor is not entitled, as against the official receiver or trustee of the bankrupt's estate, to retain the benefit of the execution or attachment, or any sums paid to avoid it, unless the execution or attachment was completed, or the sums were paid, before the commencement of the bankruptcy.

(2) Subject as follows, where any goods of a person have been taken in execution, then, if before the completion of the execution notice is given to the sheriff or other officer charged with the execution that that person has been adjudged bankrupt—

(*a*) a sheriff or other officer shall on request deliver to the official receiver or trustee of the bankrupt's estate the goods and any money seized or recovered in part satisfaction of the execution, but
(*b*) the costs of the execution are a first charge on the goods or money so delivered and the official receiver or trustee may sell the goods or a sufficient part of them for the purpose of satisfying the charge.

(3) Subject to subsection (6) below, where—

(*a*) under an execution in respect of a judgment for a sum exceeding such sum as may be prescribed for the purposes of this subsection, the goods of any person are sold or money is paid in order to avoid a sale, and
(*b*) before the end of the period of 14 days beginning with the day of the sale or payment the sheriff or other officer charged with the execution is given notice that a bankruptcy petition has been presented in relation to that person, and
(*c*) a bankruptcy order is or has been made on that petition,

the balance of the proceeds of sale or money paid, after deducting the costs of execution, shall (in priority to the claim of the execution creditor) be comprised in the bankrupt's estate.

(4) Accordingly, in the case of an execution in respect of a judgment for a sum exceeding the sum prescribed for the purposes of subsection (3), the sheriff or other officer charged with the execution—

(*a*) shall not dispose of the balance mentioned in subsection (3) at any time within the period of 14 days so mentioned or while there is pending a bankruptcy petition of which he has been given notice under that subsection, and

(b) shall pay that balance, where by virtue of that subsection it is comprised in the bankrupt's estate, to the official receiver or (if there is one) to the trustee of that estate.

(5) For the purposes of this section—

(a) an execution against goods is completed by seizure and sale or by the making of a charging order under section 1 of the Charging Orders Act 1979;

(b) an execution against land is completed by seizure, by the appointment of a receiver or by the making of a charging order under that section;

(c) an attachment of a debt is completed by the receipt of the debt.

(6) The rights conferred by subsections (1) to (3) on the official receiver or the trustee may, to such extent and on such terms as it thinks fit, be set aside by the court in favour of the creditor who has issued the execution or attached the debt.

(7) Nothing in this section entitles the trustee of a bankrupt's estate to claim goods from a person who has acquired them in good faith under a sale by a sheriff or other officer charged with an execution.

(8) Neither subsection (2) nor subsection (3) applies in relation to any execution against property which has been acquired by or has devolved upon the bankrupt since the commencement of the bankruptcy, unless, at the time the execution is issued or before it is completed—

(a) the property has been or is claimed for the bankrupt's estate under section 307 (after-acquired property), and

(b) a copy of the notice given under that section has been or is served on the sheriff or other officer charged with the execution.   **[346]**

NOTES

Commencement: 29 December 1986.

This section derived from the Insolvency Act 1985, s 179.

---

347. Distress, etc

(1) The right of any landlord or other person to whom rent is payable to distrain upon the goods and effects of an undischarged bankrupt for rent due to him from the bankrupt is available (subject to subsection (5) below) against goods and effects comprised in the bankrupt's estate, but only for 6 months' rent accrued due before the commencement of the bankruptcy.

(2) Where a landlord or other person to whom rent is payable has distrained for rent upon the goods and effects of an individual to whom a bankruptcy petition relates and a bankruptcy order is subsequently made on that petition, any amount recovered by way of that distress which—

(a) is in excess of the amount which by virtue of subsection (1) would have been recoverable after the commencement of the bankruptcy, or

(b) is in respect of rent for a period or part of a period after the distress was levied,

shall be held for the bankrupt as part of his estate.

(3) Where any person (whether or not a landlord or person entitled to rent) has distrained upon the goods or effects of an individual who is adjudged bankrupt before the end of the period of 3 months beginning with the distraint, so much of those goods or effects, or of the proceeds of their sale, as is not held for the bankrupt under subsection (2) shall be charged for the benefit of the

bankrupt's estate with the preferential debts of the bankrupt to the extent that the bankrupt's estate is for the time being insufficient for meeting those debts.

(4) Where by virtue of any charge under subsection (3) any person surrenders any goods or effects to the trustee of a bankrupt's estate or makes a payment to such a trustee, that person ranks, in respect of the amount of the proceeds of the sale of those goods or effects by the trustee or, as the case may be, the amount of the payment, as a preferential creditor of the bankrupt, except as against so much of the bankrupt's estate as is available for the payment of preferential creditors by virtue of the surrender or payment.

(5) A landlord or other person to whom rent is payable is not at any time after the discharge of a bankrupt entitled to distrain upon any goods or effects comprised in the bankrupt's estate.

(6) Where in the case of any execution—

   (*a*) a landlord is (apart from this section) entitled under section 1 of the Landlord and Tenant Act 1709 or section 102 of the County Courts Act 1984 (claims for rent where goods seized in execution) to claim for an amount not exceeding one year's rent, and

   (*b*) the person against whom the execution is levied is adjudged bankrupt before the notice of claim is served on the sheriff or other officer charged with the execution,

the right of the landlord to claim under that section is restricted to a right to claim for an amount not exceeding 6 months' rent and does not extend to any rent payable in respect of a period after the notice of claim is so served.

(7) Nothing in subsection (6) imposes any liability on a sheriff or other officer charged with an execution to account to the official receiver or the trustee of a bankrupt's estate for any sums paid by him to a landlord at any time before the sheriff or other officer was served with notice of the bankruptcy order in question.

But this subsection is without prejudice to the liability of the landlord.

(8) Nothing in this Group of Parts affects any right to distrain otherwise than for rent; and any such right is at any time exercisable without restriction against property comprised in a bankrupt's estate, even if that right is expressed by any enactment to be exercisable in like manner as a right to distrain for rent.

(9) Any right to distrain against property comprised in a bankrupt's estate is exercisable notwithstanding that the property has vested in the trustee.

(10) The provisions of this section are without prejudice to a landlord's right in a bankruptcy to prove for any bankruptcy debt in respect of rent.   **[347]**

NOTES
  Commencement: 29 December 1986.
  This section derived from the Insolvency Act 1985, s 180.

---

348. Apprenticeships, etc

(1) This section applies where—

   (*a*) a bankruptcy order is made in respect of an individual to whom another individual was an apprentice or articled clerk at the time when the petition on which the order was made was presented, and

   (*b*) the bankrupt or the apprentice or clerk gives notice to the trustee terminating the apprenticeship or articles.

(2) Subject to subsection (6) below, the indenture of apprenticeship or, as the case may be, the articles of agreement shall be discharged with effect from the commencement of the bankruptcy.

(3) If any money has been paid by or on behalf of the apprentice or clerk to the bankrupt as a fee, the trustee may, on an application made by or on behalf of the apprentice or clerk, pay such sum to the apprentice or clerk as the trustee thinks reasonable, having regard to—

    (*a*) the amount of the fee,
    (*b*) the proportion of the period in respect of which the fee was paid that has been served by the apprentice or clerk before the commencement of the bankruptcy, and
    (*c*) the other circumstances of the case.

(4) The power of the trustee to make a payment under subsection (3) has priority over his obligation to distribute the bankrupt's estate.

(5) Instead of making a payment under subsection (3), the trustee may, if it appears to him expedient to do so on an application made by or on behalf of the apprentice or clerk, transfer the indenture or articles to a person other than the bankrupt.

(6) Where a transfer is made under subsection (5), subsection (2) has effect only as between the apprentice or clerk and the bankrupt. **[348]**

NOTES
Commencement: 29 December 1986.
This section derived from the Insolvency Act 1985, s 181.

349. Unenforceability of liens on books, etc

(1) Subject as follows, a lien or other right to retain possession of any of the books, papers or other records of a bankrupt is unenforceable to the extent that its enforcement would deny possession of any books, papers or other records to the official receiver or the trustee of the bankrupt's estate.

(2) Subsection (1) does not apply to a lien on documents which give a title to property and are held as such. **[349]**

NOTES
Commencement: 29 December 1986.
This section derived from the Insolvency Act 1985, s 182.

CHAPTER VI

BANKRUPTCY OFFENCES

Preliminary

350. Scheme of this Chapter

(1) Subject to section 360(3) below, this Chapter applies where the court has made a bankruptcy order on a bankruptcy petition.

(2) This Chapter applies whether or not the bankruptcy order is annulled, but proceedings for an offence under this Chapter shall not be instituted after the annulment.

(3) Without prejudice to his liability in respect of a subsequent bankruptcy,

the bankrupt is not guilty of an offence under this Chapter in respect of anything done after his discharge; but nothing in this Group of Parts prevents the institution of proceedings against a discharged bankrupt for an offence committed before his discharge.

(4) It is not a defence in proceedings for an offence under this Chapter that anything relied on, in whole or in part, as constituting that offence was done outside England and Wales.

(5) Proceedings for an offence under this Chapter or under the rules shall not be instituted except by the Secretary of State or by or with the consent of the Director of Public Prosecutions.

(6) A person guilty of any offence under this Chapter is liable to imprisonment or a fine, or both.   **[350]**

NOTES
Commencement: 29 December 1986.
This section derived from the Insolvency Act 1985, ss 183(1)–(3), (5), (6), 192.

351. Definitions

In the following provisions of this Chapter—

    (*a*) references to property comprised in the bankrupt's estate or to property possession of which is required to be delivered up to the official receiver or the trustee of the bankrupt's estate include any property which would be such property if a notice in respect of it were given under section 307 (after-acquired property) or 308 (personal property and effects of bankrupt having more than replacement value);

    (*b*) "the initial period" means the period between the presentation of the bankruptcy petition and the commencement of the bankruptcy; and

    (*c*) a reference to a number of months or years before petition is to that period ending with the presentation of the bankruptcy petition. **[351]**

NOTES
Commencement: 29 December 1986.
This section derived from the Insolvency Act 1985, ss 184(5), 187(3)(*a*).

352. Defence of innocent intention

Where in the case of an offence under any provision of this Chapter it is stated that this section applies, a person is not guilty of the offence if he proves that, at the time of the conduct constituting the offence, he had no intent to defraud or to conceal the state of his affairs.   **[352]**

NOTES
Commencement: 29 December 1986.
This section derived from the Insolvency Act 1985, s 183(4).

Wrongdoing by the bankrupt before and after bankruptcy

353. Non-disclosure

(1) The bankrupt is guilty of an offence if—

    (*a*) he does not to the best of his knowledge and belief disclose all the property comprised in his estate to the official receiver or the trustee, or (*b*) he does not inform the official receiver or the trustee of any disposal of any property which but for the disposal would be so comprised, stating how, when, to whom and for what consideration the property was disposed of.

(2) Subsection (1)(*b*) does not apply to any disposal in the ordinary course of a business carried on by the bankrupt or to any payment of the ordinary expenses of the bankrupt or his family.

(3) Section 352 applies to this offence. **[353]**

NOTES
Commencement: 29 December 1986.
This section derived from the Insolvency Act 1985, ss 183(4), 184(1).

354. Concealment of property

(1) The bankrupt is guilty of an offence if—

(*a*) he does not deliver up possession to the official receiver or trustee, or as the official receiver or trustee may direct, of such part of the property comprised in his estate as is in his possession or under his control and possession of which he is required by law so to deliver up,

(*b*) he conceals any debt due to or from him or conceals any property the value of which is not less than the prescribed amount and possession of which he is required to deliver up to the official receiver or trustee, or

(*c*) in the 12 months before petition, or in the initial period, he did anything which would have been an offence under paragraph (*b*) above if the bankruptcy order had been made immediately before he did it.

Section 352 applies to this offence.

(2) The bankrupt is guilty of an offence if he removes, or in the initial period removed, any property the value of which was not less than the prescribed amount and possession of which he has or would have been required to deliver up to the official receiver or the trustee.

Section 352 applies to this offence.

(3) The bankrupt is guilty of an offence if he without reasonable excuse fails, on being required to do so by the official receiver or the court—

(*a*) to account for the loss of any substantial part of his property incurred in the 12 months before petition or in the initial period, or

(*b*) to give a satisfactory explanation of the manner in which such a loss was incurred. **[354]**

NOTES
Commencement: 29 December 1986.
This section derived from the Insolvency Act 1985, ss 183(4), 184(2)–(4).

355. Concealment of books and papers; falsification

(1) The bankrupt is guilty of an offence if he does not deliver up possession to the official receiver or the trustee, or as the official receiver or trustee may direct, of all books, papers and other records of which he has possession or control and which relate to his estate or his affairs.

Section 352 applies to this offence.

(2) The bankrupt is guilty of an offence if—

(*a*) he prevents, or in the initial period prevented, the production of any books, papers or records relating to his estate or affairs;

(*b*) he conceals, destroys, mutilates or falsifies, or causes or permits the concealment, destruction, mutilation or falsification of, any books, papers or other records relating to his estate or affairs;

(*c*) he makes, or causes or permits the making of, any false entries in any book, document or record relating to his estate or affairs; or

(*d*) in the 12 months before petition, or in the initial period, he did anything which would have been an offence under paragraph (*b*) or (*c*) above if the bankruptcy order had been made before he did it.

Section 352 applies to this offence.

(3) The bankrupt is guilty of an offence if—

(*a*) he disposes of, or alters or makes any omission in, or causes or permits the disposal, altering or making of any omission in, any book, document or record relating to his estate or affairs, or

(*b*) in the 12 months before petition, or in the initial period he did anything which would have been an offence under paragraph (*a*) if the bankruptcy order had been made before he did it.

Section 352 applies to this offence. **[355]**

NOTES
Commencement: 29 December 1986.
This section derived from the Insolvency Act 1985, ss 183(4), 185.

356. False statements

(1) The bankrupt is guilty of an offence if he makes or has made any material omission in any statement made under any provision in this Group of Parts and relating to his affairs.

Section 352 applies to this offence.

(2) The bankrupt is guilty of an offence if—

(*a*) knowing or believing that a false debt has been proved by any person under the bankruptcy, he fails to inform the trustee as soon as practicable; or

(*b*) he attempts to account for any part of his property by fictitious losses or expenses; or

(*c*) at any meeting of his creditors in the 12 months before petition or (whether or not at such a meeting) at any time in the initial period, he did anything which would have been an offence under paragraph (*b*) if the bankruptcy order had been made before he did it; or

(*d*) he is, or at any time has been, guilty of any false representation or other fraud for the purpose of obtaining the consent of his creditors, or any of them, to an agreement with reference to his affairs or to his bankruptcy. **[356]**

NOTES
Commencement: 29 December 1986.
This section derived from the Insolvency Act 1985, ss 183(4), 186.

357. Fraudulent disposal of property

(1) The bankrupt is guilty of an offence if he makes or causes to be made, or has in the period of 5 years ending with the commencment of the bankruptcy made or caused to be made, any gift or transfer of, or any charge on, his property.

Section 352 applies to this offence.

(2) The reference to making a transfer of or charge on any property includes causing or conniving at the levying of any execution against that property.

(3) The bankrupt is guilty of an offence if he conceals or removes, or has at any time before the commencement of the bankruptcy concealed or removed, any part of his property after, or within 2 months before, the date on which a judgment or order for the payment of money has been obtained against him, being a judgment or order which was not satisfied before the commencement of the bankruptcy.

Section 352 applies to this offence. **[357]**

NOTES

Commencement: 29 December 1986.

This section derived from the Insolvency Act 1985, ss 183(4), 187(1), (3)(*b*).

358. Absconding

The bankrupt is guilty of an offence if—

    (*a*) he leaves, or attempts or makes preparations to leave, England and Wales with any property the value of which is not less than the prescribed amount and possession of which he is required to deliver up to the official receiver or the trustee, or

    (*b*) in the 6 months before petition, or in the initial period, he did anything which would have been an offence under paragraph (*a*) if the bankruptcy order had been made immediately before he did it.

Section 352 applies to this offence. **[358]**

NOTES

Commencement: 29 December 1986.

This section derived from the Insolvency Act 1985, ss 183(4), 187(2).

359. Fraudulent dealing with property obtained on credit

(1) The bankrupt is guilty of an offence if, in the 12 months before petition, or in the initial period, he disposed of any property which he had obtained on credit and, at the time he disposed of it, had not paid for.

Section 352 applied to this offence.

(2) A person is guilty of an offence if, in the 12 months before petition or in the initial period, he acquired or received property from the bankrupt knowing or believing—

    (*a*) that the bankrupt owed money in respect of the property, and

    (*b*) that the bankrupt did not intend, or was unlikely to be able, to pay the money he so owed.

(3) A person is not guilty of an offence under subsection (1) or (2) if the disposal, acquisition or receipt of the property was in the ordinary course of a business carried on by the bankrupt at the time of the disposal, acquisition or receipt.

(4) In determining for the purposes of this section whether any property is disposed of, acquired or received in the ordinary course of a business carried on by the bankrupt, regard may be had, in particular, to the price paid for the property.

(5) In this section references to disposing of property include pawning or pledging it; and references to acquiring or receiving property shall be read accordingly. **[359]**

NOTES
Commencement: 29 December 1986.
This section derived from the Insolvency Act 1985, ss 183(4), 188.

360. Obtaining credit; engaging in business

(1) The bankrupt is guilty of an offence if—

(a) either alone or jointly with any other person, he obtains credit to the extent of the prescribed amount or more without giving the person from whom he obtains it the relevant information about his status; or

(b) he engages (whether directly or indirectly) in any business under a name other than that in which he was adjudged bankrupt without disclosing to all persons with whom he enters into any business transaction the name in which he was so adjudged.

(2) The reference to the bankrupt obtaining credit includes the following cases—

(a) where goods are bailed to him under a hire-purchase agreement, or agreed to be sold to him under a conditional sale agreement, and

(b) where he is paid in advance (whether in money or otherwise) for the supply of goods or services.

(3) A person whose estate has been sequestrated in Scotland, or who has been adjudged bankrupt in Northern Ireland, is guilty of an offence if, before his discharge, he does anything in England and Wales which would be an offence under subsection (1) if he were an undischarged bankrupt and the sequestration of his estate or the adjudication in Northern Ireland were an adjudication under this Part.

(4) For the purposes of subsection (1)(a), the relevant information about the status of the person in question is the information that he is an undischarged bankrupt or, as the case may be, that his estate has been sequestrated in Scotland and that he has not been discharged. **[360]**

NOTES
Commencement: 29 December 1986.
This section derived from the Insolvency Act 1985, s 189.

361. Failure to keep proper accounts of business

(1) Where the bankrupt has been engaged in any business for any of the period of 2 years before petition, he is guilty of an offence if he—

(a) has not kept proper accounting records throughout that period and throughout any part of the initial period in which he was so engaged, or

(b) has not preserved all the accounting records which he has kept.

(2) The bankrupt is not guilty of an offence under subsection (1)—

(*a*) if his unsecured liabilities at the commencement of the bankruptcy did not exceed the prescribed amount, or

(*b*) if he proves that in the circumstances in which he carried on business the omission was honest and excusable.

(3) For the purposes of this section a person is deemed not to have kept proper accounting records if he has not kept such records as are necessary to show or explain his transactions and financial position in his business, including—

(*a*) records containing entries from day to day, in sufficient detail, of all cash paid and received,

(*b*) where the business involved dealings in goods, statements of annual stock-takings, and

(*c*) except in the case of goods sold by way of retail trade to the actual customer, records of all goods sold and purchased showing the buyers and sellers in sufficient detail to enable the goods and the buyers and sellers to be identified.

(4) In relation to any such records as are mentioned in subsection (3), subsections (2)(*d*) and (3)(*b*) of section 355 apply with the substitution of 2 years for 12 months. **[361]**

NOTES

Commencement: 29 December 1986.

This section derived from the Insolvency Act 1985, s 190.

362. Gambling

(1) The bankrupt is guilty of an offence if he has—

(*a*) in the 2 years before petition, materially contributed to, or increased the extent of, his insolvency by gambling or by rash and hazardous speculations, or

(*b*) in the initial period, lost any part of his property by gambling or by rash and hazardous speculations.

(2) In determining for the purposes of this section whether any speculations were rash and hazardous, the financial position of the bankrupt at the time when he entered into them shall be taken into consideration. **[362]**

NOTES

Commencement: 29 December 1986.

This section derived from the Insolvency Act 1985, s 191.

CHAPTER VII

POWERS OF COURT IN BANKRUPTCY

363. General control of court

(1) Every bankruptcy is under the general control of the court and, subject to the provisions in this Group of Parts, the court has full power to decide all questions of priorities and all other questions, whether of law or fact, arising in any bankruptcy.

(2) Without prejudice to any other provision in this Group of Parts, an undischarged bankrupt or a discharged bankrupt whose estate is still being administered under Chapter IV of this Part shall do all such things as he may

be directed to do by the court for the purposes of his bankruptcy or, as the case may be, the administration of that estate.

(3) The official receiver or the trustee of a bankrupt's estate may at any time apply to the court for a direction under subsection (2).

(4) If any person without reasonable excuse fails to comply with any obligation imposed on him by subsection (2), he is guilty of a contempt of court and liable to be punished accordingly (in addition to any other punishment to which he may be subject).   **[363]**

NOTES
  Commencement: 29 December 1986.
  This section derived from the Insolvency Act 1985, s 193.

364. Power of arrest

(1) In the cases specified in the next subsection the court may cause a warrant to be issued to a constable or prescribed officer of the court—

  (a) for the arrest of a debtor to whom a bankruptcy petition relates or of an undischarged bankrupt, or of a discharged bankrupt whose estate is still being administered under Chapter IV of this Part, and
  (b) for the seizure of any books, papers, records, money or goods in the possession of a person arrested under the warrant,

and may authorise a person arrested under such a warrant to be kept in custody, and anything seized under such a warrant to be held, in accordance with the rules, until such time as the court may order.

(2) The powers conferred by subsection (1) are exercisable in relation to a debtor or undischarged or discharged bankrupt if, at any time after the presentation of the bankruptcy petition relating to him or the making of the bankruptcy order against him, it appears to the court—

  (a) that there are reasonable grounds for believing that he has absconded, or is about to abscond, with a view to avoiding or delaying the payment of any of his debts or his appearance to a bankruptcy petition or to avoiding, delaying or disrupting any proceedings in bankruptcy against him or any examination of his affairs, or
  (b) that he is about to remove his goods with a view to preventing or delaying possession being taken of them by the official receiver or the trustee of his estate, or
  (c) that there are reasonable grounds for believing that he has concealed or destroyed, or is about to conceal or destroy, any of his goods or any books, papers or records which might be of use to his creditors in the course of his bankruptcy or in connection with the administration of his estate, or
  (d) that he has, without the leave of the official receiver or the trustee of his estate, removed any goods in his possession which exceed in value such sum as may be prescribed for the purposes of this paragraph, or
  (e) that he has failed, without reasonable excuse, to attend any examination ordered by the court.   **[364]**

NOTES
  Commencement: 29 December 1986.
  This section derived from the Insolvency Act 1985, s 194.

365. Seizure of bankrupt's property

(1) At any time after a bankruptcy order has been made, the court may, on the application of the official receiver or the trustee of the bankrupt's estate, issue a warrant authorising the person to whom it is directed to seize any property comprised in the bankrupt's estate which is, or any books, papers or records relating to the bankrupt's estate or affairs which are, in the possession or under the control of the bankrupt or any other person who is required to deliver the property, books, papers or records to the official receiver or trustee.

(2) Any person executing a warrant under this section may, for the purpose of seizing any property comprised in the bankrupt's estate or any books, papers or records relating to the bankrupt's estate or affairs, break open any premises where the bankrupt or anything that may be seized under the warrant is or is believed to be and any receptacle of the bankrupt which contains or is believed to contain anything that may be so seized.

(3) If, after a bankruptcy order has been made, the court is satisfied that any property comprised in the bankrupt's estate is, or any books, papers or records relating to the bankrupt's estate or affairs are, concealed in any premises not belonging to him, it may issue a warrant authorising any constable or prescribed officer of the court to search those premises for the property, books, papers or records.

(4) A warrant under subsection (3) shall not be executed except in the prescribed manner and in accordance with its terms. **[365]**

NOTES
    Commencement: 29 December 1986.
    This section derived from the Insolvency Act 1985, s 195.

366. Inquiry into bankrupt's dealings and property

(1) At any time after a bankruptcy order has been made the court may, on the application of the official receiver or the trustee of the bankrupt's estate, summon to appear before it—

    (*a*) the bankrupt or the bankrupt's spouse or former spouse,

    (*b*) any person known or believed to have any property comprised in the bankrupt's estate in his possession or to be indebted to the bankrupt,

    (*c*) any person appearing to the court to be able to give information concerning the bankrupt or the bankrupt's dealings, affairs or property.

The court may require any such person as is mentioned in paragraph (*b*) or (*c*) to submit an affidavit to the court containing an account of his dealings with the bankrupt or to produce any documents in his possession or under his control relating to the bankrupt or the bankrupt's dealings, affairs or property.

(2) Without prejudice to section 364, the following applies in a case where—

    (*a*) a person without reasonable excuse fails to appear before the court when he is summoned to do so under this section, or

    (*b*) there are reasonable grounds for believing that a person has absconded, or is about to abscond, with a view to avoiding his appearance before the court under this section.

(3) The court may, for the purpose of bringing that person and anything in his possession before the court, cause a warrant to be issued to a constable or prescribed officer of the court—

(a) for the arrest of that person, and
(b) for the seizure of any books, papers, records, money or goods in that person's possession.

(4) The court may authorise a person arrested under such a warrant to be kept in custody, and anything seized under such a warrant to be held, in accordance with the rules, until that person is brought before the court under the warrant or until such other time as the court may order. **[366]**

NOTES
Commencement: 29 December 1986.
This section derived from the Insolvency Act 1985, s 196(1), (2).

367. Court's enforcement powers under s 366

(1) If it appears to the court, on consideration of any evidence obtained under section 366 or this section, that any person has in his possession any property comprised in the bankrupt's estate, the court may, on the application of the official receiver or the trustee of the bankrupt's estate, order that person to deliver the whole or any part of the property to the official receiver or the trustee at such time, in such manner and on such terms as the court thinks fit.

(2) If it appears to the court, on consideration of any evidence obtained under section 366 or this section, that any person is indebted to the bankrupt, the court may, on the application of the official receiver or the trustee of the bankrupt's estate, order that person to pay to the official receiver or trustee, at such time and in such manner as the court may direct, the whole or part of the amount due, whether in full discharge of the debt or otherwise as the court thinks fit.

(3) The court may, if it thinks fit, order that any person who if within the jurisdiction of the court would be liable to be summoned to appear before it under section 366 shall be examined in any part of the United Kingdom where he may be for the time being, or in any place outside the United Kingdom.

(4) Any person who appears or is brought before the court under section 366 or this section may be examined on oath, either orally or by interrogatories, concerning the bankrupt or the bankrupt's dealings, affairs and property. **[367]**

NOTES
Commencement: 29 December 1986.
This section derived from the Insolvency Act 1985, s 196(3)–(6).

368. Provision corresponding to s 366, where interim receiver appointed

(1) Sections 366 and 367 apply where an interim receiver has been appointed under section 286 as they apply where a bankruptcy order has been made, as if—

(a) references to the official receiver or the trustee were to the interim receiver, and
(b) references to the bankrupt and to his estate were (respectively) to the debtor and his property. **[368]**

NOTES
Commencement: 29 December 1986.
This section derived from the Insolvency Act 1985, s 196(7).

369. Order for production of documents by inland revenue

(1) For the purposes of an examination under section 290 (public examination of bankrupt) or proceedings under sections 366 to 368, the court may, on the application of the official receiver or the trustee of the bankrupt's estate, order an inland revenue official to produce to the court—

    (*a*) any return, account or accounts submitted (whether before or after the commencement of the bankruptcy) by the bankrupt to any inland revenue official,

    (*b*) any assessment or determination made (whether before or after the commencement of the bankruptcy) in relation to the bankrupt by any inland revenue official, or

    (*c*) any correspondence (whether before or after the commencement of the bankruptcy) between the bankrupt and any inland revenue official.

(2) Where the court has made an order under subsection (1) for the purposes of any examination or proceedings, the court may, at any time after the document to which the order relates is produced to it, by order authorise the disclosure of the document, or of any part of its contents, to the official receiver, the trustee of the bankrupt's estate or the bankrupt's creditors.

(3) The court shall not address an order under subsection (1) to an inland revenue official unless it is satisfied that that official is dealing, or has dealt, with the affairs of the bankrupt.

(4) Where any document to which an order under subsection (1) relates is not in the possession of the official to whom the order is addressed, it is the duty of that official to take all reasonable steps to secure possession of it and, if he fails to do so, to report the reasons for his failure to the court.

(5) Where any document to which an order under subsection (1) relates is in the possession of an inland revenue official other than the one to whom the order is addressed, it is the duty of the official in possession of the document, at the request of the official to whom the order is addressed, to deliver it to the official making the request.

(6) In this section "inland revenue official" means any inspector or collector of taxes appointed by the Commissioners of Inland Revenue or any person appointed by the Commissioners to serve in any other capacity.

(7) This section does not apply for the purposes of an examination under sections 366 and 367 which takes place by virtue of section 368 (interim receiver).   **[369]**

NOTES
    Commencement: 29 December 1986.
    This section derived from the Insolvency Act 1985, s 197.

370. Power to appoint special manager

(1) The court may, on an application under this section, appoint any person to be the special manager—

    (*a*) of a bankrupt's estate, or

    (*b*) of the business of an undischarged bankrupt, or

    (*c*) of the property or business of a debtor in whose case the official receiver has been appointed interim receiver under section 286.

(2) An application under this section may be made by the official receiver

or the trustee of the bankrupt's estate in any case where it appears to the official receiver or trustee that the nature of the estate, property or business, or the interests of the creditors generally, require the appointment of another person to manage the estate, property or business.

(3) A special manager appointed under this section has such powers as may be entrusted to him by the court.

(4) The power of the court under subsection (3) to entrust powers to a special manager includes power to direct that any provision in this Group of Parts that has effect in relation to the official receiver, interim receiver or trustee shall have the like effect in relation to the special manager for the purposes of the carrying out by the special manager of any of the functions of the official receiver, interim receiver or trustee.

(5) A special manager appointed under this section shall—

    (*a*) give such security as may be prescribed,

    (*b*) prepare and keep such accounts as may be prescribed, and

    (*c*) produce those accounts in accordance with the rules to the Secretary of State or to such other persons as may be prescribed. **[370]**

NOTES

Commencement: 29 December 1986.

This section derived from the Insolvency Act 1985, s 198.

371. Re-direction of bankrupt's letters, etc

(1) Where a bankruptcy order has been made, the court may from time to time, on the application of the official receiver or the trustee of the bankrupt's estate, order the Post Office to re-direct and send or deliver to the official receiver or trustee or otherwise any postal packet (within the meaning of the Post Office Act 1953) which would otherwise be sent or delivered by them to the bankrupt at such place or places as may be specified in the order.

(2) An order under this section has effect for such period, not exceeding 3 months, as may be specified in the order. **[371]**

NOTES

Commencement: 29 December 1986.

This section derived from the Insolvency Act 1985, s 199.

PART X

INDIVIDUAL INSOLVENCY: GENERAL PROVISIONS

372. Supplies of gas, water, electricity, etc

(1) This section applies where on any day ("the relevant day")—

    (*a*) a bankruptcy order is made against an individual or an interim receiver of an individual's property is appointed, or

    (*b*) a voluntary arrangement proposed by an individual is approved under Part VIII, or

    (*c*) a deed of arrangement is made for the benefit of an individual's creditors;

and in this section "the office-holder" means the official receiver, the trustee in bankruptcy, the interim receiver, the supervisor of the voluntary arrangement or the trustee under the deed of arrangement, as the case may be.

(2) If a request falling within the next subsection is made for the giving after the relevant day of any of the supplies mentioned in subsection (4), the supplier—

(a) may make it a condition of the giving of the supply that the office-holder personally guarantees the payment of any charges in respect of the supply, but

(b) shall not make it a condition of the giving of the supply, or do anything which has the effect of making it a condition of the giving of the supply, that any outstanding charges in respect of a supply given to the individual before the relevant day are paid.

(3) A request falls within this subsection if it is made—

(a) by or with the concurrence of the office-holder, and

(b) for the purposes of any business which is or has been carried on by the individual, by a firm or partnership of which the individual is or was a member, or by an agent or manager for the individual or for such a firm or partnership.

(4) The supplies referred to in subsection (2) are—

(a) a public supply of gas,

(b) a supply of electricity by an Electricity Board,

(c) a supply of water by statutory water undertakers,

(d) a supply of telecommunication services by a public telecommunications operator.

(5) The following applies to expressions used in subsection (4)—

(a) "public supply of gas" means a supply of gas by the British Gas Corporation or a public gas supplier within the meaning of Part I of the Gas Act 1986;

(b) "Electricity Board" means the same as in the Energy Act 1983; and

(c) "telecommunication services" and "public telecommunications operator" mean the same as in the Telecommunications Act 1984, except that the former does not include services consisting in the conveyance of programmes included in cable programme services (within the meaning of the Cable and Broadcasting Act 1984). **[372]**

NOTES
Commencement: 29 December 1986.
This section derived from the Insolvency Act 1985, s 200.

373. Jurisdiction in relation to insolvent individuals

(1) The High Court and the county courts have jurisdiction throughout England and Wales for the purposes of the Parts in this Group.

(2) For the purposes of those Parts, a county court has, in addition to its ordinary jurisdiction, all the powers and jurisdiction of the High Court; and the orders of the court may be enforced accordingly in the prescribed manner.

(3) Jurisdiction for the purposes of those Parts is exercised—

(a) by the High Court in relation to the proceedings which, in accordance with the rules, are allocated to the London insolvency district, and

(b) by each county court in relation to the proceedings which are so allocated to the insolvency district of that court.

(4) Subsection (3) is without prejudice to the transfer of proceedings from

one court to another in the manner prescribed by the rules; and nothing in that subsection invalidates any proceedings on the grounds that they were initiated or continued in the wrong court. **[373]**

NOTES
Commencement: 29 December 1986.
This section derived from the Insolvency Act 1985, s 201.

374. Insolvency districts

(1) The Lord Chancellor may by order designate the areas which are for the time being to be comprised, for the purposes of the Parts in this Group, in the London insolvency district and the insolvency district of each county court; and an order under this section may—

    (a) exclude any county court from having jurisdiction for the purposes of those Parts, or

    (b) confer jurisdiction for those purposes on any county court which has not previously had that jurisdiction.

(2) An order under this section may contain such incidental, supplemental and transitional provisions as may appear to the Lord Chancellor necessary or expedient.

(3) An order under this section shall be made by statutory instrument and, after being made, shall be laid before each House of Parliament.

(4) Subject to any order under this section—

    (a) the district which, immediately before the appointed day, is the London bankruptcy district becomes, on that day, the London insolvency district;

    (b) any district which immediately before that day is the bankruptcy district of a county court becomes, on that day, the insolvency district of that court, and

    (c) any county court which immediately before that day is excluded from having jurisdiction in bankruptcy is excluded, on and after that day, from having jurisdiction for the purposes of the Parts in this Group.

[374]

NOTES
Commencement: 29 December 1986.
This section derived from the Insolvency Act 1985, s 202.

375. Appeals etc from courts exercising insolvency jurisdiction

(1) Every court having jurisdiction for the purposes of the Parts in this Group may review, rescind or vary any order made by it in the exercise of that jurisdiction.

(2) An appeal from a decision made in the exercise of jurisdiction for the purposes of those Parts by a county court or by a registrar in bankruptcy of the High Court lies to a single judge of the High Court; and an appeal from a decision of that judge on such an appeal lies, with the leave of the judge or of the Court of Appeal, to the Court of Appeal.

(3) A county court is not, in the exercise of its jurisdiction for the purposes

of those Parts, to be subject to be restrained by the order of any other court, and no appeal lies from its decision in the exercise of that jurisdiction except as provided by this section. **[375]**

NOTES
Commencement: 29 December 1986.
This section derived from the Insolvency Act 1985, s 203.

376. Time-limits

Where by any provision in this Group of Parts or by the rules the time for doing anything is limited, the court may extend the time, either before or after it has expired, on such terms, if any, as it thinks fit. **[376]**

NOTES
Commencement: 29 December 1986.
This section derived from the Insolvency Act 1985, s 204.

377. Formal defects

The acts of a person as the trustee of a bankrupt's estate or as a special manager, and the acts of the creditors' committee established for any bankruptcy, are valid notwithstanding any defect in the appointment, election or qualifications of the trustee or manager or, as the case may be, of any member of the committee. **[377]**

NOTES
Commencement: 29 December 1986.
This section derived from the Insolvency Act 1985, s 205.

378. Exemption from stamp duty

Stamp duty shall not be charged on—

  (a) any document, being a deed, conveyance, assignment, surrender, admission or other assurance relating solely to property which is comprised in a bankrupt's estate and which, after the execution of that document, is or remains at law or in equity the property of the bankrupt or of the trustee of that estate,
  (b) any writ, order, certificate or other instrument relating solely to the property of a bankrupt or to any bankruptcy proceedings. **[378]**

NOTES
Commencement: 29 December 1986.
This section derived from the Insolvency Act 1985, s 206.

379. Annual report

As soon as practicable after the end of 1986 and each subsequent calendar year, the Secretary of State shall prepare and lay before each House of Parliament a report about the operation during that year of so much of this Act as is comprised in this Group of Parts, and about proceedings in the course of that year under the Deeds of Arrangement Act 1914. **[379]**

NOTES
Commencement: 29 December 1986.
This section derived from the Insolvency Act 1985, s 210.

PART XI

INTERPRETATION FOR SECOND GROUP OF PARTS

380. Introductory

The next five sections have effect for the interpretation of the provisions of this Act which are comprised in this Group of Parts; and where a definition is provided for a particular expression, it applies except so far as the context otherwise requires.   **[380]**

NOTES
Commencement: 29 December 1986.

381. "Bankrupt" and associated terminology

(1) "Bankrupt" means an individual who has been adjudged bankrupt and, in relation to a bankruptcy order, it means the individual adjudged bankrupt by that order.

(2) "Bankruptcy order" means an order adjudging an individual bankrupt.

(3) "Bankruptcy petition" means a petition to the court for a bankruptcy order.   **[381]**

NOTES
Commencement: 29 December 1986.
This section derived from the Insolvency Act 1985, s 211(1) (part).

382. "Bankruptcy debt", etc

(1) "Bankruptcy debt", in relation to a bankrupt, means (subject to the next subsection) any of the following—

(a) any debt or liability to which he is subject at the commencement of the bankruptcy,

(b) any debt or liability to which he may become subject after the commencement of the bankruptcy (including after his discharge from bankruptcy) by reason of any obligation incurred before the commencement of the bankruptcy,

(c) any amount specified in pursuance of section 39(3)(c) of the Powers of Criminal Courts Act 1973 in any criminal bankruptcy order made against him before the commencement of the bankruptcy, and

(d) any interest provable as mentioned in section 322(2) in Chapter IV of Part IX.

(2) In determining for the purposes of any provision in this Group of Parts whether any liability in tort is a bankruptcy debt, the bankrupt is deemed to become subject to that liability by reason of an obligation incurred at the time when the cause of action accrued.

(3) For the purposes of references in this Group of Parts to a debt or liability, it is immaterial whether the debt or liability is present or future, whether it is certain or contingent or whether its amount is fixed or liquidated, or is capable of being ascertained by fixed rules or as a matter of opinion; and references in this Group of Parts to owing a debt are to be read accordingly.

(4) In this Group of Parts, except in so far as the context otherwise requires, "liability" means (subject to subsection (3) above) a liability to pay money or

money's worth, including any liability under an enactment, any liability for breach of trust, any liability in contract, tort or bailment and any liability arising out of an obligation to make restitution. **[382]**

NOTES
Commencement: 29 December 1986.
This section derived from the Insolvency Act 1985, s 211(1) (part), (2), (3).

383. "Creditor", "security", etc

(1) "Creditor"—

(*a*) in relation to a bankrupt, means a person to whom any of the bankruptcy debts is owed (being, in the case of an amount falling within paragraph (*c*) of the definition in section 382(1) of "bankruptcy debt", the person in respect of whom that amount is specified in the criminal bankruptcy order in question), and

(*b*) in relation to an individual to whom a bankruptcy petition relates, means a person who would be a creditor in the bankruptcy if a bankruptcy order were made on that petition.

(2) Subject to the next two subsections and any provision of the rules requiring a creditor to give up his security for the purposes of proving a debt, a debt is secured for the purposes of this Group of Parts to the extent that the person to whom the debt is owed holds any security for the debt (whether a mortgage, charge, lien or other security) over any property of the person by whom the debt is owed.

(3) Where a statement such as is mentioned in section 269(1)(*a*) in Chapter I of Part IX has been made by a secured creditor for the purposes of any bankruptcy petition and a bankruptcy order is subsequently made on that petition, the creditor is deemed for the purposes of the Parts in this Group to have given up the security specified in the statement.

(4) In subsection (2) the reference to a security does not include a lien on books, papers or other records, except to the extent that they consist of documents which give a title to property and are held as such. **[383]**

NOTES
Commencement: 29 December 1986.
This section derived from the Insolvency Act 1985, s 211(1) (part), (5)–(7).

384. "Prescribed" and "the rules"

(1) Subject to the next subsection, "prescribed" means prescribed by the rules; and "the rules" means rules made under section 412 in Part XV.

(2) References in this Group of Parts to the amount prescribed for the purposes of any of the following provisions—

section 273;
section 346(3);
section 354(1) and (2);
section 358;
section 360(1);
section 361(2); and
section 364(2)(*d*),

and references in those provisions to the prescribed amount are to be read in accordance with section 418 in Part XV and orders made under that section.

[384]

NOTES
  Commencement: 29 December 1986.
  This section derived from the Insolvency Act 1985, ss 209(1) (part), 211(1) (part).

385. Miscellaneous definitions

(1) The following definitions have effect—

"the court", in relation to any matter, means the court to which, in accordance with section 373 in Part X and the rules, proceedings with respect to that matter are allocated or transferred;

"creditor's petition" means a bankruptcy petition under section 264(1)(*a*);

"criminal bankruptcy order" means an order under section 39(1) of the Powers of Criminal Courts Act 1973;

"debt" is to be construed in accordance with section 382(3);

"the debtor"—

(*a*) in relation to a proposal for the purposes of Part VIII, means the individual making or intending to make that proposal, and

(*b*) in relation to a bankruptcy petition, means the individual to whom the petition relates;

"debtor's petition" means a bankruptcy petition presented by the debtor himself under section 264(1)(*b*);

"dwelling house" includes any building or part of a building which is occupied as a dwelling and any yard, garden, garage or outhouse belonging to the dwelling house and occupied with it;

"estate", in relation to a bankrupt is to be construed in accordance with section 283 in Chapter II of Part IX;

"family", in relation to a bankrupt, means the persons (if any) who are living with him and are dependent on him;

"secured" and related expressions are to be construed in accordance with section 383; and

"the trustee", in relation to a bankruptcy and the bankrupt, means the trustee of the bankrupt's estate.

(2) References in this Group of Parts to a person's affairs include his business, if any.   **[385]**

NOTES
  Commencement: 29 December 1986.
  This section derived from the Insolvency Act 1985, s 211(1) (part), (4).

THE THIRD GROUP OF PARTS

MISCELLANEOUS MATTERS BEARING ON BOTH COMPANY AND
INDIVIDUAL INSOLVENCY; GENERAL INTERPRETATION;
FINAL PROVISIONS

PART XII

PREFERENTIAL DEBTS IN COMPANY AND
INDIVIDUAL INSOLVENCY

386. Categories of preferential debts

(1) A reference in this Act to the preferential debts of a company or an individual is to the debts listed in Schedule 6 to this Act (money owed to the

Inland Revenue for income tax deducted at source; VAT, car tax, betting and gaming duties; social security and pension scheme contributions; remuneration etc of employees); and references to preferential creditors are to be read accordingly.

(2) In that Schedule "the debtor" means the company or the individual concerned.

(3) Schedule 6 is to be read with Schedule 3 to the Social Security Pensions Act 1975 (occupational pension scheme contributions). **[386]**

NOTES
Commencement: 29 December 1986.
This section derived from the Companies Act 1985, ss 196(2), 475(1), and the Insolvency Act 1985, ss 23(7), 89(1), 108(3), 115(9), 166(1), Sch 4, para 1(1), Sch 6, para 15(3).

387. "The relevant date"

(1) This section explains references in Schedule 6 to the relevant date (being the date which determines the existence and amount of a preferential debt).

(2) For the purposes of section 4 in Part I (meeting to consider company voluntary arrangement), the relevant date in relation to a company which is not being wound up is—

    (a) where an administration order is in force in relation to the company, the date of the making of that order, and

    (b) where no such order has been made, the date of the approval of the voluntary arrangement.

(3) In relation to a company which is being wound up, the following applies—

    (a) if the winding up is by the court, and the winding-up order was made immediately upon the discharge of an administration order, the relevant date is the date of the making of the administration order;

    (b) if the case does not fall within paragraph (a) and the company—

        (i) is being wound up by the court, and

        (ii) had not commenced to be wound up voluntarily before the date of the making of the winding-up order,

    the relevant date is the date of the appointment (or first appointment) of a provisional liquidator or, if no such appointment has been made, the date of the winding-up order;

    (c) if the case does not fall within either paragraph (a) or (b), the relevant date is the date of the passing of the resolution for the winding up of the company.

(4) In relation to a company in receivership (where section 40 or, as the case may be, section 59 applies), the relevant date is—

    (a) in England and Wales, the date of the appointment of the receiver by debenture-holders, and

    (b) in Scotland, the date of the appointment of the receiver under section 53(6) or (as the case may be) 54(5).

(5) For the purposes of section 258 in Part VIII (individual voluntary arrangements), the relevant date is, in relation to a debtor who is not an undischarged bankrupt, the date of the interim order made under section 252 with respect to his proposal.

(6) In relation to a bankrupt, the following applies—

    (*a*) where at the time the bankruptcy order was made there was an interim receiver appointed under section 286, the relevant date is the date on which the interim receiver was first appointed after the presentation of the bankruptcy petition;

    (*b*) otherwise, the relevant date is the date of the making of the bankruptcy order.   **[387]**

NOTES

    Commencement: 29 December 1986.

    This section derived from the Companies Act 1985, ss 196(2)–(4), 475(3), (4), and the Insolvency Act 1985, ss 23(8), 115(10), Sch 4, Pt II, para 1(2), (3), Sch 6, paras 15(4), 20(3).

PART XIII

INSOLVENCY PRACTITIONERS AND THEIR QUALIFICATION

Restrictions on unqualified persons acting as liquidator, trustee in bankruptcy, etc

388. Meaning of "act as insolvency practitioner"

(1) A person acts as an insolvency practitioner in relation to a company by acting—

    (*a*) as its liquidator, provisional liquidator, administrator or administrative receiver, or

    (*b*) as supervisor of a voluntary arrangement approved by it under Part I.

(2) A person acts as an insolvency practitioner in relation to an individual by acting—

    (*a*) as his trustee in bankruptcy or interim receiver of his property or as permanent or interim trustee in the sequestration of his estate; or

    (*b*) as trustee under a deed which is a deed of arrangement made for the benefit of his creditors or, in Scotland, a trust deed for his creditors; or

    (*c*) as supervisor of a voluntary arrangement proposed by him and approved under Part VIII; or

    (*d*) in the case of a deceased individual to the administration of whose estate this section applies by virtue of an order under section 421 (application of provisions of this Act to insolvent estates of deceased persons), as administrator of that estate.

(3) References in this section to an individual include, except in so far as the context otherwise requires, references to a partnership and to any debtor within the meaning of the Bankruptcy (Scotland) Act 1985.

(4) In this section—

    "administrative receiver" has the meaning given by section 251 in Part VII;

    "company" means a company within the meaning given by section 735(1) of the Companies Act or a company which may be wound up under Part V of this Act (unregistered companies); and

    "interim trustee" and "permanent trustee" mean the same as in the Bankruptcy (Scotland) Act 1985.

(5) Nothing in this section applies to anything done by the official receiver.

[388]

NOTES
Commencement: 29 December 1986.
This section derived from the Insolvency Act 1985, s 1(2)–(6).

389. Acting without qualification an offence

(1) A person who acts as an insolvency practitioner in relation to a company or an individual at a time when he is not qualified to do so is liable to imprisonment or a fine, or to both.

(2) This section does not apply to the official receiver.   **[389]**

NOTES
Commencement: 29 December 1986.
This section derived from the Insolvency Act 1985, s 1(1).

The requisite qualification, and the means of obtaining it

390. Persons not qualified to act as insolvency practitioners

(1) A person who is not an individual is not qualified to act as an insolvency practitioner.

(2) A person is not qualified to act as an insolvency practitioner at any time unless at that time—

- (a) he is authorised so to act by virtue of membership of a professional body recognised under section 391 below, being permitted so to act by or under the rules of that body, or
- (b) he holds an authorisation granted by a competent authority under section 393.

(3) A person is not qualified to act as an insolvency practitioner in relation to another person at any time unless—

- (a) there is in force at that time security or, in Scotland, caution for the proper performance of his functions, and
- (b) that security or caution meets the prescribed requirements with respect to his so acting in relation to that other person.

(4) A person is not qualified to act as an insolvency practitioner at any time if at that time—

- (a) he has been adjudged bankrupt or sequestration of his estate has been awarded and (in either case) he has not been discharged,
- (b) he is subject to a disqualification order made under the Company Directors Disqualification Act 1986, or
- (c) he is a patient within the meaning of Part VII of the Mental Health Act 1983 or section 125(1) of the Mental Health (Scotland) Act 1984.

[390]

NOTES
Commencement: 29 December 1986.
This section derived from the Insolvency Act 1985, ss 2, 3(1).

391. Recognised professional bodies

(1) The Secretary of State may by order declare a body which appears to him to fall within subsection (2) below to be a recognised professional body for the purposes of this section.

(2) A body may be recognised if it regulates the practice of a profession and maintains and enforces rules for securing that such of its members as are permitted by or under the rules to act as insolvency practitioners—

    (*a*) are fit and proper persons so to act, and
    (*b*) meet acceptable requirements as to education and practical training and experience.

(3) References to members of a recognised professional body are to persons who, whether members of that body or not, are subject to its rules in the practice of the profession in question.

The reference in section 390(2) above to membership of a professional body recognised under this section is to be read accordingly.

(4) An order made under subsection (1) in relation to a professional body may be revoked by a further order if it appears to the Secretary of State that the body no longer falls within subsection (2).

(5) An order of the Secretary of State under this section has effect from such date as is specified in the order; and any such order revoking a previous order may make provision whereby members of the body in question continue to be treated as authorised to act as insolvency practitioners for a specified period after the revocation takes effect.   [391]

NOTES
    Commencement: 29 December 1986.
    This section derived from the Insolvency Act 1985, s 3(2)–(5).

392. Authorisation by competent authority

(1) Application may be made to a competent authority for authorisation to act as an insolvency practitioner.

(2) The competent authorities for this purpose are—

    (*a*) in relation to a case of any description specified in directions given by the Secretary of State, the body or person so specified in relation to cases of that description, and
    (*b*) in relation to a case not falling within paragraph (*a*), the Secretary of State.

(3) The application—

    (*a*) shall be made in such manner as the competent authority may direct,
    (*b*) shall contain or be accompanied by such information as that authority may reasonably require for the purpose of determining the application, and
    (*c*) shall be accompanied by the prescribed fee;

and the authority may direct that notice of the making of the application shall be published in such manner as may be specified in the direction.

(4) At any time after receiving the application and before determining it the authority may require the applicant to furnish additional information.

(5) Directions and requirements given or imposed under subsection (3) or (4) may differ as between different applications.

(6) Any information to be furnished to the competent authority under this section shall, if it so requires, be in such form or verified in such manner as it may specify.

(7) An application may be withdrawn before it is granted or refused.

(8) Any sums received under this section by a competent authority other than the Secretary of State may be retained by the authority; and any sums so received by the Secretary of State shall be paid into the Consolidated Fund.
[392]

NOTES
Commencement: 29 December 1986.
This section derived from the Insolvency Act 1985, ss 4, 11 (part).

393. Grant, refusal and withdrawal of authorisation

(1) The competent authority may, on an application duly made in accordance with section 392 and after being furnished with all such information as it may require under that section, grant or refuse the application.

(2) The authority shall grant the application if it appears to it from the information furnished by the applicant and having regard to such other information, if any, as it may have—

(*a*) that the applicant is a fit and proper person to act as an insolvency practitioner, and
(*b*) that the applicant meets the prescribed requirements with respect to education and practical training and experience.

(3) An authorisation granted under this section, if not previously withdrawn, continues in force for such period not exceeding the prescribed maximum as may be specified in the authorisation.

(4) An authorisation so granted may be withdrawn by the competent authority if it appears to it—

(*a*) that the holder of the authorisation is no longer a fit and proper person to act as an insolvency practitioner, or
(*b*) without prejudice to paragraph (*a*), that the holder—

(i) has failed to comply with any provision of this Part or of any regulations made under this Part or Part XV, or
(ii) in purported compliance with any such provision, has furnished the competent authority with false, inaccurate or misleading information.

(5) An authorisation granted under this section may be withdrawn by the competent authority at the request or with the consent of the holder of the authorisation. **[393]**

NOTES
Commencement: 29 December 1986.
This section derived from the Insolvency Act 1985, s 5.

394. Notices

(1) Where a competent authority grants an authorisation under section 393, it shall give written notice of that fact to the applicant, specifying the date on which the authorisation takes effect.

(2) Where the authority proposes to refuse an application, or to withdraw an authorisation under section 393(4), it shall give the applicant or holder of the authorisation written notice of its intention to do so, setting out particulars of the grounds on which it proposes to act.

(3) In the case of a proposed withdrawal the notice shall state the date on which it is proposed that the withdrawal should take effect.

(4) A notice under subsection (2) shall give particulars of the rights exercisable under the next two sections by a person on whom the notice is served. **[394]**

NOTES
Commencement: 29 December 1986.
This section derived from the Insolvency Act 1985, s 6.

395. Right to make representations

(1) A person on whom a notice is served under section 394(2) may within 14 days after the date of service make written representations to the competent authority.

(2) The competent authority shall have regard to any representations so made in determining whether to refuse the application or withdraw the authorisation, as the case may be. **[395]**

NOTES
Commencement: 29 December 1986.
This section derived from the Insolvency Act 1985, s 7.

396. Reference to Tribunal

(1) The Insolvency Practitioners Tribunal ("the Tribunal") continues in being; and the provisions of Schedule 7 apply to it.

(2) Where a person is served with a notice under section 394(2), he may—

    (*a*) at any time within 28 days after the date of service of the notice, or
    (*b*) at any time after the making by him of representations under section 395 and before the end of the period of 28 days after the date of the service on him of a notice by the competent authority that the authority does not propose to alter its decision in consequence of the representations,

give written notice to the authority requiring the case to be referred to the Tribunal.

(3) Where a requirement is made under subsection (2), then, unless the competent authority—

    (*a*) has decided or decides to grant the application or, as the case may be, not to withdraw the authorisation, and
    (*b*) within 7 days after the date of the making of the requirement, gives written notice of that decision to the person by whom the requirement was made,

it shall refer the case to the Tribunal.   **[396]**

NOTES
Commencement: 29 December 1986.
This section derived from the Insolvency Act 1985, ss 8(1), (2), (6), 11 (part).

397. Action of Tribunal on reference

(1) On a reference under section 396 the Tribunal shall—

    (*a*) investigate the case, and

    (*b*) make a report to the competent authority stating what would in their opinion be the appropriate decision in the matter and the reasons for that opinion,

and it is the duty of the competent authority to decide the matter accordingly.

    (2) The Tribunal shall send a copy of the report to the applicant or, as the case may be, the holder of the authorisation; and the competent authority shall serve him with a written notice of the decision made by it in accordance with the report.

    (3) The competent authority may, if he thinks fit, publish the report of the Tribunal.   **[397]**

NOTES
Commencement: 29 December 1986.
This section derived from the Insolvency Act 1985, s 8(3)–(5).

398. Refusal or withdrawal without reference to Tribunal

Where in the case of any proposed refusal or withdrawal of an authorisation either—

    (*a*) the period mentioned in section 396(2)(*a*) has expired without the making of any requirement under that subsection or of any representations under section 395, or

    (*b*) the competent authority has given a notice such as is mentioned in section 396(2)(*b*) and the period so mentioned has expired without the making of any such requirement,

the competent authority may give written notice of the refusal or withdrawal to the person concerned in accordance with the proposal in the notice given under section 394(2).   **[398]**

NOTES
Commencement: 29 December 1986.
This section derived from the Insolvency Act 1985, s 9.

PART XIV

PUBLIC ADMINISTRATION (ENGLAND AND WALES)

Official receivers

399. Appointment, etc of official receivers

(1) For the purposes of this Act the official receiver, in relation to any bankruptcy or winding up, is any person who by virtue of the following provisions of this section or section 401 below is authorised to act as the official receiver in relation to that bankruptcy or winding up.

(2) The Secretary of State may (subject to the approval of the Treasury as to numbers) appoint persons to the office of official receiver, and a person appointed to that office (whether under this section or section 70 of the Bankruptcy Act 1914)—

    (*a*) shall be paid out of money provided by Parliament such salary as the Secretary of State may with the concurrence of the Treasury direct,

    (*b*) shall hold office on such other terms and conditions as the Secretary of State may with the concurrence of the Treasury direct, and

    (*c*) may be removed from office by a direction of the Secretary of State.

(3) Where a person holds the office of official receiver, the Secretary of State shall from time to time attach him either to the High Court or to a county court having jurisdiction for the purposes of the second Group of Parts of this Act.

(4) Subject to any directions under subsection (6) below, an official receiver attached to a particular court is the person authorised to act as the official receiver in relation to every bankruptcy or winding up falling within the jurisdiction of that court.

(5) The Secretary of State shall ensure that there is, at all times, at least one official receiver attached to the High Court and at least one attached to each county court having jurisdiction for the purposes of the second Group of Parts; but he may attach the same official receiver to two or more different courts.

(6) The Secretary of State may give directions with respect to the disposal of the business of official receivers, and such directions may, in particular—

    (*a*) authorise an official receiver attached to one court to act as the official receiver in relation to any case or description of cases falling within the jurisdiction of another court;

    (*b*) provide, where there is more than one official receiver authorised to act as the official receiver in relation to cases falling within the jurisdiction of any court, for the distribution of their business between or among themselves.

(7) A person who at the coming into force of section 222 of the Insolvency Act 1985 (replaced by this section) is an official receiver attached to a court shall continue in office after the coming into force of that section as an official receiver attached to that court under this section. **[399]**

NOTES
    Commencement: 29 December 1986.
    This section derived from the Insolvency Act 1985, s 222.

---

400. Functions and status of official receivers

(1) In addition to any functions conferred on him by this Act, a person holding the office of official receiver shall carry out such other functions as may from time to time be conferred on him by the Secretary of State.

(2) In the exercise of the functions of his office a person holding the office of official receiver shall act under the general directions of the Secretary of State and shall also be an officer of the court in relation to which he exercises those functions.

(3) Any property vested in his official capacity in a person holding the office of official receiver shall, on his dying, ceasing to hold office or being otherwise

succeeded in relation to the bankruptcy or winding up in question by another
official receiver, vest in his successor without any conveyance, assignment or
transfer. **[400]**

NOTES
Commencement: 29 December 1986.
This section derived from the Insolvency Act 1985, s 223.

401. Deputy official receivers and staff

(1) The Secretary of State may, if he thinks it expedient to do so in order to
facilitate the disposal of the business of the official receiver attached to any
court, appoint an officer of his department to act as deputy to that official
receiver.

(2) Subject to any directions given by the Secretary of State under section
399 or 400, a person appointed to act as deputy to an official receiver has, on
such conditions and for such period as may be specified in the terms of his
appointment, the same status and functions as the official receiver to whom he
is appointed deputy.

Accordingly, references in this Act (except section 399(1) to (5)) to an official
receiver include a person appointed to act as his deputy.

(3) An appointment made under subsection (1) may be terminated at any
time by the Secretary of State.

(4) The Secretary of State may, subject to the approval of the Treasury as to
numbers and remuneration and as to the other terms and conditions of the
appointments, appoint officers of his department to assist official receivers in
the carrying out of their functions. **[401]**

NOTES
Commencement: 29 December 1986.
This section derived from the Insolvency Act 1985, s 224.

The Official Petitioner

402. Official Petitioner

(1) There continues to be an officer known as the Official Petitioner for the
purpose of discharging, in relation to cases in which a criminal bankruptcy
order is made, the functions assigned to him by or under this Act; and the
Director of Public Prosecutions continues, by virtue of his office, to be the
Official Petitioner.

(2) The functions of the Official Petitioner include the following—

   (*a*) to consider whether, in a case in which a criminal bankruptcy order
      is made, it is in the public interest that he should himself present a
      petition under section 264(1)(*d*) of this Act;

   (*b*) to present such a petition in any case where he determines that it is in
      the public interest for him to do so;

   (*c*) to make payments, in such cases as he may determine, towards
      expenses incurred by other persons in connection with proceedings in
      pursuance of such a petition; and

   (*d*) to exercise, so far as he considers it in the public interest to do so, any
      of the powers conferred on him by or under this Act.

(3) Any functions of the Official Petitioner may be discharged on his behalf by any person acting with his authority.

(4) Neither the Official Petitioner nor any person acting with his authority is liable to any action or proceeding in respect of anything done or omitted to be done in the discharge, or purported discharge, of the functions of the Official Petitioner.

(5) In this section "criminal bankruptcy order" means an order under section 39(1) of the Powers of Criminal Courts Act 1973. **[402]**

NOTES
Commencement: 29 December 1986.
This section derived from the Insolvency Act 1985, s 225.

Insolvency Service finance, accounting and investment

403. Insolvency Services Account

(1) All money received by the Secretary of State in respect of proceedings under this Act as it applies to England and Wales shall be paid into the Insolvency Services Account kept by the Secretary of State with the Bank of England; and all payments out of money standing to the credit of the Secretary of State in that account shall be made by the Bank of England in such manner as he may direct.

(2) Whenever the cash balance standing to the credit of the Insolvency Services Account is in excess of the amount which in the opinion of the Secretary of State is required for the time being to answer demands in respect of bankrupts' estates or companies' estates, the Secretary of State shall—

(a) notify the excess to the National Debt Commissioners, and
(b) pay into the Insolvency Services Investment Account ("the Investment Account") kept by the Commissioners with the Bank of England the whole or any part of the excess as the Commissioners may require for investment in accordance with the following provisions of this Part.

(3) Whenever any part of the money so invested is, in the opinion of the Secretary of State, required to answer any demand in respect of bankrupt's estates or companies' estates, he shall notify to the National Debt Commissioners the amount so required and the Commissioners—

(a) shall thereupon repay to the Secretary of State such sum as may be required to the credit of the Insolvency Services Account, and
(b) for that purpose may direct the sale of such part of the securities in which the money has been invested as may be necessary. **[403]**

NOTES
Commencement: 29 December 1986.
This section derived from the Insolvency Services (Accounting and Investment) Act 1970, s 1, the Insolvency Act 1976, s 3, and the Insolvency Act 1985, Sch 8, para 28.

404. Investment Account

Any money standing to the credit of the Investment Account (including any money received by the National Debt Commissioners by way of interest on or proceeds of any investment under this section) may be invested by the Commissioners, in accordance with such directions as may be given by the Treasury, in any manner for the time being specified in Part II of Schedule 1 to the Trustee Investments Act 1961. **[404]**

NOTES
Commencement: 29 December 1986.
This section derived from the Insolvency Services (Accounting and Investment) Act 1970, s 2.

405. Application of income in Investment Account; adjustment of balances

(1) Where the annual account to be kept by the National Debt Commissioners under section 409 below shows that in the year for which it is made up the gross amount of the interest accrued from the securities standing to the credit of the Investment Account exceeded the aggregate of—

> (a) a sum, to be determined by the Treasury, to provide against the depreciation in the value of the securities, and
>
> (b) the sums paid into the Insolvency Services Account in pursuance of the next section together with the sums paid in pursuance of that section to the Commissioners of Inland Revenue,

the National Debt Commissioners shall, within 3 months after the account is laid before Parliament, cause the amount of the excess to be paid out of the Investment Account into the Consolidated Fund in such manner as may from time to time be agreed between the Treasury and the Commissioners.

(2) Where the said annual account shows that in the year for which it is made up the gross amount of interest accrued from the securities standing to the credit of the Investment Account was less than the aggregate mentioned in subsection (1), an amount equal to the deficiency shall, at such times as the Treasury direct, be paid out of the Consolidated Fund into the Investment Account.

(3) If the Investment Account is insufficient to meet its liabilities the Treasury may, on being informed of the insufficiency by the National Debt Commissioners, issue the amount of the deficiency out of the Consolidated Fund and the Treasury shall certify the deficiency to Parliament.   **[405]**

NOTES
Commencement: 29 December 1986.
This section derived from the Insolvency Services (Accounting and Investment) Act 1970, s 3, and the Insolvency Act 1976, Sch 2, para 5.

406. Interest on money received by liquidators and invested

Where under rules made by virtue of paragraph 16 of Schedule 8 to this Act (investment of money received by company liquidators) a company has become entitled to any sum by way of interest, the Secretary of State shall certify that sum and the amount of tax payable on it to the National Debt Commissioners; and the Commissioners shall pay, out of the Investment Account—

> (a) into the Insolvency Services Account, the sum so certified less the amount of tax so certified, and
>
> (b) to the Commissioners of Inland Revenue, the amount of tax so certified.   **[406]**

NOTES
Commencement: 29 December 1986.
This section derived from the Insolvency Services (Accounting and Investment) Act 1970, s 4, the Insolvency Act 1976, Sch 2, para 6, and the Insolvency Act 1985, Sch 8, para 17.

407. Unclaimed dividends and undistributed balances

(1) The Secretary of State shall from time to time pay into the Consolidated Fund out of the Insolvency Services Account so much of the sums standing to the credit of that Account as represents—

    (*a*) dividends which were declared before such date as the Treasury may from time to time determine and have not been claimed, and

    (*b*) balances ascertained before that date which are too small to be divided among the persons entitled to them.

(2) For the purposes of this section the sums standing to the credit of the Insolvency Services Account are deemed to include any sums paid out of that Account and represented by any sums or securities standing to the credit of the Investment Account.

(3) The Secretary of State may require the National Debt Commissioners to pay out of the Investment Account into the Insolvency Services Account the whole or part of any sum which he is required to pay out of that account under subsection (1); and the Commissioners may direct the sale of such securities standing to the credit of the Investment Account as may be necessary for that purpose.   **[407]**

NOTES
Commencement: 29 December 1986.
This section derived from the Insolvency Services (Accounting and Investment) Act 1970, s 5, and the Insolvency Act 1976, Sch 2, para 7.

408. Recourse to Consolidated Fund

If, after any repayment due to it from the Investment Account, the Insolvency Services Account is insufficient to meet its liabilities, the Treasury may, on being informed of it by the Secretary of State, issue the amount of the deficiency out of the Consolidated Fund, and the Treasury shall certify the deficiency to Parliament.   **[408]**

NOTES
Commencement: 29 December 1986.
This section derived from the Insolvency Services (Accounting and Investment) Act 1970, s 6, and the Insolvency Act 1976, Sch 2, para 8.

409. Annual financial statement and audit

(1) The National Debt Commissioners shall for each year ending on 31st March prepare a statement of the sums credited and debited to the Investment Account in such form and manner as the Treasury may direct and shall transmit it to the Comptroller and Auditor General before the end of November next following the year.

(2) The Secretary of State shall for each year ending 31st March prepare a statement of the sums received or paid by him under section 403 above in such form and manner as the Treasury may direct and shall transmit each statement to the Comptroller and Auditor General before the end of November next following the year.

(3) Every such statement shall include such additional information as the Treasury may direct.

(4) The Comptroller and Auditor General shall examine, certify and report on every such statement and shall lay copies of it, and of his report, before Parliament.   **[409]**

NOTES
Commencement: 29 December 1986.
This section derived from the Insolvency Services (Accounting and Investment) Act 1970, s 7, and the Insolvency Act 1976, Sch 2, para 9.

Supplementary

410. Extent of this Part

This Part of this Act extends to England and Wales only. **[410]**

NOTES
Commencement: 29 December 1986.
This section derived from the Insolvency Services (Accounting and Investment) Act 1970, s 9(3), the Insolvency Act 1976, s 14(6), and the Insolvency Act 1985, s 236(3)(i).

PART XV

SUBORDINATE LEGISLATION

General insolvency rules

411. Company insolvency rules

(1) Rules may be made—

> (*a*) in relation to England and Wales, by the Lord Chancellor with the concurrence of the Secretary of State, or
>
> (*b*) in relation to Scotland, by the Secretary of State,

for the purpose of giving effect to Parts I to VII of this Act.

(2) Without prejudice to the generality of subsection (1), or to any provision of those Parts by virtue of which rules under this section may be made with respect to any matter, rules under this section may contain—

> (*a*) any such provision as is specified in Schedule 8 to this Act or corresponds to provision contained immediately before the coming into force of section 106 of the Insolvency Act 1985 in rules made, or having effect as if made, under section 663(1) or (2) of the Companies Act (old winding-up rules), and
>
> (*b*) such incidental, supplemental and transitional provisions as may appear to the Lord Chancellor or, as the case may be, the Secretary of State necessary or expedient.

(3) In Schedule 8 to this Act "liquidator" includes a provisional liquidator; and references above in this section to Parts I to VII of this Act are to be read as including the Companies Act so far as relating to, and to matters connected with or arising out of, the insolvency or winding up of companies.

(4) Rules under this section shall be made by statutory instrument subject to annulment in pursuance of a resolution of either House of Parliament.

(5) Regulations made by the Secretary of State under a power conferred by rules under this section shall be made by statutory instrument and, after being made, shall be laid before each House of Parliament.

(6) Nothing in this section prejudices any power to make rules of court.

[411]

NOTES
Commencement: 29 December 1986.
This section derived from the Insolvency Act 1985, s 106.

412. Individual insolvency rules (England and Wales)

(1) The Lord Chancellor may, with the concurrence of the Secretary of State, make rules for the purpose of giving effect to Parts VIII to XI of this Act.

(2) Without prejudice to the generality of subsection (1), or to any provision of those Parts by virtue of which rules under this section may be made with respect to any matter, rules under this section may contain—

    (*a*) any such provision as is specified in Schedule 9 to this Act or corresponds to provision contained immediately before the appointed day in rules made under section 132 of the Bankruptcy Act 1914; and

    (*b*) such incidental, supplemental and transitional provisions as may appear to the Lord Chancellor necessary or expedient.

(3) Rules under this section shall be made by statutory instrument subject to annulment in pursuance of a resolution of either House of Parliament.

(4) Regulations made by the Secretary of State under a power conferred by rules under this section shall be made by statutory instrument and, after being made, shall be laid before each House of Parliament.

(5) Nothing in this section prejudices any power to make rules of court.

[412]

NOTES
    Commencement: 29 December 1986.
    This section derived from the Insolvency Act 1985, s 207.

413. Insolvency Rules Committee

(1) The committee established under section 10 of the Insolvency Act 1976 (advisory committee on bankruptcy and winding-up rules) continues to exist for the purpose of being consulted under this section.

(2) The Lord Chancellor shall consult the committee before making any rules under section 411 or 412.

(3) Subject to the next subsection, the committee shall consist of—

    (*a*) a judge of the High Court attached to the Chancery Division;
    (*b*) a circuit judge;
    (*c*) a registrar in bankruptcy of the High Court;
    (*d*) the registrar of a county court;
    (*e*) a practising barrister;
    (*f*) a practising solicitor; and
    (*g*) a practising accountant;

and the appointment of any person as a member of the committee shall be made by the Lord Chancellor.

(4) The Lord Chancellor may appoint as additional members of the committee any persons appearing to him to have qualifications or experience that would be of value to the committee in considering any matter with which it is concerned.

[413]

NOTES
    Commencement: 29 December 1986.
    This section derived from the Insolvency Act 1985, s 226.

Fees orders

414. Fees orders (company insolvency proceedings)

(1) There shall be paid in respect of—

    (*a*) proceedings under any of Parts I to VII of this Act, and

    (*b*) the performance by the official receiver or the Secretary of State of functions under those Parts,

such fees as the competent authority may with the sanction of the Treasury by order direct.

(2) That authority is—

    (*a*) in relation to England and Wales, the Lord Chancellor, and

    (*b*) (*applies to Scotland only*).

(3) The Treasury may by order direct by whom and in what manner the fees are to be collected and accounted for.

(4) The Lord Chancellor may, with the sanction of the Treasury, by order provide for sums to be deposited, by such persons, in such manner and in such circumstances as may be specified in the order, by way of security for fees payable by virtue of this section.

(5) An order under this section may contain such incidental, supplemental and transitional provisions as may appear to the Lord Chancellor, the Secretary of State or (as the case may be) the Treasury necessary or expedient.

(6) An order under this section shall be made by statutory instrument and, after being made, shall be laid before each House of Parliament.

(7) Fees payable by virtue of this section shall be paid into the Consolidated Fund.

(8) References in subsection (1) to Parts I to VII of this Act are to be read as including the Companies Act so far as relating to, and to matters connected with or arising out of, the insolvency or winding up of companies.

(9) Nothing in this section prejudices any power to make rules of court; and the application of this section to Scotland is without prejudice to section 2 of the Courts of Law Fees (Scotland) Act 1895. **[414]**

NOTES
Commencement: 29 December 1986.
This section derived from the Insolvency Act 1985, ss 106(5), 107.

415. Fees orders (individual insolvency proceedings in England and Wales)

(1) There shall be paid in respect of—

    (*a*) proceedings under Parts VIII to XI of this Act, and

    (*b*) the performance by the official receiver or the Secretary of State of functions under those Parts,

such fees as the Lord Chancellor may with the sanction of the Treasury by order direct.

(2) The Treasury may by order direct by whom and in what manner the fees are to be collected and accounted for.

(3) The Lord Chancellor may, with the sanction of the Treasury, by order

provide for sums to be deposited, by such persons, in such manner and in such circumstances as may be specified in the order, by way of security for—

(a) fees payable by virtue of this section, and

(b) fees payable to any person who has prepared an insolvency practitioner's report under section 274 in Chapter I of Part IX.

(4) An order under this section may contain such incidental, supplemental and transitional provisions as appear to the Lord Chancellor or, as the case may be, the Treasury, necessary or expedient.

(5) An order under this section shall be made by statutory instrument and, after being made, shall be laid before each House of Parliament.

(6) Fees payable by virtue of this section shall be paid into the Consolidated Fund.

(7) Nothing in this section prejudices any power to make rules of court.

[415]

NOTES
Commencement: 29 December 1986.
This section derived from the Insolvency Act 1985, ss 207(5), 208(1)–(3), (5).

*Specification, increase and reduction of money sums relevant
in the operation of this Act*

416. Monetary limits (companies winding up)

(1) The Secretary of State may by order in a statutory instrument increase or reduce any of the money sums for the time being specified in the following provisions in the first Group of Parts—

section 117(2) (amount of company's share capital determining whether county court has jurisdiction to wind it up);

section 120(3) (the equivalent as respects sheriff court jurisdiction in Scotland);

section 123(1)(a) (minimum debt for service of demand on company by unpaid creditor);

section 184(3) (minimum value of judgment, affecting sheriff's duties on levying execution);

section 206(1)(a) and (b) (minimum value of company property concealed or fraudulently removed, affecting criminal liability of company's officer).

(2) An order under this section may contain such transitional provisions as may appear to the Secretary of State necessary or expedient.

(3) No order under this section increasing or reducing any of the money sums for the time being specified in section 117(2), 120(3) or 123(1)(a) shall be made unless a draft of the order has been laid before and approved by a resolution of each House of Parliament.

(4) A statutory instrument containing an order under this section, other than an order to which subsection (3) applies, is subject to annulment in pursuance of a resolution of either House of Parliament. **[416]**

NOTES
Commencement: 29 December 1986.
This section derived from the Companies Act 1985, s 664, and the Insolvency Act 1985, Sch 6, para 49.

417. Money sum in s 222

The Secretary of State may by regulations in a statutory instrument increase or reduce the money sum for the time being specified in section 222(1) (minimum debt for service of demand on unregistered company by unpaid creditor); but such regulations shall not be made unless a draft of the statutory instrument containing them has been approved by resolution of each House of Parliament.

[417]

NOTES
Commencement: 29 December 1986.
This section derived from the Companies Act 1985, s 667(2) (part).

418. Monetary limits (bankruptcy)

(1) The Secretary of State may by order prescribe amounts for the purposes of the following provisions in the second Group of Parts—

section 273 (minimum value of debtor's estate determining whether immediate bankruptcy order should be made; small bankruptcies level);

section 346(3) (minimum amount of judgment, determining whether amount recovered on sale of debtor's goods is to be treated as part of his estate in bankruptcy);

section 354(1) and (2) (minimum amount of concealed debt, or value of property concealed or removed, determining criminal liability under the section);

section 358 (minimum value of property taken by a bankrupt out of England and Wales, determining his criminal liability);

section 360(1) (maximum amount of credit which bankrupt may obtain without disclosure of his status);

section 361(2) (exemption of bankrupt from criminal liability for failure to keep proper accounts, if unsecured debts not more than the prescribed minimum);

section 364(2)(*d*) (minimum value of goods removed by the bankrupt, determining his liability to arrest);

and references in the second Group of Parts to the amount prescribed for the purposes of any of those provisions, and references in those provisions to the prescribed amount, are to be construed accordingly.

(2) An order under this section may contain such transitional provisions as may appear to the Secretary of State necessary or expedient.

(3) An order under this section shall be made by statutory instrument subject to annulment in pursuance of a resolution of either House of Parliament.   [418]

NOTES
Commencement: 29 December 1986.
This section derived from the Insolvency Act 1985, s 209(1) (part), (2), (3).

Insolvency practice

419. Regulations for purposes of Part XIII

(1) The Secretary of State may make regulations for the purpose of giving effect to Part XIII of this Act; and "prescribed" in that Part means prescribed by regulations made by the Secretary of State.

(2) Without prejudice to the generality of subsection (1) or to any provision

of that Part by virtue of which regulations may be made with respect to any matter, regulations under this section may contain—

> (*a*) provision as to the matters to be taken into account in determining whether a person is a fit and proper person to act as an insolvency practitioner;
>
> (*b*) provision prohibiting a person from so acting in prescribed cases, being cases in which a conflict of interest will or may arise;
>
> (*c*) provision imposing requirements with respect to—
>
>> (i) the preparation and keeping by a person who acts as an insolvency practitioner of prescribed books, accounts and other records, and
>>
>> (ii) the production of those books, accounts and records to prescribed persons;
>
> (*d*) provision conferring power on prescribed persons—
>
>> (i) to require any person who acts or has acted as an insolvency practitioner to answer any inquiry in relation to a case in which he is so acting or has so acted, and
>>
>> (ii) to apply to a court to examine such a person or any other person on oath concerning such a case;
>
> (*e*) provision making non-compliance with any of the regulations a criminal offence; and
>
> (*f*) such incidental, supplemental and transitional provisions as may appear to the Secretary of State necessary or expedient.

(3) Any power conferred by Part XIII or this Part to make regulations, rules or orders is exercisable by statutory instrument subject to annulment by resolution of either House of Parliament.

(4) Any rule or regulation under Part XIII or this Part may make different provision with respect to different cases or descriptions of cases, including different provision for different areas. **[419]**

NOTES
Commencement: 29 December 1986.
This section derived from the Insolvency Act 1985, ss 10, 11 (part).

Other order-making powers

420. Insolvent partnerships

(1) The Lord Chancellor may, by order made with the concurrence of the Secretary of State, provide that such provisions of this Act as may be specified in the order shall apply in relation to insolvent partnerships with such modifications as may be so specified.

(2) An order under this section may make different provision for different cases and may contain such incidental, supplemental and transitional provisions as may appear to the Lord Chancellor necessary or expedient.

(3) An order under this section shall be made by statutory instrument subject to annulment in pursuance of a resolution of either House of Parliament. **[420]**

NOTES
Commencement: 29 December 1986.
This section derived from the Insolvency Act 1985, s 227.

421. Insolvent estates of deceased persons

(1) The Lord Chancellor may, by order made with the concurrence of the Secretary of State, provide that such provisions of this Act as may be specified in the order shall apply to the administration of the insolvent estates of deceased persons with such modifications as may be so specified.

(2) An order under this section may make different provision for different cases and may contain such incidental, supplemental and transitional provisions as may appear to the Lord Chancellor necessary or expedient.

(3) An order under this section shall be made by statutory instrument subject to annulment in pursuance of a resolution of either House of Parliament.

(4) For the purposes of this section the estate of a deceased person is insolvent if, when realised, it will be insufficient to meet in full all the debts and other liabilities to which it is subject. **[421]**

NOTES
Commencement: 29 December 1986.
This section derived from the Insolvency Act 1985, s 228.

422. Recognised banks, etc

(1) The Secretary of State may, by order made with the concurrence of the Treasury and after consultation with the Bank of England, provide that such provisions in the first Group of Parts as may be specified in the order shall apply in relation to—

> (a) recognised banks and licensed institutions within the meaning of the Banking Act 1979, and
> (b) institutions to which sections 16 and 18 of that Act apply as if they were licensed institutions,

with such modifications as may be so specified.

(2) An order under this section may make different provision for different cases and may contain such incidental, supplemental and transitional provisions as may appear to the Secretary of State necessary or expedient.

(3) An order under this section shall be made by statutory instrument subject to annulment in pursuance of a resolution of either House of Parliament. **[422]**

NOTES
Commencement: 29 December 1986.
This section derived from the Insolvency Act 1985, s 229.

PART XVI

PROVISIONS AGAINST DEBT AVOIDANCE (ENGLAND AND WALES ONLY)

423. Transactions defrauding creditors

(1) This section relates to transactions entered into at an undervalue; and a person enters into such a transaction with another person if—

> (a) he makes a gift to the other person or he otherwise enters into a transaction with the other on terms that provide for him to receive no consideration;

(*b*) he enters into a transaction with the other in consideration of marriage; or

(*c*) he enters into a transaction with the other for a consideration the value of which, in money or money's worth, is significantly less than the value, in money or money's worth, of the consideration provided by himself.

(2) Where a person has entered into such a transaction, the court may, if satisfied under the next subsection, make such order as it thinks fit for—

(*a*) restoring the position to what it would have been if the transaction had not been entered into, and

(*b*) protecting the interests of persons who are victims of the transaction.

(3) In the case of a person entering into such a transaction, an order shall only be made if the court is satisfied that it was entered into by him for the purpose—

(*a*) of putting assets beyond the reach of a person who is making, or may at some time make, a claim against him, or

(*b*) of otherwise prejudicing the interests of such a person in relation to the claim which he is making or may make.

(4) In this section "the court" means the High Court or—

(*a*) if the person entering into the transaction is an individual, any other court which would have jurisdiction in relation to a bankruptcy petition relating to him;

(*b*) if that person is a body capable of being wound up under Part IV or V of this Act, any other court having jurisdiction to wind it up.

(5) In relation to a transaction at an undervalue, references here and below to a victim of the transaction are to a person who is, or is capable of being, prejudiced by it; and in the following two sections the person entering into the transaction is referred to as "the debtor". [423]

NOTES
Commencement: 29 December 1986.
This section derived from the Insolvency Act 1985, s 212(1), (3), (7) (part).

424. Those who may apply for an order under s 423

(1) An application for an order under section 423 shall not be made in relation to a transaction except—

(*a*) in a case where the debtor has been adjudged bankrupt or is a body corporate which is being wound up or in relation to which an administration order is in force, by the official receiver, by the trustee of the bankrupt's estate or the liquidator or administrator of the body corporate or (with the leave of the court) by a victim of the transaction;

(*b*) in a case where a victim of the transaction is bound by a voluntary arrangement approved under Part I or Part VIII of this Act, by the supervisor of the voluntary arrangement or by any person who (whether or not so bound) is such a victim; or

(*c*) in any other case, by a victim of the transaction.

(2) An application made under any of the paragraphs of subsection (1) is to be treated as made on behalf of every victim of the transaction. [424]

NOTES
Commencement: 29 December 1986.
This section derived from the Insolvency Act 1985, s 212(2).

425. Provision which may be made by order under s 423

(1) Without prejudice to the generality of section 423, an order made under that section with respect to a transaction may (subject as follows)—

    (*a*) require any property transferred as part of the transaction to be vested in any person, either absolutely or for the benefit of all the persons on whose behalf the application for the order is treated as made;

    (*b*) require any property to be so vested if it represents, in any person's hands, the application either of the proceeds of sale of property so transferred or of money so transferred;

    (*c*) release or discharge (in whole or in part) any security given by the debtor;

    (*d*) require any person to pay to any other person in respect of benefits received from the debtor such sums as the court may direct;

    (*e*) provide for any surety or guarantor whose obligations to any person were released or discharged (in whole or in part) under the transaction to be under such new or revived obligations as the court thinks appropriate;

    (*f*) provide for security to be provided for the discharge of any obligation imposed by or arising under the order, for such an obligation to be charged on any property and for such security or charge to have the same priority as a security or charge released or discharged (in whole or in part) under the transaction.

(2) An order under section 423 may affect the property of, or impose any obligation on, any person whether or not he is the person with whom the debtor entered into the transaction; but such an order—

    (*a*) shall not prejudice any interest in property which was acquired from a person other than the debtor and was acquired in good faith, for value and without notice of the relevant circumstances, or prejudice any interest deriving from such an interest, and

    (*b*) shall not require a person who received a benefit from the transaction in good faith, for value and without notice of the relevant circumstances to pay any sum unless he was a party to the transaction.

(3) For the purposes of this section the relevant circumstances in relation to a transaction are the circumstances by virtue of which an order under section 423 may be made in respect of the transaction.

(4) In this section "security" means any mortgage, charge, lien or other security. **[425]**

NOTES
Commencement: 29 December 1986.
This section derived from the Insolvency Act 1985, s 212(4)–(6), (7) (part).

PART XVII

MISCELLANEOUS AND GENERAL

426. Co-operation between courts exercising jurisdiction in relation to insolvency

(1) An order made by a court in any part of the United Kingdom in the exercise of jurisdiction in relation to insolvency law shall be enforced in any other part

of the United Kingdom as if it were made by a court exercising the corresponding jurisdiction in that other part.

(2) However, without prejudice to the following provisions of this section, nothing in subsection (1) requires a court in any part of the United Kingdom to enforce, in relation to property situated in that part, any order made by a court in any other part of the United Kingdom.

(3) The Secretary of State, with the concurrence in relation to property situated in England and Wales of the Lord Chancellor, may by order make provision for securing that a trustee or assignee under the insolvency law of any part of the United Kingdom has, with such modifications as may be specified in the order, the same rights in relation to any property situated in another part of the United Kingdom as he would have in the corresponding circumstances if he were a trustee or assignee under the insolvency law of that other part.

(4) The courts having jurisdiction in relation to insolvency law in any part of the United Kingdom shall assist the courts having the corresponding jurisdiction in any other part of the United Kingdom or any relevant country or territory.

(5) For the purposes of subsection (4) a request made to a court in any part of the United Kingdom by a court in any other part of the United Kingdom or in a relevant country or territory is authority for the court to which the request is made to apply, in relation to any matters specified in the request, the insolvency law which is applicable by either court in relation to comparable matters falling within its jurisdiction.

In exercising its discretion under this subsection, a court shall have regard in particular to the rules of private international law.

(6) Where a person who is a trustee or assignee under the insolvency law of any part of the United Kingdom claims property situated in any other part of the United Kingdom (whether by virtue of an order under subsection (3) or otherwise), the submission of that claim to the court exercising jurisdiction in relation to insolvency law in that other part shall be treated in the same manner as a request made by a court for the purpose of subsection (4).

(7) Section 38 of the Criminal Law Act 1977 (execution of warrant of arrest throughout the United Kingdom) applies to a warrant which, in exercise of any jurisdiction in relation to insolvency law, is issued in any part of the United Kingdom for the arrest of a person as it applies to a warrant issued in that part of the United Kingdom for the arrest of a person charged with an offence.

(8) Without prejudice to any power to make rules of court, any power to make provision by subordinate legislation for the purpose of giving effect in relation to companies or individuals to the insolvency law of any part of the United Kingdom includes power to make provisions for the purpose of giving effect in that part to any provision made by or under the preceding provisions of this section.

(9) An order under subsection (3) shall be made by statutory instrument subject to annulment in pursuance of a resolution of either House of Parliament.

(10) In this section "insolvency law" means—

(*a*) in relation to England and Wales, provision made by or under this Act or sections 6 to 10, 12, 19(*c*) and 20 (with Schedule 1) of the

Company Directors Disqualification Act 1986 and extending to England and Wales;

(b) in relation to Scotland, provision extending to Scotland and made by or under this Act, sections 6 to 10, 12, 15, 19(c) and 20 (with Schedule 1) of the Company Directors Disqualification Act 1986, Part XVIII of the Companies Act or the Bankruptcy (Scotland) Act 1985;

(c) in relation to Northern Ireland, provision made by or under the Bankruptcy Acts (Northern Ireland) 1857 to 1980, Part V, VI or IX of the Companies Act (Northern Ireland) 1960 or Part IV of the Companies (Northern Ireland) Order 1978;

(d) in relation to any relevant country or territory, so much of the law of that country or territory as corresponds to provisions falling within any of the foregoing paragraphs;

and references in this subsection to any enactment include, in relation to any time before the coming into force of that enactment the corresponding enactment in force at that time.

(11) In this section "relevant country or territory" means—

(a) any of the Channel Islands or the Isle of Man, or

(b) any country or territory designated for the purposes of this section by the Secretary of State by order made by statutory instrument.   **[426]**

NOTES
Commencement: 29 December 1986.
This section derived from the Insolvency Act 1985, s 213.

427. Parliamentary disqualification

(1) Where a court in England and Wales or Northern Ireland adjudges an individual bankrupt or a court in Scotland awards sequestration of an individual's estate, the individual is disqualified—

(a) for sitting or voting in the House of Lords,

(b) for being elected to, or sitting or voting in, the House of Commons, and

(c) for sitting or voting in a committee of either House.

(2) Where an individual is disqualified under this section, the disqualification ceases—

(a) except where the adjudication is annulled or the award recalled or reduced without the individual having been first discharged, on the discharge of the individual, and

(b) in the excepted case, on the annulment, recall or reduction, as the case may be.

(3) No writ of summons shall be issued to any lord of Parliament who is for the time being disqualified under this section for sitting and voting in the House of Lords.

(4) Where a member of the House of Commons who is disqualified under this section continues to be so disqualified until the end of the period of 6 months beginning with the day of the adjudication or award, his seat shall be vacated at the end of that period.

(5) A court which makes an adjudication or award such as is mentioned in subsection (1) in relation to any lord of Parliament or member of the House of Commons shall forthwith certify the adjudication or award to the Speaker of

the House of Lords or, as the case may be, to the Speaker of the House of Commons.

(6) Where a court has certified an adjudication or award to the Speaker of the House of Commons under subsection (5), then immediately after it becomes apparent which of the following certificates is applicable, the court shall certify to the Speaker of the House of Commons—

(a) that the period of 6 months beginning with the day of the adjudication or award has expired without the adjudication or award having been annulled, recalled or reduced, or

(b) that the adjudication or award has been annulled, recalled or reduced before the end of that period.

(7) Subject to the preceding provisions of this section, so much of this Act and any other enactment (whenever passed) and of any subordinate legislation (whenever made) as—

(a) makes provision for or in connection with bankruptcy in one or more parts of the United Kingdom, or

(b) makes provision conferring a power of arrest in connection with the winding up or insolvency of companies in one or more parts of the United Kingdom,

applies in relation to persons having privilege of Parliament or peerage as it applies in relation to persons not having such privilege.   **[427]**

NOTES
Commencement: 29 December 1986.
This section derived from the Insolvency Act 1985, s 214.

428. Exemptions from Restrictive Trade Practices Act

(1) No restriction in respect of any of the matters specified in the next subsection shall, on or after the appointed day, be regarded as a restriction by virtue of which the Restrictive Trade Practices Act 1976 applies to any agreement (whenever made).

(2) Those matters are—

(a) the charges to be made, quoted or paid for insolvency services supplied, offered or obtained;

(b) the terms or conditions on or subject to which insolvency services are to be supplied or obtained;

(c) the extent (if any) to which, or the scale (if any) on which, insolvency services are to be made available, supplied or obtained;

(d) the form or manner in which insolvency services are to be made available, supplied or obtained;

(e) the persons or classes of persons for whom or from whom, or the areas or places in or from which, insolvency services are to be made available or supplied or are to be obtained.

(3) In this section "insolvency services" means the services of persons acting as insolvency practitioners or carrying out under the law of Northern Ireland functions corresponding to those mentioned in section 388(1) or (2) in Part XIII, in their capacity as such; and expressions which are also used in the Act of 1976 have the same meaning here as in that Act.   **[428]**

NOTES
Commencement: 29 December 1986.
This section derived from the Insolvency Act 1985, s 217(1)–(3).

429. Disabilities on revocation of administration order against an individual

(1) The following applies where a person fails to make any payment which he is required to make by virtue of an administration order under Part VI of the County Courts Act 1984.

(2) The court which is administering that person's estate under the order may, if it thinks fit—

(a) revoke the administration order, and

(b) make an order directing that this section and section 12 of the Company Directors Disqualification Act 1986 shall apply to the person for such period, not exceeding 2 years, as may be specified in the order.

(3) A person to whom this section so applies shall not—

(a) either alone or jointly with another person, obtain credit to the extent of the amount prescribed for the purposes of section 360(1)(a) or more, or

(b) enter into any transaction in the course of or for the purposes of any business in which he is directly or indirectly engaged,

without disclosing to the person from whom he obtains the credit, or (as the case may be) with whom the transaction is entered into, the fact that this section applies to him.

(4) The reference in subsection (3) to a person obtaining credit includes—

(a) a case where goods are bailed or hired to him under a hire-purchase agreement or agreed to be sold to him under a conditional sale agreement, and

(b) a case where he is paid in advance (whether in money or otherwise) for the supply of goods or services.

(5) A person who contravenes this section is guilty of an offence and liable to imprisonment or a fine, or both. **[429]**

NOTES
Commencement: 29 December 1986.
This section derived from the Insolvency Act 1985, s 221(1), (3)–(5).

430. Provision introducing Schedule of punishments

(1) Schedule 10 to this Act has effect with respect to the way in which offences under this Act are punishable on conviction.

(2) In relation to an offence under a provision of this Act specified in the first column of the Schedule (the general nature of the offence being described in the second column), the third column shows whether the offence is punishable on conviction on indictment, or on summary conviction, or either in the one way or the other.

(3) The fourth column of the Schedule shows, in relation to an offence, the maximum punishment by way of fine or imprisonment under this Act which may be imposed on a person convicted of the offence in the way specified in relation to it in the third column (that is to say, on indictment or summarily), a reference to a period of years or months being to a term of imprisonment of that duration.

(4) The fifth column shows (in relation to an offence for which there is an entry in that column) that a person convicted of the offence after continued

contravention is liable to a daily default fine; that is to say, he is liable on a second or subsequent conviction of the offence to the fine specified in that column for each day on which the contravention is continued (instead of the penalty specified for the offence in the fourth column of the Schedule).

(5) For the purpose of any enactment in this Act whereby an officer of a company who is in default is liable to a fine or penalty, the expression "officer who is in default" means any officer of the company who knowingly and wilfully authorises or permits the default, refusal or contravention mentioned in the enactment.   **[430]**

NOTES
     Commencement: 29 December 1986.
     This section derived from the Companies Act 1985, s 730, and the Insolvency Act 1985 passim.

431. Summary proceedings

(1) Summary proceedings for any offence under any of Parts I to VII of this Act may (without prejudice to any jurisdiction exercisable apart from this subsection) be taken against a body corporate at any place at which the body has a place of business, and against any other person at any place at which he is for the time being.

(2) Notwithstanding anything in section 127(1) of the Magistrates' Courts Act 1980, an information relating to such an offence which is triable by a magistrates' court in England and Wales may be so tried if it is laid at any time within 3 years after the commission of the offence and within 12 months after the date on which evidence sufficient in the opinion of the Director of Public Prosecutions or the Secretary of State (as the case may be) to justify the proceedings comes to his knowledge.

(3) Summary proceedings in Scotland for such an offence shall not be commenced after the expiration of 3 years from the commission of the offence.

Subject to this (and notwithstanding anything in section 331 of the Criminal Procedure (Scotland) Act 1975), such proceedings may (in Scotland) be commenced at any time within 12 months after the date on which evidence in the Lord Advocate's opinion to justify the proceedings came to his knowledge or, where such evidence was reported to him by the Secretary of State, within 12 months after the date on which it came to the knowledge of the latter; and subsection (3) of that section applies for the purpose of this subsection as it applies for the purpose of that section.

(4) For purposes of this section, a certificate of the Director of Public Prosecutions, the Lord Advocate or the Secretary of State (as the case may be) as to the date on which such evidence as is referred to above came to his knowledge is conclusive evidence.   **[431]**

NOTES
     Commencement: 29 December 1986.
     This section derived from the Companies Act 1985, s 731, and the Insolvency Act 1985, s 108(1).

432. Offences by bodies corporate

(1) This section applies to offences under this Act other than those excepted by subsection (4).

(2) Where a body corporate is guilty of an offence to which this section applies and the offence is proved to have been committed with the consent or

connivance of, or to be attributable to any neglect on the part of, any director, manager, secretary or other similar officer of the body corporate or any person who was purporting to act in any such capacity he, as well as the body corporate, is guilty of the offence and liable to be proceeded against and punished accordingly.

(3) Where the affairs of a body corporate are managed by its members, subsection (2) applies in relation to the acts and defaults of a member in connection with his functions of management as if he were a director of the body corporate.

(4) The offences excepted from this section are those under sections 30, 39, 51, 53, 54, 62, 64, 66, 85, 89, 164, 188, 201, 206, 207, 208, 209, 210 and 211. **[432]**

NOTES
Commencement: 29 December 1986.
This section derived from the Insolvency Act 1985, s 230.

433. Admissibility in evidence of statements of affairs, etc

In any proceedings (whether or not under this Act)—

(*a*) a statement of affairs prepared for the purposes of any provision of this Act which is derived from the Insolvency Act 1985, and
(*b*) any other statement made in pursuance of a requirement imposed by or under any such provision or by or under rules made under this Act,

may be used in evidence against any person making or concurring in making the statement. **[433]**

NOTES
Commencement: 29 December 1986.
This section derived from the Insolvency Act 1985, s 231.

434. Crown application

For the avoidance of doubt it is hereby declared that provisions of this Act which derive from the Insolvency Act 1985 bind the Crown so far as affecting or relating to the following matters, namely—

(*a*) remedies against, or against the property of, companies or individuals;
(*b*) priorities of debts;
(*c*) transactions at an undervalue or preferences;
(*d*) voluntary arrangements approved under Part I or Part VIII, and
(*e*) discharge from bankruptcy. **[434]**

NOTES
Commencement: 29 December 1986.
This section derived from the Insolvency Act 1985, s 234.

PART XVIII

INTERPRETATION

435. Meaning of "associate"

(1) For the purposes of this Act any question whether a person is an associate of another person is to be determined in accordance with the following provisions of this section (any provision that a person is an associate of another person being taken to mean that they are associates of each other).

(2) A person is an associate of an individual if that person is the individual's husband or wife, or is a relative, or the husband or wife of a relative, of the individual or of the individual's husband or wife.

(3) A person is an associate of any person with whom he is in partnership, and of the husband or wife or a relative of any individual with whom he is in partnership; and a Scottish firm is an associate of any person who is a member of the firm.

(4) A person is an associate of any person whom he employs or by whom he is employed.

(5) A person in his capacity as trustee of a trust other than—

(a) a trust arising under any of the second Group of Parts or the Bankruptcy (Scotland) Act 1985, or
(b) a pension scheme or an employees' share scheme (within the meaning of the Companies Act),

is an associate of another person if the beneficiaries of the trust include, or the terms of the trust confer a power that may be exercised for the benefit of, that other person or an associate of that other person.

(6) A company is an associate of another company—

(a) if the same person has control of both, or a person has control of one and persons who are his associates, or he and persons who are his associates, have control of the other, or
(b) if a group of two or more persons has control of each company, and the groups either consist of the same persons or could be regarded as consisting of the same persons by treating (in one or more cases) a member of either group as replaced by a person of whom he is an associate.

(7) A company is an associate of another person if that person has control of it or if that person and persons who are his associates together have control of it.

(8) For the purposes of this section a person is a relative of an individual if he is that individual's brother, sister, uncle, aunt, nephew, niece, lineal ancestor or lineal descendant, treating—

(a) any relationship of the half blood as a relationship of the whole blood and the stepchild or adopted child of any person as his child, and
(b) an illegitimate child as the legitimate child of his mother and reputed father;

and references in this section to a husband or wife include a former husband or wife and a reputed husband or wife.

(9) For the purposes of this section any director or other officer of a company is to be treated as employed by that company.

(10) For the purposes of this section a person is to be taken as having control of a company if—

(a) the directors of the company or of another company which has control of it (or any of them) are accustomed to act in accordance with his directions or instructions, or
(b) he is entitled to exercise, or control the exercise of, one third or more of the voting power at any general meeting of the company or of another company which has control of it;

and where two or more persons together satisfy either of the above conditions, they are to be taken as having control of the company.

(11) In this section "company" includes any body corporate (whether incorporated in Great Britain or elsewhere); and references to directors and other officers of a company and to voting power at any general meeting of a company have effect with any necessary modifications. **[435]**

NOTES
Commencement: 29 December 1986.
This section derived from the Insolvency Act 1985, s 233.

436. Expressions used generally

In this Act, except in so far as the context otherwise requires (and subject to Parts VII and XI)—

"the appointed day" means the day on which this Act comes into force under section 443;

"associate" has the meaning given by section 435;

"business" includes a trade or profession;

"the Companies Act" means the Companies Act 1985;

"conditional sale agreement" and "hire-purchase agreement" have the same meanings as in the Consumer Credit Act 1974;

"modifications" includes additions, alterations and omissions and cognate expressions shall be construed accordingly;

"property" includes money, goods, things in action, land and every description of property wherever situated and also obligations and every description of interest, whether present or future or vested or contingent, arising out of, or incidental to, property;

"records" includes computer records and other non-documentary records;

"subordinate legislation" has the same meaning as in the Interpretation Act 1978; and

"transaction" includes a gift, agreement or arrangement, and references to entering into a transaction shall be construed accordingly. **[436]**

NOTES
Commencement: 29 December 1986.
This section derived from the Insolvency Act 1985, s 232 (part).

PART XIX

FINAL PROVISIONS

437. Transitional provisions, and savings

The transitional provisions and savings set out in Schedule 11 to this Act shall have effect, the Schedule comprising the following Parts—

Part I: company insolvency and winding up (matters arising before appointed day, and continuance of proceedings in certain cases as before that day);

Part II: individual insolvency (matters so arising, and continuance of bankruptcy proceedings in certain cases as before that day);

Part III: transactions entered into before the appointed day and capable of being affected by orders of the court under Part XVI of this Act;

Part IV: insolvency practitioners acting as such before the appointed day; and

Part V: general transitional provisions and savings required consequentially on, and in connection with, the repeal and replacement by this Act and the Company Directors Disqualification Act 1986 of provisions of the Companies Act, the greater part of the Insolvency Act 1985 and other enactments.   **[437]**

NOTES
Commencement: 29 December 1986.

438. Repeals

The enactments specified in the second column of Schedule 12 to this Act are repealed to the extent specified in the third column of that Schedule.   **[438]**

NOTES
Commencement: 29 December 1986.

439. Amendment of enactments

(1) The Companies Act is amended as shown in Parts I and II of Schedule 13 to this Act, being amendments consequential on this Act and the Company Directors Disqualification Act 1986.

(2) The enactments specified in the first column of Schedule 14 to this Act (being enactments which refer, or otherwise relate, to those which are repealed and replaced by this Act or the Company Directors Disqualification Act 1986) are amended as shown in the second column of that Schedule.

(3) The Lord Chancellor may by order make such consequential modifications of any provision contained in any subordinate legislation made before the appointed day and such transitional provisions in connection with those modifications as appear to him necessary or expedient in respect of—

  (*a*) any reference in that subordinate legislation to the Bankruptcy Act 1914;
  (*b*) any reference in that subordinate legislation to any enactment repealed by Part III or IV of Schedule 10 to the Insolvency Act 1985; or
  (*c*) any reference in that subordinate legislation to any matter provided for under the Act of 1914 or under any enactment so repealed.

(4) An order under this section shall be made by statutory instrument subject to annulment in pursuance of a resolution of either House of Parliament.   **[439]**

NOTES
Commencement: 29 December 1986.

440. Extent (Scotland)

(1) Subject to the next subsection, provisions of this Act contained in the first Group of Parts extend to Scotland except where otherwise stated.

(2) The following provisions of this Act do not extend to Scotland—

  (*a*) In the first Group of Parts—

        section 43;

sections 238 to 241; and
section 246;

(b) the second Group of Parts;

(c) in the third Group of Parts—

sections 399 to 402,
sections 412, 413, 415, 418, 420 and 421,
sections 423 to 425, and
section 429(1) and (2); and

(d) in the Schedules—

Parts II and III of Schedule 11; and

Schedules 12 and 14 so far as they repeal or amend enactments
which extend to England and Wales only.   **[440]**

NOTES
Commencement: 29 December 1986.
This section derived from the Insolvency Act 1985, s 236(3).

441. Extent (Northern Ireland)

(1) The following provisions of this Act extend to Northern Ireland—

(a) sections 197, 426, 427 and 428; and

(b) so much of section 439 and Schedule 14 as relates to enactments which
extend to Northern Ireland.

(2) Subject as above, and to any provision expressly relating to companies
incorporated elsewhere than in Great Britain, nothing in this Act extends to
Northern Ireland or applies to or in relation to companies registered or
incorporated in Northern Ireland.   **[441]**

NOTES
Commencement: 29 December 1986.
This section derived from the Companies Act 1985, s 745, and the Insolvency Act 1985, s 236(4).

442. Extent (other territories)

Her Majesty may, by Order in Council, direct that such of the provisions of this
Act as are specified in the Order, being provisions formerly contained in the
Insolvency Act 1985, shall extend to any of the Channel Islands or any colony
with such modifications as may be so specified.   **[442]**

NOTES
Commencement: 29 December 1986.
This section derived from the Insolvency Act 1985, s 236(5).

443. Commencement

This Act comes into force on the day appointed under section 236(2) of the
Insolvency Act 1985 for the coming into force of Part III of that Act (individual
insolvency and bankruptcy), immediately after that Part of that Act comes into
force for England and Wales.   **[443]**

NOTES
Commencement: 29 December 1986.

444. Citation

This Act may be cited as the Insolvency Act 1986.   **[444]**

NOTES
   Commencement: 29 December 1986.

SCHEDULES

SCHEDULE 1

Sections 14, 42

POWERS OF ADMINISTRATOR OR ADMINISTRATIVE RECEIVER

1. Power to take possession of, collect and get in the property of the company and, for that purpose, to take such proceedings as may seem to him expedient.

2. Power to sell or otherwise dispose of the property of the company by public auction or private contract or, in Scotland, to sell, feu, hire out or otherwise dispose of the property of the company by public roup or private bargain.

3. Power to raise or borrow money and grant security therefor over the property of the company.

4. Power to appoint a solicitor or accountant or other professionally qualified person to assist him in the performance of his functions.

5. Power to bring or defend any action or other legal proceedings in the name and on behalf of the company.

6. Power to refer to arbitration any question affecting the company.

7. Power to effect and maintain insurances in respect of the business and property of the company.

8. Power to use the company's seal.

9. Power to do all acts and to execute in the name and on behalf of the company any deed, receipt or other document.

10. Power to draw, accept, make and endorse any bill of exchange or promissory note in the name and on behalf of the company.

11. Power to appoint any agent to do any business which he is unable to do himself or which can more conveniently be done by an agent and power to employ and dismiss employees.

12. Power to do all such things (including the carrying out of works) as may be necessary for the realisation of the property of the company.

13. Power to make any payment which is necessary or incidental to the performance of his functions.

14. Power to carry on the business of the company.

15. Power to establish subsidiaries of the company.

16. Power to transfer to subsidiaries of the company the whole or any part of the business and property of the company.

17. Power to grant or accept a surrender of a lease or tenancy of any of the property of the company, and to take a lease or tenancy of any property required or convenient for the business of the company.

18. Power to make any arrangement or compromise on behalf of the company.

19. Power to call up any uncalled capital of the company.

20. Power to rank and claim in the bankruptcy, insolvency, sequestration or

liquidation of any person indebted to the company and to receive dividends, and to accede to trust deeds for the creditors of any such person.

21. Power to present or defend a petition for the winding up of the company.

22. Power to change the situation of the company's registered office.

23. Power to do all other things incidental to the exercise of the foregoing powers.

[445]

NOTES
Commencement: 29 December 1986.
This Schedule derived from the Insolvency Act 1985, Sch 3.

SCHEDULE 2
Section 55

POWERS OF A SCOTTISH RECEIVER (ADDITIONAL TO THOSE CONFERRED ON HIM BY THE INSTRUMENT OF CHARGE)

1. Power to take possession of, collect and get in the property from the company or a liquidator thereof or any other person, and for that purpose, to take such proceedings as may seem to him expedient.

2. Power to sell, feu, hire out or otherwise dispose of the property by public roup or private bargain and with or without advertisement.

3. Power to raise or borrow money and grant security therefor over the property.

4. Power to appoint a solicitor or accountant or other professionally qualified person to assist him in the performance of his functions.

5. Power to bring or defend any action or other legal proceedings in the name and on behalf of the company.

6. Power to refer to arbitration all questions affecting the company.

7. Power to effect and maintain insurances in respect of the business and property of the company.

8. Power to use the company's seal.

9. Power to do all acts and to execute in the name and on behalf of the company any deed, receipt or other document.

10. Power to draw, accept, make and endorse any bill of exchange or promissory note in the name and on behalf of the company.

11. Power to appoint any agent to do any business which he is unable to do himself or which can more conveniently be done by an agent, and power to employ and dismiss employees.

12. Power to do all such things (including the carrying out of works), as may be necessary for the realisation of the property.

13. Power to make any payment which is necessary or incidental to the performance of his functions.

14. Power to carry on the business of the company or any part of it.

15. Power to grant or accept a surrender of a lease or tenancy of any of the property, and to take a lease or tenancy of any property required or convenient for the business of the company.

16. Power to make any arrangement or compromise on behalf of the company.

17. Power to call up any uncalled capital of the company.

18. Power to establish subsidiaries of the company.

19. Power to transfer to subsidiaries of the company the business of the company or any part of it and any of the property.

20. Power to rank and claim in the bankruptcy, insolvency, sequestration or liquidation of any person or company indebted to the company and to receive dividends, and to accede to trust deeds for creditors of any such person.

21. Power to present or defend a petition for the winding up of the company.

22. Power to change the situation of the company's registered office.

23. Power to do all other things incidental to the exercise of the powers mentioned in section 55(1) of this Act or above in this Schedule.   **[446]**

NOTES

Commencement: 29 December 1986.

This Schedule derived from the Companies Act 1985, s 471(1), and the Insolvency Act 1985, s 57.

SCHEDULE 3

Section 162

ORDERS IN COURSE OF WINDING UP PRONOUNCED IN VACATION (SCOTLAND)

PART I

ORDERS WHICH ARE TO BE FINAL

Orders under section 153, as to the time for proving debts and claims.

Orders under section 195 as to meetings for ascertaining wishes of creditors or contributories.

Orders under section 198, as to the examination of witnesses in regard to the property or affairs of a company.   **[447]**

NOTES

Commencement: 29 December 1986.

This Part derived from the Companies Act 1985, Sch 16, Pt I.

PART II

ORDERS WHICH ARE TO TAKE EFFECT UNTIL MATTER DISPOSED OF BY INNER HOUSE

Orders under section 126(1), 130(2) or (3), 147, 227 or 228, restraining or permitting the commencement or the continuance of legal proceedings.

Orders under section 135(5), limiting the powers of provisional liquidators.

Orders under section 108, appointing a liquidator to fill a vacancy.

Orders under section 167 or 169, sanctioning the exercise of any powers by a liquidator, other than the powers specified in paragraphs 1, 2 and 3 of Schedule 4 to this Act.

Orders under section 158, as to the arrest and detention of an absconding contributory and his property.   **[448]**

NOTES

Commencement: 29 December 1986.

This Part derived from the Companies Act 1985, Sch 16, Pt II.

SCHEDULE 4

Sections 165, 167

POWERS OF LIQUIDATOR IN A WINDING UP

PART I

POWERS EXERCISABLE WITH SANCTION

1. Power to pay any class of creditors in full.

2. Power to make any compromise or arrangement with creditors or persons claiming to be creditors, or having or alleging themselves to have any claim (present or future, certain or contingent, ascertained or sounding only in damages) against the company, or whereby the company may be rendered liable.

3. Power to compromise, on such terms as may be agreed—

(a) all calls and liabilities to calls, all debts and liabilities capable of resulting in debts, and all claims (present or future, certain or contingent, ascertained or sounding only in damages) subsisting or supposed to subsist between the company and a contributory or alleged contributory or other debtor or person apprehending liability to the company, and

(b) all questions in any way relating to or affecting the assets or the winding up of the company,

and take any security for the discharge of any such call, debt, liability or claim and give a complete discharge in respect of it.   **[449]**

NOTES

Commencement: 29 December 1986.
This Part derived from the Companies Act 1985, ss 539(1)(*d*)–(*f*), 598(1).

PART II

POWERS EXERCISABLE WITHOUT SANCTION IN VOLUNTARY
WINDING UP, WITH SANCTION IN WINDING UP BY THE COURT

4. Power to bring or defend any action or other legal proceeding in the name and on behalf of the company.

5. Power to carry on the business of the company so far as may be necessary for its beneficial winding up.   **[450]**

NOTES

Commencement: 29 December 1986.
This Part derived from the Companies Act 1985, ss 539(1)(*a*), (*b*), 598(2).

PART III

POWERS EXERCISABLE WITHOUT SANCTION IN ANY WINDING UP

6. Power to sell any of the company's property by public auction or private contract with power to transfer the whole of it to any person or to sell the same in parcels.

7. Power to do all acts and execute, in the name and on behalf of the company, all deeds, receipts and other documents and for that purpose to use, when necessary, the company's seal.

8. Power to prove, rank and claim in the bankruptcy, insolvency or sequestration of any contributory for any balance against his estate, and to receive dividends in the bankruptcy, insolvency or sequestration in respect of that balance, as a separate debt due from the bankrupt or insolvent, and rateably with the other separate creditors.

9. Power to draw, accept, make and indorse any bill of exchange or promissory note in the name and on behalf of the company, with the same effect with respect to the company's liability as if the bill or note had been drawn, accepted, made or indorsed by or on behalf of the company in the course of its business.

10. Power to raise on the security of the assets of the company any money requisite.

11. Power to take out in his official name letters of administration to any deceased contributory, and to do in his official name any other act necessary for obtaining payment of any money due from a contributory or his estate which cannot conveniently be done in the name of the company.

In all such cases the money due is deemed, for the purpose of enabling the liquidator to take out the letters of administration or recover the money, to be due to the liquidator himself.

12. Power to appoint an agent to do any business which the liquidator is unable to do himself.

13. Power to do all such other things as may be necessary for winding up the company's affairs and distributing its assets.   **[451]**

NOTES
  Commencement: 29 December 1986.
  This Part derived from the Companies Act 1985, ss 539(2), 598(2).

SCHEDULE 5

Section 314

POWERS OF TRUSTEE IN BANKRUPTCY

PART I
POWERS EXERCISABLE WITH SANCTION

1. Power to carry on any business of the bankrupt so far as may be necessary for winding it up beneficially and so far as the trustee is able to do so without contravening any requirement imposed by or under any enactment.

2. Power to bring, institute or defend any action or legal proceedings relating to the property comprised in the bankrupt's estate.

3. Power to accept as the consideration for the sale of any property comprised in the bankrupt's estate a sum of money payable at a future time subject to such stipulations as to security or otherwise as the creditors' committee or the court thinks fit.

4. Power to mortgage or pledge any part of the property comprised in the bankrupt's estate for the purpose of raising money for the payment of his debts.

5. Power, where any right, option or other power forms part of the bankrupt's estate, to make payments or incur liabilities with a view to obtaining, for the benefit of the creditors, any property which is the subject of the right, option or power.

6. Power to refer to arbitration, or compromise on such terms as may be agreed on, any debts, claims or liabilities subsisting or supposed to subsist between the bankrupt and any person who may have incurred any liability to the bankrupt.

7. Power to make such compromise or other arrangement as may be thought expedient with creditors, or persons claiming to be creditors, in respect of bankruptcy debts.

8. Power to make such compromise or other arrangement as may be thought expedient with respect to any claim arising out of or incidental to the bankrupt's estate made or capable of being made on the trustee by any person or by the trustee on any person.   **[452]**

NOTES
  Commencement: 29 December 1986.
  This Part derived from the Insolvency Act 1985, s 160(2).

PART II

GENERAL POWERS

9. Power to sell any part of the property for the time being comprised in the bankrupt's estate, including the goodwill and book debts of any business.

10. Power to give receipts for any money received by him, being receipts which effectually discharge the person paying the money from all responsibility in respect of its application.

11. Power to prove, rank, claim and draw a dividend in respect of such debts due to the bankrupt as are comprised in his estate.

12. Power to exercise in relation to any property comprised in the bankrupt's estate any powers the capacity to exercise which is vested in him under Parts VIII to XI of this Act.

13. Power to deal with any property comprised in the estate to which the bankrupt is beneficially entitled as tenant in tail in the same manner as the bankrupt might have dealt with it.   [453]

NOTES
    Commencement: 29 December 1986.
    This Part derived from the Insolvency Act 1985, s 160(1).

PART III

ANCILLARY POWERS

14. For the purposes of, or in connection with, the exercise of any of his powers under Parts VIII to XI of this Act, the trustee may, by his official name—

    (*a*) hold property of every description,
    (*b*) make contracts,
    (*c*) sue and be sued,
    (*d*) enter into engagements binding on himself and, in respect of the bankrupt's estate, on his successors in office,
    (*e*) employ an agent,
    (*f*) execute any power of attorney, deed or other instrument;

and he may do any other act which is necessary or expedient for the purposes of or in connection with the exercise of those powers.   [454]

NOTES
    Commencement: 29 December 1986.
    This Part derived from the Insolvency Act 1985, s 160(6).

SCHEDULE 6

Section 386

THE CATEGORIES OF PREFERENTIAL DEBTS

Category 1: Debts due to Inland Revenue

1. Sums due at the relevant date from the debtor on account of deductions of income tax from emoluments paid during the period of 12 months next before that date.

The deductions here referred to are those which the debtor was liable to make under section 204 of the Income and Corporation Taxes Act 1970 (pay as you earn), less the amount of the repayments of income tax which the debtor was liable to make during that period.

2. Sums due at the relevant date from the debtor in respect of such deductions as are required to be made by the debtor for that period under section 69 of the Finance (No 2) Act 1975 (sub-contractors in the construction industry).

Category 2: Debts due to Customs and Excise

3. Any value added tax which is referable to the period of 6 months next before the relevant date (which period is referred to below as "the 6-month period").

For the purposes of this paragraph—

(a) where the whole of the prescribed accounting period to which any value added tax is attributable falls within the 6-month period, the whole amount of that tax is referable to that period; and

(b) in any other case the amount of any value added tax which is referable to the 6-month period is the proportion of the tax which is equal to such proportion (if any) of the accounting reference period in question as falls within the 6-month period;

and in sub-paragraph (a) "prescribed" means prescribed by regulations under the Value Added Tax Act 1983.

4. The amount of any car tax which is due at the relevant date from the debtor and which became due within a period of 12 months next before that date.

5. Any amount which is due—

(a) by way of general betting duty or bingo duty, or

(b) under section 12(1) of the Betting and Gaming Duties Act 1981 (general betting duty and pool betting duty recoverable from agent collecting stakes), or

(c) under section 14 of, or Schedule 2 to, that Act (gaming licence duty),

from the debtor at the relevant date and which became due within the period of 12 months next before that date.

Category 3: Social security contributions

6. All sums which on the relevant date are due from the debtor on account of Class 1 or Class 2 contributions under the Social Security Act 1975 or the Social Security (Northen Ireland) Act 1975 and which became due from the debtor in the 12 months next before the relevant date.

7. All sums which on the relevant date have been assessed on and are due from the debtor on account of Class 4 contributions under either of those Acts of 1975, being sums which—

(a) are due to the Commissioners of Inland Revenue (rather than to the Secretary of State or a Northern Ireland department), and

(b) are assessed on the debtor up to 5th April next before the relevant date,

but not exceeding, in the whole, any one year's assessment.

Category 4: Contributions to occupational pension schemes, etc

8. Any sum which is owed by the debtor and is a sum to which Schedule 3 to the Social Security Pensions Act 1975 applies (contributions to occupational pension schemes and state scheme premiums).

Category 5: Remuneration, etc, of employees

9. So much of any amount which—

(a) is owed by the debtor to a person who is or has been an employee of the debtor, and

(b) is payable by way of remuneration in respect of the whole or any part of the period of 4 months next before the relevant date,

as does not exceed so much as may be prescribed by order made by the Secretary of State.

10. An amount owed by way of accrued holiday remuneration, in respect of any period of employment before the relevant date, to a person whose employment by the debtor has been terminated, whether before, on or after that date.

11. So much of any sum owed in respect of money advanced for the purpose as has

been applied for the payment of a debt which, if it had not been paid, would have been a debt falling within paragraph 9 or 10.

12. So much of any amount which—

(*a*) is ordered (whether before or after the relevant date) to be paid by the debtor under the Reserve Forces (Safeguard of Employment) Act 1985, and

(*b*) is so ordered in respect of a default made by the debtor before that date in the discharge of his obligations under that Act,

as does not exceed such amount as may be prescribed by order made by the Secretary of State.

Interpretation for Category 5

13.—(1) For the purposes of paragraphs 9 to 12, a sum is payable by the debtor to a person by way of remuneration in respect of any period if—

(*a*) it is paid as wages or salary (whether payable for time or for piece work or earned wholly or partly by way of commission) in respect of services rendered to the debtor in that period, or

(*b*) it is an amount falling within the following sub-paragraph and is payable by the debtor in respect of that period.

(2) An amount falls within this sub-paragraph if it is—

(*a*) a guarantee payment under section 12(1) of the Employment Protection (Consolidation) Act 1978 (employee without work to do for a day or part of a day);

(*b*) remuneration on suspension on medical grounds under section 19 of that Act;

(*c*) any payment for time off under section 27(3) (trade union duties), 31(3) (looking for work, etc) or 31A(4) (ante-natal care) of that Act; or

(*d*) remuneration under a protective award made by an industrial tribunal under section 101 of the Employment Protection Act 1975 (redundancy dismissal with compensation).

14.—(1) This paragraph relates to a case in which a person's employment has been terminated by or in consequence of his employer going into liquidation or being adjudged bankrupt or (his employer being a company not in liquidation) by or in consequence of—

(*a*) a receiver being appointed as mentioned in section 40 of this Act (debenture-holders secured by floating charge), or

(*b*) the appointment of a receiver under section 53(6) or 54(5) of this Act (Scottish company with property subject to floating charge), or

(*c*) the taking of possession by debenture-holders (so secured), as mentioned in section 196 of the Companies Act.

(2) For the purposes of paragraphs 9 to 12, holiday remuneration is deemed to have accrued to that person in respect of any period of employment if, by virtue of his contract of employment or of any enactment that remuneration would have accrued in respect of that period if his employment had continued until he became entitled to be allowed the holiday.

(3) The reference in sub-paragraph (2) to any enactment includes an order or direction made under an enactment.

15. Without prejudice to paragraphs 13 and 14—

(*a*) any remuneration payable by the debtor to a person in respect of a period of holiday or of absence from work through sickness or other good cause is deemed to be wages or (as the case may be) salary in respect of services rendered to the debtor in that period, and

(*b*) references here and in those paragraphs to remuneration in respect of a period of holiday include any sums which, if they had been paid, would have been treated for the purposes of the enactments relating to social security as earnings in respect of that period.

Orders

16. An order under paragraph 9 to 12—

  (*a*) may contain such transitional provisions as may appear to the Secretary of State necessary or expedient;

  (*b*) shall be made by statutory instrument subject to annulment in pursuance of a resolution of either House of Parliament. [455]

NOTES

Commencement: 29 December 1986.

This Schedule derived from the Insolvency Act 1985, Sch 4, Pt I, Pt II, paras 2–4.

SCHEDULE 7

Section 396

INSOLVENCY PRACTITIONERS TRIBUNAL

Panels of members

1.—(1) The Secretary of State shall draw up and from time to time revise—

  (*a*) a panel of persons who are barristers, advocates or solicitors, in each case of not less than 7 years' standing, and are nominated for the purpose by the Lord Chancellor or the Lord President of the Court of Session, and

  (*b*) a panel of persons who are experienced in insolvency matters;

and the members of the Tribunal shall be selected from those panels in accordance with this Schedule.

(2) The power to revise the panels includes power to terminate a person's membership of either of them, and is accordingly to that extent subject to section 8 of the Tribunals and Inquiries Act 1971 (which makes it necessary to obtain the concurrence of the Lord Chancellor and the Lord President of the Court of Session to dismissals in certain cases).

Remuneration of members

2. The Secretary of State may out of money provided by Parliament pay to members of the Tribunal such remuneration as he may with the approval of the Treasury determine; and such expenses of the Tribunal as the Secretary of State and the Treasury may approve shall be defrayed by the Secretary of State out of money so provided.

Sittings of Tribunal

3.—(1) For the purposes of carrying out their functions in relation to any cases referred to them, the Tribunal may sit either as a single tribunal or in two or more divisions.

(2) The functions of the Tribunal in relation to any case referred to them shall be exercised by three members consisting of—

  (*a*) a chairman selected by the Secretary of State from the panel drawn up under paragraph 1(1)(*a*) above, and

  (*b*) two other members selected by the Secretary of State from the panel drawn up under paragraph 1(1)(*b*).

Procedure of Tribunal

4.—(1) Any investigation by the Tribunal shall be so conducted as to afford a reasonable opportunity for representations to be made to the Tribunal by or on behalf of the person whose case is the subject of the investigation.

(2) For the purposes of any such investigation, the Tribunal—

  (*a*) may by summons require any person to attend, at such time and place as is specified in the summons, to give evidence or to produce any books, papers and other records in his possession or under his control which the Tribunal consider it necessary for the purposes of the investigation to examine, and (*b*) may take evidence on oath, and for the purpose administer oaths, or may, instead of administering an oath, require the person examined to make and subscribe a declaration of the truth of the matter respecting which he is examined;

but no person shall be required, in obedience to such a summons, to go more than ten miles from his place of residence, unless the necessary expenses of his attendance are paid or tendered to him.

(3) Every person who—

(*a*) without reasonable excuse fails to attend in obedience to a summons issued under this paragraph, or refuses to give evidence, or

(*b*) intentionally alters, suppresses, conceals or destroys or refuses to produce any document which he may be required to produce for the purpose of an investigation by the Tribunal,

is liable to a fine.

(4) Subject to the provisions of this paragraph, the Secretary of State may make rules for regulating the procedure on any investigation by the Tribunal.

(5) In their application to Scotland, sub-paragraphs (2) and (3) above have effect as if for any reference to a summons there were substituted a reference to a notice in writing. **[456]**

NOTES
Commencement: 29 December 1986.
This Schedule derived from the Insolvency Act 1985, Sch 1.

SCHEDULE 8

Section 411

PROVISIONS CAPABLE OF INCLUSION IN COMPANY INSOLVENCY RULES

Courts

1. Provision for supplementing, in relation to the insolvency or winding up of companies, any provision made by or under section 117 of this Act (jurisdiction in relation to winding up).

2. Provision for regulating the practice and procedure of any court exercising jurisdiction for the purposes of Parts I to VII of this Act or the Companies Act so far as relating to, and to matters connected with or arising out of, the insolvency or winding up of companies, being any provision that could be made by rules of court.

Notices, etc

3. Provision requiring notice of any proceedings in connection with or arising out of the insolvency or winding up of a company to be given or published in the manner prescribed by the rules.

4. Provision with respect to the form, manner of serving, contents and proof of any petition, application, order, notice, statement or other document required to be presented, made, given, published or prepared under any enactment or subordinate legislation relating to, or to matters connected with or arising out of, the insolvency or winding up of companies.

5. Provision specifying the persons to whom any notice is to be given.

Registration of voluntary arrangements

6. Provision for the registration of voluntary arrangements approved under Part I of this Act, including provision for the keeping and inspection of a register.

Provisional liquidator

7. Provision as to the manner in which a provisional liquidator appointed under section 135 is to carry out his functions.

Conduct of insolvency

8. Provision with respect to the certification of any person as, and as to the proof that a person is, the liquidator, administrator or adminstrative receiver of a company.

9. The following provision with respect to meetings of a company's creditors, contributories or members—

(a) provision as to the manner of summoning a meeting (including provision as to how any power to require a meeting is to be exercised, provision as to the manner of determining the value of any debt or contribution for the purposes of any such power and provision making the exercise of any such power subject to the deposit of a sum sufficient to cover the expenses likely to be incurred in summoning and holding a meeting);

(b) provision specifying the time and place at which a meeting may be held and the period of notice required for a meeting;

(c) provision as to the procedure to be followed at a meeting (including the manner in which decisions may be reached by a meeting and the manner in which the value of any vote at a meeting is to be determined);

(d) provision for requiring a person who is or has been an officer of the company to attend a meeting;

(e) provision creating, in the prescribed circumstances, a presumption that a meeting has been duly summoned and held;

(f) provision as to the manner of proving the decisions of a meeting.

10.—(1) Provision as to the functions, membership and proceedings of a committee established under section 26, 49, 68, 101, 141 or 142 of this Act.

(2) The following provision with respect to the establishment of a committee under section 101, 141 or 142 of this Act, that is to say—

(a) provision for resolving differences between a meeting of the company's creditors and a meeting of its contributories or members;

(b) provision authorising the establishment of the committee without a meeting of contributories in a case where a company is being wound up on grounds including its inability to pay its debts; and

(c) provision modifying the requirements of this Act with respect to the establishment of the committee in a case where a winding-up order has been made immediately upon the discharge of an administration order.

11. Provision as to the manner in which any requirement that may be imposed on a person under any of Parts I to VII of this Act by the official receiver, the liquidator, administrator or administrative receiver of a company or a special manager appointed under section 177 is to be so imposed.

12. Provision as to the debts that may be proved in a winding up, as to the manner and conditions of proving a debt and as to the manner and expenses of establishing the value of any debt or security.

13. Provision with respect to the manner of the distribution of the property of a company that is being wound up, including provision with respect to unclaimed funds and dividends.

14. Provision which, with or without modifications, applies in relation to the winding up of companies any enactment contained in Parts VIII to XI of this Act or in the Bankruptcy (Scotland) Act 1985.

Financial provisions

15. Provision as to the amount, or manner of determining the amount, payable to the liquidator, administrator or administrative receiver of a company or a special manager

appointed under section 177, by way of remuneration for the carrying out of functions in connection with or arising out of the insolvency or winding up of a company.

16. Provision with respect to the manner in which moneys received by the liquidator of a company in the course of carrying out his functions as such are to be invested or otherwise handled and with respect to the payment of interest on sums which, in pursuance of rules made by virtue of this paragraph, have been paid into the Insolvency Services Account.

17. Provision as to the fees, costs, charges and other expenses that may be treated as the expenses of a winding up.

18. Provision as to the fees, costs, charges and other expenses that may be treated as properly incurred by the administrator or administrative receiver of a company.

19. Provision as to the fees, costs, charges and other expenses that may be incurred for any of the purposes of Part I of this Act or in the administration of any voluntary arrangement approved under that Part.

Information and records

20. Provision requiring registrars and other officers of courts having jurisdiction in England and Wales in relation to, or to matters connected with or arising out of, the insolvency or winding up of companies—

   (a) to keep books and other records with respect to the exercise of that jurisdiction, and
   (b) to make returns to the Secretary of State of the business of those courts.

21. Provision requiring a creditor, member or contributory, or such a committee as is mentioned in paragraph 10 above, to be supplied (on payment in prescribed cases of the prescribed fee) with such information and with copies of such documents as may be prescribed.

22. Provision as to the manner in which public examinations under sections 133 and 134 of this Act and proceedings under sections 236 and 237 are to be conducted, as to the circumstances in which records of such examinations or proceedings are to be made available to prescribed persons and as to the costs of such examinations and proceedings.

23. Provision imposing requirements with respect to—

   (a) the preparation and keeping by the liquidator, administrator or administrative receiver of a company, or by the supervisor of a voluntary arrangement approved under Part I of this Act, of prescribed books, accounts and other records;
   (b) the production of those books, accounts and records for inspection by prescribed persons;
   (c) the auditing of accounts kept by the liquidator, administrator or administrative receiver of a company, or the supervisor of such a voluntary arrangement; and
   (d) the issue by the administrator or administrative receiver of a company of such a certificate as is mentioned in section 22(3)(b) of the Value Added Tax Act 1983 (refund of tax in cases of bad debts) and the supply of copies of the certificate to creditors of the company.

24. Provision requiring the person who is the supervisor of a voluntary arrangement approved under Part I, when it appears to him that the voluntary arrangement has been fully implemented and that nothing remains to be done by him under the arrangement—

   (a) to give notice of that fact to persons bound by the voluntary arrangement, and
   (b) to report to those persons on the carrying out of the functions conferred on the supervisor of the arrangement.

25. Provision as to the manner in which the liquidator of a company is to act in relation to the books, papers and other records of the company, including provision authorising their disposal.

26. Provision imposing requirements in connection with the carrying out of functions

under section 7(3) of the Company Directors Disqualification Act 1986 (including, in particular, requirements with respect to the making of periodic returns).

General

27. Provision conferring power on the Secretary of State to make regulations with respect to so much of any matter that may be provided for in the rules as relates to the carrying out of the functions of the liquidator, administrator or administrative receiver of a company.

28. Provision conferring a discretion on the court.

29. Provision conferring power on the court to make orders for the purpose of securing compliance with obligations imposed by or under section 22, 47, 66, 131, 143(2) or 235 of this Act or section 7(4) of the Company Directors Disqualification Act 1986.

30. Provision making non-compliance with any of the rules a criminal offence.

31. Provision making different provision for different cases or descriptions of cases, including different provisions for different areas. **[457]**

NOTES
Commencement: 29 December 1986.
This Schedule derived from the Insolvency Act 1985, Sch 5.

SCHEDULE 9

Section 412

PROVISIONS CAPABLE OF INCLUSION IN INDIVIDUAL
INSOLVENCY RULES

Courts

1. Provision with respect to the arrangement and disposition of the business under Parts VIII to XI of this Act of courts having jurisdiction for the purpose of those Parts, including provision for the allocation of proceedings under those Parts to particular courts and for the transfer of such proceedings from one court to another.

2. Provision for enabling a registrar in bankruptcy of the High Court or a registrar of a county court having jurisdiction for the purposes of those Parts to exercise such of the jurisdiction conferred for those purposes on the High Court or, as the case may be, that county court as may be prescribed.

3. Provision for regulating the practice and procedure of any court exercising jurisdiction for the purposes of those Parts, being any provision that could be made by rules of court.

4. Provision conferring rights of audience, in courts exercising jurisdiction for the purposes of those Parts, on the official receiver and on solicitors.

Notices, etc

5. Provision requiring notice of any proceedings under Parts VIII to XI of this Act or of any matter relating to or arising out of a proposal under Part VIII or a bankruptcy to be given or published in the prescribed manner.

6. Provision with respect to the form, manner of serving, contents and proof of any petition, application, order, notice, statement or other document required to be presented, made, given, published or prepared under any enactment contained in Parts VIII to XI or subordinate legislation under those Parts or Part XV (including provision requiring prescribed matters to be verified by affidavit).

7. Provision specifying the persons to whom any notice under Parts VIII to XI is to be given.

Registration of voluntary arrangements

8. Provision for the registration of voluntary arrangements approved under Part VIII of this Act, including provision for the keeping and inspection of a register.

Interim receiver

9. Provision as to the manner in which an interim receiver appointed under section 286 is to carry out his functions, including any such provision as is specified in relation to the trustee of a bankrupt's estate in paragraph 21 or 27 below.

Receiver or manager

10. Provision as to the manner in which the official receiver is to carry out his functions as receiver or manager of a bankrupt's estate under section 287, including any such provision as is specified in relation to the trustee of a bankrupt's estate in paragraph 21 or 27 below.

Administration of individual insolvency

11. Provision with respect to the certification of the appointment of any person as trustee of a bankrupt's estate and as to the proof of that appointment.

12. The following provision with respect to meetings of creditors—

(a) provision as to the manner of summoning a meeting (including provision as to how any power to require a meeting is to be exercised, provision as to the manner of determining the value of any debt for the purposes of any such power and provision making the exercise of any such power subject to the deposit of a sum sufficient to cover the expenses likely to be incurred in summoning and holding a meeting);

(b) provision specifying the time and place at which a meeting may be held and the period of notice required for a meeting;

(c) provision as to the procedure to be followed at such a meeting (including the manner in which decisions may be reached by a meeting and the manner in which the value of any vote at a meeting is to be determined);

(d) provision for requiring a bankrupt or debtor to attend a meeting;

(e) provision creating, in the prescribed circumstances, a presumption that a meeting has been duly summoned and held; and

(f) provision as to the manner of proving the decisions of a meeting.

13. Provision as to the functions, membership and proceedings of a creditors' committee established under section 301.

14. Provision as to the manner in which any requirement that may be imposed on a person under Parts VIII to XI of this Act by the official receiver, the trustee of a bankrupt's estate or a special manager appointed under section 370 is to be so imposed and, in the case of any requirement imposed under section 305(3) (information etc to be given by the trustee to the official receiver), provision conferring power on the court to make orders for the purpose of securing compliance with that requirement.

15. Provision as to the manner in which any requirement imposed by virtue of section 310(3) (compliance with income payments order) is to take effect.

16. Provision as to the terms and conditions that may be included in a charge under section 313 (dwelling house forming part of bankrupt's estate).

17. Provision as to the debts that may be proved in any bankruptcy, as to the manner and conditions of proving a debt and as to the manner and expenses of establishing the value of any debt or security.

18. Provision with respect to the manner of the distribution of a bankrupt's estate, including provision with respect to unclaimed funds and dividends.

19. Provision modifying the application of Parts VIII to XI of this Act in relation to a debtor or bankrupt who has died.

Financial provisions

20. Provision as to the amount, or manner of determining the amount, payable to an interim receiver, the trustee of a bankrupt's estate or a special manager appointed under section 370 by way of remuneration for the performance of functions in connection with or arising out of the bankruptcy of any person.

21. Provision with respect to the manner in which moneys received by the trustee of a bankrupt's estate in the course of carrying out his functions as such are to be handled.

22. Provision as to the fees, costs, charges and other expenses that may be treated as the expenses of a bankruptcy.

23. Provision as to the fees, costs, charges and other expenses that may be incurred for any of the purposes of Part VIII of this Act or in the administration of any voluntary arrangement approved under that Part.

Information and records

24. Provision requiring registrars and other officers of courts having jurisdiction for the purposes of Parts VIII to XI—

   (*a*) to keep books and other records with respect to the exercise of that jurisdiction and of jurisdiction under the Deeds of Arrangement Act 1914, and

   (*b*) to make returns to the Secretary of State of the business of those courts.

25. Provision requiring a creditor or a committee established under section 301 to be supplied (on payment in prescribed cases of the prescribed fee) with such information and with copies of such documents as may be prescribed.

26. Provision as to the manner in which public examinations under section 290 and proceedings under sections 366 to 368 are to be conducted, as to the circumstances in which records of such examinations and proceedings are to be made available to prescribed persons and as to the costs of such examinations and proceedings.

27. Provision imposing requirements with respect to—

   (*a*) the preparation and keeping by the trustee of a bankrupt's estate, or the supervisor of a voluntary arrangement approved under Part VIII, of prescribed books, accounts and other records;

   (*b*) the production of those books, accounts and records for inspection by prescribed persons; and

   (*c*) the auditing of accounts kept by the trustee of a bankrupt's estate or the supervisor of such a voluntary arrangement.

28. Provision requiring the person who is the supervisor of a voluntary arrangement approved under Part VIII, when it appears to him that the voluntary arrangement has been fully implemented and that nothing remains to be done by him under it—

   (*a*) to give notice of that fact to persons bound by the voluntary arrangement, and

   (*b*) to report to those persons on the carrying out of the functions conferred on the supervisor of it.

29. Provision as to the manner in which the trustee of a bankrupt's estate is to act in relation to the books, papers and other records of the bankrupt, including provision authorising their disposal.

General

30. Provision conferring power on the Secretary of State to make regulations with respect to so much of any matter that may be provided for in the rules as relates to the carrying out of the functions of an interim receiver appointed under section 286, of the official receiver while acting as a receiver or manager under section 287 or of a trustee of a bankrupt's estate.

31. Provision conferring a discretion on the court.

32. Provision making non-compliance with any of the rules a criminal offence.

33. Provision making different provision for different cases, including different provision for different areas. **[458]**

NOTES

Commencement: 29 December 1986.

This Schedule derived from the Insolvency Act 1985, Sch 7.

Section 430

SCHEDULE 10

PUNISHMENT OF OFFENCES UNDER THIS ACT

Note: In the fourth and fifth columns of this Schedule, "the statutory maximum" means—

(a) in England and Wales, the prescribed sum under section 32 of the Magistrates' Courts Act 1980 (c 43), and
(b) in Scotland, the prescribed sum under s 289B of the Criminal Procedure (Scotland) Act 1975 (c 21).

Section of Act creating offence	General nature of offence	Mode of prosecution	Punishment	Daily default fine (where applicable)
12(2)	Company and others failing to state in correspondence etc that administrator appointed	Summary	One-fifth of the statutory maximum	One-fiftieth of the statutory maximum.
15(8)	Failure of administrator to register office copy of court order permitting disposal of charged property	Summary	One-fifth of the statutory maximum	One-fiftieth of the statutory maximum.
18(5)	Failure of administrator to register office copy of court order varying or discharging administration order	Summary	One-fifth of the statutory maximum	One-fiftieth of the statutory maximum.
21(3)	Administrator failing to register administration order and give notice of appointment	Summary	One-fifth of the statutory maximum	One-fiftieth of the statutory maximum.
22(6)	Failure to comply with provisions relating to statement of affairs, where administrator appointed	1. On indictment 2. Summary	A fine The statutory maximum	One-tenth of the statutory maximum.
23(3)	Administrator failing to send out, register and lay before creditors statement of his proposals	Summary	One-fifth of the statutory maximum	One-fiftieth of the statutory maximum.
24(7)	Administrator failing to file court order discharging administration order under s 24	Summary	One-fifth of the statutory maximum	One-fiftieth of the statutory maximum.
27(6)	Administrator failing to file court order discharging administration order under s 27	Summary	One-fifth of the statutory maximum	One-fiftieth of the statutory maximum.
30	Body corporate acting as receiver	1. On indictment 2. Summary	A fine The statutory maximum	
31	Undischarged bankrupt acting as receiver or manager	1. On indictment 2. Summary	2 years or a fine, or both 6 months or the statutory maximum, or both	
38(5)	Receiver failing to deliver accounts to registrar	Summary	One-fifth of the statutory maximum	One-fiftieth of the statutory maximum.

Section of Act creating offence	General nature of offence	Mode of prosecution	Punishment	Daily default fine (where applicable)
39(2)	Company and others failing to state in correspondence that receiver appointed	Summary	One-fifth of the statutory maximum	One-fiftieth of the statutory maximum.
43(6)	Administrative receiver failing to file office copy of order permitting disposal of charged property	Summary	One-fifth of the statutory maximum	One-fiftieth of the statutory maximum.
45(5)	Administrative receiver failing to file notice of vacation of office	Summary	One-fifth of the statutory maximum	One-fiftieth of the statutory maximum.
46(4)	Administrative receiver failing to give notice of his appointment	Summary	One-fifth of the statutory maximum	One-fiftieth of the statutory maximum.
47(6)	Failure to comply with provisions relating to statement of affairs, where administrative receiver appointed	1. On indictment 2. Summary	A fine The statutory maximum	One-tenth of the statutory maximum.
48(8)	Administrative receiver failing to comply with requirements as to his report	Summary	One-fifth of the statutory maximum	One-fiftieth of the statutory maximum.
51(4)	Body corporate or Scottish firm acting as receiver	1. On indictment 2. Summary	A fine The statutory maximum	
51(5)	Undischarged bankrupt acting as receiver (Scotland)	1. On indictment 2. Summary	2 years or a fine, or both 6 months or the statutory maximum, or both	
53(2)	Failing to deliver to registrar copy of instrument of appointment of receiver	Summary	One-fifth of the statutory maximum	One-fiftieth of the statutory maximum.
54(3)	Failing to deliver to registrar the court's interlocutor appointing receiver	Summary	One-fifth of the statutory maximum	One-fiftieth of the statutory maximum.
61(7)	Receiver failing to send to registrar certified copy of court order authorising disposal of charged property	Summary	One-fifth of the statutory maximum	One-fiftieth of the statutory maximum.
62(5)	Failing to give notice to registrar of cessation or removal of receiver	Summary	One-fifth of the statutory maximum	One-fiftieth of the statutory maximum.
64(2)	Company and others failing to state on correspondence etc that receiver appointed	Summary	One-fifth of the statutory maximum	One-fiftieth of the statutory maximum.
65(4)	Receiver failing to send or publish notice of his appointment	Summary	One-fifth of the statutory maximum	One-fiftieth of the statutory maximum.
66(6)	Failing to comply with provisions concerning statement of affairs, where receiver appointed	1. On indictment 2. Summary	A fine The statutory maximum	One-tenth of the statutory maximum.

Section of Act creating offence	General nature of offence	Mode of prosecution	Punishment	Daily default fine (where applicable)
67(8)	Receiver failing to comply with requirements as to his report	Summary	One-fifth of the statutory maximum	One-fiftieth of the statutory maximum.
85(2)	Company failing to give notice in Gazette of resolution for voluntary winding up	Summary	One-fifth of the statutory maximum	One-fiftieth of the statutory maximum.
89(4)	Director making statutory declaration of company's solvency without reasonable grounds for his opinion	1. On indictment 2. Summary	2 years or a fine, or both 6 months or the statutory maximum, or both	
89(6)	Declaration under section 89 not delivered to registrar within prescribed time	Summary	One-fifth of the statutory maximum	One-fiftieth of the statutory maximum.
93(3)	Liquidator failing to summon general meeting of company at each year's end	Summary	One-fifth of the statutory maximum	
94(4)	Liquidator failing to send to registrar a copy of account of winding up and return of final meeting	Summary	One-fifth of the statutory maximum	One-fiftieth of the statutory maximum.
94(6)	Liquidator failing to call final meeting	Summary	One-fifth of the statutory maximum	
95(8)	Liquidator failing to comply with s 95, where company insolvent	Summary	The statutory maximum	
98(6)	Company failing to comply with s 98 in respect of summoning and giving notice of creditors' meeting	1. On indictment 2. Summary	A fine The statutory maximum	
99(3)	Directors failing to attend and lay statement in prescribed form before creditors' meeting	1. On indictment 2. Summary	A fine The statutory maximum	
105(3)	Liquidator failing to summon company general meeting and creditors' meeting at each year's end	Summary	One-fifth of the statutory maximum	
106(4)	Liquidator failing to send to registrar account of winding up and return of final meetings	Summary	One-fifth of the statutory maximum	One-fiftieth of the statutory maximum.
106(6)	Liquidator failing to call final meeting of company or creditors	Summary	One-fifth of the statutory maximum	
109(2)	Liquidator failing to publish notice of his appointment	Summary	One-fifth of the statutory maximum	One-fiftieth of the statutory maximum.
114(4)	Directors exercising powers in breach of s 114, where no liquidator	Summary	The statutory maximum	

Section of Act creating offence	General nature of offence	Mode of prosecution	Punishment	Daily default fine (where applicable)
131(7)	Failing to comply with requirements as to statement of affairs, where liquidator appointed	1. On indictment 2. Summary	A fine The statutory maximum	One-tenth of the statutory maximum.
164	Giving, offering etc corrupt inducement affecting appointment of liquidator	1. On indictment 2. Summary	A fine The statutory maximum	
166(7)	Liquidator failing to comply with requirements of s 166 in creditors' voluntary winding up	Summary	The statutory maximum	
188(2)	Default in compliance with s 188 as to notification that company being wound up	Summary	One-fifth of the statutory maximum	One-fiftieth of the statutory maximum.
192(2)	Liquidator failing to notify registrar as to progress of winding up	Summary	One-fifth of the statutory maximum	One-fiftieth of the statutory maximum.
201(4)	Failing to deliver to registrar office copy of court order deferring dissolution	Summary	One-fifth of the statutory maximum	One-fiftieth of the statutory maximum.
203(6)	Failing to deliver to registrar copy of directions or result of appeal under s 203	Summary	One-fifth of the statutory maximum	One-fiftieth of the statutory maximum.
204(7)	Liquidator failing to deliver to registrar copy of court order for early dissolution	Summary	One-fifth of the statutory maximum	One-fiftieth of the statutory maximum.
204(8)	Failing to deliver to registrar copy of court order deferring early dissolution	Summary	One-fifth of the statutory maximum	One-fiftieth of the statutory maximum.
205(7)	Failing to deliver to registrar copy of Secretary of State's directions or court order deferring dissolution	Summary	One-fifth of the statutory maximum	One-fiftieth of the statutory maximum.
206(1)	Fraud etc in anticipation of winding up	1. On indictment 2. Summary	7 years or a fine, or both 6 months or the statutory maximum, or both	
206(2)	Privity to fraud in anticipation of winding up; fraud, or privity to fraud, after commencement of winding up	1. On indictment 2. Summary	7 years or a fine, or both 6 months or the statutory maximum, or both	
206(5)	Knowingly taking in pawn or pledge, or otherwise receiving, company property	1. On indictment 2. Summary	7 years or a fine, or both 6 months or the statutory maximum, or both	
207	Officer of company entering into transaction in fraud of company's creditors	1. On indictment 2. Summary	2 years or a fine, or both 6 months or the statutory maximum, or both	

Section of Act creating offence	General nature of offence	Mode of prosecution	Punishment	Daily default fine (where applicable)
208	Officer of company misconducting himself in course of winding up	1. On indictment 2. Summary	7 years or a fine, or both 6 months or the statutory maximum, or both	
209	Officer or contributory destroying, falsifying, etc company's books	1. On indictment 2. Summary	7 years or a fine, or both 6 months or the statutory maximum, or both	
210	Officer of company making material omission from statement relating to company's affairs	1. On indictment 2. Summary	7 years or a fine, or both 6 months or the statutory maximum, or both	
211	False representation or fraud for purpose of obtaining creditors' consent to an agreement in connection with winding up	1. On indictment 2. Summary	7 years or a fine, or both 6 months or the statutory maximum, or both	
216(4)	Contravening restrictions on re-use of name of company in insolvent liquidation	1. On indictment 2. Summary	2 years or a fine, or both 6 months or the statutory maximum, or both	
235(5)	Failing to co-operate with office-holder	1. On indictment 2. Summary	A fine The statutory maximum	One-tenth of the statutory maximum.
353(1)	Bankrupt failing to disclose property or disposals to official receiver or trustee	1. On indictment 2. Summary	7 years or a fine, or both 6 months or the statutory maximum, or both	
354(1)	Bankrupt failing to deliver property to, or concealing property from, official receiver or trustee	1. On indictment 2. Summary	7 years or a fine, or both 6 months or the statutory maximum, or both	
354(2)	Bankrupt removing property which he is required to deliver to official receiver or trustee	1. On indictment 2. Summary	7 years or a fine, or both 6 months or the statutory maximum, or both	
354(3)	Bankrupt failing to account for loss of substantial part of property	1. On indictment 2. Summary	2 years or a fine, or both 6 months or the statutory maximum, or both	
355(1)	Bankrupt failing to deliver books, papers and records to official receiver or trustee	1. On indictment 2. Summary	7 years or a fine, or both 6 months or the statutory maximum, or both	

Section of Act creating offence	General nature of offence	Mode of prosecution	Punishment	Daily default fine (where applicable)
355(2)	Bankrupt concealing, destroying etc books, papers or records, or making false entries in them	1. On indictment 2. Summary	7 years or a fine, or both 6 months or the statutory maximum, or both	
355(3)	Bankrupt disposing of, or altering, books, papers or records relating to his estate or affairs	1. On indictment 2. Summary	7 years or a fine, or both 6 months or the statutory maximum, or both	
356(1)	Bankrupt making material omission in statement relating to his affairs	1. On indictment 2. Summary	7 years or a fine, or both 6 months or the statutory maximum, or both	
356(2)	Bankrupt making false statement, or failing to inform trustee, where false debt proved	1. On indictment 2. Summary	7 years or a fine, or both 6 months or the statutory maximum, or both	
357	Bankrupt fraudulently disposing of property	1. On indictment 2. Summary	2 years or a fine, or both 6 months or the statutory maximum, or both	
358	Bankrupt absconding with property he is required to deliver to official receiver or trustee	1. On indictment 2. Summary	2 years or a fine, or both 6 months or the statutory maximum, or both	
359(1)	Bankrupt disposing of property obtained on credit and not paid for	1. On indictment 2. Summary	7 years or a fine, or both 6 months or the statutory maximum, or both	
359(2)	Obtaining property in respect of which money is owed by a bankrupt	1. On indictment 2. Summary	7 years or a fine, or both 6 months or the statutory maximum, or both	
360(1)	Bankrupt obtaining credit or engaging in business without disclosing his status or name in which he was made bankrupt	1. On indictment 2. Summary	2 years or a fine, or both 6 months or the statutory maximum, or both	
360(3)	Person made bankrupt in Scotland or Northern Ireland obtaining credit, etc in England and Wales	1. On indictment 2. Summary	2 years or a fine, or both 6 months or the statutory maximum, or both	
361(1)	Bankrupt failing to keep proper accounting records	1. On indictment 2. Summary	2 years or a fine, or both 6 months or the statutory maximum, or both	

[459]

Section of Act creating offence	General nature of offence	Mode of prosecution	Punishment	Daily default fine (where applicable)
362	Bankrupt increasing extent of insolvency by gambling	1. On indictment 2. Summary	2 years or a fine, or both 6 months or the statutory maximum, or both	
389	Acting as insolvency practitioner when not qualified	1. On indictment 2. Summary	2 years or a fine, or both 6 months or the statutory maximum, or both	
429(5)	Contravening s 429 in respect of disabilities imposed by county court on revocation of administration order	1. On indictment 2. Summary	2 years or a fine, or both 6 months or the statutory maximum, or both	
Sch 7, para 4(3)	Failure to attend and give evidence to Insolvency Practitioners Tribunal; suppressing, concealing, etc relevant documents	Summary	Level 3 on the standard scale within the meaning given by section 75 of the Criminal Justice Act 1982	

NOTES
Commencement: 29 December 1986.
This Schedule derived from the Companies Act 1985 and the Insolvency Act 1985 passim.

SCHEDULE 11

Section 437

TRANSITIONAL PROVISIONS AND SAVINGS

PART I

COMPANY INSOLVENCY AND WINDING UP

Administration orders

1.—(1) Where any right to appoint an administrative receiver of a company is conferred by any debentures or floating charge created before the appointed day, the conditions precedent to the exercise of that right are deemed to include the presentation of a petition applying for an administration order to be made in relation to the company.

(2) "Administrative receiver" here has the meaning assigned by section 251.

Receivers and managers (England and Wales)

2.—(1) In relation to any receiver or manager of a company's property who was appointed before the appointed day, the new law does not apply; and the relevant provisions of the former law continue to have effect.

(2) "The new law" here means Chapter I of Part III, and Part VI, of this Act; and "the former law" means the Companies Act and so much of this Act as replaces provisions of that Act (without the amendments in paragraphs 15 to 17 of Schedule 6 to the Insolvency Act 1985, or the associated repeals made by that Act), and any provision of the Insolvency Act 1985 which was in force before the appointed day.

(3) This paragraph is without prejudice to the power conferred by this Act under which rules under section 411 may make transitional provision in connection with the coming into force of those rules; and such provision may apply those rules in relation to the receiver or manager of a company's property notwithstanding that he was appointed before the coming into force of the rules or section 411.

Receivers (Scotland)

3.—(1) In relation to any receiver appointed under section 467 of the Companies Act before the appointed day, the new law does not apply and the relevant provisions of the former law continue to have effect.

(2) "The new law" here means Chapter II of Part III, and Part VI, of this Act; and "the former law" means the Companies Act and so much of this Act as replaces provisions of that Act (without the amendments in paragraphs 18 to 22 of Schedule 6 to the Insolvency Act 1985 or the associated repeals made by that Act), and any provision of the Insolvency Act 1985 which was in force before the appointed day.

(3) This paragraph is without prejudice to the power conferred by this Act under which rules under section 411 may make transitional provision in connection with the coming into force of those rules; and such provision may apply those rules in relation to a receiver appointed under section 467 notwithstanding that he was appointed before the coming into force of the rules or section 411.

Winding up already in progress

4.—(1) In relation to any winding up which has commenced, or is treated as having commenced, before the appointed day, the new law does not apply, and the former law continues to have effect, subject to the following paragraphs.

(2) "The new law" here means any provisions in the first Group of Parts of this Act which replace sections 66 to 87 and 89 to 105 of the Insolvency Act 1985; and "the former law" means Parts XX and XXI of the Companies Act (without the amendments in paragraphs 23 to 52 of Schedule 6 to the Insolvency Act 1985, or the associated repeals made by that Act).

Statement of affairs

5.—(1) Where a winding up by the court in England and Wales has commenced, or is treated as having commenced, before the appointed day, the official receiver or (on appeal from a refusal by him) the court may, at any time on or after that day—

(a) release a person from an obligation imposed on him by or under section 528 of the Companies Act (statement of affairs), or

(b) extend the period specified in subsection (6) of that section.

(2) Accordingly, on and after the appointed day, section 528(6) has effect in relation to a winding up to which this paragraph applies with the omission of the words from "or within" onwards.

Provisions relating to liquidator

6.—(1) This paragraph applies as regards the liquidator in the case of a winding up by the court in England and Wales commenced, or treated as having commenced, before the appointed day.

(2) The official receiver may, at any time when he is liquidator of the company, apply to the Secretary of State for the appointment of a liquidator in his (the official receiver's) place; and on any such application the Secretary of State shall either make an appointment or decline to make one.

(3) Where immediately before the appointed day the liquidator of the company has not made an application under section 545 of the Companies Act (release of liquidators), then—

(a) except where the Secretary of State otherwise directs, sections 146(1) and (2) and 172(8) of this Act apply, and section 545 does not apply, in relation to any liquidator of that company who holds office on or at any time after the appointed day and is not the official receiver;

(b) section 146(3) applies in relation to the carrying out at any time after that day by any liquidator of the company of any of his functions; and

(c) a liquidator in relation to whom section 172(8) has effect by virtue of this paragraph has his release with effect from the time specified in section 174(4)(d) of this Act.

(4) Subsection (6) of section 174 of this Act has effect for the purposes of sub-paragraph (3)(c) above as it has for the purposes of that section, but as if the reference to section 212 were to section 631 of the Companies Act.

(5) The liquidator may employ a solicitor to assist him in the carrying out of his functions without the permission of the committee of inspection; but if he does so employ a solicitor he shall inform the committee of inspection that he has done so.

Winding up under supervision of the court

7. The repeals in Part II of Schedule 10 to the Insolvency Act 1985 of references (in the Companies Act and elsewhere) to a winding up under the supervision of the court do not affect the operation of the enactments in which the references are contained in relation to any case in which an order under section 606 of the Companies Act (power to order winding up under supervision) was made before the appointed day.

Saving for power to make rules

8.—(1) Paragraphs 4 to 7 are without prejudice to the power conferred by this Act under which rules made under section 411 may make transitional provision in connection with the coming into force of those rules.

(2) Such provision may apply those rules in relation to a winding up notwithstanding that the winding up commenced, or is treated as having commenced, before the coming into force of the rules or section 411.

Setting aside of preferences and other transactions

9.—(1) Where a provision in Part VI of this Act applies in relation to a winding up or in relation to a case in which an administration order has been made, a preference given, floating charge created or other transaction entered into before the appointed day shall not be set aside under that provision except to the extent that it could have been set aside under the law in force immediately before that day, assuming for this purpose that any relevant administration order had been a winding-up order.

(2) The references above to setting aside a preference, floating charge or other transaction include the making of an order which varies or reverses any effect of a preference, floating charge or other transaction. **[460]**

NOTES
Commencement: 29 December 1986.
Paras 1, 2, 9 derived from the Insolvency Act 1985, Sch 9, paras 6, 7, 10; paras 4, 5, 7, 8 derived from the Insolvency Act 1985, Sch 9, para 9(1), (2), (6), (7); para 6 derived from the Insolvency Act 1985, Sch 9, para 9(3)–(5), (8).

PART II
INDIVIDUAL INSOLVENCY

Bankruptcy (general)

10.—(1) Subject to the following provisions of this Part of this Schedule, so much of this Act as replaces Part III of the Insolvency Act 1985 does not apply in relation to any case in which a petition in bankruptcy was presented, or a receiving order or adjudication in bankruptcy was made, before the appointed day.

(2) In relation to any such case as is mentioned above, the enactments specified in Schedule 8 to that Act, so far as they relate to bankruptcy, and those specified in Parts III and IV of Schedule 10 to that Act, so far as they so relate, have effect without the amendments and repeals specified in those Schedules.

(3) Where any subordinate legislation made under an enactment referred to in sub-paragraph (2) is in force immediately before the appointed day, that subordinate legislation continues to have effect on and after that day in relation to any such case as is mentioned in sub-paragraph (1).

11.—(1) In relation to any such case as is mentioned in paragraph 10(1) the references in any enactment or subordinate legislation to a petition, order or other matter which is provided for under the Bankruptcy Act 1914 and corresponds to a petition, order or other matter provided for under provisions of this Act replacing Part III of the Insolvency Act 1985 continue on and after the appointed day to have effect as references to the petition, order or matter provided for by the Act of 1914; but otherwise those references have effect on and after that day as references to the petition, order or matter provided for by those provisions of this Act.

(2) Without prejudice to sub-paragraph (1), in determining for the purposes of section 279 of this Act (period of bankruptcy) or paragraph 13 below whether any person was an undischarged bankrupt at a time before the appointed day, an adjudication in bankruptcy and an annulment of a bankruptcy under the Act of 1914 are to be taken into account in the same way, respectively, as a bankruptcy order under the provisions of this Act replacing Part III of the Insolvency Act 1985 and the annulment under section 282 of this Act of such an order.

12. Transactions entered into before the appointed day have effect on and after that day as if references to acts of bankruptcy in the provisions for giving effect to those transactions continued to be references to acts of bankruptcy within the meaning of the Bankruptcy Act 1914, but as if such acts included failure to comply with a statutory demand served under section 268 of this Act.

Discharge from old bankruptcy

13.—(1) Where a person—

(a) was adjudged bankrupt before the appointed day or is adjudged bankrupt on or after that day on a petition presented before that day, and

(b) that person was not an undischarged bankrupt at any time in the period of 15 years ending with the adjudication,

that person is deemed (if not previously discharged) to be discharged from his bankruptcy for the purposes of the Bankruptcy Act 1914 at the end of the discharge period.

(2) Subject to sub-paragraph (3) below, the discharge period for the purposes of this paragraph is—

(a) in the case of a person adjudged bankrupt before the appointed day, the period of 3 years beginning with that day, and

(b) in the case of a person who is adjudged bankrupt on or after that day on a petition presented before that day, the period of 3 years beginning with the date of the adjudication.

(3) Where the court exercising jurisdiction in relation to a bankruptcy to which this paragraph applies is satisfied, on the application of the official receiver, that the bankrupt has failed, or is failing, to comply with any of his obligations under the Bankruptcy Act 1914, any rules made under that Act or any such rules as are mentioned in paragraph 19(1) below, the court may order that the discharge period shall cease to run for such period, or until the fulfilment of such conditions (including a condition requiring the court to be satisfied as to any matter) as may be specified in the order.

Provisions relating to trustee

14.—(1) This paragraph applies as regards the trustee in the case of a person adjudged bankrupt before the appointed day, or adjudged bankrupt on or after that day on a petition presented before that day.

(2) The official receiver may at any time when he is the trustee of the bankrupt's estate apply to the Secretary of State for the appointment of a person as trustee instead of the official receiver; and on any such application the Secretary of State shall either make an appointment or decline to make one.

(3) Where on the appointed day the trustee of a bankrupt's estate has not made an application under section 93 of the Bankruptcy Act 1914 (release of trustee), then—

(a) except where the Secretary of State otherwise directs, sections 298(8), 304 and 331(1) to (3) of this Act apply, and section 93 of the Act of 1914 does not apply, in relation to any trustee of the bankrupt's estate who holds office on or at any time after the appointed day and is not the official receiver;

(b) section 331(4) of this Act applies in relation to the carrying out at any time on or after the appointed day by the trustee of the bankrupt's estate of any of his functions; and

(c) a trustee in relation to whom section 298(8) of this Act has effect by virtue of this paragraph has his release with effect from the time specified in section 299(3)(d).

(4) Subsection (5) of section 299 has effect for the purposes of sub-paragraph (3)(c) as it has for the purposes of that section.

(5) In the application of subsection (3) of section 331 in relation to a case by virtue of this paragraph, the reference in that subsection to section 330(1) has effect as a reference to section 67 of the Bankruptcy Act 1914.

(6) The trustee of the bankrupt's estate may employ a solicitor to assist him in the carrying out of his functions without the permission of the committee of inspection; but if he does so employ a solicitor, he shall inform the committee of inspection that he has done so.

Copyright

15. Where a person who is adjudged bankrupt on a petition presented on or after the appointed day is liable, by virtue of a transaction entered into before that day, to pay royalties or a share of the profits to any person in respect of any copyright or interest in copyright comprised in the bankrupt's estate, section 60 of the Bankruptcy Act 1914 (limitation on trustee's powers in relation to copyright) applies in relation to the trustee of that estate as it applies in relation to a trustee in bankruptcy under the Act of 1914.

Second bankruptcy

16.—(1) Sections 334 and 335 of this Act apply with the following modifications where the earlier bankruptcy (within the meaning of section 334) is a bankruptcy in relation to which the Act of 1914 applies instead of the second Group of Parts in this Act, that is to say—

   (*a*) references to property vested in the existing trustee under section 307(3) of this Act have effect as references to such property vested in that trustee as was acquired by or devolved on the bankrupt after the commencement (within the meaning of the Act of 1914) of the earlier bankruptcy; and

   (*b*) references to an order under section 310 of this Act have effect as references to an order under section 51 of the Act of 1914.

(2) Section 39 of the Act of 1914 (second bankruptcy) does not apply where a person who is an undischarged bankrupt under that Act is adjudged bankrupt under this Act.

Setting aside of preferences and other transactions

17.—(1) A preference given, assignment made or other transaction entered into before the appointed day shall not be set aside under any of sections 339 to 344 of this Act except to the extent that it could have been set aside under the law in force immediately before that day.

(2) References in sub-paragraph (1) to setting aside a preference, assignment or other transaction include the making of any order which varies or reverses any effect of a preference, assignment or other transaction.

Bankruptcy offences

18.—(1) Where a bankruptcy order is made under this Act on or after the appointed day, a person is not guilty of an offence under Chapter VI of Part IX in respect of anything done before that day; but, notwithstanding the repeal by the Insolvency Act 1985 of the Bankruptcy Act 1914, is guilty of an offence under the Act of 1914 in respect of anything done before the appointed day which would have been an offence under that Act if the making of the bankruptcy order had been the making of a receiving order under that Act.

(2) Subsection (5) of section 350 of this Act applies (instead of sections 157(2), 158(2), 161 and 165 of the Act of 1914) in relation to proceedings for an offence under that Act which are instituted (whether by virtue of sub-paragraph (1) or otherwise) after the appointed day.

Power to make rules

19.—(1) The preceding provisions of this Part of this Schedule are without prejudice to the power conferred by this Act under which rules under section 412 may make transitional provision in connection with the coming into force of those rules; and such provision may apply those rules in relation to a bankruptcy notwithstanding that it arose from a petition presented before either the coming into force of the rules or the appointed day.

(2) Rules under section 412 may provide for such notices served before the appointed day as may be prescribed to be treated for the purposes of this Act as statutory demands served under section 268.   **[461]**

NOTES

Commencement: 29 December 1986.

Paras 10–13, 15–19 derived from the Insolvency Act 1985, Sch 9, paras 11–14, 18–22; para 14 derived from the Insolvency Act 1985, Sch 9, paras 15–17.

PART III
TRANSITIONAL EFFECT OF PART XVI

20.—(1) A transaction entered into before the appointed day shall not be set aside under Part XVI of this Act except to the extent that it could have been set aside under the law in force immediately before that day.

(2) References above to setting aside a transaction include the making of any order which varies or reverses any effect of a transaction.

PART IV
INSOLVENCY PRACTITIONERS

21. Where an individual began to act as an insolvency practitioner in relation to any person before the appointed day, nothing in section 390(2) or (3) prevents that individual from being qualified to act as an insolvency practitioner in relation to that person.

PART V
GENERAL TRANSITIONAL PROVISIONS AND SAVINGS

Interpretation for this Part

22. In this Part of this Schedule, "the former enactments" means so much of the Companies Act as is repealed and replaced by this Act, the Insolvency Act 1985 and the other enactments repealed by this Act.

General saving for past acts and events

23. So far as anything done or treated as done under or for the purposes of any provision of the former enactments could have been done under or for the purposes of the corresponding provision of this Act, it is not invalidated by the repeal of that provision but has effect as if done under or for the purposes of the corresponding provision; and any order, regulation, rule or other instrument made or having effect under any provision of the former enactments shall, insofar as its effect is preserved by this paragraph, be treated for all purposes as made and having effect under the corresponding provision.

Periods of time

24. Where any period of time specified in a provision of the former enactments is current immediately before the appointed day, this Act has effect as if the corresponding provision had been in force when the period began to run; and (without prejudice to the foregoing) any period of time so specified and current is deemed for the purposes of this Act—

(a) to run from the date or event from which it was running immediately before the appointed day, and

(b) to expire (subject to any provision of this Act for its extension) whenever it would have expired if this Act had not been passed;

and any rights, priorities, liabilities, reliefs, obligations, requirements, powers, duties or exemptions dependent on the beginning, duration or end of such a period as above mentioned shall be under this Act as they were or would have been under the former enactments.

Internal cross-references in this Act

25. Where in any provision of this Act there is a reference to another such provision, and the first-mentioned provision operates, or is capable of operating, in relation to things done or omitted, or events occurring or not occurring, in the past (including in

particular past acts of compliance with any enactment, failures of compliance, contraventions, offences and convictions of offences), the reference to the other provision is to be read as including a reference to the corresponding provision of the former enactments.

Punishment of offences

26.—(1) Offences committed before the appointed day under any provision of the former enactments may, notwithstanding any repeal by this Act, be prosecuted and punished after that day as if this Act had not passed.

(2) A contravention of any provision of the former enactments committed before the appointed day shall not be visited with any severer punishment under or by virtue of this Act than would have been applicable under that provision at the time of the contravention; but where an offence for the continuance of which a penalty was provided has been committed under any provision of the former enactments, proceedings may be taken under this Act in respect of the continuance of the offence on and after the appointed day in the like manner as if the offence had been committed under the corresponding provision of this Act.

References elsewhere to the former enactments

27.—(1) A reference in any enactment, instrument or document (whether express or implied, and in whatever phraseology) to a provision of the former enactments (including the corresponding provision of any yet earlier enactment) is to be read, where necessary to retain for the enactment, instrument or document the same force and effect as it would have had but for the passing of this Act, as, or as including, a reference to the corresponding provision by which it is replaced in this Act.

(2) The generality of the preceding sub-paragraph is not affected by any specific conversion of references made by this Act, nor by the inclusion in any provision of this Act of a reference (whether express or implied, and in whatever phraseology) to the provision of the former enactments corresponding to that provision, or to a provision of the former enactments which is replaced by a corresponding provision of this Act.

Saving for power to repeal provisions in section 51

28. The Secretary of State may by order in a statutory instrument repeal subsections (3) to (5) of section 51 of this Act and the entries in Schedule 10 relating to subsections (4) and (5) of that section.

Saving for Interpretation Act 1978 ss 16, 17

29. Nothing in this Schedule is to be taken as prejudicing sections 16 and 17 of the Interpretation Act 1978 (savings from, and effect of, repeals); and for the purposes of section 17(2) of that Act (construction of references to enactments repealed and replaced, etc), so much of section 18 of the Insolvency Act 1985 as is replaced by a provision of this Act is deemed to have been repealed by this Act and not by the Company Directors Disqualification Act 1986.   [462]

NOTES
Commencement: 29 December 1986.
Para 20 derived from the Insolvency Act 1985, Sch 9, para 24; para 21 derived from the Insolvency Act 1985, Sch 9, para 1; paras 22–29 are drafting provisions.

SCHEDULE 12

Section 438

ENACTMENTS REPEALED

Chapter	Short Title	Extent of Repeal
1970 c 8	The Insolvency Services (Accounting and Investment) Act 1970	The whole Act.

Chapter	Short Title	Extent of Repeal
1976 c 60	The Insolvency Act 1976	Section 3.
1985 c 6	The Companies Act 1985	In section 463(4), the words "Subject to section 617".
		Sections 467 to 485.
		In section 486, in the definition of "company" the words "other than in Chapter II of this Part"; and the definitions of "instrument of appointment", "prescribed", "receiver" and "register of charges".
		Sections 488 to 650.
		Sections 659 to 664.
		Sections 665 to 674.
		Section 709(4).
		Section 710(4).
		Section 724.
		Schedule 16.
		In Schedule 24, the entries relating to section 467; all entries thereafter up to and including section 641(2); and the entry relating to section 710(4).
1985 c 65	The Insolvency Act 1985	Sections 1 to 11.
		Section 15.
		Section 17.
		Section 19.
		Sections 20 to 107.
		Section 108(1) and (3) to (7).
		Sections 109 to 211.
		Sections 212 to 214.
		Section 216.
		Section 217(1) to (3).
		Sections 221 to 234.
		In section 235, subsections (2) to (5).
		In section 236, subsections (3) to (5).
		In Schedule 1, paragraphs 1 to 4, and sub-paragraph (4) of paragraph 5.
		Schedules 3 to 5.
		In Schedule 6, paragraphs 5, 6, 9, 15 to 17, 20 to 22, 25 to 44 and 48 to 52.
		Schedule 7.
		In Schedule 9, paragraphs 1 and 4 to 24.
		Schedule 10.
1985 c 66	The Bankruptcy (Scotland) Act 1985	In Schedule 7, paragraphs 19 to 22.
1986 c 44	The Gas Act 1986	In Schedule 7, paragraph 31.

[463]

NOTE
Commencement: 29 December 1986.

SCHEDULE 13

Section 439(1)

CONSEQUENTIAL AMENDMENTS OF COMPANIES ACT 1985

PART I

INTERNAL AND OTHER SECTION REFERENCES AMENDED OR RE-AMENDED

Section of Act	Consequential amendment or re-amendment
Section 13(4)	After "this Act", add "and the Insolvency Act".
Section 44(7)	In paragraph (*a*), for "section 582" substitute "section 110 of the Insolvency Act".
Section 103(7)	In paragraph (*a*), the same amendment.
Section 131(7)	The same amendment.
Section 140(2)	In paragraph (*b*), for "section 518" substitute "section 123 of the Insolvency Act".
Section 153(3)	In paragraph (*f*), for "section 582" substitute "section 110 of the Insolvency Act".
	In paragraph (*g*), for "Chapter II of Part II of the Insolvency Act 1985" substitute "Part I of the Insolvency Act".
Section 156(3)	For "section 517" substitute "section 122 of the Insolvency Act".
Section 173(4)	The same amendment.
Section 196	For this section substitute—
	"196.—(1) The following applies in the case of a company registered in England and Wales, where debentures of the company are secured by a charge which, as created, was a floating charge.
	(2) If possession is taken, by or on behalf of the holders of any of the debentures, of any property comprised in or subject to the charge, and the company is not at that time in course of being wound up, the company's preferential debts shall be paid out of assets coming to the hands of the person taking possession in priority to any claims for principal or interest in respect of the debentures.
	(3) "Preferential debts" means the categories of debts listed in Schedule 6 to the Insolvency Act; and for the purposes of that Schedule "the relevant date" is the date of possession being taken as above mentioned.
	(4) Payments made under this section shall be recouped, as far as may be, out of the assets of the company available for payment of general creditors."
Section 222(4)	For "section 106 of the Insolvency Act 1985" substitute "section 411 of the Insolvency Act".
Section 225	At the end of the section add—
	"(8) At any time when an administration order is in force, under Part II of the Insolvency Act is in force this section has effect as if subsections (3) and (5) to (7) were omitted".
Section 380(4)	In paragraph (*j*), for "section 572(1)(*a*)" substitute "section 84(1)(*a*) of the Insolvency Act".
Section 441(1)	For "section 13 of the Insolvency Act 1985" substitute "section 8 of the Company Directors Disqualification Act 1986".
Section 449(1)	In paragraph (*ba*), for "section 12 or 13 of the Insolvency Act 1985" substitute "section 6, 7 or 8 of the Company Directors Disqualification Act 1986".
Section 461(6)	For "section 106 of the Insolvency Act 1985" substitute "section 411 of the Insolvency Act".

Section of Act	Consequential amendment or re-amendment
Section 462(5)	After "this Part" insert "and Part III of the Insolvency Act 1986".
Section 463(2)	For "Part XX (except section 623(4))" substitute "Part IV of the Insolvency Act (except section 185)".
Section 463(3)	For this subsection substitute— "(3) Nothing in this section derogates from the provisions of sections 53(7) and 54(6) of the Insolvency Act (attachment of floating charge on appointment of receiver), or prejudices the operation of sections 175 and 176 of that Act (payment of preferential debts in winding up)".
Section 464(6)	For "section 89 of the Insolvency Act 1985" substitute "sections 175 and 176 of the Insolvency Act".
Section 657(2)	For "subsections (3) and (5) to (7) of section 91 of the Insolvency Act 1985 and section 92 of that Act" substitute "section 178(4) and sections 179 to 182 of the Insolvency Act".
Section 658(1)	For "Subsection (7) of section 91 of the Insolvency Act 1985" substitute "Section 180 of the Insolvency Act".
Section 711(2)	In paragraph (b), for "section 600" substitute "section 109 of the Insolvency Act".
Section 733	In subsection (1), omit "295(7)". In subsection (3), for "216(3) or 295(7)" substitute "or 216(3)".

PART II

AMENDMENT OF PART XXVI (INTERPRETATION)

In Part XXVI of the Companies Act, after section 735, insert the following section—

"735A Relationship of this Act to Insolvency Act

(1) In this Act "the Insolvency Act" means the Insolvency Act 1986; and in the following provisions of this Act, namely, sections 375(1)(b), 425(6)(a), 440, 449(1)(a) and (d), 460(2), 675, 676, 677, 699(1), 728 and Schedule 21, paragraph 6(1), the words "this Act" are to be read as including Parts I to VII of that Act, sections 411, 413, 414, 416 and 417 in Part XV of that Act, and also the Company Directors Disqualification Act 1986.

(2) In sections 704(5), 706(1), 707(1), 708(1)(a) and (4), 710(5), 713(1), 729 and 732(3) references to the Companies Acts include Parts I to VII of the Insolvency Act, sections 411, 413, 414, 416 and 417 in Part XV of that Act, and also the Company Directors Disqualification Act 1986.

(3) Subsections (1) and (2) apply unless the contrary intention appears."

[464]

NOTE
  Commencement: 29 December 1986.

SCHEDULE 14

Section 439(2)

CONSEQUENTIAL AMENDMENTS OF OTHER ENACTMENTS

Enactment	Amendment
Deeds of Arrangement Act 1914 (c 47): Section 3(1)	For "Part III of the Insolvency Act 1985" substitute "Parts VIII to XI of the Insolvency Act 1986".
Section 3(4)	The same amendment.
Section 11(1) and (2)	In each subsection, the same amendment.

Enactment	Amendment
Section 15(1)	For "section 207 of the Insolvency Act 1985" substitute "section 412 of the Insolvency Act 1986".
Section 16	The same amendment as of section 3(1).
Section 23	The same amendment.
Section 30(1)	For the definition of "property" substitute– "'property' has the meaning given by section 436 of the Insolvency Act 1986".
Law of Property Act 1925 (c 20): Section 52(2)(*b*)	For "section 91 or 161 of the Insolvency Act 1985" substitute "sections 178 to 180 or sections 315 to 319 of the Insolvency Act 1986".
Land Registration Act 1925 (c 21): Section 42(2)	For "section 161 of the Insolvency Act 1985" substitute "sections 315 to 319 of the Insolvency Act 1986".
Section 112AA(3)(*a*)	For "the Insolvency Act 1985 or the Companies Act 1985" substitute "the Insolvency Act 1986".
Third Parties (Rights against Insurers) Act 1930 (c 25): Section 1	In subsection (1)(*b*), for the words from "a composition" to "that Chapter" substitute "a voluntary arrangement proposed for the purposes of Part I of the Insolvency Act 1986 being approved under that Part". In subsection (2), for "228 of the Insolvency Act 1985" substitute "421 of the Insolvency Act 1986". In subsection (3), the same amendment.
Section 2	In subsection (1), the same amendment as of section 1(2). In subsection (1A), for the words from "composition or scheme" to the end of the subsection substitute "voluntary arrangement proposed for the purposes of, and approved under, Part I or Part VIII of the Insolvency Act 1986".
Section 4	In paragraph (*b*), the same amendment as of section 1(2).
Exchange Control Act 1947 (c 14): Schedule 4	In paragraphs 6 and 8(4), for "section 120 of the Insolvency Act 1985" substitute "sections 267 to 270 of the Insolvency Act 1986".
Arbitration Act 1950 (c 27): Section 3(2)	For "committee established under section 148 of the Insolvency Act 1985" substitute "creditors' committee established under section 301 of the Insolvency Act 1986".
Agricultural Marketing Act 1958 (c 47): Schedule 2	For paragraph 4 substitute— "4.—(1) A scheme shall provide for the winding up of the board, and for that purpose may apply Part V of the Insolvency Act 1986 (winding up of unregistered companies), subject to the following modifications. (2) For the purposes of sections 221, 222 and 224 of the Act of 1986, the principal place of business of the board is deemed to be the office of the board the address of which is registered by the Minister under paragraph 3 above. (3) Section 223 does not apply.

Enactment	Amendment
	(4) Section 224 applies as if the words "or any member of it as such" were omitted. (5) A petition for winding up the board may be presented by the Minister as well as by any person authorised under Part IV of the Insolvency Act 1986 to present a petition for winding up a company".
Charities Act 1960 (c 58): Section 30(1)	For "Companies Act 1985" substitute "Insolvency Act 1986".
Licensing Act 1964 (c 26): Section 8(1)	In paragraph (*c*), for the words from "composition or scheme" to "Act 1985" substitute "voluntary arrangement proposed by the holder of the licence has been approved under Part VIII of the Insolvency Act 1986"; and for "composition or scheme" substitute "voluntary arrangement".
Section 10(5)	For the words from "composition or scheme" to "Act 1985" substitute "voluntary arrangement proposed by the holder of a justices' licence has been approved under Part VIII of the Insolvency Act 1986"; and for "composition or scheme" substitute "voluntary arrangement".
Industrial and Provident Societies Act 1965 (c 12): Section 55	For "Companies Act 1985" substitute "Insolvency Act 1986".
Medicines Act 1968 (c 67): Section 72(4)	For the words from "composition or scheme" to the end of the subsection substitute "voluntary arrangement proposed for the purposes of, and approved under, Part VIII of the Insolvency Act 1986".
Income and Corporation Taxes Act 1970 (c 10): Section 247(7)	For "Companies Act 1985" substitute "Insolvency Act 1986".
Section 265(5)	For "538 of the Companies Act 1985" substitute "145 of the Insolvency Act 1986".
Conveyancing and Feudal Reform (Scotland) Act 1970 (c 35): Schedule 3	In Standard Condition 9(2)(*b*), for "228 of the Insolvency Act 1985" substitute "421 of the Insolvency Act 1986".

Tribunals and Inquiries Act 1971 (c 62):
  Schedule 1
	For paragraph 10A substitute—
	  "10A. The Insolvency Practitioners Tribunal referred to in section 396 of the Insolvency Act 1986".

Superannuation Act 1972 (c 11): Section 5(2)	For "156 of the Insolvency Act 1985" substitute "310 of the Insolvency Act 1986"; and for "the said section 156" substitute "the said section 310".
Road Traffic Act 1972 (c 20): Section 150	In subsection (1)(*b*), for "228 of the Insolvency Act 1985" substitute "421 of the Insolvency Act 1986". In subsection (2), the same amendment.
Finance Act 1972 (c 41): Schedule 16	In paragraph 13(5), for "Companies Act 1985" substitute "Insolvency Act 1986".

Enactment	Amendment
Land Charges Act 1972 (c 61): Section 16(2)	For "207 of the Insolvency Act 1985" substitute "412 of the Insolvency Act 1986"; and for "Part III" substitute "Parts VIII to XI".
Matrimonial Causes Act 1973 (c 18): Section 39	For "section 174 of the Insolvency Act 1985" substitute "section 339 or 340 of the Insolvency Act 1986".
Powers of Criminal Courts Act 1973 (c 62): Section 39(3)	In paragraph (*d*), for "174(10) of the Insolvency Act 1985" substitute "341(4) of the Insolvency Act 1986".
Friendly Societies Act 1974 (c 46): Section 87(2)	For "Companies Act 1985" substitute "Insolvency Act 1986".
Social Security Pensions Act 1975 (c 60): Section 58	The section is to have effect as originally enacted, and without the amendment made by paragraph 26(1) of Schedule 8 to the Insolvency Act 1985.
Schedule 3	At the end of paragraph 3(1) add— "or (in the case of a company not in liquidation)— (*a*) the appointment of a receiver as mentioned in section 40 of the Insolvency Act 1986 (debenture-holders secured by floating charge), or (*b*) the appointment of a receiver under section 53(6) or 54(5) of that Act (Scottish company with property subject to floating charge), or (*c*) the taking of possession by debenture-holders (so secured) as mentioned in section 196 of the Companies Act 1985". In paragraph 4, for the words from the beginning to "Act 1985" substitute "Section 196(3) of the Companies Act 1985 and section 387 of the Insolvency Act 1986 apply as regards the meaning in this Schedule of the expression 'the relevant date'.".
Recess Elections Act 1975 (c 66): Section 1(2)	In the definition of "certificate of vacancy", for "214(6)(*a*) of the Insolvency Act 1985" substitute "427(6)(*a*) of the Insolvency Act 1986".
Policyholders Protection Act 1975 (c 75): Section 5(1)(*a*)	For "Companies Act 1985" substitute "Insolvency Act 1986".
Section 15(1)	For "532 of the Companies Act 1985" substitute "135 of the Insolvency Act 1986".
Section 16(1)(*b*)	The same amendment as of section 5(1)(*a*).
Development Land Tax Act 1976 (c 24): Section 33(1)	For "538 of the Companies Act 1985" substitute "145 of the Insolvency Act 1986".
Restrictive Trade Practices Act 1976 (c 34): Schedule 1	For paragraph 9A (inserted by Insolvency Act 1985, section 217(4)) substitute—

Enactment	Amendment
	"9A. Insolvency services within the meaning of section 428 of the Insolvency Act 1986".
Employment Protection (Consolidation) Act 1978 (c 44):	
Section 106(5)	In paragraph (b), for "228 of the Insolvency Act 1985" substitute "421 of the Insolvency Act 1986". In paragraph (c), for the words from "a composition or" to the end of the paragraph substitute "a voluntary arrangement proposed for the purposes of Part I of the Insolvency Act 1986 is approved under that Part".
Section 106(6)	The same amendment as of section 106(5)(c).
Section 122	In subsection (7), for "181 of the Insolvency Act 1985" substitute "348 of the Insolvency Act 1986"; and for "section 106" substitute "section 411". In subsection (9), for the words from "composition or scheme" to "Act 1985" substitute "voluntary arrangement proposed for the purposes of, and approved under, Part I or VIII of the Insolvency Act 1986".
Section 123(6)	For the words from "composition or scheme" to "Act 1985" substitute "voluntary arrangement proposed for the purposes of, and approved under, Part I or VIII of the Insolvency Act 1986".
Section 125(2)	For paragraph (a) substitute— "(a) the following provisions of the Insolvency Act 1986— (i) sections 175 and 176, 328 and 329, 348 and Schedule 6, and (ii) any rules under that Act applying section 348 of it to the winding up of a company; and"
Section 127(1)	In paragraph (b), for "228 of the Insolvency Act 1985" substitute "421 of the Insolvency Act 1986". In paragraph (c), for the words from "composition or" to the end of the paragraph substitute "voluntary arrangement proposed for the purposes of Part I of the Insolvency Act 1986 is approved under that Part".
Section 127(2)	In paragraph (c), the same amendment as of section 127(1)(c).
Credit Unions Act 1979 (c 34):	
Section 6(1)	For "517(1)(e) of the Companies Act 1985" substitute "122(1)(e) of the Insolvency Act 1986"; and for "517(1)(e) of the Act of 1985" substitute "122(1)(e) of the Act of 1986".
Banking Act 1979 (c 37):	
Section 6(3)	In paragraph (b), for "Part XXI of the Companies Act 1985" substitute "Part V of the Insolvency Act 1986".
Section 18	In subsection (1), for "Companies Act 1985" substitute "Insolvency Act 1986"; and in paragraph (a) of the subsection for "518" substitute "123". In subsection (2), for "Companies Act 1985" substitute "Insolvency Act 1986"; and for "Part XXI" substitute "Part V". In subsection (4)— in paragraph (a), for "Companies Act 1985" substitute "Insolvency Act 1986"; in paragraph (b), for "518 of the said Act of 1985" substitute "123 of the said Act of 1986"; and

Enactment	Amendment
Section 19	in paragraph (c), for "Part XXI of the said Act of 1985" substitute "Part V of the said Act of 1986". In subsection (2), for paragraph (ba) substitute— "(ba) in connection with any proceedings under any provision of— (i) Part XVIII or XX of the Companies Act 1985, or (ii) Parts I to VII of the Insolvency Act 1986 (other than sections 236 and 237)". In subsection (8), for paragraphs (a) and (aa) substitute— "(a) for the references in subsection (2) to Part XVIII or XX of the Companies Act 1985 and Parts I to VII of the Insolvency Act 1986, there shall be substituted references to Parts V, VI and IX of the Companies Act (Northern Ireland) 1960 (the reference to sections 236 and 237 of the Act of 1986 being disregarded)".
Section 28	In subsection (3), in paragraph (c), for "83 of the Insolvency Act 1985" substitute "95 of the Insolvency Act 1986". In subsection (4), in paragraph (a), for "Part XXI of the Companies Act 1985" substitute "Part V of the Insolvency Act 1986". In subsection (6)(b), for sub-paragraphs (ii) to (iv) substitute— "(ii) to be a member of a liquidation committee established under Part IV or V of the Insolvency Act 1986; (iii) to be a member of a creditors committee appointed under section 301 of that Act; and (iv) to be a commissioner under section 30 of the Bankruptcy (Scotland) Act 1985"; (v) to be a member of a committee of inspection appointed for the purposes of Part V or Part IX of the Companies Act (Northern Ireland) 1960; and (in the passage following sub-paragraph (iv)) for "such a committee as is mentioned in paragraph (b)(ii) or (iv) above" substitute "a liquidation committee, creditors' committee or committee of inspection". In subsection (7), in paragraph (b), for the words from "section 116(4)" to the end of the paragraph substitute "section 261(1) of the Insolvency Act 1986 to any person in whom the property of the firm is vested under section 282(4) of that Act".
Section 31(7)	For paragraph (a) substitute— "(a) for England and Wales, under sections 411 and 412 of the Insolvency Act 1986"; and in paragraph (b) for "the said section 106" substitute "section 411 of that Act".
British Aerospace Act 1980 (c 26): Section 9(1)	In paragraph (a), for "Companies Act 1985" substitute "Insolvency Act 1986".
Public Passenger Vehicles Act 1981 (c 14): Section 19(3)	In paragraph (a), for "Chapter III of Part II of the Insolvency Act 1985" substitute "Part II of the Insolvency Act 1986".

Enactment	Amendment
Finance Act 1981 (c 35):	
Section 55(4)	For "Companies Act 1985" substitute "Insolvency Act 1986".
Supreme Court Act 1981 (c 54):	
Section 40A(2)	For "section 179 of the Insolvency Act 1985" substitute "section 346 of the Insolvency Act 1986"; and for "621 of the Companies Act 1985" substitute "183 of the Insolvency Act 1986".
Trustee Savings Banks Act 1981 (c 65):	
Section 31	In paragraph (*b*), for "666 to 669 of the Companies Act 1985" substitute "221 to 224 of the Insolvency Act 1986".
Section 54(2)	For "666(6) of the Companies Act 1985" substitute "221(6) of the Insolvency Act 1986".
Iron and Steel Act 1982 (c 25):	
Schedule 4	In paragraph 3(3) after "Companies Act 1985" insert "or the Insolvency Act 1986".
Civil Jurisdiction and Judgments Act 1982 (c 27):	
Section 18(3)	In paragraph (*ba*), for "213 of the Insolvency Act 1985" substitute "426 of the Insolvency Act 1986".
Schedule 5	In paragraph (1), for "Companies Act 1985" substitute "Insolvency Act 1986".
Insurance Companies Act 1982 (c 50):	
Section 53	For "Companies Act" (the first time) substitute "Insolvency Act 1986"; and for "Companies Act" (the second time) substitute "that Act of 1986".
Section 54	In subsection (1), for "the Companies Act" (the first time) substitute "Part IV or V of the Insolvency Act 1986"; and in paragraph (*a*), for "518 or sections 667 to 669" substitute "123 or sections 222 to 224". In subsection (4) for "Companies Act" (the first time) substitute "Insolvency Act 1986".
Section 55	In subsection (5), for "subsection (3) of section 540 of the Companies Act" substitute "section 168(2) of the Insolvency Act 1986". In subsection (6), for "631 of the Companies Act" substitute "212 of the Insolvency Act 1986".
Section 56	In subsection (4), for "Section 90(5) of the Insolvency Act 1985" substitute "Section 177(5) of the Insolvency Act 1986"; and for "section 90 of the said Act of 1985" substitute "section 177 of the said Act of 1986". In subsection (7), for "section 539(1) of the Companies Act" substitute "section 167 of, and Schedule 4 to, the Insolvency Act 1986".
Section 59	In subsection (1), for "106 of the Insolvency Act 1985" substitute "411 of the Insolvency Act 1986". In subsection (2), for "106 of the Insolvency Act 1985" substitute "411 of the Insolvency Act 1986"; and for "section 89 of, and Schedule 4 to, the Insolvency Act 1985" substitute "sections 175 and 176 of, and Schedule 6 to, the Insolvency Act 1986".
Section 96(1)	In the definition of "insolvent", for "517 and 518 or section 666 of the Companies Act" substitute "122 and 123 or section 221 of the Insolvency Act 1986".

Enactment	Amendment
Finance Act 1983 (c 28): Schedule 5	In paragraph 5(4), for "Companies Act 1985" substitute "Insolvency Act 1986".
Telecommunications Act 1984 (c 12): Section 68(1)	In paragraph (*a*), for "Companies Act 1985" substitute "Insolvency Act 1986".

County Courts Act 1984 (c 28):
    Section 98
	For subsection (3) substitute—
	    "(3) The provisions of this section have effect subject to those of sections 183, 184 and 346 of the Insolvency Act 1986".

Section 102	For subsection (8) substitute— "(8) Nothing in this section affects section 346 of the Insolvency Act 1986".
Section 109(2)	For "179 of the Insolvency Act 1985" substitute "346 of the Insolvency Act 1986".
Finance Act 1985 (c 54): Section 79	Omit the word "altogether"; and after "Companies Act 1985" insert "sections 110 and 111 of the Insolvency Act 1986".
Housing Act 1985 (c 68): Schedule 18	In paragraphs 3(4) and 5(3), for "228 of the Insolvency Act 1985" substitute "421 of the Insolvency Act 1986".

[465]

NOTE
Commencement: 29 December 1986.

DERIVATION TABLE

Note: The following abbreviations are used in this Table:—

"INS 1970"	=	The Insolvency Services (Accounting and Investment) Act 1970 (c 8)
"INS 1976"	=	The Insolvency Act 1976 (c 60)
"CA"	=	The Companies Act 1985 (c 6)
"IA"	=	The Insolvency Act 1985 (c 65)
"B(Sc)"	=	The Bankruptcy (Scotland) Act 1985 (c 66)

Provision	Derivation	Provision	Derivation
1	IA s 20	45	IA s 51
2	IA s 21	46	IA s 52
3	IA s 22	47	IA s 53
4	IA s 23(1)–(6), (7) (part)	48	IA s 54
5	IA s 24	49	IA s 55
6	IA s 25	50	CA s 487
7	IA s 26	51	CA s 467
8	IA s 27	52	CA s 468
9	IA s 28	53	CA s 469; IA s 56 (part)
10	IA s 29	54	CA s 470
11	IA s 30	55	CA s 471; IA s 57
12	IA s 31	56	CA s 472
13	IA s 32	57	CA s 473; IA s 58
14	IA s 33	58	CA s 474
15	IA s 34(1)–(8), (12)	59	CA s 475; IA Sch 6 para 20(2)
16	IA s 34(9), (10)		
17	IA s 35	60	CA s 476; IA Sch 6 para 21
18	IA s 36		
19	IA s 37(1)–(3)	61	CA s 477; IA s 59
20	IA s 37(4), (5)	62	CA s 478; IA s 60, Sch 6 para 13
21	IA s 38		
22	IA s 39	63	CA s 479; IA s 61
23	IA s 40	64	CA s 480
24	IA s 41	65	CA s 481; IA s 62
25	IA s 42	66	CA s 482; IA s 63
26	IA s 43	67	CA s 482A; IA s 64
27	IA ss 34(11), 44	68	CA s 482B; IA s 65
28	CA s 488; IA s 45(1)	69	CA s 483
29	CA s 500; IA s 45(2)	70	CA ss 462(4), 484, 486 (part)
30	CA s 489		
31	CA s 490	71	CA s 485
32	CA s 491	72	CA s 724
33	IA s 46	73	CA s 501
34	IA s 47	74	CA s 502
35	CA s 492(1), (2); IA Sch 6 para 16(2)	75	CA s 503
		76	CA s 504
36	CA s 494	77	CA s 505
37	CA s 492(3); IA Sch 6 para 16(3), (4)	78	CA s 506
		79	CA s 507; IA Sch 6 para 5
38	CA s 498; IA Sch 6 para 17		
		80	CA s 508
39	CA s 493	81	CA s 509
40	CA s 196 (part); IA Sch 6 para 15(2), (3)	82	CA s 510
		83	CA s 511
41	CA s 499	84	CA s 572
42	IA s 48	85	CA s 573
43	IA s 49	86	CA s 574
44	IA s 50	87	CA s 575

Provision	Derivation	Provision	Derivation
88	CA s 576	134	IA s 68(5), (6)
89	CA s 577; IA Sch 6 para 35	135	CA s 532; IA s 69(3)
		136	IA s 70(1)–(3); 4(a), (5), (6)
90	CA s 578		
91	CA s 580	137	IA s 70(4)(b), (7)–(9)
92	CA s 581	138	CA s 535; IA s 71, Sch 6 para 30
93	CA s 584; IA Sch 6 para 36		
		139	IA s 72
94	CA s 585(1)–(4), (7)	140	IA s 73
95	IA s 83(1)–(6), (9), (10)	141	IA s 74
96	IA s 83(7) (part)	142	IA s 75
97	CA s 587; IA s 85(1)	143	IA s 69(1), (2)
98	IA s 85(2), (3), (6)–(8), (9)(a), (10)	144	CA s 537
		145	CA s 538
99	IA s 85(4), 5, (9)(b), (c), (10)	146	IA s 78
		147	CA s 549
100	CA s 589; IA Sch 6 para 37(1), (2)	148	CA s 550
		149	CA s 552; IA Sch 6 para 32
101	CA s 590; IA Sch 6 para 38(2)–(4)		
		150	CA s 553
102	IA s 83(7) (part)	151	CA s 554
103	CA s 591; IA Sch 6 para 39	152	CA s 555
		153	CA s 557
104	CA s 592	154	CA s 558
105	CA s 594; IA s 83(8)	155	CA s 559
106	CA s 595(1)–(5), (8)	156	CA s 560
107	CA s 597	157	CA s 562; IA Sch 6 para 33
108	CA s 599		
109	CA s 600	158	CA s 565
110	CA ss 582(1)–(4), (7), 593; IA Sch 6 para 40	159	CA s 566
		160	CA s 567; IA Sch 6 para 34
111	CA s 582(5), (6), (8)		
112	CA s 602	161	CA s 569
113	CA s 603	162	CA s 571
114	IA s 82	163	IA s 94
115	CA s 604	164	CA s 635
116	CA s 605	165	CA ss 539(1)(d), (e), (f), 598; IA s 84(1), Sch 6 para 41
117	CA s 512; IA Sch 6 paras 25, 26		
		166	IA s 84
118	CA s 513	167	CA s 539(1), (2), (2A), (3); IA Sch 6 para 31(2), (3)
119	CA s 514		
120	CA s 515; IA Sch 6 para 25		
		168	CA s 540(3)–(6)
121	CA s 516	169	CA s 539(4), (5); IA Sch 6 para 31(4)
122	CA s 517		
123	CA s 518; IA Sch 6 paras, 25, 27	170	CA s 636
		171	IA s 86
124	CA s 519; IA Sch 6 para 28	172	IA s 79
		173	IA s 87
125	CA s 520	174	IA s 80
126	CA s 521	175	IA s 89(1), (2)
127	CA s 522	176	IA s 89(3), (4)
128	CA s 523	177	IA s 90
129	CA s 524	178	IA s 91(1)–(4), (8)
130	CA s 525; IA Sch 6 para 29	179	IA s 91(5), (6)
		180	IA s 91(7)
131	IA s 66	181	IA s 92(1)–(4), (9), (10)
132	IA s 67	182	IA s 92(5)–(8)
133	IA s 68(1)–(4)		

Provision	Derivation	Provision	Derivation
183	CA s 621	226	CA s 671
184	CA s 622; IA Sch 6 para 25	227	CA s 672
		228	CA s 673
185	CA s 623; B(Sc) Sch 7 para 21	229	CA s 674
		230	IA ss 95(1), (2), 96(1)
186	CA s 619(4)	231	IA ss 95(1), (2), 96(2)
187	CA s 659; IA Sch 6 para 48	232	IA ss 95(1), (2), 96(3)
		233	IA ss 95, 97
188	CA s 637	234	IA ss 95(1), (2), 98
189	IA s 93	235	IA ss 95(1), (2), 99
190	CA s 638	236	IA ss 95(1), (2), 100(1), (2), (6)
191	CA s 639		
192	CA s 641	237	IA s 100(3)–(5), (7)
193	CA s 643; B(Sc) Sch 7 para 22	238	IA ss 95(1)(a), (b), 101(1) (part)–(3)
194	CA s 644	239	IA ss 95(1)(a), (b), 101(1) (part), (4)–(7), (11)
195	CA s 645		
196	CA s 646	240	IA s 101(8)–(11)
197	CA s 647	241	IA ss 95(1), 102
198	CA s 648	242	CA s 615A; B(Sc) Sch 7 para 20
199	CA s 649		
200	CA s 650	243	CA s 615B; B(Sc) Sch 7 para 20
201	CA ss 585(5), (6), 595(6), (7)		
		244	IA ss 95(1)(a), (b), 103
202	IA s 76(1)–(3), (6)	245	IA ss 95(1)(a), (b), 104
203	IA s 76(4), (5), (7)–(10)	246	IA ss 95(1)(a), (b), (2), 105
204	IA s 77		
205	IA s 81	247	IA s 108(3) (part), (4)
206	CA s 624; IA Sch 6 para 25	248	IA s 108(3) (part)
		249	IA s 108(5)
207	CA s 625; IA Sch 6 para 42	250	IA s 108(6)
		251	IA s 108(3) (part)
208	CA s 626; IA Sch 6 para 43	252	IA s 112(1) (part), (3)
		253	IA ss 110, 111(1), (2), (3) (part)
209	CA s 627		
210	CA s 628	254	IA s 111(4), (5)
211	CA s 629	255	IA s 112(1) (part), (2), (4)–(7)(a)
212	IA s 19		
213	CA s 630(1), (2); IA Sch 6 para 6(1)	256	IA s 113
		257	IA s 114(1) (part), (2), (3)
214	IA ss 12(9), 15(1)–(5), (7), Sch 9 para 4	258	IA s 115(1)–(6), (9), (10)
		259	IA s 115(7), (8)
215	CA s 630(3)–(6); IA s 15(6), Sch 6 para 6(2), (3)	260	IA s 116(1)–(3), (6), (7)
		261	IA s 116(4), (5)
		262	IA s 117
216	IA s 17, Sch 9 para 5	263	IA s 118
217	IA s 18(1) (part), (2)–(6)	264	IA s 119(1)
218	CA s 632; IA Sch 6 para 44	265	IA s 119(2), (3)
		266	IA s 119(4)–(7)
219	CA s 633	267	IA s 120(1), (2), (7)–(9)
220	CA s 665	268	IA s 120(3), (4)
221	CA s 666	269	IA s 120(5)
222	CA s 667; IA Sch 6 para 50	270	IA s 120(6)
		271	IA s 121
223	CA s 668; IA Sch 6 para 51	272	IA s 122
		273	IA s 123(1), (2), (8)
224	CA s 669; IA Sch 6 para 52	274	IA s 111(3) (part), 112(1) (part), (7)(b), 114(1) (part), 123(3)–(5)
225	CA s 670		

Provision	Derivation	Provision	Derivation
275	IA s 123(6), (7)	334	IA s 170(1)–(3)
276	IA s 124	335	IA s 170(4)–(9)
277	IA s 125	336	IA s 171
278	IA s 126(1)	337	IA s 172
279	IA s 126(2)–(5)	338	IA s 173
280	IA s 127	339	IA s 174(1) (part), (2)
281	IA s 128	340	IA s 174(1) (part), (3)–
282	IA s 129		(6), (12) (part)
283	IA s 130	341	IA s 174(7)–(11), (12)
284	IA s 131		(part)
285	IA s 132	342	IA s 175
286	IA s 133	343	IA s 176
287	IA s 134	344	IA s 177
288	IA s 135	345	IA s 178
289	IA s 136	346	IA s 179
290	IA s 137	347	IA s 180
291	IA s 138	348	IA s 181
292	IA s 139	349	IA s 182
293	IA s 140	350	IA ss 183(1)–(3), (5), (6),
294	IA s 141		192
295	IA s 142	351	IA ss 184(5), 187(3)(*a*)
296	IA s 143	352	IA s 183(4)
297	IA s 144	353	IA ss 183(4), 184(1)
298	IA s 145	354	IA ss 183(4), 184(2)–(4)
299	IA s 146	355	IA ss 183(4), 185
300	IA s 147	356	IA ss 183(4), 186
301	IA s 148	357	IA ss 183(4), 187(1)(3)(*b*)
302	IA s 149	358	IA ss 183(4), 187(2)
303	IA s 150	359	IA ss 183(4), 188
304	IA s 151	360	IA s 189
305	IA s 152	361	IA s 190
306	IA s 153	362	IA s 191
307	IA s 154(1)–(4), (7)	363	IA s 193
308	IA s 155(1), (2), (4), (5)	364	IA s 194
309	IA ss 154(5), (6), 155(3)	365	IA s 195
310	IA s 156	366	IA s 196(1), (2)
311	IA s 157	367	IA s 196(3)–(6)
312	IA s 158	368	IA s 196(7)
313	IA s 159	369	IA s 197
314	IA s 160	370	IA s 198
315	IA s 161(1)–(4), (10)	371	IA s 199
316	IA s 161(5)	372	IA s 200
317	IA s 161(6), (7)	373	IA s 201
318	IA s 161(8)	374	IA s 202
319	IA s 161(9)	375	IA s 203
320	IA s 162(1)–(4), (9), (10)	376	IA s 204
321	IA s 162(5)–(8)	377	IA s 205
322	IA s 163	378	IA s 206
323	IA s 164	379	IA s 210
324	IA s 165(1)–(4)	380	—
325	IA s 165(5), (6)	381	IA s 211(1) (part)
326	IA s 165(7), (8)	382	IA s 211(1) (part), (2), (3)
327	IA s 165(9)	383	IA s 211(1) (part), (5)–(7)
328	IA s 166(1)–(5), (7)	384	IA ss 209(1) (part),
329	IA s 166(6)		211(1) (part)
330	IA s 167	385	IA s 211(1) (part), (4)
331	IA s 168(1), (2), (4)	386	CA ss 196(2), 475(1); IA
332	IA s 168(3)		ss 23(7), 89(1), 108(3),
333	IA s 169		115(9), 166(1), Sch 4

Provision	Derivation	Provision	Derivation
	para 1(1), Sch 6 para 15(3)	428	IA s 217(1)–(3)
387	CA ss 196(2)–(4), 475(3), (4); IA ss 23(8), 115(10), Sch 4, Pt II para 1(2), (3), Sch 6 paras 15(4), 20(3)	429	IA s 221(1), (3)–(5)
		430	CA s 730; IA passim
		431	CA s 731; IA s 108(1)
		432	IA s 230
		433	IA s 231
		434	IA s 234
388	IA s 1(2)–(6)	435	IA s 233
389	IA s 1(1)	436	IA s 232 (part)
390	IA ss 2, 3(1)	437	—
391	IA s 3(2)–(5)	438	—
392	IA ss 4, 11 (part)	439	—
393	IA s 5	440	IA s 236(3)
394	IA s 6	441	CA s 745; IA s 236(4)
395	IA s 7	442	IA s 236(5)
396	IA ss 8(1), (2), (6), 11 (part)	443	—
		444	—
397	IA s 8(3)–(5)	Sch 1	IA Sch 3
398	IA s 9	Sch 2	CA s 471(1); IA s 57
399	IA s 222	Sch 3	CA Sch 16
400	IA s 223	Sch 4	
401	IA s 224	Pt I	CA ss 539(1)(*d*)–(*f*), 598(1)
402	IA s 225		
403	INS 1970 s 1; INS 1976 s 3; IA Sch 8 para 28	Pt II	CA ss 539(1)(*a*), (*b*), 598(2)
404	INS 1970 s 2	Pt III	CA ss 539(2), 598(2)
405	INS 1970 s 3; INS 1976 Sch 2 para 5	Sch 5	
406	INS 1970 s 4; INS 1976 Sch 2 para 6; IA Sch 8 para 17	Pt I	IA s 160(2)
		Pt II	IA s 160(1)
		Pt III	IA s 160(6)
407	INS 1970 s 5; INS 1976 Sch 2 para 7	Sch 6	IA Sch 4 Pt I, Pt II paras 2–4
408	INS 1970 s 6; INS 1976 Sch 2 para 8	Sch 7	IA Sch 1
409	INS 1970 s 7; INS 1976 Sch 2 para 9	Sch 8	IA Sch 5
410	INS 1970 s 9(3); INS 1976 s 14(6); IA s 236(3)(i)	Sch 9	IA Sch 7
		Sch 10	CA and IA passim
411	IA s 106	Sch 11	
412	IA s 207	para 1	IA Sch 9 para 6
413	IA s 226	2	IA Sch 9 para 7
414	IA ss 106(5), 107	3	IA Sch 9 para 8
415	IA ss 207(5), 208(1)–(3), (5)	4	IA Sch 9 para 9(1)
		5	IA Sch 9 para 9(2)
416	CA s 664; IA Sch 6 para 49	6	IA Sch 9 para 9(3)–(5), (8)
417	CA s 667(2) (part)	7	IA Sch 9 para 9(6)
418	IA s 209(1) (part), (2), (3)	8	IA Sch 9 para 9(7)
419	IA ss 10, 11 (part)	9	IA Sch 9 para 10
420	IA s 227	10	IA Sch 9 para 11
421	IA s 228	11	IA Sch 9 para 12
422	IA s 229	12	IA Sch 9 para 13
423	IA s 212(1), (3), (7) (part)	13	IA Sch 9 para 14
424	IA s 212(2)	14	IA Sch 9 paras 15, 16, 17
425	IA s 212(4)–(6), (7) (part)	15	IA Sch 9 para 18
426	IA s 213	16	IA Sch 9 para 19
427	IA s 214	17	IA Sch 9 para 20

Provision	Derivation	Provision	Derivation
18	IA Sch 9 para 21	21	IA Sch 9 para 1
19	IA Sch 9 para 22	22–28	—
20	IA Sch 9 para 24	Schs 12–14	—

[466]

DESTINATION TABLE

This table shows in column (1) the enactments repealed by the Insolvency Act 1986, s 438, Sch 12 ante (and, in certain cases where indicated by an asterisk *, provisions repealed by the Company Directors Disqualification Act 1986, s 23(2), Sch 4, post, although for the bulk of those provisions see the destination table to that Act), and in column (2) the provisions of the former Act corresponding to the repealed provisions.

In certain cases the enactment in column (1), although having a corresponding provision in column (2) is not, or is not wholly, repealed, as it is still required, or partly required, for the purposes of other legislation.

It will be observed that many of the provisions repealed by the Insolvency Act 1986 consolidate provisions formerly in the Insolvency Act 1985, which itself repealed and replaced directly, or was otherwise comparable to, older legislation. To facilitate cross reference from pre-1985 legislation through to the provisions of the 1986 Act, a comparative table delineating the destination of those provisions repealed by the 1985 Act follows this destination table. The two tables may then be used in conjunction with each other.

(1)	(2)	(1)	(2)
Insolvency Services (Accounting and Investment) Act 1970 (c 8)	Insolvency Act 1986 (c 45)	Companies Act 1985 (c 6)	Insolvency Act 1986 (c 45)
		s 471	s 55
		s 472	s 56
s 1	s 403	s 473	s 57
s 2	s 404	s 474	s 58
s 3	s 405	s 475	s 59
s 4	s 406	s 476	s 60
s 5	s 407	s 477	s 61
s 6	s 408	s 478	s 62
s 7	s 409	s 479	s 63
s 8	Spent	s 480	s 64
s 9(1), (2), (4)	Unnecessary	s 481	s 65
s 9(3)	s 410	s 482	s 66
Sch 1	Rep, 1976 c 60, s 14(4), Sch 3	s 482A	s 67
		s 482B	s 68
Sch 2	Spent	s 483	s 69
		s 485	s 71
Insolvency Act 1976 (c 60)	Insolvency Act 1986 (c 60)	s 488	s 28
		s 489	s 30
		s 490	s 31
		s 491	s 32
s 3(1), (2), (6)	Unnecessary	s 492(1), (2)	s 35
s 3(3), (4), (5)	s 403(1), (2), (3)	s 492(3)	s 37(1), (3)
s 14(6)†	s 410	s 492(4), (5)	s 37(2), (4)
Sch 2, para 5†	s 405(1)	s 493	s 39
para 6†	s 406	s 494	s 36
para 7†	s 407	s 495, 496, 497	Rep, 1985 c 65, s 235(3), Sch 10, Pt II
para 8†	s 408	s 498	s 38(1)–(3), (5)
para 9†	s 409	s 499	s 41
		s 500	s 29(1)
Companies Act 1985 (c 6)	Insolvency Act 1986 (c 45)	s 501	s 73
		s 502	s 74
		s 503	s 75
s 196(1), (2), (5)†	s 40	s 504	s 76
s 196(2)†	s 386(1)–(3)	s 505	s 77
s 196(3)†	s 387(4)(a)	s 506	s 78
s 462(4), 484, 486 (part)	s 70	s 507	s 79
s 467	s 51	s 508	s 80
s 468	s 52	s 509	s 81
s 469	s 53	s 510	s 82
s 470	s 54		

† Not repealed

(1)	(2)	(1)	(2)
Companies Act 1985 (c 6)	Insolvency Act 1986 (c 45)	Companies Act 1985 (c 6)	Insolvency Act 1986 (c 45)
s 511	s 83	s 566	s 159
s 512	s 117	s 567	s 160
s 513	s 118	s 568	Rep, 1985 c 65, s 235(3), Sch 10, Pt II
s 514	s 119	s 569	s 161
s 515	s 120	s 570	Rep, 1985 c 65, s 235(3), Sch 10, Pt IV
s 516	s 121	s 571	s 162
s 517	s 122	s 572	s 84
s 518	s 123	s 573	s 85
s 519(1)–(3), (7)	s 124(1)–(3), (5)	s 574	s 86
s 519(4), (6)	s 124(4)	s 575	s 87
s 519(5)	Rep, 1985 c 65, s 235(3), Sch 10, Pt II	s 576	s 88
s 520	s 125	s 577	s 89
s 521	s 126	s 578	s 90
s 522	s 127	s 579	Unnecessary
s 523	s 128	s 580	s 91
s 524	s 129	s 581	s 92
s 525	s 130	s 582(1), (2)	s 110(1)–(3)
s 526–531	Rep, 1985 c 65, s 235(3), Sch 10, Pt II	s 582(3), (4)	s 110(4), (5)
s 532	s 135	s 582(5), (6)	s 111(2), (3)
s 533, 534, 536	Rep, 1985 c 65, s 235(3), Sch 10, Pt II	s 582(7)	s 110(6)
		s 582(8)	s 111(4)
s 535	s 138(1)	s 583	Rep, 1985 c 65, s 235(3), Sch 10, Pt II
s 537	s 144		
s 538	s 145	s 584	s 93
s 539(1), (2)	s 167(1)	s 585(1), (2), (4), (7)	s 94(1), (2), (5), (6)
s 539(1)(a), (b)	Sch 4, Pt II	s 585(3)	s 94(3), (4)
s 539(1)(d)–(f)	Sch 4, Pt I	s 585(5)	s 201(2), (3)
s 539(2)	Sch 4, Pt III	s 585(6)	s 201(4)
s 539(2A), (3)	s 167(2), (3)	s 586	Rep, 1985 c 65, s 235(3), Sch 10, Pt II
s 540(1), (2)	Rep, 1985 c 65, s 235(3), Sch 10, Pt II	s 587	s 97
s 540(3)–(6)	s 168(2)–(5)	s 588	Rep, 1985 c 65, s 235(3), Sch 10, Pt II
s 541–548	Rep, 1985 c 65, s 235(3), Sch 10, Pts I, II	s 589	s 100
s 549	s 147	s 590(1)–(3)	s 101
s 550	s 148	s 590(4), 591(1)	Rep, 1985 c 65, s 235(3), Sch 10, Pt II
s 551	Rep, 1985 c 65, s 235(3), Sch 10, Pt II	s 591(2)	s 103
s 552	s 149	s 592	s 104
s 553	s 150	s 593	s 110
s 554	s 151	s 594	s 105(1)–(3)
s 555	s 152	s 595(1)–(5)	s 106(1)–(5)
s 556	Rep, 1985 c 65, s 235(3), Sch 10, Pt II	s 595(6), (7)	s 201(3), (4)
s 557	s 153	s 595(8)	s 106(6)
s 558	s 154	s 596	Unnecessary
s 559	s 155	s 597	s 107
s 560	s 156	s 598	s 165(2)–(6), Sch 4, Pt III
s 561	Rep, 1985 c 65, s 235(3), Sch 10, Pt II	s 599	s 108
s 562	s 157	s 600	s 109
s 563, 564	Rep, 1985 c 65, s 235(3), Sch 10, Pt II	s 601	Rep, 1985 c 65, s 235(3), Sch 10, Pt II
s 565	s 158	s 602	s 112
		s 603	s 113

(1)	(2)	(1)	(2)
Companies Act 1985 (c 6)	Insolvency Act 1986 (c 45)	Companies Act 1985 (c 6)	Insolvency Act 1986 (c 45)
s 604	s 115	s 670	s 225
s 605	s 116	s 671	s 226
s 606–615	Rep, 1985 c 65, s 235(3), Sch 10, Pt II	s 672	s 227
s 615A	s 242	s 673	s 228
s 615B	s 243	s 674	s 229
s 616–618, 619(1)–(3), (5)–(8)	Rep, 1985 c 65, s 235(3), Sch 10, Pt II	s 709(4), 710(4)	—
s 619(4)	s 186	s 724	s 72
s 620	Rep, 1985 c 65, s 235(3), Sch 10, Pt II	s 730†	s 430
		s 731†	s 431
s 621	s 183	s 741(1), (2)†	s 251
s 622	s 184	s 745†	s 441
s 623	s 185	Sch 16	Sch 3
s 624	s 206	Sch 16 (pt)	—
s 625	s 207		

(1)	(2)
Companies Consolidation (Consequential Provisions) Act 1985 (c 9)	Insolvency Act 1986 (c 45)
Sch 2 (pt)†	s 403(1)

(1)	(2)
Companies Act 1985 (c 6)	Insolvency Act 1986 (c 45)
s 626	s 208
s 627	s 209
s 628	s 210
s 629	s 211
s 630(1), (2)	s 213(1), (2)
s 630(3)–(5), (5A), (6)	s 215(1)–(6)
s 631	Rep, 1985 c 65, s 235(3), Sch 10, Pt II
s 632	s 218
s 633	s 219
s 634	Rep, 1985 c 65, s 235(3), Sch 10, Pt I
s 635	s 164
s 636	s 170
s 637	s 188
s 638	s 190
s 639	s 191
s 640	Rep, 1985 c 65, s 235(3), Sch 10, Pt II
s 641	s 192
s 642	Rep, 1985 c 65, s 235(3), Sch 10, Pt II
s 643	s 193
s 644	s 194
s 645	s 195
s 646	s 196
s 647	s 197
s 648	s 198
s 649	s 199
s 650	s 200
s 659	s 187
s 660–663	Rep, 1985 c 65, s 235(3), Sch 10, Pt II
s 664	s 416
s 665	s 220
s 666	s 221
s 667(1)	s 222(1)
s 667(2)	s 222(2), 417
s 668	s 223
s 669	s 224

(1)	(2)
Insolvency Act 1985 (c 65)	Insolvency Act 1986 (c 45)
s 1(1)	s 389(1)
s 1(2)–(4)	s 388(1)–(3)
s 1(5)	s 388(1), (4)
s 1(6)	s 388(5), 389(2)
s 2	s 390
s 3(1)	s 390(2)
s 3(2)	s 391(1), (4)
s 3(3), (5)	s 391(2), (3)
s 3(4)	s 391(5)
s 4	s 392(3)–(8)
s 5	s 393
s 6	s 394
s 7	s 395
s 8(1), (2)	s 396(2), (3)
s 8(3)–(5)	s 397(1)–(3)
s 8(6)	s 396(1)
s 9	s 398
s 10	s 419
s 11	s 392(2), 396(1), 419(1)
s 12(9)★	s 214(7)
s 15(1)–(5)	s 214(1)–(5)
s 15(6)	s 214(8), 215(5)
s 15(7)	s 214(6)
s 17	s 216
s 18★	s 217
s 19	s 212
s 20	s 1
s 21	s 2
s 22	s 3
s 23(1)–(7)	s 4
s 23(7)	s 4, 386(1), (3)

† Not repealed   ★ See notes to this table above

(1)	(2)	(1)	(2)
Insolvency Act 1985 (c 65)	Insolvency Act 1986 (c 45)	Insolvency Act 1985 (c 65)	Insolvency Act 1986 (c 45)
s 23(8)	s 387(2)	s 70(4)(a)	s 136(4)
s 24	s 5	s 70(4)(b)	s 137(1)
s 25	s 6	s 70(7), (8)	s 137(2), (3)
s 26	s 7	s 70(9)	s 137(4), (5)
s 27	s 8	s 71	s 138(2)–(6)
s 28	s 9	s 72	s 139
s 29	s 10	s 73	s 140
s 30	s 11	s 74	s 141
s 31	s 12	s 75	Scottish
s 32	s 13	s 76(1)	s 202(1), (2)
s 33	s 14	s 76(2), (3), (6)	s 202(3), (4), (5)
s 34(1)–(8)	s 15(1)–(8)	s 76(4), (5), (7)–(10)	s 203
s 34(9), (10)	s 16	s 77	s 204
s 34(11)	s 27(5)	s 78	s 146
s 34(12)	s 15(9)	s 79	s 172
s 35	s 17	s 80	s 174
s 36	s 18	s 81	s 205
s 37(1)–(3)	s 19	s 82	s 114
s 37(4), (5)	s 20	s 83(1)–(6), (9), (10)	s 95(1)–(6), (7), (8)
s 38	s 21	s 83(7)	s 96, 102, 105(4)
s 39	s 22	s 83(8)	s 105(4)
s 40	s 23	s 84	s 165(1), 166
s 41	s 24	s 85(1)	s 97
s 42	s 25	s 85(2), (3)	s 98(1), (2)
s 43	s 26	s 85(4), (5)	s 99(1), (2)
s 44(1)–(4)	s 27(1)–(4)	s 85(6), (7), (8)	s 98(3), (4), (5)
s 44(5)–(6)	s 27(6)	s 85(9)(a)	s 98(6)
s 45(1)	s 28	s 85(9)(b), (c)	s 99(3)
s 45(2)	s 29(2)	s 85(10)	s 98(6), 99(3)
s 46	s 33	s 86	s 171
s 47	s 34	s 87	s 173
s 48	s 42	s 88	Spent
s 49	s 43	s 89(1), (2)	s 175, 386
s 50	s 44	s 89(3)	s 176(1), (2)
s 51	s 45	s 89(4)	s 176(3)
s 52	s 46	s 90	s 177
s 53	s 47	s 91(1)	s 178(1), (2)
s 54	s 48	s 91(2)–(4)	s 178(3)–(5)
s 55	s 49	s 91(5), (6)	s 179(1), (2)
s 56	s 53	s 91(7)	s 180
s 57	s 55	s 91(8)	s 178(6)
s 58	s 57	s 92(1)–(4)	s 181(1)–(4)
s 59	s 61	s 92(5)–(8)	s 182(1)–(4)
s 60	s 62	s 92(9), (10)	s 181(5), (6)
s 61	s 63	s 93	s 189
s 62	s 65	s 94	s 163
s 63	s 66	s 95(1)	s 230(1), (2), 231, 232, 233(1), 234(1), 235(1), 236(1), 238(1), 239(1), 241, 244(1), 245(1), 246(1)
s 64	s 67		
s 65	s 68		
s 66	s 131		
s 67	s 132		
s 68(1)–(4)	s 133		
s 68(5), (6)	s 134	s 95(2)	s 230(3), (4), 231, 233(1), 234(1), 235(1), 236(1), 246(1)
s 69(1), (2)	s 143(1), (2)		
s 69(3)	s 135(4)		
s 70(1)–(3), (5), (6)	s 136(1)–(3), (5), (6)		

(1)	(2)	(1)	(2)
Insolvency Act 1985 (c 65)	Insolvency Act 1986 (c 45)	Insolvency Act 1985 (c 65)	Insolvency Act 1986 (c 45)
s 95(3)	s 233(1)	s 114(2), (3)	s 257(2), (3)
s 96(1)	s 230(1), (2), (5)	s 115(1)–(6)	s 258(1)–(6)
s 96(2)	s 230(3), (4), 231	s 115(7), (8)	s 259
s 96(3)	s 232	s 115(9)	s 258(7), 386(1), (3)
s 97(1), (3), (4)	s 233(2), (4), (5)	s 115(10)(a)	s 387(5)
s 97(2)	s 233(3), (5)	s 115(10)(b)	——
s 98(1)	s 234(2)	s 116(1)–(3), (6), (7)	s 260(1)–(3), (4), (5)
s 98(2)	s 234(3), (4)	s 116(4), (5)	s 261
s 99(1), (2)	s 235(2), (3)	s 117	s 262
s 99(3)	s 235(3), (4)	s 118	s 263
s 99(4)(a)	s 235(3)	s 119(1)	s 264
s 99(4)(b)	s 235(1)	s 119(2), (3)	s 265
s 99(5)	s 235(5)	s 119(4)–(7)	s 266
s 100(1)	s 236(2), (3)	s 120(1), (2), (7)–(9)	s 267(1), (2), (3)–(5)
s 100(2)	s 236(4)–(6)	s 120(3), (4)	s 268
s 100(3)	s 237(4)	s 120(5)	s 269
s 100(4), (5), (7)	s 237(1)–(3)	s 120(6)	s 270
s 100(6)	s 236(1)	s 121	s 271
s 101(1)	s 238(2), (3), 239(2), (3)	s 122	s 272
s 101(2), (3)	s 238(4), (5)	s 123(1), (8)	s 273(1)
s 101(4)–(7)	s 239(4)–(7)	s 123(2)	s 273(2)
s 101(8)	s 240(1)	s 123(3), (4), (5)	s 274(1), (2), (3)
s 101(9), (10)	s 240(2), (3)	s 123(6)	s 275(1), (2)
s 101(11)	s 239(6), 240(1)	s 123(7)	s 274(4), 275(3)
s 102	s 241	s 124	s 276
s 103	s 244	s 125	s 277
s 104	s 245(2)–(6)	s 126(1)	s 278
s 105	s 246(2), (3)	s 126(2)–(5)	s 279
s 106(1)	s 411(1), (3)	s 127	s 280
s 106(2)	s 411(2), (3)	s 128	s 281
s 106(3), (4)	s 411(4), (5)	s 129	s 282
s 106(5)	s 411(6), s 414(9)	s 130	s 283
s 107(1)	s 414(1), (2), (3), (8)	s 131	s 284
s 107(2)–(5)	s 414(4)–(7)	s 132	s 285
s 107(6)	s 414(9)	s 133	s 286
s 108(1)	s 431	s 134	s 287
s 108(3)	s 247(1), 248, 251, 386(1), (3)	s 135	s 288
s 108(4)	s 247(2)	s 136	s 289
s 108(5)	s 249	s 137	s 290
s 108(6)	s 250	s 138	s 291
s 109	Unnecessary	s 139	s 292
s 110	s 253(1), (2)	s 140	s 293
s 111(1)	s 253(1), (3)	s 141	s 294
s 111(2)	s 253(4)	s 142	s 295
s 111(3)	s 253(5), 274(3)	s 143	s 296
s 111(4), (5)	s 254	s 144	s 297
s 112(1)	s 252(1), 255(2), 274(3)	s 145	s 298
s 112(2)	s 255(1)	s 146	s 299
s 112(3)	s 252(2)	s 147	s 300
s 112(4)–(6)	s 255(3)–(5)	s 148	s 301
s 112(7)(a)	s 255(6)	s 149	s 302
s 112(7)(b)	s 274(4)	s 150	s 303
s 113(1), (2)	s 256(1)	s 151	s 304
s 113(3)–(7)	s 256(2)–(6)	s 152	s 305
s 114(1)	s 257(1), 274(5)	s 153	s 306
		s 154(1)–(4), (7)	s 307(1)–(4), (5)

(1)	(2)	(1)	(2)
Insolvency Act 1985 (c 65)	Insolvency Act 1986 (c 45)	Insolvency Act 1985 (c 65)	Insolvency Act 1986 (c 45)
s 154(5), (6)	s 309(1), (2)	s 183(4)	s 352, 353(3), 354(1), (2), 355, 356, 357(1), (3), 358, 359
s 155(1), (2), (4), (5) . .	s 308(1)–(4)		
s 155(3)	s 309(1), (2)	s 183(5), (6)	s 350(4), (5)
s 156	s 310	s 184(1)	s 353(1), (2)
s 157	s 311	s 184(2)	s 354(1)
s 158	s 312	s 184(3)	s 351(b), (c), 354(2)
s 159	s 313	s 184(4)	s 351(b), (c), 354(3)
s 160(1)	s 314(1), Sch 5, Pt II	s 184(5)	s 351(a)
s 160(2)	s 314(1), Sch 5, Pt I	s 185	s 355
s 160(3)–(5), (7)–(9) . .	s 314(2)–(4), (6)–(8)	s 185(2)(a), (d)	s 351(b), (c)
s 160(6)	s 314(5), Sch 5, Pt III	s 185(3)(b)	s 351(b), (c)
s 161(1)–(4), (10)	s 315(1), (4), (5)	s 186	s 356
s 161(5)	s 316	s 186(2)(c)	s 351(b), (c)
s 161(6), (7)	s 317	s 187(1)	s 357(1), (3)
s 161(8)	s 318	s 187(2)	s 351(b), (c), 358
s 161(9)	s 319	s 187(3)(a)	s 351(a)
s 162(1)–(4), (9), (10) . .	s 320(1)–(6)	s 187(3)(b)	s 357(2)
s 162(5)–(8)	s 321	s 188	s 359
s 163	s 322	s 188(1), (2)	s 351(b), (c)
s 164	s 323	s 189	s 360
s 165(1)–(4)	s 324	s 190	s 361
s 165(5), (6)	s 325	s 190(1)	s 351(b), (c)
s 165(7)	s 326(1)	s 191	s 362
s 165(8)	s 326(2), (3)	s 191(1)	s 351(b), (c)
s 165(9)	s 327	s 192	s 350(6)
s 166(1)	s 328(1), 386(1), (3)	s 193	s 363
s 166(2)–(5), (7)	s 328(2)–(5), (6)	s 194	s 364
s 166(6)	s 329	s 195	s 365
s 167	s 330	s 196(1)	s 366(1)
s 168(1)	s 331(1), (2)	s 196(2)	s 366(2)–(4)
s 168(2), (4)	s 331(3), (4)	s 196(3)	s 367(4)
s 168(3)	s 332	s 196(4)–(6)	s 367(1)–(3)
s 169	s 333	s 196(7)	s 368
s 170(1)–(3)	s 334	s 197	s 369
s 170(4)–(9)	s 335	s 198	s 370
s 171	s 336	s 199	s 371
s 172	s 337	s 200	s 372
s 173	s 338	s 201	s 373
s 174(1)	s 339(1), (2), 340(1), (2)	s 202	s 374
s 174(2)	s 339(3)	s 203	s 375
s 174(3), (4), (6)	s 340(3), (4), (6)	s 204	s 376
s 174(5)	s 340(5)	s 205	s 377
s 174(7)	s 341(1)	s 206	s 378
s 174(8)	s 341(2)	s 207	s 412
s 174(9)–(11)	s 341(3)–(5)	s 207(5)	s 415(7)
s 174(12)	s 340(5), 341(1), (2)	s 208	s 415(1)–(6)
s 175	s 342	s 209	s 418
s 176	s 343	s 209(1)	s 384(2)
s 177	s 344	s 210	s 379
s 178	s 345	s 211(1)	s 381, 382(1), (4), 383(1), 384(1), 385(1)
s 179	s 346		
s 180	s 347		
s 181	s 348		
s 182	s 349	s 211(2), (3)	s 382(2), (3)
s 183(1)–(3)	s 350(1)–(3)	s 211(4)	s 385(2)

(1)	(2)	(1)	(2)
Insolvency Act 1985 (c 65)	Insolvency Act 1986 (c 45)	Insolvency Act 1985 (c 65)	Insolvency Act 1986 (c 45)
s 211(5)–(7)	s 383(2)–(4)	Sch 1	Sch 7
s 212(1)	s 423(2), (3), (5)	Sch 3	Sch 1
s 212(2)	s 423(5), 424	Sch 4, Pt I	Sch 6
s 212(3)	s 423(1)	Sch 4, Pt II, para 1(1) . .	s 386(2)
s 212(4)–(6)	s 425(1)–(3)	para 1(2), (3)	s 387(3), (6)
s 212(7)	s 423(4), 425(7)	para 2	Sch 6, para 3
s 213	s 426	para 3	Sch 6, paras 13–15
s 214	s 427	para 4	Sch 6, para 16
s 216	Spent	Sch 5	Sch 8
s 217	s 428	Sch 6 (pt)	See under enactments affected
s 221	s 429	Sch 7	Sch 9
s 222	s 399	Sch 8, para 17†	s 406
s 223	s 400	Sch 8, para 28†	s 403(1)
s 224	s 401	Sch 9 (pt)	Sch 11
s 225	s 402	Sch 10	Spent
s 226	s 413		
s 227	s 420	Bankruptcy (Scotland) Act 1986 (c 66)	Insolvency Act 1986 (c 45)
s 228	s 421		
s 229	s 422	Sch 7 (pt)	s 185(1)–(3)
s 230	s 432		Remainder unnecessary
s 231	s 433		
s 232	s 436	Gas Act 1986 (c 44)	Insolvency Act 1986 (c 45)
s 233	s 435		
s 234	s 434		
s 235(2)–(5)	Unnecessary	Sch 7, para 31	s 233(3), 372(4)
s 236(1), (2)	Unnecessary		
s 236(3)	s 440		
s 236(4)	s 441		
s 236(5)	s 442		

† Not repealed

COMPARATIVE TABLE

This table shows in column (1) certain enactments within the scope of this work which were repealed by the Insolvency Act 1985, and in column (2) those provisions of that Act which replaced (generally with amendments) or were otherwise comparable with the provisions in column (1). The table does not list every enactment repealed by the 1985 Act; in particular provisions which are not reproduced in any form are omitted.

(1)	(2)	(1)	(2)
Law of Property Act 1925 (c 20)	Insolvency Act 1985 (c 65)	Companies Act 1985 (c 6)	Insolvency Act 1985 (c 65)
s 172	s 212	s 533 (1)–(6)	s 70, 72
		(7)	94
Social Security Act 1975 (c 14)		534 (b)	69 (2)
		536 (1)	79 (2), (6)
s 153 (1), (2), Sch 18	89 (1), Sch 4, Pt I, para 3 (1), Pt II, para 1 (2)	(2)	Sch 5, para 15
		(4), (5)	s 96 (2), (3)
		541	Sch 5, para 23 (a), (b)
		542	para 16
		543	para 23 (c)
Insolvency Act 1976 (c 60)		545	s 80
		546	74 (1)–(4)
s 2	Sch 5, para 2, 3	547	Sch 5, para 10
10	s 226	548	s 74 (5)
		551	98 (1)
Employment Protection (Consolidation) Act 1978 (c 44)		556	90, Sch 5, para 15
		561	100
		563	68
		564	Sch 5, para 22
s 121	Sch 4, Pt II, para 3 (1), (2)	565*	s 100 (2)
		568	81
		570	213
Employment Act 1980 (c 42)		580 (1)*	Sch 5, para 15
		583, 586	s 83
		588	85
Sch 1, para 15	Sch 4, Pt II, para 3 (2) (c)	590 (4)	Sch 5, para 10
		591 (1)	para 15
		598 (5)	s 96 (2)
Social Security and Housing Benefits Act 1982 (c 24)		601	Cf s 24, 25
		606–610	See s 88
		611	Sch 5, para 12
		612	para 14
Sch 2, para 12	Sch 4, Pt II, para 3 (2) (d)	614	s 89
		615, 616	101, 102
		617	104
Companies Act 1985 (c 6)		618, 619 (1)–(3), (5)–(8), 620	91, 92
		631	19
s 300	s 12	640	Sch 5, para 25
495–497	52–54	642	para 13
501 (1) (c)	See s 88	660	para 16
519 (5)	Sch 5, para 2	661*	s 224 (4)
526, 527	s 222	662	Sch 5, para 20
528	66	663 (1)	s 106 (1)
529 (2)	Sch 5, para 21	(3)	231
(4)	s 231	(4)	107 (1)
530	67	(5)	106 (3), 107 (4)
531	Cf s 70		

* Repealed in part

(1)	(2)	(1)	(2)
Companies Act 1985 (c 6)	Insolvency Act 1985 (c 65)	Companies Act 1985 (c 6)	Insolvency Act 1985 (c 65)
s 663 (6) 665*, 666 (7) Sch 12, Pt II	s 107 (5) Cf s 227 s 12	Sch 17 18 19 20, Pt I	Sch 5, para 10 See s 88 Sch 4 s 91, 92

* Repealed in part

PART II

COMPANY DIRECTORS DISQUALIFICATION ACT 1986

COMPANY DIRECTORS DISQUALIFICATION ACT 1986
(c 46)

ARRANGEMENT OF SECTIONS

Preliminary

Section   Para
 1 Disqualification orders: general ..   ..   [469]

Disqualification for general misconduct in connection with companies

 2 Disqualification on conviction of indictable offence   ..   ..   [470]
 3 Disqualification for persistent breaches of companies legislation   ..   ..   [471]
 4 Disqualification for fraud, etc, in winding up   ..   ..   [472]
 5 Disqualification on summary conviction ..   ..   [473]

Disqualification for unfitness

 6 Duty of court to disqualify unfit directors of insolvent companies   ..   ..   [474]
 7 Applications to court under s 6; reporting provisions   ..   ..   [475]
 8 Disqualification after investigation of company ..   ..   [476]
 9 Matters for determining unfitness of directors   ..   ..   [477]

Other cases of disqualification

10 Participation in wrongful trading ..   ..   [478]
11 Undischarged bankrupts ..   ..   [479]
12 Failure to pay under county court administration order ..   ..   [480]

Consequences of contravention

13 Criminal penalties ..   ..   [481]
14 Offences by body corporate   ..   ..   [482]
15 Personal liability for company's debts where person acts while disqualified   ..   ..   [483]

Supplementary provisions

16 Application for disqualification order   ..   ..   [484]
17 Application for leave under an order   ..   ..   [485]
18 Register of disqualification orders   ..   ..   [486]
19 Special savings from repealed enactments   ..   ..   [487]

Miscellaneous and general

20 Admissibility in evidence of statements ..   ..   [488]
21 Interaction with Insolvency Act ..   ..   [489]
22 Interpretation   ..   ..   [490]
23 Transitional provisions, savings, repeals ..   ..   [491]
24 Extent   ..   ..   [492]
25 Commencement   ..   ..   [493]
26 Citation   ..   ..   [494]

SCHEDULES:

Schedule 1—Matters for determining unfitness of directors   ..   ..   ..   [495]
Schedule 2—Savings from Companies Act 1981, ss 93, 94, and Insolvency Act
  1985, Schedule 9   ..   ..   [496]
Schedule 3—Transitional Provisions and Savings   ..   ..   [497]
Schedule 4—Repeals ..   ..   [498]

*An Act to consolidate certain enactments relating to the disqualification of persons
from being directors of companies, and from being otherwise concerned with a
company's affairs*   **[25 July 1986]**

Preliminary

1. Disqualification orders: general

(1) In the circumstances specified below in this Act a court may, and under section 6 shall, make against a person a disqualification order, that is to say an order that he shall not, without leave of the court—

    (*a*) be a director of a company, or

    (*b*) be a liquidator or administrator of a company, or

    (*c*) be a receiver or manager of a company's property, or

    (*d*) in any way, whether directly or indirectly, be concerned or take part in the promotion, formation or management of a company,

for a specified period beginning with the date of the order.

(2) In each section of this Act which gives to a court power or, as the case may be, imposes on it the duty to make a disqualification order there is specified the maximum (and, in section 6, the minimum) period of disqualification which may or (as the case may be) must be imposed by means of the order.

(3) Where a disqualification order is made against a person who is already subject to such an order, the periods specified in those orders shall run concurrently.

(4) A disqualification order may be made on grounds which are or include matters other than criminal convictions, notwithstanding that the person in respect of whom it is to be made may be criminally liable in respect of those matters. **[469]**

NOTES

Commencement: 29 December 1986.

This section derived from the Companies Act 1985, s 295(1), (2), (4), and the Insolvency Act 1985, Sch 6, para 1(1)–(3).

Disqualification for general misconduct in connection with companies

2. Disqualification on conviction of indictable offence

(1) The court may make a disqualification order against a person where he is convicted of an indictable offence (whether on indictment or summarily) in connection with the promotion, formation, management or liquidation of a company, or with the receivership or management of a company's property.

(2) "The court" for this purpose means—

    (*a*) any court having jurisdiction to wind up the company in relation to which the offence was committed, or

    (*b*) the court by or before which the person is convicted of the offence, or

    (*c*) in the case of a summary conviction in England and Wales, any other magistrates' court acting for the same petty sessions area;

and for the purposes of this section the definition of "indictable offence" in Schedule 1 to the Interpretation Act 1978 applies for Scotland as it does for England and Wales.

(3) The maximum period of disqualification under this section is—

    (*a*) where the disqualification order is made by a court of summary jurisdiction, 5 years, and

(b) in any other case, 15 years. **[470]**

NOTES
Commencement: 29 December 1986.
This section derived from the Companies Act 1985, ss 295(2), 296.

3. Disqualification for persistent breaches of companies legislation

(1) The court may make a disqualification order against a person where it appears to it that he has been persistently in default in relation to provisions of the companies legislation requiring any return, account or other document to be filed with, delivered or sent, or notice of any matter to be given, to the registrar of companies.

(2) On an application to the court for an order to be made under this section, the fact that a person has been persistently in default in relation to such provisions as are mentioned above may (without prejudice to its proof in any other manner) be conclusively proved by showing that in the 5 years ending with the date of the application he has been adjudged guilty (whether or not on the same occasion) of three or more defaults in relation to those provisions.

(3) A person is to be treated under subsection (2) as being adjudged guilty of a default in relation to any provision of that legislation if—

(a) he is convicted (whether on indictment or summarily) of an offence consisting in a contravention of or failure to comply with that provision (whether on his own part or on the part of any company), or

(b) a default order is made against him, that is to say an order under any of the following provisions—

   (i) section 244 of the Companies Act (order requiring delivery of company accounts),

  (ii) section 713 of that Act (enforcement of company's duty to make returns),

 (iii) section 41 of the Insolvency Act (enforcement of receiver's or manager's duty to make returns), or

 (iv) section 170 of that Act (corresponding provision for liquidator in winding up),

in respect of any such contravention of or failure to comply with that provision (whether on his own part or on the part of any company).

(4) In this section "the court" means any court having jurisdiction to wind up any of the companies in relation to which the offence or other default has been or is alleged to have been committed.

(5) The maximum period of disqualification under this section in 5 years.
[471]

NOTES
Commencement: 29 December 1986.
This section derived from the Companies Act 1985, ss 295(2), 297.

4. Disqualification for fraud, etc, in winding up

(1) The court may make a disqualification order against a person if, in the course of the winding up of a company, it appears that he—

(a) has been guilty of an offence for which he is liable (whether he has been convicted or not) under section 458 of the Companies Act (fraudulent trading), or (*b*) has otherwise been guilty, while an officer or liquidator of the company or receiver or manager of its property, of any fraud in relation to the company or of any breach of his duty as such officer, liquidator, receiver or manager.

(2) In this section "the court" means any court having jurisdiction to wind up any of the companies in relation to which the offence or other default has been or is alleged to have been committed; and "officer" includes a shadow director.

(3) The maximum period of disqualification under this section is 15 years.

[472]

NOTES
Commencement: 29 December 1986.
This section derived from the Companies Act 1985, ss 295(2), 298.

5. Disqualification on summary conviction

(1) An offence counting for the purposes of this section is one of which a person is convicted (either on indictment or summarily) in consequence of a contravention of, or failure to comply with, any provision of the companies legislation requiring a return, account or other document to be filed with, delivered or sent, or notice of any matter to be given, to the registrar of companies (whether the contravention or failure is on the person's own part or on the part of any company).

(2) Where a person is convicted of a summary offence counting for those purposes, the court by which he is convicted (or, in England and Wales, any other magistrates' court acting for the same petty sessions area) may make a disqualification order against him if the circumstances specified in the next subsection are present.

(3) Those circumstances are that, during the 5 years ending with the date of the conviction, the person has had made against him, or has been convicted of, in total not less than 3 default orders and offences counting for the purposes of this section; and those offences may include that of which he is convicted as mentioned in subsection (2) and any other offence of which he is convicted on the same occasion.

(4) For the purposes of this section—

(*a*) the definition of "summary offence" in Schedule 1 to the Interpretation Act 1978 applies for Scotland as for England and Wales, and
(*b*) "default order" means the same as in section 3(3)(*b*).

(5) The maximum period of disqualification under this section is 5 years.

[473]

NOTES
Commencement: 29 December 1986.
This section derived from the Companies Act 1985, ss 295(2), 299.

Disqualification for unfitness

6. Duty of court to disqualify unfit directors of insolvent companies

(1) The court shall make a disqualification order against a person in any case where, on an application under this section, it is satisfied—

(a) that he is or has been a director of a company which has at any time become insolvent (whether while he was a director or subsequently), and

(b) that his conduct as a director of that company (either taken alone or taken together with his conduct as a director of any other company or companies) makes him unfit to be concerned in the management of a company.

(2) For the purposes of this section and the next, a company becomes insolvent if—

(a) the company goes into liquidation at a time when its assets are insufficient for the payment of its debts and other liabilities and the expenses of the winding up,

(b) an administration order is made in relation to the company, or

(c) an administrative receiver of the company is appointed;

and references to a person's conduct as a director of any company or companies include, where that company or any of those companies has become insolvent, that person's conduct in relation to any matter connected with or arising out of the insolvency of that company.

(3) In this section and the next "the court" means—

(a) in the case of a person who is or has been a director of a company which is being wound up by the court, the court by which the company is being wound up.

(b) in the case of a person who is or has been a director of a company which is being wound up voluntarily, any court having jurisdiction to wind up the company,

(c) in the case of a person who is or has been a director of a company in relation to which an administration order is in force, the court by which that order was made, and

(d) in any other case, the High Court or, in Scotland, the Court of Session;

and in both sections "director" includes a shadow director.

(4) Under this section the minimum period of disqualification is 2 years, and the maximum period is 15 years.   **[474]**

NOTES
Commencement: 29 December 1986.
This section derived from the Companies Act 1985, s 295(2), and the Insolvency Act 1985, ss 12(1), (2), (7)–(9), 108(2).

7. Applications to court under s 6; reporting provisions

(1) If it appears to the Secretary of State that it is expedient in the public interest that a disqualification order under section 6 should be made against any person, an application for the making of such an order against that person may be made—

(a) by the Secretary of State, or

(b) if the Secretary of State so directs in the case of a person who is or has been a director of a company which is being wound up by the court in England and Wales, by the official receiver.

(2) Except with the leave of the court, an application for the making under that section of a disqualification order against any person shall not be made after the end of the period of 2 years beginning with the day on which the company of which that person is or has been a director became insolvent.

(3) If it appears to the office-holder responsible under this section, that is to say—

(a) in the case of a company which is being wound up by the court in England and Wales, the official receiver,

(b) in the case of a company which is being wound up otherwise, the liquidator,

(c) in the case of a company in relation to which an administration order is in force, the administrator, or

(d) in the case of a company of which there is an administrative receiver, that receiver.

that the conditions mentioned in section 6(1) are satisfied as respects a person who is or has been a director of that company, the officer-holder shall forthwith report the matter to the Secretary of State.

(4) The Secretary of State or the official receiver may require the liquidator, administrator or administrative receiver of a company, or the former liquidator, administrator or administrative receiver of a company—

(a) to furnish him with such information with respect to any person's conduct as a director of the company, and

(b) to produce and permit inspection of such books, papers and other records relevant to that person's conduct as such a director,

as the Secretary of State or the official receiver may reasonably require for the purpose of determining whether to exercise, or of exercising, any function of his under this section. **[475]**

NOTES
Commencement: 29 December 1986.
This section derived from the Insolvency Act 1985, s 12(3)–(6).

8. Disqualification after investigation of company

(1) If it appears to the Secretary of State from a report made by inspectors under section 437 of the Companies Act [or section 94 or 177 of the Financial Services Act 1986], or from information or documents obtained under section 447 or 448 of [the Companies Act or section 105 of the Financial Services Act 1986], that it is expedient in the public interest that a disqualification order should be made against any person who is or has been a director or shadow director of any company, he may apply to the court for such an order to be made against that person.

(2) The court may make a disqualification order against a person where, on an application under this section, it is satisfied that his conduct in relation to the company makes him unfit to be concerned in the management of a company.

(3) In this section "the court" means the High Court or, in Scotland, the Court of Session.

(4) The maximum period of disqualification under this section is 15 years. **[476]**

NOTES
Commencement: 29 December 1986.
This section derived from the Companies Act 1985, s 295(2), and the Insolvency Act 1985, ss 12(9), 13, 108(2).
First words in square brackets in sub-s (1) inserted by the Financial Services Act 1986, s 198(2)(a), as from 15 November 1986.
Second words in square brackets substituted by the Financial Services Act 1986, s 198(2)(b), as from 18 December 1986.

9. Matters for determining unfitness of directors

(1) Where it falls to a court to determine whether a person's conduct as a director or shadow director of any particular company or companies makes him unfit to be concerned in the management of a company, the court shall, as respects his conduct as a director of that company or, as the case may be, each of those companies, have regard in particular—

    (*a*) to the matters mentioned in Part I of Schedule 1 to this Act, and

    (*b*) where the company has become insolvent, to the matters mentioned in Part II of that Schedule;

and references in that Schedule to the director and the company are to be read accordingly.

(2) Section 6(2) applies for the purposes of this section and Schedule 1 as it applies for the purposes of sections 6 and 7.

(3) Subject to the next subsection, any reference in Schedule 1 to an enactment contained in the Companies Act or the Insolvency Act includes, in relation to any time before the coming into force of that enactment, the corresponding enactment in force at that time.

(4) The Secretary of State may by order modify any of the provisions of Schedule 1; and such an order may contain such transitional provisions as may appear to the Secretary of State necessary or expedient.

(5) The power to make orders under this section is exercisable by statutory instrument subject to annulment in pursuance of a resolution of either House of Parliament.   **[477]**

NOTES
    Commencement: 29 December 1986.
    This section derived from the Insolvency Act 1985, ss 12(9), 14.

Other cases of disqualification

10. Participation in wrongful trading

(1) Where the court makes a declaration under section 213 or 214 of the Insolvency Act that a person is liable to make a contribution to a company's assets, then, whether or not an application for such an order is made by any person, the court may, if it thinks fit, also make a disqualification order against the person to whom the declaration relates.

(2) The maximum period of disqualification under this section is 15 years.
    [478]

NOTES
    Commencement: 29 December 1986.
    This section derived from the Companies Act 1985, s 295(2), and the Insolvency Act 1985, ss 16, 108(2).

11. Undischarged bankrupts

(1) It is an offence for a person who is an undischarged bankrupt to act as director of, or directly or indirectly to take part in or be concerned in the promotion, formation or management of, a company, except with the leave of the court.

(2) "The court" for this purpose is the court by which the person was adjudged bankrupt or, in Scotland, sequestration of his estates was awarded.

(3) In England and Wales, the leave of the court shall not be given unless notice of intention to apply for it has been served on the official receiver; and it is the latter's duty, if he is of opinion that it is contrary to the public interest that the application should be granted, to attend on the hearing of the application and oppose it.   **[479]**

NOTES
   Commencement: 29 December 1986.
   This section derived from the Companies Act 1985, s 302.

12. Failure to pay under county court administration order

(1) The following has effect where a court under section 429 of the Insolvency Act revokes an administration order under Part VI of the County Courts Act 1984.

(2) A person to whom that section applies by virtue of the order under section 429(2)(*b*) shall not, except with the leave of the court which made the order, act as director or liquidator of, or directly or indirectly take part or be concerned in the promotion, formation or management of, a company.   **[480]**

NOTES
   Commencement: 29 December 1986.
   This section derived from the Insolvency Act 1985, s 221(2).

Consequences of contravention

13. Criminal penalties

If a person acts in contravention of a disqualification order or of section 12(2), or is guilty of an offence under section 11, he is liable—

   (*a*) on conviction on indictment, to imprisonment for not more than 2 years or a fine, or both; and
   (*b*) on summary conviction, to imprisonment for not more than 6 months or a fine not exceeding the statutory maximum, or both.   **[481]**

NOTES
   Commencement: 29 December 1986.
   This section derived from the Companies Act 1985, ss 295(7), 302(1), Sch 24, and the Insolvency Act 1985, s 221(5).

14. Offences by body corporate

(1) Where a body corporate is guilty of an offence of acting in contravention of a disqualification order, and it is proved that the offence occurred with the consent or connivance of, or was attributable to any neglect on the part of any director, manager, secretary or other similar officer of the body corporate, or any person who was purporting to act in any such capacity he, as well as the body corporate, is guilty of the offence and liable to be proceeded against and punished accordingly.

(2) Where the affairs of a body corporate are managed by its members, subsection (1) applies in relation to the acts and defaults of a member in connection with his functions of managements as if he were a director of the body corporate.   **[482]**

NOTES
Commencement: 29 December 1986.
This section derived from the Companies Act 1985, s 733(1)–(3), and the Insolvency Act 1985,
Sch 6, para 7.

15. Personal liability for company's debts where person acts while disqualified

(1) A person is personally responsible for all the relevant debts of a company if at any time—

(*a*) in contravention of a disqualification order or of section 11 of this Act he is involved in the management of the company, or

(*b*) as a person who is involved in the management of the company, he acts or is willing to act on instructions given without the leave of the court by a person whom he knows at that time to be the subject of a disqualification order or to be an undischarged bankrupt.

(2) Where a person is personally responsible under this section for the relevant debts of a company, he is jointly and severally liable in respect of those debts with the company and any other person who, whether under this section or otherwise, is so liable.

(3) For the purposes of this section the relevant debts of a company are—

(*a*) in relation to a person who is personally responsible under paragraph (*a*) of subsection (1), such debts and other liabilities of the company as are incurred at a time when that person was involved in the management of the company, and

(*b*) in relation to a person who is personally responsible under paragraph (*b*) of that subsection, such debts and other liabilities of the company as are incurred at a time when that person was acting or was willing to act on instructions given as mentioned in that paragraph.

(4) For the purposes of this section, a person is involved in the management of a company if he is a director of the company or if he is concerned, whether directly or indirectly, or takes part, in the management of the company.

(5) For the purposes of this section a person who, as a person involved in the management of a company, has at any time acted on instructions given without the leave of the court by a person whom he knew at that time to be the subject of a disqualification order or to be an undischarged bankrupt is presumed, unless the contrary is shown, to have been willing at any time thereafter to act on any instructions given by that person.   **[483]**

NOTES
Commencement: 29 December 1986.
This section derived from the Insolvency Act 1985, s 18(1) (part), (2)–(6).

Supplementary provisions

16. Application for disqualification order

(1) A person intending to apply for the making of a disqualification order by the court having jurisdiction to wind up a company shall give not less than 10 days' notice of his intention to the person against whom the order is sought; and on the hearing of the application the last-mentioned person may appear and himself give evidence or call witnesses.

(2) An application to a court with jurisdiction to wind up companies for the making against any person of a disqualification order under any of sections 2 to

5 may be made by the Secretary of State or the official receiver, or by the
liquidator or any past or present member or creditor of any company in relation
to which that person has committed or is alleged to have committed an offence
or other default.

(3) On the hearing of any application under this Act made by the Secretary
of State or the official receiver or the liquidator, the applicant shall appear and
call the attention of the court to any matters which seem to him to be relevant,
and may himself give evidence or call witnesses.   **[484]**

NOTES
   Commencement: 29 December 1986.
   This section derived from the Companies Act 1985, s 295(6) (part), Sch 12, paras 1–3, and the
Insolvency Act 1985, s 108(2), Sch 6, para 1(4).

17. Application for leave under an order

(1) As regards the court to which application must be made for leave under a
disqualification order, the following applies—

   (*a*) where the application is for leave to promote or form a company, it is
        any court with jurisdiction to wind up companies, and
   (*b*) where the application is for leave to be a liquidator, administrator or
        director of, or otherwise to take part in the management of a company,
        or to be a receiver or manager of a company's property, it is any court
        having jurisdiction to wind up that company.

(2) On the hearing of an application for leave made by a person against
whom a disqualification order has been made on the application of the Secretary
of State, the official receiver or the liquidator, the Secretary of State, official
receiver or liquidator shall appear and call the attention of the court to any
matters which seem to him to be relevant, and may himself give evidence or call
witnesses.   **[485]**

NOTES
   Commencement: 29 December 1986.
   This section derived from the Companies Act 1985, s 295(6) (part), Sch 12, paras 4, 5, and the
Insolvency Act 1985, s 108(2), Sch 6, paras 1(4), 14.

18. Register of disqualification orders

(1) The Secretary of State may make regulations requiring officers of courts to
furnish him with such particulars as the regulations may specify of cases in
which—

   (*a*) a disqualification order is made, or
   (*b*) any action is taken by a court in consequence of which such an order
        is varied or ceases to be in force, or
   (*c*) leave is granted by a court for a person subject to such an order to do
        any thing which otherwise the order prohibits him from doing;

and the regulations may specify the time within which, and the form and
manner in which, such particulars are to be furnished.

(2) The Secretary of State shall, from the particulars so furnished, continue
to maintain the register of orders, and of cases in which leave has been granted
as mentioned in subsection (1)(*c*), which was set up by him under section 29 of
the Companies Act 1976 and continued under section 301 of the Companies
Act 1985.

(3) When an order of which entry is made in the register ceases to be in

force, the Secretary of State shall delete the entry from the register and all particulars relating to it which have been furnished to him under this section or any previous corresponding provision.

(4) The register shall be open to inspection on payment of such fee as may be specified by the Secretary of State in regulations.

(5) Regulations under this section shall be made by statutory instrument subject to annulment in pursuance of a resolution of either House of Parliament.   **[486]**

NOTES
Commencement: 29 December 1986.
This section derived from the Companies Act 1985, s 301, and the Insolvency Act 1985, s 108(2), Sch 6, para 2.

19. Special savings from repealed enactments

Schedule 2 to this Act has effect—

> (a) in connection with certain transitional cases arising under sections 93 and 94 of the Companies Act 1981, so as to limit the power to make a disqualification order, or to restrict the duration of an order, by reference to events occurring or things done before those sections came into force,
>
> (b) to preserve orders made under section 28 of the Companies Act 1976 (repealed by the Act of 1981), and
>
> (c) to preclude any applications for a disqualification order under section 6 or 8, where the relevant company went into liquidation before 28th April 1986.   **[487]**

NOTES
Commencement: 29 December 1986.
This section derived from the Companies Act 1985, s 295(6), and see also Sch 2 to that Act.

Miscellaneous and general

20. Admissibility in evidence of statements

In any proceedings (whether or not under this Act), any statement made in pursuance of a requirement imposed by or under sections 6 to 10, 15 or 19(c) of, or Schedule 1 to, this Act, or by or under rules made for the purposes of this Act under the Insolvency Act, may be used in evidence against any person making or concurring in making the statement.   **[488]**

NOTES
Commencement: 29 December 1986.
This section derived from the Insolvency Act 1985, s 231 (part).

21. Interaction with Insolvency Act

(1) References in this Act to the official receiver, in relation to the winding up of a company or the bankruptcy of an individual, are to any person who, by virtue of section 399 of the Insolvency Act, is authorised to act as the official receiver in relation to that winding up or bankruptcy; and, in accordance with section 401(2) of that Act, references in this Act to an official receiver includes a person appointed as his deputy.

(2) Sections 6 to 10, 15, 19(*c*) and 20 of, and Schedule 1 to, this Act are deemed included in Parts I to VII of the Insolvency Act for the purposes of the following sections of that Act—

> section 411 (power to make insolvency rules);
> section 414 (fees orders);
> section 420 (orders extending provisions about insolvent companies to insolvent partnerships);
> section 422 (modification of such provisions in their application to recognised banks); and
> section 431 (summary proceedings).

(3) Section 434 of that Act (Crown application) applies to sections 6 to 10, 15, 19(*c*) and 20 of, and Schedule 1 to, this Act as it does to the provisions of that Act which are there mentioned. **[489]**

NOTES
Commencement: 29 December 1986.
This section derived from the Insolvency Act 1985, ss 106, 107, 108(1), (2), 222(1), 224(2), 227, 229, 234.

22. Interpretation

(1) This section has effect with respect to the meaning of expressions used in this Act, and applies unless the context otherwise requires.

(2) The expression "company"—

(*a*) in section 11, includes an unregistered company and a company incorporated outside Great Britain which has an established place of business in Great Britain, and

(*b*) elsewhere, includes any company which may be wound up under Part V of the Insolvency Act.

(3) Section 247 in Part VII of the Insolvency Act (interpretation for the first Group of Parts of that Act) applies as regards references to a company's insolvency and to its going into liquidation; and "administrative receiver" has the meaning given by section 251 of that Act.

(4) "Director" includes any person occupying the position of director, by whatever name called, and in sections 6 to 9 includes a shadow director.

(5) "Shadow director", in relation to a company, means a person in accordance with whose directions or instructions the directors of the company are accustomed to act (but so that a person is not deemed a shadow director by reason only that the directors act on advice given by him in a professional capacity).

(6) Section 740 of the Companies Act applies as regards the meaning of "body corporate"; and "officer" has the meaning given by section 744 of that Act.

(7) In references to legislation other than this Act—

> "the Companies Act" means the Companies Act 1985;
> "the Companies Acts" has the meaning given by section 744 of that Act; and
> "the Insolvency Act" means the Insolvency Act 1986;

and in section 3(1) and 5(1) of this Act "the companies legislation" means the Companies Acts (except the Insider Dealing Act), Parts I to VII of the Insolvency Act and, in Part XV of that Act, sections 411, 413, 414, 416 and 417.

(8) Any reference to provisions, or a particular provision, of the Companies Acts or the Insolvency Act includes the corresponding provisions or provision of the former Companies Acts (as defined by section 735(1)(c) of the Companies Act, but including also that Act itself) or, as the case may be, the Insolvency Act 1985.

(9) Any expression for whose interpretation provision is made by Part XXVI of the Companies Act (and not by subsections (3) to (8) above) is to be construed in accordance with that provision.   **[490]**

NOTES
  Commencement: 29 December 1986.
  This section derived from the Insolvency Act 1985, s 108(1)–(4).

23. Transitional provisions, savings, repeals

(1) The transitional provisions and savings in Schedule 3 to this Act have effect, and are without prejudice to anything in the Interpretation Act 1978 with regard to the effect of repeals.

(2) The enactments specified in the second column of Schedule 4 to this Act are repealed to the extent specified in the third column of that Schedule.   **[491]**

NOTES
  Commencement: 29 December 1986.

24. Extent

(1) This Act extends to England and Wales and to Scotland.

(2) Nothing in this Act extends to Northern Ireland.   **[492]**

NOTES
  Commencement: 29 December 1986.
  This section derived from the Companies Act 1985, s 745(2), and the Insolvency Act 1985, s 236(4).

25. Commencement

This Act comes into force simultaneously with the Insolvency Act 1986.   **[493]**

NOTES
  Commencement: 29 December 198

26. Citation

This Act may be cited as the Company Directors Disqualification Act 1986.
     [494]

NOTES
  Commencement: 29 December 1986.

SCHEDULES
SCHEDULE 1

Section 9

MATTERS FOR DETERMINING UNFITNESS OF DIRECTORS

PART I
MATTERS APPLICABLE IN ALL CASES

1. Any misfeasance or breach of any fiduciary or other duty by the director in relation to the company.

2. Any misapplication or retention by the director of, or any conduct by the director giving rise to an obligation to account for, any money or other property of the company.

3. The extent of the director's responsibility for the company entering into any transaction liable to be set aside under Part XVI of the Insolvency Act (provisions against debt avoidance).

4. The extent of the director's responsibility for any failure by the company to comply with any of the following provisions of the Companies Act, namely—

    (a) section 221 (companies to keep accounting records);
    (b) section 222 (where and for how long records to be kept);
    (c) section 288 (register of directors and secretaries);
    (d) section 352 (obligation to keep and enter up register of members);
    (e) section 353 (location of register of members);
    (f) sections 363 and 364 (company's duty to make annual return);
    (g) section 365 (time for completion of annual return); and
    (h) sections 399 and 415 (company's duty to register charges it creates).

5. The extent of the director's responsibility for any failure by the directors of the company to comply with section 227 (directors' duty to prepare annual accounts) or section 238 (signing of balance sheet and documents to be annexed) of the Companies Act.

PART II
MATTERS APPLICABLE WHERE COMPANY HAS BECOME INSOLVENT

6. The extent of the director's responsibility for the causes of the company becoming insolvent.

7. The extent of the director's responsibility for any failure by the company to supply any goods or services which have been paid for (in whole or in part).

8. The extent of the director's responsibility for the company entering into any transaction or giving any preference, being a transaction or preference—

    (a) liable to be set aside under section 127 or sections 238 to 240 of the Insolvency Act, or
    (b) challengeable under section 242 or 243 of that Act or under any rule of law in Scotland.

9. The extent of the director's responsibility for any failure by the directors of the company to comply with section 98 of the Insolvency Act (duty to call creditors' meeting in creditors' voluntary winding up).

10. Any failure by the director to comply with any obligation imposed on him by or under any of the following provisions of the Insolvency Act—

    (a) section 22 (company's statement of affairs in administration);
    (b) section 47 (statement of affairs to administrative receiver);
    (c) section 66 (statement of affairs in Scottish receivership);
    (d) section 99 (directors' duty to attend meeting; statement of affairs in creditors' voluntary winding up);
    (e) section 131 (statement of affairs in winding up by the court);

(*f*) section 234 (duty of any one with company property to deliver it up);
(*g*) section 235 (duty to co-operate with liquidator, etc).   **[495]**

NOTES
Commencement: 29 December 1986.
This Schedule derived from the Insolvency Act 1985, Sch 2.

SCHEDULE 2

Section 19

SAVINGS FROM COMPANIES ACT 1981 ss 93, 94, AND INSOLVENCY ACT 1985 SCHEDULE 9

1. Sections 2 and 4(1)(*b*) do not apply in relation to anything done before 15th June 1982 by a person in his capacity as liquidator of a company or as receiver or manager of a company's property.

2. Subject to paragraph 1—

   (*a*) section 2 applies in a case where a person is convicted on indictment of an offence which he committed (and, in the case of a continuing offence, has ceased to commit) before 15th June 1982; but in such a case a disqualification order under that section shall not be made for a period in excess of 5 years;

   (*b*) that section does not apply in a case where a person is convicted summarily—

   (i) in England and Wales, if he had consented so to be tried before that date, or

   (ii) in Scotland, if the summary proceedings commenced before that date.

3. Subject to paragraph 1, section 4 applies in relation to an offence committed or other thing done before 15th June 1982; but a disqualification order made on the grounds of such an offence or other thing done shall not be made for a period in excess of 5 years.

4. The powers of a court under section 5 are not exercisable in a case where a person is convicted of an offence which he committed (and, in the case of a continuing offence, had ceased to commit) before 15th June 1982.

5. For purposes of section 3(1) and section 5, no account is to be taken of any offence which was committed, or any default order which was made, before 1st June 1977.

6. An order made under section 28 of the Companies Act 1976 has effect as if made under section 3 of this Act; and an application made before 15th June 1982 for such an order is to be treated as an application for an order under the section last mentioned.

7. Where—

   (*a*) an application is made for a disqualification order under section 6 of this Act by virtue of paragraph (*a*) of subsection (2) of that section, and

   (*b*) the company in question went into liquidation before 28th April 1986 (the coming into force of the provision replaced by section 6),

the court shall not make an order under that section unless it could have made a disqualification order under section 300 of the Companies Act as it had effect immediately before the date specified in sub-paragraph (*b*) above.

8. An application shall not be made under section 8 of this Act in relation to a report made or information or documents obtained before 28th April 1986.   **[496]**

NOTES
Commencement: 29 December 1986.
This Schedule derived from the Companies Act 1985, Sch 12, Pt III, and the Insolvency Act 1985, Sch 9, paras 2, 3.

SCHEDULE 3

Section 23(1)

TRANSITIONAL PROVISIONS AND SAVINGS

1. In this Schedule, "the former enactments" means so much of the Companies Act, and so much of the Insolvency Act, as is repealed and replaced by this Act; and "the appointed day" means the day on which this Act comes into force.

2. So far as anything done or treated as done under or for the purposes of any provision of the former enactments could have been done under or for the purposes of the corresponding provision of this Act, it is not invalidated by the repeal of that provision but has effect as if done under or for the purposes of the corresponding provision; and any order, regulation, rule or other instrument made or having effect under any provision of the former enactments shall, insofar as its effect is preserved by this paragraph, be treated for all purposes as made and having effect under the corresponding provision.

3. Where any period of time specified in a provision of the former enactments is current immediately before the appointed day, this Act has effect as if the corresponding provision had been in force when the period began to run; and (without prejudice to the foregoing) any period of time so specified and current is deemed for the purposes of this Act—

(a) to run from the date or event from which it was running immediately before the appointed day, and

(b) to expire (subject to any provision of this Act for its extension) whenever it would have expired if this Act had not been passed;

and any rights, priorities, liabilities, reliefs, obligations, requirements, powers, duties or exemptions dependent on the beginning, duration or end of such a period as above mentioned shall be under this Act as they were or would have been under the former enactments.

4. Where in any provision of this Act there is a reference to another such provision, and the first-mentioned provision operates, or is capable of operating, in relation to things done or omitted, or events occuring or not occuring, in the past (including in particular past acts of compliance with any enactment, failures of compliance, contraventions, offences and convictions of offences) the reference to the other provision is to be read as including a reference to the corresponding provision of the former enactments.

5. Offences committed before the appointed day under any provision of the former enactments may, notwithstanding any repeal by this Act, be prosecuted and punished after that day as if this Act had not passed.

6. A reference in any enactment, instrument or document (whether express or implied, and in whatever phraseology) to a provision of the former enactments (including the corresponding provision of any yet earlier enactment) is to be read, where necessary to retain for the enactment, instrument or document the same force and effect as it would have had but for the passing of this Act, as, or as including, a reference to the corresponding provision by which it is replaced in this Act. **[497]**

NOTES

Commencement: 29 December 1986.

SCHEDULE 4

REPEALS

Chapter	Short Title	Extent of Repeal
1985 c 6	The Companies Act 1985	Sections 295 to 299. Section 301. Section 302. Schedule 12. In Schedule 24, the entries relating to sections 295(7) and 302(1).
1985 c 65	The Insolvency Act 1985	Sections 12 to 14. Section 16. Section 18. Section 108(2). Schedule 2. In Schedule 6, paragraphs 1, 2, 7 and 14. In Schedule 9, paragraphs 2 and 3.

[498]

NOTES
  Commencement: 29 December 1986.

DERIVATION TABLE

Note: The following abbreviations are used in this Table:—

"CA" = The Companies Act 1985 (c 6)
"IA" = The Insolvency Act 1985 (c 65)

Provision	Derivation	Provision	Derivation
1	CA s 295(1), (2), (4); IA Sch 6 para 1(1)–(3)	17	CA s 295(6) (part), Sch 12 paras 4, 5; IA s 108(2), Sch 6 paras 1(4), 14
2	CA ss 295(2), 296		
3	CA ss 295(2), 297		
4	CA ss 295(2), 298	18	CA s 301; IA s 108(2), Sch 6 para 2
5	CA ss 295(2), 299		
6	CA s 295(2); IA ss 12(1), (2), (7)–(9), 108(2)	19	CA s 295(6); and see Sch 2
7	IA s 12(3)–(6)	20	IA s 231 (part)
8	CA s 295(2); IA ss 12(9), 13, 108(2)	21	IA ss 106, 107, 108(1), (2), 222(1), 224(2), 227, 229, 234
9	IA ss 12(9), 14		
10	CA s 295(2); IA ss 16, 108(2)	22	IA s 108(1)–(4)
		23	—
11	CA s 302	24	CA s 745(2); IA s 236(4)
12	IA s 221(2)	25	—
13	CA ss 295(7), 302(1), Sch 24; IA s 221(5)	26	—
		Sch 1	IA Sch 2
14	CA s 733(1)–(3); IA Sch 6 para 7	Sch 2	CA Sch 12 Pt III; IA Sch 9 paras 2, 3
15	IA s 18(1) (part), (2)–(6)	Sch 3	—
16	CA s 295(6) (part), Sch 12 paras 1–3; IA s 108(2), Sch 6 para 1(4)	Sch 4	—

DESTINATION TABLE

This table shows in column (1) the enactments repealed by the Company Directors Disqualification Act 1986, s 23(2), Sch 4 (and, in certain cases where indicated by an asterisk*, provisions repealed by the Insolvency Act 1986, s 438, Sch 12), and in column (2) the provisions of the former Act corresponding to the repealed provisions.

In certain cases the enactment in column (1), although having a corresponding provision in column (2) is not, or is not wholly, repealed, as it is still required, or partly required, for the purposes of other legislation.

(1)	(2)	(1)	(2)
Companies Act 1985 (c 6)	Company Directors Disqualification Act 1986 (c 46)	Insolvency Act 1985 (c 65)	Company Directors Disqualification Act 1986 (c 46)
s 295(1)	s 1(1)	s 12(1), (2)	s 6(1), (4)
s 295(2)	s 1(2), (3), 2(3), 3(5), 4(3), 5(5), 6(4), 8(4), 10(2)	s 12(3)–(6)	s 7(1)–(4)
		s 12(7)	s 6(2)
s 295(3)	s 22(2)	s 12(8), (9)	s 6(3)
s 295(4)	s 1(4)	s 13	s 8
s 295(5)	Unnecessary	s 14	s 9
s 295(6)	s 16, 17, 19(a), (b)	s 16	s 10(1)
s 295(7)	s 13	s 18(1)–(5)	s 15(1)–(5)
s 296	s 2	s 18(6)	s 22(2)
s 297	s 3	s 106, 107, 108(1)* . . .	s 21, 22^x
s 298	s 4	s 108(2)	s 6(4), 8(4), 10(2), 16, 17, 18, 21, 22^x
s 299	s 5		
s 301	s 18	s 108(3), (4)*	s 22^x
s 302(1)	s 13	s 221(2)*	s 12(2)
s 302(1)–(3)	s 11(1)–(3)	s 221(5)*	s 13
s 302(4)	s 22(2)	s 222(1), 224(2), 227, 229*	s 21
s 733(1)†	s 14(1), (2)	s 231*	s 20
s 733(2), (3)†	s 14(1), (2)	s 234*	s 21
s 745(2)†	s 24	s 236(4)*	s 24
Sch 12, para 1–3	s 16(1)–(3)	Sch 2	Sch 1
para 4, 5	s 17(1), (2)	Sch 6, para 1(2), (3) . . .	s 1(1), (3)
para 6–8, 15, 16 . . .	Rep, 1985 c 65, s 235(3), Sch 10, Pt II	para 1(4)	s 16, 17
		para 2	s 18(1)
para 9–14	Sch 2, para 1–6	para 7	s 14
Sch 24 (part)	s 13	para 14	s 17(1)
		Sch 9, para 2, 3	Sch 2, para 7, 8

† Not repealed   * See notes to this table above ^{x} See specific derivation note   **[500]**

PART III

BANKRUPTCY (SCOTLAND) ACT 1985

BANKRUPTCY (SCOTLAND) ACT 1985
(c 46)

ARRANGEMENT OF SECTIONS

Administration of bankruptcy

Section		Para
1	Accountant in Bankruptcy..	[501]
2	Interim trustee	[502]
3	Permanent trustee ..	[503]
4	Commissioners	[504]

Petitions for sequestration

5 | Sequestration of the estate of living or deceased debtor .. | [505]
6 | Sequestration of other estates | [506]
7 | Meaning of apparent insolvency .. | [507]
8 | Further provisions relating to presentation of petitions .. | [508]
9 | Jurisdiction .. | [509]
10 | Concurrent proceedings for sequestration or analogous remedy | [510]
11 | Creditor's oath | [511]

Award of sequestration and appointment and resignation of interim trustee

12 | When sequestration is awarded .. | [512]
13 | Appointment and resignation of interim trustee .. | [513]
14 | Registration of court order.. | [514]
15 | Further provisions relating to award of sequestration .. | [515]
16 | Petitions for recall of sequestration | [516]
17 | Recall of sequestration | [517]

Period between award of sequestration and statutory meeting of creditors

18 | Interim preservation of estate | [518]
19 | Debtor's list of assets and liabilities | [519]
20 | Trustee's duties on receipt of list of assets and liabilities | [520]

Statutory meeting of creditors and confirmation of permanent trustee

21 | Calling of statutory meeting | [521]
22 | Submission of claims for voting purposes at statutory meeting .. | [522]
23 | Proceedings at statutory meeting before election of permanent trustee | [523]
24 | Election of permanent trustee | [524]
25 | Confirmation of permanent trustee | [525]
26 | Provisions relating to termination of interim trustee's functions | [526]
27 | Discharge of interim trustee | [527]

Replacement of permanent trustee

28 | Resignation and death of permanent trustee | [528]
29 | Removal of permanent trustee and trustee not acting .. | [529]

Election, resignation and removal of commissioners

30 | Election, resignation and removal of commissioners | [530]

Vesting of estate in permanent trustee

31 | Vesting of estate at date of sequestration .. | [531]
32 | Vesting of estate, and dealings of debtor, after sequestration .. | [532]
33 | Limitations on vesting | [533]

Safeguarding of interests of creditors of insolvent persons

34 | Gratuitous alienations | [534]

Section   Para
35   Recalling of order for payment of capital sum on divorce   ..   ..   [535]
36   Unfair preferences ..   ..   [536]

Effect of sequestration on diligence

37   Effect of sequestration on diligence   ..   ..   [537]

Administration of estate by permanent trustee

38   Taking possession of estate by permanent trustee   ..   ..   ..   [538]
39   Management and realisation of estate   ..   ..   [539]
40   Power of permanent trustee in relation to the debtor's family home   ..   ..   [540]
41   Protection of rights of spouse against arrangements intended to defeat them ..   ..   [541]
42   Contractual powers of permanent trustee   ..   ..   [542]
43   Money received by permanent trustee   ..   ..   [543]

Examination of debtor

44   Private examination   ..   ..   [544]
45   Public examination..   ..   ..   [545]
46   Provisions ancillary to sections 44 and 45   ..   ..   [546]
47   Conduct of examination   ..   ..   [547]

Submission and adjudication of claims

48   Submission of claims to permanent trustee   ..   ..   [548]
49   Adjudication of claims   ..   ..   [549]

Entitlement to vote and draw dividend

50   Entitlement to vote and draw dividend   ..   ..   [550]

Distribution of debtor's estate

51   Order of priority in distribution   ..   ..   [551]
52   Estate to be distributed in respect of accounting periods   ..   ..   [552]
53   Procedure after end of accounting period   ..   ..   ..   [553]

Discharge of debtor

54   Automatic discharge after 3 years ..   ..   [554]
55   Effect of discharge under section 54   ..   ..   [555]
56   Discharge on composition ..   ..   [556]

Discharge of permanent trustee

57   Discharge of permanent trustee   ..   ..   [557]
58   Unclaimed dividends   ..   ..   [558]

Voluntary trust deeds for creditors

59   Voluntary trust deeds for creditors   ..   ..   [559]

Miscellaneous and supplementary

60   Liabilities and rights of co-obligants   ..   ..   [560]
61   Extortionate credit transactions   ..   ..   [561]
62   Sederunt book and other documents   ..   ..   [562]
63   Power to cure defects in procedure   ..   ..   [563]
64   Debtor to co-operate with permanent trustee   ..   ..   ..   [564]
65   Arbitration and compromise   ..   ..   [565]
66   Meetings of creditors and commissioners   ..   ..   ..   [566]
67   General offences by debtor etc   ..   ..   [567]
68   Summary proceedings   ..   ..   [568]
69   Outlays of interim and permanent trustee   ..   ..   ..   [569]
70   Supplies by utilities ..   ..   [570]
71   Edinburgh Gazette ..   ..   [571]
72   Regulations ..   ..   [572]
73   Interpretation   ..   ..   [573]
74   Meaning of "associate"   ..   ..   [574]
75   Amendments, repeals and transitional provisions   ..   ..   ..   [575]
76   Receipts and expenses   ..   ..   [576]

Section   Para
77   Crown application ..   ..   [577]
78   Short title, commencement and extent   ..   ..   [578]

SCHEDULES:

Schedule 1—Determination of amount of creditor's claim ..   ..   [579]
Schedule 2—Adaptation of procedure etc. under this Act where permanent trustee
    not elected   ..   ..   [580]
Schedule 3—Preferred debts   ..   ..   [581]
Schedule 4—Discharge on composition   ..   ..   [583]
Schedule 5—Voluntary trust deeds for creditors   ..   ..   [584]
Schedule 6—Meetings of creditors and commissioners   ..   ..   [585]
Schedule 7—Consequential amendments and re-enactments   ..   ..   ..   [588]
Schedule 8—Repeals   ..   ..   [590]

An Act to reform the law of Scotland relating to sequestration and personal insolvency; and for connected purposes   [30 October 1985]

Enforcement of insolvency law in other parts of the United Kingdom: See the Involvency Act 1986, s 426, for provision for co-operation between courts exercising jurisdiction in relation to insolvency.

Drug trafficking confiscation orders: Nothing in this Act shall be taken as restricting, or enabling the restriction of, the exercise of the powers of the court under the Drug Trafficking Offences Act 1986, ss 8–12, 20–22 (enforcement of confiscation orders); see s 16(3) of that Act.

Administration of bankruptcy

1. Accountant in Bankruptcy

(1) The Accountant in Bankruptcy shall have the following general functions in the administration of sequestration and personal insolvency—

    (a) the supervision of the performance by interim trustees, permanent trustees and commissioners of the functions conferred on them by this Act and the investigation of any complaints made against them;

    (b) the maintenance of a list of persons (in this Act referred to as the "list of interim trustees") from which interim trustees shall be appointed;

    (c) the maintenance of a register (in this Act referred to as the "register of insolvencies"), in a form prescribed by the Court of Session by act of sederunt, which shall contain particulars of—

        (i) estates which have been sequestrated; and

        (ii) trust deeds which have been sent to him for registration under paragraph 5(d) of Schedule 5 to this Act; and

    (d) the preparation of an annual report which shall be presented to the Court of Session and the Secretary of State and shall contain—

        (i) statistical information relating to the state of all sequestrations of which particulars have been registered in the register of insolvencies during the year to which the report relates;

        (ii) particulars of trust deeds registered as protected trust deeds in that year; and

        (iii) particulars of the performance of the Accountant in Bankruptcy's functions under this Act.

(2) The Accountant of Court shall be the Accountant in Bankruptcy.

(3) If it appears to the Accountant in Bankruptcy that an interim trustee, permanent trustee or commissioner has failed without reasonable excuse to perform a duty imposed on him by any provision of this Act, he shall report the matter to the court which, after hearing the interim trustee, permanent trustee

or commissioner on the matter, may remove him from office or censure him or
make such other order as the circumstances of the case may require.

(4) If the Accountant in Bankruptcy has reasonable grounds to suspect that
an interim trustee, permanent trustee or commissioner has committed an
offence in the performance of his functions under this Act, or that an offence
has been committed in relation to a sequestration—

(*a*) by the debtor, in respect of his assets, his dealings with them or his
conduct in relation to his business or financial affairs; or

(*b*) by a person other than the debtor in that person's dealings with the
debtor, the interim trustee or the permanent trustee in respect of the
debtor's assets, business or financial affairs,

he shall report the matter to the Lord Advocate.

(5) The Accountant in Banruptcy shall—

(*a*) make the register of insolvencies, at all reasonable times, available
for inspection; and

(*b*) provide any person, on request, with a certified copy of any entry in
the register.

(6) The power of the Secretary of State to regulate fees under section 2 of
the Courts of Law Fees (Scotland) Act 1895 shall include power to prescribe the
fees payable in respect of any matter relating to the functions of the Accountant
in Bankruptcy.   **[501]**

NOTES
  Commencement: 1 February 1986 (sub-ss (1)(*b*), (2), (6)); 1 April 1986 (sub-ss (1)(*a*), (*c*), (*d*), (3)–
(5).
  Commencement orders: SI 1985 No 1924, SI 1986 No 1913.

2. Interim trustee

(1) In every sequestration there shall be appointed under section 13 of this Act
an interim trustee whose general functions shall be—

(*a*) to safeguard the debtor's estate pending the appointment of a
permanent trustee under this Act;

(*b*) to ascertain the reasons for the debtor's insolvency and the
circumstances surrounding it;

(*c*) to ascertain the state of the debtor's liabilities and assets;

(*d*) to administer the sequestration process pending the appointment of a
permanent trustee; and

(*e*) whether or not he is still acting in the sequestration, to supply the
Accountant in Bankruptcy with such information as the Accountant
in Bankruptcy considers necessary to enable him to discharge his
functions under this Act.

(2) A person shall be entitled to have his name included in the list of interim
trustees if, but only if, he—

(*a*) resides within the jurisdiction of the Court of Session; and

(*b*) is qualified to act as an insolvency practitioner.

(3) The Accountant in Bankruptcy shall remove a person's name from the
list of interim trustees—

(*a*) at the person's own request:

(b) if it appears to the Accountant in Bankruptcy that the person has ceased to meet either of the requirements mentioned in subsection (2) above; or

(c) if, on an application by the Accountant in Bankruptcy to the sheriff for the sheriffdom in which the person is habitually resident or his principal place of business is, or was last, situated, the sheriff is satisfied that the person is physically or mentally incapacitated from acting as interim trustee:

Provided that removal of a person's name in pursuance of paragraph (a) above shall not absolve that person, if he is acting as an interim or permanent trustee in a particular case, from continuing so to act until he has completed his duties in relation to that case:

Provided also that, until the coming into force of section 2 of the Insolvency Act 1985 (qualifications of insolvency practitioners), paragraph (b) above shall have effect as if at the end were added the words "or is not a fit and proper person to act as interim trustee".

(4) Any person aggrieved by the exclusion or removal of his name from the list of interim trustees may appeal against that exclusion or removal to the Court of Session.   **[502]**

NOTES
   Commencement: 1 February 1986 (sub-ss (2)–(4)); 1 April 1986 (sub-s (1)).
   Commencement orders: SI 1985 No 1924, SI 1986 No 1913.

3. Permanent trustee

(1) In every sequestration there shall be a permanent trustee whose general functions shall be—

(a) to recover, manage and realise the debtor's estate, whether situated in Scotland or elsewhere;

(b) to distribute the estate among the debtor's creditors according to their respective entitlements;

(c) to ascertain the reasons for the debtor's insolvency and the circumstances surrounding it;

(d) to ascertain the state of the debtor's liabilities and assets;

(e) to maintain a sederunt book during his term of office for the purpose of providing an accurate record of the sequestration process;

(f) to keep regular accounts of his intromissions with the debtor's estate, such accounts being available for inspection at all reasonable times by the commissioners (if any), the creditors and the debtor; and

(g) whether or not he is still acting in the sequestration, to supply the Accountant in Bankruptcy with such information as the Accountant in Bankruptcy considers necessary to enable him to discharge his functions under this Act.

(2) A permanent trustee in performing his functions under this Act shall have regard to advice offered to him by the commissioners (if any).

(3) If the permanent trustee has reasonable grounds to suspect that an offence has been committed in relation to a sequestration—

(a) by the debtor in respect of his assets, his dealings with them or his conduct in relation to his business or financial affairs; or (*b*) by a person other than the debtor in that person's dealings with the debtor, the interim trustee or the permanent trustee in resepct of the debtor's assets, business or financial affairs,

he shall report the matter to the Accountant in Bankruptcy.

(4) A report under subsection (3) above shall be absolutely privileged. **[503]**

NOTES
    Commencement: 1 April 1986.
    Commencement order: SI 1985 No 1924.

4. Commissioners

In any sequestration (other than one to which Schedule 2 to this Act applies) commissioners, whose general functions shall be to supervise the intromissions of the permanent trustee with the sequestrated estate and to advise him, may be elected in accordance with section 30 of this Act. **[504]**

NOTES
    Commencement: 1 April 1986.
    Commencement order: SI 1985 No 1924.

Petitions for sequestration

5. Sequestration of the estate of living or deceased debtor

(1) The estate of a debtor may be sequestrated in accordance with the provisions of this Act.

(2) The sequestration of the estate of a living debtor shall be on the petition of—

(*a*) the debtor, with the concurrence of a qualified creditor or qualified creditors;

(*b*) a qualified creditor or qualified creditors, if the debtor is apparently insolvent; or

(*c*) the trustee acting under a voluntary trust deed granted by or on behalf of the debtor whereby his estate is conveyed to the trustee for the benefit of his creditors generally (in this Act referred to as a "trust deed").

(3) The sequestration of the estate of a deceased debtor shall be on the petition of—

(*a*) an executor or a person entitled to be appointed as executor on the estate;

(*b*) a qualified creditor or qualified creditors of the deceased debtor; or

(*c*) the trustee acting under a trust deed.

(4) In this Act "qualified creditor" means a creditor who, at the date of the presentation of the petition, is a creditor of the debtor in respect of liquid or illiquid debts (other than contingent or future debts), whether secured or unsecured, which amount (or of one such debt which amounts) to not less than £750 or such sum as may be prescribed; and "qualified creditors" means creditors who at the said date are creditors of the debtor in respect of such debts as aforesaid amounting in aggregate to not less than £750 or such sum as may be prescribed.

(5) Paragraphs 1(1) and (3), 2(1)(*a*) and (2) and 6 of Schedule 1 to this Act shall apply in order to ascertain the amount of the debt or debts for the purposes

of subsection (4) above as they apply in order to ascertain the amount which a creditor is entitled to claim, but as if for any reference to the date of sequestration there were substituted a reference to the date of presentation of the petition.

(6) The petitioner shall send a copy of any petition presented under this section to the Accountant in Bankruptcy.

(7) Where, after a petition for sequestration has been presented but before the sequestration has been awarded, the debtor dies then—

    (*a*) if the petitioner was the debtor, the petition shall fall;

    (*b*) if the petitioner is a creditor, the proceedings shall continue in accordance with this Act so far as circumstances will permit.

(8) Where, after a petition for sequestration has been presented under this section but before the sequestration has been awarded, a creditor who—

    (*a*) is the petitioner or concurs in a petition by the debtor; or

    (*b*) has lodged answers to the petition,

withdraws or dies, there may be sisted in the place of—

    (i) the creditor mentioned in paragraph (*a*) above, any creditor who was a qualified creditor at the date when the petition was presented and who remains so qualified at the date of the sist;

    (ii) the creditor mentioned in paragraph (*b*) above, any other creditor.

[505]

NOTES

    Commencement: 1 April 1986.

    Commencement order: SI 1985 No 1924.

---

6. Sequestration of other estates

(1) Subject to subsection (2) below, the estate belonging to or held for or jointly by the members of any of the following entities may be sequestrated—

    (*a*) a trust in respect of debts incurred by it;

    (*b*) a partnership, including a dissolved partnership;

    (*c*) a body corporate or an unincorporated body;

    (*d*) a limited partnership (including a dissolved partnership) within the meaning of the Limited Partnerships Act 1907.

(2) It shall not be competent to sequestrate the estate of any of the following entities—

    (*a*) a company registered under the Companies Act 1985 or under the former Companies Act (within the meaning of that Act); or

    (*b*) an entity in respect of which an enactment provides, expressly or by implication, that sequestration is incompetent.

(3) The sequestration of a trust estate in respect of debts incurred by the trust shall be on the petition of—

    (*a*) a majority of the trustees, with the concurrence of a qualified creditor or qualified creditors; or

    (*b*) a qualified creditor or qualified creditors, if the trustees as such are apparently insolvent.

(4) The sequestration of the estate of a partnership shall be on the petition of—

    (*a*) the partnership, with the concurrence of a qualified creditor or qualified creditors; or (*b*) a qualified creditor or qualified creditors, if the partnership is apparently insolvent.

(5) A petition under subsection (4)(*b*) above may be combined with a petition for the sequestration of the estate of any of the partners as an individual where that individual is apparently insolvent.

(6) The sequestration of the estate of a body corporate or of an unincorporated body shall be on the petition of—

(*a*) a person authorised to act on behalf of the body, with the concurrence of a qualified creditor or qualified creditors; or

(*b*) a qualified creditor or qualified creditors, if the body is apparently insolvent.

(7) The application of this Act to the sequestration of the estate of a limited partnership shall be subject to such modifications as may be prescribed.

(8) Subsections (6) and (8) of section 5 of this Act shall apply for the purposes of this section as they apply for the purposes of that section.   **[506]**

NOTES
Commencement: 1 April 1986.
Commencement order: SI 1985 No 1924.

7. Meaning of apparent insolvency

(1) A debtor's apparent insolvency shall be constituted (or, where he is already apparently insolvent, constituted anew) whenever—

(*a*) his estate is sequestrated, or he is adjudged bankrupt in England or Wales or Northern Ireland; or

(*b*) he gives written notice to his creditors that he has ceased to pay his debts in the ordinary course of business; or

(*c*) any of the following circumstances occurs—

  (i) he grants a trust deed;

  (ii) following the service on him of a duly executed charge for payment of a debt, the days of charge expire without payment;

  (iii) following a poinding or seizure of any of his moveable property in pursuance of a summary warrant for the recovery of rates or taxes, 14 days elapse without payment;

  (iv) a decree of adjudication of any part of his estate is granted, either for payment or in security;

  (v) his effects are sold under a sequestration for rent due by him; or

  (vi) a receiving order is made against him in England or Wales,

  unless it is shown that at the time when any such circumstance occurred, the debtor was able and willing to pay his debts as they became due; or

(*d*) a creditor of the debtor, in respect of a liquid debt which amounts (or liquid debts which in aggregate amount) to not less than £750 or such sum as may be prescribed, has served on the debtor, by personal service by an officer of court, a demand in the prescribed form requiring him either to pay the debt (or debts) or to find security for its (or their) payment, and within 3 weeks after the date of service of the demand the debtor has not—

  (i) complied with the demand; or

(ii) intimated to the creditor, by recorded delivery, that he denies that there is a debt or that the sum claimed by the creditor as the debt is immediately payable.

(2) A debtor's apparent insolvency shall continue, if constituted under—

(a) subsection (1)(a) above, until his discharge; or

(b) subsection (1)(b), (c) or (d) above, until he becomes able to pay his debts and pays them as they become due.

(3) The apparent insolvency of—

(a) a partnership shall be constituted either in accordance with the foregoing provisions of this section or if any of the partners is apparently insolvent for a debt of the partnership;

(b) an unincorporated body shall be constituted if a person representing the body is apparently insolvent, or a person holding property of the body in a fiduciary capacity is apparently insolvent, for a debt of the body.

(4) Notwithstanding subsection (2) of section 6 of this Act, the apparent insolvency of an entity such as is mentioned in paragraph (a) or (b) of that subsection may be constituted (or as the case may be constituted anew) under subsection (1) above; and any reference in the foregoing provisions of this section to a debtor shall, except where the context otherwise requires, be construed as including a reference to such an entity.   **[507]**

NOTES
    Commencement: 1 April 1986.
    Commencement order: SI 1985 No 1924.

8. Further provisions relating to presentation of petitions

(1) Subject to subsection (2) below, a petition for the sequestration of a debtor's estate (other than a deceased debtor's estate) may be presented—

(a) at any time by the debtor or by a trustee acting under a trust deed; but

(b) by a qualified creditor or qualified creditors, only if the apparent insolvency founded on in the petition was constituted within 4 months before the petition is presented.

(2) A petition for the sequestration of the estate of a limited partnership may be presented within such time as may be prescribed.

(3) A petition for the sequestration of the estate of a deceased debtor may be presented—

(a) at any time by an executor or a person entitled to be appointed as executor on the estate or a trustee acting under a trust deed;

(b) by a qualified creditor or qualified creditors of the deceased debtor—

(i) in a case where the apparent insolvency of the debtor was constituted within 4 months before his death, at any time;

(ii) in any other case (whether or not apparent insolvency has been constituted), not earlier than 6 months after the debtor's death.

(4) If an executor does not petition for sequestration of the deceased debtor's estate or for the appointment of a judicial factor to administer the estate within a reasonable period after he knew or ought to have known that the estate was absolutely insolvent and likely to remain so, any intromission by him with the estate after the expiry of that period shall be deemed to be an intromission without a title.

(5) The presentation of, or the concurring in, a petition for sequestration shall bar the effect of any enactment or rule of law relating to the limitation of actions in any part of the United Kingdom.

(6) Where before sequestration is awarded it becomes apparent that a petitioning or concurring creditor was ineligible so to petition or concur he shall withdraw, or as the case may be withdraw from, the petition but another creditor may be sisted in his place. **[508]**

NOTES
Commencement: 1 April 1986.
Commencement order: SI 1985 No 1924.

9. Jurisdiction

(1) The Court of Session shall have jurisdiction in respect of the sequestration of the estate of a living debtor or of a deceased debtor if the debtor had an established place of business in Scotland, or was habitually resident there, at the relevant time.

(2) The Court of Session shall have jurisdiction in respect of the sequestration of the estate of any entity which may be sequestrated by virtue of section 6 of this Act, if the entity—

(a) had an established place of business in Scotland at the relevant time; or

(b) was constituted or formed under Scots law, and at any time carried on business in Scotland.

(3) Notwithstanding that the partner of a firm, whether alive or deceased, does not fall within subsection (1) above, the Court of Session shall have jurisdiction in respect of the sequestration of his estate if a petition has been presented for the sequestration of the estate of the firm of which he is, or was at the relevant time before his decease, a partner and the process of that sequestration is still current.

(4) The provisions of this section shall apply to the sheriff as they apply to the Court of Session but as if for the word "Scotland" wherever it occurs there were substituted the words "the sheriffdom" and in subsection (3) after the word "presented" there were inserted the words "in the sheriffdom".

(5) In this section "the relevant time" means at any time in the year immediately preceding the date of presentation of the petition or the date of death, as the case may be. **[509]**

NOTES
Commencement: 1 April 1986.
Commencement order: SI 1985 No 1924.

10. Concurrent proceedings for sequestration or analogous remedy

(1) If, in the course of sequestration proceedings, the petitioner for sequestration, the debtor or a creditor concurring in the petition (the petition in such proceedings being hereafter in this section referred to as the "instant petition") is, or becomes, aware that—

(a) another petition for sequestration of the debtor's estate is before a court or such sequestration has been awarded; or

(b) a petition for the appointment of a judicial factor on the debtor's estate is before a court or such a judicial factor has been appointed; or

(c) a petition is before a court for the winding up of the debtor under Part XX
     of the Companies Act 1985 or the debtor has been wound up under the
     said Part XX; or
(d) an application for an analogous remedy in respect of the debtor's
     estate is proceeding or such an analogous remedy is in force,

he shall as soon as possible bring that fact to the notice of the court to which the
instant petition was presented.

(2) If a petitioner (not being the debtor) or a creditor concurring in the
petition fails to comply with subsection (1) above, he may be made liable for the
expenses of presenting the petition for sequestration; and, if the debtor fails to
comply with subsection (1) above, he shall be guilty of an offence and liable, on
summary conviction, to a fine not exceeding level 5 on the standard scale.

(3) Where in the course of sequestration proceedings any of the circumstances mentioned in paragraph (a), (b) or (c) of subsection (1) above exists
then—

(a) the court to which the instant petition was presented may, on its own
     motion or at the instance of the debtor or any creditor or other person
     having an interest, allow that petition to proceed or may sist or dismiss
     it; or
(b) without prejudice to paragraph (a) above, the Court of Session may,
     on its own motion or on application by the debtor or any creditor or
     other person having an interest, direct the sheriff before whom the
     instant petition is pending, or the court before which the other petition
     is pending, to sist or dismiss the instant petition or, as the case may
     be, the other petition, or may order the petitions to be heard together.

(4) Where in respect of the same estate—

(a) a petition for sequestration is pending before a court; and
(b) an application for an analogous remedy is proceeding or an analogous
     remedy is in force,

the court, on its own motion or at the instance of the debtor or any creditor or
other person having an interest, may allow the petition for sequestration to
proceed or may sist or dismiss it.

(5) In this section "analogous remedy" means a bankruptcy order under the
Bankruptcy Act 1914 or under the Insolvency Act 1985 or an administration
order under section 112 of the County Courts Act 1984 in England and Wales
or under any enactment having the like effect in Northern Ireland or a remedy
analogous to either of the aforesaid remedies, or to sequestration, in any other
country.   **[510]**

NOTES
    Commencement: 1 April 1986.
    Commencement order: SI 1985 No 1924.
    Prospective substitution: Sub-s (1)(c) is substituted as follows by the Financial Services Act
1986, s 212(2), Sch 16, para 29, as from a date to be appointed under s 211(1) of that Act:

    "(c) a petition is before a court for the winding up of the debtor under Part IV or V of the
         Insolvency Act 1986 or section 72 of the Financial Services Act 1986;".

11. Creditor's oath

(1) Every creditor, being a petitioner for sequestration, a creditor who concurs
in a petition by a debtor or a qualified creditor who becomes sisted under
subsection (8)(i) of section 5 of this Act or under that subsection as applied by

section 6(8) of this Act, shall produce an oath in the prescribed form made by him or on his behalf.

(2) The oath may be made—

    (*a*) in the United Kingdom, before any person entitled to administer an oath there;

    (*b*) outwith the United Kingdom, before a British diplomatic or consular officer or any person authorised to administer an oath or affirmation under the law of the place where the oath is made.

(3) The identity of the person making the oath and the identity of the person before whom the oath is made and their authority to make and to administer the oath respectively shall be presumed to be correctly stated, and any seal or signature on the oath shall be presumed to be authentic, unless the contrary is established.

(4) If the oath contains any error or has omitted any fact, the court to which the petition for sequestration was presented may, at any time before sequestration is awarded, allow another oath to be produced rectifying the original oath; and this section shall apply to the making of that other oath as it applies to the making of the original oath.

(5) Every creditor must produce along with the oath an account or voucher (according to the nature of the debt) which constitutes *prima facie* evidence of the debt; and a petitioning creditor shall in addition produce such evidence as is available to him to show the apparent insolvency of the debtor. **[511]**

NOTES
    Commencement: 1 April 1986.
    Commencement order: SI 1985 No 1924.

Award of sequestration and appointment and resignation of interim trustee

12. When sequestration is awarded

(1) Where a petition for sequestration of his estate is presented by the debtor, the court shall award sequestration forthwith if the court is satisfied that the petition has been presented in accordance with the provisions of this Act unless cause is shown why sequestration cannot competently be awarded.

(2) Where a petition for sequestration of a debtor's estate is presented by a creditor or a trustee acting under a trust deed, the court to which the petition is presented shall grant warrant to cite the debtor to appear before it on such date as shall be specified in the warrant, being a date not less than 6 nor more than 14 days after the date of citation, to show cause why sequestration should not be awarded.

(3) If, on a petition for sequestration presented by a creditor or a trustee acting under a trust deed, the court is satisfied that, if the debtor has not appeared, proper citation has been made of the debtor, that the petition has been presented in accordance with the provisions of this Act and that, in the case of a petition by a creditor, the requirements of this Act relating to apparent insolvency have been fulfilled, it shall award sequestration forthwith unless—

    (*a*) cause is shown why sequestration cannot competently be awarded; or

    (*b*) the debtor forthwith pays or satisfies or produces written evidence of the payment or satisfaction of, or gives sufficient security for the payment of—

(i) the debt in respect of which he became apparently insolvent; and
(ii) any other debt due by him to the petitioner and any creditor concurring in the petition.

(4) In this Act "the date of sequestration" means if the petition for sequestration is presented by—

(*a*) the debtor, the date on which sequestration is awarded;
(*b*) a creditor or a trustee acting under a trust deed, the date on which the court grants warrant under subsection (2) above.   **[512]**

NOTES
Commencement: 1 April 1986.
Commencement order: SI 1985 No 1924.

13. Appointment and resignation of interim trustee

(1) An interim trustee shall be appointed by the court from the list of interim trustees on sequestration being awarded or as soon as may be thereafter:

Provided that, where the petition for sequestration is presented by a creditor or a trustee acting under a trust deed, an interim trustee may be so appointed before sequestration is awarded if—

(*a*) the debtor consents, or
(*b*) the Accountant in Bankruptcy, the trustee acting under the trust deed or any creditor shows cause.

(2) The court may, on an application by an interim trustee, authorise the interim trustee to resign office and, if he does so, shall appoint another person from the list of interim trustees to act in his place; and an interim trustee shall not otherwise resign office.

(3) Without prejudice to section 1(3) of this Act or to subsection (4) below, where the court is satisfied that an interim trustee—

(*a*) is unable to act (whether by, under or by virtue of a provision of this Act or from any other cause whatsoever); or
(*b*) has had his name removed from the list of interim trustees; or
(*c*) has so conducted himself that he should no longer continue to act in the sequestration,

the court, on the application of the debtor, a creditor, the Accountant in Bankruptcy or, in respect of paragraph (*a*) above, the interim trustee, shall appoint another interim trustee from that list to act in his place.

(4) Where under section 1(3) of this Act the court removes an interim trustee from office, the court, on the application of the Accountant in Bankruptcy, shall appoint another interim trustee from the list of interim trustees to act in his place.

(5) Subsect to subsection (6) below, no one shall act as interim trustee in a sequestration if he would, by virtue of section 24(2) of this Act, be disqualified from acting as permanent trustee in that sequestration; but where an interim trustee is, by virtue of this subsection, prohibited from so acting he shall forthwith make an application under subsection (3)(*a*) above.

(6) No person appointed as interim trustee under this section shall be entitled to decline to accept his appointment.

(7) Notwithstanding the provisions of paragraph (*a*) of section 18(3) of this

Act, the court may, if requested to do so in the petition for sequestration, empower the interim trustee to act as is mentioned in that paragraph.

(8) An order of the court making an appointment under this section shall be appealable only by the debtor, a creditor, the Accountant in Bankruptcy or the appointee and only on the ground that the person appointed is unable to act as mentioned in subsection (3)(*a*) above, or is not on the list of interim trustees:

Provided that such an order under subsection (3) above may also be appealed against by the displaced interim trustee on the ground that the court should not have been satisfied as is mentioned in that subsection.

(9) An interim trustee, as soon as may be after his appointment, shall notifity the debtor and the Accountant in Bankruptcy of the appointment. **[513]**

NOTES
  Commencement: 1 April 1986.
  Commencement order: SI 1985 No 1924.

14. Registration of court order

(1) The clerk of the court shall forthwith after the date of sequestration send—

  (*a*) a certified copy of the relevant court order to the keeper of the register of inhibitions and adjudications for recording in that register; and
  (*b*) a copy of the order to the Accountant in Bankruptcy.

(2) Recording under subsection (1)(*a*) above shall have the effect as from the date of sequestration of an inhibition and of a citation in an adjudication of the debtor's heritable estate at the instance of the creditors who subsequently have claims in the sequestration accepted under section 49 of this Act.

(3) The effect mentioned in subsection (2) above shall expire—

  (*a*) on the recording under section 15(5)(*a*) or 17(8)(*a*) of, or by virtue of paragraph 11 of Schedule 4 to, this Act of a certified copy of an order; or
  (*b*) subject to subsection (4) below, if the effect has not expired by virtue of paragraph (*a*) above, at the end of the period of 3 years beginning with the date of sequestration.

(4) The permanent trustee, if not discharged, shall before the end of the period of 3 years mentioned in subsection (3)(*b*) above send a memorandum in a form prescribed by the Court of Session by act of sederunt to the keeper of the register of inhibitions and adjudications for recording in that register, and such recording shall renew the effect mentioned in subsection (2) above; and thereafter the said effect shall continue to be preserved only if such a memorandum is so recorded before the expiry of every subsequent period of 3 years.

(5) In this section "relevant court order" means, if the petition for sequestration is presented by—

  (*a*) the debtor, the order of the court awarding sequestration; or
  (*b*) a creditor or the trustee acting under a trust deed, the order of the court granting warrant under section 12(2) of this Act. **[514]**

NOTES
  Commencement: 1 April 1986.
  Commencement order: SI 1985 No 1924.

15. Further provisions relating to award of sequestration

(1) Where sequestration has been awarded by the Court of Session, it shall remit the sequestration to such sheriff as in all the circumstances of the case it considers appropriate.

(2) The Court of Session may at any time after sequestration has been awarded, on application being made to it, transfer the sequestration from the sheriff before whom it is depending or to whom it has been remitted to any other sheriff.

(3) Where the court makes an order refusing to award sequestration, the petitioner or a creditor concurring in the petition for sequestration may appeal against the order within 14 days of the date of making of the order.

(4) Without prejudice to any right to bring an action of reduction of an award of sequestration, such an award shall not be subject to review otherwise than by recall under sections 16 and 17 of this Act.

(5) Where a petition for sequestration is presented by a creditor or a trustee acting under a trust deed, the clerk of the court shall—

> (a) on the final determination or abandonment of any appeal under subsection (3) above in relation to the petition, or if there is no such appeal on the expiry of the 14 days mentioned in that subsection, send a certified copy of an order refusing to award sequestration to the keeper of the register of inhibitions and adjudications for recording in that register;
>
> (b) forthwith send a copy of an order awarding or refusing to award sequestration to the Accountant in Bankruptcy.

(6) The interim trustee, as soon as an award of sequestration has been granted, shall publish a notice in the prescribed form in the Edinburgh Gazette and the London Gazette stating that sequestration has been awarded and inviting the submission of claims to him.

(7) Where sequestration has been awarded, the process of sequestration shall not fall asleep.

(8) Where a debtor learns, whether before or after the date of sequestration, that he may derive benefit from another estate, he shall as soon as practicable after that date inform—

> (a) the permanent trustee or, if the permanent trustee has not yet been elected or appointed, the interim trustee of that fact; and
>
> (b) the person who is administering that other estate of the sequestration.

(9) If the debtor fails to comply with subsection (8) above, he shall be guilty of an offence and liable, on summary conviction, to a fine not exceeding level 5 on the standard scale.   **[515]**

NOTES
  Commencement: 1 April 1986.
  Commencement order: SI 1985 No 1924.

16. Petitions for recall of sequestration

(1) A petition for recall of an award of sequestration may be presented to the Court of Session by—

(a) the debtor, any creditor or any other person having an interest (notwithstanding that he was a petitioner, or concurred in the petition, for the sequestration);

(b) the interim trustee, the permanent trustee, or the Accountant in Bankruptcy.

(2) The petitioner shall serve upon the debtor, any person who was a petitioner, or concurred in the petition, for the sequestration, the interim trustee or permanent trustee and the Accountant in Bankruptcy, a copy of the petition along with a notice stating that the recipient of the notice may lodge answers to the petition within 14 days of the service of the notice.

(3) At the same time as service is made under subsection (2) above, the petitioner shall publish a notice in the Edinburgh Gazette stating that a petition has been presented under this section and that any person having an interest may lodge answers to the petition within 14 days of the publication of the notice.

(4) Subsect to section 41(1)(b) of this Act, a petition under this section may be presented—

(a) within 10 weeks after the date of sequestration; but

(b) at any time if the petition is presented on any of the grounds mentioned in paragraphs (a) to (c) of section 17(1) of this Act.

(5) Notwithstanding that a petition has been presented under this section, the proceedings in the sequestration shall continue (subject to section 17(6) of this Act) as if that petition had not been presented until the recall is granted.

(6) Where—

(a) a petitioner under this section; or

(b) a person who has lodged answers to the petition,

withdraws or dies, any person entitled to present or, as the case may be, lodge answers to a petition under this section may be sisted in his place.   **[516]**

NOTES
Commencement: 1 April 1986.
Commencement order: SI 1985 No 1924.

17. Recall of sequestration

(1) The Court of Session may recall an award of sequestration if it is satisfied that in all the circumstances of the case (including those arising after the date of the award of sequestration) it is appropriate to do so and, without prejudice to the foregoing generality, may recall the award if it is satisfied that—

(a) the debtor has paid his debts in full or has given sufficient security for their payment;

(b) a majority in value of the creditors reside in a country other than Scotland and that it is more appropriate for the debtor's estate to be administered in that other country; or

(c) one or more other awards of sequestration of the estate or analogous remedies (as defined in section 10(5) of this Act) have been granted.

(2) Where one or more awards of sequestration of the debtor's estate have been granted, the Court may, after such intimation as it considers necessary, recall an award whether or not the one in respect of which the petition for recall was presented.

(3) On recalling an award of sequestration, the Court—

(a) shall make provision for the payment of the outlays and remuneration

of the interim trustee and permanent trustee by directing that such
payment shall be made out of the debtor's estate or by requiring any
person who was a party to the petition for sequestration to pay the
whole or any part of the said outlays and remuneration;

(b) without prejudice to subsection (7) below, may direct that payment of
the expenses of a creditor who was a petitioner, or concurred in the
petition, for sequestration shall be made out of the debtor's estate;

(c) may make any further order that it considers necessary or reasonable
in all the circumstances of the case.

(4) Subject to subsection (5) below, the effect of the recall of an award of
sequestration shall be, so far as predictable, to restore the debtor and any other
person affected by the sequestration to the position he would have been in if the
sequestration had not been awarded.

(5) A recall of an award of sequestration shall not—

(a) affect the interruption of prescription caused by the presentation of
the petition for sequestration or the submission of a claim under
section 22 or 48 of this Act;

(b) invalidate any transaction entered into before such recall by the
interim trustee or permanent trustee with a person acting in good
faith.

(6) Where the Court considers that it is inappropriate to recall or to refuse
to recall an award of sequestration forthwith, it may order that the proceedings
in the sequestration shall continue but shall be subject to such conditions as it
may think fit.

(7) The Court may make such order in relation to the expenses in a petition
for recall as it thinks fit.

(8) The clerk of court shall send—

(a) a certified copy of any order recalling an award of sequestration to the
keeper of the register of inhibitions and adjudications for recording
in that register; and

(b) a copy of any order recalling or refusing to recall an award of
sequestration, or of any order under this section 41(1)(b)(ii) of this
Act, to—

(i) the Accountant in Bankruptcy; and

(ii) the permanent trustee (if any) who shall insert it in the sederunt
book.   **[517]**

NOTES
Commencement: 1 April 1986.
Commencement order: SI 1985 No 1924.

Period between award of sequestration and statutory meeting of creditors

18. Interim preservation of estate

(1) The interim trustee may give general or particular directions to the debtor
relating to the management of the debtor's estate.

(2) In exercising the functions conferred on him by section 2(1)(a) of this
Act, an interim trustee may—

(a) require the debtor to deliver up to him any money or valuables, or any
document relating to the debtor's business or financial affairs,
belonging to or in the possession of the debtor or under his control;

(*b*) place in safe custody anything mentioned in paragraph (*a*) above;

(*c*) require the debtor to deliver up to him any perishable goods belonging to the debtor or under his control and may arrange for the sale or disposal of such goods;

(*d*) make or cause to be made an inventory or valuation of any property belonging to the debtor;

(*e*) require the debtor to implement any transaction entered into by the debtor;

(*f*) effect or maintain insurance policies in respect of the business or property of the debtor;

(*g*) close down the debtor's business.

(3) The court, on the application of the interim trustee, may—

(*a*) empower the interim trustee to—

(i) carry on any business of the debtor;

(ii) borrow money,

in so far as it is necessary for the trustee to do so to safeguard the debtor's estate;

(*b*) on cause shown, grant a warrant authorising the interim trustee to enter the house where the debtor resides or his business premises and to search for and take possession of anything mentioned in paragraphs (*a*) and (*c*) of subsection (2) above, if need be by opening shut and lock-fast places; or

(*c*) make such other order to safeguard the debtor's estate as it thinks appropriate.

(4) The court, on an application by the debtor on the grounds that a direction under subsection (1) above is unreasonable, may—

(*a*) if it considers the direction to be unreasonable, set aside the direction; and

(*b*) in any event, give such directions to the debtor regarding the management of his estate as it considers appropriate;

but, subject to any interim order of the court, the debtor shall comply with the direction appealed against pending the final determination of the appeal.

(5) The debtor shall be guilty of an offence if—

(*a*) he fails without reasonable excuse to comply with—

(i) a direction under subsection (1) or (4)(*b*) above; or

(ii) a requirement under subsection (2)(*a*), (*c*) or (*e*) above; or

(*b*) he obstructs the interim trustee where the interim trustee is acting in pursuance of subsection (3)(*b*) above.

(6) A person convicted of an offence under subsection (5) above shall be liable—

(*a*) on summary conviction to a fine not exceeding the statutory maximum or—

(i) to imprisonment for a term not exceeding 3 months; or

(ii) if he has previously been convicted of an offence inferring dishonest appropriation of property or an attempt at such appropriation, to imprisonment for a term not exceeding 6 months,

or (in the case of either sub-paragraph) to both such fine and such imprisonment; or

(b) on conviction on indictment to a fine or to imprisonment for a term not exceeding 2 years or to both.   **[518]**

NOTES
Commencement: 1 April 1986.
Commencement order: SI 1985 No 1924.

19. Debtor's list of assets and liabilities

. (1) The debtor shall deliver to the interim trustee—

    (a) if the petitioner for sequestration is the debtor, within 7 days of the appointment of the interim trustee;

    (b) if the petitioner for sequestration is a creditor or a trustee acting under a trust deed, within 7 days of the interim trustee notifying the debtor of his appointment,

a list of the debtor's assets and liabilities in the prescribed form.

    (2) If without reasonable excuse the debtor—

    (a) fails to deliver in accordance with subsection (1) above a list of assets and liabilities to the interim trustee; or

    (b) fails to disclose any material in it; or

    (c) makes a material misstatement in it,

he shall be guilty of an offence and liable on summary conviction to a fine not exceeding level 5 on the standard scale or to imprisonment for a term not exceeding 3 months or to both.   **[519]**

NOTES
Commencement: 1 April 1986.
Commencement order: SI 1985 No 1924.

20. Trustee's duties on receipt of list of assets and liabilities

(1) On receipt of the debtor's list of assets and liabilities, the interim trustee shall prepare a preliminary statement of the debtor's affairs so far as within the knowledge of the interim trustee and shall indicate in the statement whether, in his opinion, the debtor's assets are unlikely to be sufficient to pay any dividend whatsoever in respect of the debts mentioned in paragraphs (e) to (h) of section 51(1) of this Act.

    (2) The interim trustee shall, not later than 4 days before the date fixed for the statutory meeting, send to the Accountant in Bankruptcy—

    (a) a copy of the debtor's list of assets and liabilities; and

    (b) a copy of the preliminary statement of the debtor's affairs; and

    (c) written comments by the interim trustee indicating what in his opinion are the causes of the insolvency and to what extent the conduct of the debtor may have contributed to the insolvency.

    (3) The written comments made under subsection (2)(c) above shall be absolutely privileged.

    (4) The interim trustee may request—

    (a) the debtor to appear before him and to give information relating to his assets, his dealings with them or his conduct in relation to his business or financial affairs; or

    (b) the debtor's spouse or any other person who the interim trustee believes can give such information to give that information, and if the interim trustee considers it necessary he may apply to the sheriff for an order requiring the debtor, spouse or other person to appear before the sheriff for private examination.

(5) Subsections (2) to (4) of section 44 and sections 46 and 47 of this Act shall apply, subject to any necessary modifications, in respect of private examination under subsection (4) above as they apply in respect of private examination under the said subsection (2). **[520]**

NOTES
Commencement: 1 April 1986.
Commencement order: SI 1985 No 1924.

Statutory meeting of creditors and confirmation of permanent trustee

21. Calling of statutory meeting

(1) The interim trustee shall call a meeting of creditors (in this Act referred to as "the statutory meeting") to be held within 28 days, or such longer period as the sheriff on cause shown may allow, after the date of the award of sequestration.

(2) Not less than 7 days before the date fixed for the statutory meeting, the interim trustee shall notify—

(*a*) every creditor known to him; and
(*b*) the Accountancy in Bankruptcy,

of the date, time and place of the meeting, and shall in the notification to creditors invite the submission of such claims as have not already been submitted and inform them of his duties under section 23(3) and (5) of this Act.

(3) The creditors may continue the statutory meeting to a date not later than 7 days after the end of the period—

(*a*) of 28 days mentioned in subsection (1) above; or (as the case may be),
(*b*) allowed by the sheriff under that subsection. **[521]**

NOTES
Commencement: 1 April 1986.
Commencement order: SI 1985 No 1924.

22. Submission of claims for voting purposes at statutory meeting

(1) For the purposes of voting at the statutory meeting, a creditor shall submit a claim in accordance with this section to the interim trustee at or before the meeting.

(2) A creditor shall submit a claim under this section by producing to the interim trustee—

(*a*) a statement of claim in the prescribed form; and
(*b*) an account or voucher (according to the nature of the debt) which constitutes *prima facie* evidence of the debt:

Provided that the interim trustee may dispense with any requirement under this subsection in respect of any debt or any class of debt.

(3) Where a creditor neither resides nor has a place of business in the United Kingdom, the interim trustee—

(*a*) shall, if he knows where the creditor resides or has a place of business and if no notification has been given to that creditor under section

21(2) of this Act, write to him informing him that he may submit a
claim under this section;

(b) may allow the creditor to submit an informal claim in writing.

(4) A creditor who has produced a statement of claim in accordance with
subsection (2) above may at any time before the statutory meeting produce in
place of that statement of claim another such statement of claim specifying a
different amount for his claim.

(5) If a creditor produces under this section a statement of claim, account,
voucher or other evidence which is false—

(a) the creditor shall be guilty of an offence unless he shows that he
neither knew nor had reason to believe that the statement of claim,
account, voucher or other evidence was false;

(b) the debtor shall be guilty of an offence if he—

(i) knew or became aware that the statement of claim, account,
voucher or other evidence was false; and

(ii) failed as soon as practicable after acquiring such knowledge to
report it to the interim trustee or permanent trustee.

(6) A creditor may, in such circumstances as may be prescribed, state the
amount of his claim in foreign currency.

(7) The interim trustee shall, on production of any document to him under
this section, initial the document and keep a record of it stating the date when
it was produced to him, and, if requested by the sender, shall return it (if it is
not a statement of claim) to him.

(8) The submission of a claim under this section shall bar the effect of any
enactment or rule of law relating to the limitation of actions in any part of the
United Kingdom.

(9) Schedule 1 to this Act shall have effect for determining the amount in
respect of which a creditor shall be entitled to claim.

(10) A person convicted of an offence under subsection (5) above shall be
liable—

(a) on summary conviction to a fine not exceeding the statutory maximum
or—

(i) to imprisonment for a term not exceeding 3 months; or

(ii) if he has previously been convicted of an offence inferring
dishonest appropriation of property or an attempt at such
appropriation, to imprisonment for a term not exceeding 6
months,

or (in the case of either sub-paragraph) to both such fine and such
imprisonment; or

(b) on conviction on indictment to a fine or to imprisonment for a term
not exceeding 2 years or to both. **[522]**

NOTES

Commencement: 1 April 1986.

Commencement order: SI 1985 No 1924.

Sub-s (6): For the prescribed circumstances, see the Bankruptcy (Scotland) Regulations 1985, SI
1985 No 1925, reg 6, para **[1707F]** post.

23. Proceedings at statutory meeting before election of permanent trustee

(1) At the commencement of the statutory meeting, the chairman shall be the interim trustee who as chairman shall—

(a) for the purposes of subsection (2) below, accept or reject in whole or in part the claim of each creditor, and, if the amount of a claim is stated in foreign currency, he shall convert that amount into sterling, in such manner as may be prescribed, at the rate of exchange prevailing at the close of business on the date of sequestration;

(b) invite the creditors thereupon to elect one of their number as chairman in his place and shall preside over the election:

Provided that if a chairman is not elected in pursuance of this paragraph, the interim trustee shall remain the chairman throughout the meeting; and

(c) arrange for a record to be made of the proceedings at the meeting.

(2) The acceptance of a claim in whole or in part under subsection (1) above shall, subject to section 24(3) of this Act, determine the entitlement of a creditor to vote at the statutory meeting.

(3) On the conclusion of the proceedings under subsection (1) above, the interim trustee—

(a) shall make the debtor's list of assets and liabilities and the preliminary statement under section 20(1) of this Act available for inspection;

(b) shall answer to the best of his ability any questions, and shall consider any representations, put to him by the creditors relating to the debtor's assets, business or financial affairs or his conduct in relation thereto;

(c) shall, after considering any such representations as are mentioned in paragraph (b) above, indicate whether, in his opinion, the debtor's assets are unlikely to be sufficient as mentioned in section 20(1) of this Act; and

(d) shall prepare (either at or as soon as possible after the statutory meeting), a final statement of the debtor's affairs.

(4) Where the interim trustee has indicated under subsection (3)(c) above that, in his opinion, the debtor's assets are unlikely to be sufficient as mentioned in section 20(1) of this Act, he shall forthwith make a report of the proceedings at the statutory meeting to the sheriff who shall thereupon appoint the interim trustee as the permanent trustee; and the provisions of this Act shall have effect as regards the sequestration subject to such modifications, and with such further provisions, as are set out in Schedule 2 to this Act.

(5) The interim trustee shall as soon as possible after the statutory meeting send a copy of the statement prepared by him under subsection (3)(d) above, together with an intimation as to whether or not he intends to apply under section 27(1) of this Act for a certificate of discharge, to—

(a) every creditor known to him; and

(b) the Accountant in Bankruptcy. **[523]**

NOTES
Commencement: 1 April 1986.
Commencement order: SI 1985 No 1924.
Sub-s 1(a): For the prescribed manner of conversion into sterling, see the Bankruptcy (Scotland) Regulations 1985, SI 1985 No 1925, reg 7, para **[1707a]** post.

24. Election of permanent trustee

(1) Where subsection (4) of section 23 of this Act is not applicable, the creditors shall, at the conclusion of the proceedings under subsection (3) of that section, proceed at the statutory meeting to the election of the permanent trustee.

(2) None of the following persons shall be eligible for election as permanent trustee, nor shall anyone who becomes such a person after having been elected as permanent trustee be qualified to continue to act as permanent trustee—

    (*a*) the debtor;

    (*b*) a person who is not qualified to act as an insolvency practitioner or who, though qualified to act as an insolvency practitioner, is not qualified to act as such in relation to the debtor;

    (*c*) a person who holds an interest opposed to the general interests of the creditors;

    (*d*) a person who resides outwith the jurisdiction of the Court of Session.

(3) The following persons shall not be entitled to vote in the election of the permanent trustee—

    (*a*) anyone acquiring a debt due by the debtor, otherwise than by succession, after the date of sequestration;

    (*b*) any creditor to the extent that his debt is a postponed debt.

(4) If no creditor entitled to vote in the election of the permanent trustee attends the statutory meeting or if no permanent trustee is elected, the interim trustee shall forthwith—

    (*a*) so notify the Accountant in Bankruptcy; and

    (*b*) report the proceedings at the statutory meeting to the sheriff, who shall thereupon appoint the interim trustee as the permanent trustee.

(5) Where subsection (4) above applies, the provisions of this Act shall have effect as regards the sequestration subject to such modifications, and with such further provisions, as are set out in Schedule 2 to this Act.   **[524]**

NOTES
    Commencement: 1 April 1986.
    Commencement order: SI 1985 No 1924.

25. Confirmation of permanent trustee

(1) On the election of the permanent trustee—

    (*a*) the interim trustee shall forthwith make a report of the proceedings at the statutory meeting to the sheriff; and

    (*b*) the debtor, a creditor, the interim trustee, the permanent trustee or the Accountant in Bankruptcy may, within 4 days after the statutory meeting, object to any matter connected with the election; and such objection shall be by summary application to the sheriff, specifying the grounds on which the objection is taken.

(2) If there is no timeous objection under subsection (1)(*b*) above, the sheriff shall forthwith declare the elected person to be the permanent trustee; and the sheriff shall confirm his election and the sheriff clerk shall issue to him an act and warrant in a form prescribed by the Court of Session by act of sederunt and send a copy of the act and warrant to the Accountant in Bankruptcy.

(3) If there is a timeous objection under subsection (1)(*b*) above, the sheriff shall forthwith give parties an opportunity to be heard thereon and shall give his decision.

(4) If in his decision under subsection (3) above the sheriff—

(*a*) rejects the objection, subsection (2) above shall apply as if there had been no timeous objection;

(*b*) sustains the objection, he shall order the interim trustee to arrange a new meeting of or the election of a permanent trustee; and sections 23 and 24 of his Act and this section shall apply in relation to such a meeting.

(5) Any declaration, confirmation or decision of the sheriff under this section shall be final, and no expense in objecting under this section shall fall on the debtor's estate.

(6) The permanent trustee shall—

(*a*) insert a copy of the said act and warrant in the sederunt book; and

(*b*) where he is not the same person as the interim trustee, publish a notice in the Edinburgh Gazette in the prescribed form stating that he has been confirmed in office as permanent trustee. **[525]**

NOTES
Commencement: 1 April 1986.
Commencement order: SI 1985 No 1924.

26. Provisions relating to termination of interim trustee's functions

(1) Where the interim trustee does not himself become the permanent trustee, he shall, on confirmation of the permanent trustees in office, hand over to him everything in his possession which relates to the sequestration (including a copy of the debtor's list of assets and liabilities, of the statement prepared under section 23(3)(*d*), and of the written comments sent under section 20(2)(*c*) of this Act) and shall thereupon cease to act in the sequestration.

(2) Within 3 months of the confirmation in office of the permanent trustee, the interim trustee shall—

(*a*) submit to the Accountant in Bankruptcy—

(i) his accounts of his intromissions (if any) with the debtor's estate; and

(ii) a claim for outlays reasonably incurred, and for remuneration for work reasonably undertaken, by him; and

(*b*) send to the permanent trustee (unless the interim trustee has himself become the permanent trustee), a copy of what is submitted to the Accountant in Bankruptcy under paragraph (*a*) above.

(3) On a submission being made to him under subsection (2) above, the Accountant in Bankruptcy—

(*a*) shall—

(i) audit the accounts; and

(ii) issue a determination fixing the amount of the outlays and remuneration payable to the interim trustee; and

(*b*) shall send a copy of—

(i) the said determination to the interim trustee (except where the interim trustee has himself become the permanent trustee); and

(ii) the interim trustee's audited accounts and of the said determination to the permanent trustee, who shall insert the copies in the sederunt book.

(4) The interim trustee, the permanent trustee, the debtor or any creditor may appeal to the sheriff against a determination under subsection (3)(*a*)(ii) above within 14 days of its issue.

(5) The permanent trustee, on being confirmed in office, shall make such insertions in the sederunt book as are appropriate to provide a record of the sequestration process before his confirmation, but he shall make no insertion therein relating to the written comments made by the interim trustee under section 20(2)(*c*) of this Act.   **[526]**

NOTES
   Commencement: 1 April 1986.
   Commencement order: SI 1985 No 1924.

27. Discharge of interim trustee

(1) On receiving a copy of the Accountant in Bankruptcy's determination sent under subsection (3)(*b*)(i) of section 26 of this Act the interim trustee may apply to him for a certificate of discharge.

(2) The interim trustee shall send notice of an application under subsection (1) above to the debtor and to the permanent trustee and shall inform the debtor—

    (*a*) that he, the permanent trustee or any creditor may make written representations relating to the application to the Accountant in Bankruptcy within a period of 14 days after such notification;

    (*b*) that the audited accounts of his intromissions (if any) with the debtor's estate are available for inspection at the office of the interim trustee and that a copy of those accounts has been sent to the permanent trustee for insertion in the sederunt book; and

    (*c*) of the effect mentioned in subsection (5) below.

(3) On the expiry of the period mentioned in subsection (2)(*a*) above the Accountant in Bankruptcy, after considering any representations duly made to him, shall—

    (*a*) grant or refuse to grant the certificate of discharge; and

    (*b*) notify (in addition to the interim trustee) the debtor, the permanent trustee, and all creditors who have made such representations, accordingly.

(4) The interim trustee, the permanent trustee, the debtor or any creditor who has made representations under subsection (2)(*a*) above may, within 14 days after the issuing of the determination under subsection (3) above, appeal therefrom to the sheriff and if the sheriff determines that a certificate of discharge which has been refused should be granted he shall order the Accountant in Bankruptcy to grant it; and the sheriff clerk shall send a copy of the decree of the sheriff to the Accountant in Bankruptcy.

(5) The grant of a certificate of discharge under this section by the Accountant in Bankruptcy shall have the effect of discharging the interim trustee from all liability (other than any liability arising from fraud) to the creditors or to the debtor in respect of any act or omission of the interim trustee in exercising the functions conferred on him by this Act.

(6) Where a certificate of discharge is granted under this section, the permanent trustee shall make an appropriate entry in the sederunt book.

(7) Where the interim trustee has died, resigned office or been removed from office, then once the accounts of his intromissions (if any) with the debtor's

estate are or have been submitted to and audited by the Accountant in Bankruptcy, the Accountant in Bankruptcy shall issue a determination fixing the amount of the outlays and remuneration payable to the interim trustee and the provisions of subsection (4) of section 26 of his Act and the foregoing provisions of this section shall, subject to any necessary modifications, apply in relation to that interim trustee or, if he has died, to his executor as they apply in relation to an interim trustee receiving a copy of such a determination under subsection (3)(*b*)(i) of that section. **[527]**

NOTES
    Commencement: 1 April 1986.
    Commencement order: SI 1985 No 1924.

Replacement of permanent trustee

28. Resignation and death of permanent trustee

(1) The permanent trustee may resign office if—

    (*a*) the creditors, at a meeting called for the purpose, accept his resignation and thereupon elect a new permanent trustee; or

    (*b*) on an application by the permanent trustee, the sheriff is satisfied that he should be permitted to resign; but the sheriff may make the granting of an application under this paragraph subject to the election of a new permanent trustee and to such conditions as he thinks appropriate in all the circumstances of the case.

(2) Where the sheriff grants an application under paragraph (*b*) of subsection (1) above—

    (*a*) except where paragraph (*b*) below applies, the commissioners, or if there are no commissioners, the Accountant in Bankruptcy, shall call a meeting of the creditors, to be held not more than 28 days after the permanent trustee has resigned, for the election by them of a new permanent trustee;

    (*b*) if the application has been granted subject to the election of a new permanent trustee, the resigning permanent trustee shall himself call a meeting of the creditors, to be held not more than 28 days after the granting of the application, for the purpose referred to in paragraph (*a*) above.

(3) Where the commissioners become, or if there are no commissioners the Accountant in Bankruptcy becomes, aware that the permanent trustee has died, they or as the case may be the Accountant in Bankruptcy shall as soon as practicable after becoming so aware call a meeting of creditors for the election by the creditors of a new permanent trustee.

(4) The foregoing provisions of this Act relating to the election and confirmation in office of the permanent trustee shall, subject to any necessary modifications, apply in relation to the election and confirmation in office of a new permanent trustee in pursuance of subsection (1), (2) or (3) above.

(5) Where no new permanent trustee is elected in pursuance of subsection (2) or (3) above, a person nominated by the Accountant in Bankruptcy from the list of interim trustees, not being a person ineligible for election as permanent trustee under section 24(2) of this Act, shall forthwith apply to the sheriff for appointment as permanent trustee, and the sheriff shall thereupon so appoint him; and the provisions of this Act shall have effect as regards the sequestration subject to such modifications and with such further provisions as are set out in Schedule 2 to this Act.

(6) The new permanent trustee may require—

(*a*) delivery to him of all documents relating to the sequestration in the possession of the former trustee or his representatives, except the former trustee's accounts of which he shall be entitled to delivery of only a copy;

(*b*) the former trustee or his representatives to submit the trustee's accounts for audit to the commissioners or, if there are no commissioners, to the Accountant in Bankruptcy, and the commissioners or the Accountant in Bankruptcy shall issue a determination fixing the amount of the outlays and remuneration payable to the trustee or representatives in accordance with section 53 of this Act.

(7) The former trustee or his representatives, the new permanent trustee, the debtor or any creditor may appeal against a determination issued under subsection (6)(*b*) above within 14 days after it is issued—

(*a*) where it is a determination of the commissioners, to the Accountant in Bankruptcy; and

(*b*) where it is a determination of the Accountant in Bankruptcy, to the sheriff;

and the determination of the Accountant in Bankruptcy under paragraph (*a*) above shall be appealable to the sheriff. **[528]**

NOTES
Commencement: 1 April 1986.
Commencement order: SI 1985 No 1924.

29. Removal of permanent trustee and trustee not acting

(1) The permanent trustee may be removed from office—

(*a*) by the creditors (other than any such person as is mentioned in section 24(3) of this Act) at a meeting called for the purpose if they also elect forthwith a new permanent trustee; or

(*b*) without prejudice to section 1(3) of this Act, by order of the sheriff, on the application of—

(i) the Accountant in Bankruptcy;

(ii) the commissioners; or

(iii) a person representing not less than one quarter in value of the creditors,

if the sheriff is satisfied that cause has been shown on the basis of circumstances other than those to which subsection (9) below applies.

(2) The sheriff shall order any application under subsection (1)(*b*) above to be served on the permanent trustee and intimated in the Edinburgh Gazette, and before disposing of the application shall give the permanent trustee an opportunity of being heard.

(3) On an application under subsection (1)(*b*) above, the sheriff may, in ordering the removal of the permanent trustee from office, make such further order as he thinks fit or may, instead of removing the permanent trustee from office, make such other order as he thinks fit.

(4) The permanent trustee, the Accountant in Bankruptcy, the commissioners or any creditor may appeal against the decision of the sheriff on an

application under subsection (1)(*b*) above within 14 days after the date of that decision.

(5) If the permanent trustee has been removed from office under subsection (1)(*b*) above or under section 1(3) of this Act or following an appeal under subsection (4) above, the commissioners or, if there are no commissioners, the Accountant in Bankruptcy shall call a meeting of creditors, to be held not more than 28 days after such removal, for the election by them of a new permanent trustee.

(6) Without prejudice to section 1(3) of this Act, where the sheriff is satisfied of any of the circumstances to which subsection (9) below applies he may, on the application of a commissioner, the debtor, a creditor or the Accountant in Bankruptcy, and after such intimation as the sheriff considers necessary—

(*a*) declare the office of permanent trustee to have become or to be vacant; and

(*b*) make any necessary order to enable the sequestration to proceed or to safeguard the estate pending the election of a new permanent trustee;

and thereafter the commissioners or, if there are no commissioners, the Accountant in Bankruptcy shall call a meeting of creditors, to be held not more than 28 days after such declaration, for the election by them of a new permanent trustee.

(7) The foregoing provisions of this Act relating to the election and confirmation in office of the permanent trustee shall, subject to any necessary modifications, apply in relation to the election and confirmation in office of a new permanent trustee in pursuance of subsection (5) or (6) above.

(8) Subsections (5) to (7) of section 28 of this Act shall apply for the purposes of this section as they apply for the purposes of that section.

(9) The circumstances to which this subsection applies are that the permanent trustee—

(*a*) is unable to act (whether by, under or by virtue of a provision of this Act or from any other cause whatsoever other than death); or

(*b*) has so conducted himself that he should no longer continue to act in the sequestration. **[529]**

NOTES
Commencement: 1 April 1986.
Commencement order: SI 1985 No 1924.

Election, resignation and removal of commissioners

30. Election, resignation and removal of commissioners

(1) At the statutory meeting or any subsequent meeting of creditors, the creditors (other than any such person as is mentioned in section 24(3) of this Act) may, from among the creditors or their mandatories, elect one or more commissioners (or new or additional commissioners); but not more than 5 commissioners shall hold office in any sequestration at any one time.

(2) None of the following persons shall be eligible for election as a commissioner, nor shall anyone who becomes such a person after having been elected as a commissioner be entitled to continue to act as a commissioner—

(*a*) any person mentioned in paragraph (*a*) or (*c*) of section 24(2) of this Act as not being eligible for election;

(*b*) a person who is an associate of the debtor or of the permanent trustee.

(3) A commissioner may resign office at any time.

(4) Without prejudice to section 1(3) of this Act, a commissioner may be removed from office—

(a) if he is a mandatory of a creditor, by the creditor recalling the mandate and intimating in writing its recall to the permanent trustee;

(b) by the creditors (other than any such person as is mentioned in section 24(3) of this Act) at a meeting called for the purpose.   **[530]**

NOTES
Commencement: 1 April 1986.
Commencement order: SI 1985 No 1924.

Vesting of estate in permanent trustee

31. Vesting of estate at date of sequestration

(1) Subject to section 33 of this Act, the whole estate of the debtor shall vest as at the date of sequestration in the permanent trustee for the benefit of the creditors; and—

(a) the estate shall so vest by virtue of the act and warrant issued on confirmation of the permanent trustee's appointment; and

(b) the act and warrant shall, in respect of the heritable estate in Scotland of the debtor, have the same effect as if a decree of adjudication in implement of sale, as well as a decree of adjudication for payment and in security of debt, subject to no legal reversion, had been pronounced in favour of the permanent trustee.

(2) The exercise by the permanent trustee of any power conferred on him by this Act in respect of any heritable estate vested in him by virtue of the act and warrant shall not be challengeable on the ground of any prior inhibition (reserving any effect of such inhibition on ranking).

(3) Where the debtor has an uncompleted title to any heritable estate in Scotland, the permanent trustee may complete title thereto either in his own name or in the name of the debtor, but completion of title in the name of the debtor shall not validate by accretion any unperfected right in favour of any person other than the permanent trustee.

(4) Any moveable property, in respect of which but for this subsection—

(a) delivery or possession; or

(b) intimation of its assignation,

would be required in order to complete title to it, shall vest in the permanent trustee by virtue of the act and warrant as if at the date of sequestration the permanent trustee had taken delivery or possession of the property or had made intimation of its assignation to him, as the case may be.

(5) Any non-vested contingent interest which the debtor has shall vest in the permanent trustee as if an assignation of that interest had been executed by the debtor and intimation thereof made at the date of sequestration.

(6) Any person claiming a right to any estate claimed by the permanent trustee may apply to the court for the estate to be excluded from such vesting, a copy of the application being served on the permanent trustee; and the court shall grant the application if it is satisfied that the estate should not be so vested.

(7) Where any successor of a deceased debtor whose estate has been sequestrated has made up title to, or is in possession of, any part of that estate,

the court may, on the application of the permanent trustee, order the successor to convey such estate to him.

(8) In subsection (1) above the "whole estate of the debtor" means his whole estate at the date of sequestration, wherever situated, including—

(a) any income or estate vesting in the debtor on that date; and

(b) the capacity to exercise and to take proceedings for exercising, all such powers in, over, or in respect of any property as might have been exercised by the debtor for his own benefit as at, or on, the date of sequestration or might be exercised on a relevant date (within the meaning of section 32(10) of this Act). **[531]**

NOTES

Commencement: 1 April 1986.
Commencement order: SI 1985 No 1924.

32. Vesting of estate, and dealings of debtor, after sequestration

(1) Subject to subsection (2) below, any income of whatever nature received by the debtor on a relevant date, other than income arising from the estate which is vested in the permanent trustee, shall vest in the debtor.

(2) The sheriff, on the application of the permanent trustee, may, after having regard to all the circumstances, determine a suitable amount to allow for—

(a) aliment for the debtor; and

(b) the debtor's relevant obligations;

and if the debtor's income is in excess of the total amount so allowed the sheriff shall fix the amount of the excess and order it to be paid to the permanent trustee.

(3) The debtor's relevant obligations referred to in paragraph (b) of subsection (2) above are—

(a) any obligation of aliment owed by him ("obligation of aliment" having the same meaning as in the Family Law (Scotland) Act 1985);

(b) any obligation of his to make a periodical allowance to a former spouse;

but any amount allowed under that subsection for the relevant obligations need not be sufficient for compliance with a subsisting order or agreement as regards such aliment or periodical allowance.

(4) In the event of any change in the debtor's circumstances, the sheriff, on the application of the permanent trustee, the debtor or any other interested person, may vary or recall any order under subsection (2) above.

(5) Diligence in respect of a debt or obligation of which the debtor would be discharged under section 55 of this Act were he discharged under section 54 thereof shall not be competent against income vesting in him under subsection (1) above.

(6) Without prejudice to subsection (1) above, any estate, wherever situated, which—

(a) is acquired by the debtor on a relevant date; and

(b) would have vested in the permanent trustee if it had been part of the debtor's estate on the date of sequestration,

shall vest in the permanent trustee for the benefit of the creditors as at the date of acquisition; and any person who holds any such estate shall, on production to him of a copy of the act and warrant certified by the sheriff clerk confirming the permanent trustee's appointment, convey or deliver the estate to the permanent trustee:

Provided that—

(i) if such a person has in good faith and without knowledge of the sequestration conveyed the estate to the debtor or to anyone on the instructions of the debtor, he shall incur no liability to the permanent trustee except to account for any proceeds of the conveyance which are in his hands; and

(ii) this subsection shall be without prejudice to any right or interest acquired in the estate in good faith and for value.

(7) The debtor shall immediately notify the permanent trustee of any assets acquired by him on a relevant date or of any other substantial change in his financial circumstances; and, if the debtor fails to comply with this subsection, he shall be guilty of an offence and liable on summary conviction to a fine not exceeding level 5 on the standard scale or to imprisonment for a term not exceeding 3 months or to both.

(8) Subject to subsection (9) below, any dealing of or with the debtor relating to his estate vested in the permanent trustee under section 31 of this Act shall be of no effect in a question with the permanent trustee.

(9) Subsection (8) above shall not apply where the person seeking to uphold the dealing establishes—

(*a*) that the permanent trustee—

(i) which has abandoned to the debtor the property to which the dealing relates;

(ii) has expressly or impliedly authorised the dealing; or

(iii) is otherwise personally barred from challenging the dealing, or

(*b*) that the dealing is—

(i) the performance of an obligation undertaken before the date of sequestration by a person obliged to the debtor in the obligation;

(ii) the purchase from the debtor of goods for which the purchaser has given value to the debtor or is willing to give value to the permanent trustee; or

(iii) a banking transaction in the ordinary course of business between the banker and the debtor,

and that the person dealing with the debtor was, at the time when the dealing occurred, unaware of the sequestration and had at that time no reason to believe that the debtor's estate had been sequestrated or was the subject of sequestration proceedings.

(10) In this section "a relevant date" means a date after the date of sequestration and before the date on which the debtor's discharge becomes effective. **[532]**

NOTES
Commencement: 1 April 1986.
Commencement order: SI 1985 No 1924.

33. Limitations on vesting

(1) The following property of the debtor shall not vest in the permanent trustee—

(*a*) property exempted from poinding for the purpose of protecting the debtor and his family;

(*b*) property held on trust by the debtor for any other person.

(2) The vesting of a debtor's estate in a permanent trustee shall not affect the right of hypothec of a landlord.

(3) Sections 31 and 32 of this Act are without prejudice to the right of any secured creditor which is preferable to the rights of the permanent trustee. **[533]**

NOTES
Commencement: 1 April 1986.
Commencement order: SI 1985 No 1924.

Safeguarding of interests of creditors of insolvent persons

34. Gratuitous alienations

(1) Where this subsection applies, an alienation by a debtor shall be challengeable by—

(*a*) any creditor who is a creditor by virtue of a debt incurred on or before the date of sequestration, or before the granting of the trust deed or the debtor's death, as the case may be; or

(*b*) the permanent trustee, the trustee acting under the trust deed or the judicial factor, as the case may be.

(2) Subsection (1) above applies where—

(*a*) by the alienation, whether before or after the coming into force of this section, any of the debtor's property has been transferred or any claim or right of the debtor has been discharged or renounced; and

(*b*) any of the following has occurred—

(i) his estate has been sequestrated (other than, in the case of a natural person, after his death); or

(ii) he has granted a trust deed which has become a protected trust deed; or

(iii) he has died and within 12 months after his death, his estate has been sequestrated; or

(iv) he has died and within the said 12 months, a judicial factor has been appointed under section 11A of the Judicial Factors (Scotland) Act 1889 to administer his estate and the estate was absolutely insolvent at the date of death; and

(*c*) the alienation took place on a relevant day.

(3) For the purposes of paragraph (*c*) of subsection (2) above, the day on which an alienation took place shall be the day on which the alienation became completely effectual; and in that paragraph "relevant day" means, if the alienation has the effect of favouring—

(*a*) a person who is an associate of the debtor, a day not earlier than 5 years before the date of sequestration, the granting of the trust deed or the debtor's death, as the case may be; or (*b*) any other person, a day not earlier than 2 years before the said date.

(4) On a challenge being brought under subsection (1) above, the court shall grant decree of reduction or for such restoration of property to the debtor's estate or other redress as may be appropriate, but the court shall not grant such a decree if the person seeking to uphold the alienation establishes—

(*a*) that immediately, or at any other time, after the alienation the debtor's assets were greater than his liabilities; or

(*b*) that the alienation was made for adequate consideration; or

(*c*) that the alienation—

(i) was a birthday, Christmas or other conventional gift; or

(ii) was a gift made, for a charitable purpose, to a person who is not an associate of the debtor,

which having regard to all the circumstances, it was reasonable for the debtor to make:

Provided that this subsection shall be without prejudice to any right or interest acquired in good faith and for value from or through the transferee in the alienation.

(5) In subsection (4) above, "charitable purpose" means any charitable, benevolent or philanthropic purpose whether or not it is charitable within the meaning of any rule of law.

(6) For the purposes of the foregoing provisions of this section, an alienation in implementation of a prior obligation shall be deemed to be one for which there was no consideration or no adequate consideration to the extent that the prior obligation was undertaken for no consideration or no adequate consideration.

(7) This section is without prejudice to the operation of section 2 of the Married Women's Policies of Assurance (Scotland) Act 1880 (policy of assurance may be effected in trust for spouse, future spouse and children).

(8) A permanent trustee, the trustee acting under a protected trust deed and a judicial factor appointed under section 11A of the Judicial Factors (Scotland) Act 1889 shall have the same right as a creditor has under any rule of law to challenge an alienation of a debtor made for no consideration or for no adequate consideration.

(9) The permanent trustee shall insert in the sederunt book a copy of any decree under this section affecting the sequestrated estate.　　　　**[534]**

NOTES
    Commencement: 1 April 1986.
    Commencement order: SI 1985 No 1924.

35. Recalling of order for payment of capital sum on divorce

(1) This section applies where—

(*a*) a court has made an order, whether before or after the coming into force of this section, under section 5 of the Divorce (Scotland) Act 1976 or section 8(2) of the Family Law (Scotland) Act 1985, for the payment by a debtor of a capital sum or under the said section 8(2) for the transfer of property by him;

(*b*) on the date of the making of the order the debtor was absolutely insolvent or was rendered so by implementation of the order; and (*c*) within 5 years after the making of the order—

    (i) the debtor's estate has been sequestrated other than after his death; or

    (ii) he has granted a trust deed which has (whether or not within the 5 years) become a protected trust deed; or

    (iii) he has died and, within 12 months after his death, his estate has been sequestrated; or

    (iv) he has died and, within the said 12 months, a judicial factor has been appointed under section 11A of the Judicial Factors (Scotland) Act 1889 to administer his estate.

(2) Where this section applies, the court, on an application brought by the permanent trustee, the trustee acting under the trust deed or the judicial factor, may make an order for recall of the order made under the said section 5 or 8(2) and for the repayment to the applicant of the whole or part of any sum already paid, or as the case may be for the return to the applicant of all or part of any property already transferred, under that order, or, where such property has been sold, for payment to the applicant of all or part of the proceeds of sale:

Provided that before making an order under this subsection the court shall have regard to all the circumstances including, without prejudice to the generality of this proviso, the financial, and other, circumstances (in so far as made known to the court) of the person against whom the order would be made.

(3) Where an application is brought under this section in a case where the debtor's estate has been sequestrated, the permanent trustee shall insert a copy of the decree of recall in the sederunt book. **[535]**

NOTES
    Commencement: 1 April 1986.
    Commencement order: SI 1985 No 1924.

36. Unfair preferences

(1) Subject to subsection (2) below, subsection (4) below applies to a transaction entered into by a debtor, whether before or after the coming into force of this section, which has the effect of creating a preference in favour of a creditor to the prejudice of the general body of creditors, being a preference created not earlier than 6 months before—

    (*a*) the date of sequestration of the debtor's estate (if, in the case of a natural person, a date within his lifetime); or

    (*b*) the granting by him of a trust deed which has become a protected trust deed; or

    (*c*) his death where, within 12 months after his death—

        (i) his estate has been sequestrated, or

        (ii) a judicial factor has been appointed under section 11A of the Judicial Factors (Scotland) Act 1889 to administer his estate and his estate was absolutely insolvent at the date of death.

(2) Subsection (4) below shall not apply to any of the following transactions—

    (*a*) a transaction in the ordinary course of trade or business;

    (*b*) a payment in cash for a debt which when it was paid had become payable unless the transaction was collusive with the purpose of prejudicing the general body of creditors;

    (*c*) a transaction whereby the parties thereto undertake reciprocal obligations (whether the performance by the parties of their respective obligations occurs at the same time or at different times) unless the transaction was collusive as aforesaid;

    (*d*) the granting of a mandate by a debtor authorising an arrestee to pay over the arrested funds or part thereof to the arrester where—

        (i) there has been a decree for payment or a warrant for summary diligence; and

        (ii) the decree or warrant has been preceded by an arrestment on the dependence of the action or followed by an arrestment in execution.

(3) For the purposes of subsection (1) above, the day on which a preference was created shall be the day on which the preference became completely effectual.

(4) A transaction to which this subsection applies shall be challengeable by—

    (*a*) any creditor who is a creditor by virtue of a debt incurred on or before the date of sequestration, the granting of the protected trust deed or the debtor's death, as the case may be; or

    (*b*) the permanent trustee, the trustee acting under the protected trust deed, or the judicial factor, as the case may be.

(5) On a challenge being brought under subsection (4) above, the court, if satisfied that the transaction challenged is a transaction to which this section applies, shall grant decree of reduction or for such restoration of property to the debtor's estate or other redress as may be appropriate.

Provided that this subsection shall be without prejudice to any right or interest acquired in good faith and for value from or through the creditor in whose favour the preference was created.

(6) A permanent trustee, the trustee acting under a protected trust deed and a judicial factor appointed under section 11A of the Judicial Factors (Scotland) Act 1889 shall have the same right as a creditor has under any rule of law to challenge a preference created by a debtor.

(7) The permanent trustee shall insert in the sederunt book a copy of any decree under this section affecting the sequestrated estate.   **[536]**

NOTES
    Commencement: 1 April 1986.
    Commencement order: SI 1985 No 1924.

Effect of sequestration on diligence

37. Effect of sequestration on diligence

(1) The order of the court awarding sequestration shall as from the date of sequestration have the effect, in relation to diligence done (whether before or after the date of sequestration) in respect of any part of the debtor's estate, of—

    (*a*) a decree of adjudication of the heritable estate of the debtor for payment of his debts which has been duly recorded in the register of inhibitions and adjudications on that date; and

    (*b*) an arrestment in execution and decree of furthcoming, an arrestment in execution and warrant of sale, and a completed poinding,

in favour of the creditors according to their respective entitlements.

(2) No inhibition on the estate of the debtor which takes effect within the period of 60 days before the date of sequestration shall be effectual to create a preference for the inhibitor and any relevant right of challenge shall, at the date of sequestration, vest in the permanent trustee as shall any right of the inhibitor to receive payment for the discharge of the inhibition:

Provided that this subsection shall neither entitle the trustee to receive any payment made to the inhibitor before the date of sequestration nor affect the validity of anything done before that date in consideration of such payment.

(3) In subsection (2) above, "any relevant right of challenge" means any right to challenge a deed voluntarily granted by the debtor if it is a right which vested in the inhibitor by virtue of the inhibition.

(4) No arrestment or poinding of the estate of the debtor (including any estate vesting in the permanent trustee under section 32(6) of this Act) executed—

(a) within the period of 60 days before the date of sequestration and whether or not subsisting at that date; or
(b) on or after the date of sequestration,

shall be effectual to create a preference for the arrester or poinder; and the estate so arrested or poinded, or the proceeds of sale thereof, shall be handed over to the permanent trustee.

(5) An arrester or poinder whose arrestment or poinding is executed within the said period of 60 days shall be entitled to payment, out of the arrested or poinded estate or out of the proceeds of the sale thereof, of the expenses incurred—

(a) in obtaining the extract of the decree or other document on which the arrestment or poinding proceeded;
(b) in executing the arrestment or poinding; and
(c) in taking any further action in respect of the diligence.

(6) No poinding of the ground in respect of the estate of the debtor (including any estate vesting in the permanent trustee under section 32(6) of this Act) executed within the period of 60 days before the date of sequestration or on or after that date shall be effectual in a question with the permanent trustee, except for the interest on the debt of a secured creditor, being interest for the current half-yearly term and arrears of interest for one year immediately before the commencement of that term.

(7) The foregoing provisions of this section shall apply to the estate of a deceased debtor which—

(a) has been sequestrated; or
(b) was absolutely insolvent at the date of death and in respect of which a judicial factor has been appointed under section 11A of the Judicial Factors (Scotland) Act 1889,

within 12 months after his death, but as if for any reference to the date of sequestration and the debtor there were substituted respectively a reference to the date of the deceased's death and to the deceased debtor.

(8) It shall be incompetent on or after the date of sequestration for any creditor to raise or insist in an adjudication against the estate of a debtor (including any estate vesting in the permanent trustee under section 32(6) of this Act) or to be confirmed as executor-creditor on the estate.

(9) Where—

(a) a deceased debtor's estate is sequestrated; or

(b) a judicial factor is appointed under section 11A of the Judicial Factors (Scotland) Act 1889 to administer his estate (in a case where the estate is absolutely insolvent),

within 12 months after the debtor's death, no confirmation as executor-creditor on that estate at any time after the debtor's death shall be effectual in a question with the permanent trustee or the judicial factor; but the executor-creditor shall be entitled out of that estate, or out of the proceeds of sale thereof, to the expenses incurred by him in obtaining the confirmation. **[537]**

NOTES
Commencement: 1 April 1986.
Commencement order: SI 1985 No 1924.
Companies winding up: Sub-ss (1)–(6) of this section, and s 39(3), (4), (7), (8) post, applied by the Insolvency Act 1986, s 185 (so far as consistent with that Act), in the winding up of a company registered in Scotland in like manner as they apply in the sequestration of a debtor's estate, with the following substitutions, and with any other necessary modifications: for references to the debtor, the sequestration, the date of sequestration and the permanent trustee there are substituted, respectively, references to the company, the winding up, the commencement of the winding up and the liquidator.

Administration of estate by permanent trustee

38. Taking possession of estate by permanent trustee

(1) The permanent trustee shall—

(a) as soon as may be after his confirmation in office, for the purpose of recovering the debtor's estate under section 3(1)(a) of this Act, and subject to section 40 of this Act, take possession of the debtor's whole estate so far as vesting in the permanent trustee under sections 31 and 32 of this Act and any document in the debtor's possession or control relating to his assets or his business or financial affairs;

(b) make up and maintain an inventory and valuation of the estate which he shall record in the sederunt book; and

(c) forthwith thereafter send a copy of any such inventory and valuation to the Accountant in Bankruptcy.

(2) The permanent trustee shall be entitled to have access to all documents relating to the assets or the business or financial affairs of the debtor sent by or on behalf of the debtor to a third party and in that third party's hands and to make copies of any such documents.

(3) If any person obstructs a permanent trustee who is exercising, or attempting to exercise, a power conferred by subsection (2) above, the sheriff, on the application of the permanent trustee, may order that person to cease so to obstruct the permanent trustee.

(4) The permanent trustee may require delivery to him of any title deed or other document of the debtor, notwithstanding that a right of lien is claimed over the title deed or document; but this subsection is without prejudice to any preference of the holder of the lien. **[538]**

NOTES
Commencement: 1 April 1986.
Commencement order: SI 1985 No 1924.

39. Management and realisation of estate

(1) As soon as may be after his confirmation in office, the permanent trustee shall consult with the commissioners or, if there are no commissioners, with the Accountant in Bankruptcy concerning the exercise of his functions under section 3(1)(*a*) of this Act; and, subject to subsection (6) below, the permanent trustee shall comply with any general or specific directions given to him, as the case may be—

    (*a*) by the creditors;

    (*b*) on the application under this subsection of the commissioners, by the court; or

    (*c*) if there are no commissioners, by the Accountant in Bankruptcy,

as to the exercise by him of such functions.

(2) The permanent trustee may, but if there are commissioners only with the consent of the commissioners, the creditors or the court, do any of the following things if he considers that its doing would be beneficial for the administration of the estate—

    (*a*) carry on any business of the debtor;

    (*b*) bring, defend or continue any legal proceedings relating to the estate of the debtor;

    (*c*) create a security over any part of the estate;

    (*d*) where any right, option or other power forms part of the debtor's estate, make payments or incur liabilities with a view to obtaining, for the benefit of the creditors, any property which is the subject of the right, option or power.

(3) Any sale of the debtor's estate by the permanent trustee may be by either public sale or private bargain.

(4) The following rules shall apply to the sale of any part of the debtor's heritable estate over which a heritable security is held by a creditor or creditors if the rights of the secured creditor or creditors are preferable to those of the permanent trustee—

    (*a*) the permanent trustee may sell that part only with the concurrence of every such creditor unless he obtains a sufficiently high price to discharge every such security;

    (*b*) subject to paragraph (*c*) below, the following acts shall be precluded—

        (i) the taking of steps by a creditor to enforce his security over that part after the permanent trustee has intimated to the creditor that he intends to sell it;

        (ii) the commencement by the permanent trustee of the procedure for the sale of that part after a creditor has intimated to the permanent trustee that he intends to commence the procedure for its sale;

    (*c*) where the permanent trustee or a creditor has given intimation under paragraph (*b*) above, but has unduly delayed in proceeding with the sale, then, if authorised by the court in the case of intimation under—

        (i) sub-paragraph (i) of that paragraph, any creditor to whom intimation has been given may enforce his security; or

        (ii) sub-paragraph (ii) of that paragraph, the permanent trustee may sell that part.

(5) The function of the permanent trustee under section 3(1)(*a*) of this Act

to realise the debtor's estate shall include the function of selling, with or without recourse against the estate, debts owing to the estate.

(6) The permanent trustee may sell any perishable goods without complying with any directions given to him under subsection (1)(*a*) or (*c*) above if the permanent trustee considers that compliance with such directions would adversely affect the sale.

(7) The validity of the title of any purchaser shall not be challengeable on the ground that there has been a failure to comply with a requirement of this section.

(8) It shall be incompetent for the permanent trustee or an associate of his or for any commissioner, to produce any of the debtor's estate in pursuance of this section.   **[539]**

NOTES

Commencement: 1 April 1986.
Commencement order: SI 1985 No 1924.
Companies winding up: See note to s 37 ante.

40. Power of permanent trustee in relation to the debtor's family home

(1) Before the permanent trustee sells or disposes of any right or interest in the debtor's family home he shall—

(*a*) obtain the relevant consent; or
(*b*) where he is unable to do so, obtain the authority of the court in accordance with subsection (2) below.

(2) Where the permanent trustee requires to obtain the authority of the court in terms of subsection (1)(*b*) above, the court, after having regard to all the circumstances of the case, including—

(*a*) the needs and financial resources of the debtor's spouse or former spouse;
(*b*) the needs and financial resources of any child of the family;
(*c*) the interests of the creditors;
(*d*) the length of the period during which (whether before or after the relevant date) the family home was used as a residence by any of the persons referred to in paragraph (*a*) or (*b*) above,

may refuse to grant the application or may postpone the granting of the application for such period (not exceeding twelve months) as it may consider reasonable in the circumstances or may grant the application subject to such conditions as it may prescribe.

(3) Subsection (2) above shall apply—

(*a*) to an action for division and sale of the debtor's family home; or
(*b*) to an action for the purpose of obtaining vacant possession of the debtor's family home,

brought by the permanent trustee as it applies to an application under subsection (1)(*b*) above and, for the purposes of this subsection, any reference in the said subsection (2) to that granting of the application shall be construed as a reference to the granting of decree in the action.

(4) In this section—

(*a*) "family home" means any property in which, at the relevant date, the debtor had (whether alone or in common with any other person) a right or interest, being property which was occupied at that date as a residence by the debtor and his spouse or by the debtor's spouse or former spouse (in any case with or without a child of the family) or by the debtor with a child of the family;

(b) "child of the family" includes any child or grandchild of either the debtor or his spouse or former spouse, and any person who has been brought up or accepted by either the debtor or his spouse or former spouse as if he or she were a child of the debtor, spouse or former spouse whatever the age of such a child, grandchild or person may be;

(c) "relevant consent" means in relation to the sale or disposal of any right or interest in a family home—

　(i) in a case where the family home is occupied by the debtor's spouse or former spouse, the consent of the spouse, or, as the case may be, the former spouse, whether or not the family home is also occupied by the debtor;

　(ii) where sub-paragraph (i) above does not apply, in a case where the family home is occupied by the debtor with a child of the family, the consent of the debtor; and

(d) "relevant date" means the day immediately preceding the date of sequestration. **[540]**

NOTES

　Commencement: 1 April 1986.
　Commencement order: SI 1985 No 1924.

41. Protection of rights of spouse against arrangements intended to defeat them

(1) If a debtor's sequestrated estate includes a matrimonial home of which the debtor, immediately before the date of issue of the act and warrant of the permanent trustee (or, if more than one such act and warrant is issued in the sequestration, of the first such issue) was an entitled spouse and the other spouse is a non-entitled spouse—

(a) the permanent trustee shall, where he—

　(i) is aware that the entitled spouse is married to the non-entitled spouse; and

　(ii) knows where the non-entitled spouse is residing,

　inform the non-entitled spouse, within the period of 14 days beginning with that date, of the fact that sequestration of the entitled spouse's estate has been awarded, of the right of petition which exists under section 16 of this Act and of the effect of paragraph (b) below; and

(b) the Court of Session, on the petition under section 16 of this Act of the non-entitled spouse presented either within the period of 40 days beginning with that date or within the period of 10 weeks beginning with the date of sequestration may—

　(i) under section 17 of this Act recall the sequestration; or

　(ii) make such order as it thinks appropriate to protect the occupancy rights of the non-entitled spouse;

　if it satisfied that the purpose of the petition for sequestration was wholly or mainly to defeat the occupancy rights of the non-entitled spouse.

(2) In subsection (1) above—

　"entitled spouse" and "non-entitled spouse" have the same meanings as in section 6 of the Matrimonial Homes (Family Protection) (Scotland) Act 1981;

"matrimonial home" has the meaning assigned by section 22 of that Act as amended by the Law Reform (Miscellaneous Provisions) (Scotland) Act 1985; and

"occupancy rights" has the meaning assigned by section 1(4) of the said Act of 1981.   **[541]**

NOTES
Commencement: 1 April 1986.
Commencement order: SI 1985 No 1924.

42. Contractual powers of permanent trustee

(1) Subject to subsections (2) and (3) below, the permanent trustee may adopt any contract entered into by the debtor before the date of sequestration where he considers that its adoption would be beneficial to the administration of the debtor's estate, except where the adoption is precluded by the express or implied terms of the contract, or may refuse to adopt any such contract.

(2) The permanent trustee shall, within 28 days from the receipt by him of a request in writing from any party to a contract entered into by the debtor or within such longer period of that receipt as the court on application by the permanent trustee may allow, adopt or refuse to adopt the contract.

(3) If the permanent trustee does not reply in writing to the request under subsection (2) above within the said period of 28 days or longer period, as the case may be, he shall be deemed to have refused to adopt the contract.

(4) The permanent trustee may enter into any contract where he considers that this would be beneficial for the administration of the debtor's estate. **[542]**

NOTES
Commencement: 1 April 1986.
Commencement order: SI 1985 No 1924.

43. Money received by permanent trustee

(1) Subject to subsection (2) below, all money received by the permanent trustee in the exercise of his functions shall be deposited by him in the name of the debtor's estate in an appropriate bank or institution.

(2) The permanent trustee may at any time retain in his hands a sum not exceeding £200 or such other sum as may be prescribed.   **[543]**

NOTES
Commencement: 1 April 1986.
Commencement order: SI 1985 No 1924.

Examination of debtor

44. Private examination

(1) The permanent trustee may request—

    (*a*) the debtor to appear before him and to give information relating to his assets, his dealings with them or his conduct in relation to his business or financial affairs; or

    (*b*) the debtor's spouse or any other person who the permanent trustee believes can give such information (in this Act such spouse or other person being referred to as a "relevant person"), to give that information, and, if he considers it necessary, the permanent trustee may apply to the sheriff for an order to be made under subsection (2) below.

(2) Subject to section 46(2) of this Act, on application to him under subsection (1) above the sheriff may make an order requiring the debtor or a relevant person to attend for private examination before him on a date (being not earlier than 8 days nor later than 16 days after the date of the order) and at a time specified in the order.

(3) A person who fails without reasonable excuse to comply with an order made under subsection (2) above shall be guilty of an offence and liable on summary conviction to a fine not exceeding level 5 on the standard scale or to imprisonment for a term not exceeding 3 months or to both.

(4) Where the debtor is an entity whose estate may be sequestrated by virtue of section 6(1) of this Act, the references in this section and in sections 45 to 47 of this Act to the debtor shall be construed, unless the context otherwise requires, as references to a person representing the entity. **[544]**

NOTES
Commencement: 1 April 1986.
Commencement order: SI 1985 No 1924.

45. Public examination

(1) Not less than 8 weeks before the end of the first accounting period, the permanent trustee—

    (*a*) may; or
    (*b*) if requested to do so by the Accountant in Bankruptcy or the commissioners (if any) or one quarter in value of the creditors, shall,

apply to the sheriff for an order for the public examination before the sheriff of the debtor or of a relevant person relating to the debtor's assets, his dealings with them or his conduct in relation to his business or financial affairs:

Provided that, on cause shown, such application may be made by the permanent trustee at any time.

(2) Subject to section 46(2) of this Act, the sheriff, on an application under subsection (1) above, shall make an order requiring the debtor or relevant person to attend for examination before him in open court on a date (being not earlier than 8 days nor later than 16 days after the date of the order) and at a time specified in the order.

(3) On the sheriff making an order under subsection (2) above, the permanent trustee shall—

    (*a*) publish in the Edinburgh Gazette a notice in such form and containing such particulars as may be prescribed; and
    (*b*) send a copy of the said notice—

        (i) to every creditor known to the permanent trustee; and
        (ii) where the order is in respect of a relevant person, to the debtor, and

    inform the creditor and, where applicable, the debtor that he may participate in the examination.

(4) A person who fails without reasonable excuse to comply with an order made under subsection (2) above shall be guilty of an offence and liable on

summary conviction to a fine not exceeding level 5 on the standard scale or to imprisonment for a term not exceeding 3 months or to both.   **[545]**

NOTES
Commencement: 1 April 1986.
Commencement order: SI 1985 No 1924.

46. Provisions ancillary to sections 44 and 45

(1) If the debtor or relevant person is residing—

    (a) in Scotland, the sheriff may, on the application of the permanent trustee, grant a warrant which may be executed by a messenger-at-arms or sheriff officer anywhere in Scotland; or

    (b) in any other part of the United Kingdom, the Court of Session or the sheriff may, on the application of the permanent trustee, request any court having jurisdiction where the debtor or the relevant person, as the case may be, resides to take appropriate steps, which shall be enforceable by that court,

to apprehend the debtor or relevant person and have him taken to the place of the examination:

Provided that a warrant under paragraph (a) above shall not be granted nor a request under paragraph (b) above made unless the court is satisfied that it is necessary to do so to secure the attendance of the debtor or relevant person at the examination.

(2) If the debtor or a relevant person is for any good reason prevented from attending for examination, the sheriff may, without prejudice to subsection (3) below, grant a commission to take his examination (the commissioner being in this section and section 47 below referred to as an "examining commissioner").

(3) The sheriff or the examining commissioner may at any time adjourn the examination to such day as the sheriff or the examining commissioner may fix.

(4) The sheriff or the examining commissioner may order the debtor or a relevant person to produce for inspection any document in his custody or control relating to the debtor's assets, his dealings with them or his conduct in relation to his business or financial affairs, and to deliver the document or a copy thereof to the permanent trustee for further examination by him.   **[546]**

NOTES
Commencement: 1 April 1986.
Commencement order: SI 1985 No 1924.

47. Conduct of examination

(1) The examination, whether before the sheriff or an examining commissioner, shall be taken on oath.

    (2) At the examination—

    (a) the permanent trustee or a solicitor or counsel acting on his behalf and, in the case of public examination, any creditor may question the debtor or a relevant person; and

    (b) the debtor may question a relevant person,

as to any matter relating to the debtor's assets, his dealings with them or his conduct in relation to his business or financial affairs.

    (3) The debtor or a relevant person shall be required to answer any question relating to the debtor's assets, his dealings with them or his conduct in relation

to his business or financial affairs and shall not be excused from answering any such question on the ground that the answer may incriminate or tend to incriminate him or on the ground of confidentiality:

Provided that—

(*a*) a statement made by the debtor or a relevant person in answer to such a question shall not be admissible in evidence in any subsequent criminal proceedings against the person making the statement, except where the proceedings are in respect of a charge of perjury relating to the statement;

(*b*) a person subject to examination shall not be required to disclose any information which he has received from a person who is not called for examination if the information is confidential between them.

(4) Rule 65 of Schedule 1 to the Sheriff Courts (Scotland) Act 1907 (recording of evidence) shall apply in relation to the recording of evidence at the examination before the sheriff or the examining commissioner.

(5) The debtor's deposition at the examination shall be subscribed by himself and by the sheriff (or, as the case may be, the examining commissioner) and shall be inserted in the sederunt book.

(6) The permanent trustee shall insert a copy of the record of the examination in the sederunt book and send a copy of the record to the Accountant in Bankruptcy.

(7) A relevant person shall be entitled to fees or allowances in respect of his attendance at the examination as if he were a witness in an ordinary civil cause in the sheriff court:

Provided that, if the sheriff thinks that it is appropriate in all the circumstances, he may disallow or restrict the entitlement to such fees or allowances. **[547]**

NOTES
Commencement: 1 April 1986.
Commencement order: SI 1985 No 1924.

Submission and adjudication of claims

48. Submission of claims to permanent trustee

(1) Subject to subsection (2) below and subsections (8) and (9) of section 52 of this Act, a creditor in order to obtain an adjudication as to his entitlement—

(*a*) to vote at a meeting of creditors other than the statutory meeting; or

(*b*) (so far as funds are available), to a dividend out of the debtor's estate in respect of any accounting period,

shall submit a claim in accordance with this section to the permanent trustee respectively—

(i) at or before the meeting; or

(ii) not later than 8 weeks before the end of the accounting period.

(2) A claim submitted by a creditor—

(*a*) under section 22 of this Act and accepted in whole or in part by the interim trustee for the purpose of voting at the statutory meeting; or

(b) under this section and accepted in whole or in part by the permanent trustee for the purpose of voting at a meeting or of drawing a dividend in respect of any accounting period,

shall be deemed to have been re-submitted for the purpose of obtaining an adjudication as to his entitlement both to vote at any subsequent meeting and (so far as funds are available) to a dividend in respect of an accounting period, or, as the case may be, any subsequent accounting period.

(3) Subsections (2) and (3) of section 22 of this Act shall apply for the purposes of this section but as if in the proviso to subsection (2) for the words "interim trustee" there were substituted the words "permanent trustee with the consent of the commissioners, if any", and for any other reference to the interim trustee there were substituted a reference to the permanent trustee.

(4) A creditor who has submitted a claim under this section (or under section 22 of this Act, a statement of claim which has been deemed re-submitted as mentioned in subsection (2) above) may at any time submit a further claim under this section specifying a different amount for his claim:

Provided that a secured creditor shall not be entitled to produce a further claim specifying a different value for the security at any time after the permanent trustee requires the creditor to discharge, or convey or assign, the security under paragraph 5(2) of Schedule 1 to this Act.

(5) The permanent trustee, for the purpose of satisfying himself as to the validity or amount of a claim submitted by a creditor under this section, may require—

(a) the creditor to produce further evidence; or
(b) any other person who he believes can produce relevant evidence, to produce such evidence,

and, if the creditor or other person refuses or delays to do so, the permanent trustee may apply to the sheriff for an order requiring the creditor or other person to attend for his private examination before the sheriff.

(6) Sections 44(2) and (3) and 47(1) of this Act shall apply, subject to any necessary modifications, to the examination of the creditor or other person as they apply to the examination of a relevant person; and references in this subsection and subsection (5) above to a creditor in a case where the creditor is an entity mentioned in section 6(1) of this Act shall be construed, unless the context otherwise requires, as references to a person representing the entity.

(7) Subsections (5) to (10) of section 22 of this Act shall apply for the purposes of this section but as if—

(a) in subsection (5) the words "interim trustee or" were omitted;
(b) in subsection (7) for the words "interim" and "keep a record of it" there were substituted respectively the words "permanent" and "make an insertion relating thereto in the sederunt book".

(8) At any private examination under subsection (5) above, a solicitor or counsel may act on behalf of the permanent trustee or he may appear himself.

[548]

NOTES
Commencement: 1 April 1986.
Commencement order: SI 1985 No 1924.

49. Adjudication of claims

(1) At the commencement of every meeting of creditors (other than the statutory meeting), the permanent trustee shall, for the purposes of section 50 of this Act so far as it relates to voting at that meeting, accept or reject the claim of each creditor.

(2) Where funds are available for payment of a dividend out of the debtor's estate in respect of an accounting period, the permanent trustee for the purpose of determining who is entitled to such a dividend shall, not later than 4 weeks before the end of the period, accept or reject every claim submitted or deemed to have been re-submitted to him under this Act; and shall at the same time make a decision on any matter requiring to be specified under paragraph (*a*) or (*b*) of subsection (5) below.

(3) If the amount of a claim is stated in foreign currency the permanent trustee in adjudicating on the claim under subsection (1) or (2) above shall convert the amount into sterling, in such manner as may be prescribed, at the rate of exchange prevailing at the close of business on the date of sequestration.

(4) Where the permanent trustee rejects a claim, he shall forthwith notify the creditor giving reasons for the rejection.

(5) Where the permanent trustee accepts or rejects a claim, he shall record in the sederunt book his decision on the claim specifying—

    (*a*) the amount of the claim accepted by him,
    (*b*) the category of debt, and the value of any security, as decided by him, and
    (*c*) if he is rejecting the claim, his reasons therefor.

(6) The debtor or any creditor may, if dissatisfied with the acceptance or rejection of any claim (or, in relation to such acceptance or rejection, with a decision in respect of any matter requiring to be specified under subsection (5)(*a*) or (*b*) above), appeal therefrom to the sheriff—

    (*a*) if the acceptance or rejection is under subsection (1) above, within 2 weeks of that acceptance or rejection;
    (*b*) if the acceptance or rejection is under subsection (2) above, not later than 2 weeks before the end of the accounting period,

and the permanent trustee shall record the sheriff's decision in the sederunt book.

(7) Any reference in this section to the acceptance or rejection of a claim shall be construed as a reference to the acceptance or rejection of the claim in whole or in part.   **[549]**

NOTES
    Commencement: 1 April 1986.
    Commencement order: SI 1985 No 1924.
    Sub-s (3): For the prescribed manner of conversion into sterling, see the Bankruptcy (Scotland) Regulations 1985, SI 1985 No 1925, reg 7, para **[1707G]** post.

Entitlement to vote and draw dividend

50. Entitlement to vote and draw dividend

A creditor who has had his claim accepted in whole or in part by the permanent trustee or on appeal under subsection (6) of section 49 of this Act shall be entitled—

(*a*) subject to sections 29(1)(*a*) and 30(1) and (4)(*b*) of this Act, in a case where the acceptance is under (or on appeal arising from) subsection (1) of the said section 49, to vote on any matter at the meeting of creditors for the purpose of voting at which the claim is accepted; and

(*b*) in a case where the acceptance is under (or on appeal arising from) subsection (2) of the said section 49, to payment out of the debtor's estate of a dividend in respect of the accounting period for the purposes of which the claim is accepted; but such entitlement to payment shall arise only in so far as that estate has funds available to make that payment, having regard to section 51 of this Act.   **[550]**

NOTES
Commencement: 1 April 1986.
Commencement order: SI 1985 No 1924.

Distribution of debtor's estate

51. Order of priority in distribution

(1) The funds of the debtor's estate shall be distributed by the permanent trustee to meet the following debts in the order in which they are mentioned—

(*a*) the outlays and remuneration of the interim trustee in the administration of the debtor's estate;

(*b*) the outlays and remuneration of the permanent trustee in the administration of the debtor's estate;

(*c*) where the debtor is a deceased debtor, deathbed and funeral expenses reasonably incurred and expenses reasonably incurred in administering the deceased's estate;

(*d*) the expenses reasonably incurred by a creditor who is a petitioner, or concurs in the petition, for sequestration;

(*e*) preferred debts (excluding any interest which has accrued thereon to the date of sequestration);

(*f*) ordinary debts, that is to say a debt which is neither a secured debt nor a debt mentioned in any other paragraph of this subsection;

(*g*) interest at the rate specified in subsection (7) below on—

    (i) the preferred debts;
    (ii) the ordinary debts,

between the date of sequestration and the date of payment of the debt;

(*h*) any postponed debt.

(2) In this Act "preferred debt" means a debt listed in Part I of Schedule 3 to this Act; and Part II of that Schedule shall have effect for the interpretation of the said Part I.

(3) In this Act "postponed debt" means—

(*a*) a loan made to the debtor, in consideration of a share of the profits in his business, which is postponed under section 3 of the Partnership Act 1890 to the claims of other creditors;

(*b*) a loan made to the debtor by the debtor's spouse;

(*c*) a creditor's right to anything vesting in the permanent trustee by virtue of a successful challenge under section 34 of this Act or to the proceeds of sale of such a thing.

(4) Any debt falling within any of paragraphs (*c*) to (*h*) of subsection (1) above shall have the same priority as any other debt falling within the same paragraph and, where the funds of the estate are inadequate to enable the debts

mentioned in the paragraph to be paid in full, they shall abate in equal proportions.

(5) Any surplus remaining, after all the debts mentioned in this section have been paid in full, shall be made over to the debtor or to his successors or assignees; and in this subsection "surplus" includes any kind of estate but does not include any unclaimed dividend.

(6) Nothing in this section shall affect—

(a) the right of a secured creditor which is preferable to the rights of the permanent trustee; or

(b) any preference of the holder of a lien over a title deed or other document which has been delivered to the permanent trustee in accordance with a requirement under section 38(4) of this Act.

(7) The rate of interest referred to in paragraph (g) of subsection (1) above shall be whichever is the greater of—

(a) the prescribed rate at the date of sequestration; and

(b) the rate applicable to that debt apart from the sequestration. **[551]**

NOTES
Commencement: 1 April 1986 (sub-ss (1), (3)–(7)); 29 December 1986 (sub-s (2)).
Commencement orders: SI 1985 No 1924, SI 1986 No 1913.
Sub-s (7): For the prescribed rate of interest, see the Bankruptcy (Scotland) Regulations 1985, SI 1985 No 1925, reg 8, para **[1707H]** post.

52. Estate to be distributed in respect of accounting periods

(1) Subject to subsection (6) below, the permanent trustee, until the funds of the estate are exhausted, shall make up accounts of his intromissions with the debtor's estate in respect of periods of 26 weeks, the first such period commencing with the date of sequestration.

(2) In this Act "accounting period" shall be construed in accordance with subsections (1) above and (6) below.

(3) Subject to the following provisions of this section, the permanent trustee shall, if the funds of the debtor's estate are sufficient and after making allowance for future contingencies, pay under section 53(7) of this Act a dividend out of the estate to the creditors in respect of each accounting period.

(4) The permanent trustee may pay—

(a) the debts mentioned in subsection (1)(a) to (d) of section 51 of this Act, other than his own remuneration, at any time;

(b) the preferred debts at any time but only with the consent of the commissioners or, if there are no commissioners, of the Accountant in Bankruptcy.

(5) If the permanent trustee—

(a) is not ready to pay a dividend in respect of an accounting period; or

(b) considers it would be inappropriate to pay such a dividend because the expense of doing so would be disproportionate to the amount of the dividend,

he may, with the consent of the commissioners, or if there are no commissioners of the Accountant in Bankruptcy, postpone such payment to a date not later than the time for payment of a dividend in respect of the next accounting period.

(6) Where the permanent trustee considers that it would be expedient to accelerate payment of a dividend other than a dividend in respect of the first accounting period, the accounting period shall be shortened so as to end on such date as the permanent trustee, with the consent of the commissioners (if any), may specify and the next accounting period shall run from the end of that shortened period; and the permanent trustee shall record in the sederunt book the date so specified.

(7) Where an appeal is taken under section 49(6)(b) of this Act against the acceptance or rejection of a creditor's claim, the permanent trustee shall, at the time of payment of dividends and until the appeal is determined, set aside an amount which would be sufficient, if the determination in the appeal were to provide for the claim being accepted in full, to pay a dividend in respect of that claim.

(8) Where a creditor—

(a) has failed to produce evidence in support of his claim earlier than 8 weeks before the end of an accounting period on being required by the permanent trustee to do so under section 48(5) of this Act; and

(b) has given a reason for such failure which is acceptable to the permanent trustee,

the permanent trustee shall set aside, for such time as is reasonable to enable him to produce that evidence or any other evidence that will enable the permanent trustee to be satisfied under the said section 48(5), an amount which would be sufficient, if the claim were accepted in full, to pay a dividend in respect of that claim.

(9) Where a creditor submits a claim to the permanent trustee later than 8 weeks before the end of an accounting period but more than 8 weeks before the end of a subsequent accounting period in respect of which, after making allowance for contingencies, funds are available for the payment of a dividend, the permanent trustee shall, if he accepts the claim in whole or in part, pay to the creditor—

(a) the same dividend or dividends as has or have already been paid to creditors of the same class in respect of any accounting period or periods; and

(b) whatever dividend may be payable to him in respect of the said subsequent accounting period:

Provided that paragraph (a) above shall be without prejudice to any dividend which has already been paid. **[552]**

NOTES
    Commencement: 1 April 1986.
    Commencement order: SI 1985 No 1924.

53. Procedure after end of accounting period

(1) Within 2 weeks after the end of an accounting period, the permanent trustee shall in respect of that period submit to the commissioners or, if there are no commissioners, to the Accountant in Bankruptcy—

(a) his accounts of his intromissions with the debtor's estate for audit and, where funds are available after making allowance for contingencies, a scheme of division of the divisible funds; and

(b) a claim for the outlays reasonably incurred by him and for his remuneration;

and, where the said documents are submitted to the commissioners, he shall
send a copy of them to the Accountant in Bankruptcy.

(2) All accounts in respect of legal services incurred by the permanent
trustee shall, before payment thereof by him, be submitted for taxation to the
auditor of the court before which the sequestration is pending.

Provided that the permanent trustee may be authorised by the Accountant
in Bankruptcy to pay any such account without taxation.

(3) Within 6 weeks after the end of an accounting period—

    (a) the commissioners or, as the case may be, the Accountant in
        Bankruptcy shall—

        (i) audit the accounts; and
        (ii) issue a determination fixing the amount of the outlays and the
            remuneration payable to the permanent trustee; and

    (b) the permanent trustee shall make the audited accounts, scheme of
        division and the said determination available for inspection by the
        debtor and the creditors.

(4) The basis for fixing the amount of the remuneration payable to the
permanent trustee may be a commission calculated by reference to the value of
the debtor's estate which has been realised by the permanent trustee, but there
shall in any event be taken into account—

    (a) the work which, having regard to that value, was reasonably
        undertaken by him; and
    (b) the extent of his responsibilities in administering the debtor's estate.

(5) In fixing the amount of such remuneration in respect of the final
accounting period, the commissioners or, as the case may be, the Accountant in
Bankruptcy may take into account any adjustment which the commissioners or
the Accountant in Bankruptcy may wish to make in the amount of the
remuneration fixed in respect of any earlier accounting period.

(6) Not later than 8 weeks after the end of an accounting period, the
permanent trustee, the debtor or any creditor may appeal against a determination
issued under subsection (3)(a)(ii) above—

    (a) where it is a determination of the commissioners, to the Accountant
        in Bankruptcy; and
    (b) Where it is a determination of the Accountant in Bankruptcy, to the
        sheriff;

and the determination of the Accountant in Bankruptcy under paragraph (a)
above shall be appealable to the sheriff.

(7) On the expiry of the period within which an appeal may be taken under
subsection (6) above or, if an appeal is so taken, on the final determination of
the last such appeal, the permanent trustee shall pay to the creditors their
dividends in accordance with the scheme of division.

(8) Any dividend—

    (a) allocated to a creditor which is not cashed or uplifted; or
    (b) dependent on a claim in respect of which an amount has been set
        aside under subsection (7) or (8) of section 52 of this Act,

shall be deposited by the permanent trustee in an appropriate bank or institution.

(9) If a creditor's claim is revalued, the permanent trustee may—

(a) in paying any dividend to that creditor, make such adjustment to it as he considers necessary to take account of that revaluation; or

(b) require the creditor to repay to him the whole or part of a dividend already paid to him.

(10) The permanent trustee shall insert in the sederunt book the audited accounts, the scheme of division and the final determination in relation to the permanent trustee's outlays and remuneration. **[553]**

NOTES
    Commencement: 1 April 1986.
    Commencement order: SI 1985 No 1924.

Discharge of debtor

54. Automatic discharge after 3 years

(1) Subject to the following provisions of this section, the debtor shall be discharged on the expiry of 3 years from the date of sequestration.

(2) Every debtor who has been discharged under or by virtue of this section or section 75(4) of this Act may apply to the Accountant in Bankruptcy for a certificate that he has been so discharged; and the Accountant in Bankruptcy, if satisfied of such discharge, shall grant a certificate of discharge in the prescribed form.

(3) The permanent trustee or any creditor may, not later than 2 years and 9 months after the date of sequestration, apply to the sheriff for a deferment of the debtor's discharge by virtue of subsection (1) above.

(4) On an application being made to him under subsection (3) above, the sheriff shall order—

(a) the applicant to serve the application on the debtor and (if he is not himself the applicant and is not discharged) the permanent trustee; and

(b) the debtor to lodge in court a declaration—

    (i) that he has made a full and fair surrender of his estate and a full disclosure of all claims which he is entitled to make against other persons; and

    (ii) that he has delivered to the interim or permanent trustee every document under his control relating to his estate or his business or financial affairs;

and, if the debtor fails to lodge such a declaration in court within 14 days of being required to do so, the sheriff shall defer his discharge without a hearing for a period not exceeding 2 years.

(5) If the debtor lodges the declaration in court within the said period of 14 days, the sheriff shall—

(a) fix a date for a hearing not earlier than 28 days after the date of the lodging of the declaration; and

(b) order the applicant to notify the debtor and the permanent trustee or (if he has been discharged) the Accountant in Bankruptcy of the date of the hearing;

and the permanent trustee or (if he has been discharged) the Accountant in Bankruptcy shall, not later than 7 days before the date fixed under paragraph (a) above, lodge in court a report upon the debtor's assets and liabilities, his financial and business affairs and his conduct in relation thereto and upon the sequestration and his conduct in the course of it.

(6) After considering at the hearing any representations made by the applicant, the debtor or any creditor, the sheriff shall make an order either deferring the discharge for such period not exceeding 2 years as he thinks appropriate or dismissing the application:

Provided that the applicant or the debtor may appeal against an order under this subsection within 14 days after it is made.

(7) Where the discharge is deferred under subsection (4) or (6) above, the clerk of the court shall send—

(a) a certified copy of the order of the sheriff deferring discharge to the keeper of the register of inhibitions and adjudications for recording in that register; and

(b) a copy of such order to—

(i) the Accountant in Bankruptcy; and
(ii) the permanent trustee (if not discharged) for insertion in the sederunt book.

(8) A debtor whose discharge has been deferred under subsection (4) or (6) above may, at any time thereafter and provided that he lodges in court a declaration as to the matters mentioned in sub-paragraphs (i) and (ii) of paragraph (b) of the said subsection (4), petition the sheriff for his discharge; and subsections (5) to (7) above shall, with any necessary modifications, apply in relation to the proceedings which shall follow the lodging of a declaration under this subsection as they apply in relation to the proceedings which follow the timeous lodging of a declaration under the said paragraph (b).

(9) The permanent trustee or any creditor may, not later than 3 months before the end of a period of deferment, apply to the sheriff for a further deferment of the discharge; and subsections (4) to (8) above and this subsection shall apply in relation to that further deferment.   **[554]**

NOTES

Commencement: 1 April 1986.
Commencement order: SI 1985 No 1924.

55. Effect of discharge under section 54

(1) Subject to subsection (2) below, on the debtor's discharge under section 54 of this Act, the debtor shall be discharged within the United Kingdom of all debts and obligations contracted by him, or for which he was liable, at the date of sequestration.

(2) The debtor shall not be discharged by virtue of subsection (1) above from—

(a) any liability to pay a fine or other penalty due to the Crown;
(b) any liability to forfeiture of a sum of money deposited in court under section 1(3) of the Bail etc (Scotland) Act 1980;
(c) any liability incurred by reason of fraud or breach of trust;
(d) any obligation to pay aliment or any sum of an alimentary nature under any enactment or rule of law or any periodical allowance payable on divorce by virtue of a court order or under an obligation, not being aliment or a periodical allowance which could be included in the amount of a creditor's claim under paragraph 2 of Schedule 1 to this Act;

(*e*) the obligation imposed on him by section 64 of this Act.   **[555]**

NOTES
   Commencement: 1 April 1986.
   Commencement order: SI 1985 No 1924.
   Fine: This includes a confiscation order; see the Drug Trafficking Offences Act 1986, s 39(6)
(and for confiscation orders under that Act, see s 1 thereof).

56. Discharge on composition

Schedule 4 to this Act shall have effect in relation to an offer of composition by
or on behalf of the debtor to the permanent trustee in respect of his debts and
his discharge and the discharge of the permanent trustee where the offer is
approved.   **[556]**

NOTES
   Commencement: 1 April 1986.
   Commencement order: SI 1985 No 1924.

Discharge of permanent trustee

57. Discharge of permanent trustee

(1) After the permanent trustee has made a final division of the debtor's estate
and has inserted his final audited accounts in the sederunt book, he—

   (*a*) shall deposit any unclaimed dividends and any unapplied balances in
        an appropriate bank or institution;
   (*b*) shall thereafter send to the Accountant in Bankruptcy the sederunt
        book, a copy of the audited accounts and a receipt for the deposit of
        the unclaimed dividends and unapplied balances; and
   (*c*) may at the same time as sending the said documents apply to the
        Accountant in Bankruptcy for a certificate of discharge.

(2) The permanent trustee shall send notice of an application under
subsection (1)(*c*) above to the debtor and to all the creditors known to the
permanent trustee and shall inform the debtor and such creditors—

   (*a*) that they may make written representations relating to the application
        to the Accountant in Bankruptcy within a period of 14 days after such
        notification;
   (*b*) that the sederunt book is available for inspection at the office of the
        Accountant in Bankruptcy and contains the audited accounts of, and
        scheme of division in, the sequestration; and
   (*c*) of the effect mentioned in subsection (5) below.

(3) On the expiry of the period mentioned in subsection (2)(*a*) above, the
Accountant in Bankruptcy, after examining the documents sent to him and
considering any representations duly made to him, shall—

   (*a*) grant or refuse to grant the certificate of discharge; and
   (*b*) notify (in addition to the permanent trustee) the debtor and all
        creditors who have made such representations accordingly.

(4) The permanent trustee, the debtor or any creditor who has made
representations under subsection (2)(*a*) above, may within 14 days after the
issuing of the determination under subsection (3) above, appeal therefrom to
the sheriff and if the sheriff determines that a certificate of discharge which has
been refused should be granted he shall order the Accountant in Bankruptcy to

grant it; and the sheriff clerk shall send a copy of the decree of the sheriff to the Accountant in Bankruptcy.

(5) The grant of a certificate of discharge under this section by the Accountant in Bankruptcy shall have the effect of discharging the permanent trustee from all liability (other than any liability arising from fraud) to the creditors or to the debtor in respect of any act or omission of the permanent trustee in exercising the functions conferred on him by this Act including, where he was also the interim trustee, the functions conferred on him as interim trustee.

(6) Where a certificate of discharge is granted under this section, the Accountant in Bankruptcy shall make an appropriate entry in the register of insolvencies and in the sederunt book.

(7) Where the permanent trustee has died, resigned office or been removed from office, the provisions of this section shall, subject to any necessary modifications, apply in relation to that permanent trustee or, if he has died, to his executor as they apply to a permanent trustee who has made a final division of the debtor's estate in accordance with the foregoing provisions of this Act.

[557]

NOTES
   Commencement: 1 April 1986.
   Commencement order: SI 1985 No 1924.

58. Unclaimed dividends

(1) Any person, producing evidence of his right, may apply to the Accountant in Bankruptcy to receive a dividend deposited under section 57(1)(*a*) of this Act, if the application is made not later than 7 years after the date of such deposit.

(2) If the Accountant in Bankruptcy is satisfied of the applicant's right to the dividend, he shall authorise the appropriate bank or institution to pay to the applicant the amount of that dividend and of any interest which has accrued thereon.

(3) The Accountant in Bankruptcy shall, at the expiry of 7 years from the date of deposit of any unclaimed dividend or unapplied balance under section 57(1)(*a*) of this Act, hand over the deposit receipt or other voucher relating to such dividend or balance to the Secretary of State, who shall thereupon be entitled to payment of the amount due, principal and interest, from the bank or institution in which the deposit was made.   [558]

NOTES
   Commencement: 1 April 1986.
   Commencement order: SI 1985 No 1924.
   Companies winding up: This section applied, with any necessary modifications, to sums lodged in a bank or institution under the Insolvency Act 1986, s 193, and to sums deposited under the Companies Act 1985, s 430(13) (so far as it is consistent with those Acts); see s 193(3) of the 1986 Act and s 430(14) of the 1985 Act.

Voluntary trust deeds for creditors

59. Voluntary trust deeds for creditors

Schedule 5 to this Act shall have effect in relation to trust deeds executed after the commencement of this section.   [559]

NOTES
　　Commencement: 1 April 1986.
　　Commencement order: SI 1985 No 1924.

Miscellaneous and supplementary

60. Liabilities and rights of co-obligants

(1) Where a creditor has an obligant (in this section referred to as the "co-obligant") bound to him along with the debtor for the whole or part of the debt, the co-obligant shall not be freed or discharged from his liability for the debt by reason of the discharge of the debtor or by virtue of the creditor's voting or drawing a dividend or assenting to, or not opposing—

　　(a) the discharge of the debtor; or
　　(b) any composition.

(2) Where—

　　(a) a creditor has had a claim accepted in whole or in part; and
　　(b) a co-obligant holds a security over any part of the debtor's estate,

the co-obligant shall account to the permanent trustee so as to put the estate in the same position as if the co-obligant had paid the debt to the creditor and thereafter had had his claim accepted in whole or in part in the sequestration after deduction of the value of the security.

(3) Without prejudice to any right under any rule of law of a co-obligant who has paid the debt, the co-obligant may require and obtain at his own expense from the creditor an assignation of the debt on payment of the amount thereof, and thereafter may in respect of that debt submit a claim, and vote and draw a dividend, if otherwise legally entitled to do so.

(4) In this section a "co-obligant" includes a cautioner.　　　　**[560]**

NOTES
　　Commencement: 1 April 1986.
　　Commencement order: SI 1985 No 1924.

61. Extortionate credit transactions

(1) This section applies where the debtor is or has been a party to a transaction for, or involving, the provision to him of credit and his estate is sequestrated.

(2) The court may, on the application of the permanent trustee, make an order with respect to the transaction if the transaction is or was extortionate and was not entered into more than three years before the date of sequestration.

(3) For the purposes of this section a transaction is extortionate if, having regard to the risk accepted by the person providing the credit—

　　(a) the terms of it are or were such as to require grossly exorbitant payments to be made (whether unconditionally or in certain contingencies) in respect of the provision of the credit; or
　　(b) it otherwise grossly contravened ordinary principles of fair dealing; and it shall be presumed, unless the contrary is proved, that a transaction with respect to which an application is made under this section is, or as the case may be was, extortionate.

(4) An order under this section with respect to any transaction may contain such one or more of the following as the court thinks fit—

(*a*) provision setting aside the whole or part of any obligation created by the transaction;

(*b*) provision otherwise varying the terms of the transaction or varying the terms on which any security for the purposes of the transaction is held;

(*c*) provision requiring any person who is a party to the transaction to pay to the permanent trustee any sums paid to that person, by virtue of the transaction, by the debtor;

(*d*) provision requiring any person to surrender to the permanent trustee any property held by him as security for the purposes of the transaction;

(*e*) provision directing accounts to be taken between any persons.

(5) Any sums or property required to be paid or surrendered to the permanent trustee in accordance with an order under this section shall vest in the permanent trustee.

(6) Neither—

(*a*) the permanent trustee; nor

(*b*) a debtor who has not been discharged,

shall be entitled to make an application under section 139(1)(*a*) of the Consumer Credit Act 1974 (re-opening of extortionate credit agreements) for any agreement by which credit is or has been provided to the debtor to be re-opened; but the powers conferred by this section shall be exercisable in relation to any transaction concurrently with any powers exercisable under this Act in relation to that transaction as a gratuitous alienation or unfair preference.

(7) In this section "credit" has the same meaning as in the said Act of 1974. **[561]**

NOTES
Commencement: 1 April 1986.
Commencement order: SI 1985 No 1924.

62. Sederunt book and other documents

(1) Subject to subsection (2) below, whoever by virtue of this Act for the time being holds the sederunt book shall make it available for inspection at all reasonable hours by any interested person.

(2) As regards any case in which the person on whom a duty is imposed by subsection (1) above is the Accountant in Bankruptcy, the Court of Session may by act of sederunt—

(*a*) limit the period for which the duty is so imposed; and

(*b*) prescribe conditions in accordance with which the duty shall be carried out.

(3) Any entry in the sederunt book shall be sufficient evidence of the facts stated therein, except where it is founded on by the permanent trustee in his own interest.

(4) Notwithstanding any provision of this Act, the permanent trustee shall not be bound to insert in the sederunt book any document of a confidential nature.

(5) The permanent trustee shall not be bound to exhibit to any person other than a commissioner or the Accountant in Bankruptcy any document in his possession of a confidential nature.

(6) An extract from the register of insolvencies bearing to be signed by the Accountant in Bankruptcy shall be sufficient evidence of the facts stated therein.   **[562]**

NOTES
   Commencement: 1 April 1986.
   Commencement order: SI 1985 No 1924.

63. Power to cure defects in procedure

(1) The sheriff may, on the application of any person having an interest—

    (*a*) if there has been a failure to comply with any requirement of this Act or any regulations made under it, make an order waiving any such failure and, so far as practicable, restoring any person prejudiced by the failure to the position he would have been in but for the failure;

    (*b*) if for any reason anything required or authorised to be done in, or in connection with, the sequestration process cannot be done, make such order as may be necessary to enable that thing to be done.

(2) The sheriff, in an order under subsection (1) above, may impose such conditions, including conditions as to expenses, as he thinks fit and may—

    (*a*) authorise or dispense with the performance of any act in the sequestration process;

    (*b*) appoint as permanent trustee on the debtor's estate a person who would be eligible to be elected under section 24 of this Act, whether or not in place of an existing trustee;

    (*c*) extend or waive any time limit specified in or under this Act.

(3) An application under subsection (1) above—

    (*a*) may at any time be remitted by the sheriff to the Court of Session, of his own accord or on an application by any person having an interest;

    (*b*) shall be so remitted, if the Court of Session so directs on an application by any such person,

if the sheriff or the Court of Session, as the case may be, considers that the remit is desirable because of the importance or complexity of the matters raised by the application.

(4) The permanent trustee shall record in the sederunt book the decision of the sheriff or the Court of Session under this section.   **[563]**

NOTES
   Commencement: 1 April 1986.
   Commencement order: SI 1985 No 1924.

64. Debtor to co-operate with permanent trustee

(1) The debtor shall take every practicable step, and in particular shall execute any document, which may be necessary to enable the permanent trustee to perform the functions conferred on him by this Act.

(2) If the sheriff, on the application of the permanent trustee, is satisfied that the debtor has failed—

    (*a*) to execute any document in compliance with subsection (1) above, he may authorise the sheriff clerk to do so; and the execution of a document by the sheriff clerk under this paragraph shall have the like force and effect in all respects as if the document had been executed by the debtor;

(*b*) to comply in any other respect with subsection (1) above, he may order the debtor to do so.

(3) If the debtor fails to comply with an order of the sheriff under subsection (2) above, he shall be guilty of an offence.

(4) In this section "debtor" includes a debtor discharged under this Act.

(5) A person convicted of an offence under subsection (3) above shall be liable—

    (*a*) on summary conviction, to a fine not exceeding the statutory maximum or—

        (i) to imprisonment for a term not exceeding 3 months; or

        (ii) if he has previously been convicted of an offence inferring dishonest appropriation of property or an attempt at such appropriation, to imprisonment for a term not exceeding 6 months,

    or (in the case of either sub-paragraph) to both such fine and such imprisonment; or

    (*b*) on conviction on indictment to a fine or to imprisonment for a term not exceeding 2 years or to both.   **[564]**

NOTES

    Commencement: 1 April 1986.
    Commencement order: SI 1985 No 1924.

65. Arbitration and compromise

(1) The permanent trustee may (but if there are commissioners only with the consent of the commissioners, the creditors or the court)—

    (*a*) refer to arbitration any claim or question of whatever nature which may arise in the course of the sequestration; or

    (*b*) make a compromise with regard to any claim of whatever nature made against or on behalf of the sequestrated estate;

and the decree arbitral or compromise shall be binding on the creditors and the debtor.

(2) Where any claim or question is referred to arbitration under this section, the Accountant in Bankruptcy may vary any time limit in respect of which any procedure under this Act has to be carried out.

(3) The permanent trustee shall insert a copy of the decree arbitral, or record the compromise, in the sederunt book.   **[565]**

NOTES

    Commencement: 1 April 1986.
    Commencement order: SI 1985 No 1924.

66. Meetings of creditors and commissioners

Part I of Schedule 6 to this Act shall have effect in relation to meetings of creditors other than the statutory meeting; Part II of that Schedule shall have effect in relation to all meetings of creditors under this Act; and Part III of that Schedule shall have effect in relation to meetings of commissioners.   **[566]**

NOTES
    Commencement: 1 April 1986.
    Commencement order: SI 1985 No 1924.

67. General offences by debtor etc

(1) A debtor who during the relevant period makes a false statement in relation to his assets or his business or financial affairs to any creditor or to any person concerned in the administration of his estate shall be guilty of an offence, unless he shows that he neither knew nor had reason to believe that his statement was false.

(2) A debtor, or other person acting in his interest whether with or without his authority, who during the relevant period destroys, damages, conceals or removes from Scotland any part of the debtor's estate or any document relating to his assets or his business or financial affairs shall be guilty of an offence, unless the debtor or other person shows that he did not do so with intent to prejudice the creditors.

(3) A debtor who is absent from Scotland and who after the date of sequestration of his estate fails, when required by the court, to come to Scotland for any purpose connected with the administration of his estate, shall be guilty of an offence.

(4) A debtor, or other person acting in his interest whether with or without his authority, who during the relevant period falsifies any document relating to the debtor's assets or his business or financial affairs, shall be guilty of an offence, unless the debtor or other person shows that he had no intention to mislead the permanent trustee, a commissioner or any creditor.

(5) If a debtor whose estate is sequestrated—

   (a) knows that a person has falsified any document relating to the debtor's assets or his business or financial affairs; and
   (b) fails, within one month of the date of acquiring such knowledge, to report his knowledge to the interim or permanent trustee,

he shall be guilty of an offence.

(6) A person who is absolutely insolvent and who during the relevant period transfers anything to another person for an inadequate consideration or grants any unfair preference to any of his creditors shall be guilty of an offence, unless the transferor or grantor shows that he did not do so with intent to prejudice the creditors.

(7) A debtor who is engaged in trade or business shall be guilty of an offence if at any time in the period of one year ending with the date of sequestration of his estate, he pledges or disposes of, otherwise than in the ordinary course of his trade or business, any property which he has obtained on credit and has not paid for unless he shows that he did not intend to prejudice his creditors.

(8) A debtor who is engaged in trade or business shall be guilty of an offence if at any time in the period of 2 years ending with the date of sequestration, he has failed to keep or preserve such records as are necessary to give a fair view of the state of his assets or his business and financial affairs and to explain his transactions, unless he shows that such failure was neither reckless nor dishonest:

> Provided that a debtor shall not be guilty of an offence under this subsection if, at the date of sequestration, his unsecured liabilities did not exceed the prescribed amount; but, for the purposes of this proviso, if at

any time the amount of a debt (or part of a debt) over which a security is held exceeds the value of the security, that debt (or part) shall be deemed at that time to be unsecured to the extent of the excess.

(9) If a debtor, either alone or jointly with another person, obtains credit to the extent of £100 (or such other sum as may be prescribed) or more without giving the person from whom he obtained it the relevant information about his status he shall be guilty of an offence.

(10) For the purposes of subsection (9) above—

(*a*) "debtor" means—

(i) a debtor whose estate has been sequestrated, or
(ii) a person who has been adjudged bankrupt in England and Wales or Northern Ireland,

and who, in either case, has not been discharged;
(*b*) the reference to the debtor obtaining credit includes a reference to a case where goods are hired to him under a hire-purchase agreement or agreed to be sold to him under a conditional sale agreement; and
(*c*) the relevant information about the status of the debtor is the information that his estate has been sequestrated and that he has not received his discharge or, as the case may be, that he is an undischarged bankrupt in England and Wales or Northern Ireland.

(11) In this section—

(*a*) "the relevant period" means the period commencing one year immediately before the date of sequestration of the debtor's estate and ending with his discharge;
(*b*) references to intent to prejudice creditors shall include references to intent to prejudice an individual creditor.

(12) A person convicted of any offence under this section shall be liable—

(*a*) on summary conviction, to a fine not exceeding the statutory maximum or—

(i) to imprisonment for a term not exceeding 3 months; or
(ii) if he has previously been convicted of an offence inferring dishonest appropriation of property or an attempt at such appropriation, to imprisonment for a term not exceeding 6 months,

or (in the case of either sub-paragraph) to both such fine and such imprisonment; or
(*b*) on conviction on indictment to a fine or—

(i) in the case of an offence under subsection (1), (2), (4) or (7) above to imprisonment for a term not exceeding 2 years,
(ii) in any other case to imprisonment for a term not exceeding 2 years,

or (in the case of either sub-paragraph) to both such fine and such imprisonment. **[567]**

NOTES
  Commencement: 1 April 1986.
  Commencement order: SI 1985 No 1924.
  Sub-s (8): For the prescribed amount of unsecured liabilities under this subsection, see the Bankruptcy (Scotland) Regulations 1985, SI 1985 No 1925, reg 9, para **[1707I]** post.

68. Summary proceedings

(1) Summary proceedings for an offence under this Act may be commenced at any time within the period of 6 months after the date on which evidence sufficient in the opinion of the Lord Advocate to justify the proceedings comes to his knowledge.

(2) Subsection (3) of section 331 of the Criminal Procedure (Scotland) Act 1975 (date of commencement of summary proceedings) shall have effect for the purposes of subsection (1) above as it has effect for the purposes of that section.

(3) For the purposes of subsection (1) above, a certificate of the Lord Advocate as to the date on which the evidence in question came to his knowledge is conclusive evidence of the date on which it did so.   **[568]**

NOTES
  Commencement: 1 April 1986.
  Commencement order: SI 1985 No 1924.

69. Outlays of interim and permanent trustee

The Secretary of State may, by regulations, provide for the premium (or a proportionate part thereof) of any bond of caution or other security required, for the time being, to be given by an insolvency practitioner to be taken into account as part of the outlays of the insolvency practitioner in his actings as an interim trustee or permanent trustee.   **[569]**

NOTES
  Commencement: 1 April 1986.
  Commencement order: SI 1985 No 1924.

70. Supplies by utilities

(1) This section applies where on any day ("the relevant day")—

  (*a*) sequestration is awarded in a case where the petition was presented by the debtor,

  (*b*) a warrant is granted under section 12(2) of this Act in a case where the petition was presented by a creditor or a trustee acting under a trust deed; or

  (*c*) the debtor grants a trust deed,

and in this section "the office holder" means the interim trustee, the permanent trustee or the trustee acting under a trust deed, as the case may be.

(2) If a request falling within subsection (3) below is made for the giving after the relevant day of any of the supplies mentioned in subsection (4) below, the supplier—

  (*a*) may make it a condition of the giving of the supply that the office holder personally guarantees the payment of any charges in respect of the supply; and

  (*b*) shall not make it a condition of the giving of the supply, or do anything which has the effect of making it a condition of the giving of the supply, that any outstanding charges in respect of a supply given to the debtor before the relevant day are paid.

(3) A request falls within this subsection if it is made—

  (*a*) by or with the concurrence of the office holder; and

  (*b*) for the purposes of any business which is or has been carried on by or on behalf of the debtor.

(4) The supplies referred to in subsection (2) above are—

(*a*) a supply of gas by [a public gas supplier within the meaning of Part I of the Gas Act 1986];

(*b*) a supply of electricity by an Electricity Board (within the meaning of the Energy Act 1983);

(*c*) a supply of water by a water authority (within the meaning of the Water (Scotland) Act 1980);

(*d*) a supply of telecommunication services (within the meaning of the Telecommunications Act 1984) by a public telecommunications operator (within the meaning of that Act).

(5) In subsection (4) above the reference to telecommunication services does not include a reference to services consisting in the conveyance of cable programmes, that is to say programmes included in cable programme services (within the meaning of the Cable and Broadcasting Act 1984). **[570]**

NOTES
  Commencement: 1 April 1986.
  Commencement order: SI 1985 No 1924.
  Sub-s (4)(*a*): Words in square brackets in sub-s (4)(*a*) substituted by the Gas Act 1986, s 67(1), Sch 7, para 32.

71. Edinburgh Gazette

The keeper of the Edinburgh Gazette shall, on each day of its publication, send a free copy of it to—

(*a*) the Accountant in Bankruptcy; and

(*b*) the petition department of the Court of Session. **[571]**

NOTES
  Commencement: 1 April 1986.
  Commencement order: SI 1985 No 1924.

72. Regulations

Any power to make regulations under this Act shall be exercisable by statutory instrument subject to annulment in pursuance of a resolution of either House of Parliament; and the regulations may make different provision for different cases or classes of case. **[572]**

NOTES
  Commencement: 1 February 1986.
  Commencement order: SI 1985 No 1924.

73. Interpretation

(1) In this Act, unless the context otherwise requires—

  "Accountant in Bankruptcy" shall be construed in accordance with section 1 of this Act;

  "accounting period" shall be construed in accordance with section 52(1) and (6) of this Act;

  "apparent insolvency" and "apparently insolvent" shall be construed in accordance with section 7 of this Act;

  "appropriate bank or institution" means a bank or institution mentioned in section 2(1) of the Banking Act 1979 or for the time being specified in Schedule 1 to that Act;

  "act and warrant" means an act and warrant issued under section 25(2) of, or paragraph 2(2) of Schedule 2 to, this Act;

"associate" shall be construed in accordance with section 74 of this Act;

"business" means the carrying on of any activity, whether for profit or not;

"commissioner", except in the expression "examining commissioner", shall be construed in accordance with section 30(1) of this Act;

"court" means Court of Session or sheriff;

"date of sequestration" has the meaning assigned by section 12(4) of this Act;

"debtor" includes, without prejudice to the expression's generality, an entity whose estate may be sequestrated by virtue of section 6 of this Act, a deceased debtor or his executor or a person entitled to be appointed as executor to a deceased debtor;

"examination" means a public examination under section 45 of this Act or a private examination under section 44 of this Act;

"examining commissioner" shall be construed in accordance with section 46(2) of this Act;

"interim trustee' shall be construed in accordance with section 2 of this Act;

"list of interim trustees" has the meaning assigned by section 1(1)(b) of this Act;

"ordinary debt" shall be construed in accordance with section 51(1)(f) of this Act;

"permanent trustee" shall be construed in accordance with section 3 of this Act;

"postponed debt" has the meaning assigned by section 51(3) of this Act;

"preferred debt" has the meaning assigned by section 51(2) of this Act;

"prescribed" means prescribed by regulations made by the Secretary of State;

"protected trust deed" shall be construed in accordance with paragraph 8 of Schedule 5 to this Act;

"qualified creditor" and "qualified creditors" shall be construed in accordance with section 5(4) of this Act;

"qualified to act as an insolvency practitioner" means being, in accordance with section 2 of the Insolvency Act 1985 (qualifications of insolvency practitioners), so qualified:

Provided that, until the coming into force of that section the expression shall instead mean satisfying such requirements (which, without prejudice to the generality of this definition, may include requirements as to the finding of caution) as may be prescribed for the purposes of this Act;

"register of insolvencies" has the meaning assigned by section 1(1)(c) of this Act;

"relevant person" has the meaning assigned by section 44(1)(b) of this Act;

"secured creditor" means a creditor who holds a security for his debt over any part of the debtor's estate;

"security" means any security, heritable or moveable, or any right of lien, retention or preference;

"sederunt book" means the sederunt book maintained under section 3(1)(e) of this Act;

"standard scale" means the standard scale as defined in section 75(b) of the Criminal Justice Act 1982;

"statutory meeting" has the meaning assigned by section 21(1) of this Act;

"statutory maximum" has the meaning assigned by section 74(2) of the Criminal Justice Act 1982;

"trust deed" has the meaning assigned by section 5(2)(*c*) of this Act; and

"unfair preference" means a preference created as is mentioned in subsection (1) of section 36 of this Act by a transaction to which subsection (4) of that section applies.

(2) Any reference in this Act to a debtor being absolutely insolvent shall be construed as a reference to his liabilities being greater than his assets, and any reference to a debtor's estate being absolutely insolvent shall be construed accordingly.

(3) Any reference in this Act to value of the creditors is, in relation to any matter, a reference to the value of their claims as accepted for the purposes of that matter.

(4) Any reference in this Act to "the creditors" in the context of their giving consent or doing any other thing shall, unless the context otherwise requires, be construed as a reference to the majority in value of such creditors as vote in that context at a meeting of creditors.

(5) Any reference in this Act to any of the following acts by a creditor barring the effect of any enactment or rule of law relating to the limitation of actions in any part of the United Kingdom, namely—

(*a*) the presentation of a petition for sequestration;

(*b*) the concurrence in such a petition; and

(*c*) the submission of a claim,

shall be construed as a reference to that Act having the same effect, for the purposes of any such enactment or rule of law, as an effective acknowledgement of the creditor's claim; and any reference in this Act to any such enactment shall not include a reference to an enactment which implements or gives effect to any international agreement or obligation. **[573]**

NOTES

Commencement: 1 February 1986 (sub-s (1), except the definition of "preferred debt" therein, sub-ss (2), (5)); 29 December 1986 (the definition of "preferred debt" in sub-s (1)).

Commencement orders: SI 1985 No 1924, SI 1986 No 913.

74. Meaning of "associate"

(1) Subject to subsection (7) below, for the purposes of this Act any question whether a person is an associate of another person shall be determined in accordance with the following provisions of this section (any reference, whether in those provisions or in regulations under the said subsection (7), to a person being an associate of another person being taken to be a reference to their being associates of each other).

(2) A person is an associate of an individual if that person is the individual's husband or wife, or is a relative, or the husband or wife of a relative, of the individual or of the individual's husband or wife.

(3) A person is an associate of any person with whom he is in partnership, [and of any person who is an associate of any person with whom he is in partnership;] and a firm is an associate of any person who is a member of the firm.

(4) For the purposes of this section a person is a relative of an individual if he is that individual's brother, sister, uncle, aunt, nephew, niece, lineal ancestor or lineal descendant treating—

  (*a*) any relationship of the half blood as a relationship of the whole blood
and the stepchild or adopted child of any person as his child; and

  (*b*) an illegitimate child as the legitimate child of his mother and reputed
father,

and references in this section to a husband or wife include a former husband or
wife and a reputed husband or wife.

  (5) A person is an associate of any person whom he employs or by whom he
is employed; and for the purposes of this subsection any director or other officer
of a company shall be treated as employed by that company.

  [(5A) A company is an associate of another company—

  (*a*) if the same person has control of both, or a person has control of one
and persons who are his associates, or he and persons who are his
associates, have control of the other; or

  (*b*) if a group of two or more persons has control of each company, and
the groups either consist of the same persons or could be regarded as
consisting of the same persons by treating (in one or more cases) a
member of either group as replaced by a person of whom he is an
associate.

  (5B) A company is an associate of another person if that person has control
of it or if that person and persons who are his associates together have control
of it.

  (5C) For the purposes of this section a person shall be taken to have control
of a company if—

  (*a*) the directors of the company or of another company which has control
of it (or any of them) are accustomed to act in accordance with his
directions or instructions; or

  (*b*) he is entitled to exercise, or control the exercise of, one third or more
of the voting power at any general meeting of the company or of
another company which has control of it;

and where two or more persons together satisfy either of the above conditions,
they shall be taken to have control of the company.]

  (6) [In subsections (5), (5A), (5B) and (5C) above,] "company" includes any
body corporate (whether incorporated in Great Britain or elsewhere).

  (7) The Secretary of State may by regulations—

  (*a*) amend the foregoing provisions of this section so as to provide further
categories of persons who, for the purposes of this Act, are to be
associates of other persons; and

  (*b*) provide that any or all of subsections (2) to (6) above (or any subsection
added by virtue of paragraph (*a*) above) shall cease to apply, whether
in whole or in part, or shall apply subject to such modifications as he
may specify in the regulations;

and he may in the regulations make such incidental or transitional provision as
he considers appropriate.   **[574]**

NOTES

  Commencement: 1 April 1986.

  Commencement order: SI 1985 No 1924.

  The words in square brackets in sub-ss (3), (6) were substituted, and paras (5A)–(5C) were
inserted, by the Bankruptcy (Scotland) Regulations 1985, SI 1985 No 1925, reg 11, para **[1707K]**
post.

75 Amendments, repeals and transitional provisions

(1) Subject to subsection (3) below—

(a) the enactments mentioned in Part I of Schedule 7 to this Act shall have effect subject to the amendments respectively specified in that Schedule, being amendments consequential on the provisions of this Act;

(b) Part II of that Schedule, which re-enacts certain provisions of the Bankruptcy (Scotland) Act 1913 repealed by this Act, shall have effect.

(2) The enactments set out in columns 1 and 2 of Schedule 8 to this Act are, subject to subsection (3) below, hereby repealed to the extent specified in the third column of that Schedule.

(3) Subject to subsections (4) and (5) below, nothing in this Act shall affect any of the enactments repealed or amended by this Act in their operation in relation to a sequestration as regards which the award was made before the coming into force of this section.

(4) Where a debtor's estate has been sequestrated before the coming into force of this section but he has not been discharged, the debtor shall be discharged on the expiry of—

(a) 2 years after such coming into force; or

(b) 3 years after the date of sequestration,

whichever expires later:

Provided that, not later than 3 months before the date on which the debtor is due to be discharged under this subsection, the trustee in the sequestration or any creditor may apply to the sheriff for a deferment of that discharge; and subsections (4) to (8) of section 54 of this Act shall apply in relation to that application by the trustee as they apply in relation to an application under subsection (3) of that section by the permanent trustee.

(5) Section 63 of this Act shall apply in a case where before the coming into force of this section sequestration of a debtor's estate has been awarded under the Bankruptcy (Scotland) Act 1913 but the debtor has not yet been discharged, subject to the following modifications—

(a) in subsections (1)(a) and (2)(c) for the words "this Act" there shall be substituted the words "the Bankruptcy (Scotland) Act 1913";

(b) in subsections (2)(b) and (4) the word "permanent" shall be omitted; and

(c) in subsection (2)(b) for the words "24 of this Act" there shall be substituted the words "64 of the Bankruptcy (Scotland) Act 1913".

(6) The apparent insolvency of a debtor may be constituted for the purposes of this Act notwithstanding that the circumstance founded upon to constitute the apparent insolvency occurred on a date before the coming into force of section 7 of this Act; and, for those purposes, the apparent insolvency shall be deemed to have been constituted on that date:

Provided that apparent insolvency shall be constituted by virtue of this subsection only on grounds which would have constituted notour bankruptcy under the Bankruptcy (Scotland) Act 1913.

(7) Where a debtor whose estate is sequestrated after the commencement of this subsection is liable, by virtue of a transaction entered into before that date, to pay royalties or a share of the profits to any person in respect of any copyright or interest in copyright comprised in the sequestrated estate, section 102 of the Bankruptcy (Scotland) Act 1913 (trustee's powers in relation to copyright) shall apply in relation to the permanent trustee as it applied before its repeal in relation to a trustee in bankruptcy under the said Act of 1913.

(8) Where sequestration of a debtor's estate is awarded under this Act a person shall not be guilty of an offence under any provision of this Act in respect of anything done before the date of commcencement of that provision but, notwithstanding the repeal by this Act of the Bankruptcy (Scotland) Act 1913, he shall be guilty of an offence under that Act in respect of anything done before that date which would have been an offence under that Act if the award of sequestration had been made under that Act.

(9) Unless the context otherwise requires, any reference in any enactment or document to notour bankruptcy, or to a person being notour bankrupt, shall be construed as a reference to apparent insolvency, or to a person being apparently insolvent, within the meaning of section 7 of this Act.

(10) Unless the context otherwise requires, any reference in any enactment or document to a person's estate being sequestrated under the Bankruptcy (Scotland) Act 1913 shall be construed as, or as including, a reference to its being sequestrated under this Act; and analogous references shall be construed accordingly.

(11) Unless the context otherwise requires, any reference in any enactment or document to a trustee in sequestration or to a trustee in bankruptcy shall be construed as a reference to a permanent trustee, or in a case where no permanent trustee has been elected or appointed an interim trustee, within the meaning of this Act; and analogous expressions shall be construed accordingly.

(12) Unless the context otherwise requires, any reference in any enactment or document—

    (*a*) to a "gratuitous alienation" shall be construed as including a reference to an alienation challengeable under section 34(1) of this Act or under section 615A(1) of the Companies Act 1985;

    (*b*) to a "fraudulent preference" or to an "unfair preference" shall be construed as including a reference to—

        (i) an unfair preference within the meaning of this Act;

        (ii) a preference created as is mentioned in subsection (1) of section 36 of this Act (as applied by section 615B of the said Act of 1985), by a transaction to which subsection (4) of the said section 36 (as so applied) applies.   **[575]**

NOTES
    Commencement: 1 April 1986.
    Commencement order: SI 1985 No 1924.

76. Receipts and expenses

(1) Any—

    (*a*) payments received by the Secretary of State under section 58(3) of this Act; or

(*b*) amounts handed over to him in accordance with section 53 of this Act
by virtue of the insertion provided for in paragraph 9 of Schedule 2 to
this Act,

shall be paid by him into the Consolidated Fund.

(2) There shall be paid out of moneys provided by Parliament—

(*a*) any amount of outlays and remuneration payable in accordance with
section 53 of this Act by virtue of the insertion mentioned in subsection
(1)(*b*) above;

(*b*) any administrative expenses incurred by the Secretary of State under
this Act; and

(*c*) any increase attributable to this Act in the sums so payable under any
other Act.   **[576]**

77. Crown application

The application of this Act to the Crown is to the Crown as creditor only. **[577]**

78 Short title, commencement and extent

(1) This Act may be cited as the Bankruptcy (Scotland) Act 1985.

(2) This Act, except this section, shall come into force on such day as the
Secretary of State may by order made by statutory instrument appoint; and
different days may be so appointed for different purposes and for different
provisions.

(3) An order under subsection (2) above may contain such transitional
provisions and savings as appear to the Secretary of State necessary or expedient
in connection with the provisions brought into force (whether wholly or partly)
by the order.

(4) Without prejudice to section 75(3) to (5) of this Act, this Act applies to
sequestrations as regards which the petition—

(*a*) is presented on or after the date of coming into force of section 5 of
this Act; or

(*b*) was presented before, but in respect of which no award of sequestration
has been made by, that date.

(5) This Act, except the provisions mentioned in subsection (6) below,
extends to Scotland only.

(6) The provisions referred to in subsection (5) above are sections 8(5), 22(8)
(including that subsection as applied by section 48(7)), 46, 55 and 73(5),
paragraph 16(*b*) of Schedule 4 and paragraph 3 of Schedule 5.   **[578]**

SCHEDULES
SCHEDULE 1

Sections 5(5) and 22(9)

DETERMINATION OF AMOUNT OF CREDITOR'S CLAIM

Amount which may be claimed generally

1.—(1) Subject to the provisions of this Schedule, the amount in respect of which a creditor shall be entitled to claim shall be the accumulated sum of principal and any interest which is due on the debt as at the date of sequestration.

(2) If a debt does not depend on a contingency but would not be payable but for the sequestration until after the date of sequestration, the amount of the claim shall be calculated as if the debt were payable on the date of sequestration but subject to the deduction of interest at the rate specified in section 51(7) of this Act from the said date until the date for payment of the debt.

(3) In calculating the amount of his claim, a creditor shall deduct any discount (other than any discount for payment in cash) which is allowable by contract or course of dealing between the creditor and the debtor or by the usage of trade.

Claims for aliment and periodical allowance on divorce

2.—(1) A person entitled to aliment, however arising, from a living debtor as at the date of sequestration, or from a deceased debtor immediately before his death, shall not be entitled to include in the amount of his claim—

(a) any unpaid aliment for any period before the date of sequestration unless the amount of the aliment has been quantified by court decree or by any legally binding obligation which is supported by evidence in writing, and, in the case of spouses (or, where the aliment is payable to a divorced person in respect of a child, former spouses) they were living apart during that period;

(b) any aliment for any period after the date of sequestration.

(2) Sub-paragraph (1) above shall apply to a periodical allowance payable on divorce—

(a) by virtue of a court order; or

(b) under any legally binding obligation which is supported by evidence in writing,

as it applies to aliment and as if for the words from "in the case" to "they" there were substituted the words "the payer and payee".

Debts depending on contingency

3.—(1) Subject to sub-paragraph (2) below, the amount which a creditor shall be entitled to claim shall not include a debt in so far as its existence or amount depends upon a contingency.

(2) On an application by the creditor—

(a) to the permanent trustee; or

(b) if there is no permanent trustee, to the sheriff,

the permanent trustee or sheriff shall put a value on the debt in so far as it is contingent, and the amount in respect of which the creditor shall then be entitled to claim shall be that value but no more; and, where the contingent debt is an annuity, a cautioner may not then be sued for more than that value.

(3) Any interested person may appeal to the sheriff against a valuation under sub-paragraph (2) above by the permanent trustee, and the sheriff may affirm or vary that valuation.

Debts due under composition contracts

4. Where in the course of a sequestration the debtor is discharged following approval by the sheriff of a composition offered by the debtor but the sequestration is subsequently revived, the amount in respect of which a creditor shall be entitled to claim shall be the

same amount as if the composition had not been so approved less any payment already made to him under the composition contract.

Secured debts

5.—(1) In calculating the amount of his claim, a secured creditor shall deduct the value of any security as estimated by him:

Provided that if he surrenders, or undertakes in writing to surrender, a security for the benefit of the debtor's estate, he shall not be required to make a deduction of the value of that security.

(2) The permanent trustee may, at any time after the expiry of 12 weeks from the date of sequestration, require a secured creditor at the expense of the debtor's estate to discharge the security or convey or assign it to the permanent trustee on payment to the creditor of the value specified by the creditor; and the amount in respect of which the creditor shall then be entitled to claim shall be any balance of his debt remaining after receipt of such payment.

(3) In calculating the amount of his claim, a creditor whose security has been realised shall deduct the amount (less the expenses of realisation) which he has received, or is entitled to receive, from the realisation.

Valuation of claims against partners for debts of the partnership

6. Where a creditor claims in respect of a debt of a partnership, against the estate of one of its partners, the creditor shall estimate the value of—

(*a*) the debt to the creditor from the firm's estate where that estate has not been sequestrated; or
(*b*) the creditor's claim against that estate where it has been sequestrated,

and deduct that value from his claim against the partner's estate; and the amount in respect of which he shall be entitled to claim on the partner's estate shall be the balance remaining after that deduction has been made. **[579]**

NOTES
Commencement: 1 April 1986.
Commencement order: SI 1985 No 1924.

SCHEDULE 2
Sections 23(4), 24(5) and 28(5)

ADAPTATION OF PROCEDURE ETC UNDER THIS ACT WHERE PERMANENT TRUSTEE NOT ELECTED

1. Section 24(2) shall, in so far as it relates to qualifications for continuing to act as permanent trustee, apply to a permanent trustee appointed, as it applies to one elected, under this Act.

2.—(1) In place of sections 25 and 26, sub-paragraphs (2) and (3) below shall have effect.

(2) The sheriff clerk shall issue to the permanent trustee an act and warrant in such form as shall be prescribed by the Court of Session by act of sederunt.

(3) The permanent trustee, on appointment, shall make such insertions in the sederunt book as are appropriate to provide a record of the sequestration process before his appointment, but he shall make no insertion therein relating to the written comments made by the interim trustee under section 20(2)(*c*) of this Act.

3.—(1) In place of subsections (1) to (5) of section 28 sub-paragraphs (2) and (3) below shall have effect.

(2) The permanent trustee may resign office with the consent of the accountant in Bankruptcy or the sheriff.

(3) Where the permanent trustee resigns under sub-paragraph (2) above, or dies, a person nominated by the Accountant in Bankruptcy from the list of interim trustees, not being a person ineligible for election as permanent trustee under section 24(2) of this Act, shall forthwith apply to the sheriff for appointment as permanent trustee, and the sheriff shall thereupon so appoint him.

4. In section 29—

    (a) subsection (5) shall not have effect but sub-paragraph (3) of paragraph 3 above shall apply where the permanent trustee has been removed from office under subsection (1)(b) of section 29 of this Act or following an appeal under subsection (4) of that section as that sub-paragraph applies where he resigns or dies;

    (b) subsection (6) shall have effect as if for the words from "(b)" to the end there were substituted the words—

        "(b) appoint as permanent trustee a person nominated by the Accountant in Bankruptcy from the list of interim trustees, not being a person ineligible for election as permanent trustee under section 24(2) of this Act.";

    (c) subsection (7) shall not have effect; and

    (d) subsection (8) shall have effect as if for the word "(4)" there were substituted the word "(5)".

5. Where an appointment is made under paragraph 3(3), or by virtue of paragraph 4(a) or (b), above the provisions of this Act shall continue to have effect as regards the sequestration subject to such modifications and with such further provisions as are set out in this Schedule.

6. Section 30 shall not have effect, and, in any sequestration to which this Schedule applies by virtue of section 28(5) of this Act, any commissioners already holding office shall cease to do so.

7. In section 39—

    (a) in subsection (1), the reference to the permanent trustee's confirmation in office shall be construed as a reference to his receiving the act and warrant issued under paragraph 2(2) of this Schedule;

    (b) subsection (2) shall have effect as if for the words "if there are commissioners only with the consent of the commissioners, the creditors or the court" there were substituted the words "only with the consent of the Accountant in Bankruptcy".

8. Any power under section 44 or 45 to apply to the sheriff for an order requiring attendance shall be exerciseable only with the consent of the Accountant in Bankruptcy (unless, in the case of section 45(1), the Accountant in Bankruptcy has requested the application).

9. In subsection (1) of section 53 the reference to the period in respect of which submission is to be made by the permanent trustee shall, where that period is the first accounting period, be construed as including a reference to any period during which he has acted as interim trustee in the sequestration; and that section shall have effect as if after that subsection there were inserted the following subsection—

"(1A) Where the funds of the debtor's estate are insufficient to meet the amount of the outlays and remuneration of both the interim trustee and the permanent trustee—

    (a) that amount to the extent of the insufficiency shall be met by the Accountant in Bankruptcy out of money provided under section 76(2)(a) of this Act; and

    (b) the Accountant in Bankruptcy in his determination under subsection (3)(a)(ii) below shall specify the respective sums to be met out of the debtor's estate and out of money so provided:

Provided that—

    (i) no amount shall be payable by virtue of paragraph (a) above if any dividend has been paid to creditors in the sequestration; and

(ii) if any amount is paid by virtue of that paragraph and a subsequent distribution of the estate is proposed, that amount shall be handed over to the Secretary of State before such distribution is made.". **[580]**

NOTES
Commencement: 1 April 1986.
Commencement order: SI 1985 No 1924.

SCHEDULE 3

Section 51

PREFERRED DEBTS

PART I

LIST OF PREFERRED DEBTS

Debts to Inland Revenue

1.—(1) Sums due at the relevant date from the debtor on account of deductions of income tax from emoluments paid during the period of twelve months next before that date, being deductions which the debtor was liable to make under section 204 of the Income and Corporation Taxes Act 1970 (pay as you earn), less the amount of the repayments of income tax which the debtor was liable to make during that period.

(2) Sums due at the relevant date from the debtor in respect of such deductions as are required to be made by the debtor for that period under section 69 of the Finance (No 2) Act 1975 (subcontractors in the construction industry).

Debts due to Customs and Excise

2.—(1) Any value added tax which is referable to the period of six months next before the relevant date.

(2) The amount of any car tax which is due at the relevant date from the debtor and which became due within a period of twelve months next before that date.

(3) Any amount which is due—

(a) by way of general betting duty or bingo duty, or
(b) under section 12(1) of the Betting and Gaming Duties Act 1981 (general betting duty and pool betting duty recoverable from agent collecting stakes), or
(c) under section 14 of, or Schedule 2 to, that Act (gaming licence duty),

from the debtor at the relevant date and which became due within the period of twelve months next before that date.

Social Security contributions

3.—(1) All sums which on the relevant date are due from the debtor on account of Class 1 or Class 2 contributions under the Social Security Act 1975 or the Social Security (Northern Ireland) Act 1975 and which became due from the debtor in the twelve months next before the relevant date.

(2) All sums which on the relevant date have been assessed on and are due from the debtor on account of Class 4 contributions under either of the said Acts of 1975, being sums which—

(a) are due to the Commissioners of Inland Revenue (rather than to the Secretary of State or a Northern Ireland department); and
(b) are assessed on the debtor up to 5th April next before the relevant date,

but not exceeding, in the whole, any one year's assessment.

Contributions to occupational pension schemes, etc

4. Any sum which is owed by the debtor and is a sum to which Schedule 3 to the Social Security Pensions Act 1975 (contributions to occupational pension scheme and state scheme premiums) applies.

Remuneration of employees, etc

5.—(1) So much of any amount which—

(a) is owed by the debtor to a person who is or has been an employee of the debtor, and

(b) is payable by way of remuneration in respect of the whole or any part of the period of four months next before the relevant date,

as does not exceed the prescribed amount.

(2) An amount owed by way of accrued holiday remuneration, in respect of any period of employment before the relevant date, to a person whose employment by the debtor has been terminated, whether before, on or after that date.

(3) So much of any sum owed in respect of money advanced for the purpose as has been applied for the payment of a debt which, if it had not been paid, would have been a debt falling within sub-paragraph (1) or (2) above.

6. So much of any amount which—

(a) is ordered, whether before or after the relevant date, to be paid by the debtor under the Reserve Forces (Safeguard of Employment) Act 1985; and

(b) is so ordered in respect of a default made by the debtor before that date in the discharge of his obligations under that Act,

as does not exceed such amount as may be prescribed. **[581]**

NOTES

Commencement: 29 December 1986.
Commencement order: SI 1986 No 1913.

PART II
INTERPRETATION OF PART I

Meaning of "the relevant date"

7. In Part I of this Schedule "the relevant date" means—

(a) in relation to a debtor (other than a deceased debtor), the date of sequestration; and

(b) in relation to a deceased debtor, the date of his death.

Periods to which value added tax referable

8.—(1) For the purpose of paragraph 2(1) of Part I of this Schedule—

(a) where the whole of the prescribed accounting period to which any value added tax is attributable falls within the period of six months next before the relevant date ("the relevant period"), the whole amount of that tax shall be referable to the relevant period; and

(b) in any other case the amount of any value added tax which shall be referable to the relevant period shall be the proportion of the tax which is equal to such proportion (if any) of the accounting reference period in question as falls within the relevant period.

(2) In sub-paragraph (1) above "prescribed accounting period" has the same meaning as in the Value Added Tax Act 1983.

Amounts payable by way of remuneration

9.—(1) For the purposes of paragraph 5 of Part I of this Schedule a sum is payable by the debtor to a person by way of remuneration in respect of any period if—

(a) it is paid as wages or salary (whether payable for time or for piece work or earned wholly or partly by way of commission) in respect of services rendered to the debtor in that period; or

(b) it is an amount falling within sub-paragraph (2) below and is payable by the debtor in respect of that period.

(2) An amount falls within this sub-paragraph if it is—

(a) a guarantee payment under section 12(1) of the Employment Protection (Consolidation) Act 1978 (employee without work to do for a day or part of a day),

(b) remuneration on suspension on medical grounds under section 19 of that Act,

(c) any payment for the time off under section 27(3) (trade-union duties), 31(3) (looking for work, etc) or 31A(4) (ante-natal care) of that Act,

(d) . . .

(e) remuneration under a protective award made by an industrial tribunal under section 101 of the Employment Protection Act 1975 (redundancy dismissal with compensation).

(3) For the purposes of paragraph 5(2) of Part I of this Schedule, holiday remuneration shall be deemed, in the case of a person whose employment has been terminated by or in consequence of the award of sequestration of his employer's estate, to have accrued to that person in respect of any period of employment if, by virtue of that person's contract of employment or of any enactment (including an order made or direction given under any enactment), that remuneration would have accrued in respect of that period if that person's employment had continued until he became entitled to be allowed the holiday.

(4) Without prejudice to the preceding provisions of this paragraph—

(a) any remuneration payable by the debtor to a person in respect of a period of holiday or of absence from work through sickness or other good cause is deemed to be wages or, as the case may be, salary in respect of services rendered to the debtor in that period; and

(b) references in this paragraph to remuneration in respect of a period of holiday include references to any sums which, if they had been paid, would have been treated for the purposes of the enactments relating to social services as earnings in respect of that period.

Transitional Provisions

10. Regulations under paragraph 5 or 6 of Part I of this Schedule may contain such transitional provisions as may appear to the Secretary of State necessary or expedient.

[582]

NOTES
Commencement: 29 December 1986.
Commencement order: SI 1986 No 1913.
Para 9(2)(d): Repealed by the Social Security Act 1986, s 86, Sch 10, Pt IV, para 80, Sch 11.

SCHEDULE 4
Section 56

DISCHARGE ON COMPOSITION

1.—(1) At any time after the sheriff clerk issues the act and warrant to the permanent trustee, an offer of composition may be made by or on behalf of the debtor, in respect of his debts, to the permanent trustee.

(2) Any offer of composition shall specify caution or other security to be provided for its implementation.

2. The permanent trustee shall submit the offer of composition along with a report thereon to the commissioners or, if there are no commissioners, to the Accountant in Bankruptcy.

3. The commissioners or, if there are no commissioners, the Accountant in Bankruptcy—

(a) if they consider (or he considers) that the offer of composition will be timeously implemented and that, if the rules set out in section 51 of, and Schedule 1 to, this Act were applicable, its implementation would secure payment of a dividend of at least 25p in the £ in respect of the ordinary debts; and

(b) if satisfied with the caution or other security specified in the offer.

shall recommend that the offer should be placed before the creditors.

4. Where a recommendation is made that the offer of composition should be placed before the creditors, the permanent trustee shall—

    (*a*) intimate the recommendation to the debtor and record it in the sederunt book;

    (*b*) publish in the Edinburgh Gazette a notice stating that an offer of composition has been made and where its terms may be inspected;

    (*c*) invite every creditor known to him to accept or reject the offer by completing a prescribed form sent by the permanent trustee with the invitation and returning the completed form to him; and

    (*d*) send along with the prescribed form a report—

        (i) summarising the offer and the present state of the debtor's affairs and the progress in realising his estate; and

        (ii) estimating, if the offer is accepted, the expenses to be met in concluding the sequestration proceedings and the dividend which would be payable in respect of the ordinary debts if the rules set out in section 51 of, and Schedule 1 to, this Act were applied.

5.—(1) The permanent trustee shall determine from the completed prescribed forms duly received by him that the offer of composition has been accepted by the creditors, if a majority in number and not less than two-thirds in value of the creditors known to him have accepted it, and otherwise shall determine that they have rejected it.

(2) For the purposes of this paragraph, a prescribed form shall be deemed to be duly received by the permanent trustee if it is received by him not later than 14 days after the date on which it was sent to the creditor.

(3) The permanent trustee shall intimate in writing his determination under this paragraph to the debtor and any other person by whom the offer of composition was made and shall insert his determination in the sederunt book.

6. Where the permanent trustee determines that the creditors have accepted the offer of composition, he shall submit to the sheriff—

    (*a*) a statement that he has so determined;

    (*b*) a copy of the report mentioned in paragraph 4(*d*) of this Schedule; and

    (*c*) a declaration by the debtor as to the matters mentioned in sub-paragraphs (i) and (iii) of section 54(4)(*b*) of this Act.

7.—(1) The sheriff shall, on the receipt by him of the documents mentioned in paragraph 6 of this Schedule, fix a date and time for a hearing to consider whether or not to approve the offer of composition.

(2) The permanent trustee shall then send to every creditor known to him a notice in writing stating—

    (*a*) that he has determined that the creditors have accepted the offer of composition;

    (*b*) that a hearing has been fixed by the sheriff to consider whether or not to approve the offer;

    (*c*) the place, date and time of the hearing; and

    (*d*) that the recipient of the notice may make representations at the hearing as to whether or not the offer of composition should be approved.

8.—(1) At the hearing the sheriff shall examine the documents and hear any representations and thereafter shall make an order—

    (*a*) if he is satisfied that a majority in number and not less than two-thirds in value of the creditors known to the permanent trustee have accepted the offer of composition and that the terms of the offer are reasonable, approving the offer; and

    (*b*) if he is not so satisfied, refusing to approve the offer of composition.

(2) The sheriff may make an order approving the offer of composition, notwithstanding that there has been a failure to comply with any provision of this Schedule.

(3) The debtor or any creditor may within 14 days of the order being made appeal against an order approving or refusing to approve the offer of composition.

9.—(1) Where the offer of composition is approved, the permanent trustee shall—

(a) submit to the commissioners or, if there are no commissioners, to the Accountant in Bankruptcy, his accounts of his intromissions with the debtor's estate for audit and a claim for the outlays reasonably incurred by him and for his remuneration; and where the said documents are submitted to the commissioners, he shall send a copy of them to the Accountant in Bankruptcy;

(b) take all reasonable steps to ensure that the interim trustee (where he is a different person) has submitted, or submits, to the Accountant in Bankruptcy his accounts and his claim for his outlays and remuneration.

(2) Subsections (3), (4), (6) and (10) of section 53 of this Act shall apply, subject to any necessary modifications, in respect of the accounts and claim submitted under sub-paragraph (1)(a) above as they apply in respect of the accounts and claim submitted under section 53(1) of this Act.

10. As soon as the procedure under paragraph 9 of this Schedule has been completed, there shall be lodged with the sheriff clerk—

(a) by the permanent trustee, a declaration that all necessary charges in connection with the sequestration have been paid or that satisfactory provision has been made in respect of the payment of such charges;

(b) by or on behalf of the debtor, the bond of caution or other security for payment of the composition.

11. Once the documents have been lodged under paragraph 10 of this Schedule, the sheriff shall make an order discharging the debtor and the permanent trustee; and subsection (7) of section 54 of this Act shall apply in relation to an order under this paragraph as it applies in relation to an order under subsection (6) of that section.

12. An order under paragraph 11 of this Schedule discharging the permanent trustee shall have the effect of discharging him from all liability (other than any liability arising from fraud) to the creditors or to the debtor in respect of any act or omission of the permanent trustee in exercising the functions conferred on him by this Act.

13. Notwithstanding that an offer of composition has been made, the sequestration shall proceed as if no such offer of composition has been made until the discharge of the debtor becomes effective; and the sequestration shall thereupon cease.

14. A creditor who has not submitted a claim under section 48 of this Act before the sheriff makes an order approving an offer of composition shall not be entitled to make any demand against a person offering the composition on behalf of the debtor or against a cautioner in the offer; but this paragraph is without prejudice to any right of such a creditor to a dividend out of the debtor's estate equal to the dividend which creditors of the same class are entitled to receive under the composition.

15. A debtor may make two, but no more than two, offers of composition in the course of a sequestration.

16. On an order under paragraph 11 of this Schedule discharging the debtor becoming effective—

(a) the debtor shall be re-invested in his estate as existing at the date of the order;

(b) the debtor shall, subject to paragraph 14 of this Schedule, be discharged of all debts for which he was liable at the date of sequestration (other than any debts mentioned in section 55(2) of this Act); and

(c) the claims of creditors in the sequestration shall be converted into claims for their respective shares in the composition.

17.—(1) Without prejudice to any rule of law relating to the reduction of court decrees, the Court of Session, on the application of any creditor, may recall the order of the sheriff approving the offer of composition and discharging the debtor and the permanent trustee where it is satisfied—

(a) that there has been, or is likely to be, default in payment of the composition or of any instalment thereof; or

(b) that for any reason the composition cannot be proceeded with or cannot be proceeded with without undue delay or without injustice to the creditors.

(2) The effect of a decree of recall under this paragraph where the debtor has already been discharged shall be to revive the sequestration:

Provided that the revival of the sequestration shall not affect the validity of any transaction which has been entered into by the debtor since his discharge with a person who has given value and has acted in good faith.

(3) Where the permanent trustee has been discharged, the Court may, on pronouncing a decree of recall under this paragraph, appoint a judicial factor to administer the debtor's estate, and give the judicial factor such order as it thinks fit as to that administration.

(4) The clerk of the court shall send a copy of a decree of recall under this paragraph to the permanent trustee or judicial factor for insertion in the sederunt book.

18.—(1) Without prejudice to any rule of law relating to the reduction of court decrees, the Court of Session, on the application of any creditor, may reduce an order under paragraph 11 of this Schedule discharging a debtor where it is satisfied that a payment was made or a preference granted or that a payment or preference was promised for the purpose of facilitating the obtaining of the debtor's discharge.

(2) The Court may, whether or not it pronounces a decree of reduction under this paragraph, order a creditor who has received a payment or preference in connection with the debtor's discharge to surrender the payment or the value of the preference to the debtor's estate.

(3) Where the permanent trustee has been discharged, the Court may, on pronouncing a decree of reduction under this paragraph, appoint a judicial factor to administer the debtor's estate, and give the judicial factor such order as it thinks fit as to that administration.

(4) The clerk of court shall send a copy of a decree of reduction under this paragraph to the permanent trustee or judicial factor for insertion in the sederunt book.   **[583]**

NOTES
    Commencement: 1 April 1986.
    Commencement order: SI 1985 No 1924.

SCHEDULE 5

Section 59

VOLUNTARY TRUST DEEDS FOR CREDITORS

Remuneration of trustee

1. Whether or not provision is made in the trust deed for auditing the trustee's accounts and for determining the method of fixing the trustee's remuneration or whether or not the trustee and the creditors have agreed on such auditing and the method of fixing the remuneration, the debtor, the trustee or any creditor may, at any time before the final distribution of the debtor's estate among the creditors, have the trustee's accounts audited by and his remuneration fixed by the Accountant in Bankruptcy.

Registration of notice of inhibition

2.—(1) The trustee, from time to time after the trust deed has been delivered to him, may cause a notice in such form as shall be prescribed by the Court of Session by act of sederunt to be recorded in the register of inhibitions and adjudications; and such recording shall have the same effect as the recording in that register of letters of inhibition against the debtor.

(2) The trustee, after the debtor's estate has been finally distributed among his creditors or the trust deed has otherwise ceased to be operative, shall cause to be so recorded a notice in such form as shall be prescribed as aforesaid recalling the notice recorded under sub-paragraph (1) above.

Lodging of claim to bar effect of limitation of actions

3. The submission of a claim by a creditor to the trustee acting under a trust deed shall bar the effect of any enactment or rule of law relating to limitation of actions in any part of the United Kingdom.

Valuation of claims

4. Unless the trust deed otherwise provides, Schedule 1 to this Act shall apply in relation to a trust deed as it applies in relation to a sequestration but subject to the following modifications—

(a) in paragraphs 1, 2 and 5 for the word "sequestration" wherever it occurs there shall be substituted the words "granting of the trust deed";

(b) in paragraph 3—

(i) in sub-paragraph (2), for the words from the beginning of paragraph (a) to "or sheriff" there shall be substituted the words "the trustee"; and

(ii) in sub-paragraph (3), for the reference to the permanent trustee there shall be substituted a reference to the trustee;

(c) paragraph 4 shall be omitted; and

(d) in paragraph 5(2) for the references to the permanent trustee there shall be substituted references to the trustee.

Protected trust deeds

5. Paragraphs 6 and 7 of this Schedule shall apply in respect of a trust deed if—

(a) the trustee is a person who would not be disqualified under section 24(2) of this Act from acting as permanent trustee if the debtor's estate were being sequestrated;

(b) the trustee, forthwith after the trust deed has been delivered to him, both publishes in the Edinburgh Gazette and sends to every creditor known to him a notice in the prescribed form—

(i) stating that the trust deed has been granted by the debtor; and

(ii) inviting creditors, in order that paragraphs 6 and 7 of this Schedule may apply, to accede to the trust deed within 4 weeks of the date on which the notice is so published;

(c) within the said period of 4 weeks a majority in number and not less than two-thirds in value of the creditors accede to the trust deed; and

(d) the trustee immediately after the expiry of the said period sends to the Accountant in Bankruptcy for registration in the register of insolvencies a copy of the trust deed with a certificate endorsed thereon that it is a true copy and the accession of creditors as required by sub-paragraph (c) above has been obtained.

6. Where the provisions of paragraph 5 of this Schedule have been fulfilled, then—

(a) subject to paragraph 7 of this Schedule, a creditor who has not acceded to the trust deed shall have no higher right to recover his debt than a creditor who has so acceded; and

(b) the debtor may not petition for the sequestration of his estate while the trust deed subsists.

7.—(1) A qualified creditor who has not acceded to the trust deed may present a petition for sequestration of the debtor's estate—

(a) not later than 6 weeks after the date of publication of the notice under paragraph 5(b) of this Schedule; but

(b) subject to section 8(1)(b) of this Act, at any time if he avers that the provision for distribution of the estate is or is likely to be unduly prejudicial to a creditor or class of creditors.

(2) The court may award sequestration in pursuance of sub-paragraph (1)(a) above if it considers that to do so would be in the best interests of the creditors.

(3) The court shall award sequestration in pursuance of sub-paragraph (1)(*b*) above if, but only if, it is satisfied that the creditor's said averment is correct.

8. In this Act a trust deed in respect of which paragraphs 6 and 7 of this Schedule apply is referred to as a "protected trust deed".

9. Where the trustee under a protected trust deed has made the final distribution of the estate among the creditors, he shall, not more than 28 days after the final distribution, send to the Accountant in Bankruptcy for registration in the register of insolvencies—

    (*a*) a statement in the prescribed form indicating how the estate was realised and distributed; and

    (*b*) a certificate to the effect that the distribution was in accordance with the trust deed.

10. Where the trustee under a protected trust deed has obtained a discharge from the creditors who have acceded to the trust deed he shall forthwith give notice of the discharge—

    (*a*) by sending the notice by recorded delivery to every creditor known to him who has not acceded to the trust deed; and

    (*b*) by sending the notice to the Accountant in Bankruptcy who shall register the fact of the discharge in the register of insolvencies,

and, except where the court makes an order under paragraph 12 below, the sending of such notice to a creditor who has not acceded to the trust deed shall be effective to make the discharge binding upon that creditor.

Creditors not acceding to protected trust deed

11. A creditor who has not acceded to a protected trust deed may, not more than 28 days after notice has been sent under paragraph 10 above, apply to the court for an order under paragraph 12 below.

12. Where, on an application by a creditor under paragraph 11 above, the court is satisfied (on grounds other than those on which a petition under paragraph 7(1)(*b*) above was or could have been presented by that creditor) that the intromissions of the trustee under the protected trust deed with the estate of the debtor have been so unduly prejudicial to that creditor's claim that he should not be bound by the discharge it may order that he shall not be so bound.

13. Where the court makes an order under paragraph 12 above, the clerk of the court shall send a copy of the order to—

    (*a*) the trustee; and

    (*b*) the Accountant in Bankruptcy who shall register the copy of the order in the register of insolvencies.   **[584]**

NOTES
Commencement: 1 April 1986.
Commencement order: SI 1985 No 1924.

SCHEDULE 6

Section 66

MEETINGS OF CREDITORS AND COMMISSIONERS

PART I

MEETINGS OF CREDITORS OTHER THAN THE STATUTORY MEETING

Calling of meeting

1. The permanent trustee shall call a meeting of creditors if required to do so by—

    (*a*) order of the court;

    (*b*) one-tenth in number or one-third in value of the creditors;

(*c*) a commissioner; or
(*d*) the Accountant in Bankruptcy.

2. A meeting called under paragraph 1 above shall be held not later than 28 days after the issuing of the order of the court under sub-paragraph (*a*) of that paragraph or the receipt by the permanent trustee of the requirement under sub-paragraph (*b*), (*c*) or (*d*) thereof.

3. The permanent trustee or a commissioner who has given written notice to him may at any time call a meeting of creditors.

4. The permanent trustee or a commissioner calling a meeting under paragraph 1 or 3 above shall, not less than 7 days before the date fixed for the meeting, notify—

(*a*) every creditor known to him; and
(*b*) the Accountant in Bankruptcy,

of the date, time and place fixed for the holding of the meeting and its purpose.

5.—(1) Where a requirement has been made under paragraph 1 above but no meeting has been called by the permanent trustee, the Accountant in Bankruptcy may, of his own accord or on the application of any creditor, call a meeting of creditors.

(2) The Accountant in Bankruptcy calling a meeting under this paragraph shall, not less than 7 days before the date fixed for the meeting, take reasonable steps to notify the creditors of the date, time and place fixed for the holding of the meeting and its purpose.

6. It shall not be necessary to notify under paragraph 4 or 5 of this Schedule any creditor whose accepted claim is less than £50 for such sum as may be prescribed, unless the creditor has requested in writing such notification.

Role of permanent trustee at meeting

7.—(1) At the commencement of a meeting, the chairman shall be the permanent trustee who as chairman shall, after carrying out his duty under section 49(1) of this Act, invite the creditors to elect one of their number as chairman in his place and shall preside over the election.

(2) If a chairman is not elected in pursuance of this paragraph, the permanent trustee shall remain the chairman throughout the meeting.

(3) The permanent trustee shall arrange for a record to be made of the proceedings at the meeting and he shall insert the minutes of the meeting in the sederunt book.

Appeals

8. The permanent trustee, a creditor or any other person having an interest may, within 14 days after the date of a meeting called under paragraph 1 or 3 above, appeal to the sheriff against a resolution of the creditors at the meeting.   **[585]**

NOTES
Commencement: 1 April 1986.
Commencement order: SI 1985 No 1924.

PART II
ALL MEETINGS OF CREDITORS

Validity of proceedings

9. No proceedings at a meeting shall be invalidated by reason only that any notice or other document relating to the calling of the meeting which is required to be sent or given under any provision of this Act has not been received by, or come to the attention of, any creditor before the meeting.

Locus of meeting

10. Every meeting shall be held in such place (whether or not in the sheriffdom) as is, in the opinion of the person calling the meeting, the most convenient for the majority of the creditors.

Mandatories

11.—(1) A creditor may authorise in writing any person to represent him at a meeting.

(2) A creditor shall lodge any authorisation given under sub-paragraph (1) above with the interim trustee or, as the case may be, the permanent trustee before the commencement of the meeting.

(3) Any reference in paragraph 7(1) of this Schedule and the following provisions of this Part of this Schedule to a creditor shall include a reference to a person authorised by him under this paragraph.

Quorum

12. The quorum at any meeting shall be one creditor.

Voting at meeting

13. Any question at a meeting shall be determined by a majority in value of the creditors who vote on that question.

Objections by creditors

14.—(1) The chairman at any meeting may allow or disallow any objection by a creditor, other than (if the chairman is not the permanent trustee) an objection relating to a creditor's claim.

(2) Any person aggrieved by the determination of the chairman in respect of an objection may appeal therefrom to the sheriff.

(3) If the chairman is in doubt whether to allow or disallow an objection, the meeting shall proceed as if no objection had been made, except that for the purposes of appeal the objection shall be deemed to have been disallowed.

Adjournment of meeting

15.—(1) If no creditor has appeared at a meeting at the expiry of a period of half an hour after the time appointed for the commencement of the meeting, the chairman shall adjourn the meeting to such other day as the chairman shall appoint, being not less than 7 nor more than 21 days after the day on which the meeting was adjourned.

(2) The chairman may, with the consent of a majority in value of the creditors who vote on the matter, adjourn a meeting.

(3) Any adjourned meeting shall be held at the same time and place as the original meeting, unless in the resolution for the adjournment of the meeting another time or place is specified.

Minutes of meeting

16. The minutes of every meeting shall be signed by the chairman and within 14 days of the meeting a copy of the minutes shall be sent to the Accountant in Bankruptcy.**[586]**

NOTES
    Commencement: 1 April 1986.
    Commencement order: SI 1985 No 1924.

PART III

MEETING OF COMMISSIONERS

17. The permanent trustee may call a meeting of commissioners at any time, and shall call a meeting of commissioners—

(a) on being required to do so by order of the court; or

(b) on being requested to do so by the Accountant in Bankruptcy or any commissioner.

18. If the permanent trustee fails to call a meeting of commissioners within 14 days of being required or requested to do so under paragraph 17 of this Schedule, a commissioner may call a meeting of commissioners.

19. The permanent trustee shall give the commissioners at least 7 days notice of a meeting called by him, unless the commissioners decide that they do not require such notice.

20. The permanent trustee shall act as clerk at meetings and shall insert a record of the deliberations of the commissioners in the sederunt book.

21. If the commissioners are considering the performance of the functions of the permanent trustee under any provision of this Act, he shall withdraw from the meeting if requested to do so by the commissioners; and in such a case a commissioner shall act as clerk, shall transmit a record of the deliberations of the commissioners to the permanent trustee for insertion in the sederunt book and shall authenticate the insertion when made.

22. The quorum at a meeting of commissioners shall be one commissioner and the commissioners may act by a majority of the commissioners present at the meeting.

23. Any matter may be agreed by the commissioners without a meeting if such agreement is unanimous and is subsequently recorded in a minute signed by the commissioners; and that minute shall be inserted by the permanent trustee in the sederunt book.   **[587]**

NOTES
    Commencement: 1 April 1986.
    Commencement order: SI 1985 No 1924.

SCHEDULE 7
Section 75(1)

PART I

CONSEQUENTIAL AMENDMENTS

The Judicial Factors (Scotland) Act 1880 (c 4)

1. In section 3 (interpretation), for the words "section 14 or 163 of the Bankruptcy (Scotland) Act 1913" there shall be substituted the words "section 11A of the Judicial Factors (Scotland) Act 1889".

The Bankruptcy Act 1883 (c 52)

2.—(1) In subsection (1) of section 32 after the words "adjudged bankrupt" there shall be inserted the words "or his estate has been sequestrated".

(2) After subsection (2) of that section there shall be inserted the following subsection

"(2A) The disqualifications to which a debtor whose estate has been sequestrated in Scotland is subject shall cease to have effect if and when—

(a) the award of sequestration is recalled or reduced; or

(b) he is discharged under or by virtue of the Bankruptcy (Scotland) Act 1985.".

(3) After section 34 there shall be inserted the following section—

"34A. Extent of Part II

This Part of this Act (except section 34 above) shall extend to Scotland.".

The Judicial Factors (Scotland) Act 1889 (c 39)

3. In section 2, at the beginning there shall be inserted the words "Without prejudice to section 1(2) of the Bankruptcy (Scotland) Act 1985 (Accountant of Court to be Accountant in Bankruptcy),".

4. After section 11 there shall be inserted the following sections—

"11A. Application for judicial factor on estate of person deceased

(1) It shall be competent to one or more creditors of parties deceased, or to persons having an interest in the succession of such parties, in the event of the deceased having left no settlement appointing trustees or other parties having power to manage his estate or part thereof, or in the event of such parties not accepting or acting, to apply by summary petition to the Court of Session or to the sheriff of the sheriffdom within which the deceased resided or carried on business during the year immediately preceding the date of the petition, or within which heritage belonging to the deceased at the time of his death is situated, for the appointment of a judicial factor.

(2) After such intimation of the petition to the creditors of the deceased, and other persons interested, as may be considered necessary, and after hearing parties, the Court or sheriff may appoint such factor, who shall administer the estate subject to the supervision of the accountant in accordance with this Act and the Judicial Factors (Scotland) Act 1880 and relative acts of sederunt; and, if the deceased's estate is absolutely insolvent within the meaning of section 73(2) of the Bankruptcy (Scotland) Act 1985, section 51 of, and Schedule 1 to, that Act shall apply as if for references to—

    (a) the interim trustee or permanent trustee there were substituted references to the judicial factor; and

    (b) the date of sequestration there were substituted references to the date of the judicial factor's appointment.

11B. Judicial factor's duties to be regulated by act of sederunt

The Court of Session shall have full power to regulate by act of sederunt—

    (a) the caution to be found by a factor appointed under section 11A above;

    (b) the mode in which he shall proceed in realising and dividing the funds, and otherwise in the discharge of his duties; and

    (c) any other matter which they may deem necessary.".

The Conveyancing (Scotland) Act 1924 (c 27)

5. In section 44(4)(c) (limitation of effect of entries in the register of inhibitions and adjudications)—

    (a) after the words "Bankruptcy (Scotland) Act 1913" there shall be inserted the words "or the Bankruptcy (Scotland) Act 1985";

    (b) after the words "effect of recording" there shall be inserted "(a)" and after the words "as aforesaid" there shall be inserted the words "; or (b) under subsection (1)(a) of section 14 of the Bankruptcy (Scotland) Act 1985 the certified copy of an order shall have expired by virtue of subsection (3) of that section"; and

    (c) for the words "in terms of paragraph (b) of this subsection", there shall be substituted the words "in the form provided by Schedule O to this Act".

The Third Parties (Rights Against Insurers) Act 1930 (c 25)

6.—(1) In section 1(2) (rights of third parties against insurers on bankruptcy of insured), after the words "provable in bankruptcy" there shall be inserted the words "(in Scotland, any claim accepted in the sequestration)".

(2) In section 4 (application to Scotland)—

    (a) paragraph (a) shall be omitted; and

(b) in paragraph (b), for the words "one hundred and sixty-three of the Bankruptcy (Scotland) Act 1913" there shall be substituted the words "11A of the Judicial Factors (Scotland) Act 1889".

The Exchange Control Act 1947 (c 14)

7. In paragraph 7 of the Fourth Schedule (application of that Schedule to Scotland), for sub-paragraph (4) there shall be substituted the following sub-paragraph—

"(4) In paragraph 6, for the words from 'complies' to 'creditor's debt' there shall be substituted the words 'is a debt which would allow a creditor to be a qualified creditor in accordance with the requirements of subsection (4) of section 5 of the Bankruptcy (Scotland) Act 1985, be a debt in respect of which a creditor may present a petition for sequestration'."

The Conveyancing and Feudal Reform (Scotland) Act 1970 (c 35)

8. In paragraph 9(2)(b) of Schedule 3 ("insolvent" for purposes of standard condition as to default), for the words "163 of the Bankruptcy (Scotland) Act 1913" there shall be substituted the words "11A of the Judicial Factors (Scotland) Act 1889".

The Superannuation Act 1972 (c 11)

9. In section 5(2) (benefits under civil service superannuation schemes not negotiable), for the words "148" and "1913" there shall be substituted respectively, the words "32(2) and (4)" and "1985".

The Road Traffic Act 1972 (c 20)

10. In section 150(2) (effect of bankruptcy of insured or secured persons)—

(a) the words from "'company'" to "and", where it first occurs, shall be omitted; and

(b) for the words from "163" to "1913" there shall be substituted the words "11A of the Judicial Factors (Scotland) Act 1889".

The Prescription and Limitation (Scotland) Act 1973 (c 52)

11. In section 9(1), for paragraph (b) there shall be substituted the following paragraphs—

"(b) by the presentation of, or the concurring in, a petition for sequestration or by the submission of a claim under section 22 or 48 of the Bankruptcy (Scotland) Act 1985 (or those sections as applied by section 613 of the Companies Act 1985); or

(c) by a creditor to the trustee acting under a trust deed as defined in section 5(2)(c) of the Bankruptcy (Scotland) Act 1985;".

The Local Government (Scotland) Act 1973 (c 65)

12. In section 31(2) (disqualifications regarding members of local authority), for paragraph (b) there shall be substituted the following paragraph—

"(b) he is discharged under or by virtue of the Bankruptcy (Scotland) Act 1985.".

The Social Security Pensions Act 1975 (c 60)

13. In section 58 of the Social Security Pensions Act 1975 (under which Schedule 3 to that Act has effect for giving priority in bankruptcy etc. to certain debts) after the word "effect" there shall be inserted the words "for the purposes, in respect of the sequestration of estates in Scotland, of Schedule 3 to the Bankruptcy (Scotland) Act 1985 (preferred debts)"; and, for the purposes of the sequestration of a debtor's estate in Scotland, Schedule 3 to the said Act of 1975 shall have effect as if—

(i) in paragraph 3(1), for the words "a person going into liquidation or being adjudged bankrupt" there were substituted the words "the sequestration of a debtor's estate"; and

(ii) in paragraph 4, for the words "Schedule 4 to the Insolvency" there were substituted the words "Part I of Schedule 3 to the Bankruptcy (Scotland)".

The Employment Protection (Consolidation) Act 1978 (c 44)

14.—(1) In section 106(6) (payments out of fund to employees), in paragraph (b) for the words from "163" to "1913" there shall be substituted the words "11A of the Judicial Factors (Scotland) Act 1889".

(2) In section 122(8) (employee's rights on insolvency of employer), for the word "admitted" there shall be substituted the word "accepted".

(3) In section 125(2) (transfer to Secretary of State of rights and remedies), for paragraph (b) there shall be substituted the following paragraph—

"(b) section 51 of the Bankruptcy (Scotland) Act 1985; and".

(4) In section 127(2)(b) (interpretation) for the words from "163" to "1913" there shall be substituted the words "11A of the Judicial Factors (Scotland) Act 1889".

The Land Registration (Scotland) Act 1979 (c 33)

15. In section 12(3)(b) (restriction as regards indemnity in respect of registered interest in land), after the word "reduced", where it first occurs, there shall be inserted the words ", whether or not under subsection (4) of section 34, or subsection (5) of section 36, of the Bankruptcy (Scotland) Act 1985 (or either of those subsections as applied by sections 615A(4) and 615B of the Companies Act 1985, respectively),".

The Banking Act 1979 (c 37)

16. In section 28 (payments to depositors on institution's insolvency)—

(a) in subsection (6)—

    (i) in paragraph (a), after the word "proved" there shall be inserted the words "or whose claim has been accepted in the sequestration"; and

    (ii) in paragraph (b)(iii), for the words "72" and "1913" there shall be substituted, respectively, the words "30" and "1985"; and

(b) in subsection (7)(c)—

    (i) the words from "where" to "court", shall cease to have effect; and

    (ii) for the words "deed of arrangement or other settlement or arrangement by way" there shall be substituted the words "trust deed, contract of composition or offer".

The Estate Agents Act 1979 (c 38)

17. In section 23(2) (bankrupts not to engage in estate agency work), in paragraph (a) after the word "recalled" there shall be inserted the words "or reduced".

The Value Added Tax Act 1983 (c 55)

18. In section 22(4)(a)(ii) ("insolvency" for purposes of refund of tax in cases of bad debts), for the words "163 of the Bankruptcy (Scotland) Act 1913" there shall be substituted the words "11A of the Judicial Factors (Scotland) Act 1889".

19–22. . . .

The Family Law (Scotland) Act 1985 (c 37)

23. In section 14(5)(b) for the words from "sections 30" to "1913" there shall be substituted the words "section 41 of the Bankruptcy (Scotland) Act 1985".   **[588]**

NOTES

Commencement: 1 April 1986 (paras 1–12, 14(1), (2), (4), 15–23); 29 December 1986 (paras 13, 14(3)).

Commencement orders: SI 1985 No 1924, SI 1986 No 1913.

Paras 19–22: Repealed by the Insolvency Act 1986, s 438, Sch 12.

PART II

RE-ENACTMENT OF CERTAIN PROVISIONS OF BANRUPTCY (SCOTLAND) ACT 1913 (c 20)

Arrestments and Poindings

24.—(1) Subject to sub-paragraph (2) below, all arrestments and poindings which have been executed within 60 days prior to the constitution of the apparent insolvency of the debtor, or within four months thereafter, shall be ranked *pari passu* as if they had all been executed on the same date.

(2) Any such arrestment which is executed on the dependence of an action shall be followed up without undue delay.

(3) Any creditor judicially producing in a process relative to the subject of such arrestment or poinding liquid grounds of debt or decree of payment within 60 days or four months referred to in sub-paragraph (1) above shall be entitled to rank as if he had executed an arrestment or a poinding; and if the first or any subsequent arrester obtains in the meantime a decree of furthcoming, and recovers payment, or a poinding creditor carries through a sale, he shall be accountable for the sum recovered to those who, by virtue of this Act, may be eventually found to have a right to a ranking *pari passu* thereon, and shall be liable in an action at their instance for payment to them proportionately, after allowing out of the fund the expense of such recovery.

(4) Arrestments executed for attaching the same effects of the debtor after the period of four months subsequent to the constitution of his apparent insolvency shall not compete with those within the said periods prior or subsequent thereto, but may rank with each other on any reversion of the fund attached in accordance with any enactment or rule of law relating thereto.

(5) Any reference in the foregoing provisions of this paragraph to a debtor shall be construed as including a reference to an entity whose apparent insolvency may, by virtue of subsection (5) of section 7 of this Act, be constituted under subsection (1) of that section.

(6) This paragraph shall apply in respect of arrestments and poindings which have been executed either before or after the coming into force of this paragraph.

(7) The repeal of the Bankruptcy (Scotland) Act 1913 shall not affect the equalisation of arrestments and poindings (whether executed before or after the coming into force of this paragraph) in consequence of the constitution of notour bankruptcy under that Act.

Exemptions from stamp or other duties for conveyances, deeds etc relating to sequestrated estates

25. Any—

(a) conveyance, assignation, instrument, discharge, writing, or deed relating solely to the estate of a debtor which has been or may be sequestrated, either under this or any former Act, being estate which after the execution of such conveyance, assignation, instrument, discharge, writing, or deed, shall be and remain the property of such debtor, for the benefit of his creditors, or the interim or permanent trustee appointed or chosen under or by virtue of such sequestration,

(b) discharge to such debtor,

(c) deed, assignation, instrument, or writing for reinvesting the debtor in the estate,

(d) article of roup or sale, or submission,

(e) other instrument or writing whatsoever relating solely to the estate of any such debtor; and

(f) other deed or writing forming part of the proceedings ordered under sequestration,

shall be exempt from all stamp duties or other Government duty.   [589]

NOTES
　Commencement: 1 April 1986.
　Commencement order: SI 1985 No 1924.

SCHEDULE 8

Section 75(2)

REPEALS

Chapter	Short Title	Extent of Repeal
1621 c 18	The Bankruptcy Act 1621	The whole Act.
1696 c 5	The Bankruptcy Act 1696	The whole Act.
31 & 32 Vict c 101	The Titles to Land Consolidation (Scotland) Act 1868	Section 148.
44 & 45 Vict c 21	The Married Women's Property (Scotland) Act 1881	Section 1(4).
52 & 53 Vict c 39	The Judicial Factors (Scotland) Act 1889	In section 5, the words ", and of the Bankruptcy Acts and Cessio Acts," and the words "and accountant in bankruptcy respectively,". In section 14, the proviso. Sections 15 and 16. Section 22.
57 & 58 Vict c 60	The Merchant Shipping Act 1894	Section 36.
3 & 4 Geo 5 c 20	The Bankruptcy (Scotland) Act 1913	The whole Act.
10 & 11 Geo 5 c 64	The Married Women's Property (Scotland) Act 1920	In section 5, the proviso.
14 & 15 Geo 5 c 27	The Conveyancing (Scotland) Act 1924	In section 44, in subsection (4) paragraphs (*a*) and (*b*); and in subsection (6) the words "and section 44 of the Bankruptcy (Scotland) Act 1913".
20 & 21 Geo 5 c 25	The Third Parties (Rights Against Insurers) Act 1930	In section 4, paragraph (*a*).
10 & 11 Geo 6 c 47	The Companies Act 1947	Sections 91 and 115.
11 & 12 Geo 6 c 39	The Industrial Assurance and Friendly Societies Act 1948	In section 2(4), the words "where the receiving order or the award of sequestration of his estate was made after the passing of this Act".
15 & 16 Geo 6 & 1 Eliz 2 c 33	The Finance Act 1952	In section 30, subsections (4) and (6).
1965 c 25	The Finance Act 1965	In Schedule 10, paragraph 15(1).
1969 c 48	The Post Office Act 1969	In Schedule 4, paragraph 22.
1970 c 10	The Income and Corporation Taxes Act 1970	In Part II of Schedule 15, the entry relating to the Finance Act 1952.
1972 c 20	The Road Traffic Act 1972	In section 150(2), the words "'company' includes a limited partnership, and".

Chapter	Short Title	Extent of Repeal
1974 c 46	The Friendly Societies Act 1974	In section 59, in subsection (1)(*a*) the words "or bankruptcy"; in subsection (2) the words "or trustee in bankruptcy"; and subsections (3) and (4).
1975 c 14	The Social Security Act 1975	In Schedule 18, paragraph 1(1)(*b*) and (2)(*b*).
1975 c 18	The Social Security (Consequential Provisions) Act 1975	In Schedule 2, paragraph 1.
1975 c 45	The Finance (No 2) Act 1975	In section 71(6), the words "section 30 of the Finance Act 1952".
1975 c 60	The Social Security Pensions Act 1975	In Schedule 4, paragraph 1.
1976 c 24	The Development Land Tax Act 1976	In section 42, subsection (1), so far as it relates to bankruptcy in Scotland; and subsection (4)(*a*).
1976 c 60	The Insolvency Act 1976	In section 5, subsections (3) and (4). In Schedule 1, in Part I, the entries relating to the Bankruptcy (Scotland) Act 1913; and, in Part II, paragraphs 1(*a*), 2(*a*), 4 and 5(*b*).
1978 c 44	The Employment Protection (Consolidation) Act 1978	Section 121(1)(*b*).
1979 c 37	The Banking Act 1979	In section 28(7)(*c*) the words "where the sequestration is declared at an end by a competent court".
1979 c 54	The Sale of Goods Act 1979	In section 61(4), the words ", and whether he has become a notour bankrupt or not".
1980 c 55	The Law Reform (Miscellaneous Provisions) (Scotland) Act 1980	Section 12.
1981 c 59	The Matrimonial Homes (Family Protection) (Scotland) Act 1981	Section 10.
1981 c 63	The Betting and Gaming Duties Act 1981	In section 30, subsections (1) and (2).
1983 c 53	The Car Tax Act 1983	In Schedule 1, paragraph 4.
1983 c 55	The Value Added Tax Act 1983	In Schedule 7, paragraph 12.
1985 c 6	The Companies Act 1985	In section 665, the words "(whether limited or not)"; and in paragraph (*d*) the words "registered in England and Wales or Northern Ireland".

Chapter	Short Title	Extent of Repeal
1985 c 17	The Reserve Forces (Safeguard of Employment) Act 1985	In section 13, the word "—(*a*)"; the words from "or, (*b*)" to "estate,"; the word "—(i)"; and the words from "or, (ii)" to "1913,".

[590]

NOTES
    Commencement: 1 April 1986 (in part); 29 December 1986 (remainder).
    Commencement orders: SI 1985 No 1924, SI 1986 No 1913.

PART IV

INSOLVENCY STATUTORY INSTRUMENTS

Section A

Insolvency Rules 1986

Section A

Insolvency Rules 1986

SECTION A

INSOLVENCY RULES 1986
(SI 1986 No 1925)

NOTES
    Made: 10 November 1986.
    Commencement: 29 December 1986.
    Authority: Insolvency Act 1986, ss 411, 412.

ARRANGEMENT OF RULES

The First Group of Parts

Company Insolvency; Companies Winding Up
Introductory Provisions

Rule		Para
0.1	Citation and commencement	[591]
0.2	Construction and principal references	[592]
0.3	Extent	[593]

Part 1
Company Voluntary Arrangements

Chapter 1
Preliminary

1.1	Scope of this Part; interpretation	[594]

Chapter 2
Proposal by Directors

1.2	Preparation of proposal	[595]
1.3	Contents of proposal	[596]
1.4	Notice to intended nominee	[597]
1.5	Statement of affairs	[598]
1.6	Additional disclosure for assistance of nominee	[599]
1.7	Nominee's report on the proposal	[600]
1.8	Replacement of nominee	[601]
1.9	Summoning of meetings under s 3	[602]

Chapter 3
Proposal by Administrator or Liquidator (Himself the Nominee)

1.10	Preparation of proposal	[603]
1.11	Summoning of meetings under s 3	[604]

Rule   Para

CHAPTER 4

PROPOSAL BY ADMINISTRATOR OR LIQUIDATOR (ANOTHER INSOLVENCY PRACTITIONER THE NOMINEE)

1.12   Preparation of proposal and notice to nominee ..   .. [605]

CHAPTER 5

PROCEEDINGS ON A PROPOSAL MADE BY THE DIRECTORS, OR BY THE ADMINISTRATOR, OR BY THE
LIQUIDATOR

SECTION A: MEETINGS OF COMPANY'S CREDITORS AND MEMBERS
1.13   Summoning of meetings   ..   .. [606]
1.14   The chairman at meetings ..   .. [607]
1.15   The chairman as proxy-holder   ..   .. [608]
1.16   Attendance by company officers ..   .. [609]

SECTION B: VOTING RIGHTS AND MAJORITIES
1.17   Voting rights (creditors)   ..   .. [610]
1.18   Voting rights (members)   ..   .. [611]
1.19   Requisite majorities (creditors)   ..   .. [612]
1.20   Requisite majorities (members)   ..   .. [613]
1.21   Proceedings to obtain agreement on the proposal   ..   .. [614]

SECTION C: IMPLEMENTATION OF THE ARRANGEMENT
1.22   Resolutions to follow approval   ..   .. [615]
1.23   Hand-over of property etc to supervisor ..   .. [616]
1.24   Report of meetings ..   .. [617]
1.25   Revocation or suspension of the arrangement   ..   .. [618]
1.26   Supervisor's accounts and reports ..   .. [619]
1.27   Production of accounts and records to Secretary of State   ..   ..   .. [620]
1.28   Fees, costs, charges and expenses ..   .. [621]
1.29   Completion of the arrangement   ..   .. [622]

CHAPTER 6

GENERAL

1.30   False representations, etc ..   .. [623]

PART 2

ADMINISTRATION PROCEDURE

CHAPTER 1

APPLICATION FOR, AND MAKING OF, THE ORDER

2.1   Affidavit to support petition   ..   .. [624]
2.2   Independent report on company's affairs..   ..   .. [625]
2.3   Contents of affidavit   ..   .. [626]
2.4   Form of petition   ..   .. [627]
2.5   Filing of petition   ..   .. [628]
2.6   Service of petition ..   .. [629]
2.7   Manner in which service to be effected   ..   .. [630]
2.8   Proof of service   ..   .. [631]
2.9   The hearing ..   .. [632]
2.10   Notice and advertisement of administration order   ..   .. [633]

Rule   Para

CHAPTER 2

STATEMENT OF AFFAIRS AND PROPOSALS TO CREDITORS

2.11 Notice requiring statement of affairs .. .. [634]
2.12 Verification and filing .. .. [635]
2.13 Limited disclosure .. .. [636]
2.14 Release from duty to submit statement of affairs; extension of time .. .. .. [637]
2.15 Expenses of statement of affairs .. .. [638]
2.16 Statement to be annexed to proposals .. .. [639]
2.17 Notice of proposals to creditors .. .. [640]

CHAPTER 3

CREDITORS' AND COMPANY MEETINGS

SECTION A: CREDITORS' MEETINGS

2.18 Meeting to consider administrator's proposals .. .. [641]
2.19 Creditors' meetings generally .. .. [642]
2.20 The chairman at meetings .. .. [643]
2.21 Meeting requisitioned by creditors .. .. [644]
2.22 Entitlement to vote.. .. .. [645]
2.23 Admission and rejection of claims .. .. [646]
2.24 Secured creditors .. .. [647]
2.25 Holders of negotiable instruments .. .. [648]
2.26 Retention of title creditors.. .. .. [649]
2.27 Hire-purchase, conditional sale and chattel leasing agreements .. .. .. [650]
2.28 Resolutions and minutes .. .. [651]
2.29 Administrator's report .. .. [652]
2.30 Notices to creditors .. .. [653]

SECTION B: COMPANY MEETINGS

2.31 Venue and conduct of company meeting .. .. [654]

CHAPTER 4

THE CREDITORS' COMMITTEE

2.32 Constitution of committee.. .. .. [655]
2.33 Formalities of establishment .. .. [656]
2.34 Functions and meetings of the committee .. .. [657]
2.35 The chairman at meetings .. .. [658]
2.36 Quorum .. .. [659]
2.37 Committee-members' representatives .. .. [660]
2.38 Resignation.. .. .. [661]
2.39 Termination of membership .. .. [662]
2.40 Removal .. .. [663]
2.41 Vacancies .. .. [664]
2.42 Procedure at meetings .. .. [665]
2.43 Resolutions by post .. .. [666]
2.44 Information from administrator .. .. [667]
2.45 Expenses of members .. .. [668]
2.46 Members' dealings with the company .. .. [669]

CHAPTER 5

THE ADMINISTRATOR

2.47 Fixing of remuneration .. .. [670]
2.48 Recourse to meeting of creditors .. .. [671]
2.49 Recourse to the court .. .. [672]
2.50 Creditors' claim that remuneration is excessive .. .. [673]

Rule   Para
2.51   Disposal of charged property, etc ..   ..   [674]
2.52   Abstract of receipts and payments   ..   ..   [675]
2.53   Resignation ..   ..   [676]
2.54   Administrator deceased   ..   ..   [677]
2.55   Order filling vacancy   ..   ..   [678]

CHAPTER 6

VAT BAD DEBT RELIEF

2.56   Issue of certificate of insolvency   ..   ..   [679]
2.57   Notice to creditors ..   ..   [680]
2.58   Preservation of certificate with company's records   ..   ..   [681]

PART 3

ADMINISTRATIVE RECEIVERSHIP

CHAPTER 1

APPOINTMENT OF ADMINISTRATIVE RECEIVER

3.1   Acceptance of appointment   ..   ..   [682]
3.2   Notice and advertisement of appointment   ..   ..   [683]

CHAPTER 2

STATEMENT OF AFFAIRS AND REPORT TO CREDITORS

3.3   Notice requiring statement of affairs   ..   ..   [684]
3.4   Verification and filing   ..   ..   [685]
3.5   Limited disclosure ..   ..   [686]
3.6   Release from duty to submit statement of affairs; extension of time   ..   ..   [687]
3.7   Expenses of statement of affairs ..   ..   [688]
3.8   Report to creditors ..   ..   [689]

CHAPTER 3

CREDITORS' MEETING

3.9   Procedure for summoning meeting under s 48(2)   ..   ..   [690]
3.10   The chairman at the meeting   ..   ..   [691]
3.11   Voting rights   ..   ..   [692]
3.12   Admission and rejection of claims   ..   ..   [693]
3.13   Quorum   ..   ..   [694]
3.14   Adjournment   ..   ..   [695]
3.15   Resolutions and minutes ..   ..   [696]

CHAPTER 4

THE CREDITORS' COMMITTEE

3.16   Constitution of committee ..   ..   [697]
3.17   Formalities of establishment   ..   ..   [698]
3.18   Functions and meetings of the committee   ..   ..   [699]
3.19   The chairman at meetings ..   ..   [700]
3.20   Quorum   ..   ..   [701]
3.21   Committee-members' representatives   ..   ..   [702]
3.22   Resignation ..   ..   [703]
3.23   Termination of membership   ..   ..   [704]
3.24   Removal   ..   ..   [705]
3.25   Vacancies ..   ..   [706]
3.26   Procedure at meetings   ..   ..   [707]
3.27   Resolutions by post   ..   ..   [708]
3.28   Information from receiver ..   ..   [709]
3.29   Expenses of members   ..   ..   [710]
3.30   Members' dealings with the company   ..   ..   [711]

Rule　　　　　　　　　　　　　　　　　　　　　　　　　　　　　　　　　　　　Para

CHAPTER 5

THE ADMINISTRATIVE RECEIVER (MISCELLANEOUS)

3.31　Disposal of charged property　　..　　...　　..　　..　　..　　..　　..　　..　　[712]
3.32　Abstract of receipts and payments　　..　　..　　..　　..　　..　　..　　[713]
3.33　Resignation..　　..　　..　　..　　..　　..　　..　　..　　..　　..　　[714]
3.34　Receiver deceased ..　　..　　..　　..　　..　　..　　..　　..　　..　　[715]
3.35　Vacation of office　　..　　..　　..　　..　　..　　..　　..　　..　　..　　[716]

CHAPTER 6

VAT BAD DEBT RELIEF

3.36　Issue of certificate of insolvency　　..　　..　　..　　..　　..　　..　　..　　[717]
3.37　Notice to creditors ..　　..　　..　　..　　..　　..　　..　　..　　..　　[718]
3.38　Preservation of certificate with company's records　　..　　..　　..　　..　　[719]

PART 4

COMPANIES WINDING UP

CHAPTER 1

THE SCHEME OF THIS PART OF THE RULES

4.1　Voluntary winding up; winding up by the court ..　　..　　..　　..　　..　　[720]
4.2　Winding up by the court: the various forms of petition ..　　..　　..　　..　　[721]
4.3　Time-limits ..　　..　　..　　..　　..　　..　　..　　..　　..　　[722]

CHAPTER 2

THE STATUTORY DEMAND

(NO CVL APPLICATION)

4.4　Preliminary..　　..　　..　　..　　..　　..　　..　　..　　..　　[723]
4.5　Form and content of statutory demand　　..　　..　　..　　..　　..　　[724]
4.6　Information to be given in statutory demand　　..　　..　　..　　..　　..　　[725]

CHAPTER 3

PETITION TO WINDING-UP ORDER

(NO CVL APPLICATION)

(NO APPLICATION TO PETITION BY CONTRIBUTORIES)

4.7　Presentation and filing of petition　　..　　..　　..　　..　　..　　..　　[726]
4.8　Service of petition ..　　..　　..　　..　　..　　..　　..　　..　　[727]
4.9　Proof of service　　..　　..　　..　　..　　..　　..　　..　　..　　[728]
4.10　Other persons to receive copies of petition　　..　　..　　..　　..　　[729]
4.11　Advertisement of petition ..　　..　　..　　..　　..　　..　　..　　[730]
4.12　Verification of petition　　..　　..　　..　　..　　..　　..　　..　　[731]
4.13　Persons entitled to copy of petition　　..　　..　　..　　..　　..　　[732]
4.14　Certificate of compliance　　..　　..　　..　　..　　..　　..　　..　　[733]
4.15　Leave for petitioner to withdraw ..　　..　　..　　..　　..　　..　　[734]
4.16　Notice of appearance　　..　　..　　..　　..　　..　　..　　..　　[735]
4.17　List of appearances　　..　　..　　..　　..　　..　　..　　..　　[736]
4.18　Affidavit in opposition　　..　　..　　..　　..　　..　　..　　..　　[737]
4.19　Substitution of creditor or contributory for petitioner ..　　..　　..　　..　　[738]
4.20　Notice and settling of winding-up order ..　　..　　..　　..　　..　　[739]
4.21　Transmission and advertisement of order　　..　　..　　..　　..　　[740]

CHAPTER 4

PETITION BY CONTRIBUTORIES

(NO CVL APPLICATION)

4.22　Presentation and service of petition　　..　　..　　..　　..　　..　　[741]
4.23　Return of petition ..　　..　　..　　..　　..　　..　　..　　..　　[742]
4.24　Application of Rules in Chapter 3　　..　　..　　..　　..　　..　　[743]

Rule Para

CHAPTER 5

PROVISIONAL LIQUIDATOR

(NO CVL APPLICATION)

4.25	Appointment of provisional liquidator	[744]
4.26	Order of appointment	[745]
4.27	Deposit	[746]
4.28	Security	[747]
4.29	Failure to give or keep up security	[748]
4.30	Remuneration	[749]
4.31	Termination of appointment	[750]

CHAPTER 6

STATEMENT OF AFFAIRS AND OTHER INFORMATION

4.32	Notice requiring statement of affairs	[751]
4.33	Verification and filing	[752]
4.34–CVL	Statement of affairs	[753]
4.35	Limited disclosure	[754]
4.36	Release from duty to submit statement of affairs; extension of time	[755]
4.37	Expenses of statement of affairs	[756]
4.38–CVL	Expenses of statement of affairs	[757]
4.39	Submission of accounts	[758]
4.40–CVL	Submission of accounts	[759]
4.41–CVL	Expenses of preparing accounts	[760]
4.42	Further disclosure	[761]

CHAPTER 7

INFORMATION TO CREDITORS AND CONTRIBUTORIES

4.43	Reports by official receiver	[762]
4.44	Meaning of "creditors"	[763]
4.45	Report where statement of affairs lodged	[764]
4.46	Statement of affairs dispensed with	[765]
4.47	General rule as to reporting	[766]
4.48	Winding up stayed	[767]
4.49–CVL	Information to creditors and contributories	[768]

CHAPTER 8

MEETINGS OF CREDITORS AND CONTRIBUTORIES

SECTION A: RULES OF GENERAL APPLICATION

4.50	First meetings	[769]
4.51–CVL	First meeting of creditors	[770]
4.52	Business at first meetings in the liquidation	[771]
4.53–CVL	Business at meeting under s 95 or 98	[772]
4.54	General power to call meetings	[773]
4.55	The chairman at meetings	[774]
4.56–CVL	The chairman at meetings	[775]
4.57	Requisitioned meetings	[776]
4.58	Attendance at meetings of company's personnel	[777]
4.59	Notice of meetings by advertisement only	[778]
4.60	Venue	[779]
4.61	Expenses of summoning meetings	[780]
4.62–CVL	Expenses of meeting under s 98	[781]
4.63	Resolutions	[782]
4.64	Chairman of meeting as proxy-holder	[783]
4.65	Suspension and adjournment	[784]
4.66	Quorum	[785]
4.67	Entitlement to vote (creditors)	[786]
4.68–CVL	Chairman's discretion to allow vote	[787]
4.69	Entitlement to vote (contributories)	[788]
4.70	Admission and rejection of proof (creditors' meeting)	[789]
4.71	Record of proceedings	[790]

Rule   Para
                    SECTION B: WINDING UP OF RECOGNISED BANKS, ETC
4.72   Additional provisions as regards certain meetings   ..   ..   [791]

                                 CHAPTER 9

                       PROOF OF DEBTS IN A LIQUIDATION

                        SECTION A: PROCEDURE FOR PROVING

4.73   Meaning of "prove"   ..   ..   [792]
4.74   Supply of forms   ..   ..   [793]
4.75   Contents of proof ..   ..   [794]
4.76–CVL   Particulars of creditor's claim   ..   ..   [795]
4.77   Claim established by affidavit   ..   ..   [796]
4.78   Cost of proving   ..   ..   [797]
4.79   Liquidator to allow inspection of proofs ..   ..   [798]
4.80   Transmission of proofs to liquidator   ..   ..   [799]
4.81   New liquidator appointed ..   ..   [800]
4.82   Admission and rejection of proofs for dividend ..   ..   [801]
4.83   Appeal against decision on proof ..   ..   [802]
4.84   Withdrawal or variation of proof ..   ..   [803]
4.85   Expunging of proof by the court ..   ..   [804]

                        SECTION B: QUANTIFICATION OF CLAIM

4.86   Estimate of quantum   ..   ..   [805]
4.87   Negotiable instruments, etc   ..   ..   [806]
4.88   Secured creditors   ..   ..   [807]
4.89   Discounts   ..   ..   [808]
4.90   Mutual credit and set-off   ..   ..   [809]
4.91   Debt in foreign currency   ..   ..   [810]
4.92   Payments of a periodical nature   ..   ..   [811]
4.93   Interest   ..   ..   [812]
4.94   Debt payable at future time   ..   ..   [813]

                                 CHAPTER 10

                              SECURED CREDITORS

4.95   Value of security   ..   ..   [814]
4.96   Surrender for non-disclosure   ..   ..   [815]
4.97   Redemption by liquidator ..   ..   [816]
4.98   Test of security's value   ..   ..   [817]
4.99   Realisation of security by creditor   ..   ..   [818]

                                 CHAPTER 11

                               THE LIQUIDATOR

                   SECTION A: APPOINTMENT AND ASSOCIATED FORMALITIES

4.100   Appointment by creditors or contributories   ..   ..   [819]
4.101–CVL   Appointment by creditors or by the company   ..   ..   ..   [820]
4.102   Appointment by the court ..   ..   [821]
4.103–CVL   Appointment by the court ..   ..   [822]
4.104   Appointment by Secretary of State   ..   ..   [823]
4.105   Authentication of liquidator's appointment   ..   ..   [824]
4.106   Appointment to be advertised and registered   ..   ..   [825]
4.107   Hand-over of assets to liquidator ..   ..   [826]

               SECTION B: RESIGNATION AND REMOVAL; VACATION OF OFFICE

4.108   Creditors' meeting to receive liquidator's resignation   ..   ..   ..   [827]
4.109   Action following acceptance of resignation   ..   ..   [828]
4.110–CVL   Action following acceptance of resignation   ..   ..   ..   [829]
4.111   Leave to resign granted by the court   ..   ..   [830]
4.112   Advertisement of resignation   ..   ..   [831]
4.113   Meeting of creditors to remove liquidator   ..   ..   [832]
4.114–CVL   Meeting of creditors to remove liquidator ..   ..   [833]

Rule   Para
4.115   Court's power to regulate meetings under Rules 4.113, 4.114–CVL .. .. .. [834]
4.116   Procedure on removal .. .. [835]
4.117–CVL   Procedure on removal .. .. [836]
4.118   Advertisement of removal .. .. [837]
4.119   Removal of liquidator by the court .. .. [838]
4.120–CVL   Removal of liquidator by the court .. .. [839]
4.121   Release of resigning or removed liquidator .. .. [840]
4.122–CVL   Release of resigning or removed liquidator .. .. [841]
4.123   Removal of liquidator by Secretary of State .. .. [842]

SECTION C: RELEASE ON COMPLETION OF ADMINISTRATION

4.124   Release of official receiver .. .. [843]
4.125   Final meeting .. .. [844]
4.126–CVL   Final meeting .. .. [845]

SECTION D: REMUNERATION

4.127   Fixing of remuneration .. .. [846]
4.128   Other matters affecting remuneration .. .. [847]
4.129   Recourse of liquidator to meeting of creditors .. .. [848]
4.130   Recourse to the court .. .. [849]
4.131   Creditors' claim that remuneration is excessive .. .. [850]

SECTION E: SUPPLEMENTARY PROVISIONS

4.132   Liquidator deceased .. .. [851]
4.133–CVL   Liquidator deceased .. .. [852]
4.134   Loss of qualification as insolvency practitioner .. .. [853]
4.135–CVL   Loss of qualification as insolvency practitioner .. .. [854]
4.136–CVL   Vacation of office on making of winding-up order .. .. .. [855]
4.137   Notice to official receiver of intention to vacate office .. .. [856]
4.138   Liquidator's duties on vacating office .. .. [857]

SECTION F: THE LIQUIDATOR IN A MEMBERS' VOLUNTARY WINDING-UP

4.139   Appointment by the company .. .. [858]
4.140   Appointment by the court .. .. [859]
4.141   Authentication of liquidator's appointment .. .. [860]
4.142   Company meeting to receive liquidator's resignation .. .. [861]
4.143   Removal of liquidator by the court .. .. [862]
4.144   Release of resigning or removed liquidator .. .. [863]
4.145   Liquidator deceased .. .. [864]
4.146   Loss of qualification as insolvency practitioner .. .. [865]
4.147   Vacation of office on making of winding-up order .. .. [866]
4.148   Liquidator's duties on vacating office .. .. [867]

SECTION G: RULES APPLYING IN EVERY WINDING UP, WHETHER VOLUNTARY OR BY THE COURT

4.149   Power of court to set aside certain transactions .. .. [868]
4.150   Rule against solicitation .. .. [869]

CHAPTER 12

THE LIQUIDATION COMMITTEE

4.151   Preliminary .. .. [870]
4.152   Membership of committee .. .. [871]
4.153   Formalities of establishment .. .. [872]
4.154   Committee established by contributories .. .. [873]
4.155   Obligations of liquidator to committee .. .. [874]
4.156   Meetings of the committee .. .. [875]
4.157   The chairman at meetings .. .. [876]
4.158   Quorum .. .. [877]
4.159   Committee-members' representatives .. .. [878]
4.160   Resignation .. .. [879]
4.161   Termination of membership .. .. [880]
4.162   Removal .. .. [881]
4.163   Vacancy (creditor members) .. .. [882]

Rule		Para
4.164	Vacancy (contributory members)	[883]
4.165	Voting rights and resolutions	[884]
4.166–CVL	Voting rights and resolutions	[885]
4.167	Resolutions by post	[886]
4.168	Liquidator's reports	[887]
4.169	Expenses of members, etc	[888]
4.170	Dealings by committee-members and others	[889]
4.171	Composition of committee when creditors paid in full	[890]
4.172	Committee's functions vested in Secretary of State	[891]

CHAPTER 13

THE LIQUIDATION COMMITTEE WHERE WINDING UP FOLLOWS IMMEDIATELY ON ADMINISTRATION

(NO CVL APPLICATION)

4.173	Preliminary	[892]
4.174	Continuation of creditors' committee	[893]
4.175	Membership of committee	[894]
4.176	Liquidator's certificate	[895]
4.177	Obligations of liquidator to committee	[896]
4.178	Application of Chapter 12	[897]

CHAPTER 14

COLLECTION AND DISTRIBUTION OF COMPANY'S ASSETS BY LIQUIDATOR

4.179	General duties of liquidator	[898]
4.180	Manner of distributing assets	[899]
4.181	Debts of insolvent company to rank equally	[900]
4.182	Supplementary provisions as to dividend	[901]
4.183	Division of unsold assets	[902]
4.184	General powers of liquidator	[903]
4.185	Enforced delivery up of company's property	[904]
4.186	Final distribution	[905]

CHAPTER 15

DISCLAIMER

4.187	Liquidator's notice of disclaimer	[906]
4.188	Communication of disclaimer to persons interested	[907]
4.189	Additional notices	[908]
4.190	Duty to keep court informed	[909]
4.191	Application by interested party under s 178(5)	[910]
4.192	Interest in property to be declared on request	[911]
4.193	Disclaimer presumed valid and effective	[912]
4.194	Application for exercise of court's powers under s 181	[913]

CHAPTER 16

SETTLEMENT OF LIST OF CONTRIBUTORIES

(NO CVL APPLICATION)

4.195	Preliminary	[914]
4.196	Duty of liquidator to settle list	[915]
4.197	Form of list	[916]
4.198	Procedure for settling list	[917]
4.199	Application to court for variation of the list	[918]
4.200	Variation of, or addition to, the list	[919]
4.201	Costs not to fall on official receiver	[920]

CHAPTER 17

CALLS

(NO CVL APPLICATION)

4.202	Calls by liquidator	[921]
4.203	Control by liquidation committee	[922]

Rule   Para
4.204 Application to court for leave to make a call .. .. [923]
4.205 Making and enforcement of the call .. .. [924]

CHAPTER 18

SPECIAL MANAGER

4.206 Appointment and remuneration .. .. [925]
4.207 Security .. .. [926]
4.208 Failure to give or keep up security .. .. [927]
4.209 Accounting .. .. [928]
4.210 Termination of appointment .. .. [929]

CHAPTER 19

PUBLIC EXAMINATION OF COMPANY OFFICERS AND OTHERS

4.211 Order for public examination .. .. [930]
4.212 Notice of hearing .. .. [931]
4.213 Order on request by creditors or contributories .. .. [932]
4.214 Witness unfit for examination .. .. [933]
4.215 Procedure at hearing .. .. [934]
4.216 Adjournment .. .. [935]
4.217 Expenses of examination .. .. [936]

CHAPTER 20

ORDER OF PAYMENT OF COSTS, ETC, OUT OF ASSETS

4.218 General rule as to priority .. .. [937]
4.219 Winding up commencing as voluntary .. .. [938]
4.220 Saving for powers of the court .. .. [939]

CHAPTER 21

MISCELLANEOUS RULES

SECTION A: RETURN OF CAPITAL

(NO CVL APPLICATION)

4.221 Application to court for order authorising return .. .. [940]
4.222 Procedure for return .. .. [941]

SECTION B: CONCLUSION OF WINDING UP

4.223–CVL Statements to registrar of companies under s 192 .. .. [942]

SECTION C: DISSOLUTION AFTER WINDING UP

4.224 Secretary of State's directions under ss 203, 205 .. .. [943]
4.225 Procedure following appeal under s 203(4) or 205(4) .. .. .. [944]

CHAPTER 22

LEAVE TO ACT AS DIRECTOR, ETC, OF COMPANY WITH PROHIBITED NAME (SECTION 216 OF THE ACT)

4.226 Preliminary .. .. [945]
4.227 Application for leave under s 216(3) .. .. [946]
4.228 First excepted case .. .. [947]
4.229 Second excepted case .. .. [948]
4.230 Third excepted case .. .. [949]

THE SECOND GROUP OF PARTS

INDIVIDUAL INSOLVENCY; BANKRUPTCY

PART 5

INDIVIDUAL VOLUNTARY ARRANGEMENTS

5.1 Introductory .. .. [950]

Rule   Para

SECTION A: THE DEBTOR'S PROPOSAL

5.2   Preparation of proposal .. .. [951]
5.3   Contents of proposal .. .. [952]
5.4   Notice to intended nominee .. .. [953]
5.5   Application for interim order .. .. [954]
5.6   Hearing of the application.. .. .. [955]
5.7   Action to follow making of order .. .. [956]
5.8   Statement of affairs .. .. [957]
5.9   Additional disclosure for assistance of nominee .. .. [958]
5.10 Nominee's report on the proposal.. .. .. [959]
5.11 Replacement of nominee .. .. [960]

SECTION B: ACTION ON THE PROPOSAL; CREDITORS' MEETING

5.12 Consideration of nominee's report .. .. [961]
5.13 Summoning of creditors' meeting .. .. [962]
5.14 Creditors' meeting: supplementary .. .. [963]
5.15 The chairman at the meeting .. .. [964]
5.16 The chairman as proxy-holder .. .. [965]
5.17 Voting rights .. .. [966]
5.18 Requisite majorities .. .. [967]
5.19 Proceedings to obtain agreement on the proposal .. .. [968]

SECTION C: IMPLEMENTATION OF THE ARRANGEMENT

5.20 Resolutions to follow approval .. .. [969]
5.21 Hand-over of property, etc to supervisor .. .. [970]
5.22 Report of creditors' meeting .. .. [971]
5.23 Register of voluntary arrangements .. .. [972]
5.24 Reports to Secretary of State .. .. [973]
5.25 Revocation or suspension of the arrangement .. .. [974]
5.26 Supervisor's accounts and reports.. .. .. [975]
5.27 Production of accounts and records to Secretary of State .. .. .. [976]
5.28 Fees, costs, charges and expenses .. .. [977]
5.29 Completion of the arrangement .. .. [978]

SECTION D: GENERAL

5.30 False representations, etc .. .. [979]

PART 6

BANKRUPTCY

CHAPTER 1

THE STATUTORY DEMAND

6.1   Form and content of statutory demand .. .. [980]
6.2   Information to be given in statutory demand .. .. [981]
6.3   Requirements as to service .. .. [982]
6.4   Application to set aside statutory demand .. .. [983]
6.5   Hearing of application to set aside .. .. [984]

CHAPTER 2

BANKRUPTCY PETITION (CREDITOR'S)

6.6   Preliminary.. .. .. [985]
6.7   Identification of debtor .. .. [986]
6.8   Identification of debt .. .. [987]
6.9   Court in which petition to be presented .. .. [988]
6.10 Procedure for presentation and filing .. .. [989]
6.11 Proof of service of statutory demand .. .. [990]
6.12 Verification of petition .. .. [991]
6.13 Notice to Chief Land Registrar .. .. [992]
6.14 Service of petition .. .. [993]
6.15 Proof of service .. .. [994]
6.16 Death of debtor before service .. .. [995]

Rule   Para
6.17 Security for costs (s 268(2) only) ..   .. [996]
6.18 Hearing of petition ..   .. [997]
6.19 Petition against two or more debtors   ..   .. [998]
6.20 Petition by moneylender ..   .. [999]
6.21 Petition opposed by debtor   ..   .. [1000]
6.22 Amendment of petition   ..   .. [1001]
6.23 Notice by persons intending to appear   ..   .. [1002]
6.24 List of appearances   ..   .. [1003]
6.25 Decision on the hearing   ..   .. [1004]
6.26 Non-appearance of creditor   ..   .. [1005]
6.27 Vacating registration on dismissal of petition   ..   .. [1006]
6.28 Extension of time for hearing   ..   .. [1007]
6.29 Adjournment   ..   .. [1008]
6.30 Substitution of petitioner ..   .. [1009]
6.31 Change of carriage of petition   ..   .. [1010]
6.32 Petitioner seeking dismissal or leave to withdraw   ..   .. [1011]
6.33 Settlement and content of bankruptcy order   .. .   . [1012]
6.34 Action to follow making of order ..   .. [1013]
6.35 Amendment of title of proceedings   ..   .. [1014]
6.36 Old bankruptcy notices   ..   .. [1015]

CHAPTER 3

BANKRUPTCY PETITION (DEBTOR'S)

6.37 Preliminary..   ..   .. [1016]
6.38 Identification of debtor   ..   .. [1017]
6.39 Admission of insolvency ..   .. [1018]
6.40 Court in which petiton to be filed ..   .. [1019]
6.41 Statement of affairs   ..   .. [1020]
6.42 Procedure for presentation and filing   ..   .. [1021]
6.43 Notice to Chief Land Registrar   ..   .. [1022]
6.44 Report of insolvency practitioner ..   .. [1023]
6.45 Settlement and content of bankruptcy order   ..   .. [1024]
6.46 Action to follow making of order ..   .. [1025]
6.47 Amendment of title of proceedings   ..   .. [1026]
6.48 Certificate of summary administration   ..   .. [1027]
6.49 Duty of official receiver in summary administration   ..   .. [1028]
6.50 Revocation of certificate of summary administration   ..   .. [1029]

CHAPTER 4

THE INTERIM RECEIVER

6.51 Application for appointment of interim receiver   ..   .. [1030]
6.52 Order of appointment   ..   .. [1031]
6.53 Deposit   ..   .. [1032]
6.54 Security   ..   .. [1033]
6.55 Failure to give or keep up security   ..   .. [1034]
6.56 Remuneration   ..   .. [1035]
6.57 Termination of appointment   ..   .. [1036]

CHAPTER 5

DISCLOSURE BY BANKRUPT WITH RESPECT TO THE STATE OF HIS AFFAIRS

SECTION A : CREDITOR'S PETITION

6.58 Preliminary..   ..   .. [1037]
6.59 The statement of affairs   ..   .. [1038]
6.60 Verification and filing   ..   .. [1039]
6.61 Limited disclosure ..   .. [1040]
6.62 Release from duty to submit statement; extension of time   ..   ..   .. [1041]
6.63 Expenses of statement of affairs ..   .. [1042]
6.64 Requirement to submit accounts ..   .. [1043]
6.65 Submission and filing of accounts..   ..   .. [1044]
6.66 Further disclosure ..   .. [1045]

Rule   Para
SECTION B: DEBTOR'S PETITION

6.67   Preliminary .. .. [1046]
6.68   Contents of statement .. .. [1047]
6.69   Requirement to submit accounts .. .. [1048]
6.70   Submission and filing of accounts .. .. [1049]
6.71   Expenses of preparing accounts .. .. [1050]
6.72   Further disclosure .. .. [1051]

CHAPTER 6

INFORMATION TO CREDITORS

6.73   General duty of official receiver .. .. [1052]
6.74   Those entitled to be informed .. .. [1053]
6.75   Report where statement of affairs lodged .. .. [1054]
6.76   Statement of affairs dispensed with .. .. [1055]
6.77   General rule as to reporting .. .. [1056]
6.78   Bankruptcy order annulled .. .. [1057]

CHAPTER 7

CREDITORS' MEETINGS

6.79   First meeting of creditors .. .. [1058]
6.80   Business at first meeting .. .. [1059]
6.81   General power to call meetings .. .. [1060]
6.82   The chairman at a meeting .. .. [1061]
6.83   Requisitioned meetings .. .. [1062]
6.84   Attendance at meetings of bankrupt, etc .. .. [1063]
6.85   Notice of meetings by advertisement only .. .. [1064]
6.86   Venue of meetings .. .. [1065]
6.87   Expenses of summoning meetings .. .. [1066]
6.88   Resolutions .. .. [1067]
6.89   Chairman of meeting as proxy-holder .. .. [1068]
6.90   Suspension of meeting .. .. [1069]
6.91   Adjournment .. .. [1070]
6.92   Quorum .. .. [1071]
6.93   Entitlement to vote .. .. [1072]
6.94   Admission and rejection of proof .. .. [1073]
6.95   Record of proceedings .. .. [1074]

CHAPTER 8

PROOF OF BANKRUPTCY DEBTS

SECTION A: PROCEDURE FOR PROVING

6.96   Meaning of "prove" .. .. [1075]
6.97   Supply of forms .. .. [1076]
6.98   Contents of proof .. .. [1077]
6.99   Claim established by affidavit .. .. [1078]
6.100 Cost of proving .. .. [1079]
6.101 Trustee to allow inspection of proofs .. .. [1080]
6.102 Proof of licensed moneylender .. .. [1081]
6.103 Transmission of proofs to trustee .. .. [1082]
6.104 Admission and rejection of proofs for dividend .. .. .. [1083]
6.105 Appeal against decision on proof .. .. [1084]
6.106 Withdrawal or variation of proof .. .. [1085]
6.107 Expunging of proof by the court .. .. [1086]

SECTION B: QUANTIFICATION OF CLAIM

6.108 Negotiable instruments, etc .. .. [1087]
6.109 Secured creditors .. .. [1088]
6.110 Discounts .. .. [1089]
6.111 Debt in foreign currency .. .. [1090]
6.112 Payments of a periodical nature .. .. [1091]
6.113 Interest .. .. [1092]
6.114 Debt payable at future time .. .. [1093]

Rule Para

CHAPTER 9

SECURED CREDITORS

6.115 Value of security .. .. [1094]
6.116 Surrender for non-disclosure .. .. [1095]
6.117 Redemption by trustee .. .. [1096]
6.118 Test of security's value .. .. [1097]
6.119 Realisation of security by creditor .. .. [1098]

CHAPTER 10

THE TRUSTEE IN BANKRUPTCY

SECTION A: APPOINTMENT AND ASSOCIATED FORMALITIES

6.120 Appointment by creditors' meeting .. .. [1099]
6.121 Appointment by the court .. .. [1100]
6.122 Appointment by Secretary of State .. .. [1101]
6.123 Authentication of trustee's appointment .. .. [1102]
6.124 Advertisement of appointment .. .. [1103]
6.125 Hand-over of estate to trustee .. .. [1104]

SECTION B: RESIGNATION AND REMOVAL; VACATION OF OFFICE

6.126 Creditors' meeting to receive trustee's resignation .. .. .. [1105]
6.127 Action following acceptance of resignation .. .. [1106]
6.128 Leave to resign granted by the court .. .. [1107]
6.129 Meeting of creditors to remove trustee .. .. [1108]
6.130 Court's power to regulate meeting under Rule 6.129 .. .. .. [1109]
6.131 Procedure on removal .. .. [1110]
6.132 Removal of trustee by the court .. .. [1111]
6.133 Removal of trustee by Secretary of State .. .. [1112]
6.134 Advertisement of resignation or removal .. .. [1113]
6.135 Release of resigning or removed trustee .. .. [1114]

SECTION C: RELEASE ON COMPLETION OF ADMINISTRATION

6.136 Release of official receiver .. .. [1115]
6.137 Final meeting of creditors .. .. [1116]

SECTION D: REMUNERATION

6.138 Fixing of remuneration .. .. [1117]
6.139 Other matters affecting remuneration .. .. [1118]
6.140 Recourse of trustee to meeting of creditors .. .. [1119]
6.141 Recourse to the court .. .. [1120]
6.142 Creditor's claim that remuneration is excessive .. .. [1121]

SECTION E: SUPPLEMENTARY PROVISIONS

6.143 Trustee deceased .. .. [1122]
6.144 Loss of qualification as insolvency practitioner .. .. [1123]
6.145 Notice to official receiver of intention to vacate office .. .. [1124]
6.146 Trustee's duties on vacating office .. .. [1125]
6.147 Power of court to set aside certain transactions .. .. [1126]
6.148 Rule against solicitation .. .. [1127]
6.149 Enforcement of trustee's obligations to official receiver .. .. [1128]

CHAPTER 11

THE CREDITORS' COMMITTEE

6.150 Membership of creditors' committee .. .. [1129]
6.151 Formalities of establishment .. .. [1130]
6.152 Obligations of trustee to committee .. .. [1131]
6.153 Meetings of the committee .. .. [1132]
6.154 The chairman at meetings .. .. [1133]
6.155 Quorum .. .. [1134]
6.156 Committee-members' representatives .. .. [1135]

Rule		Para
6.157	Resignation ..	[1136]
6.158	Termination of membership	[1137]
6.159	Removal	[1138]
6.160	Vacancies ..	[1139]
6.161	Voting rights and resolutions	[1140]
6.162	Resolutions by post	[1141]
6.163	Trustee's reports	[1142]
6.164	Expenses of members, etc ..	[1143]
6.165	Dealings by committee-members and others	[1144]
6.166	Committee's functions vested in Secretary of State	[1145]

CHAPTER 12

SPECIAL MANAGER

6.167	Appointment and remuneration	[1146]
6.168	Security	[1147]
6.169	Failure to give or keep up security	[1148]
6.170	Accounting ..	[1149]
6.171	Termination of appointment	[1150]

CHAPTER 13

PUBLIC EXAMINATION OF BANKRUPT

6.172	Order for public examination	[1151]
6.173	Order on request by creditors	[1152]
6.174	Bankrupt unfit for examination	[1153]
6.175	Procedure at hearing	[1154]
6.176	Adjournment	[1155]
6.177	Expenses of examination ..	[1156]

CHAPTER 14

DISCLAIMER

6.178	Trustee's notice of disclaimer	[1157]
6.179	Communication of disclaimer to persons interested	[1158]
6.180	Additional notices ..	[1159]
6.181	Duty to keep court informed	[1160]
6.182	Application for leave to disclaim ..	[1161]
6.183	Application by interested party under s 316	[1162]
6.184	Interest in property to be declared on request	[1163]
6.185	Disclaimer presumed valid and effective ..	[1164]
6.186	Application for exercise of court's powers under s 320 ..	[1165]

CHAPTER 15

REPLACEMENT OF EXEMPT PROPERTY

6.187	Purchase of replacement property	[1166]
6.188	Money provided in lieu of sale	[1167]

CHAPTER 16

INCOME PAYMENTS ORDERS

6.189	Application for order	[1168]
6.190	Action to follow making of order ..	[1169]
6.191	Variation of order ..	[1170]
6.192	Order to payor of income: administration	[1171]
6.193	Review of order	[1172]

CHAPTER 17

ACTION BY COURT UNDER SECTION 369; ORDER TO INLAND REVENUE OFFICIAL

6.194	Application for order	[1173]
6.195	Making and service of the order ..	[1174]
6.196	Custody of documents	[1175]

Rule   Para

CHAPTER 18

MORTGAGED PROPERTY

6.197   Claim by mortgagee of land   ..   ..   [1176]
6.198   Power of court to order sale   ..   ..   [1177]
6.199   Proceeds of sale   ..   ..   [1178]

CHAPTER 19

AFTER-ACQUIRED PROPERTY

6.200   Duties of bankrupt in respect of after-acquired property   ..   ..   ..   [1179]
6.201   Trustee's recourse to disponee of property   ..   ..   [1180]
6.202   Expenses of getting in property for the estate   ..   ..   [1181]

CHAPTER 20

LEAVE TO ACT AS DIRECTOR, ETC

6.203   Application for leave   ..   ..   [1182]
6.204   Report of official receiver ..   ..   [1183]
6.205   Court's order on application   ..   ..   [1184]

CHAPTER 21

ANNULMENT OF BANKRUPTCY ORDER

6.206   Application for annulment   ..   ..   [1185]
6.207   Report by trustee   ..   ..   [1186]
6.208   Power of court to stay proceedings   ..   ..   [1187]
6.209   Notice to creditors who have not proved ..   ..   [1188]
6.210   The hearing..   ..   ..   [1189]
6.211   Matters to be proved under s 282(1)(*b*)   ..   ..   [1190]
6.212   Notice to creditors ..   ..   [1191]
6.213   Other matters arising on annulment ..   ..   [1192]
6.214   Trustee's final accounts   ..   ..   [1193]

CHAPTER 22

DISCHARGE

6.215   Application for suspension of discharge ..   ..   [1194]
6.216   Lifting of suspension of discharge   ..   ..   [1195]
6.217   Application by bankrupt for discharge   ..   ..   [1196]
6.218   Report of official receiver ..   ..   [1197]
6.219   Order of discharge on application   ..   ..   [1198]
6.220   Certificate of discharge   ..   ..   [1199]
6.221   Deferment of issue of order pending appeal   ..   ..   [1200]
6.222   Costs under this Chapter ..   ..   [1201]
6.223   Bankrupt's debts surviving discharge   ..   ..   [1202]

CHAPTER 23

ORDER OF PAYMENT OF COSTS, ETC, OUT OF ESTATE

6.224   General rule as to priority ..   ..   [1203]

CHAPTER 24

SECOND BANKRUPTCY

6.225   Scope of this Chapter   ..   ..   [1204]
6.226   General duty of existing trustee   ..   ..   [1205]
6.227   Delivery up to later trustee   ..   ..   [1206]
6.228   Existing trustee's expenses   ..   ..   [1207]

Rule   Para

CHAPTER 25

CRIMINAL BANKRUPTCY

6.229 Presentation of petition   .. .. [1208]
6.230 Status and functions of Official Petitioner   .. .. [1209]
6.231 Interim receivership   .. .. [1210]
6.232 Proof of bankruptcy debts and notice of order   .. .. [1211]
6.233 Meetings under the Rules ..   .. [1212]
6.234 Trustee in bankruptcy; creditors' committee; annulment of bankruptcy order   .. [1213]

CHAPTER 26

MISCELLANEOUS RULES IN BANKRUPTCY

6.235 Bankruptcy of solicitors   .. .. [1214]
6.236 Consolidation of petitions ..   .. [1215]
6.237 Bankrupt's dwelling-house and home   .. .. [1216]

THE THIRD GROUP OF PARTS

PART 7

COURT PROCEDURE AND PRACTICE

CHAPTER 1

APPLICATIONS

7.1   Preliminary ..   .. [1217]
7.2   Interpretation   .. .. [1218]
7.3   Form and contents of application ..   .. [1219]
7.4   Filing and service of application ..   .. [1220]
7.5   Other hearings *ex parte*   .. .. [1221]
7.6   Hearing of application   .. .. [1222]
7.7   Use of affidavit evidence   .. .. [1223]
7.8   Filing and service of affidavits   .. .. [1224]
7.9   Use of reports   .. .. [1225]
7.10 Adjournment of hearing; directions   .. .. [1226]

CHAPTER 2

TRANSFER OF PROCEEDINGS BETWEEN COURTS

7.11 General power of transfer ..   .. [1227]
7.12 Proceedings commenced in wrong court ..   .. [1228]
7.13 Applications for transfer   .. .. [1229]
7.14 Procedure following order for transfer   .. .. [1230]
7.15 Consequential transfer of other proceedings   .. .. [1231]

CHAPTER 3

SHORTHAND WRITERS

7.16 Nomination and appointment of shorthand writers   .. .. [1232]
7.17 Remuneration   .. .. [1233]
7.18 Cost of shorthand note   .. .. [1234]

CHAPTER 4

ENFORCEMENT PROCEDURES

7.19 Enforcement of court orders   .. .. [1235]
7.20 Orders enforcing compliance with the Rules   .. .. [1236]
7.21 Warrants (general provisions)   .. .. [1237]
7.22 Warrants under ss 134, 364   .. .. [1238]
7.23 Warrants under ss 236, 366   .. .. [1239]
7.24 Execution of warrants outside court's district   .. .. [1240]
7.25 Warrants under s 365   .. .. [1241]

Rule   Para

CHAPTER 5

COURT RECORDS AND RETURNS

7.26 Title of proceedings .. .. [1242]
7.27 Court records .. .. [1243]
7.28 Inspection of records .. .. [1244]
7.29 Returns to Secretary of State .. .. [1245]
7.30 File of court proceedings .. .. [1246]
7.31 Right to inspect the file .. .. [1247]
7.32 Filing of Gazette notices and advertisements .. .. [1248]

CHAPTER 6

COSTS AND TAXATION

7.33 Application of Rules of Supreme Court and County Court Rules .. .. [1249]
7.34 Requirement to tax costs .. .. [1250]
7.35 Procedure where taxation required .. .. [1251]
7.36 Costs of sheriff .. .. [1252]
7.37 Petitions presented by insolvents .. .. [1253]
7.38 Costs paid otherwise than out of insolvent estate .. .. .. [1254]
7.39 Award of costs against official receiver or responsible insolvency practitioner .. [1255]
7.40 Applications for costs .. .. [1256]
7.41 Costs and expenses of witnesses .. .. [1257]
7.42 Certificate of taxation .. .. [1258]

CHAPTER 7

PERSONS INCAPABLE OF MANAGING THEIR AFFAIRS

7.43 Introductory .. .. [1259]
7.44 Appointment of another person to act .. .. [1260]
7.45 Affidavit in support of application .. .. [1261]
7.46 Service of notices following appointment .. .. [1262]

CHAPTER 8

APPEALS IN INSOLVENCY PROCEEDINGS

7.47 Appeals and reviews of court orders (winding up) .. .. .. [1263]
7.48 Appeals in bankruptcy .. .. [1264]
7.49 Procedure on appeal .. .. [1265]
7.50 Appeal from Secretary of State or official receiver .. .. .. [1266]

CHAPTER 9

GENERAL

7.51 Principal court rules and practice to apply .. .. [1267]
7.52 Right of audience .. .. [1268]
7.53 Right of attendance (company insolvency) .. .. [1269]
7.54 Insolvency practitioner's solicitor .. .. [1270]
7.55 Formal defects .. .. [1271]
7.56 Restriction on concurrent proceedings and remedies .. .. .. [1272]
7.57 Affidavits .. .. [1273]
7.58 Security in court .. .. [1274]
7.59 Payment into court .. .. [1275]
7.60 Discovery .. .. [1276]
7.61 Office copies of documents .. .. [1277]

PART 8

PROXIES AND COMPANY REPRESENTATION

8.1 Definition of "proxy" .. .. [1278]
8.2 Issue and use of forms .. .. [1279]
8.3 Use of proxies at meetings .. .. [1280]
8.4 Retention of proxies .. .. [1281]
8.5 Right of inspection .. .. [1282]

Rule   Para

8.6   Proxy-holder with financial interest   ..   ..   [1283]

8.7   Company representation   ..   ..   [1284]

PART 9

EXAMINATION OF PERSONS CONCERNED IN COMPANY AND INDIVIDUAL INSOLVENCY

9.1   Preliminary ..   ..   [1285]

9.2   Form and contents of application ..   ..   [1286]

9.3   Order for examination, etc   ..   ..   [1287]

9.4   Procedure for examination   ..   ..   [1288]

9.5   Record of examination   ..   ..   [1289]

9.6   Costs of proceedings under ss 236, 366   ..   ..   [1290]

PART 10

OFFICIAL RECEIVERS

10.1   Appointment of official receivers ..   ..   [1291]

10.2   Persons entitled to act on official receiver's behalf   ..   ..   ..   [1292]

10.3   Application for directions ..   ..   [1293]

10.4   Official receiver's expenses   ..   ..   [1294]

PART 11

DECLARATION AND PAYMENT OF DIVIDEND (WINDING UP AND BANKRUPTCY)

11.1   Preliminary ..   ..   [1295]

11.2   Notice of intended dividend   ..   ..   [1296]

11.3   Final admission/rejection of proofs   ..   ..   [1297]

11.4   Postponement or cancellation of dividend   ..   ..   ..   [1298]

11.5   Decision to declare dividend   ..   ..   [1299]

11.6   Notice of declaration   ..   ..   [1300]

11.7   Notice of no, or no further, dividend   ..   ..   [1301]

11.8   Proof altered after payment of dividend ..   ..   [1302]

11.9   Secured creditors   ..   ..   [1303]

11.10   Disqualification from dividend   ..   ..   [1304]

11.11   Assignment of right to dividend   ..   ..   [1305]

11.12   Preferential creditors   ..   ..   [1306]

11.13   Debt payable at future time   ..   ..   [1307]

PART 12

MISCELLANEOUS AND GENERAL

12.1   Power of Secretary of State to regulate certain matters ..   ..   ..   [1308]

12.2   Costs, expenses, etc   ..   ..   [1309]

12.3   Provable debts   ..   ..   [1310]

12.4   Notices   ..   ..   [1311]

12.5   Evidence of proceedings at meetings   ..   ..   [1312]

12.6   Documents issuing from Secretary of State   ..   ..   ..   [1313]

12.7   Forms for use in insolvency proceedings ..   ..   [1314]

12.8   Insolvency practitioner's security ..   ..   [1315]

12.9   Time-limits ..   ..   [1316]

12.10   Service by post   ..   ..   [1317]

12.11   General provisions as to service   ..   ..   [1318]

12.12   Service outside the jurisdiction   ..   ..   [1319]

12.13   Confidentiality of documents   ..   ..   [1320]

12.14   Notices sent simultaneously to the same person ..   ..   ..   [1321]

12.15   Right to copy documents ..   ..   [1322]

12.16   Non-receipt of notice of meeting ..   ..   [1323]

12.17   Right to have list of creditors   ..   ..   [1324]

12.18   False claim of status as creditor, etc   ..   ..   [1325]

12.19   Execution overtaken by judgment debtor's insolvency ..   ..   ..   [1326]

12.20   The Gazette   ..   ..   [1327]

12.21   Punishment of offences   ..   ..   [1328]

PART 13

INTERPRETATION AND APPLICATION

13.1   Introductory   ..   ..   [1329]

13.2   "The court"; "the registrar"   ..   ..   [1330]

Rule   Para
13.3   "Give notice", etc ..   .. [1331]
13.4   Notice, etc to solicitors   ..   .. [1332]
13.5   Notice to joint liquidators, joint trustees, etc   ..   .. [1333]
13.6   "Venue"   ..   .. [1334]
13.7   "Insolvency proceedings" ..   .. [1335]
13.8   "Insolvent estate" ..   .. [1336]
13.9   "Responsible insolvency practitioner", etc   ..   .. [1337]
13.10 "Petitioner"   ..   .. [1338]
13.11 "The appropriate fee"   ..   .. [1339]
13.12 "Debt", "liability" (winding up) ..   .. [1340]
13.13 Expressions used generally   ..   .. [1341]
13.14 Application ..   .. [1342]

SCHEDULES

Schedule 1—Deposit Protection Board's Voting Rights   ..   .. [1343]
Schedule 2—Alternative Courts for Debtors' Petitions in Bankruptcy   ..   .. [1344]
Schedule 3—Shorthand Writers' Remuneration   ..   .. [1345]
Schedule 4—Forms   ..   .. [1346]
Schedule 5—Punishment of Offences under the Rules   ..   .. [1347]

INTRODUCTORY PROVISIONS

0.1. Citation and commencement

These Rules may be cited as the Insolvency Rules 1986 and shall come into force on 29th December 1986.   **[591]**

0.2. Construction of principal references

In these Rules—

> "the Act" means the Insolvency Act 1986 (any reference to a numbered section being to a section of that Act);
> "the Companies Act" means the Companies Act 1985; and
> "the Rules" means the Insolvency Rules 1986.   **[592]**

0.3. Extent

(1) Parts 1, 2 and 4 of the Rules, and Parts 7 to 13 as they relate to company insolvency, apply in relation to companies which the courts in England and Wales have jurisdiction to wind up.

(2) Part 3 of the Rules applies to administrative receivers appointed otherwise than under section 51 (Scottish receivership).

(3) Parts 5 and 6 of the Rules, and Parts 7 to 13 as they relate to individual insolvency, extend to England and Wales only.   **[593]**

THE FIRST GROUP OF PARTS

COMPANY INSOLVENCY; COMPANIES WINDING UP

PART 1

COMPANY VOLUNTARY ARRANGEMENTS

CHAPTER 1

PRELIMINARY

1.1. Scope of this Part; interpretation

(1) The Rules in this Part apply where, pursuant to Part I of the Act, it is intended to make, and there is made, a proposal to a company and its creditors

for a voluntary arrangement, that is to say, a composition in satisfaction of its debts or a scheme of arrangement of its affairs.

(2) In this Part—

    (*a*) Chapter 2 applies where the proposal for a voluntary arrangement is made by the directors of the company, and neither is the company in liquidation, nor is an administration order (under Part II of the Act) in force in relation to it;

    (*b*) Chapter 3 applies where the company is in liquidation or an administration order is in force, and the proposal is made by the liquidator or (as the case may be) the administrator, he in either case being the nominee for the purposes of the proposal;

    (*c*) Chapter 4 applies in the same case as Chapter 3, but where the nominee is an insolvency practitioner other than the liquidator or the administrator; and

    (*d*) Chapters 5 and 6 apply in all the three cases mentioned in sub-paragraphs (*a*) to (*c*) above.

(3) In Chapters 3, 4 and 5, the liquidator or the administrator is referred to as "the responsible insolvency practitioner".   **[594]**

CHAPTER 2
PROPOSAL BY DIRECTORS

1.2. Preparation of proposal

The directors shall prepare for the intended nominee a proposal on which (with or without amendments to be made under Rule 1.3 below) to make his report to the court under section 2.   **[595]**

1.3. Contents of proposal

(1) The directors' proposal shall provide a short explanation why, in their opinion, a voluntary arrangement under Part I of the Act is desirable, and give reasons why the company's creditors may be expected to concur with such an arrangement.

(2) The following matters shall be stated, or otherwise dealt with, in the directors' proposal—

    (*a*) the following matters, so far as within the directors' immediate knowledge—

        (i) the company's assets, with an estimate of their respective values,

        (ii) the extent (if any) to which the assets are charged in favour of creditors,

        (iii) the extent (if any) to which particular assets are to be excluded from the voluntary arrangement;

    (*b*) particulars of any property, other than assets of the company itself, which is proposed to be included in the arrangement, the source of such property and the terms on which it is to be made available for inclusion;

    (*c*) the nature and amount of the company's liabilities (so far as within the directors' immediate knowledge), the manner in which they are proposed to be met, modified, postponed or otherwise dealt with by means of the arrangement, and (in particular)—

(i) how it is proposed to deal with preferential creditors (defined in section 4(7)) and creditors who are, or claim to be, secured,

(ii) how persons connected with the company (being creditors) are proposed to be treated under the arrangement, and

(iii) where there are, to the directors' knowledge, any circumstances giving rise to the possibility, in the event that the company should go into liquidation, of claims under—

section 238 (transactions at an undervalue),

section 239 (preferences),

section 244 (extortionate credit transactions), or

section 245 (floating charges invalid);

and, where any such circumstances are present, whether, and if so how, it is proposed under the voluntary arrangement to make provision for wholly or partly indemnifying the company in respect of such claims;

(*d*) whether any, and if so what, guarantees have been given of the company's debts by other persons, specifying which (if any) of the guarantors are persons connected with the company;

(*e*) the proposed duration of the voluntary arrangement;

(*f*) the proposed dates of distributions to creditors, with estimates of their amounts;

(*g*) the amount proposed to be paid to the nominee (as such) by way of renumeration and expenses;

(*h*) the manner in which it is proposed that the supervisor of the arrangement should be remunerated, and his expenses defrayed;

(*j*) whether, for the purposes of the arrangement, any guarantees are to be offered by directors, or other persons, and whether (if so) any security is to be given or sought;

(*k*) the manner in which funds held for the purposes of the arrangement are to be banked, invested or otherwise dealt with pending distribution to creditors;

(*l*) the manner in which funds held for the purpose of payment to creditors, and not so paid on the termination of the arrangement, are to be dealt with;

(*m*) the manner in which the business of the company is proposed to be conducted during the course of the arrangement;

(*n*) details of any further credit facilities which it is intended to arrange for the company, and how the debts so arising are to be paid;

(*o*) the functions which are to be undertaken by the supervisor of the arrangement; and

(*p*) the name, address and qualification of the person proposed as supervisor of the voluntary arrangement, and confirmation that he is (so far as the directors are aware) qualified to act as an insolvency practitioner in relation to the company.

(3) With the agreement in writing of the nominee, the directors' proposal may be amended at any time up to delivery of the former's report to the court under section 2(2).   **[596]**

1.4. Notice to intended nominee

(1) The directors shall give to the intended nominee written notice of their proposal.

(2) The notice, accompanied by a copy of the proposal, shall be delivered

either to the nominee himself, or to a person authorised to take delivery of documents on his behalf.

(3) If the intended nominee agrees to act, he shall cause a copy of the notice to be endorsed to the effect that it has been received by him on a specified date; and the period of 28 days referred to in section 2(2) then runs from that date.

(4) The copy of the notice so endorsed shall be returned by the nominee forthwith to the directors at an address specified by them in the notice for that purpose.   [597]

1.5. Statement of affairs

(1) The directors shall, within 7 days after their proposal is delivered to the nominee, or within such longer time as he may allow, deliver to him a statement of the company's affairs.

(2) The statement shall comprise the following particulars (supplementing or amplifying, so far as is necessary for clarifying the state of the company's affairs, those already given in the directors' proposal)—

(*a*) a list of the company's assets, divided into such categories as are appropriate for easy identification, with estimated values assigned to each category;

(*b*) in the case of any property on which a claim against the company is wholly or partly secured, particulars of the claim and its amount, and of how and when the security was created;

(*c*) the names and addresses of the company's preferential creditors (defined in section 4(7)), with the amounts of their respective claims;

(*d*) the names and addresses of the company's unsecured creditors, with the amounts of their respective claims;

(*e*) particulars of any debts owed by or to the company to or by persons connected with it;

(*f*) the names and addresses of the company's members, with details of their respective shareholdings;

(*g*) such other particulars (if any) as the nominee may in writing require to be furnished for the purposes of making his report to the court on the directors' proposal.

(3) The statement of affairs shall be made up to a date not earlier than 2 weeks before the date of the notice to the nominee under Rule 1.4.

However, the nominee may allow an extension of that period to the nearest practicable date (not earlier than 2 months before the date of the notice under Rule 1.4); and if he does so, he shall give his reasons in his report to the court on the directors' proposal.

(4) The statement shall be certified as correct, to the best of their knowledge and belief, by two or more directors of the company, or by the company secretary and at least one director (other than the secretary himself).   [598]

1.6. Additional disclosure for assistance of nominee

(1) If it appears to the nominee that he cannot properly prepare his report on the basis of information in the directors' proposal and statement of affairs, he may call on the directors to provide him with—

(*a*) further and better particulars as to the circumstances in which, and the reasons why, the company is insolvent or (as the case may be) threatened with insolvency;

(*b*) particulars of any previous proposals which have been made in respect
of the company under Part I of the Act;

(*c*) any further information with respect to the company's affairs which
the nominee thinks necessary for the purposes of his report.

(2) The nominee may call on the directors to inform him, with respect to
any person who is, or at any time in the 2 years preceding the notice under Rule
1.4 has been, a director or officer of the company, whether and in what
circumstances (in those 2 years or previously) that person—

(*a*) has been concerned in the affairs of any other company (whether or
not incorporated in England and Wales) which has become insolvent,
or

(*b*) has himself been adjudged bankrupt or entered into an arrangement
with his creditors.

(3) For the purpose of enabling the nominee to consider their proposal and
prepare his report on it, the directors must give him access to the company's
accounts and records.   **[599]**

1.7. Nominee's report on the proposal

(1) With his report to the court under section 2 the nominee shall deliver—

(*a*) a copy of the directors' proposal (with amendments, if any, authorised
under Rule 1.3(3)); and

(*b*) a copy or summary of the company's statement of affairs.

(2) If the nominee makes known his opinion that meetings of the company
and its creditors should be summoned under section 3, his report shall have
annexed to it his comments on the proposal.

If his opinion is otherwise, he shall give his reasons for that opinion.

(3) The court shall cause the nominee's report to be endorsed with the date
on which it is filed in court. Any director, member or creditor of the company is
entitled, at all reasonable times on any business day, to inspect the file.

(4) The nominee shall send a copy of his report, and of his comments (if
any), to the company.   **[600]**

1.8. Replacement of nominee

Where any person intends to apply to the court under section 2(4) for the
nominee to be replaced, he shall give to the nominee at least 7 days' notice of
his application.   **[601]**

1.9. Summoning of meetings under s 3

(1) If in his report the nominee states that in his opinion meetings of the
company and its creditors should be summoned to consider the directors'
proposal, the date on which the meetings are to be held shall be not less than 14,
nor more than 28, days from that on which the nominee's report is filed in court
under Rule 1.7.

(2) Notices calling the meetings shall be sent by the nominee, at least 14
days before the day fixed for them to be held—

(*a*) in the case of the creditors' meeting, to all the creditors specified in
the statement of affairs, and any other creditors of the company of
whom he is otherwise aware; and

(b) in the case of the meeting of members of the company, to all persons who are, to the best of the nominee's belief, members of it.

(3) Each notice sent under this Rule shall specify the court to which the nominee's report under section 2 has been delivered and shall state the effect of Rule 1.19(1), (3) and (4) (requisite majorities (creditors)); and with each notice there shall be sent—

(a) a copy of the directors' proposal;
(b) a copy of the statement of affairs or, if the nominee thinks fit, a summary of it (the summary to include a list of creditors and the amount of their debts); and
(c) the nominee's comments on the proposal.   **[602]**

CHAPTER 3
PROPOSAL BY ADMINISTRATOR OR LIQUIDATOR
(HIMSELF THE NOMINEE)

1.10. Preparation of proposal

(1) The responsible insolvency practitioner's proposal shall specify—

(a) all such matters as under Rule 1.3 in Chapter 2 the directors of the company would be required to include in a proposal by them, and
(b) such other matters (if any) as the insolvency practitioner considers appropriate for ensuring that members and creditors of the company are enabled to reach an informed decision on the proposal.

(2) Where the company is being wound up by the court, the insolvency practitioner shall give notice of the proposal to the official receiver.   **[603]**

1.11. Summoning of meetings under s 3

(1) The responsible insolvency practitioner shall fix a venue for the creditors' meeting and the company meeting, and give at least 14 days' notice of the meetings—

(a) in the case of the creditors' meeting, to all the creditors specified in the company's statement of affairs, and to any other creditors of whom the insolvency practitioner is aware; and
(b) in the case of the company meeting, to all persons who are, to the best of his belief, members of the company.

(2) Each notice sent out under this Rule shall state the effect of Rule 1.19(1), (3) and (4) (requisite majorities (creditors)); and with it there shall be sent—

(a) a copy of the responsible insolvency practitioner's proposal, and
(b) a copy of the statement of affairs or, if he thinks fit, a summary of it (the summary to include a list of creditors and the amounts of their debts).   **[604]**

CHAPTER 4
PROPOSAL BY ADMINISTRATOR OR LIQUIDATOR (ANOTHER
INSOLVENCY PRACTITIONER THE NOMINEE)

1.12. Preparation of proposal and notice to nominee

(1) The responsible insolvency practitioner shall give notice to the intended nominee, and prepare his proposal for a voluntary arrangement, in the same

manner as is required of the directors, in the case of a proposal by them, under Chapter 2.

(2) Rule 1.2 applies to the responsible insolvency practitioner as it applies to the directors; and Rule 1.4 applies as regards the action to be taken by the nominee.

(3) The content of the proposal shall be as required by Rule 1.3, reading references to the directors as referring to the responsible insolvency practitioner.

(4) Rule 1.6 applies in respect of the information to be furnished to the nominee, reading references to the directors as referring to the responsible insolvency practitioner.

(5) With the proposal the responsible insolvency practitioner shall provide a copy of the company's statement of affairs.

(6) Where the company is being wound up by the court, the responsible insolvency practitioner shall send a copy of the proposal to the official receiver, accompanied by the name and address of the insolvency practitioner who has agreed to act as nominee.

(7) Rules 1.7 to 1.9 apply as regards a proposal under this Chapter as they apply to a proposal under Chapter 2. **[605]**

CHAPTER 5

PROCEEDINGS ON A PROPOSAL MADE BY THE DIRECTORS, OR BY THE ADMINISTRATOR, OR BY THE LIQUIDATOR

SECTION A: MEETINGS OF COMPANY'S CREDITORS AND MEMBERS

1.13. Summoning of meetings

(1) Subject as follows, in fixing the venue for the creditors' meeting and the company meeting, the person summoning the meeting ("the convener") shall have regard primarily to the convenience of the creditors.

(2) Meetings shall in each case be summoned for commencement between 10.00 and 16.00 hours on a business day.

(3) The meetings shall be held on the same day and in the same place, but the creditors' meeting shall be fixed for a time in advance of the company meeting.

(4) With every notice summoning either meeting there shall be sent out forms of proxy. **[606]**

NOTES
Para (4): See Sch 4, form 8.1.

1.14. The chairman at meetings

(1) Subject as follows, at both the creditors' meeting and the company meeting, and at any combined meeting, the convener shall be chairman.

(2) If for any reason he is unable to attend, he may nominate another person to act as chairman in his place; but a person so nominated must be either—

    (*a*) a person qualified to act as an insolvency practitioner in relation to the company, or (*b*) an employee of the convener or his firm who is experienced in insolvency matters.   **[607]**

1.15. The chairman as proxy-holder

The chairman shall not by virtue of any proxy held by him vote to increase or reduce the amount of the remuneration or expenses of the nominee or the supervisor of the proposed arrangement, unless the proxy specifically directs him to vote in that way.   **[608]**

1.16. Attendance by company officers

(1) At least 14 days' notice to attend the meetings shall be given by the convener—

    (*a*) to all directors of the company, and

    (*b*) to any persons in whose case the convener thinks that their presence is required as being officers of the company, or as having been directors or officers of it at any time in the 2 years immediately preceding the date of the notice.

(2) The chairman may, if he thinks fit, exclude any present or former director or officer from attendance at a meeting, either completely or for any part of it; and this applies whether or not a notice under this Rule has been sent to the person excluded.   **[609]**

SECTION B: VOTING RIGHTS AND MAJORITIES

1.17. Voting rights (creditors)

(1) Subject as follows, every creditor who was given notice of the creditors' meeting is entitled to vote at the meeting or any adjournment of it.

(2) Votes are calculated according to the amount of the creditor's debt as at the date of the meeting or, where the company is being wound up or is subject to an administration order, the date of its going into liquidation or (as the case may be) of the administration order.

(3) A creditor shall not vote in respect of a debt for an unliquidated amount, or any debt whose value is not ascertained, except where the chairman agrees to put upon the debt an estimated minimum value for the purpose of entitlement to vote.

(4) At any creditors' meeting the chairman has power to admit or reject a creditor's claim for the purpose of his entitlement to vote, and the power is exercisable with respect to the whole or any part of the claim.

(5) The chairman's decision on a creditor's entitlement to vote is subject to appeal to the court by any creditor or member of the company.

(6) If the chairman is in doubt whether a claim should be admitted or rejected, he shall mark it as objected to and allow the creditor to vote, subject to his vote being subsequently declared invalid if the objection to the claim is sustained.

(7) If on an appeal the chairman's decision is reversed or varied, or a creditor's vote is declared invalid, the court may order another meeting to be summoned, or make such other order as it thinks just.

The court's power to make an order under this paragraph is exercisable only if it considers that the matter is such as gives rise to unfair prejudice or material irregularity.

(8) An application to the court by way of appeal against the chairman's decision shall not be made after the end of the period of 28 days beginning with the first day on which each of the reports required by section 4(6) has been made to the court.

(9) The chairman is not personally liable for any costs incurred by any person in respect of an appeal under this Rule.   **[610]**

1.18. Voting rights (members)

(1) Subject as follows, members of the company at their meeting vote according to the rights attaching to their shares respectively in accordance with the articles.

(2) Where no voting rights attach to a member's shares, he is nevertheless entitled to vote either for or against the proposal or any modification of it.

(3) References in this Rule to a person's shares include any other interest which he may have as a member of the company.   **[611]**

1.19. Requisite majorities (creditors)

(1) Subject as follows, at the creditors' meeting for any resolution to pass approving any proposal or modification there must be a majority in excess of three-quarters in value of the creditors present in person or by proxy and voting on the resolution.

(2) The same applies in respect of any other resolution proposed at the meeting, but substituting one-half for three-quarters.

(3) In the following cases there is to be left out of account a creditor's vote in respect of any claim or part of a claim—

    (*a*) where written notice of the claim was not given, either at the meeting or before it, to the chairman or convenor of the meeting;
    (*b*) where the claim or part is secured;
    (*c*) where the claim is in respect of a debt wholly or partly on, or secured by, a current bill of exchange or promissory note, unless the creditor is willing—

        (i) to treat the liability to him on the bill or note of every person who is liable on it antecedently to the company, and against whom a bankruptcy order has not been made (or in the case of a company, which has not gone into liquidation), as a security in his hands, and
        (ii) to estimate the value of the security and (for the purpose of entitlement to vote, but not of any distribution under the arrangement) to deduct it from his claim.

(4) Any resolution is invalid if those voting against it include more than half in value of the creditors, counting in these latter only those—

    (*a*) to whom notice of the meeting was sent;
    (*b*) whose votes are not to be left out of account under paragraph (3); and
    (*c*) who are not, to the best of the chairman's belief, persons connected with the company.

(5) It is for the chairman of the meeting to decide whether under this Rule—

(*a*) a vote is to be left out of account in accordance with paragraph (3), or

(*b*) a person is a connected person for the purposes of paragraph (4)(*c*);

and in relation to the second of these two cases the chairman is entitled to rely on the information provided by the company's statement of affairs or otherwise in accordance with this Part of the Rules.

(6) If the chairman uses a proxy contrary to Rule 1.15, his vote with that proxy does not count towards any majority under this Rule.

(7) Paragraphs (5) to (9) of Rule 1.17 apply as regards an appeal against the decision of the chairman under this Rule.   [612]

1.20 Requisite majorities (members)

(1) Subject as follows, and to any express provision made in the articles, at a company meeting any resolution is to be regarded as passed if voted for by more than one-half of the members present in person or by proxy and voting on the resolution.

(2) In determining whether a majority for any resolution has been obtained, there is to be left out of account any vote cast in accordance with Rule 1.18(2).

(3) If the chairman uses a proxy contrary to Rule 1.15, his vote with that proxy does not count towards any majority under this Rule.   [613]

1.21 Proceedings to obtain agreement on the proposal

(1) On the day on which the meetings are held, they may from time to time be adjourned; and, if the chairman thinks fit for the purpose of obtaining the simultaneous agreement of the meetings to the proposal (with the same modifications, if any), the meetings may be held together.

(2) If on that day the requisite majority for the approval of the voluntary arrangement (with the same modifications, if any) has not been obtained from both creditors and members of the company, the chairman may, and shall if it is so resolved, adjourn the meetings for not more than 14 days.

(3) If there are subsequently further adjournments, the final adjournment shall not be to a day later than 14 days after the date on which the meetings were originally held.

(4) There shall be no adjournment of either meeting unless the other is also adjourned to the same business day.

(5) In the case of a proposal by the directors, if the meetings are adjourned under paragraph (2), notice of the fact shall be given by the nominee forthwith to the court.

(6) If following any final adjournment of the meetings the proposal (with the same modifications, if any) is not agreed by both meetings, it is deemed rejected.   [614]

Section C: Implementation of the Arrangement

1.22. Resolutions to follow approval

(1) If the voluntary arrangement is approved (with or without modifications) by the two meetings, a resolution may be taken by the creditors, where two or more insolvency practitioners are appointed to act as supervisor, on the question

whether acts to be done in connection with the arrangement may be done by any one of them, or must be done by both or all.

(2) A resolution under paragraph (1) may be passed in anticipation of the approval of the voluntary arrangement by the company meeting if that meeting has not then been concluded.

(3) If at either meeting a resolution is moved for the appointment of some person other than the nominee to be supervisor of the arrangement, there must be produced to the chairman, at or before the meeting—

   (a) that person's written consent to act (unless he is present and then and there signifies his consent), and
   (b) his written confirmation that he is qualified to act as an insolvency practitioner in relation to the company.   **[615]**

1.23. Hand-over of property etc to supervisor

(1) After the approval of the voluntary arrangement—

   (a) the directors, or
   (b) where the company is in liquidation or is subject to an administration order, and a person other than the responsible insolvency practitioner is appointed as supervisor of the voluntary arrangement, the insolvency practitioner,

shall forthwith do all that is required for putting the supervisor into possession of the assets included in the arrangement.

(2) Where the company is in liquidation or is subject to an administration order, the supervisor shall on taking possession of the assets discharge any balance due to the insolvency practitioner by way of remuneration or on account of—

   (a) fees, costs, charges and expenses properly incurred and payable under the Act or the Rules, and
   (b) any advances made in respect of the company, together with interest on such advances at the rate specified in section 17 of the Judgments Act 1838 at the date on which the company went into liquidation or (as the case may be) became subject to the administration order.

(3) Alternatively, the supervisor must, before taking possession, give the responsible insolvency practitioner a written undertaking to discharge any such balance out of the first realisation of assets.

(4) The insolvency practitioner has a charge on the assets included in the voluntary arrangement in respect of any sums due as above until they have been discharged, subject only to the deduction from realisations by the supervisor of the proper costs and expenses of such realisations.

(5) The supervisor shall from time to time out of the realisation of assets discharge all guarantees properly given by the responsible insolvency practitioner for the benefit of the company, and shall pay all the insolvency practitioner's expenses.

(6) References in this Rule to the responsible insolvency practitioner include, where a company is being wound up by the court, the official receiver, whether or not in his capacity as liquidator; and any sums due to the official receiver take priority over those due to a liquidator.   **[616]**

1.24. Report of meetings

(1) A report of the meetings shall be prepared by the person who was chairman of them.

(2) The report shall—

    (*a*) state whether the proposal for a voluntary arrangement was approved or rejected and, if approved, with what (if any) modifications;

    (*b*) set out the resolutions which were taken at each meeting, and the decision on each one;

    (*c*) list the creditors and members of the company (with their respective values) who were present or represented at the meetings, and how they voted on each resolution; and

    (*d*) include such further information (if any) as the chairman thinks it appropriate to make known to the court.

(3) A copy of the chairman's report shall, within 4 days of the meetings being held, be filed in court; and the court shall cause that copy to be endorsed with the date of filing.

(4) In respect of each of the meetings, the persons to whom notice of its result is to be sent by the chairman under section 4(6) are all those who were sent notice of the meeting under this Part of the Rules.

The notice shall be sent immediately after a copy of the chairman's report is filed in court under paragraph (3).

(5) If the voluntary arrangement has been approved by the meetings (whether or not in the form proposed), the supervisor shall forthwith send a copy of the chairman's report to the registrar of companies. **[617]**

NOTES

    Para (5): See Sch 4, form 1.1.

1.25. Revocation or suspension of the arrangement

(1) This Rule applies where the court makes an order of revocation or suspension under section 6.

(2) The person who applied for the order shall serve sealed copies of it—

    (*a*) on the supervisor of the voluntary arrangement, and

    (*b*) on the directors of the company or the administrator or liquidator (according to who made the proposal for the arrangement).

Service on the directors may be effected by service of a single copy of the order on the company at its registered office.

(3) If the order includes a direction by the court under section 6(4)(*b*) for any further meetings to be summoned, notice shall also be given (by the person who applied for the order) to whoever is, in accordance with the direction, required to summon the meetings.

(4) The directors or (as the case may be) the administrator or liquidator shall—

    (*a*) forthwith after receiving a copy of the court's order, give notice of it to all persons who were sent notice of the creditors' and company meetings or who, not having been sent that notice, appear to be affected by the order;

(b) within 7 days of their receiving a copy of the order (or within such longer period as the court may allow), give notice to the court whether it is intended to make a revised proposal to the company and its creditors, or to invite re-consideration of the original proposal.

(5) The person on whose application the order of revocation or suspension was made shall, within 7 days after the making of the order, deliver a copy of the order to the registrar of companies.   **[618]**

NOTES
    Para (5): See Sch 4, form 1.2.

1.26. Supervisor's accounts and reports

(1) Where the voluntary arrangement authorises or requires the supervisor—

    (a) to carry on the business of the company or trade on its behalf or in its name, or

    (b) to realise assets of the company, or

    (c) otherwise to administer or dispose of any of its funds,

he shall keep accounts and records of his acts and dealings in and in connection with the arrangement, including in particular records of all receipts and payments of money.

(2) The supervisor shall, not less often than once in every 12 months beginning with the date of his appointment, prepare an abstract of such receipts and payments, and send copies of it, accompanied by his comments on the progress and efficacy of the arrangement, to—

    (a) the court,

    (b) the registrar of companies,

    (c) the company,

    (d) all those of the company's creditors who are bound by the arrangement,

    (e) subject to paragraph (5) below, the members of the company who are so bound, and

    (f) if the company is not in liquidation, the company's auditors for the time being.

If in any period of 12 months he has made no payments and had no receipts, he shall at the end of that period send a statement to that effect to all those specified in sub-paragraphs (a) to (f) above.

(3) An abstract provided under paragraph (2) shall relate to a period beginning with the date of the supervisor's appointment or (as the case may be) the day following the end of the last period for which an abstract was prepared under this Rule; and copies of the abstract shall be sent out, as required by paragraph (2), within the 2 months following the end of the period to which the abstract relates.

(4) If the supervisor is not authorised as mentioned in paragraph (1), he shall, not less often than once in every 12 months beginning with the date of his appointment, send to all those specified in paragraph (2)(a) to (f) a report on the progress and efficacy of the voluntary arrangement.

(5) The court may, on application by the supervisor—

    (a) dispense with the sending under this Rule of abstracts or reports to members of the company, either altogether or on the basis that the availability of the abstract or report to members is to be advertised by the supervisor in a specified manner;

(*b*) vary the dates on which the obligation to send abstracts or reports arises.   **[619]**

NOTES
   Para (2): See Sch 4, form 1.3.

1.27. Production of accounts and records to Secretary of State

(1) The Secretary of State may at any time during the course of the voluntary arrangement or after its completion require the supervisor to produce for inspection—

(*a*) his records and accounts in respect of the arrangement, and
(*b*) copies of abstracts and reports prepared in compliance with Rule 1.26.

(2) The Secretary of State may require production either at the premises of the supervisor or elsewhere; and it is the duty of the supervisor to comply with any requirement imposed on him under this Rule.

(3) The Secretary of State may cause any accounts and records produced to him under this Rule to be audited; and the supervisor shall give to the Secretary of State such further information and assistance as he needs for the purposes of his audit.   **[620]**

1.28. Fees, costs, charges and expenses

(1) The fees, costs, charges and expenses that may be incurred for any of the purposes of the voluntary arrangement are—

(*a*) any disbursements made by the nominee prior to the approval of the arrangement, and any remuneration for his services as such agreed between himself and the company (or, as the case may be, the administrator or liquidator);
(*b*) any fees, costs, charges or expenses which—
   (i) are sanctioned by the terms of the arrangement, or
   (ii) would be payable, or correspond to those which would be payable, in an administration or winding up.   **[621]**

1.29. Completion of the arrangement

(1) Not more than 28 days after the final completion of the voluntary arrangement, the supervisor shall send to all the creditors and members of the company who are bound by it a notice that the voluntary arrangement has been fully implemented.

(2) With the notice there shall be sent to each creditor and member a copy of a report by the supervisor summarising all receipts and payments made by him in pursuance of the arrangement, and explaining any difference in the actual implementation of it as compared with the proposal as approved by the creditors' and company meetings.

(3) The supervisor shall, within the 28 days mentioned above, send to the registrar of companies and to the court a copy of the notice to creditors and members under paragraph (1), together with a copy of the report under paragraph (2).

(4) The court may, on application by the supervisor, extend the period of 28 days under paragraphs (1) and (3).   **[622]**

CHAPTER 6

GENERAL

1.30. False representations, etc

(1) A person being a past or present officer of a company commits an offence if he makes any false representation or commits any other fraud for the purpose of obtaining the approval of the company's members or creditors to a proposal for a voluntary arrangement under Part I of the Act.

(2) For this purpose "officer" includes a shadow director.

(3) A person guilty of an offence under this Rule is liable to imprisonment or a fine, or both.   **[623]**

PART 2

ADMINISTRATION PROCEDURE

CHAPTER 1

APPLICATION FOR, AND MAKING OF, THE ORDER

2.1. Affidavit to support petition

(1) Where it is proposed to apply to the court by petition for an administration order to be made in relation to a company, an affidavit complying with Rule 2.3 below must be prepared and sworn, with a view to its being filed in court in support of the petition.

(2) If the petition is to be presented by the company or by the directors, the affidavit must be made by one of the directors, or the secretary of the company, stating himself to make it on behalf of the company or, as the case may be, on behalf of the directors.

(3) If the petition is to be presented by creditors, the affidavit must be made by a person acting under the authority of them all, whether or not himself one of their number. In any case there must be stated in the affidavit the nature of his authority and the means of his knowledge of the matters to which the affidavit relates.

(4) If the petition is to be presented by the supervisor of a voluntary arrangement under Part I of the Act, it is to be treated as if it were a petition by the company.   **[624]**

2.2. Independent report on company's affairs

(1) There may be prepared, with a view to its being exhibited to the affidavit in support of the petition, a report by an independent person to the effect that the appointment of an administrator for the company is expedient.

(2) The report may be by the person proposed as administrator, or by any

other person having adequate knowledge of the company's affairs, not being a director, secretary, manager, member, or employee of the company.

(3) The report shall specify the purposes which, in the opinion of the person preparing it, may be achieved for the company by the making of an administration order, being purposes particularly specified in section 8(3). **[625]**

2.3. Contents of affidavit

(1) The affidavit shall state—
- (*a*) the deponent's belief that the company is, or is likely to become, unable to pay its debts and the grounds of that belief; and
- (*b*) which of the purposes specified in section 8(3) is expected to be achieved by the making of an administration order.

(2) There shall in the affidavit be provided a statement of the company's financial position, specifying (to the best of the deponent's knowledge and belief) assets and liabilities, including contingent and prospective liabilities.

(3) Details shall be given of any security known or believed to be held by creditors of the company, and whether in any case the security is such as to confer power on the holder to appoint an administrative receiver. If an administrative receiver has been appointed, that fact shall be stated.

(4) If any petition has been presented for the winding up of the company, details of it shall be given in the affidavit, so far as within the immediate knowledge of the deponent.

(5) If there are other matters which, in the opinion of those intending to present the petition for an administration order, will assist the court in deciding whether to make such an order, those matters (so far as lying within the knowledge or belief of the deponent) shall also be stated.

(6) If a report has been prepared for the company under Rule 2.2, that fact shall be stated. If not, an explanation shall be provided why not.   **[626]**

2.4. Form of petition

(1) If presented by the company or by the directors, the petition shall state the name of the company and its address for service, which (in the absence of special reasons to the contrary) is that of the company's registered office.

(2) If presented by a single creditor, the petition shall state his name and address for service.

(3) If the petition is presented by the directors, it shall state that it is so presented under section 9; but from and after presentation it is to be treated for all purposes as the petition of the company.

(4) If the petition is presented by two or more creditors, it shall state that it is so presented (naming them); but from and after presentation it is to be treated for all purposes as the petition of one only of them, named in the petition as petitioning on behalf of himself and other creditors. An address for service for that one shall be specified.

(5) The petition shall specify the name and address of the person proposed to be appointed as administrator; and it shall be stated that, to the best of the petitioner's knowledge and belief, the person is qualified to act as an insolvency practitioner in relation to the company.

(6) There shall be exhibited to the affidavit in support of the petition—

  (*a*) a copy of the petition;
  (*b*) a written consent by the proposed administrator to accept appointment, if an administration order is made; and
  (*c*) if a report has been prepared under Rule 2.2, a copy of it.   **[627]**

NOTES
  Para (6): See Sch 4, form 2.2.

2.5. Filing of petition

(1) The petition and affidavit shall be filed in court, with a sufficient number of copies for service and use as provided by Rule 2.6.

(2) Each of the copies delivered shall have applied to it the seal of the court and be issued to the petitioner; and on each copy there shall be endorsed the date and time of filing.

(3) The court shall fix a venue for the hearing of the petition and this also shall be endorsed on each copy of the petition issued under paragraph (2).

(4) After the petition is filed, it is the duty of the petitioner to notify the court in writing of any winding-up petition presented against the company, as soon as he becomes aware of it.   **[628]**

2.6. Service of petition

(1) In the following paragraphs of this Rule, references to the petition are to a copy of the petition issued by the court under Rule 2.5(2) together with the affidavit in support of it and the documents (other than the copy petition) exhibited to the affidavit.

(2) The petition shall be served—

  (*a*) on any person who has appointed an administrative receiver for the company, or has the power to do so;
  (*b*) if the administrative receiver has been appointed, on him;
  (*c*) if there is pending a petition for the winding up of the company, on the petitioner (and also on the provisional liquidator, if any); and
  (*d*) on the person proposed as administrator.

(3) If the petition for the making of an administration order is presented by creditors of the company, the petition shall be served on the company.   **[629]**

2.7. Manner in which service to be effected

(1) Service of the petition in accordance with Rule 2.6 shall be effected by the petitioner, or his solicitor, or by a person instructed by him or his solicitor, not less than 5 days before the date fixed for the hearing.

(2) Service shall be effected as follows—

  (*a*) on the company (subject to paragraph (3) below), by delivering the documents to its registered office;
  (*b*) on any other person (subject to paragraph (4)), by delivering the documents to his proper address;
  (*c*) in either case, in such other manner as the court may direct.

(3) If delivery to the company's registered office is not practicable, service

may be effected by delivery to its last known principle place of business in England and Wales.

(4) For the purposes of paragraph (2)(*b*), a person's proper address is any which he has previously notified as his address for service; but if he has not notified any such address, service may be effected by delivery to his usual or last known address.

(5) Delivery of documents to any place or address may be made by leaving them there, or sending them by first class post.   **[630]**

2.8. Proof of service

(1) Service of the petition shall be verified by affidavit, specifying the date on which, and the manner in which, service was effected.

(2) The affidavit, with a sealed copy of the petition exhibited to it, shall be filed in court forthwith after service, and in any event not less than one day before the hearing of the petition.   **[631]**

NOTES
 Para (1): See Sch 4, form 2.3.

2.9. The hearing

(1) At the hearing of the petition, any of the following may appear or be represented—
 (*a*) the petitioner;
 (*b*) the company;
 (*c*) any person who has appointed an administrative receiver, or has the power to do so;
 (*d*) if an administrative receiver has been appointed, he;
 (*e*) any person who has presented a petition for the winding up of the company;
 (*f*) the person proposed for appointment as administrator; and
 (*g*) with the leave of the court, any other person who appears to have an interest justifying his appearance.

(2) If the court makes an administration order, the costs of the petitioner, and of any person appearing whose costs are allowed by the court, are payable as an expense of the administration.   **[632]**

NOTES
 See Sch 4, form 2.4.

2.10. Notice and advertisement of administration order

(1) If the court makes an administration order, it shall forthwith give notice to the person appointed as administrator.

(2) Forthwith after the order is made, the administrator shall advertise its making once in the Gazette, and once in such newspaper as he thinks most appropriate for ensuring that the order comes to the notice of the company's creditors.

(3) The administrator shall also forthwith give notice of the making of the order—

(*a*) to any person who has appointed an administrative receiver, or has power to do so;

(*b*) if an administrative receiver has been appointed, to him;

(*c*) if there is pending a petition for the winding up of the company, to the petitioner (and also to the provisional liquidator, if any); and

(*d*) to the registrar of companies.

(4) Two sealed copies of the order shall be sent by the court to the administrator, one of which shall be sent by him to the registrar of companies in accordance with section 21(2).

(5) If under section 9(4) the court makes any other order, it shall give directions as to the persons to whom, and how, notice of it is to be given. **[633]**

NOTES
Para (2): See Sch 4, form 2.5.
Para (3): See Sch 4, form 2.6.
Para (4): See Sch 4, form 2.7.

CHAPTER 2

STATEMENT OF AFFAIRS AND PROPOSALS TO CREDITORS

2.11. Notice requiring statement of affairs

(1) If the administrator determines to require a statement of the company's affairs to be made out and submitted to him in accordance with section 22, he shall send notice to each of the persons whom he considers should be made responsible under that section, requiring them to prepare and submit the statement.

(2) The persons to whom the notice is sent are referred to in this Chapter as "the deponents".

(3) The notice shall inform each of the deponents—

(*a*) of the names and addresses of all others (if any) to whom the same notice has been sent;

(*b*) of the time within which the statement must be delivered;

(*c*) of the effect of section 22(6) (penalty for non-compliance); and

(*d*) of the application to him, and to each of the other deponents, of section 235 (duty to provide information, and to attend on the administrator if required).

(4) The administrator shall, on request, furnish each deponent with instructions for the preparation of the statement and with the forms required for that purpose. **[634]**

NOTES
Para (1): See Sch 4, form 2.8.

2.12. Verification and filing

(1) The statement of affairs shall be in Form 2.9, shall contain all the particulars required by that form and shall be verified by affidavit by the deponents (using the same form).

(2) The administrator may require any of the persons mentioned in section

22(3) to submit an affidavit of concurrence, stating that he concurs in the statement of affairs.

(3) An affidavit of concurrence may be qualified in respect of matters dealt with in the statement of affairs, where the maker of the affidavit is not in agreement with the deponents, or he considers the statement to be erroneous or misleading, or he is without the direct knowledge necessary for concurring with it.

(4) The statement of affairs shall be delivered to the administrator by the deponent making the affidavit of verification (or by one of them, if more than one), together with a copy of the verified statement.

(5) Every affidavit of concurrence shall be delivered by the person who makes it, together with a copy.

(6) The administrator shall file the verified copy of the statement, and the affidavits of concurrence (if any) in court.   **[635]**

2.13. Limited disclosure

(1) Where the administrator thinks that it would prejudice the conduct of the administration for the whole or part of the statement of affairs to be disclosed, he may apply to the court for an order of limited disclosure in respect of the statement, or any specified part of it.

(2) The court may on the application order that the statement or, as the case may be, the specified part of it, be not filed in court, or that it is to be filed separately and not be open to inspection otherwise than with leave of the court.

(3) The court's order may include directions as to the delivery of documents to the registrar of companies and the disclosure of relevant information to other persons.   **[636]**

2.14. Release from duty to submit statement of affairs; extension of time

(1) The power of the administrator under section 22(5) to give a release from the obligation imposed by that section, or to grant an extension of time, may be exercised at the administrator's own discretion, or at the request of any deponent.

(2) A deponent may, if he requests a release or extension of time and it is refused by the administrator, apply to the court for it.

(3) The court may, if it thinks that no sufficient cause is shown for the application, dismiss it; but it shall not do so unless the applicant has had an opportunity to attend the court for an *ex parte* hearing, of which he has been given at least 7 days' notice.
If the application is not dismissed under this paragraph, the court shall fix a venue for it to be heard, and give notice to the deponent accordingly.

(4) The deponent shall, at least 14 days before the hearing, send to the administrator a notice stating the venue and accompanied by a copy of the application, and of any evidence which he (the deponent) intends to adduce in support of it.

(5) The administrator may appear and be heard on the application; and, whether or not he appears, he may file a written report of any matters which he considers ought to be drawn to the court's attention.

If such a report is filed, a copy of it shall be sent by the administrator to the deponent, not later than 5 days before the hearing.

(6) Sealed copies of any order made on the application shall be sent by the court to the deponent and the administrator.

(7) On any application under this Rule the applicant's costs shall be paid in any event by him and, unless the court otherwise orders, no allowance towards them shall be made out of the assets. **[637]**

2.15. Expenses of statement of affairs

(1) A deponent making the statement of affairs and affidavit shall be allowed, and paid by the administrator out of his receipts, any expenses incurred by the deponent in so doing which the administrator considers reasonable.

(2) Any decision by the administrator under this Rule is subject to appeal to the court.

(3) Nothing in this Rule relieves a deponent from any obligation with respect to the preparation, verification and submission of the statement of affairs, or to the provision of information to the administrator. **[638]**

2.16. Statement to be annexed to proposals

There shall be annexed to the administrator's proposals, when sent to the registrar of companies under section 23 and laid before the creditors' meeting to be summoned under that section, a statement by him showing—

(a) details relating to his appointment as administrator, the purposes for which an administration order was applied for and made, and any subsequent variation of those purposes;

(b) the names of the directors and secretary of the company;

(c) an account of the circumstances giving rise to the application for an administration order;

(d) if a statement of affairs has been submitted, a copy or summary of it, with the administrator's comments, if any;

(e) if no statement of affairs has been submitted, details of the financial position of the company at the latest practicable date (which must, unless the court otherwise orders, be a date not earlier than that of the administration order);

(f) the manner in which the affairs of the company will be managed and its business financed, if the administrator's proposals are approved; and

(g) such other information (if any) as the administrator thinks necessary to enable creditors to decide whether or not to vote for the adoption of the proposals. **[639]**

2.17. Notice to members of proposals to creditors

The manner of publishing—

(a) under section 23(2)(b), notice to members of the administrator's proposals to creditors, and

(b) under section 25(3)(b), notice to members of substantial revisions of the proposals,

shall be by gazetting; and the notice shall also in either case be advertised once in the newspaper in which the administration order was advertised. **[640]**

CHAPTER 3

CREDITORS' AND COMPANY MEETINGS

SECTION A : CREDITORS' MEETINGS

2.18. Meeting to consider administrator's proposals

(1) Notice of the creditors' meetings to be summoned under section 23(1) shall be given to all the creditors of the company who are identified in the statement of affairs, or are known to the administrator and had claims against the company at the date of the administration order.

(2) Notice of the meeting shall also (unless the court otherwise directs) be given by advertisement in the newspaper in which the administration order was advertised.

(3) Notice to attend the meeting shall be sent out at the same time to any directors or officers of the company (including persons who have been directors or officers in the past) whose presence at the meeting is, in the administrator's opinion, required.

(4) If at the meeting there is not the requisite majority for approval of the administrator's proposals (with modifications, if any), the chairman may, and shall if a resolution is passed to that effect, adjourn the meeting for not more than 14 days.   **[641]**

NOTES

Para (3): See Sch 4, form 2.10.

2.19. Creditors' meetings generally

(1) This Rule applies to creditors' meetings summoned by the administrator under—

    (*a*) section 14(2)(*b*) (general power to summon meetings of creditors);
    (*b*) section 17(3) (requisition by creditors; direction by the court);
    (*c*) section 23(1) (to consider administrator's proposals); or
    (*d*) section 25(2)(*b*) (to consider substantial revisions).

(2) In fixing the venue for the meeting, the administrator shall have regard to the convenience of creditors.

(3) The meeting shall be summoned for commencement between 10.00 and 16.00 hours on a business day, unless the court otherwise directs.

(4) At least 21 days' notice of the meeting shall be given to all creditors who are known to the administrator and had claims against the company at the date of the administration order; and the notice shall specify the purpose of the meeting and contain a statement of the effect of Rule 2.22(1) (entitlement to vote).

(5) With the notice summoning the meeting there shall be sent out forms of proxy.

(6) If within 30 minutes from the time fixed for commencement of the meeting there is no person present to act as chairman, the meeting stands adjourned to the same time and place in the following week or, if that is not a business day, to the business day immediately following.

(7) The meeting may from time to time be adjourned, if the chairman thinks fit, but not for more than 14 days from the date on which it was fixed to commence.   **[642]**

NOTES
   Para (4): See Sch 4, form 2.11.
   Para (5): See Sch 4, form 8.2.

2.20. The chairman at meetings

(1) At any meeting of creditors summoned by the administrator, either he shall be chairman, or a person nominated by him in writing to act in his place.

(2) A person so nominated must be either—
   (a) one who is qualified to act as an insolvency practitioner in relation to the company, or
   (b) an employee of the administrator or his firm who is experienced in insolvency matters.   **[643]**

2.21. Meeting requisitioned by creditors

(1) Any request by creditors to the administrator for a meeting of creditors to be summoned shall be accompanied by—
   (a) a list of the creditors concurring with the request, showing the amounts of their respective claims in the administration;
   (b) from each creditor concurring, written confirmation of his concurrence; and
   (c) a statement of the purpose of the proposed meeting.

This paragraph does not apply if the requisitioning creditor's debt is alone sufficient, without the concurrence of other creditors.

(2) The administrator shall, if he considers the request to be properly made in accordance with section 17(3), fix a venue for the meeting, not more than 35 days from his receipt of the request, and give at least 21 days' notice of the meeting to creditors.

(3) The expenses of summoning and holding a meeting at the instance of any person other than the administrator shall be paid by that person, who shall deposit with the administrator security for their payment.

(4) The sum to be deposited shall be such as the administrator may determine, and he shall not act without the deposit having been made.

(5) The meeting may resolve that the expenses of summoning and holding it are to be payable out of the assets of the company, as an expense of the administration.

(6) To the extent that any deposit made under this Rule is not required for the payment of expenses of summoning and holding the meeting, it shall be repaid to the person who made it.   **[644]**

2.22. Entitlement to vote

(1) Subject as follows, at a meeting of creditors in administration proceedings a person is entitled to vote only if—
   (a) he has given to the administrator, not later than 12.00 hours on the business day before the day fixed for the meeting, details in writing of

the debt which he claims to be due to him from the company, and the claim has been duly admitted under the following provisions of this Rule, and

(b) there has been lodged with the administrator any proxy which he intends to be used on his behalf.

Details of the debt must include any calculation for the purposes of Rules 2.24 to 2.27.

(2) The chairman of the meeting may allow a creditor to vote, notwithstanding that he has failed to comply with paragraph (1)(a), if satisfied that the failure was due to circumstances beyond the creditor's control.

(3) The administrator or, if other, the chairman of the meeting may call for any document or other evidence to be produced to him, where he thinks it necessary for the purpose of substantiating the whole or any part of the claim.

(4) Votes are calculated according to the amount of a creditor's debt as at the date of the administration order, deducting any amounts paid in respect of the debt after that date.

(5) A creditor shall not vote in respect of a debt for an unliquidated amount, or any debt whose value is not ascertained, except where the chairman agrees to put upon the debt an estimated minimum value for the purpose of entitlement to vote and admits the claim for that purpose. **[645]**

2.23. Admission and rejection of claims

(1) At any creditors' meeting the chairman has power to admit or reject a creditor's claim for the purpose of his entitlement to vote; and the power is exercisable with respect to the whole or any part of the claim.

(2) The chairman's decision under this Rule, or in respect of any matter arising under Rule 2.22, is subject to appeal to the court by any creditor.

(3) If the chairman is in doubt whether a claim should be admitted or rejected, he shall mark it as objected to and allow the creditor to vote, subject to his vote being subsequently declared invalid if the objection to the claim is sustained.

(4) If on an appeal the chairman's decision is reversed or varied, or a creditor's vote is declared invalid, the court may order that another meeting be summoned, or make such other order as it thinks just.

(5) In the case of the meeting summoned under section 23 to consider the administrator's proposals, an application to the court by way of appeal under this Rule against a decision of the chairman shall not be made later than 28 days after the delivery of the administrator's report in accordance with section 24(4).

(6) Neither the administrator nor any person nominated by him to be chairman is personally liable for costs incurred by any person in respect of an appeal to the court under this Rule, unless the court makes an order to that effect. **[646]**

2.24. Secured creditors

At a meeting of creditors a secured creditor is entitled to vote only in respect of the balance (if any) of his debt after deducting the value of his security as estimated by him. **[647]**

2.25. Holders of negotiable instruments

A creditor shall not vote in respect of a debt on, or secured by, a current bill of exchange or promissory note, unless he is willing—

    (*a*) to treat the liability to him on the bill or note of every person who is liable on it antecedently to the company, and against whom a bankruptcy order has not been made (or, in the case of a company, which has not gone into liquidation), as a security in his hands, and

    (*b*) to estimate the value of the security and, for the purpose of his entitlement to vote, to deduct it from his claim. **[648]**

2.26. Retention of title creditors

For the purpose of entitlement to vote at a creditors' meeting in administration proceedings, a seller of goods to the company under a retention of title agreement shall deduct from his claim the value, as estimated by him, of any rights arising under that agreement in respect of goods in possession of the company. **[649]**

2.27. Hire-purchase, conditional sale and chattel leasing agreements

(1) Subject as follows, an owner of goods under a hire-purchase or chattel leasing agreement, or a seller of goods under a conditional sale agreement, is entitled to vote in respect of the amount of the debt due and payable to him by the company as at the date of the administration order.

(2) In calculating the amount of any debt for this purpose, no account shall be taken of any amount attributable to the exercise of any right under the relevant agreement, so far as the right has become exercisable solely by virtue of the presentation of the petition for an administration order or any matter arising in consequence of that, or of the making of the order. **[650]**

2.28. Resolutions and minutes

(1) At a creditors' meeting in administration proceedings, a resolution is passed when a majority (in value) of those present and voting, in person or by proxy, have voted in favour of it.

(2) The chairman of the meeting shall cause minutes of its proceedings to be entered in the company's minute book.

(3) The minutes shall include a list of the creditors who attended (personally or by proxy) and, if a creditors' committee has been established, the names and addresses of those elected to be members of the committee. **[651]**

2.29. Administrator's report

Any report by the administrator of the result of creditors' meetings held under section 23 or 25 shall have annexed to it details of the proposals which were considered by the meeting in question and of the modifications which were so considered. **[652]**

2.30. Notices to creditors

(1) Within 14 days of the conclusion of a meeting of creditors to consider the administrator's proposals or revised proposals, the administrator shall send notice of the result of the meeting (including, where appropriate, details of the proposals as approved) to every creditor who received notice of the meeting under the Rules, and to any other creditor of whom the administrator has since become aware.

(2) Within 14 days of the end of every period of 6 months beginning with the date of approval of the administrator's proposals or revised proposals, the administrator shall send to all creditors of the company a report on the progress of the administration.

(3) On vacating office the administrator shall send to creditors a report on the administration up to that time.

This does not apply where the administration is immediately followed by the company going into liquidation, nor when the administrator is removed from office by the court or ceases to be qualified as an insolvency practitioner.

[653]

NOTES

Para (1): See Sch 4, form 2.12.

SECTION B: COMPANY MEETINGS

2.31. Venue and conduct of company meeting

(1) Where the administrator summons a meeting of members of the company, he shall fix a venue for it having regard to their convenience.

(2) The chairman of the meeting shall be the administrator or a person nominated by him in writing to act in his place.

(3) A person so nominated must be either—

    (*a*) one who is qualified to act as an insolvency practitioner in relation to the company, or

    (*b*) an employee of the administrator or his firm who is experienced in insolvency matters.

(4) If within 30 minutes from the time fixed for commencement of the meeting there is no person present to act as chairman, the meeting stands adjourned to the same time and place in the following week or, if that is not a business day, to the business day immediately following.

(5) Subject as above, the meeting shall be summoned and conducted as if it were a general meeting of the company summoned under the company's articles of association, and in accordance with the applicable provisions of the Companies Act.

(6) The chairman of the meeting shall cause minutes of its proceedings to be entered in the company's minute book. **[654]**

CHAPTER 4

THE CREDITORS' COMMITTEE

2.32. Constitution of committee

(1) Where it is resolved by a creditors' meeting to establish a creditors' committee for the purposes of the administration, the committee shall consist of at least 3 and not more than 5 creditors of the company elected at the meeting.

(2) Any creditor of the company is eligible to be a member of the committee, so long as his claim has not been rejected for the purpose of his entitlement to vote.

(3) A body corporate may be a member of the committee, but it cannot act as such otherwise than by a representative appointed under Rule 2.37 below.

[655]

2.33. Formalities of establishment

(1) The creditors' committee does not come into being, and accordingly cannot act, until the administrator has issued a certificate of its due constitution.

(2) No person may act as a member of the committee unless and until he has agreed to do so; and the administrator's certificate of the committee's due constitution shall not issue unless and until at least 3 of the persons who are to be members of it have agreed to act.

(3) As and when the others (if any) agree to act, the administrator shall issue an amended certificate.

(4) The certificate, and any amended certificate, shall be filed in court by the administrator.

(5) If after the first establishment of the committee there is any change in its membership, the administrator shall report the change to the court.   [656]

NOTES
  Para (4): See Sch 4, form 2.13.
  Para (5): See Sch 4, form 2.14.

2.34. Functions and meetings of the committee

(1) The creditors' committee shall assist the administrator in discharging his functions, and act in relation to him in such manner as may be agreed from time to time.

(2) Subject as follows. meetings of the committee shall be held when and where determined by the administrator.

(3) The administrator shall call a first meeting of the committee not later than 3 months after its first establishment; and thereafter he shall call a meeting—

  (a) if so requested by a member of the committee or his representative (the meeting then to be held within 21 days of the request being received by the administrator), and

  (b) for a specified date, if the committee has previously resolved that a meeting be held on that date.

(4) The administrator shall give 7 days' written notice of the venue of any meeting to every member of the committee (or his representative designated for that purpose), unless in any case the requirement of notice has been waived by or on behalf of any member.

Waiver may be signified either at or before the meeting.   [657]

2.35. The chairman at meetings

(1) Subject to Rule 2.44(3), the chairman at any meeting of the creditors' committee shall be the administrator or a person nominated by him in writing to act.

(2) A person so nominated must be either—

(*a*) one who is qualified to act as an insolvency practitioner in relation to the company, or

(*b*) an employee of the administrator or his firm who is experienced in insolvency matters.   **[658]**

2.36. Quorum

A meeting of the committee is duly constituted if due notice of it has been given to all the members, and at least 2 members are present or represented.   **[659]**

2.37. Committee-members' representatives

(1) A member of the committee may, in relation to the business of the committee, be represented by another person duly authorised by him for that purpose.

(2) A person acting as a committee-member's representative must hold a letter of authority entitling him so to act (either generally or specially) and signed by or on behalf of the committee-member.

(3) The chairman at any meeting of the committee may call on a person claiming to act as a committee-member's representative to produce his letter of authority, and may exclude him if it appears that his authority is deficient.

(4) No member may be represented by a body corporate, or by a person who is an undischarged bankrupt, or is subject to a composition or arrangement with his creditors.

(5) No person shall—

(*a*) on the same committee, act at one and the same time as representative of more than one committee-member, or

(*b*) act both as a member of the committee and as representative of another member.

(6) Where a member's representative signs any document on the member's behalf, the fact that he so signs must be stated below his signature.   **[660]**

2.38. Resignation

A member of the committee may resign by notice in writing delivered to the administrator.   **[661]**

2.39. Termination of membership

(1) Membership of the creditors' committee is automatically terminated if the member—

(*a*) becomes bankrupt, or compounds or arranges with his creditors, or

(*b*) at 3 consecutive meetings of the committee is neither present nor represented (unless at the third of those meetings it is resolved that this Rule is not to apply in his case), or

(*c*) ceases to be, or is found never to have been, a creditor.

(2) However, if the cause of termination is the members's bankruptcy, his trustee in bankruptcy replaces him as a member of the committee.   **[662]**

2.40. Removal

A member of the committee may be removed by resolution at a meeting of creditors, at least 14 days' notice having been given of the intention to move that resolution. **[663]**

2.41. Vacancies

(1) The following applies if there is a vacancy in the membership of the creditors' committee.

(2) The vacancy need not be filled if the administrator and a majority of the remaining members of the committee so agree, provided that the total number of members does not fall below the minimum required under Rule 2.32.

(3) The administrator may appoint any creditor (being qualified under the Rules to be a member of the committee) to fill the vacancy, if a majority of the other members of the committee agree to the appointment, and the creditor concerned consents to act. **[664]**

2.42. Procedure at meetings

(1) At any meeting of the creditors' committee, each member of it (whether present himself, or by his representative) has one vote; and a resolution is passed when a majority of the members present or represented have voted in favour of it.

(2) Every resolution passed shall be recorded in writing, either separately or as part of the minutes of the meeting.

(3) A record of each resolution shall be signed by the chairman and placed in the company's minute book. **[665]**

2.43. Resolutions by post

(1) In accordance with this Rule, the administrator may seek to obtain the agreement of members of the creditors' committee to a resolution by sending to every member (or his representative designated for the purpose) a copy of the proposed resolution.

(2) Where the administrator makes use of the procedure allowed by this Rule, he shall send out to members of the committee or their representatives (as the case may be) a statement incorporating the resolution to which their agreement is sought, each resolution (if more than one) being sent out in a separate document.

(3) Any member of the committee may, within 7 business days from the date of the administrator sending out a resolution, require him to summon a meeting of the committee to consider the matters raised by the resolution.

(4) In the absence of such a request, the resolution is deemed to have been passed by the committee if and when the administrator is notified in writing by a majority of the members that they concur with it.

(5) A copy of every resolution passed under this Rule, and a note that the committee's concurrence was obtained, shall be placed in the company's minute book. **[666]**

2.44. Information from administrator

(1) Where the committee resolves to require the attendance of the administrator under section 26(2), the notice to him shall be in writing signed by the majority of the members of the committee for the time being. A member's representative may sign for him.

(2) The meeting at which the administrator's attendance is required shall be fixed by the committee for a business day, and shall be held at such time and place as he determines.

(3) Where the administrator so attends, the members of the committee may elect any one of their number to be chairman of the meeting, in place of the administrator or a nominee of his.   **[667]**

2.45. Expenses of members

(1) Subject as follows, the administrator shall out of the assets of the company defray any reasonable travelling expenses directly incurred by members of the creditors' committee or their representatives in relation to their attendance at the committee's meetings, or otherwise on the committee's business, as an expense of the administration.

(2) Paragraph (1) does not apply to any meeting of the committee held within 3 months of a previous meeting, unless the meeting in question is summoned at the instance of the administrator.   **[668]**

2.46. Members' dealings with the company

(1) Membership of the committee does not prevent a person from dealing with the company while the administration order is in force, provided that any transactions in the course of such dealings are in good faith and for value.

(2) The court may, on the application of any person interested, set aside any transaction which appears to it to be contrary to the requirements of this Rule, and may give such consequential directions as it thinks fit for compensating the company for any loss which it may have incurred in consequence of the transaction.   **[669]**

CHAPTER 5

THE ADMINISTRATOR

2.47. Fixing of remuneration

(1) The administrator is entitled to receive remuneration for his services as such.

(2) The remuneration shall be fixed either—

   (a) as a percentage of the value of the property with which he has to deal, or

   (b) by reference to the time properly given by the insolvency practitioner (as administrator) and his staff in attending to matters arising in the administration.

(3) It is for the creditors' committee (if there is one) to determine whether the remuneration is to be fixed under paragraph (2)(a) or (b) and, if under paragraph (2)(a), to determine any percentage to be applied as there mentioned.

(4) In arriving at that determination, the committee shall have regard to the following matters—

(a) the complexity (or otherwise) of the case,

(b) any respects in which, in connection with the company's affairs, there falls on the administrator any responsibility of an exceptional kind or degree,

(c) the effectiveness with which the administrator appears to be carrying out, or to have carried out, his duties as such, and

(d) the value and nature of the property with which he has to deal.

(5) If there is no creditors' committee, or the committee does not make the requisite determination, the administrator's remuneration may be fixed (in accordance with paragraph (2)) by a resolution of a meeting of creditors; and paragraph (4) applies to them as it does to the creditors' committee.

(6) If not fixed as above, the administrator's remuneration shall, on his application, be fixed by the court.

(7) Rule 4.128(2) and (3) in Part 4 of the Rules (remuneration of joint liquidators; solicitors' profit costs) applies to an administrator as it applies to a liquidator, with any necessary modifications.   [670]

2.48. Recourse to meeting of creditors

If the administrator's remuneration has been fixed by the creditors' committee, and he considers the rate or amount to be insufficient, he may request that it be increased by resolution of the creditors.   [671]

2.49. Recourse to the court

(1) If the administrator considers that the remuneration fixed for him by the creditors' committee, or by resolution of the creditors, is insufficient, he may apply to the court for an order increasing its amount or rate.

(2) The administrator shall give at least 14 days' notice of his application to the members of the creditors' committee; and the committee may nominate one or more members to appear or be represented, and to be heard, on the application.

(3) If there is no creditors' committee, the administrator's notice of his application shall be sent to such one or more of the company's creditors as the court may direct, which creditors may nominate one or more of their number to appear or be represented.

(4) The court may, if it appears to be a proper case, order the costs of the administrator's application, including the costs of any member of the creditors' committee appearing on it, or any creditor so appearing, to be paid as an expense of the administration.   [672]

2.50. Creditors' claim that remuneration is excessive

(1) Any creditor of the company may, with the concurrence of at least 25 per cent in value of the creditors (including himself), apply to the court for an order that the administrator's remuneration be reduced, on the grounds that it is, in all the circumstances, excessive.

(2) The court may, if it thinks that no sufficient cause is shown for a reduction, dismiss the application; but it shall not do so unless the applicant has

had an opportunity to attend the court for an *ex parte* hearing, of which he has been given at least 7 days' notice.

If the application is not dismissed under this paragraph, the court shall fix a venue for it to be heard, and give notice to the applicant accordingly.

(3) The applicant shall, at least 14 days before the hearing, send to the administrator a notice stating the venue and accompanied by a copy of the application, and of any evidence which the applicant intends to adduce in support of it.

(4) If the court considers the application to be well-founded, it shall make an order fixing the remuneration at a reduced amount or rate.

(5) Unless the court orders otherwise, the costs of the application shall be paid by the applicant, and are not payable as an expense of the administration.
[673]

2.51. Disposal of charged property, etc

(1) The following applies where the administrator applies to the court under section 15(2) for authority to dispose of property of the company which is subject to a security, or goods in the possession of the company under an agreement, to which that subsection relates.

(2) The court shall fix a venue for the hearing of the application, and the administrator shall forthwith give notice of the venue to the person who is the holder of the security or, as the case may be, the owner under the agreement.

(3) If an order is made under section 15(2), the administrator shall forthwith give notice of it to that person or owner.

(4) The court shall send 2 sealed copies of the order to the administrator, who shall send one of them to that person or owner.   [674]

2.52. Abstract of receipts and payments

(1) The administrator shall—
>   (*a*) within 2 months after the end of 6 months from the date of his appointment, and of every subsequent period of 6 months, and
>   (*b*) within 2 months after he ceases to act as administrator,

send to the court, and to the registrar of companies, and to each member of the creditors' committee, the requisite accounts of the receipts and payments of the company.

(2) The court may, on the administrator's application, extend the period of 2 months mentioned above.

(3) The accounts are to be in the form of an abstract showing—
>   (*a*) receipts and payments during the relevant period of 6 months, or
>   (*b*) where the administrator has ceased to act, receipts and payments during the period from the end of the last 6-month period to the time when he so ceased (alternatively, if there has been no previous abstract, receipts and payments in the period since his appointment as administrator).

(4) If the administrator makes default in complying with this Rule, he is liable to a fine and, for continued contravention, to a daily default fine.   [675]

NOTES
    Para (1): See Sch 4, form 2.15.

2.53. Resignation

(1) The administrator may give notice of his resignation on grounds of ill health or because—

    (*a*) he intends ceasing to be in practice as an insolvency practitioner, or

    (*b*) there is some conflict of interest, or change of personal circumstances, which precludes or makes impracticable the further discharge by him of the duties of administrator.

(2) The administrator may, with the leave of the court, give notice of his resignation on grounds other than those specified in paragraph (1).

(3) The administrator must give to the persons specified below at least 7 days' notice of his intention to resign, or to apply for the court's leave to do so—

    (*a*) if there is a continuing administrator of the company, to him;

    (*b*) if there is no such administrator, to the creditors' committee; and

    (*c*) if there is no such administrator and no creditors' committee, to the company and its creditors. **[676]**

NOTES
    Para (1): See Sch 4, form 2.16.
    Para (2): See Sch 4, form 2.17.

2.54. Administrator deceased

(1) Subject as follows, where the administrator has died, it is the duty of his personal representatives to give notice of the fact to the court, specifying the date of the death.
This does not apply if notice has been given under any of the following paragraphs of this Rule.

(2) If the deceased administrator was a partner in a firm, notice may be given by a partner in the firm who is qualified to act as an insolvency practitioner, or is a member of any body recognised by the Secretary of State for the authorisation of insolvency practitioners.

(3) Notice of the death may be given by any person producing to the court the relevant death certificate or a copy of it. **[677]**

2.55. Order filling vacancy

Where the court makes an order filling a vacancy in the office of administrator, the same provisions apply in respect of giving notice of, and advertising, the order as in the case of the original appointment of an administrator. **[678]**

CHAPTER 6

VAT BAD DEBT RELIEF

2.56. Issue of certificate of insolvency

(1) In accordance with this Rule, it is the duty of the administrator to issue a certificate in the terms of paragraph (*b*) of section 22(3) of the Value Added Tax Act 1983 (which specifies the circumstances in which a company is deemed insolvent for the purposes of that section) forthwith upon his forming the opinion described in that paragraph.

(2) There shall in the certificate be specified—

(*a*) the name of the company and its registered number;
(*b*) the name of the administrator and the date of his appointment;
(*c*) the date on which the certificate is issued.

(3) The certificate shall be intituled "CERTIFICATE OF INSOLVENCY FOR THE PURPOSES OF SECTION 22(3)(*b*) OF THE VALUE ADDED TAX ACT 1983".   **[679]**

2.57. Notice to creditors

(1) Notice of the issue of the certificate shall be given by the administrator within 3 months of his appointment or within 2 months of issuing the certificate, whichever is the later, to all of the company's unsecured creditors of whose address he is then aware and who have, to his knowledge, made supplies to the company, with a charge to value added tax, at any time before his appointment.

(2) Thereafter, he shall give the notice to any such creditor of whose address and supplies to the company he becomes aware.

(3) He is not under obligation to provide any creditor with a copy of the certificate.   **[680]**

2.58. Preservation of certificate with company's records

(1) The certificate shall be retained with the company's accounting records, and section 222 of the Companies Act (where and for how long records are to be kept) shall apply to the certificate as it applies to those records.

(2) It is the duty of the administrator, on vacating office, to bring this Rule to the attention of the directors or (as the case may be) any successor of his as administrator.   **[681]**

PART 3

ADMINISTRATIVE RECEIVERSHIP

CHAPTER 1

APPOINTMENT OF ADMINISTRATIVE RECEIVER

3.1. Acceptance of appointment

(1) Where a person is appointed as the sole or joint administrative receiver of a company's property under powers contained in an instrument, the appointee, if he accepts the appointment, shall within 7 days confirm his acceptance in writing to the appointer.

(2) If two or more persons are appointed jointly as administrative receivers, each of them shall confirm acceptance on his own behalf; but the appointment is effective only when all those jointly appointed have complied with this Rule.

(3) Confirmation under this Rule may be given on the appointee's behalf by a person whom he has duly authorised to give it.

(4) In confirming his acceptance, the appointee shall state—

(*a*) the time and date of his receipt of notice of the appointment, and
(*b*) the time and date of his acceptance.   **[682]**

3.2. Notice and advertisement of appointment

(1) This Rule relates to the notice which a person is required by section 46(1) to send and publish, when appointed as administrative receiver.

(2) The following matters shall be stated in the notice—

  (a) the registered name of the company, as at the date of the appointment, and its registered number;
  (b) any other name with which the company has been registered in the 12 months preceding that date;
  (c) any name under which the company has traded at any time in those 12 months, if substantially different from its then registered name;
  (d) the name and address of the administrative receiver, and the date of his appointment;
  (e) the name of the person by whom the appointment was made;
  (f) the date of the instrument conferring the power under which the appointment was made, and a brief description of the instrument;
  (g) a brief description of the assets of the company (if any) in respect of which the person appointed is not made the receiver.

(3) The administrative receiver shall cause notice of his appointment to be advertised once in the Gazette, and once in such newspaper as he thinks most appropriate for ensuring that it comes to the notice of the company's creditors.

(4) The advertisement shall state all the matters specified in sub-paragraphs (a) to (e) of paragraph (2) above.   **[683]**

CHAPTER 2

STATEMENT OF AFFAIRS AND REPORT TO CREDITORS

3.3. Notice requiring statement of affairs

(1) If the administrative receiver determines to require a statement of the company's affairs to be made out and submitted to him in accordance with section 47, he shall send notice to each of the persons whom he considers should be made responsible under that section, requiring them to prepare and submit the statement.

(2) The persons to whom the notice is sent are referred to in this Chapter as "the deponents".

(3) The notice shall inform each of the deponents—

  (a) of the names and addresses of all others (if any) to whom the same notice has been sent;
  (b) of the time within which the statement must be delivered;
  (c) of the effect of section 47(6) (penalty for non-compliance); and
  (d) of the application to him, and to each of the other deponents, of section 235 (duty to provide information, and to attend on the administrative receiver if required).

(4) The administrative receiver shall, on request, furnish each deponent with instructions for the preparation of the statement and with the forms required for that purpose.   **[684]**

NOTES
  Para (1): See Sch 4, form 3.1.

3.4. Verification and filing

(1) The statement of affairs shall be in Form 3.2, shall contain all the particulars required by that form and shall be verified by affidavit by the deponents (using the same form).

(2) The administrative receiver may require any of the persons mentioned in section 47(3) to submit an affidavit of concurrence, stating that he concurs in the statement of affairs.

(3) An affidavit of concurrence may be qualified in respect of matters dealt with in the statement of affairs, where the maker of the affidavit is not in agreement with the deponents, or he considers the statement to be erroneous or misleading, or he is without the direct knowledge necessary for concurring with it.

(4) The statement of affairs shall be delivered to the receiver by the deponent making the affidavit of verification (or by one of them, if more than one), together with a copy of the verified statement.

(5) Every affidavit of concurrence shall be delivered by the person who makes it, together with a copy.

(6) The administrative receiver shall retain the verified copy of the statement and the affidavits of concurrence (if any) as part of the records of the receivership.   **[685]**

3.5. Limited disclosure

(1) Where the administrative receiver thinks that it would prejudice the conduct of the receivership for the whole or part of the statement of affairs to be disclosed, he may apply to the court for an order of limited disclosure in respect of the statement or a specified part of it.

(2) The court may on the application order that the statement, or, as the case may be, the specified part of it, be not open to inspection otherwise than with leave of the court.

(3) The court's order may include directions as to the delivery of documents to the registrar of companies and the disclosure of relevant information to other persons.   **[686]**

3.6. Release from duty to submit statement of affairs; extension of time

(1) The power of the administrative receiver under section 47(5) to give a release from the obligation imposed by that section, or to grant an extension of time, may be exercised at the receiver's own discretion, or at the request of any deponent.

(2) A deponent may, if he requests a release or extension of time and it is refused by the receiver, apply to the court for it.

(3) The court may, if it thinks that no sufficient cause is shown for the application, dismiss it; but it shall not do so unless the applicant has had an opportunity to attend the court for an *ex parte* hearing, of which he has been given at least 7 days' notice.

If the application is not dismissed under this paragraph, the court shall fix a venue for it to be heard, and give notice to the deponent accordingly.

(4) The deponent shall, at least 14 days before the hearing, send to the receiver a notice stating the venue and accompanied by a copy of the application, and of any evidence which he (the deponent) intends to adduce in support of it.

(5) The receiver may appear and he heard on the application; and, whether or not he appears, he may file a written report of any matters which he considers ought to be drawn to the court's attention.
If such a report is filed, a copy of it shall be sent by the receiver to the deponent, not later than 5 days before the hearing.

(6) Sealed copies of any order made on the application shall be sent by the court to the deponent and the receiver.

(7) On any application under this Rule the applicant's costs shall be paid in any event by him and, unless the court otherwise orders, no allowance towards them shall be made out of the assets under the administrative receiver's control. **[687]**

3.7. Expenses of statement of affairs

(1) A deponent making the statement of affairs and affidavit shall be allowed, and paid by the administrative receiver out of his receipts, any expenses incurred by the deponent is so doing which the receiver thinks reasonable.

(2) Any decision by the receiver under this Rule is subject to appeal to the court.

(3) Nothing in this Rule relieves a deponent from any obligation with respect to the preparation, verification and submission of the statement of affairs, or to the provision of information to the receiver. **[688]**

3.8. Report to creditors

(1) If under section 48(2) the administrative receiver determines not to send a copy of his report to creditors, but to publish notice under paragraph (*b*) of that subsection, the notice shall be published in the newspaper in which the receiver's appointment was advertised.

(2) If he proposes to apply to the court to dispense with the holding of the meeting of unsecured creditors (otherwise required by section 48(2)), he shall in his report to creditors or (as the case may be) in the notice published as above, state the venue fixed by the court for the hearing of the application.

(3) Subject to any order of the court under Rule 3.5, the copy of the receiver's report which under section 48(1) is to be sent to the registrar of companies shall have attached to it a copy of any statement of affairs under section 47, and copies of any affidavits of concurrence.

(4) If the statement of affairs or affidavits of concurrence, if any, have not been submitted to the receiver by the time he sends a copy of his report to the registrar of companies, he shall send a copy of the statement and any affidavits of concurrence as soon thereafter as he receives them. **[689]**

NOTES
Para (4): See Sch 4, form 3.3.

CHAPTER 3

CREDITORS' MEETING

3.9. Procedure for summoning meeting under s 48(2)

(1) In fixing the venue for a meeting of creditors summoned under section 48(2), the administrative receiver shall have regard to the convenience of the persons who are invited to attend.

(2) The meeting shall be summoned for commencement between 10.00 and 16.00 hours on a business day, unless the court otherwise directs.

(3) At least 14 days' notice of the venue shall be given to all creditors of the company who are identified in the statement of affairs, or are known to the receiver and had claims against the company at the date of his appointment.

(4) With the notice summoning the meeting there shall be sent out forms of proxy.

(5) The notice shall include a statement to the effect that creditors whose claims are wholly secured are not entitled to attend or be represented at the meeting.

(6) Notice of the venue shall also be published in the newspaper in which the receiver's appointment was advertised.

(7) The notice to creditors and the newspaper advertisement shall contain a statement of the effect of Rule 3.11(1) below (voting rights).   **[690]**

NOTES
    Para (4): See Sch 4, form 8.3.

3.10. The chairman at the meeting

(1) The chairman at the creditors' meeting shall be the receiver, or a person nominated by him in writing to act in his place.

(2) A person so nominated must be either—

   (a) one who is qualified to act as an insolvency practitioner in relation to the company, or
   (b) an employee of the receiver or his firm who is experienced in insolvency matters.   **[691]**

3.11. Voting rights

(1) Subject as follows, at the creditors' meeting a person is entitled to vote only if—

   (a) he has given to the receiver, not later than 12.00 hours on the business day before the day fixed for the meeting, details in writing of the debt that he claims to be due to him from the company, and the claim has been duly admitted under the following provisions of this Rule, and
   (b) there has been lodged with the administrative receiver any proxy which the creditor intends to be used on his behalf.

(2) The chairman of the meeting may allow a creditor to vote, notwithstanding that he has failed to comply with paragraph (1)(a), if satisfied that the failure was due to circumstances beyond the creditor's control.

(3) The receiver or (if other) the chairman of the meeting may call for any

document or other evidence to be produced to him where he thinks it necessary for the purpose of substantiating the whole or any part of the claim.

(4) Votes are calculated according to the amount of a creditor's debt as at the date of the appointment of the receiver, after deducting any amounts paid in respect of that debt after that date.

(5) A creditor shall not vote in respect of a debt for an unliquidated amount, or any debt whose value is not ascertained, except where the chairman agrees to put upon the debt an estimated minimum value for the purpose of entitlement to vote and admits the claim for that purpose.

(6) A secured creditor is entitled to vote only in respect of the balance (if any) of his debt after deducting the value of his security as estimated by him.

(7) A creditor shall not vote in respect of a debt on, or secured by, a current bill of exchange or promissory note, unless he is willing—

> (*a*) to treat the liability to him on the bill or note of every person who is liable on it antecedently to the company, and against whom a bankruptcy order had not been made (or, in the case of a company, which has not gone into liquidation), as a security in his hands, and
>
> (*b*) to estimate the value of the security and, for the purpose of his entitlement to vote, to deduct it from his claim. **[692]**

3.12. Admission and rejection of claim

(1) At the creditors' meeting the chairman has power to admit or reject a creditor's claim for the purpose of his entitlement to vote; and the power is exercisable with respect to the whole or any part of the claim.

(2) The chairman's decision under this Rule, or in respect of any matter arising under Rule 3.11, is subject to appeal to the court by any creditor.

(3) If the chairman is in doubt whether a claim should be admitted or rejected, he shall mark it as objected to and allow the creditor to vote, subject to his vote being subsequently declared invalid if the objection to the claim is sustained.

(4) If on an appeal the chairman's decision is reversed or varied, or a creditor's vote is declared invalid, the court may order that another meeting be summoned, or make such other order as it thinks just.

(5) Neither the receiver nor any person nominated by him to be chairman is personally liable for costs incurred by any person in respect of an appeal to the court under this Rule, unless the court makes an order to that effect. **[693]**

3.13. Quorum

(1) The creditors' meeting is not competent to act unless there are present in person or by proxy at least 3 creditors (or all of the creditors, if their number does not exceed 3), being in either case entitled to vote.

(2) One person constitutes a quorum if—

> (*a*) he is himself a creditor or representative under section 375 of the Companies Act, with entitlement to vote, and he holds a number of proxies sufficient to ensure that, with his own vote, paragraph (1) is complied with, or
>
> (*b*) being the chairman or any other person, he holds that number of proxies. **[694]**

3.14. Adjournment

(1) The creditors' meeting shall not be adjourned, even if no quorum is present, unless the chairman decides that it is desirable; and in that case he shall adjourn it to such date, time and place as he thinks fit.

(2) Rule 3.9(1) and (2) applies, with necessary modifications, to any adjourned meeting.

(3) If there is no quorum, and the meeting is not adjourned, it is deemed to have been duly summoned and held.   **[695]**

3.15. Resolutions and minutes

(1) At the creditors' meeting, a resolution is passed when a majority (in value) of those present and voting in person or by proxy have voted in favour of it.

(2) The chairman of the meeting shall cause a record to be made of the proceedings, and kept as part of the records of the receivership.

(3) The record shall include a list of the creditors who attended (personally or by proxy) and, if a creditors' committee has been established, the names and addresses of those elected to be members of the committee.   **[696]**

CHAPTER 4

THE CREDITORS' COMMITTEE

3.16. Constitution of committee

(1) Where it is resolved by the creditors' meeting to establish a creditors' committee, the committee shall consist of at least 3 and not more than 5 creditors of the company elected at the meeting.

(2) Any creditor of the company is eligible to be a member of the committee, so long as his claim has not been rejected for the purpose of his entitlement to vote.

(3) A body corporate may be a member of the committee, but it cannot act as such otherwise than by a representative appointed under Rule 3.21 below.
                                               [697]

3.17. Formalities of establishment

(1) The creditors' committee does not come into being, and accordingly cannot act, until the administrative receiver has issued a certificate of its due constitution.

(2) No person may act as a member of the committee unless and until he has agreed to do so; and the receiver's certificate of the committee's due constitution shall not issue unless and until at least 3 of the persons who are to be members of it have agreed to act.

(3) As and when the others (if any) agree to act, the receiver shall issue an amended certificate.

(4) The certificate, and any amended certificate, shall be sent by the receiver to the registrar of companies.

(5) If, after the first establishment of the committee, there is any change in its membership, the receiver shall report the change to the registrar of companies.   **[698]**

NOTES
Para (4): See Sch 4, form 3.4.
Para (5): See Sch 4, form 3.5.

3.18. Functions and meetings of the committee

(1) The creditors' committee shall assist the administrative receiver in discharging his functions, and act in relation to him in such manner as may be agreed from time to time.

(2) Subject as follows, meetings of the committee shall be held when and where determined by the receiver.

(3) The receiver shall call a first meeting of the committee not later than 3 months after its establishment; and thereafter he shall call a meeting—

  (*a*) if requested by a member of the committee or his representative (the meeting then to be held within 21 days of the request being received by the receiver), and
  (*b*) for a specified date, if the committee has previously resolved that a meeting be held on that date.

(4) The receiver shall give 7 days' written notice of the venue of any meeting to every member (or his representative designated for that purpose), unless in any case the requirement of notice has been waived by or on behalf of any member.
Waiver may be signified either at or before the meeting.   **[699]**

3.19. The chairman at meetings

(1) Subject to Rule 3.28(3), the chairman at any meeting of the creditors' committee shall be the administrative receiver, or a person nominated by him in writing to act.

(2) A person so nominated must be either—

  (*a*) one who is qualified to act as an insolvency practitioner in relation to the company, or
  (*b*) an employee of the receiver or his firm who is experienced in insolvency matters.   **[700]**

3.20. Quorum

A meeting of the committee is duly constituted if due notice has been given to all the members, and at least 2 members are present or represented.   **[701]**

3.21. Committee-members' representatives

(1) A member of the committee may, in relation to the business of the committee, be represented by another person duly authorised by him for that purpose.

(2) A person acting as a committee-member's representative must hold a letter of authority entitling him so to act (either generally or specially) and signed by or on behalf of the committee-member.

(3) The chairman at any meeting of the committee may call on a person

claiming to act as a committee-member's representative to produce his letter of authority, and may exclude him if it appears that his authority is deficient.

(4) No member may be represented by a body corporate, or by a person who is an undischarged bankrupt, or is subject to a composition or arrangement with his creditors.

(5) No person shall—

    (*a*) on the same committee, act at one and the same time as representative of more than one committee-member, or

    (*b*) act both as a member of the committee and as representative of another member.

(6) where a member's representative signs any document on the member's behalf, the fact that he so signs must be stated below his signature.   **[702]**

3.22. Resignation

A member of the committee may resign by notice in writing delivered to the administrative receiver.   **[703]**

3.23. Termination of membership

(1) Membership of the creditors' committee is automatically terminated if the member—

    (*a*) becomes bankrupt, or compounds or arranges with his creditors, or

    (*b*) at 3 consecutive meetings of the committee is neither present nor represented (unless at the third of those meetings it is resolved that this Rule is not to apply in his case), or

    (*c*) ceases to be, or is found never to have been, a creditor.

(2) However, if the cause of termination is the member's bankruptcy, his trustee in bankruptcy replaces him as a member of the committee.   **[704]**

3.24. Removal

A member of the committee may be removed by resolution at a meeting of creditors, at least 14 days' notice having been given of the intention to move that resolution.   **[705]**

3.25. Vacancies

(1) The following applies if there is a vacancy in the membership of the creditors' committee.

(2) The vacancy need not be filled if the administrative receiver and a majority of the remaining members of the committee so agree, provided that the total number of members does not fall below the minimum required under Rule 3.16.

(3) The receiver may appoint any creditor (being qualified under the Rules to be a member of the committee) to fill the vacancy, if a majority of the other members of the committee agree to the appointment and the creditor concerned consents to act.   **[706]**

3.26. Procedure at meetings

(1) At any meeting of the committee, each member of it (whether present himself or by his representative) has one vote; and a resolution is passed when a majority of the members present or represented have voted in favour of it.

(2) Every resolution passed shall be recorded in writing, either separately or as part of the minutes of the meeting.

(3) A record of each resolution shall be signed by the chairman and kept as part of the records of the receivership.   [707]

3.27. Resolutions by post

(1) In accordance with this Rule, the administrative receiver may seek to obtain the agreement of members of the creditors' committee to a resolution by sending to every member (or his representative designated for the purpose) a copy of the proposed resolution.

(2) Where the receiver makes use of the procedure allowed by this Rule, he shall send out to members of the committee or their representatives (as the case may be) a statement incorporating the resolution to which their agreement is sought, each resolution (if more than one) being sent out in a separate document.

(3) Any member of the committee may, within 7 business days from the date of the receiver sending out a resolution, require him to summon a meeting of the committee to consider the matters raised by the resolution.

(4) In the absence of such a request, the resolution is deemed to have been passed by the committee if and when the receiver is notified in writing by a majority of the members that they concur with it.

(5) A copy of every resolution passed under this Rule, and a note that the committee's concurrence was obtained, shall be kept with the records of the receivership.   [708]

3.28. Information from receiver

(1) Where the committee resolves to require the attendance of the administrative receiver under section 49(2), the notice to him shall be in writing signed by the majority of the members of the committee for the time being. A member's representative may sign for him.

(2) The meeting at which the receiver's attendance is required shall be fixed by the committee for a business day, and shall be held at such time and place as he determines.

(3) Where the receiver so attends, the members of the committee may elect any one of their number to be chairman of the meeting, in place of the receiver or any nominee of his.   [709]

3.29. Expenses of members

(1) Subject as follows, the administrative receiver shall out of the assets of the company defray any reasonable travelling expenses directly incurred by members of the creditors' committee or their representatives in relation to their attendance at the committee's meetings, or otherwise on the committee's business, as an expense of the receivership.

(2) Paragraph (1) does not apply to any meeting of the committee held

within 3 months of a previous meeting, unless the meeting in question is summoned at the instance of the administrative receiver.   **[710]**

3.30. Members' dealings with the company

(1) Membership of the committee does not prevent a person from dealing with the company while the receiver is acting, provided that any transactions in the course of such dealings are entered into in good faith and for value.

(2) The court may, on the application of any person interested, set aside a transaction which appears to it to be contrary to the requirements of this Rule, and may give such consequential directions as it thinks fit for compensating the company for any loss which it may have incurred in consequence of the transaction.   **[711]**

CHAPTER 5

THE ADMINISTRATIVE RECEIVER (MISCELLANEOUS)

3.31. Disposal of charged property

(1) The following applies where the administrative receiver applies to the court under section 43(1) for authority to dispose of property of the company which is subject to a security.

(2) The court shall fix a venue for the hearing of the application, and the receiver shall forthwith give notice of the venue to the person who is the holder of the security.

(3) If an order is made under section 43(1), the receiver shall forthwith give notice of it to that person.

(4) The court shall send 2 sealed copies of the order to the receiver, who shall send one of them to that person.   **[712]**

3.32. Abstract of receipts and payments

(1) The administrative receiver shall—
    (*a*) within 2 months after the end of 12 months from the date of his appointment, and of every subsequent period of 12 months, and
    (*b*) within 2 months after he ceases to act as administrative receiver,

send to the registrar of companies, to the company and to the person by whom he was appointed, and to each member of the creditors' committee (if there is one), the requisite accounts of his receipts and payments as receiver.

(2) The court may, on the receiver's application, extend the period of 2 months referred to in paragraph (1).

(3) The accounts are to be in the form of an abstract showing—
    (*a*) receipts and payments during the relevant period of 12 months, or
    (*b*) where the receiver has ceased to act, receipts and payments during the period from the end of the last 12-month period to the time when he so ceased (alternatively, if there has been no previous abstract, receipts and payments in the period since his appointment as administrative receiver).

(4) This Rule is without prejudice to the receiver's duty to render proper accounts required otherwise than as above.

(5) If the administrative receiver makes default in complying with this Rule, he is liable to a fine and, for continued contravention, to a daily default fine.   [713]

3.33. Resignation

(1) Subject as follows, before resigning his office the administrative receiver shall give at least 7 days' notice of his intention to do so to—

(a) the person by whom he was appointed, and
(b) the company or, if it is then in liquidation, its liquidator.

(2) A notice given under this Rule shall specify the date on which the receiver intends his resignation to take effect.

(3) No notice is necessary if the receiver resigns in consequence of the making of an administration order.   [714]

3.34. Receiver deceased

If the administrative receiver dies, the person by whom he was appointed shall, forthwith on his becoming aware of the death, give notice of it to—

(a) the registrar of companies, and
(b) the company or, if it is in liquidation, the liquidator.   [715]

3.35. Vacation of office

(1) The administrative receiver, on vacating office on completion of the receivership, or in consequence of his ceasing to be qualified as an insolvency practitioner, shall forthwith give notice of his doing so—

(a) if the company is in liquidation, to the liquidator, and
(b) in any case, to the members of the creditors' committee (if any).

(2) Where the receiver's office is vacated, the notice to the registrar of companies which is required by section 45(4) may be given by means of an indorsement on the notice required by section 405(2) of the Companies Act (notice for the purposes of the register of charges).   [716]

CHAPTER 6

VAT BAD DEBT RELIEF

3.36. Issue of certificate of insolvency

(1) In accordance with this Rule, it is the duty of the administrative receiver to issue a certificate in the terms of paragraph (b) of section 22(3) of the Value Added Tax Act 1983 (which specifies the circumstances in which a company is deemed insolvent for the purposes of that section) forthwith upon his forming the opinion described in that paragraph.

(2) There shall in the certificate be specified—

(a) the name of the company and its registered number;

(b) the name of the administrative receiver and the date of his appointment; and

(c) the date on which the certificate is issued.

(3) The certificate shall be intituled "CERTIFICATE OF INSOLVENCY FOR THE PURPOSES OF SECTION 22(3)(b) OF THE VALUE ADDED TAX ACT 1983". **[717]**

3.37. Notice to creditors

(1) Notice of the issue of the certificate shall be given by the administrative receiver within 3 months of his appointment or within 2 months of issuing the certificate, whichever is the later, to all of the company's unsecured creditors of whose address he is then aware and who have, to his knowledge, made supplies to the company, with a charge to value added tax, at any time before his appointment.

(2) Thereafter, he shall give the notice to any such creditor of whose address and supplies to the company he becomes aware.

(3) He is not under obligation to provide any creditor with a copy of the certificate. **[718]**

3.38. Preservation of certificate with company's records

(1) The certificate shall be retained with the company's accounting records, and section 222 of the Companies Act (where and for how long records are to be kept) shall apply to the certificate as it applies to those records.

(2) It is the duty of the administrative receiver, on vacating office, to bring this Rule to the attention of the directors or (as the case may be) any successor of his as receiver. **[719]**

PART 4

COMPANIES WINDING UP

CHAPTER 1

THE SCHEME OF THIS PART OF THE RULES

4.1. Voluntary winding up; winding up by the court

(1) In a members' voluntary winding up, the Rules in this Part do not apply, except as follows—

(a) Chapters 9 (proof of debts in a liquidation), 10 (secured creditors) and 18 (special manager) apply wherever, and in the same way as, they apply in a creditors' voluntary winding up;

(b) Section B of Chapter 8 (additional provisions concerning meetings in relation to Bank of England and Deposit Protection Board) applies in the winding up of recognised banks, etc, whether members' or creditors' voluntary or by the court;

(c) Section F of Chapter 11 (the liquidator) applies only in a members' voluntary winding up, and not otherwise;

(d) Section G of that Chapter (court's power to set aside certain transactions; rule against solicitation) applies in any winding up, whether members' or creditors' voluntary or by the court; and

(e) Section B of Chapter 21 (liquidator's statements) applies in the same way as it applies in a creditors' voluntary winding up.

(2) Subject as follows, the Rules in this Part apply both in a creditors' voluntary winding up and in a winding up by the court; and for this purpose a winding up is treated as a creditors' voluntary if, and from the time when, the liquidator forms the opinion that the company will be unable to pay its debts in full, and determines accordingly to summon a creditors' meeting under section 95.

(3) The following Chapters, or Sections of Chapters, of this Part do not apply in a creditors' voluntary winding up—

Chapter 2—The statutory demand;

Chapter 3—Petition to winding-up order;

Chapter 4—Petition by contributories;

Chapter 5—Provisional liquidator;

Chapter 13—The liquidation committee where winding up follows imme-
     diately on administration;

Chapter 16—Settlement of list of contributories;

Chapter 17—Calls;

Chapter 19—Public examination of company officers and others; and

Chapter 21 (Section A)—Return of capital.

(4) Where at the head of any Rule, or at the end of any paragraph of a Rule, there appear the words "(NO CVL APPLICATION)", this signifies that the Rule or, as the case may be, the paragraph does not apply in a creditors' voluntary winding up.

However, this does not affect the court's power to make orders under section 112 (exercise in relation to voluntary winding up of powers available in winding up by the court).

(5) Where to any Rule or paragraph there is given a number incorporating the letters "CVL", that signifies that the Rule or (as the case may be) the paragraph applies in a creditors' voluntary winding up, and not in a winding up by the court. **[720]**

4.2. Winding up by the court: the various forms of petition

(1) Insofar as the Rules in this Part apply to winding up by the court, they apply (subject as follows) whether the petition for winding up is presented under any of the several paragraphs of section 122(1), namely—

 paragraph (*a*)—company special resolution for winding up by the court;
 paragraph (*b*)—public company without certificate under section 117 of
  the Companies Act;
 paragraph (*c*)—old public company;
 paragraph (*d*)—company not commencing business after formation, or
  suspending business;
 paragraph (*e*)—number of company's members reduced below 2;
 paragraph (*f*)—company unable to pay its debts;
 paragraph (*g*)—court's power under the "just and equitable" rule,

or under any enactment enabling the presentation of a winding-up petition.

(2) Except as provided by the following two paragraphs or by any particular Rule, the Rules apply whether the petition for winding up is presented by the company, the directors, one or more creditors, one or more contributories, the

Secretary of State, the official receiver, or any person entitled under any enactment to present such a petition.

(3) Chapter 2 (statutory demand) has no application except in relation to an unpaid creditor of the company satisfying section 123(1)(*a*) (the first of the two cases specified, in relation to England and Wales, of the company being deemed unable to pay its debts within section 122(1)(*f*)) or section 222(1) (the equivalent provision in relation to unregistered companies).

(4) Chapter 3 (petition to winding-up order) has no application to a petition for winding up presented by one or more contributories; and in relation to a petition so presented Chapter 4 has effect.   **[721]**

4.3. Time-limits

Where by any provision of the Act or the Rules about winding up, the time for doing anything is limited, the court may extend the time, either before or after it has expired, on such terms, if any, as it thinks fit.   **[722]**

CHAPTER 2

THE STATUTORY DEMAND

(NO CVL APPLICATION)

4.4. Preliminary

(1) This Chapter does not apply where a petition for the winding up of a company is presented under section 124 on or after the date on which the Rules come into force and the petition is based on failure to comply with a written demand served on the company before that date.

(2) A written demand served by a creditor on a company under section 123(1)(*a*) (registered companies) or 222(1)(*a*) (unregistered companies) is known in winding-up proceedings as "the statutory demand".

(3) The statutory demand must be dated, and be signed either by the creditor himself or by a person stating himself to be authorised to make the demand on the creditor's behalf.   **[723]**

4.5 Form and content of statutory demand

(1) The statutory demand must state the amount of the debt and the consideration for it (or, if there is no consideration, the way in which it arises).

(2) If the amount claimed in the demand includes—

  (*a*) any charge by way of interest not previously notified to the company as included in its liability, or
  (*b*) any other charge accruing from time to time,

the amount or rate of the charge must be separately identified, and the grounds on which payment of it is claimed must be stated.

In either case the amount claimed must be limited to that which has accrued due at the date of the demand.   **[724]**

NOTES
Para (1): See Sch 4, form 4.1.

4.6. Information to be given in statutory demand

(1) The statutory demand must include an explanation to the company of the following matters—

    (*a*) the purpose of the demand, and the fact that, if the demand is not complied with, proceedings may be instituted for the winding up of the company;

    (*b*) the time within which it must be complied with, if that consequence is to be avoided; and

    (*c*) the methods of compliance which are open to the company.

(2) Information must be provided for the company as to how an officer or representative of it may enter into communication with one or more named individuals, with a view to securing or compounding for the debt to the creditor's satisfaction.

In the case of any individual so named in the demand, his address and telephone number (if any) must be given. **[725]**

CHAPTER 3

PETITION TO WINDING-UP ORDER

(NO CVL APPLICATION)

(NO APPLICATION TO PETITION BY CONTRIBUTORIES)

4.7. Presentation and filing of petition

(1) The petition, verified by affidavit in accordance with Rule 4.12 below, shall be filed in court.

(2) No petition shall be filed unless there is produced with it the receipt for the deposit payable on presentation.

(3) If the petitioner is other than the company itself, there shall be delivered with the petition—

    (*a*) one copy for service on the company, and

    (*b*) one copy to be exhibited to the affidavit verifying service.

(4) There shall in any case be delivered with the petition—

    (*a*) if the company is in course of being wound up voluntarily, and a liquidator has been appointed, one copy of the petition to be sent to him;

    (*b*) if an administration order is in force in relation to the company, one copy to be sent to the administrator;

    (*c*) if an administrative receiver has been appointed in relation to the company, one copy to be sent to him;

    (*d*) if there is in force for the company a voluntary arrangement under Part I of the Act, one copy for the supervisor of the arrangement; and

    (*e*) if the company is—

        (i) a recognised bank or licensed institution within the meaning of the Banking Act 1979, or

        (ii) an institution to which sections 16 and 18 of that Act apply as if it were licensed,

    and the petitioner is not the Bank of England, one copy to be sent to the Bank.

(5) Each of the copies delivered shall have applied to it the seal of the court, and shall be issued to the petitioner.

(6) The court shall fix a venue for the hearing of the petition; and this shall be endorsed on any copy issued to the petitioner under paragraph (5).   [726]

NOTES

Para (1): See Sch 4, forms 4.1, 4.2.

4.8. Service of petition

(1) The following paragraphs apply as regards service of the petition on the company (where the petitioner is other than the company itself); and references to the petition are to a copy of the petition bearing the seal of the court in which it is presented.

(2) Subject as follows, the petition shall be served at the company's registered office, that is to say—

(*a*) the place which is specified, in the company's statement delivered under section 10 of the Companies Act as the intended situation of its registered office on incorporation, or

(*b*) if notice has been given by the company to the registrar of companies under section 287 of that Act (change of registered office), the place specified in that notice or, as the case may be, in the last such notice.

(3) Service of the petition at the registered office may be effected in any of the following ways—

(*a*) it may be handed to a person who there and then acknowledges himself to be, or to the best of the server's knowledge, information and belief is, a director or other officer, or employee, of the company; or

(*b*) it may be handed to a person who there and then acknowledges himself to be authorised to accept service of documents on the company's behalf; or

(*c*) in the absence of any such person as is mentioned in sub-paragraph (*a*) or (*b*), it may be deposited at or about the registered office in such a way that it is likely to come to the notice of a person attending at the office.

(4) If for any reason service at the registered office is not practicable, or the company has no registered office, or it is an unregistered company, the petition may be served at the company's last known principal place of business in England and Wales, or at some place in England and Wales at which it has carried on business, by handing it to such a person as is mentioned in paragraph (3)(*a*) or (*b*) above.

(5) In the case of an oversea company, service may be effected in any manner provided for by section 695 of the Companies Act.

(6) If for any reason it is impracticable to effect service as provided by paragraphs (2) to (5), the petition may be served in such other manner as the court may direct.

(7) Application for leave of the court under paragraph (6) may be made *ex parte*, on affidavit stating what steps have been taken to comply with paragraphs (2) to (5), and the reasons why it is impracticable to effect service as there provided.   [727]

4.9. Proof of service

(1) Service of the petition shall be proved by affidavit, specifying the manner of service.

(2) The affidavit shall have exhibited to it—

    (*a*) a sealed copy of the petition, and

    (*b*) if substituted service has been ordered, a sealed copy of the order;

and it shall be filed in court immediately after service. **[728]**

NOTES

    Para (1): See Sch 4, forms 4.4, 4.5.

4.10. Other persons to receive copies of petition

(1) If to the petitioner's knowledge the company is in course of being wound up voluntarily, a copy of the petition shall be sent by him to the liquidator.

(2) If to the petitioner's knowledge an administrative receiver has been appointed in relation to the company, or an administration order is in force in relation to it, a copy of the petition shall be sent by him to the receiver or, as the case may be, the administrator.

(3) If to the petitioner's knowledge there is in force for the company a voluntary arrangement under Part I of the Act, a copy of the petition shall be sent by him to the supervisor of the voluntary arrangement.

(4) If the company is a recognised bank or a licensed institution within the meaning of the Banking Act 1979, or an institution to which sections 16 and 18 of that Act apply as if it were a licensed institution, a copy of the petition shall be sent by the petitioner to the Bank of England.

This does not apply if the petitioner is the Bank of England itself.

(5) A copy of the petition which is required by this Rule to be sent shall be despatched on the next business day after the day on which the petition is served on the company. **[729]**

4.11. Advertisement of petition

(1) Unless the court otherwise directs, the petition shall be advertised once in the Gazette.

(2) The advertisement must be made to appear—

    (*a*) if the petitioner is the company itself, not less than 7 business days before the day appointed for the hearing, and

    (*b*) otherwise, not less than 7 business days after service of the petition on the company, nor less than 7 business days before the day so appointed.

(3) The court may, if compliance with paragraph (2) is not reasonably practicable, direct that advertisement of the petition be made to appear in a specified London morning newspaper, or other newspaper, instead of in the Gazette.

(4) The advertisement of the petition must state—

    (*a*) the name of the company and the address of its registered office, or—

        (i) in the case of an unregistered company, the address of its principal place of business;

    (ii) in the case of an oversea company, the address at which service of the petition was effected;

(*b*) the name and address of the petitioner;

(*c*) where the petitioner is the company itself, the address of its registered office or, in the case of an unregistered company, of its principal place of business;

(*d*) the date on which the petition was presented;

(*e*) the venue fixed for the hearing of the petition;

(*f*) the name and address of the petitioner's solicitor (if any); and

(*g*) that any person intending to appear at the hearing (whether to support or oppose the petition) must give notice of his intention in accordance with Rule 4.16.

(5) If the petition is not duly advertised in accordance with this Rule, the court may dismiss it.   **[730]**

NOTES
Para (1): See Sch 4, form 4.6.

4.12. Verification of petition

(1) The petition shall be verified by an affidavit that the statements in the petition are true, or are true to the best of the deponent's knowledge, information and belief.

(2) If the petition is in respect of debts due to different creditors, the debts to each creditor must be separately verified.

(3) The petition shall be exhibited to the affidavit verifying it.

(4) The affidavit shall be made—

(*a*) by the petitioner (or if there are two or more petitioners, any one of them), or

(*b*) by some person such as a director, company secretary or similar company officer, or a solicitor, who has been concerned in the matters giving rise to the presentation of the petition, or

(*c*) by some responsible person who is duly authorised to make the affidavit and has the requisite knowledge of those matters.

(5) Where the deponent is not the petitioner himself, or one of the petitioners, he must in the affidavit identify himself and state—

(*a*) the capacity in which, and the authority by which, he makes it, and

(*b*) the means of his knowledge of the matters sworn to in the affidavit.

(6) The affidavit is prima facie evidence of the statements in the petition to which it relates.

(7) An affidavit verifying more than one petition shall include in its title the names of the companies to which it relates and shall set out, in respect of each company, the statements relied on by the petitioner; and a clear and legible photocopy of the affidavit shall be filed with each petition which it verifies.

                                                        [731]

NOTES
Para (1): See Sch 4, forms 4.2, 4.3.

4.13. Persons entitled to copy of petition

Every director, contributory or creditor of the company is entitled to be furnished by the solicitor for the petitioner (or by the petitioner himself, if acting in person) with a copy of the petition within 2 days after requiring it, on payment of the appropriate fee. **[732]**

4.14. Certificate of compliance

(1) The petitioner or his solicitor shall, at least 5 days before the hearing of the petition, file in court a certificate of compliance with the Rules relating to service and advertisement.

(2) The certificate shall show—

    (*a*) the date of presentation of the petition,
    (*b*) the date fixed for the hearing, and
    (*c*) the date or dates on which the petition was served and advertised in compliance with the Rules.

A copy of the advertisement of the petition shall be filed in court with the certificate.

(3) Non-compliance with this Rule is a ground on which the court may, if it thinks fit, dismiss the petition. **[733]**

NOTES
    Para (1): See Sch 4, form 4.7.

4.15. Leave for petitioner to withdraw

If at least 5 days before the hearing the petitioner, on an *ex parte* application, satisfies the court that—

    (*a*) the petition has not been advertised, and
    (*b*) no notices (whether in support or in opposition) have been received by him with reference to the petition, and
    (*c*) the company consents to an order being made under this Rule,

the court may order that the petitioner has leave to withdraw the petition on such terms as to costs as the parties may agree. **[734]**

NOTES
    See Sch 4, form 4.8.

4.16. Notice of appearance

(1) Every person who intends to appear on the hearing of the petition shall give to the petitioner notice of his intention in accordance with this Rule.

(2) The notice shall specify—

    (*a*) the name and address of the person giving it, and any telephone number and reference which may be required for communication with him or with any other person (to be also specified in the notice) authorised to speak or act on his behalf;
    (*b*) whether his intention is to support or oppose the petition; and
    (*c*) the amount and nature of his debt.

(3) The notice shall be sent to the petitioner at the address shown for him in

the court records, or in the advertisement of the petition required by Rule 4.11; or it may be sent to his solicitor.

(4) The notice shall be sent so as to reach the addressee not later than 16.00 hours on the business day before that which is appointed for the hearing (or, where the hearing has been adjourned, for the adjourned hearing).

(5) A person failing to comply with this Rule may appear on the hearing of the petition only with the leave of the court. **[735]**

NOTES
Para (1): See Sch 4, form 4.9.

4.17. List of appearances

(1) The petitioner shall prepare for the court a list of the persons (if any) who have given notice under Rule 4.16, specifying their names and addresses and (if known to him) their respective solicitors.

(2) Against the name of each creditor in the list it shall be stated whether his intention is to support the petition, or to oppose it.

(3) On the day appointed for the hearing of the petition, a copy of the list shall be handed to the court before the commencement of the hearing.

(4) If any leave is given under Rule 4.16(5), the petitioner shall add to the list the same particulars in respect of the person to whom leave has been given.

[736]

NOTES
Para (1): See Sch 4, form 4.10.

4.18. Affidavit in opposition

(1) If the company intends to oppose the petition, its affidavit in opposition shall be filed in court not less than 7 days before the date fixed for the hearing.

(2) A copy of the affidavit shall be sent by the company to the petitioner, forthwith after filing. **[737]**

4.19. Substitution of creditor or contributory for petitioner

(1) This Rule applies where a person petitions and is subsequently found not entitled to do so, or where the petitioner—

    (*a*) fails to advertise his petition within the time prescribed by the Rules or such extended time as the court may allow, or

    (*b*) consents to withdraw his petition, or to allow it to be dismissed, consents to an adjournment, or fails to appear in support of his petition when it is called on in court on the day originally fixed for the hearing, or on a day to which it is adjourned, or

    (*c*) appears, but does not apply for an order in the terms of the prayer of his petition.

(2) The court may, on such terms as it thinks just, substitute as petitioner any creditor or contributory who in its opinion would have a right to present a petition, and who is desirous of prosecuting it.

(3) An order of the court under this Rule may, where a petitioner fails to advertise his petition within the time prescribed by these Rules, or consents to withdraw his petition, be made at any time. **[738]**

4.20. Notice and settling of winding-up order

(1) When a winding-up order has been made, the court shall forthwith give notice of the fact to the official receiver.

(2) The petitioner and every other person who has appeared on the hearing of the petition shall, not later than the business day following that on which the order is made, leave at the court all the documents required for enabling the order to be completed forthwith.

(3) It is not necessary for the court to appoint a venue for any person to attend to settle the order, unless in any particular case the special circumstances make an appointment necessary. **[739]**

NOTES
Para (1): See Sch 4, forms 4.11, 4.12, 4.13.

4.21. Transmission and advertisement of order

(1) When the winding-up order has been made, 3 copies of it, sealed with the seal of the court, shall be sent forthwith by the court to the official receiver.

(2) The official receiver shall cause a sealed copy of the order to be served on the company by prepaid letter addressed to it at its registered office (if any) or, if there is no registered office, at its principal or last known principal place of business.
Alternatively, the order may be served on such other person or persons, or in such other manner, as the court directs.

(3) The official receiver shall forward to the registrar of companies the copy of the order which by section 130(1) is directed to be so forwarded by the company.

(4) The official receiver shall forthwith—
   (*a*) cause the order to be gazetted, and
   (*b*) advertise the order in such local newspaper as the official receiver may select. **[740]**

CHAPTER 4

PETITION BY CONTRIBUTORIES

(NO CVL APPLICATION)

4.22. Presentation and service of petition

(1) The petition shall specify the grounds on which it is presented and the nature of the relief which is sought by the petitioner, and shall be filed in court with one copy for service under this Rule.

(2) The court shall fix a hearing for a day ("the return day") on which, unless the court otherwise directs, the petitioner and the company shall attend before the registrar in chambers for directions to be given in relation to the procedure on the petition.

(3) On fixing the return day, the court shall return to the petitioner a sealed

copy of the petition for service, endorsed with the return day and time of hearing.

(4) The petitioner shall, at least 14 days before the return day, serve a sealed copy of the petition on the company.   **[741]**

NOTES
Para (1): See Sch 4, form 4.14.

4.23. Return of petition

(1) On the return day, or at any time after it, the court shall give such directions as it thinks appropriate with respect to the following matters—

    (*a*) service of the petition, whether in connection with the venue for a further hearing, or for any other purpose;

    (*b*) whether particulars of claim and defence are to be delivered, and generally as to the procedure on the petition;

    (*c*) whether, and if so by what means, the petition is to be advertised;

    (*d*) the manner in which any evidence is to be adduced at any hearing before the judge and in particular (but without prejudice to the generality of the above) as to—

        (i) the taking of evidence wholly or in part by affidavit or orally;

        (ii) the cross-examination of any deponents to affidavits;

        (iii) the matters to be dealt with in evidence;

    (*e*) any other matter affecting the procedure on the petition or in connection with the hearing and disposal of the petition.

(2) In giving directions under paragraph (1)(*a*), the court shall have regard to whether any of the persons specified in Rule 4.10 should be served with a copy of the petition.   **[742]**

4.24. Application of Rules in Chapter 3

The following Rules in Chapter 3 apply, with the necessary modifications—

Rule 4.16 (notice of appearance);
Rule 4.17 (list of appearances);
Rule 4.20 (notice and settling of winding-up order); and
Rule 4.21 (transmission and advertisement of order).   **[743]**

Chapter 5

Provisional Liquidator

(No CVL Application)

4.25. Appointment of provisional liquidator

(1) An application to the court for the appointment of a provisional liquidator under section 135 may be made by the petitioner, or by a creditor of the company, or by a contributory, or by the company itself, or by the Secretary of State, or by any person who under any enactment would be entitled to present a petition for the winding up of the company.

(2) The application must be supported by an affidavit stating—

    (*a*) the grounds on which it is proposed that a provisional liquidator should be appointed;

(b) if some person other than the official receiver is proposed to be appointed, that the person has consented to act and, to the best of the applicant's belief, is qualified to act as an insolvency practitioner in relation to the company;

(c) whether or not the official receiver has been informed of the application and, if so, has been furnished with a copy of it;

(d) whether to the applicant's knowledge—

  (i) there has been proposed or is in force for the company a voluntary arrangement under Part I of the Act, or

  (ii) an administrator or administrative receiver is acting in relation to the company, or

  (iii) a liquidator has been appointed for its voluntary winding up; and

(e) the applicant's estimate of the value of the assets in respect of which the provisional liquidator is to be appointed.

(3) The applicant shall send copies of the application and of the affidavit in support to the official receiver, who may attend the hearing and make any representations which he thinks appropriate.

If for any reason it is not practicable to comply with this paragraph, the official receiver must be informed of the application in sufficient time for him to be able to attend.

(4) The court may on the application, if satisfied that sufficient grounds are shown for the appointment, make it on such terms as it thinks fit.   [744]

4.26. Order of appointment

(1) The order appointing the provisional liquidator shall specify the functions to be carried out by him in relation to the company's affairs.

(2) The court shall, forthwith after the order is made, send sealed copies of the order as follows—

(a) if the official receiver is appointed, two copies to him;

(b) if a person other than the official receiver is appointed—

  (i) two copies of that person, and

  (ii) one copy to the official receiver;

(c) if there is an administrative receiver acting in relation to the company, one copy to him.

(3) Of the two copies of the order sent to the official receiver under paragraph (2)(a), or to another person under paragraph (2)(b)(i), one shall in each case be sent by the recipient to the company or, if a liquidator has been appointed for the company's voluntary winding up, to him.   [745]

NOTES
    Para (1): See Sch 4, form 4.15.

4.27. Deposit

(1) Before an order appointing the official receiver as provisional liquidator is issued, the applicant for it shall deposit with him, or otherwise secure to his satisfaction, such sum as the court directs to cover the official receiver's remuneration and expenses.

(2) If the sum deposited or secured subsequently proves to be insufficient,

the court may, on application by the official receiver, order that an additional sum be deposited or secured. If the order is not complied with within 2 days after service of it on the person to whom it is directed, the court may discharge the order appointing the provisional liquidator.

(3) If a winding-up order is made after a provisional liquidator has been appointed, any money deposited under this Rule shall (unless it is required by reason of insufficiency of assets for payment of remuneration and expenses of the provisional liquidator) be repaid to the person depositing it (or as that person may direct) out of the assets, in the prescribed order of priority.   **[746]**

4.28. Security

(1) The following applies where an insolvency practitioner is appointed to be provisional liquidator under section 135.

(2) The cost of providing the security required under the Act shall be paid in the first instance by the provisional liquidator; but—

    (*a*) if a winding-up order is not made, the person so appointed is entitled to be reimbursed out of the property of the company, and the court may make an order on the company accordingly, and

    (*b*) if a winding-up order is made, he is entitled to be reimbursed out of the assets in the prescribed order of priority.   **[747]**

4.29. Failure to give or keep up security

(1) If the provisional liquidator fails to give or keep up his security, the court may remove him, and make such order as it thinks fit as to costs.

(2) If an order is made under this Rule removing the provisional liquidator, or discharging the order appointing him, the court shall give directions as to whether any, and if so what, steps should be taken for the appointment of another person in his place.   **[748]**

4.30. Remuneration

(1) The remuneration of the provisional liquidator (other than the official receiver) shall be fixed by the court from time to time on his application.

(2) In fixing his remuneration, the court shall take into account—

    (*a*) the time properly given by him (as provisional liquidator) and his staff in attending to the company's affairs;

    (*b*) the complexity (or otherwise) of the case;

    (*c*) any respects in which, in connection with the company's affairs, there falls on the provisional liquidator any responsibility of an exceptional kind or degree;

    (*d*) the effectiveness with which the provisional liquidator appears to be carrying out, or to have carried out, his duties; and

    (*e*) the value and nature of the property with which he has to deal.

(3) The provisional liquidator's remuneration (whether the official receiver or another) shall be paid to him, and the amount of any expenses incurred by him reimbursed—

    (*a*) if a winding-up order is not made, out of the property of the company (and the court may make an order on the company accordingly), and

    (*b*) if a winding-up order is made, out of the assets, in the prescribed order of priority, or, in either case (the relevant funds being insufficient), out of the deposit under Rule 4.27.

(4) Where a person other than the official receiver has been appointed provisional liquidator, and the official receiver has taken any steps for the purpose of obtaining a statement of affairs or has performed any other duty under the Rules, he shall pay the official receiver such sum (if any) as the court may direct. **[749]**

4.31. Termination of appointment

(1) The appointment of the provisional liquidator may be terminated by the court on his application, or on that of any of the persons specified in Rule 4.25(1).

(2) If the provisional liquidator's appointment terminates, in consequence of the dismissal of the winding-up petition or otherwise, the court may give such directions as it thinks fit with respect to the accounts of his administration or any other matters which it thinks appropriate.

(3) The court may under paragraph (2)—

> (*a*) direct that any expenses properly incurred by the provisional liquidator during the period of his appointment, including any remuneration to which he is entitled, be paid out of the property of the company, and
> (*b*) authorise him to retain out of that property such sums as are required for meeting those expenses.

Alternatively, the court may make such order as it thinks fit with respect to those matters. **[750]**

CHAPTER 6

STATEMENT OF AFFAIRS AND OTHER INFORMATION

4.32. Notice requiring statement of affairs

(NO CVL APPLICATION)

(1) The following applies where the official receiver determines to require a statement of the company's affairs to be made out and submitted to him in accordance with section 131.

(2) He shall send notice to each of the persons whom he considers should be made responsible under that section, requiring them to prepare and submit the statement.

(3) The persons to whom that notice is sent are referred to in this Chapter as "the deponents".

(4) The notice shall inform each of the deponents—

> (*a*) of the names and addresses of all others (if any) to whom the same notice has been sent;
> (*b*) of the time within which the statement must be delivered;
> (*c*) of the effect of section 131(7) (penalty for non-compliance); and
> (*d*) of the application to him, and to each of the other deponents, of section 235 (duty to provide information, and to attend on the official receiver if required).

(5) The official receiver shall, on request, furnish a deponent with instructions for the preparation of the statement and with the forms required for that purpose.   **[751]**

NOTES
    Para (1): See Sch 4, form 4.16.

4.33. Verification and filing

(NO CVL APPLICATION)

(1) The statement of affairs shall be in Form 4.17, shall contain all the particulars required by that form and shall be verified by affidavit by the deponents (using the same form).

(2) The official receiver may require any of the persons mentioned in section 131(3) to submit an affidavit of concurrence, stating that he concurs in the statement of affairs.

(3) An affidavit of concurrence made under paragraph (2) may be qualified in respect of matters dealt with in the statement of affairs, where the maker of the affidavit is not in agreement with the deponents, or he considers the statement to be erroneous or misleading, or he is without the direct knowledge necessary for concurring in the statement.

(4) The statement of affairs shall be delivered to the official receiver by the deponent making the affidavit of verification (or by one of them, if more than one), together with a copy of the verified statement.

(5) Every affidavit of concurrence shall be delivered to the official receiver by the person who makes it, together with a copy.

(6) The official receiver shall file the verified copy of the statement and the affidavits of concurrence (if any) in court.

(7) The affidavit may be sworn before an official receiver or a deputy official receiver, or before an officer of the Department or the court duly authorised in that behalf.   **[752]**

4.34–CVL. Statement of affairs

(1) This Rule applies with respect to the statement of affairs made out by the liquidator under section 95(3) or (as the case may be) by the directors under section 99(1).

(2) Where it is made out by the liquidator, the statement of affairs shall be delivered by him to the registrar of companies within 7 days after the creditors' meeting summoned under section 95(2).

(3) Where it is made out by the directors under section 99(1), the statement of affairs shall be delivered by them to the liquidator, when appointed; and he shall, within 7 days, deliver it to the registrar of companies.   **[753]**

NOTES
    Para (1): See Sch 4, forms 4.18, 4.19.
    Paras (2), (3): See Sch 4, form 4.20.

4.35. Limited disclosure

(NO CVL APPLICATION)

(1) Where the official receiver thinks that it would prejudice the conduct of the

liquidation for the whole or part of the statement of affairs to be disclosed, he may apply to the court for an order of limited disclosure in respect of the statement, or any specified part of it.

(2) The court may on the application order that the statement or, as the case may be, the specified part of it be not filed, or that it is to be filed separately and not be open to inspection otherwise than with leave of the court.   **[754]**

4.36. Release from duty to submit statement of affairs; extension of time

(NO CVL APPLICATION)

(1) The power of the official receiver under section 131(5) to give a release from the obligation imposed by that section, or to grant an extension of time, may be exercised at the official receiver's own discretion, or at the request of any deponent.

(2) A deponent may, if he requests a release or extension of time and it is refused by the official receiver, apply to the court for it.

(3) The court may, if it thinks that no sufficient cause is shown for the application, dismiss it; but it shall not do so unless the applicant has had an opportunity to attend the court for an *ex parte* hearing, of which he has been given at least 7 days' notice.

If the application is not dismissed under this paragraph, the court shall fix a venue for it to be heard, and give notice to the deponent accordingly.

(4) The deponent shall, at least 14 days before the hearing, send to the official receiver a notice stating the venue and accompanied by a copy of the application, and of any evidence which he (the deponent) intends to adduce in support of it.

(5) The official receiver may appear and be heard on the application; and, whether or not he appears, he may file a written report of any matters which he considers ought to be drawn to the court's attention.

If such a report is filed, a copy of it shall be sent by the official receiver to the deponent, not later than 5 days before the hearing.

(6) Sealed copies of any order made on the application shall be sent by the court to the deponent and the official receiver.

(7) On any application under this Rule the applicant's costs shall be paid in any event by him and, unless the court otherwise orders, no allowance towards them shall be made out of the assets.   **[755]**

4.37. Expenses of statement of affairs

(NO CVL APPLICATION)

(1) If any deponent cannot himself prepare a proper statement of affairs, the official receiver may, at the expense of the assets, employ some person or persons to assist in the preparation of the statement.

(2) At the request of any deponent, made on the grounds that he cannot himself prepare a proper statement, the official receiver may authorise an allowance, payable out of the assets, towards expenses to be incurred by the deponent in employing some person or persons to assist him in preparing it.

(3) Any such request by the deponent shall be accompanied by an estimate of the expenses involved; and the official receiver shall only authorise the

employment of a named person or a named firm, being in either case approved by him.

(4) An authorisation given by the official receiver under this Rule shall be subject to such conditions (if any) as he thinks fit to impose with respect to the manner in which any person may obtain access to relevant books and papers.

(5) Nothing in this Rule relieves a deponent from any obligation with respect to the preparation, verification and submission of the statement of affairs, or to the provision of information to the official receiver or the liquidator.

(6) Any payment out of the assets under this Rule shall be made in the prescribed order of priority.

(7) Paragraphs (2) to (6) of this Rule may be applied, on application to the official receiver by any deponent, in relation to the making of an affidavit of concurrence. **[756]**

4.38–CVL. Expenses of statements of affairs

(1) Payment may be made out of the company's assets, either before or after the commencement of the winding up, of any reasonable and necessary expenses of preparing the statement of affairs under section 99.

Any such payment is an expense of the liquidation.

(2) Where such a payment is made before the commencement of the winding up, the director presiding at the creditors' meeting held under section 98 shall inform the meeting of the amount of the payment and the identity of the person to whom it was made.

(3) The liquidator appointed under section 100 may make such a payment (subject to the next paragraph); but if there is a liquidation committee, he must give the committee at least 7 days' notice of his intention to make it.

(4) Such a payment shall not be made by the liquidator to himself, or to any associate of his, otherwise than with the approval of the liquidation committee, the creditors, or the court.

(5) This Rule is without prejudice to the powers of the court under Rule 4.219 (voluntary winding up superseded by winding up by the court). **[757]**

4.39. Submission of accounts

(NO CVL APPLICATION)

(1) Any of the persons specified in section 235(3) shall, at the request of the official receiver, furnish him with accounts of the company of such nature, as at such date, and for such period, as he may specify.

(2) The period specified may begin from a date up to 3 years preceding the date of the presentation of the winding-up petition, or from an earlier date to which audited accounts of the company were last prepared.

(3) The court may, on the official receiver's application, require accounts for any earlier period.

(4) Rule 4.37 applies (with the necessary modifications) in relation to accounts to be furnished under this Rule as it applies in relation to the statement of affairs.

(5) The accounts shall, if the official receiver so requires, be verified by

affidavit and (whether or not so verified) delivered to him within 21 days of the request under paragraph (1), or such longer period as he may allow.

(6) Two copies of the accounts and (where required) the affidavit shall be delivered to the offical receiver by whoever is required to furnish them; and the official receiver shall file one copy in court (with the affidavit, if any).   [758]

4.40–CVL. Submission of accounts

(1) Any of the persons specified in section 235(3) shall, at the request of the liquidator, furnish him with accounts of the company of such nature, as at such date, and for such period, as he may specify.

(2) The specified period for the accounts may begin from a date up to 3 years preceding the date of the resolution for winding up, or from an earlier date to which audited accounts of the company were last prepared.

(3) The accounts shall, if the liquidator so requires, be verified by affidavit and (whether or not so verified) delivered to him, with the affidavit if required, within 21 days from the request under paragraph (1), or such longer period as he may allow.   [759]

4.41–CVL. Expenses of preparing accounts

(1) Where a person is required under Rule 4.40–CVL to furnish accounts, the liquidator may, with the sanction of the liquidation committee (if there is one) and at the expense of the assets, employ some person or persons to assist in the preparation of the accounts.

(2) At the request of the person subject to the requirement, the liquidator may, with that sanction, authorise an allowance, payable out of the assets, towards expenses to be incurred by that person in employing others to assist him in preparing the accounts.

(3) Any such request shall be accompanied by an estimate of the expenses involved; and the liquidator shall only authorise the employment of a named person or a named firm, being in either case approved by him.   [760]

4.42. Further disclosure

(NO CVL APPLICATION)

(1) The official receiver may at any time require the deponents, or any one or more of them, to submit (in writing) further information amplifying, modifying or explaining any matter contained in the statement of affairs, or in accounts submitted in pursuance of the Act or the Rules.

(2) The information shall, if the official receiver so directs, be verified by affidavit, and (whether or not so verified) delivered to him within 21 days of the requirement under paragraph (1), or such longer period as he may allow.

(3) Two copies of the documents containing the information and (where verification is directed) the affidavit shall be delivered by the deponent to the official receiver, who shall file one copy in court (with the affidavit, if any).

                                                                        [761]

CHAPTER 7

INFORMATION TO CREDITORS AND CONTRIBUTORIES

4.43. Reports by official receiver

(NO CVL APPLICATION)

The official receiver shall, at least once after the making of the winding-up order, send a report to creditors and contributories with respect to the proceedings in the winding up, and the state of the company's affairs.   **[762]**

4.44. Meaning of "creditors"

Any reference in this Chapter to creditors is to creditors of the company who are known to the official receiver or (as the case may be) the liquidator or, where a statement of the company's affairs has been submitted, are identified in the statement.   **[763]**

4.45. Report where statement of affairs lodged

(NO CVL APPLICATION)

(1) Where a statement of affairs has been submitted and filed in court, the official receiver shall send out to creditors and contributories a report containing a summary of the statement and such observations (if any) as he thinks fit to make with respect to it, or to the affairs of the company in general.

(2) The official receiver need not comply with paragraph (1) if he has previously reported to creditors and contributories with respect to the company's affairs (so far as known to him) and he is of opinion that there are no additional matters which ought to be brought to their attention.   **[764]**

4.46. Statement of affairs dispensed with

(NO CVL APPLICATION)

(1) This Rule applies where, in the company's case, release from the obligation to submit a statement of affairs has been granted by the official receiver or the court.

(2) As soon as may be after the release has been granted, the official receiver shall send to creditors and contributories a report containing a summary of the company's affairs (so far as within his knowledge), and his observations (if any) with respect to it, or to the affairs of the company in general.

(3) The official receiver need not comply with paragraph (2) if he has previously reported to creditors and contributories with respect to the company's affairs (so far as known to him) and he is of opinion that there are no additional matters which ought to be brought to their attention.   **[765]**

4.47. General rule as to reporting

(NO CVL APPLICATION)

(1) The court may, on the official receiver's application, relieve him of any duty imposed on him by this Chapter, or authorise him to carry out the duty in a way other than there required.

(2) In considering whether to act under this Rule, the court shall have regard to the cost of carrying out the duty, to the amount of the assets available,

and to the extent of the interest of creditors or contributories, or any particular class of them **[766]**

4.48. Winding up stayed

(NO CVL APPLICATION)

(1) If proceedings in the winding up are stayed by order of the court, any duty of the official receiver to send reports under the preceding Rules in this Chapter ceases.

(2) Where the court grants a stay, it may include in its order such requirements on the company as it thinks fit with a view to bringing the stay to the notice of creditors and contributories. **[767]**

4.49–CVL. Information to creditors and contributories

The liquidator shall, within 28 days of a meeting held under section 95 or 98, send to creditors and contributories of the company—

>   (*a*) a copy or summary of the statement of affairs, and
>   (*b*) a report of the proceedings at the meeting. **[768]**

CHAPTER 8

MEETINGS OF CREDITORS AND CONTRIBUTORIES

SECTION A: RULES OF GENERAL APPLICATION

4.50 First meetings

(NO CVL APPLICATION)

(1) If under section 136(5) the official receiver decides to summon meetings of the company's creditors and contributories for the purpose of nominating a person to be liquidator in place of himself, he shall fix a venue for each meeting, in neither case more than 4 months from the date of the winding-up order.

(2) When for each meeting a venue has been fixed, notice of the meetings shall be given to the court and—

>   (*a*) in the case of the creditors' meeting, to every creditor who is known to the official receiver or is identified in the company's statement of affairs; and
>   (*b*) in the case of the contributories' meeting, to every person appearing (by the company's books or otherwise) to be a contributory of the company.

(3) Notice to the court shall be given forthwith, and the other notices shall be given at least 21 days before the date fixed for each meeting respectively.

(4) The notice to creditors shall specify a time and date, not more than 4 days before the date fixed for the meeting, by which they must lodge proofs and (if applicable) proxies, in order to be entitled to vote at the meeting; and the same applies in respect of contributories and their proxies.

(5) Notice of the meetings shall also be given by public advertisement.

(6) Where the official receiver receives a request by creditors under section 136(5)(*c*) for meetings of creditors and contributories to be summoned, and it appears to him that the request is properly made in accordance with the Act, he shall—

(a) withdraw any notices previously given by him under section 136(5)(b) (that he has decided not to summon such meetings),

(b) fix the venue of each meeting for not more than 3 months from his receipt of the creditors' request, and

(c) act in accordance with paragraphs (2) to (5) above, as if he had decided under section 136 to summon the meetings.

(7) Meetings summoned by the official receiver under this Rule are known respectively as "the first meeting of creditors" and "the first meeting of contributories", and jointly as "the first meetings in the liquidation".

(8) Where the company is a recognised bank or licensed institution under the Banking Act 1979, or an institution to which sections 16 and 18 of that Act apply as if it were a licensed institution, additional notices are required by Rule 4.72.   **[769]**

NOTES

Para (6): See Sch 4, form 4.21.

4.51–CVL. First meeting of creditors

(1) This Rule applies in the case of a meeting of creditors summoned by the liquidator under section 95 (where, in what starts as a members' voluntary winding up, he forms the opinion that the company will be unable to pay its debts) or a meeting under section 98 (first meeting of creditors in a creditors' voluntary winding up).

(2) The notice summoning the meeting shall specify a venue for the meeting and the time (not earlier than 12.00 hours on the business day before the day fixed for the meeting) by which, and the place at which, creditors must lodge proofs and (if applicable) proxies.

(3) Where the company is a recognised bank or licensed institution under the Banking Act 1979, or an institution to which sections 16 and 18 of that Act apply as if it were a licensed institution, additional notices are required by Rule 4.72.   **[770]**

4.52. Business at first meetings in the liquidation

(NO CVL APPLICATION)

(1) At the first meeting of creditors, no resolutions shall be taken other than the following—

(a) a resolution to appoint a named insolvency practitioner to be liquidator, or two or more insolvency practitioners as joint liquidators;

(b) a resolution to establish a liquidation committee;

(c) (unless it has been resolved to establish a liquidation committee) a resolution specifying the terms on which the liquidator is to be remunerated, or to defer consideration of that matter;

(d) (if, and only if, two or more persons are appointed to act jointly as liquidator) a resolution specifying whether acts are to be done by both or all of them, or by only one;

(e) (where the meeting has been requisitioned under section 136), a resolution authorising payment out of the assets, as an expense of the liquidation, of the cost of summoning and holding the meeting and any meeting of contributories so requisitioned and held;

(f) a resolution to adjourn the meeting for not more than 3 weeks;

(*g*) any other resolution which the chairman thinks it right to allow for special reasons.

(2) The same applies as regards the first meeting of contributories, but that meeting shall not pass any resolution to the effect of paragraph (1)(*c*) or (*e*).

(3) At neither meeting shall any resolution be proposed which has for its object the appointment of the official receiver as liquidator. [771]

4.53–CVL. Business at meeting under s 95 or 98

Rule 4.52(1), except sub-paragraph (*e*), applies to a creditors' meeting under section 95 or 98. [772]

4.54. General power to call meetings

(1) The official receiver or the liquidator may at any time summon and conduct meetings of creditors or of contributories for the purpose of ascertaining their wishes in all matters relating to the liquidation; and in relation to any meeting summoned under the Act or the Rules, the person summoning it is referred to as "the convener".

(2) When (in either case) a venue for the meeting has been fixed, notice of it shall be given by the convener—

(*a*) in the case of a creditors' meeting, to every creditor who is known to him or is identified in the company's statement of affairs; and

(*b*) in the case of a meeting of contributories, to every person appearing (by the company's books or otherwise) to be a contributory of the company.

(3) Notice of the meeting shall be given at least 21 days before the date fixed for it, and shall specify the purpose of the meeting.

(4) The notice shall specify a time and date, not more than 4 days before the date fixed for the meeting, by which, and the place at which, creditors must lodge proofs and proxies, in order to be entitled to vote at the meeting; and the same applies in respect of contributories and their proxies.

(NO CVL APPLICATION)

(5–CVL) The notice shall specify a time and date, not more than 4 days before that fixed for the meeting, by which, and the place at which, creditors (if not individuals attending in person) must lodge proxies, in order to be entitled to vote at the meeting.

(6) Additional notice of the meeting may be given by public advertisement if the convener thinks fit, and shall be so given if the court orders. [773]

NOTES

Para (2)(*a*): See Sch 4, form 4.22.

Para (2)(*b*): See Sch 4, form 4.23.

4.55. The chairman at meetings

(NO CVL APPLICATION)

(1) This Rule applies both to a meeting of creditors and to a meeting of contributories.

(2) Where the convener of the meeting is the official receiver, he, or a person nominated by him, shall be chairman.

A nomination under this paragraph shall be in writing, unless the nominee is another official receiver or a deputy official receiver.

(3) Where the convener is other than the official receiver, the chairman shall be he, or a person nominated in writing by him.

A person nominated under this paragraph must be either—

 (a) one who is qualified to act as an insolvency practitioner in relation to the company, or
 (b) an employee of the liquidator or his firm who is experienced in insolvency matters.   **[774]**

4.56–CVL. The chairman at meetings

(1) This Rule applies both to a meeting of creditors (except a meeting under section 98) and to a meeting of contributories.

(2) The liquidator, or a person nominated by him in writing to act, shall be chairman of the meeting.

A person nominated under this paragraph must be either—

 (a) one who is qualified to act as an insolvency practitioner in relation to the company, or
 (b) an employee of the liquidator or his firm who is experienced in insolvency matters.   **[775]**

4.57. Requisitioned meetings

(1) Any request by creditors to the liquidator (whether or not the official receiver) for a meeting of creditors or contributories, or meetings of both, to be summoned shall be accompanied by—

 (a) a list of the creditors concurring with the request and the amount of their respective claims in the winding up;
 (b) from each creditor concurring, written confirmation of his concurrence; and
 (c) a statement of the purpose of the proposed meeting.

Sub-paragraphs (a) and (b do not apply if the requisitioning creditor's debt is alone sufficient, without the concurrence of other creditors.

(2) The liquidator shall, if he considers the request to be properly made in accordance with the Act, fix a venue for the meeting, not more than 35 days from his receipt of the request.

(3) The liquidator shall give 21 days' notice of the meeting, and the venue for it, to creditors.

(4) Paragraphs (1) to (3) above apply to the requisitioning by contributories of contributories' meetings, with the following modifications—

 (a) for the reference in paragraph (1)(a) to the creditors' respective claims substitute the contributories' respective values (being the amounts for which they may vote at any meeting); and
 (b) the persons to be given notice under paragraph (3) are those appearing (by the company's books or otherwise) to be contributories of the company.

(NO CVL APPLICATION)   **[776]**

NOTES
>   Para (1): See Sch 4, form 4.21.
>   Para (4): See Sch 4, form 4.24.

4.58. Attendance at meetings of company's personnel

(1) This Rule applies to meetings of creditors and to meetings of contributories.

(2) Whenever a meeting is summoned, the convener shall give at least 21 days' notice to such of the company's personnel as he thinks should be told of, or be present at, the meeting.

"The company's personnel" means the persons referred to in paragraphs (*a*) to (*d*) of section 235(3) (present and past officers, employees, etc).

(3) If the meeting is adjourned, the chairman of the meeting shall, unless for any reason he thinks it unnecessary or impracticable, give notice of the adjournment to such (if any) of the company's personnel as he considers appropriate, being persons who were not themselves present at the meeting.

(4) The convener may, if he thinks fit, give notice to any one or more of the company's personnel that he is, or they are, required to be present at the meeting, or to be in attendance.

(5) In the case of any meeting, any one or more of the company's personnel, and any other persons, may be admitted, but—

>   (*a*) they must have given reasonable notice of their wish to be present, and
>   (*b*) it is a matter for the chairman's discretion whether they are to be admitted or not, and his decision is final as to what (if any) intervention may be made by any of them.

(6) If it is desired to put questions to any one of the company's personnel who is not present, the chairman may adjourn the meeting with a view to obtaining his attendance.

(7) Where one of the company's personnel is present at a meeting, only such questions may be put to him as the chairman may in his discretion allow.   [777]

4.59 Notice of meetings by advertisement only

(1) In the case of any meeting of creditors or contributories to be held under the Act or the Rules, the court may order that notice of the meeting be given by public advertisement, and not by individual notice to the persons concerned.

(2) In considering whether to act under this Rule, the court shall have regard to the cost of public advertisement, to the amount of the assets available, and to the extent of the interest of creditors or of contributories, or any particular class of either of them.   [778]

4.60. Venue

(1) In fixing the venue for a meeting of creditors or contributories, the convener shall have regard to the convenience of the persons (other than whoever is to be chairman) who are invited to attend.

(2) Meetings shall in all cases be summoned for commencement between the hours of 10.00 and 16.00 hours on a business day, unless the court otherwise directs.

(3) With every notice summoning a meeting of creditors or contributories there shall be sent out forms of proxy.   **[779]**

NOTES
    Para (3): See Sch 4, form 8.4 or 8.5.

4.61. Expenses of summoning meetings

(1) Subject as follows, the expenses of summoning and holding a meeting of creditors or contributories at the instance of any person other than the official receiver or the liquidator shall be paid by that person, who shall deposit with the liquidator security for their payment.

(2) The sum to be deposited shall be such as the official receiver or liquidator (as the case may be) determines to be appropriate; and neither shall act without the deposit having been made.

(3) Where a meeting of creditors is so summoned, it may vote that the expenses of summoning and holding it, and of summoning and holding any meeting of contributories requisitioned at the same time, shall be payable out of the assets, as an expense of the liquidation.

(4) Where a meeting of contributories is summoned on the requisition of contributories, it may vote that the expenses of summoning and holding it shall be payable out of the assets, but subject to the right of creditors to be paid in full, with interest.

(5) To the extent that any deposit made under this Rule is not required for the payment of expenses of summoning and holding a meeting, it shall be repaid to the person who made it.   **[780]**

4.62–CVL. Expenses of meeting under s 98

(1) Payment may be made out of the company's assets, either before or after the commencement of the winding up, of any reasonable and necessary expenses incurred in connection with the summoning, advertisement and holding of a creditors' meeting under section 98.

Any such payment is an expense of the liquidation.

(2) Where such payments are made before the commencement of the winding up, the director presiding at the creditors' meeting shall inform the meeting of their amount and the identity of the persons to whom they were made.

(3) The liquidator appointed under section 100 may make such a payment (subject to the next paragraph); but if there is a liquidation committee, he must give the committee at least 7 days' notice of his intention to make the payment.

(4) Such a payment shall not be made by the liquidator to himself, or to any associate of his, otherwise than with the approval of the liquidation committee, the creditors, or the court.

(5) This Rule is without prejudice to the powers of the court under Rule 4.219 (voluntary winding up superseded by winding up by the court).   **[781]**

4.63. Resolutions

(1) At a meeting of creditors or contributories, a resolution is passed when a majority (in value) of those present and voting, in person or by proxy, have voted in favour of the resolution.

The value of contributories is determined by reference to the number of votes conferred on each contributory by the company's articles.

(2) In the case of resolution for the appointment of a liquidator—

    (*a*) if on any vote there are two nominees for appointment, the person who obtains the most support is appointed;

    (*b*) if there are three or more nominees, and one of them has a clear majority over both or all the others together, that one is appointed; and

    (*c*) in any other case, the chairman of the meeting shall continue to take votes (disregarding at each vote any nominee who has withdrawn and, if no nominee has withdrawn, the nominee who obtained the least support last time), until a clear majority is obtained for any one nominee.

(3) The chairman may at any time put to the meeting a resolution for the joint appointment of any two or more nominees.

(4) Where a resolution is proposed which affects a person in respect of his remuneration or conduct as liquidator, or as proposed or former liquidator, the vote of that person, and of any partner or employee of his, shall not be reckoned in the majority required for passing the resolution.

This paragraph applies with respect to a vote given by a person either as creditor or contributory or as proxy for a creditor or a contributory (but subject to Rule 8.6 in Part 8 of the Rules).   **[782]**

4.64. Chairman of meeting as proxy-holder

Where the chairman at a meeting of creditors or contributories holds a proxy which requires him to vote for a particular resolution, and no other person proposes that resolution—

    (*a*) he shall himself propose it, unless he considers that there is good reason for not doing so, and

    (*b*) if he does not propose it, he shall forthwith after the meeting notify his principal of the reason why not.   **[783]**

4.65. Suspension and adjournment

(1) This Rule applies to meetings of creditors and to meetings of contributories.

(2) Once only in the course of any meeting, the chairman may, in his discretion and without an adjournment, declare the meeting suspended for any period up to one hour.

(3) The chairman at any meeting may in his discretion, and shall if the meeting so resolves, adjourn it to such time and place as seems to him to be appropriate in the circumstances.

This is subject to Rule 4.113(3) in case where the liquidator or his nominee is chairman, and a resolution has been proposed for the liquidator's removal.

(4) If within a period of 30 minutes from the time appointed for the commencement of a meeting a quorum is not present, then by virtue of this

Rule the meeting stands adjourned to such time and place as may be appointed by the chairman.

(5) An adjournment under this Rule shall not be for a period of more than 21 days; and Rule 4.60(1) and (2) applies.

(6) If there is no person present to act as chairman, some other person present (being entitled to vote) may make the appointment under paragraph (4), with the agreement of others present (being persons so entitled).

Failing agreement, the adjournment shall be to the same time and place in the next following week or, if that is not a business day, to the business day immediately following.

(7) Where a meeting is adjourned under this Rule, proofs and proxies may be used if lodged at any time up to midday on the business day immediately before the adjourned meeting.   **[784]**

4.66. Quorum

(1) A meeting is not competent to act, in the absence of a quorum, for any purpose except—

    (*a*) the election of a chairman,

    (*b*) in the case of a creditors' meeting, the admission by the chairman of proofs for the purpose of entitlement of creditors to vote, and

    (*c*) the adjournment of the meeting.

(NO CVL APPLICATION)

(2–CVL) A meeting is not competent to act, in the absence of a quorum, for any purpose except the election of a chairman, or the adjournment of the meeting.

(3) Subject to paragraph (4), a quorum is—

    (*a*) in the case of a creditor's meeting, at least 3 creditors entitled to vote, or all the creditors so entitled, if their number does not exceed 3;

    (*b*) in the case of a meeting of contributories, at least 2 contributories so entitled, or all the contributories, if their number does not exceed 2.

The references to creditors and contributories are to those present in person or by proxy, or duly represented under section 375 of the Companies Act.

(4) One person present constitutes a quorum if—

    (*a*) he is himself a creditor or representative under section 375 of the Companies Act or (as the case may be) a contributory with entitlement to vote and he holds a number of proxies sufficient to ensure that, with his own vote, paragraph (3) is complied with, or

    (*b*) being the chairman or any other person, he holds that number of proxies.   **[785]**

4.67. Entitlement to vote (creditors)

(1) Subject as follows in this Rule and the next, at a meeting of creditors a person is entitled to vote as a creditor only if—

    (*a*) there has been duly lodged (in a winding up by the court by the time and date stated in the notice of the meeting) a proof of the debt claimed to be due to him from the company, and the claim has been admitted under Rule 4.70 for the purpose of entitlement to vote, and

(b) there has been lodged, by the time and date stated in the notice of the meeting, any proxy requisite for that entitlement.

(2) The court may, in exceptional circumstances, by order declare the creditors, or any class of them, entitled to vote at creditors' meetings, without being required to prove their debts.

Where a creditor is so entitled, the court may, on the application of the liquidator, make such consequential orders as it thinks fit (as for example an order treating a creditor as having proved his debt for the purpose of permitting payment of dividend).

(3) A creditor shall not vote in respect of a debt for an unliquidated amount, or any debt whose value is not ascertained, except where the chairman agrees to put upon the debt an estimated minimum value for the purpose of entitlement to vote and admits his proof for that purpose.

(4) A secured creditor is entitled to vote only in respect of the balance (if any) of his debt after deducting the value of his security as estimated by him.

(5) A creditor shall not vote in respect of a debt on, or secured by, a current bill of exchange or promissory note, unless he is willing—

(a) to treat the liability to him on the bill or note of every person who is liable on it antecedently to the company, and against whom a bankruptcy order has not been made (or, in the case of a company, which has not gone into liquidation), as a security in his hands, and

(b) to estimate the value of the security and (for the purpose of entitlement to vote, but not for dividend) to deduct it from his proof.   [786]

4.68–CVL. Chairman's discretion to allow vote

At a creditors' meeting, the chairman may allow a creditor to vote, notwithstanding that he has failed to comply with Rule 4.67(1)(a), if satisfied that the failure was due to circumstances beyond the creditor's control.   [787]

4.69. Entitlement to vote (contributories)

At a meeting of contributories, voting rights are as at a general meeting of the company, subject to any provision in the articles affecting entitlement to vote, either generally or at a time when the company is in liquidation.   [788]

4.70. Admission and rejection of proof (creditors' meeting)

(1) At any creditors' meeting the chairman has power to admit or reject a creditor's proof for the purpose of his entitlement to vote; and the power is exercisable with respect to the whole or any part of the proof.

(2) The chairman's decision under this Rule, or in respect of any matter arising under Rule 4.67, is subject to appeal to the court by any creditor or contributory.

(3) If the chairman is in doubt whether a proof should be admitted or rejected, he shall mark it as objected to and allow the creditor to vote, subject to his vote being subsequently declared invalid if the objection to the proof is sustained.

(4) If on an appeal the chairman's decision is reversed or varied, or a creditor's vote is declared invalid, the court may order that another meeting be summoned, or make such other order as it thinks just.

(5) Neither the official receiver, nor any person nominated by him to be chairman, is personally liable for costs incurred by any person in respect of an application under this Rule; and the chairman (if other than the official receiver or a person so nominated) is not so liable unless the court makes an order to that effect.

(NO CVL APPLICATION)

(6–CVL) The liquidator or his nominee as chairman is not personally liable for costs incurred by any person in respect of an application under this Rule, unless the court makes an order to that effect.   **[789]**

4.71. Record of proceedings

(1) At any meeting, the chairman shall cause minutes of the proceedings to be kept. The minutes shall be signed by him, and retained as part of the records of the liquidation.

(2) The chairman shall also cause to be made up and kept a list of all the creditors or, as the case may be, contributories who attended the meeting.

(3) The minutes of the meeting shall include a record of every resolution passed.

(4) It is the chairman's duty to see to it that particulars of all such resolutions, certified by him, are filed in court not more than 21 days after the date of the meeting.

(NO CVL APPLICATION)   **[790]**

SECTION B: WINDING UP OF RECOGNISED BANKS, ETC

4.72. Additional provisions as regards certain meetings

(1) This Rule applies where a company goes, or proposes to go, into liquidation and it is—

  (*a*) a recognised bank or licensed institution within the meaning of the Banking Act 1979, or
  (*b*) an institution to which sections 16 and 18 of that Act apply as if it were a licensed institution.

(2) Notice of any meeting of the company at which it is intended to propose a resolution for its winding up shall be given by the directors to the Bank of England and to the Deposit Protection Board.

(3) Notice to the Bank and the Board shall be the same as given to members of the company.

(4) Where a creditors' meeting is summoned by the liquidator under section 95 or, in a creditors' voluntary winding up, is summoned under section 98, the same notice of the meeting must be given to the Bank and the Board as is given to creditors under Rule 4.51–CVL.

(5) Where the company is being wound up by the court, notice of the first meetings of creditors and contributories shall be given to the Bank and the Board by the official receiver.

(6) Where in the winding up (whether voluntary or by the court) a meeting of creditors or contributories or of the company is summoned for the purpose of—

   (*a*) receiving the liquidator's resignation, or
   (*b*) removing the liquidator, or
   (*c*) appointing a new liquidator,

the person summoning the meeting and giving notice of it shall also give notice to the Bank and the Board.

(7) The Board is entitled to be represented at any meeting of which it is required by this Rule to be given notice; and Schedule 1 to the Rules has effect with respect to the voting rights of the Board at such a meeting.   **[791]**

CHAPTER 9

PROOF OF DEBTS IN A LIQUIDATION

SECTION A: PROCEDURE FOR PROVING

4.73. Meaning of "prove"

(1) Where a company is being wound up by the court, a person claiming to be a creditor of the company and wishing to recover his debt in whole or in part must (subject to any order of the court under Rule 4.67(2)) submit his claim in writing to the liquidator. (NO CVL APPLICATION)

(2–CVL) In a voluntary winding up (whether members' or creditors') the liquidator may require a person claiming to be a creditor of the company and wishing to recover his debt in whole or in part, to submit the claim in writing to him.

(3) A creditor who claims (whether or not in writing) is referred to as "proving" for his debt; and a document by which he seeks to establish his claim is his "proof".

(4) Subject to the next paragraph, a proof must be in the form known as "proof of debt" (whether the form prescribed by the Rules, or a substantially similar form), which shall be made out by or under the directions of the creditor, and signed by him or a person authorised in that behalf. (NO CVL APPLICATION)

(5) Where a debt is due to a Minister of the Crown or a Government Department, the proof need not be in that form, provided that there are shown all such particulars of the debt as are required in the form used by other creditors, and as are relevant in the circumstances. (NO CVL APPLICATION)

(6–CVL) The creditor's proof may be in any form.

(7) In certain circumstances, specified below in this Chapter, the proof must be in the form of an affidavit.   **[792]**

NOTES
   Para (4): See Sch 4, form 4.25.

4.74. Supply of forms

(NO CVL APPLICATION)

(1) Forms of proof shall be sent out by the liquidator to every creditor of the company who is known to him, or is identified in the company's statement of affairs.

(2) The forms shall accompany (whichever is first)—

(*a*) the notice to creditors under section 136(5)(*b*) (official receiver's decision not to call meetings of creditors and contributories), or

(*b*) the first notice calling a meeting of creditors, or

(*c*) where a liquidator is appointed by the court, the notice of his appointment sent by him to creditors.

(3) Where, with the leave of the court under Rule 4.102(5), the liquidator advertises his appointment, he shall send proofs to the creditors within 4 months after the date of the winding-up order.

(4) The above paragraphs of this Rule are subject to any order of the court dispensing with the requirement to send out forms of proof, or altering the time at which the forms are to be sent.   **[793]**

4.75. Contents of proof

(NO CVL APPLICATION)

(1) The following matters shall be stated in a creditor's proof of debt—

(*a*) the creditor's name and address;

(*b*) the total amount of his claim as at the date on which the company went into liquidation;

(*c*) whether or not that amount includes outstanding uncapitalised interest;

(*d*) whether or not the claim includes value added tax;

(*e*) whether the whole or any part of the debt falls within any (and if so which) of the categories of preferential debts under section 386 of, and Schedule 6 to, the Act (as read with Schedule 3 to the Social Security Pensions Act 1975);

(*f*) particulars of how and when the debt was incurred by the company;

(*g*) particulars of any security held, the date when it was given and the value which the creditor puts upon it; and

(*h*) the name, address and authority of the person signing the proof (if other than the creditor himself).

(2) There shall be specified in the proof any documents by reference to which the debt can be substantiated; but (subject as follows) it is not essential that such documents be attached to the proof or submitted with it.

(3) The liquidator, or the chairman or convener of any meeting, may call for any document or other evidence to be produced to him, where he thinks it necessary for the purpose of substantiating the whole or any part of the claim made in the proof.   **[794]**

4.76–CVL. Particulars of creditor's claim

The liquidator, or the convener or chairman of any meeting, may, if he thinks it necessary for the purpose of clarifying or substantiating the whole or any part of a creditor's claim made in his proof, call for details of any matter specified in paragraphs (*a*) to (*h*) of Rule 4.75(1), or for the production to him of such documentary or other evidence as he may require.   **[795]**

4.77. Claim established by affidavit

(1) The liquidator may, if he thinks it necessary, require a claim of debt to be verified by means of an affidavit, for which purpose there shall be used the form known as "affidavit of debt", or a substantially similar form.

(2) An affidavit may be required notwithstanding that a proof of debt has already been lodged.

(3) The affidavit may be sworn before an official receiver or deputy official receiver, or before an officer of the Department or of the court duly authorised in that behalf. (NO CVL APPLICATION)   **[796]**

4.78. Cost of proving

(1) Subject as follows, every creditor bears the cost of proving his own debt, including such as may be incurred in providing documents or evidence under Rule 4.75(3) or 4.76–CVL.

(2) Costs incurred by the liquidator in estimating the quantum of a debt under Rule 4.86 (debts not bearing a certain value) are payable out of the assets, as an expense of the liquidation.

(3) Paragraphs (1) and (2) apply unless the court otherwise orders.   **[797]**

4.79. Liquidator to allow inspection of proofs

The liquidator shall, so long as proofs lodged with him are in his hands, allow them to be inspected, at all reasonable times on any business day, by any of the following persons—

  (a) any creditor who has submitted his proof of debt (unless his proof has been wholly rejected for purposes of dividend or otherwise);
  (b) any contributory of the company;
  (c) any person acting on behalf of either of the above.   **[798]**

4.80. Transmission of proofs to liquidator

(NO CVL APPLICATION)

(1) Where a liquidator is appointed, the official receiver shall forthwith transmit to him all the proofs which he has so far received, together with an itemised list of them.

(2) The liquidator shall sign the list by way of receipt for the proofs, and return it to the official receiver.

(3) From then on, all proofs of debt shall be sent to the liquidator, and retained by him.   **[799]**

4.81. New liquidator appointed

(1) If a new liquidator is appointed in place of another, the former liquidator shall transmit to him all proofs which he has received, together with an itemised list of them.

(2) The new liquidator shall sign the list by way of receipt for the proofs, and return it to his predecessor.   **[800]**

4.82. Admission and rejection of proofs for dividend

(1) A proof may be admitted for dividend either for the whole amount claimed by the creditor, or for part of that amount.

(2) If the liquidator rejects a proof in whole or in part, he shall prepare a

written statement of his reasons for doing so, and send it forthwith to the
creditor.　　　　　　　　　　　　　　　　　　　　　　　　　　　　**[801]**

4.83. Appeal against decision on proof

(1) If a creditor is dissatisfied with the liquidator's decision with respect to his
proof (including any decision on the question of preference), he may apply to
the court for the decision to be reversed or varied.

The application must be made within 21 days of his receiving the statement
sent under Rule 4.82(2).

(2) A contributory or any other creditor may, if dissatisfied with the
liquidator's decision admitting or rejecting the whole or any part of a proof,
make such an application within 21 days of becoming aware of the liquidator's
decision.

(3) Where an application is made to the court under this Rule, the court
shall fix a venue for the application to be heard, notice of which shall be sent by
the applicant to the creditor who lodged the proof in question (if it is not
himself) and to the liquidator.

(4) The liquidator shall, on receipt of the notice, file in court the relevant
proof, together (if appropriate) with a copy of the statement sent under Rule
4.82(2).

(5) After the application has been heard and determined, the proof shall,
unless it has been wholly disallowed, be returned by the court to the liquidator.

(6) The official receiver is not personally liable for costs incurred by any
person in respect of an application under this Rule; and the liquidator (if other
than the official receiver) is not so liable unless the court makes an order to that
effect.　　　　　　　　　　　　　　　　　　　　　　　　　　　**[802]**

4.84. Withdrawal or variation of proof

A creditor's proof may at any time, by agreement between himself and the
liquidator, be withdrawn or varied as to the amount claimed.　　　**[803]**

4.85. Expunging of proof by the court

(1) The court may expunge a proof or reduce the amount claimed—

　　(*a*) on the liquidator's application, where he thinks that the proof has
　　　　been improperly admitted, or ought to be reduced; or
　　(*b*) on the application of a creditor, if the liquidator declines to interfere
　　　　in the matter.

(2) Where application is made to the court under this Rule, the court shall
fix a venue for the application to be heard, notice of which shall be sent by the
applicant—

　　(*a*) in the case of an application by the liquidator, to the creditor who
　　　　made the proof, and
　　(*b*) in the case of an application by a creditor, to the liquidator and to the
　　　　creditor who made the proof (if not himself).　　　　　　**[804]**

Section B: Quantification of Claim

4.86. Estimate of quantum

(1) The liquidator shall estimate the value of any debt which, by reason of its being subject to any contingency or for any other reason, does not bear a certain value; and he may revise any estimate previously made, if he thinks fit by reference to any change of circumstances or to information becoming available to him.

He shall inform the creditor as to his estimate and any revision of it.

(2) Where the value of a debt is estimated under this Rule, or by the court under section 168(3) or (5), the amount provable in the winding up in the case of that debt is that of the estimate for the time being.   [805]

4.87. Negotiable instruments, etc

Unless the liquidator allows, a proof in respect of money owed on a bill of exchange, promissory note, cheque or other negotiable instrument or security cannot be admitted unless there is produced the instrument or security itself or a copy of it, certified by the creditor or his authorised representative to be a true copy.   [806]

4.88. Secured creditors

(1) If a secured creditor realises his security, he may prove for the balance of his debt, after deducting the amount realised.

(2) If a secured creditor voluntarily surrenders his security for the general benefit of creditors, he may prove for his whole debt, as if it were unsecured.
                                                                 [807]

4.89. Discounts

There shall in every case be deducted from the claim all trade and other discounts which would have been available to the company but for its liquidation, except any discount for immediate, early or cash settlement.   [808]

4.90. Mutual credit and set-off

(1) This Rule applies where, before the company goes into liquidation there have been mutual credits, mutual debts or other mutual dealings between the company and any creditor of the company proving or claiming to prove for a debt in the liquidation.

(2) An account shall be taken of what is due from each party to the other in respect of the mutual dealings, and the sums due from one party shall be set off against the sums due from the other.

(3) Sums due from the company to another party shall not be included in the account taken under paragraph (2) if that other party had notice at the time they became due that a meeting of creditors had been summoned under section 98 or (as the case may be) a petition for the winding up of the company was pending.

(4) Only the balance (if any) of the account is provable in the liquidation. Alternatively (as the case may be) the amount shall be paid to the liquidator as part of the assets.   [809]

4.91. Debt in foreign currency

(1) For the purpose of proving a debt incurred or payable in a currency other than sterling, the amount of the debt shall be converted into sterling at the official exchange rate prevailing on the date when the company went into liquidation.

(2) "The official exchange rate" is the middle market rate at the Bank of England, as published for the date in question. In the absence of any such published rate, it is such rate as the court determines. **[810]**

4.92. Payments of a periodical nature

(1) In the case of rent and other payments of a periodical nature, the creditor may prove for any amounts due and unpaid up to the date when the company went into liquidation.

(2) Where at that date any payment was accruing due, the creditor may prove for so much as would have fallen due at that date, if accruing from day to day. **[811]**

4.93. Interest

(1) Where a debt proved in the liquidation bears interest, that interest is provable as part of the debt except in so far as it is payable in respect of any period after the company went into liquidation.

(2) In the following circumstances the creditor's claim may include interest on the debt for periods before the company went into liquidation, although not previously reserved or agreed.

(3) If the debt is due by virtue of a written instrument, and payable at a certain time, interest may be claimed for the period from that time to the date when the company went into liquidation.

(4) If the debt is due otherwise, interest may only be claimed if, before that date, a demand for payment of the debt was made in writing by or on behalf of the creditor, and notice given that interest would be payable from the date of the demand to the date of payment.

(5) Interest under paragraph (4) may only be claimed for the period from the date of the demand to that of the company's going into liquidation.

(6) The rate of interest to be claimed under paragraph (3) or (4) of this Rule is the rate specified in section 17 of the Judgments Act 1838 on the date when the company went into liquidation, except that, where the case falls within paragraph (4), the rate is that specified in the notice there referred to, not exceeding the rate under the Judgments Act mentioned above. **[812]**

4.94. Debt payable at future time

A creditor may prove for a debt of which payment was not yet due on the date when the company went into liquidation, but subject to Rule 11.13 in Part 11 of the Rules (adjustment of dividend where payment made before time). **[813]**

CHAPTER 10

SECURED CREDITORS

4.95. Value of security

(1) A secured creditor may, with the agreement of the liquidator or the leave of the court, at any time alter the value which he has, in his proof of debt, put upon his security.

(2) However, if a secured creditor—

    (*a*) being the petitioner, has in the petition put a value on his security, or
    (*b*) has voted in respect of the unsecured balance of his debt,

he may re-value his security only with leave of the court. (NO CVL APPLICATION) **[814]**

4.96. Surrender for non-disclosure

(1) If a secured creditor omits to disclose his security in his proof of debt, he shall surrender his security for the general benefit of creditors, unless the court, on application by him, relieves him for the effect of this Rule on the ground that the omission was inadvertent or the result of honest mistake.

(2) If the court grants that relief, it may require or allow the creditor's proof of debt to be amended, on such terms as may be just. **[815]**

4.97. Redemption by liquidator

(1) The liquidator may at any time give notice to a creditor whose debt is secured that he proposes, at the expiration of 28 days from the date of the notice, to redeem the security at the value put upon it in the creditor's proof.

(2) The creditor then has 21 days (or such longer period as the liquidator may allow) in which, if he so wishes, to exercise his right to re-value his security (with the leave of the court, when Rule 4.95(2) applies).

If the creditor re-values his security, the liquidator may only redeem at the new value.

(3) If the liquidator redeems the security, the cost of transferring it is payable out of the assets.

(4) A secured creditor may at any time, by a notice in writing, call on the liquidator to elect whether he will or will not exercise his power to redeem the security at the value then placed on it; and the liquidator then has 6 months in which to exercise the power or determine not to exercise it. **[816]**

4.98. Test of security's value

(1) Subject as follows, the liquidator, if he is dissatisfied with the value which a secured creditor puts on his security (whether in his proof or by way of re-valuation under Rule 4.97), may require any property comprised in the security to be offered for sale.

(2) The terms of sale shall be such as may be agreed, or as the court may direct; and if the sale is by auction, the liquidator on behalf of the company, and the creditor on his own behalf, may appear and bid. **[817]**

4.99. Realisation of security by creditor

If a creditor who has valued his security subsequently realises it (whether or not at the instance of the liquidator)—

>   (*a*) the net amount realised shall be substituted for the value previously put by the creditor on the security, and
>   (*b*) that amount shall be treated in all respects as an amended valuation made by him.   **[818]**

CHAPTER 11

THE LIQUIDATOR

SECTION A : APPOINTMENT AND ASSOCIATED FORMALITIES

4.100. Appointment by creditors or contributories

(NO CVL APPLICATION)

(1) This Rule applies where a person is appointed as liquidator either by a meeting of creditors or by a meeting of contributories.

(2) The chairman of the meeting shall certify the appointment, but not unless and until the person appointed has provided him with a written statement to the effect that he is an insolvency practitioner, duly qualified under the Act to be the liquidator, and that he consents so to act.

(3) Where the chairman of the meeting is not the official receiver, he shall send the certificate to him.

(4) The official receiver shall in any case file a copy of the certificate in court; and the liquidator's appointment is effective as from the date on which the official receiver files the copy certificate in court, that date to be endorsed on the copy certificate.

(5) The certificate, so endorsed, shall be sent by the official receiver to the liquidator.   **[819]**

NOTES
    Para (2): See Sch 4, forms 4.27, 4.28.

4.101–CVL. Appointment by creditors or by the company

(1) This Rule applies where a person is appointed as liquidator either by a meeting of creditors or by a meeting of the company.

(2) Subject as follows, the chairman of the meeting shall certify the appointment, but not unless and until the person appointed has provided him with a written statement to the effect that he is an insolvency practitioner, duly qualified under the Act to be the liquidator, and that he consents so to act; the liquidator's appointment is effective from the date of the certificate.

(3) The chairman shall send the certificate forthwith to the liquidator, who shall keep it as part of the records of the liquidation.

(4) Paragraphs (2) and (3) need not be complied with in the case of a liquidator appointed by a company meeting and replaced by another liquidator appointed on the same day by a creditors' meeting.   **[820]**

NOTES
    Para (2): See Sch 4, forms 4.27, 4.28.

4.102. Appointment by the court

(NO CVL APPLICATION)

(1) This Rule applies where the liquidator is appointed by the court under section 139(4) (different persons nominated by creditors and contributories) or section 140 (liquidation following administration or voluntary arrangement).

(2) The court's order shall not issue unless and until the person appointed has filed in court a statement to the effect that he is an insolvency practitioner, duly qualified under the Act to be the liquidator, and that he consents so to act.

(3) Thereafter, the court shall send 2 copies of the order to the official receiver. One of the copies shall be sealed, and this shall be sent to the person appointed as liquidator.

(4) The liquidator's appointment takes effect from the date of the order.

(5) The liquidator shall, within 28 days of his appointment, give notice of it to all creditors and contributories of the company of whom he is aware in that period. Alternatively, if the court allows, he may advertise his appointment in accordance with the court's directions.

(6) In his notice or advertisement under this Rule the liquidator shall—

    (*a*) state whether he proposes to summon meetings of creditors and contributories for the purpose of establishing a liquidation committee, or proposes to summon only a meeting of creditors for that purpose, and

    (*b*) if he does not propose to summon any such meeting, set out the powers of the creditors under the Act to require him to summon one.   **[821]**

NOTES
Para (1): See Sch 4, forms 4.29, 4.30.

4.103–CVL. Appointment by the court

(1) This Rule applies where the liquidator is appointed by the court under section 100(3) or 108.

(2) The court's order shall not issue unless and until the person appointed has filed in court a statement to the effect that he is an insolvency practitioner, duly qualified under the Act to be the liquidator, and that he consents so to act.

(3) Thereafter, the court shall send a sealed copy of the order to the liquidator, whose appointment takes effect from the date of the order.

(4) Not later than 28 days from his appointment, the liquidator shall give notice of it to all creditors of the company of whom he is aware in that period. Alternatively, if the court allows, he may advertise his appointment in accordance with the court's directions.   **[822]**

NOTES
See Sch 4, forms 4.29, 4.30.

4.104. Appointment by Secretary of State

(NO CVL APPLICATION)

(1) This Rule applies where the official receiver applies to the Secretary of State to appoint a liquidator in place of himself, or refers to the Secretary of State the need for an appointment.

(2) If the Secretary of State makes an appointment, he shall send two copies of the certificate of appointment to the official receiver, who shall transmit one such copy to the person appointed, and file the other in court.

(3) The certificate shall specify the date from which the liquidator's appointment is to be effective.   **[823]**

4.105 Authentication of liquidator's appointment

A copy of the certificate of the liquidator's appointment or (as the case may be) a sealed copy of the court's order, may in any proceedings be adduced as proof that the person appointed is duly authorised to exercise the powers and perform the duties of liquidator in the company's winding up.   **[824]**

4.106. Appointment to be advertised and registered

(1) Subject as follows, where the liquidator is appointed by a creditors' or contributories' meeting, or by a meeting of the company, he shall, on receiving his certificate of appointment, give notice of his appointment in such newspaper as he thinks most appropriate for ensuring that it comes to the notice of the company's creditors and contributories.

(2–CVL) Paragraph (1) need not be complied with in the case of a liquidator appointed by a company meeting and replaced by another liquidator appointed on the same day by a creditors' meeting.

(3) The expense of giving notice under this rule shall be borne in the first instance by the liquidator; but he is entitled to be reimbursed out of the assets, as an expense of the liquidation.

The same applies also in the case of the notice or advertisement required where the appointment is made by the court or the Secretary of State.

(4) In the case of a winding up by the court, the liquidator shall also forthwith notify his appointment to the registrar of companies.

This applies however the liquidator is appointed.   **[825]**

NOTES
    Para (4): See Sch 4, form 4.31.

4.107. Hand-over of assets to liquidator

(NO CVL APPLICATION)

(1) This Rule applies only where the liquidator is appointed in succession to the official receiver acting as liquidator.

(2) When the liquidator's appointment takes effect, the official receiver shall forthwith do all that is required for putting him into possession of the assets.

(3) On taking possession of the assets, the liquidator shall discharge any balance due to the official receiver on account of—

    (*a*) expenses properly incurred by him and payable under the Act or the Rules, and

    (*b*) any advances made by him in respect of the assets, together with interest on such advances at the rate specified in section 17 of the Judgments Act 1838 at the date of the winding-up order.

(4) Alternatively, the liquidator may (before taking office) give to the official

receiver a written undertaking to discharge any such balance out of the first realisation of assets.

(5) The official receiver has a charge on the assets in respect of any sums due to him under paragraph (3). But, where the liquidator has realised assets with a view to making those payments, the official receiver's charge does not extend in respect of sums deductible by the liquidator from the proceeds of realisation, as being expenses properly incurred therein.

(6) The liquidator shall from time to time out of the realisation of assets discharge all guarantees properly given by the official receiver for the benefit of the estate, and shall pay all the official receiver's expenses.

(7) The official receiver shall give to the liquidator all such information relating to the affairs of the company and the course of the winding up as he (the official receiver) considers to be reasonably required for the effective discharge by the liquidator of his duties as such.

(8) The liquidator shall also be furnished with a copy of any report made by the official receiver under Chapter 7 of this Part of the Rules.   **[826]**

SECTION B: RESIGNATION AND REMOVAL; VACATION OF OFFICE

4.108. Creditors' meeting to receive liquidator's resignation

(1) Before resigning his office, the liquidator must call a meeting of creditors for the purpose of receiving his resignation. The notice summoning the meeting shall indicate that this is the purpose, or one of the purposes, of it, and shall draw the attention of creditors to Rule 4.121 or, as the case may be, Rule 4.122–CVL with respect to the liquidator's release.

(2) A copy of the notice shall at the same time also be sent to the official receiver. (NO CVL APPLICATION)

(3) The notice to creditors under paragraph (1) must be accompanied by an account of the liquidator's administration of the winding up, including—

(a) a summary of his receipts and payments, and
(b) a statement by him that he has reconciled his account with that which is held by the Secretary of State in respect of the winding up.

(4) Subject as follows, the liquidator may only proceed under this Rule on grounds of ill health or because—

(a) he intends ceasing to be in practice as an insolvency practitioner, or
(b) there is some conflict of interest or change of personal circumstances which precludes or makes impracticable the further discharge by him of the duties of liquidator.

(5) Where two or more persons are acting as liquidator jointly, any one of them may proceed under this Rule (without prejudice to the continuation in office of the other or others) on the ground that, in his opinion and that of the other or others, it is no longer expedient that there should continue to be the present number of joint liquidators.   **[827]**

NOTES
Para (1): See Sch 4, form 4.22.

4.109. Action following acceptance of resignation

(NO CVL APPLICATION)

(1) This Rule applies where a meeting is summoned to receive the liquidator's resignation.

(2) If the chairman of the meeting is other than the official receiver, and there is passed at the meeting any of the following resolutions—

(*a*) that the liquidator's resignation be accepted,
(*b*) that a new liquidator be appointed,
(*c*) that the resigning liquidator be not given his release,

the chairman shall, within 3 days, send to the official receiver a copy of the resolution.

If it has been resolved to accept the liquidator's resignation, the chairman shall send to the official receiver a certificate to that effect.

(3) If the creditors have resolved to appoint a new liquidator, the certificate of his appointment shall also be sent to the official receiver within that time; and Rule 4.100 shall be complied with in respect of it.

(4) If the liquidator's resignation is accepted, the notice of it required by section 172(6) shall be given by him forthwith after the meeting; and he shall send a copy of the notice to the official receiver.

The notice shall be accompanied by a copy of the account sent to creditors under Rule 4.108(3).

(5) The official receiver shall file a copy of the notice in court.

(6) The liquidator's resignation is effective as from the date on which the official receiver files the copy notice in court, that date to be endorsed on the copy notice.   **[828]**

NOTES

  Para (4): See Sch 4, form 4.32.

4.110–CVL. Action following acceptance of resignation

(1) This Rule applies where a meeting is summoned to receive the liquidator's resignation.

(2) If his resignation is accepted, the notice of it required by section 171(5) shall be given by him forthwith after the meeting.

(3) Where a new liquidator is appointed in place of the one who has resigned, the certificate of his appointment shall be delivered forthwith by the chairman of the meeting to the new liquidator.   **[829]**

NOTES

  Para (2): See Sch 4, form 4.33.

4.111. Leave to resign granted by the court

(1) If at a creditors' meeting summoned to accept the liquidator's resignation it is resolved that it be not accepted, the court may, on the liquidator's application, make an order giving him leave to resign.

(2) The court's order may include such provision as it thinks fit with respect to matters arising in connection with the resignation, and shall determine the date from which the liquidator's release is effective.

(3) The court shall send two sealed copies of the order to the liquidator, who shall send one of the copies forthwith to the official receiver. (NO CVL APPLICATION)

(4–CVL) The court shall send two sealed copies of the order to the liquidator, who shall forthwith send one of them to the registrar of companies.

(5) On sending notice of his resignation to the court, the liquidator shall send a copy of it to the official receiver. (NO CVL APPLICATION) **[830]**

NOTES
    Para (1): See Sch 4, form 4.34.
    Para (4): See Sch 4, form 4.35.
    Para (5): See Sch 4, form 4.36.

4.112. Advertisement of resignation

Where a new liquidator is appointed in place of one who has resigned, the former shall, in giving notice of his appointment, state that his predecessor has resigned and (if it be the case) that he has been given his release. **[831]**

4.113. Meeting of creditors to remove liquidator

(NO CVL APPLICATION)

(1) Where a meeting of creditors is summoned for the purpose of removing the liquidator, the notice summoning it shall indicate that this is the purpose, or one of the purposes, of the meeting; and the notice shall draw the attention of creditors to section 174(4) with respect to the liquidator's release.

(2) A copy of the notice shall at the same time also be sent to the official receiver.

(3) At the meeting, a person other than the liquidator or his nominee may be elected to act as chairman; but if the liquidator or his nominee is chairman and a resolution has been proposed for the liquidator's removal, the chairman shall not adjourn the meeting without the consent of at least one-half (in value) of the creditors present (in person or by proxy) and entitled to vote.

(4) Where the chairman of the meeting is other than the official receiver, and there is passed at the meeting any of the following resolutions—

    (*a*) that the liquidator be removed,
    (*b*) that a new liquidator be appointed,
    (*c*) that the removed liquidator be not given his release,

the chairman shall, within 3 days, send to the official receiver a copy of the resolution.

If it has been resolved to remove the liquidator, the chairman shall send to the official receiver a certificate to that effect.

(5) If the creditors have resolved to appoint a new liquidator, the certificate of his appointment shall also be sent to the official receiver within that time; and Rule 4.100 above shall be complied with in respect of it. **[832]**

NOTES
    Para (1): See Sch 4, form 4.22.
    Para (4): See Sch 4, form 4.37.

4.114–CVL. Meeting of creditors to remove liquidator

(1) A meeting held under section 171(2)(*b*) for the removal of the liquidator shall be summoned by him if requested by 25 per cent in value of the company's creditors, excluding those who are connected with it.

(2) The notice summoning the meeting shall indicate that the removal of the liquidator is the purpose, or one of the purposes, of the meeting; and the notice shall draw the attention of creditors to section 173(2) with respect to the liquidator's release.

(3) At the meeting, a person other than the liquidator or his nominee may be elected to act as chairman; but if the liquidator or his nominee is chairman and a resolution has been proposed for the liquidator's removal, the chairman shall not adjourn the meeting without the consent of at least one-half (in value) of the creditors present (in person or by proxy) and entitled to vote.   **[833]**

NOTES
Para (2): See Sch 4, form 4.22.

4.115. Court's power to regulate meetings under Rules 4.113, 4.114–CVL

Where a meeting under Rule 4.113 or 4.114–CVL is to be held, or is proposed to be summoned, the court may, on the application of any creditor, give directions as to the mode of summoning it, the sending out and return of forms of proxy, the conduct of the meeting, and any other matter which appears to the court to require regulation or control under this Rule.   **[834]**

4.116. Procedure on removal

(NO CVL APPLICATION)

(1) Where the creditors have resolved that the liquidator be removed, the official receiver shall file in court the certificate of removal.

(2) The resolution is effective as from the date on which the official receiver files the certificate of removal in court, and that date shall be endorsed on the certificate.

(3) A copy of the certificate, so endorsed, shall be sent by the official receiver to the liquidator who has been removed and, if a new liquidator has been appointed, to him.

(4) The official receiver shall not file the certificate in court unless and until the Secretary of State has certified to him that the removed liquidator has reconciled his account with that held by the Secretary of State in respect of the winding up.   **[835]**

4.117–CVL. Procedure on removal

Where the creditors have resolved that the liquidator be removed, the chairman of the creditors' meeting shall forthwith—

    (*a*) if at the meeting another liquidator was not appointed, send the certificate of the liquidator's removal to the registrar of companies, and

    (*b*) otherwise, deliver the certificate to the new liquidator, who shall send it to the registrar.   **[836]**

NOTES
See Sch 4, form 4.38.

4.118. Advertisement of removal

Where a new liquidator is appointed in place of one removed, the former shall, in giving notice of his appointment, state that his predecessor has been removed and (if it be the case) that he has been given his release.   **[837]**

4.119. Removal of liquidator by the court

(NO CVL APPLICATION)

(1) This Rule applies where application is made to the court for the removal of the liquidator, or for an order directing the liquidator to summon a meeting of creditors for the purpose of removing him.

(2) The court may, if it thinks that no sufficient cause is shown for the application, dismiss it; but it shall not do so unless the applicant has had an opportunity to attend the court for an *ex parte* hearing, of which he has been given at least 7 days' notice.

If the application is not dismissed under this paragraph, the court shall fix a venue for it to be heard.

(3) The court may require the applicant to make a deposit or give security for the costs to be incurred by the liquidator on the application.

(4) The applicant shall, at least 14 days before the hearing, send to the liquidator and the official receiver a notice stating the venue and accompanied by a copy of the application, and of any evidence which he intends to adduce in support of it.

(5) Subject to any contrary order of the court, the costs of the application are not payable out of the assets.

(6) Where the court removes the liquidator—

    (*a*) it shall send copies of the order of removal to him and to the official receiver;

    (*b*) the order may include such provision as the court thinks fit with respect to matters arising in connection with the removal; and

    (*c*) if the court appoints a new liquidator, Rule 4.102 applies.   **[838]**

NOTES
    Para (1): See Sch 4, form 4.39.

4.120–CVL. Removal of liquidator by the court

(1) This Rule applies where the application is made to the court for the removal of the liquidator, or for an order directing the liquidator to summon a creditors' meeting for the purpose of removing him.

(2) The court may, if it thinks that no sufficient cause is shown for the application, dismiss it; but it shall not do so unless the applicant has had an opportunity to attend the court for an *ex parte* hearing, of which he has been given at least 7 days' notice.

If the application is not dismissed under this paragraph, the court shall fix a venue for it to be heard.

(3) The court may require the applicant to make a deposit or give security for the costs to be incurred by the liquidator on the application.

(4) The applicant shall, at least 14 days before the hearing, send to the

liquidator a notice stating the venue and accompanied by a copy of the application, and of any evidence which he intends to adduce in support of it.

(5) Subject to any contrary order of the court, the costs of the application are not payable out of the assets.

(6) Where the court removes the liquidator—

(a) it shall send 2 copies of the order of removal to him, one to be sent by him forthwith to the registrar of companies, with notice of his ceasing to act;

(b) the order may include such provision as the court thinks fit with respect to matters arising in connection with the removal; and

(c) if the court appoints a new liquidator, Rule 4.103–CVL applies. **[839]**

NOTES
   Para (1): See Sch 4, form 4.39.
   Para (6)(a): See Sch 4, form 4.40.

4.121. Release of resigning or removed liquidator

(NO CVL APPLICATION)

(1) Where the liquidator's resignation is accepted by a meeting of creditors which has not resolved against his release, he has his release from when his resignation is effective under Rule 4.109.

(2) Where the liquidator is removed by a meeting of creditors which has not resolved against his release, the fact of his release shall be stated in the certificate of removal.

(3) Where—

(a) the liquidator resigns, and the creditors' meeting called to receive his resignation has resolved against his release, or

(b) he is removed by a creditors' meeting which has so resolved, or is removed by the court,

he must apply to the Secretary of State for his release.

(4) When the Secretary of State gives the release, he shall certify it accordingly, and send the certificate to the official receiver, to be filed in court.

(5) A copy of the certificate shall be sent by the Secretary of State to the former liquidator, whose release is effective from the date of the certificate.

[840]

NOTES
   Para (3): See Sch 4, form 4.41.

4.122–CVL. Release of resigning or removed liquidator

(1) Where the liquidator's resignation is accepted by a meeting of creditors which has not resolved against his release, he has his release from when he gives notice of his resignation to the registrar of companies.

(2) Where the liquidator is removed by a creditors' meeting which has not resolved against his relase, the fact of his release shall be stated in the certificate of removal.

(3) Where—

(*a*) the liquidator resigns, and the creditors' meeting called to receive his resignation has resolved against his release, or

(*b*) he is removed by a creditors' meeting which has so resolved, or is removed by the court,

he must apply to the Secretary of State for his release.

(4) When the Secretary of State gives the release, he shall certify it accordingly, and send the certificate to the registrar of companies.

(5) A copy of the certificate shall be sent by the Secretary of State to the former liquidator, whose release is effective from the date of the certificate.

[841]

NOTES
    Para (1): See Sch 4, form 4.40.
    Para (3): See Sch 4, form 4.41.

4.123. Removal of liquidator by Secretary of State

(NO CVL APPLICATION)

(1) If the Secretary of State decides to remove the liquidator, he shall before doing so notify the liquidator and the official receiver of his decision and the grounds of it, and specify a period within which the liquidator may make representations against implementation of the decision.

(2) If the Secretary of State directs the removal of the liquidator, he shall forthwith—

(*a*) file notice of his decision in court, and

(*b*) send notice to the liquidator and the official receiver.

(3) If the liquidator is removed by direction of the Secretary of State—

(*a*) Rule 4.121 applies as regards the liquidator obtaining his release, as if he had been removed by the court, and

(*b*) the court may make any such order in his case as it would have power to make if he had been so removed. [842]

SECTION C: RELEASE ON COMPLETION OF ADMINISTRATION

4.124. Release of official receiver

(NO CVL APPLICATION)

(1) The official receiver shall, before giving notice to the Secretary of State under section 174(3) (that the winding up is for practical purposes complete), send out notice of his intention to do so to all creditors who have proved their debts.

(2) The notice shall in each case be accompanied by a summary of the official receiver's receipts and payments as liquidator.

(3) The Secretary of State, when he has determined the date from which the official receiver is to have his release, shall give notice to the court that he has done so. The notice shall be accompanied by the summary referred to in paragraph (2). [843]

4.125. Final meeting

(NO CVL APPLICATION)

(1) Where the liquidator is other than the official receiver, he shall give at least 28 days' notice of the final meeting of creditors to be held under section 146. The notice shall be sent to all creditors who have proved their debts; and the liquidator shall cause it to be gazetted at least one month before the meeting is to be held.

(2) The liquidator's report laid before the meeting under that section shall contain an account of the liquidator's administration of the winding up, including—

(*a*) a summary of his receipts and payments, and

(*b*) a statement by him that he has reconciled his account with that which is held by the Secretary of State in respect of the winding up.

(3) At the final meeting, the creditors may question the liquidator with respect to any matter contained in his report, and may resolve against him having his release.

(4) The liquidator shall give notice to the court that the final meeting has been held; and the notice shall state whether or not he has been given his release, and be accompanied by a copy of the report laid before the final meeting. A copy of the notice shall be sent by the liquidator to the official receiver.

(5) If there is no quorum present at the final meeting, the liquidator shall report to the court that a final meeting was summoned in accordance with the Rules, but there was no quorum present; and the final meeting is then deemed to have been held, and the creditors not to have resolved against the liquidator having his release.

(6) If the creditors at the final meeting have not so resolved, the liquidator is released when the notice under paragraph (4) is filed in court. If they have so resolved, the liquidator must obtain his release from the Secretary of State and Rule 4.121 applies accordingly. **[844]**

NOTES
Para (1): See Sch 4, form 4.22.
Para (4): See Sch 4, form 4.42.

4.126–CVL. Final meeting

(1) The liquidator shall give at least 28 days' notice of the final meeting of creditors to be held under section 106. The notice shall be sent to all creditors who have proved their debts.

(2) At the final meeting, the creditors may question the liquidator with respect to any matter contained in the account required under the section, and may resolve against the liquidator having his release.

(3) Where the creditors have so resolved, he must obtain his release from the Secretary of State; and Rule 4.122–CVL applies accordingly. **[845]**

NOTES
Para (1): See Sch 4, form 4.22.

SECTION D: REMUNERATION

4.127. Fixing of remuneration

(1) The liquidator is entitled to receive remuneration for his services as such.

(2) The remuneration shall be fixed either—

    (a) as a percentage of the value of the assets which are realised or distributed, or of the one value and the other in combination, or

    (b) by reference to the time properly given by the insolvency practitioner (as liquidator) and his staff in attending to matters arising in the winding up.

(3) Where the liquidator is other than the official receiver, it is for the liquidation committee (if there is one) to determine whether the remuneration is to be fixed under paragraph (2)(a) or (b) and, if under paragraph (2)(a), to determine any percentage to be applied as there mentioned.

(4) In arriving at that determination, the committee shall have regard to the following matters—

    (a) the complexity (or otherwise) of the case,

    (b) any respects in which, in connection with the winding up, there falls on the insolvency practitioner (as liquidator) any responsibility of an exceptional kind or degree,

    (c) the effectiveness with which the insolvency practitioner appears to be carrying out, or to have carried out, his duties as liquidator, and

    (d) the value and nature of the assets with which the liquidator has to deal.

(5) If there is no liquidation committee, or the committee does not make the requisite determination, the liquidator's remuneration may be fixed (in accordance with paragraph (2)) by a resolution of a meeting of creditors; and paragraph (4) applies to them as it does to the liquidation committee.

(6) If not fixed as above, the liquidator's remuneration shall be in accordance with the scale laid down for the official receiver by general regulations.   **[846]**

4.128. Other matters affecting remuneration

(1) Where the liquidator sells assets on behalf of a secured creditor, he is entitled to take for himself, out of the proceeds of sale, a sum by way of remuneration equivalent to that which is chargeable in corresponding circumstances by the official receiver under general regulations.

(2) Where there are joint liquidators, it is for them to agree between themselves as to how the remuneration payable should be apportioned. Any dispute arising between them may be referred—

    (a) to the court, for settlement by order, or

    (b) to the liquidation committee or a meeting of creditors, for settlement by resolution.

(3) If the liquidator is a solicitor and employs his own firm, or any partner in it, to act on behalf of the company, profit costs shall not be paid unless this is authorised by the liquidation committee, the creditors or the court.   **[847]**

4.129. Recourse of liquidator to meeting of creditors

If the liquidator's remuneration has been fixed by the liquidation committee, and he considers the rate or amount to be insufficient, he may request that it be increased by resolution of the creditors.   **[848]**

4.130. Recourse to the court

(1) If the liquidator considers that the remuneration fixed for him by the liquidation committee, or by resolution of the creditors, or as under Rule 4.127(6), is insufficient, he may apply to the court for an order increasing its amount or rate.

(2) The liquidator shall give at least 14 days' notice of his application to the members of the liquidation committee; and the committee may nominate one or more members to appear or be represented, and to be heard, on the application.

(3) If there is no liquidation committee, the liquidator's notice of his application shall be sent to such one or more of the company's creditors as the court may direct, which creditors may nominate one or more of their number to appear or be represented.

(4) The court may, if it appears to be a proper case, order the costs of the liquidator's application, including the costs of any member of the liquidation committee appearing on it, or any creditor so appearing, to be paid out of the assets.   **[849]**

4.131. Creditors' claim that remuneration is excessive

(1) Any creditor of the company may, with the concurrence of at least 25 per cent in value of the creditors (including himself), apply to the court for an order that the liquidator's remuneration be reduced, on the grounds that it is, in all the circumstances, excessive.

(2) The court may, if it thinks that no sufficient cause is shown for a reduction, dismiss the application; but it shall not do so unless the applicant has had an opportunity to attend the court for an *ex parte* hearing, of which he has been given at least 7 days' notice.

If the application is not dismissed under this paragraph, the court shall fix a venue for it to be heard, and give notice to the applicant accordingly.

(3) The applicant shall, at least 14 days before the hearing, send to the liquidator a notice stating the venue and accompanied by a copy of the application, and of any evidence which the applicant intends to adduce in support of it.

(4) If the court considers the application to be well-founded, it shall make an order fixing the remuneration at a reduced amount or rate.

(5) Unless the court orders otherwise, the costs of the application shall be paid by the applicant, and are not payable out of the assets.   **[850]**

Section E: Supplementary Provisions

4.132. Liquidator deceased

(NO CVL APPLICATION)

(1) Subject as follows, where the liquidator (other than the official receiver)

has died, it is the duty of his personal representatives to give notice of the fact to the official receiver, specifying the date of the death.

This does not apply if notice has been given under any of the following paragraphs of this Rule.

(2) If the deceased liquidator was a partner in a firm, notice may be given to the official receiver by a partner in the firm who is qualified to act as an insolvency practitioner, or is a member of any body recognised by the Secretary of State for the authorisation of insolvency practitioners.

(3) Notice of the death may be given by any person producing to the official receiver the relevant death certificate or a copy of it.

(4) The official receiver shall give notice to the court, for the purpose of fixing the date of the deceased liquidator's release.   **[851]**

4.133–CVL. Liquidator deceased

(1) Subject as follows, where the liquidator has died, it is the duty of his personal representatives to give notice of the fact, and of the date of death, to the registrar of companies and to the liquidation committee (if any) or a member of that committee.

(2) In the alternative, notice of the death may be given—

    (*a*) if the deceased liquidator was a partner in a firm, by a partner qualified to act as an insolvency practitioner or who is a member of any body approved by the Secretary of State for the authorisation of insolvency practitioners, or

    (*b*) by any person, if he delivers with the notice a copy of the relevant death certificate.   **[852]**

NOTES
    Para (1): See Sch 4, form 4.44.

4.134. Loss of qualification as insolvency practitioner

(NO CVL APPLICATION)

(1) This Rule applies where the liquidator vacates office on ceasing to be qualified to act as an insolvency practitioner in relation to the company.

(2) He shall forthwith give notice of his doing so to the official receiver, who shall give notice to the Secretary of State.
The official receiver shall file in court a copy of his notice under this paragraph.

(3) Rule 4.121 applies as regards the liquidator obtaining his release, as if he had been removed by the court.   **[853]**

NOTES
    Para (2): See Sch 4, form 4.45.

4.135–CVL. Loss of qualification as insolvency practitioner

(1) This Rule applies where the liquidator vacates office on ceasing to be qualified to act as an insolvency practitioner in relation to the company.

(2) He shall forthwith give notice of his doing so to the registrar of companies and the Secretary of State.

(3) Rule 4.122–CVL applies as regards the liquidator obtaining his release, as if he had been removed by the court.   **[854]**

NOTES
    Para (2): See Sch 4, forms 4.46, 4.45.

4.136–CVL. Vacation of office on making of winding-up order

Where the liquidator vacates office in consequence of the court making a winding-up order against the company, Rule 4.122-CVL applies as regards his obtaining his release, as if he had been removed by the court.   **[855]**

4.137. Notice to official receiver of intention to vacate office

(NO CVL APPLICATION)

(1) Where the liquidator intends to vacate office, whether by resignation or otherwise, and there remain any unrealised assets, he shall give notice of his intention to the official receiver, informing him of the nature, value and whereabouts of the assets in question.

(2) Where there is to be a creditors' meeting to receive the liquidator's resignation, or otherwise in respect of his vacation of office, the notice to the official receiver must be given at least 21 days before the meeting.   **[856]**

4.138. Liquidator's duties on vacating office

(1) Where the liquidator ceases to be in office as such, in consequence of removal, resignation or cesser of qualification as an insolvency practitioner, he is under obligation forthwith to deliver up to the person succeeding him as liquidator the assets (after deduction of any expenses properly incurred, and distributions made, by him) and further to deliver up to that person—

  (*a*) the records of the liquidation, including correspondence, proofs and other related papers appertaining to the administration while it was within his responsibility, and
  (*b*) the company's books, papers and other records.

(2) When the winding up is for practical purposes complete, the liquidator shall forthwith file in court all proofs remaining with him in the proceedings.
(NO CVL APPLICATION)   **[857]**

SECTION F: THE LIQUIDATOR IN A MEMBERS' VOLUNTARY WINDING UP

4.139. Appointment by the company

(1) This Rule applies where the liquidator is appointed by a meeting of the company.

(2) Subject as follows, the chairman of the meeting shall certify the appointment, but not unless and until the person appointed has provided him with a written statement to the effect that he is an insolvency practitioner, duly qualified under the Act to be the liquidator, and that he consents so to act.

(3) The chairman shall send the certificate forthwith to the liquidator, who shall keep it as part of the records of the liquidation.

(4) Not later than 28 days from his appointment, the liquidator shall give notice of it to all creditors of the company of whom he is aware in that period.

[858]

NOTES
  Para (2): See Sch 4, forms 4.27, 4.28.

4.140. Appointment by the court

(1) This Rule applies where the liquidator is appointed by the court under section 108.

(2) The court's order shall not issue unless and until the person appointed has filed in court a statement to the effect that he is an insolvency practitioner, duly qualified under the Act to be the liquidator, and that he consents so to act.

(3) Thereafter, the court shall send a sealed copy of the order to the liquidator, whose appointment takes effect from the date of the order.

(4) Not later than 28 days from his appointment, the liquidator shall give notice of it to all creditors of the company of whom he is aware in that period.

[859]

NOTES
  Para (2): See Sch 4, forms 4.29, 4.30.

4.141. Authentication of liquidator's appointment

A copy of the certificate of the liquidator's appointment or (as the case may be) a sealed copy of the court's order appointing him may in any proceedings be adduced as proof that the person appointed is duly authorised to exercise the powers and perform the duties of liquidator in the company's winding up. [860]

4.142. Company meeting to receive liquidator's resignation

(1) Before resigning his office, the liquidator must call a meeting of the company for the purpose of receiving his resignation. The notice summoning the meeting shall indicate that this is the purpose, or one of the purposes, of it.

(2) The notice under paragraph (1) must be accompanied by an account of the liquidator's administration of the winding up, including—

  (*a*) a summary of his receipts and payments, and
  (*b*) a statement by him that he has reconciled his account with that which is held by the Secretary of State in respect of the winding up.

(3) Subject as follows, the liquidator may only proceed under this Rule on grounds of ill health or because—

  (*a*) he intends ceasing to be in practice as an insolvency practitioner, or
  (*b*) there is some conflict of interest or change of personal circumstances which precludes or makes impracticable the further discharge by him of the duties of liquidator.

(4) Where two or more persons are acting as liquidator jointly, any one of them may proceed under this Rule (without prejudice to the continuation in office of the other or others) on the ground that, in his opinion or that of the

other or others, it is no longer expedient that there should continue to be the present number of joint liquidators.

(5) The notice of the liquidator's resignation required by section 171(5) shall be given by him forthwith after the meeting.

(6) Where a new liquidator is appointed in place of one who has resigned, the former shall, in giving notice of his appointment, state that his predecessor has resigned.   **[861]**

NOTES
   Para (5): See Sch 4, form 4.33.

4.143. Removal of liquidator by the court

(1) This Rule applies where application is made to the court for the removal of the liquidator, or for an order directing the liquidator to summon a company meeting for the purpose of removing him.

(2) The court may, if it thinks that no sufficient cause is shown for the application, dismiss it; but it shall not do so unless the applicant has had an opportunity to attend the court for an *ex parte* hearing, of which he has been given at least 7 days' notice.

If the application is not dismissed under this paragraph, the court shall fix a venue for it to be heard.

(3) The court may require the applicant to make a deposit or give security for the costs to be incurred by the liquidator on the application.

(4) The applicant shall, at least 14 days before the hearing, send to the liquidator a notice stating the venue and accompanied by a copy of the application, and of any evidence which he intends to adduce in support of it.

Subject to any contrary order of the court, the costs of the application are not payable out of the assets.

(5) Where the court removes the liquidator—

   (a) it shall send 2 copies of the order of removal to him, one to be sent by him forthwith to the registrar of companies, with notice of his ceasing to act;

   (b) the order may include such provision as the court thinks fit with respect to matters arising in connection with the removal; and

   (c) if the court appoints a new liquidator, Rule 4.140 applies.   **[862]**

NOTES
   Para (5): See Sch 4, forms 4.39, 4.40.

4.144. Release of resigning or removed liquidator

(1) Where the liquidator resigns, he has his release from the date on which he gives notice of his resignation to the registrar of companies.

(2) Where the liquidator is removed by a meeting of the company, he shall forthwith give notice to the registrar of companies of his ceasing to act.

(3) Where the liquidator is removed by the court, he must apply to the Secretary of State for his release.

(4) When the Secretary of State gives the release, he shall certify it accordingly, and send the certificate to the registrar of companies.

(5) A copy of the certificate shall be sent by the Secretary of State to the former liquidator, whose release is effective from the date of the certificate.

[863]

NOTES
  Paras (1), (2): See Sch 4, form 4.40.
  Para (3): See Sch 4, form 4.41.

4.145. Liquidator deceased

(1) Subject as follows, where the liquidator has died, it is the duty of his personal representatives to give notice of the fact, and of the date of death, to the company's directors, or any one of them, and to the registrar of companies.

(2) In the alternative, notice of the death may be given—

  (*a*) if the deceased liquidator was a partner in a firm, by a partner qualified to act as an insolvency practitioner or who is a member of any body approved by the Secretary of State for the authorisation of insolvency practitioners, or

  (*b*) by any person, if he delivers with the notice a copy of the relevant death certificate. **[864]**

NOTES
  Para (1): See Sch 4, form 4.44.

4.146. Loss of qualification as insolvency practitioner

(1) This Rules applies where the liquidator vacates office on ceasing to be qualified to act as an insolvency practitioner in relation to the company.

(2) He shall forthwith give notice of his doing so to the registrar of companies and the Secretary of State.

(3) Rule 4.144 applies as regards the liquidator obtaining his release, as if he had been removed by the court. **[865]**

NOTES
  Para (2): See Sch 4, forms 4.45, 4.46.

4.147. Vacation of office on making of winding-up order

Where the liquidator vacates office in consequence of the court making a winding-up order against the company, Rule 4.144 applies as regards his obtaining his release, as if he had been removed by the court. **[866]**

4.148. Liquidator's duties on vacating office

Where the liquidator ceases to be in office as such, in consequence of removal, resignation or cesser of qualification as an insolvency practitioner, he is under obligation forthwith to deliver up to the person succeeding him as liquidator the assets (after deduction of any expenses properly incurred, and distributions made, by him) and further to deliver up to that person—

  (*a*) the records of the liquidation, including correspondence, proofs and other related papers appertaining to the administration while it was within his responsibility, and (*b*) the company's books, papers and other records.   **[867]**

SECTION G: RULES APPLYING IN EVERY WINDING UP, WHETHER VOLUNTARY OR BY THE COURT

4.149. Power of court to set aside certain transactions

(1) If in the administration of the estate the liquidator enters into any transaction with a person who is an associate of his, the court may, on the application of any person interested, set the transaction aside and order the liquidator to compensate the company for any loss suffered in consequence of it.

(2) This does not apply if either—
    (*a*) the transaction was entered into with the prior consent of the court, or
    (*b*) it is shown to the court's satisfaction that the transaction was for value, and that it was entered into by the liquidator without knowing, or having any reason to suppose, that the person concerned was an associate.

(3) Nothing in this Rule is to be taken as prejudicing the operation of any rule of law or equity with respect to a liquidator's dealings with trust property, or the fiduciary obligations of any person.   **[868]**

4.150. Rule against solicitation

(1) Where the court is satisfied that any improper solicitation has been used by or on behalf of the liquidator in obtaining proxies or procuring his appointment, it may order that no remuneration out of the assets be allowed to any person by whom, or on whose behalf, the solicitation was exercised.

(2) An order of the court under this Rule overrides any resolution of the liquidation committee or the creditors, or any other provision of the Rules relating to the liquidator's remuneration.   **[869]**

CHAPTER 12

THE LIQUIDATION COMMITTEE

4.151. Preliminary

(NO CVL APPLICATION)

For the purposes of this Chapter—
    (*a*) an "insolvent winding up" is where the company is being wound up on grounds which include inability to pay its debts, and
    (*b*) a "solvent winding up" is where the company is being wound up on grounds which do not include that one.   **[870]**

4.152. Membership of committee

(1) Subject to Rule 4.154 below, the liquidation committee shall consist as follows—
    (*a*) in any case of at least 3, and not more than 5, creditors of the company, elected by the meeting of creditors held under section 141 of the Act, and

(*b*) also, in the case of a solvent winding up, where the contributories' meeting held under that section so decides, of up to 3 contributories, elected by that meeting.

(NO CVL APPLICATION)

(2–CVL) The committee must have at least 3 members before it can be established.

(3) Any creditor of the company (other than one whose debt is fully secured) is eligible to be a member of the committee, so long as—

(*a*) he has lodged a proof of his debt, and
(*b*) his proof has neither been wholly disallowed for voting purposes, nor wholly rejected for purposes of distribution or dividend.

(4) No person can be a member as both a creditor and a contributory.

(5) A body corporate may be a member of the committee, but it cannot act as such otherwise than by a representative appointed under Rule 4.159.

(6) Members of the committee elected or appointed to represent the creditors are called "creditor members"; and those elected or appointed to represent the contributories are called "contributory members".

(7) Where a representative of the Deposit Protection Board exercises the right (under section 28 of the Banking Act 1979) to be a member of the committee, he is to be regarded as an additional creditor member.   [871]

4.153. Formalities of establishment

(1) The liquidation committee does not come into being, and accordingly cannot act, until the liquidator has issued a certificate of its due constitution.

(2) If the chairman of the meeting which resolves to establish the committee is not the liquidator, he shall forthwith give notice of the resolution to the liquidator (or, as the case may be, the person appointed as liquidator by that same meeting), and inform him of the names and addresses of the persons elected to be members of the committee.

(3) No person may act as a member of the committee unless and until he has agreed to do so; and the liquidator's certificate of the committee's due constitution shall not issue before the minimum number of persons (in accordance with Rule 4.152) who are to be members of it have agreed to act.

(4) As and when the others (if any) agree to act, the liquidator shall issue an amended certificate.

(5) The certificate, and any amended certificate, shall be filed in court by the liquidator.

(NO CVL APPLICATION)

(6–CVL) The certificate, and any amended certificate, shall be sent by the liquidator to the registrar of companies.

(7) If after the first establishment of the committee there is any change in its membership, the liquidator shall report the change to the court.

(NO CVL APPLICATION)

(8–CVL) If after the first establishment of the committee there is any change in its membership, the liquidator shall report the change to the registrar of companies.   **[872]**

NOTES
Para (1): See Sch 4, form 4.47.
Para (6): See Sch 4, forms 4.47, 4.48.
Para (7): See Sch 4, form 4.49.
Para (8): See Sch 4, forms 4.48, 4.49.

4.154. Committee established by contributories

(NO CVL APPLICATION)

(1) The following applies where the creditors' meeting under section 141 does not decide that a liquidation committee should be established, or decides that a committee should not be established.

(2) The meeting of contributories under that section may appoint one of their number to make application to the court for an order to the liquidator that a further creditors' meeting be summoned for the purpose of establishing a liquidation committee; and—

> (a) the court may, if it thinks that there are special circumstances to justify it, make that order, and
> (b) the creditors' meeting summoned by the liquidator in compliance with the order is deemed to have been summoned under section 141.

(3) If the creditors' meeting so summoned does not establish a liquidation committee, a meeting of contributories may do so.

(4) The committee shall then consist of at least 3, and not more than 5, contributories elected by that meeting; and Rule 4.153 applies, substituting references to contributories for references to creditors.   **[873]**

4.155. Obligations of liquidator to committee

(1) Subject as follows, it is the duty of the liquidator to report to the members of the liquidation committee all such matters as appear to him to be, or as they have indicated to him as being, of concern to them with respect to the winding up.

(2) In the case of matters so indicated to him by the committee, the liquidator need not comply with any request for information where it appears to him that—

> (a) the request is frivolous or unreasonable, or
> (b) the cost of complying would be excessive, having regard to the relative importance of the information, or
> (c) there are not sufficient assets to enable him to comply.

(3) Where the committee has come into being more than 28 days after the appointment of the liquidator, he shall report to them, in summary form, what actions he has taken since his appointment, and shall answer all such questions as they may put to him regarding his conduct of the winding up hitherto.

(4) A person who becomes a member of the committee at any time after its first establishment is not entitled to require a report to him by the liquidator, otherwise than in summary form, of any matters previously arising.

(5) Nothing in this Rule disentitles the committee, or any member of it,

from having access to the liquidator's records of the liquidation, or from seeking an explanation of any matter within the committee's responsibility. **[874]**

4.156. Meetings of the committee

(1) Subject as follows, meetings of the liquidation committee shall be held when and where determined by the liquidator.

(2) The liquidator shall call a first meeting of the committee to take place within 3 months of his appointment or of the committee's establishment (whichever is the later); and thereafter he shall call a meeting—

    (*a*) if so requested by a creditor member of the committee or his representative (the meeting then to be held within 21 days of the request being received by the liquidator), and

    (*b*) for a specified date, if the committee has previously resolved that a meeting be held on that date.

(3) The liquidator shall give 7 days' written notice of the venue of a meeting to every member of the committee (or his representative, if designated for that purpose), unless in any case the requirement of the notice has been waived by or on behalf of any member.

Waiver may be signified either at or before the meeting. **[875]**

4.157. The chairman at meetings

(1) The chairman at any meetings of the liquidation committee shall be the liquidator, or a person nominated by him to act.

(2) A person so nominated must be either—

    (*a*) one who is qualified to act as an insolvency practitioner in relation to the company, or

    (*b*) an employee of the liquidator or his firm who is experienced in insolvency matters. **[876]**

4.158. Quorum

(1) A meeting of the committee is duly constituted if due notice of it has been given to all the members, and at least 2 creditor members are present or represented.

(NO CVL APPLICATION)

(2–CVL) A meeting of the committee is duly constituted if due notice of it has been given to all the members, and at least 2 members are present or represented. **[877]**

4.159. Committee-members' representatives

(1) A member of the liquidation committee may, in relation to the business of the committee, be represented by another person duly authorised by him for that purpose.

(2) A person acting as a committee-member's representative must hold a letter of authority entitling him so to act (either generally or specially) and signed by or on behalf of the committee-member.

(3) The chairman at any meeting of the committee may call on a person claiming to act as a committee-member's representative to produce his letter of authority, and may exclude him if it appears that his authority is deficient.

(4) No member may be represented by a body corporate, or by a person who is an undischarged bankrupt or is subject to a composition or arrangement with his creditors.

(5) No person shall—

> (*a*) on the same committee, act at one and the same time as representative of more than one committee-member, or
> (*b*) act both as a member of the committee and as representative of another member.

(6) Where a member's representative signs any document on the member's behalf, the fact that he so signs must be stated below his signature. **[878]**

4.160. Resignation

A member of the liquidation committee may resign by notice in writing delivered to the liquidator. **[879]**

4.161. Termination of membership

(1) A person's membership of the liquidation committee is automatically terminated if—

> (*a*) he becomes bankrupt or compounds or arranges with his creditors, or
> (*b*) at 3 consecutive meetings of the committee he is neither present nor represented (unless at the third of those meetings it is resolved that this Rule is not to apply in his case).

(2) However, if the cause of termination is the member's bankruptcy, his trustee in bankruptcy replaces him as a member of the committee.

(3) The membership of a creditor member is also automatically terminated if he ceases to be, or is found never to have been, a creditor. **[880]**

4.162. Removal

(1) A creditor member of the committee may be removed by resolution at a meeting of creditors; and a contributory member may be removed by a resolution of a meeting of contributories.

(2) In either case, 14 days' notice must be given of the intention to move the resolution. **[881]**

4.163. Vacancy (creditor members)

(1) The following applies if there is a vacancy among the creditor members of the committee.

(2) The vacancy need not be filled if the liquidator and a majority of the remaining creditor members so agree, provided that the total number of members does not fall below the minimum required by Rule 4.152.

(3) The liquidator may appoint any creditor (being qualified under the Rules to be a member of the committee) to fill the vacancy, if a majority of the other creditor members agree to the appointment, and the creditor concerned consents to act.

(4) Alternatively, a meeting of creditors may resolve that a creditor be appointed (with his consent) to fill the vacancy. In this case, at least 14 days'

notice must have been given of the resolution to make such an appointment (whether or not of a person named in the notice).

(5) Where the vacancy is filled by an appointment made by a creditors' meeting at which the liquidator is not present, the chairman of the meeting shall report to the liquidator the appointment which has been made. **[882]**

4.164. Vacancy (contributory members)

(1) The following applies if there is a vacancy among the contributory members of the committee.

(2) The vacancy need not be filled if the liquidator and a majority of the remaining contributory members so agree, provided that, in the case of a committee of contributory members only, the total number of members does not fall below the minimum required by Rule 4.154(4) or, as the case may be, 4.171(5).

(3) The liquidator may appoint any contributory member (being qualified under the Rules to be a member of the committee) to fill the vacancy, if a majority of the other contributory members agree to the appointment, and the contributory concerned consents to act.

(4) Alternatively, a meeting of contributories may resolve that a contributory be appointed (with his consent) to fill the vacancy. In this case, at least 14 days' notice must have been given of the resolution to make such an appointment (whether or not of a person named in the notice).

(5–CVL) Where the contributories make an appointment under paragraph (4), the creditor members of the committee may, if they think fit, resolve that the person appointed ought not to be a member of the committee; and—

    (*a*) that person is not then, unless the court otherwise directs, qualified to act as a member of the committee, and

    (*b*) on any application to the court for a direction under this paragraph the court may, if it thinks fit, appoint another person (being a contributory) to fill the vacancy on the committee.

(6) Where the vacancy is filled by an appointment made by a contributories' meeting at which the liquidator is not present, the chairman of the meeting shall report to the liquidator the appointment which has been made. **[883]**

4.165. Voting rights and resolutions

(NO CVL APPLICATION)

(1) At any meeting of the committee, each member of it (whether present himself, or by his representative) has one vote; and a resolution is passed when a majority of the creditor members present or represented have voted in favour of it.

(2) Subject to the next paragraph, the votes of contributory members do not count towards the number required for passing a resolution, but the way in which they vote on any resolution shall be recorded.

(3) Paragraph (2) does not apply where, by virtue of Rule 4.154 or 4.171, the only members of the committee are contributories. In that case the committee is to be treated for voting purposes as if all its members were creditors.

(4) Every resolution passed shall be recorded in writing, either separately or

as part of the minutes of the meeting. The record shall be signed by the chairman and kept with the records of the liquidation.   **[884]**

4.166–CVL. Voting rights and resolutions

(1) At any meeting of the committee, each member of it (whether present himself, or by his representative) has one vote; and a resolution is passed when a majority of the members present or represented have voted in favour of it.

(2) Every resolution passed shall be recorded in writing, either separately or as part of the minutes of the meeting. The record shall be signed by the chairman and kept with the records of the liquidation.   **[885]**

4.167. Resolutions by post

(1) In accordance with this Rule, the liquidator may seek to obtain the agreement of members of the liquidation committee to a resolution by sending to every member (or his representative designated for the purpose) a copy of the proposed resolution.

(2) Where the liquidator makes use of the procedure allowed by this Rule, he shall send out to members of the committee or their representatives (as the case may be) a statement incorporating the resolution to which their agreement is sought, each resolution (if more than one) being set out in a separate document.

(3) Any creditor member of the committee may, within 7 business days from the date of the liquidator sending out a resolution, require him to summon a meeting of the committee to consider the matters raised by the resolution. (NO CVL APPLICATION)

(4-CVL) Any member of the committee may, within 7 business days from the date of the liquidator sending out a resolution, require him to summon a meeting of the committee to consider the matters raised by the resolution.

(5) In the absence of such a request, the resolution is deemed to have been passed by the committee if and when the liquidator is notified in writing by a majority of the creditor members that they concur with it. (NO CVL APPLI-CATION)

(6–CVL) In the absence of such a request, the resolution is deemed to have been passed by the committee if and when the liquidator is notified in writing by a majority of the members that they concur with it.

(7) A copy of every resolution passed under this Rule, and a note that the committee's concurrence was obtained, shall be kept with the records of the liquidation.   **[886]**

4.168. Liquidator's reports

(1) The liquidator shall, as and when directed by the liquidation committee (but not more often than once in any period of 2 months), send a written report to every member of the committee setting out the position generally as regards the progress of the winding up and matters arising in connection with it, to which he (the liquidator) considers the committee's attention should be drawn.

(2) In the absence of such directions by the committee, the liquidator shall send such a report not less often than once in every period of 6 months.

(3) The obligations of the liquidator under this Rule are without prejudice to those imposed by Rule 4.155. **[887]**

4.169. Expenses of members, etc

The liquidator shall defray out of the assets, in the prescribed order of priority, any reasonable travelling expenses directly incurred by members of the liquidation committee or their representatives in respect of their attendance at the committee's meetings, or otherwise on the committee's business. **[888]**

4.170. Dealings by committee-members and others

(1) This Rule applies to—

- (*a*) any member of the liquidation committee,
- (*b*) any committee-member's representative,
- (*c*) any person who is an associate of a member of the committee or a committee-member's representative, and
- (*d*) any person who has been a member of the committee at any time in the last 12 months.

(2) Subject as follows, a person to whom this Rule applies shall not enter into any transaction whereby he—

- (*a*) receives out of the company's assets any payment for services given or goods supplied in connection with the administration, or
- (*b*) obtains any profit from the administration, or
- (*c*) acquires any asset forming part of the estate.

(3) Such a transaction may be entered into by a person to whom this Rule applies—

- (*a*) with the prior leave of the court, or
- (*b*) if he does so as a matter of urgency, or by way of performance of a contract in force before the date on which the company went into liquidation, and obtains the court's leave for the transaction, having applied for it without undue delay, or
- (*c*) with the prior sanction of the liquidation committee, where it is satisfied (after full disclosure of the circumstances) that the person will be giving full value in the transaction.

(4) Where in the committee a resolution is proposed that sanction be accorded for a transaction to be entered into which, without that sanction or the leave of the court, would be in contravention of this Rule, no member of the committee, and no representative of a member, shall vote if he is to participate directly or indirectly in the transaction.

(5) The court may, on the application of any person interested—

- (*a*) set aside a transaction on the ground that it has been entered into in contravention of this Rule, and
- (*b*) make with respect to it such other order as it thinks fit, including (subject to the following paragraph) an order requiring a person to whom this Rule applies to account for any profit obtained from the transaction and compensate the estate for any resultant loss.

(6) In the case of a person to whom this Rule applies as an associate of a member of the committee or of a committee-member's representative, the court shall not make any order under paragraph (5), if satisfied that he entered into the relevant transaction without having any reason to suppose that in doing so he would contravene this Rule.

(7) The costs of an application to the court for leave under this Rule are not payable out of the assets, unless the court so orders.   **[889]**

4.171. Composition of committee when creditors paid in full

(1) This Rule applies if the liquidator issues a certificate that the creditors have been paid in full, with interest in accordance with section 189.

(2) The liquidator shall forthwith file the certificate in court. (NO CVL APPLICATION)

(3–CVL) The liquidator shall forthwith send a copy of the certificate to the registrar of companies.

(4) The creditor members of the liquidation committee cease to be members of the committee.

(5) The committee continues in being unless and until abolished by decision of a meeting of contributories, and (subject to the next paragraph) so long as it consists of at least 3 contributory members.

(6) The committee does not cease to exist on account of the number of contributory members falling below 3, unless and until 28 days have elapsed since the issue of the liquidator's certificate under paragraph (1).

But at any time when the committee consists of less than 3 contributory members, it is suspended and cannot act.

(7) Contributories may be co-opted by the liquidator, or appointed by a contributories' meeting, to be members of the committee; but the maximum number of members is 5.

(8) The foregoing Rules in this Chapter continue to apply to the liquidation committee (with any necessary modifications) as if all the members of the committee were creditor members.   **[890]**

NOTES

    Para (2): See Sch 4, form 4.50.
    Para (3): See Sch 4, form 4.51.

4.172. Committee's functions vested in Secretary of State

(NO CVL APPLICATION)

(1) At any time when the functions of the liquidation committee are vested in the Secretary of State under section 141(4) or (5), requirements of the Act or the Rules about notices to be given, or reports to be made, to the committee by the liquidator do not apply, otherwise than as enabling the committee to require a report as to any matter.

(2) Where the committee's functions are so vested under section 141(5), they may be exercised by the official receiver.   **[891]**

CHAPTER 13

THE LIQUIDATION COMMITTEE WHERE WINDING UP FOLLOWS
IMMEDIATELY ON ADMINISTRATION

(NO CVL APPLICATION)

4.173. Preliminary

(1) The rules in this Chapter apply where—

(*a*) the winding-up order has been made immediately upon the discharge of an administration order under Part II of the Act, and

(*b*) the court makes an order under section 140(1) of the Act appointing as liquidator the person who was previously the administrator.

(2) In this Chapter, "insolvent winding up", "solvent winding up", "creditor member" and "contributory member" mean the same as in Chapter 12.   **[892]**

4.174. Continuation of creditors' committee

(1) If under section 26 a creditors' committee has been established for the purposes of the administration, then (subject as follows in this Chapter) that committee continues in being as the liquidation committee for the purposes of the winding up, and—

(*a*) it is deemed to be a committee established as such under section 141, and

(*b*) no action shall be taken under subsections (1) to (3) of that section to establish any other.

(2) This Rule does not apply if, at the time when the court's order under section 140(1) is made, the committee under section 26 consists of less than 3 members; and a creditor who was, immediately before that date, a member of it, ceases to be a member on the making of the order if his debt is fully secured.

[893]

4.175. Membership of committee

(1) Subject as follows, the liquidation committee shall consist of at least 3, and not more than 5, creditors of the company, elected by the creditors' meeting held under section 26 or (in order to make up numbers or fill vacancies) by a creditors' meeting summoned by the liquidator after the company goes into liquidation.

(2) In the case of a solvent winding up, the liquidator shall, on not less than 21 days' notice, summon a meeting of contributories, in order to elect (if it so wishes) contributory members of the liquidation committee, up to 3 in number.

[894]

4.176. Liquidator's certificate

(1) The liquidator shall issue a certificate of the liquidation committee's continuance, specifying the persons who are, or are to be, members of it.

(2) It shall be stated in the certificate whether or not the liquidator has summoned a meeting of contributories under Rule 4.175(2), and whether (if so) the meeting has elected contributories to be members of the committee.

(3) Pending the issue of the liquidator's certificate, the committee is suspended and cannot act.

(4) No person may act, or continue to act, as a member of the committee unless and until he has agreed to do so; and the liquidator's certificate shall not issue until at least the minimum number of persons required under Rule 4.175 to form a committee have signified their agreement.

(5) As and when the others signify their agreement, the liquidator shall issue an amended certificate.

(6) The liquidator's certificate (or, as the case may be, the amended certificate) shall be filed by him in court.

(7) If subsequently there is any change in the committee's membership, the liquidator shall report the change to the court.   **[895]**

NOTES
> Para (1): See Sch 4, form 4.52.
> Para (5): See Sch 4, form 4.52.
> Para (7): See Sch 4, form 4.49.

4.177. Obligations of liquidator to committee

(1) As soon as may be after the issue of the liquidator's certificate under Rule 4.176, the liquidator shall report to the liquidation committee what actions he has taken since the date on which the company went into liquidation.

(2) A person who becomes a member of the committee after that date is not entitled to require a report to him by the liquidator, otherwise than in a summary form, of any matters previously arising.

(3) Nothing in this rule disentitles the committee, or any member of it, from having access to the records of the liquidation (whether relating to the period when he was administrator, or to any subsequent period), or from seeking an explanation of any matter within the committee's responsibility.   **[896]**

4.178. Application of Chapter 12

Except as provided above in this Chapter, Rules 4.155 to 4.172 in Chapter 12 apply to the liquidation committee following the issue of the liquidator's certificate under Rule 4.176, as if it had been established under section 141.
     [897]

CHAPTER 14

COLLECTION AND DISTRIBUTION OF COMPANY'S ASSETS BY
LIQUIDATOR

4.179. General duties of liquidator

(NO CVL APPLICATION)

(1) The duties imposed on the court by the Act with regard to the collection of the company's assets and their application in discharge of its liabilities are discharged by the liquidator as an officer of the court subject to its control.

(2) In the discharge of his duties the liquidator, for the purposes of acquiring and retaining possession of the company's property, has the same powers as a receiver appointed by the High Court, and the court may on his application enforce such acquisition or retention accordingly.   **[898]**

4.180. Manner of distributing assets

(1) Whenever the liquidator has sufficient funds in hand for the purpose he shall, subject to the retention of such sums as may be necessary for the expenses of the winding up, declare and distribute dividends among the creditors in respect of the debts which they have respectively proved.

(2) The liquidator shall give notice of his intention to declare and distribute a dividend.

(3) Where the liquidator has declared a dividend, he shall give notice of it to the creditors, stating how the dividend is proposed to be distributed. The notice shall contain such particulars with respect to the company, and to its assets and affairs, as will enable the creditors to comprehend the calculation of the amount of the dividend and the manner of its distribution.   **[899]**

4.181. Debts of insolvent company to rank equally

(NO CVL APPLICATION)

Debts other than preferential debts rank equally between themselves in the winding up, and, after the preferential debts, shall be paid in full unless the assets are insufficient for meeting them, in which case they abate in equal proportions between themselves.   **[900]**

4.182. Supplementary provisions as to dividend

(1) In the calculation and distribution of a dividend the liquidator shall make provision—

- (a) for any debts which appear to him to be due to persons who, by reason of the distance of their place of residence, may not have had sufficient time to tender and establish their proofs,
- (b) for any debts which are the subject of claims which have not yet been determined, and
- (c) for disputed proofs and claims.

(2) A creditor who has not proved his debt before the declaration of any dividend is not entitled to disturb, by reason that he has not participated in it, the distribution of that dividend or any other dividend declared before his debt was proved, but—

- (a) when he has proved that debt he is entitled to be paid, out of any money for the time being available for the payment of any further dividend, any dividend or dividends which he has failed to receive, and
- (b) any dividend or dividends payable under sub-paragraph (a) shall be paid before that money is applied to the payment of any such further dividend.

(3) No action lies against the liquidator for a dividend; but if he refuses to pay a dividend the court may, if it thinks fit, order him to pay it and also to pay, out of his own money—

- (a) interest on the dividend, at the rate for the time being specified in section 17 of the Judgments Act 1838, from the time when it was withheld, and
- (b) the costs of the proceedings in which the order to pay is made.   **[901]**

4.183. Division of unsold assets

Without prejudice to provisions of the Act about disclaimer, the liquidator may, with the permission of the liquidation committee, divide in its existing form amongst the company's creditors, according to its estimated value, any property which from its peculiar nature or other special circumstances cannot be readily or advantageously sold.   **[902]**

4.184. General powers of liquidator

(1) Any permission given by the liquidation committee or the court under section 167(1)(a), or under the Rules, shall not be a general permission but shall relate to a particular proposed exercise of the liquidator's power in question; and a person dealing with the liquidator in good faith and for value is not concerned to enquire whether any such permission has been given.

(2) Where the liquidator has done anything without that permission, the court or the liquidation committee may, for the purpose of enabling him to meet his expenses out of the assets, ratify what he has done; but neither shall do so unless it is satisfied that the liquidator has acted in a case of urgency and has sought ratification without undue delay.   **[903]**

4.185. Enforced delivery up of company's property

(NO CVL APPLICATION)

(1) The powers conferred on the court by section 234 (enforced delivery of company property) are exercisable by the liquidator or, where a provisional liquidator has been appointed, by him.

(2) Any person on whom a requirement under section 234(2) is imposed by the liquidator or provisional liquidator shall, without avoidable delay, comply with it.   **[904]**

4.186. Final distribution

(1) When the liquidator has realised all the company's assets or so much of them as can, in his opinion, be realised without needlessly protracting the liquidation, he shall give notice, under Part 11 of the Rules, either—

  (a) of his intention to declare a final dividend, or
  (b) that no dividend, or further dividend, will be declared.

(2) The notice shall contain all such particulars as are required by Part 11 of the rules and shall require claims against the assets to be established by a date specified in the notice.

(3) After that date, the liquidator shall—

  (a) defray any outstanding expenses of the winding up out of the assets, and
  (b) if he intends to declare a final dividend, declare and distribute that dividend without regard to the claim of any person in respect of a debt not already proved.

(4) The court may, on the application of any person, postpone the date specified in the notice.   **[905]**

CHAPTER 15

DISCLAIMER

4.187. Liquidator's notice of disclaimer

(1) Where the liquidator disclaims property under section 178, the notice of disclaimer shall contain such particulars of the property disclaimed as enable it to be easily identified.

(2) The notice shall be signed by the liquidator and filed in court, with a

copy. The court shall secure that both the notice and the copy are sealed and endorsed with the date of filing.

(3) The copy notice, so sealed and endorsed, shall be returned by the court to the liquidator as follows—

 (*a*) if the notice has been delivered at the offices of the court by the liquidator in person, it shall be handed to him,

 (*b*) if it has been delivered by some person acting on the liquidator's behalf, it shall be handed to that person, for immediate transmission to the liquidator, and

 (*c*) otherwise, it shall be sent to the liquidator by first class post.

The court shall cause to be endorsed on the original notice, or otherwise recorded on the file, the manner in which the copy notice was returned to the liquidator.

(4) For the purposes of section 178, the date of the prescribed notice is that which is endorsed on it, and on the copy, in accordance with this Rule. **[906]**

NOTES
 Para (1): See Sch 4, form 4.53.

4.188. Communication of disclaimer to persons interested

(1) Within 7 days after the day on which the copy of the notice of disclaimer is returned to him under Rule 4.187, the liquidator shall send or give copies of the notice (showing the date endorsed as required by that Rule) to the persons mentioned in paragraphs (2) to (4) below.

(2) Where the property disclaimed is of a leasehold nature, he shall send or give a copy to every person who (to his knowledge) claims under the company as underlessee or mortgagee.

(3) He shall in any case send or give a copy of the notice to every person who (to his knowledge)—

 (*a*) claims an interest in the disclaimed property, or

 (*b*) is under any liability in respect of the property, not being a liability discharged by the disclaimer.

(4) If the disclaimer is of an unprofitable contract, he shall send or give copies of the notice to all such persons as, to his knowledge, are parties to the contract or have interests under it.

(5) If subsequently it comes to the liquidator's knowledge, in the case of any person, that he has such an interest in the disclaimed property as would have entitled him to receive a copy of the notice of disclaimer in pursuance of paragraphs (2) to (4), the liquidator shall then forthwith send or give to that person a copy of the notice.

But compliance with this paragraph is not required if—

 (*a*) the liquidator is satisfied that the person has already been made aware of the disclaimer and its date, or

 (*b*) the court, on the liquidator's application, orders that compliance is not required in that particular case. **[907]**

NOTES
 Para (1): See Sch 4, form 4.53.

4.189. Additional notices

The liquidator disclaiming property may, without prejudice to his obligations under sections 178 to 180 and Rules 4.187 and 4.188, at any time give notice of the disclaimer to any persons who in his opinion ought, in the public interest or otherwise, to be informed of it.   **[908]**

NOTES
   See Sch 4, form 4.53.

4.190. Duty to keep court informed

The liquidator shall notify the court from time to time as to the persons to whom he has sent or given copies of the notice of disclaimer under the two preceding Rules, giving their names and addresses, and the nature of their respective interests.   **[909]**

4.191. Application by interested party under s 178(5)

Where, in the case of any property, application is made to the liquidator by an interested party under section 178(5) (request for decision whether the property is to be disclaimed or not), the application—

    (a) shall be delivered to the liquidator personally or by registered post, and

    (b) shall be made in the form known as "notice to elect", or a substantially similar form.   **[910]**

NOTES
   See Sch 4, form 4.54.

4.192. Interest in property to be declared on request

(1) If, in the case of property which the liquidator has the right to disclaim, it appears to him that there is some person who claims, or may claim, to have an interest in the property, he may give notice to that person calling on him to declare within 14 days whether he claims any such interest and, if so, the nature and extent of it.

(2) Failing compliance with the notice, the liquidator is entitled to assume that the person concerned has no such interest in the property as will prevent or impede its disclaimer.   **[911]**

NOTES
   Para (1): See Sch 4, form 4.55.

4.193. Disclaimer presumed valid and effective

Any disclaimer of property by the liquidator is presumed valid and effective, unless it is proved that he has been in breach of his duty with respect to the giving of notice of disclaimer, or otherwise under sections 178 to 180, or under this Chapter of the Rules.   **[912]**

4.194. Application for exercise of court's powers under s 181

(1) This Rule applies with respect to an application by any person under section 181 for an order of the court to vest or deliver disclaimed property.

(2) The application must be made within 3 months of the applicant

becoming aware of the disclaimer, or of his receiving a copy of the liquidator's notice of disclaimer sent under Rule 4.188, whichever is the earlier.

(3) The applicant shall with his application file in court an affidavit—

(*a*) stating whether he applies under paragraph (*a*) of section 181(2) (claim of interest in the property) or under paragraph (*b*) (liability not discharged);

(*b*) specifying the date on which he received a copy of the liquidator's notice of disclaimer, or otherwise became aware of the disclaimer; and

(*c*) specifying the grounds of his application and the order which he desires the court to make under section 181.

(4) The court shall fix a venue for the hearing of the application; and the applicant shall, not later than 7 days before the date fixed, give to the liquidator notice of the venue, accompanied by copies of the application and the affidavit under paragraph (3).

(5) On the hearing of the application, the court may give directions as to other persons (if any) who should be sent or given notice of the application and the grounds on which it is made.

(6) Sealed copies of any order made on the application shall be sent by the court to the applicant and the liquidator.

(7) In a case where the property disclaimed is of a leasehold nature, and section 179 applies to suspend the effect of the disclaimer, there shall be included in the court's order a direction giving effect to the disclaimer.

This paragraph does not apply if, at the time when the order is issued, other applications under section 181 are pending in respect of the same property.

[913]

CHAPTER 16

SETTLEMENT OF LIST OF CONTRIBUTORIES

(NO CVL APPLICATION)

4.195. Preliminary

The duties of the court with regard to the settling of the list of contributories are, by virtue of the Rules, delegated to the liquidator. **[914]**

4.196. Duty of liquidator to settle list

(1) Subject as follows, the liquidator shall, as soon as may be after his appointment, exercise the court's power to settle a list of the company's contributories for the purposes of section 148 and, with the court's approval, rectify the register of members.

(2) The liquidator's duties under this Rule are performed by him as an officer of the court subject to the court's control. **[915]**

4.197. Form of list

(1) The list shall identify—

(*a*) the several classes of the company's shares (if more than one), and

(b) the several classes of contributories, distinguishing between those who are contributories in their own right and those who are so as representatives of, or liable for the debts of, others.

(2) In the case of each contributory there shall in the list be stated—

(a) his address,

(b) the number and class of shares, or the extent of any other interest to be attributed to him, and

(c) if the shares are not fully paid up, the amounts which have been called up and paid in respect of them (and the equivalent, if any, where his interest is other than shares).   **[916]**

4.198. Procedure for settling list

(1) Having settled the list, the liquidator shall forthwith give notice, to every person included in the list, that he has done so.

(2) The notice given to each person shall state—

(a) in what character, and for what number of shares or what interest, he is included in the list,

(b) what amounts have been called up and paid up in respect of the shares or interest, and

(c) that in relation to any shares or interest not fully paid up, his inclusion in the list may result in the unpaid capital being called.

(3) The notice shall inform any person to whom it is given that, if he objects to any entry in, or omission from, the list, he should so inform the liquidator in writing within 21 days from the date of the notice.

(4) On receipt of any such objection, the liquidator shall within 14 days give notice to the objector either—

(a) that he has amended the list (specifying the amendment), or

(b) that he considers the objection to be not well-founded and declines to amend the list.

The notice shall in either case inform the objector of the effect of Rule 4.199.   **[917]**

4.199. Application to court for variation of the list

(1) If a person objects to any entry in, or exclusion from, the list of contributories as settled by the liquidator and, notwithstanding notice by the liquidator declining to amend the list, maintains his objection, he may apply to the court for an order removing the entry to which he objects or (as the case may be) otherwise amending the list.

(2) The application must be made within 21 days of the service on the applicant of the liquidator's notice under Rule 4.198(4).   **[918]**

4.200. Variation of, or addition to, the list

The liquidator may from time to time vary or add to the list of contributories as previously settled by him, but subject in all respects to the preceding Rules in this Chapter.   **[919]**

4.201. Costs not to fall on official receiver

The official receiver is not personally liable for any costs incurred by a person in respect of an application to set aside or vary his act or decision in settling the list of contributories, or varying or adding to the list; and the liquidator (if other than the official receiver) is not so liable unless the court makes an order to that effect.   **[920]**

CHAPTER 17

CALLS

(NO CVL APPLICATION)

4.202. Calls by liquidator

Subject as follows, the powers conferred by the Act with respect to the making of calls on contributories are exerciseable by the liquidator as an officer of the court subject to the court's control.   **[921]**

4.203. Control by liquidation committee

(1) Where the liquidator proposes to make a call, and there is a liquidation committee, he may summon a meeting of the committee for the purpose of obtaining its sanction.

(2) At least 7 days' notice of the meeting shall be given by the liquidator to each member of the committee.

(3) The notice shall contain a statement of the proposed amount of the call, and the purpose for which it is intended to be made.   **[922]**

4.204. Application to court for leave to make a call

(1) For the purpose of obtaining the leave of the court for the making of a call on any contributories of the company, the liquidator shall apply *ex parte*, supporting his application by affidavit.

(2) There shall in the application be stated the amount of the proposed call, and the contributories on whom it is to be made.

(3) The court may direct that notice of the order be given to the contributories concerned, or to other contributories, or may direct that the notice be publicly advertised.   **[923]**

NOTES
    Para (1): See Sch 4, form 4.56.
    Para (2): See Sch 4, form 4.57.

4.205. Making and enforcement of the call

(1) Notice of the call shall be given to each of the contributories concerned, and shall specify—

(a) the amount or balance due from him in respect of it, and
(b) whether the call is made with the sanction of the court or the liquidation committee.

(2) Payment of the amount due from any contributory may be enforced by order of the court.   **[924]**

NOTES
    Para (1): See Sch 4, form 4.58.
    Para (2): See Sch 4, form 4.59.

CHAPTER 18

SPECIAL MANAGER

4.206. Appointment and remuneration

(1) An application made by the liquidator under section 177 for the appointment of a person to be special manager shall be supported by a report setting out the reasons for the application.

The report shall include the applicant's estimate of the value of the assets in respect of which the special manager is to be appointed.

(2) This Chapter applies also with respect to an application by the provisional liquidator, where one has been appointed, and references to the liquidator are to be read accordingly as including the provisional liquidator. (NO CVL APPLICATION)

(3) The court's order appointing the special manager shall specify the duration of his appointment, which may be for a period of time, or until the occurrence of a specified event. Alternatively, the order may specify that the duration of the appointment is to be subject to a further order of the court.

(4) The appointment of a special manager may be renewed by order of the court.

(5) The special manager's remuneration shall be fixed from time to time by the court.

(6) The acts of the special manager are valid notwithstanding any defect in his appointment or qualifications.   **[925]**

NOTES
    Para (3): See Sch 4, form 4.60.

4.207. Security

(1) The appointment of the special manager does not take effect until the person appointed has given (or, being allowed by the court to do so, undertaken to give) security to the person who applies for him to be appointed.

(2) It is not necessary that security shall be given for each separate company liquidation; but it may be given either specially for a particular liquidation, or generally for any liquidation in relation to which the special manager may be employed as such.

(3) The amount of the security shall be not less than the value of the assets in respect of which he is appointed, as estimated by the applicant in his report under Rule 4.206.

(4) When the special manager has given security to the person applying for his appointment, that person shall file in court a certificate as to the adequacy of the security.

(5) The cost of providing the security shall be paid in the first instance by the special manager; but—

    (a) where a winding-up order is not made, he is entitled to be reimbursed out of the property of the company, and the court may make an order on the company accordingly, and

    (b) where a winding-up order is made, he is entitled to be reimbursed out of the assets in the prescribed order of priority.

(NO CVL APPLICATION)

(6–CVL) The cost of providing the security shall be paid in the first instance by the special manager; but he is entitled to be reimbursed out of the assets, in the prescribed order of priority.   **[926]**

4.208. Failure to give or keep up security

(1) If the special manager fails to give the required security within the time stated for that purpose by the order appointing him, or any extension of that time that may be allowed, the liquidator shall report the failure to the court, which may thereupon discharge the order appointing the special manager.

(2) If the special manager fails to keep up his security, the liquidator shall report his failure to the court, which may thereupon remove the special manager, and make such order as it thinks fit as to costs.

(3) If an order is made under this Rule removing the special manager, or discharging the order appointing him, the court shall give directions as to whether any, and if so what, steps should be taken for the appointment of another special manager in his place.   **[927]**

4.209. Accounting

(1) The special manager shall produce accounts, containing details of his receipts and payments, for the approval of the liquidator.

(2) The accounts shall be in respect of 3–month periods for the duration of the special manager's appointment (or for a lesser period, if his appointment terminates less than 3 months from its date, or from the date to which the last accounts were made up).

(3) When the accounts have been approved, the special manager's receipts and payments shall be added to those of the liquidator.   **[928]**

4.210. Termination of appointment

(1) The special manager's appointment terminates if the winding-up petition is dismissed or if, a provisional liquidator having been appointed, the latter is discharged without a winding-up order having been made. (NO CVL APPLICATION)

(2) If the liquidator is of opinion that the employment of the special manager is no longer necessary or profitable for the company, he shall apply to the court for directions, and the court may order the special manager's appointment to be terminated.

(3) The liquidator shall make the same application if a resolution of the creditors is passed, requesting that the appointment be terminated.   **[929]**

CHAPTER 19

PUBLIC EXAMINATION OF COMPANY OFFICERS AND OTHERS

4.211. Order for public examination

(1) If the official receiver applies to the court under section 133 for the public examination of any person, a copy of the court's order shall, forthwith after its making, be served on that person.

(2) Where the application relates to a person falling within section 133(1)(*c*) (promoters, past managers, etc), it shall be accompanied by a report by the official receiver indicating—

    (*a*) the grounds on which the person is supposed to fall within that paragraph, and

    (*b*) whether, in the official receiver's opinion, it is likely that service of the order on the person can be effected by post at a known address.

(3) If in his report the official receiver gives it as his opinion that, in a case to which paragraph (2) applies, there is no reasonable certainty that service by post will be effective, the court may direct that the order be served by some means other than, or in addition to, post.

(4) In a case to which paragraphs (2) and (3) apply, the court shall rescind the order if satisfied by the person to whom it is directed that he does not fall within section 133(1)(*c*).   **[930]**

NOTES
    Para (1): See Sch 4, form 4.61.

4.212. Notice of hearing

(1) The court's order shall appoint a venue for the examination of the person to whom it is directed ("the examinee"), and direct his attendance thereat.

(2) The official receiver shall give at least 14 days' notice of the hearing—

    (*a*) if a liquidator has been nominated or appointed, to him;

    (*b*) if a special manager has been appointed, to him; and

    (*c*) subject to any contrary direction of the court, to every creditor and contributory of the company who is known to the official receiver or is identified in the company's statement of affairs.

(3) The official receiver may, if he thinks fit, cause notice of the order to be given, by advertisement in one or more newspapers, at least 14 days before the date fixed for the hearing; but, unless the court otherwise directs, there shall be no such advertisement before at least 7 days have elapsed since the examinee was served with the order.   **[931]**

4.213. Order on request by creditors or contributories

(1) A request to the official receiver by creditors or contributories under section 133(2) shall be made in writing and be accompanied by—

    (*a*) a list of the creditors concurring with the request and the amounts of their respective claims in the liquidation or (as the case may be) of the contributories so concurring, with their respective values, and

    (*b*) from each creditor or contributory concurring, written confirmation of his concurrence.

This paragraph does not apply if the requisitioning creditor's debt or, as the case may be, requisitioning contributory's shareholding is alone sufficient, without the concurrence of others.

(2) The request must specify the name of the proposed examinee, the relationship which he has, or has had, to the company and the reasons why his examination is requested.

(3) Before an application to the court is made on the request, the requisitionists shall deposit with the official receiver such sum as the latter may

determine to be appropriate by way of security for the expenses of the hearing of a public examination, if ordered.

(4) Subject as follows, the official receiver shall, within 28 days of receiving the request, make the application to the court required by section 133(2).

(5) If the official receiver is of opinion that the request is an unreasonable one in the circumstances, he may apply to the court for an order relieving him from the obligation to make the application otherwise required by that subsection.

(6) If the court so orders, and the application for the order was made *ex parte*, notice of the order shall be given forthwith by the official receiver to the requisitionists. If the application for an order is dismissed, the official receiver's application under section 133(2) shall be made forthwith on conclusion of the hearing of the application first mentioned.   **[932]**

NOTES
    Para (1): See Sch 4, forms 4.62, 4.63.

4.214. Witness unfit for examination

(1) Where the examinee is suffering from any mental disorder or physical affliction or disability rendering him unfit to undergo or attend for public examination, the court may, on application in that behalf, either stay the order for his public examination or direct that it shall be conducted in such manner and at such place as it thinks fit.

(2) Application under this Rule shall be made—

    (*a*) by a person who has been appointed by a court in the United Kingdom or elsewhere to manage the affairs of, or to represent, the examinee, or

    (*b*) by a relative or friend of the examinee whom the court considers to be a proper person to make the application, or

    (*c*) by the official receiver.

(3) Where the application is made by a person other than the official receiver, then—

    (*a*) it shall, unless the examinee is a patient within the meaning of the Mental Health Act 1983, be supported by the affidavit of a registered medical practitioner as to the examinee's mental and physical condition;

    (*b*) at least 7 days' notice of the application shall be given to the official receiver and the liquidator (if other than the official receiver); and

    (*c*) before any order is made on the application, the applicant shall deposit with the official receiver such sum as the latter certifies to be necessary for the additional expenses of any examination that may be ordered on the application.

An order made on the application may provide that the expenses of the examination are to be payable, as to a specified proportion, out of the deposit under sub-paragraph (*c*), instead of out of the assets.

(4) Where the application is made by the official receiver it may be made *ex parte*, and may be supported by evidence in the form of a report by the official receiver to the court.   **[933]**

NOTES
    Para (1): See Sch 4, form 4.64.

4.215. Procedure at hearing

(1) The examinee shall at the hearing be examined on oath; and he shall answer all such questions as the court may put, or allow to be put, to him.

(2) Any of the persons allowed by section 133(4) to question the examinee may, with the approval of the court (made known either at the hearing or in advance of it), appear by solicitor or counsel; or he may in writing authorise another person to question the examinee on his behalf.

(3) The examinee may at his own expense employ a solicitor with or without counsel, who may put to him such questions as the court may allow for the purpose of enabling him to explain or qualify any answers given by him, and may make representations on his behalf.

(4) There shall be made in writing such record of the examination as the court thinks proper. The record shall be read over either to or by the examinee, signed by him, and verified by affidavit at a venue fixed by the court.

(5) The written record may, in any proceedings (whether under the Act or otherwise) be used as evidence against the examinee of any statement made by him in the course of his public examination.

(6) If criminal proceedings have been instituted against the examinee, and the court is of opinion that the continuance of the hearing would be calculated to prejudice a fair trial of those proceedings, the hearing may be adjourned.

[934]

NOTES
    Para (4): See Sch 4, form 4.65.

4.216. Adjournment

(1) The public examination may be adjourned by the court from time to time, either to a fixed date or generally.

(2) Where the examination has been adjourned generally, the court may at any time on the application of the official receiver or of the examinee—

> (*a*) fix a venue for the resumption of the examination, and
> (*b*) give directions as to the manner in which, and the time within which, notice of the resumed public examination is to be given to persons entitled to take part in it.

(3) Where application under paragraph (2) is made by the examinee, the court may grant it on terms that the expenses of giving the notices required by that paragraph shall be paid by him and that, before a venue for the resumed public examination is fixed, he shall deposit with the official receiver such sum as the latter considers necessary to cover those expenses.   **[935]**

NOTES
    Para (1): See Sch 4, form 4.66.
    Para (2): See Sch 4, form 4.67.

4.217. Expenses of examination

(1) Where a public examination of the examinee has been ordered by the court on a creditors' or contributories' requisition under Rule 4.213, the court may

order that the expenses of the examinaiton are to be paid, as to a specified proportion, out of the deposit under Rule 4.213(3), instead of out of the assets.

(2) In no case do the costs and expenses of a public examination fall on the official receiver personally. **[936]**

CHAPTER 20

ORDER OF PAYMENT OF COSTS, ETC, OUT OF ASSETS

4.218. General rule as to priority

(1) The expenses of the liquidation are payable out of the assets in the following order of priority—

- (*a*) expenses properly chargeable or incurred by the official receiver or the liquidator in preserving, realising or getting in any of the assets of the company;
- (*b*) any other expenses incurred or disbursements made by the official receiver or under his authority, including those incurred or made in carrying on the business of the company;
- (*c*) (i) the fee payable under any order made under section 414 for the performance by the official receiver of his general duties as official receiver;
  (ii) any repayable deposit lodged by the petitioner under any such order as security for the fee mentioned in sub-paragraph (i);
- (*d*) any other fees payable under any order made under section 414, including those payable to the official receiver, and any remuneration payable to him under general regulations;
- (*e*) the cost of any security provided by a provisional liquidator, liquidator or special manager in accordance with the Act or the Rules;
- (*f*) the remuneration of the provisional liquidator (if any);
- (*g*) any deposit lodged on an application for the appointment of a provisional liquidator;
- (*h*) the costs of the petitioner, and of any person appearing on the petition whose costs are allowed by the court;
- (*j*) the remuneration of the special manager (if any);
- (*k*) any amount payable to a person employed or authorised, under Chapter 6 of this Part of the Rules, to assist in the preparation of a statement of affairs or of accounts;
- (*l*) any allowance made, by order of the court, towards costs on an application for release from the obligation to submit a statement of affairs, or for an extension of time for submitting such a statement;
- (*m*) any necessary disbursements by the liquidator in the course of his administration (including any expenses incurred by members of the liquidation committee or their representatives and allowed by the liquidator under Rule 4.169, but not including any payment of capital gains tax in circumstances referred to in sub-paragraph (*p*) below);
- (*n*) the remuneration or emoluments of any person who has been employed by the liquidator to perform any services for the company, as required or authorised by or under the Act or the Rules;
- (*o*) the remuneration of the liquidator, up to any amount not exceeding that which is payable to the official receiver under general regulations;
- (*p*) the amount of any capital gains tax on chargeable gains accruing on the realisation of any asset of the company (without regard to whether the realisation is effected by the liquidator, a secured creditor, or a receiver or manager appointed to deal with a security);

(*q*) the balance, after payment of any sums due under sub-paragraph (*o*) above, of any remuneration due to the liquidator.

(2) The costs of employing a shorthand writer, if appointed by an order of the court made at the instance of the official receiver in connection with an examination, rank in priority with those specified in paragraph (1)(*a*). The costs of employing a shorthand writer so appointed in any other case rank after the allowance mentioned in paragraph (1)(*l*) and before the disbursements mentioned in paragraph (1)(*m*).

(3) Any expenses incurred in holding an examination under Rule 4.214 (examinee unfit), where the application for it is made by the official receiver, rank in priority with those specified in paragraph (1)(*a*).   **[937]**

4.219. Winding up commencing as voluntary

In a winding up by the court which follows immediately on a voluntary winding up (whether members' voluntary or creditors' voluntary), such remuneration of the voluntary liquidator and costs and expenses of the voluntary liquidation as the court may allow are to rank in priority with the expenses specified in Rule 4.218(1)(*a*).   **[938]**

4.220. Saving for powers of the court

(1) In a winding up by the court, the priorities laid down by Rules 4.218 and 4.219 are subject to the power of the court to make orders under section 156, where the assets are insufficient to satisfy the liabilities.

(2) Nothing in those Rules applies to or affects the power of any court, in proceedings by or against the company, to order costs to be paid by the company, or the liquidator; nor do they affect the rights of any person to whom such costs are ordered to be paid.   **[939]**

CHAPTER 21

MISCELLANEOUS RULES

SECTION A: RETURN OF CAPITAL
(NO CVL APPLICATION)

4.221. Application to court for order authorising return

(1) This Rule applies where the liquidator intends to apply to the court for an order authorising a return of capital.

(2) The application shall be accompanied by a list of the persons to whom the return is to be made.

(3) The list shall include the same details of those persons as appears in the settled list of contributories, with any necessary alterations to take account of matters after settlement of the list, and the amount to be paid to each person.

(4) Where the court makes an order authorising the return, it shall send a sealed copy of the order to the liquidator.   **[940]**

4.222. Procedure for return

(1) The liquidator shall inform each person to whom a return is made of the rate of return per share, and whether it is expected that any further return will be made.

(2) Any payments made by the liquidator by way of the return may be sent by post, unless for any reason another method of making the payment has been agreed with the payee. **[941]**

SECTION B: CONCLUSION OF WINDING UP

4.223–CVL. Statements to registrar of companies under s 192

(1) The statement which section 192 requires the liquidator to send to the registrar of companies, if the winding up is not concluded within one year from its commencement, shall be sent not more than 30 days after the expiration of that year, and thereafter not less often than 6-monthly until the winding up is concluded.

(2) For this purpose the winding up is concluded at the date of the dissolution of the company, except that if at that date any assets or funds of the company remain unclaimed or undistributed in the hands or under the control of the liquidator or any former liquidator, the winding up is not concluded until those assets or funds have either been distributed or paid into the Insolvency Services Account.

(3) Subject as above, the liquidator's final statement shall be sent forthwith after the conclusion of the winding up.

(4) Every statement sent to the registrar of companies under section 192 shall be in duplicate. **[942]**

NOTES
Para (1): See Sch 4, form 4.68.

SECTION C: DISSOLUTION AFTER WINDING UP

4.224. Secretary of State's directions under ss 203, 205

(1) Where the Secretary of State gives a direction under—
  (a) section 203 (where official receiver applies to registrar of companies for a company's early dissolution), or
  (b) section 205 (application by interested person for postponement of dissolution),
he shall send two copies of the direction to the applicant for it.

(2) Of those copies one shall be sent by the applicant to the registrar of companies, to comply with section 203(5) or, as the case may be, 205(6). **[943]**

4.225. Procedure following appeal under s 203(4) or 205(4)

Following an appeal under section 203(4) or 205(4) (against a decision of the Secretary of State under the applicable section) the court shall send two sealed copies of its order to the person in whose favour the appeal was determined; and that party shall send one of the copies to the registrar of companies to comply with section 203(5) or, as the case may be, 205(6). **[944]**

NOTES
See Sch 4, form 4.69.

CHAPTER 22

LEAVE TO ACT AS DIRECTOR, ETC, OF COMPANY WITH PROHIBITED NAME (SECTION 216 OF THE ACT)

4.226. Preliminary

The Rules in this Chapter—

- (a) relate to the leave required under section 216 (restriction on re-use of name of company in insolvent liquidation) for a person to act as mentioned in section 216(3) in relation to a company with a prohibited name, and
- (b) prescribe the cases excepted from that provision, that is to say, those in which a person to whom the section applies may so act without that leave.   **[945]**

4.227. Application for leave under s 216(3)

When considering an application for leave under section 216, the court may call on the liquidator, or any former liquidator, of the liquidating company for a report of the circumstances in which that company became insolvent, and the extent (if any) of the applicant's apparent responsibility for its doing so.   **[946]**

4.228. First excepted case

(1) Where a company ("the successor company") acquires the whole, or substantially the whole, of the business of an insolvent company, under arrangements made by an insolvency practitioner acting as its liquidator, administrator or administrative receiver, or as supervisor of a voluntary arrangement under Part I of the Act, the successor company may for the purposes of section 216 give notice under this Rule to the insolvent company's creditors.

(2) To be effective, the notice must be given within 28 days from the completion of the arrangements, to all creditors of the insolvent company of whose addresses the successor company is aware in that period; and it must specify—

- (a) the name and registered number of the insolvent company and the circumstances in which its business has been acquired by the successor company.
- (b) the name which the successor company has assumed, or proposes to assume for the purpose of carrying on the business, if that name is or will be a prohibited name under section 216, and
- (c) any change of name which it has made, or proposes to make, for that purpose under section 28 of the Companies Act.

(3) The notice may name a person to whom section 216 may apply as having been a director or shadow director of the insolvent company, and give particulars as to the nature and duration of that directorship, with a view to his being a director of the successor company or being otherwise associated with its management.

(4) If the successor company has effectively given notice under this Rule to the insolvent company's creditors, a person who is so named in the notice may act in relation to the successor company in any of the ways mentioned in section 216(3), notwithstanding that he has not the leave of the court under that section.   **[947]**

4.229. Second excepted case

(1) In the circumstances specified below, a person to whom section 216 applies as having been a director or shadow director of the liquidating company may act in any of the ways mentioned in section 216(3), notwithstanding that he has not the leave of the court under that section.

(2) Those circumstances are that—

(*a*) he applies to the court for leave, not later than 7 days from the date on which the company went into liquidation, and

(*b*) leave is granted by the court not later than 6 weeks from that date.

[948]

4.230. Third excepted case

The court's leave under section 216(3) is not required where the company there referred to, though known by a prohibited name within the meaning of the section—

(*a*) has been known by that name for the whole of the period of 12 months ending with the day before the liquidating company went into liquidation, and

(*b*) has not at any time in those 12 months been dormant within the meaning of section 252(5) of the Companies Act. **[949]**

THE SECOND GROUP OF PARTS

INDIVIDUAL INSOLVENCY; BANKRUPTCY

PART 5

INDIVIDUAL VOLUNTARY ARRANGEMENTS

5.1. Introductory

(1) The Rules in this Part apply where a debtor, with a view to an application for an interim order under Part VIII of the Act, makes a proposal to his creditors for a voluntary arrangement, that is to say, a composition in satisfaction of his debts or a scheme of arrangement of his affairs.

(2) The Rules apply whether the debtor is an undischarged bankrupt ("Case 1"), or he is not ("Case 2"). **[950]**

SECTION A: THE DEBTOR'S PROPOSAL

5.2. Preparation of proposal

The debtor shall prepare for the intended nominee a proposal on which (with or without amendments to be made under Rule 5.3(3) below) to make his report to the court under section 256. **[951]**

5.3. Contents of proposal

(1) The debtor's proposal shall provide a short explanation why, in his opinion, a voluntary arrangement under Part VIII is desirable, and give reasons why his creditors may be expected to concur with such an arrangement.

(2) The following matters shall be stated, or otherwise dealt with, in the proposal—

(*a*) the following matters, so far as within the debtor's immediate knowledge—

      (i) his assets, with an estimate of their respective values,

     (ii) the extent (if any) to which the assets are charged in favour of creditors,

   (iii) the extent (if any) to which particular assets are to be excluded from the voluntary arrangement;

(*b*) particulars of any property, other than assets of the debtor himself, which is proposed to be included in the arrangement, the source of such property and the terms on which it is to be made available for inclusion;

(*c*) the nature and amount of the debtor's liabilities (so far as within his immediate knowledge), the manner in which they are proposed to be met, modified, postponed or otherwise dealt with by means of the arrangement and (in particular)—

      (i) how it is proposed to deal with preferential creditors (defined in section 258(7)) and creditors who are, or claim to be, secured,

     (ii) how associates of the debtor (being creditors of his) are proposed to be treated under the arrangement, and

   (iii) (Case 2 only) whether there are, to the debtor's knowledge, any circumstances giving rise to the possibility, in the event that he should be adjudged bankrupt, of claims under—

> section 339 (transactions at an undervalue),
> section 340 (preferences), or
> section 343 (extortionate credit transactions),

and, where any such circumstances are present, whether, and if so how, it is proposed under the voluntary arrangement to make provision for wholly or partly indemnifying the insolvent estate in respect of such claims;

(*d*) whether any, and if so what, guarantees have been given of the debtor's debts by other persons, specifying which (if any) of the guarantors are associates of his;

(*e*) the proposed duration of the voluntary arrangements;

(*f*) the proposed dates of distributions to creditors, with estimates of their amounts;

(*g*) the amount proposed to be paid to the nominee (as such) by way of remuneration and expenses;

(*h*) the manner in which it is proposed that the supervisor of the arrangement should be remunerated, and his expenses defrayed;

(*j*) whether, for the purposes of the arrangement, any guarantees are to be offered by any persons other than the debtor, and whether (if so) any security is to be given or sought;

(*k*) the manner in which funds held for the purposes of the arrangement are to be banked, invested or otherwise dealt with pending distribution to creditors;

(*l*) the manner in which funds held for the purpose of payment to creditors, and not so paid on the termination of the arrangement, are to be dealt with;

(*m*) if the debtor has any business, the manner in which it is proposed to be conducted during the course of the arrangement;

(*n*) details of any further credit facilities which it is intended to arrange for the debtor, and how the debts so arising are to be paid;

(*o*) the functions which are to be undertaken by the supervisor of the arrangement;

(*p*) the name, address and qualification of the person proposed as supervisor of the voluntary arrangement, and confirmation that he is (so far as the debtor is aware) qualified to act as an insolvency practitioner in relation to him.

(3) With the agreement in writing of the nominee, the debtor's proposal may be amended at any time up to the delivery of the former's report to the court under section 256.   **[952]**

5.4. Notice to intended nominee

(1) The debtor shall give to the intended nominee written notice of his proposal.

(2) The notice, accompanied by a copy of the proposal, shall be delivered either to the nominee himself, or to a person authorised to take delivery of documents on his behalf.

(3) If the intended nominee agrees to act, he shall cause a copy of the notice to be endorsed to the effect that it has been received by him on a specified date.

(4) The copy of the notice so endorsed shall be returned by the nominee forthwith to the debtor at an address specified by him in the notice for that purpose.

(5) Where (in Case 1) the debtor gives notice of his proposal to the official receiver and (if any) the trustee, the notice must contain the name and address of the insolvency practitioner who has agreed to act as nominee.   **[953]**

5.5. Application for interim order

(1) An application to the court for an interim order under Part VIII of the Act shall be accompanied by an affidavit of the following matters—

    (*a*) the reasons for making the application;

    (*b*) particulars of any execution or other legal process which, to the debtor's knowledge, has been commenced against him;

    (*c*) that he is an undischarged bankrupt or (as the case may be) that he is able to petition for his own bankruptcy;

    (*d*) that no previous application for an interim order has been made by or in respect of the debtor in the period of 12 months ending with the date of the affidavit; and

    (*e*) that the nominee under the proposal (naming him) is a person who is qualified to act as an insolvency practitioner in relation to the debtor, and is willing to act in relation to the proposal.

(2) A copy of the notice to the intended nominee under Rule 5.4, endorsed to the effect that he agrees so to act, shall be exhibited to the affidavit.

(3) On receiving the application and affidavit, the court shall fix a venue for the hearing of the application.

(4) The applicant shall give at least 2 days' notice of the hearing—

    (*a*) in Case 1, to the bankrupt, the official receiver and the trustee (whichever of those three is not himself the applicant),

    (*b*) in Case 2, to any creditor who (to the debtor's knowledge) has presented a bankruptcy petition against him, and

    (*c*) in either case, to the nominee who has agreed to act in relation to the debtor's proposal.   **[954]**

5.6. Hearing of the application

(1) Any of the persons who have been given notice under Rule 5.5(4) may appear or be represented at the hearing of the application.

(2) The court, in deciding whether to make an interim order on the application, shall take into account any representation made by or on behalf of any of those persons (in particular, whether an order should be made containing such provision as is referred to in section 255(3) and (4)).

(3) If the court makes an interim order, it shall fix a venue for consideration of the nominee's report. Subject to the following paragraph, the date for that consideration shall be not later than that on which the interim order ceases to have effect under section 255(6).

(4) If under section 256(4) an extension of time is granted for filing the nominee's report, the court shall, unless there appear to be good reasons against it, correspondingly extend the period for which the interim order has effect.

[955]

5.7. Action to follow making of order

(1) Where an interim order is made, at least 2 sealed copies of the order shall be sent by the court forthwith to the person who applied for it; and that person shall serve one of the copies on the nominee under the debtor's proposal.

(2) The applicant shall also forthwith give notice of the making of the order to any person who was given notice of the hearing pursuant to Rule 5.5(4) and was not present or represented at it.   **[956]**

5.8. Statement of affairs

(1) In Case 1, if the debtor has already delivered a statement of affairs under section 272 (debtor's petition) or 288 (creditor's petition), he need not deliver a further statement unless so required by the nominee, with a view to supplementing or amplifying the former one.

(2) In Case 2, the debtor shall, within 7 days after his proposal is delivered to the nominee, or within such longer time as the latter may allow, deliver to the nominee a statement of his (the debtor's) affairs.

(3) The statement shall comprise the following particulars (supplementing or amplifying, so far as is necessary for clarifying the state of the debtor's affairs, those already given in his proposal)—

    (*a*) a list of his assets, divided into such categories as are appropriate for easy identification, with estimated values assigned to each category;

    (*b*) in the case of any property on which a claim against the debtor is wholly or partly secured, particulars of the claim and its amount, and of how and when the security was created;

    (*c*) the names and addresses of the debtor's preferential creditors (defined in section 258(7)), with the amounts of their respective claims;

    (*d*) the names and addresses of the debtor's unsecured creditors, with the amounts of their respective claims;

    (*e*) particulars of any debts owed by or to the debtor to or by persons who are associates of his;

    (*f*) such other particulars (if any) as the nominee may in writing require to be furnished for the purposes of making his report to the court on the debtor's proposal.

(4) The statement of affairs shall be made up to a date not earlier than 2 weeks before the date of the notice to the nominee under Rule 5.4.

However, the nominee may allow an extension of that period to the nearest practicable date (not earlier than 2 months before the date of the notice under Rule 5.4); and if he does so, he shall give his reason in his report to the court on the debtor's proposal.

(5) The statement shall be certified by the debtor as correct, to the best of his knowledge and belief.   **[957]**

5.9. Additional disclosure for assistance of nominee

(1) If it appears to the nominee that he cannot properly prepare his report on the basis of information in the debtor's proposal and statement of affairs, he may call on the debtor to provide him with—

> (*a*) further and better particulars as to the circumstances in which, and the reasons why, he is insolvent or (as the case may be) threatened with insolvency;
> (*b*) particulars of any previous proposals which have been made by him under Part VIII of the Act;
> (*c*) any further information with respect to his affairs which the nominee thinks necessary for the purposes of his report.

(2) The nominee may call on the debtor to inform him whether and in what circumstances he has at any time—

> (*a*) been concerned in the affairs of any company (whether or not incorporated in England and Wales) which has become insolvent, or
> (*b*) been adjudged bankrupt, or entered into an arrangement with his creditors.

(3) For the purpose of enabling the nominee to consider the debtor's proposal and prepare his report on it, the latter must give him access to his accounts and records.   **[958]**

5.10. Nominee's report on the proposal

(1) The nominee's report shall be delivered by him to the court not less than 2 days before the interim order ceases to have effect.

(2) With his report the nominee shall deliver—

> (*a*) a copy of the debtor's proposal (with amendments, if any, authorised under Rule 5.3(3)); and
> (*b*) a copy or summary of any statement of affairs provided by the debtor.

(3) If the nominee makes known his opinion that a meeting of the debtor's creditors should be summoned under section 257, his report shall have annexed to it his comments on the debtor's proposal.

If his opinion is otherwise, he shall give his reasons for that opinion.

(4) The court shall cause the nominee's report to be endorsed with the date on which it is filed in court. Any creditor of the debtor is entitled, at all reasonable times on any business day, to inspect the file.

(5) In Case 1, the nominee shall send to the official receiver—

> (*a*) a copy of the debtor's proposal,
> (*b*) a copy of his (the nominee's) report and his comments accompanying it (if any), and

(*c*) a copy or summary of the debtor's statement of affairs.

In Case 2, the nominee shall send a copy of each of those documents to any person who has presented a bankruptcy petition against the debtor.   **[959]**

5.11. Replacement of nominee

Where the debtor intends to apply to the court under section 256(3) for the nominee to be replaced, he shall give to the nominee at least 7 days' notice of his application.   **[960]**

SECTION B: ACTION ON THE PROPOSAL;
CREDITORS' MEETING

5.12. Consideration of nominee's report

(1) At the hearing by the court to consider the nominee's report, any of the persons who have been given notice under Rule 5.5(4) may appear or be represented.

(2) Rule 5.7 applies to any order made by the court at the hearing.   **[961]**

5.13. Summoning of creditors' meeting

(1) If in his report the nominee states that in his opinion a meeting of creditors should be summoned to consider the debtor's proposal, the date on which the meeting is to be held shall be not less than 14, nor more than 28, days from that on which the nominee's report is filed in court under Rule 5.10.

(2) Notices calling the meeting shall be sent by the nominee, at least 14 days before the day fixed for it to be held, to all the creditors specified in the debtor's statement of affairs, and any other creditors of whom the nominee is otherwise aware.

(3) Each notice sent under this rule shall specify the court to which the nominee's report on the debtor's proposal has been delivered and shall state the effect of Rule 5.18(1), (3) and (4) (requisite majorities); and with it there shall be sent—

    (*a*) a copy of the proposal,

    (*b*) a copy of the statement of affairs or, if the nominee thinks fit, a summary of it (the summary to include a list of the creditors and the amounts of their debts), and

    (*c*) the nominee's comments on the proposal.   **[962]**

5.14. Creditors' meeting: supplementary

(1) Subject as follows, in fixing the venue for the creditors' meeting, the nominee shall have regard to the convenience of creditors.

(2) The meeting shall be summoned for commencement between 10.00 and 16.00 hours on a business day.

(3) With every notice summoning the meeting there shall be sent out forms of proxy.   **[963]**

NOTES

    Para (3): See Sch 4, form 8.1.

5.15. The chairman at the meeting

(1) Subject as follows, the nominee shall be chairman of the creditors' meeting.

(2) If for any reason the nominee is unable to attend, he may nominate another person to act as chairman in his place; but a person so nominated must be either—

    (*a*) a person qualified to act as an insolvency practitioner in relation to the debtor, or

    (*b*) an employee of the nominee or his firm who is experienced in insolvency matters.   **[964]**

5.16. The chairman as proxy-holder

The chairman shall not by virtue of any proxy held by him vote to increase or reduce the amount of the remuneration or expenses of the nominee or the supervisor of the proposed arrangement, unless the proxy specifically directs him to vote in that way.   **[965]**

5.17. Voting rights

(1) Subject as follows, every creditor who was given notice of the creditors' meeting is entitled to vote at the meeting or any adjournment of it.

(2) In Case 1, votes are calculated according to the amount of the creditor's debt as at the date of the bankruptcy order, and in Case 2 according to the amount of the debt as at the date of the meeting.

(3) A creditor shall not vote in respect of a debt for an unliquidated amount or any debt whose value is not ascertained, except where the chairman agrees to put upon the debt an estimated minimum value for the purpose of entitlement to vote.

(4) The chairman has power to admit or reject a creditor's claim for the purpose of his entitlement to vote, and the power is exercisable with respect to the whole or any part of the claim.

(5) The chairman's decision on entitlement to vote is subject to appeal to the court by any creditor, or by the debtor.

(6) If the chairman is in doubt whether a claim should be admitted or rejected, he shall mark it as objected to and allow the creditor to vote, subject to his vote being subsequently declared invalid if the objection to the claim is sustained.

(7) If on an appeal the chairman's decision is reversed or varied, or a creditor's vote is declared invalid, the court may order another meeting to be summoned, or make such other order as it thinks just.

The court's power to make an order under this paragraph is exercisable only if it considers that the matter is such as to give rise to unfair prejudice or a material irregularity.

(8) An application to the court by way of appeal under this Rule against the chairman's decision shall not be made after the end of the period of 28 days beginning with the day on which the chairman's report to the court is made under section 259.

(9) The chairman is not personally liable for any costs incurred by any person in respect of an appeal under this Rule.   **[966]**

5.18. Requisite majorities

(1) Subject as follows, at the creditors' meeting for any resolution to pass approving any proposal or modification there must be a majority in excess of three-quarters in value of the creditors present in person or by proxy and voting on the resolution.

(2) The same applies in respect of any other resolution proposed at the meeting, but substituting one-half for three-quarters.

(3) In the following cases there is to be left out of account a creditor's vote in respect of any claim or part of a claim—

    (*a*) where written notice of the claim was not given, either at the meeting or before it, to the chairman or the nominee;

    (*b*) where the claim or part is secured;

    (*c*) where the claim is in respect of a debt wholly or partly on, or secured by, a current bill of exchange or promissory note, unless the creditor is willing—

        (i) to treat the liability to him on the bill or note of every person who is liable on it antecedently to the debtor, and against whom a bankruptcy order has not been made (or, in the case of a company, which has not gone into liquidation), as a security in his hands, and

        (ii) to estimate the value of the security and (for the purpose of entitlement to vote, but not of any distribution under the arrangement) to deduct it from his claim.

(4) Any resolution is invalid if those voting against it include more than half in value of the creditors, counting in these latter only those—

    (*a*) to whom notice of the meeting was sent;

    (*b*) whose votes are not to be left out of account under paragraph (3); and

    (*c*) who are not, to the best of the chairman's belief, associates of the debtor.

(5) It is for the chairman of the meeting to decide whether under this Rule—

    (*a*) a vote is to be left out of account in accordance with paragraph (3), or

    (*b*) a person is an associate of the debtor for the purposes of paragraph (4)(*c*);

and in relation to the second of these two cases the chairman is entitled to rely on the information provided by the debtor's statement of affairs or otherwise in accordance with this Part of the Rules.

(6) If the chairman uses a proxy contrary to Rule 5.16, his vote with that proxy does not count towards any majority under this Rule.

(7) Paragraphs (5) to (9) of Rule 5.17 apply as regards an appeal against the decision of the chairman under this Rule.   **[967]**

5.19. Proceedings to obtain agreement on the proposal

(1) On the day on which the creditors' meeting is held, it may from time to time be adjourned.

(2) If on that day the requisite majority for the approval of the voluntary arrangement (with or without modifications) has not been obtained, the chairman may, and shall if it is so resolved, adjourn the meeting for not more than 14 days.

(3) If there are subsequently further adjournments, the final adjournment shall not be to a day later than 14 days after that on which the meeting was originally held.

(4) If the meeting is adjourned under paragraph (2), notice of the fact shall be given by the chairman forthwith to the court.

(5) If following any final adjournment of the meeting the proposal (with or without modifications) is not agreed to, it is deemed rejected.   **[968]**

SECTION C: IMPLEMENTATION OF THE ARRANGEMENT

5.20. Resolutions to follow approval

(1) If the voluntary arrangement is approved (with or without modifications), a resolution may be taken by the creditors, where two or more insolvency practitioners are appointed to act as supervisor, on the question whether acts to be done in connection with the arrangement may be done by any one of them, or must be done by both or all.

(2) If at the creditors' meeting a resolution is moved for the appointment of some person other than the nominee to be supervisor of the arrangement, there must be produced to the chairman, at or before the meeting—

(*a*) that person's written consent to act (unless he is present and then and there signifies his consent), and

(*b*) his written confirmation that he is qualified to act as an insolvency practitioner in relation to the debtor.   **[969]**

5.21. Hand-over of property, etc to supervisor

(1) Forthwith after the approval of the voluntary arrangement, the debtor in Case 2, and the official receiver or trustee in Case 1, shall do all that is required for putting the supervisor into possession of the assets included in the arrangement.

(2) On taking possession of the assets in Case 1, the supervisor shall discharge any balance due to the official receiver and (if other) the trustee by way of remuneration or on account of—

(*a*) fees, costs, charges and expenses properly incurred and payable under the Act or the Rules, and

(*b*) any advances made in respect of the insolvent estate, together with interest on such advances at the rate specified in section 17 of the Judgments Act 1838 at the date of the bankruptcy order.

(3) Alternatively in Case 1, the supervisor must, before taking possession, give the official receiver or the trustee a written undertaking to discharge any such balance out of the first realisation of assets.

(4) The official receiver and (if other) the trustee has in Case 1 a charge on the assets included in the voluntary arrangement in respect of any sums due as above until they have been discharged, subject only to the deduction from realisations by the supervisor of the proper costs and expenses of realisation.

Any sums due to the official receiver take priority over those due to a trustee.

(5) The supervisor shall from time to time out of the realisation of assets discharge all guarantees properly given by the official receiver or the trustee for the benefit of the estate, and shall pay all their expenses.   **[970]**

5.22. Report of creditors' meeting

(1) A report of the creditors' meeting shall be prepared by the chairman of the meeting.

(2) The report shall—

    (*a*) state whether the proposal for a voluntary arrangement was approved or rejected and, if approved, with what (if any) modifications;

    (*b*) set out the resolutions which were taken at the meeting, and the decision on each one;

    (*c*) list the creditors (with their respective values) who were present or represented at the meeting, and how they voted on each resolution; and

    (*d*) include such further information (if any) as the chairman thinks it appropriate to make known to the court.

(3) A copy of the chairman's report shall, within 4 days of the meeting being held, be filed in court; and the court shall cause that copy to be endorsed with the date of filing.

(4) The persons to whom notice of the result is to be given, under section 259(1), are all those who were sent notice of the meeting under this Part of the Rules.

The notice shall be sent immediately after a copy of the chairman's report is filed in court under paragraph (3).   **[971]**

5.23. Register of voluntary arrangements

(1) The Secretary of State shall maintain a register of individual voluntary arrangements, and shall enter in it all such matters as are reported to him in pursuance of this Part of the Rules.

(2) The register shall be open to public inspection.   **[972]**

5.24. Reports to Secretary of State

(1) Immediately after the chairman of the creditors' meeting has filed in court a report that the meeting has approved the voluntary arrangement, he shall report to the Secretary of State the following details of the arrangement—

    (*a*) the name and address of the debtor;

    (*b*) the date on which the arrangement was approved by the creditors;

    (*c*) the name and address of the supervisor; and

    (*d*) the court in which the chairman's report has been filed.

(2) A person who is appointed to act as supervisor of an individual voluntary arrangement (whether in the first instance or by way of replacement of another person previously appointed) shall forthwith give written notice to the Secretary of State of his appointment.

If he vacates office as supervisor, he shall forthwith give written notice of that fact also to the Secretary of State.   **[973]**

5.25. Revocation or suspension of the arrangement

(1) This Rule applies where the court makes an order of revocation or suspension under section 262.

(2) The person who applied for the order shall serve sealed copies of it—

    (*a*) in Case 1, on the debtor, the official receiver and the trustee;

    (b) in Case 2, on the debtor; and

    (c) in either case on the supervisor of the voluntary arrangement.

(3) If the order includes a direction by the court under section 262(4)(b) for any further creditors' meeting to be summoned, notice shall also be given (by the person who applied for the order) to whoever is, in accordance with the direction, required to summon the meeting.

(4) The debtor (in Case 2) and the official receiver or the trustee (in Case 1) shall—

    (a) forthwith after receiving a copy of the court's order, give notice of it to all persons who were sent notice of the creditors' meeting which approved the voluntary arrangement or who, not having been sent that notice, appear to be affected by the order;

    (b) within 7 days of their receiving a copy of the order (or within such longer period as the court may allow), give notice to the court whether it is intended to make a revised proposal to creditors, or to invite reconsideration of the original proposal.

(5) The person on whose application the order of revocation or suspension was made shall, within 7 days after the making of the order, give written notice of it to the Secretary of State.   **[974]**

5.26. Supervisor's accounts and reports

(1) Where the voluntary arrangement authorises or requires the supervisor—

    (a) to carry on the debtor's business or to trade on his behalf or in his name, or

    (b) to realise assets of the debtor or (in Case 1) belonging to the estate, or

    (c) otherwise to administer or dispose of any funds of the debtor or the estate,

he shall keep accounts and records of his acts and dealings in and in connection with the arrangement, including in particular records of all receipts and payments of money.

(2) The supervisor shall, not less often than once in every 12 months beginning with the date of his appointment, prepare an abstract of such receipts and payments, and send copies of it, accompanied by his comments on the progress and efficacy of the arrangement, to—

    (a) the court,

    (b) the debtor, and

    (c) all those of the debtor's creditors who are bound by the arrangement.

If in any period of 12 months he has made no payments and had no receipts, he shall at the end of that period send a statement to that effect to all who are specified in sub-paragraphs (a) to (c) above.

(3) An abstract provided under paragraph (2) shall relate to a period beginning with the date of the supervisor's appointment or (as the case may be) the day following the end of the last period for which an abstract was prepared under this Rule; and copies of the abstract shall be sent out, as required by paragraph (2), within the 2 months following the end of the period to which the abstract relates.

(4) If the supervisor is not authorised as mentioned in paragraph (1), he shall, not less often than once in every 12 months beginning with the date of his

appointment, send to all those specified in paragraph (2)(*a*) to (*c*) a report on the progress and efficacy of the voluntary arrangement.

(5) The court may, on application by the supervisor, vary the dates on which the obligation to send abstracts or reports arises. [975]

5.27. Production of accounts and records to Secretary of State

(1) The Secretary of State may at any time during the course of the voluntary arrangement or after its completion require the supervisor to produce for inspection—

    (*a*) his records and accounts in respect of the arrangement, and
    (*b*) copies of abstracts and reports prepared in compliance with Rule 5.26.

(2) The Secretary of State may require production either at the premises of the supervisor or elsewhere; and it is the duty of the supervisor to comply with any requirement imposed on him under this Rule.

(3) The Secretary of State may cause any accounts and records produced to him under this rule to be audited; and the supervisor shall give to the Secretary of State such further information and assistance as he needs for the purposes of his audit. [976]

5.28. Fees, costs, charges and expenses

The fees, costs, charges and expenses that may be incurred for any purposes of the voluntary arrangement are—

    (*a*) any disbursements made by the nominee prior to the approval of the arrangement, and any remuneration for his services as such agreed between himself and the debtor, the official receiver or the trustee;
    (*b*) any fees, costs, charges or expenses which—

        (i) are sanctioned by the terms of the arrangement, or
        (ii) would be payable or correspond to those which would be payable, in the debtor's bankruptcy. [977]

5.29. Completion of the arrangement

(1) Not more than 28 days after the final completion of the voluntary arrangement, the supervisor shall send to all creditors of the debtor who are bound by the arrangement, and to the debtor, a notice that the arrangement has been fully implemented.

(2) With the notice there shall be sent to each of those persons a copy of a report by the supervisor summarising all receipts and payments made by him in pursuance of the arrangement, and explaining any difference in the actual implementation of it as compared with the proposal as approved by the creditors' meeting.

(3) The supervisor shall, within the 28 days mentioned above, send to the Secretary of State and to the court a copy of the notice under paragraph (1), together with a copy of the report under paragraph (2).

(4) The court may, on application by the supervisor, extend the period of 28 days under paragraphs (1) and (3). [978]

SECTION D: GENERAL

5.30. False representations, etc

(1) The debtor commits an offence if he makes any false representation or commits any other fraud for the purpose of obtaining the approval of his creditors to a proposal for a voluntary arrangement under Part VIII of the Act.

(2) A person guilty of an offence under this Rule is liable to imprisonment or a fine, or both.   [979]

PART 6

BANKRUPTCY

CHAPTER 1

THE STATUTORY DEMAND

6.1. Form and content of statutory demand

(1) A statutory demand under section 268 must be dated, and be signed either by the creditor himself or by a person stating himself to be authorised to make the demand on the creditor's behalf.

(2) The statutory demand must specify whether it is made under section 268(1) (debt payable immediately) or section 268(2) (debt not so payable).

(3) The demand must state the amount of the debt, and the consideration for it (or, if there is no consideration, the way in which it arises) and—

    (*a*) if made under section 268(1) and founded on a judgment or order of a court, it must give details of the judgment or order, and

    (*b*) if made under section 268(2), it must state the grounds on which it is alleged that the debtor appears to have no reasonable prospect of paying the debt.

(4) If the amount claimed in the demand includes—

    (*a*) any charge by way of interest not previosuly notified to the debtor as a liability of his, or

    (*b*) any other charge accruing from time to time,

the amount or rate of the charge must be separately identified, and the grounds on which payment of it is claimed must be stated.

In either case the amount claimed must be limited to that which has accrued due at the date of the demand.

(5) If the creditor holds any security in respect of the debt, the full amount of the debt shall be specified, but—

    (*a*) there shall in the demand be specified the nature of the security, and the value which the creditor puts upon it as at the date of the demand, and

    (*b*) the amount of which payment is claimed by the demand shall be the full amount of the debt, less the amount specified as the value of the security.   [980]

NOTES

Para (1): See Sch 4, forms 6.1–6.3.

6.2. Information to be given in statutory demand

(1) The statutory demand must include an explanation to the debtor of the following matters—

(*a*) the purpose of the demand, and the fact that, if the debtor does not comply with the demand, bankruptcy proceedings may be commenced against him;

(*b*) the time within which the demand must be complied with, if that consequence is to be avoided;

(*c*) the methods of compliance which are open to the debtor; and

(*d*) his right to apply to the court for the statutory demand to be set aside.

(2) The demand must specify one or more named individuals with whom the debtor may, if he wishes, enter into communication with a view to securing or compounding for the debt to the satisfaction of the creditor or (as the case may be) establishing to the creditor's satisfaction that there is a reasonable prospect that the debt will be paid when it falls due.

In the case of any individual so named in the demand, his address and telephone number (if any) must be given. **[981]**

6.3. Requirements as to service

(1) Rule 6.11 in Chapter 2 below has effect as regards service of the statutory demand, and proof of that service by affidavit to be filed with a bankruptcy petition.

(2) The creditor is, by virtue of the Rules, under an obligation to do all that is reasonable for the purpose of bringing the statutory demand to the debtor's attention and, if practicable in the particular circumstances, to cause personal service of the demand to be effected.

(3) Where the statutory demand is for payment of a sum due under a judgment or order of any court and the creditor knows, or believes with reasonable cause—

(*a*) that the debtor has absconded or is keeping out of the way with a view to avoiding service, and

(*b*) there is no real prospect of the sum due being recovered by execution or other process,

the demand may be advertised in one or more newspapers; and the time limited for compliance with the demand runs from the date of the advertisement's appearance or (as the case may be) its first appearance. **[982]**

6.4. Application to set aside statutory demand

(1) The debtor may, within the period allowed by this Rule, apply to the appropriate court for an order setting the statutory demand aside.

That period is 18 days from the date of the service on him of the statutory demand or, where the demand is advertised in a newspaper pursuant to Rule 6.3, from the date of the advertisement's appearance or (as the case may be) its first appearance.

(2) Where the creditor issuing the statutory demand is a Minister of the Crown or a Government Department and—

(*a*) the debt in respect of which the demand is made, or a part of it equal to or exceeding the bankruptcy level (within the meaning of section 267), is the subject of a judgment or order of any court, and (*b*) the statutory demand specifies the date of the judgment or order and the court in which it was obtained, but indicates the creditor's intention to present a bankruptcy petition against the debtor in the High Court,

the appropriate court under this Rule is the High Court; and in any other case it is that to which the debtor would, in accordance with paragraphs (1) and (2) of Rule 6.40 in Chapter 3 below, present his own bankruptcy petition.

(3) As from (inclusive) the date on which the application is filed in court, the time limited for compliance with the statutory demand ceases to run, subject to any order of the court under Rule 6.5(6).

(4) The debtor's application shall be supported by an affidavit—

(*a*) specifying the date on which the statutory demand came into his hands, and
(*b*) stating the grounds on which he claims that it should be set aside.

The affidavit shall have exhibited to it a copy of the statutory demand.   **[983]**

NOTES
    Para (1): See Sch 4, form 6.4.
    Para (4): See Sch 4, form 6.5.

6.5. Hearing of application to set aside

(1) On receipt of an application under Rule 6.4, the court may, if satisfied that no sufficient cause is shown for it, dismiss it without giving notice to the creditor. As from (inclusive) the date on which the application is dismissed, the time limited for compliance with the statutory demand runs again.

(2) If the application is not dismissed under paragraph (1), the court shall fix a venue for it to be heard, and shall give at least 7 days' notice of it to—

(*a*) the debtor or, if the debtor's application was made by a solicitor acting for him, to the solicitor,
(*b*) the creditor, and
(*c*) whoever is named in the statutory demand as the person with whom the debtor may enter into communication with reference to the demand (or, if more than one person is so named, the first of them).

(3) On the hearing of the application, the court shall consider the evidence then available to it, and may either summarily determine the application or adjourn it, giving such directions as it thinks appropriate.

(4) The court may grant the application if—

(*a*) the debtor appears to have a counterclaim, set-off or cross demand which equals or exceeds the amount of the debt or debts specified in the statutory demand; or
(*b*) the debt is disputed on grounds which appear to the court to be substantial; or
(*c*) it appears that the creditor holds some security in respect of the debt claimed by the demand, and either Rule 6.1(5) is not complied with in respect of it, or the court is satisfied that the value of the security equals or exceeds the full amount of the debt; or
(*d*) the court is satisfied, on other grounds, that the demand ought to be set aside.

(5) Where the creditor holds some security in respect of his debt, and Rule 6.1(5) is complied with in respect of it but the court is satisfied that the security is under-valued in the statutory demand, the creditor may be required to amend

the demand accordingly (but without prejudice to his right to present a bankruptcy petition by reference to the original demand).

(6) If the court dismisses the application, it shall make an order authorising the creditor to present a bankruptcy petition either forthwith, or on or after a date specified in the order.

A copy of the order shall be sent by the court forthwith to the creditor. **[984]**

NOTES
　Para (4): See Sch 4, form 6.6.

CHAPTER 2
BANKRUPTCY PETITION (CREDITOR'S)

6.6. Preliminary

The Rules in this Chapter relate to a creditor's petition, and the making of a bankruptcy order thereon; and in those Rules "the debt" means, except where the context otherwise requires, the debt (or debts) in respect of which the petition is presented.

Those Rules also apply to a petition under section 264(1)(c) (supervisor of, or person bound by, voluntary arrangement), with any necessary modifications. **[985]**

NOTES
　See Sch 4, forms 6.7–6.10.

6.7. Identification of debtor

(1) The petition shall state the following matters with respect to the debtor, so far as they are within the petitioner's knowledge—

　(a) his name, place of residence and occupation (if any);
　(b) the name or names in which he carries on business, if other than his true name, and whether, in the case of any business of a specified nature, he carries it on alone or with others;
　(c) the nature of his business, and the address or addresses at which he carries it on;
　(d) any name or names, other than his true name, in which he has carried on business at or after the time when the debt was incurred, and whether he has done so alone or with others;
　(e) any address or addresses at which he has resided or carried on business at or after that time, and the nature of that business.

(2) The particulars of the debtor given under this Rule determine the full title of the proceedings.

(3) If to the petitioner's personal knowledge the debtor has used any name other than the one specified under paragraph (1)(a), that fact shall be stated in the petition. **[986]**

6.8. Identification of debt

(1) There shall be stated in the petition, with reference to every debt in respect of which it is presented—

　(a) the amount of the debt, the consideration for it (or, if there is no consideration, the way in which it arises) and the fact that it is owed to the petitioner;
　(b) when the debt was incurred or became due;

(*c*) if the amount of the debt includes—

    (i) any charge by way of interest not previously notified to the debtor as a liability of his, or

    (ii) any other charge accruing from time to time,

the amount or rate of the charge (separately identified) and the grounds on which it is claimed to form part of the debt;

(*d*) either—

    (i) that the debt is for a liquidated sum payable immediately, and the debtor appears to be unable to pay it, or

    (ii) that the debt is for a liquidated sum payable at some certain, future time (that time to be specified), and the debtor appears to have no reasonable prospect of being able to pay it,

and, in either case (subject to section 269) that the debt is unsecured.

(2) Where the debt is one for which, under section 268, a statutory demand must have been served on the debtor—

(*a*) there shall be specified the date and manner of service of the statutory demand, and

(*b*) it shall be stated that, to the best of the creditor's knowledge and belief—

    (i) the demand has been neither complied with nor set aside in accordance with the Rules, and

    (ii) no application to set it aside is outstanding.

(3) If the case is within section 268(1)(*b*) (debt arising under judgment or order of court; execution returned unsatisfied), the court from which the execution or other process issued shall be specified, and particulars shall be given relating to the return. **[987]**

6.9. Court in which petition to be presented

(1) In the following cases, the petition shall be presented to the High Court—

(*a*) if the petition is presented by a Minister of the Crown or a Government Department, and either in any statutory demand on which the petition is based the creditor has indicated the intention to present a bankruptcy petition to that Court, or the petition is presented under section 268(1)(*b*), or

(*b*) if the debtor has resided or carried on business within the London insolvency district for the greater part of the 6 months immediately preceding the presentation of the petition, or for a longer period in those 6 months than in any other insolvency district, or

(*c*) if the debtor is not resident in England and Wales, or

(*d*) if the petitioner is unable to ascertain the residence of the debtor, or his place of business.

(2) In any other case the petition shall be presented to the county court for the insolvency district in which the debtor has resided or carried on business for the longest period during those 6 months.

(3) If the debtor has for the greater part of those 6 months carried on business in one insolvency district and resided in another, the petition shall be presented to the court for the insolvency district in which he has carried on business.

(4) If the debtor has during those 6 months carried on business in more than

one insolvency district, the petition shall be presented to the court for the insolvency district in which is, or has been for the longest period in those 6 months, his principal place of business.

(5) The petition shall contain sufficient information to establish that it is brought in the appropriate court.   **[988]**

6.10. Procedure for presentation and filing

(1) The petition, verified by affidavit in accordance with Rule 6.12(1) below, shall be filed in court.

(2) No petition shall be filed unless there is produced with it the receipt for the deposit payable on presentation.

(3) The following copies of the petition shall also be delivered to the court with the petition—

    (*a*) one service on the debtor, and

    (*b*) one to be exhibited to the affidavit verifying that service.

Each of these copies shall have applied to it the seal of the court, and shall be issued to the petitioner.

(4) The date and time of filing the petition shall be endorsed on the petition and on any copy issued under paragraph (3).

(5) The court shall fix a venue for hearing the petition, and this also shall be endorsed on the petition and on any copy so issued.   **[989]**

6.11. Proof of service of statutory demand

(1) Where under section 268 the petition must have been preceded by a statutory demand, there must be filed in court, with the petition, an affidavit proving service of the demand.

(2) The affidavit must have exhibited to it a copy of the demand as served.

(3) Subject to the next paragraph, if the demand has been served personally on the debtor, the affidavit must be made by the person who effected that service.

(4) If service of the demand (however effected) has been acknowledged in writing either by the debtor himself, or by some person stating himself in the acknowledgement to be authorised to accept service on the debtor's behalf, the affidavit must be made either by the creditor or by a person acting on his behalf, and the acknowledgement of service must be exhibited to the affidavit.

(5) If neither paragraph (3) nor paragraph (4) applies, the affidavit must be made by a person having direct personal knowledge of the means adopted for serving the statutory demand, and must—

    (*a*) give particulars of the steps which have been taken with a view to serving the demand, and

    (*b*) state the means whereby (those steps having been ineffective) it was sought to bring the demand to the debtor's attention, and

    (*c*) specify a date by which, to the best of the knowledge, information and belief of the person making the affidavit, the demand will have come to the debtor's attention.

(6) The steps of which particulars are given for the purposes of paragraph (5)(*a*) must be such as would have sufficed to justify an order for substituted service of a petition.

(7) If the affidavit specifies a date for the purposes of compliance with paragraph (5)(*c*), then unless the court otherwise orders, that date is deemed for the purposes of the Rules to have been the date on which the statutory demand was served on the debtor.

(8) Where the creditor has taken advantage of Rule 6.3(3) (newspaper advertisement), the affidavit must be made either by the creditor himself or by a person having direct personal knowledge of the circumstances; and there must be specified in the affidavit—

> (*a*) the means of the creditor's knowledge or (as the case may be) belief required for the purposes of that Rule, and
> (*b*) the date or dates on which, and the newspaper in which, the statutory demand was advertised under that Rule;

and there shall be exhibited to the affidavit a copy of any advertisement of the statutory demand.

(9) The court may decline to file the petition if not satisfied that the creditor has discharged the obligation imposed on him by Rule 6.3(2). **[990]**

NOTES
Para (3): See Sch 4, form 6.11.
Para (5): See Sch 4, form 6.12.

6.12. Verification of petition

(1) The petition shall be verified by an affidavit that the statements in the petition are true, or are true to the best of the deponent's knowledge, information and belief.

(2) If the petition is in respect of debts to different creditors, the debts to each creditor must be separately verified.

(3) The petition shall be exhibited to the affidavit verifying it.

(4) The affidavit shall be made—

> (*a*) by the petitioner (or if there are two or more petitioners, any one of them), or
> (*b*) by some person such as a director, company secretary or similar company officer, or a solicitor, who has been concerned in the matters giving rise to the presentation of the petition, or
> (*c*) by some responsible person who is duly authorised to make the affidavit and has the requisite knowledge of those matters.

(5) Where the maker of the affidavit is not the petitioner himself, or one of the petitioners, he must in the affidavit identify himself and state—

> (*a*) the capacity in which, and the authority by which, he makes it and
> (*b*) the means of his knowledge of the matters sworn to in the affidavit.

(6) The affidavit is prima facie evidence of the truth of the statements in the petition to which it relates.

(7) If the petition is based upon a statutory demand, and more than 4 months have elapsed between the service of the demand and the presentation of the petition, the affidavit must also state the reasons for the delay. **[991]**

NOTES
Para (1): See Sch 4, form 6.13.

6.13. Notice to Chief Land Registrar

When the petition is filed, the court shall forthwith send to the Chief Land Registrar notice of the petition together with a request that it may be registered in the register of pending actions.   **[992]**

NOTES
   See Sch 4, form 6.14.

6.14. Service of petition

(1) Subject as follows, the petition shall be served personally on the debtor by an officer of the court, or by the petitioning creditor or his solicitor, or by a person instructed by the creditor or his solicitor for that purpose; and service shall be effected by delivering to him a sealed copy of the petition.

(2) If the court is satisfied by affidavit or other evidence on oath that prompt personal service cannot be effected because the debtor is keeping out of the way to avoid service of the petition or other legal process, or for any other cause, it may order substituted service to be effected in such manner as it thinks fit.

(3) Where an order for substituted service has been carried out, the petition is deemed duly served on the debtor.   **[993]**

NOTES
   Para (3): See Sch 4, forms 6.15, 6.16.

6.15. Proof of service

(1) Service of the petition shall be proved by affidavit.

(2) The affidavit shall have exhibited to it—

   (*a*) a sealed copy of the petition, and
   (*b*) if substituted service has been ordered, a sealed copy of the order;

and it shall be filed in court immediately after service.   **[994]**

NOTES
   Para (1): See Sch 4, forms 6.17, 6.18.

6.16. Death of debtor before service

If the debtor dies before service of the petition, the court may order service to be effected on his personal representatives, or on such other persons as it thinks fit.   **[995]**

6.17. Security for costs (s 268(2) only)

(1) This Rule applies where the debt in respect of which the petition is presented is for a liquidated sum payable at some future time, it being claimed in the petition that the debtor appears to have no reasonable prospect of being able to pay it.

(2) The petitioning creditor may, on the debtor's application, be ordered to give security for the debtor's costs.

(3) The nature and amount of the security to be ordered is in the court's discretion.

(4) If an order is made under this Rule, there shall be no hearing of the petition until the whole amount of the security has been given.   **[996]**

6.18. Hearing of petition

(1) Subject as follows, the petition shall not be heard until at least 14 days have elapsed since it was served on the debtor.

(2) The court may, on such terms as it thinks fit, hear the petition at an earlier date, if it appears that the debtor has absconded, or the court is satisfied that it is a proper case for an expedited hearing, or the debtor consents to a hearing within the 14 days.

(3) Any of the following may appear and be heard, that is to say, the petitioning creditor, the debtor and any creditor who has given notice under Rule 6.23 below. **[997]**

6.19. Petition against two or more debtors

Where two or more debtors are named in the petition, and the petition has not been served on both or all of them, the petition may be heard separately or collectively as regards any of those who have been served, and may subsequently be heard (separately or collectively) as regards the others, as and when service on them is effected. **[998]**

6.20. Petition by moneylender

A petition in respect of a money lending transaction made before 27th January 1980 of a creditor who at the time of the transaction was a licensed money-lender shall at the hearing of the petition be supported by an affidavit incorporating a statement setting out in detail the particulars mentioned in section 9(2) of the Moneylenders Act 1927. **[999]**

6.21. Petition opposed by debtor

Where the debtor intends to oppose the petition, he shall not later than 7 days before the day fixed for the hearing—

(*a*) file in court a notice specifying the grounds on which he will object to the making of a bankruptcy order, and

(*b*) send a copy of the notice to the petitioning creditor or his solicitor.

[1000]

NOTES
See Sch 4, form 6.19.

6.22. Amendment of petition

With the leave of the court (given on such terms, if any, as the court thinks fit to impose), the petition may be amended at any time after presentation by the omission of any creditor or any debt. **[1001]**

6.23. Notice by persons intending to appear

(1) Every creditor who intends to appear on the hearing of the petition shall give to the petitioning creditor notice of his intention in accordance with this Rule.

(2) The notice shall specify—

(*a*) the name and address of the person giving it, and any telephone number and reference which may be required for communication with him or with any other person (to be also specified in the notice) authorised to speak or act on his behalf;

(*b*) whether his intention is to support or oppose the petition; and (*c*) the amount and nature of his debt.

(3) The notice shall be sent so as to reach the addressee not later than 16.00 hours on the business day before that which is appointed for the hearing (or, where the hearing has been adjourned, for the adjourned hearing).

(4) A person failing to comply with this Rule may appear on the hearing of the petition only with the leave of the court.   **[1002]**

NOTES
Para (1): See Sch 4, form 6.20.

6.24. List of appearances

(1) The petitioning creditor shall prepare for the court a list of the creditors (if any) who have given notice under Rule 6.23, specifying their names and addresses and (if known to him) their respective solicitors.

(2) Against the name of each creditor in the list it shall be stated whether his intention is to support the petition, or to oppose it.

(3) On the day appointed for the hearing of the petition, a copy of the list shall be handed to the court before the commencement of the hearing.

(4) If any leave is given under Rule 6.23(4), the petitioner shall add to the list the same particulars in respect of the person to whom leave has been given.
[1003]

NOTES
Para (1): See Sch 4, form 6.21.

6.25. Decision on the hearing

(1) On the hearing of the petition, the court may make a bankruptcy order if satisfied that the statements in the petition are true, and that the debt on which it is founded has not been paid, or secured or compounded for.

(2) If the petition is brought in respect of a judgment debt, or a sum ordered by any court to be paid, the court may stay or dismiss the petition on the ground that an appeal is pending from the judgment or order, or that execution of the judgment has been stayed.

(3) A petition preceded by a statutory demand shall not be dismissed on the ground only that the amount of the debt was over-stated in the demand, unless the debtor, within the time allowed for complying with the demand, gave notice to the creditor disputing the validity of the demand on that ground; but, in the absence of such notice, the debtor is deemed to have complied with the demand if he has, within the time allowed, paid the correct amount.   **[1004]**

NOTES
Para (2): See Sch 4, form 6.22.

6.26. Non-appearance of creditor

If the petitioning creditor fails to appear on the hearing of the petition, no subsequent petition against the same debtor, either alone or jointly with any other person, shall be presented by the same creditor in respect of the same debt, without the leave of the court to which the previous petition was presented.   **[1005]**

6.27. Vacating registration on dismissal of petition

If the petition is dismissed or withdrawn by leave of the court, an order shall be made at the same time permitting vacation of the registration of the petition as a pending action; and the court shall send to the debtor two sealed copies of the order. **[1006]**

NOTES
See Sch 4, form 6.22.

6.28. Extension of time for hearing

(1) The petitioning creditor may, if the petition has not been served, apply to the court to appoint another venue for the hearing.

(2) The application shall state the reasons why the petition has not been served.

(3) No costs occasioned by the application shall be allowed in the proceedings except by order of the court.

(4) If the court appoints another day for the hearing, the petitioning creditor shall forthwith notify any creditor who has given notice under Rule 6.23. **[1007]**

6.29. Adjournment

(1) If the court adjourns the hearing of the petition, the following applies.

(2) Unless the court otherwise directs, the petitioning creditor shall forthwith send—

   (*a*) to the debtor, and
   (*b*) where any creditor has given notice under Rule 6.23 but was not present at the hearing, to him,

notice of the making of the order of adjournment. The notice shall state the venue for the adjourned hearing. **[1008]**

NOTES
Para (1): See Sch 4, form 6.23.
Para (2): See Sch 4, form 6.24.

6.30. Substitution of petitioner

(1) This Rule applies where a creditor petitions and is subsequently found not entitled to do so, or where the petitioner—

   (*a*) consents to withdraw his petition or to allow it to be dismissed, or consents to an adjournment, or fails to appear in support of his petition when it is called on in court on the day originally fixed for the hearing, or on a day to which it is adjourned, or
   (*b*) appears, but does not apply for an order in the terms of the prayer of his petition.

(2) The court may, on such terms as it thinks just, order that there be substituted as petitioner any creditor who—

   (*a*) has under Rule 6.23 given notice of his intention to appear at the hearing,
   (*b*) is desirous of prosecuting the petition, and
   (*c*) was, at the date on which the petition was presented, in such a position in relation to the debtor as would have enabled him (the

creditor) on that date to present a bankruptcy petition in respect of a debt or debts owed to him by the debtor, paragraphs (*a*) to (*d*) of section 267(2) being satisfied in respect of that debt or those debts.

[1009]

6.31. Change of carriage of petition

(1) On the hearing of the petition, any person who claims to be a creditor of the debtor, and who has given notice under Rule 6.23 of his intention to appear at the hearing, may apply to the court for an order giving him carriage of the petition in place of the petitioning creditor, but without requiring any amendment of the petition.

(2) The court may, on such terms as it thinks just, make a change of carriage order if satisfied that—

    (*a*) the applicant is an unpaid and unsecured creditor of the debtor, and
    (*b*) the petitioning creditor either—

        (i) intends by any means to secure the postponement, adjournment or withdrawal of the petition, or
        (ii) does not intend to prosecute the petition, either diligently or at all.

(3) The court shall not make the order if satisfied that the petitioning creditor's debt has been paid, secured or compounded for by means of—

    (*a*) a disposition of property made by some person other than the debtor, or
    (*b*) a disposition of the debtor's own property made with the approval of, or ratified by, the court.

(4) A change of carriage order may be made whether or not the petitioning creditor appears at the hearing.

(5) If the order is made, the person given the carriage of the petition is entitled to rely on all evidence previously adduced in the proceedings (whether by affidavit or otherwise).   **[1010]**

6.32. Petitioner seeking dismissal or leave to withdraw

(1) Where the petitioner applies to the court for the petition to be dismissed, or for leave to withdraw it, he must, unless the court otherwise orders, file in court an affidavit specifying the grounds of the application and the circumstances in which it is made.

(2) If, since the petition was filed, any payment has been made to the petitioner by way of settlement (in whole or in part) of the debt or debts in respect of which the petition was brought, or any arrangement has been entered into for securing or compounding it or them, the affidavit must state—

    (*a*) what dispositions of property have been made for the purposes of the settlement or arrangement, and
    (*b*) whether, in the case of any disposition, it was property of the debtor himself, or of some other person, and

(c) whether, if it was property of the debtor, the disposition was made with the approval of, or has been ratified by, the court (if so, specifying the relevant court order).

(3) No order giving leave to withdraw shall be given before the petition is heard. **[1011]**

NOTES
  Para (3): See Sch 4, form 6.22.

6.33. Settlement and content of bankruptcy order

(1) The bankruptcy order shall be settled by the court.

(2) The order shall—

(a) state the date of the presentation of the petition on which the order is made, and the date and time of the making of the order, and
(b) contain a notice requiring the bankrupt, forthwith after service of the order on him, to attend on the official receiver at the place stated in the order.

(3) Subject to section 346 (effect of bankruptcy on enforcement procedures), the order may include provision staying any action or proceeding against the bankrupt.

(4) Where the petitioning creditor is represented by a solicitor, the order shall be endorsed with the latter's name, address, telephone number and reference (if any). **[1012]**

NOTES
  Para (1): See Sch 4, form 6.25.

6.34. Action to follow making of order

(1) At least two sealed copies of the bankruptcy order shall be sent forthwith by the court to the official receiver, who shall forthwith send one of them to the bankrupt.

(2) Subject to the next paragraph, the official receiver shall—

(a) send notice of the making of the order to the Chief Land Registrar, for registration in the register of writs and orders affecting land,
(b) cause the order to be advertised in such local paper as the official receiver thinks fit, and
(c) cause the order to be gazetted.

(3) The court may, on the application of the bankrupt or a creditor, order the official receiver to suspend action under paragraph (2), pending a further order of the court.

An application under this paragraph shall be supported by an affidavit stating the grounds on which it is made.

(4) Where an order is made under paragraph (3), the applicant for the order shall forthwith deliver a copy of it to the official receiver. **[1013]**

NOTES
  Para (2): See Sch 4, form 6.26.

6.35. Amendment of title of proceedings

(1) At any time after the making of a bankruptcy order, the official receiver or the trustee may apply to the court for an order amending the full title of the proceedings.

(2) Where such an order is made, the official receiver shall forthwith send notice of it to the Chief Land Registrar, for corresponding amendment of the register; and, if the court so directs he shall also cause notice of the order to be gazetted, and to be advertised in such local newspaper as the official receiver thinks fit.   **[1014]**

6.36. Old bankruptcy notices

(1) Subject as follows, a person who has before the appointed day for the purposes of the Act served a bankruptcy notice under the Bankruptcy Act 1914 may, on or after that day, proceed on the notice as if it were a statutory demand duly served under Chapter 1 of this Part of the Rules.

(2) The conditions of the application of this Rule are that—

    (*a*) the debt in respect of which the bankruptcy notice was served has not been paid, secured or compounded for in the terms of the notice and the Act of 1914;

    (*b*) the date by which compliance with the notice was required was not more than 3 months before the date of presentation of the petition; and

    (*c*) there has not, before the appointed day, been presented any bankruptcy petition with reference to an act of bankruptcy arising from non-compliance with the bankruptcy notice.

(3) If before, on or after the appointed day, application is made (under the Act of 1914) to set the bankruptcy notice aside, that application is to be treated, on and after that day, as an application duly made (on the date on which it was in fact made) to set aside a statutory demand duly served on the date on which the bankruptcy notice was in fact served.   **[1015]**

CHAPTER 3

BANKRUPTCY PETITION (DEBTOR'S)

6.37. Preliminary

The Rules in this Chapter relate to a debtor's petition, and the making of a bankruptcy order thereon.   **[1016]**

NOTES
   See Sch 4, form 6.27.

6.38. Identification of debtor

(1) The petition shall state the following matters with respect to the debtor—

    (*a*) his name, place of residence and occupation (if any);

    (*b*) the name or names in which he carries on business, if other than his true name, and whether, in the case of any business of a specified nature, he carries it on alone or with others;

    (*c*) the nature of his business, and the address or addresses at which he carries it on;

    (*d*) any name or names, other than his true name, in which he has carried on business in the period in which any of his bankruptcy debts were incurred and, in the case of any such business, whether he has carried it on alone or with others; and

(e) any address or addresses at which he has resided or carried on business during that period, and the nature of that business.

(2) The particulars of the debtor given under this Rule determine the full title of the proceedings.

(3) If the debtor has at any time used a name other than the one given under paragraph (1)(a), that fact shall be stated in the petition. **[1017]**

6.39. Admission of insolvency

(1) The petition shall contain the statement that the petitioner is unable to pay his debts, and a request that a bankruptcy order be made against him.

(2) If within the period of 5 years ending with the date of the petition the petitioner has been adjudged bankrupt, or has made a composition with his creditors in satisfaction of his debts or a scheme of arrangement of his affairs, or he has entered into any voluntary arrangement or been subject to an administration order under Part VI of the County Courts Act 1984, particulars of these matters shall be given in the petition. **[1018]**

6.40. Court in which petition to be filed

(1) In the following cases, the petition shall be presented to the High Court—

(a) if the debtor has resided or carried on business in the London insolvency district for the greater part of the 6 months immediately preceding the presentation of the petition, or for a longer period in those 6 months than in any other insolvency district, or

(b) if the debtor is not resident in England and Wales.

(2) In any other case, the petition shall (subject to paragraph (3) below), be presented to the debtor's own county court, which is—

(a) the county court for the insolvency district in which he has resided or carried on business for the longest period in those 6 months, or

(b) if he has for the greater part of those 6 months carried on business in one insolvency district and resided in another, the county court for that in which he has carried on business, or

(c) if he has during those 6 months carried on business in more than one insolvency district, the county court for that in which is, or has been for the longest period in those 6 months, his principal place of business.

(3) If, in the case not falling within paragraph (1), it is more expedient for the debtor with a view to expediting his petition, it may be presented to whichever county court is specified by Schedule 2 to the Rules as being, in relation to the debtor's own county court, the nearest full-time court.

(4) The petition shall contain sufficient information to establish that it is brought in the appropriate court. **[1019]**

6.41. Statement of affairs

(1) The petition shall be accompanied by a statement of the debtor's affairs, verified by affidavit.

(2) Section B of Chapter 5 below applies with respect to the statement of affairs. **[1020]**

NOTES
  Para (1): See Sch 4, form 6.28.

6.42. Procedure for presentation and filing

(1) The petition and the statement of affairs shall be filed in court, together with three copies of the petition, and two copies of the statement. No petition shall be filed unless there is produced with it the receipt for the deposit payable on presentation.

(2) The court may hear the petition forthwith. If it does not do so, it shall fix a venue for the hearing.

(3) Of the three copies of the petition delivered—

  (a) one shall be returned to the petitioner, endorsed with any venue fixed;
  (b) another, so endorsed, shall be retained by the court, to be sent to the official receiver if he is appointed interim receiver or a bankruptcy order is made; and
  (c) the remaining copy shall be retained by the court, to be sent to an insolvency practitioner (if appointed under section 273(2)).

(4) Of the two copies of the statement of affairs—

  (a) one shall be retained by the court, to be sent to the official receiver if he is appointed interim receiver or a bankruptcy order is made; and
  (b) the other shall be retained by the court to be sent to the insolvency practitioner (if appointed).

(5) The affidavit verifying the debtor's statement of affairs may be sworn before an officer of the court duly authorised in that behalf.   **[1021]**

6.43. Notice to Chief Land Registrar

When the petition is filed, the court shall forthwith send to the Chief Land Registrar notice of the petition, for registration in the register of pending actions.   **[1022]**

NOTES
  See Sch 4, form 6.14.

6.44. Report of insolvency practitioner

(1) If the court under section 273(2) appoints an insolvency practitioner to act in the debtor's case, it shall forthwith—

  (a) send to the person appointed—

    (i) a sealed copy of the order of appointment, and
    (ii) copies of the petition and statement of affairs,

  (b) fix a venue for the insolvency practitioner's report to be considered, and
  (c) send notice of the venue to the insolvency practitioner and the debtor.

(2) The insolvency practitioner shall file his report in court with one copy, and send one copy of it to the debtor, so as to be in his hands not less than 3 days before the date fixed for consideration of the report.

(3) The debtor is entitled to attend when the report is considered, and shall attend if so directed by the court. If he attends, the court shall hear any representations which he makes with respect to any of the matters dealt with in the report.

(4) If the official receiver is appointed interim receiver or a bankruptcy order is made, a copy of the insolvency practitioner's report, the debtor's petition and his statement of affairs shall be sent by the court to the official receiver.   **[1023]**

6.45. Settlement and content of bankruptcy order

(1) The bankruptcy order shall be settled by the court.

(2) The order shall—

    (*a*) state the date of the presentation of the petition on which the order is made, and the date and time of the making of the order, and

    (*b*) contain a notice requiring the bankrupt, forthwith after the service of the order on him, to attend on the official receiver at the place stated in the order.

(3) Subject to section 346 (effect of bankruptcy on enforcement procedures), the order may include provisions staying any action or proceeding against the bankrupt.

(4) Where the bankrupt is represented by a solicitor, the order shall be endorsed with the latter's name, address, telephone number and reference.

[1024]

6.46. Action to follow making of order

(1) At least two sealed copies of the bankruptcy order shall be sent forthwith by the court to the official receiver, who shall forthwith send one of them to the bankrupt.

(2) Subject to the next paragraph, the official receiver shall—

    (*a*) send notice of the making of the order to the Chief Land Registrar, for registration in the register of writs and orders affecting land,

    (*b*) cause the order to be advertised in such local paper as the official receiver thinks fit, and

    (*c*) cause notice of the order to be gazetted.

(3) The court may, on the application of the bankrupt or a creditor, order the official receiver to suspend action under paragraph (2), pending a further order of the court.

An application under this paragraph shall be supported by an affidavit stating the grounds on which it is made.

(4) Where an order is made under paragraph (3), the applicant shall forthwith deliver a copy of it to the official receiver.   **[1025]**

6.47. Amendment of title of proceedings

(1) At any time after the making of the bankruptcy order, the official receiver or the trustee may apply to the court for an order amending the full title of the proceedings.

(2) Where such an order is made, the official receiver shall forthwith send notice of it to the Chief Land Registrar, for corresponding amendment of the register; and, if the court so directs, he shall also—

    (*a*) cause notice of the order to be gazetted, and
    (*b*) cause notice of the order to be advertised in such local paper as the official receiver thinks appropriate.   **[1026]**

6.48. Certificate of summary administration

(1) If the court under section 275 issues a certificate for the summary administration of the bankrupt's estate, the certificate may be included in the bankruptcy order.

(2) If the certificate is not so included, the court shall forthwith send copies of it to the official receiver and the bankrupt.   **[1027]**

NOTES
    Para (1): See Sch 4, form 6.30.

6.49. Duty of official receiver in summary administration

(1) Where a trustee has been appointed, the official receiver shall send a copy of the certificate of summary administration (whether or not included in the bankruptcy order) to him.

(2) Within 12 weeks after the issue of the certificate the official receiver shall (insofar as he has not already done so) give notice to creditors of the making of the bankruptcy order.   **[1028]**

6.50. Revocation of certificate of summary administration

(1) The court may under section 275(3) revoke a certificate for summary administration, either of its own motion or on the application of the official receiver.

(2) If the official receiver applies for the certificate to be revoked, he shall give at least 14 days' notice of the application to the bankrupt.

(3) If the court revokes the certificate, it shall forthwith give notice to the official receiver and the bankrupt.

(4) If at the time of revocation there is a trustee other than the official receiver, the official receiver shall send a copy of the court's notice to him.

[1029]

NOTES
    Para (1): See Sch 4, form 6.31.

6.51. Application for appointment of interim receiver

(1) An application to the court for the appointment of an interim receiver under section 286 may be made by a creditor or by the debtor, or by an insolvency practitioner appointed under section 273(2).

(2) The application must be supported by an affidavit stating—

- (*a*) the grounds on which it is proposed that the interim receiver should be appointed,
- (*b*) whether or not the official receiver has been informed of the application and, if so, has been furnished with a copy of it,
- (*c*) whether to the applicant's knowledge there has been proposed or is in force a voluntary arrangement under Part VIII of the Act, and
- (*d*) the applicant's estimate of the value of the property or business in respect of which the interim receiver is to be appointed.

(3) If an insolvency practitioner has been appointed under section 273, and it is proposed that he (and not the official receiver) should be appointed interim receiver, and it is not the insolvency practitioner himself who is the applicant under this Rule, the affidavit under paragraph (2) must state that he has consented to act.

(4) The applicant shall send copies of the application and the affidavit to the person proposed to be appointed interim receiver. If that person is the official receiver and an insolvency practitioner has been appointed under section 273 (and he is not himself the applicant), copies of the application and affidavit shall be sent by the applicant to the insolvency practitioner.

If, in any case where a copy of the application is to be sent to a person under this paragraph, it is for any reason not practicable to send a copy, that person must be informed of the application in sufficient time to enable him to be present at the hearing.

(5) The official receiver and (if appointed) the insolvency practitioner may attend the hearing of the application and make representations.

(6) The court may on the application, if satisfied that sufficient grounds are shown for the appointment, make it on such terms as it thinks fit. **[1030]**

6.52. Order of appointment

(1) The order appointing the interim receiver shall state the nature and a short description of the property of which the person appointed is to take possession, and the duties to be performed by him in relation to the debtor's affairs.

(2) The court shall, forthwith after the order is made, send 2 sealed copies of it to the person appointed interim receiver (one of which shall be sent by him forthwith to the debtor). **[1031]**

NOTES

Para (1): See Sch 4, form 6.32.

6.53. Deposit

(1) Before an order appointing the official receiver as interim receiver is issued, the applicant for it shall deposit with him, or otherwise secure to his satisfaction, such sum as the court directs to cover his remuneration and expenses.

(2) If the sum deposited or secured subsequently proves to be insufficient, the court may, on application by the official receiver, order that an additional sum be deposited or secured. If the order is not complied with within 2 days after service on the person to whom the order is directed, the court may discharge the order appointing the interim receiver.

(3) If a bankruptcy order is made after an interim receiver has been appointed, any money deposited under this Rule shall (unless it is required by reason of insufficiency of assets for payment of remuneration and expenses of the interim receiver, or the deposit was made by the debtor out of his own property) be repaid to the person depositing it (or as that person may direct) out of the bankrupt's estate, in the prescribed order of priority.   **[1032]**

6.54. Security

(1) The following applies where an insolvency practitioner is appointed to be interim receiver under section 286(2).

(2) The cost of providing the security required under the Act shall be paid in the first instance by the interim receiver; but—

    (*a*) if a bankruptcy order is not made, the person so appointed is entitled to be reimbursed out of the property of the debtor, and the court may make an order on the debtor accordingly, and

    (*b*) if a bankruptcy order is made, he is entitled to be reimbursed out of the estate in the prescribed order of priority.   **[1033]**

6.55. Failure to give or keep up security

(1) If the interim receiver fails to give or keep up his security, the court may remove him, and make such order as it thinks fit as to costs.

(2) If an order is made under this Rule removing the interim receiver, or discharging the order appointing him, the court shall give directions as to whether any, and if so what, steps should be taken for the appointment of another person in his place.   **[1034]**

6.56. Remuneration

(1) The remuneration of the interim receiver (other than the official receiver) shall be fixed by the court from time to time on his application.

(2) In fixing the interim receiver's remuneration, the court shall take into account—

    (*a*) the time properly given by him (as interim receiver) and his staff in attending to the debtor's affairs,

    (*b*) the complexity (or otherwise) of the case,

    (*c*) any respects in which, in connection with the debtor's affairs, there falls on the interim receiver any responsibility of an exceptional kind or degree,

    (*d*) the effectiveness with which the interim receiver appears to be carrying out, or to have carried out, his duties as such, and (*e*) the value and nature of the property with which he has to deal.

(3) The interim receiver's remuneration (whether the official receiver or another) shall be paid to him, and the amount of any expenses incurred by him reimbursed—

    (*a*) if a bankruptcy order is not made, out of the property of the debtor (and the court may make an order on the debtor accordingly), and

    (*b*) if a bankruptcy order is made, out of the estate in the prescribed order of priority,

or, in either case (the relevant funds being insufficient), out of the deposit under Rule 6.53. **[1035]**

6.57. Termination of appointment

(1) The appointment of the interim receiver may be terminated by the court on his application, or on that of the official receiver, the debtor or any creditor.

(2) If the interim receiver's appointment terminates, in consequence of the dismissal of the bankruptcy petition or otherwise, the court may give such directions as it thinks fit with respect to the accounts of his administration and any other matters which it thinks appropriate.

(3) The court may under paragraph (2)—

    (*a*) direct that any expenses properly incurred by the interim receiver during the period of his appointment, and any remuneration to which he is entitled, be paid out of property of the debtor, and

    (*b*) authorise him to retain out of that property such sums as are required for meeting his expenses and remuneration.

Alternatively, the court may make such order as it thinks fit with respect to those matters. **[1036]**

CHAPTER 5

DISCLOSURE BY BANKRUPT WITH RESPECT TO THE STATE OF HIS AFFAIRS

SECTION A: CREDITORS PETITION

6.58. Preliminary

The Rules in this Section apply with respect to the statement of affairs required by section 288(1) to be submitted by the bankrupt, following a bankruptcy order made on a creditor's petition, and the further and other disclosure which is required of him in that case. **[1037]**

6.59. The statement of affairs

The bankrupt's statement of affairs shall be in Form 6.33, and contain all the particulars required by that form. **[1038]**

NOTES

    See Sch 4, form 6.33.

6.60. Verification and filing

(1) The bankrupt shall be furnished by the official receiver with instructions for the preparation of his statement of affairs, and the forms required for that purpose.

(2) The statement of affairs shall be verified by affidavit and delivered to the official receiver, together with one copy.

(3) The official receiver shall file the verified statement in court.

(4) The affidavit may be sworn before an official receiver or a deputy official receiver, or before an officer of the Department or the court duly authorised in that behalf. **[1039]**

6.61. Limited disclosure

(1) Where the official receiver thinks that it would prejudice the conduct of the bankruptcy for the whole or part of the statement of affairs to be disclosed, he may apply to the court for an order of limited disclosure in respect of the statement, or any specified part of it.

(2) The court may on the application order that the statement or, as the case may be, the specified part of it be not filed in court, or that it is to be filed separately and not be open to inspection otherwise than with leave of the court.
[1040]

6.62. Release from duty to submit statement of affairs; extension of time

(1) The power of the official receiver under section 288(3) to release the bankrupt from his duty to submit a statement of affairs, or to grant an extension of time, may be exercised at the official receiver's own discretion, or at the bankrupt's request.

(2) The bankrupt may, if he requests a release or extension of time and it is refused by the official receiver, apply to the court for it.

(3) The court may, if it thinks that no sufficient cause is shown for the application, dismiss it; but it shall not do so unless the bankrupt has had an opportunity to attend the court for an *ex parte* hearing, of which he has been given at least 7 days' notice.

If the application is not dismissed under this paragraph, the court shall fix a venue for it to be heard, and give notice to the bankrupt accordingly.

(4) The bankrupt shall, at least 14 days before the hearing, send to the official receiver a notice stating the venue and accompanied by a copy of the application, and of any evidence which he (the bankrupt) intends to adduce in support of it.

(5) The official receiver may appear and be heard on the application; and, whether or not he appears, he may file a written report of any matters which he considers ought to be drawn to the court's attention.

If such a report is filed, a copy of it shall be sent by the official receiver to the bankrupt, not later than 5 days before the hearing.

(6) Sealed copies of any order made on the application shall be sent by the court to the bankrupt and the official receiver.

(7) On any application under this Rule the bankrupt's costs shall be paid in any event by him and, unless the court otherwise orders, no allowance towards them shall be made out of the estate. **[1041]**

6.63. Expenses of statement of affairs

(1) If the bankrupt cannot himself prepare a proper statement of affairs, the official receiver may, at the expense of the estate, employ some person or persons to assist in the preparation of the statement.

(2) At the request of the bankrupt, made on the grounds that he cannot himself prepare a proper statement, the official receiver may authorise an allowance payable out of the estate (in accordance with the prescribed order of priority) towards expenses to be incurred by the bankrupt in employing some person or persons to assist him in preparing it.

(3) Any such request by the bankrupt shall be accompanied by an estimate of the expenses involved; and the official receiver shall only authorise the employment of a named person or a named firm, being in either case approved by him.

(4) An authorisation given by the official receiver under this Rule shall be subject to such conditions (if any) as he thinks fit to impose with respect to the manner in which any person may obtain access to relevant books and papers.

(5) Nothing in this Rule relieves the bankrupt from any obligation with respect to the preparation, verification and submission of his statement of affairs, or to the provision of information to the official receiver or the trustee.

[1042]

6.64 Requirement to submit accounts

(1) The bankrupt shall, at the request of the official receiver, furnish him with accounts relating to his affairs of such nature, as at such date and for such period as he may specify.

(2) The period specified may begin from a date up to 3 years preceding the date of the presentation of the bankruptcy petition.

(3) The court may, on the official receiver's application, require accounts in respect of any earlier period.

(4) Rule 6.63 applies (with the necessary modifictions) in relation to accounts to be furnished under this Rule as it applies in relation to the statement of affairs. **[1043]**

6.65. Submission and filing of accounts

(1) The accounts to be furnished under Rule 6.64 shall, if the official receiver so requires, be verified by affidavit, and (whether or not so verified) delivered to him within 21 days of the request under Rule 6.64(1), or such longer period as he may allow.

(2) Two copies of the accounts and (where required) the affidavit shall be delivered by the bankrupt to the official receiver, who shall file one copy in court (with the affidavit, if any). **[1044]**

6.66. Further disclosure

(1) The official receiver may at any time require the bankrupt to submit (in writing) further information amplifying, modifying or explaining any matter contained in his statement of affairs, or in accounts submitted in pursuance of the Act or the Rules.

(2) The information shall, if the official receiver so directs, be verified by affidavit, and (whether or not so verified) delivered to him within 21 days of the requirement under this Rule, or such longer period as he may allow.

(3) Two copies of the documents containing the information and (where verification is directed) the affidavit shall be delivered by the bankrupt to the official receiver, who shall file one copy in court (with the affidavit, if any).

[1045]

SECTION B: DEBTORS PETITION

6.67. Preliminary

The Rules in this Section apply with respect to the statement of affairs required in the case of a person petitioning for a bankruptcy order to be made against him, and the further disclosure which is required of him in that case.   **[1046]**

6.68. Contents of statement

The statement of affairs required by Rule 6.41 to accompany the debtor's petition shall be in Form 6.28, and contain all the particulars required by that form.   **[1047]**

NOTES
   See Sch 4, form 6.28.

6.69. Requirement to submit accounts

(1) The bankrupt shall, at the request of the official receiver, furnish him with accounts relating to his affairs of such nature, as at such date and for such period as he may specify.

(2) The period specified may begin from a date up to 3 years preceding the date of the presentation of the bankruptcy petition.

(3) The court may, on the official receiver's application, require accounts in respect of any earlier period.   **[1048]**

6.70. Submission and filing of accounts

(1) The accounts to be furnished under Rule 6.69 shall, if the official receiver so requires, be verified by affidavit, and (whether or not so verified) delivered to him within 21 days of the request under Rule 6.69, or such longer period as he may allow.

(2) Two copies of the accounts and (where required) the affidavit shall be delivered by the bankrupt to the official receiver, who shall file one copy in court (with the affidavit, if any).   **[1049]**

6.71. Expenses of preparing accounts

(1) If the bankrupt cannot himself prepare proper accounts under Rule 6.69, the official receiver may, at the expense of the estate, employ some person or persons to assist in their preparation.

(2) At the request of the bankrupt, made on the grounds that he cannot himself prepare the accounts, the official receiver may authorise an allowance payable out of the estate (in accordance with the prescribed order of priority) towards expenses to be incurred by the bankrupt in employing some person or persons to assist him in their preparation.

(3) Any such request by the bankrupt shall be accompanied by an estimate of the expenses involved; and the official receiver shall only authorise the employment of a named person or a named firm, being in either case approved by him.

(4) An authorisation given by the official receiver under this Rule shall be subject to such conditions (if any) as he thinks fit to impose with respect to the manner in which any person may obtain access to relevant books and papers.

(5) Nothing in this Rule relieves the bankrupt from any obligation with respect to the preparation and submission of accounts, or to the provision of information to the official receiver or the trustee. **[1050]**

6.72. Further disclosure

(1) The official receiver may at any time require the bankrupt to submit (in writing) further information amplifying, modifying or explaining any matter contained in his statement of affairs, or in accounts submitted in pursuance of the Act or the Rules.

(2) The information shall, if the official receiver so directs, be verified by affidavit, and (whether or not so verified) delivered to him within 21 days from the date of the requirement under paragraph (1), or such longer period as he may allow.

(3) Two copies of the documents containing the information and (where verification is directed) the affidavit shall be delivered by the bankrupt to the official receiver, who shall file one copy in court, with the affidavit (if any).
[1051]

CHAPTER 6
INFORMATION TO CREDITORS

6.73. General duty of official receiver

In accordance with this Chapter, the official receiver shall, at least once after the making of the bankruptcy order, send a report to creditors with respect to the bankruptcy proceedings, and the state of the bankrupt's affairs. **[1052]**

6.74. Those entitled to be informed

Any reference in this Chapter to creditors is to creditors of the bankrupt who are known to the official receiver or, where the bankrupt has submitted a statement of affairs, are identified in the statement. **[1053]**

6.75. Report where statement of affairs lodged

(1) Where the bankrupt has submitted a statement of affairs, and it has been filed in court, the official receiver shall send out to creditors a report containing a summary of the statement and such observations (if any) as he thinks fit to make with respect to it or to the bankrupt's affairs generally.

(2) The official receiver need not comply with paragraph (1) if he has previously reported to creditors with respect to the bankrupt's affairs (so far as known to him) and he is of opinion that there are no additional matters which ought to be brought to their attention. **[1054]**

6.76. Statement of affairs dispensed with

(1) This Rule applies where the bankrupt has been released from the obligation to submit a statement of affairs.

(2) As soon as may be after the release has been granted, the official receiver shall send to creditors a report containing a summary of the bankrupt's affairs (so far as within his knowledge), and his observations (if any) with respect to it or the bankrupt's affairs generally.

(3) The official receiver need not comply with paragraph (2) if he has previously reported to creditors with respect to the bankrupt's affairs (so far as known to him) and he is of opinion that there are no additional matters which ought to be brought to their attention.   **[1055]**

6.77. General rule as to reporting

(1) The court may, on the official receiver's application relieve him of any duty imposed on him by this Chapter of the Rules, or authorise him to carry out the duty in a way other than there required.

(2) In considering whether to act as above, the court shall have regard to the cost of carrying out the duty, to the amount of the funds available in the estate, and to the extent of the interest of creditors or any particular class of them.   **[1056]**

6.78. Bankruptcy order annulled

If the bankruptcy order is annulled, the duty of the official receiver to send reports under the preceding Rules in this Chapter ceases.   **[1057]**

CHAPTER 7
Creditors' Meetings

6.79. First meeting of creditors

(1) If under section 293(1) the official receiver decides to summon a meeting of creditors, he shall fix a venue for the meeting, not more than 4 months from the date of the bankruptcy order.

(2) When a venue has been fixed, notice of the meeting shall be given—

    (*a*) to the court, and
    (*b*) to every creditor of the bankrupt who is known to the official receiver or is identified in the bankrupt's statement of affairs.

(3) Notice to the court shall be given forthwith; and the notice to creditors shall be given at least 21 days before the date fixed for the meeting.

(4) The notice to creditors shall specify a time and date, not more than 4 days before the date fixed for the meeting, by which they must lodge proofs and (if applicable) proxies, in order to be entitled to vote at the meeting.

(5) Notice of the meeting shall also be given by public advertisement.

(6) Where the official receiver receives a request by a creditor under section 294 for a meeting of creditors to be summoned, and it appears to him that the request is properly made in accordance with the Act, he shall—

(*a*) withdraw any notice already given by him under section 293(2) (that he has decided not to summon such a meeting), and

(*b*) fix the venue of the meeting for not more than 3 months from his receipt of the creditor's request, and

(*c*) act in accordance with paragraphs (2) to (5) above, as if he had decided under section 293(1) to summon the meeting.

(7) A meeting summoned by the official receiver under section 293 or 294 is known as "the first meeting of creditors". **[1058]**

NOTES
See Sch 4, form 6.34.

6.80. Business at first meeting

(1) At the first meeting of creditors, no resolutions shall be taken other than the following—

(*a*) a resolution to appoint a named insolvency practitioner to be trustee in bankruptcy or two or more named insolvency practitioners as joint trustees;

(*b*) a resolution to establish a creditors' committee;

(*c*) (unless it has been resolved to establish a creditors' committee) a resolution specifying the terms on which the trustee is to be remunerated, or to defer consideration of that matter;

(*d*) (if, and only if, two or more persons are appointed to act jointly as trustee) a resolution specifying whether acts are to be done by both or all of them, or by only one;

(*e*) (where the meeting has been requisitioned under section 294) a resolution authorising payment out of the estate, as an expense of the bankruptcy, of the cost of summoning and holding the meeting;

(*f*) a resolution to adjourn the meeting for not more than 3 weeks:

(*g*) any other resolution which the chairman thinks it right to allow for special reasons.

(2) No resolution shall be proposed which has for its object the appointment of the official receiver as trustee. **[1059]**

6.81. General power to call meetings

(1) The official receiver or the trustee may at any time summon and conduct meetings of creditors for the purpose of ascertaining their wishes in all matters relating to the bankruptcy.

In relation to any meeting of creditors, the person summoning it is referred to as "the convener".

(2) When a venue for the meeting has been fixed, notice of the meeting shall be given by the convener to every creditor who is known to him or is identified in the bankrupt's statement of affairs.

The notice shall be given at least 21 days before the date fixed for the meeting.

(3) The notice to creditors shall specify the purpose for which the meeting is summoned, and a time and date (not more than 4 days before the meeting) by

which creditors must lodge proxies and those who have not already lodged proofs must do so, in order to be entitled to vote at the meeting.

(4) Additional notice of the meeting may be given by public advertisement if the convener thinks fit, and shall be so given if the court so orders.   **[1060]**

NOTES
Para (2): See Sch 4, form 6.35.

6.82. The chairman at a meeting

(1) Where the convener of a meeting is the official receiver, he, or a person nominated by him, shall be chairman.

A nomination under this paragraph shall be in writing, unless the nominee is another official receiver or a deputy official receiver.

(2) Where the convener is other than the official receiver, the chairman shall be he, or a person nominated by him in writing to act.

A person nominated under this paragraph must be either—

(a) one who is qualified to act as an insolvency practitioner in relation to the bankrupt, or

(b) an employee of the trustee or his firm who is experienced in insolvency matters.   **[1061]**

6.83. Requisitioned meetings

(1) A request by creditors to the official receiver for a meeting of creditors to be summoned shall be accompanied by—

(a) a list of the creditors concurring with the request and the amount of their respective claims in the bankruptcy,

(b) from each creditor concurring, written confirmation of his concurrence, and

(c) a statement of the purpose of the proposed meeting.

Sub-paragraphs (a) and (b) do not apply if the requisitioning creditor's debt is alone sufficient, without the concurrence of other creditors.

(2) The official receiver, if he considers the request to be properly made in accordance with the Act, shall—

(a) fix a venue for the meeting, to take place not more than 35 days from the receipt of the request, and

(b) give 21 days' notice of the meeting, and of the venue for it, to creditors.

(3) Where a request for a creditors' meeting is made to the trustee, this Rule applies to him as it does to the official receiver.   **[1062]**

NOTES
Para (1): See Sch 4, form 6.34.

6.84. Attendance at meetings of bankrupt, etc

(1) Whenever a meeting of creditors is summoned, the convener shall give at least 21 days' notice of the meeting to the bankrupt.

(2) If the meeting is adjourned, the chairman of the meeting shall (unless for any reason it appears to him to be unnecessary or impracticable) give notice of the fact to the bankrupt, if the latter was not himself present at the meeting.

(3) The convener may, if he thinks fit, give notice to the bankrupt that he is required to be present, or in attendance.

(4) In the case of any meeting, the bankrupt or any other person may, if he has given reasonable notice of his wish to be present, be admitted; but this is at the discretion of the chairman.

The chairman's decision is final as to what (if any) intervention may be made by the bankrupt, or by any other person admitted to the meeting under this paragraph.

(5) If the bankrupt is not present, and it is desired to put questions to him, the chairman may adjourn the meeting with a view to obtaining his attendance.

(6) Where the bankrupt is present at a creditor's meeting, only such questions may be put to him as the chairman may in his discretion allow. **[1063]**

NOTES
    Para (1): see Sch 4, form 6.36.

6.85. Notice of meetings by advertisement only

(1) In the case of any meeting to be held under the Act or the Rules, the court may order that notice of it be given by public advertisement, and not by individual notice to the persons concerned.

(2) In considering whether to act under this Rule, the court shall have regard to the cost of public advertisement, to the amount of the funds available in the estate, and to the extent of the interest of creditors or any particular class of them. **[1064]**

6.86. Venue of meetings

(1) In fixing the venue for a meeting of creditors, the person summoning the meeting shall have regard to the convenience of the creditors.

(2) Meetings shall in all cases be summoned for commencement between the hours of 10.00 and 16.00 hours on a business day, unless the court otherwise directs.

(3) With every notice summoning a creditors' meeting there shall be sent out forms of proxy. **[1065]**

NOTES
    Para (1): See Sch 4, form 8.5.

6.87. Expenses of summoning meetings

(1) Subject to paragraph (3) below, the expenses of summoning and holding a meeting of creditors at the instance of any person other than the official receiver or the trustee shall be paid by that person, who shall deposit security for their payment with the trustee or, if no trustee has been appointed, with the official receiver.

(2) The sum to be deposited shall be such as the trustee or (as the case may be) the official receiver determines to be appropriate; and neither shall act without the deposit having been made.

(3) Where a meeting is so summoned, it may vote that the expenses of summoning and holding it shall be payable out of the estate, as an expense of the bankruptcy.

(4) To the extent that any deposit made under this Rule is not required for the payment of expenses of summoning and holding the meeting, it shall be repaid to the person who made it.   **[1066]**

6.88. Resolutions

(1) At a meeting of creditors, a resolution is passed when a majority (in value) of those present and voting, in person or by proxy, have voted in favour of the resolution.

(2) In the case of a resolution for the appointment of a trustee—

    (*a*) if on any vote there are two nominees for appointment, the person who obtains the most support is appointed;

    (*b*) if there are three or more nominees, and one of them has a clear majority over both or all the others together, that one is appointed; and

    (*c*) in any other case the chairman shall continue to take votes (disregarding at each vote any nominee who has withdrawn and, if no nominee has withdrawn, the nominee who obtained the least support last time), until a clear majority is obtained for any one nominee.

(3) The chairman may at any time put to the meeting a resolution for the joint appointment of any two or more nominees.

(4) Where a resolution is proposed which affects a person in respect of his remuneration or conduct as trustee, or as proposed or former trustee, the vote of that person, and of any partner or employee of his, shall not be reckoned in the majority required for passing the resolution.

This paragraph applies with respect to a vote given by a person either as creditor or as proxy for a creditor (but subject to Rule 8.6 in Part 8 of the Rules). **[1067]**

6.89. Chairman of meeting as proxy-holder

Where the chairman as a meeting holds a proxy for a creditor, which requires him to vote for a particular resolution, and no other person proposes that resolution—

    (*a*) he shall himself propose it, unless he considers that there is good reason for not doing so, and

    (*b*) if he does not propose it, he shall forthwith after the meeting notify his principal of the reason why not.   **[1068]**

6.90. Suspension of meeting

Once only in the course of any meeting, the chairman may, in his discretion and without an adjournment declare the meeting suspended for any period up to one hour.   **[1069]**

6.91. Adjournment

(1) The chairman at any meeting may, in his discretion, and shall if the meeting so resolves, adjourn it to such time and place as seems to him to be appropriate in the circumstances.

This is subject to Rule 6.129(3) in a case where the trustee or his nominee is chairman and a resolution has been proposed for the trustee's removal.

(2) If within a period of 30 minutes from the time appointed for the commencement of a meeting a quorum is not present, then by virtue of this

Rule the meeting stands adjourned to such time and place as may be appointed by the chairman.

(3) An adjournment under this Rule shall not be for a period of more than 21 days; and Rule 6.86(1) and (2) applies with regard to the venue of the adjourned meeting.

(4) If there is no person present to act as chairman, some other person present (being entitled to vote) may make the appointment under paragraph (2), with the agreement of others present (being persons so entitled).

Failing agreement, the adjournment shall be to the same time and place in the next following week or, if that is not a business day, to the business day immediately following.

(5) Where a meeting is adjourned under this Rule, proofs and proxies may be used if lodged at any time up to midday on the business day immediately before the adjourned meeting. **[1070]**

6.92. Quorum

(1) A creditors' meeting is not competent to act for any purpose, except—

    (a) the election of a chairman;
    (b) the admission by the chairman of creditors' proofs, for the purpose of their entitlement to vote, and
    (c) the adjournment of the meeting,

unless there are present in person or by proxy at least 3 creditors, or all the creditors, if their number does not exceed 3, being in either case persons entitled to vote.

(2) One person present constitutes a quorum if—

    (a) he is himself a creditor with entitlement to vote and he holds a number of proxies sufficient to ensure that, with his own vote, paragraph (1) of this Rule is complied with, or
    (b) being the chairman or any other person, he holds that number of proxies. **[1071]**

6.93. Entitlement to vote

(1) Subject as follows, at a meeting of creditors a person is entitled to vote as a creditor only if—

    (a) there has been duly lodged, by the time and date stated in the notice of the meeting, a proof of the debt claimed to be due to him from the bankrupt, and the claim has been admitted under Rule 6.94 for the purpose of entitlement to vote, and
    (b) there has been lodged, by that time and date, any proxy requisite for that entitlement.

(2) The court may, in exceptional circumstances, by order declare the creditors, or any class of them, entitled to vote at creditors' meetings, without being required to prove their debts.

Where a creditor is so entitled, the court may, on the application of the trustee, make such consequential orders as it thinks fit (as for example an order treating a creditor as having proved his debt for the purpose of permitting payment of dividend).

(3) A creditor shall not vote in respect of a debt for an unliquidated amount,

or any debt whose value is not ascertained, except where the chairman agrees to put upon the debt an estimated minimum value for the purpose of entitlement to vote and admits his proof for that purpose.

(4) A secured creditor is entitled to vote only in respect of the balance (if any) of his debt after deducting the value of his security as estimated by him.

(5) A creditor shall not vote in respect of a debt on, or secured by, a current bill of exchange or promissory note, unless he is willing—

  (*a*) to treat the liability to him on the bill or note of every person who is liable on it antecedently to the bankrupt, and against whom a bankruptcy order has not been made (or, in the case of a company, which has not gone into liquidation), as a security in his hands, and
  (*b*) to estimate the value of the security and (for the purpose of entitlement to vote, but not for dividend) to deduct it from his proof.   **[1072]**

6.94. Admission and rejection of proof

(1) At any creditors' meeting the chairman has power to admit or reject a creditor's proof for the purpose of his entitlement to vote; and the power is exercisable with respect to the whole or any part of the proof.

(2) The chairman's decision under this Rule, or in respect of any matter arising under Rule 6.93, is subject to appeal to the court by any creditor, or by the bankrupt.

(3) If the chairman is in doubt whether a proof should be admitted or rejected, he shall mark it as objected to and allow the creditor to vote, subject to his vote being subsequently declared invalid if the objection to the proof is sustained.

(4) If on an appeal the chairman's decision is reversed or varied, or a creditor's vote is declared invalid, the court may order that another meeting be summoned, or make such other order as it thinks just.

(5) Neither the official receiver nor any person nominated by him to be chairman is personally liable for costs incurred by any person in respect of an application to the court under this Rule; and the chairman (if other than the official receiver or a person so nominated) is not so liable unless the court makes an order to that effect.   **[1073]**

6.95. Record of proceedings

(1) The chairman at any creditors' meeting shall cause minutes of the proceedings at the meeting, signed by him, to be retained by him as part of the records of the bankruptcy.

(2) He shall also cause to be made up and kept a list of all the creditors who attended the meeting.

(3) The minutes of the meeting shall include a record of every resolution passed; and it is the chairman's duty to see to it that particulars of all such resolutions, certified by him, are filed in court not more than 21 days after the date of the meeting.   **[1074]**

CHAPTER 8

PROOF OF BANKRUPTCY DEBTS

SECTION A: PROCEDURE FOR PROVING

6.96. Meaning of "prove"

(1) A person claiming to be a creditor of the bankrupt and wishing to recover his debt in whole or in part must (subject to any order of the court under Rule 6.93(2)) submit his claim in writing to the official receiver, where acting as receiver and manager, or to the trustee.

(2) The creditor is referred to as "proving" for his debt; and the document by which he seeks to establish his claim is his "proof".

(3) Subject to the next two paragraphs, the proof must be in the form known as "proof of debt" (whether the form prescribed by the Rules, or a substantially similar form), which shall be made out by or under the directions of the creditor, and signed by him or a person authorised in that behalf.

(4) Where a debt is due to a Minister of the Crown or a Government Department, the proof need not be in that form, provided that there are shown all such particulars of the debt as are required in the form used by other creditors, and as are relevant in the circumstances.

(5) Where an existing trustee proves in a later bankruptcy under section 335(5), the proof must be in Form 6.38.

(6) In certain circumstances, specified below in this Chapter, the proof must be in the form of an affidavit.   **[1075]**

NOTES
Para (3): See Sch 4, form 6.37.
Para (5): See Sch 4, form 6.38.
Para (6): See Sch 4, form 6.39.

6.97. Supply of forms

(1) Forms to be used for the purpose of proving bankruptcy debts shall be sent out by the official receiver or the trustee to every creditor of the bankrupt who is known to the sender, or is identified in the bankrupt's statement of affairs.

(2) The forms shall accompany (whichever is first)—

    (*a*) the notice to creditors under section 293(2) (official receiver's decision not to call meeting of creditors), or

    (*b*) the first notice called a meeting of creditors, or

    (*c*) where a certificate of summary administration has been issued by the court, the notice sent by the official receiver under Rule 6.49(2), or

    (*d*) where a trustee is appointed by the court, the notice of his appointment sent by him to creditors.

(3) Where, with the leave of the court under section 297(7), the trustee advertises his appointment, he shall send proofs to the creditors within 4 months after the date of the bankruptcy order.

(4) The above paragraphs of this Rule are subject to any order of the court dispensing with the requirement to send out forms of proof, or altering the time at which the forms are to be sent.   **[1076]**

6.98. Contents of proof

(1) The following matters shall be stated in a creditor's proof of debt—

   (*a*) the creditor's name and address;
   (*b*) the total amount of his claim as at the date of the bankruptcy order;
   (*c*) whether or not that amount includes outstanding uncapitalised interest;
   (*d*) whether or not the claim includes value added tax;
   (*e*) whether the whole or any part of the debt falls within any (and if so which) of the categories of preferential debts under section 386 of, and Schedule 6 to, the Act (as read with Schedule 3 to the Social Security Pensions Act 1975);
   (*f*) particulars of how and when the debt was incurred by the debtor;
   (*g*) particulars of any security held, the date when it was given and the value which the creditor puts upon it; and
   (*h*) the name, address and authority of the person signing the proof (if other than the creditor himself).

(2) There shall be specified in the proof any documents by reference to which the debt can be substantiated; but (subject as follows) it is not essential that such documents be attached to the proof or submitted with it.

(3) The trustee, or the convener or chairman of any meeting, may call for any document or other evidence to be produced to him, where he thinks it necessary for the purpose of substantiating the whole or any part of the claim made in the proof.   **[1077]**

6.99. Claim established by affidavit

(1) The trustee may, if he thinks it necessary, require a claim of debt to be verified by affidavit, for which purpose there shall be used the form known as "affidavit of debt".

(2) An affidavit may be required notwithstanding that a proof of debt has already been lodged.

(3) The affidavit may be sworn before an official receiver or a deputy official receiver, or before an officer of the Department or of the court duly authorised in that behalf.   **[1078]**

NOTES
  Para (1): See Sch 4, form 6.39.

6.100. Cost of proving

(1) Subject as follows, every creditor bears the cost of proving his own debt, including such as may be incurred in providing documents or evidence under Rule 6.98(3).

(2) Costs incurred by the trustee in estimating the value of a bankruptcy debt under section 322(3) (debts not bearing a certain value) fall on the estate, as an expense of the bankruptcy.

(3) Paragraphs (1) and (2) apply unless the court otherwise orders.   **[1079]**

6.101. Trustee to allow inspection of proofs

The trustee shall, so long as proofs lodged with him are in his hands, allow them to be inspected, at all reasonable times on any business day, by any of the following persons—

> (a) any creditor who has submitted his proof of debt (unless his proof has been wholly rejected for purposes of dividend or otherwise),
>
> (b) the bankrupt, and
>
> (c) any person acting on behalf of either of the above.   **[1080]**

6.102. Proof of licensed moneylender

A proof of debt in respect of a moneylending transaction made before 27th January 1980, where the creditor was at the time of the transaction a licensed moneylender, shall have endorsed on or annexed to it a statement setting out in detail the particulars mentioned in section 9(2) of the Moneylenders Act 1927.

[1081]

6.103. Transmission of proofs to trustee

(1) Where a trustee is appointed, the official receiver shall forthwith transmit to him all the proofs which he has so far received, together with an itemised list of them.

(2) The trustee shall sign the list by way of receipt for the proofs, and return it to the official receiver.

(3) From then on, all proofs of debt shall be sent to the trustee and retained by him.   **[1082]**

6.104. Admission and rejection of proofs for dividend

(1) A proof may be admitted for dividend either for the whole amount claimed by the creditor, or for part of that amount.

(2) If the trustee rejects a proof in whole or in part, he shall prepare a written statement of his reasons for doing so, and send it forthwith to the creditor.

[1083]

6.105. Appeal against decision on proof

(1) If a creditor is dissatisfied with the trustee's decision with respect to his proof (including any decision on the question of preference), he may apply to the court for the decision to be reversed or varied.

The application must be made within 21 days of his receiving the statement sent under Rule 6.104(2).

(2) The bankrupt or any other creditor may, if dissatisfied with the trustee's decision admitting or rejecting the whole or any part of a proof, make such an application within 21 days of becoming aware of the trustee's decision.

(3) Where application is made to the court under this Rule, the court shall fix a venue for the application to be heard, notice of which shall be sent by the applicant to the creditor who lodged the proof in question (if it is not himself) and to the trustee.

(4) The trustee shall, on receipt of the notice, file in court the relevant proof, together (if appropriate) with a copy of the statement sent under Rule 6.104(2).

(5) After the application has been heard and determined, the proof shall, unless it has been wholly disallowed, be returned by the court to the trustee.

(6) The official receiver is not personally liable for costs incurred by any person in respect of an application under this Rule; and the trustee (if other than the official receiver) is not so liable unless the court makes an order to that effect.   **[1084]**

6.106. Withdrawal or variation of proof

A creditor's proof may at any time, by agreement between himself and the trustee, be withdrawn or varied as to the amount claimed.   **[1085]**

6.107. Expunging of proof by the court

(1) The court may expunge a proof or reduce the amount claimed—

> (a) on the trustee's application, where he thinks that the proof has been improperly admitted, or ought to be reduced; or
> (b) on the application of a creditor, if the trustee declines to interfere in the matter.

(2) Where application is made to the court under this Rule, the court shall fix a venue for the application to be heard, notice of which shall be sent by the applicant—

> (a) in the case of an application by the trustee, to the creditor who made the proof, and
> (b) in the case of an application by a creditor, to the trustee and to the creditor who made the proof (if not himself).   **[1086]**

Section B: Quantification of Claim

6.108. Negotiable instruments, etc

Unless the trustee allows, a proof in respect of money owed on a bill of exchange, promissory note, cheque or other negotiable instrument or security cannot be admitted unless there is produced the instrument or security itself or a copy of it, certified by the creditor or his authorised representative to be a true copy.
        [1087]

6.109. Secured creditors

(1) If a secured creditor realises his security, he may prove for the balance of his debt, after deducting the amount realised.

(2) If a secured creditor voluntarily surrenders his security for the general benefit of creditors, he may prove for his whole debt, as if it were unsecured.
        [1088]

6.110. Discounts

There shall in every case be deducted from the claim all trade and other discounts which would have been available to the bankrupt but for his bankruptcy, except any discount for immediate, early or cash settlement. **[1089]**

6.111. Debt in foreign currency

(1) For the purpose of proving a debt incurred or payable in a currency other than sterling, the amount of the debt shall be converted into sterling at the official exchange rate prevailing on the date of the bankruptcy order.

(2) "The official exchange rate" is the middle market rate at the Bank of England, as published for the date in question. In the absence of any such published rate, it is such rate as the court determines. **[1090]**

6.112. Payments of a periodical nature

(1) In the case of rent and other payments of a periodical nature, the creditor may prove for any amounts due and unpaid up to the date of the bankruptcy order.

(2) Where at that date any payment was accruing due, the creditor may prove for so much as would have fallen due at that date, if accruing from day to day. **[1091]**

6.113. Interest

(1) In the following circumstances the creditor's claim may include interest on the debt for periods before the bankruptcy order, although not previously reserved or agreed.

(2) If the debt is due by virtue of a written instrument and payable at a certain time, interest may be claimed for the period from that time to the date of the bankruptcy order.

(3) If the debt is due otherwise, interest may only be claimed if, before the presentation of the bankruptcy petition, a demand for payment was made in writing by or on behalf of the creditor, and notice given that interest would be payable from the date of the demand to the date of payment.

In that case interest may be claimed under this Rule for the period from the date of the demand to that of the bankruptcy order.

(4) The rate of interest to be claimed under this Rule is the rate specified in section 17 of the Judgments Act 1838 on the date of the bankruptcy order; except that, where the case falls within paragraph (3), the rate is that specified in the notice there referred to, not exceeding the rate under the Judgments Act as mentioned above. **[1092]**

6.114. Debt payable at future time

A creditor may prove for a debt of which payment was not yet due at the date of the bankruptcy order, but subject to Rule 11.13 in Part 11 of the Rules (adjustment of dividend where payment made before time). **[1093]**

CHAPTER 9

SECURED CREDITORS

6.115. Value of security

(1) A secured creditor may, with the agreement of the trustee or the leave of the court, at any time alter the value which he has, in his proof of debt, put upon his security.

(2) However, if a secured creditor—

(*a*) being the petitioner, has in the petition put a value on his security, or

(*b*) has voted in respect of the unsecured balance of his debt,

he may re-value his security only with leave of the court.   **[1094]**

6.116. Surrender for non-disclosure

(1) If a secured creditor omits to disclose his security in his proof of debt, he shall surrender his security for the general benefit of creditors, unless the court, on application by him, relieves him from the effect of this Rule on the ground that the omission was inadvertent or the result of honest mistake.

(2) If the court grants that relief, it may require or allow the creditor's proof of debt to be amended, on such terms as may be just.   **[1095]**

6.117. Redemption by trustee

(1) The trustee may at any time give notice to a creditor whose debt is secured that he proposes, at the expiration of 28 days from the date of the notice, to redeem the security at the value put upon it in the creditor's proof.

(2) The creditor then has 21 days (or such longer period as the trustee may allow) in which, if he so wishes, to exercise his right to re-value his security (with the leave of the court, where Rule 6.115(2) applies).

If the creditor re-values his security, the trustee may only redeem at the new value.

(3) If the trustee redeems the security, the cost of transferring it is borne by the estate.

(4) A secured creditor may at any time, by a notice in writing, call on the trustee to elect whether he will or will not exercise his power to redeem the security at the value then placed on it; and the trustee then has 6 months in which to exercise the power or determine not to exercise it.   **[1096]**

6.118. Test of security's value

(1) Subject as follows, the trustee, if he is dissatisfied with the value which a secured creditor puts on his security (whether in his proof or by way of re-valuation under Rule 6.117), may require any property comprised in the security to be offered for sale.

(2) The terms of sale shall be such as may be agreed, or as the court may direct; and if the sale is by auction, the trustee on behalf of the estate, and the creditor on his own behalf, may appear and bid.

(3) This Rule does not apply if the security has been re-valued and the re-valuation has been approved by the court.   **[1097]**

6.119. Realisation of security by creditor

If a creditor who has valued his security subsequently realises it (whether or not at the instance of the trustee)—

(*a*) the net amount realised shall be substituted for the value previously put by the creditor on the security, and

(*b*) that amount shall be treated in all respects as an amended valuation made by him.   **[1098]**

CHAPTER 10

THE TRUSTEE IN BANKRUPTCY

SECTION A: APPOINTMENT AND ASSOCIATED FORMALITIES

6.120. Appointment by creditors' meeting

(1) This rule applies where a person has been appointed trustee by resolution of a creditors' meeting.

(2) The chairman of the meeting shall certify the appointment, but not unless and until the person to be appointed has provided him with a written statement to the effect that he is an insolvency practitioner, duly qualified under the Act to act as trustee in relation to the bankrupt, and that he consents so to act.

(3) The chairman (if not himself the official receiver) shall send the certificate to the official receiver.

(4) The official receiver shall in any case file a copy of the certificate in court; and the trustee's appointment is effective as from the date on which the official receiver files the copy certificate in court, that date to be endorsed on the copy certificate.

The certificate, so endorsed, shall be sent by the official receiver to the trustee. **[1099]**

NOTES
Para (2): See Sch 4, forms 6.40, 6.41.

6.121. Appointment by the court

(1) This Rule applies where the court under section 297(3), (4) or (5) appoints the trustee.

(2) The court's order shall not issue unless and until the person appointed has filed in court a statement to the effect that he is an insolvency practitioner, duly qualified under the Act to be the trustee, and that he consents so to act.

(3) Thereafter, the court shall send 2 copies of the order to the official receiver. One of the copies shall be sealed, and this shall be sent by him to the person appointed as trustee.

(4) The trustee's appointment takes effect from the date of the order. **[1100]**

NOTES
Para (1): See Sch 4, forms 6.42, 6.43.

6.122. Appointment by Secretary of State

(1) This rule applies where the official receiver—

   (a) under section 295 or 300, refers to the Secretary of State the need for an appointment of a trustee, or
   (b) under section 296, applies to the Secretary of State to make the appointment.

(2) If the Secretary of State makes an appointment he shall send two copies of the certificate of appointment to the official receiver, who shall transmit one such copy to the person appointed, and file the other copy in court.

The certificate shall specify the date from which the trustee's appointment is to be effective.   **[1101]**

6.123. Authentication of trustee's appointment

Where a trustee is appointed under any of the 3 preceding Rules, a sealed copy of the order of appointment or (as the case may be) a copy of the certificate of his appointment may in any proceedings be adduced as proof that he is duly authorised to exercise the powers and perform the duties of trustee of the bankrupt's estate.   **[1102]**

6.124. Advertisement of appointment

(1) Where the trustee is appointed by a creditors' meeting, he shall, forthwith after receiving his certificate of appointment, give notice of his appointment in such newspaper as he thinks most appropriate for ensuring that it comes to the notice of the bankrupt's creditors.

(2) The expense of giving the notice shall be borne in the first instance by the trustee; but he is entitled to be reimbursed by the estate, as an expense of the bankruptcy.

The same applies also in the case of the notice or advertisement under section 296(4) (appointment of trustee by Secretary of State), and of the notice or advertisement under section 297(7) (appointment by the court).   **[1103]**

6.125. Hand-over of estate to trustee

(1) This Rule applies only where—

    (*a*) the bankrupt's estate vests in the trustee under Chapter IV of Part IX of the Act, following a period in which the official receiver is the receiver and manager of the estate according to section 287, or

    (*b*) the trustee is appointed in succession to the official receiver acting as trustee.

(2) When the trustee's appointment takes effect, the official receiver shall forthwith do all that is required for putting him into possession of the estate.

(3) On taking possession of the estate, the trustee shall discharge any balance due to the official receiver on account of—

    (*a*) expenses properly incurred by him and payable under the Act or the Rules, and

    (*b*) any advances made by him in respect of the estate, together with interest on such advances at the rate specified in section 17 of the Judgments Act 1838 on the date of the bankruptcy order.

(4) Alternatively, the trustee may (before taking office) give to the official receiver a written undertaking to discharge any such balance out of the first realisation of assets.

(5) The official receiver has a charge on the estate in respect of any sums due to him under paragraph (3). But, where the trustee has realised assets with a view to making those payments, the official receiver's charge does not extend in respect of sums deductible by the trustee from the proceeds of realisation, as being expenses properly incurred therein.

(6) The trustee shall from time to time out of the realisation of assets discharge all guarantees properly given by the official receiver for the benefit of the estate, and shall pay all the official receiver's expenses.

(7) The official receiver shall give to the trustee all such information, relating to the affairs of the bankrupt and the course of the bankruptcy, as he (the official receiver) considers to be reasonably required for the effective discharge by the trustee of his duties in relation to the estate.

(8) The trustee shall also be furnished with any report of the official receiver under Chapter 6 of this Part of the Rules. **[1104]**

SECTION B: RESIGNATION AND REMOVAL; VACATION OF OFFICE

6.126. Creditors' meeting to receive trustee's resignation

(1) Before resigning his office, the trustee must call a meeting of creditors for the purpose of receiving his resignation. Notice of the meeting shall be sent to the official receiver at the same time as it is sent to creditors.

(2) The notice to creditors must be accompanied by an account of the trustee's administration of the bankrupt's estate, including—

> (*a*) a summary of his receipts and payments and
> (*b*) a statement by him that he has reconciled his account with that which is held by the Secretary of State in respect of the bankruptcy.

(3) Subject as follows, the trustee may only proceed under this Rule on grounds of ill health or because—

> (*a*) he intends ceasing to be in practice as an insolvency practitioner, or
> (*b*) there is some conflict of interest or change of personal circumstances which precludes or makes impracticable the further discharge by him of the duties of trustee.

(4) Where two or more persons are acting as trustee jointly, any one of them may proceed under this Rule (without prejudice to the continuation in office of the other or others) on the ground that, in his opinion and that of the other or others, it is no longer expedient that there should continue to be the present number of joint trustees. **[1105]**

6.127. Action following acceptance of resignation

(1) Where a meeting of creditors is summoned for the purpose of receiving the trustee's resignation, the notice summoning it shall indicate that this is the purpose, or one of the purposes, of the meeting; and the notice shall draw the attention of creditors to Rule 6.135 with respect to the trustee's release.

(2) A copy of the notice shall at the same time also be sent to the official receiver.

(3) Where the chairman of the meeting is other than the official receiver, and there is passed at the meeting any of the following resolutions—

> (*a*) that the trustee's resignation be accepted,
> (*b*) that a new trustee be appointed,
> (*c*) that the resigning trustee be not given his release,

the chairman shall, within 3 days, send to the official receiver a copy of the resolution.

If it has been resolved to accept the trustee's resignation, the chairman shall send to the official receiver a certificate to that effect.

(4) If the creditors have resolved to appoint a new trustee, the certificate of

his appointment shall also be sent to the official receiver within that time; and Rule 6.120 above shall be complied with in respect of it.

(5) If the trustee's resignation is accepted, the notice of it required by section 298(7) shall be given by him forthwith after the meeting; and he shall send a copy of the notice to the official receiver.

The notice shall be accompanied by a copy of the account sent to creditors under Rule 6.126(2).

(6) The official receiver shall file a copy of the notice in court.

(7) The trustee's resignation is effective as from the date on which the official receiver files the copy notice in court, that date to be endorsed on the copy notice.   **[1106]**

NOTES
    Para (1): See Sch 4, form 6.35.
    Para (3): See Sch 4, form 6.44.

6.128. Leave to resign granted by the court

(1) If at a creditors' meeting summoned to accept the trustee's resignation it is resolved that it be not accepted, the court may, on the trustee's application, make an order giving him leave to resign.

(2) The court's order under this Rule may include such provision as it thinks fit with respect to matters arising in connection with the resignation, and shall determine the date from which the trustee's release is effective.

(3) The court shall send two sealed copies of the order to the trustee, who shall send one of the copies forthwith to the official receiver.

(4) On sending notice of his resignation to the court, as required by section 298(7), the trustee shall send a copy of it to the official receiver.   **[1107]**

NOTES
    Para (1): See Sch 4, form 6.45.
    Para (4): See Sch 4, form 6.46.

6.129. Meeting of creditors to remove trustee

(1) Where a meeting of creditors is summoned for the purpose of removing the trustee, the notice summoning it shall indicate that this is the purpose, or one of the purposes, of the meeting; and the notice shall draw the attention of creditors to section 299(3) with respect to the trustee's release.

(2) A copy of the notice shall at the same time also be sent to the official receiver.

(3) At the meeting, a person other than the trustee or his nominee may be elected to act as chairman; but if the trustee or his nominee is chairman and a resolution has been proposed for the trustee's removal, the chairman shall not adjourn the meeting without the consent of at least one-half (in value) of the creditors present (in person or by proxy) and entitled to vote.

(4) Where the chairman of the meeting is other than the official receiver, and there is passed at the meeting any of the following resolutions—

   (*a*) that the trustee be removed,
   (*b*) that a new trustee be appointed,

(*c*) that the removed trustee be not given his release,

the chairman shall, within 3 days, send to the official receiver a copy of the resolution.

If it has been resolved to remove the trustee, the chairman shall send to the official receiver a certificate to that effect.

(5) If the creditors have resolved to appoint a new trustee, the certificate of his appointment shall also be sent to the official receiver within that time; and Rule 6.120 shall be complied with in respect of it. **[1108]**

NOTES
    Para (1): See Sch 4, form 6.35.
    Para (4): See Sch 4, form 6.47.

6.130. Court's power to regulate meeting under Rule 6.129

Where a meeting under Rule 6.129 is to be held, or is proposed to be summoned, the court may on the application of any creditor give directions as to the mode of summoning it, the sending out and return of forms of proxy, the conduct of the meeting, and any other matter which appears to the court to require regulation or control. **[1109]**

6.131. Procedure on removal

(1) Where the creditors have resolved that the trustee be removed, the official receiver shall file the certificate of removal in court.

(2) The resolution is effective as from the date on which the official receiver files the certificate of removal in court, and that date shall be endorsed on the certificate.

(3) A copy of the certificate, so endorsed, shall be sent by the official receiver to the trustee who has been removed and, if a new trustee has been appointed, to him.

(4) The official receiver shall not file the certificate in court until the Secretary of State has certified to him that the removed trustee has reconciled his account with that held by the Secretary of State in respect of the bankruptcy. **[1110]**

6.132. Removal of trustee by the court

(1) This Rule applies where application is made to the court for the removal of the trustee, or for an order directing the trustee to summon a meeting of creditors for the purpose of removing him.

(2) The court may, if it thinks that no sufficient cause is shown for the application, dismiss it; but it shall not do so unless the applicant has had an opportunity to attend the court for an ex parte hearing, of which he has been given at least 7 days' notice.

If the application is not dismissed under this paragraph, the court shall fix a venue for it to be heard.

(3) The applicant shall, at least 14 days before the hearing, send to the trustee and the official receiver notice stating the venue so fixed; and the notice shall be accompanied by a copy of the application, and of any evidence which the applicant intends to adduce in support of it.

(4) Subject to any contrary order of the court, the costs of the application do not fall on the estate.

(5) Where the court removes the trustee—

    (*a*) it shall send copies of the order of removal to him and to the official receiver;

    (*b*) the order may include such provision as the court thinks fit with respect to matters arising in connection with the removal; and

    (*c*) if the court appoints a new trustee, Rule 6.121 applies.   **[1111]**

NOTES
   Para (1): See Sch 4, form 6.48.

6.133. Removal of trustee by Secretary of State

(1) If the Secretary of State decides to remove the trustee, he shall before doing so notify the trustee and the official receiver of his decision and the grounds of it, and specify a period within which the trustee may make representations against implementation of the decision.

(2) If the Secretary of State directs the removal of the trustee, he shall forthwith—

    (*a*) file notice of his decision in court, and

    (*b*) send notice to the trustee and the official receiver.

(3) If the trustee is removed by direction of the Secretary of State, the court may make any such order in his case as it would have power to make if he had been removed by itself.   **[1112]**

6.134. Advertisement of resignation or removal

Where a new trustee is appointed in place of one who has resigned or been removed, the new trustee shall, in the advertisement of his appointment, state that his predecessor has resigned or, as the case may be, been removed and (if it be the case) that he has been given his release.   **[1113]**

6.135. Release of resigning or removed trustee

(1) Where the trustee's resignation is accepted by a meeting of creditors which has not resolved against his release, he has his release from when his resignation is effective under Rule 6.127.

(2) Where the trustee is removed by a meeting of creditors which has not resolved against his release, the fact of his release shall be stated in the certificate of removal.

(3) Where—

    (*a*) the trustee resigns, and the creditors' meeting called to receive his resignation has resolved against his release, or

    (*b*) he is removed by a creditors' meeting which has so resolved, or is removed by the court,

he must apply to the Secretary of State for his release.

(4) When the Secretary of State gives the release, he shall certify it accordingly, and send the certificate to the official receiver, to be filed in court.

(5) A copy of the certificate shall be sent by the Secretary of State to the former trustee, whose release is effective from the date of the certificate. **[1114]**

NOTES

    Para (1): See Sch 4, form 6.49.

SECTION C: RELEASE ON COMPLETION OF ADMINISTRATION

6.136. Release of offical receiver

(1) The official receiver shall, before giving notice to the Secretary of State under section 299(2) (that the administration of the estate is for practical purposes complete), send out notice of his intention to do so to all creditors who have proved their debts, and to the bankrupt.

(2) The notice shall in each case be accompanied by a summary of the official receiver's receipts and payments as trustee.

(3) The Secretary of State, when he has under section 299(2) determined the date from which the official receiver is to have his release, shall give notice to the court that he has done so. The notice shall be accompanied by the summary referred to in paragraph (2).   **[1115]**

6.137. Final meeting of creditors

(1) Where the trustee is other than the official receiver, he shall give at least 28 days' notice of the final meeting of creditors to be held under section 331. The notice shall be sent to all creditors who have proved their debts, and to the bankrupt.

(2) The trustee's report laid before the meeting under that section shall include—

    (*a*) a summary of his receipts and payments, and
    (*b*) a statement by him that he has reconciled his account with that which is held by the Secretary of State in respect of the bankruptcy.

(3) At the final meeting, the creditors may question the trustee with respect to any matter contained in his report, and may resolve against him having his release.

(4) The trustee shall give notice to the court that the final meeting has been held; and the notice shall state whether or not he has been given his release, and be accompanied by a copy of the report laid before the final meeting. A copy of the notice shall be sent by the trustee to the official receiver.

(5) If there is no quorum present at the final meeting, the trustee shall report to the court that a final meeting was summoned in accordance with the Rules, but there was no quorum present; and the final meeting is then deemed to have been held, and the creditors not to have resolved against the trustee having his release.

(6) If the creditors at the final meeting have not so resolved, the trustee is released when the notice under paragraph (4) is filed in court. If they have so

resolved, the trustee must obtain his release from the Secretary of State, as provided by Rule 6.135.   **[1116]**

NOTES
   Para (1): See Sch 4, form 6.35.
   Para (4): See Sch 4, form 6.50.

Section D: Remuneration

6.138. Fixing of remuneration

(1) The trustee is entitled to receive remuneration for his services as such.

(2) The remuneration shall be fixed either—

  (a) as a percentage of the value of the assets in the bankrupt's estate which are realised or distributed, or of the one value and the other in combination, or

  (b) by reference to the time properly given by the insolvency practitioner (as trustee) and his staff in attending to matters arising in the bankruptcy.

(3) Where the trustee is other than the official receiver, it is for the creditors' committee (if there is one) to determine whether his remuneration is to be fixed under paragraph (2)(a) or (b) and, if under paragraph (2)(a), to determine any percentage to be applied as there mentioned.

(4) In arriving at that determination, the committee shall have regard to the following matters.—

  (a) the complexity (or otherwise) of the case,

  (b) any respects in which, in connection with the administration of the estate, there falls on the insolvency practitioner (as trustee) any responsibility of an exceptional kind or degree,

  (c) the effectiveness with which the insolvency practitioner appears to be carrying out, or to have carried out, his duties as trustee, and

  (d) the value and nature of the assets in the estate with which the trustee has to deal.

(5) If there is no creditors' committee, or the committee does not make the requisite determination, the trustee's remuneration may be fixed (in accordance with paragraph (2)) by a resolution of a meeting of creditors; and paragraph (4) applies to them as it does to the creditors' committee.

(6) If not fixed as above, the trustee's remuneration shall be on the scale laid down for the official receiver by general regulations.   **[1117]**

6.139. Other matters affecting remuneration

(1) Where the trustee sells assets on behalf of a secured creditor, he is entitled to take for himself, out of the proceeds of sale, a sum by way of remuneration equivalent to the remuneration chargeable in corresponding circumstances by the official receiver under general regulations.

(2) Where there are joint trustees, it is for them to agree between themselves as to how the remuneration payable should be apportioned. Any dispute arising between them may be referred—

  (a) to the court, for settlement by order, or

(*b*) to the creditors' committee or a meeting of creditors, for settlement by resolution.

(3) If the trustee is a solicitor and employs his own firm, or any partner in it, to act on behalf of the estate, profit costs shall not be paid unless this is authorised by the creditors' committee, the creditors or the court.   **[1118]**

6.140. Recourse of trustee to meeting of creditors

If the trustee's remuneration has been fixed by the creditors' committee, and he considers the rate or amount to be insufficient, he may request that it be increased by resolution of the creditors.   **[1119]**

6.141. Recourse to the court

(1) If the trustee considers that the remuneration fixed for him by the creditors' committee, or by resolution of the creditors, or as under Rule 6.138(6), is insufficient, he may apply to the court for an order increasing its amount or rate.

(2) The trustee shall give at least 14 days' notice of his application to the members of the creditors' committee; and the committee may nominate one or more members to appear or be represented, and to be heard, on the application.

(3) If there is no creditors' committee, the trustee's notice of his application shall be sent to such one or more of the bankrupt's creditors as the court may direct, which creditors may nominate one or more of their number to appear or be represented.

(4) The court may, if it appears to be a proper case, order the costs of the trustee's application, including the costs of any member of the creditors' committee appearing on it, or any creditor so appearing, to be paid out of the estate.   **[1120]**

6.142. Creditor's claim that remuneration is excessive

(1) Any creditor of the bankrupt may, with the concurrence of at least 25 per cent in value of the creditors (including himself), apply to the court for an order that the trustee's remuneration be reduced, on the grounds that it is, in all the circumstances, excessive.

(2) The court may, if it thinks that no sufficient cause is shown for the application, dismiss it; but it shall not do so unless the applicant has had an opportunity to attend the court for an ex parte hearing, of which he has been given at least 7 days' notice.

If the application is not dismissed under this paragraph, the court shall fix a venue for it to be heard.

(3) The applicant shall, at least 14 days before the hearing, send to the trustee a notice stating the venue so fixed; and the notice shall be accompanied by a copy of the application, and of any evidence which the applicant intends to adduce in support of it.

(4) If the court considers the application to be well-founded, it shall make an order fixing the remuneration at a reduced amount or rate.

(5) Unless the court orders otherwise, the costs of the application shall be paid by the applicant, and do not fall on the estate.   **[1121]**

SECTION E: SUPPLEMENTARY PROVISIONS

6.143. Trustee deceased

(1) Subject as follows, where the trustee (other than the official receiver) has died, it is the duty of his personal representatives to give notice of the fact to the official receiver, specifying the date of the death.

This does not apply if notice has been given under any of the following paragraphs of this Rule.

(2) If the deceased trustee was a partner in a firm, notice may be given to the official receiver by a partner in the firm who is qualified to act as an insolvency practitioner, or is a member of any body recognised by the Secretary of State for the authorisation of insolvency practitioners.

(3) Notice of the death may be given by any person producing to the official receiver the relevant death certificate or a copy of it.

(4) The official receiver shall give notice to the court, for the purpose of fixing the date of the deceased trustee's release in accordance with section 299(3)(a).   **[1122]**

6.144. Loss of qualification as insolvency practitioner

(1) This Rule applies where the trustee vacates office, under section 298(6), on his ceasing to be qualified to act as an insolvency practitioner in relation to the bankrupt.

(2) The trustee vacating office shall forthwith give notice of his doing so to the official receiver, who shall give notice to the Secretary of State.

The official receiver shall file in court a copy of his notice under this paragraph.

(3) Rule 6.135 applies as regards the trustee obtaining his release, as if he had been removed by the court.   **[1123]**

NOTES
    Para (2): See Sch 4, form 6.51.

6.145. Notice to official receiver of intention to vacate office

(1) Where the trustee intends to vacate office, whether by resignation or otherwise, and there remain in the estate any unrealised assets, he shall give notice of his intention to the official receiver, informing him of the nature, value and whereabouts of the assets in question.

(2) Where there is to be a creditors' meeting to receive the trustee's resignation, or otherwise in respect of his vacation of office, the notice to the official receiver must be given at least 21 days before the meeting.   **[1124]**

6.146. Trustee's duties on vacating office

(1) Where the trustee ceases to be in office as such, in consequence of removal, resignation or cesser of qualification as an insolvency practitioner, he is under obligation forthwith to deliver up to the person succeeding him as trustee the assets of the estate (after deduction of any expenses properly incurred, and distributions made, by him) and further to deliver up to that person—

   (*a*) the records of the bankruptcy, including correspondence, proofs and other related papers appertaining to the bankruptcy while it was within his responsibility, and

   (*b*) the bankrupt's books, papers and other records.

(2) When the administration of the bankrupt's estate is for practical purposes complete, the trustee shall forthwith file in court all proofs remaining with him in the proceedings.   **[1125]**

6.147. Power of court to set aside certain transactions

(1) If in the administration of the estate the trustee enters into any transaction with a person who is an associate of his, the court may, on the application of any person interested, set the transaction aside and order the trustee to compensate the estate for any loss suffered in consequence of it.

   (2) This does not apply if either—

   (*a*) the transaction was entered into with the prior consent of the court, or

   (*b*) it is shown to the court's satisfaction that the transaction was for value, and that it was entered into by the trustee without knowing, or having any reason to suppose, that the person concerned was an associate.

(3) Nothing in this Rule is to be taken as prejudicing the operation of any rule of law or equity with respect to a trustee's dealings with trust property, or the fiduciary obligations of any person.   **[1126]**

6.148. Rule against solicitation

(1) Where the court is satisfied that any improper solicitation has been used by or on behalf of the trustee in obtaining proxies or procuring his appointment, it may order that no remuneration out of the estate be allowed to any person by whom, or on whose behalf, the solicitation was exercised.

(2) An order of the court under this Rule overrides any resolution of the creditors' committee or the creditors, or any other provision of the Rules relating to the trustee's remuneration.   **[1127]**

6.149. Enforcement of trustee's obligations to official receiver

(1) The court may, on the application of the official receiver, make such orders as it thinks necessary for enforcement of the duties of the trustee under section 305(3) (information and assistance to be given; production and inspection of books and records relating to the bankruptcy).

(2) An order of the court under this Rule may provide that all costs of and incidental to the official receiver's application shall be borne by the trustee.

          [1128]

CHAPTER 11

THE CREDITORS' COMMITTEE

6.150. Membership of creditors' committee

(1) The creditors' committee shall consist of at least 3, and not more than 5, members.

(2) All the members of the committee must be creditors of the bankrupt; and any creditor (other than one who is fully secured) may be a member, so long as—

> (a) he has lodged a proof of his debt, and
> (b) his proof has neither been wholly disallowed for voting purposes, nor wholly rejected for the purposes of distribution or dividend.

(3) A body corporate may be a member of the committee, but it cannot act as such otherwise than by a representative appointed under Rule 6.156.   **[1129]**

6.151. Formalities of establishment

(1) The creditors' committee does not come into being, and accordingly cannot act, until the trustee has issued a certificate of its due constitution.

(2) If the chairman of the creditors' meeting which resolves to establish the committee is not the trustee, he shall forthwith give notice of the resolution to the trustee (or, as the case may be, the person appointed as trustee by that same meeting), and inform him of the names and addresses of the persons elected to be members of the committee.

(3) No person may act as a member of the committee unless and until he has agreed to do so; and the trustee's certificate of the committee's due constitution shall not issue before at least 3 persons elected to be members of it have agreed to act.

(4) As and when the others (if any) agree to act, the trustee shall issue an amended certificate.

(5) The certificate, and any amended certificate, shall be filed in court by the trustee.

(6) If after the first establishment of the committee there is any change in its membership, the trustee shall report the change to the court.   **[1130]**

NOTES
  Paras (1), (4): See Sch 4, form 6.52.
  Para (6): See Sch 4, form 6.53.

6.152. Obligations of trustee to committee

(1) Subject as follows, it is the duty of the trustee to report to the members of the creditors' committee all such matters as appear to him to be, or as they have indicated to him as being, of concern to them with respect to the bankruptcy.

(2) In the case of matters so indicated to him by the committee, the trustee need not comply with any request for information where it appears to him that—

> (a) the request is frivolous or unreasonable, or
> (b) the cost of complying would be excessive, having regard to the relative importance of the information, or
> (c) the estate is without funds sufficient for enabling him to comply.

(3) Where the committee has come into being more than 28 days after the appointment of the trustee, the latter shall report to them, in summary form, what actions he has taken since his appointment, and shall answer such questions as they may put to him regarding his conduct of the bankruptcy hitherto.

(4) A person who becomes a member of the committee at any time after its first establishment is not entitled to require a report to him by the trustee, otherwise than in summary form, of any matters previously arising.

(5) Nothing in this Rule disentitles the committee, or any member of it, from having access to the trustee's records of the bankruptcy, or from seeking an explanation of any matter within the committee's responsibility.   **[1131]**

6.153. Meetings of the committee

(1) Subject as follows, meetings of the creditors' committee shall be held when and where determined by the trustee.

(2) The trustee shall call a first meeting of the committee to take place within 3 months of his appointment or of the committee's establishment (whichever is the later); and thereafter he shall call a meeting—

(a) if so requested by a member of the committee or his representative (the meeting then to be held within 21 days of the request being received by the trustee), and

(b) for a specified date, if the committee has previously resolved that a meeting be held on that date.

(3) The trustee shall give 7 days' notice in writing of the venue of any meeting to every member of the committee (or his representative, if designated for that purpose), unless in any case the requirement of the notice has been waived by or on behalf of any member.

Waiver may be signified either at or before the meeting.   **[1132]**

6.154. The chairman at meetings

(1) The chairman at any meeting of the creditors' committee shall be the trustee, or a person appointed by him in writing to act.

(2) A person so nominated must be either—

(a) one who is qualified to act as an insolvency practitioner in relation to the bankrupt, or

(b) an employee of the trustee or his firm who is experienced in insolvency matters.   **[1133]**

6.155. Quorum

A meeting of the committee is duly constituted if due notice of it has been given to all the members and at least 2 of the members are present or represented.

[1134]

6.156. Committee-members' representatives

(1) A member of the creditors' committee may, in relation to the business of the committee, be represented by another person duly authorised by him for that purpose.

(2) A person acting as a committee-member's representative must hold a letter of authority entitling him so to act (either generally or specially). The letter must be signed by or on behalf of the committee-member.

(3) The chairman at any meeting of the committee may call on a person claiming to act as a committee-member's representative to produce his letter of authority, and may exclude him if it appears that his authority is deficient.

(4) No member may be represented by a body corporate, or by a person who is an undischarged bankrupt or is subject to a composition or arrangement with his creditors.

(5) No person shall—

(a) on the same committee, act at one and the same time as representative of more than one committee-member, or

(b) act both as a member of the committee and as representative of another member.

(6) Where the representative of a committee-member signs any document on the latter's behalf, the fact that he so signs must be stated below his signature.   **[1135]**

6.157. Resignation

A member of the creditors' committee may resign by notice in writing delivered to the trustee.   **[1136]**

6.158. Termination of membership

(1) A person's membership of the creditors' committee is automatically terminated if—

(a) he becomes bankrupt or compounds or arranges with his creditors, or

(b) at 3 consecutive meetings of the committee he is neither present nor represented (unless at the third of those meetings it is resolved that this Rule is not to apply in his case), or

(c) he ceases to be, or is found never to have been, a creditor.

(2) However, if the cause of termination is the member's bankruptcy, his trustee in bankruptcy replaces him as a member of the committee.   **[1137]**

6.159. Removal

A member of the creditors' committee may be removed by resolution at a meeting of creditors, at least 14 days' notice having been given of the intention to move that resolution.   **[1138]**

6.160. Vacancies

(1) The following applies if there is a vacancy in the membership of the creditors' committee.

(2) The vacancy need not be filled if the trustee and a majority of the remaining committee-members so agree, provided that the number of members does not fall below the minimum required by Rule 6.150(1).

(3) The trustee may appoint any creditor (being qualified under the Rules to be a member of the committee) to fill the vacancy, if a majority of the other members of the committee agree to the appointment and the creditor concerned consents to act.

(4) Alternatively, a meeting of creditors may resolve that a creditor be appointed (with his consent) to fill the vacancy. In this case at least 14 days' notice must have been given of a resolution to make such an appointment (whether or not of a person named in the notice).

(5) Where the vacancy is filled by an appointment made by a creditors'

meeting at which the trustee is not present, the chairman of the meeting shall report to the trustee the appointment which has been made. **[1139]**

6.161. Voting rights and resolutions

(1) At any meeting of the committee, each member (whether present himself, or by his representative) has one vote; and a resolution is passed when a majority of the members present or represented have voted in favour of it.

(2) Every resolution passed shall be recorded in writing, either separately or as part of the minutes of the meeting. The record shall be signed by the chairman and kept with the records of the bankruptcy. **[1140]**

6.162. Resolutions by post

(1) In accordance with this Rule, the trustee may seek to obtain the agreement of members of the creditors' committee to a resolution by sending to every member (or his representative designated for the purpose) a copy of the proposed resolution.

(2) Where the trustee makes use of the procedure allowed by this Rule, he shall send out to members of the committee or their representatives (as the case may be) a statement incorporating the resolution to which their agreement is sought, each resolution (if more than one) being set out in a separate document.

(3) Any member of committee may, within 7 days from the date of the trustee sending out a resolution, require the trustee to summon a meeting of the committee to consider the matters raised by the resolution.

(4) In the absence of such a request, the resolution is deemed to have been carried in the committee if and when the trustee is notified in writing by a majority of the members that they concur with it.

(5) A copy of every resolution passed under this Rule, and a note that the concurrence of the committee was obtained, shall be kept with the records of the bankruptcy. **[1141]**

6.163. Trustee's reports

(1) The trustee shall, as and when directed by the creditors' committee (but not more often than once in any period of 2 months), send a written report to every member of the committee setting out the position generally as regards the progress of the bankruptcy and matters arising in connection with it, to which he (the trustee) considers the committee's attention should be drawn.

(2) In the absence of any such directions by the committee, the trustee shall send such a report not less often than once in every period of 6 months.

(3) The obligations of the trustee under this Rule are without prejudice to those imposed by Rule 6.152. **[1142]**

6.164. Expenses of members etc

The trustee shall defray out of the estate, in the prescribed order of priority, any reasonable travelling expenses directly incurred by members of the creditors' committee or their representatives in respect of their attendance at the committee's meetings, or otherwise on the committee's business. **[1143]**

6.165. Dealings by committee-members and others

(1) This Rule applies to—

    (*a*) any member of the creditors' committee,

    (*b*) any committee-member's representative,

    (*c*) any person who is an associate of a member of the committee or a committee-members's representative, and

    (*d*) any person who has been a member of the committee at any time in the last 12 months.

(2) Subject as follows, a person to whom this Rule applies shall not enter into any transaction whereby he—

    (*a*) receives out of the estate any payment for services given or goods supplied in connection with the estate's administration, or

    (*b*) obtains any profit from the administration, or

    (*c*) acquires any asset forming part of the estate.

(3) Such a transaction may be entered into by a person to whom this Rule applies—

    (*a*) with the prior leave of the court, or

    (*b*) if he does so as a matter of urgency, or by way of performance of a contract in force before the commencement of the bankruptcy, and obtains the court's leave for the transaction, having applied for it without undue delay, or

    (*c*) with the prior sanction of the creditors' committee, where it is satisfied (after full disclosure of the circumstances) that the person will be giving full value in the transaction.

(4) Where in the committee a resolution is proposed that sanction be accorded for a transaction to be entered into which, without that sanction or the leave of the court, would be in contravention of this Rule, no member of the committee, and no representative of a member, shall vote if he is to participate directly or indirectly in the transaction.

(5) The court may, on the application of any person interested—

    (*a*) set aside a transaction on the ground that it has been entered into in contravention of this Rule, and

    (*b*) make with respect to it such other order as it thinks fit, including (subject to the following paragraph) an order requiring a person to whom this Rule applies to account for any profit obtained from the transaction and compensate the estate for any resultant loss.

(6) In the case of a person to whom this Rule applies as an associate of a member of the committee or of a committee-member's representative, the court shall not make any order under paragraph (5), if satisfied that he entered into the relevant transaction without having any reason to suppose that in doing so he would contravene this Rule.

(7) The costs of an application to the court for leave under this Rule do not fall on the estate, unless the court so orders.   **[1144]**

6.166. Committee's functions vested in Secretary of State

(1) At any time when the functions of the creditors' committee are vested in the Secretary of State under section 302(1) or (2), requirements of the Act or the Rules about notices to be given, or reports to be made, to the committee by the

trustee do not apply, otherwise than as enabling the committee to require a report as to any matter.

(2) Where the committee's functions are so vested under section 302(2), they may be exercised by the official receiver. **[1145]**

CHAPTER 12

SPECIAL MANAGER

6.167. Appointment and remuneration

(1) An application made by the official receiver or trustee under section 370 for the appointment of a person to be special manager shall be supported by a report setting out the reasons for the application.

The report shall include the applicant's estimate of the value of the estate, property or business in respect of which the special manager is to be appointed.

(2) The court's order appointing the special manager shall specify the duration of his appointment, which may be for a period of time, or until the occurrence of a specified event. Alternatively, the order may specify that the duration of the appointment is to be subject to a further order of the court.

(3) The appointment of a special manager may be renewed by order of the court.

(4) The special manager's remuneration shall be fixed from time to time by the court. **[1146]**

NOTES
Para (2): See Sch 4, form, 6.54.

6.168. Security

(1) The appointment of the special manager does not take effect until the person appointed has given (or, being allowed by the court to do so, undertaken to give) security to the person who applies for him to be appointed.

(2) It is not necessary that security shall be given for each separate bankruptcy; but it may be given either specially for a particular bankruptcy, or generally for any bankruptcy in relation to which the special manager may be employed as such.

(3) The amount of the security shall be not less than the value of the estate, property or business in respect of which he is appointed, as estimated by the applicant in his report under Rule 6.167(1).

(4) When the special manager has given security to the person applying for his appointment, that person's certificate as to the adequacy of the security shall be filed in court.

(5) The cost of providing the security shall be paid in the first instance by the special manager; but—

(a) where a bankruptcy order is not made, he is entitled to be reimbursed out of the property of the debtor, and the court may make an order on the debtor accordingly, and

(b) where a bankrupcy order is made, he is entitled to be reimbursed out of the estate in the prescribed order of priority. **[1147]**

6.169. Failure to give or keep up security

(1) If the special manager fails to give the required security within the time stated for that purpose by the order appointing him, or any extension of that time that may be allowed, the official receiver or trustee (as the case may be) shall report the failure to the court, which may thereupon discharge the order appointing the special manager.

(2) If the special manager fails to keep up his security, the official receiver or trustee shall report his failure to the court, which may thereupon remove the special manager, and make such order as it thinks fit as to costs.

(3) If an order is made under this Rule removing the special manager, or discharging the order appointing him, the court shall give directions as to whether any, and if so what, steps should be taken for the appointment of another special manager in his place.   **[1148]**

6.170. Accounting

(1) The special manager shall produce accounts, containing details of his receipts and payments, for the approval of the trustee.

(2) The accounts shall be in respect of 3-month periods for the duration of the special manager's appointment (or for a lesser period, if his appointment terminates less than 3 months from its date, or from the date to which the last accounts were made up).

(3) When the accounts have been approved, the special manager's receipts and payments shall be added to those of the trustee.   **[1149]**

6.171. Termination of appointment

(1) The special manager's appointment terminates if the bankruptcy petition is dismissed or if, an interim receiver having been appointed, the latter is discharged without a bankruptcy order having been made.

(2) If the official receiver or the trustee is of opinion that the employment of the special manager is no longer necessary or profitable for the estate, he shall apply to the court for directions, and the court may order the special manager's appointment to be terminated.

(3) The official receiver or the trustee shall make the same application if a resolution of the creditors is passed, requesting that the appointment be terminated.   **[1150]**

CHAPTER 13

PUBLIC EXAMINATION OF BANKRUPT

6.172. Order for public examination

(1) If the official receiver applies to the court, under section 290, for the public examination of the bankrupt, a copy of the court's order shall, forthwith after its making, be sent by the official receiver to the bankrupt.

(2) The order shall appoint a venue for the hearing, and direct the bankrupt's attendance thereat.

(3) The official receiver shall give at least 14 days' notice of the hearing—

(*a*) if a trustee has been nominated or appointed, to him;

(*b*) if a special manager has been appointed, to him; and

(*c*) subject to any contrary direction of the court, to every creditor of the bankrupt who is known to the official receiver or is identified in the bankrupt's statement of affairs.

(4) The official receiver may, if he thinks fit, cause notice of the order to be given, by public advertisement in one or more newspapers, at least 14 days before the day fixed for the hearing. **[1151]**

NOTES
Para (1): See Sch 4, form 6.55.

6.173. Order on request by creditors

(1) A request by a creditor to the official receiver, under section 290(2), for the bankrupt to be publicly examined shall be made in writing and be accompanied by—

(*a*) a list of the creditors concurring with the request and the amount of their respective claims in the bankruptcy,

(*b*) from each creditor concurring, written confirmation of his concurrence, and

(*c*) a statement of the reasons why the examination is requested.

Sub-paragraphs (*a*) and (*b*) do not apply if the requisitioning creditor's debt is alone sufficient, without the concurrence of others.

(2) Before an application to the court is made on the request, the requisitionist shall deposit with the official receiver such sum as the latter may determine to be appropriate by way of security for the expenses of the hearing of a public examination, if ordered.

(3) Subject as follows, the official receiver shall, within 28 days of receiving the request, make the application to the court required by section 290(2).

(4) If the official receiver is of opinion that the request is an unreasonable one in the circumstances, he may apply to the court for an order relieving him from the obligation to make the application otherwise required by that subsection.

(5) If the court so orders, and the application for the order was made *ex parte*, notice of the order shall be given forthwith by the official receiver to the requisitionist. If the application for an order is dismissed, the official receiver's application under section 290(2) shall be made forthwith on conclusion of the hearing of the application first mentioned. **[1152]**

NOTES
Para (1): See Sch 4, form 6.56.

6.174. Bankrupt unfit for examination

(1) Where the bankrupt is suffering from any mental disorder or physical affliction or disability rendering him unfit to undergo or attend for public examination, the court may, on application in that behalf, either stay the order for his public examination or direct that it shall be conducted in such manner and at such place as it thinks fit.

(2) Application under this Rule shall be made—

(*a*) by a person who has been appointed by a court in the United Kingdom or elsewhere to manage the affairs of, or to represent, the bankrupt, or

(*b*) by a relative or friend of the bankrupt whom the court considers to be a proper person to make the application, or

(*c*) by the official receiver.

(3) Where the application is made by a person other than the official receiver, then—

(*a*) it shall, unless the bankrupt is a patient within the meaning of the Mental Health Act 1983, be supported by the affidavit of a registered medical practitioner as to the bankrupt's mental and physical condition;

(*b*) at least 7 days' notice of the application shall be given to the official receiver and the trustee (if any); and

(*c*) before any order is made on the application, the applicant shall deposit with the official receiver such sum as the latter certifies to be necessary for the additional expenses of any examination that may be ordered on the application.

An order made on the application may provide that the expenses of the examination are to be payable, as to a specified proportion, out of the deposit under sub-paragraph (*c*), instead of out of the estate.

(4) Where the application is made by the official receiver, it may be made *ex parte*, and may be supported by evidence in the form of a report by the official receiver to the court. **[1153]**

NOTES
Para (1): See Sch 4, form 6.57.

6.175. Procedure at hearing

(1) The bankrupt shall at the hearing be examined on oath; and he shall answer all such questions as the court may put, or allow to be put, to him.

(2) Any of the persons allowed by section 290(4) to question the bankrupt may, with the approval of the court (made known either at the hearing or in advance of it), appear by solicitor or counsel; or he may in writing authorise another person to question the bankrupt on his behalf.

(3) The bankrupt may at his own expense employ a solicitor with or without counsel, who may put to him such questions as the court may allow for the purpose of enabling him to explain or qualify any answers given by him, and may make representations on his behalf.

(4) There shall be made in writing such record of the examination as the court thinks proper. The record shall be read over either to or by the bankrupt, signed by him, and verified by affidavit at a venue fixed by the court.

(5) The written record may, in any proceedings (whether under the Act or otherwise) be used as evidence against the bankrupt of any statement made by him in the course of his public examination.

(6) If criminal proceedings have been instituted against the bankrupt, and the court is of opinion that the continuance of the hearing would be calculated to prejudice a fair trial of those proceedings, the hearing may be adjourned.

[1154]

6.176. Adjournment

(1) The public examination may be adjourned by the court from time to time, either to a fixed date or generally.

(2) Where the examination has been adjourned generally, the court may at the time on the application of the official receiver or of the bankrupt—

    (*a*) fix a venue for the resumption of the examination, and

    (*b*) give directions as to the manner in which, and the time within which, notice of the resumed public examination is to be given to persons entitled to take part in it.

(3) Where application under paragraph (2) is made by the bankrupt, the court may grant it on terms that the expenses of giving the notices required by that paragraph shall be paid by him and that, before a venue for the resumed public examination is fixed, he shall deposit with the official receiver such sum as the latter considers necessary to cover those expenses.

(4) Where the examination is adjourned generally, the official receiver may, there and then, make application under section 279(3) (suspension of automatic discharge). **[1155]**

6.177. Expenses of examination

(1) Where a public examination of the bankrupt has been ordered by the court on a creditors' requisition under Rule 6.173, the court may order that the expenses of the examination are to be paid, as to a specified proportion, out of the deposit under Rule 6.173(2), instead of out of the estate.

(2) In no case do the costs and expenses of a public examination fall on the official receiver personally. **[1156]**

CHAPTER 14
DISCLAIMER

6.178. Trustee's notice of disclaimer

(1) Where the trustee disclaims property under section 315, the notice of disclaimer shall contain such particulars of the property disclaimed as enable it to be easily identified.

(2) The notice shall be signed by the trustee and filed in court, with a copy. The court shall secure that both the notice and the copy are sealed and endorsed with the date of filing.

(3) The copy notice, so sealed and endorsed, shall be returned by the court to the trustee as follows—

    (*a*) if the notice has been delivered at the offices of the court by the trustee in person, it shall be handed to him, (*b*) if it has been delivered by some person acting on the trustee's behalf, it shall be handed to that person, for immediate transmission to the trustee, and

(*c*) otherwise, it shall be sent to the trustee by first class post.

The court shall cause to be endorsed on the original notice, or otherwise recorded on the file, the manner in which the copy notice was returned to the trustee.

(4) For the purposes of section 315, the date of the prescribed notice is that which is endorsed on it, and on the copy, in accordance with this Rule.   **[1157]**

NOTES

Para (1): See Sch 4, form 6.61.

6.179. Communication of disclaimer to persons interested

(1) Within 7 days after the day on which a copy of the notice of disclaimer is returned to him, the trustee shall send or give copies of the notice (showing the date endorsed as required by Rule 6.178) to the persons mentioned in paragraphs (2) to (5) below.

(2) Where the property disclaimed is of a leasehold nature, he shall send or give a copy to every person who (to his knowledge) claims under the bankrupt as underlessee or mortgagee.

(3) Where the disclaimer is of property in a dwelling-house, he shall send or give a copy to every person who (to his knowledge) is in occupation of, or claims a right to occupy, the house.

(4) He shall in any case send or give a copy of the notice to every person who (to his knowledge)—

(*a*) claims an interest in the disclaimed property, or

(*b*) is under any liability in respect of the property, not being a liability discharged by the disclaimer.

(5) If the disclaimer is of an unprofitable contract, he shall send or give copies of the notice to all such persons as, to his knowledge, are parties to the contract or have interests under it.

(6) If subsequently it comes to the trustee's knowledge, in the case of any person, that he has such an interest in the disclaimed property as would have entitled him to receive a copy of the notice of disclaimer in pursuance of paragraphs (2) to (5), the trustee shall then forthwith send or give to that person a copy of the notice.

But compliance with this paragraph is not required if—

(*a*) the trustee is satisfied that the person has already been made aware of the disclaimer and its date, or

(*b*) the court, on the trustee's application, orders that compliance is not required in that particular case.   **[1158]**

6.180. Additional notices

The trustee disclaiming property may, without prejudice to his obligations under sections 315 to 319 and Rules 6.178 and 6.179, at any time give notice of the disclaimer to any persons who in his opinion ought, in the public interest or otherwise, to be informed of it.   **[1159]**

6.181. Duty to keep court informed

The trustee shall notify the court from time to time as to the persons to whom he has sent or given copies of the notice of disclaimer under the two preceding Rules, giving their names and addresses, and the nature of their respective interests. **[1160]**

6.182. Application for leave to disclaim

(1) Where under section 315(4) the trustee requires the leave of the court to disclaim property claimed for the bankrupt's estate under section 307 or 308, he may apply for that leave *ex parte*.

(2) The application must be accompanied by a report—

    (*a*) giving such particulars of the property proposed to be disclaimed as enable it to be easily identified,

    (*b*) setting out the reasons why, the property having been claimed for the estate, the court's leave to disclaim is now applied for, and

    (*c*) specifying the persons (if any) who have been informed of the trustee's intention to make the application.

(3) If it is stated in the report that any person's consent to the disclaimer has been signified, a copy of that consent must be annexed to the report.

(4) The court may, on consideration of the application, grant the leave applied for; and it may, before granting leave—

    (*a*) order that notice of the application be given to all such persons who, if the property is disclaimed, will be entitled to apply for a vesting or other order under section 320, and

    (*b*) fix a venue for the hearing of the application under section 315(4).

[1161]

6.183. Application by interested party under s 316

(1) The following applies where, in the case of any property, application is made to the trustee by an interested party under section 316 (request for decision whether the property is to be disclaimed or not).

(2) The application—

    (*a*) shall be delivered to the trustee personally or by registered post, and

    (*b*) shall be made in the form known as "notice to elect", or a substantially similar form.

(3) This paragraph applies in a case where the property concerned cannot be disclaimed by the trustee without the leave of the court.

If within the period of 28 days mentioned in section 316(1) the trustee applies to the court for leave to disclaim, the court shall extend the time allowed by that section for giving notice of disclaimer to a date not earlier than the date fixed for the hearing of the application. **[1162]**

NOTES

    Para (2): See Sch 4, form 6.62.

6.184. Interest in property to be declared on request

(1) If, in the case of property which the trustee has the right to disclaim, it appears to him that there is some person who claims, or may claim, to have an interest in the property, he may give notice to that person calling on him to

declare within 14 days whether he claims any such interest and, if so, the nature and extent of it.

(2) Failing compliance with the notice, the trustee is entitled to assume that the person concerned has no such interest in the property as will prevent or impede its disclaimer. **[1163]**

NOTES
   Para (1): See Sch 4, form 6.63.

6.185. Disclaimer presumed valid and effective

Any disclaimer of property by the trustee is presumed valid and effective, unless it is proved that he has been in breach of his duty with respect to the giving of notice of disclaimer, or otherwise under sections 315 to 319, or under this Chapter of the Rules. **[1164]**

6.186. Application for exercise of court's powers under s 320

(1) This Rule applies with respect to an application by any person under section 320 for an order of the court to vest or deliver disclaimed property.

(2) The application must be made within 3 months of the applicant becoming aware of the disclaimer, or of his receiving a copy of the trustee's notice of disclaimer sent under Rule 6.179, whichever is the earlier.

(3) The applicant shall with his application file an affidavit—

   (a) stating whether he applies under paragraph (a) of section 320(2) (claim of interest in the property), under paragraph (b) (liability not discharged) or under paragraph (c) (occupation of dwelling-house);
   (b) specifying the date on which he received a copy of the trustee's notice of disclaimer, or otherwise became aware of the disclaimer; and
   (c) specifying the grounds of his application and the order which he desires the court to make under section 320.

(4) The court shall fix a venue for the hearing of the application; and the applicant shall, not later than 7 days before the date fixed, give to the trustee notice of the venue, accompanied by copies of the application and the affidavit under paragraph (3).

(5) On the hearing of the application, the court may give directions as to other persons (if any) who should be sent or given notice of the application and the grounds on which it is made.

(6) Sealed copies of any order made on the application shall be sent by the court to the applicant and the trustee.

(7) In a case where the property disclaimed is of a leasehold nature, or is property in a dwelling-house, and section 317 or (as the case may be) section 318 applies to suspend the effect of the disclaimer, there shall be included in the court's order a direction giving effect to the disclaimer.

This paragraph does not apply if, at the time when the order is issued, other applications under section 320 are pending in respect of the same property.

[1165]

6.187. Purchase of replacement property

(1) A purchase of replacement property under section 308(3) may be made either before or after the realisation by the trustee of the value of the property vesting in him under the section.

(2) The trustee is under no obligation, by virtue of the section, to apply funds to the purchase of a replacement for property vested in him, unless and until he has sufficient funds in the estate for that purpose. **[1166]**

6.188. Money provided in lieu of sale

(1) The following applies where a third party proposes to the trustee that he (the former) should provide the estate with a sum of money enabling the bankrupt to be left in possession of property which would otherwise be made to vest in the trustee under section 308.

(2) The trustee may accept that proposal, if satisfied that it is a reasonable one, and that the estate will benefit to the extent of the value of the property in question less the cost of a reasonable replacement. **[1167]**

CHAPTER 16

INCOME PAYMENTS ORDERS

6.189. Application for order

(1) Where the trustee applies for an income payments order under section 310, the court shall fix a venue for the hearing of the application.

(2) Notice of the application, and of the venue, shall be sent by the trustee to the bankrupt at least 28 days before the day fixed for the hearing, together with a copy of the trustee's application and a short statement of the grounds on which it is made.

(3) The notice shall inform the bankrupt that—

    (*a*) unless at least 7 days before the date fixed for the hearing he sends to the court and to the trustee written consent to an order being made in the terms of the application, he is required to attend the hearing, and

    (*b*) if he attends, he will be given an opportunity to show cause why the order should not be made, or an order should be made otherwise than as applied for by the trustee. **[1168]**

NOTES
    Para (2): See Sch 4, form 6.64.

6.190. Action to follow making of order

(1) Where the court makes an income payments order, a sealed copy of the order shall, forthwith after it is made, be sent by the trustee to the bankrupt.

(2) If the order is made under section 310(3)(*b*), a sealed copy of the order shall also be sent by the trustee to the person to whom the order is directed. **[1169]**

NOTES
    Para (1): See Sch 4, forms 6.65, 6.66.

6.191. Variation of order

(1) If an income payments order is made under section 310(3)(*a*), and the bankrupt does not comply with it, the trustee may apply to the court for the order to be varied, so as to take effect under section 310(3)(*b*) as an order to the payor of the relevant income.

(2) The trustee's application under this Rule may be made *ex parte*.

(3) Sealed copies of any order made on the application shall, forthwith after it is made, be sent by the court to the trustee and the bankrupt.

(4) In the case of an order varying or discharging an income payments order made under section 310(3)(*b*), an additional sealed copy shall be sent to the trustee, for transmission forthwith to the payor of the relevant income.   **[1170]**

NOTES
    Para (1): See Sch 4, form 6.67.

6.192. Order to payor of income: administration

(1) Where a person receives notice of an income payments order under section 310(3)(*b*), with reference to income otherwise payable by him to the bankrupt, he shall make the arrangements requisite for immediate compliance with the order.

(2) When making any payment to the trustee, he may deduct the appropriate fee towards the clerical and administrative costs of compliance with the income payments order.

He shall give to the bankrupt a written statement of any amount deducted by him under this paragraph.

(3) Where a person receives notice of an income payments order imposing on him a requirement under section 310(3)(*b*), and either—

    (*a*) he is then no longer liable to make to the bankrupt any payment of income, or

    (*b*) having made payments in compliance with the order, he ceases to be so liable,

he shall forthwith give notice of that fact to the trustee.   **[1171]**

6.193. Review of order

(1) Where an income payments order is in force, either the trustee or the bankrupt may apply to the court for the order to be varied or discharged.

(2) If the application is made by the trustee, Rule 6.189 applies (with any necessary modification) as in the case of an application for an income payments order.

(3) If the application is made by the bankrupt, it shall be accompanied by a short statement of the grounds on which it is made.

(4) The court may, if it thinks that no sufficient cause is shown for the application, dismiss it; but it shall not do so unless the applicant has had an opportunity to attend the court for an *ex parte* hearing, of which he has been given at least 7 days' notice.

If the application is not dismissed under this paragraph, the court shall fix a venue for it to be heard.

(5) At least 28 days before the date fixed for the hearing, the applicant shall send to the trustee or the bankrupt (whichever of them is not himself the applicant) notice of the venue, accompanied by a copy of the application.

Where the applicant is the bankrupt, the notice shall be accompanied by a copy of the statement of grounds under paragraph (3).

(6) The trustee may, if he thinks fit, appear and be heard on the application; and, whether or not he intends to appear, he may, not less than 7 days before the date fixed for the hearing, file a written report of any matters which he considers ought to be drawn to the court's attention.

If such a report is filed, a copy of it shall be sent by the trustee to the bankrupt.

(7) Sealed copies of any order made on the application shall, forthwith after the order is made, be sent by the court to the trustee, the bankrupt and the payor (if other than the bankrupt). **[1172]**

NOTES
Para (7): See Sch 4, form 6.66.

CHAPTER 17

ACTION BY COURT UNDER SECTION 369
ORDER TO INLAND REVENUE OFFICIAL

6.194. Application for order

(1) An application by the official receiver or the trustee for an order under section 369 (order to inland revenue official to produce documents) shall specify (with such particularity as will enable the order, if made, to be most easily complied with) the documents whose production to the court is desired, naming the official to whom the order is to be addressed.

(2) The court shall fix a venue for the hearing of the application.

(3) Notice of the venue, accompanied by a copy of the application, shall be sent by the applicant to the Commissioners of Inland Revenue ("the Commissioners") at least 28 days before the hearing.

(4) The notice shall require the Commissioners, not later than 7 days before the date fixed for the hearing of the application, to inform the court whether they consent or object to the making of an order under the section.

(5) If the Commissioners consent to the making of an order, they shall inform the court of the name of the official to whom it should be addressed, if other than the one named in the application.

(6) If the Commissioners object to the making of an order, they shall secure that an officer of theirs attend the hearing of the application and, not less than 7 days before it, deliver to the court a statement in writing of their grounds of objection.

A copy of the statement shall be sent forthwith to the applicant. **[1173]**

6.195. Making and service of the order

(1) If on the hearing of the application it appears to the court to be a proper case, the court may make the order applied for, with such modifications (if any) as appear appropriate having regard to any representations made on behalf of the Commissioners.

(2) The order—

    (*a*) may be addressed to an inland revenue official other than the one named in the application,

    (*b*) shall specify a time, not less than 28 days after service on the official to whom the order is addressed, within which compliance is required, and

    (*c*) may include requirements as to the manner in which documents to which the order relates are to be produced.

(3) A sealed copy of the order shall be served by the applicant on the official to whom it is addressed.

(4) If the official is unable to comply with the order because he has not the relevant documents in his possession, and has been unable to obtain possession of them he shall deliver to the court a statement in writing as to the reasons for his non-compliance.

A copy of the statement shall be sent forthwith by the official to the applicant.   **[1174]**

NOTES
    Para (1): See Sch 4, form 6.69.

6.196. Custody of documents

Where in compliance with an order under section 369 original documents are produced, and not copies, any person who, by order of the court under section 369(2) (authorised disclosure to persons with right of inspection), has them in his possession or custody is reponsible to the court for their safe keeping and return as and when directed.   **[1175]**

CHAPTER 18

MORTGAGED PROPERTY

6.197. Claim by mortgagee of land

(1) Any person claiming to be the legal or equitable mortgagee of land belonging to the bankrupt may apply to the court for an order directing that the land be sold.

    "Land" includes any interest in, or right over, land.

(2) The court, if satisfied as to the applicant's title, may direct accounts to be taken and enquiries made to ascertain—

    (*a*) the principal, interest and costs due under the mortgage, and

    (*b*) where the mortgagee has been in possession of the land or any part of it, the rents and profits, dividends, interest, or other proceeds received by him or on his behalf.

Directions may be given by the court under this paragraph with respect to any mortgage (whether prior or subsequent) on the same property, other than that of the applicant.

(3) For the purpose of those accounts and enquiries, and of making title to the purchaser, any of the parties may be examined by the court, and shall produce on oath before the court all such documents in their custody or under their control relating to the estate of the bankrupt as the court may direct.

The court may under this paragraph authorise the service of interrogatories on any party.

(4) In any proceedings between a mortgagor and mortgagee, or the trustee of either of them, the court may order accounts to be taken and enquiries made in like manner as in the Chancery Division of the High Court.   **[1176]**

6.198. Power of court to order sale

(1) The court may order that the land, or any specified part of it, be sold; and any party bound by the order and in possession of the land or part, or in receipt of the rents and profits from it, may be ordered to deliver up possession or receipt to the purchaser or to such other person as the court may direct.

(2) The court may permit the person having the conduct of the sale to sell the land in such manner as he thinks fit. Alternatively, the court may direct that the land be sold as directed by the order.

(3) The court's order may contain directions—

   (a) appointing the persons to have the conduct of the sale;
   (b) fixing the manner of sale (whether by contract conditional on the court's approval, private treaty, public auction, or otherwise);
   (c) settling the particulars and conditions of sale;
   (d) obtaining evidence of the value of the property, and fixing a reserve or minimum price;
   (e) requiring particular persons to join in the sale and conveyance;
   (f) requiring the payment of the purchase money into court, or to trustees or others;
   (g) if the sale is to be by public auction, fixing the security (if any) to be given by the auctioneer, and his remuneration.

(4) The court may direct that, if the sale is to be by public auction, the mortgagee may appear and bid on his own behalf.   **[1177]**

6.199. Proceeds of sale

(1) The proceeds of sale shall be applied—

   (a) first, in payment of the expenses of the trustee, of and occasioned by the application to the court, of the sale and attendance thereat, and of any costs arising from the taking of accounts, and making of enquiries, as directed by the court under Rule 6.197; and
   (b) secondly, in payment of the amount found due to any mortgagee, for principal, interest and costs;

and the balance (if any) shall be retained by or paid to the trustee.

(2) Where the proceeds of the sale are insufficient to pay in full the amount found due to the mortgagee, he is entitled to prove as a creditor for any deficiency, and to receive dividends rateably with other creditors, but not so as to disturb any dividend already declared.   **[1178]**

CHAPTER 19

AFTER-ACQUIRED PROPERTY

6.200. Duties of bankrupt in respect of after-acquired property

(1) The notice to be given by the bankrupt to the trustee, under section 333(2), of property acquired by, or devolving upon, him, or of any increase of his income, shall be given within 21 days of his becoming aware of the relevant facts.

(2) Having served notice in respect of property acquired by or devolving upon him, the bankrupt shall not, without the trustee's consent in writing, dispose of it within the period of 42 days beginning with the date of the notice.

(3) If the bankrupt disposes of property before giving the notice required by this Rule or in contravention of paragraph (2), it is his duty forthwith to disclose to the trustee the name and address of the disponee, and to provide any other information which may be necessary to enable the trustee to trace the property and recover it for the estate.

(4) Subject as follows, paragraphs (1) to (3) do not apply to property acquired by the bankrupt in the ordinary course of a business carried on by him.

(5) If the bankrupt carries on a business, he shall, not less often than 6-monthly, furnish to the trustee information with respect to it, showing the total of goods bought and sold (or, as the case may be, services supplied) and the profit or loss arising from the business.

The trustee may require the bankrupt to furnish fuller details (including accounts) of the business carried on by him.   **[1179]**

6.201. Trustee's recourse to disponee of property

(1) Where property has been disposed of by the bankrupt, before giving the notice required by Rule 6.200 or otherwise in contravention of that Rule, the trustee may serve notice on the disponee, claiming the property as part of the estate by virtue of section 307(3).

(2) The trustee's notice under this Rule must be served within 28 days of his becoming aware of the disponee's identity and an address at which he can be served.   **[1180]**

6.202. Expenses of getting in property for the estate

Any expenses incurred by the trustee in acquiring title to after-acquired property shall be paid out of the estate, in the prescribed order of priority.   **[1181]**

CHAPTER 20

LEAVE TO ACT AS DIRECTOR, ETC

6.203. Application for leave

(1) An application by the bankrupt for leave, under section 11 of the Company Directors Disqualification Act 1986, to act as director of, or to take part or be concerned in the promotion, formation or management of a company, shall be supported by an affidavit complying with this Rule.

(2) The affidavit must identify the company and specify—

(*a*) the nature of its business or intended business, and the place or places where that business is, or is to be, carried on,

(*b*) whether it is, or is to be, a private or a public company,

(*c*) the persons who are, or are to be, principally responsible for the conduct of its affairs (whether as directors, shadow directors, managers or otherwise),

(*d*) the manner and capacity in which the applicant proposes to take part or be concerned in the promotion or information of the company or, as the case may be, its management, and

(*e*) the emoluments and other benefits to be obtained from the directorship.

(3) If the company is already in existence, the affidavit must specify the date of its incorporation and the amount of its nominal and issued share capital; and if not, it must specify the amount, or approximate amount, of its proposed commencing share capital, and the sources from which that capital is to be obtained.

(4) Where the bankrupt intends to take part or be concerned in the promotion or information of a company, the affidavit must contain an undertaking by him that he will, within not less than 7 days of the company being incorporated, file in court a copy of its memorandum of association and certificate of incorporation under section 13 of the Companies Act.

(5) The court shall fix a venue for the hearing of the bankrupt's application, and give notice to him accordingly. **[1182]**

6.204. Report of official receiver

(1) The bankrupt shall, not less than 28 days before the date fixed for the hearing, give to the official receiver and the trustee notice of the venue, accompanied by copies of the application and the affidavit under Rule 6.203.

(2) The official receiver may, not less than 14 days before the date fixed for the hearing, file in court a report of any matters which he considers ought to be drawn to the court's attention. A copy of the report shall be sent by him, forthwith after it is filed, to the bankrupt and to the trustee.

(3) The bankrupt may, not later than 7 days before the date of the hearing, file in court a notice specifying any statements in the official receiver's report which he intends to deny or dispute.

If he gives notice under this paragraph, he shall send copies of it, not less than 4 days before the date of the hearing, to the official receiver and the trustee.

(4) The official receiver and the trustee may appear on the hearing of the application, and may make representations and put to the bankrupt such questions as the court may allow. **[1183]**

6.205. Court's order on application

(1) If the court grants the bankrupt's application for leave under section 11 of the Company Directors Disqualification Act 1986, its order shall specify that which by virtue of the order the bankrupt has leave to do.

(2) The court may at the same time, having regard to any representations made by the trustee on the hearing of the application—

(*a*) include in the order provision varying an income payments order already in force in respect of the bankrupt, or

(*b*) if no income payments order is in force, make one.

(3) Whether or not the application is granted, copies of the order shall be sent by the court to the bankrupt, the trustee and the official receiver.   **[1184]**

CHAPTER 21

ANNULMENT OF BANKRUPTCY ORDER

6.206. Application for annulment

(1) An application to the court under section 282(1) for the annulment of a bankruptcy order shall specify whether it is made—

> (*a*) under subsection (1)(*a*) of the section (claim that the order ought not to have been made), or
> (*b*) under subsection (1)(*b*) (debts and expenses of the bankruptcy all paid or secured).

(2) The application shall, in either case, be supported by an affidavit stating the grounds on which it is made; and, where it is made under section 282(1)(*b*), there shall be set out in the affidavit all the facts by reference to which the court is, under the Act and the Rules, required to be satisfied before annulling the bankruptcy order.

(3) A copy of the application and supporting affidavit shall be filed in court; and the court shall give to the applicant notice of the venue fixed for the hearing.

(4) The applicant shall, not less than 28 days before the hearing, give to the official receiver and (if other) the trustee notice of the venue, accompanied by copies of the application and the affidavit under paragraph (2).   **[1185]**

6.207. Report by trustee

(1) The following applies where the application is made under section 282(1)(*b*) (debts and expenses of the bankruptcy all paid or secured).

(2) Not less than 21 days before the date fixed for the hearing, the trustee or, if no trustee has been appointed, the official receiver shall file in court a report with respect to the following matters—

> (*a*) the circumstances leading to the bankrutpcy;
> (*b*) (in summarised form) the extent of the bankrupt's assets and liabilities at the date of the bankruptcy order and at the date of the present application;
> (*c*) details of creditors (if any) who are known to him to have claims, but have not proved; and
> (*d*) such other matters as the person making the report considers to be, in the circumstances, necessary for the information of the court.

(3) The report shall include particulars of the event (if any) to which, and the manner in which, the debts and expenses of the bankruptcy have been paid or secured.

In so far as debts and expenses are unpaid but secured, the person making the report shall state in it whether and to what extent he considers the security to be satisfactory.

(4) A copy of the report shall be sent to the applicant at least 14 days before the date fixed for the hearing; and he may, if he wishes, file further affidavits in answer to statements made in the report.

Copies of any such affidavits shall be sent by the applicant to the official receiver and (if other) the trustee.

(5) If the trustee is other than the official receiver, a copy of his report shall be sent to the official receiver at least 21 days before the hearing. The official receiver may then file an additional report, a copy of which shall be sent to the applicant at least 7 days before the hearing.   **[1186]**

6.208. Power of court to stay proceedings

(1) The court may, in advance of the hearing, make an interim order staying any proceedings which it thinks ought, in the circumstances of the application, to be stayed.

(2) Application for an interim order under this Rule may be made *ex parte*.
                                                                            [1187]

6.209. Notice to creditors who have not proved

Where the application for annulment is made under section 282(1)(*b*) and it has been reported to the court under Rule 6.207 that there are known creditors of the bankrupt who have not proved, the court may—

>   (*a*) direct the trustee to send notice of the application to such of those creditors as the court thinks ought to be informed of it, with a view to their proving their debts (if they so wish) within 21 days, and
>   (*b*) direct the trustee to advertise the fact that the application has been made, so that creditors who have not proved may do so within a specified time, and
>   (*c*) adjourn the application meanwhile, for any period not less than 35 days.   **[1188]**

6.210. The hearing

(1) The trustee shall attend the hearing of the application.

(2) The official receiver, if he is not the trustee, may attend, but is not required to do so unless he has filed a report under Rule 6.207.

(3) If the court makes an order on the application, it shall send copies of the order to the applicant, the official receiver and (if other) the trustee.   **[1189]**

NOTES
    Para (3): See Sch 4, form 6.71.

6.211. Matters to be proved under s 282(1)(*b*)

(1) This rule applies with regard to the matters which must, in an application under section 282(1)(*b*), be proved to the satisfaction of the court.

(2) Subject to the following paragraph, all bankruptcy debts which have been proved must have been paid in full.

(3) If a debt is disputed, or a creditor who has proved can no longer be traced, the bankrupt must have given such security (in the form of money paid into court, or a bond entered into with approved sureties) as the court considers adequate to satisfy any sum that may subsequently be proved to be due to the creditor concerned and (if the court thinks fit) costs.

(4) Where under paragraph (3) security has been given in the case of an untraced creditor, the court may direct that particulars of the alleged debt, and the security, be advertised in such manner as it thinks fit.

If advertisement is ordered under this paragraph, and no claim on the security is made within 12 months from the date of the advertisement (or the first advertisement, if more than one), the court shall, on application in that behalf, order the security to be released. **[1190]**

6.212. Notice to creditors

(1) Where the official receiver has notified creditors of the debtor's bankruptcy, and the bankruptcy order is annulled, he shall forthwith notify them of the annulment.

(2) Expenses incurred by the official receiver in giving notice under this Rule are a charge in his favour on the property of the former bankrupt, whether or not actually in his hands.

(3) Where any property is in the hands of a trustee or any person other than the former bankrupt himself, the official receiver's charge is valid subject only to any costs that may be incurred by the trustee or that other person in effecting realisation of the property for the purpose of satisfying the charge. **[1191]**

6.213. Other matters arising on annulment

(1) In an order under section 282 the court shall include provision permitting vacation of the registration of the bankruptcy petition as a pending action, and of the bankruptcy order, in the register of writs and orders affecting land.

(2) The court shall forthwith give notice of the making of the order to the Secretary of State.

(3) The former bankrupt may require the Secretary of State to give notice of the making of the order—
    (a) in the Gazette, or
    (b) in any newspaper in which the bankruptcy order was advertised, or
    (c) in both.

(4) Any requirement by the former bankrupt under paragraph (3) shall be addressed to the Secretary of State in writing. The Secretary of State shall notify him forthwith as to the cost of the advertisement, and is under no obligation to advertise until that sum has been paid.

(5) Where the former bankrupt has died, or is a person incapable of managing his affairs (within the meaning of Chapter 7 in Part 7 of the Rules), the references to him in paragraphs (3) and (4) are to be read as referring to his personal representative or, as the case may be, a person appointed by the court to represent or act for him. **[1192]**

6.214. Trustee's final account

(1) Where a bankruptcy order is annulled under section 282, this does not of itself release the trustee from any duty or obligation, imposed on him by or under the Act or the Rules, to account for all his transactions in connection with the former bankrupt's estate.

(2) The trustee shall submit a copy of his final account to the Secretary of State, as soon as practicable after the court's order annulling the bankruptcy order; and he shall file a copy of the final account in court.

(3) The final account must include a summary of the trustee's receipts and payments in the administration, and contain a statement to the effect that he

has reconciled his account with that which is held by the Secretary of State in respect of the bankruptcy.

(4) The trustee is released from such time as the court may determine, having regard to whether—

(*a*) paragraph (2) of this Rule has been complied with, and

(*b*) any security given under Rule 6.11(3) has been, or will be, released.

[1193]

CHAPTER 22

DISCHARGE

6.215. Application for suspension of discharge

(1) The following applies where the official receiver applies to the court for an order under section 279(3) (suspension of automatic discharge), but not where he makes that application, pursuant to Rule 6.176(4), on the adjournment of the bankrupt's public examination.

(2) The official receiver shall with his application file a report setting out the reasons why it appears to him that such an order should be made.

(3) The court shall fix a venue for the hearing of the application, and give notice of it to the official receiver, the trustee and the bankrupt.

(4) Copies of the official receiver's report under this Rule shall be sent by him to the trustee and the bankrupt, so as to reach them at least 21 days before the date fixed for the hearing.

(5) The bankruptcy may, not later than 7 days before the date of the hearing, file in court a notice specifying any statements in the official receiver's report which he intends to deny or dispute.

If he gives notice under this paragraph, he shall send copies of it, not less than 4 days before the date of the hearing, to the official receiver and the trustee.

(6) If on the hearing the court makes an order suspending the bankrupt's discharge, copies of the order shall be sent by the court to the official receiver, the trustee and the bankrupt. [1194]

NOTES

Para (6): See Sch 4, form 6.72.

6.216. Lifting of suspension of discharge

(1) Where the court has made an order under section 279(3) that the relevant period (that is to say, the period after which the bankrupt may under that section have his discharge) shall cease to run, the bankrupt may apply to it for the order to be discharged.

(2) The court shall fix a venue for the hearing of the application; and the bankrupt shall, not less than 28 days before the date fixed for hearing, give notice of the venue to the official receiver and the trustee, accompanied in each case by a copy of the application.

(3) The official receiver and the trustee may appear and be heard on the bankrupt's application; and, whether or not he appears, the official receiver may file in court a report of any matters which he considers ought to be drawn to the court's attention.

(4) If the court's order under section 279(3) was for the relevant period to cease to run until the fulfilment of specified conditions, the court may request a report from the official receiver as to whether those conditions have or have not been fulfilled.

(5) If a report is filed under paragraph (3) or (4), copies of it shall be sent by the official receiver to the bankrupt and the trustee, not later than 14 days before the hearing.

(6) The bankrupt may, not later than 7 days before the date of the hearing, file in court a notice specifying any statements in the official receiver's report which he intends to deny or dispute.

If he gives notice under this paragraph, he shall send copies of it, not less than 14 days before the date of the hearing, to the official receiver and the trustee.

(7) If on the bankrupt's application the court discharges the order under section 279(3) (being satisfied that the relevant period should begin to run again), it shall issue to the bankrupt a certificate that it has done so, with effect from a specified date. **[1195]**

NOTES

Para (7): See Sch 4, forms 6.73, 6.74.

6.217. Application by bankrupt for discharge

(1) If the bankrupt applies under section 280 for an order discharging him from bankruptcy, he shall give to the official receiver notice of the application, and deposit with him such sum as the latter may require to cover his costs of the application.

(2) The court, if satisfied that paragraph (1) has been complied with, shall fix a venue for the hearing of the application, and give at least 42 days' notice of it to the official receiver and the bankrupt.

(3) The official receiver shall give notice accordingly—
 (*a*) to the trustee, and
 (*b*) to every creditor who, to the official receiver's knowledge, has a claim outstanding against the estate which has not been satisfied.

(4) Notices under paragraph (3) shall be given not later than 14 days before the date fixed for the hearing of the bankrupt's application. **[1196]**

6.218. Report of official receiver

(1) Where the bankrupt makes an application under section 280, the official receiver shall, at least 21 days before the date fixed for the hearing of the application, file in court a report containing the following information with respect to the bankrupt—
 (*a*) any failure by him to comply with his obligations under Parts VIII to XI of the Act;
 (*b*) the circumstances surrounding the present bankruptcy, and those surrounding any previous bankruptcy of his;
 (*c*) the extent to which, in the present and in any previous bankruptcy, his liabilities have exceeded his assets; and
 (*d*) particulars of any distribution which has been, or is expected to be, made to creditors in the present bankruptcy or, if such is the case, that there has been and is to be no distribution;

and the official receiver shall include in his report any other matters which in his opinion ought to be brought to the court's attention.

(2) The official receiver shall send a copy of the report to the bankrupt and the trustee, so as to reach them at least 14 days before the date of the hearing of the application under section 280.

(3) The bankrupt may, not later than 7 days before the date of the hearing, file in court a notice specifying any statements in the official receiver's report which he intends to deny or dispute.

If he gives notice under this paragraph, he shall send copies of it, not less than 4 days before the date of the hearing, to the official receiver and the trustee.

(4) The official receiver, the trustee and any creditor may appear on the hearing of the bankrupt's application, and may make representations and put to the bankrupt such questions as the court may allow.   **[1197]**

NOTES
    Para (3): See Sch 4, form 6.75.

6.219. Order of discharge on application

(1) An order of the court under section 280(2)(*b*) (discharge absolutely) or (*c*) (discharge subject to conditions with respect to income or property) shall bear the date on which it is made, but does not take effect until such time as it is drawn up by the court.

(2) The order then has effect retrospectively to the date on which it was made.

(3) Copies of any order made by the court on an application by the bankrupt for discharge under section 280 shall be sent by the court to the bankrupt, the trustee and the official receiver.   **[1198]**

NOTES
    Para (1): See Sch 4, form 6.76.

6.220. Certificate of discharge

(1) Where it appears to the court that a bankrupt is discharged, whether by expiration of time or otherwise, the court shall, on his application, issue to him a certificate of his discharge, and the date from which it is effective.

(2) The discharged bankrupt may require the Secretary of State to give notice of the discharge—

    (*a*) in the Gazette, or
    (*b*) in any newspaper in which the bankruptcy was advertised, or
    (*c*) in both.

(3) Any requirement by the former bankrupt under paragraph (2) shall be addressed to the Secretary of State in writing. The Secretary of State shall notify him forthwith as to the cost of the advertisement, and is under no obligation to advertise until that sum has been paid.

(4) Where the former bankrupt has died, or is a person incapable of managing his affairs (within the meaning of Chapter 7 in Part 7 of the Rules),

the references to him in paragraphs (2) and (3) are to be read as referring to his personal representative or, as the case may be, a person appointed by the court to represent or act for him.   **[1199]**

NOTES
    Para (1): See Sch 4, form 6.77.

6.221. Deferment of issue of order pending appeal

An order made by the court on an application by the bankrupt for discharge under section 280 shall not be issued or gazetted until the time allowed for appealing has expired or, if an appeal is entered, until the appeal has been determined.   **[1200]**

6.222. Costs under this Chapter

In no case do any costs or expenses arising under this Chapter fall on the official receiver personally.   **[1201]**

6.223. Bankrupt's debts surviving discharge

Discharge does not release the bankrupt from any obligation arising under a confiscation order made under section 1 of the Drug Trafficking Offences Act 1986.   **[1202]**

CHAPTER 23

ORDER OF PAYMENT OF COSTS, ETC, OUT OF ESTATE

6.224. General rule as to priority

(1) The expenses of the bankruptcy are payable out of the estate in the following order of priority—

  (*a*) expenses properly chargeable or incurred by the official receiver or the trustee in preserving, realising or getting in any of the assets of the bankrupt, including those incurred in acquiring title to after-acquired property;

  (*b*) any other expenses incurred or disbursements made by the official receiver or under his authority, including those incurred or made in carrying on the business of a debtor or bankrupt;

  (*c*) (i) the fee payable under any order made under section 415 for the performance by the official receiver of his general duties as official receiver;

   (ii) any repayable deposit lodged by the petitioner under any such order as security for the fee mentioned in sub-paragraph (i) (except where the deposit is applied to the payment of the remuneration of an insolvency practitioner appointed under section 273 (debtor's petition));

  (*d*) any other fees payable under any order made under section 415, including those payable to the official receiver, and any remuneration payable to him under general regulations;

  (*e*) the cost of any security provided by an interim receiver, trustee or special manager in accordance with the Act or the Rules;

  (*f*) the remuneration of the interim receiver (if any);

  (*g*) any deposit lodged on an application for the appointment of an interim receiver;

(*h*) the costs of the petitioner, and of any person appearing on the petition whose costs are allowed by the court;

(*j*) the remuneration of the special manager (if any);

(*k*) any amount payable to a person employed or authorised, under Chapter 5 of this Part of the Rules, to assist in the preparation of a statement of affairs or of accounts;

(*l*) any allowance made, by order of the court, towards costs on an application for release from the obligation to submit a statement of affairs, or for an extension of time for submitting such a statement;

(*m*) any necessary disbursements by the trustee in the course of his administration (including any expenses incurred by members of the creditors' committee or their representatives and allowed by the trustee under Rule 6.164, but not including any payment of capital gains tax in circumstances referred to in sub-paragraph (*p*) below);

(*n*) the remuneration or emoluments of any person (including the bankrupt) who has been employed by the trustee to perform any services for the estate, as required or authorised by or under the Act or the Rules;

(*o*) the remuneration of the trustee, up to any amount not exceeding that which is payable to the official receiver under general regulations;

(*p*) the amount of any capital gains tax on chargeable gains accruing on the realisation of any asset of the bankrupt (without regard to whether the realisation is affected by the trustee, a secured creditor, or a receiver or manager appointed to deal with a security);

(*q*) the balance, after payment of any sums due under sub-paragraph (*o*) above, of any remuneration due to the trustee.

(2) The costs of employing a shorthand writer, if appointed by an order of the court made at the instance of the official receiver in connection with an examination, rank in priority with those specified in paragraph (1)(*a*). The costs of employing a shorthand writer so appointed in any other case rank after the allowance mentioned in paragraph (1)(*l*) and before the disbursements mentioned in paragraph (1)(*m*).

(3) Any expenses incurred in holding an examination under Rule 6.174 (examinee unfit), where the application for it is made by the official receiver, rank in priority with those specified in paragraph (1)(*a*). **[1203]**

CHAPTER 24

SECOND BANKRUPTCY

6.225. Scope of this Chapter

(1) The Rules in this Chapter relate to the manner in which, in the case of a second bankruptcy, the trustee in the earlier bankruptcy is to deal with property and money to which section 334(3) applies, until there is a trustee of the estate in the later bankruptcy.

(2) "The earlier bankruptcy", "the later bankruptcy" and "the existing trustee" have the meanings given by section 334(1). **[1204]**

6.226. General duty of existing trustee

(1) Subject as follows, the existing trustee shall take into his custody or under his control all such property and money, in so far as he has not already done so as part of his duties as trustee in the earlier bankruptcy.

(2) Where any of that property consists of perishable goods, or goods the value of which is likely to diminish if they are not disposed of, the existing trustee has power to sell or otherwise dispose of those goods.

(3) The proceedings of any such sale or disposal shall be held, under the existing trustee's control, with the other property and money comprised in the bankrupt's estate.   **[1205]**

6.227. Delivery up to later trustee

The existing trustee shall, as and when requested by the trustee for the purposes of the later bankruptcy, deliver up to the latter all such property and money as is in his custody or under his control in pursuance of Rule 6.226.   **[1206]**

6.228. Existing trustee's expenses

Any expenses incurred by the existing trustee in compliance with section 335(1) and this Chapter of the Rules shall be defrayed out of, and are a charge on, all such property and money as is referred to in section 334(3), whether in the hands of the existing trustee or of the trustee for the purposes of the later bankruptcy.   **[1207]**

CHAPTER 25

CRIMINAL BANKRUPTCY

6.229. Presentation of petition

(1) In criminal bankruptcy, the petition under section 264(1)(*d*) shall be presented to the High Court, and accordingly Rule 6.9 in Chapter 2 (court in which other petitions to be presented) does not apply.

(2) This does not affect the High Court's power to order that the proceedings be transferred.   **[1208]**

NOTES
   Para (1): See Sch 4, form 6.79.

6.230. Status and functions of Official Petitioner

(1) Subject as follows, the Official Petitioner is to be regarded for all purposes of the Act and the Rules as a creditor of the bankrupt.

(2) He may attend or be presented at any meeting of creditors, and is to be given any notice under the Act or the Rules which is required or authorised to be given to creditors; and the requirements of the Rules as to the lodging or use of proxies do not apply.   **[1209]**

6.231. Interim receivership

Chapter 4 of this Part of the Rules applies in criminal bankruptcy only in so far as it provides for the appointment of the official receiver as interim receiver.
          [1210]

6.232. Proof of bankruptcy debts and notice of order

(1) The making of a bankruptcy order on a criminal bankruptcy petition does not affect the right of creditors to prove for their debts arising otherwise than in consequence of the criminal proceedings.

(2) A person specified in a criminal bankruptcy order as having suffered loss or damage shall be treated as a creditor of the bankrupt; and a copy of the order is sufficient evidence of his claim, subject to its being shown by any party to the bankruptcy proceedings that the loss or damage actually suffered was more or (as the case may be) less than the amount specified in the order.

(3) The requirements of the Rules with respect to the proof of debts do not apply to the Official Petitioner.

(4) In criminal bankruptcy, the forms to be used by any person for the purpose of proving bankruptcy debts shall be set out by the official receiver, not less than 12 weeks from the making of the bankruptcy order, to every creditor who is known to him, or is identified in the bankrupt's statement of affairs.

(5) The official receiver shall, within those 12 weeks, send to every such creditor notice of the making of the bankruptcy order. **[1211]**

6.233. Meetings under the Rules

(1) The following Rules in Chapter 6 of this Part do not apply in criminal bankruptcy—

    Rules 6.79 and 6.80 (first meeting of creditors, and business threat);
    Rule 6.82(2) (the chairman, if other than the official receiver);
    Rule 6.88(2) and (3) (resolution for appointment of trustee).

(2) Rule 6.97 (supply of forms for proof of debts) does not apply. **[1212]**

6.234. Trustee in bankruptcy; creditors' committee; annulment of bankruptcy order

(1) Chapter 11 of this Part of the Rules does not apply in criminal bankruptcy, except Rules 6.136 (release of official receiver) and 6.147 (power of court to set aside transactions).

(2) Chapter 12 (creditors' committee) does not apply.

(3) Chapter 21 (annulment of bankruptcy order) applies to an application to the court under section 282(2) as it applies to an application under section 282(1), with any necessary modifications. **[1213]**

CHAPTER 26

MISCELLANEOUS RULES IN BANKRUPTCY

6.235. Bankruptcy of solicitors

Where a bankruptcy order is made against a solicitor, or such an order made against a solicitor is rescinded or annulled, the court shall forthwith give notice to the Secretary of the Law Society of the order that it has made. **[1214]**

6.236. Consolidation of petitions

Where two or more bankruptcy petitions are presented against the same debtor, the court may order the consolidation of the proceedings, on such terms as it thinks fit. **[1215]**

6.237. Bankrupt's dwelling-house and home

(1) This Rule applies where the trustee applies to the court under section 313 for an order imposing a charge on property consisting of an interest in a dwelling-house.

(2) The bankrupt's spouse or former spouse shall be made respondent to the application; and the court may, if it thinks fit, direct other persons to be made respondents also, in respect of any interest which they may have in the property.

(3) The trustee shall make a report to the court, containing the following particulars—

    (a) the extent of the bankrupt's interest in the property which is the subject of the application; and

    (b) the amount which, at the date of the application, remains owing to unsecured creditors of the bankrupt.

(4) The terms of the charge to be imposed shall be agreed between the trustee and the bankrupt or, failing agreement, shall be settled by the court.

(5) The rate of interest applicable under section 313(2) is the rate specified in section 17 of the Judgments Act 1838 on the day on which the charge is imposed, and the rate so applicable shall be stated in the court's order imposing the charge.

(6) The court's order shall also—

    (a) describe the property to be charged;

    (b) state whether the title to the property is registered and, if it is, specify the title number;

    (c) set out the extent of the bankrupt's interest in the property which has vested in the trustee;

    (d) indicate, by reference to the amount which remains owing to unsecured creditors of the bankrupt, the amount of the charge to be imposed;

    (e) set out the conditions (if any) imposed by the court under section 3(1) of the Charging Orders Act 1979;

    (f) provide for any property comprised in the charge to vest again in the bankrupt as from a specified date.

(7) Unless the court is of the opinion that a different date is appropriate, the date under paragraph (6)(f) shall be that of the registration of the charge in accordance with section 3(2) of the Charging Orders Act 1979.

(8) The trustee shall, forthwith after the making of the court's order, send notice of it and its effect to the Chief Land Registrar.   **[1216]**

THE THIRD GROUP OF PARTS

PART 7

COURT PROCEDURE AND PRACTICE

CHAPTER 1

APPLICATIONS

7.1. Preliminary

This Chapter applies to any application made to the court under the Act or Rules except a petition for—

(*a*) an administration order under Part II,
(*b*) a winding-up order under Part IV, or
(*c*) a bankruptcy order under Part IX

of the Act. **[1217]**

7.2. Interpretation

(1) In this Chapter, except in so far as the context otherwise requires—

"originating application" means an application to the court which is not an application in pending proceedings before the court; and "ordinary application" means any other application to the court.

(2) Every application shall be in the form appropriate to the application concerned. **[1218]**

NOTES
See Sch 4, forms 7.1, 7.2.

7.3. Form and contents of application

(1) Each application shall be in writing and shall state—

(*a*) the names of the parties;
(*b*) the nature of the relief or order applied for or the directions sought from the court;
(*c*) the names and addresses of the persons (if any) on whom it is intended to serve the application or that no person is intended to be served;
(*d*) where the Act or Rules require that notice of the application is to be given to specified persons, the names and addresses of all those persons (so far as known to the applicant); and
(*e*) the applicant's address for service.

(2) An originating application shall set out the grounds on which the applicant claims to be entitled to the relief or order sought.

(3) The application must be signed by the applicant if he is acting in person or, when he is not so acting, by or on behalf of his solicitor. **[1219]**

7.4. Filing and service of application

(1) The application shall be filed in court, accompanied by one copy and a number of additional copies equal to the number of persons who are to be served with the application.

(2) Subject as follows in this Rule and the next, or unless the Rule under which the application is brought provides otherwise, or the court otherwise orders, upon the presentation of the documents mentioned in paragraph (1) above, the court shall fix a venue for the application to be heard.

(3) Unless the court otherwise directs, the applicant shall serve a sealed copy of the application, endorsed with the venue for the hearing, on the respondent named in the application (or on each respondent if more than one).

(4) The court may give any of the following directions—

(*a*) that the application be served upon persons other than those specified by the relevant provision of the Act or Rules;
(*b*) that the giving of notice to any person may be dispensed with;
(*c*) that notice be given in some way other than that specified in paragraph (3).

(5) Unless the provision of the Act or Rules under which the application is made provides otherwise, and subject to the next paragraph, the application must be served at least 14 days before the date fixed for the hearing.

(6) Where the case is one of urgency, the court may (without prejudice to its general power to extend or abridge time limits)—

(a) hear the application immediately, either with or without notice to, or the attendance of, other parties, or

(b) authorise a shorter period of service than that provided for by paragraph (5);

and any such application may be heard on terms providing for the filing or service of documents, or the carrying out of other formalities, as the court thinks fit.   **[1220]**

7.5. Other hearings ex parte

(1) Where the relevant provisions of the Act or Rules do not require service of the application on, or notice of it to be given to, any person, the court may hear the application *ex parte*.

(2) Where the application is properly made *ex parte*, the court may hear it forthwith, without fixing a venue as required by Rule 7.4(2).

(3) Alternatively, the court may fix a venue for the application to be heard, in which case Rule 7.4 applies (so far as relevant).   **[1221]**

7.6. Hearing of application

(1) Unless allowed or authorised to be made otherwise, every application before the registrar shall, and every application before the judge may, be heard in chambers.

(2) Unless either—

(a) the judge has given a general or special direction to the contrary, or

(b) it is not within the registrar's power to make the order required.

the jurisdiction of the court to hear and determine the application may be exercised by the registrar, and the application shall be made to the registrar in the first instance.

(3) Where the application is made to the registrar he may refer to the judge any matter which he thinks should properly be decided by the judge, and the judge may either dispose of the matter or refer it back to the registrar with such directions as he thinks fit.

(4) Nothing in the Rule precludes an application being made directly to the judge in a proper case.   **[1222]**

7.7. Use of affidavit evidence

(1) In any proceedings evidence may be given by affidavit unless by any provision of the Rules it is otherwise provided or the court otherwise directs; but the court may, on the application of any party, order the attendance for cross-examination of the person making the affidavit.

(2) Where, after such an order has been made, the person in question does not attend, his affidavit shall not be used in evidence without the leave of the court.   **[1223]**

7.8. Filing and service of affidavits

(1) Unless the provision of the Act or Rules under which the application is made provides otherwise, or the court otherwise allows—

    (*a*) if the applicant intends to rely at the first hearing on affidavit evidence, he shall file the affidavit or affidavits (if more than one) in court and serve a copy or copies on the respondent, not less than 14 days before the date fixed for the hearing, and

    (*b*) where a respondent to an application intends to oppose it and to rely for that purpose on affidavit evidence, he shall file the affidavit or affidavits (if more than one) in court and serve a copy or copies on the applicant, not less than 7 days before the date fixed for the hearing.

(2) Any affidavit may be sworn by the applicant or by the respondent or by some other person possessing direct knowledge of the subject matter of the application. **[1224]**

7.9. Use of reports

(1) A report may be filed in court instead of an affidavit—

    (*a*) in any case, by the official receiver (whether or not he is acting in any capacity mentioned in sub-paragraph (*b*)), or a deputy official receiver, or

    (*b*) unless the application involves other parties or the court otherwise orders, by—

        (i) an administrator, a liquidator or a trustee in bankruptcy,

        (ii) a provisional liquidator or an interim receiver,

        (iii) a special manager, or

        (iv) an insolvency practitioner appointed under section 273(2).

(2) In any case where a report is filed instead of an affidavit, the report shall be treated for the purposes of Rule 7.8(1) and any hearing before the court as if it were an affidavit.

(3) Any report filed by the official receiver in accordance with the Act or the Rules is prima facie evidence of any matter contained in it. **[1225]**

7.10. Adjournment of hearing; directions

(1) The court may adjourn the hearing of an application on such terms (if any) as it thinks fit.

(2) The court may at any time give such directions as it thinks fit as to—

    (*a*) service or notice of the application on or to any person, whether in connection with the venue of a resumed hearing or for any other purpose;

    (*b*) whether particulars of claim and defence are to be delivered and generally as to the procedure on the application;

    (*c*) the manner in which any evidence is to be adduced at a resumed hearing and in particular (but without prejudice to the generality of this sub-paragraph) as to—

        (i) the taking of evidence wholly or in part by affidavit or orally;

        (ii) the cross-examination either before the judge or registrar on the hearing in court or in chambers, of any deponents to affidavits;

        (iii) any report to be given by the official receiver or any person mentioned in Rule 7.9(1)(*b*);

    (*d*) the matters to be dealt with in evidence. **[1226]**

CHAPTER 2
TRANSFER OF PROCEEDINGS BETWEEN COURTS

7.11. General power of transfer

(1) Where winding-up or bankruptcy proceedings are pending in the High Court, the court may order them to be transferred to a specified county court.

(2) Where winding-up or bankruptcy proceedings are pending in a county court, the court may order them to be transferred either to the High Court or to another county court.

(3) In any case where proceedings are transferred to a county court, the transfer must be to a court which has jurisdiction to wind up companies or, as the case may be, jurisdiction in bankruptcy.

(4) Where winding-up or bankruptcy proceedings are pending in a county court, a judge of the High Court may order them to be transferred to that Court.

(5) A transfer of proceedings under this Rule may be ordered—

   (*a*) by the court of its own motion, or
   (*b*) on the application of the official receiver, or
   (*c*) on the application of a person appearing to the court to have an interest in the proceedings.

(6) A transfer of proceedings under this Rule may be ordered notwithstanding that the proceedings commenced before the coming into force of the Rules.

[1227]

7.12. Proceedings commenced in wrong court

Where winding-up or bankruptcy proceedings are commenced in a court which is, in relation to those proceedings, the wrong court, that court may—

   (*a*) order the transfer of the proceedings to the court in which they ought to have been commenced;
   (*b*) order that the proceedings be continued in the court in which they have been commenced; or
   (*c*) order the proceedings to be struck out.   **[1228]**

7.13. Applications for transfer

(1) An application by the official receiver for proceedings to be transferred shall be made with a report by him—

   (*a*) setting out the reasons for the transfer, and
   (*b*) including a statement either that the petitioner consents to the transfer, or that he has been given at least 14 days' notice of the official receiver's application.

(2) If the court is satisfied from the official receiver's report that the proceedings can be conducted more conveniently in another court, the proceedings shall be transferred to that court.

(3) Where an application for the transfer of proceedings is made otherwise than by the official receiver, at least 14 days' notice of the application shall be given by the applicant—

(a) to the official receiver attached to the court in which the proceedings are pending, and

(b) to the official receiver attached to the court to which it is proposed that they should be transferred. **[1229]**

7.14. Procedure following order for transfer

(1) Subject as follows, the court making an order under Rule 7.11 shall forthwith send to the transferee court a sealed copy of the order, and the file of the proceedings.

(2) On receipt of these, the transferee court shall forthwith send notice of the transfer to the official receivers attached to that court and the transferor court respectively.

(3) Paragraph (1) does not apply where the order is made by the High Court under Rule 7.11(4). In that case—

(a) the High Court shall send sealed copies of the order to the county court from which the proceedings are to be transferred, and to the official receivers attached to that court and the High Court respectively, and

(b) that county court shall send the file of the proceedings to the High Court.

(4) Following compliance with this Rule, if the official receiver attached to the court to which the proceedings are ordered to be transferred is not already, by virtue of directions given by the Secretary of State under section 399(6)(a), the official receiver in relation to those proceedings, he becomes, in relation to those proceedings, the official receiver in place of the official receiver attached to the other court concerned. **[1230]**

7.15. Consequential transfer of other proceedings

(1) This Rule applies where—

(a) an order for the winding up of a company, or a bankruptcy order in the case of an individual, has been made by the High Court, or

(b) in either such case, a provisional liquidator or (as the case may be) an interim receiver has been appointed, or

(c) winding-up or bankruptcy proceedings have been transferred to that Court from a county court.

(2) A judge of any Division of the High Court may, of his own motion, order the transfer to that Division of any such proceedings as are mentioned below and are pending against the company or individual concerned ("the insolvent") either in another Division of the High Court or in a court in England and Wales other than the High Court.

(3) Proceedings which may be so transferred are those brought by or against the insolvent for the purpose of enforcing a claim against the insolvent estate, or brought by a person other than the insolvent for the purpose of enforcing any such claim (including in either case proceedings of any description by a debenture-holder or mortgagee).

(4) Where proceedings are transferred under this Rule, the registrar may (subject to general or special directions of the judge) dispose of any matter arising in the proceedings which would, but for the transfer, have been disposed of in chambers or, in the case of proceedings transferred from a county court, by the registrar of that court. **[1231]**

CHAPTER 3

SHORTHAND WRITERS

7.16. Nomination and appointment of shorthand writers

(1) In the High Court the judge and, in a county court, the registrar may in writing nominate one or more persons to be official shorthand writers to the court.

(2) The court may, at any time in the course of insolvency proceedings, appoint a shorthand writer to take down the evidence of a person examined under section 133, 236, 290 or 366.

(3) Where the official receiver applies to the court for an order appointing a shorthand writer, he shall name the person he proposes for appointment; and that appointment shall be made, unless the court otherwise orders.   **[1232]**

NOTES
    Para (1): See Sch 4, form 7.3.
    Para (2): See Sch 4, form 7.4.

7.17. Remuneration

(1) The remuneration of a shorthand writer appointed in insolvency proceedings shall be paid by the party at whose instance the appointment was made, or out of the insolvent estate, or otherwise, as the court may direct.

(2) The remuneration payable shall be calculated in accordance with Schedule 3 to the Rules.   **[1233]**

7.18. Cost of shorthand note

Where in insolvency proceedings the court appoints a shorthand writer on the application of the official receiver, in order that a written record may be taken of the evidence of a person to be examined, the cost of the written record is deemed an expense of the official receiver in the proceedings.   **[1234]**

CHAPTER 4

ENFORCEMENT PROCEDURES

7.19 Enforcement of court orders

(1) In any insolvency proceedings, orders of the court may be enforced in the same manner as a judgment to the same effect.

(2) Where an order in insolvency proceedings is made, or any process is issued, by a county court ("the primary court"), the order or process may be enforced, executed and dealt with by any other county court ("the secondary court"), as if it had been made or issued for the enforcement of a judgment or order to the same effect made by the secondary court.

This applies whether or not the secondary court has jurisdiction to take insolvency proceedings.   **[1235]**

7.20. Orders enforcing compliance with the Rules

(1) The court may, on application by the competent person, make such orders as it thinks necessary for the enforcement of obligations falling on any person in accordance with—

(*a*) section 22, 47 or 131 (duty to submit statement of affairs in administration, administrative receivership or winding up),

(*b*) section 143(2) (liquidator to furnish information, books, papers, etc), or

(*c*) section 235 (duty of various persons to co-operate with office-holder).

(2) The competent person for this purpose is—

(*a*) under section 22, the administrator,

(*b*) under section 47, the administrative receiver,

(*c*) under section 131 or 143(2), the official receiver, and

(*d*) under section 235, the official receiver, the administrator, the administrative receiver, the liquidator or the provisional liquidator, as the case may be.

(3) An order of the court under this Rule may provide that all costs of and incidental to the application for it shall be borne by the person against whom the order is made.   **[1236]**

7.21. Warrants (general provisions)

(1) A warrant issued by the court under any provision of the Act shall be addressed to such officer of the High Court or of a county court (whether or not having jurisdiction in insolvency proceedings) as the warrant specifies, or to any constable.

(2) The persons referred to in sections 134(2), 236(5), 364(1), 365(3) and 366(3) (court's powers of enforcement) as the prescribed officer of the court are—

(*a*) in the case of the High Court, the tipstaff and his assistants of the court, and

(*b*) in the case of a county court, the registrar and the bailiffs.

(3) In this Chapter references to property include books, papers and records.   **[1237]**

7.22. Warrants under ss 134, 364

When a person is arrested under a warrant issued by the court under section 134 (officer of company failing to attend for public examination), or section 364 (arrest of debtor or bankrupt)—

(*a*) the officer apprehending him shall give him into the custody of the governor of the prison named in the warrant, who shall keep him in custody until such time as the court otherwise orders and shall produce him before the court as it may from time to time direct; and

(*b*) any property in the arrested person's possession which may be seized shall be—

    (i) lodged with, or otherwise dealt with as instructed by, whoever is specified in the warrant as authorised to receive it, or

    (ii) kept by the officer seizing it pending the receipt of written orders from the court as to its disposal,

as may be directed by the court in the warrant.   **[1238]**

NOTES

  See Sch 4, forms 7.6, 7.7.

7.23. Warrants under ss 236, 366

(1) When a person is arrested under a warrant issued under section 236 (inquiry into insolvent company's dealings) or 366 (the equivalent in bankruptcy), the officer arresting him shall forthwith bring him before the court issuing the warrant in order that he may be examined.

(2) If he cannot immediately be brought up for examination, the officer shall deliver him into the custody of the governor of the prison named in the warrant, who shall keep him in custody and produce him before the court as it may from time to time direct.

(3) After arresting the person named in the warrant, the officer shall forthwith report to the court the arrest or delivery into custody (as the case may be) and apply to the court to fix a venue for the person's examination.

(4) The court shall appoint the earliest practicable time for the examination, and shall—

    (*a*) direct the governor of the prison to produce the person for examination at the time and place appointed, and

    (*b*) forthwith give notice of the venue to the person who applied for the warrant.

(5) Any property in the arrested person's possession which may be seized shall be—

    (*a*) lodged with, or otherwise dealt with as instructed by, whoever is specified in the warrant as authorised to receive it, or

    (*b*) kept by the officer seizing it pending the receipt of written orders from the court as to its disposal,

as may be directed by the court. **[1239]**

NOTES

    Para (1): See Sch 4, form 7.8.
    Para (2): See Sch 4, form 7.9.
    Para (4): See Sch 4, form 7.9.

7.24. Execution of warrants outside court's district

(1) This Rule applies where a warrant for a person's arrest has been issued in insolvency proceedings by a county court ("the primary court") and is addressed to another county court ("the secondary court") for execution in its district.

(2) The secondary court may send the warrant to the registrar of any other county court (whether or not having jurisdiction to take insolvency proceedings) in whose district the person to be arrested is or is believed to be, with a notice to the effect that the warrant is transmitted to that court under this Rule for execution in its district at the request of the primary court.

(3) The court receiving a warrant transmitted by the secondary court under this Rule shall apply its seal to the warrant, and secure that all such steps are taken for its execution as would be appropriate in the case of a warrant issued by itself. **[1240]**

NOTES

    Para (1): See Sch 4, form 7.10.

7.25. Warrants under s 365

(1) A warrant issued under section 365(3) (search of premises not belonging to the bankrupt) shall authorise any person executing it to seize any property of the bankrupt found as a result of the execution of the warrant.

(2) Any property seized under a warrant issued under section 365(2) or (3) shall be—

    (*a*) lodged with, or otherwise dealt with as instructed by, whoever is specified in the warrant as authorised to receive it, or

    (*b*) kept by the officer seizing it pending the receipt of written orders from the court as to its disposal,

as may be directed by the warrant. **[1241]**

NOTES
    Para (2): See Sch 4, forms 7.12, 7.13.

CHAPTER 5

COURT RECORDS AND RETURNS

7.26. Title of proceedings

(1) Every proceeding under Parts I to VII of the Act shall, with any necessary additions, be intituled "IN THE MATTER OF . . . (naming the company to which the proceedings relate) AND IN THE MATTER OF THE INSOLVENCY ACT 1986".

(2) Every proceeding under Parts IX to XI of the Act shall be intituled "IN BANKRUPTCY". **[1242]**

7.27. Court records

The court shall keep records of all insolvency proceedings, and shall cause to be entered in the records the taking of any step in the proceedings, and such decisions of the court in relation thereto, as the court thinks fit. **[1243]**

7.28. Inspection of records

(1) Subject as follows, the court's records of insolvency proceedings shall be open to inspection by any person.

(2) If in the case of a person applying to inspect the records the registrar is not satisfied as to the propriety of the purpose for which inspection is required, he may refuse to allow it. The person may then apply forthwith and *ex parte* to the judge, who may refuse the inspection, or allow it on such terms as he thinks fit.

(3) The judge's decision under paragraph (2) is final. **[1244]**

7.29. Returns to Secretary of State

(1) The court shall from time to time send to the Secretary of State the following particulars relating to winding-up and bankruptcy proceedings—

    (*a*) the full title of the proceedings, including the number assigned to each case;

    (*b*) where a winding-up or bankruptcy order has been made, the date of the order.

(2) The Secretary of State may, on the request of any person, furnish him with particulars sent by the court under this Rule.   **[1245]**

7.30. File of court proceedings

(1) In respect of all insolvency proceedings, the court shall open and maintain a file for each case; and (subject to directions of the registrar) all documents relating to such proceedings shall be placed on the relevant file.

(2) No proceedings shall be filed in the Central Office of the High Court.

[1246]

7.31. Right to inspect the file

(1) In the case of any insolvency proceedings, the following have the right, at all reasonable times, to inspect the court's file of the proceedings—

   (*a*) the person who, in relation to those proceedings, is the responsible insolvency practitioner;
   (*b*) any duly authorised officer of the Department; and
   (*c*) any person stating himself in writing to be a creditor of the company to which, or the individual to whom, the proceedings relate.

(2) The same right of inspection is exercisable—

   (*a*) in proceedings under Parts I to VII of the Act, by every person who is, or at any time has been, a director or officer of the company to which the proceedings relate, or who is a member of the company or a contributory in its winding up;
   (*b*) in proceedings with respect to a voluntary arrangement proposed by a debtor under Part VIII of the Act, by the debtor;
   (*c*) in bankruptcy proceedings, by—
      (i) the bankrupt,
      (ii) any person against whom, or by whom, a bankruptcy petition has been presented, and
      (iii) any person who has been served, in accordance with Chapter 1 of Part 6 of the Rules, with a statutory demand.

(3) The right of inspection conferred as above on any person may be exercised on his behalf by a person properly authorised by him.

(4) Any person may, by special leave of the court, inspect the file.

(5) The right of inspection conferred by this Rule is not exercisable in the case of documents, or parts of documents, as to which the court directs (either generally or specially) that they are not to be made open to inspection without the court's leave.

An application for a direction of the court under this paragraph may be made by the official receiver, by the person who in relation to any proceedings is the responsible insolvency practitioner, or by any party appearing to the court to have an interest.

(6) If, for the purpose of powers conferred by the Act or the Rules, the Secretary of State, the Department or the official receiver requires to inspect the file of any insolvency proceedings, and requests the transmission of the file, the court shall comply with the request (unless the file is for the time being in use for the court's own purposes).

(7) Paragraphs (2) and (3) of Rule 7.28 apply in respect of the court's file of any proceedings as they apply in respect of court records.   **[1247]**

7.32. Filing of Gazette notices and advertisements

(1) In any court in which insolvency proceedings are pending, an officer of the court shall file a copy of every issue of the Gazette which contains an advertisement relating to those proceedings.

(2) Where there appears in a newspaper an advertisement relating to insolvency proceedings pending in any court, the person inserting the advertisement shall file a copy of it in that court.

The copy of the advertisement shall be accompanied by, or have endorsed on it, such particulars as are necessary to identify the proceedings and the date of the advertisement's appearance.

(3) An officer of any court in which insolvency proceedings are pending shall from time to time file a memorandum giving the dates of, and other particulars relating to, any notice published in the Gazette, and any newspaper advertisements, which relate to proceedings so pending.

The officer's memorandum is prima facie evidence that any notice or advertisement mentioned in it was duly inserted in the issue of the newspaper or the Gazette which is specified in the memorandum.   **[1248]**

CHAPTER 6
COSTS AND TAXATION

7.33. Application of Rules of Supreme Court and County Court Rules

Subject to provision to inconsistent effect made as follows in this Chapter—

> (*a*) Order 62 of the Rules of the Supreme Court applies to insolvency proceedings in the High Court, and
> (*b*) Order 38 of the County Court Rules applies to such proceedings in a county court,

in either case, with any necessary modifications.   **[1249]**

7.34. Requirement to tax costs

(1) Subject as follows, where any costs, charges or expenses of any person are payable out of the insolvent estate, the responsible insolvency practitioner may agree them with the person entitled to payment or may require them to be taxed by the court to which the insolvency proceedings are allocated or, where in relation to a company there is no such court, by a court having jurisdiction to wind up the company.

(2) If a liquidation or creditors' committee established in insolvency proceedings (except administrative receivership) resolves that any such costs, charges or expenses be taxed, the insolvency practitioner shall require taxation.

(3) Where the costs, charges or expenses of any person employed by an insolvency practitioner in insolvency proceedings are required to be taxed, this does not preclude the insolvency practitioner from making payments on account to such person on the basis of an undertaking by that person to repay immediately any money which may, on taxation, prove to have been overpaid, with interest at the rate specified in section 17 of the Judgments Act 1838 on the

date payment was made and for the period from the date of payment to that of repayment.

(4) In any proceedings before the court, including proceedings on a petition, the court may order costs to be taxed.

(5) Unless otherwise directed or authorised, the costs of a trustee in bankruptcy or a liquidator are to be allowed on the standard basis.

(6) This Rule applies additionally (with any necessary modifications) to winding-up and bankruptcy proceedings commenced before the coming into force of the Rules.   **[1250]**

7.35. Procedure where taxation required

(1) Before taxing the costs of any person employed in insolvency proceedings by a responsible insolvency practitioner, the taxing officer shall require a certificate of employment, which shall be endorsed on the bill and signed by the insolvency practitioner.

(2) The certificate shall include—
   (a) the name and address of the person employed,
   (b) details of the functions to be carried out under the employment, and
   (c) a note of any special terms of remuneration which have been agreed.

(3) Every person whose costs are required to be taxed in insolvency proceedings shall, on being required in writing to do so by the insolvency practitioner, deliver his bill of costs to the taxing officer for taxation.

(4) If that person does not so deliver his bill within 3 months of the requirement under paragraph (3), or within such further time as the court, on application, may grant, the insolvency practitioner may deal with the insolvent estate without regard to any claim by that person, whose claim is forfeited.

(5) Where in any such case such a claim lies additionally against an insolvency practitioner in his personal capacity, that claim is also forfeited.
          [1251]

7.36. Costs of sheriff

(1) Where a sheriff—
   (a) is required under section 184(2) or 346(2) to deliver up goods or money, or
   (b) has under section 184(3) or 346(3) deducted costs from the proceeds of an execution or money paid to him,
the responsible insolvency practitioner may require in writing that the sheriff's bill of costs be taxed.

(2) Where such a requirement is made, Rule 7.35(4) applies.

(3) Where, in the case of a deduction under paragraph (1)(b), any amount is disallowed on taxation, the sheriff shall forthwith pay a sum equal to that amount to the insolvency practitioner for the benefit of the insolvent estate.
          [1252]

7.37. Petitions presented by insolvents

(1) In any case where a petition is presented by a company or individual ("the insolvent") against himself, any solicitor acting for the insolvent shall in his bill

of costs give credit for any sum or security received from the insolvent as a deposit on account of the costs and expenses to be incurred in respect of the filing and prosecution of the petition; and the deposit shall be noted by the taxing officer on the taxing certificate.

(2) Paragraph (3) applies where a petition is presented by a person other than the insolvent to whom the petition relates and before it is heard the insolvent presents a petition for the same order, and that order is made.

(3) Unless the court considers that the insolvent estate has benefited by the insolvent's conduct, or that there are otherwise special circumstances justifying the allowance of costs, no costs shall be allowed to the insolvent or his solicitor out of the insolvent estate.   **[1253]**

7.38. Costs paid otherwise than out of the insolvent estate

Where a bill of costs is taxed under an order of the court directing that the costs are to be paid otherwise than out of the insolvent estate, the taxing officer shall note on the certificate of taxation by whom, or the manner in which, the costs are to be paid.   **[1254]**

7.39. Award of costs against official receiver or responsible insolvency practitioner

Without prejudice to any provision of the Act or Rules by virtue of which the official receiver is not in any event to be liable for costs and expenses, where the official receiver or a responsible insolvency practitioner is made a party to any proceedings on the application of another party to the proceedings, he shall not be personally liable for costs unless the court otherwise directs.   **[1255]**

7.40. Applications for costs

(1) This Rule applies where a party to, or person affected by, any proceedings in an insolvency—

   (*a*) applies to the court for an order allowing his costs, or part of them, incidental to the proceedings, and
   (*b*) that application is not made at the time of the proceedings.

(2) The person concerned shall serve a sealed copy of his application on the responsible insolvency practitioner, and, in a winding up by the court or bankruptcy, on the official receiver.

(3) The insolvency practitioner and, where appropriate, the official receiver may appear on the application.

(4) No costs of or incidental to the application shall be allowed to the applicant unless the court is satisfied that the application could not have been made at the time of the proceedings.   **[1256]**

7.41. Costs and expenses of witnesses

(1) Except as directed by the court, no allowance as a witness in any examination or other proceedings before the court shall be made to the bankrupt or an officer of the insolvent company to which the proceedings relate.

(2) A person presenting any petition in insolvency proceedings shall not be regarded as a witness on the hearing of the petition, but the taxing officer may allow his expenses of travelling and subsistence.   **[1257]**

7.42. Certificate of taxation

(1) A certificate of taxation of the taxing officer is final and conclusive as to all matters which have not been objected to in the manner provided for under the rules of the court.

(2) Where it is proved to the satisfaction of a taxing officer that a certificate of taxation has been lost or destroyed, he may issue a duplicate.

(3) "Certificate of taxation" includes, for the purposes of the Rules, an order of the registrar in a county court.   **[1258]**

CHAPTER 7

PERSONS INCAPABLE OF MANAGING THEIR AFFAIRS

7.43. Introductory

(1) The Rules in this Chapter apply where in insolvency proceedings it appears to the court that a person affected by the proceedings is one who is incapable of managing and administering his property and affairs either—

  (*a*) by reason of mental disorder within the meaning of the Mental Health Act 1983, or
  (*b*) due to physical affliction or disability.

(2) The person concerned is referred to as "the incapacitated person".
        [1259]

7.44. Appointment of another person to act

(1) The court may appoint such person as it thinks fit to appear for, represent or act for the incapacitated person.

(2) The appointment may be made either generally or for the purpose of any particular application or proceeding, or for the exercise of particular rights or powers which the incapacitated person might have exercised but for his incapacity.

(3) The court may make the appointment either of its own motion or on application by—

  (*a*) a person who has been appointed by a court in the United Kingdom or elsewhere to manage the affairs of, or to represent, the incapacitated person, or
  (*b*) any relative or friend of the incapacitated person who appears to the court to be a proper person to make the application, or
  (*c*) the official receiver, or
  (*d*) the person who, in relation to the proceedings, is the responsible insolvency practitioner.

(4) Application under paragraph (3) may be made *ex parte*; but the court may require such notice of the application as it thinks necessary to be given to the person alleged to be incapacitated, or any other person, and may adjourn the hearing of the application to enable the notice to be given.   **[1260]**

NOTES
    Para (1): See Sch 4, form 7.19.

7.45. Affidavit in support of application

(1) Except where made by the official receiver, an application under Rule 7.44(3) shall be supported by an affidavit of a registered medical practitioner as to the mental or physical condition of the incapacitated person.

(2) In the excepted case, a report made by the official receiver is sufficient.

[1261]

7.46. Service of notices following appointment

Any notice served on, or sent to, a person appointed under Rule 7.44 has the same effect as if it had been served on, or given to, the incapacitated person.

[1262]

CHAPTER 8

APPEALS IN INSOLVENCY PROCEEDINGS

7.47. Appeals and reviews of court orders (winding up)

(1) Every court having jurisdiction under the Act to wind up companies may review, rescind or vary any order made by it in the exercise of that jurisdiction.

(2) An appeal from a decision made in the exercise of that jurisdiction by a county court or by a registrar of the High Court lies to a single judge of the High Court; and an appeal from a decision of that judge on such an appeal lies, with the leave of that judge or the Court of Appeal, to the Court of Appeal.

(3) A county court is not, in the exercise of its jurisdiction to wind up companies, subject to be restrained by the order of any other court, and no appeal lies from its decision in the exercise of that jurisdiction except as provided by this Rule.

(4) Any application for the rescission of a winding-up order shall be made within 7 days after the date on which the order was made. **[1263]**

7.48. Appeals in bankruptcy

(1) In bankruptcy proceedings, an appeal lies at the instance of the Secretary of State from any order of the court made on an application for the rescission or annulment of a bankruptcy order, or for a bankrupt's discharge.

(2) In the case of an order made by a county court or by a registrar of the High Court, the appeal lies to a single judge of the High Court; and an appeal from a decision of that judge on such an appeal lies, with the leave of that judge or the Court of Appeal, to the Court of Appeal. **[1264]**

7.49. Procedure on appeal

(1) Subject as follows, the procedure and practice of the Supreme Court relating to appeals to the Court of Appeal apply to appeals in insolvency proceedings.

(2) In relation to any appeal to a single judge of the High Court under section 375(2) (individual insolvency) or Rule 7.47(2) above (company insolvency), any reference in the Rules of the Supreme court to the Court of Appeal is replaced by a reference to that judge.

(3) In insolvency proceedings, the procedure under Order 59 of the Rules of

the Supreme Court (appeal to the Court of Appeal) is by application, and not by summons.   **[1265]**

7.50. Appeal against decision of Secretary of State or official receiver

An appeal under the Act or the Rules against a decision of the Secretary of State or the official receiver shall be brought within 28 days of the notification of the decision.   **[1266]**

CHAPTER 9

GENERAL

7.51. Principal court rules and practice to apply

Except so far as inconsistent with the Insolvency Rules, the Rules of the Supreme Court and the practice of the High Court apply to insolvency proceedings in the High Court, and the County Court Rules and the practice of the county court apply to insolvency proceedings in a county court, in either case with any necessary modifications.   **[1267]**

7.52. Right of audience

(1) Official receivers and deputy official receivers have right of audience in insolvency proceedings, whether in the High Court or a county court.

(2) Subject as above, rights of audience in insolvency proceedings are the same as obtained before the coming into force of the Rules.   **[1268]**

7.53. Right of attendance (company insolvency)

(1) Subject as follows, in company insolvency proceedings any person stating himself in writing, in records kept by the court for that purpose, to be a creditor or member of the company or, where the company is being wound up, a contributory, is entitled, at his own cost, to attend in court or in chambers at any stage of the proceedings.

(2) Attendance may be by the person himself, or his solicitor.

(3) A person so entitled may request the court in writing to give him notice of any step in the proceedings; and, subject to his paying the costs involved and keeping the court informed as to his address, the court shall comply with the request.

(4) If the court is satisfied that the exercise by a person of his rights under this Rule has given rise to costs for the insolvent estate which would not otherwise have been incurred and ought not, in the circumstances, to fall on that estate, it may direct that the costs be paid by the person concerned, to an amount specified.

The person's rights under this Rule are in abeyance so long as those costs are not paid.

(5) The court may appoint one or more persons to represent the creditors, the members or the contributories of an insolvent company, or any class of them, to have the rights conferred by this Rule, instead of the rights being exercisable by any or all of them individually.

If two or more persons are appointed under this paragraph to represent the same interest, they must (if at all) instruct the same solicitor.   **[1269]**

7.54. Insolvency practitioner's solicitor

Where in any proceedings the attendance of the responsible insolvency practitioner's solicitor is required, whether in court or in chambers, the insolvency practitioner himself need not attend, unless directed by the court.

[1270]

7.55. Formal defects

No insolvency proceedings shall be invalidated by any formal defect or by any irregularity, unless the court before which objection is made considers that substantial injustice has been caused by the defect or irregularity, and that the injustice cannot be remedied by any order of the court. **[1271]**

7.56. Restriction on concurrent proceedings and remedies

Where in insolvency proceedings the court makes an order staying any action, execution or other legal process against the property of a company, or against the property or person of an individual debtor or bankrupt, service of the order may be effected by sending a sealed copy of the order to whatever is the address for service of the plaintiff or other party having the carriage of the proceedings to be stayed. **[1272]**

7.57. Affidavits

(1) Subject as follows, the rules and practice obtaining in the High Court with regard to affidavits, their form and contents, and the procedure governing their use, are to be taken as applicable in all insolvency proceedings in any court.

(2) In applying RSC Order 41 (which relates to affidavits generally), there are to be disregarded provisions which are inconsistent with, or necessarily excluded by, the following paragraphs of this Rule.

(3) Where in insolvency proceedings an affidavit is made by the official receiver or the responsible insolvency practitioner, the deponent shall state the capacity in which he makes it, the position which he holds, and the address at which he works.

(4) Notwithstanding RSC Order 41 Rule 8 (affidavit not to be sworn before party's own solicitor), a creditor's affidavit of debt may be sworn before his own solicitor.

(5) The official receiver, any deputy official receiver, or any officer of the court duly authorised in that behalf, may take affidavits and declarations.

[1273]

7.58. Security in court

(1) Where security has to be given to the court (otherwise than in relation to costs), it may be given by guarantee, bond or the payment of money into court.

(2) A person proposing to give a bond as security shall give notice to the party in whose favour the security is required, and to the court, naming those who are to be sureties to the bond.

(3) The court shall forthwith give notice to both the parties concerned of a venue for the execution of the bond and the making of any objection to the sureties.

(4) The sureties shall make an affidavit of their sufficiency (unless dispensed

with by the party in whose favour the security is required) and shall, if required
by the court, attend the court to be cross-examined.   **[1274]**

7.59. Payment into court

The Rules of the Supreme Court and the County Court Rules relating to
payment into and out of court of money lodged in court as security for costs
apply, in the High Court and a county court respectively, to money lodged in
court under the Rules.   **[1275]**

7.60. Discovery

(1) Any party to insolvency proceedings may, with the leave of the court,
administer interrogatories to, or obtain discovery from, any other party to those
proceedings.

(2) Application under this Rule may be made *ex parte*.   **[1276]**

7.61. Office copies of documents

(1) Any person who has under the Rules the right to inspect the court file of
insolvency proceedings may require the court to provide him with an office copy
of any document from the file.

(2) A person's rights under this Rule may be exercised on his behalf by his
solicitor.

(3) An office copy provided by the court under this Rule shall be in such
form as the registrar thinks appropriate, and shall bear the court's seal.   **[1277]**

PART 8
PROXIES AND COMPANY REPRESENTATION

8.1. Definition of "proxy"

(1) For the purposes of the Rules, a proxy is an authority given by a person
("the principal") to another person ("the proxy-holder") to attend a meeting
and speak and vote as his representative.

(2) Proxies are for use at creditors', company or contributories' meetings
under the Act or the Rules.

(3) Only one proxy may be given by a person for any one meeting at which
he desires to be represented; and it may only be given to one person, being an
individual aged 18 or over. But the principal may specify one or more other
such individuals to be proxy-holder in the alternative, in the order in which they
are named in the proxy.

(4) Without prejudice to the generality of paragraph (3), a proxy for a
particular meeting may be given to whoever is to be the chairman of the
meeting; and for a meeting held as part of the proceedings in a winding up by
the court, or in a bankruptcy, it may be given to the official receiver.

(5) A proxy requires the holder to give the principal's vote on matters
arising for determination at the meeting, or to abstain, either as directed or in
accordance with the holder's own discretion; and it may authorise or require
the holder to propose, in the principal's name, a resolution to be voted on by the
meeting.   **[1278]**

NOTES
See Sch 4, forms 8.1 to 8.5.

8.2. Issue and use of forms

(1) When notice is given of a meeting to be held in insolvency proceedings, and forms of proxy are sent out with the notice, no form so sent out shall have inserted in it the name or description of any person.

(2) No form of proxy shall be used at any meeting except that which is sent out with the notice summoning the meeting, or a substantially similar form.

(3) A form of proxy shall be signed by the principal, or by some person authorised by him (either generally or with reference to a particular meeting). If the form is signed by a person other than the principal, the nature of the person's authority shall be stated. **[1279]**

8.3. Use of proxies at meetings

(1) A proxy given for a particular meeting may be used at any adjournment of that meeting.

(2) Where the official receiver holds proxies for use at any meeting, his deputy, or any other official receiver, may act as proxy-holder in his place.

Alternatively, the official receiver may in writing authorise another officer of the Department to act for him at the meeting and use the proxies as if that other officer were himself proxy-holder.

(3) Where the responsible insolvency practitioner holds proxies to be used by him as chairman of a meeting, and some other person acts as chairman, the other person may use the insolvency practitioner's proxies as if he were himself proxy-holder. **[1280]**

8.4. Retention of proxies

(1) Subject as follows, proxies used for voting at any meeting shall be retained by the chairman of the meeting.

(2) The chairman shall deliver the proxies, forthwith after the meeting, to the responsible insolvency practitioner (where that is someone other than himself). **[1281]**

8.5. Right of inspection

(1) The responsible insolvency practitioner shall, so long as proxies lodged with him are in his hands, allow them to be inspected, at all reasonable times on any business day, by—

    (a) the creditors, in the case of proxies used at a meeting of creditors, and
    (b) a company's members or contributories, in the case of proxies used at a meeting of the company or of its contributories.

(2) The reference in paragraph (1) to creditors is—

    (a) in the case of a company in liquidation or of an individual's bankruptcy, those creditors who have proved their debts, and
    (b) in any other case, persons who have submitted in writing a claim to be creditors of the company or individual concerned;

but in neither case does it include a person whose proof or claim has been wholly rejected for purposes of voting, dividend or otherwise.

(3) The right of inspection given by this Rule is also exercisable—

(*a*) in the case of an insolvent company, by its directors, and
(*b*) in the case of an insolvent individual, by him.

(4) Any person attending a meeting in insolvency proceedings is entitled, immediately before or in the course of the meeting, to inspect proxies and associated documents to be used in connection with that meeting.   **[1282]**

8.6. Proxy-holder with financial interest

(1) A proxy-holder shall not vote in favour of any resolution which would directly or indirectly place him, or any associate of his, in a position to receive any remuneration out of the insolvent estate, unless the proxy specifically directs him to vote in that way.

(2) This Rule applies also to any person acting as chairman of a meeting and using proxies in that capacity; and in its application to him, the proxy-holder is deemed an associate of his.   **[1283]**

8.7. Company representation

(1) Where a person is authorised under section 375 of the Companies Act to represent a corporation at a meeting of creditors or of the company or its contributories, he shall produce to the chairman of the meeting a copy of the resolution from which he derives his authority.

(2) The copy resolution must be under the seal of the corporation, or certified by the secretary or a director of the corporation to be a true copy.   **[1284]**

PART 9

EXAMINATION OF PERSONS CONCERNED IN COMPANY AND INDIVIDUAL INSOLVENCY

9.1. Preliminary

(1) The Rules in this Part relate to applications to the court for an order under—

(*a*) section 236 (inquiry into company's dealings when it is, or is alleged to be, insolvent), or
(*b*) section 366 (inquiry in bankruptcy, with respect to the bankrupt's dealings).

(2) The following definitions apply—

(*a*) the person in respect of whom an order is applied for is "the respondent";
(*b*) "the applicable section" is section 236 or section 366, according to whether the affairs of a company or those of a bankrupt or (where the application under section 366 is made by virtue of section 368) a debtor are in question;
(*c*) the company or, as the case may be, the bankrupt or debtor concerned is "the insolvent".   **[1285]**

NOTES
See Sch 4, form 9.1.

9.2. Form and contents of application

(1) The application shall be in writing, and be accompanied by a brief statement of the grounds on which it is made.

(2) The respondent must be sufficiently identified in the application.

(3) It shall be stated whether the application is for the respondent—
- (*a*) to be ordered to appear before the court, or
- (*b*) to answer interrogatories (if so, particulars to be given of the matters in respect of which answers are required), or
- (*c*) to submit affidavits (if so, particulars to be given of the matters to which he is required to swear), or
- (*d*) to produce books, papers or other records (if so, the items in question to be specified),

or for any two or more of those purposes.

(4) The application may be made *ex parte*. **[1286]**

9.3. Order for examination, etc

(1) The court may, whatever the purpose of the application, make any order which it has power to make under the applicable section.

(2) The court, if it orders the respondent to appear before it, shall specify a venue for his appearance, which shall be not less than 14 days from the date of the order.

(3) If he is ordered to submit affidavits, the order shall specify—
- (*a*) the matters which are to be dealt with in his affidavits, and
- (*b*) the time within which they are to be submitted to the court.

(4) If the order is to produce books, papers or other records, the time and manner of compliance shall be specified.

(5) The order must be served forthwith on the respondent; and it must be served personally, unless the court otherwise orders. **[1287]**

9.4. Procedure for examination

(1) At any examination of the respondent, the applicant may attend in person, or be represented by a solicitor with or without counsel, and may put such questions to the respondent as the court may allow.

(2) Any other person who could have applied for an order under the applicable section in respect of the insolvent's affairs may, with the leave of the court and if the applicant does not object, attend the examination and put questions to the respondent (but only through the applicant).

(3) If the respondent is ordered to answer interrogatories, the court shall direct him as to the questions which he is required to answer, and as to whether his answers (if any) are to be made on affidavit.

(4) Where application has been made under the applicable section on information provided by a creditor of the insolvent, that creditor may, with the leave of the court and if the applicant does not object, attend the examination and put questions to the respondent (but only through the applicant).

(5) The respondent may at his own expense employ a solicitor with or without counsel, who may put to him such questions as the court may allow for

the purpose of enabling him to explain or qualify any answers given by him, and may make representations on his behalf.

(6) There shall be made in writing such record of the examination as the court thinks proper. The record shall be read over either to or by the respondent and signed by him at a venue fixed by the court.

(7) The written record may, in any proceedings (whether under the Act or otherwise) be used as evidence against the respondent of any statement made by him in the course of his examination. **[1288]**

9.5. Record of examination

(1) Unless the court otherwise directs, the written record of the respondent's examination, and any answer given by him to interrogatories, and any affidavits submitted by him in compliance with an order of the court under the applicable section, shall not be filed in court.

(2) The written record, answers and affidavits shall not be open to inspection, without an order of the court, by any person other than—

(a) the applicant for an order under the applicable section, or

(b) any person who could have applied for such an order in respect of the affairs of the same insolvent.

(3) Paragraph (2) applies also to so much of the court file as shows the grounds of the application for an order under the applicable section and to any copy of proposed interrogatories.

(4) The court may from time to time give directions as to the custody and inspection of any documents to which this Rule applies, and as to the furnishing of copies of, or extracts from, such documents. **[1289]**

9.6. Costs of proceedings under ss 236, 366

(1) Where the court has ordered an examination of any person under the applicable section, and it appears to it that the examination was made necessary because information had been unjustifiably refused by the respondent, it may order that the costs of the examination be paid by him.

(2) Where the court makes an order against a person under—

(a) section 237(1) or 367(1) (to deliver up property in his possession which belongs to the insolvent), or

(b) section 237(2) or 367(2) (to pay any amount in discharge of a debt due to the insolvent).

the costs of the application for the order may be ordered by the court to be paid by the respondent.

(3) Subject to paragraphs (1) and (2) above, the applicant's costs shall, unless the court otherwise orders, be paid out of the insolvent estate.

(4) A person summoned to attend for examination under this Chapter shall be tendered a reasonable sum in respect of travelling expenses incurred in connection with his attendance. Other costs falling on him are at the court's discretion.

(5) Where the examination is on the application of the official receiver otherwise than in the capacity of liquidator or trustee, no order shall be made for the payment of costs by him. **[1290]**

PART 10

OFFICIAL RECEIVERS

10.1. Appointment of official receivers

Judicial notice shall be taken of the appointment under sections 399 to 401 of official receivers and deputy official receivers **[1291]**

10.2. Persons entitled to act on official receiver's behalf

(1) In the absence of the official receiver authorised to act in a particular case, an officer authorised in writing for the purpose by the Secretary of State, or by the official receiver himself, may, with the leave of the court, act on the official receiver's behalf and in his place—

    (a) in any examination under section 133, 236, 290 or 366, and
    (b) in respect of any application to the court.

    (2) In case of emergency, where there is no official receiver capable of acting, anything to be done by, to or before the official receiver may be done by, to or before the registrar of the court. **[1292]**

10.3. Application for directions

The official receiver may apply to the court for directions in relation to any matter arising in insolvency proceedings **[1293]**

10.4. Official receiver's expenses

(1) Any expenses incurred by the official receiver (in whatever capacity he may be acting) in connection with proceedings taken against him in insolvency proceedings are to be treated as expenses of the insolvency proceedings.

    "Expenses" includes damages.

    (2) In respect of any sums due to him under paragraph (1), the official receiver has a charge on the insolvent estate. **[1294]**

PART 11

DECLARATION AND PAYMENT OF DIVIDEND
(WINDING UP AND BANKRUPTCY)

11.1. Preliminary

(1) The Rules in this Part relate to the declaration and payment of dividends in companies winding up and in bankruptcy.

    (2) The following definitions apply—

    (a) "the insolvent" means the company in liquidation or, as the case may be, the bankrupt; and
    (b) "creditors" means those creditors of the insolvent of whom the responsible insolvency practitioner is aware, or who are identified in the insolvent's statement of affairs **[1295]**

11.2. Notice of intended dividend

(1) Before declaring a dividend, the responsible insolvency practitioner shall give notice of his intention to do so to all creditors who have not proved their debts.

(2) The notice shall specify a date ("the last date for proving") up to which proofs may be lodged. The date shall be the same for all creditors, and not less than 21 days from that of the notice.

(3) The insolvency practitioner shall in the notice state his intention to declare a dividend (specified as interim or final, as the case may be) within the period of 4 months from the last date for proving.   **[1296]**

11.3. Final admission/rejection of proofs

(1) The responsible insolvency practitioner, shall within 7 days from the last date of proving, deal with every creditor's proof (in so far as not already dealt with) by admitting or rejecting it in whole or in part, or by making such provision as he thinks fit in respect of it.

(2) The insolvency practitioner is not obliged to deal with proofs lodged after the last date for proving; but he may do so, if he thinks fit.   **[1297]**

11.4. Postponement or cancellation of dividend

If in the period of 4 months referred to in Rule 11.2(3)—

- (a) the responsible insolvency practitioner has rejected a proof in whole or in part and application is made to the court for his decision to be reversed or varied, or
- (b) application is made to the court for the insolvency practitioner's decision on a proof to be reversed or varied, or for a proof to be expunged, or for a reduction of the amount claimed,

the insolvency practitioner may postpone or cancel the dividend.   **[1298]**

11.5. Decision to declare dividend

(1) If the responsible insolvency practitioner has not, in the 4-month period referred to in Rule 11.2(3), had cause to postpone or cancel the dividend, he shall within that period proceed to declare the dividend of which he gave notice under that Rule.

(2) Except with the leave of the court, the insolvency practitioner shall not declare the dividend so long as there is pending any application to the court to reverse or vary a decision of his on a proof, or to expunge a proof or to reduce the amount claimed.

If the court gives leave under this paragraph, the insolvency practitioner shall make such provision in respect of the proof in question as the court directs.

[1299]

11.6. Notice of declaration

(1) The responsible insolvency practitioner shall give notice of the dividend to all creditors who have proved their debts.

(2) The notice shall include the following particulars relating to the insolvency and the administration of the insolvent estate—

- (a) amounts realised from the sale of assets, indicating (so far as practicable) amounts raised by the sale of particular assets;
- (b) payments made by the insolvency practitioner in the administration of the insolvent estate;
- (c) provision (if any) made for the unsettled claims, and funds (if any) retained for particular purposes;

(*d*) the total amount to be distributed, and the rate of dividend;
(*e*) whether, and if so when, any further dividend is expected to be declared.

(3) The dividend may be distributed simultaneously with the notice declaring it.

(4) Payment of dividend may be made by post, or arrangements may be made with any creditor for it to be paid to him in another way, or held for his collection.

(5) Where a dividend is paid on a bill of exchange or other negotiable instrument, the amount of the dividend shall be endorsed on the instrument, or on a certified copy of it, if required to be produced by the holder for that purpose. **[1300]**

11.7. Notice of no, or no further, dividend

If the responsible insolvency practitioner gives notice to creditors that he is unable to declare any dividend or (as the case may be) any further dividend, the notice shall contain a statement to the effect either—

(*a*) that no funds have been realised, or
(*b*) that the funds realised have already been distributed or used or allocated for defraying the expenses of administration. **[1301]**

11.8. Proof altered after payment of dividend

(1) If after payment of dividend the amount claimed by a creditor in his proof is increased, the creditor is not entitled to disturb the distribution of the dividend; but he is entitled to be paid, out of any money for the time being available for the payment of any further dividend, any dividend or dividends which he has failed to receive.

(2) Any dividend or dividends payable under paragraph (1) shall be paid before the money there referred to is applied to the payment of any such further dividend.

(3) If, after a creditor's proof has been admitted, the proof is withdrawn or expunged, or the amount of it is reduced, the creditor is liable to repay to the responsible insolvency practitioner, for the credit of the insolvent estate, any amount overpaid by way of dividend. **[1302]**

11.9. Secured creditors

(1) The following applies where a creditor re-values his security at a time when a dividend has been declared.

(2) If the revaluation results in a reduction of his unsecured claim ranking for dividend, the creditor shall forthwith repay to the responsible insolvency practitioner, for the credit of the insolvent estate, any amount received by him as dividend in excess of that to which he would be entitled having regard to the revaluation of the security.

(3) If the revaluation results in an increase of his unsecured claim, the creditor is entitled to receive from the insolvency practitioner, out of any money for the time being available for the payment of a further dividend, before any such further dividend is paid, any dividend or dividends which he has failed to receive, having regard to the revaluation of the security.

However, the creditor is not entitled to disturb any dividend declared (whether or not distributed) before the date of the revaluation.   **[1303]**

11.10. Disqualification from dividend

If a creditor contravenes any provision of the Act or the Rules relating to the valuation of securities, the court may, on the application of the responsible insolvency practitioner, order that the creditor be wholly or partly disqualified from participation in any dividend.   **[1304]**

11.11. Assignment of right to dividend

(1) If a person entitled to a dividend gives notice to the responsible insolvency practitioner that he wishes the dividend to be paid to another person, or that he has assigned his entitlement to another person, the insolvency practitioner shall pay the dividend to that other accordingly.

(2) A notice given under this Rule must specify the name and address of the person to whom payment is to be made.   **[1305]**

11.12 Preferential creditors

(1) Subject as follows, the Rules in this Part apply with respect to any distribution made in the insolvency to preferential creditors, with such adaptations as are appropriate considering that such creditors are of a limited class.

(2) The notice by the responsible insolvency practitioner under Rule 11.2, where a dividend is to be declared for preferential creditors, need only be given to those creditors in whose case he has reason to believe that their debts are preferential.   **[1306]**

11.13. Debt payable at future time

(1) Where a creditor has proved for a debt of which payment is not due at the date of the declaration of dividend, he is entitled to dividend equally with other creditors, but subject as follows.

(2) For the purpose of dividend (and for no other purpose), the amount of the creditor's admitted proof (or, if a distribution has previously been made to him, the amount remaining outstanding in respect of his admitted proof) shall be reduced by an amount calculated as follows—

$$\frac{I \times M}{12}$$

where I is 5 per cent and M is the number of months (expressed, if need be, as, or as including, fractions of months) between the declaration of dividend and the date when payment of the creditor's debt would otherwise be due.

(3) Other creditors are not entitled to interest out of surplus funds under section 189(2) or (as the case may be) 328(4) until any creditor to whom paragraphs (1) and (2) apply has been paid the full amount of his debt.   **[1307]**

PART 12

MISCELLANEOUS AND GENERAL

12.1. Power of Secretary of State to regulate certain matters

(1) Pursuant to paragraph 27 of Schedule 8 to the Act, and paragraph 30 of Schedule 9 to the Act, the Secretary of State may make regulations with respect

to the following matters arising in companies winding up and individual bankruptcy—

   (*a*) the preparation and keeping by liquidators, trustees, provisional liquidators, interim receivers and the official receiver, of books, accounts and other records, and their production to such persons as may be authorised or required to inspect them;
   (*b*) the auditing of liquidators' and trustees' accounts;
   (*c*) the manner in which liquidators and trustees are to act in relation to the insolvent company's or bankrupt's books, papers and other records, and the manner of their disposal by the responsible insolvency practitioner or others;
   (*d*) the supply—
      (i) in company insolvency, by the liquidator to creditors and members of the company, contributories in its winding up and the liquidation committee, and
      (ii) in individual insolvency, by the trustee to creditors and the creditors' committee,

   of copies of documents relating to the insolvency and the affairs of the insolvent company or individual (on payment, in such cases as may be specified by the regulations, of the specified fee);
   (*e*) the manner in which insolvent estates are to be distributed by liquidators and trustees, including provision with respect to unclaimed funds and dividends;
   (*f*) the manner in which moneys coming into the hands of a liquidator or trustee in the course of his administration are to be handled and, in the case of a liquidator, invested, and the payment of interest on sums which, in pursuance of regulations made by virtue of this sub-paragraph, have been paid into the Insolvency Services Account;
   (*g*) the amount (or the manner of determining the amount) to be paid to the official receiver by way of remuneration when acting as provisional liquidator, liquidator, interim receiver or trustee.

(2) Any reference in paragraph (1) to a trustee includes a reference to the official receiver when acting as receiver and manager under section 287.

(3) Regulations made pursuant to paragraph (1) may—

   (*a*) confer a discretion on the court;
   (*b*) make non-compliance with any of the regulations a criminal offence;
   (*c*) make different provision for different cases, including different provision for different areas. **[1308]**

12.2. Costs, expenses, etc

All fees, costs, charges and other expenses incurred in the course of winding up or bankruptcy proceedings are to be regarded as expenses of the winding up or, as the case may be, of the bankruptcy. **[1309]**

12.3. Provable debts

(1) Subject as follows, in both winding up and bankruptcy, all claims by creditors are provable as debts against the company or, as the case may be, the bankrupt, whether they are present or future, certain or contingent, ascertained or sounding only in damages.

(2) The following are not provable—

(*a*) in bankruptcy, any fine imposed for an offence, and any obligation arising under an order made in family or domestic proceedings;

(*b*) in winding up or bankruptcy, any obligation arising under a confiscation order made under section 1 of the Drug Trafficking Offences Act 1986.

"Fine", domestic proceedings" and "family proceedings" have the meanings given by section 281(8) of the Act (which applies the Magistrates' Courts Act 1980 and the Matrimonial and Family Proceedings Act 1984).

(3) Nothing in this Rule prejudices any enactment or rule of law under which a particular kind of debt is not provable, whether on grounds of public policy or otherwise.   **[1310]**

12.4. Notices

(1) All notices required or authorised by or under the Act or the Rules to be given must be in writing, unless it is otherwise provided, or the court allows the notice to be given in some other way.

(2) Where in any proceedings a notice is required to be sent or given by the official receiver or by the responsible insolvency practitioner, the sending or giving of it may be proved by means of a certificate—

(*a*) in the case of the official receiver, by him or a member of his staff, and

(*b*) in the case of the insolvency practitioner, by him, or his solicitor, or a partner or an employee of either of them,

that the notice was duly posted.

(3) In the case of a notice to be sent or given by a person other than the official receiver or insolvency practitioner, the sending or giving of it may be proved by means of a certificate by that person that he posted the notice, or instructed another person (naming him) to do so.

(4) A certificate under this Rule may be endorsed on a copy or specimen of the notice to which it relates.   **[1311]**

12.5. Evidence of proceedings at meetings

(1) A minute of proceedings at a meeting (held under the Act or the Rules) of a person's creditors, or of the members of a company, or of the contributories in a company's liquidation, signed by a person describing himself as, or appearing to be, the chairman of that meeting is admissible in insolvency proceedings without further proof.

(2) The minute is prima facie evidence that—

(*a*) the meeting was duly convened and held,

(*b*) all resolutions passed at the meeting were duly passed, and

(*c*) all proceedings at the meeting duly took place.   **[1312]**

12.6. Documents issuing from Secretary of State

(1) Any document purporting to be, or to contain, any order, directions or certificate issued by the Secretary of State shall be received in evidence and deemed to be or (as the case may be) contain that order or certificate, or those directions, without further proof, unless the contrary is shown.

(2) Paragraph (1) applies whether the document is signed by the Secretary of State himself or an officer on his behalf.

(3) Without prejudice to the foregoing, a certificate signed by the Secretary of State or an officer on his behalf and confirming—

    (*a*) the making of any order,

    (*b*) the issuing of any document, or

    (*c*) the exercise of any discretion, power or obligation arising or imposed under the Act or the Rules,

is conclusive evidence of the matters dealt with in the certificate. **[1313]**

12.7. Forms for use in insolvency proceedings

(1) The forms contained in Schedule 4 to the Rules shall be used in and in connection with, insolvency proceedings, whether in the High Court or a county court.

(2) The forms shall be used with such variations, if any, as the circumstances may require.

(3) Where any form contained in Schedule 4 is substantially the same as one used for a corresponding purpose under the law and practice obtaining before the coming into force of the Rules, the latter may continue to be used (with the necessary modifications) until the Lord Chancellor otherwise directs. **[1314]**

12.8. Insolvency practitioner's security

(1) Wherever under the Rules any person has to appoint, or certify the appointment of, an insolvency practitioner to any office, he is under a duty to satisfy himself that the person appointed or to be appointed has security for the proper performance of his functions.

(2) It is the duty—

    (*a*) of the creditors' committee in companies administration, administrative receivership and bankruptcy,

    (*b*) of the liquidation committee in companies winding up, and

    (*c*) of any committee of creditors established for the purposes of a voluntary arrangement under Part I or VIII of the Act,

to review from time to time the adequacy of the responsible insolvency practitioner's security.

(3) In any insolvency proceedings the cost of the responsible insolvency practitioner's security shall be defrayed as an expense of the proceedings. **[1315]**

12.9. Time-limits

The provisions of Order 3 of the Rules of the Supreme Court, except Rules 3 and 6, apply as regards computation of time in respect of anything required or authorised by the Rules to be done. **[1316]**

12.10. Service by post

(1) For a document to be properly served by post, it must be contained in an envelope addressed to the person on whom service is to be effected, and pre-paid for either first or second class post.

(2) Where first class post is used, the document is treated as served on the second business day after the date of posting, unless the contrary is shown.

(3) Where second class post is used, the document is treated as served on the fourth business day after the date of posting, unless the contrary is shown.

(4) The date of posting is presumed, unless the contrary is shown, to be the date shown in the post-mark on the envelope in which the document is contained.   **[1317]**

12.11. General provisions as to service

(1) Subject as follows, Order 65 of the Rules of the Supreme Court applies as regards any matter relating to the service of documents and the giving of notice in insolvency proceedings.

(2) In Order 65 Rule 7, the expression "other originating process" does not include any application in insolvency proceedings.

(3) Order 65 Rule 9 does not apply.

(4) In Order 65 Rule 10, the expression "process" includes any application in insolvency proceedings.   **[1318]**

12.12. Service outside the jurisdiction

(1) Order 11 of the Rules of the Supreme Court, and the corresponding County Court Rules, do not apply in insolvency proceedings.

(2) A bankruptcy petition may, with the leave of the court, be served outside England and Wales in such manner as the court may direct.

(3) Where for the purposes of insolvency proceedings any process or order of the court, or other document, is required to be served on a person who is not in England and Wales, the court may order service to be effected within such time, on such person, at such place and in such manner as it thinks fit, and may also require such proof of service as it thinks fit.

(4) An application under this Rule shall be supported by an affidavit stating—
   (*a*) the grounds on which the application is made, and
   (*b*) in what place or country the person to be served is, or probably may be found.   **[1319]**

12.13. Confidentiality of documents

(1) Where in insolvency proceedings the responsible insolvency practitioner considers, in the case of a document forming part of the records of the insolvency, that—
   (*a*) it should be treated as confidential, or
   (*b*) it is of such a nature that its disclosure would be calculated to be injurious to the interests of the insolvent's creditors or, in the case of a company's insolvency, its members or the contributories in its winding up,
he may decline to allow it to be inspected by a person who would otherwise be entitled to inspect it.

(2) The persons to whom the insolvency practitioner may under this Rule refuse inspection include the members of a liquidation committee or a creditors' committee.

(3) Where under this Rule the insolvency practitioner determines to refuse

inspection of a document, the person wishing to inspect it may apply to the court for that determination to be overruled; and the court may either overrule it altogether, or sustain it subject to such conditions (if any) as it thinks fit to impose. **[1320]**

12.14. Notices sent simultaneously to the same person

Where under the Act or the Rules a document of any description is to be sent to a person (whether or not as a member of a class of persons to whom that same document is to be sent), it may be sent as an accompaniment to any other document or information which the person is to receive, with or without modification or adaptation of the form applicable to that document. **[1321]**

12.15. Right to copy documents

Where the Rules confer a right for any person to inspect documents, the right includes that of taking copies of those documents, on payment—

(*a*) in the case of documents on the court's file of proceedings, of the fee chargeable under any order made under section 130 of the Supreme Court Act 1981 or under section 128 of the County Courts Act 1984, and

(*b*) otherwise, of the appropriate fee. **[1322]**

12.16. Non-receipt of notice of meeting

Where in accordance with the Act or the Rules a meeting of creditors or other persons is summoned by notice, the meeting is presumed to have been duly summoned and held, notwithstanding that not all those to whom the notice is to be given have received it. **[1323]**

12.17. Right to have list of creditors

(1) This Rule applies in any of the following proceedings—

(*a*) proceedings under Part II of the Act (company administration),
(*b*) a creditors' voluntary winding up, or a winding up by the court, and
(*c*) proceedings in bankruptcy.

(2) In any such proceedings a creditor who under the Rules has the right to inspect documents on the court file also has the right to require the responsible insolvency practitioner to furnish him with a list of the insolvent's creditors and the amounts of their respective debts.

This does not apply if a statement of the insolvent's affairs has been filed in court or, in the case of a creditors' voluntary winding up, been delivered to the registrar of companies.

(3) The insolvency practitioner, on being required by any person to furnish the list, shall send it to him, but is entitled to charge the appropriate fee for doing so. **[1324]**

12.18. False claim of status as creditor, etc

(1) Where the Rules provide for creditors, members of a company or contributories in a company's winding up a right to inspect any documents, whether on the court's file or in the hands of a responsible insolvency practitioner or other person, it is an offence for a person, with the intention of obtaining a sight of documents which he has not under the Rules any right to inspect, falsely to claim a status which would entitle him to inspect them.

(2) A person guilty of an offence under this Rule is liable to imprisonment or a fine, or both.   **[1325]**

12.19. Execution overtaken by judgment debtor's insolvency

(1) This Rule applies where execution has been taken out against property of a judgment debtor, and notice is given to the sheriff or other officer charged with the execution—

    (*a*) under section 184(1) (that a winding-up order has been made against the debtor, or that a provisional liquidator has been appointed, or that a resolution for voluntary winding up has been passed); or

    (*b*) under section 184(4) (that a winding-up petition has been presented or a winding-up order made, or that a meeting has been called at which there is to be proposed a resolution for voluntary winding up, or that such a resolution has been passed); or

    (*c*) under section 346(2) (that the judgment debtor has been adjudged bankrupt); or

    (*d*) under section 346(3)(*b*) (that a bankruptcy petition has been presented in respect of him).

(2) Subject as follows, the notice shall be in writing and be delivered by hand, at, or sent by recorded delivery to, the office of the under-sheriff or (as the case may be) of the officer charged with the execution.

(3) Where the execution is in a county court, and the officer in charge of it is the registrar of that court, then if—

    (*a*) there is filed in that court in respect of the judgment debtor a winding-up or bankruptcy petition, or

    (*b*) there is made by that court in respect of him a winding-up order or an order appointing a provisional liquidator, or a bankruptcy order or an order appointing an interim receiver,

section 184 or (as the case may be) 346 is deemed satisfied as regards the requirement of a notice to be served on, or given to, the officer in charge of the execution.   **[1326]**

12.20. The Gazette

(1) A copy of the Gazette containing any notice required by the Act or the Rules to be gazetted is evidence of any facts stated in the notice.

(2) In the case of an order of the court notice of which is required by the Act or the Rules to be gazetted, a copy of the Gazette containing the notice may in any proceedings be produced as conclusive evidence that the order was made on the date specified in the notice.

(3) Where an order of the court which is gazetted has been varied, and where any matter has been erroneously or inaccurately gazetted, the person whose responsibility it was to procure the requisite entry in the Gazette shall forthwith cause the variation of the order to be gazetted or, as the case may be, a further entry to be made in the Gazette for the purpose of correcting the error or inaccuracy.   **[1327]**

12.21. Punishment of offences

(1) Schedule 5 to the Rules has effect with respect to the way in which contraventions of the Rules are punishable on conviction.

(2) In relation to an offence under a provision of the Rules specified in the first column of the Schedule (the general nature of the offence being described in the second column), the third column shows whether the offence is punishable on conviction on indictment, or on summary conviction, or either in the one way or the other.

(3) The fourth column shows, in relation to an offence, the maximum punishment by way of fine or imprisonment which may be imposed on a person convicted of the offence in the way specified in relation to it in the third column (that is to say, on indictment or summarily), a reference to a period of years or months being to a term of imprisonment of that duration.

(4) The fifth column shows (in relation to an offence for which there is an entry in that column) that a person convicted of the offence after continued contravention is liable to a daily default fine; that is to say, he is liable on a second or subsequent conviction of the offence to the fine specified in that column for each day on which the contravention is continued (instead of the penalty specified for the offence in the fourth column of the Schedule).

(5) Section 431 (summary proceedings), as it applies to England and Wales, has effect in relation to offences under the Rules as to offences under the Act.

[1328]

PART 13

INTERPRETATION AND APPLICATION

13.1. Introductory

This Part of the Rules has effect for their interpretation and application; and any definition given in this Part applies except, and in so far as, the context otherwise requires.   **[1329]**

13.2. "The court"; "the registrar"

(1) Anything to be done under or by virtue of the Act or the Rules by, to or before the court may be done by, to or before a judge or the registrar.

(2) The registrar may authorise any act of a formal or administrative character which is not by statute his responsibility to be carried out by the chief clerk or any other officer of the court acting on his behalf, in accordance with directions given by the Lord Chancellor.

(3) In individual insolvency proceedings, "the registrar" means a Registrar in Bankruptcy of the High Court, or the registrar or deputy registrar of a county court.

(4) In company insolvency proceedings in the High Court, "the registrar" means—

  (a) subject to the following paragraph, a Registrar in Bankruptcy of the High Court;
  (b) where the proceedings are in the District Registry of Birmingham, Bristol, Cardiff, Leeds, Liverpool, Manchester, Newcastle-upon-Tyne or Preston, the District Registrar.

(5) In company insolvency proceedings in a county court, "the registrar" means the officer of the court whose duty it is to exercise the functions which in the High Court are exercised by a registrar.   **[1330]**

13.3. "Give notice", etc

(1) A reference in the Rules to giving notice, or to delivering, sending or serving any document, means that the notice or document may be sent by post, unless under a particular Rule personal service is expressly required.

(2) Any form of post may be used, unless under a particular Rule a specified form is expressly required.

(3) Personal service of a document is permissible in all cases.

(4) Notice of the venue fixed for an application may be given by service of the sealed copy of the application under Rule 7.4(3). **[1331]**

13.4. Notice, etc to solicitors

Where under the Act or the Rules a notice or other document is required or authorised to be given to a person, it may, if he has indicated that his solicitor is authorised to accept service on his behalf, be given instead to the solicitor. **[1332]**

13.5. Notice to joint liquidators, joint trustees, etc

Where two or more persons are acting jointly as the responsible insolvency practitioner in any proceedings, delivery of a document to one of them is to be treated as delivery to them all. **[1333]**

13.6. "Venue"

References to the "venue" for any proceeding or attendance before the court, or for a meeting, are to the time, date and place for the proceeding, attendance or meeting. **[1334]**

13.7. "Insolvency proceedings"

"Insolvency proceedings" means any proceedings under the Act or the Rules. **[1335]**

13.8. "Insolvent estate"

References to "the insolvent estate" are—

- (*a*) in relation to a company insolvency, the company's assets, and
- (*b*) in relation to an individual insolvency, the bankrupt's estate or (as the case may be) the debtor's property. **[1336]**

13.9. "Responsible insolvency practitioner", etc

(1) In relation to any insolvency proceedings, "the responsible insolvency practitioner" means—

- (*a*) the person acting in a company insolvency, as supervisor of a voluntary arrangement under Part I of the Act, or as administrator, administrative receiver, liquidator or provisional liquidator;
- (*b*) the person acting in an individual insolvency, as the supervisor of a voluntary arrangement under Part VIII of the Act, or as trustee or interim receiver;
- (*c*) the official receiver acting as receiver and manager of a bankrupt's estate.

(2) Any reference to the liquidator, provisional liquidator, trustee or interim

receiver includes the official receiver when acting in the relevant capacity.

13.10. "Petitioner"

In winding up and bankruptcy, references to "the petitioner" or "the petitioning creditor" include any person who has been substituted as such, or been given carriage of the petition. **[1338]**

13.11. "The appropriate fee"

"The appropriate fee" means—

    (*a*) in Rule 6.192(2) (payor under income payments order entitled to clerical etc costs), 50 pence; and

    (*b*) in other cases, 15 pence per A4 or A5 page, and 30 pence per A3 page. **[1339]**

13.12. "Debt", "liability" (winding up)

(1) "Debt", in relation to the winding up of a company, means (subject to the next paragraph) any of the following—

    (*a*) any debt or liability to which the company is subject at the date on which it goes into liquidation;

    (*b*) any debt or liability to which the company may become subject after that date by reason of any obligation incurred before that date; and

    (*c*) any interest provable as mentioned in rule 4.93(1).

(2) In determining for the purposes of any provision of the Act or the Rules about winding up, whether any liability in tort is a debt provable in the winding up, the company is deemed to become subject to that liability by reason of an obligation incurred at the time when the cause of action accrued.

(3) For the purposes of references in any provision of the Act or the Rules about winding up to a debt or liability, it is immaterial whether the debt or liability is present or future, whether it is certain or contingent, or whether its amount is fixed or liquidated, or is capable of being ascertained by fixed rules or as a matter of opinion; and references in any such provision to owing a debt are to be read accordingly.

(4) In any provision of the Act or the Rules about winding up, except in so far as the context otherwise requires, "liability" means (subject to paragraph (3) above) a liability to pay money or money's worth, including any liability under an enactment, any liability for breach of trust, any liability in contract, tort or bailment, and any liability arising out of an obligation to make restitution. **[1340]**

13.13. Expressions used generally

(1) "Business day"—

    (*a*) in relation to the High Court has the same meaning as in Order 65, Rule 5(4) of the Rules of the Supreme Court, and

    (*b*) in relation to a county court means any day on which the court office is open in accordance with Order 2, Rule 2 of the County Court Rules.

(2) "The Department" means the Department of Trade and Industry.

(3) "File in court" means deliver to the court for filing.

(4) "The Gazette" means the London Gazette.

(5) "General regulations" means regulations made by the Secretary of State under Rule 12.1.

(6) "Prescribed order of priority" means the order of priority of payments laid down by Chapter 20 of Part 4 of the Rules, or Chapter 23 of Part 6.   **[1341]**

13.14. Application

(1) Subject to paragraph (2) of this Rule, and save where otherwise expressly provided, the Rules apply—
- (a) to administrative receivers appointed on or after the day on which the Rules come into force,
- (b) to bankruptcy proceedings where the bankruptcy petition is presented on or after the day on which the Rules come into force, and
- (c) to all other insolvency proceedings commenced on or after that day.

(2) The Rules also apply to winding-up and bankruptcy proceedings commenced before that day to which provisions of the Act are applied by Schedule 11 to the Act, to the extent necessary to give effect to those provisions.   **[1342]**

SCHEDULE 1

Rule 4.72(7)

DEPOSIT PROTECTION BOARD'S VOTING RIGHTS

1. This Schedule applies as does rule 4.72.

2. In relation to any meeting at which the Deposit Protection Board is under Rule 4.72 entitled to be represented, the Board may submit in the liquidation, instead of a proof, a written statement of voting rights ("the statement").

3. The statement shall contain details of—
- (a) the names of creditors of the company in respect of whom an obligation of the Board has arisen or may reasonably be expected to arise as a result of the liquidation or proposed liquidation;
- (b) the amount of the obligation so arising; and
- (c) the total amount of all such obligations specified in the statement.

4. The Board's statement shall, for the purpose of voting at a meeting (but for no other purpose), be treated in all respects as if it were a proof.

5. Any voting rights which a creditor might otherwise exercise at a meeting in respect of a claim against the company are reduced by a sum equal to the amount of that claim in relation to which the Board, by virtue of its having submitted a statement, is entitled to exercise voting rights at that meeting.

6. The Board may from time to time submit a further statement, and, if it does so, that statement supersedes any statement previously submitted.   **[1343]**

SCHEDULE 2

Rule 6.40(3)

ALTERNATIVE COURTS FOR DEBTORS' PETITIONS IN BANKRUPTCY

Debtor's own county court	*Nearest full-time court*
ABERDARE	CARDIFF
ABERYSTWYTH	CARDIFF
ASHTON UNDER LYNE & STALYBRIDGE	MANCHESTER

Debtor's own county court	*Nearest full-time court*
AYLESBURY	LUTON
BANBURY	LUTON or GLOUCESTER
BANGOR	BIRKENHEAD
BARNSLEY	SHEFFIELD
BARNSTAPLE	EXETER
BARROW IN FURNESS	BLACKPOOL
BATH	BRISTOL
BEDFORD	LUTON
BLACKBURN	PRESTON
BLACKWOOD	CARDIFF
BOSTON	NOTTINGHAM
BRIDGEND	CARDIFF
BRIDGWATER	BRISTOL
BURNLEY	BOLTON or PRESTON
BURTON ON TRENT	LEICESTER
BURY ST. EDMUNDS	CAMBRIDGE
CANTERBURY	CROYDON or ROMFORD
CARLISLE	PRESTON or BLACKPOOL
CARMARTHEN	CARDIFF
CHELMSFORD	SOUTHEND
CHELTENHAM	GLOUCESTER
CHESTER	BIRKENHEAD
CHESTERFIELD	SHEFFIELD
COLCHESTER	SOUTHEND
COVENTRY	BIRMINGHAM
CREWE	STOKE
DARLINGTON	MIDDLESBOROUGH
DERBY	NOTTINGHAM
DEWSBURY	LEEDS
DONCASTER	SHEFFIELD
DUDLEY	BIRMINGHAM
DURHAM	NEWCASTLE
EASTBOURNE	BRIGHTON
GREAT GRIMSBY	HULL
GREAT YARMOUTH	NORWICH
GUILDFORD	CROYDON
HALIFAX	LEEDS
HARROGATE	LEEDS
HASTINGS	BRIGHTON
HAVERFORDWEST	CARDIFF
HEREFORD	GLOUCESTER
HERTFORD	LUTON
HUDDERSFIELD	LEEDS
IPSWICH	NORWICH or SOUTHEND
KENDAL	BLACKPOOL

Debtor's own county court	*Nearest full-time court*
KIDDERMINSTER	BIRMINGHAM
KING'S LYNN	NORWICH
LANCASTER	BLACKPOOL
LEOMINSTER	GLOUCESTER
LINCOLN	NOTTINGHAM
MACCLESFIELD	STOKE
MAIDSTONE	CROYDON
MEDWAY	CROYDON
MERTHYR TYDFIL	CARDIFF
MILTON KEYNES	LUTON
NEATH	CARDIFF
NEWBURY	READING
NEWPORT (GWENT)	CARDIFF
NEWPORT (I.O.W.)	SOUTHAMPTON
NORTHAMPTON	LUTON
OXFORD	READING
PETERBOROUGH	CAMBRIDGE
PONTYPRIDD	CARDIFF
PORTMADOC	BIRKENHEAD or STOKE
ROCHDALE	BOLTON
RHYL	BIRMINGHAM
SALISBURY	BOURNEMOUTH or SOUTHAMPTON
SCARBOROUGH	YORK, HULL or MIDDLESBOROUGH
SCUNTHORPE	HULL
SHREWSBURY	STOKE
ST. ALBANS	LUTON
STAFFORD	STOKE
STOCKTON ON TEES	MIDDLESBOROUGH
STOCKPORT	MANCHESTER
STOURBRIDGE	BIRMINGHAM
SUNDERLAND	NEWCASTLE
SWANSEA	CARDIFF
SWINDON	GLOUCESTER
TAUNTON	EXETER
TORQUAY	EXETER
TRURO	PLYMOUTH
TUNBRIDGE WELLS	CROYDON
WAKEFIELD	LEEDS
WARRINGTON	SALFORD
WARWICK	BIRMINGHAM
WELSHPOOL	STOKE
WEST BROMWICH	BIRMINGHAM
WEYMOUTH	BOURNEMOUTH

Debtor's own county court	*Nearest full-time court*
WIGAN	BOLTON
WINCHESTER	SOUTHAMPTON
WORCESTER	GLOUCESTER
WORKINGTON	PRESTON
WREXHAM	BIRKENHEAD or STOKE
YEOVIL	EXETER or BRISTOL

[1344]

SCHEDULE 3

Rule 7.17

SHORTHAND WRITERS' REMUNERATION

1. For attendance	£51.80
2. Per folio of written record	72.3p plus 4p per folio for all copies.
3. Travelling time	£5.44 per hour after first hour of each journey.

4. In addition to the items in paragraphs 1 to 3, the following London weighting allowances (see note below) are payable in relation to the location of the court or other place concerned—

Inner	Intermediate	Outer
£7.33 per day	£4.20 per day	£3.08 per day

5. The amounts shown in paragraph 4 are subject to a maximum annual allowance of—

Inner	Intermediate	Outer
£1,465	£840	£615

Note:

The area at which London weighting allowances are payable is determined as follows:

(a) Inner

The area within a radius of 5 miles from Charing Cross (statue of King Charles I).

(b) Intermediate

The area outside that specified in paragraph (*a*) but within a radius of 10 miles from Charing Cross.

(c) Outer

    (i) The area outside those specified in paragraphs (*a*) and (*b*) but within a radius of 18 miles from Charing Cross; or

    (ii) the former Borough of St Albans, Herts; or

    (iii) the former Urban District of Slough, Bucks; or

    (iv) the following towns whose boundary is intersected by the 18 miles radius from Charing Cross:—

Abbots Langley
Chertsey
Egham
Fetcham
Godstone
Hatfield
Redhill
Rickmansworth
South Ockenden
Stone
Swanscombe
Weybridge

[1345]

SCHEDULE 4

Rule 12.7

FORMS

Index

PART 1: COMPANY VOLUNTARY ARRANGEMENTS
FORM NO   TITLE

1.1   Report of a meeting approving voluntary arrangement
1.2   Order of revocation or suspension of voluntary arrangement
1.3   Voluntary arrangement's supervisor's abstract of receipts and payments
1.4   Notice of completion of voluntary arrangment

PART 2: ADMINISTRATION PROCEDURE

2.1   Petition for administration order
2.2   Consent of administrator(s) to act
2.3   Affidavit of service of petition for administration order
2.4   Administration order
2.5   Notice of administration order (for newspapers)
2.6   Notice of administration order
2.7   Copy of administration order to registrar of companies
2.8   Notice requiring submission of administration statement of affairs
2.9   Statement of affairs
2.10   Notice to directors and others to attend meeting of creditors
2.11   Notice of meetings in administration proceedings
2.12   Report of meeting of creditors
2.13   Certificate of constitution [amended certificate] of creditors' committee
2.14   Notice by administrator of a change in committee membership
2.15   Administrator's abstract of receipts and payments
2.16   Notice to court of resignation of administrator under Rule 2.52 of the Insolvency Rules 1986
2.17   Notice of resignation by administrator pursuant to Rule 2.52(2) of the Insolvency Rules 1986
2.18   Notice of order to deal with charged property
2.19   Notice of discharge of administration order
2.20   Notice of variation of administration order
2.21   Statement of administrator's proposals
2.22   Statement of revised proposals and notice of meeting to consider them
2.23   Notice of result of meeting of creditors

PART 3: ADMINISTRATIVE RECEIVERSHIP

3.1   Notice requiring submission of administrative receivership statement of affairs
3.2   Statement of affairs
3.3   Statement of affairs in administrative receivership following report to creditors
3.4   Certificate of constitution [amended certificate] of creditors' committee
3.5   Administrative receiver's report as to change in membership of creditors' committee
3.6   Receiver or manager or administrative receiver's abstract of receipts and payments
3.7   Notice of administrative receiver's death

FORM NO TITLE

3.8 Notice of order to dispose of charged property
3.9 Notice of resignation of administrative receiver pursuant to section 45(1) of Insolvency Act 1986
3.10 Administrative receiver's report

PART 4: COMPANIES WINDING UP

4.1 Statutory demand under section 123(1)(*a*) or 222(1)(*a*) of the Insolvency Act 1986
4.2 Winding-up petition
4.3 Affidavit verifying winding-up petition
4.4 Affidavit of service of winding-up petition at registered office
4.5 Affidavit of service of winding-up petition other than at registered office or on an oversea company
4.6 Advertisement of winding-up petition
4.7 Certificate that relevant provisions of Rules have been complied with
4.8 Order for leave to withdraw winding-up petition
4.9 Notice of intention to appear on petition
4.10 List of persons intending to appear on the hearing of the petition
4.11 Order for winding up by the court
4.12 Order for winding up by the court following upon the discharge of an administration order
4.13 Notice to official receiver of winding-up order
4.14 Petition by contributory
4.15 Order of appointment of provisional liquidator
4.16 Notice to deponent requiring preparation and submission of statement of company's affairs
4.17 Statement of affairs [s.131 IA86—winding up by court]
4.18 Statement of affairs [s.95 IA86—voluntary liquidator]
4.19 Statement of affairs [s.99 IA86—creditors' voluntary winding up]
4.20 Statement of affairs under s.95/s.99 to registrar of companies
4.21 Request by creditors for a meeting of the company's creditors [and contributories]
4.22 Notice to creditors of meeting of creditors
4.23 Notice to contributories of meeting of contributories
4.24 Request by contributory/contributories for a meeting of the company's contributories
4.25 Proof of debt—general form
4.26 Affidavit of debt
4.27 Certificate of appointment of liquidator by meeting
4.28 Certificate of appointment of two or more liquidators by meeting
4.29 Order of court appointing liquidator
4.30 Order of court appointing two or more liquidators
4.31 Notice of appointment of liquidator in winding up by the court (for registrar of companies)
4.32 Notice to court of registration of liquidator following meeting of creditors
4.33 Notice of resignation as voluntary liquidator under s.171(5) of the Insolvency Act 1986
4.34 Order of court giving liquidator leave to resign
4.35 Order of court granting voluntary liquidator leave to resign
4.36 Notice to court of resignation of liquidator following leave of the court
4.37 Certificate of removal of liquidator
4.38 Certificate of removal of voluntary liquidator
4.39 Order of court removing liquidator or directing liquidator to summon a meeting of creditors for purpose of his removal
4.40 Notice of ceasing to act as voluntary liquidator
4.41 Liquidator's application to the Secretary of State for his release
4.42 Notice to court of final meeting of creditors

FORM NO   TITLE

4.43   Notice to registrar of companies of final meeting of creditors
4.44   Notice of death of liquidator
4.45   Notice to official receiver or Secretary of State by liquidator on loss of
            qualification as insolvency practitioner
4.46   Notice of vacation of office by voluntary liquidator
4.47   Certificate of constitution [amended certificate] of liquidation committee
4.48   Notice of constitution of liquidation committee
4.49   Report by liquidator of any change in membership of liquidation committee
4.50   Liquidator's certificate that creditors paid in full
4.51   Certificate that creditors have been paid in full
4.52   Liquidator's certificate of continuance of liquidation committee
4.53   Notice of disclaimer under section 178 of the Insolvency Act 1986
4.54   Notice to elect
4.55   Notice of intended disclaimer to interested party
4.56   Affidavit of liquidator in support of application for call
4.57   Order giving leave to make a call
4.58   Notice of call sanctioned by the court or the liquidation committee to be
            sent to contributory
4.59   Order for payment of call due from contributory
4.60   Order of appointment of special manager
4.61   Order of public examination
4.62   Notice to official receiver by creditor requesting him to make application
            for the holding of a public examination
4.63   Notice to official receiver by contributory requesting him to make
            application for the holding of a public examination
4.64   Order as to examination of person who is suffering from mental disorder or
            physical affliction or disability
4.65   Affidavit of verification of record of the public examination
4.66   Order of adjournment of public examination
4.67   Order appointing time for proceeding with public examination adjourned
            generally
4.68   Liquidator's statement of receipts and payments
4.69   Order of court on appeal against Secretary of State's decision under section
            203(4) or 205(4) of the Insolvency Act 1986
4.70   Members' voluntary winding up declaration of solvency embodying a
            statement of assets and liabilities
4.71   Return of final meeting in a members' voluntary winding up
4.72   Return of final meeting in creditors' voluntary winding up

PART 6: BANKRUPTCY

6.1   Statutory demand under section 268(1)(*a*) Insolvency Act 1986—debt for
            liquidated sum payable immediately
6.2   Statutory demand under section 268(1)(*a*) Insolvency Act 1986—debt for
            liquidated sum payable immediately following a judgment or order of the
            court
6.3   Statutory demand under section 268(2) Insolvency Act 1986—debt payable
            at future date
6.4   Application to set aside statutory demand
6.5   Affidavit in support of application to set aside statutory demand
6.6   Order setting aside statutory demand
6.7   Creditor's bankruptcy petition on failure to comply with a statutory demand
            for a liquidated sum payable immediately
6.8   Creditor's bankruptcy petition on failure to comply with a statutory demand
            for a liquidated sum payable at a future date
6.9   Creditor's bankruptcy petition where execution or other process on a
            judgment has been returned unsatisfied in whole or part
6.10   Bankruptcy petition for default in connection with voluntary arrangement

FORM NO   TITLE

6.11   Affidavit of personal service of statutory demand
6.12   Affidavit of substituted service of statutory demand
6.13   Affidavit of truth of statements in bankruptcy petition
6.14   Application for registration of a petition in bankruptcy against an individual
            under Land Charges Act 1972
6.15   Order for substituted service of a bankruptcy petition
6.16   Substituted service of bankruptcy petition—notice in Gazette
6.17   Affidavit of personal service of bankruptcy petition
6.18   Affidavit of substituted service of bankruptcy petition
6.19   Notice by debtor of intention to oppose bankruptcy petition
6.20   Notice of intention to appear on bankruptcy petition
6.21   List of creditors intending to appear on hearing of the bankruptcy petition
6.22   Dismissal or withdrawal of bankruptcy petition
6.23   Order of adjournment of bankruptcy petition
6.24   Notice to debtor and creditors of order of adjournment of bankruptcy
            petition
6.25   Bankruptcy order on creditor's petition
6.26   Application for registration of a bankruptcy order against an individual
            under the Land Charges Act 1972
6.27   Debtor's bankruptcy petition
6.28   Debtor's petition statement of affairs
6.29   Order of appointment of insolvency practitioner to prepare a report under
            section 274(1) of the Insolvency Act 1986
6.30   Bankruptcy order on debtor's petition
6.31   Revocation of certificate of summary administration
6.32   Order of appointment of interim receiver
6.33   Bankrupt's statement of affairs
6.34   Request by creditor(s) for a meeting of the bankrupt's creditors
6.35   Notice to creditors of meeting of creditors
6.36   Notice to bankrupt of meeting of creditors
6.37   Proof of debt
6.38   Proof by an existing trustee as a claim in later bankruptcy
6.39   Affidavit of debt
6.40   Certificate of appointment of trustee by creditors' meeting
6.41   Certificate of appointment of two or more trustees by creditors' meeting
6.42   Order of court appointing trustee
6.43   Order of court appointing two or more trustees
6.44   Notice to court of resignation of trustee following meeting of creditors
6.45   Order of court giving trustee leave to resign
6.46   Notice to court of resignation of trustee following leave of the court
6.47   Certificate of removal of trustee
6.48   Order of court removing trustee or directing trustee to summon a meeting of
            creditors for the purpose of his removal
6.49   Trustee's application to the Secretary of State for his release
6.50   Notice to court of final meeting of creditors
6.51   Notice to official receiver by trustee on loss of qualification as insolvency
            practitioner
6.52   Certificate of constitution [amended certificate] of creditors' committee
6.53   Report by trustee of any change in membership of creditors' committee
6.54   Order of appointment of special manager
6.55   Order for public examination of the bankrupt
6.56   Request by creditor(s) for the holding of a public examination of the
            bankrupt
6.57   Order as to examination of bankrupt who is suffering from mental disorder
            or physical affliction or disability
6.58   Affidavit of verification of record of the public examination of the bankrupt
6.59   Order of adjournment of public examination of bankrupt
6.60   Order appointing time for proceeding with public examination of bankrupt
            adjourned generally

FORM NO   TITLE

6.61   Notice of disclaimer under section 315 of the Insolvency Act 1986
6.62   Notice to elect
6.63   Notice of intended disclaimer to interested party
6.64   Notice to bankrupt of an application under section 310 of the Insolvency
            Act 1986 for an income payments order
6.65   Order for income claimed under section 310(3)(*a*) of the Insolvency Act 1986
6.66   Order for income claimed under section 310(3)(*b*) of the Insolvency Act 1986
6.67   Order converting income payments order made under section 310(1)(*a*) to
            an order under section 310(3)(*b*) of the Insolvency Act 1986
6.68   Discharge or variation of order for income claimed under section 310 of the
            Insolvency Act 1986
6.69   Order under section 369(1) of the Insolvency Act 1986
6.70   Order under section 369(2) of the Insolvency Act 1986
6.71   Order of annulment under section 282 of the Insolvency Act 1986
6.72   Order of suspension of discharge under section 279(3) of the Insolvency Act
            1986
6.73   Order of court lifting suspension of discharge
6.74   Certificate that order suspending discharge has been lifted
6.75   Notice to court by bankrupt that he intends to dispute statements made by
            official receiver in his report under section 289(2) of the Insolvency Act 1986
6.76   Order granting absolute/suspended discharge under section 280(2)(*b*) or (*c*)
            of the Insolvency Act 1986
6.77   Certificate of discharge
6.78   Notice to existing trustee of the presentation of a petition for a later
            bankruptcy
6.79   Criminal bankruptcy petition
6.80   Order to Post Office under section 371 of the Insolvency Act 1986

PART 7: COURT PROCEDURE AND PRACTICE

7.1   Originating application
7.2   Ordinary application
7.3   Declaration by official shorthand writer
7.4   Appointment of shorthand writer to take examination under the Insolvency
            Act 1986
7.5   Declaration by shorthand writer
7.6   Warrant for failure to attend examination under section 133 of the Insolvency
            Act 1986
7.7   Warrant of arrest etc under section 364 of the Insolvency Act 1986
7.8   Warrant of arrest etc under section 236 or 366 of the Insolvency Act 1986
7.9   Order for production of person arrested under warrant issued under section
            236 or 366 of the Insolvency Act 1986
7.10   Warrant to registrar of court in whose district a person against whom a
            warrant of arrest has been issued is believed to be
7.11   Endorsement of warrant of arrest issued by a court to which the same has
            been sent for execution by the court which originally issued it
7.12   Warrant of seizure of property under section 365 of the Insolvency Act 1986
7.13   Search warrant under section 365 of the Insolvency Act 1986
7.14   Order of discharge from custody under the Insolvency Act 1986 [General]
7.15   Affidavit in support of application for committal of bankrupt or other person
            under section 291, 312 or 333 of the Insolvency Act 1986
7.16   Affidavit in support of application for committal of the bankrupt under
            section 363 of the Insolvency Act 1986
7.17   Warrant of committal for contempt
7.18   Order of discharge from custody on contempt
7.19   Order appointing person to act for incapacitated person

FORM NO   TITLE

PART 8: PROXIES AND COMPANY REPRESENTATION

8.1   Proxy—company or individual voluntary arrangements
8.2   Proxy—administration
8.3   Proxy—administrative receivership
8.4   Proxy—winding up by the court or bankruptcy
8.5   Proxy—members' or creditors' voluntary winding up

PART 9: EXAMINATION OF PERSONS CONCERNED IN COMPANY AND
INDIVIDUAL INSOLVENCY

9.1   Order under section 236 or 366 of the Insolvency Act 1986

                                                                    [1346]

Rule 12.21

SCHEDULE 5

PUNISHMENT OF OFFENCES UNDER THE RULES

Note: In the fourth and fifth columns of this Schedule, "the statutory maximum" means the prescribed sum under section 32 of the Magistrates' Courts Act 1980 (c.43).

Rule creating offence.	General nature of offence.	Mode of prosecution.	Punishment.	Daily default fine (where applicable).
In Part 1, Rule 1.30.	False representation or fraud for purpose of obtaining members' or creditors' consent to proposal for voluntary arrangement.	1. On indictment. 2. Summary.	7 years or a fine, or both. 6 months or the statutory maximum, or both.	
In Part 2, Rule 2.52(4).	Administrator failing to send notification as to progress of administration.	Summary.	One-fifth of the statutory maximum.	One-fiftieth of the statutory maximum.
In Part 3, Rule 3.32(5).	Administrative receiver failing to send notification as to progress of receivership.	Summary.	One-fifth of the statutory maximum.	One-fiftieth of the statutory maximum.
In Part 5, Rule 5.30.	False representation or fraud for purpose of obtaining creditors' consent to proposal for voluntary arrangement.	1. On indictment. 2. Summary.	7 years or a fine, or both. 6 months or the statutory maximum, or both.	
In Part 12, Rule 12.18.	False representation of status for purpose of inspecting documents.	1. On indictment. 2. Summary.	2 years or a fine, or both. 6 months or the statutory maximum, or both.	

[1347]

Section B

Other Statutory Instruments

England and Wales

SECTION B
OTHER STATUTORY INSTRUMENTS
ENGLAND AND WALES

COMPANIES (WINDING UP) RULES 1949
(SI 1949 No 330)

NOTES
   Made: 23 February 1949.
   Authority: Companies Act 1948, s 365(1). These Rules now have effect as if made under the Companies Act 1985, s 663(1).

Court and Chambers

6. Proceeding in Courts other than High Court

(1) In Courts other than the High Court the following matters and applications to the Court shall be heard in open Court—

   (*a*) Petitions.
   (*b*) Public Examinations.
   (*c*) Applications under sub-section (1) of section 334 of the Act.
   (*d*) Applications to rectify the Register.
   (*e*) Appeals from the Official Receiver and Board of Trade.
   (*f*) Appeals from any decision or act of the Liquidator.
   (*g*) Applications relating to the admission or rejection of proofs.
   (*h*) ...
   (*i*) Applications under section 352 of the Act.
   (*j*) Applications under section 343 of the Act.
   (*k*)–(*m*) ...
   (*n*) Applications for the committal of any person to prison for contempt.
   (*o*) Such matters and applications as the Judge may from time to time by any general or special order direct to be heard in open Court.
   [(*p*). ...

(2) Any other matter or application may be heard and determined in Chambers.   **[1347A]**

NOTES
   Sub-paras (*h*), (*k*)–(*m*), (*p*) revoked by the Companies (Winding up) (Amendment) Rules 1986, SI 1986 No 619, r 2; sub-para (*p*) previously added by SI 1977 No 1395.
   Ss 334, 343, 352 of the Act: ie the Companies Act 1948. See now the Companies Act 1985, ss 632, 633, 642, 651.

Proceedings by or against directors, promoters and officers

68. Applications by or against delinquent directors, officers and promoters

(1) [An application made to the court under any of the following provisions—

   (*a*)   sections 296 to 299 of the Act,
   (*b*)   sections 630 and 631 of the Act,
   (*c*)   section 727 of the Act,
   (*d*)   section 15 of the Insolvency Act 1985,

shall in any court other than the High Court be made by motion to the court.]

In the High Court, the application shall be made by a summons returnable in the first instance in Chambers. The summons shall state the nature of the declaration or order for which application is made, and the grounds of the application, and, unless otherwise ordered, shall be served, in the manner in which an originating summons is required by the Rules of the Supreme Court to be served, on every person against whom an order is sought, not less than [fourteen days] before the day named in the summons for hearing the application. Where any such application is made by summons no affidavit or report shall be filed before the return of the summons.

(2) On the return of the summons the Court may give such directions as it shall think fit as to whether points of claim and defence are to be delivered, as to the taking of evidence wholly or in part by affidavit or orally, as to the cross examination either before the Judge on the hearing in Court or in Chambers of any deponents to affidavits in support of or in opposition to the application, as to any report it may require the Official Receiver or Liquidator to make and generally as to the procedure on the summons and for the hearing thereof.

(3) Where any such order as is mentioned in paragraph (2) of this Rule has directed that points of claim and defence shall be delivered then if subsequently to such order and before the summons has been set down for trial or adjourned to the Judge either party wishes to apply for any further direction as to any interlocutory matter or thing he shall restore the summons to the Registrar's list and shall give two clear day's notice in writing to the other party stating the grounds of the application. A copy of such notice shall be filed with the Registrar two clear days before the day for which the summons is restored.   **[1347B]**

NOTES

Sub-para (1): the words in the first pair of square brackets were substituted by the Companies (Winding up) (Amendment) Rules 1986, SI 1986 No 619, r 3; the words in the second pair of square brackets were substituted by SI 1979 No 209.

The Act: Companies Act 1985.

[70. Hearing of application

Where any application under sections 296 to 299 of the Act is made or heard after a public examination under section 563 of the Act has been held before the Registrar or any of the persons mentioned in subsection (7) of section 564 of the Act then such application shall be heard and determined by such Registrar or other person unless the Judge shall otherwise direct.   **[1347C]**

NOTES

Substituted by the Companies (Winding up) (Amendment) Rules 1986, SI 1986 No 619, r 4.

The Act: Companies Act 1985.

ADMINISTRATIVE RECEIVERS (VALUE ADDED TAX CERTIFICATES) RULES 1986
(SI 1986 No 385)

NOTES

Made: 27 February 1986.

Authority: Insolvency Act 1985, s 106. These Rules now have effect as if made under the Insolvency Act 1986, ss 411, 414(*a*).

ARRANGEMENT OF RULES

Rule   Para
1   Citation and commencement   ..   .. [1348]
2   Application of these Rules ..   .. [1349]
3   Issue of certificate of insolvency   ..   .. [1350]
4   Form of certificate   ..   .. [1351]
5   Notification to creditors   ..   .. [1352]
6   Preservation of certificate with company's records   ..   .. [1353]

1. Citation and commencement

(1) These Rules may be cited as the Administrative Receivers (Value Added Tax Certificates) Rules 1986 and shall come into force on 1st April 1986.

(2) In these Rules references to "the 1983 Act" are to the Value Added Tax Act 1983. **[1348]**

NOTES
Commencement: 1 April 1986.

2. Application of these Rules

These Rules apply to a company for the purposes of section 22 of the 1983 Act where a person is appointed to act as its administrative receiver except where such a person is appointed under section 467 of the Companies Act 1985 (power to appoint receivers under the law of Scotland). **[1349]**

NOTES
Commencement: 1 April 1986.
1983 Act: Value Added Tax Act 1983.

3. Issue of certificate of insolvency

In accordance with this Rule, it is the duty of the administrative receiver to issue a certificate in the terms of paragraph (*b*) of section 22(3) of the 1983 Act (which specifies the circumstances in which a company is deemed insolvent for the purposes of the section) forthwith upon his forming the opinion described in that paragraph. **[1350]**

NOTES
Commencement: 1 April 1986.
1983 Act: Value Added Tax Act 1983.

4. Form of certificate

(1) There shall in the certificate be specified:—

> (*a*) the name of the company and its registered number;
> (*b*) the full name of the administrative receiver and the date of his appointment as such; and
> (*c*) the date on which the certificate is issued.

(2) The certificate shall be intituled "CERTIFICATE OF INSOLVENCY FOR THE PURPOSES OF SECTION 22(3)(*b*) OF THE VALUE ADDED TAX ACT 1983". **[1351]**

NOTES
Commencement: 1 April 1986.

5. Notification to creditors

(1) Notice of the issue of the certificate shall be given by the administrative receiver within 3 months of his appointment or within 2 months of issuing the certificate, whichever is the later, to all of the company's unsecured creditors of whose address he is then aware and who have, to his knowledge, made supplies to the company, with a charge to value added tax, at any time before his appointment.

(2) Thereafter, he shall give the notice to any such creditor of whose address and supplies to the company he becomes aware.

(3) He is not under obligation to provide any creditor with a copy of the certificate. **[1352]**

NOTES
Commencement: 1 April 1986.

6. Preservation of certificate with company's records

The certificate shall be retained with the company's accounting records, and section 222 of the Companies Act 1985 (where and for how long records are to be kept) applies to the certificate as it applies to those records. **[1353]**

NOTES
Commencement: 1 April 1986.

INSOLVENT COMPANIES (DISQUALIFICATION OF UNFIT DIRECTORS) PROCEEDINGS RULES 1986
(1986 No 612)

NOTES
Made: 25 March 1986.
Authority: Insolvency Act 1985, s 106. These Rules now have effect as if made under the Insolvency Act 1986, ss 411, 414(9).

ARRANGEMENT OF RULES

Rule   Para

Rule		Para
1	Citation, commencement and interpretation	[1354]
2	Form of application	[1355]
3	The case against the respondent	[1356]
4	Endorsement on summons	[1357]
5	Service and acknowledgement	[1358]
6	Evidence	[1359]
7	The hearing of the application	[1360]
8	Commencement of disqualification order	[1361]
9	Setting aside of disqualification order	[1362]

1. Citation, commencement and interpretation

(1) These Rules may be cited as the Insolvent Companies (Disqualification of Unfit Directors) Proceedings Rules 1986 and shall come into force on 28th April 1986.

(2) In these Rules, "the Companies Act" means the Companies Act 1985, "the Insolvency Act" means the Insolvency Act 1985, and "Registrar" has the same meaning as in the Companies (Winding-up) Rules 1949.

(3) These Rules apply with respect to an application for a disqualification order against any person ("the respondent"), where made—

    (*a*) by the Secretary of State or the official receiver under section 12(3) of the Insolvency Act (on the grounds of the person's association with insolvent companies), or

    (*b*) by the Secretary of State under section 13 of that Act (alleged expedient in the public interest, following report of inspectors under section 437 of the Companies Act, or information or documents obtained under section 447 or 448 of that Act).   **[1354]**

NOTES
    Commencement: 28 April 1986.
    Insolvency Act 1985, ss 12(3), 13: See now the Company Directors Disqualification Act 1986, ss 7(1), 8 respectively.

2. Form of application

An application to which these Rules apply shall be made—

    (*a*) in the High Court, by originating summons (Form 10 in Appendix A to the Rules of the Supreme Court, with such adaptation as may be appropriate), and

    (*b*) in a county court, by originating application, such an application being nevertheless referred to in these Rules as a summons;

and the Rules of the Supreme Court 1965 or (as the case may be) the County Court Rules 1981 apply accordingly, except where these Rules make provision to inconsistent effect.   **[1355]**

NOTES
    Commencement: 28 April 1986.

3. The case against the respondent

(1) There shall, at the time when the summons is issued, be filed evidence in support of the application for a disqualification order; and copies of the evidence shall be served with the summons on the respondent.

(2) The evidence shall be by one or more affidavits, except where the applicant is the official receiver, in which case it may be in the form of a written report (with or without affidavits by other persons) which shall be treated as if it had been verified by affidavit by him.

(3) There shall in the affidavits or (as the case may be) the official receiver's report be included a statement of the matters by reference to which the respondent is alleged to be unfit to be concerned in the management of a company.   **[1356]**

NOTES
    Commencement: 28 April 1986.

4. Endorsement on summons

There shall on the summons be endorsed information to the respondent as follows—

    (*a*) that, in accordance with the relevant enactments, the court has power to impose disqualifications as follows—

        (i) where the application is under section 12 of the Insolvency Act, for a period of not less than 2, and up to 15, years; and

       (ii) where the application is under section 13 of the Act, for a period up to 15 years;

(b) that the application for a disqualification order may, in accordance with these Rules, be heard and determined summarily, without further or other notice to the respondent, and that, if it is so heard and determined, the court may impose disqualification for a period up to 5 years; and

(c) that if at the hearing of the application the court, on the evidence then before it, is minded to impose, in the respondent's case, disqualification for any period longer than 5 years, it will not make a disqualification order on that occasion but will adjourn the application to be heard (with further evidence, if any) at a later date to be notified.   **[1357]**

NOTES

Commencement: 28 April 1986.

Insolvency Act 1985, s 12: See now the Insolvency Act 1986, s 214(7) and the Company Directors Disqualification Act 1986, ss 6, 7.

Insolvency Act 1985, s 13: See now the Company Directors Disqualification Act 1986, s 8.

5. Service and acknowledgement

(1) The summons shall be served on the respondent by sending it by first class post to his last-known address; and the date of service shall, unless the contrary is shown, be deemed to be the 7th day next following that on which the summons was posted.

(2) Where any process or order of the court or other document is required under proceedings subject to these Rules to be served on any person who is not in England and Wales, the court may order service on him of that process or order or other document to be effected within such time and in such manner as it thinks fit, and may also require such proof of service as it thinks fit.

(3) The summons served on the respondent shall be accompanied by a form of acknowledgement of service, to be returned by him to the court within 14 days from the date of service, and for this purpose the practice and procedure of the High Court relating to acknowledgements of service shall apply to an application for an order under these Rules both in the High Court and, with such modifications as are required, in the County Court, save that any reference to Form 15 in Appendix A to the Rules of the Supreme Court 1965 shall relate to the form as modified by these Rules.

(4) The form of acknowledgement of service shall state that the respondent should indicate—

(a) whether he contests the application on the grounds that, in the case of any particular company—

(i) he was not a director or shadow director of the company at a time when conduct of his, or of other persons, in relation to that company is in question, or

(ii) his conduct as director or shadow director of that company was not as alleged in support of the application for a disqualification order,

(b) whether, in the case of any conduct of his, he disputes the allegation that it makes him unfit to be concerned in the management of a company, and

(c) whether he, while not resisting the application for a disqualification order, intends to adduce mitigating factors with a view to justifying only a short period of disqualification.   **[1358]**

NOTES

Commencement: 28 April 1986.

6. Evidence

(1) The respondent may, within 28 days from the date of service of the summons, file affidavit evidence in opposition to the application and shall forthwith serve upon the applicant a copy of such service.

(2) The applicant may within 14 days from receiving the copy of the respondent's evidence file further evidence in reply and shall forthwith serve a copy of that evidence upon the repondent. **[1359]**

NOTES

Commencement: 28 April 1986.

7. The hearing of the application

(1) The date fixed for the hearing of the application shall be not less than 8 weeks from the date of issue of the summons.

(2) The hearing shall in the first instance be before the Registrar in open court.

(3) The Registrar shall either determine the case summarily, or adjourn it for further consideration (by himself or another registrar or, if he thinks it is a fit case for the judge, by him).

(4) If he determines the case summarily, he may make a disqualification order against the respondent, whether or not the latter appears, and whether or not he has completed and returned the acknowledgement of service of the summons, or filed evidence under Rule 6.

However, the Registrar shall not then impose a period of disqualification longer than 5 years.

(5) The Registrar shall adjourn the case for further consideration if—

(*a*) he forms the provisional opinion that a disqualification order ought to be made, and that a period of disqualification longer than 5 years is appropriate, or
(*b*) he is of opinion that questions of law or fact arise which are not suitable for summary determination.

(6) Where the case is adjourned as above, the Registrar shall specify whether the adjourned hearing is to be before a registrar or the judge and give directions as to the following matters—

(*a*) the manner in which, and the time within which, notice of the adjournment and the reasons for it is to be given to the respondent,
(*b*) the filing and exchange of evidence by the applicant or the respondent,
(*c*) such other matters as the Registrar thinks necessary or expedient with a view to an expeditious disposal of the application, and
(*d*) the time and place of the adjourned hearing. **[1360]**

NOTES

Commencement: 28 April 1986.

8. Commencement of disqualification order

Unless the court otherwise orders, a disqualification order takes effect at the beginning of the 21st day after the day on which the order is made.   **[1361]**

NOTES
Commencement: 28 April 1986.

9. Setting aside of disqualification order

Any disqualification order made in the absence of the respondent may be set aside or varied by the court on such terms as it thinks just.   **[1362]–[1367]**

NOTES
Commencement: 28 April 1986.

INSOLVENCY PRACTITIONERS TRIBUNAL (CONDUCT OF INVESTIGATIONS) RULES 1986
(SI 1986 No 952)

NOTES
Made: 5 June 1986.
Authority: Insolvency Act 1985, Sch 1, para 4(4). These Rules now have effect as if made under the Insolvency Act 1986, Sch 7, para 4(4).

ARRANGEMENT OF RULES

Rule   Para
1   Citation, commencement and interpretation .. .. [1368]
2   Reference to the tribunal .. .. [1369]
3   Statement of the applicant .. .. [1370]
4   Appointment of solicitors and counsel to the tribunal .. .. [1371]
5   Investigation by the tribunal .. .. [1372]
6   Methods of inquiry by the tribunal .. .. [1373]
7   Taking of evidence .. .. [1374]
8   Final representations .. .. [1375]
9   Representation at a hearing .. .. [1376]
10   Service of written representations .. .. [1377]
11   Hearings in public or in private .. .. [1378]
12   Notices .. .. [1379]
13   Time limits .. .. [1380]
14   Powers of chairman .. .. [1381]
15   Period within which report to be made .. .. [1382]
16   Scottish Cases .. .. [1383]

1. Citation, commencement and interpretation

(1) These Rules may be cited as the Insolvency Practitioners Tribunal (Conduct of Investigations) Rules 1986 and shall come into force on 1st July 1986.

(2) In these Rules:

(*a*) references to "the Act" are references to the Insolvency Act 1985;

(*b*) "the applicant" means an applicant for authorisation under section 5 of the Act or, where it is proposed to withdraw an authorisation granted under that section, the holder of the authorisation;

(*c*) "Treasury Solicitor" means the Solicitor for the affairs of Her Majesty's Treasury as provided in the Treasury Solicitor Act 1876; and (*d*) "a Scottish case" means any case where at the time of the reference of the case of the Tribunal the applicant is either habitually resident in or has his principal place of business in Scotland.   **[1368]**

NOTES
Commencement: 1 July 1986.
Insolvency Act 1985: references within this statutory instrument to the Insolvency Act 1985 may now be construed as references to the Insolvency Act 1986.

2. Reference to the tribunal

(1) On referring a case to the tribunal under section 8(2) of the Act the relevant authority shall—

(*a*) send to the tribunal a copy of the written notice served by it on the applicant in pursuance of section 6(2) of the Act, together with a copy of the notification by the applicant that he wishes the case to be referred to the tribunal, and

(*b*) give notice to the applicant of the date on which the case has been referred by it to the tribunal and of the address to which any statement notice or other document required by these Rules to be given or sent to the tribunal is to be given or sent.

(2) Within 21 days of referring the case to the tribunal the relevant authority shall send to the tribunal such further information and copies of such other documents and records as it considers would be of assistance to the tribunal, and shall, at the same time, send to the applicant such further information and copies of such other documents and records; or, if there is no such information or copies, the relevant authority shall within the said period notify the tribunal and the applicant to that effect.   **[1369]**

NOTES
Commencement: 1 July 1986.
Ss 6(2), 8(2) of the Act: see now the Insolvency Act 1986, ss 394(2), 396(3) respectively.

3. Statement of the applicant

(1) Within 21 days after the relevant authority has sent to the applicant the material mentioned in Rule 2(2) or, as the case may be, after it has sent to him the notification mentioned in that Rule, the applicant shall send to the tribunal a statement of his grounds for requiring the case to be investigated by the tribunal specifying—

(*a*) which matters of fact (if any) contained in the written notice served on him under section 6(2) of the Act he disputes,

(*b*) any other matters which he considers should be drawn to the attention of the tribunal, and

(*c*) the names and addresses of any witnesses whose evidence he wishes the tribunal to hear.

(2) The applicant shall, on sending the statement referred to in paragraph (1) of this Rule to the tribunal, send a copy to the relevant authority.   **[1370]**

NOTES
Commencement: 1 July 1986.
S 6(2) of the Act: see now the Insolvency Act 1986, s 394(2).

4. Appointment of solicitors and counsel to the tribunal

At any time after the case has been referred to it the tribunal may appoint the Treasury Solicitor and Counsel, or, in Scottish cases, may request the Treasury

Solicitor to appoint a solicitor and may appoint Counsel, to exercise the functions of:—

> (*a*) assisting the tribunal in seeking and presenting evidence in accordance with the requirements of the tribunal; and
> (*b*) representing the public interest in relation to the matters before the tribunal. **[1371]**

NOTES
Commencement: 1 July 1986.

5. Investigation by the tribunal

After the receipt of the statement referred to in Rule 3 or, if no such statement is received, after the expiry of the period referred to in that Rule the tribunal shall investigate the case and make a report by carrying out such inquiries as it thinks appropriate for that purpose into and concerning the information, documents, records and matters placed before it under the provisions of Rules 2 and 3 above; and in carrying out such inquiries the requirements set out in the following Rules shall apply. **[1372]**

NOTES
Commencement: 1 July 1986.

6. Methods of inquiry by the tribunal

(1) As soon as practicable after the tribunal has considered the subject matter of the investigation it shall notify the relevant authority and the applicant of the manner in which it proposes to conduct its inquiries and in particular whether oral evidence is to be taken.

(2) The tribunal shall give the relevant authority and the applicant a reasonable opportunity of making representations on the manner in which it proposes to conduct its inquiries and such representations may be made orally or in writing at the option of the relevant authority or the applicant as the case may be.

(3) After considering any representations that may be made under paragraph (2) above the tribunal shall notify the relevant authority and the applicant whether and, if so, in what respects, it has decided to alter the manner in which it proposes to carry out its inquiries.

(4) If at any subsequent stage in the investigation the tribunal proposes to make any material change in the manner in which its inquiries are to be carried out it shall notify the relevant authority and the applicant and the provisions of paragraphs (2) and (3) above shall apply accordingly. **[1373]**

NOTES
Commencement: 1 July 1986.

7. Taking of evidence

When in the carrying out of its inquiries the tribunal:—

> (*a*) wishes to examine a witness orally:—
>> (i) it shall give notice to the applicant and the relevant authority of the time and place at which the examination will be held, and
>> (ii) the applicant and the relevant authority shall be entitled to be present at the examination by the tribunal of any witness and to

put such additional questions to him as may appear to the
tribunal to be relevant to the subject matter of the investigation;
or

(b) takes into consideration documentary evidence or evidence in the
form of computer or other non documentary records not placed before
the tribunal under the provisions of Rules 2 and 3 above, the tribunal
shall give the applicant and the relevant authority an opportunity of
inspecting that evidence and taking copies or an appropriate record
thereof.   **[1374]**

NOTES
Commencement: 1 July 1986.

8. Final representations

After the tribunal has completed the taking of such evidence as it considers
necessary for the purpose of the investigation it shall give the applicant and the
relevant authority a reasonable opportunity of making representations on the
evidence and on the subject matter of the investigation generally. Such
representations may be made orally or in writing at the option of the applicant
or, as the case may be, of the relevant authority.   **[1375]**

NOTES
Commencement: 1 July 1986.

9. Representation at a hearing

At the hearing of oral representations or the taking of oral evidence—

(a) the applicant may be represented by Counsel or solicitor, or by any
other person allowed by the tribunal to appear on his behalf; and
(b) the relevant authority may be represented by Counsel or solicitor or
by any officer of the relevant authority.   **[1376]**

NOTES
Commencement: 1 July 1986.

10. Service of written representations

Where the relevant authority or the applicant makes any written representations
to the tribunal in the course of its investigation the relevant authority or, as the
case may be, the applicant shall send a copy of such representations to the
other.   **[1377]**

NOTES
Commencement: 1 July 1986.

11. Hearings in public or in private

(1) The tribunal shall conduct its investigation in private and, save to the extent
that these Rules provide for the hearing of oral representations or for the taking
of oral evidence and the applicant requests that any such hearing be in public,
no person other than those specified in Rule 9 above or having the leave of the
tribunal shall be entitled to be present at any such hearing.

(2) Nothing in this Rule shall prevent a member of the Council on Tribunals
or of its Scottish Committee from attending in his capacity as such a member
any such hearing.   **[1378]**

NOTES
Commencement: 1 July 1986.

12. Notices

Any notice or other document required by these Rules to be given or sent may be given or sent by first class post. **[1379]**

NOTES
Commencement: 1 July 1986.

13. Time limits

The tribunal may in any investigation permit the relevant authority or the applicant to send any document or perform any act after the time prescribed in the Rules for so sending or performing and such permission may be granted after any such time has expired. **[1380]**

NOTES
Commencement: 1 July 1986.

14. Powers of chairman

Anything required or authorised to be done by the tribunal in the course of an investigation may be done by the chairman except—

    (*a*) the settling of the manner in which the tribunal is to conduct its investigation,

    (*b*) the hearing or consideration of any representations made by the relevant authority or the applicant, and

    (*c*) the taking of evidence, whether orally or in the form of documents or non-documentary records. **[1381]**

NOTES
Commencement: 1 July 1986.

15. Period within which report to be made

(1) The tribunal shall make its report on the case to the relevant authority no later than four months after the date on which the case is referred to it under section 8(2) of the Act unless the relevant authority, on the application of the tribunal, permits the report to be made within such further period as the relevant authority may notify in writing to the tribunal.

(2) The relevant authority may only permit the report to be made within the further period referred to in paragraph (1) above where it appears to that authority that, through exceptional circumstances, the tribunal will be unable to make its report within the period of four months referred to in paragraph (1) above. **[1382]**

NOTES
Commencement: 1 July 1986.
S 8(2) of the Act: See now the Insolvency Act 1986, s 396(3).

16. Scottish Cases

Any hearing or oral representations under Rule 6(2) or 8 or any examination of a witness under Rule 7(*a*) in a Scottish case shall be made or held in Scotland unless the applicant consents to any such hearing or examination taking place elsewhere. **[1383]**

NOTES
Commencement: 1 July 1986.

INSOLVENCY PRACTITIONERS (RECOGNISED PROFESSIONAL BODIES) ORDER 1986
(1986 No 1764)

NOTES
Made: 10 October 1986.
Authority: Insolvency Act 1985, ss 3(2), 10. This Order now has effect as if made under the Insolvency Act 1986, ss 391(1), (4), 419.

1. This Order may be cited as the Insolvency Practitioners (Recognised Professional Bodies) Order 1986 and shall come into force on 10th November 1986.   **[1384]**

NOTES
Commencement: 10 November 1986.

2. The bodies specified in the Schedule to this Order are hereby declared to be recognised professional bodies for the purposes of section 3 of the Insolvency Act 1985.   **[1385]**

NOTES
Commencement: 10 November 1986.
Insolvency Act 1985, s 3: see now the Insolvency Act 1986, ss 390(2), 391.

SCHEDULE
Article 2

RECOGNISED PROFESSIONAL BODIES

The Chartered Association of Certified Accountants

The Insolvency Practitioners Association

The Institute of Chartered Accountants in England and Wales

The Institute of Chartered Accountants in Ireland

The Institute of Chartered Accountants of Scotland

The Law Society

The Law Society of Scotland   **[1386]**

NOTES
Commencement: 10 November 1986.

INSOLVENCY REGULATIONS 1986
(SI 1986 No 1994)

NOTES
Made: 20 November 1986.
Authority: Insolvency Rules 1986, SI 1986 No 1925, r 12.1, and the Insolvency Act 1986, ss 411, 412, Sch 8, para 27, Sch 9, para 30.

ARRANGEMENT OF REGULATIONS

PART 1

GENERAL

Regulation   Para
1   Short title and commencement .. .. [1387]
2   Interpretation and application .. .. [1388]

PART 2

COMPANIES WINDING UP BY THE COURT AND BANKRUPTCY

3   Introductory .. .. [1389]

ACCOUNTS, BOOKS AND OTHER RECORDS AND AUDITING OF ACCOUNTS

4   Payments into Insolvency Services Account .. .. [1390]
5   Payments out of Insolvency Services Account .. .. [1391]
6   Local bank account .. .. [1392]
7   Retention by responsible insolvency practitioner of money without paying it into the
     Insolvency Services Account .. .. [1393]
8   Administrative records .. .. [1394]
9   Financial records .. .. [1395]
10   Responsible insolvency practitioner carrying on business .. .. [1396]
11   Certification of balance in Insolvency Services Account .. .. [1397]
12   Audit of accounts of responsible insolvency practitioner .. .. [1398]
13   Responsible insolvency practitioner to send copy of accounts .. .. .. [1399]

DISPOSAL OF INSOLVENT'S BOOKS, PAPERS AND OTHER RECORDS

14   .. .. [1400]

DIVIDENDS TO CREDITORS OF AN INSOLVENT AND RETURNS OF CAPITAL TO CONTRIBUTORIES OF A COMPANY

15   Payment .. .. [1401]

UNCLAIMED FUNDS AND DIVIDENDS

16   Payment of unclaimed or undistributed assets, dividends or other money on dissolution
     of Company .. .. [1402]
17   Claiming money paid into the Insolvency Services Account .. .. [1403]

INVESTMENT OR OTHERWISE HANDLING OF FUNDS IN WINDING UP OF COMPANIES AND PAYMENT OF INTEREST

18   .. .. [1404]

REMUNERATION OF OFFICIAL RECEIVER

19   Official receiver's remuneration while acting as liquidator or trustee calculated as a
     percentage of the value of assets realised or distributed .. .. [1405]
20   Official receiver's general remuneration while acting as interim receiver, provisional
     liquidator, liquidator or trustee .. .. [1406]
21   Official receiver's remuneration while acting as liquidator, provisional liquidator,
     trustee or interim receiver for the transfer or conveyance of property subject to a
     charge .. .. [1407]
22   Official receiver's remuneration while acting as liquidator or provisional liquidator for
     payments into the Insolvency Services Account from realisation of property charged .. [1408]

Regulation   Para

PART 3
COMPANIES VOLUNTARY WINDING UP

23   Introductory ..   .. [1409]

ACCOUNTS, BOOKS AND OTHER RECORDS AND AUDITING OF ACCOUNTS

24   Payments into the Insolvency Services Account ..   .. [1410]
25   Application by liquidator for payments out of Insolvency Services Account   .. [1411]
26   Administrative records   ..   .. [1412]
27   Financial records   ..   .. [1413]
28   Liquidator carrying on business   ..   .. [1414]
29   Certification of balance in Insolvency Services Account ..   .. [1415]
30   Audit of liquidator's accounts   ..   .. [1416]
31   Liquidator to send copy of statement containing information as to pending
     liquidations ..   .. [1417]

DISPOSAL OF COMPANY'S BOOKS, PAPERS AND OTHER RECORDS

32   ..   .. [1418]

UNCLAIMED FUNDS AND DIVIDENDS

33   ..   .. [1419]

INVESTMENT OR OTHERWISE HANDLING OF FUNDS IN VOLUNTARY WINDING UP OF COMPANIES

34   Investment of assets in Government securities and sale of securities   ..   .. [1420]
35   Liquidator to provide information to Secretary of State ..   .. [1421]

PART 4
TRANSITIONAL PROVISIONS

36   ..   .. [1422]
     The Schedule—Forms Relating to Accounts and Application for Payable Order
     for Payment of Dividends ..   .. [1423]

PART 1
GENERAL

1. Short title and commencement

These Regulations may be cited as the Insolvency Regulations 1986 and shall
come into force on 29th December 1986.   **[1387]**

NOTES
    Commencement: 29 December 1986.

---

2. Interpretation and application

(1) In these Regulations—

    "creditors' committee" means any committee established under section
      301;
    "the solvent" means the company which is being wound up by the court,
      or the bankrupt or his estate, as the case may be;

"liquidation committee" means in Part 2 of these Regulations any committee established under section 141 and in Part 3 any committee established under section 101;

"local bank" means any recognised bank in England and Wales within the meaning of the Banking Act 1979 in, or in the neighbourhood of, the insolvency district, or the district in respect of which the court has winding up jurisdiction, in which the proceedings are taken, or in the locality in which any business of the insolvent is carried on;

"local bank account" means a current account opened with a local bank under Regulation 6(1) below;

"responsible insolvency practitioner" means—

(a) in winding up, the liquidator; and

(b) in bankruptcy, the trustee,

and includes the official receiver when he is the liquidator or trustee or while acting as a receiver or manager under section 287;

"the Rules" means the Insolvency Rules 1986; and

"trustee" means trustee of a bankrupt's estate;

and other expressions used in these Regulations and defined by the Rules have the meanings assigned to them by the Rules.

(2) A form referred to in these Regulations by number means the Form so numbered in the Schedule to these Regulations.

(3) A rule referred to in these Regulations by number means the Rule so numbered in the Rules.

(4) Any application to be made to the Secretary of State or to the Department or anything required to be sent to the Secretary of State or to the Department under these Regulations shall be addressed to the Department of Trade and Industry, Insolvency Service, Gavrelle House, 2–14 Bunhill Row, London EC1Y 8LL.

(5) Subject to Regulation 36 below, these Regulations apply—

(a) to bankruptcy proceedings where the bankruptcy petition is presented on or after the day on which the Regulations come into force; and

(b) to winding-up proceedings commenced on or after that day. **[1388]**

NOTES
Commencement: 29 December 1986.

PART 2

COMPANIES WINDING UP BY THE COURT AND BANKRUPTCY

3. Introductory

This Part of these Regulations—

(a) in the case of company insolvency, relates to companies which are being wound up by the court and which the courts in England and Wales have jurisdiction to wind up; and

(b) in bankruptcy, extends to England and Wales only. **[1389]**

ACCOUNTS, BOOKS AND OTHER RECORDS AND AUDITING OF ACCOUNTS

4. Payments into Insolvency Services Account

(1) Subject to Regulation 6 below, every responsible insolvency practitioner shall pay all money received by him in the course of carrying out his functions

as such without any deduction into the Insolvency Services Account kept by the Secretary of State with the Bank of England.

(2) Every responsible insolvency practitioner shall remit the money received by him under paragraph (1) above once every 14 days, or forthwith if £5,000 or more has been received.

(3) Every remittance of money under paragraph (2) above shall be—

(*a*) paid in through the Bank Giro system; or
(*b*) sent direct to the Bank of England, Threadneedle Street, London EC2R 8AH, by cheque drawn in favour of the "Insolvency Services Account" and crossed "A/C payee only" "Bank of England",

and the responsible insolvency practitioner shall on request be given by the Department a receipt for the money so paid.

(4) Every remittance of money under paragraph (2) above shall be accompanied by forms obtainable on application from the Department for that purpose or by forms which are substantially similar.   **[1390]**

NOTES
Commencement: 29 December 1986.

5. Payments out of Insolvency Services Account

(1) Every responsible insolvency practitioner shall, on application to the Department on a requisition form obtainable on application from the Department or on a form which is substantially similar, be repaid all necessary disbursements made by him, and expenses properly incurred by him, in the course of his administration to the date of his vacation of office out of any moneys standing to the credit of the insolvent in the Insolvency Services Account.

(2) Every application under paragraph (1) above shall give details of all disbursements and expenses claimed.

(3) Every responsible insolvency practitioner who vacates office shall be repaid by any succeeding responsible insolvency practitioner, or if none by the official receiver, out of any funds available for the purpose any necessary disbursements made by him and any expenses properly incurred by him but not repaid before he vacates office.

(4) Every responsible insolvency practitioner shall, on application on a requisition form obtainable from the Department or on a form which is substantially similar, obtain cheques, money orders or payable orders to the order of the payee for sums which become payable on account of the insolvent for delivery by the responsible insolvency practitioner to the persons to whom the payments are to be made.   **[1391]**

NOTES
Commencement: 29 December 1986.

6. Local bank account

(1) Any responsible insolvency practitioner who intends to exercise his power to carry on the business of the insolvent may apply to the Secretary of State for authorisation to open a local bank account, and the Secretary of State may authorise him to make his payments into and out of a specified bank, subject to

a limit, instead of into and out of the Insolvency Services Account if satisfied that an adminstrative advantage will be derived from having such an account.

(2) Money received by a responsible insolvency practitioner relating to the purpose for which the account was opened may be paid into the local bank account to the credit of the insolvent to which the account relates.

(3) Where a responsible insolvency practitioner opens a local bank account, he shall open and maintain clearly named local bank accounts in the name of each separate insolvent of which he is the responsible insolvency practitioner and where money is provided for a specific purpose it shall be clearly identifiable in a separate account.

(4) Every responsible insolvency practitioner shall keep proper records including documentary evidence of all money paid into and out of every local bank account opened and maintained under this Regulation.

(5) Every responsible insolvency practitioner shall pay without deduction any surplus over any authorised limit in pursuance of an application under paragraph (1) above into the Insolvency Services Account in accordance with Regulation 4 above.

(6) As soon as the responsible insolvency practitioner ceases to carry on the business of the insolvent or vacates office or an authorisation given in pursuance of an application under paragraph (1) above is withdrawn, he shall close the account and remit any balance to the Insolvency Services Account in accordance with Regulation 4 above. **[1392]**

NOTES
Commencement: 29 December 1986.

7. Retention by responsible insolvency practitioner of money without paying it into the Insolvency Services Account

If a responsible insolvency practitioner at any time fails to pay into the Insolvency Services Account any money which should have been paid into that account under these Regulations, then, unless he explains that failure to the satisfaction of the Secretary of State, he shall pay interest on the amount which he has failed to pay into that account at the rate of 20 per cent per annum and shall be liable to pay any expenses occasioned by reason of his default. **[1393]**

NOTES
Commencement: 29 December 1986.

8. Administrative records

The responsible insolvency practitioner shall prepare and keep administrative records in relation to each separate insolvent containing—

(a) the minutes of the proceedings at any meeting of creditors and contributories including a record of every resolution passed at the meeting;

(b) the minutes of the proceedings at any meeting of the creditors' committee and the liquidation committee;

(c) the record of every resolution passed at any meeting of the creditors' committee and the liquidation committee;

(d) a copy of every resolution passed under Rules 4.167 and 6.162 (resolutions by post) and a note that the concurrence of the relevant committee was obtained; and (*e*) any other matters that may be necessary to give an accurate record of his administration.   **[1394]**

NOTES
Commencement: 29 December 1986.
Rules: Insolvency Rules 1986, SI 1986 No 1925.

9. Financial records

(1) The responsible insolvency practitioner shall prepare and keep separate financial records in respect of each insolvent, and shall, subject to Regulation 10 below as to trading accounts, from day to day enter in those records all the receipts and payments made by him.

(2) The responsible insolvency practitioner shall submit the financial records to the creditors' committee or the liquidation committee, as the case may be, when required, who if they are not satisfied with their contents may so inform the Secretary of State, giving the reasons for their dissatisfaction, and request him to cause any relevant account sent to him under Regulation 12(1) below to be audited.   **[1395]**

NOTES
Commencement: 29 December 1986.

10. Responsible insolvency practitioner carrying on business

Where the responsible insolvency practitioner carries on any business of the insolvent, he shall—

(*a*) keep a separate and distinct account of the trading, including where appropriate particulars of all local bank account transactions; and

(*b*) incorporate in the financial records required to be kept under Regulation 9 above the total weekly amounts of the receipts and payments made by him in relation to the account kept under paragraph (*a*) above.   **[1396]**

NOTES
Commencement: 29 December 1986.

11. Certification of balance in Insolvency Services Account

Where a responsible insolvency practitioner desires to have a certificate of the balance standing to the credit of the insolvent in the Insolvency Services Account, he shall make a written application to the Secretary of State.   **[1397]**

NOTES
Commencement: 29 December 1986.

12. Audit of accounts of responsible insolvency practitioner

(1) Every responsible insolvency practitioner shall every year during his tenure of office send to the Secretary of State an account in relation to each insolvent of his receipts and payments as responsible insolvency practitioner.

(2) The account shall be in Form 1, shall be certified by the responsible insolvency practitioner and shall be accompanied by the bank statements relating to any local bank account in the name of the insolvent.

(3) The first account so sent shall be accompanied by a summary of the insolvent's statement of affairs (if any) submitted under the Act showing the

amounts of any assets realised and explaining the reasons for any non-realisation of any assets not realised.

(4) Where a statement of affairs has not been so submitted, the account so sent shall be accompanied by a summary of all known assets and the amounts actually realised, and a summary of all known assets not realised and their value, with reasons for any non-realisation.

(5) Subject to paragraph (6) below, the responsible insolvency practitioner shall send the account in respect of the first year within 30 days of the expiration of the period of 12 months from the date of the bankruptcy or winding-up order and the other accounts within 30 days of the expiration of every period of 12 months thereafter until he vacates office.

(6) Within 14 days of vacating office the responsible insolvency practitioner shall send to the Secretary of State an account of his receipts and payments in respect of the period since the date of the last account so sent or, if no such account has been sent, an account of his receipts and payments in respect of the whole period of his office, accompanied by such a summary as is referred to in paragraph (3) or (4) above.

(7) Any account sent to the Secretary of State under paragraph (1) above shall, if he so requires, be audited, but, whether or not the Secretary of State requires the account to be audited, the responsible insolvency practitioner shall—

    (*a*) send to the Secretary of State on demand any vouchers and information relating to the account; and

    (*b*) produce on demand to the Secretary of State, and allow him to inspect, any accounts, books and other records kept by the responsible insolvency practitioner, and this duty to produce and inspect shall extend to production and inspection at the premises of the responsible insolvency practitioner. **[1398]**

NOTES
Commencement: 29 December 1986.

13. Responsible insolvency practitioner to send copy of accounts

(1) Every responsible insolvency practitioner shall, on request from the bankrupt or any creditor of the insolvent or any director of the company being wound up or any contributory for a copy of an account of his receipts and payments as responsible insolvency practitioner for any period, including future periods, send such a copy free of charge to the person making the request.

(2) The copy of the account shall be sent within 14 days of the responsible insolvency practitioner sending the account to the Secretary of State under Regulation 12(1) above or of the receipt of the request, whichever is the later.
[1399]

NOTES
Commencement: 29 December 1986.

DISPOSAL OF INSOLVENT'S BOOKS, PAPERS AND OTHER RECORDS

14. A liquidator or trustee, on the authorisation of the official receiver, during his tenure of office or on vacating office, or the official receiver while acting as liquidator or trustee, at any time may sell, destroy or otherwise dispose of the books, papers and other records of the insolvent.   **[1400]**

DIVIDENDS TO CREDITORS OF AN INSOLVENT AND RETURNS OF CAPITAL TO CONTRIBUTORIES OF A COMPANY

15. Payment

(1) A responsible insolvency practitioner shall pay every dividend by payable order on HM Paymaster General which will be prepared by the Department on the application of the responsible insolvency practitioner and transmitted to him for distribution amongst the creditors.

(2) The application for a payable order for a payment of dividend shall be made in Form 2 and shall be accompanied by a certified list of all proofs of debts admitted for dividend in whole or in part and, at the request of the Secretary of State, by the said proofs.

(3) A responsible insolvency practitioner in the case of a company shall pay every return of capital to contributories by payable order, which shall be prepared by the Department on application on a form obtainable from the Department for that purpose or on a form which is substantially similar and shall be accompanied by a copy of any order of the court authorising the return together with a schedule setting out the names and addresses of the persons to whom the return is to be paid and the amount of money payable to each person.

(4) The responsible insolvency practitioner shall enter the total amount of every dividend and of every return to contributories that he desires to pay under paragraphs (1) and (3) above in the records to be kept under Regulation 9 above in one sum.

(5) The responsible insolvency practitioner, on the expiration of six months from the last day of the month of issue, shall destroy any lapsed payable orders which have become invalid after first preparing a list of their numbers, names of payees and amounts.

(6) The responsible insolvency practitioner shall send the list mentioned in paragraph (5) above to the Department.

(7) On the responsible insolvency practitioner vacating office he shall send to the Department any valid unclaimed payable orders for dividends or returns to contributories after defacing them by cutting off the bottom right hand corner.   **[1401]**

NOTES
Commencement: 29 December 1986.

UNCLAIMED FUNDS AND DIVIDENDS

16. Payment of unclaimed or undistributed assets, dividends or other money on dissolution of company

Notwithstanding anything in these Regulations, any moneys in the hands of any or any former responsible insolvency practitioner in the case of a company which has been dissolved at the date of the dissolution of the company or his earlier vacation of office, representing unclaimed or undistributed assets of the company or dividends or held by the company in trust in respect of dividends or other sums due to any person as a member or former member of the company, shall forthwith be paid by him into the Insolvency Services Account.   **[1402]**

NOTES
  Commencement: 29 December 1986.

17. Claiming money paid into the Insolvency Services Account

(1) Any person claiming to be entitled to any moneys paid into the Insolvency Services Account may apply to the Secretary of State for payment, supported by such evidence of the claim as the Secretary of State may require.

(2) Any person dissatisfied with the decision of the Secretary of State in respect of his claim made under this Regulation may appeal to the court. **[1403]**

NOTES
  Commencement: 29 December 1986.

INVESTMENT OR OTHERWISE HANDLING OF FUNDS IN WINDING UP OF COMPANIES
AND PAYMENT OF INTEREST

18. (1) When in a winding up of a company the cash balance standing to the credit of the company in the account in respect of that company kept by the Secretary of State is in excess of the amount which, in the opinion of the responsible insolvency practitioner, is required for the immediate purposes of the liquidation and should be invested, he may request the Secretary of State to invest the amount not so required in Government securities, to be placed to the credit of that account for the company's benefit.

(2) When any part of the money so invested is, in the opinion of the responsible insolvency practitioner, required for the immediate purposes of the liquidation, he may request the Secretary of State to raise such sum as may be required by the sale of such part of those securities as may be necessary.

(3) The request of the responsible insolvency practitioner under paragraph (1) or (2) above shall be in writing addressed to the Department and shall be sufficient authority to the Secretary of State for the investment or sale, as the case may be.

(4) In cases where investments have been made at the request of the responsible insolvency practitioner in pursuance of paragraph (1) above and additional sums to the amounts so invested, including moneys received under paragraph (7) below, are paid into the Insolvency Services Account to the credit of the company, a written request shall be given to the Secretary of State by the responsible insolvency practitioner if it is desired that these additional sums should be invested.

(5) When the amount of the sums paid into the Insolvency Services Account standing to the credit of a company in the account in respect of that company kept by the Secretary of State exceeds £2,000, and the responsible insolvency practitioner gives notice to him that the excess is not required for the immediate purposes of the liquidation, the company is entitled to interest from the date of receipt of the notice by the Secretary of State on the excess at the rate of $3\frac{1}{2}$ per cent per annum.

(6) In cases where the company is entitled to interest under paragraph (5) above and additional sums are paid into the Insolvency Services Account to the credit of the company and further notice is given to the Secretary of State by the responsible insolvency practitioner that these additional sums are not required for the immediate purposes of the liquidation, the company is then entitled to interest on the additional sums in accordance with paragraph (5) above.

(7) All moneys received in respect of investments and interest earned under this Regulation shall be paid into the Insolvency Services Account to the credit of the company.   **[1404]**

NOTES
    Commencement: 29 December 1986.

REMUNERATION OF OFFICIAL RECEIVER

19. Official receiver's remuneration while acting as liquidator or trustee calculated as a percentage of the value of assets realised or distributed

Subject to Regulation 22 below, when he is the liquidator or trustee of the insolvent, the official receiver's remuneration for his services as such shall be calculated on the scales in the Table below, as a percentage of the value of the assets of the insolvent realised (after deducting any sums paid to secured creditors in respect of their securities and any sums spent out of money received in carrying on the business of the insolvent) and of the assets distributed to the insolvent's creditors (including payments made in respect of preferential debts) and, in the case of a company, to contributories.

TABLE

The realisation scale

i	on the first £5,000 or fraction thereof	20%
ii	on the next £5,000 or fraction thereof	15%
iii	on the next £90,000 or fraction thereof	10%
iv	on all further sums realised	5%

The distribution scale

i	on the first £5,000 or fraction thereof	10%
ii	on the next £5,000 or fraction thereof	7½%
iii	on the next £90,000 or fraction thereof	5 %
iv	on all further sums distributed	2½%

[1405]

NOTES
    Commencement: 29 December 1986.

20. Official receiver's general remuneration while acting as interim receiver, provisional liquidator, liquidator or trustee

(1) When he is an interim receiver appointed under section 286 or the provisional liquidator of a company being wound up or where as official receiver he performs any duty as liquidator or trustee for which remuneration is not provided in these Regulations or a fee is not provided under any order made under section 414 or 415, the official receiver's remuneration for the services provided by himself and his officers in that capacity shall be calculated on the total hourly rate as specified in the Tables below.

(2) Table 1 shall be used when calculating the remuneration of the official receiver of the London insolvency district and Table 2 shall be used when calculating the remuneration of the official receiver of any other district.

(3) The Tables referred to in paragraphs (1) and (2) above are—

TABLE 1

Official	*Total hourly rate in pounds*
Official Receiver	33
Deputy/Assistant Official Receiver	26
Senior Examiner	22
Examiner	18

TABLE 2

Official	*Total hourly rate in pounds*
Official Receiver	24
Deputy/Assistant Official Receiver	19
Senior Examiner	16
Examiner	13

[1406]

NOTES
Commencement: 29 December 1986.

21. Official receiver's remuneration while acting as liquidator, provisional liquidator, trustee or interim receiver for the transfer or conveyance of property subject to a charge

When he is a liquidator, provisional liquidator, trustee or interim receiver appointed under section 286, the official receiver's remuneration for the transfer or conveyance at the request of a secured creditor or a receiver appointed by such a creditor of property subject to any charge over the property created by the insolvent shall be 0.5 per cent of the sale price of the property or £110, whichever is the greater. **[1407]**

NOTES
Commencement: 29 December 1986.

22. Official receiver's remuneration while acting as liquidator or provisional liquidator for payments into the Insolvency Services Account from realisation of property charged

When he is a liquidator or provisional liquidator, the official receiver's remuneration for payments made by him as such into the Insolvency Services Account from the realisation of property of the company—

(a) for secured creditors (other than a creditor who holds a floating charge on the company's undertaking or property) shall be calculated on the realisation scale set out in the Table in Regulation 19 above in the manner set out in that Regulation; and

(b) for creditors who hold a floating charge on the company's undertaking or property shall be calculated on both the scales and in the manner set out in that Regulation. **[1408]**

NOTES
Commencement: 29 December 1986.

PART 3
COMPANIES VOLUNTARY WINDING UP

23. Introductory

This Part of these Regulations relates to companies which are being wound up voluntarily and which the courts in England and Wales have jurisdiction to wind up.   **[1409]**

NOTES
Commencement: 29 December 1986.

ACCOUNTS, BOOKS AND OTHER RECORDS AND AUDITING OF ACCOUNTS

24. Payments into the Insolvency Services Account

The liquidator of a company shall, within 14 days of the expiration of the period of 6 months from the date of his appointment and of every period of 6 months thereafter until he vacates office, pay into the Insolvency Services Account to the credit of the company the balance of funds in his hands or under his control relating to the company, including any unclaimed or undistributed assets or dividends, but excluding such part (if any) as he considers necessary to retain for the immediate purposes of the liquidation.   **[1410]**

NOTES
Commencement: 29 December 1986.

25. Application by liquidator for payments out of Insolvency Services Account

A liquidator who requires to make payments out of any moneys standing to the credit of the company in the Insolvency Services Account, either by way of distribution or in respect of the expenses of insolvency proceedings, shall apply in writing to the Secretary of State who may either authorise payment to the liquidator of the sum required by him, or may direct cheques to be issued to the liquidator for delivery by him to the persons to whom the payments are to be made.   **[1411]**

NOTES
Commencement: 29 December 1986.

26. Administrative records

Regulation 8, in so far as it relates to companies, applies to a creditors' voluntary winding up.   **[1412]**

NOTES
Commencement: 29 December 1986.

27. Financial records

(1) In a creditors' voluntary winding up, the liquidator shall prepare and keep such financial records of each company as the liquidation committee, or if there is no such committee, as the creditors direct, and shall, subject to Regulation 10 above as to trading accounts applied by Regulation 28 below, from day to day

enter in those records all the receipts and payments, including those relating to the Insolvency Services Account, made by him.

(2) The liquidator shall submit the records required to be kept under paragraph (1) above to the liquidation committee, or if there is no such committee, to the creditors, when required for inspection.   **[1413]**

NOTES
Commencement: 29 December 1986.

28. Liquidator carrying on business

Regulation 10 applies to a creditors' voluntary winding up.   **[1414]**

NOTES
Commencement: 29 December 1986.

29. Certification of balance in Insolvency Services Account

Regulation 11 applies.   **[1415]**

NOTES
Commencement: 29 December 1986.

30. Audit of liquidator's accounts

(1) The liquidator shall, if required by the Secretary of State at any time, send to him an account in relation to a company of his receipts and payments as liquidator.

(2) Each account shall be certified by the liquidator.

(3) Any account sent to the Secretary of State under paragraph (1) above shall, if he so requires, be audited, but, whether or not the Secretary of State requires the account to be audited, the liquidator shall—

  (a) send to the Secretary of State on demand any vouchers and information relating to the account; and
  (b) produce on demand to the Secretary of State, and allow him to inspect, any accounts, books and other records kept by the liquidator, and this duty to produce and inspect shall extend to production and inspection at the premises of the liquidator.   **[1416]**

NOTES
Commencement: 29 December 1986.

31. Liquidator to send copy of statement containing information as to pending liquidations

(1) Every liquidator shall, on request from any creditor, contributory or director of the company being wound up for a copy of a statement for any period, including future periods, sent to the registrar of companies under section 192, send such a copy free of charge to the person making the request.

(2) The copy of the statement shall be sent within 14 days of the liquidator sending the statement to the registrar or of the receipt of the request, whichever is the later.   **[1417]**

NOTES
Commencement: 29 December 1986.

DISPOSAL OF COMPANY'S BOOKS, PAPERS AND OTHER RECORDS

32. The person who was last liquidator of a company which has been dissolved may, at any time after the expiration of a period of one year from the date of dissolution, destroy or otherwise dispose of the books, papers and other records of the company.   **[1418]**

NOTES
Commencement: 29 December 1986.

UNCLAIMED FUNDS AND DIVIDENDS

33. Regulations 16 and 17 apply.   **[1419]**

NOTES
Commencement: 29 December 1986.

INVESTMENT OR OTHERWISE HANDLING OF FUNDS IN VOLUNTARY WINDING UP OF COMPANIES

34. Investment of assets in Government securities and sale of securities

Regulation 18 applies with the addition of the following paragraphs—

"(8) Any money invested or deposited at interest by a liquidator shall be deemed to be money under his control, and when such money forms part of the balance of funds in his hands or under his control relating to the company required to be paid into the Insolvency Services Account under Regulation 24 below, the liquidator shall realise the investment or withdrawn the deposit and shall pay the proceeds into that account:

Provided that where the money is invested in Government securities, such securities may, with the permission of the Secretary of State, be transferred to the control of the Secretary of State instead of being forthwith realised and the proceeds paid into the Insolvency Services Account.

(9) If and when the money represented by the securities is required wholly or in part for the immediate purposes of the liquidation, the Secretary of State may realise the securities wholly or in part and pay the proceeds of the realisation into the Insolvency Services Account in accordance with paragraph (7) above and deal with it in the same way as other monies paid into that Account may be dealt with.".   **[1420]**

NOTES
Commencement: 29 December 1986.

35. Liquidator to provide information to Secretary of State

(1) A liquidator or former liquidator, whether the winding up has been concluded under Rule 4.223 or not, shall, within 14 days of a request by the Secretary of State, give the Secretary of State particulars of any money in his hands or under his control representing unclaimed or undistributed assets of the company or dividends or held by the company in trust in respect of dividends or other sums due to any person as a member or former member of the company and such other particulars as the Secretary of State may require for the purpose of ascertaining or getting in any money payable into the Insolvency Services Account.

(2) The particulars referred to in paragaph (1) above shall, if the Secretary of State so requires, be certified by the liquidator, or former liquidator, as the case may be. **[1421]**

NOTES
Commencement: 29 December 1986.
Rules: Insolvency Rules 1986, SI 1986 No 1925.

PART 4

TRANSITIONAL PROVISIONS

36. (1) Regulations 5(1), (2) and (4), 6, 11, 15(1)–(4), 25 and 29 above apply where any application is made under those Regulations on or after 29th December 1986.

(2) Regulation 12 applies to any account required to be sent to the Secretary of State except an account due to be sent to him under the existing law before 29th December 1986 or for a period which includes that day.

(3) Regulation 14 applies to any disposal on or after 29th December 1986.

(4) Regulations 18, 30 and 34, so far as Regulation 34 applies Regulation 18(1)–(7), apply where any request or requirement is made or any notice is given under those Regulations on or after 29th December 1986. **[1422]**

NOTES
Commencement: 29 December 1986.

THE SCHEDULE

Regulations 12(2) and 15(2)

NOTES
The forms themselves are not reproduced in this work, but their numbers and descriptions are listed below.

FORMS RELATING TO ACCOUNTS AND APPLICATION FOR PAYABLE ORDER
FOR PAYMENT OF DIVIDENDS

FORM NO	TITLE
1	Liquidator/Trustee Receipts and Payments Account
2	Application to the Department of Trade and Industry for the Issue of Payable Orders for the payment of dividend to the Trustee or Liquidator

[1423]

NOTES
Commencement: 29 December 1986.

INSOLVENCY PRACTITIONERS REGULATIONS 1986
(SI 1986 No 1995)

NOTES
Made: 20 November 1986.
Authority: Insolvency Act 1985, ss 4, 5, 10; Insolvency Act 1986, ss 390, 392, 393, 419.

ARRANGEMENT OF REGULATIONS

PART I

INTRODUCTORY

Regulation   Para
1   Citation, commencement and interpretation   ..   ..   [1424]

PART II

AUTHORISATION OF INSOLVENCY PRACTITIONERS

2   Revocation ..   ..   [1425]
3   Application of this Part   ..   ..   [1426]
4   Matters for determining whether an applicant is fit and proper ..   ..   [1427]
5   Education   ..   ..   [1428]
6   Practical training and experience ..   ..   [1429]
7   Fees ..   ..   [1430]
8   Maximum period of authorisation ..   ..   [1431]

PART III

THE REQUIREMENTS FOR SECURITY AND CAUTION FOR THE PROPER PERFORMANCE OF THE FUNCTIONS OF AN INSOLVENCY PRACTITIONER

9   Application of this Part   ..   ..   [1432]
10   Requirements for security or caution   ..   ..   [1433]
11   Exceptions in relation to requirements for security or caution ..   ..   [1434]
12   Registration and filing requirements in England and Wales   ..   ..   [1435]
13   Registration and filing requirements in Scotland ..   ..   [1436]

PART IV

RECORDS TO BE KEPT BY INSOLVENCY PRACTITIONERS

14   Application of this Part   ..   ..   [1437]
15   The records to be kept   ..   ..   [1438]
16   Inspection of records   ..   ..   [1439]
17   Notification ..   ..   [1440]
18   Preservation of records   ..   ..   [1441]

SCHEDULES

Schedule 1—Academic Qualifications   ..   ..   [1442]
Schedule 2—Requirements for Security or Caution ..   ..   ..   [1445]
Schedule 3—Form of Record ..   ..   [1447]

PART I

INTRODUCTORY

1. Citation, commencement and interpretation

(1) These Regulations may be cited as the Insolvency Practitioners Regulations 1986.

(2) These Regulations shall come into force on 29th December 1986.

(3) In these Regulations except where the context otherwise requires:—

"Act" means the Insolvency Act 1986;

"application" means an application made by an individual to the competent authority for authorisation under section 393 of the Act to act as an insolvency practitioner;

"the Bankruptcy Act" means the Bankruptcy (Scotland) Act 1985;

"commencement date" means the date on which these Regulations come into force;

"insolvency practitioner" shall be construed in accordance with section 388 of the Act;

"the insolvency legislation" means the following enactments:—

the Act;

the Insolvency Act 1985;

Parts XVIII to XXI of the Companies Act 1985;

Part VII of the Employment Protection (Consolidation) Act 1978;

the Bankruptcy Act 1914;

the Deeds of Arrangement Act 1914;

the Bankruptcy Act;

the Bankruptcy (Scotland) Act 1913; and

the provisions of the enactments repealed by Schedule 1 to the Companies Consolidation (Consequential Provisions) Act 1985 relating to insolvency;

"business" includes the carrying on of any trade, profession or vocation and the discharge of the functions relating to any office or employment;

"insolvency practice" means the carrying on of the business of acting as an insolvency practitioner or in a corresponding capacity under the law of any country or territory outside Great Britain, and for this purpose acting as an insolvency practitioner shall include acting as a trustee in sequestration or a judicial factor on the bankrupt estate of a deceased person;

"office-holder" means a person who acts or has acted as an insolvency practitioner, a trustee in sequestration, or a judicial factor on the bankrupt estate of a deceased person or in a corresponding capacity under the law of any country or territory outside Great Britain;

"insolvency work experience" means engagement in work related to the administration of the estate of persons in respect of which an office-holder has been appointed;

"higher insolvency work experience" means engagement in work related to the administration of the estates of persons in respect of which an office-holder has been appointed where the work involves the management or supervision of the conduct of a case on behalf of that office-holder;

"associate" shall be construed in accordance with section 435 of the Act;

"Crown employment" shall be construed in accordance with section 12(2) of the Employment Protection Act 1975;

"interim trustee", "permanent trustee" and "trust deed for creditors" have the same meanings as in the Bankruptcy Act;

"insolvency proceedings" means any of the proceedings under the Act and the Bankruptcy Act in which a person may be appointed to act as an insolvency practitioner;

"Accountant in Bankruptcy" shall be construed in accordance with section 1 of the Bankruptcy Act. **[1424]**

NOTES

Commencement: 29 December 1986.

PART II

AUTHORISATION OF INSOLVENCY PRACTITIONERS

2. Revocation

(1) The Insolvency Practitioners (Authorisation by Relevant Authority) Regulations 1986 (the "former Regulations") are hereby revoked.

(2) Notwithstanding paragraph (1) the former Regulations shall continue to apply and have effect in relation to any application made to a relevant authority before the commencement date for authorisation under section 5 of the Insolvency Act 1985 to act as an insolvency practitioner in respect of which:—

    (*a*) no authorisation has been granted; or

    (*b*) no written notice under section 8(4) of that Act has been given by the relevant authority; or

    (*c*) no written notice under section 9 of that Act has been given by the authority,

before the commencement date. **[1425]**

NOTES

    Commencement: 29 December 1986.

3. Application of this Part

The Regulations within this Part apply in relation to:—

    (*a*) any applications made to a competent authority on or after the commencement date; and

    (*b*) any withdrawal of an authorisation granted by a competent authority or the relevant authority under section 5 of the Insolvency Act 1985 pursuant to a notice under section 394(2) of the Act given on or after the commencement date. **[1426]**

NOTES

    Commencement: 29 December 1986.

    The Act: Insolvency Act 1986.

4. Matters for determining whether an applicant is fit and proper

(1) Without prejudice to the generality of section 393(2)(*a*) or (4)(*a*) of the Act, in determining whether an applicant is a fit and proper person to act as an insolvency practitioner the matters to be taken into account shall include:—

    (*a*) whether the applicant has been convicted of any offence involving fraud or other dishonesty or violence;

    (*b*) whether the applicant has contravened any provision in any enactment contained in the insolvency legislation or in subordinate legislation made under any such enactment or any provision of the law of a country or territory outside Great Britain which corresponds to such legislation;

    (*c*) whether the applicant has engaged in any practices in the course of carrying on business appearing to be deceitful or oppressive or otherwise unfair or improper, whether unlawful or not, or which otherwise cast doubt upon his probity or competence for discharging the duties of an insolvency practitioner;

    (*d*) whether in respect of any insolvency practice carried on by the applicant at the date of or at any time prior to the making of the application there were established adequate systems of control of the practice and adequate records relating to the practice, including accounting records, and whether such systems of control and records have been or were maintained on an adequate basis;

(*e*) whether the insolvency practice of the applicant is, has been or, where the applicant is not yet carrying on such a practice, will be, carried on with the independence, integrity and the professional skills appropriate to the range and scale of the practice and the proper performance of the duties of an insolvency practitioner;

(*f*) whether the applicant in any case where he has acted as an insolvency practitioner, has failed to disclose fully to such persons as might reasonably be expected to be affected thereby circumstances where there is or appears to be a conflict of interest between his so acting and any interest of his own whether personal, financial or otherwise without having received such consent as might be appropriate to his acting or continuing to act despite the existence of such circumstances.

(2) In this Regulation "applicant" includes, where it is proposed to withdraw any authorisation on the grounds that the holder is not a fit and proper person, the holder of the authorisation. **[1427]**

NOTES
Commencement: 29 December 1986.
The Act: Insolvency Act 1986.

5. Education

(1) The requirements in respect of education which are prescribed for the purposes of section 393(2)(*b*) of the Act are that the applicant possesses one or more of the academic qualifications listed in Part I of the Schedule to these Regulations or such other academic or professional qualifications as shall indicate the attainment of an equivalent level of education to that attested by that qualification or, as the case may be, those qualifications.

(2) The provisions of this Regulation apply only in relation to:—

(*a*) an applicant who shall not have attained the age of 35 on or before 15th December 1986; and

(*b*) who has not held an authorisation granted under section 393 of the Act or section 5 of the Insolvency Act 1985. **[1428]**

NOTES
Commencement: 29 December 1986.
The Act: Insolvency Act 1986.

6. Practical training and experience

(1) In this Regulation paragraphs (2) to (6) apply in relation to any applications other than those specified in paragraph (7).

(2) The requirements with respect to practical training and experience which are prescribed for the purposes of section 393(2)(*b*) of that Act are either that:—

(*a*) the applicant has been appointed an office-holder in not less than 30 cases within the period of 10 years immediately prior to the making of his application; or

(*b*) the applicant:—

   (i) was first employed by a person carrying on insolvency practice in that practice not later than 10 years prior to the making of his application; and

   (ii) within the period of 10 years referred to in sub-paragraph (*a*) above has acquired not less than 7,000 hours of insolvency work experience whether in the employment of a person carrying on an insolvency practice or as an office-holder; and

   (iii) satisfies the condition set out in sub-paragraph (*c*) below;

  (*c*) the condition referred to in sub-paragraph (2)(*b*)(iii) is that the applicant must show he satisfies one of the following three requirements:—

   (i) he has been appointed an office-holder in at least 5 cases within the period of 5 years immediately prior to the making of his application; or

   (ii) he has acquired 1,000 hours or more of higher insolvency work experience within such period; or

   (iii) he can show that within such period he has achieved one of the following combinations of appointments as an office-holder and hours acquired of higher insolvency work experience:—

     (*a*) not less than 4 cases and 200 hours
     (*b*) not less than 3 cases and 400 hours
     (*c*) not less than 2 cases and 600 hours
     (*d*) not less than 1 case and 800 hours

(3) In determining whether an applicant falls within paragraph (2) above:—

  (*a*) no account shall be taken of any case where:—

   (i) he was appointed to the office of receiver or to a corresponding office under the law of a country or territory outside Great Britain by or on behalf of a creditor who at the time of appointment was an associate of the applicant; or

   (ii) in a members' voluntary winding up or in a corresponding procedure under the laws of a country or territory outside Great Britain, he was appointed liquidator at a general meeting where his associates were entitled to exercise or control the exercise of one third or more of the voting power at that general meeting;

  (*b*) where the applicant has been an office-holder in relation to:—

   (i) two or more companies which were associates at the time of appointment; or

   (ii) two or more individuals who were carrying on business in partnership with each other at the time of appointment:—

he shall be treated as having held office in only one case in respect of all offices held in relation to the companies which were associates or in respect of all offices held in relation to the individuals who were in partnership as the case may be.

(4) Where in order to satisfy all or any of the requirements set out in paragraph (2) above an applicant relies on appointment as an office-holder or the acquisition of insolvency work experience or higher insolvency work experience in relation to cases under the laws of a country or territory outside Great Britain, he shall demonstrate that he has no less than 1,400 hours of insolvency work experience or higher insolvency work experience in cases under the law of England and Wales or Scotland acquired within the period of the two

years immediately prior to the making of his application and that where appropriate he has a good command of the English language.

(5) For the purposes of sub-paragraph (2)(*b*) employment by a person carrying on insolvency practice includes Crown employment in the Insolvency Service of the Department of Trade and Industry.

(6) For the purposes of paragraph (2) above a person carrying on insolvency practice includes a firm or partnership.

(7) Where an application is made by a person who, at the time of making the application, is the holder of an authorisation granted by a competent authority or relevant authority the requirements with respect to practical training and experience which are prescribed for the purposes of section 393(2)(*b*) of the Act are that the applicant has been appointed an office-holder in at least one case under the law of England and Wales or Scotland within the period from the commencement of that authorisation to the making of the application and in determining whether an applicant falls within this paragraph the provisions of paragraph (3) above shall apply.   **[1429]**

NOTES
　　Commencement: 29 December 1986.
　　The Act: Insolvency Act 1986.

7. Fees

The fee to accompany any application to which the Regulations in this Part apply shall be £200.   **[1430]**

NOTES
　　Commencement: 29 December 1986.

8. Maximum period of authorisation

No authorisation granted pursuant to an application to which the Regulations in this Part apply shall continue in force for a period of more than 3 years from the date on which it is granted.   **[1431]**

NOTES
　　Commencement: 29 December 1986.

PART III

THE REQUIREMENTS FOR SECURITY AND CAUTION FOR THE PROPER PERFORMANCE OF THE FUNCTIONS OF AN INSOLVENCY PRACTITIONER

9. Application of this Part

(1) Save as provided in paragraph (2) of this Regulation the Regulations in this Part apply in relation to any person appointed on or after the commencement date to act as an insolvency practitioner in relation to any person or company.

(2) The Regulations in this Part shall not apply in relation to any insolvency practitioner appointed on or after the commencement date—

　　(*a*) to act as

　　　　(i) a liquidator in any winding up to which paragraph 4(1) of Schedule 11 to the Act applies; or

    (ii) permanent trustee in the sequestration of the estate of any person, on whose estate the insolvency practitioner has, before the commencement date, been appointed to act as interim trustee; or

  (*b*) in any bankruptcy to which paragraph 10(1) of Schedule 11 to the Act applies.   **[1432]**

NOTES

  Commencement: 29 December 1986.

  The Act: Insolvency Act 1986.

10. Requirements for security or caution

(1) For the purposes of section 390(3)(*b*) of the Act the requirements in respect of security or caution for the proper performance of the functions of an insolvency practitioner are that:—

  (*a*) there is in force at the time when an insolvency practitioner is appointed to act a bond which complies with the requirement set out in Part I of Schedule 2 to these Regulations under which the surety or cautioner is liable in the general penalty sum of £250,000; and

  (*b*) there is issued under that bond as soon as reasonably possible after the appointment of the practitioner a certificate of specific penalty in respect of the practitioner acting in relation to that person or company under which the specific penalty sum is not less than the value of that person's assets estimated in accordance with Part II of the said Schedule; and

  (*c*) where, at any time before the practitioner obtains his release or discharge in respect of his acting in relation to that person or company he forms the opinion that the value of the assets comprised in the estate of that person or company is higher than the value estimated for the purposes of paragraph (*b*) above, there is issued forthwith a further certificate of specific penalty in respect of the practitioner acting in relation to that person or company under which the penalty sum is not less than that higher value [or £5,000,000 whichever shall be the less].

    (2) The bond referred to in paragraph (1) shall be retained by the recognised professional body or, as the case may be, the competent authority by which the practitioner has been authorised to act as an insolvency practitioner.   **[1433]**

NOTES

  Commencement: 29 December 1986.

  Para (1): words in square brackets in sub-para (*c*) added by SI 1986 No 2247 with effect from 29 December 1986.

  The Act: Insolvency Act 1986.

11. Exceptions in relation to requirements for security or caution

Where a practitioner who is appointed to be—

  (*a*) provisional liquidator in the winding up by the court of a company is subsequently appointed to be liquidator of that company; or

  (*b*) liquidator in a voluntary winding up of a company is subsequently appointed to be liquidator in the winding up of that company by the court; or

  (*c*) interim trustee in the sequestration of the estate of any person is subsequently appointed to be permanent trustee in the sequestration of the estate of that person; or (*d*) an administrator of a company is subsequently appointed to be a liquidator of that company pursuant to section 140 of the Act,

and a certificate of specific penalty is issued under Regulation 10(*b*) in respect of the earlier or earliest such appointment, it shall not be necessary for such a certificate to be issued in respect of the subsequent appointment of the practitioner in any of those circumstances. **[1434]**

NOTES
Commencement: 29 December 1986.
The Act: Insolvency Act 1986.

12. Registration and filing requirements in England and Wales

(1) Where a practitioner is appointed to act in relation to a company as a liquidator in a voluntary winding up or as an administrative receiver, he shall within 14 days of receipt of the certificate deliver to the registrar of companies for registration a copy of any certificate and of any further certificate of specific penalty issued in respect of his so acting.

(2) Where a practitioner is appointed to act in relation to a company or another person in any capacity specified in section 388(1) or (2) of the Act other than one specified in paragraph (1) above he shall, within 14 days, file in the court having jurisdiction in relation to that person under the Act any certificate and any further certificate of specific penalty issued in respect of his so acting.

(3) In this Regulation a "company" means a company which the courts in England and Wales have jurisdiction to wind up and "administrative receiver" means such a receiver appointed otherwise than under section 51 of the Act (appointment of receivers under the law of Scotland). **[1435]**

NOTES
Commencement: 29 December 1986.
The Act: Insolvency Act 1986.

13. Registration and filing requirements in Scotland

(1) Where a person is appointed to act as an administrative receiver or, in relation to a company, as a liquidator, provisional liquidator, administrator or supervisor of a voluntary arrangement approved under Part I of the Act, he shall retain in the sederunt book kept under Rule 7.33 of the Insolvency (Scotland) Rules 1986 the principal copy of any certificate and of any further certificate of specific penalty issued in respect of his so acting and shall, within 14 days of the receipt of such certificate or further certificate, deliver a copy of it to the Registrar of Companies for registration.

(2) Where a practitioner is appointed to act as interim trustee or permanent trustee or as trustee under a trust deed for creditors, he shall retain in the sederunt book kept for those proceedings the principal copy of any certificate and of any further certificate of specific penalty issued in respect of his so acting and shall, within 14 days of the receipt of such certificate or further certificate, deliver a copy of it to the Accountant in Bankruptcy for retention by him.

(3) In this Regulation:—

(*a*) "company" means a company which the courts in Scotland have jurisdiction to wind up and (*b*) "administrative receiver" means a receiver appointed under section 51 of the Act (appointment of receivers under the law of Scotland) who is an administrative receiver. **[1436]**

NOTES
Commencement: 29 December 1986.
The Act: Insolvency Act 1986.

PART IV

RECORDS TO BE KEPT BY INSOLVENCY PRACTITIONERS

14. Application of this Part

(1) Save as provided in paragraph (2) of this Regulation the Regulations in this Part apply in relation to any person appointed on or after the commencement date to act as an insolvency practitioner in relation to any person.

(2) The Regulations in this Part shall not apply in the case of the appointment of an insolvency practitioner to whom Regulation 9(2) applies.

[1437]

NOTES
Commencement: 29 December 1986.

15. The records to be kept

In respect of the estate of each person in relation to whom an insolvency practitioner acts in any of the capacities specified in section 388 of the Act and in respect of the security or caution maintained by the practitioner for the proper performance of his functions in relation to that estate in compliance with section 390(3) of the Act, the practitioner shall maintain a record in the form set out in Schedule 3 to these Regulations and shall make forthwith upon the occurrence of any events specified in that form the appropriate entry in the record. **[1438]**

NOTES
Commencement: 29 December 1986.
The Act: Insolvency Act 1986.

16. Inspection of records

(1) The records maintained pursuant to this Part shall be produced by the insolvency practitioner to the authorising body or any duly appointed representative of such a body on the giving by the body or its representative of reasonable notice to the practitioner: and for the purposes of this Part the "authorising body" in relation to any practitioner shall be the professional body by virtue of membership of which that practitioner is authorised to act, or the competent authority which granted his authorisation, whichever the case may be.

(2) The records maintained by any insolvency practitioner authorised by virtue of membership of a professional body recognised under section 391 of the Act shall be produced by that practitioner to the Secretary of State on the giving by the Secretary of State of reasonable notice to the practitioner.

(3) Where the records are maintained in a non-documentary form references to their production include references to producing a copy of the records in legible form. **[1439]**

NOTES
Commencement: 29 December 1986.

17. Notification

The insolvency practitioner shall notify the authorising body of the place where the records required to be maintained under this Part are so maintained and the place (if different) where and the manner in which they are to be produced pursuant to Regulation 16 above. **[1440]**

NOTES
Commencement: 29 December 1986.

18. Preservation of records

The insolvency practitioner shall preserve every record required to be maintained under this Part for a period of 10 years from the date on which the practitioner is granted his release or discharge in respect of that estate or the date on which any security or caution maintained in respect of that estate expired or otherwise ceased to have effect whichever shall be the later. **[1441]**

NOTES
Commencement: 29 December 1986.

SCHEDULES
SCHEDULE 1

Regulation 5

ACADEMIC QUALIFICATIONS

PART I

1. A degree (other than an honorary degree) conferred by a University in the United Kingdom or Republic of Ireland or by the Council for National Academic Awards.

2. A General Certificate of Education or a Senior Certificate from a Secondary Education Board listed in Part II of this Schedule, in five subjects which must include:—

  (a) English Language;
  (b) 2 Advanced level passes or Higher grade passes obtained in one sitting in subjects included in the list in Part III of this Schedule ("acceptable subjects");
  (c) 2 other Ordinary level or Ordinary grade passes at appropriate grades (see note 1) in acceptable subjects or Advanced level or Higher grade passes in acceptable subjects.

NOTE 1: The appropriate grades are grades A, B and C at the Ordinary level of the GCE or where relevant Grades 1 to 6 at that level. **[1442]**

NOTES
Commencement: 29 December 1986.

PART II

Associated Examining Board
University of Cambridge Local Examination Syndicate
University of Durham
Joint Matriculation Board
University of London
Department of Education or Ministry of Education, Northern Ireland
Northern Ireland General Certificate of Education Examinations Board
Oxford and Cambridge Schools Examination Board
University of Oxford Delegacy of Local Examinations
Southern Universities' Joint Board for Schools Examinations
Welsh Joint Education Committee
Scottish Examination Board   **[1443]**

NOTES
    Commencement: 29 December 1986.

PART III

Mathematics
Sciences
Modern Languages
Welsh
Gaelic
Classics
History
Geography
Economics and Politics
English Literature
Law
Music
Religious Knowledge
Modern Studies
General Studies
Principles of Accounts
Theatre Studies
Design
Home Economics   **[1444]**

NOTES
    Commencement: 29 December 1986.

SCHEDULE 2
Regulation 10

REQUIREMENTS FOR SECURITY OR CAUTION

PART I

The bond referred to in Regulation 10 shall be a bond in a form approved by the Secretary
of State which contains provision whereby:—

    (i) a surety or cautioner undertakes to be jointly and severally liable with the insolvency practitioner for the proper performance by the practitioner of the duties and obligations imposed upon the practitioner by the Act or the Bankruptcy Act and the subordinate legislation made under the Act or the Bankruptcy Act,

    (ii) the liability of the surety or cautioner and the practitioner is in both a general penalty sum and a specific penalty sum in respect of each person in respect of whom the practitioner acts and is limited to a sum equivalent to the losses caused by the fraud and dishonesty of the practitioner,

    (iii) a certificate is issued by the surety accepting liability in respect of the practitioner acting in relation to a particular person in the amount of the specific penalty, and

    (iv) any claims made under the bond are made firstly in respect of the specific penalty sum. **[1445]**

NOTES

Commencement: 29 December 1986.

The Act: Insolvency Act 1986.

PART II

1. Subject to paragraph 3 below for the purposes of [Regulation 10(1)(*b*)] the value of a person's assets shall be:—

    (*a*) where the practitioner is appointed to act as:—

        (i) an interim receiver;

        (ii) a trustee in bankruptcy;

        (iii) an administrator of the estate of a deceased individual;

        (iv) a supervisor of a voluntary arrangement approved by a company under Part I of the Act;

        (v) a supervisor of a voluntary arrangement proposed by an individual and approved under Part VIII of the Act;

        (vi) a provisional liquidator;

        (vii) a liquidator;

        (viii) an administrator appointed under Part II of the Act;

        (ix) an interim or permanent trustee in sequestration;

        (x) a trustee under a trust deed for creditors, the value at the date of the appointment of the practitioner estimated by him having regard (where appropriate) to paragraph 2 of this Part of the Schedule;

    (*b*) where the practitioner is appointed to act as an administrative receiver an amount equivalent to that part of the assets of the company to which the practitioner is appointed which at the date of the appointment would appear to be available for the unsecured creditors of the company, whether in respect of the preferential debts of the company or otherwise, were the company to go into liquidation at the date of the appointment.

2. In estimating the value of a person's assets, the practitioner shall have regard to:—

    (*a*) in a case specified in subparagraphs 1(*a*)(i)-(vii) and (x) above, the estimated value of those assets disclosed in any statement of affairs in respect of such cases and any comments of creditors or the official receiver on that statement; and

    (*b*) in a case specified in subparagraph 1(*a*)(viii), the estimated value of the assets of the company as disclosed in any report on the company's affairs prepared pursuant to [Rule 2.2] of the Insolvency Rules 1986 or, as the case may be, pursuant to Rule 2.1 of the Insolvency (Scotland) Rules 1986;

    (*c*) in a case specified in subparagraph 1(*a*)(ix) the estimated value of those assets disclosed, as the case may be, by the most recently available of—

        (i) the debtor's list of assets and liabilities under section 19 of the Bankruptcy Act;

        (ii) the preliminary statement under section 20 of that Act; or

(iii) the final statement of the debtor's affairs by the interim trustee under section 23 of that Act.

3. In any case where the value of a person's assets estimated in accordance with paragraphs 1 and 2 above is less than £5,000 the value of those assets shall for the purposes of this Part of the Schedule, be deemed to be £5,000.

[4. In any case where the value of a person's assets estimated in accordance with paragraphs 1 and 2 above is more than £5,000,000 the value of those assets shall, for the purposes of this Part of the Schedule, be deemed to be £5,000,000.]   **[1446]**

NOTES
Commencement: 29 December 1986.
Paras 1, 2: words in square brackets substituted by SI 1986 No 2247 with effect from 29 December 1986.
Para 4: added by SI 1986 No 2247 with effect from 29 December 1986.

SCHEDULE 3

Regulation 15

FORM OF RECORD

[1447]

NOTES
The form itself is not reproduced in this work.
Commencement: 29 December 1986.

INSOLVENCY PROCEEDINGS (MONETARY LIMITS) ORDER 1986
(SI 1986 No 1996)

NOTES
Made: 20 November 1986.
Authority: Insolvency Act 1986, ss 416, 418, Sch 6, paras 9, 12.

ARRANGEMENT OF ARTICLES

Article	Para
1	[1448]
2	[1449]
3	[1450]
4	[1451]
Schedule—Part I—Increases of Monetary Amounts in First Group of Parts of Insolvency Act 1986	[1452]
Part II—Monetary Amounts for Purposes of Second Group of Parts of Insolvency Act 1986	[1453]

1. (1) This Order may be cited as the Insolvency Proceedings (Monetary Limits) Order 1986 and shall come into operation on 29th December 1986.

(2) In this Order "the Act" means the Insolvency Act 1986.   **[1448]**

NOTES
Commencement: 29 December 1986.

2. (1) The provisions in the first Group of Parts of the Act (companies winding up) set out in column 1 of Part 1 of the Schedule to this Order (shortly described in column 2) are hereby amended by substituting for the amounts specified in column 3 in relation to those provisions the amounts specified in column 4.

(2) The sum specified in column 4 of Part I of the Schedule in relation to section 184(3) of the Act is not to affect any case where the goods are sold or payment to avoid sale is made, before the coming into force of the increase.

[1449]

NOTES
>Commencement: 29 December 1986.
>The Act: Insolvency Act 1986.

3. The amounts prescribed for the purposes of the provisions in the second Group of Parts of the Act (bankruptcy) set out in column 1 of Part II of the Schedule to this Order (shortly described in column 2) are the amounts specified in column 3 in relation to those provisions. **[1450]**

NOTES
>Commencement: 29 December 1986.
>The Act: Insolvency Act 1986.

4. The amount prescribed for the purposes of paragraphs 9 and 12 of Schedule 6 to the Act (maximum amount for preferential status of employees' claims for remuneration and under the Reserve Forces (Safeguard of Employment) Act 1985) is £800. **[1451]**

NOTES
>Commencement: 29 December 1986.
>The Act: Insolvency Act 1986.

SCHEDULE

Article 2   PART I

INCREASES OF MONETARY AMOUNTS IN FIRST GROUP OF PARTS OF INSOLVENCY ACT 1986

. . . **[1452]**

NOTES
>Commencement: 29 December 1986.
>This Part amends the Insolvency Act 1986, ss 184, 206.

Article 3   PART II

MONETARY AMOUNTS FOR PURPOSES OF SECOND GROUP OF PARTS OF INSOLVENCY ACT 1986

Section of the Act (1)	Short Description (2)	Monetary Amount (3)
273(1)(a)	Maximum level of unsecured bankruptcy debts on debtor's petition for case to be referred to insolvency practitioner to assess possibility of voluntary arrangement with creditors.	£20,000
273(1)(b)	Minimum potential value of bankrupt's estate for case to be referred as described above.	£2,000

Section of the Act (1)	Short Description (2)	Monetary Amount (3)
346(3)	Minimum amount of judgment, determining whether amount recovered on sale of debtor's goods is to be treated as part of his estate in bankruptcy.	£500
354(1) and (2)	Minimum amount of concealed debt, or value of property concealed or removed, determining criminal liability under the section.	£500
358	Minimum value of property taken by a bankrupt out of England and Wales, determining his criminal liability.	£500
360(1)	Maximum amount of credit which bankrupt may obtain without disclosure of his status.	£250
361(2)	Exemption of bankrupt from criminal liability for failure to keep proper accountancy records, if unsecured liabilities not more than the prescribed minimum.	£20,000
364(2)(d)	Minimum value of goods removed by the bankrupt, determining his liability to arrest.	£500

[1453]

NOTES
  Commencement: 29 December 1986.

ADMINISTRATION OF INSOLVENT ESTATES OF DECEASED PERSONS ORDER 1986
(SI 1986 No 1999)

NOTES
  Made: 21 November 1986.
  Authority: Insolvency Act 1986, s 421.

ARRANGEMENT OF ARTICLES

Article		Para
1		[1454]
2		[1455]
3		[1456]
4		[1457]
5		[1458]
6		[1459]

SCHEDULES

Schedule 1—Provisions of the Act applying with relevant modifications to the Administration in bankruptcy of insolvent estates of deceased persons dying before presentation of a bankruptcy petition
  Part I—General modifications of Provisions of the Act .. .. [1460]
  Part II—Provisions of the Act not included in Part III of this Schedule .. .. [1461]
  Part III—Provisions of Part VIII of the Act relating to individual voluntary Arrangements .. .. [1462]
Schedule 2—Death of debtor after presentation of a bankruptcy petition .. .. [1463]
Schedule 3—Forms relating to Administration in Bankruptcy of Insolvent Estates of Deceased Debtors (Sch 1, Part II, paras 1, 5-7, 15, Sch 2, para 1) .. .. [1464]

1. This Order may be cited as the Administration of Insolvent Estates of Deceased Persons Order 1986 and shall come into force on 29th December 1986. **[1454]**

NOTES
Commencement: 29 December 1986.

2. In this Order—

"the Act" means the Insolvency Act 1986;

"insolvency administration order" means an order for the administration in bankruptcy of the insolvent estate of a deceased debtor (being an individual at the date of his death);

"insolvency administration petition" means a petition for an insolvency administration order; and

"the Rules" means the Insolvency Rules 1986. **[1455]**

NOTES
Commencement: 29 December 1986.

3. (1) The provisions of the Act specified in Parts II and III of Schedule 1 to this Order shall apply to the administration in bankruptcy of the insolvent estates of deceased persons dying before presentation of a bankruptcy petition with the modifications specified in those Parts and with any further such modifications as may be necessary to render them applicable to the estate of a deceased person and in particular with the modifications specified in Part I of that Schedule, and the provisions of the Rules, the Insolvency Regulations 1986 and any order made under section 415 of the Act (fees and deposits) shall apply accordingly.

(2) In the case of any conflict between any provision of the Rules and any provision of this Order, the latter provision shall prevail. **[1456]**

NOTES
Commencement: 29 December 1986.
The Act: Insolvency Act 1986.
Rules: Insolvency Rules 1986, SI 1986 No 1925.

4. (1) Where the estate of a deceased person is insolvent and is being administered otherwise than in bankruptcy, subject to paragraphs (2) and (3) below, the same provisions as may be in force for the time being under the law of bankruptcy with respect to the assets of individuals adjudged bankrupt shall apply to the administration of the estate with respect to the respective rights of secured and unsecured creditors, to debts and liabilities provable, to the valuation of future and contingent liabilities and to the priorities of debts and other payments.

(2) The reasonable funeral, testamentary and administration expenses have priority over the preferential debts listed in Schedule 6 to the Act.

(3) Section 292(2) of the Act shall not apply. **[1457]**

NOTES
Commencement: 29 December 1986.
The Act: Insolvency Act 1986.

5. (1) If a debtor by or against whom a bankruptcy petition has been presented dies, the proceedings in the matter shall, unless the court otherwise orders, be continued as if he were alive, with the modifications specified in Schedule 2 to this Order.

(2) The reasonable funeral and testamentary expenses have priority over the preferential debts listed in Schedule 6 to the Act.

(3) If a debtor dies after presentation of a bankruptcy petition but before service, the court may order service to be effected on his personal representative or such other person as it thinks fit.   **[1458]**

NOTES
  Commencement: 29 December 1986.
  The Act: Insolvency Act 1986.

6. . . .   **[1459]**

NOTES
  Commencement: 29 December 1986..
  This article amends the Insolvency Act 1986, s 385.

SCHEDULES

SCHEDULE 1

Order 3

PROVISIONS OF THE ACT APPLYING WITH RELEVANT MODIFICATIONS TO THE ADMINISTRATION IN BANKRUPTCY OF INSOLVENT ESTATES OF DECEASED PERSONS DYING BEFORE PRESENTATION OF A BANKRUPTCY PETITION

PART I

GENERAL MODIFICATIONS OF PROVISIONS OF THE ACT

Except in so far as the context otherwise requires, for any such reference as is specified in column 1 of the Table set out below there shall be substituted the reference specified in column 2.

Table

Reference in provision of the Act specified in Part II of this Schedule (1)	Substituted references (2)
the bankrupt; the debtor.	the deceased debtor or his personal representative (or if there is no personal representative such person as the court may order) as the case may require.
the bankrupt's estate.	the deceased debtor's estate.
the commencement of the bankruptcy.	the date of the insolvency administration order.
a bankruptcy order.	an insolvency administration order.
an individual being adjudged bankrupt.	an insolvency administration order being made.
a debtor's petition.	a petition by the personal representative of a deceased debtor for an insolvency administration order.

[1460]

NOTES
   Commencement: 29 December 1986.
   The Act: Insolvency Act 1986.

PART II

PROVISIONS OF THE ACT NOT INCLUDED IN PART III OF THIS SCHEDULE

The following provisions of the Act shall apply:—

1. Section 264 with the following modifications:—

   (a) the words "against an individual" shall be omitted;
   (b) at the end of paragraph 1(a) there shall be added the words "in Form 1 set out in Schedule 3 to the Administration of Insolvent Estates of Deceased Persons Order 1986";
   (c) paragraph 1(b) shall be omitted;
   (d) in paragraph 1(c) after the words "Part VIII" there shall be added the words "in Form 2 set out in the said Schedule 3";
   (e) at the end of paragraph 1(d) there shall be added the words "in Form 3 set out in the said Schedule 3 in any case where a creditor could present such a petition under paragraph (a) above"; and
   (f) at the end of subsection (2) there shall be added the words "in Form 4 set out in the said Schedule 3".

2. Section 266 with the following modifications:—

   (a) for subsection (1) there shall be substituted the following:—

   "(1) An insolvency administration petition shall, unless the court otherwise directs, be served on the personal representative and shall be served on such other persons as the court may direct."; and

   (b) in subsection (3) for the words "bankruptcy petition" there shall be substituted the words "petition to the court for an insolvency administration order with or without costs".

3. Section 267 with the following modifications to subsection (2):—

   (a) before the words "at the time" there shall be inserted the words "had the debtor been alive"; and
   (b) for paragraphs (a) to (d) there shall be substituted the following:—

   "(a) the amount of the debt, or the aggregate amount of the debts, owed by the debtor would have been equal to or exceeded the bankruptcy level, or
     (b) the debt, or each of the debts, owed by the debtor would have been for a liquidated sum payable to the petitioning creditor, or one or more of the petitioning creditors, either immediately or at some certain future time, and would have been unsecured.".

4. Section 269 with the modification that in subsection (2) for the words "sections 267 to 270" there shall be substituted the words "section 267 and this section".

5. Section 271 as if for that section there were substituted the following:—

"271.—(1) The court may make an insolvency administration order on a petition for such an order under section 264(1) if it is satisfied—

   (a) that the debt, or one of the debts, in respect of which the petition was presented is a debt which,

     (i) having been payable at the date of the petition or having since become payable, has neither been paid nor secured or compounded for; or
     (ii) has no reasonable prospect of being able to be paid when it falls due; and

   (b) that there is a reasonable probability that the estate will be insolvent.

(2) A petition for an insolvency administration order shall not be presented to the court after proceedings have been commenced in any court of justice for the administration of the deceased debtor's estate.

(3) Where proceedings have been commenced in any such court for the administration of the deceased debtor's estate, that court may, if satisfied that the estate is insolvent, transfer the proceedings to the court exercising jurisdiction for the purposes of the Parts in the second Group of Parts.

(4) Where proceedings have been transferred to the court exercising jurisdiction for the purposes of the Parts in the second Group of Parts, that court may make an insolvency administration order in Form 5 set out in Schedule 3 to the Administration of Insolvent Estates of Deceased Persons Order 1986 as if a petition for such an order had been presented under section 264.

(5) Nothing in sections 264, 266, 267, 269 or 271 or 273 shall invalidate any payment made or any act or thing done in good faith by the personal representative before the date of the insolvency administration order.".

6. Section 272(1) with the following modifications:—

   (a) after the word "petition" there shall be inserted the words "in Form 6 set out in Schedule 3 to the Administration of Insolvent Estates of Deceased Persons Order 1986"; and

   (b) for the words "debtor is unable to pay his debts" there shall be substituted the words "estate of a deceased debtor is insolvent".

7. Section 273 as if for that section there were substituted the following:—
    "273. The court shall make an insolvency administration order in Form 4 set out in Schedule 3 to the Administration of Insolvent Estates of Deceased Persons Order 1986 on the hearing of a petition presented under section 272 if it is satisfied that the deceased debtor's estate is insolvent.".

8. Section 276(2).

9. Section 277.

10. Section 278 except paragraph (b) as if for paragraph (a) there were substituted the following:—

    "(a) commences with the day on which the insolvency administration order is made;".

11. Section 282(1) and (4).

12. Sections 283 to 285 with the modification that they shall have effect as if the petition had been presented and the insolvency administration order had been made on the date of death of the deceased debtor, and with the following modifications to section 283:—

   (a) in subsection (2)(b), for the words "bankrupt and his family" there shall be substituted the words "family of the deceased debtor"; and

   (b) after subsection (4) there shall be added the following subsection:—
    "(4A) References in any of this Group of Parts to property, in relation to a deceased debtor, include the capacity to exercise and take proceedings for exercising all such powers over or in respect of property as might have been exercised by his personal representative for the benefit of the estate on the date of the insolvency administration order and as are specified in subsection (4) above.".

13. Section 286(1) and (3) to (8).

14. Section 287.

15. Section 288 with the modification that for subsections (1) and (2) there shall be substituted the following:—
    "(1) Where an insolvency administration order has been made, the personal representative, or if there is no personal representative such person as the court may on the application of the official receiver direct, shall submit to the official

receiver a statement of the deceased debtor's affairs containing particulars of the assets and liabilities of the estate as at the date of the insolvency administration order together with other particulars of the affairs of the deceased debtor in Form 7 set out in Schedule 3 to the Administration of Insolvent Estates of Deceased Persons Order 1986 or as the official receiver may require.

(2) The statement shall be submitted before the end of the period of fifty-six days beginning with the date of a request by the official receiver for the statement or such longer period as he or the court may allow.".

16. Section 289 as if for that section there were substituted the following:—
"289. The official receiver is not under any duty to investigate the conduct and affairs of the deceased debtor unless he thinks fit but may make such report (if any) to the court as he thinks fit.".

17. Section 291.

18. Sections 292 to 302, except section 297(4), with the modification that, where a meeting of creditors is summoned for the purposes of any provision in those sections, the rules regarding the trustee in bankruptcy and the creditors' committee shall apply accordingly.

19. Sections 303 and 304.

20. Section 305 with the modification that after subsection (4) there shall be added the following subsection:—
"(5) In the exercise of his functions under this section where an insolvency administration order has been made, the trustee shall have regard to any claim by the personal representative to payment of reasonable funeral, testamentary and administration expenses incurred by him in respect of the deceased debtor's estate or, if there is no such personal representative, to any claim by any other person to payment of any such expenses incurred by him in respect of the estate provided that the trustee has sufficient funds in hand for the purpose, and such claims shall have priority over the preferential debts listed in Schedule 6 to this Act.".

21. Section 306.

22. Section 307 with the modification that in subsection (1) for the words "commencement of the bankruptcy" there shall be substituted the words "date of death of the deceased debtor".

23. Sections 308 to 327.

24. Sections 328 and 329 with the modification that for the words "commencement of the bankruptcy", wherever they occur, there shall be substituted the words "date of death of the deceased debtor".

25. Section 330 with the modification that in subsection (5) for the words "the bankrupt is entitled to the surplus" there shall be substituted the words "the surplus shall be paid to the personal representative unless the court otherwise orders".

26. Sections 331 to 340.

27. Section 341 with the modification that in subsection (1)(*a*) for the words "day of the presentation of the bankruptcy petition" onwards there shall be substituted the words "date of death of the deceased debtor".

28. Sections 342 to 349, 350(1), (2), (4) to (6) and 351 except paragraphs (*a*) and (*b*).

29. Section 359 with the following modifications:—
  (*a*) subsection (1), and the reference to that subsection in subsection (3), shall be omitted; and
  (*b*) in subsection (2), for the words "petition or in the initial period" there shall be substituted the words "the date of death of the deceased debtor".

30. Sections 363 and 365 to 381.

31. Section 382 with the modification that in the definition of "bankruptcy debt" for the words "commencement of the bankruptcy", wherever they occur, there shall be substituted the words "date of death of the deceased debtor".

32. Sections 383 and 384.

33. Section 385 with the modification that at the end of the definition of "the court" there shall be added the words "and subject thereto "the court" means the court within the jurisdiction of which the debtor resided or carried on business for the greater part of the six months immediately prior to his death".

34. Section 386.

35. Section 387(1), (5) and (6) with the modification that in subsection (6)(*a*) and (*b*) for the reference to the making of the bankruptcy order there shall be substituted a reference to the date of death of the deceased debtor.

36. Sections 388 to 410, 412, 413, 415, 418 to 420, 423 to 426, 428, 430 to 436 and 437 so far as it relates to Parts II, except paragraph 13, IV and V of Schedule 11 to the Act.

[1461]

NOTES
    Commencement: 29 December 1986.
    The Act: Insolvency Act 1986.

PART III

PROVISIONS OF PART VIII OF THE ACT RELATING TO INDIVIDUAL VOLUNTARY ARRANGE-
MENTS

The following provisions of the Act shall apply where the court has made an interim order under section 252 of the Act in respect of an individual who subsequently dies:—

1. Section 256 with the modification that where the individual dies before he has submitted the document and statement referred to in subsection (2), after subsection (1) there shall be added the following subsections:—

> "(1A) The nominee shall after the death of the individual comes to his knowledge give notice to the court that the individual has died.
> (1B) After receiving such a notice the court shall discharge the order mentioned in subsection (1) above.".

2. Section 257 with the modification that where the individual dies before a creditors' meeting has been held then no such meeting shall be held and, if the individual was at the date of his death an undischarged bankrupt, the personal representative shall give notice of the death to the trustee of his estate and the official receiver.

3. Sections 258 and 259.

4. Sections 260 to 262 with the modification that they shall cease to apply on or after the death of the individual.

5. Section 263 with the modification that where the individual dies after a voluntary arrangement has been approved, then—

> (*a*) in subsection (3), for the words "debtor, any of his" there shall be substituted the words "personal representative of the deceased debtor, any of the deceased debtor's"; and
> (*b*) the supervisor shall give notice to the court that the individual has died. **[1462]**

NOTES
Commencement: 29 December 1986.
The Act: Insolvency Act 1986.

SCHEDULE 2

Order 5

DEATH OF DEBTOR AFTER PRESENTATION OF A BANKRUPTCY PETITION

Modifications

1. For subsections (1) and (2) of section 288 of the Act there shall be substituted the following:—

"(1) Where a bankruptcy order has been made otherwise than on a debtor's petition and the debtor has subsequently died without submitting a statement of his affairs to the official receiver, the personal representative or such other person as the court, on the application of the official receiver, may direct shall submit to the official receiver a statement of the deceased debtor's affairs containing particulars of the assets and liabilities of the estate as at the date of the order together with other particulars of the affairs of the deceased debtor in Form 7 set out in Schedule 3 to the Administration of Insolvent Estates of Deceased Persons Order 1986 or as the official receiver may require, and the Rules shall apply to such a statement as they apply to an ordinary statement of affairs of a debtor.

(2) The statement shall be submitted before the end of the period of fifty-six days beginning with the date of a request by the official receiver for the statement or such longer period as he or the court may allow.".

2. At the end of section 330(4)(*b*) of the Act there shall be added the words "and of the personal representative of a debtor dying after the presentation of a bankruptcy petition in respect of reasonable funeral and testamentary expenses of which notice has not already been given to the trustee".   **[1463]**

NOTES
Commencement: 29 December 1986.
The Act: Insolvency Act 1986.

SCHEDULE 3

FORMS RELATING TO ADMINISTRATION IN BANKRUPTCY OF INSOLVENT ESTATES OF DECEASED DEBTORS (SCH 1, PART II, PARAS 1, 5-7, 15, SCH 2, PARA 1)

NOTES
The forms themselves are not set out in this work, but their numbers and descriptions are listed below.

FORM NO	TITLE
1	Creditor's Petition for Insolvency Administration Order
2	Petition for Insolvency Administration Order by Supervisor of Voluntary Arrangement or Person Bound by it
3	Criminal Bankruptcy Petition for an Insolvency Administration Order
4	Insolvency Administration Order
5	Insolvency Administration Order on Transfer of Proceedings
6	Petition by Personal Representative for Insolvency Administration Order
7	Statement of Affairs (Deceased Insolvent)

[1464]–[1471]

NOTES
Commencement: 29 December 1986.

INSOLVENCY FEES ORDER 1986
(SI 1986 No 2030)

NOTES
    Made: 24 November 1986.
    Authority: Bankruptcy Act 1914, s 133, the Insolvency Act 1986, ss 414, 415 and the Public
Offices Fees Act 1879, s 2.

ARRANGEMENT OF ARTICLES

Article   Para
  1   Citation, Commencement and Application   ..   .. [1472]
  2   Interpretation   ..   .. [1473]

Fees payable in company and individual insolvency proceedings

  3   ..   .. [1474]
  4   ..   .. [1475]
  5   ..   .. [1476]
  6   ..   .. [1477]

Deposits on presentation of bankruptcy or winding-up petition

  7   ..   .. [1478]
  8   ..   .. [1479]
  9   ..   .. [1480]
 10   ..   .. [1481]
 11   ..   .. [1482]
 12   Fees payable to insolvency practitioner appointed under section 273   ..   ..   .. [1473]
 13   Revocation   ..   .. [1484]

Schedule—Fee Payable under Insolvency Act 1986
    Part I—Company Insolvency, Companies Winding-up   ..   .. [1485]
    Part II—Insolvency of Individuals; Bankruptcy   ..   .. [1486]

1. Citation, Commencement and Application

(1) This Order may be cited as the Insolvency Fees Order 1986 and shall come into force on 29th December 1986.

(2) This Order applies to proceedings under the Insolvency Act 1986 and the Insolvency Rules 1986 where—

(*a*) in the case of bankruptcy proceedings, the petition was presented on or after the day on which this Order comes into force, and

(*b*) in the case of any other proceedings, those proceedings commenced on or after that day.

(3) This Order extends to England and Wales only.   **[1472]**

NOTES
    Commencement: 29 December 1986.

2. Interpretation

In this Order, unless the context otherwise requires—

(*a*) "the Act" means the Insolvency Act 1986 (any reference to a numbered section being to a section of that Act);

(*b*) "the Rules" means the Insolvency Rules 1986 (any reference to a numbered rule being to a rule so numbered in the Rules);

(c) "the Regulations" means the Insolvency Regulations 1986 (any reference to a numbered regulation being to a regulation so numbered in the Regulations). **[1473]**

NOTES
Commencement: 29 December 1986.

Fees payable in company and individual insolvency proceedings

3. The fees to be charged in respect of proceedings under Parts I to VII of the Act (Company Insolvency; Companies Winding Up), and the performance by the official receiver or Secretary of State of functions under those Parts, shall be those set out in Part I of the Schedule to this Order. **[1474]**

NOTES
Commencement: 29 December 1986.
The Act: Insolvency Act 1986.

4. The fees to be charged in respect of proceedings under Parts VIII to XI of the Act (Insolvency of Individuals; Bankruptcy) and the performance by the official receiver or Secretary of State of functions under those Parts, shall be those set out in Part II of the Schedule to this Order. **[1475]**

NOTES
Commencement: 29 December 1986.
The Act: Insolvency Act 1986.

5.—(1) All fees shall be taken in cash.

(2) When a fee is paid to an officer of a court the person paying the fee shall inform the officer whether the fee relates to a company insolvency proceeding or an individual insolvency proceeding. **[1476]**

NOTES
Commencement: 29 December 1986.

6. Where Value Added Tax is chargeable in respect of the provision of a service for which a fee is prescribed in the Schedule, there shall be payable in addition to that fee the amount of the Value Added Tax. **[1477]**

NOTES
Commencement: 29 December 1986.

Deposits on presentation of bankruptcy or winding-up petition

7. The following 5 Articles apply where it is intended to present to the court a winding-up or bankruptcy petition under the Act. **[1478]**

NOTES
Commencement: 29 December 1986.
The Act: Insolvency Act 1986.

8.—(1) Before a winding-up or bankruptcy petition can be presented the appropriate deposit (as specified in Article 9 below) must be paid to the court in which the petition is to be presented.

(2) That deposit is security—

(*a*) for Fee No. 1 listed in Part I of the Schedule to this Order or Fee No. 2 listed in Part II of that Schedule, as the case may be (each such fee being referred to in this Order as "the administration fee"), or

(*b*) where an insolvency practitioner is appointed under section 273, for the payment of his fee under Article 12 below.   **[1479]**

NOTES
Commencement: 29 December 1986.
S 273: Insolvency Act 1986, s 273.

9. The appropriate deposit referred to in Article 8 is—

(*a*) in relation to a winding-up petition to be presented under the Act, £200;

(*b*) in relation to a bankruptcy petition to be presented under section 264(1)(*b*), £100;

(*c*) in relation to a bankruptcy petition to be presented under section 264(1)(*a*), (*c*) or (*d*), £200.   **[1480]**

NOTES
Commencement: 29 December 1986.
S 264(1); the Act: Insolvency Act 1986.

10. The court shall (except in a case falling within Article 12 below) transmit the deposit paid to the official receiver attached to the court.   **[1481]**

NOTES
Commencement: 29 December 1986.

11.—(1) In the circumstances specified in this Article a deposit made under Article 8 above is to be repaid to the person who made it.

(2) Where a winding-up or bankruptcy petition under the Act is dismissed or withdrawn the deposit shall be repaid in full, unless—

(*a*) a winding-up or bankruptcy order has been made, or

(*b*) a fee has become payable to an insolvency practitioner under Article 12 below.

(3) If the assets of the company being wound up are, or (as the case may be) the bankrupt's estate is, sufficient to pay the whole or part of the relevant administration fee, then the deposit shall be repaid to the extent that it is not required for payment of that fee.

(4) Where a winding-up or bankruptcy order is annulled, rescinded or recalled, the deposit shall be repaid to the extent that it is not required for payment of the relevant administration fee, unless a fee has become payable to an insolvency practitioner under Article 12 below.   **[1482]**

NOTES
Commencement: 29 December 1986.
The Act: Insolvency Act 1986.

12. Fees payable to insolvency practitioner appointed under section 273

Where the court appoints an insolvency practitioner under section 273(2) to prepare and submit a report under section 274 the court shall, on submission of that report, pay to the practitioner a fee of £100 (that sum being inclusive of Value Added Tax).   **[1483]**

13. Revocation

Fee No. 6 in Table B in the Schedule to the Bankruptcy Fees Order 1984 (fee payable on application to the Department of Trade and Industry to search public records) is hereby revoked.   **[1484]**

SCHEDULE

FEES PAYABLE UNDER INSOLVENCY ACT 1986

PART I

Article 3

COMPANY INSOLVENCY, COMPANIES WINDING-UP

No of Fee	Description of Proceeding	Amount £
1	For the performance by the official receiver of his general duties as official receiver on the making of a winding-up order......................	490.00
2	For all official stationery, printing, postage and tele-phone charges, including notices to creditors and contributories in respect of the first meetings of creditors and contributories and of sittings of the court—	
	(i) for a number of creditors and contributories not exceeding 25..................	135.00
	(ii) for every additional 10 creditors and contri-butories or part thereof	30.00
3	(*a*) Where the official receiver decides to summon meetings of creditors and contributories under section 136(4), for the holding of those meetings	50.00
	(*b*) Where any other meetings of creditors and contributories are held by the official receiver, for summoning and holding the meetings—	
	(i) for a number of creditors and contributories not exceeding 25..................	120.00
	(ii) for every additional 10 creditors and contri-butories or part thereof	15.00
4	On any application to the court for the rescission or recall of a winding-up order where the offical receiver attends or makes a report to the court	67.00
	for each further attendance or report	35.00
5	Where the official receiver supervises a special manager or the carrying on of a company's business—for each week or part thereof	67.00
6	For taking an affidavit, affirmation or declaration, except affidavits of debt—	
	(i) for each person making the same	3.00

No of Fee	Description of Proceeding	Amount £
	(ii) for each exhibit or schedule to be marked . .	0.75
7	On the insertion in the Gazette by the Secretary of State or the official receiver of any notice authorised by the Act or the Rules	16.25
8	On each application by a liquidator to the Secretary of State or to the official receiver to exercise the powers of a creditors' committee by virtue of section 141(5) or rule 4.172	21.00
9	On an application to the Secretary of State under regulation 5, 15 and 25 for a payment from the Insolvency Services Account or for the re-issue of a cheque, money order or payable order in respect of moneys standing to the credit of the Insolvency Services Account, for each cheque, money order or payable order issued or re-issued	0.50
10	For the performance by the Secretary of State of his general duties under the Act, the Rules and the Regulations in relation to the administration of the affairs of companies which are being wound-up by the court, a fee in accordance with the following scale, calculated on the amount paid into the Insolvency Services Account by liquidators under regulations 4 and 16 (after deducting any sums paid to secured creditors in respect of their securities and any sums spent out of money received in carrying on the business of the company):—	
	(i) on the first £50,000 or fraction thereof	per cent 10.00
	(ii) on the next £50,000 or fraction thereof . . .	per cent 7.50
	(iii) on the next £400,000 or fraction thereof . . .	per cent 6.50
	(iv) on the next £500,000 or fraction thereof . . .	per cent 3.75
	(v) on the next £4,000,000 or fraction thereof . .	per cent 2.00
	(vi) on all further amounts	per cent 1.00
11	For the performance by the Secretary of State of his general duties under the Act, the Rules and the Regulations in relation to the administration of the affairs of companies which are being wound-up voluntarily, the following fees calculated on payments into the Insolvency Services Account by liquidators under regulations 24 and 33:—	
	(1) Where the money consists of unclaimed dividends	per cent 1.25
	(2) Where the money consists of undistributed funds or balances:—	
	(i) on the first £50,000 or fraction thereof	per cent 1.25
	(ii) on all further amounts	per cent 0.75
	but so that the total fee payable under this sub-paragraph (2) shall not exceed £7,500.	
12	On the amount expended on any purchase of Government securities (including the renewal of Treasury Bills) pursuant to a request made under regulation 18 or 34 .	per cent 0.375

NOTES
  Commencement: 29 December 1986.
  The Act; ss 136(4), 141(5): Insolvency Act 1986.
  The Rules; r 4.172: Insolvency Rules 1986, SI 1986 No 1925.
  The Regulations; regs 4, 5, 15, 16, 18, 24, 25, 33, 34: Insolvency Regulations 1986, SI 1986
No 1994.

PART II

Article 4

INSOLVENCY OF INDIVIDUALS; BANKRUPTCY

No of Fee	Description of Proceeding	Amount £
1	On registration with the Secretary of State of an individual voluntary arrangement under Part VIII of the Act	27.50
2	For the performance by the official receiver of his general duties as official receiver on the making of a bankruptcy order	245.00
3	For all official stationery, printing, postage and telephone charges, including notices to creditors in respect of the first meeting of creditors and of sittings of the court—	
	(i) for a number of creditors not exceeding 25 .	135.00
	(ii) for every additional 10 creditors or part thereof	30.00
4	(a) Where the official receiver decides to summon a meeting of creditors under section 293(1), for the holding of that meeting	50.00
	(b) Where any other meeting of creditors is held by the official receiver, for summoning and holding the meeting—	
	(i) for a number of creditors not exceeding 25 .	120.00
	(ii) for every additional 10 creditors or part thereof	15.00
5	On the payments made by the official receiver into the Insolvency Services Account as a result of the performance of his functions as receiver and manager under section 287 (after deducting any sums paid to secured creditors in respect of their securities and any sums spent in carrying on the business of the debtor) a fee in accordance with the following scale—	
	(i) on the first £5,000 or fraction thereof	per cent 20.00
	(ii) on the next £5,000 or fraction thereof	per cent 15.00
	(iii) on the next £90,000 or fraction thereof . . .	per cent 10.00
	(iv) on all further sums	per cent 5.00
6	Where the official receiver, acting as receiver and manager under section 287, makes any payment to creditors, a fee of one-half the scale fee calculated under Fee No. 5 on the amount of the payment.	

No of Fee	Description of Proceeding	Amount £
7	On any application to the court for the rescission or annulment of a bankruptcy order or relating to the discharge of a bankrupt, where the official receiver attends or makes a report to the court	67.00
	for each further attendance or report	35.00
8	Where the official receiver supervises a special manager or the carrying on of a debtor's business—for each week or part thereof	67.00
9	For taking an affidavit, affirmation or declaration, except affidavits of debt—	
	(i) for each person making the same	3.00
	(ii) for each exhibit or schedule to be marked . .	0.75
10	On the insertion in the Gazette by the Secretary of State or the official receiver of any notice authorised by the Act or the Rules	16.25
11	On each application by a trustee to the Secretary of State or to the official receiver to exercise the powers of a creditors' committee by virtue of section 302 or rule 6.166	21.00
12	On an application to the Secretary of State under regulation 5 and 15 for a payment from the Insolvency Services Account or for the re-issue of a cheque, money order or payable order in respect of moneys standing to the credit of the Insolvency Services Account, for each cheque, money order or payable order issued or re-issued	0.50
13	For the performance by the Secretary of State of his general duties under the Act, the Rules and the Regulations in relation to the administration of the estates of individuals, a fee in accordance with the following scale, calculated on the amount paid into the Insolvency Service Account by trustees under regulation 4 and by the official receiver as receiver and manager under section 287 (after deducting any sums paid to secured creditors in respect of their securities and any sums spent out of money received in carrying on the business of the debtor):—	
	(a) on the first £50,000 or fraction thereof	per cent 10.00
	(b) on the next £50,000 or fraction thereof	per cent 7.50
	(c) on the next £400,000 or fraction thereof	per cent 6.50
	(d) on the next £500,000 or fraction thereof	per cent 3.75
	(e) on the next £4,000,000 or fraction thereof	per cent 2.00
	(f) on all further amounts	per cent 1.00

[1486]

NOTES

Commencement: 29 December 1986.

The Act; ss 287, 293(1), 302: Insolvency Act 1986.

Rules; r 6.166: Insolvency Rules 1986, SI 1986 No 1925.

Regulations; regs 4, 5, 15: Insolvency Regulations 1986, SI 1986 No 1994.

COMPANIES (DISQUALIFICATION ORDERS) REGULATIONS 1986
(SI 1986 No 2067)

NOTES
Made: 27 November 1986.
Authority: Companies Act 1985, s 301 and the Company Directors Disqualification Act 1986, s 18.

ARRANGEMENT OF REGULATIONS

Regulation   Para
1   Citation, commencement and interpretation   ..   .. [1487]
2   Revocation   ..   .. [1488]

Particulars to be furnished by officers of the court

3   ..   .. [1489]
4   ..   .. [1490]
5   ..   .. [1491]
6   ..   .. [1492]

Schedules 1–4—Forms ..   .. [1493]

1. Citation, commencement and interpretation

(1) These Regulations may be cited as the Companies (Disqualification Orders) Regulations 1986 and shall come into operation on 29th December 1986.

    (2) In these Regulations—

        "the Act" means the Company Directors Disqualification Act 1986;
        "disqualification order" means an order of the court under any of sections 2 to 6, 8 and 10 of the Act;
        "grant of leave" means a grant by the court of leave under section 17 of the Act to any person in relation to a disqualification order.   **[1487]**

NOTES
Commencement: 29 December 1986.

2. Revocation

The Companies (Register of Disqualification Orders) (Fee) Regulations 1977 and the Companies (Disqualification Orders) Regulations 1985 are hereby revoked.   **[1488]**

NOTES
Commencement: 29 December 1986.

Particulars to be furnished by officers of the court

3. These Regulations apply in relation to a disqualification order made after the coming into operation of these Regulations and to a grant of leave, or any action taken by a court in consequence of which a disqualification order is varied or ceases to be in force, made or taken after that date, in relation to a disqualification order made before, on or after that date.   **[1489]**

NOTES
Commencement: 29 December 1986.

4.—(1) The following officers of the court shall furnish to the Secretary of State the particulars specified in Regulation 5(*a*) to (*c*) below in the form and manner there specified:

(*a*) where a disqualification order is made by the Crown Court, the Chief Clerk;

(*b*) where a disqualification order or grant of leave is made by the High Court, the Chief Clerk;

(*c*) where a disqualification order or grant of leave is made by a county court, the Chief Clerk;

(*d*) where a disqualification order is made by a magistrates' court, the Clerk to the Justices;

(*e*) where a disqualification order is made by the High Court of Justiciary, the Deputy Principal Clerk of Justiciary;

(*f*) where a disqualification order or grant of leave is made by a sheriff court, the sheriff clerk; and

(*g*) where a disqualification order or grant of leave is made by the Court of Session, the Deputy Principal Clerk of Session.

(2) Where a disqualification order is made by any of the courts mentioned in paragraph (1) above and subsequently any action is taken by a court in consequence of which that order is varied or ceases to be in force, the officer of the first-mentioned court specified in paragraph (1) above shall furnish to the Secretary of State the particulars specified in Regulation 5(*d*) below in the form and manner there specified.   **[1490]**

NOTES
Commencement: 29 December 1986.

5. The form in which the particulars are to be furnished is—

(*a*) that set out in Schedule 1 to these Regulations with such variations as circumstances require when the person against whom the disqualification order is made is an individual, and the particulars contained therein are the particulars specified for that purpose;

(*b*) that set out in Schedule 2 to these Regulations with such variations as circumstances require when the person against whom the disqualification order is made is a body corporate, and the particulars contained therein are the particulars specified for that purpose;

(*c*) that set out in Schedule 3 to these Regulations with such variations as circumstances require when a grant of leave is made by the court, and the particulars contained therein are the particulars specified for that purpose;

(*d*) that set out in Schedule 4 to these Regulations with such variations as circumstances require when any action is taken by a court in consequence of which a disqualification order is varied or ceases to be in force, and the particulars contained therein are the particulars specified for that purpose.   **[1491]**

NOTES
Commencement: 29 December 1986.

6. The time within which a prescribed officer is to furnish the Secretary of State with the said particulars shall be a period of fourteen days beginning with the day on which the disqualification order or grant of leave is made, or any action is taken by a court in consequence of which the disqualification order is varied or ceases to be in force, as the case may be. **[1492]**

NOTES
Commencement: 29 December 1986.

SCHEDULES 1–4

Regulation 5

NOTES
The forms themselves are not reproduced in this work, but their numbers and descriptions are listed below.

FORM NO	TITLE
DO1	Particulars of a disqualification order made against an individual
DO2	Particulars of a disqualification order made against a body corporate
DO3	Particulars of the grant of leave in relation to a disqualification order
DO4	Particulars of the variation or cessation of a disqualification order **[1493]**

NOTES
Commencement: 29 December 1986.

CO-OPERATION OF INSOLVENCY COURTS (DESIGNATION OF RELEVANT COUNTRIES AND TERRITORIES) ORDER 1986
(SI 1986 No 2123)

NOTES
Made: 29 December 1986.
Authority: Insolvency Act 1986, s 426(11).

1. This Order may be cited as the Co-operation of Insolvency Courts (Designation of Relevant Countries and Territories) Order 1986 and shall come into force on 29th December 1986 **[1494]**

NOTES
Commencement: 29 December 1986.

2. The countries and territories specified in the Schedule to this Order are hereby designated relevant countries and territories for the purposes of section 426 of the Insolvency Act 1986. **[1495]**

NOTES
Commencement: 29 December 1986.

SCHEDULE

Article 2

Relevant Countries and Territories

ANGUILLA
AUSTRALIA
THE BAHAMAS
BERMUDA
BOTSWANA
CANADA
CAYMAN ISLANDS
FALKLAND ISLANDS
GIBRALTAR
HONG KONG
REPUBLIC OF IRELAND
MONTSERRAT
NEW ZEALAND
ST. HELENA
TURKS AND CAICOS ISLANDS
TUVALU
VIRGIN ISLANDS

[1496]

NOTES
Commencement: 29 December 1986.

INSOLVENT COMPANIES (REPORTS ON CONDUCT OF DIRECTORS) NO 2 RULES 1986
(SI 1986 No 2134)

NOTES
Made: 4 December 1986.
Authority: Insolvency Act 1985, s 106; Insolvency Act 1986, s 411; Company Directors Disqualification Act 1986, s 21.

ARRANGEMENT OF RULES

Rule	Para
1 Citation, commencement and interpretation	[1497]
2 Revocation	[1498]
3 Reports required under section 7(3) of the Act	[1499]
4 Return by office-holder	[1500]
5 Enforcement of section 7(4)	[1501]
6 Transitional provisions	[1502]
Schedule—Forms	[1503]

1. Citation, commencement and interpretation

(1) These Rules may be cited as the Insolvent Companies (Reports on Conduct of Directors) No 2 Rules 1986.

(2) These Rules shall come into force on 29th December 1986, and that day is referred to in these Rules as "the commencement date".

(3) In these Rules references to "the Act" are references to the Company Directors Disqualification Act 1986. **[1497]**

NOTES
Commencement: 20 December 1986.

2. Revocation

The Insolvent Companies (Reports on Conduct of Directors) Rules 1986 are hereby revoked. **[1498]**

NOTES
Commencement: 29 December 1986.

3. Reports required under section 7(3) of the Act

(1) This Rule applies to any report made to the Secretary of State under section 7(3) of the Act by—

(*a*) the liquidator of a company registered in England and Wales which passes a resolution for voluntary winding up on or after the commencement date;

(*b*) an administrative receiver of a company appointed otherwise than under section 51 of the Insolvency Act 1986 (power to appoint receivers under the law of Scotland) on or after the commencement date; or

(*c*) the administrator of a company registered in England and Wales in respect of which the court makes an administration order on or after the commencement date.

(2) Such a report shall be made in the Form D1, D2 or D6 set out in the Schedule hereto, as the case may be, and in the manner and to the extent required by the applicable form. **[1499]**

NOTES
Commencement: 29 December 1986.
S 7(3) of the Act: Company Directors Disqualification Act 1986, s 7(3).

4. Return by office-holder

(1) This Rule applies where it appears to a liquidator of a company as mentioned in Rule 3(1)(*a*), to an administrative receiver as mentioned in Rule 3(1)(*b*), or to an administrator as mentioned in Rule 3(1)(*c*) (each of whom is here referred to as "the office-holder") that the company has at any time become insolvent within the meaning of section 6(2) of the Act.

(2) Subject as follows there may be furnished to the Secretary of State by an office-holder at any time during the period of 6 months from the relevant date (defined in paragraph 4 below) a return with respect to every person who—

(*a*) was, on the relevant date a director or shadow director of the company, or

(*b*) had been a director or shadow director of the company at any time in the 3 years immediately preceding that date.

(3) The return shall be made in the Form D3, D4, D5 or D7 set out in the Schedule hereto, as the case may be, and in the manner and to the extent required by the applicable form.

(4) For the purposes of this Rule, "the relevant date" means—

(*a*) in the case of a company in creditors' voluntary winding up (there having been no declaration of solvency by the directors under section

89 of the Insolvency Act 1986) the date of the passing of the resolution
for voluntary winding up,

(*b*) in the case of a company in members' voluntary winding up the date
on which the liquidator forms the opinion that, at the time when the
company went into liquidation, its assets were insufficient for the
payment of its debts and other liabilities and the expenses of winding
up,

(*c*) in the case of the administrative receiver, the date of his appointment,

(*d*) in the case of the administrator, the date of the administration order
made in relation to the company,

and for the purposes of sub-paragraph (*c*) above the only appointment of an
administrative receiver to be taken into account in determining the relevant
date shall be that appointment which is not that of a successor in office to an
administrative receiver who has vacated office either by death or pursuant to
section 45 of the Insolvency Act 1986.

(5) It shall be the duty of the responsible office-holder to furnish a return
complying with the provisions of paragraphs 3 and 4 of this Rule to the Secretary
of State not later than the expiry of the period of 6 months from the relevant
date where no return has been so furnished by a day one week before the expiry
of that period: and for the purposes of this paragraph the responsible office-
holder shall be the person in office in relation to the company on the day
specified above or where no person is in office on that day the office-holder who
vacated office nearest to that day.

(6) A return need not be provided under this Rule if an office-holder has,
since the relevant date, made reports to the Secretary of State under section 7(3)
of the Act with respect to all the persons falling within paragraph (2) and (apart
from this paragraph) required to be the subject of return.

(7) If a responsible office-holder without reasonable excuse fails to comply
with the duty imposed by paragraph (5) of the Rule, he is liable to a fine not
exceeding £400 and, for continued contravention, to a daily default fine not
exceeding £40.   **[1500]**

NOTES

Commencement: 29 December 1986.

S 6(2) of the Act: Company Directors Disqualification Act 1986, s 6(2).

5. Enforcement of section 7(4)

(1) This Rule applies where under section 7(4) of the Act (power to call on
liquidators, former liquidators and others to provide information) the Secretary
of State or the official receiver requires a person—

(*a*) to furnish him with information with respect to a person's conduct as
director or shadow director of a company, and

(*b*) to produce and permit inspection of relevant books, papers and other
records.

(2) On the application of the Secretary of State or (as the case may be) the
official receiver, the court may make an order directing compliance within such
period as may be specified.

(3) The court's order may provide that all costs of and incidental to the
application shall be borne by the person to whom the order is directed.   **[1501]**

NOTES

Commencement: 29 December 1986.

S 7(4) of the Act: Company Directors Disqualification Act 1986, s 7(4).

6. Transitional provisions

Notwithstanding Rule 2 the provisions of Rules 2 and 3 of the Insolvent Companies (Reports on Conduct of Directors) Rules 1986 shall continue to apply, and have effect in relation to—

    (*a*) any report to which the provisions of Rule 2 of those Rules apply, and

    (*b*) any interim return required to be made by Rule 3 of those Rules.

[1502]

NOTES

    Commencement: 29 December 1986.

SCHEDULE

Rules 3(2) and 4(3)

NOTES

    The forms themselves are not set out in this work, but their numbers and descriptions are listed below.

FORM NO	TITLE
COMPANIES IN VOLUNTARY LIQUIDATION	
D1	Report on Conduct of Directors under Section 7(3) of the Company Directors Disqualification Act 1986
D2	Report on Conduct of Directors by an Administrative Receiver under Section 7(3) of the Company Directors Disqualification Act 1986
COMPANIES IN CREDITORS' VOLUNTARY LIQUIDATION	
D3	Return of Directors under Rule 4 of the Insolvent Companies (Report on Conduct of Directors) No 2 Rules 1986
COMPANIES IN VOLUNTARY LIQUIDATION WHICH BEGAN AS MEMBERS VOLUNTARY LIQUIDATION BUT INSOLVENT	
D4	Return of Directors under Rule 4 of the Insolvent Companies (Report on Conduct of Directors) No 2 Rule 1986
D5	Return of Directors by an Administrative Receiver under Rule 4 of the Insolvent Companies (Report on Conduct of Directors) No 2 Rules 1986
D6	Report on Conduct of Directors by an Administrator under Section 7(3) of the Company Directors Disqualification Act 1986
D7	Return of Directors by an Administrator under Rule 4 of the Insolvent Companies (Report on Conduct of Directors) No 2 Rules 1986

[1503]

NOTES

    Commencement: 29 December 1986

INSOLVENT PARTNERSHIPS ORDER 1986
(SI 1986 No 2142)

NOTES

    Made: 8 December 1986.

    Authority: Insolvency Act 1986, s 420; Company Directors Disqualification Act 1986, s 21(2).

ARRANGEMENT OF ARTICLES

PART 1

GENERAL

Article		Para
1	Short title, commencement and extent	[1504]
2	Interpretation	[1505]
3	Members or other persons having control or management of business of insolvent partnership	[1506]
4	Verification of petition for winding up insolvent partnership	[1507]
5	Application of Insolvency Rules, Insolvency Regulations and Insolvency Fees Order to Provisions of the Act applied in relation to insolvent partnerships	[1508]
6	Application of provisions of the Company Directors Disqualification Act 1986 in relation to insolvent partnerships	[1509]

PART 2

WINDING UP OF INSOLVENT PARTNERSHIP ONLY

7	.. ..	[1510]

PART 3

WINDING UP OF INSOLVENT PARTNERSHIP INVOLVING INSOLVENCY PETITIONS AGAINST TWO OR MORE INSOLVENT MEMBERS

8	Application of provisions of the Act with modifications	[1511]
9	Priority of expenses of insolvency proceedings where insolvency orders are made in relation to an insolvent partnership	[1512]
10	Priority of debts where insolvency orders are made in relation to an insolvent partnership	[1513]
11	Voluntary arrangements in relation to winding up and bankruptcy of members of insolvent partnerships	[1514]
12	Winding up of unregistered companies which are members of an insolvent partnership	[1515]

PART 4

INSOLVENCY PROCEEDINGS AGAINST MEMBERS OF INSOLVENT PARTNERSHIP NOT INVOLVING THE WINDING UP OF THE PARTNERSHIP AS AN UNREGISTERED COMPANY

13	Insolvency petitions by individual members	[1516]
14	Insolvency proceedings against persons found to be members of an insolvent partnership	[1517]

PART 5

SUPPLEMENTAL AND TRANSITIONAL PROVISIONS

15	.. ..	[1518]

SCHEDULES

Schedule 1—Provisions of Part V of the Act applying with relevant Modifications in relation to the Winding Up of Insolvent Partnerships where the Petitioner does not present an Insolvency Petition against an Insolvent Member .. .. [1519]

Schedule 2—Modifications to Provisions of the Act applying in relation to Insolvent Partnerships where the Partnership is Wound Up as an Unregistered Company and the Petitioner presents an Insolvency Petition against two or more Insolvent Members .. ..

Part I—Insolvent Partnerships (art 8(1)(*b*)) .. .. [1520]

Part II—Corporate Members (art 8(2)) .. .. [1521]

Para
Part III—Individual Members (art 8(2)) .. .. [1522]
Schedule 3—Forms relating to Insolvent Partnerships .. .. [1523]

PART 1

GENERAL

1. Short title, commencement and extent

(1) This Order may be cited as the Insolvent Partnerships Order 1986 and shall come into force on 29th December 1986.

(2) This Order—

(a) in the case of company insolvency and insolvent partnerships being wound up under Part V of the Act as unregistered companies, relates to companies which the courts in England and Wales have jurisdiction to wind up; and

(b) in the case of individual insolvency, extends to England and Wales only. **[1504]**

NOTES
Commencement: 29 December 1986.
The Act: Insolvency Act 1986.

2. Interpretation

(1) In this Order—

"the Act" means the Insolvency Act 1986;

"corporate member" means an insolvent member which is a company;

"individual member" means an insolvent member who is an individual;

"insolvent member" means a member of an insolvent partnership, against whom an insolvency petition is being or has been presented;

"insolvency order" means—

(a) in the case of an insolvent partnership or a corporate member, a winding-up order; and

(b) in the case of an individual member, a bankruptcy order;

"insolvency petition" means—

(a) in the case of a petition presented against a corporate member, a petition for its winding up by the court; and

(b) in the case of a petition presented against an individual member, a petition to the court for a bankruptcy order to be made against the individual,

where the petition is presented in conjunction with a petition for the winding up of the partnership by the court as an unregistered company under the Act; and

"responsible insolvency practitioner" means—

(a) in winding up, the liquidator; and

(b) in bankruptcy, the trustee,

and in either case includes the official receiver when so acting.

(2) The definitions in paragraph (1) above other than the first definition shall be added to those in section 436 of the Act.

(3) A Form referred to in this Order by number means the Form so numbered in Schedule 3 to this Order. **[1505]**

NOTES
Commencement: 29 December 1986.

3. Members or other persons having control or management of business of insolvent partnership

Where an insolvent partnership is being wound up under Part V of the Act as an unregistered company, any member or former member of the partnership or any other person who has or has had control or management of the partnership business—

(a) shall for the purposes of the provisions of the Act and the Company Directors Disqualification Act 1986 applied by this Order be deemed to be an officer and director of the company; and

(b) shall deliver up to the liquidator of the partnership for the purposes of the exercise of the liquidator's functions under the provisions referred to in paragraph (a) above possession of any partnership property within the meaning of the Partnership Act 1890 which he holds for the purposes of the partnership.   **[1506]**

NOTES
Commencement: 29 December 1986.
The Act: Insolvency Act 1986.

4. Verification of petition for winding up insolvent partnership

Every affidavit verifying the petition for the winding up of an insolvent partnership under Part V of the Act shall include the names in full and addresses of all members of the partnership so far as known to the petitioner.   **[1507]**

NOTES
Commencement: 29 December 1986.
The Act: Insolvency Act 1986.

5. Application of Insolvency Rules, Insolvency Regulations and Insolvency Fees Order to Provisions of the Act applied in relation to insolvent partnerships

(1) The Insolvency Rules 1986, the Insolvency Regulations 1986 and the Insolvency Fees Order 1986 apply with the necessary modifications for the purpose of giving effect to the provisions of Parts I and IV to XI of the Act which are applied in relation to insolvent partnerships with the modifications specified in this Order.

(2) In the case of any conflict between any provision of the Insolvency Rules 1986 and any provision of this Order, the latter provision shall prevail.

(3) Sections 414(4) and 415(3) of the Act shall apply with the following modifications:—

(a) where an order provides for any sum to be deposited on presentation of a winding-up or bankruptcy petition, that sum shall, in the case of an insolvent partnership, only be required to be deposited in respect of the petition for winding up the partnership; and

(b) production of any receipt for the sum deposited upon presentation of the petition for winding-up the partnership shall suffice for the filing in court of an insolvency petition against an insolvent member. **[1508]**

NOTES
Commencement: 29 December 1986.
The Act: Insolvency Act 1986.

6. Application of provisions of the Company Directors Disqualification Act 1986 in relation to insolvent partnerships

Where an insolvent partnership is wound up as an unregistered company under Part V of the Act, the provisions of sections 6 to 10, 15, 19(c) and 20 of, and Schedule 1 to, the Company Directors Disqualification Act 1986 apply in relation to the partnership as if any member of the partnership were a director of a company, and the partnership were a company as defined by section 22(2)(b) of that Act. **[1509]**

NOTES
Commencement: 29 December 1986.
The Act: Insolvency Act 1986.

PART 2

WINDING UP OF INSOLVENT PARTNERSHIP ONLY

7. The provisions of Part V of the Act specified in Schedule 1 to this Order shall apply in relation to the winding up of insolvent partnerships as unregistered companies with the modifications specified in that Schedule where no insolvency petition is presented by the petitioner against an insolvent member. **[1510]**

NOTES
Commencement: 29 December 1986.
The Act: Insolvency Act 1986.

PART 3

WINDING UP OF INSOLVENT PARTNERSHIP INVOLVING INSOLVENCY PETITIONS AGAINST TWO OR MORE INSOLVENT MEMBERS

8. Application of provisions of the Act with modifications

(1) Sections 220(1)and 221 of the Act shall apply in relation to the winding up of insolvent partnerships as unregistered companies where an insolvency petition is presented by the petitioner against two or more insolvent members, with the following modifications:—

    (a) in section 220(1), before the words "any association" there shall be inserted the words "any insolvent partnership,";

    (b) for section 221(1) there shall be substituted the following:—
"(1) Subject to the provisions of this Part, any insolvent partnership which has a principal place of business in England and Wales may be wound up as an unregistered company under this Act; and all the provisions of this Act and the Companies Act about winding up apply to the winding up of such a partnership as an unregistered company with the exceptions and additions mentioned in the following subsections and in Part I of Schedule 2 to the Insolvent Partnerships Order 1986."; and

    (c) for section 221(5) there shall be substituted the following:—
"(5) The circumstances in which an insolvent partnership may be wound up are that the partnership is unable to pay its debts.".

(2) All the provisions of the Act and the Companies Act about winding up of companies by the court shall apply in relation to the winding up of a corporate member where the insolvent partnership is wound up as an unregistered company under paragraph (1) above with the modifications specified in Part II

of Schedule 2 to this Order, and all the provisions of the Act about bankruptcy of individuals shall apply in relation to the bankruptcy of an individual member, with the modifications specified in Part III of Schedule 2 to this Order. **[1511]**

NOTES
 Commencement: 29 December 1986.
 The Act: Insolvency Act 1986.

9. Priority of expenses of insolvency proceedings where insolvency orders are made in relation to an insolvent partnership

(1) The provisions of paragraphs (2) to (5) below shall apply as regards priority of expenses of insolvency proceedings, where insolvency orders are made in relation to an insolvent partnership, incurred up to and including the date of the appointment of a person to act as liquidator of the partnership and to act as the responsible insolvency practitioner in relation to any insolvent member against whom an insolvency order has been made.

(2) The joint estate of an insolvent partnership shall be applicable in the first instance in payment of the joint expenses of the insolvency proceedings in winding up the partnership, and the separate estate of each insolvent member shall be applicable in the first instance in payment of the separate expenses of the insolvency proceedings relating to that member.

(3) Where the joint estate of the partnership is insufficient for the payment in full of the joint expenses of the insolvency proceedings in winding up the partnership incurred up to and including the date mentioned in paragraph (1) above, the unpaid balance shall be apportioned equally between the separate estates of the insolvent members and form part of the expenses to be paid out of those estates.

(4) Where any separate estate of an insolvent member is insufficient for the payment in full of the expenses of the insolvency proceedings so incurred to be paid out of that estate, the unpaid balance shall form part of the expenses to be paid out of the joint estate of the partnership.

(5) Where after the transfer of any unpaid balance in accordance with the preceding paragraphs of this Article any estate is insufficient for the payment in full of the expenses to be paid out of that estate, the balance then remaining unpaid shall be apportioned equally between the other estates, and if after such an apportionment one or more estates are insufficient for the payment in full of the expenses to be paid out of those estates, the total of the unpaid balances of the expenses to be paid out of those estates shall continue to be apportioned equally between the other estates until provision is made for the payment in full of the expenses or there is no estate available for the payment of the balance finally remaining unpaid, in which case it abates in equal proportions between the estates which are then insufficient.

(6) The provisions of paragraphs (2) above and (7) and (8) below shall apply as regards priority of expenses of insolvency proceedings, where insolvency orders are made in relation to an insolvent partnership, incurred after the date of the appointment of a person to act as liquidator of the partnership and to act as the responsible insolvency practitioner in relation to any insolvent member against whom an insolvency order has been made.

(7) Where the joint estate of the partnership is insufficient for the payment in full of the joint expenses of the insolvency proceedings in winding up the partnership incurred after the date mentioned in paragraph (6) above, the

unpaid balance shall be apportioned between the separate estates of the insolvent members and form part of the expenses to be paid out of those estates in such proportions as the liquidation committee established for the partnership and any corporate member sanctions or the court, on application by the liquidator of the partnership or any person interested, orders.

(8) With the sanction of the liquidation committee established for the partnership and any corporate member, or with the leave of the court obtained on application, the responsible insolvency practitioner may—

    (*a*) pay out of the joint estate of the partnership as part of the expenses to be paid out of the estate any expenses so incurred for any separate estate of an insolvent member; or

    (*b*) pay out of any separate estate of an insolvent member any part of the expenses so incurred for the joint estate of the partnership which affects that separate estate. **[1512]**

NOTES
   Commencement: 29 December 1986.

10. Priority of debts where insolvency orders are made in relation to an insolvent partnership

(1) The provisions of this Article shall apply as regards priority of debts, where insolvency orders are made against an insolvent partnership and an insolvent member.

(2) The joint estate of an insolvent partnership shall be applicable in the first instance in payment of the joint debts due to the creditors of the partnership other than those to be postponed under section 3 of the Partnership Act 1890 or any provision of the Act or any other Act, and the separate estate of each insolvent member shall be applicable in the first instance in payment of the separate debts of that member, other than those to be postponed as mentioned above.

(3) Any surplus remaining after the payment of the separate debts of any insolvent member out of his separate estate, in accordance with paragraph (2) above, shall, without the prior payment of any interest under section 189 or 328(4) of the Act, as the case may be, form part of the joint estate of the partnership and be applied in payment of the joint debts due to the creditors of the partnership.

(4) Any surplus remaining after the payment of the joint debts of the partnership out of its joint estate in accordance with paragraphs (2) and (3) above shall form part of the separate estate of each partner in proportion to the right and interest of each such partner in the joint estate:

Provided that in the case of a partner against whom an insolvency order has not been made, before any part of the surplus shall form part of his separate estate interest shall be paid out of his share on the joint debts of the partnership to the creditors of the partnership, in pursuance of section 189 of the Act.

(5) Distinct accounts shall be kept of the joint estate and of the separate estate or estates.

(6) Subject to the provisions of this Article and of the Act and of any order made under it and of any other Act all debts of the partnership other than preferential debts rank equally between themselves.

(7) Nothing in this Article shall alter the effect of section 3 of the Partnership Act 1890 or any rule of law.

(8) Neither the official receiver, the Secretary of State nor a responsible insolvency practitioner shall be entitled to remuneration or fees under the Insolvency Rules 1986, the Insolvency Regulations 1986 or the Insolvency Fees Order 1986 for his services in connection with the transfer of a surplus from a seperate estate of an insolvent member to the joint estate or from the joint estate to a separate estate under this Article.

(9) If any two or more members of an insolvent partnership constitute a separate partnership, the creditors of such separate partnership shall be deemed to be a separate set of creditors and subject to the same statutory provisions as the separate creditors of any member of the insolvent partnership.

(10) Where any surplus remains after the administration of the estate of a separate partnership, the surplus shall be carried over to the separate estates of the partners in that partnership according to their respective rights and interests in it.   **[1513]**

NOTES
    Commencement: 29 December 1986.
    The Act: Insolvency Act 1986.

11. Voluntary arrangements in relation to winding up and bankruptcy of members of insolvent partnerships

Part I of the Act (Company voluntary arrangements) shall apply to corporate members, and Part VIII (Individual voluntary arrangements) shall apply to individual members, where insolvency orders are made against the partnership and an insolvent member, with the modification that any reference to the creditors of the company or of the debtor, as the case may be, includes a reference to the creditors of the partnership.   **[1514]**

NOTES
    Commencement: 29 December 1986.
    The Act: Insolvency Act 1986.

12. Winding up of unregistered companies which are members of an insolvent partnership

Where an insolvent partnership or other body which may be wound up under Part V of the Act as an unregistered company is itself a member of an insolvent partnership being so wound up, Article 8(1) above shall apply in relation to the latter insolvent partnership as though the former body were a corporate member of that partnership.   **[1515]**

NOTES
    Commencement: 29 December 1986.
    The Act: Insolvency Act 1986.

PART 4

INSOLVENCY PROCEEDINGS AGAINST MEMBERS OF INSOLVENT PARTNERSHIP NOT INVOLVING THE WINDING UP OF THE PARTNERSHIP AS AN UNREGISTERED COMPANY

13. Insolvency petitions by individual members

(1) Where all the members of an insolvent partnership are individual members and none of them is a limited partner, a petition in Form 8 for bankruptcy orders to be made against all of them may be presented to the court by the individual members jointly under section 264 of the Act without the partnership being wound up as an unregistered company under Part V of the Act.

(2) The petition—

    (*a*) shall contain a request that the trustee shall wind up the partnership business and administer the partnership property; and

    (*b*) shall be accompanied by an affidavit made by the partner who signs the petition, showing that all the partners concur in the presentation of the petition.

(3) Where bankruptcy orders are made on a petition presented under paragraph (1) above, the provisions of Articles 3(*b*), 8(2) and 9 to 11 above shall apply with the necessary modifications in relation to the individual members.

(4) For any reference to a meeting involving the creditors of any individual members summoned under section 136(4) of the Act in paragraphs 16 and 21 in Part III of Schedule 2 to this Order applied by virtue of paragraph (3) above there shall be substituted a reference to a meeting of all the creditors of the individual members, and any reference to a liquidation committee shall be omitted.

(5) For section 272 of the Act there shall be substituted the following:—
    "272. A joint debtor's petition in Form 8 in Schedule 3 to the Insolvent Partnerships Order 1986 may be presented to the court by individual members only on the grounds that the partnership is unable to pay its debts.".

(6) Any reference in section 288 of the Act referred to in paragraph 12 of the said Part III as applied by virtue of paragraph (3) above to a statement of affairs shall include a reference to an additional statement of the affairs of the partnership. **[1516]**

NOTES
    Commencement: 29 December 1986.
    The Act: Insolvency Act 1986.

14. Insolvency proceedings against persons found to be members of an insolvent partnership

(1) Where at any time after a winding-up or bankruptcy petition has been presented to the court against any insolvent member the attention of the court is drawn to the fact that the person in question is a member of an insolvent partnership, the court may make an order as to the future conduct of the insolvency proceedings and any such order may apply any provisions of this Order with any necessary modifications.

(2) Where a bankruptcy petition has been presented against more than one

individual in the circumstances mentioned in paragraph (1) above, the court may give such directions for consolidating the proceedings, or any of them, as it thinks just.

(3) Any order or directions under paragraph (1) or (2) above may be made or given on the application of the official receiver, any responsible insolvency practitioner or any other interested person and may include provisions as to the administration of the estate of the partnership, and in particular as to the joint estate of the partnership and any separate estate of any member.   **[1517]**

NOTES
     Commencement: 29 December 1986.

PART 5

SUPPLEMENTAL AND TRANSITIONAL PROVISIONS

15. (1) This Order does not apply in relation to any case in which a petition for a winding-up order or a bankruptcy petition was presented against a partnership or a member of a partnership under the law in force immediately before 29th December 1986 or in which any bankruptcy proceedings under the Bankruptcy Act 1914 were pending on that date against any member, whether or not in the name of the partnership, and where this Order does not apply the law in force immediately before 29th December 1986 continues to have effect.

(2) The reference in paragraph (1) above to pending bankruptcy proceedings includes a reference to any case in which a bankruptcy notice against the partnership or a member of it was served.

(3) Nothing in this Order is to be taken as preventing a petition being presented against an insolvent partnership under section 18 of the Banking Act 1979 or under section 53 or 54 of the Insurance Companies Act 1982 or under any other enactment or as preventing any creditor or creditors owed one or more debts by an insolvent partnership from presenting a petition under the Act against one or more members of the partnership without including the others and without presenting a petition for the winding up of the partnership as an unregistered company, and in such a case the debt or debts shall be treated as a debts or debts of the member in question.   **[1518]**

NOTES
     Commencement: 29 December 1986.
     The Act: Insolvency Act 1986.

SCHEDULES

SCHEDULE 1

Order 7

PROVISIONS OF PART V OF THE ACT APPLYING WITH RELEVANT MODIFICATIONS IN RELATION TO THE WINDING UP OF INSOLVENT PARTNERSHIPS WHERE THE PETITIONER DOES NOT PRESENT AN INSOLVENCY PETITION AGAINST AN INSOLVENT MEMBER

The following provisions of Part V of the Act shall apply with the modifications mentioned in this Schedule:—

1. Section 220(1) with the modification that before the words "any association" there shall be inserted the words "any insolvent partnership,".

2. Section 221 with the modification that after subsection (7) there shall be added the following subsections:—

"(8) A petition in Form 1 in Schedule 3 to the Insolvent Partnerships Order 1986 for winding up an insolvent partnership may be presented by the liquidator of a corporate partner (or of a former corporate partner) or the trustee of a bankrupt partner's (or of a former bankrupt partner's) estate, if the ground of the petition is one of the circumstances in which, under subsection (5), the court may make a winding-up order against an unregistered company.

(9) Where a winding-up order is made against an insolvent partnership after the presentation of a petition under subsection (8), the court may appoint as liquidator of the partnership the person who is the liquidator of the corporate partner (or former corporate partner) or the trustee of the bankrupt partner's (or former bankrupt partner's) estate who presented the petition; and where the court makes an appointment under this subsection, section 140(3) applies as if an appointment had been made under that section.

(10) Subject to the provisions of section 124(3) as modified by paragraph 5 of Part II of Schedule 2 to the Insolvent Partnerships Order 1986, and of section 272 as modified by paragraph 8 of Part III of that Schedule, a petition for winding up an insolvent partnership may be presented by the partnership or any member of it if—

  (*a*) the partnership consists of not less than 8 members; or
  (*b*) in the case of a petition presented by a member, he presents with the leave of the court obtained on an application by the member a petition for the winding up of the partnership after a written demand in Form 2 in Schedule 3 to the Insolvent Partnerships Order 1986 has been served on the partnership in respect of a joint debt or debts exceeding £750 then due by the partnership but paid by the member, other than out of money belonging to the partnership, and the court is satisfied when granting leave to present the petition that—

    (i) the member has obtained a judgment, decree or order of any court against the partnership for reimbursement to him of the amount of the joint debt or debts so paid; and
    (ii) all reasonable steps (other than insolvency proceedings) have been taken by the member to enforce that judgment, decree or order.

(11) Where a winding-up petition is presented under subsection (8), in the event of the partnership assets being insufficient to satisfy the costs of the liquidator or trustee as petitioner the costs may be paid out of the assets of the corporate or individual member, as the case may be, as part of the expenses of the liquidation or bankruptcy, in the same order of priority as expenses properly chargeable or incurred by the liquidator or trustee in getting in any of the assets of the member.

(12) Where an insolvent partnership has a principal place of business within the insolvency district of a county court, a petition for the winding up of the partnership may be presented to that court.".

3. Section 222 with the modification that in paragraph (1)(*a*) after the words "prescribed form" there shall be inserted the words "with such variations as circumstances may require,". **[1519]**

NOTES
  Commencement: 29 December 1986.

SCHEDULE 2
Order 8

MODIFICATIONS TO PROVISIONS OF THE ACT APPLYING IN RELATION TO INSOLVENT PARTNERSHIPS WHERE THE PARTNERSHIP IS WOUND UP AS AN UNREGISTERED COMPANY AND THE PETITIONER PRESENTS AN INSOLVENCY PETITION AGAINST TWO OR MORE INSOLVENT MEMBERS

PART I
INSOLVENT PARTNERSHIPS (ART 8(1)(*B*))

Section 117

  1. After subsection (6) there shall be added the following subsections:—

"(7) The court only has jurisdiction to wind up an insolvent partnership if the partnership has carried on business in England and Wales at any time in the period of 3 years ending with the day on which the petition for winding it up was presented.

(8) Where a petition is presented to the court for the bankruptcy of an individual member of an insolvent partnership, the court only has jurisdiction to wind up the partnership if it has jurisdiction in England and Wales for the purposes of the Parts in the second Group of Parts of this Act.

(9) Where an insolvent partnership has a principal place of business within the insolvency district of a county court, a petition for the winding up of the partnership may be presented to that court.".

Section 124

2. For section 124 there shall be substituted the following:—

"124.—(1) An application to the court for the winding up of an insolvent partnership shall be by petition in Form 4 in Schedule 3 to the Insolvent Partnerships Order 1986 presented by any creditor or creditors to whom the partnership is indebted in respect of a liquidated sum payable immediately.

(2) The petition shall be presented at the same time and to the same court as any insolvency petition against an insolvent member.

(3) The petition shall be advertised in Form 5 in the said Schedule 3.

(4) At any time after the presentation of the petition the petitioner may, with the leave of the court obtained on application and on such terms as it thinks just, add other partners as parties to the proceedings in relation to the insolvent partnership.

(5) Any partner or person against whom a winding-up or bankruptcy petition has been presented in relation to the insolvent partnership is entitled to appear and to be heard on any petition for the winding up of the partnership.

(6) The petition shall contain particulars of other petitions being presented in relation to the partnership against insolvent members, identifying the members concerned.

(7) The court shall fix a venue for the hearing of the petition in advance of that fixed for the hearing of any petition against an insolvent member.

(8) The petitioner may withdraw the petition if—

   (a) he withdraws at the same time every petition which he has presented against any insolvent member; and
   (b) he gives notice to the court at least 3 days before the date appointed for the hearing of the petition of his intention to withdraw the petition.

(9) Where notice is given under subsection (8), the court may, on such terms as it thinks just, substitute as petitioner any creditor of the partnership who in its opinion would have a right to present the petition and at the same time substitute him as petitioner in respect of every petition which the petitioner has presented against an insolvent member, and if the court makes such a substitution the petition in question will not be withdrawn.".

Section 125

3. For subsection (2) there shall be substituted the followng:—

"(2) An order under subsection (1) may contain directions as to the future conduct of any insolvency proceedings in existence against any insolvent member in respect of whom an insolvency order has been made.".

Section 133

4.(a) For subsection (3) there shall be substituted the following:—

   "(3) On an application under subsection (1), the court shall, subject to subsection (5), direct that a public examination of the person to whom the application relates shall be held on a day appointed by the court; and that person shall attend on that day and be publicly examined as to the promotion, formation or management of the partnership or of an insolvent member or both or as to the conduct of their business and affairs, or of his conduct or dealings in relation to the partnership or any insolvent member."; and

(*b*) after subsection (4) there shall be added the following subsection:—

"(5) Where the court has already directed on a previous application in proceedings in relation to an insolvent member that a public examination of the person to whom the application under subsection (1) relates shall be held, the court may decline to direct that a further public examination of that person shall be held.".

Section 136

5 (*a*) For subsection (4) there shall be substituted the following:—

"(*4*) When he is the liquidator of an insolvent partnership, the official receiver shall, in the period of 4 months beginning with the day on which the winding-up order was made against the partnership, summon and hold a single meeting of the creditors of the partnership and of any insolvent member against whom an insolvency order has been made, for the purpose of choosing a person to be liquidator of the partnership in place of the official receiver and to act as the responsible insolvency practitioner in relation to that insolvent member.

(4A) Any such single meeting of creditors held under subsection (4) shall be conducted as if the creditors of the partnership and of any such insolvent member were a single set of creditors."; and

(*b*) subsections (5) and (6) shall be omitted.

Section 137

6. (*a*) In subsection (2), for the words from the beginning to "those meetings" there shall be substituted the words "Where at the meeting held under section 136(4) no person is chosen to be liquidator of the insolvent partnership and to act as the responsible insolvency practitioner in relation to any insolvent member as a result of that meeting"; and

(*b*) the reference in subsection (5) to the summoning of a general meeting of creditors shall be construed as a reference to the summoning of a single meeting of the creditors of the insolvent partnership and of the insolvent members against whom insolvency orders have been made.

Section 139 onwards in Part IV

7. Any reference in section 139 and the subsequent sections in Part IV of the Act, applied by virtue of this Order with the modifications in this Part of this Schedule, to the summoning of separate meetings of the creditors and contributories shall include a reference to the summoning of a single meeting of the creditors of the insolvent partnership and of any insolvent member against whom an insolvency order has been made and to the summoning of separate meetings, at the discretion of the liquidator, of the creditors of the partnership or of any such insolvent member, and to the summoning of a single meeting of the contributories of the partnership and of any corporate member against whom an insolvency order has been made and to the summoning of separate meetings of contributories of the partnership or of any such corporate member at the discretion of the liquidator.

Section 139

8. For section 139 there shall be substituted the following:—

"(1) This section applies where an insolvent partnership is being wound up by the court and a single meeting of creditors of the partnership and of any insolvent member against whom an insolvency order has been made is summoned for the purpose of choosing a person to be liquidator of the partnership and to act as the responsible insolvency practitioner in relation to any such insolvent member.

(2) The creditors at their meeting may nominate a person to be the liquidator of the

partnership and to act as the responsible insolvency practitioner in relation to any such insolvent member.

(3) If a responsible insolvency practitioner when acting as liquidator of an insolvent partnership is of the opinion at any time that there is a conflict of interest between his functions as liquidator of the partnership and responsible insolvency practitioner in relation to any insolvent member against whom an insolvency order has been made, he may apply to the court for directions, and in such a case the court may, without prejudice to the generality of its power to give directions, appoint one or more other insolvency practitioners in his place to act as liquidator of the partnership or as responsible insolvency practitioner in relation to any such insolvent member, or as both.".

Section 140

9. Section 140 shall be omitted.

Section 141

10. (*a*) For subsection (1) there shall be substituted the following:—

>   "(*1*) Where a winding-up order has been made by the court in England and Wales in relation to an insolvent partnership and a single meeting of creditors has been summoned for the purpose of choosing a person to be liquidator of the partnership and to act as the responsible insolvency practitioner in relation to any insolvent member against whom an insolvency order has been made, the meeting may establish a committee ("the liquidation committee"), consisting of creditors of the partnership or of such insolvent members, or of both, for the partnership and for any corporate member to exercise the functions conferred on it by or under this Act.";

>   (*b*) in subsection (2), for the words "separate general meetings of the company's creditors and contributories" there shall be substituted the words "a single general meeting of the creditors of the partnership and of any insolvent member against whom an insolvency order has been made"; and

>   (*c*) for subsection (3) there shall be substituted the following:—

>   "(3) The court may at any time, on application by a creditor of the partnership or of any insolvent member, appoint additional members of the liquidation committee, and if it does so the limit on the maximum number of members of the committee specified in the Insolvency Rules 1986 shall be increased by the number of additional members appointed by the court.".

Section 143

11. After subsection (1) there shall be added the following subsection:—

"(1A) In carrying out his functions in regard to the distribution of the assets of an insolvent partnership, the liquidator shall have regard to the provisions of Articles 9 and 10 of the Insolvent Partnerships Order 1986 (relating to priority of expenses and debts respectively).".

Section 154

12. At the end there shall be added the words "having regard in relation to insolvent partnerships to the provisions of Articles 9 and 10 of the Insolvent Partnerships Order 1986 (relating to priority of expenses and debts respectively)".

Section 168

13. (*a*) In subsection (2)—

>   (*i*) the words "or contributories" where they secondly occur shall be omitted; and

>   (*ii*) the words "or contributories (as the case may be)" shall be omitted; and

>   (*b*) at the end of subsection (3) there shall be added the words "or in relation to any insolvency proceedings in respect of any insolvent member, and any order made on such an application may contain directions as to the future conduct of any insolvency proceedings in existence against any insolvent member in respect of whom an insolvency order has been made".

Section 172

14. (*a*) For subsection (2) there shall be substituted the following:—

"(2) Subject as follows, the liquidator or provisional liquidator of an insolvent partnership may be removed from office only by an order of the court.";

(*b*) subsection (3) shall be omitted; and
(*c*) for subsection (6) there shall be substituted the following:—

"(6) A liquidator of an insolvent partnership may, with the leave of the court, or, if appointed by the Secretary of State, of the Secretary of State, resign his office by giving notice of his resignation to the court.".

Section 174(4)

15. (*a*) In paragraph (*a*), the words "who has been removed from office by a general meeting of creditors that has not resolved against his release or" shall be omitted;

(*b*) for paragraph (*b*) there shall be substituted the following:—

"(b) in the case of a person who has been removed from office by the court or by the Secretary of State, or who has vacated office under section 172(5), such time as the Secretary of State may, on an application by that person, determine;"; and

(*c*) for paragraph (*c*) there shall be substituted the following:—

"(c) in the case of a person who has resigned as liquidator of an insolvent partnership, such time as may be directed by the court or, if he was appointed by the Secretary of State, such time as the Secretary of State may, on an application by that person, determine;".

Section 189

16. After subsection (5) there shall be added the following subsection:—

"(6) The provisions of this section are subject to Article 10 of the Insolvent Partnerships Order 1986 (relating to priority of debts).".

Section 222(1)

17. For that subsection there shall be substituted the following:—

"(1) An insolvent partnership is deemed (for the purposes of section 221) unable to pay its debts if there is a creditor, by assignment or otherwise, to whom the partnership owes a joint debt in a sum exceeding £750 then due and—

(a) the creditor has served on the partnership, by leaving at its principal place of business in England and Wales, or by delivering to a partner or any person having at the time of service control or management of the partnership business there, or by otherwise serving in such manner as the court may approve or direct, a written demand in Form 3 in Schedule 3 to the Insolvent Partnerships Order 1986, and the creditor has also served on any two or more insolvent members demands in accordance with paragraph 4 of Part II and paragraph 5 of Part III of Schedule 2 to that Order, requiring the partnership and its members to pay the sum due to the creditor, and
(b) the partnership and its members have for 3 weeks after the service of the demands, or the last of them if served at different times, neglected to pay the sum or to secure or compound for it to the reasonable satisfaction of the creditor.".

Section 223 and 224

18. Sections 223 and 224 shall be omitted.   **[1520]**

NOTES
Commencement: 29 December 1986.
The Act: Insolvency Act 1986.

PART II
CORPORATE MEMBERS (ART 8(2))

Section 73

1. For section 73 there shall be substituted the following:—

"73. A corporate member may be wound up by the court (Chapter VI).".

Section 117

2. The court only has jurisdiction under section 117 to wind up a corporate member if it has jurisdiction to wind up the partnership under the section as modified by paragraph 1 of Part I of this Schedule.

Section 122

3. For that section there shall be substituted the following:—

"122. A corporate member may be wound up by the court if it is unable to pay its debts.".

Section 123

4. (*a*) For subsection (1) there shall be substituted the following:—

"(*1*) A corporate member is deemed unable to pay its debts if a creditor (by assignment or otherwise) to whom the partnership owes a joint debt in a sum exceeding £750 then due has served on the company and the partnership, by leaving in the case of service on the company at the company's registered office and in the case of service on the partnership by leaving at its principal place of business in England and Wales or by delivering to a partner or any person having at the time of service control or management of the partnership business there, or by otherwise serving in such manner as the court may approve or direct, a written demand in Form 3 in Schedule 3 to the Insolvent Partnerships Order 1986 requiring the company and the partnership to pay the sum so due and the company and the partnership have for 3 weeks after the relevant demand has been served neglected to pay the sum or to secure or compound for it to the reasonable satisfaction of the creditor."; and

(*b*) after subsection (3) there shall be added the following subsection:—

"(4) A corporate member is also deemed unable to pay its debts if the court has made a winding-up order against the partnership.".

Section 124

5. For section 124 there shall be substituted the following:—

"124.—(1) An application to the court for the winding up of a corporate member shall be by petition in Form 6 in Schedule 3 to the Insolvent Partnerships Order 1986 presented by that member or any creditor or creditors to whom the partnership is indebted in respect of a liquidated sum payable immediately.

(2) The petition shall be presented at the same time and to the same court as the petition for the winding up of the insolvent partnership.

(3) A petition by a corporate member may be presented only on the grounds that the partnership is unable to pay its debts and if—

(*a*) petitions are at the same time presented for insolvency orders against the partnership and every other member; and

(*b*) each member is willing for an insolvency order to be made against him and the petition contains a statement to this effect.

(4) The petition shall be advertised in Form 5 in the said Schedule 3.

(5) At any time after presentation of the petition the petitioner may, with the leave of the court obtained on application and on such terms as it thinks just, add other partners as parties to the proceedings in relation to the insolvent partnership.

(6) The petition shall contain particulars of other petitions being presented in relation to the partnership, identifying the partnership and members concerned.

(7) The petitioner may withdraw the petition if—

(*a*) he withdraws at the same time every other petition which he has presented against the partnership and any other insolvent member, unless the court is satisfied on application made to it by the petitioner that, because of difficulties of serving the petition or for any other reason, the continuance of that petition would be likely to prejudice or delay the proceedings on the petition which he has presented against the partnership or on any petition which he has presented against any other insolvent member; and

(*b*) he gives notice to the court at least 3 days before the date appointed for the hearing of the petition of his intention to withdraw the petition.

(8) Where notice is given under subsection (7) the court may, on such terms as it thinks just, substitute as petitioner any creditor of the partnership who in its opinion would have a right to present the petition and who has been substituted by the court as petitioner in respect of the petition for winding up the partnership and the same time substitute him as petitioner in respect of every petition which the petitioner has presented against other corporate members, and if the court makes such a substitution the petition in question will not be withdrawn.".

Section 125

6. For subsection (2) there shall be substituted the following:—

"(2) On the hearing of a winding-up petition against a corporate member the petitioner shall draw the court's attention to the result of the hearing on the winding-up petition against the partnership, and, subject to subsection (3), if a winding-up order has been made against the partnership the court shall make a winding-up order against any corporate member in respect of whom an insolvency petition has been presented.

(3) The court may dismiss a petition against a corporate member who is a limited partner, if—

(*a*) he lodges in court for the benefit of the creditors of the partnership sufficient money or security to the court's satisfaction to meet his limited liability for the debts and obligations of the partnership; or

(*b*) he satisfies the court that he is no longer under any liability in respect of the debts and obligations of the partnership.".

Section 131(2)

7. In paragraph (*a*) there shall be added at the end of the words ", specifying the corporate member's interest in the assets of the insolvent partnership and specifying those debts and liabilities which are attributable to the separate and joint estates respectively".

Section 133

8. (*a*) For subsection (3) there shall be substituted the following:—

"(*3*) On an application under subsection (1), the court shall, subject to subsection (5), direct that a public examination of the person to whom the application relates shall be held on a day appointed by the court; and that person shall attend on that day and be publicly examined as to the promotion, formation or management of the corporate member, the partnership or any other corporate member, or all of them, or as to the conduct of their business and affairs, or of his conduct or dealings in relation to the partnership or any other insolvent member."; and

(*b*) after subsection (4) there shall be added the following:—

"(5) Where the court has already directed on a previous application in proceedings in relation to the partnership or another insolvent member that a public examination of the person to whom the application under subsection (1) relates shall be held, the court may decline to direct that a further public examination of that person shall be held.".

Section 136

9. (*a*) Any reference in section 136(4) and the subsequent sections in Part IV of the Act, applied by virtue of this Order with the modifications in this Part of this Schedule to the summoning of separate meetings of the creditors and contributories or a general meeting of creditors shall include a reference to the summoning of a meeting or meetings held pursuant to paragraphs 5 to 10 of Part I of this Schedule; and

(*b*) subsections (5) and (6) shall be omitted.

Section 140

10. Section 140 shall be omitted.

Section 143

11. After subsection (1) there shall be added the following subsection:—

"(1A) In carrying out his functions in regard to the distribution of the assets of a corporate member, the liquidator shall have regard to the provisions of Articles 9 and 10 of the Insolvent Partnerships Order 1986 (relating to priority of expenses and debts respectively).".

Section 154

12. At the end there shall be added the words "having regard in relation to corporate members to the provisions of Articles 9 and 10 of the Insolvent Partnerships Order 1986 (relating to priority of expenses and debts respectively)".

Section 168

13. In subsection (2)—

(*a*) the words "or contributories" where they secondly occur shall be omitted; and
(*b*) the words "or contributories (as the case may be)" shall be omitted.

Section 172

14. (*a*) For subsection (2) there shall be substituted the following:—

"(2) Subject as follows, the liquidator or provisional liquidator of a corporate member may be removed from office only by an order of the court.";

(*b*) subsection (3) shall be omitted; and
(*c*) for subsection (6) there shall be substituted the following:—

"(6) A liquidator of a corporate member may, with the leave of the court, or, if appointed by the Secretary of State, of the Secretary of State, resign his office by giving notice of his resignation to the court.".

Section 174(4)

15. (*a*) In paragraph (*a*), the words "who has been removed from office by a general meeting of creditors that has not resolved against his release or" shall be omitted;

(*b*) for paragraph (*b*) there shall be substituted the following:—

"(*b*) in the case of a person who has been removed from office by the court or by the Secretary of State, or who has vacated office under section 172(5), such time as the Secretary of State may, on an application by that person, determine;"; and

(*c*) for paragraph (*c*) there shall be substituted the following:—

"(*c*) in the case of a person who has resigned as liquidator of a corporate member, such time as may be directed by the court or, if he was appointed by the Secretary of State, such time as the Secretary of State may, on an application by that person, determine,".

Section 189

16. After subsection (5) there shall be added the following subsection:—

"(6) The provisions of this section are subject to Article 10 of the Insolvent Partnerships Order 1986 (relating to priority of debts).".   **[1521]**

NOTES
Commencement: 29 December 1986.
The Act: Insolvency Act 1986.

PART III

INDIVIDUAL MEMBERS (ART 8(2))

Section 264

1. (*a*) For subsection (1) there shall be substituted the following:—

"(*1*) A petition in Form 7 in Schedule 3 to the Insolvent Partnerships Order 1986 for a bankruptcy order to be made against an individual member of an insolvent partnership may be presented to the court in accordance with the following provisions of this Part by one of the individual's creditors or jointly by more than one of them, and no petition can be presented under the following provisions of this Part against the partnership or against the partners in the name of the firm."; and

(*b*) after subsection (1) there shall be added the following subsections:—

"(1A) The petition shall be presented at the same time and to the same court as the petition for the winding up of the partnership.

(1B) At any time after presentation of the petition the petitioner may, with the leave of the court obtained on application and on such terms as it thinks just, add other partners as parties to the proceedings in relation to the insolvent partnership.

(1C) The petition shall contain particulars of other petitions being presented in relation to the partnership, identifying the partnership and members concerned.

(1D) The petitioner may withdraw the petition if—

(*a*) he withdraws at the same time every other petition which he has presented against the partnership and any other insolvent member, unless the court is satisfied on application made to it by the petitioner that, because of difficulties of serving the petition or for any other reason, the continuance of that petition would be likely to prejudice or delay the proceedings on the petition which he has presented against the partnership or on any petition which he has presented against any other insolvent member; and

(*b*) he gives notice to the court at least 3 days before the date appointed for the hearing of the petition of his intention to withdraw the petition.

(1E) Where notice is given under subsection (1D) the court may, on such terms as it thinks just, substitute as petitioner any creditor of the partnership who in its opinion would have a right to present the petition and who has been substituted by the court as petitioner in respect of the petition for winding up the partnership and at the same time substitute him as petitioner in respect of every petition which the petitioner has presented against other individual members, and if the court makes such a substitution the petition in question will not be withdrawn.".

Section 265

2. For that section there shall be substituted the following:—

"265. A bankruptcy petition shall not be presented to the court under section 264 against an individual member unless the court has jurisdiction to wind up the partnership.".

Section 266

3. Subsection (1) shall be omitted.

Section 267

4. (*a*) In subsection (1) for the words "debts owed by the debtor" there shall be substituted the words "joint debts owed by the insolvent partnership";

(*b*) in subsection (2)(*b*) for all the words after "creditors" to the end of the sub-paragraph there shall be substituted the word "immediately"; and

(c) in subsection (2)(c):—

> (i) for the word "debtor" there shall be substituted the words "individual member"; and
>
> (ii) the words "either" and "or to have no reasonable prospect of being able to pay" shall be omitted.

Section 268

5. (a) In subsection (1) for the words from the beginning to paragraph (a) there shall be substituted the words "(1) For the purposes of section 267(2)(c), the individual member appears to be unable to pay a debt if, but only if, the debt is payable immediately and";

(b) for subsection (1)(a) there shall be substituted the following:—

> "(a) the petitioning creditor to whom the insolvent partnership owes a joint debt has served on the individual member a demand (known as "the statutory demand"), and on the partnership a demand (known as "the written demand"), in Form 3 in Schedule 3 to the Insolvent Partnerships Order 1986 requiring the member and the partnership to pay the debt or to secure or compound for it to the reasonable satisfaction of the creditor at least 3 weeks have elapsed since the relevant demand was served and both the demands have not been complied with or the demand against the member has not been set aside in accordance with the rules,";

(c) subsection (1)(b) shall be omitted; and

(d) for subsection (2) there shall be substituted the following:—

> "(2) For the purposes of section 267(2)(c), the individual member also appears to be unable to pay a debt if the court has made a winding-up order against the partnership.
>
> (3) Where the petitioning creditor has obtained a judgment, decree or order of any court against the individual member or against the partnership, the statutory demand may be served at the principal place of business of the partnership in England and Wales on the individual member or on any partner or any other person having at the time of service control or management of the partnership business there:
>
>> Provided that such service shall not be effective service of the statutory demand on any person unless the creditor was at the time of such service entitled to issue execution or other process against the property of the member or of the partnership, as the case may be, in respect of the judgment, decree or order in question.".

Sections 269 and 270

6. Sections 269 and 270 shall be omitted.

Section 271

7. (a) In subsection (1) the word "either" and paragraph (b) shall be omitted;

(b) for subsections (2) and (3) there shall be substituted the following:—

> "(2) The court may dismiss the petition if no winding-up order has been made against the insolvent partnership."; and

(c) after subsection (2) there shall be added the following subsections:—

> "(2A) On the hearing of the petition the petitioner shall draw the court's attention to the result of the hearing on the winding-up petition against the partnership, and, subject to subsection (2B), if a winding-up order has been made against the partnership the court shall make a bankruptcy order against any individual member in respect of whom an insolvency petition has been presented.
>
> (2B) The court may dismiss a petition against an individual member who is a limited partner, if—
>
>> (a) he lodges in court for the benefit of the creditors of the partnership sufficient money or security to the court's satisfaction to meet his limited liability for the debts and obligations of the partnership; or

(*b*) he satisfies the court that he is no longer under any liability in respect of the debts and obligations of the partnership.".

Section 272

8. For section 272 there shall be substituted the following:—

"272. A debtor's petition in Form 7 in Schedule 3 to the Insolvent Partnerships Order 1986 may be presented to the court by an individual member only on the grounds that the partnership is unable to pay its debts and if—

(*a*) petitions are at the same time presented for insolvency orders against the partnership and every other member; and

(*b*) each member is willing for an insolvency order to be made against him and the petition contains a statement to this effect.".

Section 273 and 277

9. Sections 273 to 277 shall be omitted.

Sections 283

10. Subsection (2) shall be omitted so far as it relates to partnership property.

Section 284(6)

11. At the end there shall be added the words "other than a disposition made by an individual member of property held by him on trust for the partnership".

Section 288(2)

12. (*a*) In subsection (1), the words "otherwise than on a debtor's petition" shall be omitted; and

(*b*) in subsection (2)(*a*) after the word "prescribed" there shall be inserted the words ", specifying the individual member's interest in the assets of the insolvent partnership and specifying those debts and liabilities which are attributable to the separate and joint estates respectively".

Section 290

13. (*a*) For subsection (3) there shall be substituted the following:—

"(3) On an application under subsection (1), the court shall, subject to subsection (4A), direct that a public examination of the individual member shall be held on a day appointed by the court; and the individual member shall attend on that day and be publicly examined as to his affairs, dealings and property and to those of the partnership or of another insolvent member or both."; and

(*b*) after subsection (4) there shall be added the following subsection:—

"(4A) Where the court has already directed on a previous application in proceedings in relation to the partnership or another insolvent member that a public examination of the person to whom the application under subsection (1) relates shall be held, the court may decline to direct that a further public examination of that person shall be held.".

Section 292(1)

14. The words "(whether the first such trustee or a trustee appointed to fill any vacancy)" and paragraph (*c*) shall be omitted.

Section 293 and 294

15. Sections 293 and 294 shall be omitted.

Section 295

16. (*a*) In subsection (1), for the words "if a meeting summoned under section 293 or 294" there shall be substituted the words "When a meeting involving the creditors of any individual member summoned under section 136(4) as applied with modifications in relation to insolvent partnerships by paragraph 5 of Part I of Schedule 2 to the Insolvent Partnerships Order 1986"; and

(*b*) in subsection (4) the words "in a case in which no notice has been given under section 293(2)" shall be omitted.

Section 297

17. Section 297 shall be omitted.

Section 298

18. (*a*) In subsection (1), the words "or by" to the end of the subsection shall be omitted;

    (*b*) subsections (3) and (4) shall be omitted; and

    (*c*) for subsection (7) there shall be substituted the following:—

> "(7) The trustee of the estate of an individual member may, with the leave of the court, or, if appointed by the Secretary of State, of the Secretary of State, resign his office by giving notice of his resignation to the court.".

Section 299(3)

19.(*a*) In paragraph (*a*), the words "who has been removed from office by a general meeting of the bankrupt's creditors that has not resolved against his release or" shall be omitted;

    (*b*) for paragraph (*b*) there shall be substituted the following:—

> "(*b*) in the case of a person who has been removed from office by the court or by the Secretary of State, or who has vacated office under section 298(6), such time as the Secretary of State may, on an application by that person, determine;"; and

    (*c*) for paragraph (*c*) there shall be substituted the following:—

> "(*c*) in the case of a person who has resigned as trustee of the estate of an individual member, such time as may be directed by the court or, if he was appointed by the Secretary of State, such time as the Secretary of State may, on an application by that person, determine;".

Section 300

20. (*a*) Subsections (3) to (5) shall be omitted and for subsection (2) there shall be substituted the following:—

> "(2) The official receiver may refer the need for an appointment to the Secretary of State and shall be trustee of the estate of the individual member until the vacancy is filled."; and

    (*b*) in subsections (6) and (7) for the words "(4) or (5)" there shall be substituted the word "(2)".

Section 301

21. (*a*) For subsection (1) there shall be substituted the following:—

> "(*1*) Subject as follows, a general meeting involving the creditors of any individual member summoned under section 136(4), as applied with modifications in relation to insolvent partnerships by paragraph 5 of Part I of Schedule 2 to the Insolvent Partnerships Order 1986, may establish a committee (known as "the creditors' committee") composed of the same persons as the liquidation committee established under section 141, as applied with modifications in relation to insolvent partnerships by paragraph 10 of the said Part I, to exercise the functions conferred on it by or under this Act."; and

    (*b*) in subsection (2), for the words "of the bankrupt's creditors" there shall be substituted the words "involving the creditors of any such individual member".

Section 305

22. After subsection (2) there shall be added the following subsection:—

> "(2A) In carrying out his functions in regard to the distribution of the estate of the individual member, the trustee shall have regard to the provisions of

Articles 9 and 10 of the Insolvent Partnerships Order 1986 (relating to priority of expenses and debts respectively).".

Section 328

23. After subsection (6) there shall be added the following subsection:—

"(7) The provisions of this section are subject to the provisions of Article 10 of the Insolvent Partnerships Order 1986 (relating to priority of debts).".

Section 330(5)

24. For that subsection there shall be substituted the following:—

"(5) If a surplus remains after payment in full and with interest of all the creditors in accordance with Articles 9 and 10 of the Insolvent Partnerships Order 1986 (relating to priority of expenses and debts respectively), it shall be applied in accordance with those Articles.".   **[1522]**

NOTES
> Commencement: 29 December 1986.
> The Act: Insolvency Act 1986.

SCHEDULE 3

Order 13(1), Sch 1, para 2, Sch 2, Part I, paras 2, 17, Part II, paras 4, 5, Part III, paras 1, 5, 8

NOTES
> The forms themselves are not set out in this work, but their numbers and descriptions are listed below.

-

FORM NO	TITLE
1	Liquidator's or Trustee's Petition to Wind Up Partnership
2	Written Demand by Member
3	Written/Statutory Demand by Creditor
4	Petition to Wind Up Partnership (Presented in Conjunction with Petitions Against Members)
5	Advertisement of Winding-Up Petition(s) Against Partnership (And Any Corporate Members)
6	Petition to Wind Up Corporate Member (Presented in Conjunction with Petition Against Partnership)
7	Bankruptcy Petition Against Individual Member (Presented in Conjunction With Petition Against Partnership)
8	Joint Bankruptcy Petition Against Individual Members

[1523]

NOTES
> Commencement: 29 December 1986.

Section C

Insolvency (Scotland) Rules 1986

SECTION C

INSOLVENCY (SCOTLAND) RULES 1986
(1986 No 1915 (S 139))

NOTES
   Made: 10 November 1986.
   Commencement: 29 December 1986.
   Authority: Insolvency Act 1986, s 411.

ARRANGEMENT OF THE RULES

INTRODUCTORY PROVISIONS

Rule			Para
0.1	Citation and commencement	.. ..	[1524]
0.2	Interpretation	.. ..	[1525]
0.3	Application ..	.. ..	[1516]

PART 1
COMPANY VOLUNTARY ARRANGEMENTS

CHAPTER 1
PRELIMINARY

1.1	Scope of this Part; interpretation ..	.. ..	[1527]

CHAPTER 2
PROPOSAL BY DIRECTORS

1.2	Preparation of proposal	.. ..	[1528]
1.3	Contents of proposal	.. ..	[1529]
1.4	Notice to intended nominee	.. ..	[1530]
1.5	Statement of affairs	.. ..	[1531]
1.6	Additional disclosure for assistance of nominee ..	.. .. ..	[1532]
1.7	Nominee's report on the proposal..	.. ..	[1533]
1.8	Replacement of nominee ..	.. ..	[1534]
1.9	Summoning of meetings under section 3 ..	.. ..	[1535]

CHAPTER 3
PROPOSAL BY ADMINISTRATOR OR LIQUIDATOR WHERE HE IS THE NOMINEE

1.10	Preparation of proposal	.. ..	[1536]
1.11	Summoning of meetings under section 3 ..	.. ..	[1537]

CHAPTER 4
PROPOSAL BY ADMINISTRATOR OR LIQUIDATOR WHERE ANOTHER INSOLVENCY PRACTITIONER IS THE NOMINEE

1.12	Preparation of proposal and notice to nominee ..	.. ..	[1538]

Rule   Para

CHAPTER 5

MEETINGS

1.13 General ..   ..   [1539]
1.14 Summoning of meetings ..   ..   [1540]
1.15 Attendance by company officers ..   ..   [1541]
1.16 Adjournments ..   ..   [1542]
1.17 Report of meetings ..   ..   [1543]

CHAPTER 6

IMPLEMENTATION OF THE VOLUNTARY ARRANGEMENT

1.18 Resolutions to follow approval ..   ..   [1544]
1.19 Hand-over of property, etc to supervisor ..   ..   [1545]
1.20 Revocation or suspension of the arrangement ..   ..   [1546]
1.21 Supervisor's accounts and reports ..   ..   [1547]
1.22 Fees, costs, charges and expenses ..   ..   [1548]
1.23 Completion of the arrangement ..   ..   [1549]
1.24 False representations, etc ..   ..   [1550]

PART 2

ADMINISTRATION PROCEDURE

CHAPTER 1

APPLICATION FOR, AND MAKING OF, THE ORDER

2.1 Independent report on company's affairs ..   ..   [1551]
2.2 Notice of petition ..   ..   [1552]
2.3 Notice and advertisement of administration order   ..   ..   ..   [1553]

CHAPTER 2

STATEMENT OF AFFAIRS AND PROPOSALS TO CREDITORS

2.4 Notice requiring statement of affairs   ..   ..   [1554]
2.5 Form of the statement of affairs ..   ..   [1555]
2.6 Expenses of statement of affairs ..   ..   [1556]
2.7 Statement to be annexed to proposals   ..   ..   [1557]
2.8 Notices of proposals to members ..   ..   [1558]

CHAPTER 3

MEETINGS AND NOTICES

2.9 General ..   ..   [1559]
2.10 Meeting to consider administrator's proposals ..   ..   [1560]
2.11 Retention of title creditors ..   ..   [1561]
2.12 Hire purchase, conditional sale and hiring agreements ..   ..   ..   [1562]
2.13 Report of meetings ..   ..   [1563]
2.14 Notices to creditors ..   ..   [1564]

CHAPTER 4

THE CREDITORS' COMMITTEE

2.15 Application of provisions in Part 3 (Receivers) ..   ..   [1565]

Rule   Para

CHAPTER 5

THE ADMINISTRATOR

2.16   Remuneration .. .. [1566]
2.17   Abstract of receipts and payments .. .. [1567]
2.18   Resignation from office .. .. [1568]
2.19   Administrator deceased .. .. [1569]
2.20   Order filling vacancy .. .. [1570]

CHAPTER 6

VAT BAD DEBT RELIEF

2.21   Application of provisions in Part 3 (Receivers) .. .. [1571]

PART 3

RECEIVERS

CHAPTER 1

APPOINTMENT

3.1   Acceptance of appointment .. .. [1572]

CHAPTER 2

STATEMENT OF AFFAIRS

3.2   Notice requiring statement of affairs .. .. [1573]
3.3   Expenses of statement of affairs .. .. [1574]

CHAPTER 3

THE CREDITORS' COMMITTEE

3.4   Constitution of committee .. .. [1575]
3.5   Functions of the committee .. .. [1576]
3.6   Application of provisions relating to liquidation committee .. .. .. [1577]
3.7   Information from receiver .. .. [1578]
3.8   Members' dealings with the company .. .. [1579]

CHAPTER 4

MISCELLANEOUS

3.9   Abstract of receipts and payments .. .. [1580]
3.10   Receiver deceased .. .. [1581]
3.11   Vacation of office .. .. [1582]

CHAPTER 5

VAT BAD DEBT RELIEF

3.12   Issue of certificate of insolvency .. .. [1583]
3.13   Notice to creditors .. .. [1584]
3.14   Preservation of certificate with company's records .. .. .. [1585]

Rule   Para

PART 4

WINDING UP BY THE COURT

CHAPTER 1

PROVISIONAL LIQUIDATOR

4.1   Appointment of provisional liquidator   ..   .. [1586]
4.2   Order of appointment   ..   .. [1587]
4.3   Caution   ..   .. [1588]
4.4   Failure to find or to maintain caution   ..   .. [1589]
4.5   Remuneration   ..   .. [1590]
4.6   Termination of appointment   ..   .. [1591]

CHAPTER 2

STATEMENT OF AFFAIRS

4.7   Notice requiring statement of affairs   ..   .. [1592]
4.8   Form of the statement of affairs   ..   .. [1593]
4.9   Expenses of statement of affairs   ..   .. [1594]

CHAPTER 3

INFORMATION

4.10 Information to creditors and contributories   ..   .. [1595]
4.11 Information to registrar of companies   ..   .. [1596]

CHAPTER 4

MEETINGS OF CREDITORS AND CONTRIBUTORIES

4.12 First meetings in the liquidation   ..   .. [1597]
4.13 Other meetings   ..   .. [1598]
4.14 Attendance at meetings of company's personnel   ..   .. [1599]

CHAPTER 5

CLAIMS IN LIQUIDATION

4.15 Submission of claims   ..   .. [1600]
4.16 Application of the Bankruptcy Act   ..   .. [1601]
4.17 Claims in foreign currency   ..   .. [1602]

CHAPTER 6

THE LIQUIDATOR

SECTION A: APPOINTMENT AND FUNCTIONS OF LIQUIDATOR

4.18 Appointment of liquidator by the court   ..   .. [1603]
4.19 Appointment by creditors or contributories   ..   .. [1604]
4.20 Authentication of liquidator's appointment   ..   .. [1605]
4.21 Hand-over of assets to liquidator   ..   .. [1606]
4.22 Taking possession and realisation of the company's assets   ..   .. [1607]

Rule   Para

Section B: Removal and Resignation; Vacation of Office

4.23 Summoning of meeting for removal of liquidator .. .. [1608]
4.24 Procedure on liquidator's removal .. .. [1609]
4.25 Release of liquidator on removal .. .. [1610]
4.26 Removal of liquidator by the court .. .. [1611]
4.27 Advertisement of removal .. .. [1612]
4.28 Resignation of liquidator .. .. [1613]
4.29 Action following acceptance of liquidator's resignation .. .. .. [1614]
4.30 Leave to resign granted by the Court .. .. [1615]

Section C: Release on Completion of Winding Up

4.31 Final meeting .. .. [1616]

Section D: Outlays and Remuneration

4.32 Determination of amount of outlays and remuneration .. .. .. [1617]
4.33 Recourse of liquidator to meeting of creditors .. .. [1618]
4.34 Recourse to the court .. .. [1619]
4.35 Creditors' claim that remuneration is excessive .. .. [1620]

Section E: Supplementary Provisions

4.36 Liquidator deceased .. .. [1621]
4.37 Loss of qualification as insolvency practitioner .. .. [1622]
4.38 Power of court to set aside certain transactions .. .. [1623]
4.39 Rule against solicitation .. .. [1624]

Chapter 7

The Liquidation Committee

4.40 Preliminary .. .. [1625]
4.41 Membership of committee .. .. [1626]
4.42 Formalities of establishment .. .. [1627]
4.43 Committee established by contributories .. .. [1628]
4.44 Obligations of liquidator to committee .. .. [1629]
4.45 Meetings of the committee .. .. [1630]
4.46 The chairman at meetings .. .. [1631]
4.47 Quorum .. .. [1632]
4.48 Committee members' representatives .. .. [1633]
4.49 Resignation .. .. [1634]
4.50 Termination of membership .. .. [1635]
4.51 Removal .. .. [1636]
4.52 Vacancy (creditor members) .. .. [1637]
4.53 Vacancy (contributory members) .. .. [1638]
4.54 Voting rights and resolutions .. .. [1639]
4.55 Resolutions by post .. .. [1640]
4.56 Liquidator's reports .. .. [1641]
4.57 Expenses of members, etc .. .. [1642]
4.58 Dealings by committee members and others .. .. [1643]
4.59 Composition of committee when creditors paid in full .. .. .. [1644]

Chapter 8

The Liquidation Committee where Winding Up Follows Immediately on Administration

4.60 Preliminary .. .. [1645]
4.61 Continuation of creditors' committee .. .. [1646]
4.62 Membership of committee .. .. [1647]
4.63 Liquidator's certificate .. .. [1648]

Rule Para
4.64 Obligations of liquidator to committee .. .. [1649]
4.65 Application of Chapter 7 .. .. [1650]

CHAPTER 9

DISTRIBUTION OF COMPANY'S ASSETS BY LIQUIDATOR

4.66 Order of priority in distribution .. .. [1651]
4.67 Order of priority of expenses of liquidation .. .. [1652]
4.68 Application of the Bankruptcy Act .. .. [1653]

CHAPTER 10

SPECIAL MANAGER

4.69 Appointment and remuneration .. .. [1654]
4.70 Caution .. .. [1655]
4.71 Failure to find or to maintain caution .. .. [1656]
4.72 Accounting .. .. [1657]
4.73 Termination of appointment .. .. [1658]

CHAPTER 11

PUBLIC EXAMINATION OF COMPANY OFFICERS AND OTHERS

4.74 Notice of order for public examination .. .. [1659]
4.75 Order on request by creditors or contributories .. .. [1660]

CHAPTER 12

MISCELLANEOUS

4.76 Limitation .. .. [1661]
4.77 Dissolution after winding up .. .. [1662]

CHAPTER 13

COMPANY WITH PROHIBITED NAME

4.78 Preliminary .. .. [1663]
4.79 Application for leave under section 216(3) .. .. [1664]
4.80 First excepted case .. .. [1665]
4.81 Second excepted case .. .. [1666]
4.82 Third excepted case .. .. [1667]

PART 5

CREDITORS' VOLUNTARY WINDING UP

5 Application of Part 4 .. .. [1668]

PART 6

MEMBERS' VOLUNTARY WINDING UP

6 Application of Part 4 .. .. [1669]

Rule   Para

PART 7

PROVISIONS OF GENERAL APPLICATION

CHAPTER 1

MEETINGS

7.1	Scope of Chapter 1	[1670]
7.2	Summoning of meetings	[1671]
7.3	Notice of meeting	[1672]
7.4	Additional notices in certain cases	[1673]
7.5	Chairman of meetings	[1674]
7.6	Meetings requisitioned	[1675]
7.7	Quorum	[1676]
7.8	Adjournment	[1677]
7.9	Entitlement to vote (creditors)	[1678]
7.10	Entitlement to vote (members and contributories)	[1679]
7.11	Chairman of meeting as proxy holder	[1680]
7.12	Resolutions	[1681]
7.13	Report of meeting	[1682]

CHAPTER 2

PROXIES AND COMPANY REPRESENTATION

7.14	Definition of "proxy"	[1683]
7.15	Form of proxy	[1684]
7.16	Use of proxy at meeting	[1685]
7.17	Retention of proxies	[1686]
7.18	Right of inspection	[1687]
7.19	Proxy-holder with financial interest	[1688]
7.20	Representation of corporations	[1689]

CHAPTER 3

MISCELLANEOUS

7.21	Giving of notices, etc	[1690]
7.22	Sending by post	[1691]
7.23	Certificate of giving notice, etc	[1692]
7.24	Validity of proceedings	[1693]
7.25	Evidence of proceedings at meetings	[1694]
7.26	Right to list of creditors and copy documents	[1695]
7.27	Confidentiality of documents	[1696]
7.28	Insolvency practitioner's caution	[1697]
7.29	Punishment of offences	[1698]
7.30	Forms for use in insolvency proceedings	[1699]
7.31	Fees, expenses, etc	[1700]
7.32	Power of court to cure defects in procedure	[1701]
7.33	Sederunt book	[1702]

SCHEDULES

Schedule 1—Modifications of Part 4 in relation to creditors' voluntary winding up   [1703]
Schedule 2—Application of Part 4 in relation to members' voluntary winding up   [1704]
Schedule 3—Deposit Protection Board's voting rights   [1705]
Schedule 4—Punishment of offences under the Rules   [1706]
Schedule 5—Forms   [1707]

INTRODUCTORY PROVISIONS

0.1. Citation and commencement

These Rules may be cited as the Insolvency (Scotland) Rules 1986 and shall
come into operation on 29th December 1986.   **[1524]**

0.2. Interpretation

(1) In these Rules

"the Act" means the Insolvency Act 1986;

"the Companies Act" means the Companies Act 1985;

"the Bankruptcy Act" means the Bankruptcy (Scotland) Act 1985;

"the Rules" means the Insolvency (Scotland) Rules 1986;

"accounting period" in relation to the winding up of a company, shall be construed in accordance with section 52(1) and (6) of the Bankruptcy Act as applied by Rule 4.68;

"business day" means any day other than a Saturday, a Sunday, Christmas Day, Good Friday or a day which is a bank holiday in any part of Great Britain;

"company" means a company which the courts in Scotland have jurisdiction to wind up;

"insolvency proceedings" means any proceedings under the first group of Parts in the Act or under these Rules;

"receiver" means a receiver appointed under section 51 (Receivers (Scotland)); and

"responsible insolvency practitioner" means, in relation to any insolvency proceedings, the person acting as supervisor of a voluntary arrangement under Part I of the Act, or as administrator, receiver, liquidator or provisional liquidator.

(2) In these Rules, unless the context otherwise requires, any reference—

(*a*) to a section is a reference to a section of the Act;

(*b*) to a Rule is a reference to a Rule of the Rules;

(*c*) to a Part or a Schedule is a reference to a Part of, or Schedule to, the Rules;

(*d*) to a Chapter is a reference to a Chapter of the Part in which that reference is made.   **[1525]**

0.3. Application

These Rules apply—

(*a*) to receivers appointed, and

(*b*) to all other insolvency proceedings which are commenced,

on or after the date on which the Rules come into operation.   **[1526]**

PART 1

COMPANY VOLUNTARY ARRANGEMENTS

CHAPTER 1

PRELIMINARY

1.1. Scope of this Part; interpretation

(1) The Rules in this Part apply where, pursuant to Part 1 of the Act, it is intended to make and there is made a proposal to a company and to its creditors for a voluntary arrangement, that is to say, a composition in satisfaction of its debts or a scheme of arrangement of its affairs.

(2) In this Part—

(*a*) Chapter 2 applies where the proposal for a voluntary arrangement is made by the directors of the company, and neither is the company in liquidation nor is an administration order under Part II of the Act in force in relation to it;

(*b*) Chapter 3 applies where the company is in liquidation or an administration order is in force and the proposal is made by the liquidator or (as the case may be) the administrator, he in either case being the nominee for the purposes of the proposal;

(*c*) Chapter 4 applies in the same case as Chapter 3, but where the nominee is an insolvency practitioner other than the liquidator or administrator; and

(*d*) Chapters 5 and 6 apply in all of the three cases mentioned in sub-paragraphs (*a*) to (*c*) above.

(3) In Chapters 3, 4 and 5 the liquidator or the administrator is referred to as the "responsible insolvency practitioner".   **[1527]**

CHAPTER 2

PROPOSAL BY DIRECTORS

1.2. Preparation of proposal

The directors shall prepare for the intended nominee a proposal on which (with or without amendments to be made under Rule 1.3 above) to make his report to the court under section 2.   **[1528]**

1.3. Contents of proposal

(1) The directors' proposal shall provide a short explanation why, in their opinion, a voluntary arrangement under Part I of the Act is desirable, and give reasons why the company's creditors may be expected to concur with such an arrangement.

(2) The following matters shall be stated, or otherwise dealt with, in the directors' proposal—

(*a*) the following matters, so far as within the directors' immediate knowledge—

(i) the company's assets, with an estimate of their respective values;

(ii) the extent (if any) to which the assets are subject to any security in favour of any creditors;

(iii) the extent (if any) to which particular assets of the company are to be excluded from the voluntary arrangement;

(*b*) particulars of any property other than assets of the company itself, which is proposed to be included in the arrangement, the source of such property and the terms on which it is to be made available for inclusion;

(*c*) the nature and amount of the company's liabilities (so far as within the directors' immediate knowledge), the manner in which they are proposed to be met, modified, postponed or otherwise dealt with by means of the arrangement, and (in particular)—

(i) how it is proposed to deal with preferential creditors (defined in section 386) and creditors who are, or claim to be, secured;

(ii) how persons connected with the company (being creditors) are proposed to be treated under the arrangement; and

      (iii) whether there are, to the directors' knowledge, any circumstances giving rise to the possibility, in the event that the company should go into liquidation, of claims under—

            section 242 (gratuitous alienations),
            section 243 (unfair preferences),
            section 244 (extortionate credit transactions), or
            section 245 (floating charges invalid);

and, where any such circumstances are present, whether, and if so how, it is proposed under the voluntary arrangement to make provision for wholly or partly indemnifying the company in respect of such claims;

(*d*) whether any, and if so what, cautionary obligations (including guarantees) have been given of the company's debts by other persons, specifying which (if any) of the cautioners are persons connected with the company;

(*e*) the proposed duration of the voluntary arrangement;

(*f*) the proposed dates of distributions to creditors, with estimates of their amounts;

(*g*) the amount proposed to be paid to the nominee (as such) by way of remuneration and expenses;

(*h*) the manner in which it is proposed that the supervisor of the arrangement should be remunerated and his expenses defrayed;

(*i*) whether, for the purposes of the arrangement, any cautionary obligations (including guarantees) are to be offered by directors, or other persons, and whether (if so) any security is to be given or sought;

(*j*) the manner in which funds held for the purposes of the arrangement are to be banked, invested or otherwise dealt with pending distribution to creditors;

(*k*) the manner in which funds held for the purpose of payment to creditors, and not so paid on the termination of the arrangement, are to be dealt with;

(*l*) the manner in which the business of the company is being and is proposed to be conducted during the course of the arrangement;

(*m*) details of any further credit facilities which it is intended to arrange for the company and how the debts so arising are to be paid;

(*n*) the functions which are to be undertaken by the supervisor of the arrangement;

(*o*) the name, address and qualification of the person proposed as supervisor of the voluntary arrangement, and confirmation that he is (so far as the directors are aware) qualified to act as an insolvency practitioner in relation to the company.

(3) With the agreement in writing of the nominee, the directors' proposal may be amended at any time up to delivery of the former's report to the court under section 2(2).   **[1529]**

1.4. Notice to intended nominee

(1) The directors shall give to the intended nominee written notice of their proposal.

(2) The notice, accompanied by a copy of the proposal, shall be delivered either to the nominee himself, or to a person authorised to take delivery of documents on his behalf.

(3) If the intended nominee agrees to act, he shall cause a copy of the notice

to be endorsed to the effect that it has been received by him on a specified date; and the period of 28 days referred to in section 2(2) then runs from that date.

(4) The copy of the notice so endorsed shall be returned by the nominee forthwith to the directors at an address specified by them in the notice for that purpose.   **[1530]**

1.5. Statement of affairs

(1) The directors shall, within 7 days after their proposal is delivered to the nominee, or within such longer time as he may allow, deliver to him a statement of the company's affairs.

(2) The statement shall comprise the following particulars (supplementing or amplifying, so far as is necessary for clarifying the state of the company's affairs, those already given in the directors' proposal)—

- (*a*) a list of the company's assets, divided into such categories as are appropriate for easy identification, with estimated values assigned to each category;
- (*b*) in the case of any property on which a claim against the company is wholly or partly secured, particulars of the claim and its amount and of how and when the security was created;
- (*c*) the names and addresses of the company's preferential creditors (defined in section 386), with the amounts of their respective claims;
- (*d*) the names and addresses of the company's unsecured creditors, with the amounts of their respective claims;
- (*e*) particulars of any debts owed by or to the company to or by persons connected with it;
- (*f*) the names and addresses of the company's members and details of their respective shareholdings; and
- (*g*) such other particulars (if any) as the nominee may in writing require to be furnished for the purposes of making his report to the court on the directors' proposal.

(3) The statement of affairs shall be made up to a date not earlier than 2 weeks before the date of the notice given by the directors to the nominee under Rule 1.4. However the nominee may allow an extension of that period to the nearest practicable date (not earlier than 2 months before the date of the notice under Rule 1.4); and if he does so, he shall give his reasons in his report to the court on the directors' proposal.

(4) The statement shall be certified as correct, to the best of their knowledge and belief, by two or more directors of the company or by the company secretary and at least one director (other than the secretary himself).   **[1531]**

1.6. Additional disclosure for assistance of nominee

(1) If it appears to the nominee that he cannot properly prepare his report on the basis of information in the directors' proposal and statement of affairs, he may call on the directors to provide him with—

- (*a*) further and better particulars as to the circumstances in which, and the reasons why, the company is insolvent or (as the case may be) threatened with insolvency;
- (*b*) particulars of any previous proposals which have been made in respect of the company under Part I of the Act;
- (*c*) any further information with respect to the company's affairs which the nominee thinks necessary for the purposes of his report.

(2) The nominee may call on the directors to inform him, with respect to any person who is, or at any time in the 2 years preceding the notice under Rule 1.4 has been, a director or officer of the company, whether and in what circumstances (in those 2 years or previously) that person—

(a) has been concerned in the affairs of any other company (whether or not incorporated in Scotland) which has become insolvent, or

(b) has had his estate sequestrated, granted a trust deed for his creditors, been adjudged bankrupt or compounded or entered into an arrangement with his creditors.

(3) For the purpose of enabling the nominee to consider their proposal and prepare his report on it, the directors must give him access to the company's accounts and records. **[1532]**

1.7. Nominee's report on the proposal

(1) With his report to the court under section 2 the nominee shall lodge—

(a) a copy of the directors' proposal (with amendments, if any, authorised under Rule 1.3(3));

(b) a copy or summary of the company's statement of affairs.

(2) If the nominee makes known his opinion that meetings of the company and its creditors should be summoned under section 3, his report shall have annexed to it his comments on the proposal. If his opinion is otherwise, he shall give his reasons for that opinion.

(3) The nominee shall send a copy of his report and of his comments (if any) to the company. Any director, member or creditor of the company is entitled, at all reasonable times on any business day, to inspect the report and comments. **[1533]**

1.8. Replacement of nominee

Where any person intends to apply to the court under section 2(4) for the nominee to be replaced he shall give to the nominee at least 7 days' notice of his application. **[1534]**

1.9. Summoning of meetings under section 3

(1) If in his report the nominee states that in his opinion meetings of the company and its creditors should be summoned to consider the directors' proposal, the date on which the meetings are to be held shall be not less than 14, nor more than 28 days from the date on which he lodged his report in court under section 2.

(2) The notice summoning the meeting shall specify the court in which the nominee's report under section 2 has been lodged and with each notice there shall be sent—

(a) a copy of the directors' proposal;

(b) a copy of the statement of affairs or, if the nominee thinks fit, a summary of it (the summary to include a list of creditors and the amount of their debts); and

(c) the nominee's comments on the proposal.　　　**[1535]**

CHAPTER 3

PROPOSAL BY ADMINISTRATOR OR LIQUIDATOR WHERE HE IS THE NOMINEE

1.10. Preparation of proposal

The responsible insolvency practitioner's proposal shall specify—

(a) all such matters as under Rule 1.3 in Chapter 2 the directors of the company would be required to include in a proposal by them, and

(b) such other matters (if any) as the insolvency practitioner considers appropriate for ensuring that members and creditors of the company are enabled to reach an informed decision on the proposal.　**[1536]**

1.11. Summoning of meetings under section 3

(1) The responsible insolvency practitioner shall give at least 14 days' notice of the meetings of the company and of its creditors under section 3(2).

(2) With each notice summoning the meeting, there shall be sent—

(a) a copy of the responsible insolvency practitioner's proposal; and

(b) a copy of the company's statement of affairs or, if he thinks fit, a summary of it (the summary to include a list of the creditors and the amount of their debts).　**[1537]**

CHAPTER 4

PROPOSAL BY ADMINISTRATOR OR LIQUIDATOR WHERE ANOTHER INSOLVENCY PRACTITIONER IS THE NOMINEE

1.12. Preparation of proposal and notice to nominee

(1) The responsible insolvency practitioner shall give notice to the intended nominee, and prepare his proposal for a voluntary arrangement, in the same manner as is required of the directors in the case of a proposal by them, under Chapter 2.

(2) Rule 1.2 applies to the responsible insolvency practitioner as it applies to the directors; and Rule 1.4 applies as regards the action to be taken by the nominee.

(3) The content of the proposal shall be as required by Rule 1.3, reading references to the directors as referring to the responsible insolvency practitioner.

(4) Rule 1.6 applies, in respect of the information to be provided to the nominee, reading references to the directors as referring to the responsible insolvency practitioner.

(5) With the proposal the responsible insolvency practitioner shall provide a copy of the company's statement of affairs.

(6) Rules 1.7 to 1.9 apply as regards a proposal under this Chapter as they apply to a proposal under Chapter 2.　　　**[1538]**

CHAPTER 5

MEETINGS

1.13. General

The provisions of Chapter 1 of Part 7 (Meetings) shall apply with regard to the meetings of the company and of the creditors which are summoned under section 3, subject to Rules 1.9. 1.11 and 1.12(6) and the provisions in this Chapter.   **[1539]**

1.14. Summoning of meetings

(1) In fixing the date, time and place for the creditors' meeting and the company meeting, the person summoning the meetings ("the convenor") shall have regard primarily to the convenience of the creditors.

(2) The meetings shall be held on the same day and in the same place, but the creditors' meeting shall be fixed for a time in advance of the company meeting.   **[1540]**

1.15. Attendance by company officers

(1) At least 14 days' notice to attend the meetings shall be given by the convenor to—

    (*a*) all directors of the company, and

    (*b*) any persons in whose case the convenor thinks that their presence is required as being officers of the company or as having been directros or officers of it at any time in the 2 years immediately preceding the date of the notice.

(2) The chairman may, if he thinks fit, exclude any present or former director or officer from attendance at a meeting, either completely or for any part of it; and this applies whether or not a notice under this Rule has been sent to the person excluded.   **[1541]**

1.16. Adjournments

(1) On the day on which the meetings are held, they may from time to time be adjourned; and, if the chairman thinks fit for the purpose of obtaining the simultaneous agreement of the meetings to the proposal (with the same modifications, if any), the meetings may be held together.

(2) If on that day the requisite majority for the approval of the voluntary arrangement (with the same modifications, if any) has not been obtained from both creditors and members of the company, the chairman may, and shall, if it is so resolved, adjourn the meetings for not more than 14 days.

(3) If there are subsequently further adjournments, the final adjournment shall not be to a day later than 14 days after the date on which the meetings were originally held.

(4) There shall be no adjournment of either meeting unless the other is also adjourned to the same business day.

(5) In the case of a proposal by the directors, if the meetings are adjourned under paragraph (2), notice of the fact shall be given by the nominee forthwith to the court.

(6) If following any final adjournment of the meetings the proposal (with the same modifications, if any) is not agreed by both meetings, it is deemed rejected.   **[1542]**

1.17. Report of meetings

(1) A report of the meetings shall be prepared by the person who was chairman of them.

(2) The report shall—

> (a) state whether the proposal for a voluntary arrangement was approved or rejected and, if approved, with what (if any) modifications;
>
> (b) set out the resolutions which were taken at each meeting, and the decision on each one;
>
> (c) list the creditors and members of the company (with their respective values) who were present or represented at the meeting, and how they voted on each resolution; and
>
> (d) include such further information (if any) as the chairman thinks it appropriate to make known to the court.

(3) A copy of the chairman's report shall, within 4 days of the meetings being held, be lodged in court.

(4) In respect of each of the meetings the persons to whom notice of the result of the meetings is to be sent under section 4(6) are all those who were sent notice of the meeting. The notice shall be sent immediately after a copy of the chairman's report is lodged in court under paragraph (3).

(5) If the voluntary arrangement has been approved by the meetings (whether or not in the form proposed) the chairman shall forthwith send a copy of the report to the registrar of companies.   **[1543]**

CHAPTER 6
IMPLEMENTATION OF THE VOLUNTARY ARRANGEMENT

1.18. Resolutions to follow approval

(1) If the voluntary arrangement is approved (with or without modifications) by the two meetings, a resolution may be taken by the creditors, where two or more insolvency practitioners are appointed to act as supervisor, on the question whether acts to be done in connection with the arrangement may be done by one of them or are to be done by both or all.

(2) A resolution under paragraph (1) may be passed in anticipation of the approval of the voluntary arrangement by the company meeting if such meeting has not at that time been concluded.

(3) If at either meeting a resolution is moved for the appointment of some person other than the nominee to be supervisor of the arrangement, there must be produced to the chairman, at or before the meeting—

> (a) that person's written consent to act (unless the person is present and then and there signifies his consent), and
>
> (b) his written confirmation that he is qualified to act as an insolvency practitioner in relation to the company.   **[1544]**

1.19. Hand-over of property, etc to supervisor

(1) After the approval of the voluntary arrangement, the directors or, where—

    (*a*) the company is in liquidation or is subject to an administration order, and

    (*b*) a person other than the responsible insolvency practitioner is appointed as supervisor of the voluntary arrangement,

the responsible insolvency practitioner, shall forthwith do all that is required for putting the supervisor into possession of the assets included in the arrangement.

(2) Where paragraph (1)(*a*) and (*b*) applies, the supervisor shall, on taking possession of the assets, discharge any balance due to the responsible insolvency practitioner by way of remuneration or on account of—

    (*a*) fees, costs, charges and expenses properly incurred and payable under the Act or the Rules, and

    (*b*) any advances made in respect of the company, together with interest on such advances at the official rate (within the meaning of Rule 4.66(2)(*b*)) ruling at the date on which the company went into liquidation or (as the case may be) became subject to the administration order.

(3) Alternatively, the supervisor shall, before taking possession, give the responsible insolvency practitioner a written undertaking to discharge any such balance out of the first realisation of assets.

(4) The sums due to the responsible insolvency practitioner as above shall be paid out of the assets included in the arrangement in priority to all other sums payable out of those assets, subject only to the deduction from realisations by the supervisor of the proper costs and expenses of such realisations.

(5) The supervisor shall from time to time out of the realisation of assets discharge all cautionary obligations (including guarantees) properly given by the responsible insolvency practitioner for the benefit of the company and shall pay all the responsible insolvency practitioner's expenses.   **[1545]**

1.20. Revocation or suspension of the arrangement

(1) This Rule applies where the court makes an order of revocation or suspension under section 6.

(2) The person who applied for the order shall serve copies of it—

    (*a*) on the supervisor of the voluntary arrangement, and

    (*b*) on the directors of the company or the administrator or liquidator (according to who made the proposal for the arrangement).

Service on the directors may be effected by service of a single copy of the order on the company at its registered office.

(3) If the order includes a direction given by the court, under section 6(4)(*b*), for any further meetings to be summoned, notice shall also be given by the person who applied for the order to whoever is, in accordance with the direction, required to summon the meetings.

(4) The directors or (as the case may be) the administrator or liquidator shall—

(a) forthwith after receiving a copy of the court's order, give notice of it to all persons who were sent notice of the creditors' and the company meetings or who, not having been sent that notice, appear to be affected by the order; and

(b) within 7 days of their receiving a copy of the order (or within such longer period as the court may allow), give notice to the court whether it is intended to make a revised proposal to the company and its creditors, or to invite re-consideration of the original proposal.

(5) The person on whose application the order of revocation or suspension was made shall, within 7 days after the making of the order, deliver a copy of the order to the registrar of companies.   **[1546]**

NOTES

Para (5): See Sch 5, form 1.2 (Scot).

1.21. Supervisor's accounts and reports

(1) Where the voluntary arrangement authorises or requires the supervisor—

(a) to carry on the business of the company, or to trade on its behalf or in its name, or

(b) to realise assets of the company, or

(c) otherwise to administer or dispose of any of its funds,

he shall keep accounts and records of his acts and dealings in and in connection with the arrangement, including in particular records of all receipts and payments of money.

(2) The supervisor shall, not less often than once in every 12 months beginning with the date of his appointment, prepare an abstract of such receipts and payments and send copies of it, accompanied by his comments on the progress and efficacy of the arrangement, to—

(a) the court,

(b) the registrar of companies,

(c) the company,

(d) all those of the company's creditors who are bound by the arrangement,

(e) subject to paragraph (5) below, the members of the company who are so bound, and

(f) where the company is not in liquidation, the company's auditors for the time being.

If in any period of 12 months he has made no payments and had no receipts, he shall at the end of that period send a statement to that effect to all those specified in sub-paragraphs (a) to (f) above.

(3) An abstract provided under paragraph (2) shall relate to a period beginning with the date of the supervisor's appointment or (as the case may be) the day following the end of the last period for which an abstract was prepared under this Rule; and copies of the abstract shall be sent out, as required by paragraph (2), within the two months following the end of the period to which the abstract relates.

(4) If the supervisor is not authorised as mentioned in paragraph (1), he shall, not less often than once in every 12 months beginning with the date of his appointment, send to all those specified in paragraphs 2(a) to (f) a report on the progress and efficacy of the voluntary arrangement.

(5) The court may, on application by the supervisor,—

    (*a*) dispense with the sending under this Rule of abstracts or reports to members of the company, either altogether or on the basis that the availability of the abstract or report to members on request is to be advertised by the supervisor in a specified manner;

    (*b*) vary the dates on which the obligation to send abstracts or reports arises. **[1547]**

1.22. Fees, costs, charges and expenses

The fees, costs, charges and expenses that may be incurred for any of the purposes of a voluntary arrangement are—

    (*a*) any disbursements made by the nominee prior to the approval of the arrangement, and any remuneration for his services as is agreed between himself and the company (or, as the case may be, the administrator or liquidator);

    (*b*) any fees, costs, charges or expenses which—

        (i) are sanctioned by the terms of the arrangement, or

        (ii) would be payable, or correspond to those which would be payable, in an administration or winding up. **[1548]**

1.23. Completion of the arrangement

(1) Not more than 28 days after the final completion of the voluntary arrangement, the supervisor shall send to all creditors and members of the company who are bound by it a notice that the voluntary arrangement has been fully implemented.

(2) With the notice there shall be sent to each creditor and member a copy of a report by the supervisor, summarising all receipts and payments made by him in pursuance of the arrangement, and explaining any difference in the actual implementation of it as compared with the proposal approved by the creditors' and company meetings.

(3) The supervisor shall, within the 28 days mentioned above, send to the registrar of companies and to the court a copy of the notice to creditors and members under paragraph (1), together with a copy of the report under paragraph (2).

(4) The court may, on application by the supervisor, extend the period of 28 days under paragraphs (1) or (3). **[1549]**

NOTES
    Para (3): See Sch 5, form 1.4 (Scot).

1.24. False representations, etc

(1) A person being a past or present officer of a company commits an offence if he make any false representation or commits any other fraud for the purpose of obtaining the approval of the company's members or creditors to a proposal for a voluntary arrangement under Part I of the Act.

(2) For this purpose "officer" includes a shadow director.

(3) A person guilty of an offence under this Rule is liable to imprisonment or a fine, or both. **[1550]**

PART 2

ADMINISTRATION PROCEDURE

CHAPTER 1

APPLICATION FOR, AND MAKING OF, THE ORDER

2.1. Independent report on company's affairs

(1) Where it is proposed to apply to the court by way of petition for an administration order to be made under section 8 in relation to a company, there may be prepared in support of the petition a report by an independent person to the effect that the appointment of an administrator for the company is expedient.

(2) The report may be by the person proposed as administrator, or by any other person having adequate knowledge of the company's affairs, not being a director, secretary, manager, member or employee of the company.

(3) The report shall specify which of the purposes specified in section 8(3) may, in the opinion of the person preparing it, be achieved for the company by the making of an administration order in relation to it.   **[1551]**

2.2. Notice of petition

(1) Under section 9(2)(a), notice of the petition shall forthwith be given by the petitioner to the person who has appointed, or is or may be entitled to appoint, an administrative receiver, and to the following persons—

    (a) an administrative receiver, if appointed;

    (b) if a petition for the winding up of the company has been presented but no order for winding up has yet been made, the petitioner under that petition;

    (c) a provisional liquidator, if appointed;

    (d) the person proposed in the petition to be the administrator;

    (e) the registrar of companies;

    (f) the Keeper of the Register of Inhibitions and Adjudications for recording in that register; and

    (g) the company, if the petition for the making of an administration order is presented by the directors or by a creditor or creditors of the company.

(2) Notice of the petition shall also be given to the persons upon whom the court orders that the petition be served.   **[1552]**

2.3. Notice and advertisement of administration order

(1) If the court makes an administration order, it shall forthwith give notice of the order to the person appointed as administrator.

(2) Under section 21(1)(a) the administrator shall forthwith after the order is made, advertise the making of the order once in the Edinburgh Gazette and once in a newspaper circulating in the area where the company has its principal place of business or in such newspaper as he thinks most appropriate for ensuring that the order comes to the notice of the company's creditors.

(3) Under section 21(2), the administrator shall send a notice with a copy of the court's order certified by the clerk of court to the registrar of companies, and in addition shall send a copy of the order to the following persons—

(*a*) any person who has appointed an administrative receiver, or has power to do so;

(*b*) an administrative receiver, if appointed;

(*c*) a petitioner in a petition for the winding up of the company, if that petition is pending;

(*d*) any provisional liquidator of the company, if appointed; and

(*e*) the Keeper of the Register of Inhibitions and Adjudications for recording in that register.

(4) If the court dismisses the petition under section 9(4) or discharges the administration order under section 18(3) or 24(5), the petitioner or, as the case may be, the administrator shall—

(*a*) forthwith send a copy of the court's order dismissing the petition or effecting the discharge to the Keeper of the Register of Inhibitions and Adjudications for recording in that register; and

(*b*) within 14 days after the date of making of the order, send a notice with a copy, certified by the clerk of court, of the court's order dismissing the petition or effecting the discharge to the registrar of companies.

(5) Paragraph (4) is without prejudice to any order of the court as to the persons by and to whom, and how, notice of any order made by the court under section 9(4), 18 or 24 is to be given and to section 18(4) or 24(6) (notice by administrator of court's order discharging administration order).   **[1553]**

NOTES
  Para (3): See Sch 5, form 2.2 (Scot).
  Para (4): See Sch 5, forms 2.3 (Scot), 2.4 (Scot).

CHAPTER 2

STATEMENT OF AFFAIRS AND PROPOSALS TO CREDITORS

2.4. Notice requiring statement of affairs

(1) This Rule and Rules 2.5 and 2.6 apply where the administrator decides to require a statement as to the affairs of the company to be made out and submitted to him in accordance with section 22.

(2) The administrator shall send to each of the persons upon whom he decides to make such a requirement under section 22, a notice in the form required by Rule 7.30 and Schedule 5 requiring him to make out and submit a statement of affairs.

(3) Any person to whom a notice is sent under this Rule is referred to in this Chapter as "a deponent".   **[1554]**

NOTES
  Para (2): See Sch 5, form 2.5 (Scot).

2.5. Form of the statement of affairs

(1) The statement of affairs shall be in the form required by Rule 7.30 and Schedule 5.

(2) The administrator shall insert any statement of affairs submitted to him in the sederunt book.   **[1555]**

NOTES
    Para (1): See Sch 5, form 2.6 (Scot).

2.6. Expenses of statement of affairs

(1) A deponent who makes up and submits to the administrator a statement of affairs shall be allowed and be paid by the administrator out of his receipts, any expenses incurred by the deponent in so doing which the administrator considers to be reasonable.

(2) Any decision by the administrator under this Rule is subject to appeal to the court.

(3) Nothing in this Rule relieves a deponent from any obligation to make up and submit a statement of affairs, or to provide information to the administrator.   **[1556]**

2.7. Statement to be annexed to proposals

There shall be annexed to the administrator's proposals, when sent to the registrar of companies under section 23 and laid before the creditors' meeting to be summoned under that section, a statement by him showing—

   (*a*) details relating to his appointment as administrator, the purposes for which an administration order was applied for and made, and any subsequent variation of those purposes;
   (*b*) the names of the directors and secretary of the company;
   (*c*) an account of the circumstances giving rise to the application for an administration order;
   (*d*) if a statement of affairs has been submitted, a copy or summary of it with the administrator's comments, if any;
   (*e*) if no statement of affairs has been submitted, details of the financial position of the company at the latest practicable date (which must, unless the court otherwise orders, be a date not earlier than that of the administration order);
   (*f*) the manner in which the affairs of the company will be managed and its business financed, if the administrator's proposals are approved; and
   (*g*) such other information (if any) as the administrator thinks necessary to enable creditors to decide whether or not to vote for the adoption of the proposals.   **[1557]**

2.8. Notices of proposals to members

Any notice required to be published by the administrator—

   (*a*) under section 23(2)(*b*) (notice of address for members of the company to write for a copy of the administrator's statement of proposals), and
   (*b*) under section 25(3)(*b*) (notice of address for members of the company to write for a copy of the administrator's statement of proposed revisions to the proposals),

shall be inserted once in the Edinburgh Gazette and once in the newspaper in which the administrator's appointment was advertised.   **[1558]**

CHAPTER 3
MEETINGS AND NOTICES

2.9. General

The provisions of Chapter 1 of Part 7 (Meetings) shall apply with regard to meetings of the company's creditors or members which are summoned by the administrator, subject to the provisions in this Chapter.   **[1559]**

2.10. Meeting to consider administrator's proposals

(1) The administrator shall give at least 14 days' notice to attend the meeting of the creditors under section 23(1) to any directors or officers of the company (including persons who have been directors or officers in the past) whose presence at the meeting is, in the administrator's opinion, required.

(2) If at the meeting there is not the requisite majority for approval of the administrator's proposals (with modifications, if any), the chairman may, and shall if a resolution is passed to that effect, adjourn the meeting for not more than 14 days   **[1560]**

2.11. Retention of title creditors

For the purpose of entitlement to vote at a creditors' meeting in administration proceedings, a seller of goods to the company under a retention of title agreement shall deduct from his claim the value, as estimated by him, of any rights arising under that agreement in respect of goods in the possession of the company.

[1561]

2.12. Hire-purchase, conditional sale and hiring agreements

(1) Subject as follows, an owner of goods under a hire-purchase agreement or under an agreement for the hire of goods for more than 3 months, or a seller of goods under a conditional sale agreement, is entitled to vote in respect of the amount of the debt due and payable to him by the company as at the date of the administration order.

(2) In calculating the amount of any debt for this purpose, no account shall be taken of any amount attributable to the exercise of any right under the relevant agreement, so far as the right has become exercisable solely by virtue of the presentation of the petition for an administration order or any matter arising in consequence of that or of the making of the order.   **[1562]**

2.13. Report of meetings

Any report by the administrator of the proceedings of creditors' meetings held under section 23(1) or 25(2) shall have annexed to it details of the proposals which were considered by the meeting in question and of any modifications which were also considered.   **[1563]**

2.14. Notices to creditors

(1) Within 14 days after the conclusion of a meeting of creditors to consider the administrator's proposals or proposed revisions under section 23(1) or 25(2), the administrator shall send notice of the result of the meeting (including, where appropriate, details of the proposals as approved) to every creditor to whom notice of the meeting was sent and to any other creditor of whom the administrator has become aware since the notice was sent.

(2) Within 14 days after the end of every period of 6 months beginning with the date of approval of the administrator's proposals or proposed revisions, the administrator shall send to all creditors of the company a report on the progress of the administration.

(3) On vacating office, the administrator shall send to creditors a report on the administration up to that time. This does not apply where the administration is immediately followed by the company going into liquidation, nor where the administrator is removed from office by the court or ceases to be qualified to act as an insolvency practitioner.   **[1564]**

CHAPTER 4

THE CREDITORS' COMMITTEE

2.15. Application of provisions in Part 3 (Receivers)

(1) Chapter 3 of Part 3 (The creditors' committee) shall apply with regard to the creditors' committee in the administration as it applies to the creditors' committee in receivership, subject to the modifications specified below and to any other necessary modifications.

(2) For any reference in the said Chapter 3, or in any provision of Chapter 7 of Part 4 as applied by Rule 3.6, to the receiver, receivership or the creditors' committee in receivership, there shall be substituted a reference to the administrator, the administration and the creditors' committee in the administration.

(3) In Rule 3.4(1) and 3.7(1), for the reference to section 68 or 68(2), there shall be substituted a reference to section 26 or 26(2).

(4) For Rule 3.5 there shall be substituted the following rule:—

"3.5.   Functions of the Committee

The creditors' committee shall assist the administrator in discharging his functions and shall act in relation to him in such manner as may be agreed from time to time.".   **[1565]**

CHAPTER 5

THE ADMINISTRATOR

2.16. Remuneration

(1) The administrator's remuneration shall be determined from time to time by the creditors' committee or, if there is no creditors' committee, by the court, and shall be paid out of the assets as an expense of the administration.

(2) The basis for determining the amount of the remuneration payable to the administrator may be a commission calculated by reference to the value of the company's property with which he has to deal, but there shall in any event be taken into account—

  (a) the work which, having regard to that value, was reasonably undertaken by him; and
  (b) the extent of his responsibilities in administering the company's assets.

(3) Rules 4.32 to 4.34 of Chapter 6 of Part 4 shall apply to an administration as they apply to a liquidation but as if for any reference to the liquidator or the

liquidation committee there was substituted a reference to the administrator or the creditors committee. **[1566]**

2.17. Abstract of receipts and payments

(1) The administrator shall—

    (*a*) within 2 months after the end of 6 months from the date of his appointment, and of every subsequent period of 6 months, and

    (*b*) within 2 months after he ceases to act as administrator,

send to the court, and to the registrar of companies, and to each member of the creditors' committee, the requisite accounts of the receipts and payments of the company.

(2) The court may, on the administrator's application, extend the period of 2 months mentioned in paragraph (1).

(3) The amounts are to be in the form of an abstract showing—

    (*a*) receipts and payments during the relevant period of 6 months, or

    (*b*) where the administrator has ceased to act, receipts and payments during the period from the end of the last 6 month period to the time when he so ceased (alternatively, if there has been no previous abstract, receipts and payments in the period since his appointment as administrator).

(4) If the administrator makes default in complying with this Rule, he is liable to a fine and, for continued contravention, to a daily default fine. **[1567]**

NOTES
    Paras (1), (3): See Sch 5, form 2.9 (Scot).

2.18. Resignation from office

(1) The administrator may give notice of his resignation on grounds of ill health or because—

    (*a*) he intends ceasing to be in practice as an insolvency practitioner, or

    (*b*) there is some conflict of interest or change of personal circumstances, which precludes or makes impracticable the further discharge by him of the duties of administrator.

(2) The administrator may, with the leave of the court, give notice of his resignation on grounds other than those specified in paragraph (1).

(3) The administrator must give to the persons specified below at least 7 days' notice of his intention to resign, or to apply for the court's leave to do so—

    (*a*) if there is a continuing administrator of the company, to him;

    (*b*) if there is no such administrator, to the creditors' committee; and

    (*c*) if there is no such administrator and no creditors' committee, to the company and its creditors. **[1568]**

NOTES
    Para (1): See Sch 5, form 2.13 (Scot).

2.19. Administrator deceased

(1) Subject to the following paragraph, where the administrator has died, it is the duty of his executors or, where the deceased administrator was a partner in a firm, of a partner of that firm to give notice of that fact to the court, specifying

the date of the death. This does not apply if notice has been given under the following paragraph.

(2) Notice of the death may also be given by any person producing to the court a copy of the death certificate. **[1569]**

2.20. Order filling vacancy

Where the court makes an order filling a vacancy in the office of administrator, the same provisions apply in respect of giving notice of, and advertising, the appointment as in the case of the original appointment of an administrator.
[1570]

CHAPTER 6

VAT BAD DEBT RELIEF

2.21. Application of provisions in Part 3 (Receivers)

Chapter 5 of Part 3 (VAT bad debt relief) shall apply to an administrator as it applies to an administrative receiver, subject to the modification that, for any reference to the administrative receiver, there shall be substituted a reference to the administrator. **[1571]**

PART 3

RECEIVERS

CHAPTER 1

APPOINTMENT

3.1. Acceptance of appointment

(1) Where a person has been appointed a receiver by the holder of a floating charge under section 53, his acceptance (which need not be in writing) of that appointment for the purposes of paragraph (*a*) of section 53(6) shall be intimated by him to the holder of the floating charge or his agent within the period specified in that paragraph and he shall, as soon as possible after his acceptance, endorse a written docquet to that effect on the instrument of appointment.

(2) The written docquet evidencing receipt of the instrument of appointment, which is required by section 53(6)(*b*), shall also be endorsed on the instrument of appointment,

(3) The receiver shall, as soon as possible after his acceptance of the appointment, deliver a copy of the endorsed instrument of appointment to the holder of the floating charge or his agent.

(4) This Rule shall apply in the case of the appointment of joint receivers as it applies to the appointment of a receiver, except that, where the docquet of acceptance required by paragraph (1) is endorsed by each of the joint receivers, or two or more of them, on the same instrument of appointment, it is the joint receiver who last endorses his docquet of acceptance who is required to send a copy of the instrument of appointment to the holder of the floating charge or his agent under paragraph (3). **[1572]**

CHAPTER 2
STATEMENT OF AFFAIRS

3.2. Notice requiring statement of affairs

(1) Where the receiver decides to require from any person or persons a statement as to the affairs of the company to be made out and submitted to him in accordance with section 66, he shall send to each of those persons a notice in the form required by Rule 7.30 and Schedule 5 requiring him to make out and submit a statement of affairs in the form prescribed by the Receivers (Scotland) Regulations 1986.

(2) Any person to whom a notice is sent under this Rule is referred to in this Chapter as "a deponent".

(3) The receiver shall insert any statement of affairs submitted to him in the sederunt book. **[1573]**

NOTES
    Para (1): See Sch 5, para 3.1 (Scot).

3.3. Expenses of statement of affairs

(1) A deponent who makes up and submits to the receiver a statement of affairs shall be allowed and be paid by the receiver, as an expense of the receivership, any expenses incurred by the deponent in so doing which the receiver considers to be reasonable.

(2) Any decision by the receiver under this Rule is subject to appeal to the court.

(3) Nothing in this Rule relieves a deponent from any obligation to make up and submit a statement of affairs, or to provide information to the receiver. **[1574]**

CHAPTER 3
THE CREDITORS' COMMITTEE

3.4. Constitution of committee

(1) Where it is resolved by the creditors' meeting to establish a creditors' committee under section 68, the committee shall consist of at least 3 and not more than 5 creditors of the company elected at the meeting.

(2) Any creditor of the company who has lodged a claim is eligible to be a member of the committee, so long as his claim has not been rejected for the purpose of his entitlement to vote.

(3) A body corporate or a partnership may be a member of the committee, but it cannot act as such otherwise than by a representative appointed under Rule 7.20, as applied by Rule 3.6. **[1575]**

3.5. Functions of the committee

In addition to the functions conferred on it by the Act, the creditors' committee shall represent to the receiver the views of the unsecured creditors and shall act in relation to him in such manner as may be agreed from time to time. **[1576]**

3.6. Application of provisions relating to liquidation committee

(1) Chapter 7 of Part 4 (The liquidation committee) shall apply with regard to the creditors' committee in the receivership and its members as it applies to the liquidation committee and the creditor members thereof, subject to the modifications specified below and to any other necessary modifications.

(2) For any reference in the said Chapter 7 to—

    (*a*) the liquidator or the liquidation committee, there shall be substituted a reference to the receiver or to the creditors' committee;

    (*b*) to the creditor member, there shall be substituted a reference to a creditor.

and any reference to a contributory member shall be disregarded.

(3) In Rule 4.42(3) and 4.52(2), for the reference to Rule 4.41(1), there shall be substituted a reference to Rule 3.4(1).

(4) In Rule 4.57,

    (*a*) for the reference to an expense of the liquidation, there shall be substituted a reference to an expense of the receivership;

    (*b*) at the end of that Rule there shall be inserted the following:—

    "This does not apply to any meeting of the committee held within 3 months of a previous meeting, unless the meeting in question is summoned at the instance of the receiver.".

(5) The following Rules shall not apply, namely—

Rules 4.40, 4.41, 4.43 to 4.44, 4.53, 4.56, 4.58 and 4.59.   **[1577]**

3.7. Information from receiver

(1) Where the committee resolves to require the attendance of the receiver under section 68(2), the notice to him shall be in writing signed by the majority of the members of the committee for the time being or their representatives.

(2) The meeting at which the receiver's attendance is required shall be fixed by the committee for a business day, and shall be held at such time and place as he determines.

(3) Where the receiver so attends, the members of the committee may elect any one of their number to be chairman of the meeting, in place of the receiver or any nominee of his.   **[1578]**

3.8. Members' dealings with the company

(1) Membership of the committee does not prevent a person from dealing with the company while the receiver is acting, provided that any transactions in the course of such dealings are entered into on normal commercial terms.

(2) The court may, on the application of any person interested, set aside a transaction which appears to it to be contrary to the requirements of this Rule, and may give such consequential directions as it thinks fit for compensating the company for any loss which it may have incurred in consequence of the transaction.   **[1579]**

CHAPTER 4

MISCELLANEOUS

3.9. Abstract of receipts and payments

(1) The receiver shall—

(*a*) within 2 months after the end of 12 months from the date of his appointment, and of every subsequent period of 12 months, and

(*b*) within 2 months after he ceases to act as receiver,

send the requisite accounts of his receipts and payments as receiver to—

(i) the registrar of companies,

(ii) the holder of the floating charge by virtue of which he was appointed,

(iii) the members of the creditors' committee (if any),

(iv) the company or, if it is in liquidation, the liquidator.

(2) The court may, on the receiver's application, extend the period of 2 months referred to in paragraph (1).

(3) The accounts are to be in the form of an abstract showing—

(*a*) receipts and payments during the relevant period of 12 months, or

(*b*) where the receiver has ceased to act, receipts and payments during the period from the end of the last 12-month period to the time when he so ceased (alternatively, if there has been no previous abstract, receipts and payments in the period since his appointment as receiver).

(4) This Rule is without prejudice to the receiver's duty to render proper accounts required otherwise than as above.

(5) If the receiver makes default in complying with this Rule, he is liable to a fine and, for continued contravention, to a daily default fine. **[1580]**

NOTES
Para (1): See Sch 5, form 3.2 (Scot).

3.10. Receiver deceased

If the receiver dies, the holder of the floating charge by virtue of which he was appointed shall, forthwith on his becoming aware of the death, give notice of it to—

(*a*) the registrar of companies,

(*b*) the members of the creditors' committee (if any),

(*c*) the company or, if it is in liquidation, the liquidator,

(*d*) the holder of any other floating charge and any receiver appointed by him. **[1581]**

3.11. Vacation of office

The receiver, on vacating office on completion of the receivership or in consequence of his ceasing to be qualified as an insolvency practitioner, shall, in addition to giving notice to the registrar of companies under section 62(5), give notice of his vacating office, within 14 days thereof, to—

(*a*) the holder of the floating charge by virtue of which he was appointed,

(*b*) the members of the creditors' committee (if any),

(*c*) the company of, if it is in liquidation, the liquidator,

(*d*) the holder of any other floating charge and any receiver appointed by him. **[1582]**

CHAPTER 5

VAT BAD DEBT RELIEF

3.12. Issue of certificate of insolvency

(1) In accordance with this Rule, it is the duty of the administrative receiver to issue a certificate in the terms of paragraph (*b*) of section 22(3) of the Value Added Tax Act 1983 (which specifies the circumstances in which a company is deemed insolvent for the purposes of that section) forthwith upon his forming the opinion described in that paragraph.

(2) There shall in the certificate be specified—

    (*a*) the name of the company and its registered number;

    (*b*) the name of the administrative receiver and the date of his appointment; and

    (*c*) the date on which the certificate is issued.

(3) The certificate shall be entitled "CERTIFICATE OF INSOLVENCY FOR THE PURPOSES OF SECTION 22(3)(*b*) OF THE VALUE ADDED TAX ACT 1983".   **[1583]**

3.13. Notice to creditors

(1) Notice of the issue of the certificate shall be given by the administrative receiver within 3 months of his appointment or within 2 months of issuing the certificate, whichever is the later, to all of the company's unsecured creditors of whose address he is then aware and who have, to his knowledge, made supplies to the company, with a charge to value added tax, at any time before his appointment.

(2) Thereafter, he shall give the notice to any such creditor of whose address and supplies to the company he becomes aware.

(3) He is not under obligation to provide any creditor with a copy of the certificate.   **[1584]**

3.14. Preservation of certificate with company's records

(1) The certificate shall be retained with the company's accounting records, and section 222 of the Companies Act (where and for how long records are to be kept) shall apply to the certificate as it applies to those records.

(2) It is the duty of the administrative receiver, on vacating office, to bring this Rule to the attention of the directors or (as the case may be) any successor of his as receiver.   **[1585]**

PART 4

WINDING UP BY THE COURT

CHAPTER 1

PROVISIONAL LIQUIDATOR

4.1. Appointment of provisional liquidator

An application to the court for the appointment of a provisional liquidator under section 135 may be made by the petitioner in the winding up, or by a creditor of the company, or by a contributory, or by the company itself, or by any person who under any enactment would be entitled to present a petition for the winding up of the company **[1586]**

4.2. Order of appointment

(1) The provisional liquidator shall forthwith after the order appointing him is made, give notice of his appointment to—

    (a) the registrar of companies;
    (b) the company; and
    (c) any receiver of the whole or any part of the property of the company.

(2) The provisional liquidator shall advertise his appointment in accordance with any directions of the court. **[1587]**

4.3. Caution

The cost of providing the caution required by the provisional liquidator under the Act shall unless the court otherwise directs be—

    (a) if a winding up order is not made, reimbursed to him out of the property of the company, and the court may make an order against the company accordingly, and
    (b) if a winding up order is made, reimbursed to him as an expense of the liquidation. **[1588]**

4.4. Failure to find or to maintain caution

(1) If the provisional liquidator fails to find or to maintain his caution, the court may remove him and make such order as it thinks fit as to expenses.

(2) If an order is made under this Rule removing the provisional liquidator, or discharging the order appointing him, the court shall give directions as to whether any, and if so what, steps should be taken for the appointment of another person in his place. **[1589]**

4.5. Remuneration

(1) The remuneration of the provisional liquidator shall be fixed by the court from time to time.

(2) Section 53(4) of the Bankruptcy Act shall apply to determine the basis for fixing the amount of the remuneration of the provisional liquidator, subject to the modifications specified in Rule 4.16(2) and to any other necessary modifications.

(3) The provisional liquidator's remuneration shall, unless the court otherwise directs, be paid to him, and the amount of any expenses incurred by him reimbursed—

    (a) if a winding up order is not made, out of the property of the company (and the court may make an order against the company accordingly), and (*b*) if a winding up order is made, as an expense of the liquidation. **[1590]**

4.6. Termination of appointment

(1) The appointment of the provisional liquidator may be terminated by the court on his application, or on that of any of the persons entitled to make application for his appointment under Rule 4.1.

(2) If the provisional liquidator's appointment terminates, in consequence of the dismissal of the winding up petition or otherwise, the court may give such directions as it thinks fit with respect to—

(*a*) the accounts of his administration;
(*b*) the expenses properly incurred by the provisional liquidator; or
(*c*) any other matters which it thinks appropriate

and, without prejudice to the power of the court to make an order against any other person, may direct that any expenses properly incurred by the provisional liquidator during the period of his appointment, including any remuneration to which he is entitled, be paid out of the property of the company, and authorise him to retain out of that property such sums as are required for meeting those expenses.   **[1591]**

CHAPTER 2

STATEMENT OF AFFAIRS

4.7. Notice requiring statement of affairs

(1) This Chapter applies where the liquidator or, in a case where a provisional liquidator is appointed, the provisional liquidator decides to require a statement as to the affairs of the company to be made out and submitted to him in accordance with section 131.

(2) In this Chapter the expression "liquidator" includes "provisional liquidator".

(3) The liquidator shall send to each of the persons upon whom he decides to make such a requirement under section 131, a notice in the form required by Rule 7.30 and Schedule 5 requiring him to make out and submit a statement of affairs.

(4) Any person to whom a notice is sent under this Rule is referred to in this Chapter as "a deponent".
          [1592]

4.8. Form of the statement of affairs

(1) The statement of affairs shall be in the form required by Rule 7.30 and Schedule 5.

(2) The liquidator shall insert any statement of affairs submitted to him in the sederunt book.   **[1593]**

4.9. Expenses of statement of affairs

(1) At the request of any deponent, made on the grounds that he cannot himself prepare a proper statement of affairs, the liquidator may authorise an allowance towards expenses to be incurred by the deponent in employing some person or persons to be approved by the liquidator to assist the deponent in preparing it.

(2) Any such request by the deponent shall be accompanied by an estimate of the expenses involved.

(3) An authorisation given by the liquidator under this Rule shall be subject to such conditions (if any) as he thinks fit to impose with respect to the manner in which any person may obtain access to relevant books and papers.

(4) Nothing in this Rule relieves a deponent from any obligation to make up and submit a statement of affairs, or to provide information to the liquidator.

(5) Any allowance by the liquidator under this Rule shall be an expense of the liquidation.

(6) The liquidator shall intimate to the deponent whether he grants or refuses his request for an allowance under this Rule and where such request is refused the deponent affected by the refusal may appeal to the court not later than 14 days from the date intimation of such refusal is made to him.   **[1594]**

CHAPTER 3
INFORMATION

4.10. Information to creditors and contributories

(1) The liquidator shall report to the creditors, and, except where he considers it would be inappropriate to do so, the contributories with respect to the proceedings in the winding up within six weeks after the end of each accounting period or he may submit such a report to a meeting of creditors or of contributories held within such period.

(2) Any reference in this Rule to creditors is to persons known to the liquidator to be creditors of the company.

(3) Where a statement of affairs has been submitted to him, the liquidator may send out to creditors and contributories with the next convenient report to be made under paragraph (1) a summary of the statement and such observations (if any) as he thinks fit to make with respect to it.   **[1595]**

4.11. Information to registrar of companies

The statement which section 192 requires the liquidator to send to the registrar of companies if the winding up is not concluded within one year from its commencement, shall be sent not more than 30 days after the expiration of that year and thereafter at 6 monthly intervals until the winding up is concluded in the form required by Rule 7.30 and Schedule 5 and shall contain the particulars specified therein.   **[1596]**

NOTES
See Sch 5, forms 4.5 (Scot), 4.6 (Scot).

CHAPTER 4
MEETING OF CREDITORS AND CONTRIBUTORIES

4.12. First meetings in the liquidation

(1) This Rule applies where under section 138(3) the interim liquidator summons meetings of the creditors and the contributories of the company for the purpose of choosing a person to be liquidator of the company in place of the interim liquidator.

(2) Meetings summoned by the interim liquidator under that section are known respectively as "the first meeting of creditors" and "the first meeting of contributories", and jointly as "the first meetings in the liquidation".

(3) Subject as follows, no resolutions shall be taken at the first meeting of creditors other than the following:—

    (*a*) a resolution to appoint one or more named insolvency practitioners to be liquidator or, as the case may be, joint liquidators and, in the case of joint liquidators, whether any act required or authorised to be done by the liquidator is to be done by both or all of them, or by any one or more;

    (*b*) a resolution to establish a liquidation committee under section 142(1);

    (*c*) unless a liquidation committee is to be established, a resolution specifying the terms on which the liquidator is to be remunerated, or to defer consideration of that matter;

    (*d*) a resolution to adjourn the meeting for not more than 3 weeks;

    (*e*) any other resolution which the chairman considers it right to allow for special reason.

(4) This rule also applies with respect to the first meeting of contributories except that that meeting shall not pass any resolution to the effect of paragraph (3)(*c*).   **[1597]**

4.13. Other meetings

(1) The liquidator shall summon a meeting of the creditors in each year during which the liquidation is in force.

(2) Subject to the above provision, the liquidator may summon a meeting of the creditors or of the contributories at any time for the purpose of ascertaining their wishes in all matters relating to the liquidation.   **[1598]**

4.14. Attendance at meetings of company's personnel

(1) This Rule applies to meetings of creditors and to meetings of contributories.

(2) Whenever a meeting is summoned, the liquidator may, if he thinks fit, give at least 21 days' notice to any one or more of the company's personnel that he is or they are required to be present at the meeting or be in attendance.

(3) In this Rule, "the company's personnel" means the persons referred to in paragraphs (*a*) to (*d*) of section 253(3) (present and past officers, employees, etc).

(4) The liquidator may authorise payment to any person whose attendance is requested at a meeting under this Rule of his reasonable expenses incurred in travelling to the meeting and any payment so authorised shall be an expense of the liquidation.

(5) In the case of any meeting, any of the company's personnel may, if he has given reasonable notice of his wish to be present, be admitted to take part; but this is at the discretion of the chairman of the meeting, whose decision as to what (if any) intervention may be made by any of them is final.

(6) If it is desired to put questions to any of the company's personnel who are not present, the meeting may be adjourned with a view to obtaining his attendance.

(7) Where one of the company's personnel is present at a meeting, only such questions may be put to him as the chairman may in his discretion allow. **[1599]**

CHAPTER 5

CLAIMS IN LIQUIDATION

4.15. Submission of claims

(1) A creditor, in order to obtain an adjudication as to his entitlement—

    (*a*) to vote at any meeting of the creditors in the liquidation; or

    (*b*) to a dividend (so far as funds are available) out of the assets of the company in respect of any accounting period,

shall submit his claim to the liquidator—

    (*a*) at or before the meeting; or, as the case may be,

    (*b*) not later than 8 weeks before the end of the accounting period.

(2) A creditor shall submit his claim by producing to the liquidator—

    (*a*) a statement of claim in the form required by Rule 7.30 and Schedule 5; and

    (*b*) an account or voucher (according to the nature of the debt claimed) which constitutes *prima facie* evidence of the debt,

but the liquidator may dispense with any requirement of this paragraph in respect of any debt or any class of debt.

(3) A claim submitted by a creditor, which has been accepted in whole or in part by the liquidator for the purpose of voting at a meeting or of drawing a dividend in respect of any accounting period, shall be deemed to have been resubmitted for the purpose of obtaining an adjudication as to his entitlement both to vote at any subsequent meeting and (so far as funds are available) to a dividend in respect of an accounting period or, as the case may be, any subsequent accounting period.

(4) A creditor, who has submitted a claim, may at any time submit a further claim specifying a different amount for his claim:

Provided that a secured creditor shall not be entitled to produce a further claim specifying a different value for the security at any time after the liquidator has required the creditor to discharge, or convey or assign, the security under paragraph 5(2) of Schedule 1 to the Bankruptcy Act, as applied by the following Rule.

(5) Votes are calculated according to the amount of a creditor's debt as at the date of the commencement of the winding up within the meaning of section 129, deducting any amounts paid in respect of that debt after that date.

(6) In this Rule and in Rule 4.16, including the provisions of the Bankruptcy Act applied by that Rule, any reference to the liquidator includes a reference to the chairman of the meeting. **[1600]**

4.16. Application of the Bankruptcy Act

(1) Subject to the provisions in this Chapter, the following provisions of the Bankruptcy Act shall apply in relation to a liquidation of a company in like manner as they apply in a sequestration of a debtor's estate, subject to the modifications specified in paragraph (2) and to any other necessary modifications—

    (*a*) section 22(5) and (10) (criminal offence in relation to producing false claims or evidence);

    (*b*) section 48(5), (6) and (8), together with sections 44(2) and (3) and 47(1) as applied by those sections (further evidence in relation to claims);

    (*c*) section 49 (adjudication of claim);

    (*d*) section 50 (entitlement to vote and draw dividend);

    (*e*) section 60 (liabilities and rights of co-obligants); and

    (*f*) Schedule 1 except paragraphs 2, 4 and 6 (determination of amount of creditor's claim).

(2) For any reference in the provisions of the Bankruptcy Act, as applied by these rules, to any expression in column 1 below, there shall be substituted a reference to the expression in column 2 opposite thereto—

Column 1	*Column 2*
Interim trustee	Liquidator
Permanent trustee	Liquidator
Sequestration	Liquidation
Date of sequestration	Date of commencement of winding up within the meaning of section 129
Debtor	Company
Debtor's assets	Company's assets
Accountant in Bankruptcy	The court
Commissioners	Liquidation committee
Sheriff	The court
Preferred debts	Preferential debts within the meaning of section 386 **[1601]**

4.17. Claims in foreign currency

(1) A creditor may state the amount of his claim in a currency other than sterling where—

    (*a*) his claim is constituted by decree or other order made by a court ordering the company to pay to the creditor a sum expressed in a currency other than sterling, or

    (*b*) where it is not so constituted, his claim arises from a contract or bill of exchange in terms of which payment is or may be required to be made by the company to the creditor in a currency other than sterling.

(2) Where a claim is stated in currency other than sterling for the purpose of the preceding paragraph, it shall be converted into sterling at the rate of exchange for that other currency at the mean of the buying and selling spot rates prevailing in the London market at the close of business on the date of commencement of winding up.   **[1602]**

CHAPTER 6

THE LIQUIDATOR

SECTION A: APPOINTMENT AND FUNCTIONS OF LIQUIDATOR

4.18. Appointment of liquidator by the court

(1) This Rule applies where a liquidator is appointed by the court under section 138(1) (appointment of interim liquidator), 138(5) (no person appointed or nominated by the meetings of creditors and contributories), 139(4) (different

persons nominated by creditors and contributories) or 140(1) or (2) (liquidation following administration or voluntary arrangement).

(2) The court shall not make the appointment unless and until there is lodged in court a statement to the effect that the person to be appointed is an insolvency practitioner, duly qualified under the Act to be the liquidator, and that he consents so to act.

(3) Thereafter the courts shall send a copy of the order to the liquidator, whose appointment takes effect from the date of the order.

(4) The liquidator shall—

    (*a*) within 7 days of his appointment, give notice of it to the registrar of companies; and

    (*b*) within 28 days of his appointment, give notice of it to the creditors and contributories or, if the court so permits, he shall advertise his appointment in accordance with the directions of the court.

(5) In any notice or advertisement to be given by him under this Rule, the liquidator shall—

    (*a*) state whether he intends to summon meetings of creditors and contributories for the purpose of establishing a liquidation committee or whether he proposes to summon only a meeting of creditors for that purpose; and

    (*b*) if he does not propose to summon any meeting, set out the powers of the creditors under section 142(3) to require him to summon such a meeting.   **[1603]**

4.19. Appointment by creditors or contributories

(1) This Rule applies where a person is nominated for appointment as liquidator under section 139(2) either by a meeting of creditors or by a meeting of contributories.

(2) Subject to section 139(4) the interim liquidator, as chairman of the meeting, or, where the interim liquidator is nominated as liquidator, the chairman of the meeting, shall certify the appointment of a person as liquidator by the meeting but not until and unless the person to be appointed has provided him with a written statement to the effect that he is an insolvency practitioner, duly qualified under the Act to be the liquidator and that he consents so to act.

(3) The appointment of the liquidator shall be effective as from the date when his appointment is certified under paragraph (2) by the chairman of the meeting of the creditors or, where no person has been nominated to be liquidator by that meeting, the chairman of the meeting of the contributories and this date shall be stated in the certificate.

(4) The liquidator shall—

    (*a*) within 7 days of his appointment, give notice of his appointment to the court and to the registrar of companies; and

    (*b*) within 28 days of his appointment, give notice of it in a newspaper circulating in the area where the company has its principal place of business, or in such newspaper as he thinks most appropriate for ensuring that it comes to the notice of the company's creditors and contributories.

(5) The provisions of Rule 4.18(5) shall apply to any notice given by the liquidator under this Rule.

(6) Paragraphs (4) and (5) need not be complied with in the case of a liquidator appointed by a company meeting and replaced by another liquidator appointed on the same day by a creditors' meeting.   **[1604]**

NOTES
Para (4): See Sch 5, form 4.9 (Scot).

4.20. Authentication of liquidator's appointment

A copy certified by the clerk of the court of any order of court appointing the liquidator or, as the case may be, a copy, certified by the chairman of the meeting which appointed the liquidator, of the certificate of the liquidator's appointment under Rule 4.19(2), shall be sufficient evidence for all purposes and in any proceedings that he has been appointed to exercise the powers and perform the duties of liquidator in the winding up of the company.   **[1605]**

4.21. Hand-over of assets to liquidator

(1) This Rule applies where a person appointed as liquidator ("the succeeding liquidator") succeeds a previous liquidator ("the former liquidator") as the liquidator.

(2) When the succeeding liquidator's appointment takes effect, the former liquidator shall forthwith do all that is required for putting the succeeding liquidator into possession of the assets.

(3) The former liquidator shall give to the succeeding liquidator all such information, relating to the affairs of the company and the course of the winding up, as the succeeding liquidator considers to be reasonably required for the effective discharge by him of his duties as such and shall hand over all books, accounts, statements of affairs, statements of claim and other records and documents in his possession relating to the affairs of the company and its winding up.   **[1606]**

4.22. Taking possession and realisation of the company's assets

(1) Sections 38 and 39(4) and (7) of the Bankruptcy Act shall apply in relation to a liquidation of a company as it applies in relation to a sequestration of a debtor's estate, subject to the modifications specified in paragraph (2) and Rule 4.16(2) and to any other necessary modifications.

(2) For subsection (1) of section 38, there shall be substituted the following section—

"(1) The liquidator shall—
    (a) as soon as may be after his appointment take possession of the whole assets of the company and any property, books, papers or records in the possession or control of the company or to which the company appears to be entitled; and
    (b) make up and maintain an inventory and valuation of the assets which he shall retain in the sederunt book.".   **[1607]**

SECTION B: REMOVAL AND RESIGNATION; VACATION OF OFFICE

4.23. Summoning of meeting for removal of liquidator

(1) Subject to section 172(3) and without prejudice to any other method of summoning the meeting, a meeting of creditors for the removal of the liquidator

in accordance with section 172(2) shall be summoned by the liquidator if requested to do so by not less than one quarter in value of the creditors.

(2) Where a meeting of creditors is summoned especially for the purpose of removing the liquidator in accordance with section 172(2), the notice summoning it shall draw attention to section 174(4)(*a*) or (*b*) with respect to the liquidator's release.

(3) At the meeting, a person other than the liquidator or his nominee may be elected to act as chairman; but if the liquidator or his nominee is chairman and a resolution has been proposed for the liquidator's removal, the chairman shall not adjourn the meeting without the consent of at least one-half (in value) of the creditors present (in person or by proxy) and entitled to vote.

(4) Where a meeting is to be held or is proposed to be summoned under this Rule, the court may, on the application of any creditor, give directions as to the mode of summoning it, the sending out and return of forms of proxy, the conduct of the meeting, and any other matter which appears to the court to require regulation or control under this Rule.   **[1608]**

4.24. Procedure on liquidator's removal

(1) Where the creditors have resolved that the liquidator be removed, the chairman of the creditors' meeting shall forthwith—

- (*a*) if, at the meeting, another liquidator was not appointed, send a certificate of the liquidator's removal to the court and to the registrar of companies, and
- (*b*) otherwise, deliver the certificate to the new liquidator, who shall forthwith send it to the court and to the registrar of companies.

(2) The liquidator's removal is effective as from such date as the meeting of the creditors shall determine, and this shall be stated in the certificate of removal.   **[1609]**

4.25. Release of liquidator on removal

(1) Where the liquidator has been removed by a creditors' meeting which has not resolved against his release, the date on which he has his release in terms of section 174(4)(*a*) shall be stated in the certificate of removal before a copy of it is sent to the court and to the registrar of companies under Rule 4.24(1).

(2) Where the liquidator is removed by a creditors' meeting which has resolved against his release, or is removed by the court, he must apply to the Accountant of Court for his release.

(3) When the Accountant of Court releases the former liquidator, he shall—

- (*a*) issue a certificate of release to the new liquidator who shall send a copy of it to the court and to the registrar of companies, and
- (*b*) send a copy of the certificate to the former liquidator,

and in this case release of the former liquidator is effective from the date of the certificate.   **[1610]**

NOTES

  Para (2): See Sch 5, form 4.12 (Scot).
  Para (3): See Sch 5, forms 4.13 (Scot), 4.14 (Scot).

4.26. Removal of liquidator by the court

(1) This Rule applies where application is made to the court for the removal of the liquidator, or for an order directing the liquidator to summon a meeting of creditors for the purpose of removing him.

(2) The court may require the applicant to make a deposit or give caution for the expenses to be incurred by the liquidator on the application.

(3) The applicant shall, at least 14 days before the hearing, send to the liquidator a notice stating its date, time and place and accompanied by a copy of the application, and of any evidence which he intends to adduce in support of it.

(4) Subject to any contrary order of the court, the expenses of the application are not payable as an expense of the liquidation.

(5) Where the court removes the liquidator—

    (a) it shall send two copies of the order of removal to him;

    (b) the order may include such provision as the court thinks fit with respect to matters arising in connection with the removal; and

    (c) if the court appoints a new liquidator, Rule 4.18 applies,

and the liquidator, on receipt of the two court orders under sub-paragraph (a), shall send one copy of the order to the registrar of companies, together with a notice of his ceasing to act as a liquidator.   **[1611]**

NOTES
    Para (5): See Sch 5, form 4.11 (Scot).

4.27. Advertisement of removal

Where a new liquidator is appointed in place of the one removed, Rules 4.19 to 4.21 shall apply to the appointment of the new liquidator except that the notice to be given by the new liquidator under Rule 4.19(4) shall also state—

    (a) that his predecessor as liquidator has been removed; and

    (b) whether his predecessor has been released.   **[1612]**

NOTES
    See Sch 5, form 4.9 (Scot).

4.28. Resignation of liquidator

(1) Before resigning his office under section 172(6) the liquidator shall call a meeting of creditors for the purpose of receiving his resignation.

(2) The notice summoning the meeting shall draw attention to section 174(4)(c) and Rule 4.29(4) with respect of the liquidator's release and shall also be accompanied by an account of the liquidator's administration of the winding up, including a summary of his receipts and payments.

(3) Subject to paragraph (4), the liquidator may only proceed under this Rule on the grounds of ill health or because—

    (a) he intends ceasing to be in practice as an insolvency practitioner; or

    (b) there has been some conflict of interest or change of personal circumstances which precludes or makes impracticable the further discharge by him of the duties of the liquidator.

(4) Where two or more persons are acting as liquidator jointly, any one of

them may resign (without prejudice to the continuation in office of the other or others) on the ground that, in his opinion and that of the other or others, it is no longer expedient that there should continue to be the present number of joint liquidators   **[1613]**

4.29. Action following acceptance of liquidator's resignation

(1) This Rule applies where a meeting is summoned to receive the liquidator's resignation.

(2) If the liquidator's resignation is accepted, it is effective as from such date as the meeting of the creditors may determine and that date shall be stated in the notice given by the liquidator under paragraph (3).

(3) The liquidator, whose resignation is accepted, shall forthwith after the meeting give notice of his resignation to the court as required by section 172(6) and shall send a copy of it to the registrar of companies.

(4) The meeting of the creditors may grant the liquidator his release from such date as thay may determine. If the meeting resolves against the liquidator having his release, Rule 4.25(2) and (3) shall apply.

(5) Where the creditors have resolved to appoint a new liquidator in place of the one who has resigned, Rules 4.19 to 4.21 shall apply to the appointment of the new liquidator, except that the notice to be given by the new liquidator under Rule 4.19(4) shall also state that his predecessor as liquidator has resigned and whether he has been released.   **[1614]**

4.30. Leave to resign granted by the court

(1) If at a creditors' meeting summoned to receive the liquidator's resignation, it is resolved that it be not accepted, the court may, on the liquidator's application, make an order giving him leave to resign.

(2) The court's order under this Rule may include such provision as it thinks fit with respect to matters arising in connection with the resignation including the notices to be given to the creditors and the registrar of companies and shall determine the date from which the liquidator's release is effective.   **[1615]**

SECTION C: RELEASE ON COMPLETION OF WINDING UP

4.31. Final meeting

(1) The liquidator shall give at least 28 days' notice of the final meeting of creditors to be held under section 146. The notice shall be sent to all creditors whose claims in the liquidation have been accepted.

(2) The liquidator's report laid before the meeting shall contain an account of his administration of the winding up, including a summary of his receipts and payments.

(3) At the final meeting, the creditors may question the liquidator with respect to any matter contained in his report, and may resolve against the liquidator having his release.

(4) The liquidator shall within 7 days of the meeting give notice to the court and to the registrar of companies under section 172(8) that the final meeting has been held and the notice shall state whether or not he has been released, and be accompanied by a copy of the report laid before the meeting.

(5) If there is no quorum present at the final meeting, the liquidator shall report to the court that a final meeting was summoned in accordance with the Rules, but that there was no quorum present; and the final meeting is then deemed to have been held and the creditors not to have resolved against the liquidator being released.

(6) If the creditors at the final meeting have not resolved against the liquidator having his release, he is released in terms of section 174(4)(*d*)(ii) when he vacates office under section 172(8). If they have so resolved he shall apply for his release to the Accountant of Court, and Rules 4.25(2) and (3) shall apply accordingly   **[1616]**

NOTES
   Para (4): See Sch 5, form 4.17 (Scot).

Section D: Outlays and Remuneration

4.32. Determination of amount of outlays and remuneration

(1) Subject to the provisions of Rules 4.33 to 4.35, claims by the liquidator for the outlays reasonably incurred by him and for his remuneration shall be made in accordance with section 53 of the Bankruptcy Act as applied by Rule 4.68 and as further modified by paragraphs (2) and (3) below.

(2) After section 53(1) of the Bankruptcy Act, there shall be inserted the following subsection—

"(1A) The liquidator may, at any time before the end of an accounting period, submit to the liquidation committee (if any) an interim claim in respect of that period for the outlays reasonably incurred by him and for his remuneration and the liquidation committee may make an interim determination in relation to the amount of the outlays and remuneration payable to the liquidator and, where they do so, they shall take into account that interim determination when making their determination under subsection (3)(*a*)(ii).".

(3) In section 53(6) of the Bankruptcy Act, for the reference to "subsection (3)(*a*)(ii)" there shall be substituted a reference to "subsection (1A) or (3)(*a*)(ii)".   **[1617]**

4.33. Recourse of liquidator to meeting of creditors

If the liquidator's remuneration has been fixed by the liquidation committee and he considers the amount to be insufficient, he may request that it be increased by resolution of the creditors.   **[1618]**

4.34. Recourse to the court

(1) If the liquidator considers that the remuneration fixed for him by the liquidation committee, or by resolution of the creditors, is insufficient, he may apply to the court for an order increasing its amount or rate.

(2) The liquidator shall give at least 14 days' notice of his application to the members of the liquidation committee; and the committee may nominate one or more members to appear or be represented, and to be heard, on the application.

(3) If there is no liquidation committee, the liquidator's notice of his application shall be sent to such one or more of the company's creditors as the

court may direct, which creditors may nominate one or more of their number to appear or be represented.

(4) The court may, if it appears to be a proper case, order the expenses of the liquidator's application, including the expenses of any member of the liquidation committee appearing on it, or any creditor so appearing, to be paid as an expense for the liquidation. **[1619]**

4.35. Creditors' claim that remuneration is excessive

(1) If the liquidator's remuneration has been fixed by the liquidation committee or by the creditors, any creditor or creditors of the company representing in value at least 25 per cent of the creditors may apply to the court for an order that the liquidator's remuneration be reduced, on the grounds that it is, in all the circumstances, excessive.

(2) If the court considers the application to be well-founded, it shall make an order fixing the remuneration at a reduced amount or rate.

(3) Unless the court orders otherwise, the expenses of the application shall be paid by the applicant, and are not payable as an expense of the liquidation.

[1620]

Section E: Supplementary Provisions

4.36. Liquidator deceased

(1) Subject to the following paragraph, where the liquidator has died, it is the duty of his executors or, where the deceased liquidator was a partner in a firm, of a partner in that firm to give notice of that fact to the court and to the registrar of companies, specifying the date of death. This does not apply if notice has been given under the following paragraph.

(2) Notice of the death may also be given by any person producing to the court and to the registrar of companies a copy of the death certificate. **[1621]**

4.37. Loss of qualification as insolvency practitioner

(1) This Rule applies where the liquidator vacates office on ceasing to be qualified to act as an insolvency practitioner in relation to the company.

(2) He shall forthwith give notice of his doing so to the court and to the registrar of companies.

(3) Rule 4.25(2) and (3) apply as regards the liquidator obtaining his release, as if he had been removed by the court. **[1622]**

4.38. Power of court to set aside certain transactions

(1) If in the course of the liquidation the liquidator enters into any transaction with a person who is an associate of his, the court may, on the application of any person interested, set the transaction aside and order the liquidator to compensate the company for any loss suffered in consequence of it.

(2) This does not apply if either—

  (*a*) the transaction was entered into with the prior consent of the court, or

  (*b*) it is shown to the court's satisfaction that the transaction was for value, and that it was entered into by the liquidator without knowing, or having any reason to suppose, that the person concerned was an associate.

(3) Nothing in this Rule is to be taken as prejudicing the operation of any rule of law with respect to a trustee's dealings with trust property, or the fiduciary obligations of any person.   **[1623]**

4.39. Rule against solicitation

(1) Where the court is satisfied that any improper solicitation has been used by or on behalf of the liquidator in obtaining proxies or procuring his appointment, it may order that no remuneration be allowed as an expense of the liquidation to any person by whom, or on whose behalf, the solicitation was exercised.

(2) An order of the court under this Rule overrides any resolution of the liquidation committee or the creditors, or any other provision of the Rules relating to the liquidator's remuneration.   **[1624]**

CHAPTER 7

THE LIQUIDATION COMMITTEE

4.40. Preliminary

For the purposes of this Chapter—
  (*a*) an "insolvent winding up" takes place where a company is being wound up on grounds which include its inability to pay its debts, and
  (*b*) a "solvent winding up" takes place where a company is being wound up on grounds which do not include that one.   **[1625]**

4.41. Membership of committee

(1) Subject to Rule 4.43 below, the liquidation committee shall consist as follows—
  (*a*) in the case of any winding up, of at least 3 and not more than 5 creditors of the company, elected by the meeting of creditors held under section 138 or 142 of the Act, and also
  (*b*) in the case of a solvent winding up where the contributories' meeting held under either of those sections so decides, up to 3 contributories, elected by that meeting.

(2) Any creditor of the company (other than one whose debt is fully secured and who has not agreed to surrender his security to the liquidator) is eligible to be a member of the committee, so long as—
  (*a*) he has lodged a claim of his debt in the liquidation, and
  (*b*) his claim has neither been wholly rejected for voting purposes, nor wholly rejected for the purposes of his entitlement so far as funds are available to a dividend.

(3) No person can be a member as both a creditor and a contributory.

(4) A body corporate or a partnership may be a member of the committee, but it cannot act as such otherwise than by a member's representative appointed under Rule 4.48 below.

(5) In this Chapter, members of the committee elected or appointed by a creditors' meeting are called "creditor members", and those elected or appointed by contributories' meeting are called "contributory members".

(6) Where the Deposit Protection Board exercises the right (under section 28 of the Banking Act 1979) to be a member of the committee, the Board is to be regarded as an additional creditor member.   **[1626]**

4.42. Formalities of establishment

(1) The liquidation committee shall not come into being, and accordingly cannot act, until the liquidator has issued a certificate of its due constitution.

(2) If the chairman of the meeting which resolves to establish the committee is not the liquidator, he shall forthwith give notice of the resolution to the liquidator (or, as the case may be, the person appointed as liquidator by the same meeting), and inform him of the names and addresses of the persons elected to be members of the committee.

(3) No person may act as a member of the committee unless and until he has agreed to do so; and the liquidator's certificate of the committee's due constitution shall not be issued until at least the minimum number of persons in accordance with Rule 4.41 who are to be members of it have agreed to act, but shall be issued forthwith thereafter.

(4) As and when the others (if any) agree to act, the liquidator shall issue an amended certificate.

(5) The certificate (and any amended certificate) shall be sent by the liquidator to the registrar of companies.

(6) If after the first establishment of the committee there is any change in its membership, the liquidator shall report the change to the registrar of companies.   **[1627]**

NOTES
    Paras (3), (4): See Sch 5, form 4.20 (Scot).
    Paras (5), (6): See Sch 5, form 4.22 (Scot).

4.43. Committee established by contributories

(1) The following applies where the creditors' meeting under section 138 or 142 of the Act does not decide that a liquidation committee should be established or decides that a liquidation committee should not be established.

(2) A meeting of contributories under section 138 or 142 may appoint one of their number to make application to the court for an order to the liquidator that a further creditors' meeting be summoned for the purpose of establishing a liquidation committee; and

    (a) the court may, if it thinks that there are special circumstances to justify it, make that order, and
    (b) the creditors' meeting summoned by the liquidator in compliance with the order is deemed to have been summoned under section 142.

(3) If the creditors' meeting so summoned does not establish a liquidation committee, a meeting of contributories may do so.

(4) The committee shall then consist of at least 3, and not more than 5, contributories elected by that meeting; and Rule 4.42 shall apply to such a committee with the substitution of references to contributories for references to creditors.   **[1628]**

4.44. Obligations of liquidator to committee

(1) Subject as follows, it is the duty of the liquidator to report to the members of the liquidation committee all such matters as appear to him to be, or as they have indicated to him as being, of concern to them with respect to the winding up.

(2) In the case of matters so indicated to him by the committee, the liquidator need not comply with any request for information where it appears to him that—

> (a) the request is frivolous or unreasonable, or
> (b) the cost of complying would be excessive, having regard to the relative importance of the information, or
> (c) there are not sufficient assets to enable him to comply.

(3) Where the committee has come into being more than 28 days after the appointment of the liquidator, he shall report to them, in summary form, what actions he has taken since his appointment, and shall answer all such questions as they may put to him regarding his conduct of the winding up hitherto.

(4) A person who becomes a member of the committee at any time after its first establishment is not entitled to require a report to him by the liquidator, otherwise than in summary form, of any matters previously arising.

(5) Nothing in this Rule disentitles the committee, or any member of it, from having access to the liquidator's cash book and sederunt book, or from seeking an explanation of any matter within the committee's responsibility.

[1629]

4.45. Meetings of the committee

(1) Subject as follows, meetings of the liquidation committee shall be held when and where determined by the liquidator.

(2) The liquidator shall call a first meeting of the committee to take place within 3 months of his appointment or of the committee's establishment (whichever is the later); and thereafter he shall call a meeting—

> (a) if so requested by a creditor member of the committee or his representative (the meeting then to be held within 21 days of the request being received by the liquidator), and
> (b) for a specified date, if the committee has previously resolved that a meeting be held on that day.

(3) The liquidator shall give 7 days' written notice of the time and place of any meeting to every member of the committee (or his representative, if designated for that purpose), unless in any case the requirement of the notice has been waived by or on behalf of any member. Waiver may be signified either at or before the meeting.   **[1630]**

4.46. The chairman at meetings

(1) The chairman at any meeting of the liquidation committee shall be the liquidator, or a person nominated by him to act.

(2) A person so nominated must be either—

> (a) a person who is qualified to act as an insolvency practitioner in relation to the company, or

(*b*) an employee of the liquidator or his firm who is experienced in insolvency matters. **[1631]**

4.47. Quorum

A meeting of the committee is duly constituted if due notice of it has been given to all the members, and at least 2 creditor members or, in the case of a committee of contributories, 2 contributory members are present or represented. **[1632]**

4.48. Committee members' representatives

(1) A member of the liquidation committee may, in relation to the business of the committee, be represented by another person duly authorised by him for that purpose.

(2) A person acting as a committee-member's representative must hold a mandate entitling him so to act (either generally or specially) and signed by or on behalf of the committee member.

(3) The chairman at any meeting of the committee may call on a person claiming to act as a committee-member's representative to produce his mandate and may exclude him if it appears that his mandate is deficient.

(4) No member may be represented by a body corporate or by a partnership, or by an undischarged bankrupt.

(5) No person shall—

(*a*) on the same committee, act at one and the same time as representative of more than one committee-member, or
(*b*) act both as a member of the committee and as representative of another member.

(6) Where a member's representative signs any document on the member's behalf, the fact that he so signs must be stated below his signature. **[1633]**

4.49. Resignation

A member of the liquidation committee may resign by notice in writing delivered to the liquidator. **[1634]**

4.50. Termination of membership

Membership of the liquidation committee of any person is automatically terminated if—

(*a*) his estate is sequestrated or becomes bankrupt or grants a trust deed for the benefit of or makes a composition with his creditors, or
(*b*) at 3 consecutive meetings of the committee he is neither present nor represented (unless at the third of those meetings it is resolved that this Rule is not to apply in his case), or
(*c*) that creditor being a creditor member, he ceases to be, or is found never to have been a creditor. **[1635]**

4.51. Removal

A creditor member of the committee may be removed by resolution at a meeting of creditors; and a contributory member may be removed by a resolution of a meeting of contributories. **[1636]**

4.52. Vacancy (creditor members)

(1) The following applies if there is a vacancy among the creditor members of the committee.

(2) The vacancy need not be filled if the liquidator and a majority of the remaining creditor members so agree, provided that the total number of members does not fall below the minimum required by Rule 4.41(1).

(3) The liquidator may appoint any creditor, who is qualified under the Rules to be a member of the committee, to fill the vacancy, if a majority of the other creditor members agrees to the appointment, and the creditor concerned consents to act.

(4) Alternatively, a meeting of creditors may resolve that a creditor be appointed (with his consent) to fill the vacancy. In this case, at least 14 days' notice must have been given of the resolution to make such an appointment (whether or not of a person named in the notice).

(5) Where the vacancy is filled by an appointment made by a creditors' meeting at which the liquidator is not present, the chairman of the meeting shall report to the liquidator the appointment which has been made.   **[1637]**

4.53. Vacancy (contributory members)

(1) The following applies if there is a vacancy among the contributory members of the committee.

(2) The vacancy need not be filled if the liquidator and the majority of the remaining contributory members so agree, provided that, in the case of a committee of contributory members only, the total number of members does not fall below the minimum required by Rule 4.41(1) or, as the case may be, 4.59(4).

(3) The liquidator may appoint any contributory member (being qualified under the Rules to be a member of the committee) to fill the vacancy, if a majority of the other contributory members agree to the appointment, and the contributory concerned consents to act.

(4) Alternatively, a meeting of contributories may resolve that a contributory be appointed (with his consent) to fill the vacancy. In this case, at least 14 days' notice must have been given of the resolution to make such an appointment (whether or not of a person named in the notice).

(5) Where the vacancy is filled by an appointment made by a contributories' meeting at which the liquidator is not present, the chairman of the meeting shall report to the liquidator the appointment which has been made.   **[1638]**

4.54. Voting rights and resolutions

(1) At any meeting of the committee, each member of it (whether present himself, or by his representative) has one vote; and a resolution is passed when a majority of the creditor members present or represented have voted in favour of it.

(2) Subject to the next paragraph, the votes of contributory members do not count towards the number required for passing a resolution, but the way in which they vote on any resolution shall be recorded.

(3) Paragraph (2) does not apply where, by virtue of Rule 4.43(4) or 4.59,

the only members of the committee are contributories. In that case the committee is to be treated for voting purposes as if all its members were creditors.

(4) Every resolution passed shall be recorded in writing, either separately or as part of the minutes of the meeting. The record shall be signed by the chairman and kept as part of the sederunt book.　**[1639]**

4.55. Resolutions by post

(1) In accordance with this Rule, the liquidator may seek to obtain the agreement of members of the liquidation committee to a resolution by sending to every member (or his representative designated for the purpose) a copy of the proposed resolution.

(2) Where the liquidator makes use of the procedure allowed by this Rule, he shall send out to members of the committee or their representatives (as the case may be) a statement incorporating the resolution to which their agreement is sought, each resolution (if more than one) being set out in a separate document.

(3) Any creditor member of the committee may, within 7 business days from the date of the liquidator sending out a resolution, require him to summon a meeting of the committee to consider the matters raised by the resolution.

(4) In the absence of such a request, the resolution is deemed to have been passed by the committee if and when the liquidator is notified in writing by a majority of the creditor members that they concur with it.

(5) A copy of every resolution passed under this Rule, and a note that the committee's concurrence was obtained, shall be kept in the sederunt book.
[1640]

4.56. Liquidator's reports

(1) The liquidator shall, as and when directed by the liquidation committee (but not more often than once in any period of 2 months), send a written report to every member of the committee setting out the position generally as regards the progress of the winding up and matters arising in connection with it, to which the liquidator considers the committee's attention should be drawn.

(2) In the absence of such directions by the committee, the liquidator shall send such a report not less often than once in every period of 6 months.

(3) The obligations of the liquidator under this Rule are without prejudice to those imposed by Rule 4.44.　**[1641]**

4.57. Expenses of members, etc

(1) The liquidator shall defray any reasonable travelling expenses directly incurred by members of the liquidation committee or their representatives in respect of their attendance at the committee's meetings, or otherwise on the committee's business, as an expense of the liquidation.

(2) Paragraph (1) does not apply to any meeting of the committee held within 3 months of a previous meeting.　**[1642]**

4.58. Dealings by committee-members and others

(1) This Rule applies to—

(a) any member of the liquidation committee;

(b) any committee-member's representative;

(c) any person who is an associate of a member of the committee or of a committee-member's representative; and

(d) any person who has been a member of the committee at any time in the last 12 months.

(2) Subject as follows, a person to whom this Rule applies shall not enter into any transaction whereby he—

(a) receives out of the company's assets any payment for services given or goods supplied in connection with the liquidation, or

(b) obtains any profit from the liquidation, or

(c) acquires any part of the company's assets.

(3) Such a transaction may be entered into by a person to whom this Rule applies—

(a) with the prior leave of the court, or

(b) if he does so as a matter of urgency, or by way of performance of a contract in force before the date on which the company went into liquidation, and obtains the court's leave for the transaction, having applied for it without undue delay, or

(c) with the prior sanction of the liquidation committee, where it is satisfied (after full disclosure of the circumstances) that the transaction will be on normal commercial terms.

(4) Where in the committee a resolution is proposed that sanction be accorded for a transaction to be entered into which, without that sanction or the leave of the court, would be in contravention of this Rule, no member of the committee, and no representative of a member, shall vote if he is to participate directly or indirectly in the transaction.

(5) The court may, on the application of any person interested,—

(a) set aside a transaction on the ground that it has been entered into in contravention of this Rule, and

(b) make with respect to it such other order as it thinks fit, including (subject to the following paragraph) an order requiring a person to whom this Rule applies to account for any profit obtained from the transaction and compensate the company's assets for any resultant loss.

(6) In the case of a person to whom this Rule applies as an associate of a member of the committee or of a committee-member's representative, the court shall not make any order under paragraph (5), if satisfied that he entered into the relevant transaction without having any reason to suppose that in doing so he would contravene this Rule.

(7) The expenses of an application to the court for leave under this Rule are not payable as an expense of the liquidation, unless the court so orders.   **[1643]**

4.59. Composition of committee when creditors paid in full

(1) This Rule applies if the liquidator issues a certificate that the creditors have been paid in full, with interest in accordance with section 189.

(2) The liquidator shall forthwith send a copy of the certificate to the registrar of companies.

(3) The creditor members of the liquidation committee shall cease to be members of the committee.

(4) The committee continues in being unless and until abolished by decision of a meeting of contributories, and (subject to the next paragraph) so long as it consists of at least 2 contributory members.

(5) The committee does not cease to exist on account of the number of contributory members falling below 2, unless and until 28 days have elapsed since the issue of the liquidator's certificate under paragraph (1), but at any time when the committee consists of less than 2 contributory members, it is suspended and cannot act.

(6) Contributories may be co-opted by the liquidator, or appointed by a contributories' meeting, to be members of the committee; but the maximum number of members is 5.

(7) The foregoing Rules in this Chapter continue to apply to the liquidation committee (with any necessary modifications) as if all the members of the committee were creditor members. **[1644]**

NOTES

Para (2): see Sch 5, form 4.24 (Scot).

CHAPTER 8

THE LIQUIDATION COMMITTEE WHERE WINDING UP FOLLOWS IMMEDIATELY ON ADMINISTRATION

4.60. Preliminary

(1) The Rules in this Chapter apply where—
- (*a*) the winding up order has been made immediately upon the discharge of an administration order under Part II of the Act, and
- (*b*) the court makes an order under section 140(1) appointing as liquidator the person who was previously the administrator.

(2) In this Chapter the expressions "insolvent winding up", "solvent winding up", "creditor member", and "contributory member" each have the same meaning as in Chapter 7. **[1645]**

4.61. Continuation of creditors' committee

(1) If under section 26 a creditors' committee has been established for the purposes of the administration, then (subject as follows in this Chapter) that committee continues in being as the liquidation committee for the purposes of the winding up, and—
- (*a*) it is deemed to be a committee established as such under section 142, and
- (*b*) no action shall be taken under subsections (1) to (4) of that section to establish any other.

(2) This Rule does not apply if, at the time when the court's order under section 140(1) is made, the committee under section 26 consists of less than 3 members; and a creditor who was, immediately before the date of that order, a member of such a committee ceases to be a member on the making of the order if his debt is fully secured (and he has not agreed to surrender his security to the liquidator). **[1646]**

4.62. Membership of committee

(1) Subject as follows, the liquidation committee shall consist of at least 3, and not more than 5, creditors of the company, elected by the creditors' meeting held under section 26 or (in order to make up numbers or fill vacancies) by a creditors' meeting summoned by the liquidator after the company goes into liquidation.

(2) In the case of a solvent winding up, the liquidator shall, on not less than 21 days' notice, summon a meeting of contributories, in order to elect (if it so wishes) contributory members of the liquidation committee, up to 3 in number.
[1647]

4.63. Liquidator's certificate

(1) The liquidator shall issue a certificate of the liquidation committee's continuance specifying the persons who are, or are to be, members of it.

(2) It shall be stated in the certificate whether or not the liquidator has summoned a meeting of contributories under Rule 4.62(2), and whether (if so) the meeting has elected contributories to be members of the committee.

(3) Pending the issue of the liquidator's certificate, the committee is suspended and cannot act.

(4) No person may act, or continue to act, as a member of the committee unless and until he has agreed to do so; and the liquidator's certificate shall not be issued until at least the minimum number of persons required under Rule 4.62 to form a committee elected, whether under Rule 4.62 above or under section 26, have signified their agreement.

(5) As and when the others signify their agreement, the liquidator shall issue an amended certificate.

(6) The liquidator's certificate (or, as the case may be, the amended certificate) shall be sent by him to the registrar of companies.

(7) If subsequently there is any change in the committee's membership, the liquidator shall report the change to the registrar of companies.   **[1648]**

NOTES
   Para (5): See Sch 5, form 4.21 (Scot).
   Paras (6), (7): See Sch 5, form 4.22 (Scot).

4.64. Obligations of liquidator to committee

(1) As soon as may be after the issue of the liquidator's certificate under Rule 4.63, the liquidator shall report to the liquidation committee what actions he has taken since the date on which the company went into liquidation.

(2) A person who becomes a member of the committee after that date is not entitled to require a report to him by the liquidator, otherwise than in a summary form, of any matters previously arising.

(3) Nothing in this Rule disentitles the committee, or any member of it, from having access to the sederunt book (whether relating to the period when he was administrator, or to any subsequent period), or from seeking an explanation of any matter within the committee's responsibility.   **[1649]**

4.65. Application of Chapter 7

Except as provided elsewhere in this Chapter, Rules 4.44 to 4.59 of Chapter 7 shall apply to a liquidation committee established under this Chapter from the date of issue of the certificate under Rule 4.63 as if it had been established under section 142.   **[1650]**

NOTES

See Sch 5, form 4.21 (Scot).

CHAPTER 9

DISTRIBUTION OF COMPANY'S ASSETS BY LIQUIDATOR

4.66. Order of priority in distribution

(1) The funds of the company's assets shall be distributed by the liquidator to meet the following expenses and debts in the order in which they are mentioned—

    (*a*) the expenses of the liquidation;

    (*b*) any preferential debts within the meaning of section 386 (excluding any interest which has been accrued thereon to the date of commencement of the winding up within the meaning of section 129);

    (*c*) ordinary debts, that is to say a debt which is neither a secured debt nor a debt mentioned in any other sub-paragraph of this paragraph;

    (*d*) interest at the official rate on—

        (i) the preferential debts, and
        (ii) the ordinary debts,

    between the said date of commencement of the winding up and the date of payment of the debt; and

    (*e*) any postponed debt.

(2) In the above paragraph—

    (*a*) "postponed debt" means a creditor's right to any alienation which has been reduced or restored to the company's assets under section 242 or to the proceeds of sale of such an alienation; and

    (*b*) "official rate" shall be construed in accordance with subsection (4) of section 189 and, for the purposes of paragraph (*a*) of that subsection, as applied to Scotland by subsection (5), the rate specified in the Rules shall be 15 per centum per annum.

(3) The expenses of the liquidation mentioned in sub-paragraph (*a*) of paragraph (1) are payable in the order of priority mentioned in Rule 4.67.

(4) Subject to the provisions of section 175, any debt falling within any of sub-paragraphs (*b*) to (*e*) of paragraph (1) shall have the same priority as any other debt falling within the same sub-paragraph and, where the funds of the company's assets are inadequate to enable the debts mentioned in this sub-paragraph to be paid in full, they shall abate in equal proportions.

(5) Any surplus remaining, after all expenses and debts mentioned in paragraph (1) have been paid in full, shall (unless the articles of the company otherwise provide) be distributed among the members according to their rights and interests in the company.

(6) Nothing in this Rule shall affect—

(a) the right of a secured creditor which is preferable to the rights of the liquidator; or

(b) any preference of the holder of a lien over a title deed or other document which has been delivered to the permanent trustee in accordance with a requirement under section 38(4) of the Bankruptcy Act, as applied by Rule 4.22.   **[1651]**

4.67. Order of priority of expenses of liquidation

(1) Subject to section 156 and paragraph (2), the expenses of the liquidation are payable out of the assets in the following order of priority—

(a) any outlays properly chargeable or incurred by the provisional liquidator or liquidator in carrying out his functions in the liquidation, except those outlays specifically mentioned in the following sub-paragraphs;

(b) the cost, or proportionate cost, of any caution provided by a provisional liquidator, liquidator or special manager in accordance with the Act or the Rules;

(c) the remuneration of the provisional liquidator (if any);

(d) the expenses of the petitioner in the liquidation, and of any person appearing in the petition whose expenses are allowed by the court;

(e) the remuneration of the special manager (if any);

(f) any allowance made by the liquidator under Rule 4.9(1) (expenses of statement of affairs);

(g) the remuneration or emoluments of any person who has been employed by the liquidator to perform any services for the company, as required or authorised by or under the Act or the Rules;

(h) the remuneration of the liquidator determined in accordance with Rule 4.32;

(i) the amount of any capital gains tax on chargeable gains accruing on the realisation of any asset of the company (without regard to whether the realisation is effected by the liquidator, a secured creditor or otherwise).

(2) In any winding up by the court which follows immediately on a voluntary winding up (whether members' voluntary or creditors' voluntary), such outlays and remuneration of the voluntary liquidator as the court may allow, shall have the same priority as the outlays mentioned in sub-paragraph (a) of paragraph (1).

(3) Nothing in this Rule applies to or affects the power of any court, in proceedings by or against the company, to order expenses to be paid by the company, or the liquidator; nor does it affect the rights of any person to whom such expenses are ordered to be paid.   **[1652]**

4.68. Application of the Bankruptcy Act

(1) Sections 52, 53 and 58 of the Bankruptcy Act shall apply in relation to the liquidation of a company as they apply in relation to a sequestration of a debtor's estate, subject to the modifications specified in Rules 4.16(2) and 4.32(2) and (3) and the following paragraph and to any other necessary modifications.

(2) In section 52, the following modifications shall be made:

(a) in subsection (4)(a) for the reference to "the debts mentioned in subsection (1)(a) to (d)", there shall be substituted a reference to the expenses of the winding up mentioned in Rule 4.67(1)(a);

(b) in subsection (5), the words "with the consent of the commissioners or if there are no commissioners of the Accountant in Bankruptcy" should be deleted; and

(c) in subsection (7) and (8) for the references to section 48(5) and 49(6)(b) there should be substituted a reference to those sections as applied by Rule 4.16(1). **[1653]**

CHAPTER 10

SPECIAL MANAGER

4.69. Appointment and remuneration

(1) This Chapter applies to an application under section 177 by the liquidator or, where one has been appointed, by the provisional liquidator for the appointment of a person to be special manager (references in this Chapter to the liquidator shall be read as including the provisional liquidator).

(2) An application shall be supported by a report setting out the reasons for the appointment. the report shall include the applicant's estimate of the value of the assets in respect of which the special manager is to be appointed.

(3) The order of the court appointing the special manager shall specify the duration of his appointment, which may be for a period of time or until the occurrence of a specified event. Alternatively the order may specify that the duration of the appointment is to be subject to a further order of the court.

(4) The appointment of a special manager may be renewed by order of the court.

(5) The special manager's remuneration shall be fixed from time to time by the court.

(6) The acts of the special manager are valid notwithstanding any defect in his appointment or qualifications. **[1654]**

4.70. Caution

(1) The appointment of the special manager does not take effect until the person appointed has found (or, being allowed by the court to do so, has undertaken to find) caution to the person who applies for him to be appointed.

(2) It is not necessary that caution be found for each separate company liquidation; but it may be found either specially for a particular liquidation, or generally for any liquidation in relation to which the special manager may be employed as such.

(3) The amount of the caution shall be not less than the value of the assets in respect of which he is appointed, as estimated by the applicant in his report under Rule 4.69.

(4) When the special manager has found caution to the person applying for his appointment, that person shall certify the adequacy of the security and notify the court accordingly.

(5) The cost of finding caution shall be paid in the first instance by the special manager; but—

(a) where a winding up order is not made, he is entitled to be reimbursed out of the property of the company, and the court may make an order on the company accordingly, and (*b*) where a winding up order has been or is subsequently made, he is entitled to be reimbursed as an expense of the liquidation.   **[1655]**

4.71. Failure to find or to maintain caution

(1) If the special manager fails to find the required caution within the time stated for that purpose by the order appointing him, or any extension of that time that may be allowed, the liquidator shall report the failure to the court, which may thereupon discharge the order appointing the special manager.

(2) If the special manager fails to maintain his caution the liquidator shall report his failure to the court, which may thereupon remove the special manager and make such order as it thinks fit as to expenses.

(3) If an order is made under this Rule removing the special manager, or recalling the order appointing him, the court shall give directions as to whether any, and if so what, steps should be taken to appoint another special manager in his place.   **[1656]**

4.72. Accounting

(1) The special manager shall produce accounts containing details of his receipts and payments for the approval of the liquidator.

(2) The accounts shall be in respect of 3-month periods for the duration of the special manager's appointment (or for a lesser period if his appointment terminates less than 3 months from its date, or from the date to which the last accounts were made up).

(3) When the accounts have been approved, the special manager's receipts and payments shall be added to those of the liquidator.   **[1657]**

4.73. Termination of appointment

(1) The special manager's appointment terminates if the winding up petition is dismissed or, if a provisional liquidator having been appointed, he is discharged without a winding up order having been made.

(2) If the liquidator is of opinion that the employment of the special manager is no longer necessary or profitable for the company, he shall apply to the court for directions, and the court may order the special manager's appointment to be terminated.

(3) The liquidator shall make the same application if a resolution of the creditors is passed, requesting that the appointment be terminated.   **[1658]**

CHAPTER 11

PUBLIC EXAMINATION OF COMPANY OFFICERS AND OTHERS

4.74. Notice of order for public examination

Where the court orders the public examination of any person under section 133(1), then, unless the court otherwise directs, the liquidator shall give at least 14 days' notice of the time and place of the examination to the persons specified in paragraphs (*c*) to (*e*) of section 133(4) and the liquidator may, if he thinks fit, cause notice of the order to be given, by public advertisement in one or more newspapers circulating in the area of the principal place of business of the company, at least 14 days before the date fixed for the examination but there

shall be no such advertisement before at least 7 days have elapsed from the date
when the person to be examined was served with the order. **[1659]**

4.75. Order on request by creditors or contributories

(1) A request to the liquidator by a creditor or creditors or contributory or
contributories under section 133(2) shall be made in writing and be accompanied
by—

    (*a*) a list of the creditors (if any) concurring with the request and the
        amounts of their respective claims in the liquidation, or (as the case
        may be) of the contributories (if any) so concurring, with their
        respective values, and

    (*b*) from each creditor or contributory concurring, written confirmation
        of his concurrence.

(2) The request must specify the name of the proposed examinee, the
relationship which he has, or has had, to the company and the reasons why his
examination is requested.

(3) Before an application to the court is made on the request, the
requisitionists shall deposit with the liquidator such sum as the latter may
determine to be appropriate by way of caution for the expenses of the hearing
of a public examination, if ordered.

(4) Subject as follows, the liquidator shall, within 28 days of receiving the
request, make the application to the court required by section 133(2).

(5) If the liquidator is of opinion that the request is an unreasonable one in
the circumstances, he may apply to the court for an order relieving him from
the obligation to make the application required by that subsection.

(6) If the court so orders, and the application for the order was made ex
parte, notice of the order shall be given forthwith by the liquidator to the
requisitionists. If the application for an order is dismissed, the liquidator's
application under section 133(2) shall be made forthwith on conclusion of the
hearing of the application first mentioned.

(7) Where a public examination of the examinee has been ordered by the
court on a creditors' or contributories' requisition under this Rule the court may
order that the expenses of the examination are to be paid, as to a specified
proportion, out of the caution under paragraph (3), instead of out of the assets.
[1660]

CHAPTER 12

MISCELLANEOUS

4.76. Limitation

The provisions of section 8(5) and 22(8), as read with section 73(5), of the
Bankruptcy (Scotland) Act 1985 (presentation of petition or submission of claim
to bar effect of limitation of actions) shall apply in relation to the liquidation as
they apply in relation to a sequestration, subject to the modifications specified
in Rule 4.16(2) and to any other necessary modifications. **[1661]**

4.77. Dissolution after winding up

Where the court makes an order under section 204(5) or 205(5), the person on whose application the order was made shall deliver to the registrar of companies a copy of the order.   **[1662]**

CHAPTER 13

COMPANY WITH PROHIBITED NAME

4.78. Preliminary

The rules of this Chapter—

    (*a*) relate to the leave required under section 216 (restriction on re-use of name of company in insolvent liquidation) for a person to act as mentioned in section 216(3) in relation to a company with a prohibited name, and

    (*b*) prescribe the cases excepted from that provision, that is to say, those in which a person to whom the section applies may so act without that leave.   **[1663]**

4.79. Application for leave under section 216(3)

When considering an application for leave under section 216, the court may call on the liquidator, or any former liquidator, of the liquidating company for a report of the circumstances in which that company became insolvent, and the extent (if any) of the applicant's apparent responsibility for its doing so. **[1664]**

4.80. First excepted case

Where a company ("the successor company") acquires the whole, or substantially the whole, of the business of an insolvent company, under arrangements made by an insolvency practitioner acting as its liquidator, administrator or receiver, or as supervisor of a voluntary arrangement under Part I of the Act, the successor company may for the purposes of section 216 give notice under this Rule to the insolvent company's creditors.

    (2) To be effective, the notice must be given within 28 days from the completion of the arrangements to all creditors of the insolvent company of whose addresses the successor is aware in that period; and it must specify—

    (*a*) the name and registered number of the insolvent company and the circumstances in which its business has been acquired by the successor company,

    (*b*) the name which the successor company has assumed, or proposes to assume for the purpose of carrying on the business, if that name is or will be a prohibited name under section 216, and

    (*c*) any change of name which it has made, or proposes to make, for that purpose under section 28 of the Companies Act.

    (3) The notice may name a person to whom section 216 may apply as having been a director or shadow director of the insolvent company, and give particulars as to the nature and duration of that directorship, with a view to his being a director of the successor company or being otherwise associated with its management.

    (4) If the successor company has effectively given notice under this Rule to the insolvent company's creditors, a person who is so named in the notice may act in relation to the successor company in any of the ways mentioned in section

216(3), notwithstanding that he has not the leave of the court under that section. **[1665]**

4.81. Second excepted case

(1) In the circumstances specified below, a person to whom section 216 applies as having been a director or shadow director of the liquidating company may act in any of the ways mentioned in section 216(3), notwithstanding that he has not the leave of the court under that section.

(2) Those circumstances are that—

- (*a*) he applies to the court for leave, not later than 7 days from the date on which the company went into liquidation, and
- (*b*) leave is granted by the court not later than 6 weeks from that date.

[1666]

4.82. Third excepted case

The court's leave under section 216(3) is not required where the company there referred to, though known by a prohibited name within the meaning of the section,

- (*a*) has been known by that name for the whole of the period of 12 months ending with the day before the liquidating company went into liquidation, and
- (*b*) has not at any time in those 12 months been dormant within the meaning of section 252(5) of the Companies Act. **[1667]**

PART 5

CREDITORS' VOLUNTARY WINDING UP

5. Application of Part 4

The provisions of Part 4 shall apply in a creditors' voluntary winding up of a company as they apply in a winding up by the court subject to the modifications specified in Schedule 1 and to any other necessary modifications. **[1668]**

PART 6

MEMBERS' VOLUNTARY WINDING UP

6. Application of Part 4

The provisions of Part 4, which are specified in Schedule 2, shall apply in relation to a members' voluntary winding up of a company as they apply in a winding up by the court, subject to the modifications specified in Schedule 2 and to any other necessary modifications. **[1669]**

PART 7

PROVISIONS OF GENERAL APPLICATION

CHAPTER 1

MEETINGS

7.1. Scope of Chapter 1

This Chapter applies to any meetings held in insolvency proceedings other than meetings of a creditors' committee in administration or receivership, or of a liquidation committee.

(2) The Rules in this Chapter shall apply to any such meeting subject to any contrary provision in the Act or in the Rules, or to any direction of the court.

[1670]

7.2. Summoning of meetings

(1) In fixing the date, time and place for a meeting, the person summoning the meeting ("the convenor") shall have regard to the convenience of the persons who are to attend.

(2) Meetings shall in all cases be summoned for commencement between 10.00 and 16.00 hours on a business day, unless the court otherwise directs.

[1671]

7.3. Notice of meeting

(1) The convenor shall give not less than 21 days' notice of the date, time and place of the meeting to every person known to him as being entitled to attend the meeting.

(2) In paragraph (1), for the reference to 21 days, there shall be substituted a reference to 14 days in the following cases:—

    (*a*) any meeting of the company or of its creditors summoned under section 3 (to consider directors' proposals for voluntary arrangement);

    (*b*) a meeting of the creditors under section 23(1)(*b*) or 25(2)(*b*) (to consider administrator's proposals or proposed revisions); and

    (*c*) a meeting of creditors under section 67(2) (meeting of unsecured creditors in receivership).

(3) The convenor may also publish notice of the date, time and place of the meeting in a newspaper circulating in the area of the principal place of business of the company or in such other newspaper as he thinks most appropriate for ensuring that it comes to the notice of the persons who are entitled to attend the meeting. In the case of a creditors' meeting summoned by the administrator under section 23(1)(*b*), the administrator shall publish such a notice.

(4) Any notice under this Rule shall state—

    (*a*) the purpose of the meeting;

    (*b*) the persons who are entitled to attend and vote at the meeting;

    (*c*) the effects of Rule 7.9 or, as the case may be, 7.10 (Entitlement to Vote) and of the relevant provisions of Rule 7.12 (Resolutions);

    (*d*) in the case of a meeting of creditors or contributories, that proxies may be lodged at or before the meeting and the place where they may be lodged; and

    (*e*) in the case of a meeting of creditors, that claims may be lodged by those who have not already done so at or before the meeting and the place where they may be lodged.

Where a meeting of creditors is summoned specially for the purpose of removing the liquidator in accordance with section 171(2) or 172(2), or of receiving his resignation under Rule 4.28, the notice summoning it shall also include the information required by Rule 4.23(2) or, as the case may be, 4.28(2).

(5) With the notice given under paragraph (1), the convenor shall also send out a proxy form.

(6) In the case of any meeting of creditors or contributories, the court may order that notice of the meeting be given by public advertisement in such form

as may be specified in the order and not by individual notice to the persons concerned. In considering whether to make such an order, the court shall have regard to the cost of the public advertisement, to the amount of the assets available and to the extent of the interest of creditors or contributories or any particular class of either.   **[1672]**

7.4. Additional notices in certain cases

(1) This Rule applies where a company goes, or proposes to go, into liquidation and it is—

   (*a*) a recognised bank or licensed institution within the meaning of the Banking Act 1979, or
   (*b*) an institution to which sections 16 and 18 of that Act apply as if it were a licensed institution.

(2) Notice of any meeting of the company at which it is intended to propose a resolution for its voluntary winding up shall be given by the directors to the Bank of England ("the Bank") and to the Deposit Protection Board ("the Board") as such notice is given to members of the company.

(3) Where a creditors' meeting is summoned by the liquidator under section 95 or 98, the same notice of meeting must be given to the Bank and Board as is given to the creditors under this Chapter.

(4) Where the company is being wound up by the court, notice of the first meetings of creditors and contributories within the meaning of Rule 4.12 shall be given to the Bank and the Board by the liquidator.

(5) Where in any winding up a meeting of creditors or contributories is summoned for the purpose of—

   (*a*) receiving the liquidator's resignation or
   (*b*) removing the liquidator, or
   (*c*) appointing a new liquidator,

the person summoning the meeting and giving notice of it shall also give notice to the Bank and the Board.

(6) The Board is entitled to be represented at any meeting of which it is required by this Rule to be given notice; and Schedule 3 has effect with respect to the voting rights of the Board at such a meeting.   **[1673]**

7.5. Chairman of meetings

(1) The chairman at any meeting of creditors in insolvency proceedings shall be the responsible practitioner, or a person nominated by him in writing.

(2) A person nominated under this Rule must be either—

   (*a*) a person who is qualified to act as an insolvency practitioner in relation to the company, or
   (*b*) an employee of the administrator, receiver or liquidator, as the case may be, or his firm who is experienced in insolvency matters.

(3) This Rule also applies to meetings of contributories in a liquidation.

(4) At the first meeting of creditors or contributories in a winding up by the court, the interim liquidator shall be the chairman except that, where a resolution is proposed to appoint the interim liquidator to be the liquidator, another person may be elected to act as chairman for the purpose of choosing the liquidator.

(5) The Rule is subject to Rule 4.23(3) (meeting for removal of liquidator).

[1674]

7.6. Meetings requisitioned

(1) Subject to paragraph (8), this Rule applies to any request by a creditor or creditors for a meeting of creditors—

    (*a*) to an administrator under section 17(3), or

    (*b*) to a liquidator under section 142(3), 171(3) or 172(3)

or under any other provision of the Act or the Rules.

(2) Any such request shall be accompanied by—

    (*a*) a list of any creditors concurring with the request, showing the amounts of the respective claims against the company of the creditor making the request and the concurring creditors;

    (*b*) from each creditor concurring, written confirmation of his concurrence; and

    (*c*) a statement of the purpose of the proposed meeting.

(3) If the administrator or, as the case may be, the liquidator considers the request to be properly made in accordance with the Act or the Rules, he shall summon a meeting of the creditors to be held on a date not more than 35 days from the date of his receipt of the request.

(4) Expenses of summoning and holding a meeting under this Rule shall be paid by the creditor making the request, who shall deposit with the administrator caution for their payment.

(5) The sum to be deposited shall be such as the administrator or, as the case may be, the liquidator may determine and he shall not act without the deposit having been made.

(6) The meeting may resolve that the expenses of summoning and holding it are to be payable out of the assets of the company as an expense of the administration or, as the case may be, the liquidation.

(7) To the extent that any caution deposited under this Rule is not required for the payment of expenses of summoning and holding the meeting, it shall be repaid to the person or persons who made it.

(8) This Rule applies to requests by a contributory or contributories for a meeting of contributories, with the modification that, for the reference in paragraph (2) to the creditors' respective claims, there shall be substituted a reference to the contributories' respective values (being the amounts for which they may vote at any meeting).

(9) This Rule is without prejudice to the powers of the court under Rule 4.67(2) (voluntary winding up succeeded by winding up by the court).   **[1675]**

7.7. Quorum

(1) Subject to the next paragraph, a quorum is—

    (*a*) in the case of a creditors' meeting, at least one creditor entitled to vote;

    (*b*) in the case of a meeting of contributories, at least 2 contributories so entitled, or all the contributories, if their number does not exceed 2.

(2) For the purposes of this Rule, the reference to the creditor or contributories necessary to constitute a quorum is not confined to those persons present or duly represented under section 375 of the Companies Act but includes those represented by proxy by any person (including the chairman). **[1676]**

7.8. Adjournment

(1) This Rule applies to meetings of creditors and to meetings of contributories.

(2) If, within a period of 30 minutes from the time appointed for the commencement of a meeting, a quorum is not present, then, unless the chairman otherwise decides, the meeting shall be adjourned to the same time and place in the following week or, if that is not a business day, to the business day immediately following.

(3) In the course of any meeting, the chairman may, in his discretion, and shall, if the meeting so resolves, adjourn it to such date, time and place as seems to him to be appropriate in the circumstances.

(4) Paragraph (3) is subject to Rule 4.23(3) where the liquidator or his nominee is chairman and a resolution has been proposed for the liquidator's removal.

(5) An adjournment under paragraph (1) or (2) shall not be for a period of more than 21 days.

(6) Where a meeting is adjourned, any proxies given for the original meeting may be used at the adjourned meeting. **[1677]**

7.9. Entitlement to vote (creditors)

(1) This Rule applies to a creditors' meeting in any insolvency proceedings.

(2) A creditor is entitled to vote at any meeting if he has submitted his claim to the responsible insolvency practitioner and his claim has been accepted in whole or in part.

(3) Chapter 5 of Part 4 (claims in liquidation) shall apply for the purpose of determining a creditor's entitlement to vote at any creditors' meeting in any insolvency proceedings as it applies for the purpose of determining a creditor's entitlement to vote at a meeting of creditors in a liquidation, subject to the modifications specified in the following paragraphs and to any other necessary modification.

(4) For any reference in the said Chapter 5, or in any provision of the Bankruptcy Act as applied by Rule 4.16(1), to—

(a) the liquidator, there shall be substituted a reference to the supervisor, administrator or receiver, as the case may be;
(b) the liquidation, there shall be substituted a reference to the voluntary arrangement, administration or receivership as the case may be;
(c) the date of commencement of winding up, there shall be substituted a reference—

(i) in the case of a meeting in a voluntary arrangement, to the date of the meeting or, where the company is being wound up or is subject to an administration order, the date of its going into liquidation or, as the case may be, of the administration order; and

      (ii) in the case of a meeting in the administration or receivership, to the date of the administration order or, as the case may be, the date of appointment of the receiver;

(5) In the application to meetings of creditors other than in liquidation proceedings of Schedule 1 to the Bankruptcy Act, paragraph 5(2) and (3) (secured creditors) shall not apply.

(6) This Rule is subject to Rule 7.4(6) and Schedule 3.   **[1678]**

7.10. Entitlement to vote (members and contributories)

(1) Members of a company or contributories at their meetings shall vote according to their rights attaching to their shares respectively in accordance with the articles of association.

(2) In the case of a meeting of members of the company in a voluntary arrangement, where no voting rights attach to a member's share, he is nevertheless entitled to vote either for or against the proposal or any modification of it.

(3) Reference in this Rule to a person's share include any other interests which he may have as a member of the company.   **[1679]**

7.11. Chairman of meeting as proxy holder

(1) Where the chairman at a meeting of creditors or contributories holds a proxy which requires him to vote for a particular resolution and no other person proposes that resolution—

    (a) he shall propose it himself, unless he considers that there is good reason for not doing so, and

    (b) if he does not propose it, he shall forthwith after the meeting notify the person who granted him the proxy of the reason why he did not do so.

(2) At any meeting in a voluntary arrangement, the chairman shall not, by virtue of any proxy by him, vote to increase or reduce the amount of the remuneration or expenses of the nominee or the supervisor of the proposed arrangement, unless the proxy specifically directs him to vote in that way.

[1680]

7.12. Resolutions

(1) Subject to any contrary provision in the Act or the Rules, at any meeting of creditors, contributories or members of a company, a resolution is passed when a majority in value of those voting, in person or by proxy, have voted in favour of it.

(2) In a voluntary arrangement, at a creditors' meeting for any resolution to pass approving any proposal or modification, there must be at least three quarters in value of the creditors present or represented and voting, in person or by proxy, in favour of the resolution.

(3) In a liquidation, in the case of a resolution for the appointment of a liquidator—

    (a) if, on any vote, there are two nominees for appointment, the person for whom a majority in value has voted shall be appointed;

(*b*) if there are three or more nominees, and one of them has a clear majority over both or all the others together, that one is appointed; and

(*c*) in any other case, the chairman of the meeting shall continue to take votes (disregarding at each vote any nominee who has withdrawn and, if no nominee has withdrawn, the nominee who obtained the least support last time), until a clear majority is obtained for any one nominee.

The chairman may, at any time, put to the meeting a resolution for the joint appointment of any two or more nominees.

(4) Where a resolution is proposed which affects a person in respect of his remuneration or conduct as a responsible insolvency practitioner, the vote of that person, or of his firm or of any partner or employee of his shall not be reckoned in the majority required for passing the resolution. This paragraph applies with respect to a vote given by a person either as creditor or contributory or member or as proxy for a creditor, contributory, or member. **[1681]**

7.13. Report of meeting

(1) The chairman at any meeting shall cause a report to be made of the proceedings at the meeting which shall be signed by him.

(2) The report of the meeting shall include—

(*a*) a list of all the creditors or, as the case may be, contributories who attended the meeting, either in person or by proxy;

(*b*) a copy of every resolution passed; and

(*c*) if the meeting established a creditors' committee or a liquidation committee, as the case may be, a list of the names and addresses of those elected to be members of the committee.

(3) The chairman shall keep a copy of the report of the meeting as part of the sederunt book in the insolvency proceedings. **[1682]**

CHAPTER 2

PROXIES AND COMPANY REPRESENTATION

7.14. Definition of "proxy"

(1) For the purposes of the Rules, a person ("the principal") may authorise another person ("the proxy-holder") to attend, speak and vote as his representative at meetings of creditors or contributories or of the company in insolvency proceedings, and any such authority is referred to as a proxy.

(2) A proxy may be given either generally for all meetings in insolvency proceedings or specifically for any meeting or class of meetings.

(3) Only one proxy may be given by the principal for any one meeting; and it may only be given to one person, being an individual aged 18 or over. The principal may nevertheless nominate one or more other such persons to be proxy-holder in the alternative in the order in which they are named in the proxy.

(4) Without prejudice to the generality of paragraph (3), a proxy, for a particular meeting may be given to whoever is to be the chairman of the meeting.

(5) A proxy may require the holder to vote on behalf of the principal on matters arising for determination at any meeting, or to abstain, either as directed or in accordance with the holder's own discretion; and it may authorise or require the holder to propose, in the principal's name, a resolution to be voted on by the meeting.   **[1683]**

7.15. Form of proxy

(1) With every notice summoning a meeting of creditors or contributories or of the company in insolvency proceedings there shall be sent out forms of proxy.

(2) A form of proxy shall not be sent out with the name or description of any person inserted in it.

(3) A proxy shall be in the form sent out with the notice summoning the meeting or in a form substantially to the same effect.

(4) A form of proxy shall be filled out and signed by the principal, or by some person acting under his authority and, where it is signed by someone other than the principal, the nature of his authority shall be stated on the form. **[1684]**

7.16. Use of proxy at meeting

(1) A proxy given for a particular meeting may be used at any adjournment of that meeting.

(2) A proxy may be lodged at or before the meeting at which it is to be used.

(3) Where the responsible insolvency practitioner holds proxies to be used by him as chairman of the meeting, and some other person acts as chairman, the other person may use the insolvency practitioner's proxies as if he were himself proxy-holder.   **[1685]**

7.17. Retention of proxies

(1) Proxies used for voting at any meeting shall be retained by the chairman of the meeting.

(2) The chairman shall deliver the proxies forthwith after the meeting to the responsible insolvency practitioner (where he was not the chairman).

(3) The responsible insolvency practitioner shall retain all proxies in the sederunt book.   **[1686]**

7.18. Right of inspection

(1) The responsible insolvency practitioner shall, so long as proxies lodged with him are in his hands, allow them to be inspected at all reasonable times on any business day, by—
   (a) the creditors, in the case of proxies used at a meeting of creditors,
   (b) a company's members or contributories, in the case of proxies used at a meeting of the company or of its contributories.

(2) The reference in paragraph (1) to creditors is—
   (a) in the case of a company in liquidation, those creditors whose claims have been accepted in whole or in part, and
   (b) in any other case, persons who have submitted in writing a claim to be creditors of the company concerned,

but in neither case does it include a person whose claim has been wholly rejected for purposes of voting, dividend or otherwise.

(3) The right of inspection given by this Rule is also exercisable, in the case of an insolvent company, by its directors.

(4) Any person attending a meeting in insolvency proceedings is entitled immediately before or in the course of the meeting, to inspect proxies and associated documents to be used in connection with that meeting. **[1687]**

7.19. Proxy-holder with financial interest

(1) A proxy-holder shall not vote in favour of any resolution which would directly or indirectly place him, or any associate of his, in a position to receive any remuneration out of the insolvent estate, unless the proxy specifically directs him to vote in that way.

(2) This Rule applies also to any person acting as chairman of a meeting and using proxies in that capacity; and in its application to him, the proxy-holder is deemed an associate of his. **[1688]**

7.20. Representation of corporations

(1) Where a person is authorised under section 375 of the Companies Act to represent a corporation at a meeting of creditors or contributories, he shall produce to the chairman of the meeting a copy of the resolution from which he derives his authority.

(2) The copy resolution must be executed in accordance with the provisions of section 36(3) of the Companies Act, or certified by the secretary or a director of the corporation to be a true copy. **[1689]**

CHAPTER 3
MISCELLANEOUS

7.21. Giving of notices, etc

(1) All notices required or authorised by or under the Act or the Rules to be given, sent or delivered must be in writing, unless it is otherwise provided, or the court allows the notice to be sent or given in some other way.

(2) Any reference in the Rules to giving, sending or delivering a notice or any such document means, without prejudice to any other way and unless it is otherwise provided, that the notice or document may be sent by post, and that, subject to Rule 7.22, any form of post may be used. Personal service of the notice or document is permissible in all cases.

(3) Where under the Act or the Rules a notice or other document is required or authorised to be given, sent or delivered by a person ("the sender") to another ("the recipient"), it may be given, sent or delivered by any person duly authorised by the sender to do so to any person duly authorised by the recipient to receive or accept it.

(4) Where two or more persons are acting jointly as the responsible insolvency practitioner in any proceedings, the giving, sending or delivering of

a notice or document to one of them is to be treated as the giving, sending or delivering of a notice or document to each or all.   **[1690]**

7.22. Sending by post

(1) For a document to be properly sent by post, it must be contained in an envelope addressed to the person to whom it is to be sent, and pre-paid for either first or second class post.

(2) Where first class post is used, the document is to be deemed to be received on the second business day after the date of posting, unless the contrary is shown.

(3) Where second class post is used, the document is to be deemed to be received on the fourth business day after the date of posting, unless the contrary is shown.   **[1691]**

7.23. Certificate of giving notice, etc

(1) Where in any proceedings a notice or document is required to be given, sent or delivered by the responsible insolvency practitioner, the date of giving, sending or delivery of it may be proved by means of a certificate signed by him or on his behalf by his solicitor, or a partner or an employee of either of them, that the notice or document was duly given, posted or otherwise sent, or delivered on the date stated in the certificate.

(2) In the case of a notice or document to be given, sent or delivered by a person other than the responsible insolvency practitioner, the date of giving, sending or delivery of it may be proved by means of a certificate by that person that he gave, posted or otherwise sent or delivered the notice or document on the date stated in the certificate, or that he instructed another person (naming him) to do so.

(3) A certificate under this Rule may be endorsed on a copy of the notice to which it relates.

(4) A certificate purporting to be signed by or on behalf of the responsible insolvency practitioner, or by the person mentioned in paragraph (2), shall be deemed, unless the contrary is shown, to be sufficient evidence of the matters stated therein.   **[1692]**

7.24. Validity of proceedings

Where in accordance with the Act or the Rules a meeting of creditors or other persons is summoned by notice, the meeting is presumed to have been duly summoned and held, notwithstanding that not all those to whom the notice is to be given have received it.   **[1693]**

7.25. Evidence of proceedings at meetings

A report of proceedings at a meeting of the company or of the company's creditors or contributories in any insolvency proceedings, which is signed by a person describing himself as the chairman of that meeting, shall be deemed, unless the contrary is shown, to be sufficient evidence of the matters contained in that report.   **[1694]**

7.26. Right to list of creditors and copy documents

(1) Paragraph (2) applies to—

    (*a*) proceedings under Part II of the Act (company administration), and
    (*b*) proceedings in a creditors' voluntary winding up, or a winding up by the court.

(2) Subject to Rule 7.27, in any such proceedings, a creditor who has the right to inspect documents also has the right to require the responsible insolvency practitioner to furnish him with a list of the company's creditors and the amounts of their respective debts.

(3) Subject to Rule 7.27, where a person has the right to inspect documents, the right includes that of taking copies of those documents, on payment of the appropriate fee.

(4) In this Rule, the appropriate fee means 15 pence per A4 or A5 page and 30 pence per A3 page. **[1695]**

7.27. Confidentiality of documents

(1) Where, in any insolvency proceedings, the responsible insolvency practitioner considers, in the case of a document forming part of the records of those proceedings—

    (*a*) that it should be treated as confidential, or
    (*b*) that it is of such a nature that its disclosure would be calculated to be injurious to the interests of the company's creditors or, in the case of the winding up of a company, its members or the contributories in its winding up,

he may decline to allow it to be inspected by a person who would otherwise be entitled to inspect it.

(2) The persons who may be refused the right to inspect documents under this Rule by the responsible insolvency practitioner include the members of a creditors' committee in administration or in receivership, or of a liquidation committee.

(3) Where under this Rule the responsible insolvency practitioner refuses inspection of a document, the person who made that request may apply to the court for an order to overrule the refusal and the court may either overrule it altogether, or sustain it, either unconditionally or subject to such conditions, if any, as it thinks fit to impose. **[1696]**

7.28. Insolvency practitioner's caution

(1) Wherever under the Rules any person has to appoint, or certify the appointment of, an insolvency practitioner to any office, he is under a duty to satisfy himself that the person appointed or to be appointed has caution for the proper performance of his functions.

(2) It is the duty—

    (*a*) of the creditors' committee in administration or in receivership,
    (*b*) of the liquidation committee in companies winding up, and

(c) of any committee of creditors established for the purposes of a voluntary arrangement under Part I of the Act,

to review from time to time the adequacy of the responsible insolvency practitioner's caution.

(3) In any insolvency proceedings the cost of the responsible insolvency practitioner's caution shall be paid as an expense of the proceedings.   **[1697]**

7.29. Punishment of offences

(1) Schedule 4 has effect with respect to the way in which contraventions of the Rules are punishable on conviction.

(2) In that Schedule—

(a) the first column specifies the provision of the Rules which creates an offence;

(b) in relation to each such offence, the second column describes the general nature of the offence;

(c) the third column indicates its mode of trial, that is to say whether the offence is punishable on conviction on indictment, or on summary conviction, or either in the one way or the other;

(d) the fourth column shows the maximum punishment by way of fine or imprisonment which may be imposed on a person convicted of the offence in the mode of trial specified in relation to it in the third column (that is to say, on indictment or summarily), a reference to a period of years or months being to a maximum term of imprisonment of that duration; and

(e) the fifth column shows (in relation to an offence for which there is an entry in that column) that a person convicted of the offence after continued contravention is liable to a daily default fine; that is to say, he is liable on a second or subsequent conviction of the offence to the fine specified in that column for each day on which the contravention is continued (instead of the penalty specified for the offence in the fourth column of that Schedule).

(3) Section 431 (summary proceedings), as it applies to Scotland, has effect in relation to offences under the Rules as to offences under the Act.   **[1698]**

7.30. Forms for use in insolvency proceedings

The forms contained in Schedule 5, with such variations as circumstances require, are the forms to be used for the purposes of the provisions of the Act or the Rules which are referred to in those forms.   **[1699]**

7.31. Fees, expenses, etc

All fees, costs, charges and other expenses incurred in the course of insolvency proceedings are to be regarded as expenses of those proceedings.   **[1700]**

7.32. Power of court to cure defects in procedure

(1) Section 63 of the Bankruptcy Act (power of court to cure defects in procedure) shall apply in relation to any insolvency proceedings as it applies in relation to sequestration, subject to the modifications specified in paragraph (2) and to any other necessary modifications.

(2) For any reference in the said section 63 to any expression in column 1

below, there shall be substituted a reference to the expression in column 2 opposite thereto—

Column 1	Column 2
This Act or any regulations made under it	The Act or the Rules
Permanent trustee	Responsible insolvency practitioner
Sequestration process	Insolvency proceedings
Debtor	Company
Sheriff	The court
Person who would be eligible to be elected under section 24 of this Act	Person who would be eligible to act as a responsible insolvency practitioner

[1701]

7.33. Sederunt book

(1) The responsible insolvency practitioner shall maintain a sederunt book during his term of office for the purpose of providing an accurate record of the administration of each insolvency proceedings.

(2) Without prejudice to the generality of the above paragraph, there shall be inserted in the sederunt book a copy of anything required to be recorded in it by any provision of the Act or of the Rules.

(3) The responsible insolvency practitioner shall make the sederunt book available for inspection at all reasonable hours by any interested person.

(4) Any entry in the sederunt book shall be sufficient evidence of the facts stated therein, except where it is founded on by the responsible insolvency practitioner in his own interest. **[1702]**

SCHEDULE 1

Rule 5

MODIFICATIONS OF PART 4 IN RELATION TO CREDITORS' VOLUNTARY WINDING UP

1. The following paragraphs describe the modifications to be made to the provisions of Part 4 in their application by Rule 5 to a creditors' voluntary winding up of a company.

General

2. Any reference, in any provision in Part 4, which is applied to a creditors' voluntary winding up, to any other Rule is a reference to that Rule as so applied. .

Chapter 1 (Provisional liquidator)

3. This Chapter shall not apply.

Chapter 2 (Statement of affairs)

Rules 4.7 and 4.8

4. For these Rules, there shall be substituted the following—

"**4.7.**—(1) This Rule applies with respect to the statement of affairs made out by the liquidator under section 95(3) (or as the case may be) by the directors under section 99(1).

(2) The statement of affairs shall be in the form required by Rule 7.30 and Schedule 5.

(3) Where the statement of affairs is made out by the directors under section 99(1), it shall be sent by them to the liquidator, when appointed.

(4) The liquidator shall insert a copy of the statement of affairs made out under this Rule in the sederunt book.".

Rule 4.9

5. For this Rule, there shall substituted—

"*Expenses of statement of affairs*

4.9.—(1) Payment may be made as an expense of the liquidation, either before or after the commencement of the winding up, of any reasonable and necessary expenses of preparing the statement of affairs under section 99.

(2) Where such a payment is made before the commencement of the winding up, the director presiding at the creditors' meeting held under section 98 shall inform the meeting of the amount of the payment and the identity of the person to whom it was made.

(3) The liquidator appointed under section 100 may make such a payment (subject to the next paragraph); but if there is a liquidation committee, he must give the committee at least 7 days' notice of his intention to make it.

(4) Such a payment shall not be made by the liquidator to himself, or to any associate of his, otherwise than with the approval of the liquidation committee, the creditors, or the court.

(5) This Rule is without prejudice to the powers of the court under Rule 4.67(2) (voluntary winding up succeeded by winding up by the court).".

Chapter 3 (Information)
Rule 4.10

6. For this Rule, there shall be substituted the following—

"*Information to creditors and contributories*

4.10. The liquidator shall, within 28 days of a meeting held under section 95 or 98, send to creditors and contributories of the company—

    (*a*) a copy or summary of the statement of affairs, and
    (*b*) a report of the proceedings at the meeting.".

Chapter 4 (Meetings of creditors and contributories)
Rule 4.12

7. This Rule shall not apply.

Rule 4.14

8. After this Rule, there shall be inserted the following—

"*Expenses of meeting under section 98*

4.14A.—(1) Payment may be made out of the company's assets as an expense of the liquidation, either before or after the commencement of the winding up, of any reasonable and necessary expenses incurred in connection with the summoning, advertisement and holding of a creditors' meeting under section 98.

(2) Where any such payments are made before the commencement of the winding up, the director presiding at the creditors' meeting shall inform the meeting of their amount and the identity of the persons to whom they were made.

(3) The liquidator appointed under section 100 may make such a payment (subject to the next paragraph); but if there is a liquidation committee, he must give the committee at least 7 days' notice of his intention to make the payment.

(4) Such a payment shall not be made by the liquidator to himself, or to any associate of his, otherwise than with the approval of the liquidation committee, the creditors, or the court.

(5) This Rule is without prejudice to the powers of the court under Rule 4.67(2) (voluntary winding up succeeded by winding up by the court).".

Rule 4.15

9. In paragraph (5), for the reference to section 129, there shall be substituted a reference to section 86.

Rule 4.16

10. In paragraph (2), for the reference to section 129, there shall be substituted a reference to section 86.

Chapter 6 (The liquidator)

Rule 4.18

11.—(1) For paragraph (1), there shall be substituted the following—

"(1) This Rule applies where the liquidator is appointed by the court under section 100(3) or 108.".

(2) Paragraphs 4(*a*) and 5 shall be deleted.

Rule 4.19

12.—(1) For paragraphs (1) to (3) there shall be substituted the following—

"(1) This Rule applies where a person is nominated for appointment as liquidator under section 100(1) either by a meeting of the creditors or by a meeting of the company.

(2) Subject as follows, the chairman of the meeting shall certify the appointment, but not unless and until the person to be appointed has provided him with a written statement to the effect that he is an insolvency practitioner, duly qualified under the Act to be the liquidator and that he consents so to act. The liquidator's appointment is effective from the date of the certificate.

(3) The chairman shall forthwith send the certificate to the liquidator, who shall keep it in the sederunt book.".

(2) Paragraphs 4(*a*) and (5) shall not apply.

(3) In paragraph (6), for the reference to paragraphs (4) and (5), there shall be substituted a reference to paragraphs (3) and (4).

Rule 4.23

13.—(1) In paragraph (1), for the references to section 172(2) and (3), there shall be substituted a reference to section 171(2) and (3).

(2) In paragraph (2), for the references to section 172(2) and 174(4)(*a*) or (*b*), there shall be substituted a reference to section 171(2) and 173(2)(*a*) or (*b*).

Rule 4.24

14. In this Rule the references to the court shall be deleted.

Rule 4.25

15. In paragraph (1), for the reference to section 174(4)(*a*), there shall be substituted a reference to section 173(2)(*a*), and the reference to the court shall be deleted.

Rule 4.28

16.—(1) In paragraph (1), for the reference to section 172(6), there shall be substituted a reference to section 171(5).

(2) In paragraph (2), for the reference to section 174(4)(c), there shall be substituted a reference to section 173(2)(c).

Rule 4.29

17. In this Rule for paragraph (3) there shall be substituted the following—

"(3) The liquidator, whose resignation is accepted, shall forthwith after the meeting give notice of his resignation to the registrar of companies as required by section 171(5).".

Rule 4.31

18. For this Rule, substitute the following—

"Final Meeting

4.31.—(1) The liquidator shall give at least 28 days' notice of the final meeting of creditors to be held under section 106. The notice shall be sent to all creditors whose claims in the liquidation have been accepted.

(2) At the final meeting, the creditors may question the liquidator with respect to any matter contained in the account required under that section and may resolve against the liquidator having his release.

(3) The liquidator shall, within 7 days of the meeting, give notice to the registrar of companies under section 171(6) that the final meeting has been held. The notice shall state whether or not he has been released.

(4) If the creditors at the final meeting have not resolved against the liquidator having his release, he is released in terms of section 173(2)(e)(ii) when he vacates office under section 171(6). If they have so resolved, he must obtain his release from the Accountant of Court and Rule 4.25(2) and (3) shall apply accordingly.".

NOTES
Para (3): See Sch 5, form 4.17 (Scot).

Rule 4.36

19. For the reference to the court there shall be substituted a reference to the liquidation committee (if any) or a member of that committee.

Rule 4.37

20.—(1) In paragraph (2), the reference to the court shall be omitted.

(2) At the end of this Rule, there shall be inserted the following—

"Vacation of office on making of winding up order

4.37A. Where the liquidator vacates office in consequence of the court making a winding up order against the company, Rule 4.25(2) and (3) apply as regards the liquidator obtaining his release, as if he had been removed by the court.".

Chapter 7 (The liquidation committee)

Rule 4.40

21. This Rule shall not apply.

Rule 4.41

21. For paragraph (1) there shall be substituted the following—

"(1) The committee must have at least 3 members before it can be established.".

Rule 4.43

23. This Rule shall not apply.

Rule 4.47

24. For this Rule, there shall be substituted the following—

"*Quorum*

4.47. A meeting of the committee is duly constituted if due notice of it has been given to all the members and at least 2 members are present or represented.".

Rule 4.53

25. After paragraph (4) there shall be inserted the following—

"(4A) Where the contributories made an appointment under paragraph (4), the creditor members of the committee may, if they think fit, resolve that the person appointed ought not to be a member of the committee; and—

(a) that person is not then, unless the court otherwise directs, qualified to act as a member of the committee, and

(b) on any application to the court for a direction under this paragraph the court may, if it thinks fit, appoint another person (being a contributory) to fill the vacancy on the committee.".

Rule 4.54

26. Paragraphs (2) and (3) shall not apply.

Rule 4.55

27. In paragraphs (3) and (4), the word "creditor" shall be omitted.

Chapter 8 (The liquidation committee where winding up follows immediately on administration)

28. This Chapter shall not apply.

Chapter 9 (Distribution of company's assets by liquidator)

Rule 4.66

29.—(1) At the beginning of paragraph (1), insert the following—

"Subject to the provision of section 107,".

(2) In paragraph (1)(b), for the reference to section 129, there shall be substituted a reference to section 86.

Chapter 10 (Special manager)

Rule 4.70

30. For paragraph (5), there shall be substituted the following—

"(5) The cost of finding caution shall be paid in the first instance by the special manager; but he is entitled to be reimbursed out of the assets as an expense of the liquidation.".

Rule 4.71

31. Paragraph (1) shall not apply.

Chapter 11 (Public examination of company officers and others)

32. This Chapter shall not apply.

Chapter 12 (Miscellaneous)
Rule 4.77

33. This Rule shall not apply. **[1703]**

SCHEDULE 2

Rule 6

APPLICATION OF PART 4 IN RELATION TO MEMBERS' VOLUNTARY WINDING UP

1. The following paragraphs describe the provisions of Part 4 which, subject to the modifications set out in those paragraphs and any other necessary modifications, apply to a members' voluntary winding up.

General

2. Any reference in any provision of Part 4, which is applied to a members' voluntary winding up, to any other Rule is a reference to that Rule as so applied.

Chapter 3 (Information)
Rule 4.11

3. This Rule shall apply.

Chapter 6 (The liquidator)
Rule 4.18

4.—(1) This Rule shall apply subject to the following modifications.

(2) For paragraph (1), there shall be substituted the following—

"(1) This Rule applies where the liquidator is appointed by the court under section 108.".

(3) Paragraphs 4 and 5 shall be deleted.

Rule 4.19

5.—(1) This Rule shall apply subject to the following modifications.

(2) For paragraphs (1) to (3) there shall be substituted the following—

"(1) This Rule applies where the liquidator is appointed by a meeting of the company.

(2) Subject as follows, the chairman of the meeting shall certify the appointment, but not unless and until the person to be appointed has provided him with a written statement to the effect that he is an insolvency practitioner, duly qualified under the Act to be the liquidator and that he consents so to act. The liquidator's appointment is effective from the date of the certificate.

(3) The chairman shall forthwith send the certificate to the liquidator, who shall keep it in the sederunt book.".

NOTES
Paras (2), (3): See Sch 5, form 4.8 (Scot).

(3) Paragraphs 4(*a*), (5) and (6) shall be deleted.

Rules 4.20 to 4.22

6. These Rules shall apply.

Rule 4.26

7. This Rule shall apply except that in paragraph (1) for the reference to "creditors" there shall be substituted the words "the company".

Rule 4.27

8. This Rule shall apply.

Rule 4.28

9.—(1) This Rule shall apply subject to the following modifications.

(2) In paragraph (1)—

  (*a*) for the reference to section 172(6), there shall be substituted a reference to section 171(5), and

  (*b*) for the reference to a meeting of creditors, there shall be substituted a reference to a meeting of the company.

(3) In paragraph (2)—

  (*a*) for reference to section 174(4)(*c*) there shall be substituted a reference to section 173(2)(*c*), and

  (*b*) for the reference to Rule 4.29(4), there shall be substituted a reference to Rule 4.28A.

(4) After paragraph (4) there shall be inserted the following paragraphs—

"(5) The notice of the liquidator's resignation required by section 171(5) shall be given by him to the registrar of companies forthwith after the meeting.

(6) Where a new liquidator is appointed in place of the one who has resigned, the former shall, in giving notice of his appointment, state that his predecessor has resigned and whether he has been released.".

(5) After this Rule, there shall be inserted the following Rule—

"*Release of resigning or removed liquidator*

4.28A.—(1) Where the liquidator resigns, he has his release from the date on which he gives notice of his resignation to the registrar of companies.

(2) Where the liquidator is removed by a meeting of the company, he shall forthwith give notice to the registrar of companies of his ceasing to act.

(3) Where the liquidator is removed by the court, he must apply to the Accountant of Court for his release.

(4) Where the Accountant of Court gives the release, he shall certify it accordingly, and send the certificate to the registrar of companies.

(5) A copy of the certificate shall be sent by the Accountant of Court to the former liquidator, whose release is effective from the date of the certificate.".

Rule 4.36

10. This Rule shall apply, except that for any reference to the court, there shall be substituted a reference to the directors of the company or any one of them.

Rule 4.37

11.—(1) This Rule shall apply subject to the following modifications.

(2) In paragraph (2), the reference to the court shall be omitted.

(3) For paragraph (3), there shall be substituted the following—

"(3) Rule 4.28A applies as regards the liquidator obtaining his release, as if he had been removed by the court.".

(4) At the end of this Rule, there shall be inserted the following—

"*Vacation of office on making of winding up order*

4.37A. Where the liquidator vacates office in consequence of the court making a winding up order against the company, Rule 4.28A applies as regards the liquidator obtaining his release, as if he had been removed by the court.".

Rule 4.38

12. This Rule shall apply.

Rule 4.39

13. This Rule shall apply.

Chapter 10 (Special manager)

14.—(1) This Chapter shall apply subject to the following modifications.

(2) In Rule 4.70 for paragraph (5), there shall be substituted the following—

"(5) The cost of finding caution shall be paid in the first instance by the special manager; but he is entitled to be reimbursed out of the assets as an expense of the liquidation.".

(3) In Rule 4.71, paragraph (1) shall not apply.   **[1704]**

SCHEDULE 3

Rule 7.4(6)

DEPOSIT PROTECTION BOARD'S VOTING RIGHTS

1. This Schedule applies where Rule 7.4 does.

2. In relation to any meeting at which the Deposit Protection Board is under Rule 7.4 entitled to be represented, the Board may submit in the liquidation, instead of a claim, a written statement of voting rights ("the statement").

3. The statement shall contain details of—

   (a) the names of creditors of the company in respect of whom an obligation of the Board has arisen or may reasonably be expected to arise as a result of the liquidation or proposed liquidation;
   (b) the amount of the obligation so arising; and
   (c) the total amount of all such obligations specified in the statement.

4. The Board's statement shall, for the purpose of voting at a meeting (but for no other purpose), be treated in all respects as if it were a claim.

5. Any voting rights which a creditor might otherwise exercise at a meeting in respect of a claim against the company are reduced by a sum equal to the amount of that claim in relation to which the Board, by virtue of its having submitted a statement, is entitled to exercise voting rights at that meeting.

6. The Board may from time to time submit a further statement, and, if it does so, that statement supersedes any statement previously submitted.   **[1705]**

SCHEDULE 4

Rule 7.29

PUNISHMENT OF OFFENCES UNDER THE RULES

Note: In the fourth and fifth columns of this Schedule, "the statutory maximum" means the prescribed sum under section 289B(6) of the Criminal Procedure (Scotland) Act 1975 (c 21).

Rule creating offence	*General nature of offence*	*Mode of prosecution*	*Punishment*	*Daily default fine (where applicable)*
In Part 1, Rule 1.24	False representation or fraud for purpose of obtaining members' or creditors' consent to proposal for voluntary arrangement	1. On indictment 2. Summary	7 years or a fine, or both 6 months or the statutory maximum, or both	
In Part 2, Rule 2.17(4)	Administrator failing to send notification as to progress of administration	Summary	One-fifth of the statutory maximum	One-fiftieth of the statutory maximum
In Part 3, Rule 3.9(5)	Receiver failing to send notification as to progress of receivership	Summary	One-fifth of the statutory maximum	One-fiftieth of the statutory maximum

[1706]

SCHEDULE 5

Rule 7.30

NOTES
The forms themselves are not reproduced in this work, but their numbers and descriptions are listed below.

FORMS

Index

PART 1:   COMPANY VOLUNTARY ARRANGEMENTS

FORM NO   TITLE
1.1 (Scot)   Notice of report of a meeting approving voluntary arrangement.
1.2 (Scot)   Notice of order of revocation or suspension of voluntary arrangement.
1.3 (Scot)   Notice of voluntary arrangement supervisor's abstract of receipts and payments.
1.4 (Scot)   Notice of completion of voluntary arrangement.

PART 2:   ADMINISTRATION PROCEDURE

2.1 (Scot)   Notice of petition for administration order.
2.2 (Scot)   Notice of administration order.
2.3 (Scot)   Notice of dismissal of petition for administration order.

2.4 (Scot)	Notice of discharge of administration order.
2.5 (Scot)	Notice requiring submission of administration statement of affairs.
2.6 (Scot)	Statement of affairs.
2.7 (Scot)	Notice of statement of administrator's proposals.
2.8 (Scot)	Notice of result of meeting of creditors.
2.9 (Scot)	Administrator's abstract of receipts and payments.
2.10 (Scot)	Statement of administrator's proposed revisions and notice of meeting to consider them.
2.11 (Scot)	Notice of order to deal with secured property.
2.12 (Scot)	Notice of variation of administration order.
2.13 (Scot)	Notice to court of resignation of administrator.

PART 3:	RECEIVERS
3.1 (Scot)	Notice requiring submission of receivership statement of affairs.
3.2 (Scot)	Receiver's abstract of receipts and payments.
3.3 (Scot)	Notice of receiver's death.
3.4 (Scot)	Notice of authorisation to dispose of secured property.
3.5 (Scot)	Notice of receiver's report.

PART 4:	WINDING UP
4.1 (Scot)	Statutory demand.
4.2 (Scot)	Notice of winding up order.
4.3 (Scot)	Notice requiring submission of Statement of Affairs in a liquidation.
4.4 (Scot)	Statement of Affairs.
4.5 (Scot)	Liquidator's statement of receipts and payments.
4.6 (Scot)	Notice of liquidator's statement of receipts and payments.
4.7 (Scot)	Statement of claim by creditor.
4.8 (Scot)	Certificate of appointment of liquidator.
4.9 (Scot)	Notice of appointment of liquidator.
4.10 (Scot)	Certificate of removal of liquidator.
4.11 (Scot)	Notice of removal of liquidator.
4.12 (Scot)	Application by liquidator to the Accountant of Court for his release.
4.13 (Scot)	Certificate by the Accountant of Court of release of the liquidator.
4.14 (Scot)	Notice of certificate of release of liquidator.
4.15 (Scot)	Notice to court of resignation of liquidator.
4.16 (Scot)	Notice of resignation of liquidator.
4.17 (Scot)	Notice of final meeting of creditors.
4.18 (Scot)	Notice of death of liquidator.
4.19 (Scot)	Notice of vacation of office by liquidator.
4.20 (Scot)	Certificate of constitution of creditors'/liquidation committee.
4.21 (Scot)	Liquidator's certificate of continuance of liquidation committee.
4.22 (Scot)	Notice of constitution/continuance of liquidation/creditors' committee.
4.23 (Scot)	Liquidator's certificate that creditors paid in full.
4.24 (Scot)	Notice of certificate that creditors have been paid in full.
4.25 (Scot)	Declaration of solvency.
4.26 (Scot)	Return of final meeting in a voluntary winding up.
4.27 (Scot)	Notice of court's order sisting proceedings in winding up by the Court.
4.28 (Scot)	Notice under section 204(6) or 205(6).

Section D

Other Statutory Instruments

Scotland

SECTION D
OTHER STATUTORY INSTRUMENTS
SCOTLAND

BANKRUPTCY (SCOTLAND) REGULATIONS 1986
(1985 No 1925 (S 147))

NOTES

Made: 4 December 1985.

Authority: Bankruptcy (Scotland) Act 1985, ss 6(7), 7(1)(*d*), 8(2), 11(1), 15(6), 19(1), 22(2)(*a*), (6), 23(1)(*a*), 25(6)(*b*), 45(3)(*a*), 48(7), 49(3), 51(7)(*a*), 54(2), 67(8), 69, 73, 74, Sch 4, para 4(*c*), Sch 5, para 5(*b*), 9(*a*).

ARRANGEMENT OF REGULATIONS

Regulation		Para
1	Citation and commencement	[1707A]
2	Interpretation	[1707B]

Qualification to act as insolvency practitioner

3	..	[1707C]
4	..	[1707D]
5	Forms	[1707E]
6	Claims in foreign currency	[1707F]
7	Conversion of foreign currency claims ..	[1707G]
8	Interest on claims in sequestration	[1707H]
9	Amount of unsecured liabilities ..	[1707I]
10	Premium of bond of caution	[1707J]
11	Definition of "associate" ..	[1707K]
12	Application of the Act to limited partnerships ..	[1707L]
	Schedule—List of Forms	[1707M]

1. Citation and commencement

These regulations may be cited as the Bankruptcy (Scotland) Regulations 1985 and shall come into operation, for the purposes of regulations 3 and 4 of these regulations, on 1st February 1986 and for all other purposes, on 1st April 1986.

[1707A]

2. Interpretation

In these regulations—

"the Act" means the Bankruptcy (Scotland) Act 1985; and

"the 1907 Act" means the Limited Partnerships Act 1907.   **[1707B]**

NOTES

Commencement: See reg 1 ante.

Qualification to act as insolvency practitioner

3.—(1) A person shall be qualified to act as an insolvency practitioner for the purposes of the Act, until the coming into force of section 2 of the Insolvency Act 1985 only if he satisfies the following requirements:—

    (*a*) he is an individual;

(*b*) he holds a certificate entitling him, or is otherwise entitled, at the relevant time, to practise as a member of a relevant professional body or, in any other case, he has, at the relevant time, a minimum of 5 years' experience as an insolvency practitioner;

(*c*) he finds caution in accordance with the provisions of regulation 4 of these regulations; and

(*d*) he is not an undischarged bankrupt.

(2) For the purposes of paragraph (1) above—

(*a*) the expression "the relevant time" means any time at which a person acts as an insolvency practitioner or has, or seeks to have, his name included in the list of interim trustees;

(*b*) the expression "a relevant professional body" means—

The Law Society of Scotland
The Institute of Chartered Accountants of Scotland
The Insolvency Practitioners Association
The Chartered Association of Certified Accountants
The Law Society
The Institute of Chartered Accountants in England and Wales
The Institute of Chartered Accountants in Ireland;

(*c*) a person shall be treated as having a minimum of 5 years' experience as an insolvency practitioner if he has, in not less than 10 cases in the previous 5 years, acted—

(i) as a liquidator, receiver or trustee in bankruptcy or trustee under a trust deed or other voluntary arrangement for the benefit of creditors or a judicial factor under section 163 of the Bankruptcy (Scotland) Act 1913, or under section 11A of the Judicial Factors (Scotland) Act 1889 or in any similar capacity in any member state of the European Communities; or

(ii) as a senior assistant or deputy to any of those persons; and

(*d*) an undischarged bankrupt means a person who has not been discharged after his estate has been sequestrated or he has been adjudged bankrupt or he has granted a trust deed for the benefit of his creditors or he has been subject, in any other country, to any procedure similar to sequestration, bankruptcy or the granting of a trust deed for creditors.   **[1707C]**

NOTES
Commencement: 1 February 1986; see reg 1 ante.

4.—(1) For the purposes of regulation 3(1)(*c*) of these regulations, a person shall be qualified to act as an insolvency practitioner in the circumstances set out in the following paragraphs if he finds caution in accordance with the following provisions of this regulation.

(2) A person shall be qualified to act as an interim trustee if he lodges with the Accountant in Bankruptcy at the time of his application for his name to be included in the list of interim trustees and, for as long as his name remains on that list, maintains in force a bond (hereinafter referred to as "a global bond")

in terms of which it is provided that, whenever he is appointed as an interim trustee in a sequestration, the amount of caution in respect of his actings or omissions as interim trustee shall be not less than the net value of the debtor's assets in the sequestration as estimated by the interim trustee.

(3) Subject to paragraph (4) below, a person shall be qualified to act as a permanent trustee in a sequestration, if, for as long as he acts as such trustee, he has and maintains in force—

    (a) in the case where he has acted as the interim trustee in the sequestration, the global bond referred to in paragraph (2) above, which provides for caution, or

    (b) a bond of caution, which he lodges with the sheriff clerk, before the issue of the act and warrant in his favour,

in respect of his actings or omissions as a permanent trustee for such amount as shall be not less than the net value of the debtor's assets in the final statement of the debtor's affairs prepared by the interim trustee under section 23(3)(d) of the Act.

(4) A person shall be qualified to act as a trustee under a protected trust deed, if, for as long as he acts as such trustee, he has and maintains in force a bond of caution or a global bond referred to in paragraph (2) above which provides for caution in respect of his actings or omissions as such trustee for such amount as shall not be less than the value of the debtor's assets conveyed to him under the trust deed.

(5) In this regulation, the expression "net value of the debtor's assets" means the value of the debtor's assets under deduction of any security which is not surrendered to the insolvency practitioner.   **[1707D]**

NOTES
    Commencement: 1 February 1986; see reg 1 ante.

5. Forms

The forms set out in the Schedule to these regulations are the forms prescribed for the purposes of the provisions of the Act referred to therein.   **[1707E]**

NOTES
    Commencement: See reg 1 ante.

6. Claims in foreign currency

A creditor may state the amount of his claim in foreign currency for the purposes of section 22(6), or that section as applied by section 48(7), of the Act, where—

    (a) his claim is constituted by decree or other order made by a court ordering the debtor to pay to the creditor a sum expressed in foreign currency; or, where it is not so constituted,

    (b) his claim arises from a contract or bill of exchange in terms of which payment is or may be required to be made by the debtor to the creditor in foreign currency.   **[1707F]**

7. Conversion of foreign currency claims

For the purposes of sections 23(1)(*a*) and 49(3) of the Act, the manner of conversion into Sterling of the amount of a claim stated in foreign currency shall be at the rate of exchange for that currency at the mean of the buying and selling spot rates prevailing at the close of business on the date of sequestration in the London market as published in any national newspaper   **[1707G]**

8. Interest on claims in sequestration

The prescribed rate of interest for the purposes of section 51(7) of the Act (interest on preferred debts and ordinary debts between the date of sequestration and the date of payment of the debt) is 15 *per centum per annum.*   **[1707H]**

9. Amount of unsecured liabilities

The amount of the unsecured liabilities of the debtor, for the purposes of section 67(8) of the Act (the offence of failing to keep proper records), shall be £20,000.
                                                                                       [1707I]

10. Premium of bond of caution

Any premium (or a proportionate part thereof) of any bond of caution or other security required to be given by an insolvency practitioner in respect of his actings as an interim trustee or a permanent trustee in any sequestration in which he is elected or appointed may be taken into account as part of his outlays in that sequestration.   **[1707J]**

11. (*Amends the Bankruptcy (Scotland) Act 1985, s 74, para* **[574]** *ante.*)
                                                                                       [1707K]

12. Application of the Act to limited partnerships

(1) The application of the Act to the sequestration of the estate of a limited partnership shall be subject to the modifications specified in this regulation.

(2) Any reference in the Act to a partnership (other than in section 6(1)) or to a firm shall be construed as including a reference to a limited partnership.

(3) In the application of section 9 of the Act to limited partnerships, the Court of Session and the Sheriff shall have jurisdiction in respect of the sequestration of the estate of a limited partnership if it is registered in Scotland for the purposes of the 1907 Act and, in the case of the sheriff, if it has an established place of business within the sheriffdom.

(4) For the purposes of section 8(2) of the Act, a petition for the sequestration of the estate of a limited partnership may be presented—

    (*a*) by a qualified creditor or qualified creditors only if the apparent insolvency founded on in the petition was constituted within four months before the date of presentation of the petition; or

    (*b*) at any time by any other person.

(5) Without prejudice to the provisions of sections 14(1), 15(5) and 17(8) of the Act, the clerk of court shall send a copy of every court order mentioned in those sections to the Registrar of Limited Partnerships in Scotland. **[1707L]**

NOTES
    Commencement: 1 April 1986; see reg 1 ante.
    The Act: Bankruptcy (Scotland) Act 1985.
    1907 Act: Limited Partnerships Act 1907.

SCHEDULE

Regulation 5

LIST OF FORMS

NOTES
    The forms themselves are not reproduced in this work, but their numbers and descriptions are listed below.

FORM NO	PURPOSE
1	Statutory demand for payment of debt.
2	Oath by creditor.
3	Notice by the interim trustee in the Edinburgh Gazette and the London Gazette.
4	List of the assets and liabilities of the debtor.
5	Statement of claim by creditor.
6	Notice by permanent trustee in the Edinburgh Gazette of confirmation in office.
7	Notice by permanent trustee in the Edinburgh Gazette of public examination of the debtor or a relevant person.
8	Certificate of discharge of debtor.
9	Acceptance or rejection by creditor of an offer of composition.
10	Notice in Edinburgh Gazette by trustee under a trust deed for the benefit of creditors.
11	Statement of realisation and distribution of estate under a protected trust deed. **[1707M]**

ADMINISTRATIVE RECEIVERS (VALUE ADDED TAX CERTIFICATES) (SCOTLAND) RULES 1986
(1986 No 304 (S 23))

NOTES
    Made: 20 February 1986.
    Authority: Insolvency Act 1985, s 106, Sch 5, para 23(*d*). This statutory instrument now has effect as if made under the Insolvency Act 1986, ss 411, 414, Sch 8, para 23(*d*).

ARRANGEMENT OF RULES

Rule		Para
1	Citation, commencement and interpretation	.. [1708]
2	Application of these Rules	.. [1709]
3	Issue of certificate of insolvency	.. [1710]
4	Form of certificate	.. [1711]
5	Notification to creditors	.. [1712]
6	Preservation of certificate with company's records	.. [1713]

1. Citation, commencement and interpretation

(1) These Rules may be cited as the Administrative Receivers (Value Added Tax Certificates) (Scotland) Rules 1986 and shall come into operation on 1st April 1986.

(2) In these Rules references to "the 1983 Act" are to the Value Added Tax Act 1983, and the expression "administrative receiver" has the same meaning as in Part II of the Insolvency Act 1985.   **[1708]**

NOTES
    Commencement: 1 April 1986.

2. Application of these Rules

These Rules apply to a company for the purposes of section 22 of the 1983 Act where a person is appointed to act as its administrative receiver under section 467 of the Companies Act 1985 (power to appoint receivers under the law of Scotland).   **[1709]**

NOTES
    Commencement: 1 April 1986.
    1983 Act: Value Added Tax Act 1983.

3. Issue of certificate of insolvency

In accordance with this Rule, it is the duty of the administrative receiver to issue a certificate in the terms of paragraph (*b*) of section 22(3) of the 1983 Act (which specifies the circumstances in which a company is deemed insolvent for the purposes of the section) forthwith upon his forming the opinion described in that paragraph.   **[1710]**

NOTES
    Commencement: 1 April 1986.
    1983 Act: Value Added Tax Act 1983.

4. Form of certificate

(1) There shall be specified in the certificate—

(a) the name of the company and its registered number;
(b) the full name of the administrative receiver and the date of his appointment as such; and
(c) the date on which the certificate is issued.

(2) The certificate shall be intituled "CERTIFICATE OF INSOLVENCY FOR THE PURPOSES OF SECTION 22(3)(b) OF THE VALUE ADDED TAX ACT 1983". **[1711]**

NOTES
Commencement: 1 April 1986.

5. Notification to creditors

(1) Notice of the issue of the certificate shall be given by the administrative receiver, within 3 months of his appointment or within 2 months of issuing the certificate whichever is the later, to all of the company's unsecured creditors of whose address he is then aware and who have, to his knowledge, made supplies to the company, with a charge to value added tax, at any time before his appointment.

(2) Thereafter, he shall give the notice to any such creditor of whose address and supplies to the company he becomes aware.

(3) He is not under obligation to provide any creditor with a copy of the certificate. **[1712]**

NOTES
Commencement: 1 April 1986.

6. Preservation of certificate with company's records

The certificate shall be retained with the company's accounting records, and section 222 of the Companies Act 1985 (where and for how long records are to be kept) applies to the certificate as it applies to those records. **[1713]–[1716]**

NOTES
Commencement: 1 April 1986.

BANKRUPTCY (SCOTLAND) AMENDMENT REGULATIONS 1986
(1986 No 1914 (S 138))

NOTES
Made: 10 November 1986.
Authority: Bankruptcy (Scotland) Act 1985, ss 67(9), 73, Sch 3, paras 5(1), 6.

ARRANGEMENT OF REGULATIONS

Regulation		Para
1 Citation and commencement	.. ..	.. [1717]
2 Interpretation	.. ..	.. [1718]
3 Amendments	.. ..	.. [1719]
4 Revocation ..	.. ..	.. [1720]

1. Citation and commencement

These regulations may be cited as the Bankruptcy (Scotland) Amendment Regulations 1986 and shall come into operation on 29th December 1986. **[1717]**

NOTES
Commencement: 29 December 1986.

2. Interpretation

In these regulations,

"the Act" means the Bankruptcy (Scotland) Act 1985; and
"the principal regulations" means the Bankruptcy (Scotland) Regulations 1985. **[1718]**

NOTES
Commencement: 29 December 1986.

3. Amendments

There shall be inserted after regulation 12 of the principal regulations, the following regulations:—

"13. Obtaining of credit

The sum which is prescribed for the purposes of section 67(9) of the Act (the offence of obtaining credit) shall be £250 instead of £100.

14. Preference for remuneration of employees, etc

The amount which is prescribed for the purposes of paragraphs 5(1) and 6 of Schedule 3 to the Act (the maximum amount which can be claimed as a preferred debt by an employee by way of remuneration or by a person under the Reserve Forces (Safeguard of Employment) Act 1985) shall be £800.". **[1719]**

NOTES
Commencement: 29 December 1986.
Principal regulations: SI 1985 No 1925.
The Act: Bankruptcy (Scotland) Act 1985.

4. Revocation

Regulations 3 and 4 of the principal regulations are hereby revoked. **[1720]**

NOTES
Commencement: 29 December 1986.

INSOLVENT COMPANIES (REPORTS ON CONDUCT OF DIRECTORS) (No 2) (SCOTLAND) RULES 1986
(1986 No 1916 (S 140))

NOTES
Made: 10 November 1986.
Authority: Insolvency Act 1985, s 106; Insolvency Act 1986, s 411; Company Directors Disqualification Act 1986, s 21(2).

ARRANGEMENT OF RULES

Rule   Para
1   Citation, commencement and interpretation   ..   .. [1721]
2   Reports required under section 7(3) of the Act   ..   .. [1722]
3   Return by office-holder   ..   .. [1723]
4   Enforcement of section 7(4)   ..   .. [1724]
5   Revocation and transitional provisions   ..   .. [1725]

Schedule—Forms   ..   .. [1726]

1. Citation, commencement and interpretation

(1) These Rules may be cited as the Insolvent Companies (Reports on Conduct of Directors) (No. 2) (Scotland) Rules 1986.

(2) These Rules shall come into operation on 29th December 1986.

(3) In these Rules—

"the Act" means the Company Directors Disqualification Act 1986,
"commencement date" means the date on which these Rules come into operation, and
"a company" means a company which the courts in Scotland have jurisdiction to wind up.   **[1721]**

NOTES
    Commencement: 29 November 1986.

2. Reports required under section 7(3) of the Act

(1) This Rule applies to any report made to the Secretary of State under section 7(3) of the Act by—

    (*a*) the liquidator of a company which is being wound up by an order of the court made on or after the commencement date;

    (*b*) the liquidator of a company which passes a resolution for voluntary winding up on or after that date;

    (*c*) a receiver of a company, appointed under section 51 of the Insolvency Act 1986 (power to appoint receivers under the law of Scotland) on or after that date, who is an administrative receiver; or

    (*d*) an administrator of a company in relation to which an administration order is made on or after that date.

(2) Such a report shall be made in the Form D1 (Scot), D2 (Scot) or D5 (Scot) set out in the Schedule hereto, as the case may be, and in the manner and to the extent required by the applicable form.   **[1722]**

NOTES
    Commencement: 29 November 1986.
    The Act: Company Directors Disqualification Act 1986.

3. Return by office-holder

(1) This Rule applies where it appears to a liquidator of a company as mentioned in Rule 2(1)(*a*) or (*b*), to an administrative receiver as mentioned in Rule 2(1)(*c*) or to an administrator as mentioned in Rule 2(1)(*d*) (each of whom is referred to hereinafter as "the office-holder") that the company has at any time become insolvent within the meaning of section 6(2) of the Act.

(2) Subject as follows, there may be furnished to the Secretary of State by

an office-holder, at any time during the period of 6 months from the relevant date, a return with respect to every person who—

(*a*) was, on the relevant date, a director or shadow director of the company, or

(*b*) had been a director or shadow director of the company at any time in the three years immediately preceding that date.

(3) The return shall be made in the Form D3 (Scot), D4 (Scot) or D6 (Scot) set out in the Schedule hereto, as the case may be, and in the manner and to the extent required by the applicable form.

(4) For the purposes of this Rule, "the relevant date" means—

(*a*) in the case of a company in liquidation (except in the case mentioned in paragraph (4)(*b*) below), the date on which the company goes into liquidation within the meaning of section 247(2) of the Insolvency Act 1986,

(*b*) in the case of a company in members' voluntary winding up, the date on which the liquidator forms the opinion that, at the time when the company went into liquidation, its assets were insufficient for the payment of its debts and other liabilities and the expenses of winding up,

(*c*) in the case of the administrative receiver, the date of his appointment,

(*d*) in the case of the administrator, the date of the administration order made in relation to the company,

and for the purposes of sub-paragraph (*c*) above the only appointment of an administrative receiver to be taken into account in determining the relevant date shall be that appointment which is not that of a successor in office to an administrative receiver who has vacated office either by death or pursuant to section 62 of the Insolvency Act 1986.

(5) It shall be the duty of the responsible office-holder to furnish a return complying with the provisions of paragraphs (3) and (4) of this Rule to the Secretary of State not later than the expiry of the period of 6 months from the relevant date, where no return has been so furnished by a day one week before the expiry of that period; and for the purposes of this paragraph the responsible office-holder shall be the person in office in relation to the company on the day specified above or, where no person is in office on that day, the office-holder who vacated office nearest to that day.

(6) A return need not be provided under this Rule if the office-holder has, since the relevant date, made reports to the Secretary of State under section 7(3) of the Act with respect to all the persons falling within paragraph (2) and (apart from this paragraph) required to be the subject of return.

(7) If a responsible office-holder without reasonable excuse fails to comply with the duty imposed by paragraph (5) of this Rule, he is liable on summary conviction to a fine not exceeding £400 and, for continued contravention, to a daily default fine not exceeding £40.   **[1723]**

NOTES
Commencement: 29 November 1986.
The Act: Company Directors Disqualification Act 1986.

4. Enforcement of section 7(4)

(1) This Rule applies where, under section 7(4) of the Act (power to call on liquidators, former liquidators and others to provide information), the Secretary of State requires a person—

(a) to furnish him with information with respect to a person's conduct as director or shadow director of a company, and

(b) to produce and permit inspection of relevant books, papers and other records.

(2) On the application of the Secretary of State, the court may make an order directing compliance within such period as may be specified.

(3) The court's order may provide that all expenses of and incidental to the application shall be borne by the person to whom the order is directed.　**[1724]**

NOTES
Commencement: 29 November 1986.
The Act: Company Directors Disqualification Act 1986.

5. Revocation and transitional provisions

(1) The Insolvent Companies (Reports on Conduct of Directors) (Scotland) Rules 1986 ("the former Rules") are hereby revoked.

(2) Notwithstanding paragraph (1), the provisions of Rules 2 and 3 of the former Rules shall continue to apply and have effect in relation to—

(a) any report to which the provisions of Rule 2 of those Rules applies, and

(b) any interim return required to be made by Rule 3 of those Rules.

[1725]

NOTES
Commencement: 29 November 1986.

SCHEDULE

Rules 2(2) and 3(3)

FORMS

NOTES
The forms themselves are not reproduced in this work, but their numbers and descriptions are listed below.

FORM NO	TITLE
D1 (Scot)	Companies in Liquidation: Report on Conduct of Directors under Section 7(3) of the Company Directors' Disqualification Act 1986.
D2 (Scot)	Report on Conduct of Directors by an Administrative Receiver under Section 7(3) of the Company Directors' Disqualification Act 1986.
D3 (Scot)	Companies in Liquidation: Return of Directors under Rule 3 of the Insolvent Companies (Reports on Conduct of Directors) (No. 2) (Scotland) Rules 1986.
D4 (Scot)	Return of the Directors by an Administrative Receiver under Rule 3 of the Insolvent Companies (Reports on Conduct of Directors) (No. 2) (Scotland) Rules 1986.
D5 (Scot)	Report on Conduct of Directors by an Administrator under Section 7(3) of the Company Directors' Disqualification Act 1986.
D6 (Scot)	Return of Directors by an Administrator under Rule 3 of the Insolvent Companies (Reports on Conduct of Directors) (No. 2) (Scotland) Rules 1986.

[1726]

RECEIVERS (SCOTLAND) REGULATIONS 1986
(1986 No 1917 (S 141))

NOTES
    Made: 10 November 1986.
    Authority: Insolvency Act 1986, ss 53(1), (6), 54(3), 62(1), (5), 65(1)(*a*), 66(1), 67(2)(*b*), 70(1), 71.

ARRANGEMENT OF REGULATIONS

Regulation   Para
1   Citation and commencement   ..   .. [1727]
2   Interpretation   ..   .. [1728]
3   Forms   ..   .. [1729]
4   Instrument of appointment ..   .. [1730]
5   Joint receivers   ..   .. [1731]
6   Resignation ..   .. [1732]
7   Report to creditors ..   .. [1733]

        Schedule—Forms   ..   .. [1734]

1. Citation and commencement

These regulations may be cited as the Receivers (Scotland) Regulations 1986
and shall come into operation on 29th December 1986.   **[1727]**

NOTES
    Commencement: 29 December 1986.

2. Interpretation

In these regulations, "the Act" means the Insolvency Act 1986.   **[1728]**

NOTES
    Commencement: 29 December 1986.

3. Forms

The forms set out in the Schedule to these regulations, with such variations as
circumstances require, are the forms prescribed for the purposes of the
provisions of the Act which are referred to in these forms.   **[1729]**

NOTES
    Commencement: 29 December 1986.
    The Act: Insolvency Act 1986.

4. Instrument of appointment

The certified copy instrument of appointment of a receiver which is required to
be submitted to the registrar of companies by or on behalf of the person making
the appointment under section 53(1) of the Act shall be certified to be a correct
copy by or on behalf of that person.   **[1730]**

NOTES
    Commencement: 29 December 1986.
    The Act: Insolvency Act 1986.

5. Joint receivers

Where two or more persons are appointed joint receivers by the holder of a floating charge under section 53 of the Act, subsection (6) of that section shall apply subject to the following modifications:—

(a) the appointment of any of the joint receivers shall be of no effect unless the appointment is accepted by all of them in accordance with paragraph (a) of that subsection and Rule 3.1 of the Insolvency (Scotland) Rules 1986; and

(b) their appointment as joint receivers shall be deemed to be made on the day on and at the time at which the instrument of appointment is received by the last of them, as evidenced by the written docquet required by paragraph (b) of that subsection. **[1731]**

NOTES
Commencement: 29 December 1986.
The Act: Insolvency Act 1986.

6. Resignation

For the purposes of section 62(1) of the Act, a receiver, who wishes to resign his office, shall give at least 7 days' notice of his resignation to—

(a) the holder of the floating charge by virtue of which he was appointed;

(b) the holder of any other floating charge and any receiver appointed by him;

(c) the members of any committee of creditors established under section 68 of the Act; and

(d) the company, or if it is then in liquidation, its liquidator,

and the notice shall specify the date on which the resignation takes effect.
[1732]

NOTES
Commencement: 29 December 1986.
The Act: Insolvency Act 1986.

7. Report to creditors

Where the receiver determines to publish a notice under paragraph (b) of section 67(2) of the Act, the notice shall be published in a newspaper circulating in the area where the company has its principal place of business or in such other newspaper as he thinks most appropriate for ensuring that it comes to the notice of the unsecured creditors of the company. **[1733]**

NOTES
Commencement: 29 December 1986.
The Act: Insolvency Act 1986.

SCHEDULE

Regulation 3

FORMS

NOTES
The forms themselves are not reproduced in this work, but their numbers and descriptions are listed below.

FORM NO	TITLE
1 (Scot)	Notice of appointment of a receiver by the holder of a floating charge.

2 (Scot)	Notice of appointment of a receiver by the court.
3 (Scot)	Notice of the receiver ceasing to act or of his removal.
4 (Scot)	Notice of appointment of receiver.
5 (Scot)	Statement of affairs.

[1734]

NOTES

Commencement: 29 December 1986.

INSURANCE COMPANIES (WINDING UP) (SCOTLAND) RULES 1986

(1986 No 1918 (S 142))

NOTES

Made: 10 November 1986.

Authority: Insolvency Act 1986, s 411; Insurance Companies Act 1982, s 59.

ARRANGEMENT OF THE RULES

Rules   Para

1	Citation and commencement	[1735]
2	Interpretation	[1736]
3	Application	[1737]
4	Policyholders Protection Board	[1738]
5	Separation of long term and other business in winding up	[1739]
6	Valuation of general business policies	[1740]
7	Valuation of long term policies: no stop order	[1741]
8	Valuation of long term policies: stop order made	[1742]
9	Attribution of liabilities to the long term business	[1743]
10	Attribution of assets to the long term business	[1744]
11	Excess of long term business assets	[1745]
12	Actuarial advice	[1746]
13	Utilisation of excess of assets	[1747]
14	Special bank account	[1748]
15	Custody of assets	[1749]
16	Maintenance of accounting, valuation and other records	[1750]
17	Additional powers in relation to the long term business	[1751]
18	Accounts and audit	[1752]
19	Caution for long term and other business	[1753]
20	Claims	[1754]
21	Failure to pay premiums	[1755]
22	Notice of valuation of policy	[1756]
23	Dividends to creditors	[1757]
24	Meetings of creditors	[1758]
25	Apportionment of expenses of liquidation	[1759]
26	Notice of stop order	[1760]

Schedule 1—General Business Policies .. [1761]

Schedule 2—Rules For Valuing Non-Linked Policies, Non-Linked Deferred Annuity Policies, Non-Linked Annuities In Payment And Capital Redemption Policies .. [1762]

Schedule 3—Rule For Valuing Life Policies And Deferred Annuity Policies Which Are Linked Policies .. [1763]

Schedule 4—Rules For Valuing Long Term Policies Which Are Not Dealt With In Schedules 2 and 3 .. [1764]

Para
Schedule 5—Rules For Valuing Long Term Policies Where A Stop Order Has Been
Made ..   .. [1765]
Schedule 6—Notice Of Order Pronounced Under Section 56(2) Of The Insurance
Companies Act 1982 For Cessation Of Long Term Business   ..   ..   .. [1766]

1. Citation and commencement

These Rules may be cited as the Insurance Companies (Winding Up) (Scotland)
Rules 1986 and shall come into operation on 29th December 1986.   **[1735]**

NOTES
Commencement: 29 December 1986.

2. Interpretation

(1) In these Rules, unless the context or subject matter requires—

"the Act of 1923" means the Industrial Assurance Act 1923;
"the Act of 1982" means the Insurance Companies Act 1982;
"the Act of 1985" means the Companies Act 1985;
"the Act of 1986" means the Insolvency Act 1986;
"company" means an insurance company which is being wound up;
"excess of long term business assets" means the amount, if any, by which
the value as at the date of the winding up order of the assets representing
the fund or funds maintained by the company in respect of its long term
business exceeds the value as at that date of the liabilities of the company
attributable to that business;
"excess of the other business assets" means the amount, if any, by which
the value as at the date of the winding up order of the assets of the
company which do not represent the fund or funds maintained by the
company in respect of its long term business exceeds the value as at that
date of the liabilities of the company (other than liabilities in respect of
share capital) which are not attributable to that business;
"general business policy" means a policy the effecting of which by the
company constitutes the carrying on of general business;
"the Industrial Assurance Acts" means the Act of 1923 and the Industrial
Assurance and Friendly Societies Act 1929;
"insurance company" means an insurance company to which Part II of
the Act of 1982 applies and to which these Rules apply;
"linked liability" means any liability under a policy the effecting of which
constitutes the carrying on of long term insurance business the amount
of which is determined by reference to—

(*a*) the value of property and any description (whether or not
specified in the policy),
(*b*) fluctuations in the value of such property,
(*c*) income from any such property, or
(*d*) fluctuations in an index of the value of such property;

"linked policy" means a policy which provides for linked liabilities and a
policy which, when made, provided for linked liabilities shall be deemed
to be a linked policy even if the policy holder has elected to convert his
rights under the policy so that at the date of the winding up order there
are no longer linked liabilities under the policy;
"long term policy" means a policy the effecting of which by the company
constitutes the carrying on of long term business;
"non-linked policy" means a policy which is not a linked policy;

"other business", in relation to a company carrying on long term business, means such of the business of the company as is not long term business;
"the Policyholders Protection Board" or "the Board" means the Policyholders Protection Board established by the Policyholders Protection Act 1975;
"the principal Rules" means the Insolvency (Scotland) Rules 1986;
"stop order" in relation to a company means an order of the court, made under section 56(2) of the Act of 1982, ordering the liquidator to stop carrying on the long term business of the company;
"unit" in relation to a linked policy means any unit (whether or not described as a unit in the policy) by reference to the numbers and value of which the amount of the linked liabilities under the policy at any time is measured.

(2) Unless the context otherwise requires, words or expressions contained in these Rules have the same meaning as in the principal Rules, the Act of 1986 or the Act of 1982 respectively. **[1736]**

NOTES
Commencement: 29 December 1986.

3. Application

(1) These Rules apply in relation to an insurance company which the courts in Scotland have jurisdiction to wind up.

(2) These Rules apply to proceedings for the winding up of such an insurance company which commence on or after the date on which these Rules come into operation.

(3) These Rules supplement the principal Rules which also apply to the proceedings in the winding up of such an insurance company under the Act of 1986 as they apply to proceedings in the winding up of any company under that Act but, in the event of conflict between these Rules and the principal Rules, these Rules prevail. **[1737]**

NOTES
Commencement: 29 December 1986.
Act 1986: Insolvency Act 1986.
Principal Rules: SI 1986 No 1915.

4. Policyholders Protection Board

In any proceedings for the appointment of a liquidator by the court under—

    (*a*) section 138(5) of the Act of 1986 (appointment of liquidator by the court where no person is appointed or nominated by the meeting of creditors and contributories),

    (*b*) section 139(4) of that Act (appointment of liquidator by the court where conflict between creditors and contributories), or

    (*c*) section 140 of that Act (appointment of liquidator by the court following administration or voluntary arrangement),

the Policyholders Protection Board shall be entitled to appear and make representations as to the person to be appointed. **[1738]**

NOTES
Commencement: 29 December 1986.
Act of 1986: Insolvency Act 1986.

5. Separation of long term and other business in winding up

(1) This rule applies in the case of a company carrying on long term business.

(2) The assets of the company which in accordance with section 55(3) and (4) of the Act of 1982 are available for meeting the liabilities of the company attributable to its long term business shall, under section 148 of the Act of 1986, be applied in discharge of those liabilities as though those assets and those liabilities were the assets and liabilities of a separate company.

(3) The assets of the company which in accordance with section 55(3) and (4) of the Act of 1982 are available for meeting the liabilities of the company attributable to its other business shall, under section 148 of the Act of 1986, be applied in discharge of those liabilities as though those assets and those liabilities were the assets and liabilities of a separate company.   **[1739]**

NOTES
Commencement: 29 December 1986.
Act of 1982: Insurance Companies Act 1982.
Act of 1986: Insolvency Act 1986.

6. Valuation of general business policies

Except in relation to the amounts which have fallen due for payment before the date of the winding up order, the holder of a general business policy shall be accepted as a creditor in relation to his policy, without submitting or lodging a claim, for an amount equal to the value of the policy and for this purpose the value of the policy shall be determined in accordance with Schedule 1.   **[1740]**

NOTES
Commencement: 29 December 1986.

7. Valuation of long term policies: no stop order

(1) This rule applies in relation to the long term business of a company where no stop order has been made.

(2) In relation to a claim under a policy which has fallen due for payment before the date of the winding up order, a policy holder shall be accepted as a creditor without submitting or lodging a claim for such amount as appears from the records of the company to be due in respect of that claim.

(3) In all other respects a policy holder shall be accepted as a creditor in relation to his policy, without submitting or lodging a claim, for an amount equal to the value of the policy and for this purpose the value of a policy of any class shall be determined in the manner applicable to policies of that class provided by Schedules 2, 3 and 4.

(4) This rule applies in relation to a person entitled to apply for a free paid-up policy under section 24 of the Act of 1923 and to whom no such policy has been issued before the date of the winding up order (whether or not it was applied for) as if such a policy had been issued immediately before the date of the winding up order—

    (*a*) for the minimum amount determined in accordance with section 24(2) of the Act of 1923; or

    (*b*) if the liquidator is satisfied that it was the practice of the company during the 5 years immediately before the date of the winding up order to issue policies under the said section 24 in excess of the minimum amounts so determined, for the amount determined in accordance with that practice.   **[1741]**

NOTES
Commencement: 29 December 1986.
Act of 1923: Industrial Assurance Act 1923.

8. Valuation of long term policies: stop order made

(1) This rule applies in relation to the long term busines of a company where a stop order has been made.

(2) In relation to a claim under a policy which has fallen due for payment on or after the date of the winding up order and before the date of the stop order, a policy holder shall be accepted as a creditor, without submitting or lodging a claim, for such amount as appears from the records of the company and of the liquidator to be due in respect of that claim.

(3) In all other respects a policy holder shall be accepted as a creditor in relation to his policy, without submitting or lodging a claim, for an amount equal to the value of the policy and for this purpose the value of a policy of any class shall be determined in the manner applicable to policies of that class provided by Schedule 5.

(4) Paragraph (4) of rule 7 applies for the purpose of this rule as if references to the date of the winding up order (other than those in sub-paragraph (*b*) of that paragraph) were references to the date of the stop order.   **[1742]**

NOTES
Commencement: 29 December 1986.

9. Attribution of liabilities to the long term business

(1) This rule applies in the case of a company carrying on long term business if, at the date of the winding up order, there are liabilities of the company in respect of which it is not clear from the accounting and other records of the company whether they are or are not attributable to the company's long term business.

(2) The liquidator shall, in such manner and according to such accounting principles as he shall determine, identify the liabilities referred to in paragraph (1) as attributable or not attributable to the long term business of a company and those liabilities shall for the purposes of the winding up be deemed as at the date of the winding up order to be so attributable or not, as the case may be.

(3) In making his determination under this rule, the liquidator may determine that some liabilities are attributable to the company's long term business and that others are not or he may determine that a part of a liability is attributable to the long term business of the company and that the remainder of that liability is not and he may use one method for some of the liabilities and the other method for the remainder of them.   **[1743]**

NOTES
Commencement: 29 December 1986.

10. Attribution of assets to the long term business

(1) This rule applies in the case of a company carrying on long term business if at the date of the winding up order there are assets of the company in respect of which—

    (*a*) it is not clear from the accounting and other records of the company whether they do or do not represent the fund or funds maintained by the company in respect of its long term business; and

    (*b*) it cannot be inferred from the source of the income out of which those assets were provided whether they do or do not represent those funds.

(2) Subject to paragraph (6), the liquidator shall determine which, if any, of the assets referred to in paragraph (1) are attributable to those funds and which, if any, are not and those assets shall, for the purposes of the winding up, be deemed as at the date of the winding up order to represent those funds or not in accordance with the determination of the liquidator.

(3) For the purpose of paragraph (2) the liquidator may—

    (*a*) determine that some of those assets shall be attributable to those funds and that others of them shall not (the first method); or

    (*b*) determine that a part of the value of one of those assets shall be attributable to those funds and that the remainder of that value shall not (the second method),

and he may use the first method for some of those assets and the second method for others of them.

    (4)(*a*) In making the attribution, the objective of the liquidator shall, in the first instance, be so far as possible to reduce any deficit that may exist, at the date of the winding up order and before any attribution is made, either in the company's long term business or in its other business.

    (*b*) If there is a deficit in both the long term business of the company and its other business, the attribution shall be in the ratio that the amount of the one deficit bears to the amount of the other until the deficits are eliminated.

    (*c*) Thereafter, the attribution shall be in the ratio which the aggregate amount of the liabilities attributable to the long term business of the company bears to the aggregate amount of the liabilities not so attributable.

(5) For the purpose of paragraph (4), the value of a liability of the company shall, if it falls to be valued under rule 6 or 7, have the same value as it has under that rule but otherwise it shall have such value as would have been included in relation to it in a balance sheet of the company prepared under section 17 of the Act of 1982 as at the date of the winding up order and, for the purpose of determining the ratio referred to in paragraph (4) but not for the purpose of determining the amount of any deficit therein referred to, the net balance of shareholders' funds shall be included in the liabilities not attributable to the company's long term business.

(6) Notwithstanding anything in the preceding paragraphs of this rule, the court may order that the determination of which, if any, of the assets referred to in paragraph (1) are attributable to the fund or funds maintained by the company in respect of its long term business and which, if any, are not, shall be made in such manner and by such methods as the court may direct or the court may itself make the determination.   **[1744]**

NOTES
Commencement: 29 December 1986.
Act of 1982: Insurance Companies Act 1982.

11. Excess of long term business assets

Where the company is one carrying on long term business, for the purpose of determining the amount, if any, of the excess of the long term business assets, there shall be included amongst the liabilities of the company attributable to its long term business an amount determined by the liquidator in respect of liabilities and expenses likely to be incurred in connection with the transfer of the long term business of the company as a going concern to another insurance company, being liabilities not included in the valuation of the long term policies made in pursuance of rule 7.   **[1745]**

NOTES
Commencement: 29 December 1986.

12. Actuarial advice

(1) Before—

   (a) determining the value of a policy in accordance with Schedules 1 to 5 (other than paragraph 2 of Schedule 1);

   (b) identifying long term assets and liabilities in accordance with rules 9 and 10;

   (c) determining the amount, if any, of the excess of the long term business assets in accordance with rule 11; or

   (d) determining the terms on which he will accept payment of overdue premiums under rule 21(1) and the amount and nature of any recompense under rule 21(2),

the liquidator shall obtain and consider advice thereon (including an estimate of any value or amount required to be determined) from an actuary.

(2) Before seeking, for the purpose of valuing a policy, the direction of the court as to the assumption of a particular rate of interest or the employment of any rates of mortality or disability, the liquidator shall obtain and consider advice thereon from an actuary.   **[1746]**

NOTES
Commencement: 29 December 1986.

13. Utilisation of excess of assets

(1) Except at the direction of the court—

   (a) no distribution may be made out of and no transfer to another insurance company may be made of any part of the excess of the long term business assets which has been transferred to the other business; and

   (b) no distribution may be made out of and no transfer to another insurance company may be made of any part of the excess of the other business assets which has been transferred to the long term business.

(2) Before giving a direction under paragraph (1), the court may require the liquidator to advertise the proposal to make a distribution or a transfer in such a manner as the court shall direct.   **[1747]**

NOTES
Commencement: 29 December 1986.

14. Special bank account

(1) The liquidator of a company carrying on long term business in whose case no stop order has been made may open any special bank account which he is authorised to open for the purpose of the liquidation and he may pay into such an account any moneys which form part of the assets representing the fund or funds maintained by the company in respect of its long term business.

(2) All payments out of any such special bank account shall be made by cheque payable to order and every cheque shall have marked or written on the face of it the name of the company and shall be signed by the liquidator or by any special manager appointed under section 56(3) of the Act 1982.   **[1748]**

NOTES
Commencement: 29 December 1986.
Act of 1982: Insurance Companies Act 1982.

15. Custody of assets

(1) The Secretary of State may, in the case of a company carrying on long term business in whose case no stop order has been made, require that the whole or a specified proportion of the assets representing the fund or funds maintained by the company in respect of its long term business shall be held by a person approved by him for the purpose as trustee for the company.

(2) No assets held by a person as trustee for a company in compliance with a requirement imposed under this rule shall, so long as the requirement is in force, be released except with the consent of the Secretary of State, but they may be transposed by the trustee into other assets by any transaction or series of transactions on the written instructions of the liquidator.

(3) The liquidator may not, except with the consent of the Secretary of State, grant any security over assets which are held by a person as trustee for the company in compliance with a requirement imposed under this rule. **[1749]**

NOTES
Commencement: 29 December 1986.

16. Maintenance of accounting, valuation and other records

The liquidator of a company carrying on long term business in whose case no stop order has been made shall, with a view to the long term business of the company being transferred to another insurance company, maintain such minute books and accounting, valuation and other records as will enable such other insurance company upon the transfer being effected to comply with the requirements of the provisions of the Act of 1982 relating to accounts and statements of insurance companies.   **[1750]**

NOTES
Commencement: 29 December 1986.
Act of 1982: Insurance Companies Act 1982.

17. Additional powers in relation to the long term business

The liquidator of a company carrying on long term business shall, so long as no stop order has been made, have power to do all such things as may be necessary to the performance of his duties under section 56(2) of the Act of 1982, but the Secretary of State may require him—

> (*a*) not to make investments of a specified class or description;
>
> (*b*) to realise, before the expiration of a specified period (or such longer period as the Secretary of State may allow), the whole or a specified proportion of investments of a specified class or description held by the liquidator when the requirement is imposed.   **[1751]**

NOTES
   Commencement: 29 December 1986.
   Act of 1982: Insurance Companies Act 1982.

18. Accounts and audit

(1) The liquidator of a company carrying on long term business in whose case no stop order has been made shall supply the Secretary of State, at such times or intervals as he shall specify, with such accounts as he may specify and audited in such manner as he may require and with such information about specified matters and verified in such specified manner as he may require.

(2) The liquidator of such a company shall, if required to do so by the Secretary of State, instruct an actuary to investigate the financial condition of the long term business of the company and to report thereon in such manner as the Secretary of State may specify.

(3) The liquidator of such a company shall, at the expiration of six months from the date of the winding up order and at the expiration of every six months thereafter, prepare a summary of his receipts and payments in the course of carrying on the long term business of the company during that period, procure that the summary be examined and verified by a person qualified under section 389 of the Act of 1985 to audit the accounts of companies and transmit to the Secretary of State one copy of the summary verified as aforesaid.

(4) The liquidator shall make available a copy of the summary for inspection by any person.   **[1752]**

NOTES
   Commencement: 29 December 1986.
   Act of 1985: Companies Act 1985.

19. Caution for long term and other business

Where a company carries on long term business and—

> (*a*) no stop order has been made; and
>
> (*b*) a special manager has been appointed,

rule 4.70 of the principal Rules applies separately to the Company's long term business and to its other business.   **[1753]**

NOTES
   Commencement: 29 December 1986.
   Principal Rules: SI 1986 No 1915.

20. Claims

(1) This rule applies to a company carrying on long term business.

(2) The liquidator may, in relation to the long term business of the company and to its other business, fix different days on or before which the creditors of

the company, who are required to submit or lodge claims, are to do so and he may fix one of those days without at the same time fixing the other.

(3) In submitting or lodging a claim, a creditor may claim the whole or any part of such claim as attributable to the long term business of the company or to its other business or he may make no such attribution.

(4) When he accepts any claim in whole or in part, the liquidator shall state in writing how much of what he accepts is attributable to the long term business of the company and how much to the other business of the company.   **[1754]**

NOTES
Commencement: 29 December 1986.

21. Failure to pay premiums

(1) The liquidator may, in the course of carrying on the long term business of the company and on such terms as he thinks fit, accept payment of a premium even though the payment is tendered after the date on which under the terms of the policy it was finally due to be paid.

(2) The liquidator may, in the course of carrying on the long term business of the company and having regard to the general practice of insurers, recompense a policy holder whose policy has lapsed in consequence of a failure to pay any premium by issuing a free paid-up policy for reduced benefits or otherwise as the liquidator thinks fit.   **[1755]**

NOTES
Commencement: 29 December 1986.

22. Notice of valuation of policy

(1) The liquidator shall give notice of the value of each general business policy, as determined by him in accordance with rule 6, to the persons appearing from the records of the company or otherwise to be entitled to an interest in that policy and he shall do so in such manner as the court may direct.

(2) In the case of a company carrying on long term business, if the liquidator, before a stop order is made in relation to the company, summons a separate general meeting of creditors in respect of liabilities of the company attributable to its long term business, he shall give notice to the persons appearing from the records of the company or otherwise to be entitled to a payment under or to an interest in a long term policy of the amount of that payment or the value of that policy as determined by him in accordance with rule 7(2) or (3) as the case may be and he shall give that notice with the notice summoning the meeting.

(3) If a stop order is made in relation to the company, the liquidator shall give notice to all the persons appearing from the records of the company, or otherwise, to be entitled to a payment under, or to an interest in, a long term policy of the amount of that payment or the value of that policy as determined by him, in accordance with rule 8(2) or (3), as the case may be, and he shall give that notice in such manner as the court may direct.

(4) Any person to whom notice is so given shall be bound by the value so determined unless and until the court otherwise orders.

(5) Paragraphs (2) and (3) of this rule have effect as though references therein to persons appearing to be entitled to an interest in a long term policy and to the value of that policy included respectively references to persons

appearing to be entitled to apply for a free paid-up policy under section 24 of the Act of 1923 and to the value of that entitlement under rule 7 (in the case of paragraph (2) of this rule) or under rule 8 (in the case of paragraph (3) of this rule). **[1756]**

NOTES
Commencement: 29 December 1986.
Act of 1923: Industrial Assurance Act 1923.

23. Dividends to creditors

(1) This rule applies in the case of a company carrying on long term business.

(2) The procedure for payment of dividends to creditors under Chapter 9 of Part 4 of the principal Rules applies separately in relation to the two separate companies assumed for the purpose of rule 5.

(3) The court may, at any time before the making of a stop order, permit a dividend to be declared and paid on such terms as it thinks fit in respect only of debts which fell due for payment before the date of the winding up order or, in the case of claims under long term policies, which have fallen due for payment on or after the date of the winding up order. **[1757]**

NOTES
Commencement: 29 December 1986.

24. Meetings of creditors

(1) In the case of a company carrying on long term business, Chapter 4 and rule 4.31 of Part 4 and Chapters 1 and 2 of Part 7 of the principal Rules apply to each separate general meeting of the creditors summoned under the Act of 1986 or the principal Rules.

(2) In relation to any such separate meeting—

    (*a*) rule 7.6(6) of the principal Rules has effect as if the reference therein to assets of the company was a reference to the assets available under section 55 of the Act of 1982 for meeting the liabilities of the company owed to the creditors summoned to the meeting, and

    (*b*) rule 7.12 of the principal Rules applies as if the reference therein to value in relation to a creditor who is not, by virtue of rule 6, 7 or 8, required to submit or lodge a claim, was a reference to the value most recently notified to him under rule 22 or, if the court has determined a different value in accordance with rule 22(4), as if it were a reference to that different value. **[1758]**

NOTES
Commencement: 29 December 1986.
Act of 1982: Insurance Companies Act 1982.
Act of 1986: Insolvency Act 1986.
Principal Rules: SI 1986 No 1915.

25. Apportionment of expenses of liquidation

(1) Rule 4.67 of the principal Rules applies separately to the assets of the long term business of the company and to the assets of the other business of the company.

(2) Where any fee, expense, cost, charge, outlay or remuneration does not

relate exclusively to the assets of the company's long term business or to the assets of the company's other business, the liquidator shall apportion it amongst those assets in such manner as he shall determine.   **[1759]**

NOTES
Commencement: 29 December 1986.
Principal Rules: SI 1986 No 1915.

26. Notice of stop order

(1) When a stop order has been made in relation to the company, the clerk of court shall, on the same day, send—

(a) to the liquidator,
(b) to the registrar of companies for Scotland, and
(c) to such other person as the court may direct,

a certified copy of the stop order.

(2) The liquidator shall forthwith after receiving a certified copy give notice of the order in the Form in Schedule 6—

(a) in the Edinburgh Gazette, and
(b) in the newspaper in which the winding up order was advertised.

[1760]

NOTES
Commencement; 29 December 1986.

SCHEDULE 1

Rules 6 and 12

GENERAL BUSINESS POLICIES

1.—(1) This paragraph applies in relation to periodic payments under a general business policy which fall due for payment after the date of the winding up order where the event giving rise to the liability to make the payments occurred before the date of the winding up order.

(2) The value to be attributed to such periodic payments shall be determined on such actuarial principles and assumptions in regard to all relevant factors as the court shall direct.

2.—(1) This paragraph applies in relation to liabilities under a general business policy not dealt with by paragraph 1.

(2) The value to be attributed to those liabilities shall—

(a) if the terms of the policy provide for a repayment of premium upon the early termination of the policy or the policy is expressed to run from one definite date to another or the policy may be terminated by any of the parties with effect from a definite date, be the greater of the following two amounts—

(i) the amount (if any) which, under the terms of the policy, should have been repayable on early termination of the policy had the policy terminated on the date of the winding up order, and

(ii) where the policy is expressed to run from one definite date to another or may be terminated by any of the parties with effect from a definite date, such proportion of the last premium paid as is proportionate to the unexpired portion of the period in respect of which that premium was paid; and

(b) in any other case, be a just estimate of that value.   **[1761]**

NOTES
Commencement: 29 December 1986.

SCHEDULE 2

Rules 7(3) and 12

RULES FOR VALUING NON-LINKED POLICIES, NON-LINKED DEFERRED ANNUITY
POLICIES, NON-LINKED ANNUITIES IN PAYMENT AND CAPITAL REDEMPTION POLICIES

General

1.—(1) In valuing a policy—

    (*a*) where it is necessary to calculate the present value of future payments by or to the company, interest shall be assumed at such rate or rates as the court may direct;

    (*b*) where relevant the rate of mortality and the rates of disability to be employed shall be such rates as the court may consider appropriate after taking into account—

        (i) relevant published tables of rates of mortality and rates of disability, and

        (ii) the rates of mortality and the rates of disability experienced in connection with similar policies issued by the company;

    (*c*) there shall be determined—

        (i) the present value of the ordinary benefits,

        (ii) a reserve for options,

        (iii) a reserve for expenses, and

        (iv) if further fixed premiums fall due to be paid under the policy on or after the date of the winding up order, the present value of the modified net premiums;

and for the purpose of this Schedule a premium is a fixed premium if the amount of it is determined by the terms of the policy and it cannot be varied.

(2) Where under the terms of the policy or on the basis of the company's established practice the policy holder has a right to receive or an expectation of receiving benefits additional to the minimum benefits guaranteed under those terms the court shall determine rates of interest, mortality and disability under paragraph (1) which will result in the inclusion in the present value of the ordinary benefits and in the present value of the modified net premiums of such margin, if any, as the court may consider appropriate to provide for that right or expectation in respect of the period after the date of the winding up order.

Present value of the ordinary benefits

2.—(1) Ordinary benefits are the benefits which will become payable to the policy holder on or after the date of the winding up order without his having to exercise any option under the policy (including any bonus or addition to the sum assured or the amount of annuity declared before the date of the winding up order) and for this purpose "option" includes a right to surrender the policy.

(2) The present value of the ordinary benefits shall be the value at the date of the winding up order of the reversion in the ordinary benefits according to the contingency upon which those benefits are payable, calculated on the basis of the rates of interest, mortality and disability referred to in paragraph 1.

Reserve for options

3. The amount of the reserve for options shall be the amount which, in the opinion of the liquidator, arrived at on appropriate assumptions in regard to all relevant factors, is necessary to be provided at the date of the winding up order (in addition to the amount of the present value of the ordinary benefits) to cover the additional liabilities likely to arise upon the exercise on or after that date by the policy holder of any option conferred upon him by the terms of the policy or, in the case of an industrial assurance policy, by the Industrial Assurance Acts other than an option whereby the policy holder can secure a guaranteed cash payment within the period of 12 months beginning with that date.

Reserve for expenses

4.—(1) The amount of the reserve for expenses is the amount which, in the opinion of the liquidator, is necessary to be provided at the date of the winding up order for meeting future expenses.

(2) In this paragraph "future expenses" means such part of the expenses likely to be incurred after that date in the fulfilling by the liquidator, or by any transferee from the liquidator of the long term business of the company, of the obligations of that business as is appropriate to the policy and which cannot be met out of the amounts, if any, by which the actual premiums payable under that policy after that date exceed the amounts of the modified net premiums which correspond to those actual premiums.

Net premiums

5.—(1) For the purpose of determining the present value of the modified premiums, a net premium shall be determined in relation to each actual premium paid or payable under the policy in such a way that—

(*a*) the net premiums, if they had been payable when the corresponding actual premiums were or are payable, would, on the basis of the rates of interest, mortality and disability referred to in paragraph 1, have been sufficient when the policy was issued to provide for the benefits under the policy according to the contingencies on which they are payable, exclusive of any addition for profits, expenses or other charges, and

(*b*) the ratio between the counts of any two net premiums is the same as the ratio between the amounts of the two actual premiums to which they correspond (any actual premium which includes a loading for unusual risks assumed by the company in respect of a part only of the term of the policy being treated for this purpose as if it did not include that loading).

(2) For the purposes of this paragraph, where at any time after the policy was issued the terms of the policy have been varied (otherwise than by the surrender of the policy in consideration of the issue of a new policy), it shall be assumed that the policy when it was issued provided for those variations to take effect at the time when they did in fact take effect.

Modified net premiums

6.—(1) A modified net premium shall be determined in relation to each net premium by making an addition to each net premium such that—

(*a*) the additions, if each was payable when the corresponding actual premium was or is payable, would, on the basis of the rates of interest, mortality and disability referred to in paragraph 1, have been sufficient to compensate for the acquisition expenses relating to the policy; and

(*b*) the ratio between the amounts of any two modified net premiums is the same as the ratio between the amounts of the two net premiums to which they correspond.

(2) For this purpose the acquisition expenses relating to the policy shall be taken to be 3.5 per cent (or the defined percentage if it be lower than 3.5 per cent) of the relevant capital sum under the contract and for this purpose—

(*a*) "the defined percentage" is the percentage arrived at by taking (for all policies which in the opinion of the liquidator have the same or similar characteristics to the policy in question, and which he considers appropriate to be taken notice of for this purpose), the average of the percentages of the relevant capital sums under those policies that represent the acquisition expenses for which, after allowing for the effects of taxation, allowance is made in the premiums actually payable; and

(*b*) "the relevant capital sum" in relation to any policy is—

(i) for whole life assurances, the sum assured,

(ii) for policies where a sum is payable on maturity (including policies where a sum is also payable on earlier death), the sum payable on maturity,

    (iii) for temporary assurances, the sum assured on the date of the winding up order,

    (iv) for deferred annuity policies, the capitalised value on the date on which the first payment is due to be made of the payments due to be made under the policy calculated on the basis of the rates of interest, mortality and disability referred to in paragraph 1 or, if the terms of the policy include a right on the part of the policy holder to surrender the policy on that date for a cash payment greater than the said capitalised value, the amount of that cash payment, and

    (v) for capital redemption policies, the sum payable at the end of the contract period.

(3) Where the amount of a modified net premium calculated in accordance with sub-paragraphs (1) and (2) is greater than the amount of the actual premium to which it corresponds, then the amount of that modified net premium shall be the amount of that actual premium and not the amount calculated in accordance with sub-paragraphs (1) and (2).

Present value of the modified net premiums

7. The present value of the modified net premiums shall be the value as at the date of the winding up order, calculated on the basis of the rates of interest, mortality and disability referred to in paragraph 1, of the modified net premiums payable after that date on the assumption that they are payable as and when the corresponding actual premiums are payable.

Value of the policy

8.—(1) Subject to sub-paragraph (2)—

    (*a*) if no further fixed premiums fall due to be paid under the policy on or after the date of the winding up order, the value of the policy shall be the aggregate of—

        (i) the present value of the ordinary benefits,

        (ii) the reserve for options,

        (iii) the reserve for expenses, and

        (iv) where under the terms of the policy or on the basis of the company's established practice the policy holder has a right to receive or an expectation of receiving benefits additional to the ordinary benefits, such amount (if any) as the court may determine to reflect that right or expectation in respect of the period ending with the date of the winding up order;

    (*b*) if further fixed premiums fall due to be so paid and the aggregate value referred to in sub-paragraph (*a*) exceeds the present value of the modified net premiums, the value of the policy shall be the amount of that excess; and

    (*c*) if further fixed premiums fall due to be so paid and that aggregate does not exceed the present value of the modified net premiums, the policy shall have no value.

(2) Where the policy holder has a right conferred upon him by the terms of the policy or by the Industrial Assurance Acts whereby the policy holder can secure a guaranteed cash payment within the period of 12 months beginning with the date of the winding up order, the liquidator shall determine the amount which in his opinion it is necessary to provide at that date to cover the liabilities which will accrue when that option is exercised (on the assumption that it will be exercised) and the value of the policy shall be that amount if it exceeds the value of the policy (if any) determined in accordance with sub-paragraph (1).   **[1762]**

NOTES

Commencement: 29 December 1986.

SCHEDULE 3

Rules 7(3) and 12

RULES FOR VALUING LIFE POLICIES AND DEFERRED ANNUITY POLICIES WHICH ARE
LINKED POLICIES

1.—(1) Subject to sub-paragraph (2), the value of the policy shall be the aggregate of the value of the linked liabilities (calculated in accordance with paragraph 2 or 4) and the value of other than linked liabilities (calculated in accordance with paragraph 5) except where that aggregate is a negative amount in which case the policy shall have no value.

(2) Where the terms of the policy include a right whereby the policy holder can secure a guaranteed cash payment within the period of 12 months beginning with the date of the winding up order then, if the amount which in the opinion of the liquidator is necessary to be provided at that date to cover any liabilities which will accrue when that option is exercised (on the assumption that it will be exercised) is greater than the value determined under sub-paragraph (1) of this paragraph, the value of the policy shall be that greater amount.

2.—(1) Where linked liabilities are expressed in terms of units the value of those liabilities shall, subject to paragraph 3, be the amount arrived at by taking the product of the number of units of each class of units allocated to the policy on the date of the winding up order and the value of each such unit on that date and then adding those products.

(2) For the purposes of sub-paragraph (1)—

(a) where under the terms of the policy the value of a unit at any time falls to be determined by reference to the value at that time of the assets of a particular fund maintained by the company in relation to that and other policies, the value of a unit on the date of the winding up order shall be determined by reference to the net realisable value of the assets credited to that fund on that date (after taking account of disposal costs, any tax liabilities resulting from the disposal of assets insofar as they have not already been provided for by the company and any other amounts which under the terms of those policies are chargeable to the fund), and

(b) in any other case, the value of a unit on the date of the winding up shall be the value which would have been ascribed to each unit credited to the policy holder, after any deductions which may be made under the terms of the policy, for the purpose of determining the benefits payable under the policy on the date of the winding up order had the policy matured on that date.

3.—(1) This paragraph applies where—

(a) paragraph 2(2)(a) applies and the company has a right under the terms of the policy to make periodic withdrawals from the fund referred to in that paragraph or to retain any part of the income accruing in respect of the assets of that fund; or

(b) paragraph 2(2)(b) applies and the company has a right under the terms of the policy to receive the whole or any part of any distributions made in respect of the units referred to in that paragraph; or

(c) paragraph 2(2)(a) or 2(2)(b) applies and the company has a right under the terms of the policy to make periodic cancellations of a proportion of the number of units credited to the policy.

(2) Where this paragraph applies the value of the linked liabilities calculated in accordance with paragraph 2(1) shall be reduced by an amount calculated in accordance with sub-paragraph (3) of this paragraph.

(3) The said amount is—

(a) where this paragraph applies by virtue of head (a) or (b) of sub-paragraph (1), the value as at the date of the winding up order, calculated on actuarial principles, of the future income of the company in respect of the units in question arising from the rights referred to in head (*a*) or (*b*) of sub-paragraph (1) as the case may be; or

(*b*) where this paragraph applies by virtue of head (*c*) of sub-paragraph (1), the value as at the date of the winding up order, calculated on actuarial principles, of the liabilities of the company in respect of the units which fall to be cancelled in the future under the right referred to in head (*c*) of sub-paragraph (1).

(4) In calculating any amount in accordance with sub-paragraph (3) there shall be disregarded—

(*a*) such parts of the rights referred to in the relevant head of sub-paragraph (1) which in the opinion of the liquidator constitutes appropriate provision for future expenses and mortality risks; and

(*b*) such part of those rights (if any) which the court considers to constitute appropriate provision for any right or expectation of the policy holder to receive benefits additional to the benefits guaranteed under the terms of the policy.

(5) In determining the said amount—

(*a*) interest shall be assumed at such rate or rates as the court may direct; and

(*b*) where relevant the rates of mortality and the rates of disability to be employed shall be such rates as the court may consider appropriate after taking into account—

(i) relevant published tables of rates of mortality and rates of disability, and

(ii) the rates of mortality and the rates of disability experienced in connection with similar policies issued by the company.

4. Where the linked liabilities are not expressed in terms of units, the value of those liabilities shall be the value which would have been ascribed to those liabilities had the policy matured on the date of the winding up order.

5.—(1) The value of any liabilities other than linked liabilities including reserves for future expenses, options and guarantees shall be determined on actuarial principles and appropriate assumptions in regard to all relevant factors including the assumption of such rate or rates of interest, mortality and disability as the court may direct.

(2) In valuing liabilities under this paragraph, credit shall be taken for those parts of future premiums which do not fall to be applied in the allocation of future units to the policy and for any rights of the company which have been disregarded under paragraph 3(4)(*a*) in valuing the linked liabilities. **[1763]**

NOTES
Commencement: 29 December 1986.

SCHEDULE 4
Rules 7(3) and 12

RULES FOR VALUING LONG TERM POLICIES WHICH ARE NOT DEALT WITH IN
SCHEDULES 2 AND 3

The value of a long term policy not covered by Schedule 2 or 3 shall be determined on such actuarial principles and assumptions in regard to all relevant factors as the court shall determine. **[1764]**

NOTES
Commencement: 29 December 1986.

SCHEDULE 5

Rules 8(3) and 12

RULES FOR VALUING LONG TERM POLICIES WHERE A STOP ORDER HAS BEEN MADE

1. Subject to paragraphs 2 and 3, in valuing a policy Schedule 2, 3 or 4 shall apply according to the class of that policy as if those Schedules were herein repeated but with a view to a fresh valuation of each policy on appropriate assumptions in regard to all relevant factors and subject to the following modifications—

(*a*) references to the stop order shall be substituted for references to the winding up order;

(*b*) in paragraph 3 of Schedule 2 for the words "whereby the policy holder can secure a guaranteed cash payment within the period of 12 months beginning with that date." there shall be substituted the words "to surrender the policy which can be exercised on that date.";

(*c*) in paragraph 4(2) of Schedule 2 for the words "likely to be incurred" there shall be substituted the words "which were likely to have been incurred" and for the words "cannot be met" there shall be substituted the words "could not have been met";

(*d*) paragraph 8(2) of Schedule 2 shall be omitted; and

(*e*) paragraph 1(2) of Schedule 3 shall be omitted.

2.—(1) This paragraph applies where the policy holder has a right conferred upon him under the terms of the policy or by the Industrial Assurance Acts to surrender the policy and that right is exercisable on the date of the stop order.

(2) Where this paragraph applies and the amount required, at the date of the stop order, to provide for the benefits payable upon surrender of the policy on the assumption that the policy is surrendered on the date of the stop order is greater than the value of the policy determined in accordance with paragraph 1, the value of the policy shall, subject to paragraph 3, be the said amount so required.

(3) Where any part of the surrender value is payable after the date of the stop order, sub-paragraph (2) shall apply but the value therein referred to shall be discounted at such rate of interest as the court may direct.

3.—(1) This paragraph applies in the case of a linked policy where—

(*a*) the terms of the policy include a guarantee that the amount assured will on maturity of the policy be worth a minimum amount calculable in money terms; or

(*b*) the terms of the policy include a right on the part of the policy holder to surrender the policy and a guarantee that the payment on surrender will be worth a minimum amount calculable in money terms and that right is exercisable on or after the date of the stop order.

(2) Where this paragraph applies the value of the policy shall be the greater of the following two amounts—

(*a*) the value the policy would have had at the date of the stop order had the policy been a non-linked policy, that is to say, had the linked liabilities provided by the policy not been so provided but the policy had otherwise been on the same terms; and

(*b*) the value the policy would have had at the date of the stop order had the policy not included any guarantees of payments on maturity or surrender worth a minimum amount calculable in money terms. **[1765]**

NOTES
Commencement: 29 December 1986.

SCHEDULE 6

Rule 26(2)

NOTICE OF ORDER PRONOUNCED UNDER SECTION 56(2) OF THE INSURANCE COMPANIES ACT 1982 FOR CESSATION OF LONG TERM BUSINESS

Name of Company

Address of Registered Office

On . . . ., the Court . . . ., under section 56(2) of the Insurance Companies Act 1982, ordered the cessation of the long term business of the above company.

Date

Signed . . . .

Liquidator

[1766]

<hr>

NOTES

Commencement: 29 December 1986.

PART V

MISCELLANEOUS

Section A

Other Legislation

SECTION A
OTHER LEGISLATION

DEEDS OF ARRANGEMENT ACT 1914
(c 47)

ARRANGEMENT OF SECTIONS

PART I
APPLICATION OF ACT

Section   Para
1   Deeds of arrangement to which Act applies   ..   ..   [1767]

PART II
AVOIDANCE OF ARRANGEMENT WHERE STATUTORY CONDITIONS NOT COMPLIED WITH

2   Avoidance of unregistered deeds of arrangement ..   ..   [1768]
3   Avoidance of deeds of arrangement unless assented to by a majority of the creditors .. [1769]

PART III
REGISTRATION OF DEEDS OF ARRANGEMENT

5   Mode of registration..   ..   ..   [1770]
6   Form of register   ..   ..   [1771]
7   Rectification of register   ..   ..   [1772]
8   Time for registration   ..   ..   [1773]
9   Inspection of register and registered deeds   ..   ..   [1774]
10 Local registration of copy of deeds ..   ..   [1775]

PART IV
PROVISIONS AS TO TRUSTEES

11 Security by trustee ..   ..   [1776]
12 Penalty on trustee acting when deed of arrangement void   ..   ..   ..   [1777]
13 Transmission of accounts to Board of Trade   ..   ..   [1778]
14 Transmission of accounts to creditors   ..   ..   [1779]
15 Audit of accounts   ..   ..   [1780]
16 Payment of undistributed moneys into court   ..   ..   [1781]
17 Preferential payment to creditor an offence   ..   ..   [1782]
19 Provisions for the protection of trustees under void deeds   ..   ..   [1783]
20 Notice to creditors of avoidance of deed   ..   ..   [1784]
21 Payment of expenses incurred by trustees ..   ..   [1785]
22 Application of Part IV   ..   ..   [1786]

PART V
GENERAL

23 Courts in which applications for enforcement of trusts to be made   ..   ..   [1787]
24 Relation to bankruptcy law ..   ..   [1788]
25 Office copies ..   ..   [1789]
26 Fees ..   ..   [1790]
27 Report by Board of Trade   ..   ..   [1791]
29 Affidavits ..   ..   [1792]

Section   Para
30 Interpretation of terms   ..   .. [1793]
32 Short title, extent and commencement   ..   .. [1794]

An Act to consolidate the Law relating to Deeds of Arrangement [10 August 1914]

NOTES
    This Act should be considered along with the Insolvency Act 1986, ss 252–263 which deal with individual voluntary arrangements. Section 260(3) of the 1986 Act provides that the Deeds of Arrangement Act 1914 does not apply to an approved voluntary arrangement. The 1986 Act therefore provides a debtor with an alternative to a deed of arrangement.

PART I

APPLICATION OF ACT

1. Deeds of arrangement to which Act applies

(1) A deed of arrangement to which this Act applies shall include any instrument of the classes hereinafter mentioned whether under seal or not—

  (*a*) made by, for or in respect of the affairs of a debtor for the benefit of his creditors generally;
  (*b*) made by, for or in respect of the affairs of a debtor who was insolvent at the date of the execution of the instrument for the benefit of any three or more of his creditors:

otherwise than in pursuance of the law for the time being in force relating to bankruptcy.

  (2) The classes of instrument hereinbefore referred to are—

  (*a*) an assignment of property;
  (*b*) a deed of or agreement for a composition;

and in cases where creditors of the debtor obtain any control over his property or business—

  (*c*) a deed of inspectorship entered into for the purpose of carrying on or winding up a business;
  (*d*) a letter of licence authorising the debtor or any other person to manage, carry on, realise or dispose of a business with a view to the payment of debts; and
  (*e*) any agreement or instrument entered into for the purpose of carrying on or winding up the debtor's business, or authorising the debtor or any other person to manage, carry on, realise or dispose of the debtor's business with a view to the payment of his debts.   **[1767]**

PART II

AVOIDANCE OF ARRANGEMENT WHERE STATUTORY CONDITIONS NOT COMPLIED WITH

2. Avoidance of unregistered deeds of arrangement

A deed of arrangement shall be void unless it is registered with the Registrar of Bills of Sale under this Act within seven clear days after the first execution thereof by the debtor or any creditor, or if it is executed in any place out of England, then within seven clear days after the time at which it would, in the ordinary course of post, arrive in England, if posted within one week after the execution thereof, and unless it bears such . . . stamp as is provided by this Act.

[1768]

NOTES

Words omitted repealed by the Finance Act 1949, s 52, Sch 11, Part V.

3. Avoidance of deeds of arrangement unless assented to by a majority of the creditors

(1) A deed of arrangement, which either is expressed to be or is in fact for the benefit of a debtor's creditors generally, shall be void unless, before or within twenty-one days after the registration thereof, or within such extended time as the High Court or the court having jurisdiction *in bankruptcy in* [for the purposes of [Parts VIII to XI of the Insolvency Act 1986] in relation to] the district in which the debtor resided or carried on business at the date of the execution of the deed may allow, it has received the assent of a majority in number and value of the creditors of the debtor.

(2) The list of creditors annexed to the affidavit of the debtor filed on the registration of the deed of arrangement shall be prima facie evidence of the names of the creditors and the amounts of their claims.

(3) The assent of a creditor for the purposes of subsection (1) of this section shall be established by his executing the deed of arrangement or sending to the trustee his assent in writing attested by a witness, but not otherwise.

(4) The trustee shall file with the Registrar of Bills of Sale at the time of the registration of a deed of arrangement, or, in the case of a deed of arrangement assented to after registration, within twenty-eight days after registration or within such extended time as the High Court or the court having jurisdiction *in bankruptcy in* [for the purposes of [Parts VIII to XI of the Insolvency Act 1986] in relation to] the district in which the debtor resided or carried on business at the date of the execution of the deed may allow, a statutory declaration by the trustee that the requisite majority of the creditors of the debtor have assented to the deed of arrangement, which declaration shall, in favour of a purchaser for value, be conclusive evidence, and, in other cases, be prima facie evidence, of the fact declared.

(5) In calculating a majority of creditors for the purposes of this section, a creditor holding security upon the property of the debtor shall be reckoned as a creditor only in respect of the balance (if any) due to him after deducting the value of such security, and creditors whose debts amount to sums not exceeding ten pounds shall be reckoned in the majority in value but not in the majority in number.

[1769]

NOTES

Sub-ss (1), (4): words in italics repealed with savings and first words in square brackets substituted with savings by the Insolvency Act 1985, s 235, Sch 8, para 2 and the Insolvency Act 1986, s 437, Sch 11; further amended by the Insolvency Act 1986, s 349(2), Sch 14.

PART III

REGISTRATION OF DEEDS OF ARRANGEMENT

5. Mode of registration

(1) The registration of a deed of arrangement under this Act shall be effected in the following manner:—

A true copy of the deed, and of every schedule or inventory thereto annexed, or therein referred to, shall be presented to and filed with the registrar within seven clear days after the execution of the deed . . . , together with an affidavit verifying the time of execution, and containing a description of the residence and occupation of the debtor, and of the place or places where his business is carried on, and an affidavit by the debtor stating the total estimated amount of property and liabilities included under the deed, the total amount of the composition (if any) payable thereunder, and the names and addresses of his creditors.

(2) No deed shall be registered under this Act unless the original of the deed, duly stamped with the proper inland revenue duty . . . , is produced to the registrar at the time of such registration. **[1770]**

NOTES
Sub-s (1): words omitted repealed by the Administration of Justice Act 1925, s 29, Sch 5.
Sub-s (2): words omitted repealed by the Finance Act 1949, s 52(10), Sch 11.

6. Form of register

The registrar shall keep a register wherein shall be entered, as soon as conveniently may be after the presentation of a deed for registration, an abstract of the contents of every deed of arrangement registered under this Act, containing the following and any other prescribed particulars:—

(*a*) The date of the deed;

(*b*) The name, address, and description of the debtor, and the place or places where his business was carried on at the date of the execution of the deed, and the title of the firm or firms under which the debtor carried on business, and the name and address of the trustee (if any) under the deed;

(*c*) . . .

(*d*) The date of registration;

(*e*) The amount of property and liabilities included under the deed, as estimated by the debtor. **[1771]**

NOTES
Words omitted repealed by the Administration of Justice Act 1925, s 22(3), Sch 5.

7. Rectification of register

The High Court or a judge thereof, upon being satisfied that the omission to register a deed of arrangement within the time required by this Act or that the omission or mis-statement of the name, residence, or description of any person was accidental, or due to inadvertence, or to some cause beyond the control of the debtor and not imputable to any negligence on his part, may, on the application of any party interested, and on such terms and conditions as are just and expedient, extend the time for registration, or order the omission or mis-statement to be supplied or rectified by the insertion in the register of the true name, residence, or description. **[1772]**

8. Time for registration

Where the time for registering a deed of arrangement expires on a Sunday, or other day on which the registration office is closed, the registration shall be valid if made on the next following day on which the office is open. **[1773]**

9. Inspection of register and registered deeds

Any person shall be entitled, at all reasonable times, to search the register on payment of [5p], or such other fee as may be prescribed, and subject to such regulations as may be prescribed, and shall be entitled, at all reasonable times, to inspect, examine, and make extracts from any registered deed of arrangement, without being required to make a written application or to specify any particulars in reference thereto, upon payment of [5p], or such other fee as may be prescribed, for each deed of arrangement inspected:

Provided that the extracts shall be limited to the dates of execution and of registration, the names, addresses, and descriptions of the debtor and of the parties to the deed, a short statement of the nature and effect of the deed, and any other prescribed particulars.   **[1774]**

NOTES

Amended by virtue of the Decimal Currency Act 1969, s 10.

10. Local registration of copy of deeds

(1) Where the place of business or residence of the debtor who is one of the parties to a deed of arrangement, or who is referred to therein, is situate in some place outside the London bankruptcy district, the registrar shall, within three clear days after registration, and in accordance with the prescribed directions, transmit a copy of the deed to the registrar of the county court in the district of which such place of business or residence is situate.

(2) Every copy so transmitted shall be filed, kept and indexed by the registrar of the county court in the prescribed manner, and any person may search, inspect, make extracts from, and obtain copies of, the registered copy, in the like manner and upon the like terms, as to payment or otherwise, as near as may be, as in the case of deeds registered under this Act.   **[1775]**

PART IV

PROVISIONS AS TO TRUSTEES

11. Security by trustee

(1) The trustee under a deed of arrangement shall, within seven days from the date on which the statutory declaration certifying the assent of the creditors is filed, give security in the prescribed manner to the registrar of the court having jurisdiction *in bankruptcy in* [for the purposes of [Parts VIII to XI of the Insolvency Act 1986] in relation to] the district in which the debtor resided or carried on business at the date of the execution of the deed, or, if he then resided or carried on business in the *London bankruptcy district* [London insolvency district], to the senior bankruptcy registrar of the High Court, in a sum equal to the estimated assets available for distribution amongst the unsecured creditors as shown by the affidavit filed on registration, to administer the deed properly and account fully for the assets which come to his hands, unless a majority in number and value of the debtor's creditors, either by resolution passed at a meeting convened by notice to all the creditors, or by writing addressed to the trustee, dispense with his giving such security;

Provided that, when such a dispensation has been so given, the trustee shall forthwith make and file with the Registrar of Bills of Sale a statutory declaration to that effect, which declaration shall, in favour of a purchaser for value, be conclusive evidence, and, in other cases, be prima facie evidence, of the facts declared.

(2) If a trustee under a deed of arrangement fails to comply with the requirements of this section, the court having jurisdiction *in bankruptcy in* [for the purposes of [Parts VIII to XI of the Insolvency Act 1986] in relation to] the district in which the debtor resided or carried on business at the date of the execution of the deed, on the application of any creditor and after hearing such persons as it may think fit, may declare the deed of arrangement to be void or may make an order appointing another trustee in the place of the trustee appointed by the deed of arrangement.

(3) A certificate that the security required by this section has been given by a trustee, signed by the registrar to whom it was given and filed with the Registrar of Bills of Sale, shall be conclusive evidence of the fact.

(4) All moneys received by a trustee under a deed of arrangement shall be banked by him to an account to be opened in the name of the debtor's estate.

(5) In calculating a majority of creditors for the purposes of this section, a creditor holding security upon the property of the debtor shall be reckoned as a creditor only in respect of the balance (if any) due to him after deducting the value of such security, and creditors whose debts amount to sums not exceeding ten pounds shall be reckoned in the majority in value but not in the majority in number. **[1776]**

NOTES
Sub-ss (1), (2): words in italics repealed with savings and first words in square brackets substituted with savings by the Insolvency Act 1985, s 235, Sch 8, para 2 and the Insolvency Act 1986, s 437, Sch 11; further amended by the Insolvency Act 1986, s 439(2), Sch 14.

12. Penalty on trustee acting when deed of arrangement void

If a trustee acts under a deed of arrangement—

(*a*) after it has to his knowledge become void by reason of non-compliance with any of the requirements of this Act or any enactment repealed by this Act; or

(*b*) after he has failed to give security within the time and in the manner provided for by this Act or any enactment repealed by this Act,

he shall be liable on summary conviction to a fine not exceeding five pounds for every day between the date on which the deed became void or the expiration of the time within which security should have been given, as the case may be, and the last day on which he is proved to have acted as trustee, unless he satisfies the court before which he is accused that his contravention of the law was due to inadvertence, or that his action has been confined to taking such steps as were necessary for the protection of the estate. **[1777]**

13. Transmission of accounts to Board of Trade

(1) Every trustee under a deed of arrangement shall, at such times as may be prescribed, transmit to the Board of Trade, or as they direct, an account of his receipts and payments as trustee, in the prescribed form and verified in the prescribed manner.

(2) If any trustee fails to transmit such account, he shall be liable on summary conviction to a fine not exceeding five pounds for each day during which the default continues, *and the judge of the High Court to whom bankruptcy*

business has been assigned may, for the purpose of enforcing the provisions of the last preceding subsection, exercise, on the application of the Board of Trade, all the powers conferred on the court by subsection (5) of section one hundred and five of the Bankruptcy Act 1914 in cases of bankruptcy [and, in addition, shall be guilty of contempt of court and liable to be punished accordingly].

(3) The accounts transmitted to the Board of Trade in pursuance of this section shall be open to inspection by the debtor or any creditor or other person interested on payment of the prescribed fee, and copies of or extracts from the accounts shall, on payment of the prescribed fee, be furnished to the debtor, the creditors, or any other persons interested.

(4) In this section the expression "trustee" shall include any person appointed to distribute a composition or to act in any fiduciary capacity under any deed of arrangements . . .		**[1778]**

NOTES
Sub-s (2): words in italics repealed with savings and words in square brackets substituted with savings by the Insolvency Act 1985, s 235, Sch 8, para 2 and the Insolvency Act 1986, s 437, Sch 11.
Sub-s (4): words omitted repealed by the Administration of Justice Act 1925, s 29, Sch 5.

14. Transmission of accounts to creditors

Every trustee under a deed of arrangement shall, at the expiration of six months from the date of the registration of the deed, and thereafter at the expiration of every subsequent period of six months until the estate has been finally wound up, send to each creditor who has assented to the deed a statement in the prescribed form of the trustee's accounts and of the proceedings under the deed down to the date of the statement, and shall, in his affidavit verifying his accounts transmitted to the Board of Trade, state whether or not he has duly sent such statements, and the dates on which the statements were sent; and, if a trustee fails to comply with any of the provisions of this section, *the High Court may, for the purpose of enforcing those provisions, exercise on the application of the Board of Trade all the powers conferred on the court by subsection (5) of section one hundred and five of the Bankruptcy Act 1914 in cases of bankruptcy* [he shall be guilty of contempt of court and liable to be punished accordingly].		**[1779]**

NOTES
Words in italics repealed with savings and words in square brackets substituted with savings by the Insolvency Act 1985, s 235, Sch 8, para 2 and the Insolvency Act 1986, s 437, Sch 11.

15. Audit of accounts

(1) Where, in the course of the administration of the estate of a debtor who has executed a deed of arrangement, or within twelve months from the date when the final accounts of the estate were rendered to the Board of Trade, an application in writing is made to the Board by a majority in number and value of the creditors who have assented to the deed for an official audit of the trustee's accounts, the Board may cause the trustee's accounts to be audited, and in such case *all the provisions of the Bankruptcy Act 1914* [any rules made under [section 412 of the Insolvency Act 1986]] relating to the institution and enforcement of an audit of the accounts of a trustee in bankruptcy (including the provisions as to fees) shall, with necessary modifications, apply to the audit of the trustee's accounts, and the Board shall have power on the audit to require production of a certificate for the taxed costs of any solicitor whose costs have been paid or charged by the trustee, and to disallow the whole or any part of any costs in respect of which no certificate is produced.

(2) The Board of Trade may determine how and by what parties the costs, charges and expenses of and incidental to the audit (including any prescribed fees chargeable in respect thereof) are to be borne, whether by the applicants or by the trustee or out of the estate, and may, before granting an application for an audit, require the applicants to give security for the costs of the audit. **[1780]**

NOTES
Words in italics repealed and first words in square brackets substituted with savings by the Insolvency Act 1985, s 235, Sch 8, para 2 and the Insolvency Act 1986, s 437, Sch 11; further amended by the Insolvency Act 1986, s 439(2), Sch 14.

16. Payment of undistributed moneys into court

At any time after the expiration of two years from the date of the registration of a deed of arrangement, the court having jurisdiction *in bankruptcy in* [for the purposes of [Parts VIII to XI of the Insolvency Act 1986] in relation to] the district in which the debtor resided or carried on business at the date of the execution of the deed may, on the application of the trustee or a creditor, or on the application of the debtor, order that all moneys representing unclaimed dividends and undistributed funds then in the hands of the trustee or under his control be [paid into the Supreme Court or, if a county court has jurisdiction in the matter, into that court]. **[1781]**

NOTES
Words in italics repealed with savings and first words in square brackets substituted with savings by the Insolvency Act 1985, s 235, Sch 8, para 2 and the Insolvency Act 1986, s 437, Sch 11, Part II; further amended by the Insolvency Act 1986, s 439(2), Sch 14; final amendment in square brackets made by the Administration of Justice Act 1965, ss 17(1), 18, Sch 1.

17. Preferential payment to creditor an offence

If a trustee under a deed of arrangement pays to any creditor out of the debtor's property a sum larger in proportion to the creditor's claim than that paid to other creditors entitled to the benefit of the deed, then, unless the deed authorises him to do so, or unless such payments are either made to a creditor entitled to enforce his claim by distress or are such as would be lawful in a bankruptcy, he shall be guilty of a misdemeanour. **[1782]**

19. Provisions for the protection of trustees under void deeds

(1) Where a deed of arrangement is void by reason that the requisite majority of creditors have not assented thereto, or, in the case of a deed for the benefit of three or more creditors, by reason that the debtor was insolvent at the time of the execution of the deed and that the deed was not registered as required by this Act, but is not void for any other reason, and a *receiving order* [bankruptcy order] is made against the debtor upon a petition presented after the lapse of three months from the execution of the deed, the trustee under the deed shall not be liable to account to the trustee in the bankruptcy for any dealings with or payments made out of the debtor's property which would have been proper if the deed had been valid, if he proves that at the time of such dealings or payments he did not know, and had no reason to suspect, that the deed was void.

(2) Where a receiving order is made against a debtor under subsection (5) of section one hundred and seven of the Bankruptcy Act 1914 this section shall apply if the receiving order was made after the lapse of three months from the execution of the deed. **[1783]**

NOTES
   Sub-s (1): words in italics repealed with savings and words in square brackets substituted with savings by the Insolvency Act 1985, s 235, Sch 8, para 2 and the Insolvency Act 1986, s 437, Sch 11.
   Sub-s (2): repealed with savings by the Insolvency Act 1985, s 235, Sch 10, Part III and the Insolvency Act 1986, s 437, Sch 11.

20. Notice to creditors of avoidance of deed

When a deed of arrangement is void by virtue of this Act for any reason other than that, being for the benefit of creditors generally, it has not been registered within the time allowed for the purpose by this Act, the trustee shall, as soon as practicable after he has become aware that the deed is void, give notice in writing thereof to each creditor whose name and address he knows, and file a copy of the notice with the Registrar of Bills of Sale, and, if he fails to do so, he shall be liable on summary conviction to a fine not exceeding [level 2 on the standard scale].   **[1784]**

NOTES
   Maximum fine increased by the Criminal Justice Act 1977, s 31(6), and converted to a level on the standard scale by the Criminal Justice Act 1982, ss 37, 46.

21. Payment of expenses incurred by trustees

Where a deed of arrangement is avoided by reason of the bankruptcy of the debtor, any expenses properly incurred by the trustee under the deed in the performance of any of the duties imposed on him by this Act shall be allowed or paid him by the trustee in the bankruptcy as a first charge on the estate.
    [1785]

22. Application of Part IV

The provisions of this Part of this Act, except such of those provisions—

   (*a*) as relate to the transmission of accounts to the Board of Trade;

   (*b*) as provide for the protection of trustees under void deeds;

   (*c*) as require a notice to be given to creditors of avoidance of deeds;

   (*d*) as provide for the payment of expenses incurred by trustees;

shall not apply to a deed of arrangement made for the benefit of any three or more of the debtor's creditors unless it is in fact for the benefit of the debtor's creditors generally.   **[1786]**

PART V

GENERAL

23. Courts in which applications for enforcement of trusts to be made

Any application by the trustee under a deed of arrangement, which either is expressed to be or is in fact for the benefit of the debtor's creditors generally, or by the debtor or by any creditor entitled to the benefit of such a deed of arrangement, for the enforcement of the trusts or the determination of questions under it, shall be made to the court having jurisdiction *in bankruptcy in* [for the purposes of [Parts VIII to XI of the Insolvency Act 1986] in relation to] the district in which the debtor resided or carried on business at the date of the execution of the deed:

   Provided that any question as to whether any person claiming to be a creditor entitled to the benefit of a deed of arrangement is so entitled may, subject to rules made under this Act, be decided either by the court having such jurisdiction as aforesaid or by the High Court.   **[1787]**

NOTES

Words in italics repealed with savings and first words in square brackets substituted with savings by the Insolvency Act 1985, s 235, Sch 8, para 2 and the Insolvency Act 1986, s 437, Sch 11, Part II; further amended by the Insolvency Act 1986, s 439(2), Sch 14.

24. Relation to bankruptcy law

(1) If the trustee under a deed of arrangement, which either is expressed to be or is in fact for the benefit of the debtor's creditors generally, serves in the prescribed manner on any creditor of the debtor notice in writing of the execution of the deed and of the filing of the statutory declaration certifying the creditors' assents with an intimation that the creditor will not after the expiration of one month from the service of the notice be entitled to present a bankruptcy petition against the debtor founded on the execution of the deed or on any other act committed by him in the course or for the purpose of the proceedings preliminary to the execution of the deed as an act of bankruptcy, that creditor shall not, after the expiration of that period, unless the deed becomes void, be entitled to present a bankruptcy petition against the debtor founded on the execution of the deed or any act so committed by him as an act of bankruptcy.

(2) Where such a deed of arrangement as aforesaid has become void by virtue of this Act or any enactment repealed by this Act, the fact that a creditor has assented to the deed shall not disentitle him to present a bankruptcy petition founded on the execution of the deed of arrangement as an act of bankruptcy.

(3) Save as otherwise expressly provided by this Act, nothing in this Act shall be construed as repealing or shall affect any provision of the law for the time being in force in relation to bankruptcy or shall give validity to any deed or instrument which by law is *an act of bankruptcy or* void or voidable.   **[1788]**

NOTES

Words in italics repealed with savings by the Insolvency Act 1985, s 235, Sch 10, Part III and the Insolvency Act 1986, s 437, Sch 11.

25. Office copies

Subject to the provisions of this Act, and to any rules made thereunder, any person shall be entitled to have an office copy of, or extract from, any deed registered under this Act, upon paying for it at the like rate as for office copies of judgments of the High Court, and any copy or extract purporting to be an office copy or extract shall, in all courts and before all arbitrators or other persons, be admitted as prima facie evidence thereof, and of the fact and date of registration as shown thereon.   **[1789]**

26. Fees

(1) There shall be taken, in respect of the registration of deeds of arrangement, and in respect of any office copies or extracts, or official searches made by the registrar, such fees as may be from time to time prescribed; and nothing in this Act contained shall make it obligatory on the registrar to do, or permit to be done, any act in respect of which any fee is specified or prescribed, except on payment of such fee.

(2) . . .   **[1790]**

NOTES

Sub-s (2): repealed by the Statute Law Revision Act 1927.

27. Report by Board of Trade

The general annual report which, by section one hundred and thirty-six of the Bankruptcy Act 1914, the Board of Trade is required to cause to be prepared and laid before Parliament, shall include a report of proceedings under this Act . . .

[1791]

NOTES

Words omitted repealed by the Administration of Justice Act 1925, s 29, Sch 5; repealed with savings by the Insolvency Act 1985, s 235, Sch 10, Part III and the Insolvency Act 1986, s 437, Sch 11.

29. Affidavits

An affidavit required by or for the purposes of this Act may be sworn before a Master of the Supreme Court or before any person empowered to take affidavits in the Supreme Court or before any other person before whom such an affidavit may, by any law for the time being in force, be sworn . . .   **[1792]**

NOTES

Words omitted repealed by the Administration of Justice Act 1925, s 29, Sch 5.

30. Interpretation of terms

(1) In this Act; unless the context otherwise requires,—

"Creditors generally" includes all creditors who may assent to, or take the benefit of, a deed of arrangement;

. . .

["property" has the meaning given by section 436 of the Insolvency Act 1986];

"Rules" includes forms.

(2) For the purpose of determining the number of creditors for whose benefit a deed is made, any two or more joint creditors shall be treated as a single creditor.   **[1793]**

NOTES

Words omitted repealed by the Administration of Justice Act 1925, s 29, Sch 5; definition "property" substituted by the Insolvency Act 1986, s 439(2), Sch 14.

32. Short title, extent and commencement

(1) This Act may be cited as the Deeds of Arrangement Act 1914.

(2) This Act shall not extend to Scotland or Ireland.

(3) . . .   **[1794]**

NOTES

Sub-s (3): repealed by the Statute Law Revision Act 1927.

THIRD PARTIES (RIGHTS AGAINST INSURERS) ACT 1930
(c 25)

ARRANGEMENT OF SECTIONS

Section		Para
1 Rights of third parties against insurers on bankruptcy, etc, of the insured	..	.. [1795]
2 Duty to give necessary information to third parties	.. ..	.. [1796]
3 Settlement between insurers and insured persons ..	.. ..	.. [1797]
5 Short title	.. ..	.. [1798]

An Act to confer on third parties rights against insurers of third-party risks in the event of the insured becoming insolvent, and in certain other events

[10 July 1930]

1. Rights of third parties against insurers on bankruptcy, etc, of the insured

(1) Where under any contract of insurance a person (hereinafter referred to as the insured) is insured against liabilities to third parties which he may incur, then—

(a) in the event of the insured becoming bankrupt or making a composition or arrangement with his creditors; or

(b) in the case of the insured being a company, in the event of a winding-up order [or an administration order] being made, or a resolution for a voluntary winding-up being passed, with respect to the company, or of a receiver or manager of the company's business or undertaking being duly appointed, or of possession being taken, by or on behalf of the holders of any debentures secured by a floating charge, of any property comprised in or subject to the charge [or of [a voluntary arrangement proposed for the purposes of Part I of the Insolvency Act 1986 being approved under that Part]];

if, either before or after that event, any such liability as aforesaid is incurred by the insured, his rights against the insurer under the contract in respect of the liability shall, notwithstanding anything in any Act or rule of law to the contrary, be transferred to and vest in the third party to whom the liability was so incurred.

(2) Where *an order is made under section one hundred and thirty of the Bankruptcy Act 1914 for the administration of the estate of a deceased debtor according to the law of bankruptcy* [the estate of any person falls to be administered in accordance with an order under section [421 of the Insolvency Act 1986]], then, if any debt provable in bankruptcy is owing by the deceased in respect of a liability against which he was insured under a contract of insurance as being a liability to a third party, the deceased debtor's rights against the insurer under the contract in respect of that liability shall, notwithstanding anything in *the said Act* [any such order], be transferred to and vest in the person to whom the debt is owing.

(3) In so far as any contract of insurance made after the commencement of this Act in respect of any liability of the insured to third parties purports, whether directly or indirectly, to avoid the contract or to alter the rights of the parties thereunder upon the happening to the insured of any of the events specified in paragraph (a) or paragraph (b) of subsection (1) of this section or upon the *making of an order under section one hundred and thirty of the Bankruptcy*

Act 1914, in respect of his estate [estate of any person falling to be administered in accordance with an order under section [421 of the Insolvency Act 1986]], the contract shall be of no effect.

(4) Upon a transfer under subsection (1) or subsection (2) of this section, the insurer shall, subject to the provisions of section three of this Act, be under the same liability to the third party as he would have been under to the insured, but—

    (*a*) if the liability of the insurer to the insured exceeds the liability of the insured to the third party, nothing in this Act shall affect the rights of the insured against the insurer in respect of the excess; and

    (*b*) if the liability of the insurer to the insured is less than the liability of the insured to the third party, nothing in this Act shall affect the rights of the third party against the insured in respect of the balance.

(5) For the purposes of this Act, the expression "liabilities to third parties", in relation to a person insured under any contract of insurance, shall not include any liability of that person in the capacity of insurer under some other contract of insurance.

(6) This Act shall not apply—

    (*a*) where a company is wound up voluntarily merely for the purposes of reconstruction or of amalgamation with another company; or

    (*b*) to any case to which subsections (1) and (2) of section seven of the Workmen's Compensation Act 1925 applies.   **[1795]**

NOTES

    Sub-s (1): first and second words in square brackets added with savings by the Insolvency Act 1985, s 235, Sch 8, para 7 and the Insolvency Act 1986, s 437, Sch 11; other amendment in square brackets made by the Insolvency Act 1986, s 439(2), Sch 14.

    Sub-s (2): words in italics repealed with savings and first and final words in square brackets substituted with savings by the Insolvency Act 1985, s 235, Sch 8, para 7 and the Insolvency Act 1986, s 437, Sch 11; second words in square brackets substituted by the Insolvency Act 1986, s 439(2), Sch 14.

    Sub-s (3): first words in italics repealed with savings and first words in square brackets substituted with savings by the Insolvency Act 1985, s 235, Sch 8, para 7 and the Insolvency Act 1986, s 437, Sch 11; further amended by the Insolvency Act 1986, s 439(2), Sch 14.

2. Duty to give necessary information to third parties

(1) In the event of any person becoming bankrupt or making a composition or arrangement with his creditors, or in the event of *an order being made under section one hundred and thirty of the Bankruptcy Act 1914, in respect of the estate of any person* [the estate of any person falling to be administered in accordance with an order under section [421 of the Insolvency Act 1986]], or in the event of a winding-up order [or an administration order] being made, or a resolution for a voluntary winding-up being passed, with respect to any company or of a receiver or manager of the company's business or undertaking being duly appointed or of possession being taken by or on behalf of the holders of any debentures secured by a floating charge of any property comprised in or subject to the charge it shall be the duty of the bankrupt, debtor, personal representative of the deceased debtor or company, and, as the case may be, of the trustee in bankruptcy, trustee, liquidator, [administrator,] receiver, or manager, or person in possession of the property to give at the request of any person claiming that the bankrupt, debtor, deceased debtor, or company is under a liability to him such information as may reasonably be required by him for the purpose of ascertaining whether any rights have been transferred to and vested in him by this Act and for the purpose of enforcing such rights, if any, and any contract of

insurance, in so far as it purports, whether directly or indirectly, to avoid the contract or to alter the rights of the parties thereunder upon the giving of any such information in the events aforesaid or otherwise to prohibit or prevent the giving thereof in the said events shall be of no effect.

[(1A) The reference in subsection (1) of this section to a trustee includes a reference to the supervisor of a [voluntary arrangement proposed for the purposes of, and approved under, Part I or Part VIII of the Insolvency Act 1986].]

(2) If the information given to any person in pursuance of subsection (1) of this section discloses reasonable ground for supposing that there have or may have been transferred to him under this Act rights against any particular insurer, that insurer shall be subject to the same duty as is imposed by the said subsection on the persons therein mentioned.

(3) The duty to give information imposed by this section shall include a duty to allow all contracts of insurance, receipts for premiums, and other relevant documents in the possession or power of the person on whom the duty is so imposed to be inspected and copies thereof to be taken.   **[1796]**

NOTES

Commencement: 29 December 1986 (sub-s (1A)); before 1 January 1970 (remainder).

Sub-s (1): first words in italics repealed with savings and first and final words in square brackets prospectively substituted or added with savings by the Insolvency Act 1985, s 235, Sch 8, para 7 and the Insolvency Act 1986, s 437, Sch 11; other amendment made by the Insolvency Act 1986, s 439(2), Sch 14.

Sub-s (1A): added with savings by the Insolvency Act 1985, s 235, Sch 8, para 7 and the Insolvency Act 1986, s 437, Sch 11; amended by the Insolvency Act 1986, s 439(2), Sch 14.

3. Settlement between insurers and insured persons

Where the insured has become bankrupt or where in the case of the insured being a company, a winding-up order [or an administration order] has been made or a resolution for a voluntary winding-up has been passed, with respect to the company, no agreement made between the insurer and the insured after liability has been incurred to a third party and after the commencement of the bankruptcy or winding-up [or the day of the making of the administration order], as the case may be, nor any waiver, assignment, or other disposition made by, or payment made to the insured after the commencement [or day] aforesaid shall be effective to defeat or affect the rights transferred to the third party under this Act, but those rights shall be the same as if no such agreement, waiver, assignment, disposition or payment had been made.   **[1797]**

NOTES

Words in square brackets added with savings by the Insolvency Act 1985, s 235, Sch 8, para 7 and the Insolvency Act 1986, s 437, Sch 11.

5. Short title

This Act may be cited as the Third Parties (Rights Against Insurers) Act 1930.

[1798]

MATRIMONIAL CAUSES ACT 1973
(c 18)

An Act to consolidate certain enactments relating to matrimonial proceedings, maintenance agreements, and declarations of legitimacy, validity of marriage and British nationality, with amendments to give effect to recommendations of the Law Commission [23 May 1973]

PART II

FINANCIAL RELIEF FOR PARTIES TO MARRIAGE AND CHILDREN OF FAMILY

Miscellaneous and supplemental

39. Settlement, etc, made in compliance with a property adjustment order may be avoided on bankruptcy of settlor

The fact that a settlement or transfer of property had to be made in order to comply with a property adjustment order shall not prevent that settlement or transfer from being *a settlement of property to which section 42(1) of the Bankruptcy Act 1914 (avoidance of certain settlements) applies* [a transaction in respect of which an order may be made under . . . [section 339 or 340 of the Insolvency Act 1986] (transactions at an undervalue and preferences)]. **[1799]**

NOTES

Commencement: 1 January 1974.
Commencement order: SI 1973 No 1972.
This section derived from the Matrimonial Proceedings and Property Act 1970, s 23.
First words in italics repealed with savings and first words in square brackets substituted with savings by the Insolvency Act 1985, s 235, Sch 8, para 23 and the Insolvency Act 1986, s 437, Sch 11; words omitted repealed and subsequent words in square brackets substituted by the Insolvency Act 1986, s 439(2), Sch 14.

POWERS OF CRIMINAL COURTS ACT 1973
(c 62)

An Act to consolidate certain enactments relating to the powers of courts to deal with offenders and defaulters, to the treatment of offenders and to arrangements for persons on bail [25 October 1973]

PART I

POWERS OF COURTS TO DEAL WITH OFFENDERS

Criminal bankruptcy orders

39. Criminal bankruptcy orders against convicted persons

(1) Where a person is convicted of an offence before the Crown Court and it appears to the court that—

(a) as a result of the offence, or of that offence taken together with any other relevant offence or offences, loss or damage (not attributable to personal injury) has been suffered by one or more persons whose identity is known to the court; and

(b) the amount, or aggregate amount, of the loss or damage exceeds £15,000;

the court may, in addition to dealing with the offender in any other way (but not if it makes a compensation order against him), make a criminal bankruptcy order against him in respect of the offence or, as the case may be, that offence and the other relevant offence or offences.

(2) In subsection (1) above "other relevant offence or offences" means an offence or offences of which the person in question is convicted in the same proceedings or which the court takes into consideration in determining his sentence.

(3) A criminal bankruptcy order shall specify—

(a) the amount of the loss or damage appearing to the court to have resulted from the offence or, if more than one, each of the offences;

(b) the person or persons appearing to the court to have suffered that loss or damage;

(c) the amount of that loss or damage which it appears to the court that that person, or each of those persons, has suffered; and

(d) *the date which is to be the relevant date for the purpose of the exercise by the High Court of its powers under paragraph 10 of Schedule 2 to this Act in relation to dispositions made by the offender, being* [for the purposes of section [341(4) of the Insolvency Act 1986]] the date which appears to the court to be the earliest date on which the offence or, if more than one, the earliest of the offences, was committed.

(4) A criminal bankruptcy order may be made against two or more offenders in respect of the same loss or damage.

(5) Schedule 2 to this Act shall have effect in relation to criminal bankruptcy orders and the operation of the enactments relating to bankruptcy in a case where such an order has been made, and also for supplementing those enactments in relation to dispositions made by an offender against whom such an order has been made.

(6) The Secretary of State may by order direct that subsection (1) above shall be amended by substituting, for the amount specified in that subsection as originally enacted or as previously amended under this subsection, such amount as may be specified in the order. **[1800]**

NOTES

Commencement: 1 July 1974.

This section derived from the Criminal Justice Act 1972, s 7(1)-(6).

Sub-s (3): in para (d) first words in italics repealed with savings and first words in square brackets substituted with savings by the Insolvency Act 1985, s 235, Sch 8, para 24 and the Insolvency Act 1986, s 437, Sch 11; second words in square brackets substituted by the Insolvency Act 1986, s 439(2), Sch 14.

Sub-s (5): repealed with savings by the Insolvency Act 1985, s 235, Sch 10, Part III and the Insolvency Act 1986, s 437, Sch 11.

EMPLOYMENT PROTECTION (CONSOLIDATION) ACT 1978
(c 44)

ARRANGEMENT OF SECTIONS

PART VII

INSOLVENCY OF EMPLOYER

Section   Para
122 Employee's rights on insolvency of employer   ..   .. [1801]
123 Payment of unpaid contributions to occupational pension scheme   ..   ..   .. [1802]

Section   Para
124   Complaint to industrial tribunal   ..   .. [1803]
125   Transfer to Secretary of State of rights and remedies   ..   .. [1804]
126   Power of Secretary of State to obtain information in connection with applications   .. [1805]
127   Interpretation of ss 122 to 126   ..   .. [1806]

An Act to consolidate certain enactments relating to the rights of employees arising out of their employment; and certain enactments relating to the insolvency of employers; to industrial tribunals; to recoupment of certain benefits; to conciliation officers; and to the Employment Appeal Tribunal   [31 July 1978]

PART VII

INSOLVENCY OF EMPLOYER

122. Employee's rights on insolvency of employer

(1) If on an application made to him in writing by an employee the Secretary of State is satisfied—

(a) that the employer of that employee has become insolvent; and

[(*aa*) that the employment of the employee has been terminated; and]

(b) that on the relevant date the employee was entitled to be paid the whole or part of any debt to which this section applies,

the Secretary of State shall, subject to the provisions of this section, pay the employee out of the Redundancy Fund the amount to which in the opinion of the Secretary of State the employee is entitled in respect of that debt.

[(2) In this section "the relevant date"—

(a) in relation to arrears of pay (not being remuneration under a protective award made under section 101 of the Employment Protection Act 1975) and to holiday pay, means the date on which the employer became insolvent;

(b) in relation to such an award and to a basic award of compensation for unfair dismissal, means whichever is the latest of—

(i) the date on which the employer became insolvent;
(ii) the date of the termination of the employee's employment; and
(iii) the date on which the award was made;

(c) in relation to any other debt to which this section applies, means whichever is the later of the dates mentioned in sub-paragraphs (i) and (ii) of paragraph (*b*).]

(3) This section applies to the following debts:—

[(*a*) any arrears of pay in respect of one or more (but not more than eight) weeks;]

(b) any amount which the employer is liable to pay the employee for the period of notice required by section 49(1) or (2) or for any failure of the employer to give the period of notice required by section 49(1);

[(*c*) any holiday pay—

(i) in respect of a period or periods of holiday not exceeding six weeks in all; and
(ii) to which the employee became entitled during the twelve months ending with the relevant date;]

(*d*) any basic award of compensation for unfair dismissal (within the meaning of section 72);

(*e*) any reasonable sum by way of reimbursement of the whole or part of any fee or premium paid by an apprentice or articled clerk.

[(4) For the purposes of this section, the following amounts shall be treated as arrears of pay, namely—

(*a*) a guarantee payment;

(*b*) remuneration on suspension on medical grounds under section 19;

(*c*) any payment for time off under section 27(3) or 31(3) or 31A(4);

(*d*) remuneration under a protective award made under section 101 of the Employment Protection Act 1975;

(*e*) statutory sick pay, payable under Part I of the Social Security and Housing Benefits Act 1982.]

(5) The total amount payable to an employee in respect of any debt mentioned in subsection (3), where the amount of that debt is referable to a period of time, shall not exceed *[£152.00]* [£155.00] in respect of any one week or, in respect of a shorter period, an amount bearing the same proportion to *[£145.00]* [£152.00] as that shorter period bears to a week.

(6) The Secretary of State may vary the limit referred to in subsection (5) after a review under section 148, by order made in accordance with that section.

(7) A sum shall be taken to be reasonable for the purposes of subsection (3)(*e*) in a case where a trustee in bankruptcy or liquidator has been or is required to be appointed if it is admitted to be reasonable by the trustee in bankruptcy or liquidator under [section [348 of the Insolvency Act 1986] (effect of bankruptcy on apprenticeships etc.), whether as originally enacted or as applied to the winding up of a company by rules under [section 411] of that Act].

(8) Subsection (7) shall not apply to Scotland, but in Scotland a sum shall be taken to be reasonable for the purposes of subsection (3)(*e*) in a case where a trustee in bankruptcy or liquidator has been or is required to be appointed if it is admitted by the trustee in bankruptcy or the liquidator for the purposes of the bankruptcy or winding up.

(9) The provisions of subsections (10) and (11) shall apply in a case where one of the following officers (hereafter in this section referred to as the "relevant officer") has been or is required to be appointed in connection with the employer's insolvency, that is to say, a trustee in bankruptcy, a liquidator, [an administrator,] a receiver or manager, or a trustee under a composition or arrangement between the employer and his creditors or under a trust deed for his creditors executed by the employer; and in this subsection ["trustee", in relation to a composition or arrangement, includes the supervisor of a [voluntary arrangement proposed for the purposes of, and approved under, Part I or VIII of the Insolvency Act 1986]].

(10) Subject to subsection (11), the Secretary of State shall not in such a case make any payment under this section in respect of any debt until he has received a statement from the relevant officer of the amount of that debt which appears to have been owed to the employee on the relevant date and to remain unpaid; and the relevant officer shall, on request by the Secretary of State, provide him, as soon as reasonably practicable, with such a statement.

(11) Where—

    (*a*) [the application for a payment under this section has been] received by the Secretary of State, but no such payment has been made;

    (*b*) the Secretary of State is satisfied that a payment under this section should be made; and

    (*c*) it appears to the Secretary of State that there is likely to be [unreasonable] delay before he receives a statement about the debt in question,

then, the Secretary of State may, if the applicant so requests or, if the Secretary of State thinks fit, without such a request, make a payment under this section, notwithstanding that no such statement has been received.   **[1801]**

NOTES

    Commencement: 1 December 1982 (sub-s (2)); 1 November 1978 (remainder).

    Commencement order: SI 1982 No 1656.

    This section derived from the Employment Protection Act 1975, s 64.

    Sub-s (1): para (*aa*) added by the Insolvency Act 1985, s 218(2).

    Sub-s (2): substituted by the Insolvency Act 1985, s 218(3).

    Sub-s (3): paras (*a*),(*c*) substituted by the Employment Act 1982, s 21, Sch 3, para 4.

    Sub-s (4): substituted by the Insolvency Act 1985, s 218(4); para (*e*) prospectively repealed by the Social Security Act 1986, s 86, Sch 11, as from a day to be appointed.

    Sub-s (5): words in italics substituted by SI 1984 No 2019 and revoked with savings by SI 1985 No 2032, arts 1(2), 3(6); subsequent words in square brackets substituted with savings by SI 1985 No 2032, arts 2, 3(2), (6).

    Sub-s (7): first amendment in square brackets made by the Insolvency Act 1985, s 218(5); further amended by the Insolvency Act 1986, s 439(2), Sch 14.

    Sub-s (9): first amendment in square brackets made by the Insolvency Act 1985, s 218(6); further amended by the Insolvency Act 1986, s 439(2), Sch 14.

    Sub-s (11): amended by the Employment Act 1982, s 21, Sch 3, para 5.

123. Payment of unpaid contributions to occupational pension scheme

(1) If, on application made to him in writing by the person competent to act in respect of an occupational pension scheme [or a personal pension scheme], the Secretary of State is satisfied that an employer has become insolvent and that at the time that he did so there remained unpaid relevant contributions falling to be paid by him to the scheme, the Secretary of State shall, subject to the provisions of this section, pay into the resources of the scheme out of the Redundancy Fund the sum which in his opinion is payable in respect of the unpaid relevant contributions.

(2) In this section "relevant contributions" means contributions falling to be paid by an employer *in accordance with an occupational pension scheme* [to an occupational pension scheme or a personal pension scheme], either on his own account or on behalf of an employee; and for the purposes of this section a contribution of any amount shall not be treated as falling to be paid on behalf of an employee unless a sum equal to that amount has been deducted from the pay of the employee by way of a contribution from him.

(3) The sum payable under this section in respect of unpaid contributions of an employer on his own account to an occupational pension scheme [or a personal pension scheme] shall be the least of the following amounts—

    (*a*) the balance of relevant contributions remaining unpaid on the date when he became insolvent and payable by the employer on his own account to the scheme in respect of the twelve months immediately preceding that date;

    (*b*) the amount certified by an actuary to be necessary for the purpose of meeting the liability of the scheme on dissolution to pay the benefits provided by the scheme to or in respect of the employees of the employer;

(c) an amount equal to ten per cent of the total amount of remuneration paid or payable to those employees in respect of the twelve months immediately preceding the date on which the employer became insolvent.

(4) For the purposes of subsection (3)(*c*), "remuneration" includes holiday pay, *maternity pay* [statutory sick pay, statutory maternity pay under Part V of the Social Security Act 1986, maternity pay under Part III of this Act] and any such payment as if referred to in *section 121 (2)* [section 122(4)].

(5) Any sum payable under this section in respect of unpaid contributions on behalf of an employee shall not exceed the amount deducted from the pay of the employee in respect of the employee's contributions to the *occupational pension* scheme during the twelve months immediately preceding the date on which the employer became insolvent.

(6) The provisions of subsections (7) to (9) shall apply in a case where one of the following officers (hereafter in this section referred to as the "relevant officer") has been or is required to be appointed in connection with the employer's insolvency, that is to say, a trustee in bankruptcy, a liquidator, [an administrator] a receiver or manager, or a trustee under a composition or arrangement between the employer and his creditors or under a trust deed for his creditors executed by the employer; and in this subsection *"liquidator" and "receiver" include the Official Receiver in his capacity as a provisional liquidator or interim receiver* ["trustee", in relation to a composition or arrangement, includes the supervisor of a [voluntary arrangement proposed for the purposes of, and approved under, Part I or VIII of the Insolvency Act 1986].]

(7) Subject to subsection (9), the Secretary of State shall not in such a case make any payment under this section in respect of unpaid relevant contributions until he has received a statement from the relevant officer of the amount of relevant contributions which appear to have been unpaid on the date on which the employer became insolvent and to remain unpaid; and the relevant officer shall, on request by the Secretary of State provide him, as soon as reasonably practicable, with such a statement.

(8) Subject to subsection (9), an amount shall be taken to be payable, paid or deducted as mentioned in subsection (3)(*a*) or (*c*) or subsection (5), only if it is so certified by the relevant officer.

(9) Where—
  (a) [the application for a payment under this section has been] received by the Secretary of State, but no such payment has been made;
  (b) the Secretary of State is satisfied that a payment under this section should be made; and
  (c) it appears to the Secretary of State that there is likely to be [unreasonable] delay before he receives a statement of certificate about the contributions in question,

then, the Secretary of State may, if the applicants so request or, if the Secretary of State thinks fit, without such a request, make a payment under this section, notwithstanding that no such statement or certificate has been received. **[1802]**

NOTES
  Commencement: 1 November 1978.
  This section derived from the Employment Protection Act 1975, s 65.
  Sub-ss (1), (3): words in square brackets prospectively added by the Social Security Act 1986, s 86, Sch 10, Part I, para 31, as from a day to be appointed.
  Sub-s (2): words in italics prospectively repealed and subsequent words in square brackets

prospectively substituted by the Social Security Act 1986, s 86, Sch 10, Part I, para 31, as from a day to be appointed.

Sub-s (4): first words in italics prospectively repealed and first words in square brackets prospectively substituted by the Social Security Act 1986, s 86, Sch 10, Part IV, para 76 as from 6 April 1987; second words in italics repealed and second words in square brackets substituted with savings by the Insolvency Act 1985, s 235, Sch 8, para 31 and the Insolvency Act 1986, s 437, Sch 11.

Sub-s (5): words in italics prospectively repealed by the Social Security Act 1986, s 86, Sch 11, as from a day to be appointed.

Sub-s (6): first words in square brackets added by the Insolvency Act 1985, s 235, Sch 8, para 31; first words in italics repealed with savings and second words in square brackets substituted with savings by the Insolvency Act 1985, s 235, Sch 8, para 31, and the Insolvency Act 1986, s 437, Sch 11; final amendment in square brackets made by the Insolvency Act 1986, s 439(2), Sch 14.

Sub-s (9): amended by the Employment Act 1982, s 21, Sch 3, para 5.

124. Complaint to industrial tribunal

(1) A person who has applied for a payment under section 122 may, within the period of three months beginning with the date on which the decision of the Secretary of State on that application was communicated to him or, if that is not reasonably practicable, within such further period as is reasonable, present a complaint to an industrial tribunal that—

(*a*) the Secretary of State has failed to make any such payment; or

(*b*) any such payment made by the Secretary of State is less than the amount which should have been paid.

(2) Any persons who are competent to act in respect of an occupational pension scheme [or a personal pension scheme] and who have applied for a payment to be made under section 123 into the resources of the scheme may, within the period of three months beginning with the date on which the decision of the Secretary of State on that application was communicated to them, or, if that is not reasonably practicable, within such further period as is reasonable, present a complaint to an industrial tribunal that—

(*a*) the Secretary of State has failed to make any such payment; or

(*b*) any such payment made by him is less than the amount which should have been paid.

(3) Where an industrial tribunal finds that the Secretary of State ought to make a payment under section 122 or 123, it shall make a declaration to that effect and shall also declare the amount of any such payment which it finds the Secretary of State ought to make.   **[1803]**

NOTES

Commencement: 1 November 1978.

This section derived from the Employment Protection Act 1975, s 66.

Sub-s (2): words in square brackets prospectively added by the Social Security Act 1986, s 86, Sch 10, Part I, para 31, as from a day to be appointed.

125. Transfer to Secretary of State of rights and remedies

(1) Where, in pursuance of section 122, the Secretary of State makes any payment to an employee in respect of any debt to which that section applies—

(*a*) any rights and remedies of the employee in respect of that debt (or, if the Secretary of State has paid only part of it, in respect of that part) shall, on the making of the payment, become rights and remedies of the Secretary of State; and

(*b*) any decision of an industrial tribunal requiring an employer to pay that debt to the employee shall have the effect that the debt or, as the case may be, that part of it which the Secretary of State has paid, is to be paid to the Secretary of State.

(2) There shall be included among the rights and remedies which become rights and remedies of the Secretary of State in accordance with subsection (1)(*a*) any right to be paid in priority to other creditors of the employer in accordance with—

(*a*) section 33 of the Bankruptcy Act 1914;

[(*a*) sections 89, 166 and 181 of, and Schedule 4 to, the Insolvency Act 1985 and any rules under that Act applying the said section 181 to the winding up of a company; and]

[(*a*) the following provisions of the Insolvency Act 1986—

(i) sections 175 and 176, 328 and 329, 348 and Schedule 6, and

(ii) any rules under that Act applying section 348 of it to the winding up of a company; and]

(*b*) section 118 of the Bankruptcy (Scotland) Act 1913; and

[(*c*) section 614 of the Companies Act 1985, with Schedule 19 to that Act]

and the Secretary of State shall be entitled to be so paid in priority to any other unsatisfied claim of the employee; and in computing for the purposes of any of those provisions any limit on the amount of sums to be so paid any sums paid to the Secretary of State shall be treated as if they had been paid to the employee.

(3) Where in pursuance of section 123 the Secretary of State makes any payment into the resources of an occupational pension scheme [or a personal pension scheme] in respect of any contributions to the scheme, any rights and remedies in respect of those contributions belonging to the persons competent to act in respect of the scheme shall, on the making of the payment, become rights and remedies of the Secretary of State.

(4) Any sum recovered by the Secretary of State in exercising any right or pursuing any remedy which is his by virtue of this section shall be paid into the Redundancy Fund. **[1804]**

NOTES

Commencement: 1 November 1978.

This section derived from the Employment Protection Act 1975, s 67.

Sub-s (2): para (*a*) substituted with savings by the Insolvency Act 1985, s 235, Sch 8, para 31 and the Insolvency Act 1986, s 437, Sch 11, further substituted by the Insolvency Act 1986, s 439(2), Sch 14; para (*c*) substituted by the Companies Consolidation (Consequential Provisions) Act 1985, s 30, Sch 2, repealed with savings by the Insolvency Act 1985, s 235, Sch 10, Part IV and the Insolvency Act 1986, s 437, Sch 11.

Sub-s (3): prospectively amended by the Social Security Act 1986, s 86, Sch 10, Part I, para 31, as from a day to be appointed.

126. Power of Secretary of State to obtain information in connection with applications

(1) Where an application is made to the Secretary of State under section 122 or 123 in respect of a debt owed, or contributions to an occupational pension scheme [or a personal pension scheme] falling to be made, by an employer, the Secretary of State may require—

(*a*) the employer to provide him with such information as the Secretary of State may reasonably require for the purpose of determining whether the application is well-founded; and

(*b*) any person having the custody or control of any relevant records or other documents to produce for examination on behalf of the Secretary of State any such document in that person's custody or under his control which is of such a description as the Secretary of State may require.

(2) Any such requirement shall be made by notice in writing given to the person on whom the requirement is imposed and may be varied or revoked by a subsequent notice so given.

(3) If a person refuses or wilfully neglects to furnish any information or produce any document which he has been required to furnish or produce by a notice under this section he shall be liable on summary conviction to a fine not exceeding [level 3 on the standard scale].

(4) If a person, in purporting to comply with a requirement of a notice under this section, knowingly or recklessly makes any false statement he shall be liable on summary conviction to a fine not exceeding [level 5 on the standard scale].

[1805]

NOTES
Commencement: 1 November 1978.
This section derived from the Employment Protection Act 1975, s 68.
Sub-s (1): words in square brackets prospectively added by the Social Security Act 1986, s 86, Sch 10, Part I, para 31, as from a day to be appointed.
Sub-ss (3), (4): maximum fine increased and converted to a level on the standard scale by the Criminal Justice Act 1982, ss 37, 38, 46.

127. Interpretation of ss 122 to 126

(1) For the purposes of sections 122 to 126, an employer shall be taken to be insolvent if, but only if, in England and Wales,—

(*a*) he becomes bankrupt or makes composition or arrangement with his creditors or a receiving order is made against him;

(*b*) *he has died and an order is made under section 130 of the Bankruptcy Act 1914 for the administration of his estate according to the law of bankruptcy, or by virtue of an order of the court his estate is being administered in accordance with rules set out in Part I of Schedule 1 to the Administration of Estates Act 1925; or*

[(*a*) he has been adjudged bankrupt or has made a composition or arrangement with his creditors;

(*b*) he has died and his estate falls to be administered in accordance with an order under section [421 of the Insolvency Act 1986]; or]

(*c*) where the employer is a company, a winding up order [or an administration order] is made or a resolution for voluntary winding up is passed with respect to it, or a receiver or manager of its undertaking is duly appointed, or possession is taken, by or on behalf of the holders of any debentures secured by a floating charge, of any property of the company comprised in or subject to the charge [or a [voluntary arrangement proposed for the purposes of Part I of the Insolvency Act 1986 is approved under that Part]].

(2) For the purposes of sections 122 to 126, an employer shall be taken to be insolvent if, but only if, in Scotland,—

(*a*) an award of sequestration is made on his estate or he executes a trust deed for his creditors or enters into a composition contract;

(*b*) he has died and a judicial factor appointed under section 163 of the Bankruptcy (Scotland) Act 1913 is required by that section to divide his insolvent estate among his creditors; or (*c*) where the employer is a company, a winding-up order is made or a resolution for voluntary winding up is passed with respect to it or a receiver of its undertaking is duly appointed.

(3) In sections 122 to 126—

"holiday pay" means—
(*a*) pay in respect of a holiday actually taken; or
(*b*) any accrued holiday pay which under the employee's contract of employment would in the ordinary course have become payable to him in respect of the period of a holiday if his employment with the employer had continued until he became entitled to a holiday;
"occupational pension scheme" means any scheme or arrangement which provides or is capable of providing, in relation to employees in any description of employment, benefits (in the form of pensions or otherwise) payable to or in respect of any such employees on the termination of their employment or on their death or retirement;
["personal pension scheme" means any scheme or arrangement which is comprised in one or more instruments or agreements and which has, or is capable of having, effect so as to provide benefits, in the form of pensions or otherwise, payable on death or retirement to or in respect of employees who have made arrangements with the trustees or managers of the scheme for them to become members of the scheme;]

and any reference in those sections to the resources of *such* a scheme is a reference to the funds out of which the benefits provided by the scheme are from time to time payable.   **[1806]**

NOTES
Commencement: 1 November 1978.
This section derived from the Employment Protection Act 1975, s 69.
Sub-s (1): paras (*a*), (*b*) substituted with savings by the Insolvency Act 1985, s 235, Sch 8, para 31 and the Insolvency Act 1986, s 437, Sch 11; words in square brackets in para (*b*) substituted by the Insolvency Act 1986, s 439(2), Sch 14; in para (*c*) first and second amendments in square brackets made with savings by the Insolvency Act 1985, s 235, Sch 8, para 31 and the Insolvency Act 1986, s 437, Sch 11; third words in square brackets substituted by the Insolvency Act 1986, s 439(2), Sch 14.
Sub-s (3): definition in square brackets prospectively added and word in italics prospectively repealed by the Social Security Act 1986, s 86, Sch 10, Part I, para 31, Sch 11, as from a day to be appointed.

BANKING ACT 1979
(c 37)

An Act to regulate the acceptance of deposits in the course of a business; to confer functions on the Bank of England with respect to the control of institutions carrying on deposit-taking businesses; to give further protection to persons who are depositors with such institutions; to make provision with respect to advertisements inviting the making of deposits; to restrict the use of names and descriptions associated with banks and banking; to prohibit fraudulent inducement to make a deposit; to amend the Consumer Credit Act 1974 and the law with respect to instruments to which section 4 of the Cheques Act 1957 applies; to repeal certain enactments relating to banks and banking; and for purposes connected therewith   [4 April 1979]

PART I

CONTROL OF DEPOSIT-TAKING

Powers of the Bank

18. Winding up on petition from the Bank

[(1) On a petition presented by the Bank by virtue of this section, the court having jurisdiction under the [Insolvency Act 1986] may wind up a recognised bank or licensed institution under that Act if—

> (*a*) the institution is unable to pay its debts within the meaning of section [123] of that Act; or
> (*b*) the court is of the opinion that it is just and equitable that the institution should be wound up;

and for the purposes of such a petition an institution which defaults in an obligation to pay any sum due and payable to a depositor shall be deemed to be unable to pay its debts as mentioned in paragraph (*a*) above.

(2) If a petition is presented by the Bank by virtue of this section for the winding up of a recognised bank or licensed institution which is a partnership (whether limited or not), the court has jurisdiction, and the [Insolvency Act 1986] has effect, as if the institution concerned were an unregistered company within the meaning of [Part V] of that Act.]

(3) If and so long as an institution which was formerly a recognised bank or licensed institution—

> (*a*) is neither recognised nor licensed, but
> (*b*) continues to have any liability in respect of any deposit for which it had a liability at a time when it was recognised or licensed,

the provisions of this section shall apply in relation to it as if it were a licensed institution.

[(4) In its application to Northern Ireland, this section shall have effect—

> (*a*) with the substitution of a reference to the Companies Act (Northern Ireland) 1960 for any reference to the [Insolvency Act 1986];
> (*b*) with the substitution of a reference to section 211 of the said Act of 1960 for the reference to section [123 of the said Act of 1986];
> (*c*) with the substitution of a reference to Part IX of the said Act of 1960 for the reference to [Part V of the said Act of 1986]; and
> (*d*) with the insertion in subsection (2) after the words "(whether limited or not)" of the words "then, notwithstanding section 348(*d*) of the Companies Act (Northern Ireland) 1960 (exclusion of partnerships etc. having less than eight members)".]   **[1807]**

NOTES

   Commencement: 1 July 1985 (sub-s (2)); 1 October 1979 (remainder).
   Commencement order: SI 1979 No 938.
   Sub-ss (1), (2), (4): substituted by the Insolvency Act 1985, s 219; amended by the Insolvency Act 1986, s 439(2), Sch 14.

PART II

THE DEPOSIT PROTECTION SCHEME

Payments out of the fund

28. Payments to depositors when institution becomes insolvent

(1) Subject to the provisions of this section, if at any time an institution becomes insolvent and at that time—

    (a) it is a recognised bank or licensed institution which is not excluded from being a contributory institution by an order under section 23 (2) above; or

    (b) it is neither recognised nor licensed but is an institution which was formerly a recognised bank or licensed institution and, at the time when it ceased to have either recognition or a licence, was not excluded as mentioned in paragraph (a) above;

the Board shall as soon as practicable pay out of the Fund to a depositor who has a protected deposit with that institution an amount equal to three-quarters of his protected deposit.

(2) The Board may decline to make any payment under subsection (1) above to a person who, in the opinion of the Board, had any responsibility for, or may have profited directly or indirectly from, the circumstances giving rise to the institution's financial difficulties.

(3) For the purposes of this Part of this Act, a body corporate becomes insolvent—

    (a) on the making of a winding-up order against it; or

    (b) on the passing of a resolution for a creditors' voluntary winding up; [or

    (c) on the holding of a creditors' meeting summoned under section [95 of the Insolvency Act 1986] (effect of insolvency on members' voluntary winding up);]

or, in the case of a body corporate formed under the law of a country or territory outside the United Kingdom, on the occurrence of an event which appears to the Board to correspond under that law with either of the events specified above.

(4) For the purposes of this Part of this Act, a partnership becomes insolvent—

    (a) on the making of a winding-up order against the firm under [Part V of the Insolvency Act 1986] or the Companies Act (Northern Ireland) 1960 (unregistered companies); or

    (b) in England and Wales, on the making of a *receiving order* [bankruptcy order] against the firm; or

    (c) in Scotland, on the making of an award of sequestration on the estate of the partnership; or

    (d) in Northern Ireland, on the making of an order of adjudication of bankruptcy against any of the partners;

or, in the case of a partnership whose principal place of business is in a country or territory outside the United Kingdom, on the occurrence of an event which appears to the Board to correspond under the law of that country or territory with any of the events specified above.

(5) For the purposes of this Part of this Act, an unincorporated institution which is formed under the law of another member State and is not a partnership

becomes insolvent on the occurrence of an event which, under the law of that member State, appears to the Board to correspond, as near as may be, with any of the events specified in paragraphs (*a*) and (*b*) of subsection (3) or paragraphs (*a*) to (*d*) of subsection (4) above.

(6) Notwithstanding that the Board may not yet have made or become liable to make a payment under this section, in relation to an institution falling within subsection (1) above,—

(*a*) the Board shall at all times be entitled to receive any notice or other document required to be sent to a creditor of the institution whose debt has been proved; and

(*b*) a duly authorised representative of the Board shall be entitled—

(i) to attend any meeting of creditors of the institution;

(ii) *to be a member of any committee of inspection appointed under section 20 of the Bankruptcy Act 1914;*

[(ii) to be a member of a liquidation committee established under Part IV or V of the Insolvency Act 1986;]

[(iii) to be a member of a creditors committee appointed under section 301 of that Act; and]

(iv) *to be a member of any committee of inspection appointed by virtue of [Part XX or Part XXI of the Companies Act 1985] or the Companies Act (Northern Ireland) 1960;*

[(iv) to be a commissioner under section 30 of the Bankruptcy (Scotland) Act 1985;]

[(v) to be a member of a committee of inspection appointed for the purposes of Part V or Part IX of the Companies Act (Northern Ireland) 1960;]

but where a representative of the Board exercises the right to be a member of a *committee of inspection* [a liquidation committee, creditors' committee or committee of inspection] or to be a commissioner by virtue of paragraph (*b*) above, he may not be removed except with the consent of the Board and, for the purposes of any provision made by or under any enactment or Northern Ireland legislation which specifies a minimum or maximum number of members of such committee or such commission, his appointment hereunder shall be disregarded.

(7) In relation to an insolvent institution which is a partnership, any reference in this Part of this Act to the liquidator shall be construed, where the case so requires, as a reference—

(*a*) to the trustee in bankruptcy or, in Northern Ireland, the official assignee in bankruptcy; or

(*b*) in England and Wales, where no adjudication of bankruptcy occurs, to any trustee appointed in pursuance of a composition or scheme of arrangement to administer the firm's property or manage its business or distribute the composition and, where an adjudication of bankruptcy is annulled under *subsection (2) of section 21 of the Bankruptcy Act 1914, to any person in whom the property of the firm is vested under that subsection; or* [section 261(1) of the Insolvency Act 1986 to any person in whom the property of the firm is vested under section 282(4) of that Act]

(*c*) in Scotland, where the sequestration is declared at an end by a competent court, to any trustee or other person appointed to administer the firm's property or manage its business or distribute a composition in pursuance of any deed of arrangement or other settlement or arrangement by way of composition between the firm and its creditors. **[1808]**

NOTES

Commencement: 19 February 1982.

Commencement order: SI 1982 No 188.

Sub-s (3): para (c) amended with savings by the Insolvency Act 1985, s 235, Sch 8, para 32 and the Insolvency Act 1986, s 437, Sch 11; words in square brackets substituted by the Insolvency Act 1986, s 439(2), Sch 14.

Sub-s (4): first amendment in square brackets made by the Insolvency Act 1986, s 439(2), Sch 14; words in italics repealed with savings and final words in square brackets substituted with savings by the Insolvency Act 1985, s 235, Sch 8, para 32 and the Insolvency Act 1986, s 437, Sch 11.

Sub-s (6): sub-para (ii) substituted with savings by the Insolvency Act 1985, s 235, Sch 8, para 32 and the Insolvency Act 1986, ss 437, 439(2), Schs 11, 14; sub-para (iii) substituted by the Insolvency Act 1986, s 439(2), Sch 14; sub-para (iv) amended by the Companies Consolidation (Consequential Provisions) Act 1985, s 30, Sch 2, substituted with savings by the Insolvency Act 1985, s 235, Sch 8, para 32 and the Insolvency Act 1986, ss 437, 439(2), Schs 11, 14; sub-para (v) added by the Insolvency Act 1986, s 439(2), Sch 14; words "committee of inspection" substituted with savings by subsequent words in square brackets by the Insolvency Act 1986, ss 437, 439(2), Schs 11, 14.

Sub-s (7): words in italics repealed with savings and words in square brackets substituted with savings by the Insolvency Act 1985, s 235, Sch 8, para 32 and the Insolvency Act 1986, ss 437, 439(2), Schs 11, 14.

31. Liability of insolvent institutions in respect of payments made by the Board

(1) This section applies where—

    (*a*) an institution is insolvent; and

    (*b*) the Board have made, or are under a liability to make, a payment under section 28 above by virtue of the institution becoming insolvent;

and in the following provisions of this section a payment falling within paragraph (*b*) above is referred to as an "insolvency payment" and the person to whom such a payment has been or is to be made is referred to as "the depositor".

(2) Where this section applies—

    (*a*) the institution concerned shall become liable to the Board, as in respect of a contractual debt incurred immediately before the institution became insolvent, for an amount equal to the amount of the insolvency payment;

    (*b*) the liability of the institution to the depositor in respect of any deposit or deposits of his (in this section referred to as "the liability to the depositor") shall be reduced by an amount equal to the insolvency payment made or to be made to him by the Board; and

    (*c*) the duty of the liquidator of the insolvent institution to make payments to the Board on account of the liability referred to in paragraph (*a*) above (in this section referred to as "the liability to the Board") and to the depositor on account of the liability to him (after taking account of paragraph (*b*) above) shall be varied in accordance with subsection (3) below.

(3) The variation referred to in subsection (2) (*c*) above is as follows—

    (*a*) in the first instance the liquidator shall pay to the Board instead of to the depositor any amount which, apart from this section, would be payable on account of the liability to the depositor, except in so far as that liability relates to a secured deposit or a deposit which had an original term to maturity of more than five years or a deposit which is not a sterling deposit; and (*b*) if at any time the total amount paid to the Board by virtue of paragraph (*a*) above and in respect of the liability to the Board equals the amount of the insolvency payment made to the depositor, the liquidator shall thereafter pay to the depositor instead of to the Board any amount which, apart from this section, would be payable to the Board in respect of the liability to the Board.

(4) In the case of a deposit which, for the purposes of section 30 above, is held on trust for a person absolutely entitled to it as against the trustees or, as the case may be, for two or more persons so entitled jointly, any reference in the preceding provisions of this section to the liability to the depositor shall be construed as a reference to the liability of the institution concerned to the trustees.

(5) The Board may by notice in writing served on the liquidator of an insolvent institution require him, at such time or times and at such place as may be specified in the notice—

(*a*) to furnish to the Board such information, and
(*b*) to produce to the Board such books or papers specified in the notice,

as the Board may reasonably require to enable them to carry out their functions under this Part of this Act.

(6) Where, as a result of an institution having become insolvent, any books or papers have come into the possession of the Official Receiver or, in Northern Ireland, the official assignee for company liquidations or in bankruptcy, he shall permit any person duly authorised by the Board to inspect the books or papers for the purpose of establishing—

(*a*) the identity of those of the institution's depositors to whom the Board are liable to make a payment under section 28 above; and
(*b*) the amount of the protected deposit held by each of those depositors.

(7) Rules may be made—

(a) for England and Wales, under [section 663 of the Companies Act 1985] and section 132 of the Bankruptcy Act 1914;
[(*a*) for England and Wales, under sections 411 and 412 of the Insolvency Act 1986];
(*b*) for Scotland, under section 365 of the Companies Act 1948 and section 32 of the Sheriff Courts (Scotland) Act 1971; and
(*c*) for Northern Ireland, under section 317 of the Companies Act (Northern Ireland) 1960 and section 55 of the Judicature (Northern Ireland) Act 1978;

for the purpose of integrating the procedure provided for in this section into the general procedure on winding-up or bankruptcy. **[1809]**

NOTES
  Commencement: 19 February 1982.
  Commencement order: SI 1982 No 188.
  Sub-s (7): para (*a*) amended by the Companies Consolidation (Consequential Provisions) Act 1985, s 30, Sch 2; substituted with savings by the Insolvency Act 1986, ss 437, 439(2), Schs 11, 14.

INSURANCE COMPANIES ACT 1982
(c 50)

ARRANGEMENT OF SECTIONS

PART II

REGULATION OF INSURANCE COMPANIES

Winding up

Section		Para
53	Winding up of insurance companies under Companies Acts	.. [1810]
54	Winding up on petition of Secretary of State	.. [1811]
55	Winding up of insurance companies with long term business	.. [1812]
56	Continuation of long term business of insurance companies in liquidation ..	.. [1813]
57	Subsidiary companies	.. [1814]
58	Reduction of contracts as alternative to winding up	.. [1815]
59	Winding up rules	.. [1816]

PART V

SUPPLEMENTARY PROVISIONS

Interpretation

		Para
95	Insurance business	.. [1823]
96	General interpretation	.. [1824]

An Act to consolidate the Insurance Companies Acts 1974 and 1981
[28 October 1982]

PART II

REGULATION OF INSURANCE COMPANIES

Winding up

53. Winding up of insurance companies under Companies Acts

The court may order the winding up, in accordance with the [Insolvency Act 1986] or, as the case may be, the Companies Act (Northern Ireland) 1960, of an insurance company to which this Part of this Act applies and the provisions of [that Act of 1986] or, as the case may be, that Act of 1960 shall apply accordingly subject to the modification that the company may be ordered to be wound up on the petition of ten or more policy holders owning policies of an aggregate value of not less than £10,000.

Such a petition shall not be presented except by leave of the court, and leave shall not be granted until a prima facie case has been established to the satisfaction of the court and until security for costs for such amount as the court may think reasonable has been given. **[1810]**

NOTES
Commencement: 28 January 1983.
This section derived from the Insurance Companies Act 1974, s 45 and the Insurance Companies Act 1980, Sch 1, para 20.
Amended by the Insolvency Act 1986, s 439(2), Sch 14.
Companies Act: Companies Act 1985.

54. Winding up on petition of Secretary of State

(1) The Secretary of State may present a petition for the winding up, in accordance with [Part IV or V of the Insolvency Act 1986], of an insurance company to which this Part of this Act applies, being a company which may be wound up by the court under the provisions of that Act, on the ground—

(a) that the company is unable to pay its debts within the meaning of section [123 or sections 222 to 224] of that Act;

(b) that the company has failed to satisfy an obligation to which it is or was subject by virtue of this Act or any enactment repealed by this Act or by the Insurance Companies Act 1974; or

(c) that the company, being under the obligation imposed by [sections 221 and 222 of the Companies Act] with respect to the keeping of accounting records, has failed to satisfy that obligation or to produce records kept in satisfaction of that obligation and that the Secretary of State is unable to ascertain its financial position.

(2) The Secretary of State may present a petition for the winding up, in accordance with the Companies Act (Northern Ireland) 1960, of an insurance company to which this Part of this Act applies, being a company which may be wound up by the court under the provisions of that Act, on the ground—

(a) that the company is unable to pay its debts within the meaning of sections 210 and 211 or section 349 of that Act;

(b) that the company has failed to satisfy an obligation to which it is or was subject by virtue of this Act or any enactment repealed by this Act or by the Insurance Companies Act 1980; or

(c) that the company, being under an obligation imposed by Article 25 of the Companies (Northern Ireland) Order 1978 with respect to the keeping of accounting records, has failed to satisfy that obligation or to produce records kept in satisfaction of that obligation and that the Secretary of State is unable to ascertain its financial position;

and subsection (3) of section 163 of the said Act of 1960 shall have effect in relation to such an insurance company as if any reference to the Department of Commerce for Northern Ireland were a reference to the Secretary of State.

(3) In any proceedings on a petition to wind up an insurance company presented by the Secretary of State under subsection (1) or (2) above, evidence that the company was insolvent—

(a) at the close of the period to which—

(i) the accounts and balance sheet of the company last deposited under section 22 above; or

(ii) any statement of the company last deposited under section 25 above,

relate; or

(b) at any date or time specified in a requirement under section 42 or 44 above,

shall be evidence that the company continues to be unable to pay its debts, unless the contrary is proved.

(4) If, in the case of an insurance company to which this Part of this Act applies, being a company which may be wound up by the court under the provisions of the [Insolvency Act 1986] or, as the case may be, the Companies Act (Northern Ireland) 1960, it appears to the Secretary of State that it is expedient in the public interest that the company should be wound up, he may,

unless the company is already being wound up by the court, present a petition for it to be so wound up if the court thinks it just and equitable for it to be so wound up.

(5) Where a petition for the winding up of an insurance company to which this Part of this Act applies is presented by a person other than the Secretary of State, a copy of the petition shall be served on him and he shall be entitled to be heard on the petition.   **[1811]**

NOTES

Commencement: 28 January 1983.

This section derived from the Insurance Companies Act 1974, s 46, the Companies Act 1976, Sch 2, the Insurance Copanies Act 1980, Sch 1, para 21 and the Insurance Companies Act 1981, Sch 4, para 9.

Sub-s (1): first and second amendments in square brackets made by the Insolvency Act 1986, s 439(2), Sch 14, final amendment in square brackets made by the Companies Consolidation (Consequential Provisions) Act 1985, s 30, Sch 2.

Sub-s (4): amended by the Insolvency Act 1986, s 439(2), Sch 14.

Companies Act: Companies Act 1985.

55. Winding up of insurance companies with long term business

(1) No insurance company to which this Part of this Act applies which is an unincorporated body and carries on long term business shall be made the subject of bankruptcy proceedings or, in Scotland, sequestration proceedings.

(2) No insurance company to which this Part of this Act applies which carries on long term business shall be wound up voluntarily.

(3) Section 29(1) above shall not have effect in relation to the winding up of a company to which section 28(1) above applies but, subject to subsection (4) below and to rules made by virtue of section 59(2) below, in any such winding up—

   (*a*) the assets representing the fund or funds maintained by the company in respect of its long term business shall be available only for meeting the liabilities of the company attributable to that business;
   (*b*) the other assets of the company shall be available only for meeting the liabilities of the company attributable to its other business.

(4) Where the value of the assets mentioned in either paragraph of subsection (3) above exceeds the amount of the liabilities mentioned in that paragraph the restriction imposed by that subsection shall not apply to so much of those assets as represents the excess.

(5) In relation to the assets falling within either paragraph of subsection (3) above the creditors mentioned in *subsections [(1) to (3) of section 540]* [section 168(2) of the Insolvency Act 1986] or, as the case may be, paragraphs (1) and (2) of Article 73 of the Companies (Northern Ireland) Order 1978 shall be only those who are creditors in respect of liabilities falling within that paragraph; and any general meetings of creditors summoned for the purposes of that section shall accordingly be separate general meetings of the creditors in respect of the liabilities falling within each paragraph.

(6) Where under section [212 of the Insolvency Act 1986] or section 299(1) of the Companies Act (Northern Ireland) 1960 (defalcations of directors etc. disclosed in course of winding up) a court orders any money or property to be repaid or restored to a company or any sum to be contributed to its assets then, if and so far as the wrongful act which is the reason for the making of the order related to assets representing a fund or funds maintained by the company in

respect of its long term business, the court shall include in the order a direction that the money, property or contribution shall be treated for the purposes of this Act as assets of that fund or those funds and this Act shall have effect accordingly.   **[1812]**

NOTES

Commencement: 28 January 1983.

This section derived from the Insurance Companies Act 1974, s 47 and the Insurance Companies Act 1980, Sch 1, para 22.

Sub-s (5): first amendment in square brackets made by the Companies Consolidation (Consequential Provisions) Act 1985, s 30, Sch 2; words in italics repealed with savings by the Insolvency Act 1985, s 235, Sch 8, para 37, Sch 10, Part II and the Insolvency Act 1986, s 437, Sch 11; second amendment in square brackets made by the Insolvency Act 1986, s 439(2), Sch 14.

Sub-s (6): amended by the Insolvency Act 1986, s 439(2), Sch 14.

56. Continuation of long term business of insurance companies in liquidation

(1) This section has effect in relation to the winding up of an insurance company to which this Part of this Act applies, being a company carrying on long term business.

(2) The liquidator shall, unless the court otherwise orders, carry on the long term business of the company with a view to its being transferred as a going concern to another insurance company, whether an existing company or a company formed for that purpose; and, in carrying on that business as aforesaid, the liquidator may agree to the variation of any contracts of insurance in existence when the winding up order is made but shall not effect any new contracts of insurance.

(3) If the liquidator is satisfied that the interests of the creditors in respect of liabilities of the company attributable to its long term business require the appointment of a special manager of the company's long term business, he may apply to the court, and the court may on such application appoint a special manager of that business to act during such time as the court may direct, with such powers, including any of the powers of a receiver or manager, as may be entrusted to him by the court.

(4) *[Section 556(3)] of the [Companies Act]* [Section 177(5) of the Insolvency Act 1986] or, in the case of a special manager appointed in proceedings in Northern Ireland, subsections (2) and (3) of section 236A of the Companies Act (Northern Ireland) 1960 (special manager to give security and receive remuneration) shall apply to a special manager appointed under subsection (3) above as they apply to a special manager appointed under *[section 556 of the Companies Act]* [section 177 of the said Act of 1986] or, as the case may be, section 236A of the said Act of 1960.

(5) The court may, if it thinks fit and subject to such conditions (if any) as it may determine, reduce the amount of the contracts made by the company in the course of carrying on its long term business.

(6) The court may, on the application of the liquidator, a special manager appointed under subsection (3) above or the Secretary of State, appoint an independent actuary to investigate the long term business of the company and to report to the liquidator, the special manager or the Secretary of State, as the case may be, on the desirability or otherwise of that business being continued and on any reduction in the contracts made in the course of carrying on that business that may be necessary for its successful continuation.

(7) Notwithstanding [section 167 of, and Schedule 4 to, the Insolvency Act 1986] or, as the case may be, section 227(1) of the said Act of 1960 (which requires a liquidator to obtain the sanction of the court or *committee of inspection* [a specified committee] for the bringing of legal proceedings in the name of and on behalf of the company) the liquidator may without any such sanction make an application in the name of and on behalf of the company under section 49 above.

(8) In this section "the court" means the court having jurisdiction to wind up the company.   **[1813]**

NOTES
   Commencement: 28 January 1983.
   This section derived from the Insurance Companies Act 1974, s 48 and the Insurance Companies Act 1980, Sch 1, para 23.
   Sub-s (4): first, second and fourth amendments in square brackets made by the Companies Consolidation (Consequential Provisions) Act 1985, s 30, Sch 2; first and second words in italics repealed with savings by the Insolvency Act 1985, s 235, Sch 8, para 37, Sch 10, Part II and the Insolvency Act 1986, s 437, Sch 11; third and final amendments in square brackets made by the Insolvency Act 1986, s 439(2), Sch 14.
   Sub-s (7): first amendment in square brackets made by the Insolvency Act 1986, s 439(2), Sch 14; words in italics repealed with savings and final words in square brackets substituted with savings by the Insolvency Act 1985, s 235, Sch 8, para 37 and the Insolvency Act 1986, s 437, Sch 11.
   Companies Act: Companies Act 1985.

57. Subsidiary companies

(1) Where the insurance business or any part of the insurance business of an insurance company has been transferred to an insurance company to which this Part of this Act applies under an arrangement in pursuance of which the first-mentioned company (in this section called the subsidiary company) or the creditors thereof has or have claims against the company to which the transfer was made (in this section called the principal company), then, if the principal company is being wound up by *or under the supervision of* the court, the court shall, subject to the provisions of this section, order the subsidiary company to be wound up in conjunction with the principal company, and may by the same or any subsequent order appoint the same person to be liquidator for the two companies, and make provision for such other matters as may seem to the court necessary, with a view to the companies being wound up as if they were one company.

(2) The commencement of the winding up of the principal company shall, save as otherwise ordered by the court, be the commencement of the winding up of the subsidiary company.

(3) In adjusting the rights and liabilities of the members of the several companies between themselves, the court shall have regard to the constitution of the companies, and to the arrangements entered into between the companies, in the same manner as the court has regard to the rights and liabilities of different classes of contributories in the case of the winding up of a single company, or as near thereto as circumstances admit.

(4) Where any company alleged to be subsidiary is not in process of being wound up at the same time as the principal company to which it is subsidiary, the court shall not direct the subsidiary company to be wound up unless, after hearing all objections (if any) that may be urged by or on behalf of the company against its being wound up, the court is of the opinion that the company is subsidiary to the principal company, and that the winding up of the company in conjunction with the principal company is just and equitable.

(5) An application may be made in relation to the winding up of any subsidiary company in conjunction with a principal company by any creditor of, or person interested in, the principal or subsidiary company.

(6) Where a company stands in the relation of a principal company to one company, and in the relation of a subsidiary company to some other company, or where there are several companies standing in the relation of subsidiary companies to one principal company, the court may deal with any number of such companies together or in separate groups, as it thinks most expedient, upon the principles laid down in this section.   **[1814]**

NOTES

Commencement: 28 January 1983.
This section derived from the Insurance Companies Act 1974, s 49.
Sub-s (1): words in italics repealed with savings by the Insolvency Act 1985, s 235, Sch 10, Part II and the Insolvency Act 1986, s 437, Sch 11.

58. Reduction of contracts as alternative to winding up

In the case of an insurance company which has been proved to be unable to pay its debts, the court may, if it thinks fit, reduce the amount of the contracts of the company on such terms and subject to such conditions as the court thinks just, in place of making a winding up order.   **[1815]**

NOTES

Commencement: 28 January 1983.
This section derived from the Insurance Companies Act 1974, s 50.

59. Winding up rules

(1) Rules may be made under *section [663] of the [Companies Act]* [section [411 of the Insolvency Act 1986]] or section 317 of the Companies Act (Northern Ireland) 1960 (general rules about winding up) for determining the amount of the liabilities of an insurance company to policy holders of any class or description for the purpose of proof in a winding up and generally for carrying into effect the provisions of this Part of this Act with respect to the winding up of insurance companies.

(2) Without prejudice to the generality of subsection (1) above, rules under *section [663 of the Companies Act]* [section [411 of the Insolvency Act 1986]] or, as the case may be, section 317 of the said Act of 1960 may make provision for all or any of the following matters—

(a) the identification of the assets and liabilities falling within either paragraph of subsection (3) of section 55 above;

(b) the apportionment between the assets falling within paragraphs (a) and (b) of that subsection of the costs, charges and expenses of the winding up and of any debts of the company having priority under *section [614 of, and Schedule 19 to, the Companies Act]* [sections 175 and 176 of, and Schedule 6 to, the Insolvency Act 1986], or, as the case may be, section 287 of the said Act of 1960;

(c) the determination of the amount of liabilities of any description falling within either paragraph of that subsection for the purpose of establishing whether or not there is any such excess in respect of that paragraph as is mentioned in subsection (4) of section 55 above;

(d) the application of assets within paragraph (a) of the said subsection (3) for meeting the liabilities within that paragraph;

(e) the application of assets representing any such excess as is mentioned in the said subsection (4).   **[1816]–[1822]**

NOTES
Commencement: 28 January 1983.
This section derived from the Insurance Act 1974, s 51 and the Insurance Companies Act 1980, Sch 1, para 24.
Sub-s (1): first and second amendments in square brackets made by the Companies Consolidation (Consequential Provisions) Act 1985, s 30, Sch 2; first words in italics repealed with savings and third words in square brackets substituted with savings by the Insolvency Act 1985, s 235, Sch 8, para 37, Sch 10, Part II and the Insolvency Act 1986, s 437, Sch 11; final amendment in square brackets made by the Insolvency Act 1986, s 439(2), Sch 14.
Sub-s (2): first and fourth amendments in square brackets made by the Companies Consolidation (Consequential Provisions) Act 1985, s 30, Sch 2; first words in italics repealed with savings and second words in square brackets substituted with savings by the Insolvency Act 1985, s 235, Sch 8, para 37(4)(*a*), Sch 10, Part II and the Insolvency Act 1986, s 437, Sch 11; third and final amendments in square brackets made by the Insolvency Act 1986, s 439(2), Sch 14; second words in italics repealed with savings by the Insolvency Act 1985, s 235, Sch 8, para 37(4)(*b*), Sch 10, Part II and the Insolvency Act 1986, s 437, Sch 11.

PART V

SUPPLEMENTARY PROVISIONS

Interpretation

95. Insurance business

For the purposes of this Act "insurance business" includes—

(*a*) the effecting and carrying out, by a person not carrying on a banking business, of contracts for fidelity bonds, performance bonds, administration bonds, bail bonds or customs bonds or similar contracts of guarantee, being contracts effected by way of business (and not merely incidentally to some other business carried on by the person effecting them) in return for the payment of one or more premiums;

(*b*) the effecting and carrying out of tontines;

(*c*) the effecting and carrying out, by a body (not being a body carrying on a banking business) that carries on business which is insurance business apart from this paragraph, of—

   (i) capital redemption contracts;

   (ii) contracts to manage the investments of pension funds (other than funds solely for the benefit of its own officers or employees and their dependants or, in the case of a company, partly for the benefit of officers or employees and their dependants of its subsidiary or holding company or a subsidiary of its holding company);

(*d*) the effecting and carrying out of contracts to pay annuities on human life. **[1823]**

NOTES
Commencement: 28 January 1983.
This section derived from the Insurance Companies Act 1981, s 34.

96. General interpretation

(1) In this Act, unless the context otherwise requires—

"actuary" means an actuary possessing the prescribed qualifications;
"annuities on human life" does not include superannuation allowances and annuities payable out of any fund applicable solely to the relief and maintenance of persons engaged or who have been engaged in any particular profession, trade or employment, or of the dependants of such persons;

"body corporate" does not include a corporation sole or a Scottish firm but includes a body incorporated outside the United Kingdom;

"chief executive" has the meaning given in section 7 above;

["the Companies Act" means the Companies Act 1985];

"contract of insurance" includes any contract the effecting of which constitutes the carrying on of insurance business by virtue of section 95 above;

"controller" has the meaning given in section 7 above;

"court" means the High Court of Justice in England or, in the case of an insurance company registered or having its head office in Scotland, the Court of Session or, in the case of an insurance company registered or having its head office in Northern Ireland, the High Court of Justice in Northern Ireland;

"deed of settlement", in relation to an insurance company, includes any instrument constituting the company;

"director" includes any person occupying the position of director by whatever name called;

"enactment" includes an enactment of the Parliament of Northern Ireland and a Measure of the Northern Ireland Assembly;

"financial year" means, subject to section 69 above, each period of twelve months at the end of which the balance of the accounts of the insurance company is struck or, if no such balance is struck, the calendar year;

"former Companies Acts" means the Companies Act 1929 or the Companies Act (Northern Ireland) 1932 and any enactment repealed by that Act of 1929 or, as the case may be, that Act of 1932 or by the Companies (Consolidation) Act 1908 [and the Companies Acts 1948 to 1983];

"general business" has the meaning given in section 1 above;

"holding company" shall be construed in accordance with section [736] of the [Companies Act] or section 148 of the Companies Act (Northern Ireland) 1960;

"industrial assurance business" has the meaning given in section 1(2) of the Industrial Assurance Act 1923 or Articles 2(2) and 3(1) of the Industrial Assurance (Northern Ireland) Order 1979;

"insolvent" means in relation to an insurance company at any relevant date, that if proceedings had been taken for the winding up of the company the court could, in accordance with the provisions of sections [122 and 123 or section 221 of the Insolvency Act 1986] or, as the case may be, sections 210 and 211 or section 349 of the Companies Act (Northern Ireland) 1960, hold or have held that the company was at that date unable to pay its debts;

"insurance company" means a person or body of persons (whether incorporated or not) carrying on insurance business;

"life policy" means any instrument by which the payment of money is assured on death (except death by accident only) or the happening of any contingency dependent on human life, or any instrument evidencing a contract which is subject to payment of premiums for a term dependent on human life;

"long term business" has the meaning given in section 1 above;

"long term policy holder" means a policy holder in respect of a policy the effecting of which by the insurer constituted the carrying on of long term business;

"main agent" has the meaning given in section 7 above;

"manager", except in section 56, has the meaning given in section 7 above;

"margin of solvency", "United Kingdom margin of solvency" and "Community margin of solvency" shall be construed in accordance with section 32 above;

"mortgage", in relation to Scotland, means a heritable security within the meaning of section 9(8) of the Conveyancing and Feudal Reform (Scotland) Act 1970;

"ordinary long-term insurance business" means long term business that is not industrial assurance business;

"policy"—

(*a*) in relation to ordinary long-term insurance business and industrial assurance business, includes an instrument evidencing a contract to pay an annuity upon human life;

(*b*) in relation to insurance business of any other class includes any policy under which there is for the time being an existing liability already accrued or under which a liability may accrue; and

(*c*) in relation to capital redemption business, includes any policy, bond, certificate, receipt or other instrument evidencing the contract with the company;

"policy holder" means the person who for the time being is the legal holder of the policy for securing the contract with the insurance company or, in relation to capital redemption business, means the person who for the time being is the legal holder of the policy, bond, certificate, receipt or other instrument evidencing the contract with the company, and—

(*a*) in relation to such ordinary long-term insurance business or industrial assurance business as consists in the granting of annuities upon human life, includes an annuitant; and

(*b*) in relation to insurance business of any kind other than such as is mentioned in the foregoing paragraph or capital redemption business, includes a person to whom, under a policy, a sum is due or a periodic payment is payable;

"prescribed" means prescribed by regulations under this Act;

"registered society" means a society registered or deemed to be registered under the Industrial and Provident Societies Act 1965 or the Industrial and Provident Societies Act (Northern Ireland) 1969;

"registrar of companies" has the [the same meaning as in] the [Companies Act] and "registrar of companies in Northern Ireland" means the registrar of companies within the meaning of section 399(1) of the Companies Act (Northern Ireland) 1960;

"subsidiary", except in section 57, shall be construed in accordance with section [736] of the [Companies Act] or section 148 of the Companies Act (Northern Ireland) 1960;

"supervisory authority", in relation to a member State other than the United Kingdom, means the authority responsible in that State for supervising insurance companies;

"underwriter" includes any person named in a policy or other contract of insurance as liable to pay or contribute towards the payment of the sum secured by the policy or contract;

"valuation regulations" means regulations under section 90 above;

"vessel" includes hovercraft.

(2) References in this Act to a fund or funds maintained in respect of long term business are references to a fund or funds maintained under section 28(1)(*b*) above and in sections 48(3) and 55(6) above include references to a fund

or funds maintained under section 3(1) of the Insurance Companies Act 1958 or section 14(1) of the Insurance Companies Act (Northern Ireland) 1968.

(3) A person shall not be deemed to be within the meaning of any provision of this Act a person in accordance with whose directions or instructions the directors of a company or other body corporate or any of them are accustomed to act by reason only that the directors of the company or body act on advice given by him in a professional capacity.

(4) Any reference in this Act to an enactment of the Paraliament of Northern Ireland or a Measure of the Northern Ireland Assembly shall include a reference to any enactment re-enacting it with or without modifications.

[1824]–[1828]

NOTES
Commencement: 28 January 1983.
This section derived from the Insurance Companies Act 1974, s 85, the Insurance Companies Act 1980, Sch 1, para 35 and the Insurance Companies Act 1981, s 35(1), Sch 4, para 15.
Sub-s (1): definition "the Companies Act" added and definitions "holding company", "former Companies Acts", "registrar of companies" and "subsidiary" amended by the Companies Consolidation (Consequential Provisions) Act 1985, s 30, Sch 2; definition "insolvent" amended by the Insolvency Act 1986, s 439(2), Sch 14.

FINANCIAL SERVICES ACT 1986
(c 60)

ARRANGEMENT OF SECTIONS

Part I

REGULATION OF INVESTMENT BUSINESS

Chapter VII Winding Up and Administration Orders

Section   Para
72   Winding up orders   ..   .. [1829]
73   Winding up orders: Northern Ireland   ..   .. [1830]
74   Administration orders   ..   .. [1831]

An Act to regulate the carrying on of investment business; to make related provision with respect to insurance business and business carried on by friendly societies; to make new provision with respect to the official listing of securities, offers of unlisted securities, takeover offers and insider dealing; to make provision as to the disclosure of information obtained under enactments relating to fair trading, banking companies and insurance; to make provision for securing reciprocity with other countries in respect of facilities for the provision of financial services; and for connected purposes [7 November 1986]

Part I

REGULATION OF INVESTMENT BUSINESS

Chapter VII Winding Up and Administration Orders

72. Winding up orders

(1) On a petition presented by the Secretary of State by virtue of this section, the court having jurisdiction under the Insolvency Act 1986 may wind up an

authorised person or appointed representative to whom this subsection applies if—

(a) the person is unable to pay his debts within the meaning of section 123 or, as the case may be, section 221 of that Act; or

(b) the court is of the opinion that it is just and equitable that the person should be wound up.

(2) Subsection (1) above applies to any authorised person, any person whose authorisation is suspended under section 28 above or who is the subject of a direction under section 33(1)(b) above or any appointed representative who is—

(a) a company within the meaning of section 735 of the Companies Act 1985;

(b) an unregistered company within the meaning of section 220 of the Insolvency Act 1986;

(c) an oversea company within the meaning of section 744 of the Companies Act 1985; or

(d) a partnership.

(3) For the purposes of a petition under subsection (1) above a person who defaults in an obligation to pay any sum due and payable under any investment agreement shall be deemed to be unable to pay his debts.

(4) Where a petition is presented under subsection (1) above for the winding up of a partnership on the ground mentioned in paragraph (b) of subsection (1) above or, in Scotland, on a ground mentioned in paragraph (a) or (b) of that subsection, the court shall have jurisdiction and the Insolvency Act 1986 shall have effect as if the partnership were an unregistered company within the meaning of section 220 of that Act.

(5) The Secretary of State shall not present a petition under subsection (1) above for the winding up of any person who is an authorised person by virtue of membership of a recognised self-regulating organisation or certification by a recognised professional body and is subject to the rules of the organisation or body in the carrying on of all investment business carried on by him, unless that organisation or body has consented to his doing so.   **[1829]**

NOTES

Commencement: To be appointed.

This Act extends to Northern Ireland.

73. Winding up orders: Northern Ireland

(1) On a petition presented by the Secretary of State by virtue of this section, the High Court in Northern Ireland may wind up an authorised person or appointed representative to whom this subsection applies if—

(a) the person is unable to pay his debts within the meaning of Article 480 or, as the case may be, Article 616 of the Companies (Northern Ireland) Order 1986; or

(b) the court is of the opinion that it is just and equitable that the person should be wound up.

(2) Subsection (1) above applies to any authorised person, any person whose authorisation is suspended under section 28 above or who is the subject of a direction under section 33(1)(b) above or any appointed representative who is—

(a) a company within the meaning of Article 3 of the Companies (Northern Ireland) Order 1986;

(*b*) an unregistered company within the meaning of Article 615 of that Order; or

(*c*) a Part XXIII company within the meaning of Article 2 of that Order; or

(*d*) a partnership.

(3) For the purposes of a petition under subsection (1) above a person who defaults in an obligation to pay any sum due and payable under any investment agreement shall be deemed to be unable to pay his debts.

(4) Where a petition is presented under subsection (1) above for the winding up of partnership on the ground mentioned in paragraph (*b*) of subsection (1) above, the High Court in Northern Ireland shall have jurisdiction and the Companies (Northern Ireland) Order 1986 shall have effect as if the partnership were an unregistered company within the meaning of Article 615 of that Order.

(5) The Secretary of State shall not present a petition under subsection (1) above for the winding up of any person who is an authorised person by virtue of membership of a recognised self-regulating organisation or certification by a recognised professional body and is subject to the rules of the organisation or body in the carrying on of all investment business carried on by him, unless that organisation or body has consented to his doing so.   **[1830]**

NOTES
Commencement: To be appointed.
This Act extends to Northern Ireland.

74. Administration orders

A petition may be presented under section 9 of the Insolvency Act 1986 (applications for administration orders) in relation to a company to which section 8 of that Act applies which is an authorised person, a person whose authorisation is suspended under section 28 above or who is the subject of a direction under section 33(1)(*b*) above or an appointed representative—

(*a*) in the case of an authorised person who is an authorised person by virtue of membership of a recognised self-regulating organisation or certification by a recognised professional body, by that organisation or body; and

(*b*) in the case of an appointed representative or an authorised person who is not authorised as mentioned in paragraph (*a*) above or is so authorised but is not subject to the rules of the organisation or body in question in the carrying on of all investment business carried on by him, by the Secretary of State.   **[1831]–[1833]**

NOTES
Commencement: To be appointed.
This Act extends to Northern Ireland.

Section B

Other Statutory Instruments

SECTION B
OTHER STATUTORY INSTRUMENTS

DEEDS OF ARRANGEMENT RULES 1925
(SR & O 1925 No 795)

NOTES

    Made: 10 August 1925.
    Authority: Deeds of Arrangement Act 1914; Administration of Justice Act 1925, s 22.

ARRANGEMENT OF RULES

PART I

Rule		Para
1	Short title and commencement	[1834]
2	Repeal	[1835]
3	Interpretation	[1836]
4	Forms	[1837]

PART II

REGISTRATION OF DEEDS

		Para
5	Affidavits Forms 4, 5, 6	[1838]
6	Indorsement on copy of deed for filing	[1839]
7	Execution of Deed by Trustee prior to registration	[1840]
8	Certificate of registration on original deed	[1841]

SEARCHES AND EXTRACTS

		Para
9	Extracts from filed copy of deed	[1842]
10	Search and inspection in County Court	[1843]

TRANSMISSION OF COPIES TO COUNTY COURTS

		Para
11	Indorsement to be made on copies transmitted to County Court Registrars	[1844]
12	Transmission of copy by post	[1845]
13	Copies to be numbered and filed in County Court Office	[1846]
14	Extra copies of Deed to be furnished in certain cases	[1847]
15	Index to be kept in County Court Office	[1848]
16	Office copies and searches	[1849]

PART III

PROCEDURE

		Para
17	Applications, how to be made	[1850]
18	Applications, to whom to be made	[1851]
19	Evidence	[1852]
20	Affidavits by parties other than applicant	[1853]
21	Chambers and adjournment to Court	[1854]
22	Service of application under s 11 (2) Form (of order) 12	[1855]
23	Application to determine liability on bond	[1856]

Rule Para

PART IV

TRUSTEES

24 Security by trustee .. .. [1857]
25 Copy affidavit of debtor to be filed on giving security .. .. [1858]
26 Certificate that security given and copy order to be sent to Registrar .. .. .. [1859]
27 Notice by new Trustee of appointment .. .. [1860]
28 Notice to creditor of execution of Deed, &c .. .. [1861]
29 Audit of Trustee's accounts .. .. [1862]
30 Certificate of audit .. .. [1863]

PART V

ACCOUNTS

31 Transmission of Accounts .. .. [1864]
32 Receipts and payments .. .. [1865]
33 Trading account .. .. [1866]
34 Petty expenses .. .. [1867]
35 Realisations .. .. [1868]
36 Dividends .. .. [1869]
37 Partnership accounts .. .. [1870]
38 Imperfect accounts .. .. [1871]
39 Affidavit of no receipts or payments .. .. [1872]
40 Affidavit verifying final account .. .. [1873]
41 Summary of accounts or modified forms of account in particular cases .. .. .. [1874]
42 Swearing affidavits respecting accounts .. .. [1875]

APPENDIX FORMS

[1876]

PART I

1. Short title and commencement

These Rules may be cited as "The Deeds of Arrangement Rules 1925." They shall come into operation on the first day of October, one thousand nine hundred and twenty-five. **[1834]**

2. Repeal

The Deeds of Arrangement Rules 1915 are hereby annulled, provided that such annulment shall not affect anything done or suffered before the commencement of these Rules under any Rule annulled by these Rules, and that no Rule or practice repealed by the said Rules, or any of them, shall be revived by reason of the annulment effected by these Rules. **[1835]**

3. Interpretation

In these Rules unless the context or subject-matter otherwise requires:—

"The Act" means the Deeds of Arrangement Act 1914 as amended by the Administration of Justice Act 1925.

"Debtor" means any person by for or in respect of whose affairs a deed of arrangement as defined by the Act shall be made or entered into, and includes a firm of persons in co-partnership.

"Deed" means any deed of arrangement as defined by the Act.

"Judge" means in the case of the High Court the Judge to whom the bankruptcy business is for the time being assigned, and in the case of a County Court the Judge of the County Court having bankruptcy jurisdiction in the district in which the debtor resided or carried on business at the date of the execution of the deed.

"Registrar of the Court" means a Registrar in bankruptcy of the High Court if the debtor resided or carried on business in the London Bankruptcy District at the date of the execution of the deed, or if he did not then reside or carry on business within that district the Registrar or deputy Registrar of the County Court having bankruptcy jurisdiction in the district in which the debtor resided or carried on business at the said date.

"County Court Registrar" means any Registrar of a County Court to whom a copy of a registered deed is transmitted pursuant to Section 10 of the Act.

"Registrar" means the Registrar of Deeds of Arrangement appointed by the Board of Trade. **[1836]**

NOTES
S 10 of the Act: Deeds of Arrangement Act 1914.

4. Forms

(1) The Forms in the Appendix where applicable and where they are not applicable Forms of a like character with such variations as circumstances may require shall be used. Where such Forms are applicable any costs occasioned by the use of any other or more prolix Forms shall be borne by or disallowed to the party using the same unless the Court shall otherwise direct.

(2) The Board of Trade may from time to time alter any Forms which relate to matters of an administrative and not of a judicial character, or substitute new Forms in lieu thereof. Where the Board of Trade alters any Form or substitutes a new Form in lieu of one prescribed by these Rules such altered or substituted Form shall be published in the London Gazette. **[1837]**

PART II

REGISTRATION OF DEEDS

5. Affidavits Forms 4, 5, 6

The affidavits to be made pursuant to Section 5 of the Act shall be filed with the Registrar. **[1838]**

NOTES
S 5 of the Act: Deeds of Arrangement Act 1914.

6. Indorsement on copy of deed for filing

Upon every copy of a deed which is presented for filing there shall be indorsed, by the person who presents it, the name of the debtor, the date of the deed and of the filing thereof, the total amount of duty with which the deed is stamped, and a certificate signed by the solicitor of the debtor or the person who presents the copy for filing certifying that the copy is a correct copy of the deed. **[1839]**

7. Execution of Deed by Trustee prior to registration

An assignment of property by a debtor to a trustee or assignee for the benefit of his creditors shall not be registered under the Act unless it appears from the assignment that it has been or purports to have been executed, or (if not made by deed) signed by the trustee or assignee: and it shall be the duty of the Registrar, before registering such an assignment, to satisfy himself that the assignment purports to have been duly executed or signed as the case may be by the trustee or assignee thereunder. **[1840]**

NOTES

The Act: Deeds of Arrangement Act 1914.

8. Certificate of registration on original deed

When a deed is registered under the Act there shall be written on the original deed a certificate stating that the deed has been duly registered as prescribed by the Act, and the date of registration. Such certificate shall be sealed with the seal of the Registrar. **[1841]**

NOTES

The Act: Deeds of Arrangement Act 1914.

SEARCHES AND EXTRACTS

9. Extracts from filed copy of deed

Extracts from the filed copy of a deed shall be limited to the date of execution and registration, the names, addresses, and descriptions of the debtor and the parties to the deed, and a short statement of the nature and effect of the deed. **[1842]**

10. Search and inspection in County Court

The County Court Registrar shall allow any person to search the index kept by him at any time during which he is required by the County Court Rules for the time being in force to keep his office open, and to make the same extracts as are permitted by the last preceding rule upon payment by such person of the prescribed fee. The County Court Registrar shall also, if required, cause an office copy to be made of any copy of a deed filed in his office, and shall mark and seal the same upon payment of the prescribed fee. **[1843]**

TRANSMISSION OF COPIES TO COUNTY COURTS

11. Indorsement to be made on copies transmitted to County Court Registrars

Upon every copy of a deed which pursuant to the Act is transmitted to a County Court Registrar there shall be written copies of every indorsement or certificate written on the original deed or on the filed copy thereof. Such copies shall be signed by the Registrar or by some other person duly authorised by him. **[1844]**

NOTES

The Act: Deeds of Arrangement Act 1914.

12. Transmission of copy by post

The copy of a deed which pursuant to the Act is required to be transmitted to a County Court Registrar may be transmitted to him by post.   **[1845]**

NOTES
    The Act: Deeds of Arrangement Act 1914.

13. Copies to be numbered and filed in County Court Office

The County Court Registrar shall number the copies of deeds received by him in the order in which they shall respectively be received, and shall file and keep them in his office.   **[1846]**

14. Extra copies of Deed to be furnished in certain cases

Where a debtor who is one of the parties to a Deed of Arrangement or who is referred to therein has a place of business or residence situate in some place outside the London Bankruptcy District, there shall be furnished to the Registrar sufficient copies of the Deed of Arrangement to enable him to transmit a copy to the Registrar of the County Court of each district in which such place of business or residence is situate.   **[1847]**

15. Index to be kept in County Court Office

The County Court Registrar shall keep an index, alphabetically arranged, in which he shall enter, under the first letter of the surname of the debtor, such surname, with his christian name, address, and description, and the number which has been affixed to the copy.   **[1848]**

16. Office copies and searches

The provisions of Sections 9 and 25 of the Act shall apply to all documents filed with the Registrar pursuant to the Act or these Rules.   **[1849]**

NOTES
    The Act: Deeds of Arrangement Act 1914.

PART III

PROCEDURE

17. Applications, how to be made

All applications other than applications under Section 7 of the Act which by the Act or these Rules are directed or allowed to be made to the High Court or the County Court having jurisdiction in bankruptcy in the district in which the debtor resided or carried on business at the date of the execution of the deed shall be deemed to be proceedings in bankruptcy, and subject to the Act and these Rules shall be made in accordance with and in the manner prescribed for proceedings under the [Parts VIII to XI of the Insolvency Act 1986] and the [Insolvency Rules] for the time being in force, with such variations as the circumstances may require, and shall be supported by affidavit. Provided that applications for extension of time for procuring the assent of creditors to a deed under Section 3 (1) or for filing the statutory declaration required by Section 3 (4) may be made ex parte and without affidavit unless the Court shall in any case otherwise order.   **[1850]**

NOTES
   The Act: Deeds of Arrangement Act 1914.
   Amended by The Insolvency (Amendment of Subordinate Legislation) Order 1986, SI 1986 No 2001, art 2, Schedule.

18. Applications, to whom to be made

The application (except in cases within the proviso to Section 23 of the Act) shall be made to the Registrar of the Court who shall cause the same, together with the affidavits in support, to be filed, and shall appoint a day for the hearing not earlier than 14 days from the filing of the application. In cases within such proviso the application may be made as in these Rules provided either to the Registrar of the Court or to a Registrar of the High Court. The Registrar to whom the application is made may direct notice of the application to be served on such person or persons as he thinks fit, but in the absence of any special direction by him, the notice, together with copies of the affidavits in support, shall be served, when the application is made by the trustee, on the debtor and any creditor or other person to be affected thereby, and, when made by the debtor, on the trustee and on any creditor or other person to be affected thereby, and, when made by a creditor, on the trustee and the debtor.   **[1851]**

NOTES
   The Act: Deeds of Arrangement Act 1914.

19. Evidence

The evidence to be used on the application shall, unless the Court otherwise orders, be given by affidavit, but any opposite party may require, by notice in writing addressed to any deponent or his solicitor, the attendance of such deponent for cross-examination.   **[1852]**

20. Affidavits by parties other than applicant

All affidavits intended to be used by any party to such application, other than the applicant, shall be filed in the Court, and copies served on the applicant not less than four days before the day appointed for the hearing of the application.
      [1853]

21. Chambers and adjournment to Court

All such applications as are referred to in the preceding Rules shall be heard and determined by the Registrar of the Court in Chambers, but he may in any case, and shall at the request of any party thereto, adjourn the application to be heard and determined by the Judge in Court.   **[1854]**

22. Service of application under s 11 (2) Form (of order) 12

Notice of any application under Section 11 (2) of the Act to declare a deed void, or appoint another trustee, shall be served on the trustee named in the deed not less than eight days before the day appointed for the hearing.   **[1855]**

NOTES
   The Act: Deeds of Arrangement Act 1914.

23. Application to determine liability on bond

If a trustee fails to pay to a Guarantee Society, party to a bond given by him under Rule 24, the annual premium payable by him within fourteen days of the date when such premium becomes payable, or if the Society refuses to accept such premium, the Society may apply to the Registrar of the Court to determine its liability under the bond, and the Registrar of the Court, if satisfied by affidavit that default in payment of the premium has been made by the trustee, or that the refusal of the Society to accept the premium in order that its liability may be determined is reasonable, may order that, as from the date of expiration of the year for which the last premium was paid, or as from the date of the order, whichever may be the later date, all further liability of the Society shall cease and determine, save and except in respect of any loss or damage occasioned by any act or default of the said trustee in relation to his duties as such trustee as aforesaid previously to such cesser and determination of liability, and the Registrar of the Court may exercise any of the powers conferred by Section 11 (2) of the Act. Notice of any application under this rule shall be served on the three largest creditors named in the affidavit filed on registration of the deed not less than eight days before the day appointed for hearing the application, and any of such creditors may appear and be heard thereon, and Rules 17 to 21 inclusive shall, so far as applicable, be observed.   **[1856]**

NOTES
   The Act: Deeds of Arrangement Act 1914.

PART IV

TRUSTEES

24. Security by trustee

The security to be given by the trustee under a Deed of Arrangement pursuant to Section 11 (1) of the Act shall be by bond of a Guarantee Society. The Guarantee Society named in such bond shall be a Society whose bonds are accepted by the Registrar of the Court to whom security is given. Pending the preparation of the bond, a cover note shall be accepted by the Registrar of the Court as temporary security.   **[1857]**

NOTES
   The Act: Deeds of Arrangement Act 1914.

25. Copy affidavit of debtor to be filed on giving security

Every trustee on giving security for the due administration of the deed and for accounting fully for the assets pursuant to Section 11 (1) of the Act, shall produce and hand to the Registrar of the Court to whom the security is to be given an office copy of the affidavit of the debtor filed on the registration of the deed and the Registrar of the Court shall file such office copy.   **[1858]**

NOTES
   The Act: Deeds of Arrangement Act 1914.

26. Certificate that security given and copy order to be sent to Registrar

When security has been given by a trustee pursuant to Section 11 (1) of the Act, the Registrar of the Court to whom it is given shall, within three days after receipt thereof, send to the Registrar a certificate signed by him certifying that the security has been given and the Registrar shall forthwith file the same. The Registrar of the Court shall also send to the Registrar within three days after any order made under Section 11 (2) has been perfected a copy of such order.   **[1859]**

27. Notice by new Trustee of appointment

Where a new trustee of a deed has been appointed he shall forthwith send to the Registrar a notice of his appointment, giving his full name and address, and showing how and when the appointment has been made, and the Registrar shall forthwith file the same.   **[1860]**

28. Notice to creditor of execution of Deed, &c

Notice under Section 24 (1) of the Act to a creditor of the execution of a deed and of the filing of the certificate of the assents of creditors thereto shall be sent by prepaid registered post addressed to such creditor at the address mentioned in the affidavit of the debtor filed on the registration of the deed, and service shall be deemed to have been made on the day on which the notice was posted.
                    [1861]

29. Audit of Trustee's accounts

Where the Board of Trade cause a trustee's accounts to be audited, he shall, within seven days of service upon him by registered post of an order made by the Board of Trade directing him so to do, deliver to the Board of Trade copies of all the accounts transmitted by him to the Board pursuant to Section 13 of the Act, together with an account in similar form from the date to which the last account extended to the date of the order.   Such copies and account shall be sent together with an affidavit verifying the same.   **[1862]**

30. Certificate of audit

The account as audited and the auditor's certificate or observations thereon shall be filed and kept by the Board of Trade, and shall be open to the inspection of any creditor or of the trustee, who shall be at liberty to take a copy of such certificate or observations.   A certified copy of the certificate or observations shall be supplied to the trustee or to any creditor on application.   **[1863]**

PART V

ACCOUNTS

31. Transmission of Accounts

(1) The accounts of receipts and payments to be transmitted to the Board of Trade by every trustee under a Deed shall be on sheets 13 inches by 16 inches.

(2) In the case of a deed executed by the debtor prior to 1st April, 1914, such accounts shall be transmitted within 30 days of the 1st day of January in every year and shall be verified by affidavit.

(3) In the case of a deed executed by the debtor on or after 1st April, 1914, the first account shall commence at the date of execution, and be brought down to the end of 12 months from the date of registration thereof, and shall be

transmitted within 30 days from the expiration of such 12 months and the subsequent accounts shall be transmitted at intervals of 12 months. Each account shall be brought down to the end of the period of 12 months for which it is sent, and shall be verified by affidavit.

(4) The trustee shall stamp the accounts transmitted by him to the Board of Trade with a stamp equivalent to the amount of the prescribed fee. **[1864]**

NOTES
   Para (1): amended by SR & O 1941 No 1253.

32. Receipts and payments

In the account each receipt and payment must be entered in such a manner as sufficiently to explain its nature. **[1865]**

33. Trading account

When the trustee carries on a business, a trading account must be forwarded as a distinct account, and the totals of receipts and payments on the trading account must alone be set out in the yearly account. The Trading Account shall be on sheets 13 inches by 16 inches. **[1866]**

34. Petty expenses

Petty expenses must be entered in the accounts in sufficient detail to show that no estimated charges are made. **[1867]**

35. Realisations

Where property has been realised, the gross proceeds of sale must be entered under receipts in the account, and the necessary disbursements and charges incidental to sales must be entered as payments. **[1868]**

36. Dividends

Where dividends or instalments of composition are distributed under the Deed, the total amount of each dividend or instalment of composition must be entered in the trustee's accounts as one sum, and the trustee shall forward to the Board of Trade (1) with each account in which a charge in respect of dividend or composition appears a statement showing the amount of the claim of each creditor, and the amount of dividend or composition payable to each creditor, distinguishing in such statement the dividends or instalments of composition paid and those remaining unpaid; and (2) with his final account a complete statement in similar form showing the amount of the claim and the full amount of dividend or composition paid to or reserved for each creditor. Such statement shall be on sheets 13 inches by 8 inches. **[1869]**

37. Partnership accounts

Where the deed has been made by a firm of debtors in partnership, distinct accounts shall be transmitted of the joint estate and of each of the separate estates. **[1870]**

38. Imperfect accounts

Where it appears to the Board of Trade that the account transmitted by a trustee under a Deed of Arrangement is incomplete, or requires amendment or explanation, the Board of Trade may require such account to be completed or amended, or require the trustee to furnish explanations with reference to any of the entries appearing therein; and any such requirement by the Board of Trade may be enforced in the same manner as the transmission of accounts under Section 13.   **[1871]**

NOTES
  S 13: Deeds of Arrangement Act 1914, s 13.

39. Affidavit of no receipts or payments

Where a trustee has not since the date of his becoming trustee, or since the last time that his accounts have been transmitted, as the case may be, received or paid any money on account of the debtor's estate he shall, at the period when he is required to transmit his accounts to the Board of Trade, forward to the Board of Trade an affidavit of no receipts or payments.   **[1872]**

40. Affidavit verifying final account

As soon as a trustee has realised all the property included in any Deed of Arrangement, or so much thereof as can probably be realised, and has distributed a final dividend, or final instalment of composition, or in any other case as soon as the trusts of the Deed and the obligations of the trustee have been completely fulfilled, the trustee shall forthwith transmit his final account together with an affidavit verifying the same.   **[1873]**

41. Summary of accounts or modified forms of account in particular cases

In any particular case in which it shall appear to the Board of Trade that an account of receipts and payments in the form and containing the particulars specified in these Rules may for special reasons be dispensed with, the Board of Trade may permit the trustee to transmit, instead of accounts in the form therein specified, such a summary of his accounts or modified statement of accounts as to the Board of Trade shall appear sufficient.   **[1874]**

42. Swearing affidavits respecting accounts

All affidavits required by or made in pursuance of Section 13 of the Act, or these Rules, shall, if sworn in any place in England or Wales, be sworn before a Commissioner for Oaths, before a Justice of the Peace for that place or before a Master of the Supreme Court; and may, if sworn in any place out of England and Wales, be sworn before any person having authority to administer an oath in that place.   **[1875]**

NOTES
  S 13 of the Act: Deeds of Arrangement Act 1914.

Appendix Forms

NOTES
  The forms themselves are not reproduced in this work, but their numbers and descriptions are listed below.

FORM	TITLE
1	General title
2	Assent of Creditors to deed
3	Statutory declaration by Trustee as to assents of Creditors
4	Affidavit of execution by Debtor

5	Affidavit of execution where deed is first executed by a Creditor
6	Debtor's affidavit, with schedule of Creditors
7	Form of register to be kept by Registrar
8	Statutory declaration by Trustee that Creditors have dispensed with security
9	Security by Trustee: form of bond
10	Security by Trustee: cover note
11	Certificate by Registrar of the Court that security has been given by Trustee
12	Order declaring deed void or appointing new Trustee
13	Statement of accounts to be sent to Creditors pursuant to Section 14
14	Notice to Creditors by Trustee under Section 24(1)
15	Trustee's account of receipts and payments
16	Affidavit verifying Trustee's account (deeds executed before 1st April, 1914)
17	Affidavit verifying Trustee's account (deeds executed on and after 1st April, 1914)
18	Trustee's trading account
19	List of dividends or compositions
20	Affidavit verifying Trustee's final account

[1876]

NOTES
    Ss 14, 24(1): Deeds of Arrangement Act 1914, ss 14, 24(1).

DEEDS OF ARRANGEMENT FEES ORDER 1984
(SI 1984 No 887)

NOTES
    Made: 20 June 1984.
    Authority: Administration of Justice Act 1925, s 22(4); Supreme Court Act 1981, s 130; Public Offices Fees Act 1879, s 2.

1. This Order may be cited as the Deeds of Arrangement Fees Order 1984 and shall come into operation on 1st August 1984. **[1877]**

NOTES
    Commencement: 1 August 1984.

2. In this Order, unless the context otherwise requires—

(a) "the Act" means the Deeds of Arrangement Act 1914 as amended by the Administration of Justice Act 1925, and "the Rules" means the Deeds of Arrangement Rules 1925,
"the bankruptcy fee" means the fee payable on a similar proceeding in bankruptcy under any order made under [section 415(1) and (2) of the Insolvency Act 1986],
"the Supreme Court fee" means the fee payable on a similar document or proceeding under any order other than this one made under section 130 of the Supreme Court Act 1981;

(b) expressions used in this Order shall have the same meaning as in the Act or in the Rules;

(c) a section referred to by number means the section so numbered in the Act;

(d) a rule referred to by number means the rule so numbered in the Rules; and

(*e*) a fee referred to by number means the fee so numbered in the Schedule
to this Order.   **[1878]**

NOTES
Commencement: 1 August 1984.
Amended by the Insolvency (Amendment of Subordinate Legislation) Order 1986, SI 1986 No
2001, art 2, Schedule.

3. (1) The fees set out in column 2 of the Schedule to this Order shall be taken
in respect of the items in column 1 thereof, and the documents to be stamped
shall be those prescribed in column 3 thereof.

(2) The fees in Part I of the Schedule to this Order shall be taken in the
office of the Registrar of the Court, those in Part II by the Registrar and those
in Part III by the Department of Trade and Industry.

(3) The fees shall be taken in cash.   **[1879]**

NOTES
Commencement: 1 August 1984.

4. The Deeds of Arrangement Fees Order 1980 and the Deeds of Arrangement
Fees (Amendment) Order 1982 are hereby revoked save as to any fee or
percentage due or payable before the commencement of this Order.   **[1880]**

NOTES
Commencement: 1 August 1984.

SCHEDULE
Article 3

PART I

Column 1	Column 2	Column 3
	£	
1. On an application under section 11(1) to give security under a deed of arrangement, for taking security and giving certificate—		
(*a*) where the estimated assets available for distribution amongst the unsecured creditors, as shown by the affidavit filed on registration, are less than £100;	0.50	The application
(*b*) otherwise.	1.00	The application
2.(*a*) On an application to the court for extension of time under section 3(1) or 3(4);	The bankruptcy fee	The application
(*b*) on an application by a creditor for a declaration under section 11(2), or an order under section 16; and	The bankruptcy fee	The application
(*c*) on an application by any person under section 23.	The bankruptcy fee	The application
3. On any other document or proceeding not otherwise provided for in this part of this Schedule.	The Supreme Court fee	The document or any document relating to the proceeding

[1881]

NOTES
    Commencement: 1 August 1984.
    Ss 3, 11, 16, 23: Deeds of Arrangement Act 1914.

PART II

Column 1	Column 2	Column 3
	£	
4. On filing with the Registrar a deed where the total estimated amount of property included therein or the total amount of composition thereunder appears from the affidavit of the debtor to be—		
(*a*) £1,000 or less;	8.25	The copy deed
(*b*) over £1,000 and not over £2,500;	14.00	The copy deed
(*c*) over £2,500 and not over £5,000;	22.00	The copy deed
(*d*) over £5,000.	27.50	The copy deed
5. On filing with the Registrar any deed not covered by Fee No. 4.	11.00	The copy deed
6. On a certificate of registration of an original deed endorsed thereon.	1.50	The certificate
7. On filing with the Registrar a statutory declaration, affidavit or notice pursuant to the Act or Rules.	1.10	The declaration, affidavit or notice
8. On searching the register and on inspecting the filed copy, including taking the limited extract under section 9 and rule 9 (for every name inspected).	1.10	The search form

[1882]

NOTES
    Commencement: 1 August 1984.
    The Act: Deeds of Arrangement Act 1914.
    The Rules: Deeds of Arrangement Rules 1925, SR & O 1925 No 795.

PART III

Column 1	Column 2	Column 3
	£	
9. On an account transmitted by a trustee under section 13—		
(*a*) where the gross amount of the assets realised and brought to credit, or of the composition distributed (in the case of a composition) during the period of account does not exceed £1,000 on every £100 or part thereof;	2.25	The account
(*b*) where the gross amount exceeds £1,000;	22.00	The account
and in addition for every £100 or part thereof exceeding £1,000.	1.50	The account

Column 1	Column 2	Column 3
	£	
10. On an application to inspect the accounts of a trustee under section 13(3).	1.50	The application
11. On an application for an official audit of a trustee's accounts under section 15(1).	7.00	The application
12. On the audit of a trustee's accounts under section 15(1)—		
(*a*) where the amount brought to credit after deduction of the amount received and spent in carrying on the business, and of the amount paid to secured creditors out of the proceeds of their securities does not exceed £5,000, on every £100 or part thereof;	7.00	The account
(*b*) where the amount so brought to credit exceeds £5,000;	350.00	The account
and in addition for every £100 or part thereof exceeding £5,000. Note: The minimum fee for Fee No. 12(a) shall be £35.00 and in calculating Fee No. 12(a) or (b) credit shall be given for any amount paid for Fee No. 9.	3.50	The account
13. On copies of documents supplied—		
(*a*) per foolscap or A4 ISO page;	0.35	The copy
(*b*) all larger pages.	0.70	The copy

[1883]

NOTES
  Commencement: 1 August 1984.
  Ss 13, 15: Deeds of Arrangement Act 1914.

INSURANCE COMPANIES (WINDING-UP) RULES 1985
(SI 1985 No 95)

NOTES
  Made: 25 January 1985.
  Authority: Companies Act 1985, s 663(1); Insurance Companies Act 1982, s 59.

ARRANGEMENT OF RULES

CITATION AND COMMENCEMENT

Rule   Para
1   [1884]

INTERPRETATION

2   [1885]

Rule		Para
	APPLICATION	
3		[1886]
	APPOINTMENT OF LIQUIDATOR	
4		[1887]
	SEPARATION OF LONG TERM AND OTHER BUSINESS IN WINDING-UP	
5		[1888]
	VALUATION OF GENERAL BUSINESS POLICIES	
6		[1889]
	VALUATION OF LONG TERM POLICIES	
7		[1890]
8		[1891]
	ATTRIBUTION OF ASSETS AND LIABILITIES TO THE LONG TERM BUSINESS	
9		[1892]
10		[1893]
	EXCESS OF LONG TERM BUSINESS ASSETS	
11		[1894]
	ACTUARIAL ADVICE	
12		[1895]
	UTILISATION OF EXCESS OF ASSETS	
13		[1896]
	SPECIAL BANK ACCOUNT	
14		[1897]
	CUSTODY OF ASSETS	
15		[1898]
	MAINTENANCE OF ACCOUNTING, VALUATION AND OTHER RECORDS	
16		[1899]

Rule   Para

ADDITIONAL POWERS IN RELATION TO THE LONG TERM BUSINESS

17   [1900]

ACCOUNTS AND AUDIT

18   [1901]

SECURITY BY LIQUIDATOR AND SPECIAL MANAGER

20   [1902]

PROOF OF DEBTS

21   [1903]

FAILURE TO PAY PREMIUMS

22   [1904]

NOTICE OF VALUATION OF POLICY

23   [1905]

DIVIDENDS TO CREDITORS

24   [1906]

MEETINGS OF CREDITORS

25   [1907]

REMUNERATION OF LIQUIDATOR CARRYING ON LONG TERM BUSINESS

26   [1908]

APPOINTMENT OF COSTS PAYABLE OUT OF THE ASSETS

27   [1909]

NOTICE OF STOP ORDER

28   [1910]

SCHEDULES

Schedule 1—General business policies   ..   .. [1911]
Schedule 2—Rules for valuing non-linked life policies, non-linked deferred annuity
   policies, non-linked annuities in payment and capital redemption policies   .. [1912]
Schedule 3—Rules for valuing life policies and deferred annuity policies which are
   linked policies   ..   .. [1913]
Schedule 4—Rules for valuing long term policies which are not dealt with in
   Schedules 2 and 3   ..   .. [1914]
Schedule 5—Rules for valuing long term policies where a stop order has been
   made ..   .. [1915]
Schedule 6   ..   .. [1916]

CITATION AND COMMENCEMENT

1. These Rules may be cited as the Insurance Companies (Winding-Up) Rules 1985 and shall come up into operation on 1st March 1985.   **[1884]**

NOTES
Commencement: 1 March 1985.

INTERPRETATION

2.—(1) In these Rules, unless the context or subject-matter otherwise requires:—

"the Act of 1923" means the Industrial Assurance Act 1923;
. . .
"the Act of 1982" means the Insurance Companies Act 1982;
["the Act of 1985" means the Companies Act 1985;
"the Act of 1986" means the Insolvency Act 1986;]
"company" means an insurance company which is being wound up;
"excess of the long term business assets" means the amount, if any, by which the value as at the date of the winding-up order of the assets representing the fund or funds maintained by the company in respect of its long term business exceeds the value as at that date of the liabilities of the company attributable to that business;
"excess of the other business assets" means the amount, if any, by which the value as at the date of the winding-up order of the assets of the company which do not represent the fund or funds maintained by the company in respect of its long term business exceeds the value as at that date of the liabilities of the company (other than liabilities in respect of share capital) which are not attributable to that business;
"general business policy" means a policy the effecting of which by the company constitutes the carrying on of general business;
["the general regulations" means the Insolvency Regulations 1986;]
"the Industrial Assurance Acts" means the Act of 1923 and the Industrial Assurance and Friendly Societies Act 1929;
"insurance company" means an insurance company to which Part II of the Act of 1982 applies;
"linked liability" means any liability under a policy the effecting of which constitutes the carrying on of long term insurance business the amount of which is determined by reference to:—

(a) the value of property of any description (whether or not specified in the policy);
(b) fluctuations in the value of such property,
(c) income from any such property, or
(d) fluctuations in an index of the value of such property;

"linked policy" means a policy which provides for linked liabilities and a policy which when made provided for linked liabilities shall be deemed to be a linked policy even if the policy holder has elected to convert his rights under the policy so that at the date of the winding-up order there are no longer linked liabilities under the policy;
"long term policy" means a policy the effecting of which by the company constitutes the carrying on of long term business;
"non-linked policy" means a policy which is not a linked policy;
"other business", in relation to a company carrying on long term business, means such of the business of the company as is not long term business;

["the principal Rules" means the Insolvency Rules 1986;]
"stop order" in relation to a company means an order of the court, made under section 56(2) of the Act of 1982, ordering the Liquidator to stop carrying on the long term business of the company;
"unit" in relation to a linked policy means any unit (whether or not described as a unit in the policy) by reference to the numbers and value of which the amount of the linked liabilities under the policy at any time is measured.

(2) Unless the context otherwise requires words or expressions contained in these Rules bear the same meaning as in the principal Rules [the general regulations], . . . the Act of 1982, [the Act of 1986] or any statutory modification thereof respectively.   **[1885]**

NOTES
Commencement: 1 March 1985.
Amended by the Insurance Companies (Winding-up) (Amendment) Rules 1986, SI 1986 No 2002, r 4.
General Regulations 1986: Insolvency Regulations 1986, SI 1986 No 1994.
Principal Rules: Insolvency Rules 1986, SI 1986 No 1925.

APPLICATION

3.—(1) These Rules apply to proceedings for the winding-up of an insurance company which commence on or after the date on which these Rules come into operation.

(2) These Rules supplement the principal Rules [and the general regulations] which continue to apply to the proceedings in the winding-up of an insurance company under [the Act of 1986] as they apply to proceedings in the winding-up of any company under that Act but in the event of conflict between these Rules and the principal Rules [or the general regulations] these Rules prevail.
                                                                        [1886]

NOTES
Commencement: 1 March 1985.
Para (2): amended by the Insurance Companies (Winding-up) (Amendment) Rules 1986, SI 1986 No 2002, r 3.
Principal Rules: Insolvency Rules 1986, SI 1986 No 1925.
General Regulations: Insolvency Regulations 1986, SI 1986 No 1994.
Act of 1986: Insolvency Act 1986.

APPOINTMENT OF LIQUIDATOR

4. [Where the court considers the appointment of a liquidator under—

    (*a*) section 139(4) of the Act of 1986 (court appointment of liquidator where conflict between creditors and contributories), or

    (*b*) section 140 of that Act (court appointment of liquidator following administration or voluntary arrangement),

the Policyholders Protection Board may appear on the application or (as the case may be) the petition, and make representations as to the person to be appointed.]   **[1887]**

NOTES
Commencement: 29 December 1986.
Substituted by the Insurance Companies (Winding-up) (Amendment) Rules 1986, SI 1986 No 2002, r 6.
Act of 1986: Insolvency Act 1986.

SEPARATION OF LONG TERM AND OTHER BUSINESS IN WINDING-UP

5.—(1) This Rule applies in the case of a company carrying on long term business.

(2) The assets of the company which in accordance with sections 55(3) and (4) of the Act of 1982 are available for meeting the liabilities of the company attributable to its long term business shall, in pursuance of [section 148 of the Act of 1986], be applied in discharge of those liabilities as though those assets and those liabilities were the assets and liabilities of a separate company.

(3) The assets of the company which in accordance with sections 55(3) and (4) of the Act of 1982 are available for meeting the liabilities of the company attributable to its other business shall, in pursuance of [section 148 of the Act of 1986], be applied in discharge of those liabilities as though those assets and those liabilities were the assets and liabilities of a separate company.   **[1888]**

NOTES
    Commencement: 1 March 1985.
    Paras (2), (3): amended by the Insurance Companies (Winding-up) (Amendment) Rules 1986, SI 1986 No 2002, r 7.
    Act of 1982: Insurance Companies Act 1982.
    Act of 1986: Insolvency Act 1986.

VALUATION OF GENERAL BUSINESS POLICIES

6. Except in relation to amounts which have fallen due for payment before the date of the winding-up order, the holder of a general business policy shall be admitted as a creditor in relation to his policy without proof for an amount equal to the value of the policy and for this purpose the value of a policy shall be determined in accordance with Schedule 1.   **[1889]**

NOTES
    Commencement: 1 March 1985.

VALUATION OF LONG TERM POLICIES

7.—(1) This Rule applies in relation to a company's long term business where no stop order has been made.

(2) In relation to a claim under a policy which has fallen due for payment before the date of the winding-up order, a policy holder shall be admitted as a creditor without proof for such amount as appears from the records of the company to be due in respect of that claim.

(3) In all other respects a policy holder shall be admitted as a creditor in relation to his policy without proof for an amount equal to the value of the policy and for this purpose the value of a policy of any class shall be determined in the manner applicable to policies of that class provided by Schedules 2, 3 and 4.

(4) This Rule applies in relation to a person entitled to apply for a free paid-up policy under section 24 of the Act of 1923 and to whom no such policy has been issued before the date of the winding-up order (whether or not it was applied for) as if such a policy had been issued immediately before the date of the winding-up order—

(*a*) for the minimum amount determined in accordance with section 24(2) of the Act of 1923, or

(*b*) if the Liquidator is satisfied that it was the practice of the company during the five years immediately before the date of the winding-up order to issue policies under the said section 24 in excess of the minimum amounts so determined, for the amount determined in accordance with that practice. **[1890]**

NOTES
Commencement: 1 March 1985.
Act of 1923: Industrial Assurance Act 1923.

8.—(1) This Rule applies in relation to a company's long term business where a stop order has been made.

(2) In relation to a claim under a policy which has fallen due for payment on or after the date of the winding-up order and before the date of the stop order, a policy holder shall be admitted as a creditor without proof for such amount as appears from the records of the company and of the Liquidator to be due in respect of that claim.

(3) In all other respects a policy holder shall be admitted as a creditor in relation to his policy without proof for an amount equal to the value of the policy and for this purpose the value of a policy of any class shall be determined in the manner applicable to policies of that class provided by Schedule 5.

(4) Paragraph (4) of Rule 7 applies for the purposes of this Rule as if references to the date of the winding-up order (other than that in sub-paragraph (*b*) of that paragraph) were references to the date of the stop order. **[1891]**

NOTES
Commencement: 1 March 1985.

ATTRIBUTION OF ASSETS AND LIABILITIES TO THE LONG TERM BUSINESS

9.—(1) This Rule applies in the case of a company carrying on long term business if at the date of the winding-up order there are liabilities of the company in respect of which it is not clear from the accounting and other records of the company whether they are or are not attributable to the company's long term business.

(2) The Liquidator shall, in such manner and according to such accounting principles as he shall determine, identify the liabilities referred to in paragraph (1) as attributable or not attributable to a company's long term business and those liabilities shall for the purposes of the winding-up be deemed as at the date of the winding-up order to be so attributable or not as the case may be.

(3) In making his determination under this Rule the Liquidator may determine that some liabilities are attributable to the company's long term business and that others are not or he may determine that a part of a liability is attributable to the company's long term business and that the remainder of that liability is not and he may use one method for some of the liabilities and the other method for the remainder of them. **[1892]**

NOTES
Commencement: 1 March 1985.

10.—(1) This Rule applies in the case of a company carrying on long term business if at the date of the winding-up order there are assets of the company in respect of which—

    (*a*) it is not clear from the accounting and other records of the company whether they do or do not represent the funds maintained by the company in respect of its long term business, and

    (*b*) it cannot be inferred from the source of the income out of which those assets were provided whether they do or do not represent those funds.

(2) Subject to paragraph (6) the Liquidator shall determine which (if any) of the assets referred to in paragraph (1) are attributable to those funds and which (if any) are not and those assets shall, for the purposes of the winding-up, be deemed as at the date of the winding-up order to represent those funds or not in accordance with the Liquidator's determination.

(3) For the purposes of paragraph (2) the Liquidator may:—

    (*a*) determine that some of those assets shall be attributable to those funds and that others of them shall not (the first method); or

    (*b*) determine that a part of the value of one of those assets shall be attributable to those funds and that the remainder of that value shall not (the second method).

and he may use the first method for some of those assets and the second method for others of them.

(4)(*a*) In making the attribution the Liquidator's objective shall in the first instance be so far as possible to reduce any deficit that may exist, at the date of the winding-up order and before any attribution is made, either in the company's long term business or in its other business.

    (*b*) If there is a deficit in both the company's long term business and its other business the attribution shall be in the ratio that the amount of the one deficit bears to the amount of the other until the deficits are eliminated.

    (*c*) Thereafter the attribution shall be in the ratio which the aggregate amount of the liabilities attributable to the company's long term business bears to the aggregate amount of the liabilities not so attributable.

(5) For the purpose of paragaph (4) the value of a liability of the company shall, if it falls to be valued under Rule 6 or 7, have the same value as it has under that Rule but otherwise it shall have such value as would have been included in relation to it in a balance sheet of the company prepared in pursuance of section 17 of the Act of 1982 as at the date of the winding-up order and, for the purpose of determining the ratio referred to in paragraph (4) but not for the purpose of determining the amount of any deficit therein referred to, the net balance of shareholders' funds shall be included in the liabilities not attributable to the company's long term business.

(6) Notwithstanding anything in the preceding paragraphs of this Rule the court may order that the determination of which (if any) of the assets referred to in paragraph (1) are attributable to the fund or funds maintained by the company in respect of its long term business and which (if any) are not shall be made in such manner and by such methods as the court may direct or the court may itself make the determination.   **[1893]**

NOTES

    Commencement: 1 March 1985.

Act of 1982: Insurance Companies Act 1982.

EXCESS OF LONG TERM BUSINESS ASSETS

11. Where the company is one carrying on long term business, for the purpose of determining the amount, if any, of the excess of the long term business assets, there shall be included amongst the liabilities of the company attributable to its long term business an amount determined by the Liquidator in respect of liabilities and expenses likely to be incurred in connection with the transfer of the company's long term business as a going concern to another insurance company being liabilities not included in the valuation of the long term policies made in pursuance of Rule 7.   **[1894]**

NOTES
Commencement: 1 March 1985.

ACTUARIAL ADVICE

12.—(1) Before determining the value of a policy in accordance with Schedules 1 to 5 (other than paragraph 2 of Schedule 1), before identifying long term assets and liabilities in accordance with Rules 9 and 10 and before determining the amount (if any) of the excess of the long term business assets in accordance with Rule 11, and before determining the terms on which he will accept payment of overdue premiums under Rule 22(1) and the amount and nature of any compensation under Rule 22(2), the Liquidator shall obtain and consider advice thereon (including an estimate of any value or amount required to be determined) from an actuary.

(2) Before seeking, for the purpose of valuing a policy, the direction of the court as to the assumption of a particular rate of interest or the employment of any rates of mortality or disability, the Liquidator shall obtain and consider advice thereon from an actuary.   **[1895]**

NOTES
Commencement: 1 March 1985.

UTILISATION OF EXCESS OF ASSETS

13.—(1) Except at the direction of the court
   (*a*) no distribution may be made out of and no transfer to another insurance company may be made of any part of the excess of the long term business assets which has been transferred to the other business, and
   (*b*) no distribution may be made out of and no transfer to another insurance company may be made of any part of the excess of the other business assets which has been transferred to the long term business.

(2) Before giving a direction under paragraph (1) the court may require the Liquidator to advertise the proposal to make a distribution or a transfer in such manner as the court shall direct.   **[1896]**

NOTES
Commencement: 1 March 1985.

SPECIAL BANK ACCOUNT

14.—(1) In the case of a company carrying on long term business, in whose case no stop order has been made, [Regulation 6 of the general regulations] applies only in relation to the company's other business.

(2) The Liquidator of such a company may open any [local bank account] which he is authorised to open by the Secretary of State and he may pay into such an account any moneys which form part of the assets representing the fund or funds maintained by the company in respect of its long term business.

(3) All payments out of any such special bank account shall be made by cheque payable to order and every cheque shall have marked or written on the face of it the name of the company and shall be signed by the Liquidator or by any special manager appointed under section 56(3) of the Act of 1982 . . . .

[1897]

NOTES
    Commencement: 1 March 1985.
    Amended by the Insurance Companies (Winding-up) (Amendment) Rules 1986, SI 1986 No 2002, r 8.
    General regulations: Insolvency Regulations 1986, SI 1986 No 1994.
    Act of 1982: Insurance Companies Act 192.

CUSTODY OF ASSETS

15.—(1) The Secretary of State may, in the case of a company carrying on long term business in whose case no stop order has been made, require that the whole or a specified proportion of the assets representing the fund or funds maintained by the company in respect of its long term business shall be held by a person approved by him for the purpose as trustee for the company.

(2) No assets held by a person as trustee for a company in compliance with a requirement imposed under this Rule shall, so long as the requirement is in force, be released except with the consent of the Secretary of State but they may be transposed by the trustee into other assets by any transaction or series of transactions on the written instructions of the Liquidator.

(3) The Liquidator may not grant any mortgage or charge of assets which are held by a person as trustee for the company in compliance with a requirement imposed under this Rule except with the consent of the Secretary of State.

[1898]

NOTES
    Commencement: 1 March 1985.

MAINTENANCE OF ACCOUNTING, VALUATION AND OTHER RECORDS

16.—(1) In the case of a company carrying on long term business, in whose case no stop order has been made, [Regulation 9 of the general regulations] applies only in relation to the company's other business.

(2) The Liquidator of such a company shall, with a view to the long term business of the company being transferred to another insurance company, maintain such minute books and accounting, valuation and other records as will enable such other insurance company upon the transfer being effected to comply with the requirements of the provisions of the Act of 1982 relating to accounts and statements of insurance companies.   **[1899]**

NOTES
Commencement: 1 March 1985.
Para 1: amended by the Insurance Companies (Winding-up) (Amendment) Rules 1986, SI 1986
No 2002, r 9.
General regulations: Insolvency Regulations 1986, SI 1986 No 1994.
Act of 1982: Insurance Companies Act 1982.

ADDITIONAL POWERS IN RELATION TO THE LONG TERM BUSINESS

17.—(1) In the case of a company carrying on long term business, in whose case a stop order has been made, [Regulation 18 of the general regulations] applies only in relation to the company's other business.

(2) The Liquidator of a company carrying on long term business shall, so long as no stop order has been made, have power to do all such things as may be necessary to the performance of his duties under section 56(2) of the Act of 1982 but the Secretary of State may require him—

- (*a*) not to make investments of a specified class or description,
- (*b*) to realise, before the expiration of a specified period (or such longer period as the Secretary of State may allow), the whole or a specified proportion of investments of a specified class or description held by the Liquidator when the requirement is imposed. **[1900]**

NOTES
Commencement: 1 March 1985.
Para (1): amended by the Insurance Companies (Winding-up) (Amendment) Rules 1986, SI 1986 No 2002, r 10.
General regulations: Insolvency Regulations 1986, SI 1986 No 1994.
Act of 1982: Insurance Companies Act 1982.

ACCOUNTS AND AUDIT

18.—(1) In the case of a company carrying on long term business, in whose case no stop order has been made, [Regulations 9(2), 10, 12 and 13 of the general regulations] apply only in relation to the company's other business.

(2) The Liquidator of such a company shall supply the Secretary of State, at such times or intervals as he shall specify, with such accounts as he may specify and audited in such manner as he may require and with such information about specified matters and verified in such specified manner as he may require.

(3) The Liquidator of such a company shall, if required to do so by the Secretary of State, instruct an actuary to investigate the financial condition of the company's long term business and to report thereon in such manner as the Secretary of State may specify.

(4) The Liquidator of such a company shall, at the expiration of six months from the date of the winding-up order and at the expiration of every six months thereafter, prepare a summary of his receipts and payments in the course of carrying on the long term business of the company during that period, procure that the summary be examined and verified by a person qualified under [section 389 of the Act of 1985] to audit the accounts of companies and transmit to the Secretary of State two copies of the summary verified as aforesaid.

(5) The Secretary of State shall file one of these copies with the Registrar and that copy shall be open to the inspection of any person on payment of the same fee as is payable with respect to the inspection of the file of proceedings under [any order made under section 130 of the Supreme Court Act 1981 or under section 128 of the County Courts Act 1984]. **[1901]**

NOTES
    Commencement: 1 March 1985.
    Paras (1), (4), (5): amended by the Insurance Companies (Winding-up) (Amendment) Rules
1986, SI 1986 No 2002, r 11.
    General regulations: Insolvency Regulations 1986, SI 1986 No 1994.
    Act of 1985: Companies Act 1985.

SECURITY BY LIQUIDATOR AND SPECIAL MANAGER

20. In the case of a company carrying on long term business, in whose case no stop order has been made, [Rule 4.207] of the principal Rules applies separately to the company's long term business and to its other business.   **[1902]**

NOTES
    Commencement: 1 March 1985.
    Amended by the Insurance Companies (Winding-up) (Amendment) Rules 1986, SI 1986 No
2002, r 13.
    Principal Rules: Insolvency Rules 1986, SI 1986 No 1925.

PROOF OF DEBTS

21.—(1) This Rule applies in the case of a company carrying on long term business.

(2) The Liquidator may in relation to the company's long term business and to its other business fix different days on or before which the creditors of the company who are required to prove their debts or claims are to prove their debts or claims and he may fix one of those days without at the same time fixing the other.

(3) In submitting a proof of any debt a creditor may claim the whole or any part of such debt as attributable to the company's long term business or to its other business or he may make no such attribution.

(4) When he admits any debt in whole or in part the Liquidator shall state in writing how much of what he admits is attributable to the company's long term business and how much to the company's other business.   **[1903]**

NOTES
    Commencement: 1 March 1985.

FAILURE TO PAY PREMIUMS

22.—(1) The Liquidator may in the course of carrying on the company's long term business and on such terms as he thinks fit accept payment of a premium even though the payment is tendered after the date on which under the terms of the policy it was finally due to be paid.

(2) The Liquidator may in the course of carrying on the company's long term business, and having regard to the general practice of insurers, compensate a policy holder whose policy has lapsed in consequence of a failure to pay any premium by issuing a free paid-up policy for reduced benefits or otherwise as the Liquidator thinks fit.   **[1904]**

NOTES
    Commencement: 1 March 1985.

NOTICE OF VALUATION OF POLICY

23.—(1) The Liquidator shall give notice of the value of each general business policy, as determined by him in accordance with Rule 6, to the persons appearing from the records of the company or otherwise to be entitled to an interest in that policy and he shall do so in such manner as the court may direct.

(2) In the case of a company carrying on long term business, if the Liquidator, before a stop order is made in relation to the company, summons a separate general meeting of creditors in respect of liabilities of the company attributable to its long term business in pursuance of [section 168 of the Act of 1986] as that section has effect by virtue of section 55(5) of the Act of 1982, he shall give notice in Form No. 1 set out in Schedule 6 to the persons appearing from the records of the company or otherwise to be entitled to a payment under or to an interest in a long term policy of the amount of that payment or the value of that policy as determined by him in accordance with Rules 7(2) or (3) as the case may be and he shall give that notice with the notice summoning the meeting.

(3) If a stop order is made in relation to the company the Liquidator shall give notice to all the persons appearing from the records of the company or otherwise to be entitled to a payment under or to an interest in a long term policy of the amount of that payment or the value of that policy as determined by him in accordance with Rules 8(2) or (3) as the case may be and he shall give that notice in such manner as the court may direct.

(4) Any person to whom notice is so given shall be bound by the value so determined unless and until the court otherwise orders.

(5) Paragraphs (2) and (3) of this Rule have effect as though references therein to persons appearing to be entitled to an interest in a long term policy and to the value of that policy included respectively references to persons appearing to be entitled to apply for a free paid-up policy under section 24 of the Act of 1923 and to the value of that entitlement under Rule 7 (in the case of paragraph (2) of this Rule) or under Rule 8 (in the case of paragraph (3) of this Rule). **[1905]**

NOTES
 Commencement: 1 March 1985.
 Para (2): amended by the Insurance Companies (Winding-up) (Amendment) Rules 1986, SI 1986 No 2002, r 14.
 Act of 1923: Industrial Assurance Act 1923.
 Act of 1982: Insurance Companies Act 1982.
 Act of 1986: Insolvency Act 1986.

DIVIDENDS TO CREDITORS

24.—(1) This Rule applies in the case of a company carrying on long term business.

(2) [Part II] of the principal Rules applies separately in relation to the two separate companies assumed for the purposes of Rule 5.

(3) The court may, at any time before the making of a stop order, permit a dividend to be declared and paid on such terms as it thinks fit in respect only of debts which fell due for payment before the date of the winding-up order or, in the case of claims under long term policies, which have fallen due for payment on or after the date of the winding-up order. **[1906]**

NOTES
Commencement: 1 March 1985.
Para (2): amended by the Insurance Companies (Winding-up) (Amendment) Rules 1986, SI
1986 No 2002, r 15.
Principal Rules: Insolvency Rules 1986, SI 1986 No 1925.

MEETINGS OF CREDITORS

25.—(1) In the case of a company carrying on long term business, [Chapter 8 of Part 4 and Part 8 of the principal Rules (so far as relating to winding up by the court)] apply to each separate general meeting of the creditors summoned under [section 168 of the Act of 1986] as that section has effect by virtue of section 55(5) of the Act of 1982.

(2) In relation to any such separate meeting—

(a) Rule 132(2) of the principal Rules has effect as if the reference therein to assets of the company were a reference to the assets available under section 55 of the Act of 1982 for meeting the liabilities of the company owed to the creditors summoned to the meeting, and

(b) Rule 134 of the principal Rules applies as if the reference therein to value in relation to a creditor who is not, by virtue of Rule 6, 7 or 8 required to prove his debt, were a reference to the value most recently notified to him under Rule 23 or, if the court has determined a different value in accordance with Rule 23(4), as if it were a reference to that different value.   **[1907]**

NOTES
Commencement: 1 March 1985.
Para (1): amended by the Insurance Companies (Winding-up) (Amendment) Rules 1986, SI
1986 No 2002, r 16.
Principal Rules: Insolvency Rules 1986, SI 1986 No 1925.
Act of 1986: Insolvency Act 1986.
Act of 1982: Insurance Companies Act 1982.

REMUNERATION OF LIQUIDATOR CARRYING ON LONG TERM BUSINESS

26.—[(1) So long as no stop order has been made in relation to a company carrying on long term business, the Liquidator is entitled to receive remuneration for his services as such in relation to the carrying on of that business as provided for in this Rule.

(2) The remuneration shall be fixed by the liquidation committee by reference to the time properly given by the Liquidator and his staff in attending to matters arising in the winding up.

(3) If there is no liquidation committee, or the committee does not make the requisite determination, the Liquidator's remuneration may be fixed (in accordance with paragraph (2)) by a resolution of a meeting of creditors.

(4) If not fixed as above, the Liquidator's remuneration shall be in accordance with the scale laid down for the Official Receiver by the general regulations.

(5) If the Liquidator's remuneration has been fixed by the liquidation committee, and the Liquidator considers the amount to be insufficient, he may request that it be increased by resolution of the creditors.]   **[1908]**

NOTES
Commencement: 29 December 1986.
Substituted by the Insurance Companies (Winding-up) (Amendment) Rules 1986, SI 1986 No 2002, r 17.

APPOINTMENT OF COSTS PAYABLE OUT OF THE ASSETS

27.—(1) [Rule 4.218] of the principal Rules applies separately to the assets of the company's long term business and to the assets of the company's other business.

(2) But where any fee, expense, cost, charge, disbursement or remuneration does not relate exclusively to the assets of the company's long term business or to the assets of the company's other business the Liquidator shall apportion it amongst those assets in such manner as he shall determine.   **[1909]**

NOTES
Commencement: 1 March 1985.
Para (1): amended by the Insurance Companies (Winding-up) (Amendment) Rules 1986, SI 1986 No 2002, r 18.
Principal Rules: Insolvency Rules 1986, SI 1986 No 1925.

NOTICE OF STOP ORDER

28.—(1) When a stop order has been made in relation to the company the Registrar shall, on the same day, send to the Official Receiver a notice informing him that the stop order has been pronounced.

(2) The notice shall be in Form No 2 set out in Schedule 6 with such variation as circumstances may require.

(3) Three copies of the stop order sealed with the seal of the court shall forthwith be sent by post or otherwise by the Registrar to the Official Receiver.

(4) The Official Receiver shall cause a sealed copy of the order to be served upon the Liquidator by prepaid letter or upon such other person or persons, or in such other manner as the court may direct, and shall forward a copy of the order to the registrar of companies.

[(5) The Liquidator shall forthwith on receipt of a sealed copy of the order—

    (*a*) cause notice of the order in Form No 3 set out in Schedule 6 to be gazetted, and

    (*b*) advertise the making of the order in the newspaper in which the winding-up order was advertised by notice in Form No 4 set out in Schedule 6.]   **[1910]**

NOTES
Commencement: 29 December 1986 (para (5)); 1 March 1985 (remainder).
Para (5): substituted for existing paras (5), (6) by the Insurance Companies (Winding-up) (Amendment) Rules 1986, SI 1986 No 2002, r 19.

SCHEDULES

SCHEDULE 1

GENERAL BUSINESS POLICIES

1.—(1) This paragraph applies in relation to periodic payments under a general business policy which fall due for payment after the date of the winding-up order where the event giving rise to the liability to make the payments occurred before the date of the winding-up order.

(2) The value to be attributed to such periodic payments shall be determined on such actuarial principles and assumptions in regard to all relevant factors as the court shall direct.

2.—(1) This paragraph applies in relation to liabilities under a general business policy not dealt with by paragraph 1.

(2) The value to be attributed to those liabilities shall:—

(a) if the terms of the policy provide for a repayment of premium upon the early termination of the policy or the policy is expressed to run from one definite date to another or the policy may be terminated by any of the parties with effect from a definite date, be the greater of the following two amounts:—

   (i) the amount (if any) which under the terms of policy would have been repayable on early termination of the policy had the policy terminated on the date of the winding-up order, and
   (ii) where the policy is expressed to run from one definite date to another or may be terminated by any of the parties with effect from a definite date, such proportion of the last premium paid as is proportionate to the unexpired portion of the period in respect of which that premium was paid; and

(b) in any other case, be a just estimate of that value.   **[1911]**

NOTES
   Commencement: 1 March 1985.

SCHEDULE 2

RULES FOR VALUING NON-LINKED LIFE POLICIES, NON-LINKED DEFERRED ANNUITY POLICIES, NON-LINKED ANNUITIES IN PAYMENT AND CAPITAL REDEMPTION POLICIES

General

1.—(1) In valuing a policy:—

(a) where it is necessary to calculate the present value of future payments by or to the company interest shall be assumed at such rate or rates as the court may direct;

(b) where relevant the rates of mortality and the rates of disability to be employed shall be such rates as the court may consider appropriate after taking into account:—

   (i) relevant published tables of rates of mortality and rates of disability, and
   (ii) the rates of mortality and the rates of disability experienced in connection with similar policies issued by the company;

(c) there shall be determined:—

   (i) the present value of the ordinary benefits,
   (ii) a reserve for options,
   (iii) a reserve for expenses, and
   (iv) if further fixed premiums fall due to be paid under the policy on or after the date of the winding-up order, the present value of the modified net premiums;

and for the purpose of this Schedule a premium is a fixed premium if the amount of it is determined by the terms of the policy and it cannot be varied.

(2) Where under the terms of the policy or on the basis of the company's established practice the policy holder has a right to receive or an expectation of receiving benefits additional to the minimum benefits guaranteed under those terms the court shall determine rates of interest, mortality and disability under paragraph (1) which will result in the inclusion in the present value of the ordinary benefits and in the present value of the modified net premiums of such margin (if any) as the court may consider appropriate to provide for that right or expectation in respect of the period after the date of the winding-up order.

Present value of the ordinary benefits

2.—(1) Ordinary benefits are the benefits which will become payable to the policy holder on or after the date of the winding-up order without his having to exercise any option under the policy (including any bonus or addition to the sum assured or the amount of annuity declared before the date of the winding-up order) and for this purpose "option" includes a right to surrender the policy.

(2) The present value of the ordinary benefits shall be the value at the date of the winding-up order of the reversion in the ordinary benefits according to the contingency upon which those benefits are payable calculated on the basis of the rates of interest mortality and disability referred to in paragraph 1.

Reserve for options

3. The amount of the reserve for options shall be the amount which, in the opinion of the Liquidator, arrived at on appropriate assumptions in regard to all relevant factors, is necessary to be provided at the date of the winding-up order (in addition to the amount of the present value of the ordinary benefits) to cover the additional liabilities likely to arise upon the exercise on or after that date by the policy holder of any option conferred upon him by the terms of the policy or, in the case of an industrial insurance policy, by the Industrial Assurance Acts other than an option whereby the policy holder can secure a guaranteed cash payment within the period of 12 months beginning with that date.

Reserve for expenses

4.—(1) The amount of the reserve for expenses is the amount which, in the opinion of the Liquidator, is necessary to be provided at the date of the winding-up order for meeting future expenses.

(2) In this paragraph "future expenses" means such part of the expenses likely to be incurred after that date in the fulfilling by the Liquidator or by any transferee from the Liquidator of the company's long term business of the obligations of that business as is appropriate to the policy and which cannot be met out of the amounts (if any) by which the actual premiums payable under that policy after that date exceed the amounts of the modified net premiums which correspond to those actual premiums.

Net premiums

5.—(1) For the purpose of determining the present value of the modified net premiums a net premium shall be determined in relation to each actual premium paid or payable under the policy in such a way that:—

    (a) the net premiums, if they had been payable when the corresponding actual premiums were or are payable, would, on the basis of the rates of interest, mortality and disability referred to in paragraph 1, have been sufficient when the policy was issued to provide for the benefits under the policy according to the contingencies on which they are payable, exclusive of any addition for profits, expenses or other charges, and

    (b) the ratio between the amounts of any two net premiums is the same as the ratio between the amounts of the two actual premiums to which they correspond (any actual premium which includes a loading for unusual risks assumed by the company in respect of part only of the term of the policy being treated for this purpose as if it did not include that loading).

(2) For the purposes of this paragraph, where at any time after the policy was issued the terms of the policy have been varied (otherwise than by the surrender of the policy in consideration of the issue of a new policy), it shall be assumed that the policy when it was issued provided for those variations to take effect at the time when they did in fact take effect.

Modified net premiums

6.—(1) A modified net premium shall be determined in relation to each net premium by making an addition to each net premium such that:—

    (a) the additions, if each was payable when the corresponding actual premium was or is payable, would, on the basis of the rates of interest, mortality and disability referred to in paragraph 1, have been sufficient to compensate for the acquisition expenses relating to the policy, and

(b) the ratio between the amounts of any two modified net premiums is the same as the ratio between the amounts of the two net premiums to which they correspond.

(2) For this purpose the acquisition expenses relating to the policy shall be taken to be 3.5 per cent (or the defined percentage if it be lower than 3.5 per cent) of the relevant capital sum under the contract and for this purpose:—

(a) "the defined percentage" is the percentage arrived at by taking (for all policies which in the opinion of the Liquidator have the same or similar characteristics to the policy in question, and which he considers appropriate to be taken notice of for this purpose), the average of the percentages of the relevant capital sums under those policies that represent the acquisition expenses for which, after allowing for the effects of taxation, allowance is made in the premiums actually payable; and

(b) "the relevant capital sum" in relation to any policy is:—

   (i) for whole life assurances, the sum assured,
   (ii) for policies where a sum is payable on maturity (including policies where a sum is also payable on earlier death), the sum payable on maturity,
   (iii) for temporary assurances, the sum assured on the date of the winding-up order,
   (iv) for deferred annity policies, the capitalised value on the date on which the first payment is due to be made of the payments due to be made under the policy calculated on the basis of the rates of interest, mortality and disability referred to in paragraph 1 or, if the terms of the policy include a right on the part of the policy holder to surrender the policy on that date for a cash payment greater than the said capitalised value, the amount of that cash payment, and
   (v) for capital redemption policies, the sum payable at the end of the contract period.

(3) Where the amount of a modified net premium calculated in accordance with sub-paragraphs (1) and (2) is greater than the amount of the actual premium to which it corresponds then the amount of that modified net premium shall be the amount of that actual premium and not the amount calculated in accordance with sub-paragraphs (1) and (2).

Present value of the modified net premiums

7. The present value of the modified net premiums shall be the value as at the date of the winding-up order, calculated on the basis of the rates of interest, mortality and disability referred to in paragraph 1, of the modified net premiums payable after that date on the assumption that they are payable as and when the corresponding actual premiums are payable.

Value of the policy

8.—(1) Subject to sub-paragraph (2):—

(a) if no further fixed premiums fall due to be paid under the policy on or after the date of the winding-up order, the value of the policy shall be the aggregate of:—

   (i) the present value of the ordinary benefits,
   (ii) the reserve for options,
   (iii) the reserve for expenses, and
   (iv) where under the terms of the policy or on the basis of the company's established practice the policy holder has a right to receive or an expectation of receiving benefits additional to the ordinary benefits, such amount (if any) as the court may determine to reflect that right or expectation in respect of the period ending with the date of the winding-up order;

(b) if further fixed premiums fall due to be so paid and the aggregate value referred to in sub-paragraph (a) exceeds the present value of the modified net premiums, the value of the policy shall be the amount of that excess; and

(c) if further fixed premiums fall due to be so paid and that aggregate does not exceed the present value of the modified net premiums, the policy shall have not value.

(2) Where the policy holder has a right conferred upon him by the terms of the policy or by the Industrial Assurance Acts whereby the policy holder can secure a guaranteed cash payment within the period of 12 months beginning with the date of the winding-up order, the Liquidator shall determine the amount which in his opinion it is necessary to provide at that date to cover the liabilities which will accrue when that option is exercised (on the assumption that it will be exercised) and the value of the policy shall be that amount if it exceeds the value of the policy (if any) determined in accordance with sub-paragraph (1).   **[1912]**

NOTES
Commencement: 1 March 1985.

SCHEDULE 3
RULES FOR VALUING LIFE POLICIES AND DEFERRED ANNUITY POLICIES WHICH ARE LINKED POLICIES

1.—(1) Subject to sub-paragraph (2) the value of the policy shall be the aggregate of the value of the linked liabilities (calculated in accordance with paragraph 2 or 4) and the value of other than linked liabilities (calculated in accordance with paragraph 5) except where that aggregate is a negative amount in which case the policy shall have no value.

(2) Where the terms of the policy include a right whereby the policy holder can secure a guaranteed cash payment within the period of 12 months beginning with the date of the winding-up order then, if the amount which in the opinion of the Liquidator is necessary to be provided at that date to cover any liabilities which will accrue when that option is exercised (on the assumption that it will be exercised) is greater than the value determined under sub-paragraph (1) of this paragraph, the value of the policy shall be that greater amount.

2.—(1) Where the linked liabilities are expressed in terms of units the value of those liabilities shall, subject to paragraph 3, be the amount arrived at by taking the product of the number of units of each class of units allocated to the policy on the date of the winding-up order and the value of each such unit on that date and then adding those products.

(2) For the purposes of sub-paragraph (1):—

(i) where under the terms of the policy the value of a unit at any time falls to be determined by reference to the value at that time of the assets of a particular fund maintained by the company in relation to that and other policies, the value of a unit on the date of the winding-up order shall be determined by reference to the net realisable value of the assets credited to that fund on that date (after taking account of disposal costs, any tax liabilities resulting from the disposal of assets insofar as they have not already been provided for by the company and any other amounts which under the terms of those policies are chargeable to the fund), and

(ii) in any other case, the value of a unit on the date of the winding-up order shall be the value which would have been ascribed to each unit credited to the policy holder, after any deductions which may be made under the terms of the policy, for the purpose of determining the benefits payable under the policy on the date of the winding-up order had the policy matured on that date.

3.—(1) This paragraph applies where—

(a) paragraph 2(2)(i) applies and the company has a right under the terms of the policy either to make periodic withdrawals from the fund referred to in that paragraph or to retain any part of the income accruing in respect of the assets of that fund, or

(b) paragraph 2(2)(ii) applies and the company has a right under the terms of the policy to receive the whole or any part of any distributions made in respect of the units referred to in that paragraph or

(c) paragraph 2(2)(i) or paragraph 2(2)(ii) applies and the company has a right under the terms of the policy to make periodic cancellations of a proportion of the number of units credited to the policy.

(2) Where this paragraph applies the value of the linked liabilities calculated in accordance with paragraph 2(1) shall be reduced by an amount calculated in accordance with sub-paragraph (3) of this paragraph.

(3) The said amount is—

(a) where this paragraph applies by virtue of head (a) or (b) of sub-paragraph (1), the value as at the date of the winding up order, calculated on actuarial principles, of the future income of the company in respect of the units in question arising from the rights referred to in head (a) or (b) of sub-paragraph (1) as the case may be, or

(b) where this paragraph applies by virtue of head (c) of sub-paragraph (1), the value as at the date of the winding-up order, calculated on actuarial principles, of the liabilities of the company in respect of the units which fall to be cancelled in the future under the right referred to in head (c) of sub-paragraph (1).

(4) In calculating any amount in accordance with sub-paragraph (3) there shall be disregarded:—

(a) such part of the rights referred to in the relevant head of sub-paragraph (1) which in the opinion of the Liquidator constitutes appropriate provision for future expenses and mortality risks, and

(b) such part of those rights (if any) which the court considers to constitute appropriate provision for any right or expectation of the policyholder to receive benefits additional to the benefits guaranteed under the terms of the policy.

(5) In determining the said amount:—

(a) interest shall be assumed at such rate or rates as the court may direct, and

(b) where relevant the rates of mortality and the rates of disability to be employed shall be such rates as the court may consider appropriate after taking into account:—

(i) relevant published tables of rates of mortality and rates of disability, and

(ii) the rates of mortality and the rates of disability experienced in connection with similar policies issued by the company,

4. Where the linked liabilities are not expressed in terms of units the value of those liabilities shall be the value which would have been ascribed to those liabilities had the policy matured on the date of the winding-up order.

5.—(1) The value of any liabilities other than linked liabilities including reserves for future expenses, options and guarantees shall be determined on actuarial principles and appropriate assumptions in regard to all relevant factors including the assumption of such rate or rates of interest, mortality and disability as the court may direct.

(2) In valuing liabilities under this paragraph credit shall be taken for those parts of future premiums which do not fall to be applied in the location of further units to the policy and for any rights of the company which have been disregarded under paragraph 3(4)(a) in valuing the linked liabilities. **[1913]**

NOTES
Commencement: 1 March 1985.

SCHEDULE 4
RULES FOR VALUING LONG TERM POLICIES WHICH ARE NOT DEALT WITH IN SCHEDULES 2 AND 3

The value of a long term policy not covered by Schedule 2 or 3 shall be determined on such actuarial principles and assumptions in regard to all relevant factors as the court shall determine. **[1914]**

NOTES
Commencement: 1 March 1985.

SCHEDULE 5
RULES FOR VALUING LONG TERM POLICIES WHERE A STOP ORDER HAS BEEN MADE

1. Subject to paragraphs 2 and 3, in valuing a policy Schedules 2, 3 or 4 shall apply according to the class of that policy as if those Schedules were herein repeated but with a view to a fresh valuation of each policy on appropriate assumptions in regard to all relevant factors and subject to the following modifications:—

(a) references to the stop order shall be substituted for references to the winding-up order,

(b) in paragraph 3 of Schedule 2 for the words "whereby the policy holder can secure a guaranteed cash payment within the period of 12 months beginning with that date" there shall be substituted the words "to surrender the policy which can be exercised on that date",

(c) in paragraph 4(2) of Schedule 2 for the words "likely to be incurred" there shall be substituted the words "which were likely to have been incurred" and for the words "cannot be met" there shall be substituted the words "could not have been met".

(d) paragraph 8(2) of Schedule 2 shall be deleted, and

(e) paragraph 1(2) of Schedule 3 shall be deleted.

2.—(1) This paragraph applies where the policy holder has a right conferred upon him under the terms of the policy or by the Industrial Assurance Acts to surrender the policy and that right is exercisable on the date of the stop order.

(2) Where this paragraph applies and the amount required at the date of the stop order to provide for the benefits payable upon surrender of the policy on the assumption that the policy is surrendered on the date of the stop order is greater than the value of the policy determined in accordance with paragraph 1 the value of the policy shall, subject to paragraph 3, be the said amount so required.

(3) Where any part of the surrender value is payable after the date of the stop order sub-paragraph (2) shall apply but the value therein referred to shall be discounted at such rate of interest as the court may direct.

3.—(1) This paragraph applies in the case of a linked policy where:—

(a) the terms of the policy include a guarantee that the amount assured will on maturity of the policy be worth a minimum amount calculable in money terms, or

(b) the terms of the policy include a right on the part of the policy holder to surrender the policy and a guarantee that the payment on surrender will be worth a minimum amount calculable in money terms and that right is exercisable on or after the date of the stop order.

(2) Where this paragraph applies the value of the policy shall be the greater of the following two amounts:—

(a) the value the policy would have had at the date of the stop order had the policy been a non-linked policy, that is to say, had the linked liabilities provided by the policy not been so provided but the policy had otherwise been on the same terms, and

(b) the value the policy would have had at the date of the stop order had the policy not included any guarantees of payments on maturity or surrender worth a minimum amount calculable in money terms. **[1915]**

NOTES
Commencement: 1 March 1985.

SCHEDULE 6

NOTES
The forms themselves are not reproduced in this work, but their numbers and descriptions are listed below.

FORM NO	TITLE
1	Notice of meeting of long term business creditors
2	Notification to Official Receiver of Order pronounced under section 56(2) of the Insurance Companies Act 1982
3	Notice for London Gazette: Notice of Order pronounced under section 56(2) of the Insurance Companies Act 1982 for cessation of long term business
4	Notice for newspaper: Notice of Order pronounced under section 56(2) of the Insurance Companies Act 1982 for cessation of long term business **[1916]**

NOTES
Commencement: 1 March 1985.
Forms 1, 4: amended by the Insurance Companies (Winding-up) (Amendment) Rules 1986, SI 1986 No 2002, r 20.

INSURANCE COMPANIES (WINDING-UP) (AMENDMENT) RULES 1986
(SI 1986 No 2002)

NOTES
Made: 21 November 1986.
Authority: Insurance Companies Act 1982, s 59; Insolvency Act 1986, s 411.

ARRANGEMENT OF RULES

Rule		Para
1	Citation and commencement	[1917]
2	Interpretation	[1918]
3	Application	[1919]
4	Amendment of Rule 2 (Interpretation)	[1920]
5	Amendment of Rule 3 (Application)	[1921]
6	Amendment of Rule 4 (Appointment of Liquidator)	[1922]
7	Amendment of Rule 5 (Separation of long term and other business in winding up)	[1923]
8	Amendment of Rule 14 (Special bank account)	[1924]
9	Amendment of Rule 16 (Maintenance of accounting, valuation and other records)	[1925]
10	Amendment of Rule 17 (Additional powers in relation to the long term business)	[1926]
11	Amendment of Rule 18 (Accounts and audit)	[1927]
12	Deletion of Rule 19 (Special Manager)	[1928]
13	Amendment of Rule 20 (Security by liquidator and special manager)	[1929]
14	Amendment of Rule 23 (Notice of valuation of policy)	[1930]
15	Amendment of Rule 24 (Dividends to creditors)	[1931]
16	Amendment of Rule 25 (Meetings of creditors)	[1932]
17	Amendment of Rule 26 (Remuneration of liquidator carrying on long term business)	[1933]
18	Amendment of Rule 27 (Apportionment of costs payable out of the assets)	[1934]
19	Amendment of Rule 28 (Notice of stop order)	[1935]
20	Amendment of Schedule 6 (Forms)	[1936]

1. Citation and commencement

These Rules may be cited as the Insurance Companies (Winding-up)

(Amendment) Rules 1986 and shall come into force on 29th December 1986.

[1917]

NOTES
Commencement: 29 December 1986.

2. Interpretation

In these Rules, except where the context otherwise requires, references to numbered Rules, Schedules and Forms are references to the Rules, Schedules and Forms so numbered in the Insurance Companies (Winding-up) Rules 1985.

[1918]

NOTES
Commencement: 29 December 1986.
Insurance Companies (Winding-up) Rules 1985: SI 1985 No 95.

3. Application

(1) These Rules apply to proceedings for the winding up of an insurance company which the courts in England and Wales have jurisdiction to wind up which commence on or after the date on which these Rules come into force.

(2) The Insurance Companies (Winding-up) Rules 1985 shall have effect in relation to such proceedings with the amendments set out below in these Rules.

[1919]

NOTES
Commencement: 29 December 1986.

4. Amendment of Rule 2 (Interpretation)

. . .

[1920]

NOTES
Commencement: 29 December 1986.
This rule amends SI 1985 No 95, r 2.

5. Amendment of Rule 3 (Application)

. . .

[1921]

NOTES
Commencement: 29 December 1986.
This rule amends SI 1985 No 95, r 3.

6. Amendment of Rule 4 (Appointment of Liquidator)

. . .

[1922]

NOTES
Commencement: 29 December 1986.
This rule substitutes SI 1985 No 95, r 4.

7. Amendment of Rule 5 (Separation of long term and other business in winding up)

. . .

[1923]

NOTES
Commencement: 29 December 1986.

This rule amends SI 1985 No 95, r 5.

8. Amendment of Rule 14 (Special bank account)

. . .   **[1924]**

NOTES
    Commencement: 29 December 1986.
    This rule amends SI 1985 No 95, r 14.

9. Amendment of Rule 16 (Maintenance of accounting, valuation and other records)

. . .   **[1925]**

NOTES
    Commencement: 29 December 1986.
    This rule amends SI 1985 No 95, r 16.

10. Amendment of Rule 17 (Additional powers in relation to the long term business)

. . .   **[1926]**

NOTES
    Commencement: 29 December 1986.
    This rule amends SI 1985 No 95, r 17.

11. Amendment of Rule 18 (Accounts and audit)

. . .   **[1927]**

NOTES
    Commencement: 29 December 1986.
    This rule amends SI 1985 No 95, r 18.

12. Deletion of Rule 19 (Special Manager)

. . .   **[1928]**

NOTES
    Commencement: 29 December 1986.
    This rule revokes SI 1985 No 95, r 19.

13. Amendment of Rule 20 (Security by liquidator and special manager)

. . .   **[1929]**

NOTES
    Commencement: 29 December 1986.
    This rule amends SI 1985 No 95, r 20.

14. Amendment of Rule 23 (Notice of valuation of policy)

. . .   **[1930]**

NOTES
    Commencement: 29 December 1986.
    This rule amends SI 1985 No 95, r 23.

15. Amendment of Rule 24 (Dividends to creditors)

. . .   **[1931]**

NOTES
Commencement: 29 December 1986.
This rule amends SI 1985 No 95, r 24.

16. Amendment of Rule 25 (Meetings of creditors)

. . .   **[1932]**

NOTES
Commencement: 29 December 1986.
This rule amends SI 1985 No 95, r 25.

17. Amendment of Rule 26 (Remuneration of liquidator carrying on long term business)

. . .   **[1933]**

NOTES
Commencement: 29 December 1986.
This rule substitutes SI 1985 No 95, r 26.

18. Amendment of Rule 27 (Apportionment of costs payable out of the assets)

. . .   **[1934]**

NOTES
Commencement: 29 December 1986.
This rule amends SI 1985 No 95, r 27.

19. Amendment of Rule 28 (Notice of stop order)

. . .   **[1935]**

NOTES
Commencement: 29 December 1986.
This rule amends SI 1985 No 95, r 28.

20. Amendment of Schedule 6 (Forms)

. . .   **[1936]**

NOTES
Commencement: 29 December 1986.
This rule amends SI 1985 No 95, Sch 6, Forms 1, 4.

Section C

Practice Directions

SECTION C
PRACTICE DIRECTIONS

Companies Court: Petitions (No 2 of 1986) [1986] 1 WLR 1428

Company—Winding up—Petition—Companies Court Registrar hearing petitions in open court—Solicitors' right of audience

With effect from the commencement of the Hilary Sittings 1987, the list of winding up petitions, at present heard by the judge acting as Companies Court judge of the term on a Monday, will be heard by the Companies Court Registrar on a Wednesday. The registrar will sit in court on a Wednesday each week of the term when he will hear all unopposed petitions and related applications other than those for relief under section 522 of the Companies Act 1985 or for the restraint of advertisement of a petition. In accordance with *Practice Direction (Solicitors: Right of Audience)* [1986] 1 WLR 545 of 9 May 1986, solicitors, properly robed, will be permitted rights of audience before the registrar.

The Companies Court judge of the term will continue to sit on a Monday each week of the term when he will deal with (1) petitions to confirm reductions of capital and/or share premium account (2) petitions to sanction schemes of arrangement (3) motions and (4) opposed winding-up petitions which have been adjourned to him by the registrar.

By direction of the Vice-Chancellor.

22 October 1986 **[1937]**

Companies Court: Insolvency (No 3 of 1986) [1987] 1 WLR 53

Company—Companies Court—Insolvency—Applications for hearing in open court—Directions for certain applications to be heard by Chief Clerk—Insolvency Act 1986 (c 45), ss 5(3), 14(3), 18(3), 127—Insolvency Rules 1986 (SI 1986 No 1925)

1 As from 29 December 1986 the following applications shall be made direct to the judge and, unless otherwise ordered, shall be heard in open court: (i) applications to commit any person to prison for contempt; (ii) applications for urgent interlocutory relief (eg applications pursuant to section 127 of the Insolvency Act 1986 prior to any winding up order being made); (iii) applications to restrain the presentation or advertisement of a petition to wind up; (iv) petitions for administration orders or an interim order upon such a petition; (v) applications after an administration order had been made pursuant to section 14(3) of the Act (for directions) or section 18(3) of the Act (to vary or discharge the order); (vi) applications pursuant to section 5(3) of the Act (to stay a winding up or discharge an administration order or for directions) where a voluntary arrangement has been approved; (vii) appeals from a decision made by a county court or by a registrar of the High Court.

2 Subject to 4 below all other applications shall be made to the registrar in the first instance who may give any necessary directions and may, in the exercise of his discretion, either hear and determine it himself or refer it to the judge.

3 The following matters will also be heard in open court: (i) petitions to wind up (whether opposed or unopposed); (ii) public examinations; (iii) all matters and applications heard by the judge except those referred by the registrar to be heard in chambers or so directed by the judge to be heard.

4 In accordance with directions given by the Lord Chancellor the registrar has authorised certain applications to be dealt with by the Chief Clerk of the Companies Court pursuant to rule 13.2(2) of the Insolvency Rules 1986 (SI 1986 No 1925). The applications are (*a*) to extend or abridge time prescribed by the Rules in connection with winding up (rule 4.3); (*b*) for substituted service of winding up petitions (rule 4.8(6)); (*c*) to withdraw petitions (rule 4.15); (*d*) for the substitution of a petitioner (rule 4.19); (*e*) for directions on a petition presented by a contributory (rule 4.22(2)); (*f*) by the official receiver for limited disclosure of a statement of affairs (rule 4.35); (*g*) by the official receiver for relief from duties imposed upon him by the Rules (rule 4.47); (*h*) by the official receiver for leave to give notice of a meeting by advertisement only (rule 4.59); (*i*) by a liquidator for relief from the requirement to send out forms or proof of debt (rule 4.74(4)); (*j*) to expunge or reduce a proof of debt (rule 4.85); (*k*) to appoint a liquidator in either a compulsory or a voluntary winding up (rules 4.102 and 4.103); (*l*) for leave to a liquidator to resign (rule 4.111); (*m*) by a liquidator for leave to make a return of capital (rule 4.221); (*n*) to transfer proceedings from the High Court to the county courts (rule 7.11); (*o*) for leave to amend any originating application.

5 The practice directions dated 15 October 1979, *Practice Direction (Companies Court: Chief Clerk)* [1979] 1 WLR 1416; and 3 March 1982, *Practice Direction (Companies Court: Chief Clerk) (No 2)* [1982] 1 WLR 389 are hereby revoked.

By direction of the Vice-Chancellor.

10 December 1986 **[1938]**

Bankruptcy Court: Petition (No 3 of 1986) [1987] 1 WLR 81

Bankruptcy—Petition—Creditor's petition—New form of bankruptcy petition— Completion of form—Insolvency Rules 1986 (SI 1986 No 1925), r 6

To help practitioners to complete the new forms of a creditor's bankruptcy petition, attention is drawn to the following points:

1 The petition does not require dating, signing or witnessing.

2 In the title it is only necessary to recite the debtor's name eg Re John William Smith or Re J W Smith (male). Any alias or trading name will appear in the body of the petition. This also applies to all other statutory forms other than those which require the "full title".

3 Where the petition is based on a statutory demand, only the debt claimed in the demand may be included in the petition, except that interest or other charges which have accrued since the date of the demand to the date of the petition may be added: see the Insolvency Rules 1986, rule 6.8(1)(c) read with rule 6.1(4).

4 When completing paragraph 2 of the petition, attention is drawn to rule 6.8(1)(a) to (c), particularly where the "aggregate sum" is made up of a number of debts.

5 Date of service of the statutory demand (paragraph 4 of the petition):

(*a*) In the case of personal service, the date of service as set out in the affidavit of service should be recited and whether service is effected *before/after* 16.00 hours on Monday to Friday or *before/after* 12.00 hours on Saturday: see RSC Ord 65, r 7.

(*b*) In the case of substituted service (otherwise than by advertisement), the date alleged in the affidvit of service should be recited. (As to the date alleged see *Practice Note (Bankruptcy: Substituted Service)* [1987] 1 WLR 82.

(*c*) In the strictly limited case of substituted service by advertisement under rule 6.3 of the Insolvency Rules 1986, the date to be alleged is the date of the advertisement's appearance or, as the case may be, its first appearance: see rules 6.3(3) and 6.11(8) of the Insolvency Rules 1986.

6 There is no need to include in the preamble to or at the end of the petition details of the person authorised to present the petition.

7 Certificates at the end of the petition:

(*a*) The period of search for prior petitions has been reduced to *three* years.

(*b*) Where a statutory demand is based wholly or in part on a county court judgment, the following certificate, which replaces the affidavit of county court search, is to be added:

> "I/We certify that on the   day of   19   I/We attended on the   County Court and was/were informed by an officer of the Court that no money had been paid into Court in the action or matter   v
> Plaint No   pursuant to the Statutory demand."

This certificate will not be required when the demand also requires payment of a separate debt, not based on a county court judgment, the amount of which exceeds the bankruptcy level (at present £750).

8 Deposit on petition:

The deposit will now be taken by the court and forwarded to the official receiver. The petition fee and deposit should be handed to the Supreme Court Accounts Office, Fee Stamping Rooms, who will record the receipt and will impress two entries on the original petition, one in respect of the court fee and the other in respect of the deposit. Cheque(s) for the whole amount should be made payable to "HM Paymaster General".

18 December 1986 **[1939]**

Bankruptcy Court: Service (No 4 of 1986) [1987] 1 WLR 82

Bankruptcy—Practice—Service—Substituted service of statutory demand and petition—Insolvency Rules 1986 (SI 1986 No 1925), rr 6.3, 6.11, 6.14, 615

Statutory demands

1 The creditor is under an obligation to do all that is reasonable to bring the statutory demand to the debtor's attention and, if practicable, to cause personal service to be effected. Where it is not possible to effect prompt personal service, service may be effected by other means such as first class post or insertion through a letter box.

2 Advertisement can only be used as a means of substituted service where (*a*) the demand is based on a judgment or order of any court; (*b*) the debtor has absconded or is keeping out of the way with a view to avoiding service and (*c*) there is no real prospect of the sum due being recovered by execution or other process.

As there is no statutory form of advertisement, the court will accept an advertisement in the following form:

<u>STATUTORY DEMAND</u>

(Debt for liquidated sum payable immediately following a Judgment or Order of the Court) _____

To (block letters)
of

TAKE NOTICE that a Statutory Demand has been issued by
Name of creditor
Address

The creditor demands payment of £   the amount now due on a Judgment/Order of the (High Court of Justice   Division)
(County Court) dated the   day of   19

The Statutory Demand is an important document and it is deemed to have been served on you on the date of the first appearance of this advertisement. You <u>must</u> deal with this demand within 21 days of the service upon you or you could be made bankrupt and your property and goods taken away from you. If you are in any doubt as to your position, you should seek advice <u>immediately</u> from a solicitor or your nearest Citizen's Advice Bureau.

The Statutory Demand can be obtained or is available for inspection and collection from:

Name
Address

(Solicitor for) the creditor

Tel. No.   Reference

<u>You have only 21 days from the date of the first appearance of this advertisement before the creditor may present a bankruptcy petition</u>

3 In all cases where substituted service is effected, the creditor must have taken all those steps which would suffice to justify the court making an order for substituted service of a petition. The steps to be taken to obtain an order for substituted service are set out below. Practitioners are reminded that failure to comply with the requirements of this practice note may result in the court declining to file the petition: rule 6.11(5)(*a*) of the Insolvency Rules 1986.

Order for substituted service of a bankruptcy petition
4 In most cases, the following evidence will suffice to justify an order for substituted service:

    (*a*) One personal call at the residence and place of business of the debtor where both are known or at either of such places as is known. Where it is known that the debtor has more than one residential or business address, personal calls should be made at all addresses.

    (*b*) Should the creditor fail to effect service, a first class prepaid letter should be written to the debtor referring to the call(s) the purpose of the same and the failure to meet with the debtor, adding that a further call will be made for the same purpose on the   day of 19   at   hours at   (place). At least two business days notice should be given of the appointment and copies of the letter sent to all known addresses of the debtor. The appointment letter should also state that (i) in the event of the time and place not being convenient, the debtor is to name some other time and place reasonably convenient for the purpose. (ii) (Statutory demands) if the debtor fails to keep the appointment the creditor proposes to serve the debtor by [advertisement, see paragraph 2, ante p 82F–G] [post] [insertion through a letter box] or as the case may be, and that, in the event of a bankruptcy petition being presented, the court will be asked to treat such service as service of the demand on the debtor. (iii) (Petitions) if the debtor fails to keep the appointment, application will be made to the court for an order for substituted service either by advertisement, or in such other manner as the court may think fit.

(c) In attending any appointment made by letter, inquiry should be made as to whether the debtor has received all letters left for him. If the debtor is away, inquiry should also be made as to whether or not letters are being forwarded to an address within the jurisdiction (England and Wales) or elsewhere.

(d) If the debtor is represented by a solicitor, an attempt should be made to arrange an appointment for personal service through such solicitor. Practitioners are reminded that the rules provide for a solicitor accepting service of a statutory demand on behalf of his client but there is no similar provision in respect of service of a bankruptcy petition.

(e) The supporting affidavit should deal with all the above matters including all relevant facts as to the debtor's whereabouts and whether the appointment letter(s) have been returned.

5 Where the court makes an order for substituted service by first class ordinary post, the order will normally provide that service be deemed to be effected on the seventh day after posting. Practitioners serving a statutory demand by post may consider using the same method of calculating service.

18 December 1986　　　　　　　　　　　　　　　　　　　**[1940]**

Bankruptcy Court: Service (No 5 of 1986) [1987] 1 WLR 85

Bankruptcy—Practice—Service—Proof of service of statutory demand—Insolvency Rules 1986 (SI 1986 No 1925), r 6.11

1 Rule 6.11(3) of the Insolvency Rules 1986 provides that, if the statutory demand has been served personally, the affidavit of service must be made by the person who effected that service. Rule 6.11(4) provides that, if service of the demand (however effected) has been acknowledged in writing, the affidavit of service must be made by the creditor or by a person acting on his behalf. Rule 6.11(5) provides that, if neither paragraphs (3) or (4) apply, the affidavit must be made by a person having direct knowledge of the means adopted for serving the demand.

2 Form 6.11 (affidavit of personal service of the statutory demand).
This form should only be used where the demand has been served personally and acknowledged in writing: rule 6.11(4). If the demand has not been acknowledged in writing, the affidavit should be made by the process server and paragraphs 2 and 3 (part) of Form 6.11 should be omitted: rule 6.11(3).

3 Form 6.12 (affidavit of substituted service of the statutory demand).
This form can be used whether or not service of the demand has been acknowledged in writing. Paragraphs 4 and 5 (part) provide for the alternatives. Practitioners are reminded, however, that the appropriate person to make the affidavit may not be the same in both cases. If the demand has been acknowledged in writing, the appropriate person is the creditor or a person acting on his behalf. If the demand has not been acknowledged, that person must be someone having direct knowledge of the means adopted for serving the demand.

Practitioners may find it more convenient to allow process servers to carry out the necessary investigation whilst reserving to themselves the service of the demand. In these circumstances paragraph 1 should be deleted and the following paragraph substituted: "1 Attempts have been made to serve the demand, full details of which are set out in the accompanying affidavit of . . ."

31 December 1986 **[1941]**

Bankruptcy Court: Statutory demand (No 1 of 1987) [1987] 1 WLR 119

Bankruptcy—Practice—Statutory demand—Application to set aside statutory demand—Procedure—Extension of time—Insolvency Rules 1986 (SI 1986 No 1925), rr 6.4, 6.5, 7.4(1)

Application to set aside statutory demand

1 The application (Form 6.4) and affidavit in support (Form 6.5) exhibiting a copy of the statutory demand must be filed in court within 18 days of service of the statutory demand on the debtor. Where service is effected by advertisement in a newspaper the period of 18 days is calculated from the date of the first appearance of the advertisement: see *Practice Note (Bankruptcy: Substituted Service)* [1987] 1 WLR 82. Three copies of each document must be lodged with the application to enable the court to serve notice of the hearing date on the applicant, the creditor and the person named in Part B of the statutory demand.

2 Where, to avoid expense, copies of the documents are not lodged with the application, any order of the registrar fixing a venue is conditional upon copies of the documents being lodged on the next business day after the registrar's order otherwise the application will be deemed to have been dismissed.

3 Where the statutory demand is based on a judgment or order, the court will not at this stage go behind the judgment or order and inquire into the validity of the debt nor, as a general rule, will it adjourn the application to await the result of an application to set aside the judgment or order.

4 When the debtor (*a*) claims to have a counterclaim, set off or cross demand (whether or not he could have raised it in the action in which the judgment or order was obtained) which equals or exceeds the amount of the debt or debts specified in the statutory demand or (*b*) disputes the debt (not being a debt subject to a judgment or order) the court will normally set aside the statutory demand if, in its opinion, on the evidence there is a genuine triable issue.

5 *Applications for an extension of time to apply to set aside a statutory demand*
Each term two judges of the Chancery Division will sit to hear insolvency cases, one of whom ("the bankruptcy judge") will be primarily concerned to hear cases affecting individual debtors.

After the expiration of 18 days from the date of service of the statutory demand, the debtor must apply for an extension of time if he wishes to apply to set aside the demand. The application for extension of time and (if necessary) to restrain the presentation of a bankruptcy petition should be made to the bankruptcy judge, but in cases of urgency and where the bankruptcy judge is not available the application may be made to the judge hearing ordinary motions. (This requirement will appear in a practice direction to be published).

Paragraphs 1 and 2 of Form 6.5 (affidavit in support of application to set aside statutory demand) should be used in support of the application for extension of time with the following additional paragraphs:

"3. That to the best of my knowledge and belief the creditor(s) named in the demand has/have not presented a petition against me.

"4. That the reasons for my failure to apply to set aside the demand within 18 days after service are as follows: . . .

"5. Unless restrained by injunction the creditor(s) may present a bankruptcy petition against me."

(The fee on the application will be £15)

6 January 1987 **[1942]**

Bankruptcy Court: Proof of debt (No 1 of 1986) [1987] 1 WLR 120

Bankruptcy—Debt—Proof of debt—Certificate proving debt still unpaid—Filing and form of certificate—Bankruptcy Act 1914 (4 & 5 Geo 5, c 59), s 5(2)— Insolvency Act 1986 (c 45), s 271(1) (L 14) Bankruptcy Rules 1952 (SI 1952 No 2113), r 167—Insolvency Rules 1986 (SI 1986 No 1925), r 6.25(1)

On the hearing of a petition for a bankruptcy order, to satisfy the court that the debt on which the petition is founded has not been paid or secured or compounded for the court will normally accept as sufficient a certificate signed by the person representing the petitioning creditor in the following form:

"I certify that I have/my firm has made inquiries of the petitioning creditor(s) within the last business day prior to the hearing/adjourned hearing and to the best of my knowledge and belief the debt on which the petition is founded is still due and owing and has not been paid or secured or compounded for (save as to   )
      "Signed .... Dated ...."

For the convenience of practitioners this certificate will be printed on the attendance slips. It will be filed after the hearing. A fresh certificate will be required on each adjourned hearing.

This practice note will take effect on 29 December 1986, when the Insolvency Act 1986 and Insolvency Rules 1986 come into effect, in respect of all petitions heard on or after that date whether or not presented and filed earlier.

25 November 1986 **[1943]**

[Practice Directions reproduced with the permission of the Incorporated Council of Law Reporting for England Advocates]

INDEX

References are to paragraph numbers

A

ABSCONDING
offence, [358]

ACCOUNTANT
bankruptcy, in, Scotland, [501]

ACCOUNTS
deeds of arrangement, [1864]–[1875]
expenses of preparing, [760]
failure to keep, [361]
Insolvency Services. *See* Insolvency Services
receivership, delivery to registrar, [38]
special manager, [928]
submission of, [758], [759]
supervisor, of, [619], [975]

ADJUSTMENT ORDER
avoidance on bankruptcy of settlor, [1799]

ADMINISTRATION
company meetings—
conduct of, [654]
venue of, [654]
creditors' committee—
chairman, [658]
constitution, [655]
formalities of establishment, [656]
functions, [657]
information from administrator, [667]
meetings, [657]
members—
dealings with company, [669]
expenses, [668]
removal, [663]
representatives, [660]
resignation, [661]
procedure, [665]
quorum, [659]
resolutions by post, [666]
termination of membership, [662]
vacancies, [664]
creditors' meetings—
administrator's proposals, to consider, [641]
administrator's report, [652]
chairman, [643]
chattel leasing agreements, [650]
claims—
administration of, [646]
rejection of, [646]
conditional sale agreements, [650]
entitlement to vote, [645]
generally, [642]
hire-purchase agreements, [650]
minutes, [651]
negotiable instruments, holders of, [648]
notices to creditors, [653]
requisitioned by creditors, [644]
resolutions, [651]
retention of title creditors, [649]
secured creditors, [647]
forms, [1346]
liquidator, appointment by court following, [140]

ADMINISTRATION—*continued*
order. *See* Administration order
public. *See* Public admininstration
Scotland, [1551]–[1571]
statement of affairs—
expenses of, [638]
extension of time, [637]
filing, [635]
limited disclosure, [636]
notice requiring, [634]
proposals—
notice to creditors, [640]
to be annexed to, [639]
release from duty to submit, [637]
verification, [635]
VAT bad debt relief—
certificate of insolvency—
issue of, [679]
notice to creditors, [680]
preservation with company's records, [681]

ADMINISTRATION ORDER
advertisement of, [633]
application for—
company's affairs, independent report on, [625]
effect of, [10]
petition, by—
affidavit to support—
contents, [626]
generally, [624]
filing of, [628]
form, [627]
generally, [9]
hearing, [632]
service of—
generally, [629]
manner in which effected, [630]
proof of, [631]
court's power to make, [8]
creditors—
committee, establishment of, [26]
protection of interests of, [27]
discharge of, [18]
effect of, [11]
failure to pay under, [480]
investment business, [1831]–[1833]
members, protection of interests of, [27]
notice of, [633]
notification of, [12]
purposes of, [8]
revocation of, disabilities on, [429]
variation of, [18]
See also Administrator

ADMINISTRATIVE RECEIVER. *See* Receiver

ADMINISTRATOR
appointment of, [13]
court, recourse to, [672]
creditors' meeting, recourse to, [671]

ADMINISTRATOR—*continued*
death of, [13], [20], [667]
general duties, [17]
information to be given by, [21], [667]
meaning, [8]
order filling vacancy, [678]
payments, abstract of, [675]
powers—
  charged property, dealing with—
    disposal of, [674]
    generally, [15]
    Scotland, in, [16]
  general, [14]
  generally, [445]
proposals of—
  creditor's meeting, consideration by, [24]
  notice to members of, [640]
  statement of, [23]
  substantial revisions, approval of, [25]
receipts, abstract of, [675]
release of, [20]
remuneration-
  excessive, creditors' claim that, [673]
  fixing of, [670]
report, [652]
resignation, [676]
statement of affairs to be submitted to, [22]
vacation of office, [19]
voluntary arrangement, proposal for—
  meetings, summoning of, [604]
  notice to nominee, [605]
  preparation of, [603], [605]
See also Administration order

ADVERTISEMENT
administration order, of, [633]
administrative receiver, appointment of, [683]
creditors' meeting, notice of, [778]
liquidator—
  appointment of, [825]
  removal of, [837]
  resignation of, [831]
petition to winding up order, of, [730]
trustee in bankruptcy—
  appointment of, [1103]
  removal of, [1113]
  resignation of, [1113]
winding up order, of, [740]

AFFAIRS
persons incapable of managing, [1259]–[1262]
statement of. *See* Statement of affairs

AFFIDAVIT
court procedure, [1273]
deeds of arrangement, [1792]
petition for adminstration order, to support—
  contents, [626]
  generally, [624]
proof of debt, establishment of claim, [796]
winding up, with regard to, [200]

AGENCY
administrative receiver, [44]
receiver, Scotland, [57]

ALIENATION
gratuitous, [242], [534]

ANNULMENT OF BANKRUPTCY
ORDER. *See* Bankruptcy

APPEAL
court exercising insolvency jurisdiction, from, [375]
decision on proof, against, [802]
insolvency proceedings, [1263]–[1266]
order, from, Scotland, [162]

APPRENTICESHIP
prior transactions, adjustment of, [348]

ARBITRATION
Scotland, [565]

ARRANGEMENT
deeds of. *See* Deeds of arrangement
voluntary. *See* Voluntary arrangement

ARREST
absconding contributory, of, powers of court, [158]
court's power of, [364]

ASSETS
application of, powers of court, [148]
debts of insolvent company to rank equally, [900]
distribution—
  final, [905]
  manner of, [899]
dividend, supplementary provisions as to, [901]
employees, power to make over to, [187]
enforced delivery up of, [904]
liquidator—
  general duties, [898]
  general powers, [903]
  hand-over to, [826]
list of—
  debtor, of, [519]
  trustee's duties on receipt of, [520]
payment of debts out of, subject to floating charge, [40]

ASSIGNMENT
book debts, of, avoidance of, [344]

ASSOCIATE
meaning, [435], [574]

ATTACHMENT
avoidance of, [128]
effect of, [183]

AUDIT
Insolvency Services Account, [409]

AUTHORISATION
insolvency practitioner, of. *See* Insolvency

AVOIDANCE
debt, [423]–[425]

B

BAD DEBT RELIEF. *See* Value Added Tax

BANK
administration order, court's power to make, [8]
payment of money due to company into, [151]
recognised, [422]
winding up on petition from, [1807]

BANKRUPT
contract to which party, [345]
director, leave to act as, [1182]–[1184]

BANKRUPT—*continued*
dwelling house of, [1216]
estate of. *See* Bankrupt's estate
letters of, re-direction of, [371]
meaning, [381]
occupation, rights of, [337]
parliamentary disqualification, [427]
premises occupied by, payments in respect of, [338]
public examination of—
  bankrupt unfit for, [1153]
  creditors, order on request by, [1152]
  expenses, [1156]
  generally, [290]
  hearing—
    adjournment, [1155]
    procedure at, [1154]
  order for, [1151]
spouse of—
  debts to, [329]
  occupation, rights of, [336]
trustee in bankruptcy, duties in relation to, [333]
undischarged. *See* Undischarged bankrupt

BANKRUPT'S ESTATE
after-acquired property, [307], [309]
bankrupt—
  official receiver, duties in relation to, [291]
  public examination of, [290]
control—
  acquisition by trustee, [311]
  surrender to trustee, [312]
disclaimer—
  disclaimed property, court order vesting, [320], [321]
  dwelling house, [318]
  general power, [315]
  land subject to rentcharge, [319]
  leaseholds—
    generally, [317]
    vesting of, [321]
  trustee's decision, notice requiring, [316]
dispositions of property, restrictions on, [284]
distribution of—
  bankrupt's home, distribution of, [332]
  criminal bankruptcy, [327]
  debts—
    priority of, [328]
    proof of, [322]
    spouse, to, [329]
  dividend, distribution by means of, [324]
  final, [330]
  final meeting, [331]
  mutual credit, [323]
  property in specie, [326]
  set-off, [323]
  stay of, in case of second bankruptcy, [334]
  unsatisfied creditors, claims by, [325]
earlier and later estates, adjustment between, [335]
home—
  charge on, [313]
  saving for, [332]
income payments orders, [310]
interim receiver, power to appoint, [286]
meaning, [283]
official receiver—
  duties of bankrupt in relation to, [291]

BANKRUPT'S ESTATE—*continued*
official receiver—*continued*
  investigatory duties of, [289]
  proceedings, restriction on, [285]
  remedies, [285]
  statement of affairs, [288]
  summary administration, [275]
  trustee, powers of, [314]
  receivership pending appointment of, [287]
vesting in trustee—
  excess value, certain items of, [308], [309]
  generally, [306]

BANKRUPTCY
after-acquired property—
  bankrupt, duties of, [1179]
  disponee of property, trustee's recourse to, [1180]
  expenses, [1181]
  generally, [307]
apprenticeship, [348]
commencement, [278]
continuance, [278]
contributory, of, effect of, [82]
costs, order of payment out of estate, [1203]
court, powers of—
  arrest, [364]
  bankrupt's letters, re-direction of, [371]
  dealings, inquiry into, [366], [367]
  enforcement powers, [367]
  general control, [363]
  Inland Revenue, production of documents by, [369]
  interim receiver, appointment of, [368]
  property—
    inquiry into, [366], [367]
    seizure of, [365]
  special manager, power to appoint, [370]
creditors' committee—
  chairman, [1133]
  formalities of establishment, [1130]
  meetings, [1132]
  members—
    dealings by, [1144]
    expenses, [1143]
    removal, [1138]
    representatives, [1135]
    resignation, [1136]
  membership of—
    generally, [1129]
    termination of, [1137]
  quorum, [1134]
  resolutions—
    generally, [1140]
    post, by, [1141]
  Secretary of State, functions vested in, [1145]
  trustee—
    obligations of, [1131]
    reports, [1142]
  vacancies, [1139]
  voting rights, [1140]
creditors' meeting—
  adjournment, [1070]
  attendance at, [1063]
  business, [1059]
  chairman, [1061]
  entitlement to vote, [1072]

BANKRUPTCY—*continued*
  creditors' meeting—*continued*
    expenses of summoning, [1066]
    first, [1058]
    general power to call, [1060]
    notice by advertisement only, [1064]
    proof—
      admission of, [1073]
      rejection of, [1073]
    proxy-holder, chairman as, [1068]
    quorum, [1071]
    record of proceedings, [1074]
    requisitioned, [1062]
    resolutions, [1067]
    suspension of, [1069]
    venue, [1065]
  criminal—
    annulment of order, [1213]
    convicted person, order against, [1800]
    creditors' committee, [1213]
    distribution in, [327]
    interim receivership, [1210]
    meetings, [1212]
    notice of order, [1211]
    Official Petitioner—
      functions of, [1209]
      status of, [1209]
    petition, presentation of, [1208]
    proof of debts, [1211]
    trustee in bankruptcy, [1213]
  debt, meaning, [382]
  discharge—
    appeal, deferment of issue of order pending, [1200]
    application–
      bankrupt, by, [1196]
      order on, [1198]
    bankrupt's debts surviving, [1202]
    certificate of, [1199]
    costs, [1201]
    effect of, [281]
    official receiver, report of, [1197]
    order of court, by, [280]
    suspension of—
      application for, [1194]
      lifting of, [1195]
  disclaimer—
    additional notices, [1159]
    application—
      interested party, by, [1162]
      leave to disclaim, for, [1161]
    communication to persons interested, [1158]
    court's powers, application for exercise of, [1165]
    duty to keep court informed, [1160]
    interest in property, declaration on request, [1163]
    presumed valid and effective, [1164]
    trustee's notice of, [1157]
  distress, [347]
  duration, [279]
  enforcement procedures, [346]
  exempt property, replacement of—
    money provided in lieu of sale, [1167]
    purchase, [1166]
  forms, [1346]
  income payments order—
    action to follow making of, [1169]

BANKRUPTCY—*continued*
  income payments order—*continued*
    administration, [1171]
    application for, [1168]
    generally, [310]
    payor of income, order to, [1171]
    review of, [1172]
    variation of, [1170]
  information to creditors—
    bankruptcy order annulled, [1057]
    official receiver, general duty of, [1052]
    reporting, general rule as to, [1056]
    statement of affairs—
      dispensed with, [1055]
      report where lodged, [1054]
    those entitled to be informed, [1053]
  Inland Revenue official, order to—
    application for, [1173]
    documents, custody of, [1175]
    making of, [1174]
    service of, [1174]
  interpretation, [380]–[385]
  monetary limits, [418], [1450], [1453]
  mortgaged property—
    court's power to order sale, [1177]
    mortgagee of land, claim by, [1176]
    proceeds of sale, [1178]
  offences. *See* Offences
  order—
    annulment of—
      application for, [1185]
      court's powers, [282], [1187]
      criminal bankruptcy, [1213]
      hearing, [1189]
      matters to be proved, [1190]
      notice to creditors—
        generally, [1191]
        who have not proved, [1188]
      other matters arising, [1192]
      trustee—
        final accounts, [1193]
        report by, [1186]
    criminal, petition based on, [277]
    meaning, [381]
  petition. *See* Petition
  proof of debts—
    certificate, [1943]
    procedure for proving—
      affidavit, claim established by, [1078]
      costs, [1079]
      proof—
        appeal against decision on, [1084]
        contents of, [1077]
        dividend, admission and rejection for, [1083]
        expunging by court, [1086]
        licensed moneylender, of, [1081]
        transmission to trustee, [1082]
        trustee to allow inspection of, [1080]
        variation of, [1085]
        withdrawal of, [1085]
      prove, meaning, [1075]
      supply of forms, [1076]
    quantification of claim—
      debt payable at future time, [1093]
      discounts, [1089]
      foreign currency, debt in, [1090]
      interest, [1092]
      negotiable instruments, [1087]

BANKRUPTCY—*continued*
proof of debts—*continued*
quantification of claim—*continued*
payments of periodical nature, [1091]
secured creditors, [1088]
Scotland, in. *See* Scotland
second—
existing trustee—
expenses, [1207]
general duty of, [1205]
later trustee, delivery up to, [1206]
scope of Chapter, [1204]
stay of distribution in case of, [334]
secured creditors—
non-disclosure, surrender for, [1095]
redemption by trustee, [1096]
security—
realisation by creditor, [1098]
test of value, [1097]
value of, [1094]
solicitor, of, [1214]
special manager—
accounting, [1149]
appointment, [1146]
remuneration, [1146]
security—
failure to give or keep up, [1148]
generally, [1147]
termination of appointment, [1150]
statement of affairs. *See* Statement of affairs
statutory demand—
application to set aside—
generally, [983]
hearing of, [984]
practice direction, [1942]
content of, [980]
form of, [980]
information to be given in, [981]
proof of service, [990]
service—
proof of, [1941]
requirements as to, [982]
substituted, [1940]
trustee in. *See* Trustee in bankruptcy

BOARD OF TRADE
deeds of arrangement, report on, [1791]

BODY CORPORATE
offences by, [432], [482]
receiver, disqualification from acting as, [30]

BOOKS
book debts, avoidance of general assignment of, [344]
company, of. *See* Company
concealment of, [355]
inspection of, by creditors, [155]
sederunt, [562], [1702]

BUSINESS
accounts of, failure to keep, [361]
engaging in, offence in respect of, [360]
insurance, [1823]
voluntary winding up, effect of, [87]

BUSINESS DAY
meaning, [251]

C

CALLS
court's power to make, [150], [923]
enforcement of, [924]
liquidation committee, control by, [922]
liquidator, by, [921]
making of, [924]
orders for, [161]

CAPITAL
return of, [940]–[941]

CAUTION
insolvency practitioner, of, [1432]–[1436], [1445], [1697]
premium of bond of, [1707J]

CERTIFICATE
insolvency, of. *See* Certificate of insolvency
proof of debt still unpaid, [1943]
value added tax, [1348]–[1353], [1708]–[1713]

CERTIFICATE OF INSOLVENCY
issue of, [679], [717]
notice to creditors, [680], [718]
preservation with company's records, [681], [719]

CHAIRMAN
creditors' committee, [658], [700]
creditors' meeting. *See* Creditors' meeting
liquidation committee, of, [876]
See also Proxy

CHARGE
bankrupt's home, on, [313]
floating. *See* Floating charge
preferential, on goods distrained, [176]
voluntary arrangement, [621], [977]

CHARGED PROPERTY. *See* Property

CHATTEL LEASING AGREEMENT
goods possessed under, administrator's power to deal with, [15], [16]
meaning, [251]
owner of goods under, at creditors' meeting, [650]

CHIEF LAND REGISTRAR
notice to, [992], [1022]

CLAIM
adjudication of, [549]
admission of, [646], [693]
determination of amount of, [579]
foreign currency—
conversion of, [1707G]
quantification of, [810], [1090]
Scotland, in, [1707F], [1707G]
quantification of—
bankruptcy, in case of. *See* Bankruptcy
discounts, [808]
estimate of quantum, [805]
foreign currency, debt in, [810], [1090]
future time, debt payable at, [813]
interest, [812]
mutual credit, [809]
negotiable instruments, [806]
payments of periodical nature, [811]
secured creditors, [807]
set-off, [809]
rejection of, [646], [693]

CLAIM—*continued*
submission to permanent trustee, [548]
unsatisfied creditor, by, [325]

CO-OBLIGANTS
liabilities of, [560]
rights of, [560]

COMMISSION
evidence, for receiving, [197]

COMMISSIONERS
bankruptcy in Scotland. *See* Scotland

COMMITTEE
creditors, of. *See* Creditors' committee
Insolvency Rules, [413]
liquidation. *See* Liquidation committee

COMPANY
assets. *See* Assets
books of—
evidence, to be, [191]
falsification of, [209]
liens on, unenforceability of, [246], [349]
connected with, meaning, [249]
dealings, inquiry into—
court's enforcement powers, [237]
generally, [236]
director. *See* Director
dissolution after winding up—
early—
generally, [202]
notice under s 202, consequence of, [203]
Scotland, [204]
otherwise than under ss 202–204, [205]
procedure following appeal, [944]
Secretary of State's directions, [943]
voluntary winding up, [201]
insolvency rules, [411], [457]
insurance. *See* Insurance company
investigation of, disqualification of director
after, [476]
leave to proceed, costs of application for,
Scotland, [199]
legislation, disqualification of director for
breaches of, [471]
limited, formerly unlimited, contributories of,
[77]
liquidator, appointment of, [820]
meaning, [70], [490]
meetings–
attendance at, [157]
conduct of, [654]
venue, [654]
members. *See* Members
names, restriction on re-use of, [216]
officers. *See* Officers
overseas, may be wound up though dissolved,
[225]
property of—
acceptance of shares as consideration for
sale of, [110]
distribution of, [107]
getting in, [234]
winding up by court—
custody, [144]
vesting in liquidator, [145]
registered under Companies Act, [83]
representation, [1284], [1346]
statement of affairs. *See* Statement of affairs

COMPANY—*continued*
status of, effect of voluntary winding up on,
[87]
unlimited, formerly limited, contributories of,
[78]
unregistered. *See* Unregistered company
voluntary arrangement. *See* Voluntary arrangement
voluntary winding up. *See* Voluntary winding
up
winding-up. *See* Winding-up

COMPROMISE
Scotland, [565]

CONCEALMENT
books, of, [355]
papers, of, [355]
property, of, [354]

CONDITIONAL SALE AGREEMENT
goods possessed under, administrator's power
to deal with, [15], [16]
seller of goods under, at creditors' meeting,
[650]

CONSOLIDATED FUND
recourse to, [408]

CONTRACT
bankrupt party to, [345]
liability for—
administrative receiver, [44]
manager, [37]
receiver, [37], [57]
rescission by court, [186]

CONTRIBUTORIES
bankruptcy, effect of, [82]
company registered under Companies Act,
[83]
death of member, in case of, [81]
information to, [762]–[768]
liability—
director—
past, [76]
unlimited liability, with, [75]
limited company formerly unlimited, [77]
nature of, [80]
past members, [74]
present members, [74]
shareholders, [76]
unlimited company formerly limited, [78]
liquidation committee established by, [873]
liquidator—
appointment of, [819]
choice of, [139]
meaning, [79], [251]
public examination, order on request by, [932]
settlement of list of—
addition to, [919]
costs, [920]
form of, [916]
liquidator, duty to settle, [915]
preliminary, [914]
procedure for settling, [917]
variation of—
application to court, [918]
generally, [919]
unregistered company, winding up of, [226]

CONTRIBUTORIES—*continued*
  winding up by court—
    absconding contributor, power to arrest, [158]
    adjustment of rights, [154]
    debts due to company, [149]
    order to be conclusive evidence, [152]
    settlement of list, [148]
  wishes of, meetings to ascertain, [195]
  See also Creditors' meeting

CONTROL
  bankrupt's estate, of. *See* Bankrupt's estate
  general control of court, [363]

CONVICTED PERSON
  criminal bankruptcy order against, [1800]

CORRUPTION
  appointment of liquidator, inducement affecting, [164]

COSTS
  bankrupt's estate, order of payment out of, [1203]
  court procedure, [1249]–[1258]
  generally, [1309]
  leave to proceed, application for, [199]
  proof of debt, [797]
  settlement of list of contributories, [920]
  voluntary arrangement, [621], [977]
  winding up—
    commencing as voluntary, [938]
    court, saving for powers of, [939]
    priority, general rule as to, [937]

COUNTRIES
  relevant, co-operation of insolvency courts, [1494]–[1496]

COUNTY COURT
  administration order. *See* Adminstration order
  deeds of arrangement, transmission of copies, [1844]–[1849]
  winding up by—
    case stated for High Court, [119]
    jurisdiction, [117]

COURT
  administration order, making of. *See* Administration order
  administrator's recourse to, [672]
  affidavits, [1273]
  alternative, for debtor's petition in bankruptcy, [1344]
  appeal. *See* Appeal
  applications, [1217]–[1226]
  attendance, right of, [1269]
  audience, right of, [1268]
  bankruptcy, power in respect of. *See* Bankruptcy
  bankruptcy order, power to annul, [282]
  co-operation, [426], [1494]–[1496]
  companies—
    dealings, inquiry into, enforcement powers, [237]
    insolvency, [1938]
    petitions, [1937]
  concurrent proceedings, restriction on, [1272]
  contract, rescission of, [186]
  costs, [1249]–[1258]

COURT—*continued*
  county. *See* County court
  discharge by order of, [280]
  disclaimer, powers in respect of—
    generally, [181]
    leaseholds, [182]
  discovery, [1276]
  documents—
    judicial notice of, [196]
    office copies of, [1277]
  enforcement proceedings, [1235]–[1241]
  expunging of proof by, [804]
  formal defects, [1271]
  forms, [1346]
  individual voluntary arrangement. *See* Voluntary arrangement
  insolvency jurisdiction, exercising, appeals from, [375]
  insolvency practitioner's solicitor, [1270]
  liquidator—
    appointment of, [821]
    leave to resign granted by, [830]
    removal by, [838], [839]
  manager, powers regarding. *See* Manager
  meaning, [1330]
  mortgaged property, power to order sale, [1177]
  order. *See* Order
  payment into, [1275]
  persons incapable of managing affairs, [1259]–[1262]
  principal rules and practice to apply, [1267]
  proceedings. *See* Proceedings
  receiver, powers regarding. *See* Receiver
  records, [1242]–[1248]
  relevant countries and territories, co-operation of, [1494]–[1496]
  remedies, restriction on, [1272]
  returns of Secretary of State, [1245]
  security in, [1274]
  shorthand writers, [1232]–[1234], [1345]
  special manager, power to appoint, [177], [370]
  taxation, [1249]–[1258]
  trustee in bankruptcy—
    appointment of, [1100]
    general control of, [303]
    removal of, [1111]
  unfit director, duty to disqualify, [474], [475]
  voluntary winding up—
    proceedings, power to control, [113]
    reference of questions, [112]
  winding up by. *See* Winding up

COURT OF SESSION
  winding up by, [120]

CREDIT
  extortionate credit transactions, [244], [343], [561]
  fraudulent dealing with property obtained on, [359]
  mutual—
    bankrupt's estate, distribution of, [323]
    quantification of claim, [809]
  obtaining, [360], [1719]

CREDITORS
  administrator's proposals to, notice to members of, [640]

CREDITORS—*continued*
bankruptcy petition. *See* Petition
committee. *See* Creditors' committee
false claim of status as, [1325]
false representations to, [211]
fraud of, transactions in, [207]
information to, [762]–[768], [1052]–[1057]
inspection of books by, [155]
interests of, protection of, [27]
liquidator, appointment of, [819], [820]
list of, right to have, [1324]
meaning, [383], [763]
meeting. *See* Creditors' meeting
not proving in time, court's power to exclude, [153]
public examination, order on request by, [932]
retention of title, [649]
Scotland. *See* Scotland
secured. *See* Secured creditors
security, with, [269]
transactions defrauding, [423]–[425]
trustee in bankruptcy, appointment of, [294]
unsatisfied, claims by, [325]
voluntary arrangement, proceedings on proposal—
requisite majorities, [612]
voting rights, [610]
voluntary winding up. *See* Creditors' voluntary winding up
wishes of, meetings to ascertain, [195]

CREDITORS' COMMITTEE
administrative receiver, attendance of, [49]
bankruptcy, in case of. *See* Bankruptcy
chairman, [658], [700]
constitution, [655], [697]
criminal bankruptcy, [1213]
establishment of, [26], [68]
formalities of establishment, [656], [698]
functions, [657], [699]
information—
administrator, from, [667]
receiver, from, [709]
meetings, [657], [699]
members—
dealings with company, [669], [711]
expenses of, [668], [710]
removal, [663], [705]
representatives of, [660], [702]
resignation, [661], [703]
procedure, [665], [707]
quorum, [659], [701]
representative of committee-member, [660], [702]
resolutions by post, [666], [708]
termination of membership, [662], [704]
trustee in bankruptcy. *See* Trustee in bankruptcy
vacancies, [664], [706]

CREDITORS' MEETING
adjournment, [695], [784]
administrator—
proposals of, consideration of, [24], [641]
recourse to meeting, [671]
report of, [652]
advertisement, notice by, [778]
bankruptcy, in case of. *See* Bankruptcy
business—
first meeting, at, [771]

CREDITOR'S MEETING—*continued*
business—*continued*
meeting under s 95 or 98, at, [772]
chairman—
creditors' voluntary winding up, [775]
discretion to allow vote, [787]
generally, [643], [691], [774]
proxy-holder, as, [783]
chattel leasing agreement, owner of goods under, [650]
claims—
admission of, [646], [693]
rejection of, [646], [693]
company's personnel, attendance at meetings of, [777]
conditional sale agreement, seller of goods under, [650]
entitlement to vote—
contributories, [788]
creditors, [786]
generally, [645]
expenses—
creditors' voluntary winding up, [781]
summoning, of, [780]
first—
business at, [771]
generally, [769], [770]
general power to call, [773]
generally, [642]
hire-purchase agreement, owner of goods under, [650]
individual voluntary arrangement. *See* Voluntary arrangement
liquidator—
choice of, [139]
resignation, to receive, [827]
minutes, [651], [696]
negotiable instruments, holders of, [648]
notices to creditors, [653]
procedure for summoning, [690]
proceedings, record of, [790]
proof—
admission of, [789]
rejection of, [789]
quorum, [694], [785]
requisitioned—
creditors, by, [644]
generally, [776]
resolutions, [651], [696], [782]
retention of title creditors, [649]
Scotland, [566], [585], [586]
secured creditors, [647]
suspension, [784]
trustee in bankruptcy, appointment of, [1099]
venue, [779]
voluntary winding up. *See* Creditors' voluntary winding up
voting rights, [692]

CREDITORS' VOLUNTARY WINDING UP
application of Chapter, [97]
creditors' meeting. *See* Creditors' meeting
directors—
cesser of powers, [103]
statement of affairs to be laid before creditors, [99]
final meeting prior to dissolution, [106]

CREDITORS' VOLUNTARY WINDING UP—*continued*
general company meeting at each year's end, [105]
information to creditors and contributories, [768]
liquidation committee, appointment of, [101]
liquidator—
 appointment of, [100], [820], [822]
 deceased, [852]
 insolvency practitioner, loss of qualification as, [854]
 meeting to remove, [833]
 powers and duties, [166]
 release of, [841]
 removal of—
  court, by, [839]
  procedure, [836]
 resignation, action following, [829]
 vacancy in office of, [104]
 vacation of office, [855]
meeting of creditors—
 each year's end, at, [105]
 generally, [98]
 winding up converted under s 96, where, [102]
members' voluntary winding up—
 conversion of, [96]
 distinction between, [90]
Scotland, in, [1668]
statement of affairs—
 accounts–
  expenses of preparing, [760]
  submission of, [759]
 expenses, [757]
 generally, [753]

CRIMINAL BANKRUPTCY. *See* Bankruptcy

CROWN
 application, [434], [577]

CURRENCY. *See* Foreign currency

D

DEALINGS
 bankrupt, of, inquiry into, [366]

DEATH
 administrative receiver, of, [715]
 administrator, of, [13], [20], [677]
 liquidator, of, [851], [852], [864]
 member, of, contributories in case of, [81]
 permanent trustee, of, [528]
 trustee in bankruptcy, of, [1122]

DEBENTURE
 secured—
  meaning, [70]
  series of, meaning, [70]

DEBTOR
 bankruptcy petition. *See* Petition
 individual voluntary arrangement. *See* Voluntary arrangement
 judgment, execution overtaken by insolvency of, [1326]
 Scotland. *See* Scotland

DEBTS
 avoidance, [423]–[425]
 bad debt relief. *See* Value added tax
 bankruptcy, meaning, [382]
 book, avoidance of general assignment of, [344]
 due from contributory to company, [149]
 foreign currency, in, [810], [1090]
 future time, payable at, [813], [1093]
 inability to pay, meaning, [123]
 insolvent company, of, ranking equally, [900]
 interest on, [189]
 meaning, [1340]
 payment out of assets, subject to floating charge, [40]
 personal liability for, [217], [483]
 preferential—
  categories of, [386], [455]
  general provision, [175]
  preferential charge on goods distrained, [176]
  relevant date, meaning, [387]
  Scotland, [581], [582]
 priority of—
  generally, [328]
  Scotland, [59]
 proof of—
  affidavit, claim established by, [796]
  appeal against decision on, [802]
  bankruptcy, in case of. *See* Bankruptcy
  contents of, [794]
  cost of proving, [797]
  creditor's claim, particulars of, [795]
  criminal bankruptcy, [1211]
  dividend—
   admission for, [801]
   rejection for, [801]
  expunging by court, [804]
  generally, [322], [1310]
  liquidator—
   inspection of proof allowed by, [798]
   new, appointment of, [800]
   transmission of proofs to, [799]
  prove, meaning, [792]
  quantification of claim. *See* Claim
  supply of forms, [793]
  variation of, [803]
  withdrawal of, [803]
 spouse, to, [329]
 unregistered company, inability to pay. *See* Unregistered company

DECEASED PERSON
 insolvent estate of, [421], [1454]–[1464]

DEEDS OF ARRANGEMENT
 accounts, [1864]–[1875]
 affidavits, [1792]
 avoidance of, [1768]–[1769]
 bankruptcy law, relation to, [1788]
 Board of Trade, report by, [1791]
 copies—
  office, [1789]
  transmission to county court, [1844]–[1849]
 enforcement, [1787]
 extracts, [1842]
 fees, [1790], [1877]–[1883]
 office copies, [1789]
 procedure, [1850]–[1856]

DEEDS OF ARRANGEMENTS—*continued*
registration, [1770]–[1775], [1838]–[1841]
searches, [1843]
trustees, provisions as to, [1776]–[1786], [1857]–[1863]

DEFAULT
voluntary arrangement, in connection with, [276]

DEPOSIT PROTECTION BOARD
payments out of fund, [1808]–[1809]
voting rights, [1343], [1705]

DILIGENCE
effect of, [185]
sequestration, effect of, [537]

DIRECTIONS
manager, for, application to court, [35]
receiver, for, application to court, [35]

DIRECTOR
bankrupt, leave to act, [1182]–[1184]
cesser of powers, [103]
company with prohibited name, leave to act as—
application for, [946]
excepted case—
first, [947]
second, [948]
third, [949]
preliminary, [945]
conduct of, report on, [1497]–[1503], [1721]–[1726]
delinquent—
summary remedy against, [212]
winding up application by or against, [1347B]
disqualification of—
body corporate, offences by, [482]
Company Directors Disqualification Act 1986—
commencement, [493]
derivation table, [499]
destination table, [500]
extent, [492]
interaction with Insolvency Act, [489]
interpretation, [490]
repealed enactments, [487], [491], [498]
savings, [491], [496], [497]
transitional provisions, [491], [497]
company's debts, personal liability for, [483]
fraud, for, [472]
indictable offence, on conviction of, [470]
officer of court, particulars to be furnished by, [1487]–[1493]
order—
application for, [484]
county court administration, failure to pay under, [480]
criminal penalties for contravention, [481]
generally, [469]
leave under, application for, [485]
register of, [486]
persistent breaches of legislation, for, [471]
statements, admissibility in evidence of, [488]
summary conviction, on, [473]
undischarged bankrupt, [479]

DIRECTOR—*continued*
disqualification of—*continued*
unfitness, for—
application to court, [475]
disqualification order—
commencement of, [1361]
setting aside, [1362]
duty of court, [474]
evidence, [1359]
form of application, [1355]
hearing of application, [1360]
investigation of company, after, [476]
matters for determining, [477], [495]
respondent, case against, [1356]
summons—
acknowledgement of service, [1358]
endorsement on, [1357]
service, [1358]
wrongful trading, participation in, [478]
meaning, [490]
past, liability as contributory, [76]
shadow, meaning, [251], [490]
statement of affairs to be laid before creditors, [99]
unlimited liability, with, liability as contributory, [75]
voluntary arrangement, proposal for. *See* Voluntary arrangement

DISCHARGE FROM BANKRUPTCY. *See* Bankruptcy

DISCLAIMER
additional notices, [908]
bankruptcy, in case of. *See* Bankruptcy
communication to persons interested, [907]
court, powers of—
application for exercise of, [913]
generally, [181]
leasehold, in case of, [182]
disclaimed property, court order vesting, [320], [321]
duty to keep court informed, [909]
dwelling house, of, [318]
general power, [315]
interest in property, declaration on request, [911]
interested party, application by, [910]
land subject to rentcharge, [180], [319]
leasehold, of—
court, powers of, [182]
generally, [179], [317]
vesting of, [321]
liquidator's notice of, [906]
onerous property, power to disclaim, [178]
presumed valid and effective, [912]
trustee's decision, notice requiring, [316]

DISCLOSURE
limited, of statement of affairs, [636], [686], [754]

DISCOUNTS
quantification of claim, [808], [1089]

DISCOVERY
court procedure, [1276]

DISQUALIFICATION OF DIRECTOR. *See* Director

DISSOLUTION AFTER WINDING UP. *See* Company

DISTRIBUTION. *See* Bankrupt's Estate

DIVIDENDS
declaration of, [1295]–[1307]
distribution by way of, [324]
entitlement to vote and draw, [550]
Insolvency Services Account, [407]
payment of, [1295]–[1307], [1401]
supplementary provisions as to, [901]
unclaimed, [193], [1402]

DIVORCE
recalling of order for payment of capital sum on, [535]

DOCUMENTS
confidentiality of, [1320], [1696]
copies of, [1695]
court, judicial notice of, [196]
Inland Revenue, production by, [369]
office copies of, [1277]
right to copy, [1322]
Scotland, [562]
Secretary of State, issuing from, [1313]
stamp duty, exempt from, [190]

DWELLING HOUSE
bankrupt, of, [1216]
disclaimer of, [318]
occupation, rights of—
bankrupt, [337]
bankrupt's spouse, [336]

E

ELECTRICITY
supplies of, [233], [372]

EMPLOYEES
assets, power to make over, [187]
industrial tribunal, complaint to, [1803]
insolvent employer, rights against, [1801]
occupational pension scheme, payment of unpaid contributions to, [1802]
remuneration of, preference for, [1719]
Secretary of State—
information, power to obtain, [1805]
rights and remedies, transfer to, [1804]

EMPLOYER
insolvent, employee's rights against, [1801]

ENFORCEMENT
calls, of, [924]
court procedures, [1235]–[1241]
deeds of arrangement, [1787]
procedures, [346]

ESTATE
bankrupt, of. *See* Bankrupt's estate
deceased person, of, [421], [1454]–[1464]
insolvent, meaning, [1336]
interim preservation of, [518]

EVIDENCE
commission for receiving, [197]
company's books to be, [191]
disqualified director, with respect to, [488]
order on contributory to be conclusive, [152]
proceedings, of, [1312], [1694]
statement of affairs, admissibility of, [433]

EXAMINATION
application—
contents of, [1286]
form of, [1286]
costs of proceedings, [1290]
debtor, of—
conduct of, [547]
private, [544], [546]
public, [545], [546]
forms, [1346]
order for, [1287]
persons in Scotland, of, court order for, [198]
preliminary, [1285]
procedure for, [1288]
public. *See* Public examination
record of, [1289]

EXECUTION
effect of, [183]

EXEMPT PROPERTY. *See* Property

EXPENSES
creditors—
committee members, of, [668], [710]
meeting, of, [780], [781]
generally, [1309]
official receiver, of, [1294]
public examination, of, [936], [1156]
Scotland, [576], [1700]
statement of affairs, of, [638], [688], [756], [757]
voluntary arrangement. [621], [977]
voluntary winding up, of, [115]
winding up, of, payment of, [156]

F

FALSE REPRESENTATIONS
creditors, to, [211]
voluntary arrangement, [623], [979]

FALSIFICATION
offence, [355]

FEES
appropriate, meaning, [1339]
deeds of arrangement, [1790], [1877]–[1883]
insolvency, [1472]–[1486]
insolvency practitioner, of, [1430]
orders, company insolvency proceedings, [414]
Scotland, [1700]
voluntary arrangement, [621], [977]

FINANCIAL STATEMENT
Insolvency Services Account, [409]

FIXED SECURITY
meaning, [70]

FLOATING CHARGE
avoidance of, [245]
holder of, appointment of receiver by, Scotland, [53]
meaning, [70], [251]
payment of debts out of assets subject to, [40]

FOREIGN CURRENCY
claim in—
conversion of, [1707G]
Scotland, [1707F], [1707G]
debt in, [810], [1090]

FORMS
administrative receivership, [1346]
bankruptcy, [1346]
company representation, [1346]
court procedure and practice, [1346]
examination, [1346]
insolvency proceedings, for use in, [1314]
liquidation, [1346]
prescription of, Scotland, [71]
proxies, [1346]
Scotland—
  bankruptcy, [1707E], [1707M]
  prescription of, [71]
  proceedings, for use in, [1699]
voluntary arrangements, [1346]
winding up, [1346]

FRAUD
creditors, of, transactions in, [207]
disqualification of director for, [472]
transactions defrauding creditors, [423]–[425]
winding up, in anticipation of, [206]

FRAUDULENT TRADING
generally, [213]
proceedings, [215]

G

GAMBLING
offence, [362]

GAS
supplies of, [233], [372]

GAZETTE
Edinburgh, [571]
notice in, [1327]

GOODS
distrained, preferential charge on, [176]
execution against, [183]

H

HEARING
petition for administration order, of, [632]
public examination. *See* Public examination

HIGH COURT
winding up by—
  case stated, [119]
  jurisdiction, [117]

HIRE-PURCHASE AGREEMENT
goods possessed under, administrator's power
  to deal with, [15], [16]
owner of goods under, at creditors' meeting,
  [650]

HOME
bankrupt, of—
  charge on, [313]
  generally, [1216]
  saving for, [332]

I

INCOME PAYMENTS ORDER. *See* Bankruptcy

INDIVIDUAL
administration order against, disabilities on
  revocation, [429]

INDIVIDUAL—*continued*
bankrupt. *See* Bankrupt
incapable of managing affairs, [1259]–[1262]
insolvency rules, [412], [458]
insolvent, jurisdiction in relation to, [373]
voluntary arrangement. *See* Voluntary arrangement

INDUSTRIAL TRIBUNAL
complaint to, [1803]

INFORMATION
administrative receiver, to be given by, [46],
  [709]
administrator, to be given by, [21], [667]
bankruptcy. *See* Bankruptcy
contributories, to, [762]–[768]
creditors, to, [762]–[768], [1052]–[1057]
pending liquidation, as to, [192]
receiver, to be given by, Scotland, [65]
statutory demand, to be given in, [725]

INLAND REVENUE
official, order to, [1173]–[1175]
production of documents by, order for, [369]

INNER HOUSE
orders taking effect until matter disposed of
  by, [448]

INQUIRY
bankrupt's dealings and property, into, [366]
company's dealings, into—
  court's enforcement powers, [237]
  generally, [236]

INSOLVENCY
Act of 1986—
  amendment of enactments, [439], [464],
    [465]
  citation, [444]
  commencement, [443]
  comparative table, [468]
  consequential amendments, [439], [464],
    [465]
  derivation table, [466]
  destination table, [467]
  enactments repealed, [438], [463]
  interaction with Company Directors Dis-
    qualification Act 1986, [489]
  repeals, [438], [463]
  savings, [437], [460]–[462]
  transitional provisions, [437], [460]–[462]
annual report, [379]
appeal in proceedings, [1263]–[1266]
co-operation between courts, [426]
Companies Court, [1938]
company, of, effect of, [95]
debt avoidance, [423]–[425]
deceased person, estate of, [421], [1454]–[1464]
districts, [374]
employer, of, employee's rights on, [1801]
expressions used generally, [436]
extent—
  Northern Ireland, [441]
  other territories, [442]
  Scotland, [440]
fees, [1472]–[1486]
fees orders, [414]
formal defects, [377]
forms for use in proceedings, [1314]

INSOLVENCY—*continued*
  insolvent individual, jurisdiction in relation to, [373]
  judgment debtor, of, execution overtaken by, [1326]
  meaning, [247]
  partnership, [420], [1504]–[1523]
  practice, [419]
  practice direction, [1938]
  practitioner—
    act as, meaning, [388]
    acting without qualification, offence, [389]
    action on report of, [274]
    appointment by court, [273]
    audit of accounts, [1398]
    authorisation—
      competent authority, by, [392]
      education, [1428], [1442]
      fees, [1430]
      fit and proper applicant, [1427]
      grant of, [393]
      maximum period of, [1431]
      notices, [394]
      practical training and experience, [1429]
      refusal of, [393]
      representations, right to make, [395]
      revocation, [1425]
      tribunal—
        action on reference, [397]
        investigations, conduct of, [1368]–[1383]
        members, [456]
        procedure, [456]
        reference to, [396]
        refusal without reference to, [398]
        sittings, [456]
        withdrawal without reference to, [398]
      withdrawal of, [393]
    business carried on by, [1396]
    caution, requirements for, [1432]–[1436], [1445], [1697]
    copy of accounts sent out by, [1399]
    liquidator, loss of qualification, [853], [854], [865]
    persons not qualified to act as, [390]
    qualification to act as, [1707C–1707D]
    recognised professional bodies, [391], [1384]–[1386]
    records, [1437]–[1441], [1447]
    responsible, [1337]
    retention of money by, [1393]
    Scotland, [1707C–1707D]
    security, requirements for, [1315], [1432]–[1436], [1445]
    solicitor of, [1270]
    trustee in bankruptcy, loss of qualification, [1123]
  proceedings, meaning, [1335]
  public administration. *See* Public administration
  recognised banks, [422]
  rules. *See* Rules
  services. *See* Insolvency services
  time-limits, [376]
INSOLVENCY SERVICES
  account—
    certification of balance in, [1397]
    claiming money paid into, [1403]

INSOLVENCY SERVICES—*continued*
  account—*continued*
    generally, [403]
    payments into, [1390]
    payments out of, [1391]
    unclaimed dividends, [407]
    undistributed balances, [407]
  extent of Part, [410]
  investment account—
    adjustment of balances, [405]
    annual financial statement, [409]
    application of, [405]
    audit, [409]
    Consolidated Fund, recourse to, 408
    generally, [404]
    interest, [406]
INSPECTION
  books, of, by creditors, [155]
INSTRUMENT OF APPOINTMENT
  meaning, [70]
INSURANCE COMPANY
  administration order, court's power to make, [8]
  business, [1823]
  winding up, [1735]–[1766], [1810]–[1816], [1884]–[1916], [1917]–[1936]
INSURERS
  third parties' rights against, [1795]–[1798]
INTEREST
  claim in sequestration, on, [1707H]
  debts, on, [189]
  Insolvency Services Account, on, [406]
  official rate, [189], [251]
  quantification of claim, [812], [1092]
INTERESTS
  creditors, of, protection of, [27]
  members, of, protection of, [27]
INTERIM RECEIVER
  appointment of, [286], [368], [1030]
  criminal bankruptcy, [1210]
  deposit, [1032]
  order of appointment, [1031]
  remuneration, [1035]
  security—
    failure to give or keep up, [1034]
    generally, [1033]
  termination of appointment, [1036]
INVESTIGATION
  disqualification of director after, [476]
  official receiver, by, [289]
  winding up by court. *See* Winding up
INVESTMENT ACCOUNT. *See* Insolvency services
INVESTMENT BUSINESS
  administration order, [1831]–[1833]
  winding up orders—
    generally, [1829]
    Northern Ireland, [1830]

J

JURISDICTION
  insolvency courts, co-operation of, [1494]–[1496]

JURISDICTION—*continued*
  insolvent individual, in relation to, [373]
  service outside, [1319]

L

LAND
  rentcharge, subject to, disclaimer in case of,
    [180], [319]

LEASEHOLD
  disclaimer of—
    court, powers of, [182]
    generally, [179]

LETTERS
  bankrupt, of, re-direction of, [371]

LIABILITIES
  co-obligant, of, [560]
  contract, for. *See* Contract
  contributories, of. *See* Contributories
  list of—
    debtor, of, [519]
    trustee's duties on receipt of, [520]
  meaning, [1340]
  personal—
    company's debts, for, [483]
    debts, for, [217]
  unsecured, amount of, Scotland, [1707I]

LICENSED MONEYLENDER. *See* Money-
    lender

LIEN
  books, on, unenforceability of, [246], [349]

LIMITED COMPANY
  formerly unlimited, contributories of, [77]

LIMITED PARTNERSHIP
  sequestration of estate of, [1707L]

LIQUIDATION
  delegation of court's powers to, [160]
  forms, [1346]
  go into, meaning, [247]
  notification that company is in, [188]
  pending, information as to, [192]
  proof of debts. *See* Debts

LIQUIDATION COMMITTEE
  appointment of, [101]
  calls, control of, [922]
  chairman, [876]
  composition of, when creditors paid in full,
    [890]
  contributories, established by, [873]
  formalities of establishment, [872]
  liquidator—
    obligations of, [874]
    reports, [887]
  meetings, [875]
  members—
    dealings by, [889]
    expenses, [888]
    removal, [881]
    representatives, [878]
    resignation, [879]
  membership—
    generally, [871]
    termination of, [880]
  preliminary, [870]
  quorum, [877]

LIQUIDATION COMMITTEE—*continued*
  resolutions—
    creditors' voluntary winding up, [885]
    generally, [884]
    post, by, [886]
  Scotland, in, [142], [1265]–[1644], [1645]–
    [1650]
  Secretary of State, functions vested in, [891]
  termination of membership, [880]
  vacancy—
    contributory members, [883]
    creditor members, [882]
  voting rights, [884], [885]
  winding up by court, [141], [142]
  winding up following immediately on admin-
      istration—
    application of provisions, [897]
    creditors' committee, continuation of, [893]
    liquidator—
      certificate, [895]
      obligations of, [896]
    membership, [894]
    preliminary, [892]

LIQUIDATOR
  appointment of—
    advertisement, [825]
    authentication of, [824]
    company, by, [820]
    contributories, by, [819]
    contributories' meeting, choice at, [139]
    corrupt inducement affecting, [164]
    court, by—
      administration, following, [140]
      creditors' voluntary winding up, [822]
      generally, [821]
      voluntary arrangement, following, [140]
      voluntary winding up, in, [108]
    creditors—
      by, [819], [820]
      meeting of, choice at, [139]
      voluntary winding up, [100]
    members' voluntary winding up, [91], [858],
      [859]
    notice of, [109]
    official receiver, functions of, [136]
    provisional, [135]
    registration, [825]
    Scotland, in, [138], [1603]–[1607]
    Secretary of State, by, [137], [823]
  assets, collection and distribution of. *See*
      Assets
  calls by, [921]
  deceased, [851], [852]
  final meeting, [844], [845]
  functions of—
    company property—
      custody of, [144]
      vesting in liquidator, [145]
    final meeting, duty to summon, [146]
    general, [143]
  insolvency practitioner, loss of qualification
      as, [853], [854]
  joint, notice to, [1333]
  members' voluntary winding up. *See* Mem-
      bers' voluntary winding up
  none appointed or nominated by company,
      [114]

LIQUIDATOR—*continued*
powers and duties—
  returns, enforcement of duty to make, [170]
  sanction—
    exercisable with, [449]
    exercisable without, [450], [451]
  supplementary, [168], [169]
  winding up—
    court, by, [167]
    creditors', [166]
    voluntary, [165]
provisional—
  appointment of, [135], [744]
  deposit, [746]
  order of appointment, [745]
  remuneration, [749]
  Scotland, in, [1586]–[1591]
  security—
    failure to give or keep up, [748]
    generally, [747]
  termination of appointment, [750]
release of—
  voluntary winding up, [173]
  winding up by court, [174]
removal of—
  advertisement, [837]
  court's power to regulate meetings, [834]
  court, by, [108], [838], [839]
  meeting of creditors, [832], [833]
  procedure on, [835], [836]
  Secretary of State, by, [842]
  winding up—
    court, by, [172]
    voluntary, [171]
remuneration—
  excessive, creditors' claim that, [850]
  fixing of, [846]
  other matters affecting, [847]
  recourse—
    court, to, [849]
    meeting of creditors, to, [848]
resignation—
  action following acceptance of, [828], [829]
  advertisement of, [831]
  creditors' meeting to receive, [827]
  leave to resign granted by court, [830]
Scotland, in. *See* Scotland
security, redemption of, [816]
settlement of list of contributories, [915]
style of, [163]
summary remedy against, [212]
title of, [163]
vacancy in office of—
  creditors' voluntary winding up, [104]
  members' voluntary winding up, [92]
  voluntary winding up, [171]
  winding up by court, [172]
vacation of office—
  duties on, [857]
  official receiver, notice to, [856]
  winding-up order, on making of, [855]
voluntary arrangement, proposal for—
  meetings, summoning of, [604]
  notice to nominee, [605]
  preparation of, [603], [605]

LORD ORDINARY
  winding up, power to remit to, [121]

M

MANAGER
  appointment out of court—
    contracts, liability for, [37]
    directions, application to court for, [35]
    invalid appointment, liability for, [34]
    receivership accounts, delivery to registrar,
      [38]
    remuneration, court's power to fix, [36]
    time from which appointment effective,
      [33]
  extent of Chapter, [28]
  floating charge, payment of debts out of assets
    subject to, [40]
  formal defects, [377]
  meaning, [29]
  notification of appointment, [39]
  returns, enforcement of duty to make, [41]
  special. *See* Special manager
  undischarged bankrupt, disqualification from
    acting, [31]
  See also Receiver

MATRIMONIAL CAUSES
  bankruptcy of settlor, effect of, [1799]

MEETING
  adjourned, resolutions passed at, [194]
  company—
    attendance at, [157]
    conduct of, [654]
    venue, [654]
  contributories' wishes, to ascertain, [195]
  creditors' wishes, to ascertain, [195]
  creditors, of. *See* Creditors' meeting
  evidence of proceedings at, [1312]
  final, [331], [844], [845]
  non-receipt of notice of, [1323]
  Scotland, in, [1670]–[1689]
  trustee in bankruptcy, appointment of. *See*
    Trustee in bankruptcy
  See also Proxy

MEMBERS
  dealings with company, [669]
  death of, contributories in case of, [81]
  interests of, protection of, [27]
  meaning, [250]
  notice to, of proposals to creditors, [640]
  past, liability as contributories, [74]
  present, liability as contributories, [74]
  prosecution of, [218], [219]
  voluntary arrangement, proceedings on pro-
    posal—
    requisite majorities, [613]
    voting rights, [611]
  voluntary winding up. *See* Members' volun-
    tary winding up

MEMBERS' VOLUNTARY WINDING UP
  creditors' voluntary winding up—
    conversion to, [96]
    distinction between, [90]
  insolvency of company, effect of, [95]
  liquidator—
    appointment of, [91], [858], [859]
    authentication of appointment, [860]
    deceased, [864]
    duties on vacating office, [867]

MEMBERS' VOLUNTARY WINDING UP—*continued*
  liquidator—*continued*
    insolvency practitioner, loss of qualification as, [865]
    release, [863]
    removal, [862]
    resignation, [861]
    vacancy in office of, power to fill, [92]
    vacation of office, [866]
  meeting—
    final, prior to dissolution, [94]
    general company, at each year's end, [93]
  Scotland, in, [1669]

MISCONDUCT
  winding up, in course of, [208]

MONEYLENDER
  petition by, [999]
  proof of, [1081]

MONEYS
  company, due to, courts's power to order payment into bank, [151]
  distribution of, Scotland, [60]

MUTUAL CREDIT. *See* Credit

N

NAMES
  company, restriction on re-use of, [216]

NEGOTIABLE INSTRUMENTS
  holders of, [648]
  quantification of claim, [806], [1087]

NOMINEE
  voluntary arrangement. *See* Voluntary arrangement

NON-DISCLOSURE
  offence, [353]
  surrender of security for, [815]

NORTHERN IRELAND
  extent, [441]
  winding up order, [1830]

NOTICE
  administration order, of, [633]
  administrative receiver, appointment of, [683]
  administrator's proposals to creditors, of, [640]
  appointment of liquidator, of, [109]
  creditors' meeting, following, [653]
  Gazette, in, [1327]
  generally, [1311]
  give notice, meaning, [1331]
  insolvency practitioner, authorisation of, [394]
  joint liquidator, to, [1333]
  joint trustees, to, [1333]
  judicial, of court documents, [196]
  meeting, of, non-receipt of, [1323]
  Scotland, in, [1690]–[1692]
  sent simultaneously to same person, [1321]
  solicitor, to, [1332]
  statement of affairs, requiring, [634], [684]
  trustee's decision, requiring, [316]
  voluntary arrangement, proposal by directors, [597]

NOTIFICATION
  administration order, of, [12]

NOTIFICATION—*continued*
  company in liquidation, of, [188]
  manager, appointment of, [39]
  receiver, appointment of, [39], [64]

O

OCCUPATION, RIGHTS OF
  bankrupt, of, [337]
  bankrupt's spouse, [336]

OCCUPATIONAL PENSION SCHEME
  payment of unpaid contributions to, [1802]

OFFENCES
  absconding, [358]
  bodies corporate, by, [432], [482]
  business—
    engaging in, [360]
    proper accounts of, failure to keep, [361]
  company's books, falsification of, [209]
  concealment—
    books, of, [355]
    papers, of, [355]
    property, of, [354]
  credit—
    obtaining, [360]
    property obtained on, fraudulent dealing with, [359]
  creditors—
    false representations to, [211]
    transactions in fraud of, [207]
  definitions, [351]
  false statements, [356]
  falsification, [355]
  fraud—
    creditors, of, transactions in, [207]
    winding up, in anticipation of, [206]
  gambling, [362]
  indictable, disqualification of director on conviction, [470]
  innocent intention, defence of, [352]
  misconduct in course of winding up, [208]
  non-disclosure, [353]
  proper accounts of business, failure to keep, [361]
  property—
    concealment of, [354]
    credit, obtained on, fraudulent dealing with, [359]
    fraudulent disposal of, [357]
  punishment of, [430], [459], [1328], [1347], [1698], [1706]
  scheme of Chapter, [350]
  statement of affairs, material omissions from, [210]
  See also Proceedings

OFFICE COPY
  meaning, [251]

OFFICE-HOLDER
  acts, validity of, [232]
  administrator. *See* Administrator
  conduct of director, report on, [1500], [1723]
  duty to co-operate with, [235]
  liquidator. *See* Liquidator
  meaning, [233]
  qualified insolvency practitioner, as, [230]
  two or more persons, appointment of, [231]

OFFICERS
delinquent—
prosecution of, [218], [219]
winding up application by or against, [1347B]
public examination. *See* Public examination
voluntary arrangement, proceedings on proposal, attendance at, [609]

OFFICIAL PETITIONER
functions of, [402], [1209]
status of, [1209]

OFFICIAL RECEIVER
appointment of, [399], [1291]
bankrupt's duties in relation to, [291]
court's power to appoint, [32]
deputy, [401]
directions, application for, [1293]
expenses, [1294]
functions of, [400]
information to creditors, [1052]
investigation by, [132]
investigatory duties of, [289]
office of liquidator, functions in relation to, [136]
persons entitled to act on behalf of, [1292]
release of, [843], [1115]
remuneration of, [1405]–[1408]
reports by, [762]
staff, [401]
status of, [400]
trustee in bankruptcy—
enforcement of obligations to, [1128]
intention to vacate office, notice of, [1124]

ORDER
adjustment, avoidance on bankruptcy of settlor, [1799]
administration. *See* Administration order
administrator, filling vacancy in office of, [678]
bankruptcy. *See* Bankruptcy
criminal bankruptcy, against convicted person, [1800]
disqualification. *See* Director
examination of persons in Scotland, for, [198]
fees, [414]
final, [447]
income payments. *See* Bankruptcy
individual voluntary arrangement. *See* Voluntary arrangement
Inland Revenue official, to, [1173]–[1175]
Inner House, taking effect until matter disposed of by, [448]
public examination, for, [930]
substituted service of bankruptcy petition, [1940]
winding up by court. *See* Winding up

OVERSEAS
affidavit, [200]
company may be wound up though dissolved, [225]

P

PAPERS
concealment of, [355]

PARLIAMENT
disqualification of bankrupt, [427]

PARTNERSHIP
insolvent, [420], [1504]–[1523]
limited, sequestration of estate of, [1707L]

PAYMENTS
administrative receiver, of, [713]
administrator, duties of, [675]
into court, [1275]
periodical nature, of, [811], [1091]
premises occupied by bankrupt, in respect of, [338]

PENALTIES
criminal, contravention of disqualification order, [481]

PETITION
administration order, application for. *See* Administration order
bank, from, winding up on, [1807]
bankruptcy—
consolidation of, [1215]
creditor, of—
amendment of, [1001]
bankruptcy order—
action to follow making of, [1013]
content of, [1012]
settlement, [1012]
change of carriage of, [1010]
Chief Land Registrar, notice to, [992]
court in which presented, [988]
debt, identification of, [987]
debtor—
death before service, [995]
identification of, [986]
opposed by, [1000]
two or more, against, [998]
expedited, [270]
filing, [989]
grounds of, [267]
hearing—
adjournment, [1008]
decision on, [1004]
extension of time for, [1007]
generally, [997]
inability to pay, meaning, [268]
list of appearances, [1003]
moneylender, by, [999]
non-appearance of creditor, [1005]
notice by persons intending to appear, [1002]
old bankruptcy notices, [1015]
petitioner—
dismissal, seeking, [1011]
leave to withdraw, seeking, [1011]
substitution of, [1009]
practice direction, [1939]
preliminary, [985]
presentation, [989]
proceedings on, [271]
proceedings, amendment of title of, [1014]
proof of service, [994]
security—
costs, for, [996]
creditor with, [269]
service of, [993]
statement of affairs. *See* Statement of affairs

PETITION—*continued*
  bankruptcy—*continued*
    creditor, of—*continued*
      statutory demand—
        generally, [268]
        proof of service, [990]
        vacating registration on dismissal, [1006]
        verification, [991]
      debtor, conditions to be satisfied in respect
        of, [265]
    debtor, of—
      admission of insolvency, [1018]
      alternative courts for, [1344]
      bankruptcy order—
        action to follow making of, [1025]
        content of, [1024]
        proceedings, amendment of title of,
          [1026]
        settlement, [1024]
        summary administration, [1027]–
          [1029]
      Chief Land Registrar, notice to, [1022]
      court in which filed, [1019]
      filing, [1021]
      grounds of, [272]
      identification of debtor, [1017]
      insolvency practitioner—
        action on report of, [274]
        appointment by court, [273]
        report of, [1023]
      preliminary, [1016]
      presentation, [1021]
      statement of affairs. *See* Statement of
        affairs
      summary administration, [275]
      other preliminary conditions, [266]
      Scotland. *See* Scotland
      substituted service, [1940]
      who may present, [264]
    Companies Court, [1937]
    criminal bankruptcy order, based on, [277]
    meaning, [381]
    practice direction, [1937]
    winding up. *See* Winding up

PETITIONER
  meaning, [1338]

POST
  service by, [1317]

PRACTICE DIRECTIONS
  insolvency, [1938]
  petitions, [1937], [1939]
  proof of debt, [1943]
  statutory demand—
    application to set aside, [1942]
    service—
      proof of, [1941]
      substituted, [1940]

PRACTITIONER. *See* Insolvency

PREFERENCES
  adjustment of, [340]
  application to court for order, [239]
  orders, [241], [342]
  relevant time, meaning, [240], [341]
  unfair, [243]

PREFERENTIAL DEBTS. *See* Debts

PREMISES
  bankrupt, occupied by, payments in respect
    of, [338]

PRESCRIBED
  meaning, [70], [251], [384]

PROCEEDINGS
  company, against, power of court to stay or
    restrain, [126]
  concurrent, restriction on, [1272]
  court's power to control, [113]
  courts other than High Court, in, [1347A]
  evidence of, [1312], [1694]
  forms for use in, [1699]
  restriction on, [285]
  summary, [431]
  trading—
    fraudulent, [215]
    wrongful, [215]
  transfer between courts, [1227]–[1231]
  unregistered company, court's power to stay,
    sist or restrain, [227]
  validity of, [1693]

PROFESSIONAL BODY
  recognised, [391], [1384]–[1386]

PROMOTERS
  delinquent, application by or against, [1347B]

PROOF
  creditors' meeting—
    admission, [789]
    rejection, [789]
  debts, of. *See* Debts

PROPERTY
  adjustment order, avoidance on bankruptcy
    of settlor, [1799]
  after-acquired, [307], [1179]–[1181]
  assets. *See* Assets
  bankrupt, of, inquiry into, [366]
  charged—
    administrative receiver's power to dispose
      of, [43], [712]
    administrator's power to deal with—
      disposal of, [674]
      generally, [15]
      Scotland, in, [16]
  company, of. *See* Company
  concealment of, [354]
  credit, obtained on, fraudulent dealing with,
    [359]
  disposal of interest in , Scotland, [61]
  dispositions of—
    avoidance of, [127]
    restrictions on, [284]
  exempt, replacement of—
    money provided in lieu of sale, [1167]
    purchase, [1166]
  fraudulent disposal of, [357]
  in specie, distribution of, [326]
  mortgaged, [1176]–[1178]
  onerous, power to disclaim, [178]

PROPOSAL FOR VOLUNTARY AR-
  RANGEMENT. *See* Voluntary arrangement

PROSECUTION
  delinquent officers, of, [218], [219]
  members of company, of, [218], [219]

PROVISIONAL LIQUIDATOR. *See* Liquidator

PROXY
  forms—
    generally, [1346]
    issue of, [1279]
    use of, [1279]
  holder with financial interest, [1283]
  inspection, right of, [1282]
  meaning, [1278]
  meeting, use at, [1280]
  retention of, [1281]

PUBLIC ADMINISTRATION
  Insolvency Services. *See* Insolvency services
  Official Petitioner, [402]
  official receiver. *See* Official receiver

PUBLIC EXAMINATION
  adjournment, [935]
  bankrupt, of. *See* Bankrupt
  contributories, order on request by, [932]
  creditors, order on request by, [932]
  expenses, [936]
  hearing—
    notice of, [931]
    procedure at, [934]
  officers, of, [133]
  order for, [930]
  witness unfit for, [933]

PUNISHMENT
  offences, of, [430], [459], [1328], [1347], [1698], [1706]

R

RECEIPTS
  administrative receiver, of, [713]
  administrator, duties of, [675]
  Scotland, [576]

RECEIVER
  accounts, delivery to registrar, [38]
  administrative—
    agency, [44]
    appointment of—
      acceptance of, [682]
      advertisement of, [683]
      notice of, [683]
    charged property, power to dispose of, [43], [712]
    contracts, liability for, [44]
    creditors' committee—
      attendance at, [49]
      chairman, [700]
      constitution, [697]
      formalities of establishment, [698]
      functions, [699]
      information from receiver, [709]
      meetings, [699]
      members—
        dealings with company, [711]
        expenses, [710]
        removal, [705]
        representatives, [702]
        resignation, [703]

RECEIVER—*continued*
  administrative—*continued*
    creditors' committee—*continued*
      procedure, [707]
      quorum, [701]
      resolutions by post, [708]
      termination of membership, [704]
      vacancies, [706]
    creditors' meeting—
      adjournment, [695]
      chairman, [691]
      claims—
        admission of, [693]
        rejection of, [693]
      minutes, [696]
      procedure for summoning, [690]
      quorum, [694]
      resolutions, [696]
      voting rights, [692]
    deceased, [715]
    forms, [1346]
    general powers, [42]
    information to be given by, [46]
    meaning, [29], [251]
    payments, abstract of, [713]
    powers of, [445]
    receipts, abstract of, [713]
    report by, [48]
    report to creditors, [689]
    resignation, [714]
    statement of affairs—
      expenses of, [688]
      extension of time, [687]
      filing, [685]
      limited disclosure, [686]
      notice requiring, [684]
      release from duty to submit, [687]
      submission of, [47]
      verification, [685]
    VAT bad debt relief—
      certificate of insolvency—
        issue of, [717]
        preservation with company's records, [719]
      notice to creditors, [718]
    vacation of office, [45], [716]
    value added tax certificate, [1348]–[1353], [1708]–[1713]
  appointed out of court—
    contracts, liability for, [37]
    directions, application to court for, [35]
    invalid appointment, liability for, [34]
    receivership accounts, delivery to registrar, [38]
    remuneration, court's power to fix, [36]
    time from which appointment effective, [33]
  body corporate, disqualification from acting, [30]
  contracts, liability for, [37]
  cross-border operation of provisions, [72]
  directions, application to court for, [35]
  disqualifications—
    body corporate, [30]
    undischarged bankrupt, [31]
  extent of Chapter, [28]
  floating charge, payment of debts out of assets subject to, [40]

RECEIVER—*continued*
　interim. *See* Interim receiver
　invalid appointment, liability for, [34]
　meaning, [29], [70], [251]
　notification of appointment, [39]
　official. *See* Official receiver
　remuneration, court's power to fix, [36]
　returns, enforcement of duty to make, [41]
　Scotland, in—
　　agency, [57]
　　appointment of—
　　　cessation of, [62]
　　　circumstances justifying, [52]
　　　court, by, [54]
　　　holder of charge, mode of appointment
　　　　by, [53]
　　　notification of, [64]
　　　power to appoint, [51]
　　committee of creditors, [68]
　　company's statement of affairs, [66]
　　contracts, liability for, [57]
　　court, powers of, [63]
　　cross-border operation of provisions, [72]
　　distribution of moneys, [60]
　　extent of Chapter, [50]
　　forms, prescription of, [71]
　　information to be given by, [65]
　　interpretation, [70]
　　powers of, [55]
　　precedence, [56]
　　priority of debts, [59]
　　property, disposal of interest in, [61]
　　remuneration, [58]
　　report by, [67]
　　returns, enforcement of duty to make, [69]
　Scottish, powers of, [446]
　time from which appointment effective, [33]
　undischarged bankrupt, disqualification from
　　acting, [31]
　See also Manager

RECEIVERSHIP
　trustee, pending appointment of, [287]

RECORDS
　certificate of insolvency preserved with, [681],
　　[719]
　court, [1242]–[1248]
　insolvency practitioner, of, [1437]–[1441],
　　[1447]

REGISTER
　charges, of, meaning, [70]
　disqualification orders, of, [486]

REGISTRAR
　meaning, [1330]
　receivership accounts, delivery of, [38]

REGISTRAR OF COMPANIES
　statements to, [942]

REGISTRATION
　deeds of arrangement, [1770]–[1775], [1838]–
　　[1841]
　liquidator, appointment of, [825]

RELEVANT TIME
　meaning, [240]

REMEDIES
　bankrupt's estate, in respect of, [285]
　restriction on, [1272]

REMUNERATION
　administrator, of—
　　excessive, creditors' claim that, [673]
　　fixing of, [670]
　employees, of, preference for, [1719]
　interim receiver, of, [1035]
　liquidator, of. *See* Liquidator
　manager, of, court's power to fix, [36]
　official receiver, of, [1405]–[1408]
　provisional liquidator, of, [749]
　receiver, of—
　　court's power to fix, [36]
　　Scotland, [58]
　shorthand writers, of, [1233], [1345]
　special manager, of, [925]
　trustee in bankruptcy. *See* Trustee in bank-
　　ruptcy

RENT
　distress, [347]

RENTCHARGE
　land subject to, disclaimer in case of, [180],
　　[319]

REPORT
　administration order, application for, [625]
　administrative receiver, by, [48], [689]
　administrator, of, [652]
　annual, [379]
　conduct of director, on, [1497]–[1503], [1721]–
　　[1726]
　insolvency practitioner, of, action on report
　　of, [274]
　nominee, of, on proposal for voluntary arrang-
　　ment, [600]
　official receiver, by, [762]
　receiver, by, Scotland, [67]
　voluntary arrangement—
　　meetings, [617]
　　supervisor, of, [619]

REPORTING
　general rule as to, [766]

REPRESENTATIONS. *See* False representa-
　tions

REPRESENTATIVE
　company, of, [1284], [1346]
　creditors' committee member, of, [660]

RESOLUTION
　adjourned meeting, passed at, [194]
　creditors' committee, of, [666], [708]
　creditors' meeting, of, [651], [696], [782]
　liquidation committee, of. *See* Liquidation
　　committee
　voluntary winding up, for. *See* Voluntary
　　winding up

RESTRICTIVE TRADE PRACTICES ACT
　exemptions from, [428]

RETENTION OF TITLE AGREEMENT
　goods possessed under, administrator's power
　　to deal with, [15], [16]
　meaning, [251]

RETURNS
　liquidator's duty to make, enforcement of,
　　[170]
　manager's duty to make, enforcement of, [41]

RETURNS—*continued*
  receiver's duty to make, enforcement of, [41], [69]
  Secretary of State, of, [1245]
RULES
  commitee, [413]
  company insolvency, [411], [457]
  individual insolvency, [412], [458]
  meaning, [251], [384]

S

SCOTLAND
  administration procedure, [1551]–[1571]
  bankruptcy in—
    accountant in bankruptcy, [501]
    Act of 1985—
      amendments, [575]
      commencement, [578]
      consequential amendments, [588]
      extent, [578]
      re-enactments, [589]
      repeals, [575], [590]
      short title, [578]
      transitional provisions, [575]
    arbitration, [565]
    associate, meaning, [574]
    award of sequestration—
      court order, registration of, [514]
      further provisions relating to, [515]
      period between statutory meeting and, [518]–[520]
      recall of—
        generally, [517]
        petitions for, [516]
      time of, [512]
    bond of caution, premium of, [1707J]
    claims—
      adjudication of, [549]
      determination of amount of, [579]
      foreign currency—
        generally, [1707F]
        conversion of, [1707G]
      sequestration, in, interest on, [1707H]
      submission to permanent trustee, [548]
    co-obligants—
      liabilities of, [560]
      rights of, [560]
    commissioners—
      election, [530]
      functions of, [504]
      meetings of, [566], [587]
      removal of, [530]
      resignation of, [530]
    compromise, [565]
    credit, obtaining of, [1719]
    creditors—
      meetings of, [566], [585], [586]
      voluntary trust deeds for, [559], [584]
    Crown application, [577]
    debtor—
      co-operation with permanent trustee, [564]
      discharge of—
        automatic, [554]
        composition, on, [556]
        effect of, [555]

SCOTLAND—*continued*
  bankruptcy in—*continued*
    debtor—*continued*
      distribution of estate—
        accounting periods, [552]
        order of priority, [551]
        procedure after end of accounting periods, [553]
      general offences by, [567]
    defects in procedure, power to cure, [563]
    diligence, effect of sequestration on, [537]
    discharge—
      composition, on, [583]
      interim trustee, of, [527]
    dividend, entitlement to vote and draw, [550]
    divorce, recalling of order for payment of capital sum on, [535]
    documents, [562]
    Edinburgh Gazette, [571]
    employees, preference for remuneration of, [1719]
    examination of debtor—
      conduct of, [547]
      private, [544], [546]
      public, [545], [546]
    expenses, [576]
    extortionate credit transactions, [561]
    forms, [1707E], [1707M]
    gratuitous alienations, [534]
    interim preservation of estate, [518]
    interim trustee—
      appointment of, [502], [513]
      discharge of, [527]
      outlays by, [569]
      resignation of, [513]
      termination of functions, [526]
    interpretation, [573], [582]
    limited partnerships, [1707L]
    list of assets and liabilities—
      debtor, of, [519]
      trustee's duties on receipt of, [520]
    meetings—
      commissioners, of, [566], [587]
      creditors, of, [566], [585], [586]
    permanent trustee—
      administration of estate by—
        contractual powers, [542]
        debtor's family home, [540]
        management, [539]
        money received, [543]
        realisation, [539]
        spouse, protection of rights of, [541]
        taking possession of estate, [538]
      confirmation of, [525]
      death of, [528]
      debtor to co-operate with, [564]
      discharge of, [557]
      election of, [524]
      functions of, [503]
      not acting, [529]
      not elected, [580]
      outlays by, [569]
      removal of, [529]
      resignation of, [528]
      submission of claims to, [548]
      vesting of estate in—
        after sequestration, [532]
        date of sequestration, at, [531]
        limitations on, [533]

SCOTLAND—*continued*
  bankruptcy in—*continued*
    petition for sequestration—
      analogous remedy, [510]
      apparent insolvency, meaning, [507]
      concurrent proceedings, [510]
      creditor's oath, [511]
      deceased debtor, estate of, [505]
      further provisions relating to, [508]
      jurisdiction, [509]
      living debtor, estate of, [505]
      other estates, [506]
    preferred debts, [581], [582]
    receipts, [576]
    regulations, [572]
    sederunt book, [562]
    sequestration—
      interest on claims in, [1707H]
      limited partnerships, [1707L]
    statutory meeting of creditors—
      calling of, [521]
      period between award of sequestration
        and, [518]–[520]
      proceedings at, [523]
      submission of claims for voting purposes,
        [522]
    summary proceedings, [568]
    unclaimed dividends, [558]
    unfair preferences, [536]
    unsecured liabilities, amount of, [1707I]
    utilities, supplies by, [570]
  charged property, administrator's power to
    deal with, [16]
  company meetings, attendance at, [157]
  creditors, right to list of, [1695]
  cross-border operation of provisions, [72]
  defects in procedure, [1701]
  Deposit Protection Board's voting rights,
    [1705]
  diligence, effect of, [185]
  director, report on conduct of, [1721]–[1726]
  documents—
    confidentiality of, [1696]
    copies of, [1695]
  early dissolution, [204]
  examination of persons in, court order for,
    [198]
  expenses, [1700]
  fees, [1700]
  forms—
    bankruptcy, [1707E], [1707M]
    prescription of, [71]
    proceedings, for use in, [1699]
  gratuitous alienations, [242]
  insolvency practitioner—
    caution, [1697]
    qualification to act as, [1707C–1707D]
  insurance company, winding up, [1735]–
    [1766]
  leave to proceed, costs of application for, [199]
  liquidation committee, [142], [1625]–[1644],
    [1645]–[1650]
  liquidator—
    appointment of, [138], [1603]–[1607]
    provisional, [1586]–[1591]
    release of, [1616]
    removal of, [1608]–[1612]
    remuneration, [1617]–[1620]
    resignation of, [1613]–[1615]

SCOTLAND—*continued*
  liquidator—*continued*
    supplementary powers, [169], [1621]–[1624]
    meetings, [1670]–[1689]
    notices, [1690]–[1692]
    orders—
      appeals from, [162]
      calls on contributories, for, [161]
      Inner House, taking effect until matter
        disposed of by, [448]
      vacation, winding up pronounced in, [447]
    proceedings—
      court's power to control, [113]
      evidence of, [1694]
      forms for use in, [1699]
      validity of, [1693]
    punishment of offences, [1698], [1706]
    receiver. *See* Receiver
    sederunt book, [562], [1702]
    unclaimed dividends, [193]
    unfair preferences, [243]
    value added tax certificates, [1708]–[1713]
    voluntary arrangements, [1527]–[1550]
    voluntary winding up—
      creditors, of, [1668]
      members, of, [1669]
    winding up by court—
      claims in liquidation, [1600]–[1602]
      Court of Session, [120]
      dissolution after, [1662]
      distribution of assets, [1651]–[1653]
      information, [1595]–[1596]
      limitation, [1661]
      liquidation committee, [1625]–[1644],
        [1645]–[1650]
      liquidator, [1603]–[1624]
      Lord Ordinary, power to remit to, [121]
      meetings of creditors and contributories,
        [1597]–[1599]
      prohibited name, company with, [1663]–
        [1667]
      provisional liquidator, [1586]–[1591]
      public examination, [1659]–[1660]
      sheriff court, [120]
      special manager, [1654]–[1658]
      statement of affairs, [1592]–[1594]

SECOND BANKRUPTCY. *See* Bankruptcy

SECRETARY OF STATE
  creditors' committee, exercise of functions of,
    [302]
  dissolution after winding up, [943]
  documents issuing from, [1313]
  employment protection—
    information, power to obtain, [1805]
    rights and remedies, transfer of, [1804]
  liquidator—
    appointment of, [137], [823]
    removal of, [842]
  power to regulate certain matters, [1308]
  returns, [1245]
  trustee, appointment of, [296]
  trustee in bankruptcy—
    appointment of, [1101]
    removal of, [1112]
  voluntary arrangement, production of ac-
    counts and records, [620], [976]

SECURED CREDITORS
bankruptcy, in case of. *See* Bankruptcy
creditors' meeting, [647]
liquidator, redemption by, [816]
meaning, [248]
non-disclosure, surrender for, [815]
quantification of claim, [807], [1088]
realisation of security, [818]
value of security—
  generally, [814]
  test of, [817]

SECURED DEBENTURE
meaning, [70]
series of, meaning, [70]

SECURITY
court, in, [1274]
creditor with, [269]
fixed, meaning, [70]
insolvency practitioner, of, [1315], [1432]–
  [1436], [1445]
interim receiver—
  failure to give or keep up, [1034]
  generally, [1033]
meaning, [383]
provisional liquidator—
  failure to give or keep up, [748]
  generally, [747]
realisation by creditor, [818]
special manager—
  failure to keep up, [927]
  generally, [926]
value of—
  generally, [814]
  test of, [817]

SEQUESTRATION. *See* Scotland

SERVICE
general provisions as to, [1318]
outside jurisdiction, [1319]
post, by, [1317]
statutory demand, of—
  proof of, [1941]
  substituted, [1940]
substituted—
  petition, of, [1940]
  statutory demand, of, [1940]

SET-OFF
mutual dealings, [323]
quantification of claim, [809]

SETTLOR
bankruptcy of, avoidance of adjustment order
  on, [1799]

SHAREHOLDERS
contributories, liability as, [76]

SHARES
acceptance of, as consideration for sale of
  company property, [110]
transfers of, avoidance of, after winding-up
  resolution, [88]

SHERIFF
duties of, [184]

SHERIFF COURT
winding up by, [120]

SHORTHAND WRITERS
appointment of, [1232]
nomination of, [1232]
remuneration, [1233], [1345]

SOLICITATION
rule against, [869]

SOLICITOR
bankruptcy of, [1214]
insolvency practitioner, of, [1270]
notice to, [1332]

SOLVENCY
statutory declaration of, [89]

SPECIAL MANAGER
accounting, [928]
appointment of, [925]
bankruptcy, in case of. *See* Bankruptcy
court's power to appoint, [177], [370]
formal defects, [377]
remuneration, [925]
security—
  failure to give or keep up, [927]
  generally, [926]
termination of appointment, [929]

SPOUSE
bankrupt, of—
  debts to, [329]
  occupation, rights of, [336]

STAFF
official receiver, of, [401]

STAMP DUTY
documents exempt from, [190]

STATEMENT
administrator's proposals, of, [23]
admissibility in evidence of, [488]
affairs, of. *See* Statement of affairs
false, [356]
financial. *See* Financial statement
registrar of companies, to, [942]

STATEMENT OF AFFAIRS
administrative receiver, submission to, [47]
administrator, submission to, [22]
admissibility in evidence, [433]
bankrupt's estate, [288]
bankruptcy—
  creditor's petition—
    accounts—
      requirement to submit, [1043]
      submission and filing of, [1044]
    expenses, [1042]
    extension of time, [1041]
    filing, [1039]
    further disclosure, [1045]
    generally, [1038]
    limited disclosure, [1040]
    preliminary, [1037]
    release from duty to submit, [1041]
    verification, [1039]
  debtor's petition—
    accounts—
      expenses of preparing, [1050]
      requirement to submit, [1048]
      submission and filing of, [1049]
    contents of, [1047]
    further disclosure, [1051]

STATEMENT OF AFFAIRS—*continued*
  bankruptcy—*continued*
    debtor's petition—*continued*
      generally, [1020]
      preliminary, [1046]
  creditors' voluntary winding up. *See* Creditors' voluntary winding up
  directors to lay before creditors, [99]
  dispensed with, [765]
  expenses of, [638], [688]
  extension of time, [637], [687]
  filing, [635], [685]
  individual voluntary arrangement, [957]
  limited disclosure, [636], [686]
  material omissions from, [210]
  notice requiring, [634], [684]
  proposals—
    notice to creditors, [640]
    to be annexed to, [639]
  receiver, submission to, Scotland, [66]
  release from duty to submit, [637], [687]
  report where lodged, [764]
  verification, [635], [685]
  voluntary arrangement, proposal by directors, [598]
  winding up—
    accounts, submission of, [758]
    court, by, [131]
    expenses, [756]
    extension of time, [755]
    filing, [752]
    further disclosure, [761]
    limited disclosure, [754]
    notice requiring, [751]
    release from duty to submit, [755]
    verification, [752]

STATUTORY DEMAND
  bankruptcy. *See* Bankruptcy
  winding up. *See* Winding up

SUMMARY CONVICTION
  disqualification of director for, [473]

SUPERVISION
  approved voluntary arrangement, [263]

SUPERVISOR
  voluntary arrangement—
    accounts, [619], [975]
    hand-over of property etc to, [616], [970]
    reports, [619], [975]

T

TAXATION
  costs, of, [1249]–[1258]

TERRITORIES
  relevant, co-operation of insolvency courts, [1494]–[1496]

THIRD PARTIES
  insurers, rights against, [1795]–[1798]

TIME-LIMITS
  generally, [376], [1316]

TITLE
  retention of. *See* Retention of title agreement

TRADING
  fraudulent—
    generally, [213]
    proceedings, [215]
  wrongful—
    generally, [214]
    proceedings, [215]

TRANSACTIONS
  defrauding creditors, [423]–[425]
  extortionate credit, [244], [343], [561]
  undervalue, at—
    adjustment of, [339]
    generally, [238]
    orders, [241], [342]
    relevant time, meaning, [240], [341]

TRIBUNAL
  industrial, complaint to, [1803]
  insolvency practitioner, authorisation of. *See* Insolvency

TRUSTEE IN BANKRUPTCY
  appointment of—
    advertisement of, [1103]
    authentication of, [1102]
    court, by, [1100]
    creditors' meeting, by, [1099]
    Secretary of State, by, [1101]
  appointments, power to make, [292]
  bankrupt's duties in relation to, [333]
  certain transactions, power of court to set aside, [1126]
  creditors' committee—
    court, general control by, [303]
    generally, [301]
    Secretary of State, exercise of functions, [302]
  criminal bankruptcy, [1213]
  deceased, [1122]
  formal defects, [377]
  general functions of, [305]
  hand-over of estate to, [1104]
  insolvency practitioner, loss of qualification as, [1123]
  interim. *See* Scotland
  joint, notice to, [1333]
  liability of, [304]
  meeting—
    creditors' power to requisition, [294]
    failure to appoint trustee, [295]
    first trustee, summoned to appoint, [293]
  official receiver, enforcement of obligations to, [1128]
  permanent. *See* Scotland
  powers—
    ancillary, [454]
    general, [453]
    sanction, exercisable with, [452]
  receivership pending appointment of, [287]
  release of, [299], [1114]–[1116]
  removal of—
    advertisement of, [1113]
    court, by, [1111]
    generally, [298]
    meeting of creditors to remove, [1108]–[1109]
    procedure on, [1110]
    Secretary of State, by, [1112]

TRUSTEE IN BANKRUPTCY—*continued*
  remuneration—
    excessive, creditors' claim that, [1121]
    fixing of, [1117]
    other matters affecting, [1118]
    recourse—
      court, to, [1120]
      meeting of creditors, to, [1119]
  resignation—
    action following acceptance of, [1106]
    advertisement of, [1113]
    creditors' meeting to receive, [1105]
    leave granted by court, [1107]
  Secretary of State, appointment by, [296]
  solicitation, rule against, [1127]
  special cases, [297]
  vacancy in office of, [300]
  vacation of office, [298], [1124]–[1125]
  See also Bankrupt's estate

U

UNDERVALUE
  transactions at. *See* Transactions

UNDISCHARGED BANKRUPT
  debtor as, individual voluntary arrangement,
      [261]
  director, disqualification from acting as, [479]
  manager, disqualification from acting as, [31]
  receiver, disqualification from acting as, [31]

UNFITNESS OF DIRECTOR. *See* Director

UNLIMITED COMPANY
  formerly limited, contributories of, [78]

UNREGISTERED COMPANY
  debts, inability to pay—
    debt remaining unsatisfied after action
        brought, [223]
    other cases, [224]
    unpaid creditor for £750 or more, [222]
  meaning, [220]
  winding up—
    contributories, [226]
    cumulative provisions, [229]
    dissolved overseas company, [225]
    generally, [221]
    order, actions stayed on, [228]
    proceedings, court's power to stay, sist or
        restrain, [227]

UNSECURED LIABILITIES
  amount of, Scotland, [1707I]

V

VACATION
  winding up pronounced in, orders in course
      of, [447]

VALUE ADDED TAX
  bad debt relief—
    certificate of insolvency—
      issue of, [679], [717]
      preservation with company's records,
          [681], [719]
    notice to creditors, [680], [718]
  certificate, [1348]–[1353], [1708]–[1713]

VENUE
  meaning, [1334]

VOLUNTARY ARRANGEMENT
  approval, effect of, [5]
  decisions—
    challenge of, [6]
    meetings, of, [4]
  default in connection with, [276]
  forms, [1346]
  individual—
    accounts—
      production to Secretary of State, [976]
      supervisor, of, [975]
    approved—
      implementation of, [263]
      supervision of, [263]
    charges, [977]
    completion of, [978]
    costs, [977]
    creditors' meeting—
      agreement on proposal, proceedings to
          obtain, [968]
      chairman—
        generally, [964]
        proxy-holder, as, [965]
      challenge of, [262]
      decisions of, [258]
      nominee's report, consideration of, [961]
      report of—
        decisions, [259]
        generally, [971]
      requisite majorities, [967]
      summoning of, [257], [962]
      supplementary, [963]
      voting rights, [966]
    debtor as undischarged bankrupt, [261]
    debtor's proposal—
      approval, effect of, [260]
      contents of, [952]
      nominee, report of, [256], [959]
      preparation of, [951]
    expenses, [977]
    false representations, [979]
    fees, [977]
    generally, [950]
    hearing of application, [955]
    interim order—
      application for, [253]
      cases in which made, [255]
      effect of application, [254]
      generally, [252]
    nominee—
      additional disclosure for assistance of,
          [958]
      consideration of report of, [961]
      intended, notice to, [953]
      replacement of, [960]
      report on proposal, [256], [959]
    order—
      action to follow making of, [956]
      interim, application for, [954]
    records, [976]
    register of, [972]
    resolutions to follow approval, [969]
    revocation of, [974]
    Secretary of State, report to, [973]
    statement of affairs, [957]
    supervisor—
      accounts, [975]
      hand-over of property to, [970]
      reports, [975]

VOLUNTARY ARRANGEMENT—*continued*
  individual—*continued*
    suspension of, [974]
  liquidator, appointment by court following, [140]
  meaning, [1]
  meetings—
    decisions of, [4]
    summoning of, [3]
  nominee—
    administrator, not, procedure where, [2]
    liquidator, not, procedure where, [2]
    meaning, [1]
  proposal—
    administrator, by—
      meetings, summoning of, [604]
      notice to nominee, [605]
      preparation, [603], [605]
    directors, by—
      contents, [596]
      meetings, summoning of, [602]
      nominee—
        additional disclosure for assistance of, [599]
        intended, notice to, [597]
        replacement of, [601]
        report of, [600]
      preparation, [595]
      statement of affairs, [598]
    implementation of, [7]
    liquidator, by—
      meetings, summoning of, [604]
      notice to nominee, [605]
      preparation, [603], [605]
    nominee—
      administrator, not, procedure where, [2]
      liquidator, not, procedure where, [2]
    proceedings on—
      accounts—
        production to Secretary of State, [620]
        supervisor, of, [619]
      agreement, to obtain, [614]
      arrangement—
        completion of, [622]
        revocation of, [618]
        suspension of, [618]
      charges, [621]
      costs, [621]
      expenses, [621]
      false representations, [623]
      fees, [621]
      meetings of creditors and members—
        chairman at, [607]
        company officers, attendance by, [609]
        proxy-holder, chairman as, [608]
        summoning of, [606]
      records, production to Secretary of State, [620]
      report—
        meetings, of, [617]
        supervisor, of, [619]
      requisite majorities—
        creditors, [612]
        members, [613]
      resolutions to follow approval, [615]
      supervisor—
        accounts, [619]

VOLUNTARY ARRANGEMENT—*contin-ued*
  proposal—*continued*
    proceedings on—*continued*
      supervisor—*continued*
        hand-over of property etc to, [616]
        reports, [619]
      voting rights—
        creditors, [610]
        members, [611]
    who may propose, [1]
  Scotland, in, [1527]–[1550]

VOLUNTARY WINDING UP
  accounts, [1410]–[1417]
  arrangement under s 110, dissent from, [111]
  books, disposal of, [1418]
  business, effect on, [87]
  circumstances giving rise to, [84]
  commencement of, [86]
  company's property, distribution of, [107]
  court—
    appointment of liquidator, [108]
    power to control proceedings, Scotland, [113]
    reference of questions to, [112]
    removal of liquidator, [108]
  creditors, of. *See* Creditors' voluntary winding up
  dissolution of company after, [201]
  expenses, [115]
  funds—
    investment of, [1420]–[1421]
    unclaimed, [1419]
  generally, [720]
  liquidator—
    appointment by court, [108]
    none appointed or nominated by company, [114]
    notice of appointment, [109]
    powers and duties, [165]
    release of, [173]
    removal by court, [108]
    removal of, [171]
    vacation of office, [171]
  members, of. See Members' voluntary winding up
  papers, disposal of, [1418]
  resolution for—
    avoidance of share transfers after, [88]
    meaning, [84]
    notice of, [85]
  saving for certain rights, [116]
  shares, acceptance of, [110]
  solvency, statutory declaration of, [89]
  status of company, effect on, [87]

VOTING RIGHTS
  creditors' meeting, [692]
  Deposit Protection Board, of, [1343], [1705]
  liquidation committee, [884], [885]
    creditors, [610]
    members, [611]

W

WATER
  supplies of, [233], [372]

WINDING UP
  affidavits, [200]

WINDING UP—*continued*
alternative modes of, [73]
application—
　delinquent directors, officers and pro-
　　moters, by or against, [1347B]
　hearing of, [1347C]
assets—
　collection and distribution of. *See* Assets
　power to make over to employees, [187]
attachment, effect of, [183]
bank, on petition from, [1807]
calls. *See* Calls
capital, return of, [940]–[941]
certain transactions, court's power to set aside,
　[868]
commission for receiving evidence, [197]
company in liquidation, notification of, [188]
company's books to be in evidence, [191]
conclusion of, [942]
contract, rescission by court, [186]
contributories—
　bankruptcy, effect of, [82]
　company registered under Companies Act,
　　[83]
　death of member, in case of, [81]
　information to, [762]–[768]
　liability—
　　director—
　　　past, [76]
　　　unlimited liability, with, [75]
　　limited company formerly unlimited, [77]
　　nature of, [80]
　　past members, [74]
　　present members, [74]
　　shareholders, [76]
　　unlimited company formerly limited, [78]
　meaning, [79]
meetings to ascertain wishes of, [195]
settlement of list of—
　addition to, 919
　costs, [920]
　form of, [916]
　liquidator, duty to settle, [915]
　preliminary, [914]
　procedure for settling, [917]
　variation of—
　　application to court, [918]
　　generally, [919]
costs—
　court, saving for powers of, [939]
　priority, general rule as to, [937]
　winding up commencing as voluntary, [938]
court, by—
　administrative records, [1394]
　application for, [124]
　attachments, avoidance of, [128]
　books, disposal of, [1400]
　calls—
　　contributories, on, orders for, [161]
　　power to make, [150]
　circumstances giving rise to, [122]
　commencement of, [129]
　county court—
　　case stated for High Court, [119]
　　jurisdiction, [117]
　dividends—
　　payment, [1401]
　　unclaimed, [1402]

WINDING UP—*continued*
court, by—*continued*
　general powers of court—
　　assets, application of, [148]
　　calls, power to make, [150]
　　company meetings, attendance at, [157]
　　contributories—
　　　absconding, power to arrest, [158]
　　　adjustment of rights of, [154]
　　　debts due from, to company, [149]
　　　order on, to be conclusive evidence,
　　　　[152]
　　　settlement of list of, [148]
　　creditors—
　　　inspection of books by, [155]
　　　not proving in time, power to exclude,
　　　　[153]
　　cumulative nature of, [159]
　　expenses, payment of, [156]
　　liquidator, delegation of powers to, [160]
　　money due to company, payment into
　　　bank of, [151]
　　sist, power to, [147]
　　stay, power to, [147]
　generally, [720]
　High Court—
　　case stated for, [119]
　　jurisdiction, [117]
　inability to pay debts, meaning, [123]
　investigation procedures—
　　company's statement of affairs, [131]
　　enforcement of s 133, [134]
　　official receiver, investigation by, [132]
　　public examination of officers, [133]
　investment of funds, [1404]
　jurisdiction—
　　county court, [117]
　　Court of Session, [120]
　　High Court, [117]
　　sheriff court, [120]
　liquidator—
　　appointment of—
　　　contributories' meeting, choice at,
　　　　[139]
　　　court, by, following administration or
　　　　voluntary arrangement, [140]
　　　creditors' meeting, choice at, [139]
　　　official receiver, functions of, [136]
　　　provisional, [135]
　　　Scotland, in, [138]
　　　Secretary of State, by, [137]
　　functions of—
　　　custody of company property, [144]
　　　final meeting, duty to summon, [146]
　　　general, [143]
　　　vesting of company property in liqui-
　　　　dator, [145]
　　powers and duties, [167]
　　release of, [174]
　　removal of, [172]
　　vacation of office, [172]
　Lord Ordinary, power to remit winding up
　　to, [121]
　official receiver—
　　investigation by, [132]
　　office of liquidator, functions in relation
　　　to, [136]
　　remuneration of, [1405]–[1408]

WINDING UP—*continued*
  court, by—*continued*
    orders—
      appeals from, [162]
      calls on contributories, for, [161]
      consequences of, [130]
      contributories, on, as conclusive evidence, [152]
    papers, disposal of, [1400]
    petition—
      powers on hearing of, [125]
      various forms of, [721]
    proceedings against company, power to stay or restrain, [126]
    property dispositions, avoidance of, [127]
    responsible insolvency practitioner—
      audit of accounts of, [1398]
      business carried on by, [1396]
      copies of accounts, [1399]
      retention of money by, [1393]
    Scotland, in. *See* Scotland
    unclaimed funds, [1402]–[1403]
    wrong court, proceedings taken in, [118]
  court documents, judicial notice of, [196]
  creditors—
    information to, [762]–[768]
    meeting. *See* Creditors' meeting
    wishes, meetings to ascertain, [195]
  debts, interest on, [189]
  diligence, effect of, [185]
  director of company with prohibited name, leave to act as. *See* Director
  disclaimer. *See* Disclaimer
  dissolution after. *See* Company
  evidence—
    commission for receiving, [197]
    company's books to be, [191]
  examination of persons in Scotland, court order for, [198]
  execution, effect of, [183]
  forms, [1346]
  fraud in anticipation of, [206]
  individual voluntary arrangement. *See* Voluntary arrangement
  insurance company, [1735]–[1766], [1810]–[1816], [1884]–[1916], [1917]–[1936]
  leave to proceed, application for, costs of, [199]
  liquidation committee. *See* Liquidation committee
  liquidator. See Liquidator
  meetings—
    adjourned, resolutions passed at, [194]
    wishes of creditors or contributories, to ascertain, [195]
  misconduct in course of, [208]
  monetary limits, [1449], [1452]
  official receiver, reports by, [762]
  order—
    advertisement of, [740]
    investment business, [1829], [1830]
    Northern Ireland, [1830]
    notice of, [739]
    petition to. *See* petition *post*
    settling of, [739]
    transmission, [740]
  pending liquidations, information as to, [192]
  petition—
    advertisement of, [730]

WINDING UP—*continued*
  order—*continued*
    petition—*continued*
      affidavit in opposition, [737]
      appearance—
        list of, [736]
        notice of, [735]
      application of Rules, [743]
      certificate of compliance, [733]
      contributories, by—
        application of Rules, [743]
        presentation of, [741]
        return of, [742]
        service of, [741]
      copies of—
        other persons to receive, [729]
        persons entitled to, [732]
      court's powers on hearing, [125]
      filing of, [726]
      leave for petitioner to withdraw, [734]
      petitioner—
        contributory, substitution of, [738]
        creditor, substitution of, [738]
        leave to withdraw, [734]
      presentation of, [726], [741]
      proof of service, [728]
      return of, [742]
      service of, [727], [742]
      various forms of, [721]
      verification of, [731]
  preferential charge on goods distrained, [176]
  preferential debts—
    general provision, [175]
    preferential charge on goods distrained, [176]
  proceedings in courts other than High Court, in, [1347A]
  proof of debts. *See* Debts
  provisional liquidator. *See* Liquidator
  public examination of company officers. *See* Public examination
  quantification of claim. *See* Claim
  registrar of companies, statements to, [942]
  report—
    official receiver, by, [762]
    where statement of affairs lodged, [764]
  reporting, general rule as to, [766]
  secured creditors. *See* Secured creditors
  sheriff, duties of, [184]
  solicitation, rule against, [869]
  special manager. *See* Special manager
  stamp duty, documents exempt from, [190]
  statement of affairs. *See* Statement of affairs
  statutory demand—
    content of, [724]
    form of, [724]
    information to be given in, [725]
    preliminary, [723]
  stayed, [767]
  time limits, [722]
  unclaimed dividends, [193]
  unregistered company, of. *See* Unregistered company
  vacation, pronounced in, orders in course of, [447]
  voluntary. *See* Voluntary winding up

WITNESS
  examination, unfit for, [933]

WRONGFUL TRADING
  disqualification of director for participating in, [478]

WRONGFUL TRADING—*continued*
  generally, [214]
  proceedings, [215]